WILEY

GAAP
2002

Interpretation and Application of
GENERALLY ACCEPTED
ACCOUNTING PRINCIPLES
2002

Subscriber
Update
Service

BECOME A SUBSCRIBER!
Did you purchase this product from a bookstore?

If you did, it's important for you to become a subscriber. John Wiley & Sons, Inc. may publish, on a periodic basis, supplements and new editions to reflect the latest changes in the subject matter that you *need to know* in order stay competitive in this ever-changing industry. By contacting the Wiley office nearest you, you'll receive any current update at no additional charge. In addition, you'll receive future updates and revised or related volumes on a 30-day examination review.

If you purchased this product directly from John Wiley & Sons, Inc., we have already recorded your subscription for this update service.

To become a subscriber, please call **1-800-225-5945** or send your name, company name (if applicable), address, and the title of the product to:

mailing address:
> **Supplement Department**
> **John Wiley & Sons, Inc.**
> **One Wiley Drive**
> **Somerset, NJ 08875**

e-mail: **subscriber@wiley.com**
fax: **1-732-302-2300**
online: **www.wiley.com**

For customers outside the United States, please contact the Wiley office nearest you:

Professional & Reference Division
John Wiley & Sons Canada, Ltd.
22 Worcester Road
Rexdale, Ontario M9W 1L1
CANADA
(416) 675-3580
Phone: 1-800-567-4797
Fax: 1-800-565-6802
canada@jwiley.com

Jacaranda Wiley Ltd.
PRT Division
P.O. Box 174
North Ryde, NSW 2113
AUSTRALIA
Phone: (02) 805-1100
Fax: (02) 805-1597
headoffice@jacwiley.com.au

John Wiley & Sons, Ltd.
Baffins Lane
Chichester
West Sussex, PO19 1UD
ENGLAND
Phone: (44) 1243 779777
Fax: (44) 1243 770638
cs-books@wiley.co.uk

John Wiley & Sons (SEA) Pte. Ltd.
2 Clementi Loop #02-01
SINGAPORE 129809
Phone: 65 463 2400
Fax: 65 463 4605; 65 463 4604
wiley@singnet.com.sg

WILEY

GAAP
2002

Interpretation and Application of
GENERALLY ACCEPTED
ACCOUNTING PRINCIPLES
2002

Patrick R. Delaney   Ralph Nach
Barry J. Epstein   Susan Weiss Budak

JOHN WILEY & SONS, INC.
New York • Chichester • Weinheim • Brisbane • Singapore • Toronto

To order books or for customer service, call (800)-CALL WILEY (225-5945)

ISBN 0-471-43516-3

Printed in the United States of America
10 9 8 7 6 5 4 3 2

CONTENTS

ABOUT THE AUTHORS

Patrick R. Delaney, PhD, CPA, was the Arthur Andersen LLP Alumni Professor of Accountancy and Chair of the Department of Accountancy at Northern Illinois University. He received his PhD in Accountancy from the University of Illinois. Professor Delaney served as a Faculty Resident with Arthur Andersen LLP. He was the author of *CPA Examination Review*, 2-volume and 4-part sets, including the related components of the Wiley CPA preparation system. He was past president of the Rockford Chapter, Institute of Management Accountants; served on Illinois CPA Society Committees (previously as Vice-President and member, Board of Directors; Chairman of Accounting Principles Committee; chair of the Relations with Accounting Educators and Students Committee; and chair of Educator CPA Issues Committee); and had served on numerous other professional committees. He was a member of the American Accounting Association, American Institute of Certified Public Accountants, and the Institute of Management Accountants. Professor Delaney had published in *The Accounting Review* and was the recipient of NIU's Excellence in Teaching Award and the Illinois CPA Society's Outstanding Educator Award.

Barry J. Epstein, PhD, CPA, is a partner with the Chicago-based firm Gleeson, Sklar, Sawyers & Cumpata, LLP, where he specializes in technical consultation on accounting and auditing matters and corporate governance, as well as litigation matters including accountants' malpractice, contractual dispute resolution, and commercial damages modeling. He has previously served in senior technical and litigation consulting positions with several regional and national CPA firms, as a corporate finance executive, and as a college professor. Dr. Epstein has authored or coauthored six books (including *Wiley IAS Interpretation and Application*) and several articles, and coauthored a weekly business column for an international newspaper. He served on several state and national technical committees, including the AICPA's Board of Examiners, and has lectured widely on technical accounting and auditing topics over most of his thirty-five-year career, which has been primarily in public accounting. Dr. Epstein holds a doctorate from the University of Pittsburgh, as well as degrees from DePaul University and the University of Chicago. He is a member of the Illinois CPA Society, the AICPA, and the American Accounting Association.

Susan Weiss Budak, CPA, is a consultant and author. As a consultant, she has worked primarily with the FASB, the American Institute of Certified Public Accountants, Blackbaud, and the National Center for Education Statistics (NCES). Prior to becoming self-employed, Ms. Budak worked for the FASB and GASB as a project manager on research and technical activities. Her work at FASB included the contributions, financial statement display, and investment parts of the FASB not-for-profit organizations project. At the GASB, she worked on the GASB reporting model for public colleges and universities. Ms. Budak has also held positions as assistant controller and director of accounting services at Northwestern University in Evanston, Illinois, and senior accountant at Deloitte & Touche in Chicago, Illinois. Ms. Budak received her MM from the Kellogg Graduate School of Management and her BBA from Loyola University. She has coauthored five books on not-for-profit organizations.

Ralph Nach, CPA, is a managing director with the Chicago office of American Express Tax & Business Services, Inc. where he serves as a technical consultant and as the director of professional development. Mr. Nach has been a public accounting practitioner for 25 years, during which he has specialized in accounting, auditing, and financial reporting issues. Mr. Nach holds a BSBA with honors from the Walter E. Heller School of Business Administration of Roosevelt University in Chicago, and is a CPA in Illinois. Previously Mr. Nach worked for a "Big 5" CPA firm and taught graduate accounting and finance at Northwestern University. Mr. Nach has coauthored several other books and speaks nationally on accounting and auditing topics. He is a member of the American Institute of Certified Public Accountants and its Educational Management Exchange Subcommittee (EDMAX), and the Illinois CPA Society, where he has served as a chairman and/or member of numerous committees.

ACKNOWLEDGEMENT

We greatly appreciate the previous contributions by James R. Adler who was a co-author of Wiley GAAP through 2000.

PREFACE

GAAP: Interpretation and Application provides analytical explanations and copious illustrations of all current generally accepted accounting principles. The book integrates principles promulgated by all the relevant standard-setting bodies—the FASB, including its Emerging Issues Task Force's consensus summaries and discussion issues, and the AICPA's Accounting Standards Executive Committee (AcSEC) These materials are synthesized into a user-oriented topical format, eliminating the need for readers to first be knowledgeable about the names or numbers of the salient professional standards.

The focus of the book is the practitioner and the myriad practical problems faced in applying GAAP. Accordingly, meaningful, "real world"- type examples abound, guiding users in the application of GAAP to complex fact situations that must be dealt with in the actual practice of accounting In addition to this emphasis, a major strength of the book is that it does explain the theory of GAAP in sufficient detail to serve as a valuable adjunct to accounting textbooks. Not merely a reiteration of currently promulgated GAAP, it provides the user with the underlying conceptual basis for the rules, to enable the reasoning by analogy that is so necessary in dealing with a complex, fast-changing world of commercial arrangements and transaction structures. It is based on the authors' belief that proper application of GAAP demands an understanding of the logical underpinnings of its technical requirements.

Each chapter of this book, or major section thereof, provides an overview discussion of the perspective and key issues associated with the topics covered; a listing of the professional pronouncements which guide practice; and a detailed discussion of the concepts and the accompanying examples. A comprehensive checklist, following the main text, offers practical guidance to preparing financial statements in accordance with GAAP, with supplemental insights into SEC-mandated disclosures as needed. Usability is enhanced by the comprehensive index, and by the exhaustive listing of professional pronouncements which are keyed to both the text in this book and to the codification of accounting standards prepared by the FASB (i.e., the *Current Text*).

The authors' wish is that this book will serve practitioners, faculty, and student, as a reliable reference tool, to facilitate their understanding of, and ability to apply, the complexities of the authoritative literature. Comments from readers, both as to errors and omissions and as to proposed improvements for future editions, should be addressed to Barry J. Epstein, c/o John Wiley & Sons, Inc., 155 N. 3rd Street, Suite 502, DeKalb, Illinois 60115, prior to May 15, 2002, for consideration for the 2003 edition.

Barry J. Epstein
Susan Weiss Budak
Ralph Nach
August 1, 2001

AUTHORITATIVE ACCOUNTING PRONOUNCEMENTS

Listed below are all of the authoritative accounting pronouncements **currently in effect** as we go to press. The current text refers to the FASB's *Accounting Standards—Current Text,* which is divided into two volumes: General Standards and Industry Standards. These volumes as well as two volumes of Original Pronouncements may be ordered from the AICPA (800-862-4272) or FASB (203-847-0700). The Emerging Issues Task Force Abstracts, which are in a separate book, may be ordered from the FASB. AICPA Statements of Position by the Accounting Standards Executive Committee may be ordered from the AICPA. These are available individually or in the publication entitled *AICPA Technical Practice Aids.* Places in this text where the pronouncements are discussed may be found by referencing the last column in the listings below.

Pronouncement Abbreviations

The following is a key to the abbreviations used throughout the book to refer to authoritative pronouncements:

Pronouncement	*Abbreviation*
Accounting Principles Board Opinion	APB
Accounting Research Bulletin	ARB
Statements of Financial Accounting Concepts	SFAC
Statements of Financial Accounting Standards	SFAS
Financial Accounting Standards Board Interpretation	FASB I
FASB Technical Bulletin	FASB TB
EITF Discussion of Technical Matters	D
Emerging Issues Task Force Issue	EITF
AICPA Accounting Interpretation	AICPA AIN
AICPA Audit and Accounting Guide	AICPA AAG
AICPA Practice Bulletin of Accounting Standards Executive Committee (AcSEC)	AICPA PB
AICPA Statements of Position	SOP

Accounting Research Bulletins (ARB), Accounting Procedures Committee, AICPA (1953-1959)			
*Number**	*Title*	*Current text reference*	*GAAP Interp. & Applic. page reference*
43	Restatement and Revision of Accounting Research Bulletins Nos. 1-42 (originally issued 1939-1953)		
	Ch. 1 Prior Bulletins	A31, B50, C08, C23, R36, R70, R75	746
	Ch. 2 Form of Statements	F43	55
	Ch. 3 Working Capital	B05, I78	43, 46, 165, 169, 532, 534
	Ch. 4 Inventory Pricing	I78	233, 242, 256, 571
	Ch. 7 Capital Accounts	C20, Q15	788
	Ch. 9 Depreciation	D40	
	Ch. 10 Taxes	T10	537

---

* *Missing numbers throughout this listing represent pronouncements that have been completely superseded.*

(FASB cont.)

Number	Title	Current text reference	GAAP Interp. & Applic. page reference
72	Accounting for Certain Acquisitions of Banking or Thrift Institutions	B50, Bt7, I60	381, 918, 923, 931, 932, 934, 935
73	Reporting a Change in Accounting for Railroad Track Structures	A06, A35	
75	Deferral of the Effective Date of Certain Accounting Requirements for Pension Plans of State and Local Governmental Entities	Pe5	
78	Classification of Obligations That Are Callable by the Creditor	B05	535
79	Elimination of Certain Disclosures for Business Combinations by Nonpublic Enterprises	B50	
80	Accounting for Futures Contracts (in effect until June 15, 2000)		174, 226, 227, 228
84	Induced Conversions of Convertible Debt	D10, L35	548, 569
85	Yield Test for Determining Whether a Convertible Security Is a Common Stock Equivalent		
86	Accounting for the Costs of Computer Software to Be Sold, Leased, or Otherwise Marketed	Co2, R50	397, 957, 959, 962, 969, 1006
87	Employers' Accounting for Pensions	B50, C59, I67, P16, Re6	70, 702, 705, 707, 708, 709, 710, 712, 714, 716, 718, 721, 722, 723, 724, 725, 729, 730, 731, 750, 1061
88	Employers' Accounting for Settlements and Curtailments of Defined Benefit Pension Plans and for Termination Benefits	P16, P40	702, 709, 721, 724, 729
89	Financial Reporting and Changing Prices	C28	
90	Regulated Enterprises—Accounting for Abandonments and Disallowances of Plant Costs	Re6	
91	Accounting for Nonrefundable Fees and Costs Associated with Originating or Acquiring Loans	Bt7, D22, Fi4, I80, In6, L10, L20, Mo4	157, 229, 918, 936, 974, 984, 996
92	Regulated Enterprises—Accounting for Phase-in Plans	D40, Re6	1038
93	Recognition of Depreciation by Not-for-Profit Organizations	D40	1015, 1023
94	Consolidation of All Majority-Owned Subsidiaries	C51, I82, L10	401, 421, 451, 504, 505, 518, 527, 1029
95	Statement of Cash Flows	A06, A10, C25, De4, F60, I27, I73, Oi5	43, 99, 105, 937

(FASB TB cont.)

Number	Title	Current text reference	GAAP Interp. & Applic. page reference
87-2	Computation of a Loss on an Abandonment	Re6	
87-3	Accounting for Mortgage Servicing Fees and Rights	Mo4	931, 936, 996
88-1	Issues Relating to Accounting for Leases	L10	606, 630
88-2	Definition of a Right of Setoff (Reference APB Opinion 10, para 7)		
90-1	Accounting for Separately Priced Extended Warranty and Product Maintenance Contracts	R75	294
94-1	Application of Statement 115 to Debt Securities in a Troubled Debt Restructuring	I80	164, 413
97-1	Accounting under Statement 123 for Certain Employee Stock Purchase Plans with a Look-Back Option	C36	775, 812

Financial Accounting Standards Board (FASB) **Statements of Financial Accounting Concepts (1978-2001)**			
1	Objectives of Financial Reporting by Business Enterprises	--	16, 23, 99
2	Qualitative Characteristics of Accounting Information	--	17, 24
4	Objectives of Financial Reporting by Nonbusiness Organizations	--	
5	Recognition and Measurement in Financial Statements of Business Enterprises		17, 27, 99, 271, 399, 467, 475, 476, 964
6	Elements of Financial Statements	V18	17, 28, 38, 39, 64, 161, 399, 558, 639, 642, 733
7	Using Cash Flow Information and Present Value in Accounting Measurements		17, 31, 356, 371, 372, 639, 1014, 1039

Emerging Issues Task Force Issues (1984-2001)			
84-1	Tax Reform Act of 1984; Deferred Income Taxes of Stock Life Insurance Companies	Resolved by SFAS 109.	
84-2	Tax Reform Act of 1984; Deferred Income Taxes Relating to Domestic International Sales Corporations	Resolved by SFAS 109.	
84-3	Convertible Debt "Sweeteners"	Resolved by SFAS 84.	
84-4	Acquisition, Development, and Construction Loans	Resolved by Practice Bulletin 1.	333, 929
84-5	Sale of Marketable Securities with a Put Option	Partially nullified by SFAS 140; see also SFAS 133.	449
84-6	Termination of Defined Benefit Pension Plans	Consensus nullified by SFAS 88.	
84-7	Termination of Interest Rate Swaps	Partially nullified and partially resolved by SFAS 133.	227
84-8	Variable Stock Purchase Warrants Given by Suppliers to Customers	Affected by SFAS 123. See Issue 96-18.	
84-9	Deposit Float of Banks	Superseded by Practice Bulletin 1.	930

(EITF cont.)

(*EITF cont.*)

(EITF cont.)

Number	Title	Status	GAAP Interp. & Applic. page reference
90-4	Earnings-Per-Share Treatment of Tax Benefits for Dividends on Stock Held by an Employee Stock Ownership Plan	Nullified by SFAS 128. Additional guidance in Issue 92-3.	
90-5	Exchanges of Ownership Interests between Entities under Common Control	Consensus reached.	506, 523
90-6	Accounting for Certain Events Not Addressed in Issue 87-11 Relating to an Acquired Operating Unit to Be Sold	Consensus reached. See also Issue 87-11. Affected by SFAS 121.	468, 523
90-7	Accounting for a Reload Stock Option	Consensus reached; see also Issue 84-18 and FASB Interpretation 44.	801
90-8	Capitalization of Costs to Treat Environmental Contamination	Consensus reached. See Issue 89-13.	393
90-9	Changes to Fixed Employee Stock Option Plans as a Result of Restructuring	Consensus nullified by FASB Interpretation 44.	801
90-10	Accounting for a Business Combination Involving a Majority-Owned Investee of a Venture Capital Company	No resolution.	
90-11	Accounting for Exit and Entrance Fees Incurred in a Conversion from the Savings Association Insurance Fund to the Bank Insurance Fund	Deemed no longer technically helpful.	
90-12	Allocating Basis to Individual Assets and Liabilities for Transactions within the Scope of Issue 88-16	Consensus reached.	506, 523
90-13	Accounting for Simultaneous Common Control Mergers	Consensus reached. See Issue 86-29.	506, 523
90-14	Unsecured Guarantee by Parent of Subsidiary's Lease Payment in a Sale-Leaseback Transaction	Consensus reached.	622
90-15	Impact of Nonsubstantive Lessors, Residual Value Guarantees, and Other Provisions in Leasing Transactions	Consensus reached; see also Issues 96-21 and 97-1, and SFAS 140.	524, 527, 622, 625
90-16	Accounting for Discontinued Operations Subsequently Retained	Consensus affected by SFAS 121.	97
90-17	Hedging Foreign Currency Risks with Purchased Options	Superseded by SFAS 133.	226, 902
90-18	Effect of a "Removal of Accounts" Provision on the Accounting for a Credit Card Securitization	Consensus reached. See D-52.	935
90-19	Convertible Bonds with Issuer Option to Settle for Cash upon Conversion	Consensus reached; affected by SFAS 128 and partially affirmed by SFAS 133.	573
90-20	Impact of an Uncollateralized Irrevocable Letter of Credit on a Real Estate Sale-Leaseback Transaction	Consensus reached.	332, 623

(EITF cont.)

Number	Title	Status	GAAP Interp. & Applic. page reference
90-21	Balance Sheet Treatment of a Sale of Mortgage Servicing Rights with a Sub-servicing Agreement	Consensus reached. See Issues 88-18, 95-5, and D-52.	935
90-22	Accounting for Gas-Balancing Arrangements	No resolution; see SFAS 133.	
91-1	Hedging Intercompany Foreign Currency Risks	Consensus nullified by SFAS 133.	217, 902, 905
91-2	Debtor's Accounting for Forfeiture of Real Estate Subject to a Nonrecourse Mortgage	No consensus reached.	332
91-3	Accounting for Income Tax Benefits from Bad Debts of a Savings and Loan Association	Resolved by SFAS 109.	
91-4	Hedging Foreign Currency Risks with Complex Options and Similar Transactions	Resolved by SFAS 133.	
91-5	Nonmonetary Exchange of Cost-Method Investments	Consensus reached. Affected by SFAS 115 and 130.	524
91-6	Revenue Recognition of Long-Term Power Sales Contracts	Consensus partially nullified by SFAS 133.	287
91-7	Accounting for Pension Benefits Paid by Employers after Insurance Companies Fail to Provide Annuity Benefits	Consensus reached.	731
91-8	Application of FASB Statement 96 to a State Tax Based on the Greater of a Franchise Tax or an Income Tax	Consensus modified by SFAS 109.	
91-9	Revenue and Expense Recognition for Freight Services in Process	Consensus reached.	294
91-10	Accounting for Tax Increment Financing Entities and Special Assessments	Consensus reached.	393
92-1	Allocation of Residual Value or First-Loss Guarantee to Minimum Lease Payments in Leases Involving Land and Building(s)	Consensus reached.	623
92-2	Measuring Loss Accruals by Transferors for Transfers of Receivables with Recourse	Consensus reached. Additional guidance provided by SEC. See also Issue 88-11. Issue affected by SFAS 140.	156
92-3	Earnings-Per-Share Treatment of Tax Benefits for Dividends on Unallocated Stock Held by an Employee Stock Ownership Plan (Consideration of the Implications of FASB Statement 109 on Issue 2 of EITF Issue 90-4)	Consensus affected by SOP 93-6.	833
92-4	Accounting for a Change in Functional Currency When an Economy Ceases to Be Considered Highly Inflationary	Consensus reached. See Issue 92-8.	905

(EITF cont.)

Number	Title	Status	GAAP Interp. & Applic. page reference
94-7	Accounting for Financial Instruments Indexed to, and Potentially Settled in, a Company's Own Stock	Codified by Issue 96-13.	
94-8	Accounting for Conversion of a Loan into a Debt Security in a Debt Restructuring	Consensus reached.	573
94-9	Determining a Normal Servicing Fee Rate for the Sale of an SBA Loan	Consensus nullified by SFAS 125.	
94-10	Accounting by a Company for the Income Tax Effects of Transactions among or with Its Shareholders under FASB Statement 109	Consensus reached.	683
95-1	Revenue Recognition on Sales with a Guaranteed Minimum Resale Value	Consensus reached; see also SFAS 133.	624
95-2	Determination of What Constitutes a Firm Commitment for Foreign Currency Transactions Not Involving a Third Party	Consensus nullified by SFAS 133.	905
95-3	Recognition of Liabilities in Connection with a Purchase Business Combination	Consensus reached. See Issue 95-14.	97, 525
95-4	Revenue Recognition on Equipment Sold and Subsequently Repurchased Subject to an Operating Lease	Consensus reached.	624
95-5	Determination of What Risks and Rewards, If Any, Can Be Retained and Whether Any Unresolved Contingencies May Exist in a Sale of Mortgage Loan Servicing Rights	Consensus reached.	229
95-6	Accounting by a Real Estate Investment Trust for an Investment in a Service Corporation	Consensus reached.	332
95-7	Implementation Issues Related to the Treatment of Minority Interests in Certain Real Estate Investment Trusts	Consensus reached.	333
95-8	Accounting for Contingent Consideration Paid to the Shareholders of an Acquired Enterprise in a Purchase Business Combination	Consensus reached.	528
95-9	Accounting for Tax Effects of Dividends in France in Accordance with FASB Statement 109	Consensus reached.	
95-10	Accounting for Tax Credits Related to Dividend Payments in Accordance with FASB Statement 109	Consensus reached. See Issue 95-20.	684
95-11	Accounting for Derivative Instruments Containing Both a Written Option-Based Component and a Forward-Based Component	Resolved by SFAS 133.	

(EITF cont.)

(EITF cont.)

EITF DISCUSSION OF TECHNICAL MATTERS

Listed below are EITF documents that contain discussion by the Emerging Issues Task Force of technical matters that have long-term relevance and do not relate specifically to a numbered EITF Issue. The more important of these are briefly annotated.

This established the status in the GAAP hierarchy of EITF consensuses, how changes to conform thereto should be accounted for, and related matters.

This establishes that the former practice of accruing a bad debt provision at least inception, which would then be offset by unearned income consistent with other initial direct costs, is inappropriate.

This clarified that other interest recognition methods (Rule of 78s, etc.) would not be acceptable alternatives to the (effective rate) interest method.

This addressed the need for disclosure of post-balance-sheet date events in the specific context of the sharp stock market decline which occurred in late 1987.

Establishes that compensation cost accrued pursuant to FASB I 28 should not later be reversed if rights were canceled as a result of a proposed SEC rule change.

This clarified the distinctions between SFAS 6, dealing with classification of short-term debt as noncurrent under defined circumstances, and FASB TB 79-3, which addresses the potential need to classify long-term debt having a subjective acceleration clause as current.

This responded to several specific circumstances illustrating application of the SFAS 98 requirement that precludes sale-leaseback accounting (with attendant gain or loss recognition) when there is any continuing involvement by the seller other than that of a normal lessee.

Number	Title
D-27	Accounting for the Transfer of Excess Pension Assets to a Retiree Health Care Benefits Account

This states that the transfer of excess pension assets, whether or not made pursuant to the Revenue Reconciliation (Tax) Act of 1990, should be recognized as a negative contribution to the pension fund and a positive contribution to the health care plan; no gain or loss arises from this transaction.

D-30 Adjustment Due to Effect of a Change in Tax Laws or Rates

This simply reinforced the SFAS 109 requirement that the effect of changes in laws or rates is to be recognized when enacted.

D-31 Temporary Differences Related to LIFO Inventory and Tax-to-Tax Differences

This clarified that differences between tax and book LIFO inventory valuations must be tax effected. It also reinforced the rule that only book tax differences are temporary differences under SFAS 109; thus differences between "outside basis" and "inside basis" would not give rise to deferred taxes to be recognized in the financial statements.

D-32 Intraperiod Tax Allocation of the Tax Effect of Pretax Income from Continuing Operations

This item states that while the tax effect of pretax income from continuing operations would not be affected by other items (e.g., extraordinary items) on the income statement, the tax effect of a loss from continuing operations would consider the tax effects of other items, per paragraph 140 of SFAS 109.

D-33 Timing of Recognition of Tax Benefits for Prereorganization Temporary Differences and Carryforwards

This expands the requirements under SFAS 109, relevant to pre- and postacquisition carryforwards, to also apply to pre- and postreorganization carryforwards.

D-34 Accounting for Reinsurance: Questions and Answers about FASB Statement 113

D-35 FASB Staff Views on Issue 93-6, *Accounting for Multiple-Year Retrospectively-Rated Contracts by Ceding and Assuming Enterprises*

D-36 Selection of Discount Rates Used for Measuring Defined Benefit Pension Obligations and Obligations of Postretirement Benefit Plans other than Pensions

This sets forth the SEC's position that discount rates be reflective of current rates as of the balance sheet date.

D-39 Questions Related to the Implementation of FASB Statement 115

This responded to a number of specific factual situations later subsumed by subsequent professional pronouncements.

D-42 The Effect on the Calculation of Earnings Per Share for the Redemption or Induced Conversion of Preferred Stock

This sets forth the SEC staff position that any excess of fair value of consideration transferred over the carrying value of the preferred stock would be accounted for similar to dividends paid to the preferred stockholders for purposes of computing EPS, including when there is a negative excess amount.

D-43 Assurance That a Right of Setoff Is Enforceable in a Bankruptcy under FASB Interpretation 39

This clarifies the "enforceable at law" as used to define a right of setoff encompasses that the right would be upheld in bankruptcy.

D-44 Recognition of Other-Than-Temporary Impairment upon the Planned Sale of a Security Whose Cost Exceeds Fair Value

When there is no expectation of price recovery before a planned sale after the balance sheet date, the decline in fair value should be deemed other than temporary for purposes of loss recognition.

Number	*Title*
D-45	Implementation of FASB Statement 121 for Assets to Be Disposed Of

For purposes of reporting assets to be disposed of at the lower of carrying amount or fair value less costs to sell, carrying amount is acquisition cost net of accumulated depreciation or other basis adjustment as of the date management commits to a plan to dispose of the asset, before any adjustment for the decision to dispose.

D-46   Accounting for Limited Partnership Investments

The SEC's position is that the equity method should be used for investments in limited partnerships unless "minor," meaning under about a 3 to 5% interest.

D-47   Accounting for the Refund of Bank Insurance Fund and Savings Association Insurance Fund Premiums

D-49   Classifying Net Appreciation on Investments of a Donor-Restricted Endowment Fund

D-50   Classification of Gains and Losses from the Termination of an Interest Rate Swap Designated to Commercial Paper

D-51   The Applicability of FASB Statement 115 to Desecuritizations of Financial Assets

The matter of descuritizations was not addressed by either SFAS 115 or 125, but this topic states that, analogizing from the guidance in SFAS 125 on securitizations, no gain or loss would be recognized if a transferor of a securitized pool of assets receives only the underlying loans in exchange. Also, if the assets received are held to maturity, the mere fact of the descuritization transaction would not contradict the intent to hold to maturity.

D-53   Computation of Earnings Per Share for a Period That Includes a Redemption on an Induced Conversion of a Portion of a Class of Preferred Stock

This is a further consideration of the matter addressed at D-42; this topic states that any excess in the context of a partial redemption would be attributed fully to the shares redeemed.

D-54   Accounting by the Purchaser for a Seller's Guarantee of the Adequacy of Liabilities for Losses and Loss Adjustment Expenses of an Insurance Enterprise Acquired in a Purchase Business Combination

D-55   Determining a Highly Inflationary Economy under FASB Statement 52

D-56   Accounting for a Change in Functional Currency and Deferred Taxes When an Economy Becomes Highly Inflationary

D-57   Accounting Issues Relating to the Deposit Insurance Funds Act of 1996

D-58   Effect on Pooling-of-Interests Accounting of Certain Contingently Exercisable Options to Buy Equity Securities

Guidance was superseded by EITF 97-9.

D-61   Classification by the Issuer of Redeemable Instruments That Are Subject to Remarketing Agreements

Long-term debt which the holder has the ability to put back to the issuer, even if the issuer has a "best efforts" remarketing agreement which likely would result in any redeemed debt being immediately resold, must be reported by the issuer as a current obligation.

Number	*Title*
D-69	Gain Recognition on Transfers of Financial Assets under FASB Statement 125

This topic expressed the SEC's concern that gain recognition in situations in which financial assets are sold or securitized with some assets being retained or liabilities incurred was being computed on a discretionary basis; it stresses that the provisions of SFAS 125 are not elective in nature. The fair value allocation methodology to be used is set forth in SFAS 125, and any assumptions made are to be consistently applied over time and adequately disclosed.

D-70	Questions Related to the Implementation of FASB Statement 131

This addresses certain questions arising from the requirement to disclose results of operations on a segment basis. It underscores the requirement that disclosures be consistent with how the chief operating decision maker of the reporting entity evaluates the performance of the segments. It also clarifies that the threshold for segment disclosure, by evaluating the contribution of the segment versus that of the total enterprise, is not altered by the fact that segment results may internally be evaluated by inconsistent criteria by management.

D-71	Accounting Issues Relating to the Introduction of the European Economic and Monetary Union (EMU)

This holds that costs incurred to adapt recordkeeping systems to the new Euro currency are to be expensed as incurred. This conclusion was reached by analogizing from the position taken with regard to Y2K software repairs and upgrades in EITF 96-14. Also, this topic reports the SEC position that comparative financial reports including periods before the Euro was adopted may incorporate restatements of prior periods' results using the Euro exchange rates as of January 1, 1999, with full disclosure being made. Finally, it reports the FASB's belief that cumulative translation adjustments (pertaining to consolidated subsidiaries or equity investees) would not be affected by the Euro adoption.

D-72	Effect of Contracts That May Be Settled in Stock or Cash on the Computation of Diluted Earnings Per Share

This addresses an inconsistency between SFAS 128 (which gives credence to past experience in deciding whether contracts that may be settled in cash or common stock should be deemed potential common stock for diluted EPS computation purposes) and EITF 96-13 (which gives no weight to past experience regarding treatment of freestanding contracts which would be optionally settled in the entity's stock). It concludes that adjustments similar to those specified by SFAS 128 should be made, when warranted by past experience, for those set forth in EITF 96-13 as well. However, since this matter is to be further deliberated, this guidance is said to be nonauthoritative.

D-73	Reclassification and Subsequent Sales of Securities in Connection with the Adoption of FASB Statement 133

Pertaining to the SFAS 133 transition provision that permits transfers from held-to-maturity to other classifications without "tainting" other held-to-maturity securities, this states that if financial assets transferred are later sold in the same reporting quarter, the transfer must be to the trading category. Any gain or loss as of the date of the reclassification must be taken into income as part of the cumulative effect of adopting SFAS 133, and not included as realized gain or loss from trading for the quarter.

D-74	Issues Concerning the Scope of the AICPA Guide on Investment Companies

AICPA STATEMENTS OF POSITION (1974-2001)

Audit and Accounting Guides

Agricultural Producers and Agricultural Cooperatives
Airlines
Audit Sampling
Auditing Derivative Instruments, Hedging Activities, and Investments in Securities
Banks and Savings Institutions
Brokers and Dealers in Securities
Casinos
Certain Nonprofit Organizations
Colleges and Universities
Common Interest Realty Associations
Consideration of Internal Control in a Financial Statement Audit
Construction Contractors
Credit Unions
Employee Benefit Plans
Entities With Oil and Gas Producing Activities
Federal Government Contractors
Finance Companies
Health Care Organizations
Investment Companies
Life and Health Insurance Entities
Not-for-Profit Organizations
Personal Financial Statements
Property and Liability Insurance Companies
Prospective Financial Information
State and Local Governmental Units

Stock Life Insurance Companies
Use of Real Estate Appraisal Information
Voluntary Health and Welfare Organizations

OTHER GAAP SOURCES

Issues Papers of the Accounting Standards Division

Issues Papers of the AICPA's Accounting Standards Division primarily identify financial accounting and reporting issues that the Division believed needed addressing by the Financial Accounting Standards Board. These pronouncements constitute generally accepted accounting principles but are not mandatory.

Title	*Date Issued*
Accounting for Changes in Estimates	12/15/78
Accounting for Allowances for Losses on Certain Real Estate and Loan and Receivables Collateralized by Real Estate	6/21/79
Joint Venture Accounting	7/17/79
"Push Down" Accounting	10/30/79
Accounting in Consolidation for Issuances of a Subsidiary Stock	6/30/80
Certain Issues That Affect Accounting for Minority Interest in Consolidated Financial Statements	3/17/81
Depreciation of Income-Producing Real Estate	11/16/81
The Acceptability of "Simplified LIFO" for Financial Reporting Purposes	10/14/82
Accounting for Employee Capital Accumulation Plans	11/4/82
Computation of Premium Deficiencies in Insurance Enterprises	3/26/84
Accounting by Stock Life Insurance Companies for Annuities, Universal Life, and Related Products and Accounting for Nonguaranteed-Premium Products	11/5/84
Identification and Discussion of Certain Financial Accounting and Reporting Issues Concerning LIFO Inventories	11/30/84
Accounting for Options	3/6/86
The Use of Discounting in Financial Reporting for Monetary Items with Uncertain Terms other than Those Covered by Existing Authoritative Literature	9/9/87
Quasi Reorganizations	10/28/88

Practice Bulletins

1. Purpose and Scope of AcSEC Practice Bulletins and Procedures for Their Issuance

Title	*Date Issued*
ACRS Lives and GAAP	11/23/81
Accounting by Colleges and Universities for Compensated Absences	9/13/82
ADC Arrangements	2/10/86

2. Elimination of Profits Resulting from Intercompany Transfers of LIFO Inventories — 11/87
4. Accounting for Foreign Debt/Equity Swaps — 5/88
5. Income Recognition on Loans to Financially Troubled Countries — 7/88
6. Amortization of Discounts on Certain Acquired Loans — 8/89
8. Application of FASB Statement 97 to Insurance Enterprises — 11/90
11. Accounting for Preconfirmation Contingencies in Fresh Start Reporting — 3/94
13. Direct Response Advertising and Probable Future Benefits — 12/94
14. Accounting and Reporting by Limited Liability Companies and Limited Liability Partnerships — 4/95
15. Accounting by the Issuer of Surplus Notes — 1/95

Websites

See page 21.

WILEY

GAAP
2002

Interpretation and Application of
GENERALLY ACCEPTED
ACCOUNTING PRINCIPLES
2002

1 RESEARCHING GAAP PROBLEMS

DEVELOPMENT OF GAAP

What Is GAAP?

Generally accepted accounting principles (GAAP) are concerned with the measurement of economic activity, the time when such measurements are made and recorded, the disclosures surrounding these activities, and the preparation and presentation of summarized economic information in the form of financial statements. GAAP develops when questions arise about how to best accomplish those activities—measurement, timing of recognition, disclosure, or presentation. In response to those questions, either GAAP is promulgated via official pronouncements of authoritative bodies empowered to create it, or it evolves over time when authoritative bodies fail to respond. Thus, GAAP is a reaction to and a product of the economic environment in which it is developed. As such, the development of accounting and financial reporting standards has somewhat lagged the progression of increasingly intricate economic structures and transactions.

In APB 4, the Accounting Principles Board stated

> ***Generally accepted accounting principles*** *therefore is a technical term in financial accounting. Generally accepted accounting principles encompass the conventions, rules, and procedures necessary to define accepted accounting practice at a particular time. The standard of "generally accepted accounting principles" includes not only broad guidelines of general application, but also detailed practices and procedures.*
>
> *Generally accepted accounting principles are conventional—that is, they become generally accepted by agreement (often tacit agreement) rather than by formal derivation from a set of postulates or basic concepts. The principles have developed on the basis of experience, reason, custom, usage, and, to a significant extent, practical necessity.*

Accounting principles are usually directed toward solutions that are objective, conservative, and verifiable. There are two broad categories of accounting principles—recognition and disclosure. Recognition principles determine the timing and measurement of items that enter the accounting cycle and impact the financial statements. These are quantitative standards that require economic information to be reflected numerically.

Disclosure principles deal with factors that are not always numerical. Disclosures involve qualitative information that is an essential ingredient of a full set of financial statements. Their absence would make the financial statements created by recognition principles misleading by themselves. Disclosure principles complement recognition principles by explaining assumptions underlying the numerical information and giving other information on accounting policies, contingencies, uncertainties, etc., which are essential ingredients in the analytical process of accounting.

The Hierarchy of GAAP

The Auditing Standards Board (ASB) is the senior authoritative organization in the promulgation of generally accepted auditing standards. Those standards require that an audit report should express an opinion about whether the financial statements "present fairly in conformity with generally accepted accounting principles." Thus, the ASB endeavored to define the meaning of that phrase and to delineate the sources of GAAP. The determination of which accounting principle is applicable under a particular set of conditions may be difficult or even impossible without a determination of the hierarchy of GAAP by an authoritative body.

In AU 411 (SAS 69), the ASB identified the following as the sources of established generally accepted accounting principles:

A. Accounting principles promulgated by a body designated by the AICPA Council to establish such principles, pursuant to rule 203 [ET section 203.01] of the AICPA Code of Professional Conduct.
B. Pronouncements of bodies, composed of expert accountants, that deliberate accounting issues in public forums for the purpose of establishing accounting principles or describing existing accounting practices that are generally accepted, provided those pronouncements have been exposed for public comment and have been cleared by a body referred to in category A.
C. Pronouncements of bodies, organized by a body referred to in category A and composed of expert accountants, that deliberate accounting issues in public forums for the purpose of interpreting or establishing accounting principles or describing existing accounting practices that are generally accepted, or pronouncements referred to in category B that have been cleared by a body referred to in category A but have not been exposed for public comment.
D. Practices or pronouncements that are widely recognized as being generally accepted because they represent prevalent practice in a particular industry, or the knowledgeable application to specific circumstances of pronouncements that are generally accepted.

Compliance with accounting pronouncements included in category A is mandatory. An auditor should not express an unqualified opinion if the financial statements contain a material departure from category A pronouncements unless, due to unusual circumstances, adherence to the pronouncements would make the statements misleading. Rule 203 implies that application of officially established accounting principles almost always results in fair presentation in conformity with generally accepted accounting principles.

If an accounting treatment is not specified by a pronouncement covered by Rule 203, the accountant/auditor should proceed next to categories B, C, or D using the treatment specified by the source in the highest category. If an accounting pronouncement in category B, C, or D is relevant to the circumstances, an auditor must follow that pronouncement or be able to justify the conclusion that another treatment is generally accepted.

For financial statements of entities other than governmental entities[1]

    a. Category A, officially established accounting principles, consists of Financial Accounting Standards Board (FASB) Statements of Financial Accounting Standards and Interpretations, Accounting Principles Board (APB) Opinions, and AICPA Accounting Research Bulletins.

    b. Category B consists of FASB Technical Bulletins and, if cleared by the FASB, AICPA Industry Audit and Accounting Guides and AICPA Statements of Position.

    c. Category C consists of AICPA Accounting Standards Executive Committee (AcSEC) Practice Bulletins that have been cleared by the FASB and consensus positions of the FASB Emerging Issues Task Force.

    d. Category D includes AICPA accounting interpretations and implementation guides (Qs and As) published by the FASB staff, and practices that are widely recognized and prevalent either generally or in the industry.

In the absence of any source of established accounting principles, other accounting literature may be considered. These would include APB Statements, AICPA Issues Papers, FASB Statements of Financial Accounting Concepts, International Accounting Standards Committee Statements of International Accounting Standards, Governmental Accounting Standards Board Statements, Interpretations and Technical Bulletins, Technical Information Service Inquiries and Replies included in AICPA Technical Practice Aids, pronouncements of other professional associations or regulatory agencies, and accounting textbooks and articles. The use of those other sources depends upon their relevance to particular circumstances, the

---

[1] *The description of a governmental entity, which was agreed to in a joint meeting of the FASB and GASB Boards in 1996, states*

    Public corporations and bodies corporate and politic are governmental organizations. Other organizations are governmental organizations if they have one or more of the following characteristics:

      a. Popular election of officers or appointment (or approval) of a controlling majority of the members of the organization's governing body by officials of one or more state or local governments;

      b. The potential for unilateral dissolution by a government with the net assets reverting to a government; or

      c. The power to enact and enforce a tax levy.

    Furthermore, organizations are presumed to be governmental if they have the ability to issue directly (rather than through a state or municipal authority) debt that pays interest exempt from federal taxation. However, organizations possessing only that ability (to issue tax-exempt debt) and none of the other governmental characteristics may rebut the presumption that they are governmental if their determination is supported by compelling relevant evidence.

*This publication does not describe GAAP for governmental entities. Readers who are interested in learning more should consult the Wiley publication, **GAAP for Governments.***

specificity of the guidance, and the general recognition of the author or issuing organization as an authority. This would mean that FASB publications in this category would be more influential in establishing an acceptable accounting practice than would an accounting textbook. Guidance in this category would require more judgment and a broader search of literature than would be true in the other three categories.

Who Created GAAP?

Committee on Accounting Procedure. The first serious attempt to create generally accepted accounting principles began in 1930, primarily as a consequence of the stock market crash of the 1920s and the widespread perception that an absence of uniform and stringent financial reporting requirements had contributed to that crash. The American Institute of Accountants, later to become the American Institute of Certified Public Accountants (AIPCA), created a special committee to work with the New York Stock Exchange toward the goal of establishing standards for accounting procedures. The special committee recommended five rules to the Exchange which later (in 1938) were published as Accounting Research Bulletin (ARB) 1 of the Committee on Accounting Procedure. The Committee subsequently published 51 such bulletins, including Accounting Research Bulletin 43, which consolidated and superseded Bulletins 1-42. The Committee was also instrumental in attempting to achieve uniformity in accounting terminology. However, the Committee's limited resources and lack of serious research efforts in support of its pronouncements were questioned in the late 1950s, particularly as a number of very complex controversial topics loomed on the horizon.

Accounting Principles Board. The profession's response was to substitute the Accounting Principles Board (APB) for the Committee on Accounting Procedure, in order to facilitate the development of principles based primarily on the research of the Accounting Research Division. Under this new strategy, the Division was to undertake extensive and exhaustive research, publish its findings, and then permit the Accounting Principles Board to take the lead in the discussions that would ensue concerning accounting principles and practices. The Board's authority was enforced primarily through prestige and Rule 203 of the Code of Professional Ethics. Furthermore, formal approval of Board issuances by the Securities and Exchange Commission (SEC) gave additional support to its activities.

During the fourteen years of the Board, 31 opinions and 4 statements were issued. They dealt with amendments of Accounting Research Bulletins, opinions on the form and content of financial statements, and issuances requiring changes in both the recognition and disclosure principles of the profession. However, the Board did not utilize the Accounting Research Division, which published fifteen research studies during its lifetime. Both the Board and the Division acted independently in selecting topics for their respective agendas. The Board issued pronouncements in areas where little research had been done, and the Division performed research studies without seeking to be all-inclusive or exhaustive in analysis. The Accounting Principles Board did not operate differently than the Committee on Accounting Procedure.

Financial Accounting Standards Board. As a result of these operational problems and based on the recommendations of the Wheat Study Group, the Financial Accounting Standards Board (FASB) was formed in 1972. The Board consists of seven full-time members; they have diverse backgrounds with three coming from public accounting, two from private industry and one each from academia and an oversight body. The Board is assisted by a staff of professionals who conduct research and work directly with the Board. Although there is some controversy and disagreement as to its activities and pronouncements, the FASB continues to operate with the confidence of accounting practitioners and various business organizations.[2]

The FASB is recognized as authoritative through Financial Reporting Release No. 1 by the Securities and Exchange Commission and through Rule 203, Rules of Conduct by the AICPA.

The FASB is an independent body relying on the Financial Accounting Foundation for selection of its members and receipt of its budgets. Funds are raised from contributions made to the Foundation. The Board of Trustees of the Foundation is made up from members of the

> American Accounting Association
> American Institute of Certified Public Accountants
> Association for Investment Management and Research
> Financial Executives Institute
> Government Finance Officers Association
> Institute of Management Accountants
> National Association of State Auditors, Comptrollers, and Treasurers
> Securities Industry Association

There is also a Financial Accounting Standards Advisory Council that has responsibility for consulting with the Board on major areas of inquiry and analysis.

The Board issues several types of pronouncements. Statements of Financial Accounting Standards and Interpretations are the most important of these because they are category A GAAP. Interpretations are used to clarify or elaborate on existing Statements or pronouncements of predecessor bodies. Technical Bulletins, which are category B GAAP, usually address issues not covered directly by existing

---

[2] *To date, the FASB has issued 140 Statements on Financial Accounting Standards, 44 Interpretations, and 52 Technical Bulletins, and devoted substantial time and resources towards developing a Conceptual Framework for Financial Accounting, which has resulted in the issuance of 7 Concepts Statements. (Since a number of standards have been superseded and a few more have been withdrawn, the number of standards, interpretations, etc., which remain in force are somewhat fewer than the total promulgated. However, the preponderance of GAAP extant is the product of the FASB, and not of its predecessors.)*

standards and are primarily used to provide guidance where it is not expected to be costly or create a major change. Bulletins are discussed at Board meetings and subject to Board veto. Both Bulletins and Interpretations are designed to be responsive to implementation and practice problems on relatively narrow subjects.

American Institute of Certified Public Accountants (AICPA). The Accounting Standards Executive Committee (AcSEC) is the senior technical committee at the AICPA. It is composed of fifteen volunteer members, representative of industry, academia, analysts, and both national and regional public accounting firms. All AcSEC members are CPAs and members of the AICPA.

AcSEC is authorized to set accounting standards and to speak for the AICPA on accounting matters. The accounting standards that AcSEC issues are prepared largely through the work of AICPA committees and task forces. AcSEC issues Statements of Position (SOPs) and industry audit and accounting guides, which are reviewed and cleared by the FASB and thus are category B GAAP. SOPs provide guidance on financial accounting and reporting issues. Industry audit and accounting guides provide guidance to auditors in examining and reporting on financial statements of entities in specific industries and provide standards on accounting problems unique to a particular industry. AcSEC Practice Bulletins (category C GAAP) usually provide guidance on very narrowly defined accounting issues. AcSEC's standards-setting activities are often industry-specific or narrow in their scope, unlike the majority of FASB's projects, which are broader in scope.

AcSEC also issues technical practice aids and issues papers. Technical Practice Aids are answers published by the AICPA Technical Information Service to questions about accounting and auditing standards. AICPA Issues Papers are research documents about accounting and reporting problems that the AICPA believes should be resolved by the FASB. They provide information about alternative accounting treatments used in practice. These two AICPA publications, which are not approved by the FASB, have no authoritative status but can be helpful in understanding and resolving issues for which there is no authoritative literature. However, because the AICPA is the primary professional organization of accountants, those who depart from guidance in their nonauthoritative publications must be prepared to justify that departure based upon the facts and circumstances of the particular situation.

Emerging Issues Task Force (EITF). The Emerging Issues Task Force (EITF) was formed in 1984 by the FASB in order to assist the Board in identifying current or emerging issues and implementation problems that may need to be placed on the agenda of the Board. Task Force members are drawn primarily from public accounting firms but also include individuals who would be aware of issues and practices that should be considered by the group. The Task Force meets every other month with persons representing the SEC and FASB in attendance for discussion but not voting purposes.

For each agenda item, an issues paper is developed by members, their firms, or the FASB staff. After discussion by the Task Force, a consensus may be reached on the issue, in which case further action by the FASB is not needed. An EITF consensus is category C GAAP. If no consensus is reached, the problem may end up on the Board agenda or be resolved by the SEC or AICPA. It is also possible that no consensus is reached and the issue remains unresolved with no organization currently working on the problem. These may be in especially narrow areas having little broad-based interest. Occasionally, the FASB may include a narrow issue in the scope of a broader project and reaffirm or supersede the work of the Task Force.

The FASB publishes a volume of EITF Abstracts, which are summaries of each issue paper and the results of Task Force discussion. A listing of the Issues considered by the Emerging Issues Task Force and the status concerning resolution of each issue appears in the front of this publication following other more authoritative pronouncements.

The SEC believes that a Task Force consensus is GAAP for public companies, and they will question any accounting that differs from it. Remember, although EITF pronouncements are technically category C GAAP, they are so specialized that there is really no category A or B GAAP on their topics. In addition, the SEC feels that the EITF works to supply a forum to discuss accounting concerns and to assist in providing advice in a public forum. Thus, they are supportive of the Task Force work.

The EITF has been severely criticized for promulgating GAAP without sufficient due process procedures. Only a limited audience is aware of each issue, and the period of exposure is sometimes very brief. However, the Task Force resolves problems in an environment where delay would often result in widespread and divergent practices of accounting becoming entrenched. The guidance provided is often on narrow issues that are of immediate interest and importance.

As part of the issuances and consensus underlying the Emerging Issues Task Force (EITF) pronouncements, the FASB has also released discussions on various technical topics. These issuances are FASB staff announcements and SEC staff announcements that are discussed at EITF meetings. They represent discussions of technical matters that are deemed important by the FASB or SEC staff and do not relate specifically to a numbered EITF issue. These are designed to help and provide guidance on the application of relevant accounting concepts. A listing of the EITF Discussion Issues, with a short summary of each, appears in the front of this publication following the listing of the EITF Issues.

How is GAAP Created?

The FASB and AICPA adhere to rigorous "due process" when creating new guidance in category A and category B GAAP. The goal is to involve experts who would be affected by the newly issued guidance so that the standards created will result in information that reports economic activity as objectively as possible without attempting to influence behavior in any particular direction. Ultimately, how-ever, the guidance is the judgment of the FASB or the AICPA, based on research, public input, and deliberation. The process described below is the FASB's proce-dures; the AICPA follows similar procedures in its projects.

The FASB receives requests for new standards from all parts of its diverse con-stituency, including auditors, industry groups, the EITF, and the SEC. Requests for action include both suggestions for new topics and suggestions for reconsideration of existing pronouncements. For each major project it adds to its technical agenda, the FASB begins by appointing an advisory task force of approximately fifteen out-side experts. Care is taken to ensure that various points of view are represented on the task force. The task force meets with and advises the Board and staff on the definition and scope of the project and the nature and extent of any additional re-search that may be needed. The FASB and its staff then meet to debate the signifi-cant issues in the project and to arrive at tentative conclusions. As it does so, the FASB and its staff study existing literature on the subject and conduct or commis-sion any additional research as may be necessary. The task force meetings and the Board meetings are open to public observation and a public record is maintained.

If the accounting problem being considered by the Board is especially complex, the FASB will begin by publishing a Discussion Memorandum or other discussion document. The discussion document generally sets forth the definition of the prob-lem, the scope of the project, and the financial accounting and reporting issues; dis-cusses research findings and relevant literature; and presents alternative solutions to the issues under consideration and the arguments and implications relative to each. It is distributed to interested parties by request and available on the FASB website. The document is prepared by the FASB staff with the advice and assistance of the task force. It specifies a deadline for written comments and often contains an invi-tation to present viewpoints at a public hearing.

Any individual or organization may request to speak at the public hearing, which is conducted by the FASB and the staff assigned to the project. Public ob-servers are welcome. After each individual speaks, the FASB and staff ask ques-tions. Questions are based on written material submitted by the speakers prior to the hearing as well as on the speaker's oral comments. In addition to the hearing, the staff analyzes all the written comments submitted. The FASB members study this analysis and read the comment letters to help them in reaching conclusions. The hearing transcript and written comments become part of the public record.

After the comment letters and oral presentations responding to the discussion document are considered, formal deliberations begin. (If the accounting problem is not as complex and no discussion document was issued, the due process begins at this point.) The FASB deliberates at meetings that are open to public observation, although observers do not participate in the discussions. The agenda for each meeting is announced in advance. Prior to each Board meeting, the staff presents a written analysis and recommendations of the issues to be discussed. During the meeting, the staff presents orally a summary of the written materials and the Board discusses each issue presented. The Board meets as many times as is necessary to resolve the issues.

When the Board has reached tentative conclusions on all the issues in the project, the staff prepares an Exposure Draft. The Exposure Draft sets forth the Board's conclusions about the proposed standards of financial accounting and reporting, the proposed effective date and method of transition, background information, and an explanation of the basis for the Board's conclusions. The Board reviews, and if necessary, revises, the Exposure Draft. Then, a vote is taken about whether the Exposure Draft can be published for public comment. Five of the seven Board members must vote to approve an Exposure Draft for issuance for comment. If five votes are not obtained, the FASB holds additional meetings and redrafts the Exposure Draft.

Any individual or organization can provide comments about the conclusions in the Exposure Draft during the exposure period, which is generally sixty days or more. The Board may also decide to have a public hearing to hear constituents' views. At the conclusion of the comment period, all comment letters and oral presentations are analyzed by the staff, and the Board members read the letters and the staff analysis. Then, the Board is ready to redeliberate the issues, with the goal of issuing final accounting standards.

As in the earlier process, all Board meetings are open to the public. During these meetings, the Board considers the comments received and may revise their earlier conclusions. If substantial modifications are made, the Board will issue a revised Exposure Draft for additional public comment. If so, the Board also may decide that another public hearing is necessary. When the Board is satisfied that all reasonable alternatives have been adequately considered, the staff drafts a final pronouncement for the Board's vote. Five votes are required for adoption of a pronouncement. Once issued, the standards become GAAP after the effective date stated in the pronouncement.

Materiality

Materiality as a concept has great significance in understanding, researching, and implementing GAAP. Each Statement of Financial Accounting Standards (SFAS) issued by the FASB concludes by stating that the provisions of the statement are not applicable to immaterial items.

Materiality is defined by the FASB as the magnitude of an omission or misstatement in the financial statements that makes it probable that a reasonable person relying on those statements would have been influenced by the information or made a different judgment if the correct information had been known. Thus, materiality judgments are primarily quantitative in nature. However, the nature of a transaction or event can affect a determination of whether that transaction or event is material. For example, a transaction that, if recorded, changes a profit to a loss or changes compliance with ratios in a debt covenant to noncompliance would be material even if it involved an otherwise immaterial amount. Also, a transaction that might be judged immaterial if it occurred as part of routine operations may be material if it occurs in abnormal circumstances.

Another factor in judging materiality is the degree of precision that is possible to attain when making an estimate. For example, accounts payable can usually be estimated more accurately than a possible loss from the incurrence of an environmental liability. An error that would be material in estimating accounts payable might be acceptable in estimating the contingency.

Materiality as a criterion has both qualitative and quantitative aspects. Certain events or transactions may be deemed to be material because of the nature of the item, regardless of the dollar amounts involved, and thus to require disclosure under any circumstance. The enactment of prohibition (outlawing the sale of most alcoholic beverages) was a significant event to companies that produced and sold such products. Offers to buy or sell assets for more or less than book value, litigation proceedings against the company pursuant to price-fixing or antitrust allegations, and active negotiations involving future profitability are all examples of items that would not be capable of being evaluated for materiality based solely upon numerical calculations.

Quantitatively, materiality has been defined in a few accounting standards. For example, in SFAS 131, *Disclosures about Segments of an Enterprise and Related Information*, a material segment or customer is defined as 10% or more of revenues. In general, FASB has resisted requests to define materiality.

The Securities and Exchange Commission has in several of its pronouncements defined materiality as 1% of total assets for receivables from officers and stockholders, 5% of total assets for separate balance sheet disclosure of items, and 10% of total revenues for disclosure of oil and gas producing activities.

Material information is that information whose absence makes the financial statements misleading. However, that definition does not sufficiently explain the concept to provide guidance in distinguishing material information from immaterial information. The individual accountant must exercise professional judgment in evaluating information and concluding on its materiality.

Standards Overload

In recent years a complaint has arisen that there are too many accounting standards and too many organizations issuing pronouncements that create accounting standards. Some say solutions are needed to reduce and simplify existing GAAP either for all entities or at least for those entities where enforcement of such standards is not cost justified. Both the FASB and the AICPA have undertaken studies in order to seek to simplify or eliminate certain accounting principles.

A list of onerous standards will vary depending upon personal preferences and problems. Generally, standards that are complicated, such as those on leases and income taxes, will find their way onto nearly everyone's list.

The search for simplicity is not an easy process. Complex business and economic activities may not lend themselves to simple accounting standards to measure and disclose them. If simplicity means having to make an incorrect measurement, many users will have to choose between erroneous financial statements, which do not reflect economic reality, and complicated accounting standards. A reduction in standards could ultimately reduce the quality of financial reporting.

Some have suggested that different entities should follow different standards. Differential standards require a selection of a system by which to categorize entities by the standards they should follow. Some recommend a size test with large entities following complete standards and small entities following a simpler set of standards. Size might be determined by assets, sales, net worth, or number of owners. Another possibility is an ownership test, with public companies following a different and more comprehensive set of standards than privately owned businesses. However, different disclosure standards may reduce the quantity of financial information available for certain entities as well as the quality of that information. Different recognition standards again may create erroneous financial statements in terms of economic reality. However, the difficulty in making a selection of which entities apply which standards and the added complexity caused by two sets of different standards obviously compounds the standard overload problem instead of reducing it.

The search for simpler accounting standards is not hopeless, however. Where research shows that disclosures are not utilized or understood by the users of financial data, such disclosures can be dropped. If recognition standards differentiate between events that are clearly not different from an economic viewpoint, those standards add nonessential complications and can be amended. For example, all business combinations constitute an economic union and the terms purchase and pooling have no meaning in economic theory. Also, all leases give rise to liabilities, as future obligations, and assets, as future economic benefits. The differentiation of some leases as capital and others as operating may be a highly subjective concept.

The search for easier, simpler, and fewer accounting standards will continue. Certain differential standards in terms of disclosures have already been adopted, allowing nonpublic entities to avoid disclosing earnings per share, segment data, certain benefit information, and retroactive effects of a business combination. As the FASB considers future pronouncements on accounting standards, the issue of cost-benefit and applicability to all segments of the profession will be considerations. The standards overload issue will not fade away because there are numerous problems with the potential solutions that have been suggested.

RESEARCHING PUBLISHED GAAP

Researching Authoritative Sources of GAAP

Researching the appropriate GAAP to answer an accounting question begins with the analysis of publications issued by the entities that set the accounting standards in the GAAP hierarchy—the FASB, the AICPA, and the EITF.

The FASB publishes two sets of books (both looseleaf and bound) that can assist in researching accounting issues. (These and other materials are now also available on CD-ROM.) The *Current Text* integrates all of the currently recognized category A GAAP alphabetically in topic order (e.g., Accounting Changes, Business Combinations, etc.). The AICPA Research Bulletins, APB Opinions, and FASB Statements and Interpretations have been combined to create this integrated document. Supplemental guidance from the AICPA Accounting Interpretations and FASB Technical Bulletins are also incorporated. All the materials have been edited down from the original pronouncements and thus may lack the clarity that can be obtained only from the unedited version. Descriptive material including reasons for conclusions is missing. Each paragraph in the *Current Text* is referenced back to the original pronouncement for research or follow-up. The first volume of the *Current Text* deals with general standards, and the second volume contains standards for specialized industries.

The *Original Pronouncements* contains all of the AICPA Accounting Research Bulletins, Interpretations and Terminology Bulletins, the APB Opinions, Statements and Interpretations, the FASB Standards, Interpretations, Concepts, Technical Bulletins, and Exposure Drafts. The first volume contains only FASB Statements. The second volume contains all of the other pronouncements. Paragraphs containing accounting principles that have been superseded or dropped are shaded in order to make the user aware. Those changes are identified in detail by a status page placed at the beginning of each pronouncement that can reference the user to other areas and pronouncements.

Essentially, if you need a quick answer to a specific question, the *Current Text* can be accessed quickly. If you need to understand the answer and the reasons for it, the *Original Pronouncements* will afford you the opportunity to study the area in depth.

The FASB also publishes the *EITF Abstracts* (category C GAAP). Each EITF issue discussed by the Task Force is included in the book, regardless of whether a consensus was reached, in the order in which they were added to the EITF agenda. A status section at the end of each issue indicates whether the consensus has been superseded or remains relevant and whether any additional EITF discussion is planned.

The AICPA publishes all its outstanding Statements of Position (category B GAAP) and Practice Bulletins (category C GAAP) in *AICPA Technical Practice Aids.* That book is set up similar to FASB's *Original Pronouncements,* with the

SOPs and Practice Bulletins included in the order in which they were issued. There are 22 audit and accounting guides (category B GAAP). They are

- Agricultural Producers and Cooperatives
- Airlines
- Banks and Savings Institutions
- Brokers and Dealers in Securities
- Casinos
- Common Interest Realty Associations
- Consideration of Internal Control in a Financial Statement Audit
- Construction Contractors
- Credit Unions
- Derivative Instruments, Hedging Activities, and Investments in Securities
- Employee Benefit Plans
- Entities with Oil and Gas Producing Activities
- Federal Government Contractors
- Finance Companies
- Health Care Organizations
- Investment Companies
- Life and Health Insurance Entities
- Not-for-Profit Organizations
- Personal Financial Statements
- Property and Liability Insurance Companies
- Prospective Financial Information
- State and Local Governmental Units
- Use of Real Estate Appraisal Information

These publications are available in soft-cover and on CD-ROM.

Nonpromulgated GAAP

Not all GAAP came about because of a deliberation process and issuance of pronouncements by authoritative bodies. Certain principles and practices evolved into current acceptability without adopted standards. Depreciation methods such as straight-line and declining balance are both acceptable, as are inventory costing methods such as LIFO and FIFO. There are, however, no definitive pronouncements that can be found to state this. There are many disclosure principles that evolved into general accounting practice because they were required by the SEC in documents submitted to them. Among these are reconciling the actual rate with the statutory rate used in determining income tax expense, when not otherwise obvious from the financial statements themselves. Even much of the form and content of balance sheets and income statements has evolved over the years.

Researching nonpromulgated GAAP consists of reviewing pronouncements in areas similar to those being researched, and careful reading of the relevant portions of the FASB Conceptual Framework (Appendix). Understanding concepts and intentions espoused by the deliberative authorities can give the essential clues to a logical formulation of alternatives and conclusions regarding problems that have not yet been addressed by these authorities.

Both the AICPA and the FASB publish a myriad of nonauthoritative literature. The FASB publishes the documents it uses in its due process: Discussion Memorandums, Invitations to Comment, Exposure Drafts, and Preliminary Views. It also publishes research reports, *Status Report,* and implementation guidance. The AICPA publishes its Exposure Drafts, as well as Issues Papers, its comment letters on proposals of other standard-setting bodies, and the *Journal of Accountancy.* Listings of their publications are available at their websites. (A list of website addresses is located at the end of this chapter, immediately before the Appendix.)

The Securities and Exchange Commission issues Staff Accounting Bulletins and makes rulings on individual cases that come before it, which create and impose accounting standards on those whose financial statements are submitted to the Commission. The SEC, through acts passed by Congress, has broad powers to prescribe accounting practices and methods for all statements filed with it. Although it has usually preferred to encourage the development of standards in the private sector by deferring to the AICPA and FASB, the SEC has occasionally adopted policies that conflict with established standards. In each case, the result has been a veto by the SEC of the standard, and the AICPA or FASB has withdrawn or amended the standard to conform to SEC policy. However, the history of the SEC is one of cooperative assistance in the formulation of accounting standards. Congressional committees have been critical of the SEC in instances where they felt that too much power was ceded to the profession itself without adequate oversight by the Commission.

The American Accounting Association is an organization consisting primarily of accounting educators. It is devoted to encouraging research into accounting theory and practice. The issuances of the AAA tend to be normative, that is, prescribing what GAAP ought to be like, rather than explaining current standards. However, the monographs, committee reports, and *The Accounting Review* published by the AAA may be useful sources for research into applicable accounting standards.

Governmental agencies such as the Government Accounting Office and the Cost Accounting Standards Board have offered certain publications that may assist in researching written standards. Also, industry organizations and associations may be other helpful sources.

Certain publications are helpful in identifying practices used by entities that may not be promulgated as standards. The AICPA publishes an annual survey of the accounting and disclosure policies of many public companies in *Accounting Trends and Techniques* and maintains a library of financial statements that can be accessed through a computerized search process (NAARS). EDGAR (Electronic Data Gathering, Analysis, and Retrieval) publishes the SEC filing of public companies, which includes the companies' financial statements. Through selection of keywords and/or topics, these services can provide information on whether other entities have had similar problems and the methods used in accounting for them.

Researching Using This Publication

This publication can assist in researching generally accepted accounting principles in order to find technical answers to specific inquiries. A listing of all authoritative accounting pronouncements **still in effect** appears in numerical order in the front of this publication immediately following the table of contents. The listed pronouncements are referenced both to the *Current Text* published by the FASB and to pages in this publication. Using this list, you can trace to or from this publication to both the original pronouncements and/or the *Current Text*. The reader can therefore find more detail on each and every topic covered in this publication and also be aware of which topics and pronouncements are not covered within this publication at all. This should make research cross-referencing quick and reliable.

With respect to the EITF pronouncements, the current status of each issues paper is indicated; that is, whether superseded, resolved, or consensus reached by the EITF. The reader can identify any or all of the EITF issues papers that would be relevant to the current research. We have included EITF issues for which a consensus was reached in this publication at the end of the chapters to which they relate. The consensuses for some pervasive issues are included within the chapters themselves. Because EITF issues are generally on narrow issues, there is often no category A or B GAAP that would apply. Accordingly, EITF consensus represents the highest level of GAAP available for each topic. The inclusion in this publication of EITF summaries is recognizing the relative importance of these consensuses.

The reader, therefore, can be directed by this publication to the specific professional authoritative literature concerning the area of inquiry. In a like manner, the reader of the professional literature can use the listing of authoritative accounting pronouncements to quickly locate the pages in this publication relevant to each specific pronouncement.

The Conceptual Framework

The FASB has issued seven pronouncements called Statements of Financial Accounting Concepts (SFAC) in a series designed to constitute a foundation of financial accounting standards. The framework is designed to prescribe the nature, function, and limits of financial accounting and to be used as a guideline that will lead to consistent standards. These conceptual statements do not establish accounting standards or disclosure practices for particular items. They are not enforceable under the Rules of Conduct of the Code of Professional Ethics.

Of the seven SFAC, the fourth, *Objectives of Financial Reporting by Nonbusiness Organizations*, is not covered here due to its specialized nature.

SFAC 1, *Objectives of Financial Reporting by Business Enterprises*, identified three objectives of financial reporting. The objectives are to provide useful information for economic decisions, to provide understandable information capable of predicting cash flows, and to provide relevant information about economic resources and the transactions, events, and circumstances that change them.

SFAC 2, *Qualitative Characteristics of Accounting Information*, identifies the qualities that make information useful. Under a cost-benefit constraint, the primary qualities of useful information are that it be relevant and reliable. Relevant information is timely and either aids in predicting the future or in providing knowledge of the past (feedback value). Reliable information is verifiable and neutral and it faithfully represents events. In addition, such information must be comparable, consistent, and understandable.

SFAC 3, *Elements of Financial Statements of Business Enterprises*, has been replaced by SFAC 6. SFAC 6 amended this statement to include financial reporting by not-for-profit organizations.

SFAC 5, *Recognition and Measurement in Financial Statements of Enterprises*, sets forth recognition criteria that determine what information should be in financial statements and the timing of when that information will appear. A full set of such statements would show financial position at the end of a period, earnings, comprehensive income and cash flows for the period, and investments by and distributions to owners during the period.

SFAC 6, *Elements of Financial Statements*, defines ten elements as the basic components of financial statements. Three of these elements (assets, liabilities, and equity) relate to the balance sheet and are discussed in depth in Chapter 2, Balance Sheet. Five elements (revenues, expenses, gains, losses, and comprehensive income) relate to the performance of an entity over time and are discussed in Chapter 3, Statements of Income and Comprehensive Income. The remaining two elements (investments by owners and distributions to owners) relate to the transfer between a business enterprise and its owners and are discussed in Chapter 17, Stockholders' Equity.

SFAC 7, *Using Cash Flow Information and Present Value in Accounting Measurements*, provides a framework for using future cash flows as the basis for accounting measurements either at initial recognition or when assets are remeasured at fair value (fresh-start measurements). It also provides a framework for using the interest method of amortization. It provides the principles that govern measurement using present value, especially when the amount of future cash flows, their timing, or both are uncertain. However, it does not address recognition questions, such as which transactions and events should be valued using present value measures or when fresh-start measurements are appropriate.

The appendix to this chapter discusses SFAC 1, 2, 5, 6, and 7 in greater detail.

Solving GAAP Problems

The methods that are employed in solving existing accounting problems can be summarized in the following steps:

1. **Research published GAAP.** A search should be initiated at the highest level of published accounting standards, following the levels and sources of principles according to Statement on Auditing Standards 69. The researcher should look for specific pronouncements and issuances level by level. In the absence of pronouncements directly applicable to the topic, the investigation should be broadened to include related and analogous topics. Analysis of the economic factors influencing the transaction will help in the broader search.

2. **Research other literature.** Other literature beyond that recognized by SAS 69 may consist of periodical literature and general industry publications. These may be important since not all principles are promulgated and successful practice is a source of accounting standards.

3. **Research practice.** Inquiries of other entities regarding the accounting practices they follow may indicate a potential solution or at least allow consideration of alternatives.

4. **Use theory.** When published standards, other literature, and practice fail to provide the answers to problems, the researcher must fall back on accounting theory. The conceptual framework, textbooks, appendices to official pronouncements, FASB discussion memorandums, and the like are sources of theory to be analyzed. The use of theory constrained by the economic factors underlying the problem being researched may succeed in clarifying issues and alternatives when no other guidance is available.

Examples of unsolved accounting problems and potential solutions follow.

Example involving equity method

The equity method of accounting for investments in partnerships and significantly influenced and controlled corporations is in accordance with accounting principles stated in APB 18. However, there is no clearly defined solution to the problem of how to account for issuances of additional shares or interests by the investee. Assume the following:

A Company forms B Company by depositing $100,000. B then sells additional stock to outsiders, reducing A's percentage of ownership to 25%, for a total of $4,900,000. A under the equity method would see its investment account rise from $100,000 to $1,250,000 (or 25% of [$100,000 + $4,900,000]).

A did not do anything that constitutes an earning process. Furthermore, a capital transaction of an investee could have been a capital transaction by the investor. The increase in investment may be seen as a capital transaction and an increase in paid-in capital.

Another argument is that A owned 100% of an entity and now owns only 25%. Essentially, A could have sold its investment directly but chose instead to have the investment sold indirectly by the investee. Under this theory, the increase in investment may be seen as a sale by A of part of its investment, which resulted in a gain, or as a revenue transaction to be reported in the income statement.

There are various writings in accounting literature that speak on both sides of this question. Although, in general, most textbooks show the increase as a capital transaction, the Internal Revenue Service may tax it. The Securities and Exchange Commission in Staff Accounting Bulletin 51 states that it will accept both methods, and the AICPA in Issues Paper, Accounting in Consolidation for Issuances of a Subsidiary's Stock, states a preference for the revenue transaction method.

The issue is whether A's original acquisition was a bargain purchase (no revenue to be recognized) or the subsequent sale was an earning process (revenue is realized). The issue may revolve around what activities A pursued prior to B issuing its stock that may have caused the value of B's stock to rise. Such activities may qualify for revenue recognition.

Example involving consolidations

In consolidations of less than 100% ownership of a subsidiary, the question arises as to the use of the parent or entity theories of combination. Assume the following:

A Company purchases 80% of B Company for $46,000 when B has total book value of $50,000. Since 80% of $50,000 is $40,000, there is a $6,000 differential to be accounted for. Under the parent theory, since cost exceeds book value by $6,000, the entire amount represents either an identified or unidentified (goodwill) asset to be accounted for in the future. Under the entity theory, since 80% created a $6,000 value, then the entire value must be $7,500, of which $6,000 is attributed to the majority interest and $1,500 belongs to the minority interest.

Under the parent theory, the implied additional value is not acceptable because there is no cost associated with it. Under the entity theory, recognition of only the actual differential denies the market implication of value. There is no authoritative literature that speaks to these issues although the parent theory is derived from the proprietary theory (view everything from the standpoint of the owner), while the entity theory (view everything from the standpoint of the entity as a whole) is a predominant accounting concept.

Generally, if the additional value of $6,000 is unidentified (goodwill), the cost issue becomes persuasive because of the concept of acquisition of unidentifiable intangibles. If the additional value is identified, practice would push the value down to the subsidiary by entering the $7,500 increase in assets and increase in equity. B would then have a total book value of $57,500 and 80% of it would equal the investment of A of $46,000. The accounting then is B's accounting for its own asset. The argument justifying this is that the legal form of the various entities, A and B, is immaterial. A new economic entity began with A's purchase of the stock of B and the same thing could have been accomplished through a partnership to which assets were transferred or by a liquidation of B into a new corporation, with a stepped-up basis for assets. Substance over form would support equal accounting regardless of the form of the transaction.

There are, however, many who would support neither the push-down nor the implied value recognition. The answer is not definitive because there has yet to be a pronouncement on the parent and entity theories of consolidation.

Example involving cancelable leases

A lease that is cancelable is not covered by SFAS 13, *Accounting for Leases*. However, assume that a firm has no intention of canceling the lease; would this intention alone be sufficient to cause capitalization of the asset and obligation, assuming the criteria were met? Most accountants would probably agree that the intention of the pronouncement would be met by such capitalization.

In a peculiar situation, assume a construction company bidding for state projects must maintain a 2:1 current ratio in order to obtain such jobs. The company has various equipment subject to cancelable leases, which otherwise would qualify as capital leases. If the leases are capitalized, the ratio falls below 2 to 1, causing cancellation of the leases due to lack of construction jobs. If the leases are not capitalized, the ratio is above 2 to 1, and the company would intend to keep the equipment for the entire lease without cancellation. Such an accounting dilemma is conceivable, and the solution may not exist. However, since bidding does not guarantee getting a contract, the intention of the lessee with respect to cancellation is unclear at the time of bidding, and most likely, the leases would not be capitalized at that time.

Example involving stock-based compensation plans

Such plans exist when companies reward employees by giving them stock or the right to benefit from the change in market price of the company's stock or both. There are two types of plans: (1) compensatory—the employee gets compensation and the company records an expense and liability, and (2) noncompensatory—no accounting recognition.

If a compensation plan is initiated at the then-fair market value of the stock, no compensation can be reported because such compensation is measured only from the amount of the discount (market price less exercise price offered). Therefore, no discount means no accounting even though the plan is compensatory. So the difference between compensatory and noncompensatory plans can be meaningless (APB 25).

However, in practice many plans exist. These include incentive plans, option plans, stock appreciation rights plans, phantom stock plans, restricted plans, and others. Let's look at two examples.

1. A nonqualified stock option plan
2. A stock appreciation right plan

The substance of these two plans is essentially the same because economic benefits that may be received by the employee can be identical.

Assume that both plans are issued at an exercise price equal to the market price of the stock and that market price increases over time. Under the nonqualified plan, although compensatory, the compensation is measured at the date of grant which is the date of issuance. No compensation would ever be recorded, and the increase in market value would be ignored. The employee could exercise the option and sell the stock, earning the profit while the corporation would ignore the "cost."

Under the stock appreciation right, the employee gets the profit directly from the corporation without buying and then selling the stock. However, when the amount of market appreciation is paid out, the corporation records the compensation as the excess of the market price over the exercise price of the SAR.

These two plans are virtually identical, yet the accounting for them is different. Furthermore, the first plan could give the employee a fixed number of shares while the second plan could be identical except the shares may be reduced based upon some contingency. Obviously, the first plan would be more valuable than the second because of no contingency in it to the employee. The stock plan is a more valuable award to the employee than the stock appreciation right. Under current accounting, the plan would cost zero while the right would cost the entire amount of the employee's gain.

Unfortunately, the form of the transaction prevails over the economic substance, although it clearly shouldn't. The corporation can influence its accounting recognized costs by how the plan is structured. For over a decade, the FASB attempted to resolve this problem via its project on stock-based compensation. The FASB's solution was so contentious that the FASB ultimately backed away from its proposal, stating that the nature of the debate ultimately threatened the future of accounting standards-setting in the private sector. When it issued SFAS 123 in 1994, the FASB required only certain disclosures about the fair value of stock-based compensation rather than its initial proposal, which required recognition of the fair-value-based measure as an expense.

Solutions to GAAP problems may not be definitive and may not be obtainable by looking up a pronouncement. The theory of accounting and analysis of the economic factors may be the path to their solution.

Accounting Websites

AICPA Online	http://www.aicpa.org	Includes accounting news section; CPE information; section on professional ethics; information on relevant Congressional/Executive actions; online publications, such as the *Journal of Accountancy*; Accounting Standards Executive Committee; also has links to other organizations
American Accounting Association	http://www.rutgers.edu/accounting/raw/aaa	Accounting news; publications; faculty information; searchable; links to other sites
Electronic Accountant	http://www.electronicaccountant.com	Includes Internet Tax Research; Career Center; discussions on accounting. auditing, financial planning, and other topics; searchable
FASB	http://www.fasb.org	Information on FASB; includes list of new pronouncements/statements; summaries of selected projects; summaries/status of all FASB statements
GASB	http://www.gasb.org	Information on GASB; new GASB documents; summaries/status of all GASB statements; proposed statements; technical bulletins; interpretations
NASBA	http://www.nasba.org	National State Boards of Accountancy; includes listings for all state organizations and publications
Pro2Net	http://www.pro2net.com	Includes news, research, products available for purchase; jobs database; on-line tax forms; John Wiley GAAP book is searchable on-line; links to FASB and GASB
Rutgers Accounting Web	http://www.accounting.rutgers.edu	Includes links to journals and publications, software, publishers, educational institutions, government agencies, more
SEC	http://www.sec.gov	SEC digest and statements; EDGAR searchable database; information on current SEC rule-making; links to other sites

APPENDIX

CONCEPTUAL FRAMEWORK

Components of the Conceptual Framework

The components of the conceptual framework for financial accounting and reporting include objectives, qualitative characteristics, elements, recognition, measurement, financial statements, earnings, funds flow, and liquidity. The relationship between these components is illustrated in the following diagram taken from a FASB Invitation to Comment, *Financial Statements and Other Means of Financial Reporting*.

In the diagram, components to the left are more basic and those to the right depend on components to their left. Components are closely related to those above or below them.

The most basic component of the conceptual framework is the objectives. The objectives underlie the other phases and are derived from the needs of those for whom financial information is intended. The qualitative characteristics are the criteria to be used in choosing and evaluating accounting and reporting policies.

Elements of financial statements are the components from which financial statements are created. They include assets, liabilities, equity, investments by owners, distributions to owners, comprehensive income, revenues, expenses, gains, and losses. In order to be included in financial statements, an element must meet criteria for recognition and possess a characteristic that can be reliably measured.

**Conceptual Framework
for Financial Accounting and Reporting**

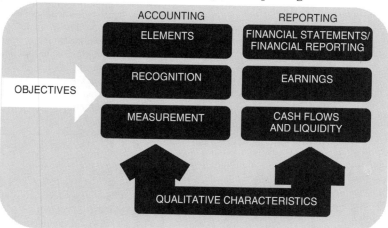

Reporting or display considerations are concerned with what information should be provided, who should provide it, and where it should be displayed. How the financial statements (financial position, earnings, and cash flow) are presented is the focal point of this part of the conceptual framework project.

Unlike a Statement of Financial Accounting Standards (SFAS), a Statement of Financial Accounting Concepts (SFAC) does not establish GAAP. Since GAAP may be inconsistent with the principles set forth in the conceptual framework, the FASB expects to reexamine existing accounting standards. Until that time, a SFAC does not require a change in existing GAAP. SFAC do not amend, modify, or interpret existing GAAP, nor do they justify changing GAAP based upon interpretations derived from them.

SFAC 1: Objectives of Financial Reporting by Business Enterprises

SFAC 1 identifies the objectives (purposes) of financial reporting and indicates that these objectives apply to all financial reporting; they are not limited to financial statements. Financial reporting includes the financial statements and other forms of communication that provide accounting information (corporate annual reports, prospectuses, annual reports filed with the Securities and Exchange Commission, news releases, and management forecasts).

SFAC 1 identifies three objectives of financial reporting. The **first objective** of financial reporting is to provide information that is useful in making business and economic decisions. Users of financial information are divided into internal and external groups. Internal users include management and directors of the business enterprise. Internal reports tend to provide information that is more detailed than the information available to or used by external users. External users include both individuals who have or intend to have a direct economic interest in a business and those who have an indirect interest because they advise or represent those individuals with a direct interest. These users include owners, lenders, suppliers, potential investors and creditors, employees, customers, financial analysts and advisors, brokers, underwriters, stock exchanges, lawyers, economists, taxing authorities, regulatory authorities, legislators, financial press and reporting agencies, labor unions, trade associations, business researchers, teachers, students, and the public. SFAC 1 is directed at general-purpose external financial reporting by a business enterprise as it relates to the ability of that enterprise to generate favorable cash flows. External users' needs are emphasized because these users lack the authority to obtain the financial information they want and need from an enterprise. Thus, external users must rely on the information provided to them by management.

The **second objective** of financial reporting is to provide understandable information that will aid investors and creditors in predicting the future cash flows of a firm. Investors and creditors want information about cash flows because the expectation of cash flows affects a firm's ability to pay interest and dividends, which in turn affects the market price of that firm's stocks and bonds.

The **third objective** of financial reporting is to provide information relative to an enterprise's economic resources, the claims to those resources (obligations), and the effects of transactions, events, and circumstances that change resources and claims to resources. A description of these informational needs follows:

- **Economic resources, obligations, and owners' equity.** This information provides the users of financial reporting with a measure of future cash flows and an indication of the firm's strengths, weaknesses, liquidity, and solvency.
- **Economic performance and earnings.** Past performance provides an indication of a firm's future performance. Furthermore, earnings based upon accrual accounting provide a better indicator of economic performance and future cash flows than do current cash receipts and disbursements. Accrual basis earnings are a better indicator because a charge for recovery of capital (depreciation/amortization) is made in determining these earnings. The relationship between earnings and economic performance results from the matching of the costs and benefits (revenues) of economic activity during a given period by means of accrual accounting. Over the life of an enterprise, economic performance can be determined by net cash flows or by total earnings since the two measures would be equal.
- **Liquidity, solvency, and funds flows.** Information about cash and other funds flows from borrowings, repayments of borrowings, expenditures, capital transactions, economic resources, obligations, owners' equity, and earnings may aid the user of financial reporting information in assessing a firm's liquidity or solvency.
- **Management stewardship and performance.** The assessment of a firm's management with respect to the efficient and profitable use of the firm's resources is usually made on the basis of economic performance as reported by periodic earnings. Because earnings are affected by factors other than current management performance, earnings may not be a reliable indicator of management performance.
- **Management explanations and interpretations.** Management is responsible for the efficient use of a firm's resources. Thus, it acquires knowledge about the enterprise and its performance that is unknown to the external user. Explanations by management concerning the financial impact of transactions, events, circumstances, uncertainties, estimates, judgments, and any effects of the separation of the results of operations into periodic measures of performance enhance the usefulness of financial information.

SFAC 2: Qualitative Characteristics of Accounting Information

The purpose of financial reporting is to provide decision makers with useful information. When accounting choices are to be made by individuals or by standard-setting bodies, those choices should be based upon the usefulness of that information to the decision-making process. This SFAC identifies the qualities or characteristics that make information useful in the decision-making process. It also establishes a terminology and set of definitions to provide a greater understanding of the characteristics. The following diagram from SFAC 2 summarizes the qualitative characteristics of accounting information:

A Hierarchy of Accounting Qualities

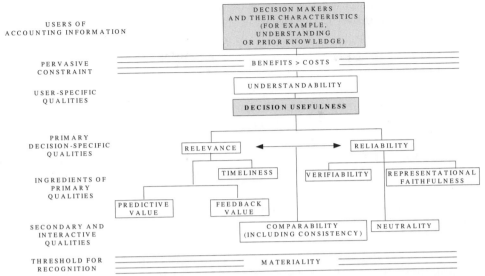

Usefulness for decision making. This is the most important characteristic of information. Information must be useful to be beneficial to the user. To be useful, accounting information must be both relevant and reliable. Both of these characteristics are affected by the completeness of the information provided.

Relevance. Information is relevant to a decision if it makes a difference to the decision maker in his/her ability to predict events or to confirm or correct expectations. Relevant information will reduce the decision maker's assessment of the uncertainty of the outcome of a decision even though it may not change the decision itself. Information is relevant if it provides knowledge concerning past events (feedback value) or future events (predictive value) and if it is timely. Disclosure requirement information such as segment reporting and interim earnings reports is relevant because it provides information about past events and it improves the predictability of future events. The predictive value of accounting information does not imply that such information is a prediction. The predictive value refers to the utility that a piece of information has as an input into a predictive model. Although timeliness alone will not make information relevant, information must be timely to be relevant. It must be available before it loses its ability to influence the decision maker.

Reliability. Financial statements are an abstraction of the activities of a business enterprise. They simplify the activities of the actual firm. To be reliable, financial statements must portray the important financial relationships of the firm itself. Information is reliable if it is verifiable and neutral and if users can depend on it to represent that which it is intended to represent (representational faithfulness).

Information may not be representationally faithful if it is biased. Bias is the tendency for an accounting measure to be consistently too high or too low. Bias may arise because the measurer does not use the measurement method properly or because the measurement method does not represent what it purports to represent.

Verifiability means that several independent measures will obtain the same accounting measure. An accounting measure that can be repeated with the same result (consensus) is desirable because it serves to detect and reduce measurer bias. Cash is highly verifiable. Inventories and depreciable assets tend to be less verifiable because alternative valuation methods exist. The direct verification of an accounting measure would serve to minimize measurer bias and measurement bias. The verification of the procedures used to obtain the measure would minimize measurer bias only. Finally, verifiability does not guarantee representational faithfulness or relevance.

The characteristic of **neutrality** means that accounting information should serve to communicate without attempting to influence behavior in a particular direction. This does not mean that accounting should not influence behavior or that it should affect everyone in the same way. It means that information should not favor certain interest groups. The effect of lease capitalization on leasing firms would not be a valid argument to oppose the requirement that certain leases be recorded as direct financing-type leases.

To be useful, accounting information should be **comparable**. The characteristic of comparability allows the users of accounting information to assess the similarities and differences either among different entities for the same time period or for the same entity over different time periods. Comparisons are usually made on the basis of quantifiable measurements of a common characteristic. Therefore, to be comparable, the measurements used must be reliable with respect to the common characteristic. Noncomparability can result from the use of different inputs, procedures, or systems of classification. Noncomparability can also arise when the data measurements lack representational faithfulness.

The characteristic of **consistency** also contributes to information usefulness. Consistency is an interperiod comparison that requires the use of the same accounting principles from one period to another. Although a change of an accounting principle to a more preferred method results in inconsistency, the change is acceptable if the effect of the change is disclosed. Consistency does not insure comparability. If the measurements used are not representationally faithful, comparability will not be achieved.

Trade-offs. Although it is desirable that accounting information contain the characteristics that have been identified above, not all of these characteristics are compatible. Often, one characteristic may be obtained only by sacrificing another. The trade-offs that must be made are determined on the basis of the relative importance of the characteristics. This relative importance, in turn, is dependent upon the nature of the users and their particular needs.

Constraints. The qualitative characteristics of useful accounting information are subject to two constraints: the **materiality** and the **relative cost benefit** of that information. An item of information is material and should be reported if it is significant enough to have an effect on the decision maker. Materiality requires judgment. It is dependent upon the relative size of an item, the precision with which the item can be estimated, and the nature of the item. No general standards of materiality are provided (although an appendix to SFAC 2 lists several guidelines that have been applied).

Accounting information provides the user with certain benefits. Associated with this benefit, however, is the cost of using that information and of providing it to the user. Information should be provided only if its benefits exceed its cost. Unfortunately, it is difficult to value the benefit of accounting information. It is also difficult to determine whether the burden of the cost of disclosure and the benefits of such disclosure are distributed fairly.

Role of conservatism. Any discussion of the qualitative characteristics of accounting information would be incomplete without some reference to the doctrine of conservatism. Conservatism is a reaction to uncertainty. For many years, accountants have been influenced by conservatism. Conservatism in accounting may mislead users if it results in a deliberate understatement of net assets and net income. Such understatement is undertaken to minimize the risk of uncertainty to outside lenders. Unfortunately, such understatements often lead to overstatements in subsequent years, produce biased financial statements, and conflict with the characteristics of representational faithfulness, neutrality, and comparability.

SFAC 5: Recognition and Measurement in Financial Statements of Business Enterprises

SFAC 5 indicates that financial statements are the principal means of communicating useful financial information. A full set of such statements contains

- Financial position at end of the period
- Earnings for the period
- Comprehensive income for the period
- Cash flows during the period
- Investments by and distributions to owners during the period

Financial statements result from simplifying, condensing, and aggregating transactions. Therefore, no one financial statement provides sufficient information by itself and no one item or part of each statement can summarize the information.

A statement of financial position provides information about an entity's assets, liabilities, and equity. Earnings is a measure of entity performance during a period. It is similar to net income but excludes accounting adjustments from earlier periods such as cumulative effect changes in accounting principles. Comprehensive income comprises all recognized changes in equity other than those arising from investments by and distributions to owners. The FASB has provided in SFAS 130 that comprehensive income be disclosed either as part of the income statement or in a separate statement of financial performance. A statement of cash flows reflects receipts and payments of cash by major sources and uses including operating, financing, and investing activities. The investments by and distributions to owners reflect the capital transactions of an entity during a period.

Income is determined by the concept of financial capital maintenance which means that only if the money amount of net assets increases during a period (excluding capital transactions) is there a profit. For recognition in financial statements, subject to both cost-benefit and materiality constraints, an item must meet the following criteria:

1. **Definition**—Meet the definition of an element in financial statements
2. **Measurability**—Have a relevant attribute measurable with sufficient reliability
3. **Relevance**
4. **Reliability**

Items reported in the financial statements are based on historical cost, replacement cost, market value, net realizable value, and present value of cash flows. Price level changes are not recognized in these statements and conservatism guides the application of recognition criteria.

SFAC 6: Elements of Financial Statements

SFAC 6 defines ten interrelated elements that are used in the financial statements of business enterprises:

1. **Assets**—Probable future economic benefits obtained or controlled by a particular entity as a result of past transactions or events
2. **Liabilities**—Probable future sacrifices of economic benefits arising from present obligations of a particular entity to transfer assets or provide services to other entities in the future as a result of past transactions or events
3. **Equity (net assets)**—The residual interest in the assets that remains after deducting its liabilities. In a business enterprise, equity is the ownership interest.
4. **Revenues**—Inflows or other enhancements of assets of an entity or settlement of its liabilities (or a combination of both) from delivering or producing goods, rendering services, or other activities that constitute the entity's ongoing major and central operations
5. **Expenses**—Outflows or other using up of assets or incurrences of liabilities (or a combination of both) from delivering or producing goods, rendering services, or carrying out other activities that constitute the entity's ongoing major and central operations
6. **Gains**—Increases in equity (net assets) from peripheral or incidental transactions of an entity and from all other transactions and other events

and circumstances affecting the entity except those that result from revenues or investments by owners

7. **Losses**—Decreases in equity (net assets) from peripheral or incidental transactions of an entity and from all other transactions and other events and circumstances affecting the entity except those that result from expenses or distributions to owners

8. **Comprehensive income**—The change in equity of a business enterprise during a period from transactions and other events and circumstances from sources other than investments by owners or distributions to owners

9. **Investments by owners**—Increases in equity of a particular business enterprise resulting from transfers to it for the purpose of increasing ownership interests

10. **Distributions to owners**—Decreases in the equity of a particular business enterprise resulting from transferring assets, rendering services, or incurring liabilities to owners

The various elements articulate; that is, a change in element causes an offsetting change in another item of the same type or causes another element to change by the same amount. For example, a purchase of a building for cash and a mortgage note increases an asset (building), decreases another asset (cash), and increases a liability (mortgage note). A diagram from SFAC 6 that illustrates the articulation of the elements is included below.

In this publication, assets, liabilities, and equity are described more fully in Chapter 2, Balance Sheet. Revenues, expenses, gains, losses, and comprehensive income are described in Chapter 3, Statements of Income and Comprehensive Income. Investments by owners and distributions to owners are described in Chapter 17, Stockholders' Equity.

SFAC 6 also defines several significant financial accounting and reporting terms that are used in the Concepts Statements (and FASB pronouncements issued after the Concepts Statements). An **event** is a happening of consequence to an entity. It can be an internal event (the use of raw materials) or an external event with another entity (the purchase of labor) or with the environment in which the business operates (a technological advance by a competitor). A **transaction** is a particular kind of event. It is an external event that involves transferring something of value to another entity. **Circumstances** are a condition, or set of conditions, that create situations that might otherwise have not occurred and might not have been anticipated. **Accrual accounting** attempts to record the financial effects on a entity of transactions and other events and circumstances that have consequences for the entity in the periods in which those transactions, events, and circumstances occur rather than in the periods in which cash is received or paid by the entity. Thus, accrual accounting is based not only on cash transactions but also on credit transactions, bartering, changes in prices, changes in the form of assets or liabilities, and other transactions, events and circumstances that involve no current cash transfers

All transactions and other events and circumstances that affect a business enterprise during a period

A. All changes in assets and liabilities not accompanied by changes in equity

B. All changes in assets or liabilities accompanied by changes in equity

C. Changes within equity that do not affect assets or liabilities

1. Ex-changes of assets for assets

2. Ex-changes of liabilities for liabilities

3. Acquisi-tions of assets by incurring liabilities

4. Settle-ments of liabilities by trans-ferring assets

1. Comprehensive income

2. All changes in equity from transfers between a business enterprise and its owners

a. Revenues

b. Gains

c. Expenses

d. Losses

a. Invest-ments by owners

b. Distri-butions to owners

but will have cash consequences in the future. **Accrual** is the accounting process of recognizing the effects of future cash receipts and payments in the current period. **Deferral** is the accounting process of recognizing a liability resulting from a current cash receipt or an asset resulting from a current cash payment. **Realization** is the process of converting noncash assets into cash. **Recognition** is the process of formally incorporating a transaction or other event into the financial statements. **Matching** is the simultaneous recognition of the revenues and expenses that result directly and jointly from the same transaction or other event. **Allocation** is the process of assigning expenses to periods when the transactions or events that cause the using up of the benefits cannot be identified or can be identified but the actual amount of benefit used up cannot be reliably measured.

SFAC 6 also discusses the elements used in the financial statements of not-for-profit organizations. Of the ten elements, seven are used by not-for-profit organizations. The three omitted are investments by owners, distributions to owners, and comprehensive income. Those are omitted because not-for-profit organizations do not have owners. The seven remaining elements are defined for not-for-profit organizations the same as they are for business enterprises. The net assets (equity) of not-for-profit organizations is divided into three classes—unrestricted, temporarily restricted, and permanently restricted—based on the existence or absence of donor-imposed restrictions. A portion of Chapter 23, Specialized Industry GAAP, describes the accounting and reporting of not-for-profit organizations.

SFAC 7: Using Cash Flow Information and Present Value in Accounting Measurements

SFAC 7 provides a framework for using future cash flows as the basis for accounting measurements either at initial recognition or when assets are remeasured at fair value (fresh-start measurements). It also provides a framework for using the interest method of amortization. It provides the principles that govern measurement using present value, especially when the amount of future cash flows, their timing, or both are uncertain. However, it does not address recognition questions, such as which transactions and events should be valued using present value measures or when fresh-start measurements are appropriate.

Fair value is the objective for most measurements at initial recognition and for fresh-start measurements in subsequent periods. At initial recognition, the cash paid or received (historical cost or proceeds) is usually assumed to be fair value, absent evidence to the contrary. For fresh-start measurements, a price that is observed in the marketplace for an essentially similar asset or liability is fair value. If purchase prices and market prices are available, there is no need to use alternative measurement techniques to approximate fair value. However, if alternative measurement techniques must be used for initial recognition and fresh-start measurements, those techniques should attempt to capture the elements that taken together would comprise a market price if one existed. The objective is to estimate the price likely to exist in the marketplace, if there were a marketplace—fair value.

SFAC 7 states that the only objective of using present value in accounting measurements is fair value. It is necessary to capture, to the extent possible, the economic differences in the marketplace between sets of estimated future cash flows. A present value measurement that fully captures those differences must include the following elements:

a. An estimate of the future cash flow, or in more complex cases, series of future cash flows at different times
b. Expectations about possible variations in the amount or timing of those cash flows
c. The time value of money, represented by the risk-free rate of interest
d. The risk premium—the price for bearing the uncertainty inherent in the asset or liability
e. Other factors, including illiquidity and market imperfections

How SFAC 7 measures differ from currently utilized present value techniques. Current present value techniques typically use a single set of estimated cash flows and a single discount (interest) rate. In current present value techniques, adjustments for factors b. through e. described in the previous paragraph are incorporated in the selection of the discount rate. In the SFAC 7 approach, only the third factor listed (the time value of money) is included in the discount rate; the other factors cause adjustments in arriving at risk-adjusted expected cash flows. SFAC 7 introduces the expected cash flow approach, which focuses on the range of possible estimated cash flows and their respective probabilities.

When computing present value, current techniques use the cash flows most likely to occur. SFAC 7 uses expected cash flow. The difference is the value that should be assigned to the cash flows other than the most-likely one. To illustrate, a cash flow might be $100, $200, or $300 with probabilities of 10%, 50%, and 40%, respectively. The most-likely cash flow is the one with 50% probability, or $200. The expected cash flow is $230 ($100 x .1 + $200 x .5 + $300 x .4).

The SFAC 7 method can also accommodate uncertainty in the timing of cash flows. Current techniques cannot; choosing one of the possible receipt dates is required. For example, a cash flow of $10,000 may be received in one year, two years, or three years with probabilities of 15%, 60%, and 25%, respectively. Current present value techniques would compute the present value using the most likely time for the payment—two years. The example below shows the computation of present value using the SFAC 7 method. Again, the expected present value of $8,973 differs from the traditional notion of a best estimate of $9,027 (the 60% probability) in this example.

Present value of $10,000 in 1 year at 5%	$9,523	
Adjusted for 15% probability		$1,428
Present value of $10,000 in 2 years at 5.25%	$9,027	
Adjusted for 60% probability		5,416
Present value of $10,000 in 3 years at 5.5%	$8,516	
Adjusted for 25% probability		2,129
Expected present value		$8,973

Measuring liabilities. The measurement of liabilities involves different problems from the measurement of assets; however, the underlying objective is the same. When using present value techniques to estimate the fair value of a liability, the objective is to estimate the value of the assets required currently to (1) settle the liability with the holder or (2) transfer the liability to an entity of comparable credit standing. To estimate the fair value of an entity's notes or bonds payable, accountants look to the price at which other entities are willing to hold the entity's liabilities as assets. For example, the proceeds of a loan are the price that a lender paid to hold the borrower's promise of future cash flows as an asset.

The most relevant measurement of an entity's liabilities should always reflect the credit standing of the entity. An entity with a good credit standing will receive more cash for its promise to pay than an entity with a poor credit standing. For example, if two entities both promise to pay $750 in three years with no stated interest payable in the interim, Entity A, with a good credit standing, might receive about $630 (a 6% interest rate). Entity B, with a poor credit standing, might receive about $533 (a 12% interest rate). Each entity initially records its respective liability at fair value, which is the amount of proceeds received—an amount that incorporates that entity's credit standing.

Present value techniques can also be used to value a guarantee of a liability. Assume that Entity B in the above example owes Entity C. If Entity A were to assume the debt, it would want to be compensated $630—the amount that it could get in the marketplace for its promise to pay $750 in three years. The difference between what Entity A would want to take the place of Entity B ($630) and the amount that Entity B receives ($533) is the value of the guarantee ($97).

Interest method of allocation. SFAC 7 describes the factors that suggest that an interest method of allocation should be used. It states that the interest method of allocation is more relevant than other methods of cost allocation when it is applied to assets and liabilities that exhibit one or more of the following characteristics:

a. The transaction is, in substance, a borrowing and lending transaction.
b. Period-to-period allocation of similar assets or liabilities employs an interest method.
c. A particular set of estimated future cash flows is closely associated with the asset or liability.
d. The measurement at initial recognition was based on present value.

Accounting for changes in expected cash flows. If the timing or amount of estimated cash flows changes and the asset or liability is not remeasured at a fresh-start measure, the interest method of allocation should be altered by a catch-up approach. That approach adjusts the carrying amount to the present value of the revised estimated future cash flows, discounted at the original effective interest rate.

Example of the relevance of present values. A measurement based on the present value of estimated future cash flows provides more relevant information than a measurement based on the undiscounted sum of those cash flows. For example, consider the following four future cash flows, all of which have an undiscounted value of $100,000:

a. Asset A has a fixed contractual cash flow of $100,000 due tomorrow. The cash flow is certain of receipt.

b. Asset B has a fixed contractual cash flow of $100,000 due in twenty years. The cash flow is certain of receipt.

c. Asset C has a fixed contractual cash flow of $100,000 due in twenty years. The amount that ultimately will be received is uncertain. There is an 80% probability that the entire $100,000 will be received. There is a 20% probability that $80,000 will be received.

d. Asset D has an *expected* cash flow of $100,000 due in twenty years. The amount that ultimately will be received is uncertain. There is a 25% probability that $120,000 will be received. There is a 50% probability that $100,000 will be received. There is a 25% probability that $80,000 will be received.

Assuming a 5% risk-free rate of return, the present values of the assets are

a. Asset A has a present value of $99,986. The time value of money assigned to the one-day period is $14 [$100,000 x .05/365 days]

b. Asset B has a present value of $37,689 [$100,000/(1 + .05)^{20}]

c. Asset C has a present value of $36,181 [(100,000 x .8 + 80,000 x .2)/(1 + .05)^{20}]

d. Asset D has a present value of $37,689 [($120,000 x .25 + 100,000 x .5 + 80,000 x .25)/(1 + .05)^{20}]

Although each of those assets has the same undiscounted cash flows, few would argue that they are economically the same or that a rational investor would pay the same price for each. Investors require compensation for the time value of money. They also require a risk premium. That is, given a choice between Asset B with expected cash flows that are certain and Asset D with cash flows of the same expected amount that are uncertain, investors will place a higher value on Asset B, even though they have the same expected present value. SFAC 7 says that the risk premium should be subtracted from the expected cash flows before applying the discount rate. Thus, if the risk premium for Asset D was $500, the risk-adjusted present values would be \$37,500 [{(\$120,000 x .25 + 100,000 x .5 + 80,000 x .25) − 500}/(1 + .05)^{20}].

Practical matters. Like any accounting measurement, the application of an expected cash flow approach is subject to a cost-benefit constraint. The cost of obtaining additional information must be weighed against the additional reliability that information will bring to the measurement. As a practical matter, an entity that uses present value measurements often has little or no information about some or all of the assumptions that investors would use in assessing the fair value of an asset or a liability. Instead, the entity must use the information that is available to it without undue cost and effort when it develops cash flow estimates. The entity's own assumptions about future cash flows can be used to estimate fair value using present value techniques, as long as there are no contrary data indicating that investors would use different assumptions. However, if contrary data exist, the entity must adjust its assumptions to incorporate that market information.

2 BALANCE SHEET

PERSPECTIVE AND ISSUES

Balance sheets (also known as statements of financial position) present information about assets, liabilities, and shareholders' equity (also known as net assets, net worth, or, if appropriate, partner's capital) and their relationships to each other. They reflect an entity's resources (assets) and its financing structure (liabilities and equity) in conformity with generally accepted accounting principles. The balance sheet reports the aggregate effect of transactions at a **point in time**, whereas the income statement, statement of retained earnings, and statement of cash flows report the effect of transactions over a **period of time.**

For years, users of financial statements put more emphasis on the income statement than on the balance sheet. Investors' main concern was the short-run maximization of earnings per share. During the late 1960s and early 1970s company growth and desirability was measured by earnings growth. But the combination of inflation and recession during the 1970s and the emphasis in the FASB's Conceptual Framework Project on the asset-liability approach to theory brought about a rediscovery of the balance sheet. This shift toward the balance sheet has marked a departure from the traditional transaction-based concept of income toward a capital maintenance concept proposed by economists. Under this approach to income measurement, the amount of beginning net assets would be compared to the amount of ending net assets, and the difference would be adjusted for dividends and capital transactions. Only to the extent that an entity maintained its net assets (after adjusting for capital transactions) would income be earned. By using a capital maintenance concept, investors can better predict the overall profit potential of the firm.

Financial statements should provide information that helps users make rational investment, credit, or economic decisions. The balance sheet must be studied in order to measure a firm's liquidity, financial flexibility and ability to generate profits, pay debts when due, and pay dividends. A firm's liquidity refers to the timing of cash flows in the normal course of business. Liquidity indicates the firm's ability to meet its obligations as they fall due. The concept of financial flexibility is broader than the concept of liquidity. Financial flexibility is a company's ability to take effective actions to alter the amounts and timing of cash flows so it can respond to unexpected needs and opportunities. Financial flexibility includes the ability to issue new capital or unused lines of credit.

The rights of the shareholders of a firm and the rights of other capital-supplying parties (bondholders and creditors) of a firm are many and varied. The disclosure of these rights is an important objective in the presentation of financial statements. The rights of shareholders and creditors are mutually exclusive claims against the entity's assets, and the rights of creditors (liabilities) take precedence over the rights of shareholders (equity). Both sources of capital are concerned with two basic rights: the right to share in the cash or property disbursements (interest and dividends) and the right to share in the assets in the event of liquidation

Although a balance sheet shows an entity's financial position, it does not purport to report the entity's value. It cannot for reasons that include

- The values of certain assets, such as human resources, secret processes, and competitive advantages are not included in a balance sheet despite the fact that they have value and will generate future cash flows.
- The values of other assets are measured at historical cost, rather than market value or specific value to the entity. For example, property and equipment are measured at original cost reduced by depreciation, but the underlying asset's value can significantly exceed that adjusted cost and the asset may continue to be productive even though fully depreciated.
- The values of most liabilities are measured at the present value of cash flows at the date the liability was incurred rather than at the current market rate. When market rates increase, the value of a below-market interest rate is not recognized in the balance sheet, nor is the loss from paying a rate in excess of market rate if interest rates fall.

In recent years, the FASB standards have increasingly used fair value as the relevant measure in the balance sheet. For example, SFAS 115, *Accounting for Certain Investments in Debt and Equity Securities,* changed the relevant measure for most securities held as assets to fair value from the lower of cost or market. SFAS 133, *Accounting for Derivative Instruments and Hedging Activities,* requires derivative financial instruments to be reported at fair value. Prior to that pronouncement, most derivatives were not reported on the balance sheet at all. A project currently on the FASB agenda proposes that certain liabilities be reported at fair value as well. Measuring more assets and liabilities at fair value enhances the ability of a balance sheet to report the entity's value.

In many industries, balance sheets are classified into categories. Assets are classified as "current" if they are reasonably expected to be converted into cash, sold, or consumed either in one year or in the operating cycle, whichever is longer. Liabilities are classified as "current" if they are expected to be liquidated through the use of current assets or the creation of other current liabilities.

In some industries, the concept of working capital (current assets less current liabilities) has little importance and the balance sheet is not classified. Such industries are broker-dealer, investment companies, real estate companies, and utilities. Personal financial statements are unclassified for the same reason.

Sources of GAAP					
ARB	*APB*	*SFAS*	*FASB I*	*TB*	*SFAC*
43, Ch. 2, 3A	6, 10, 12, 21, 22	5, 6, 12, 57, 78, 95, 115, 130	8, 39	793	6

DEFINITIONS OF TERMS

Assets. Probable future economic benefits obtained or controlled by a particular entity as a result of past transactions or events (SFAC 6).

The following three characteristics must be present for an item to qualify as an asset:

1. The asset must provide probable future economic benefit that enables it to provide future net cash inflows.
2. The entity must be able to receive the benefit and restrict other entities' access to that benefit.
3. The event that provides the entity with the right to the benefit has occurred.

Those three characteristics must be present if an item is to meet the definition of an asset. Assets have other characteristics, but those characteristics are not essential to the definition. For example, most assets are exchangeable, legally enforceable, or tangible. But an item can still be an asset even if it cannot be exchanged as long as the entity that owns it can use it in a manner that generates future cash flows or other benefits. Similarly, rights to an item need not be legally enforceable if the rights can be enforced in other ways, such as by using social or moral persuasion.

Finally, items need not be tangible. Securities, patents, and similar ownership rights are assets despite the fact that they cannot be touched or seen.

The characteristic possessed by all assets is service potential (also called future economic benefit); the ability to provide directly or indirectly services or benefits to the owner of the asset, usually in the form of future cash inflows. Once recognized, an asset remains on a balance sheet until the asset is exchanged for another or used to settle a liability, its future economic benefits are used up, or the asset can no longer provide future benefits (obsolescence).

Liabilities. Probable future sacrifices of economic benefits arising from present obligations of a particular entity to transfer assets or provide services to other entities in the future as a result of past transactions or events (SFAC 6).

The following three characteristics must be present for an item to qualify as a liability:

1. A liability requires that the entity settle a present obligation by the probable future transfer of an asset on demand, when a specified event occurs, or at a particular date.
2. The obligation cannot be avoided.
3. The event that obligates the entity has occurred.

Liabilities usually result from transactions in which entities obtain economic resources. For example, trade payables result from purchasing raw materials; salaries and wages payable result from using employees' time, and notes payable result from obtaining cash from a lender. Other liabilities may arise from nonreciprocal transfers such as the declaration of dividends to the owners of the entity or the pledge of assets to charitable organizations. An entity may involuntarily incur a liability. A liability may be imposed on the entity by government or by the court system in the form of taxes, fines, or levies. A liability may arise from price changes or interest rate changes.

Liabilities are imposed by agreement, by law, by court, by equitable or constructive obligation, and by business ethics and custom. Liabilities may be legally enforceable or they may be equitable obligations that arise from social, ethical, or moral requirements.

Liabilities continue in existence until the entity is no longer responsible for discharging them. Most liabilities are discharged either by transferring an asset or incurring another liability. However, some liabilities simply expire. For example, warranty liabilities are estimates of goods that will be returned for repair or replacement or cash that will have to be paid to a dissatisfied customer. At the end of the warranty period, any remaining liability simply is written off.

Equity. The residual interest in the assets that remains after deducting its liabilities. In a business enterprise, the equity is the ownership interest (SFAC 6).

Equity of a business enterprise is the source of enterprise distributions to the owners. Distributions of enterprise assets to owners are voluntary. Equity is increased by owners' investments and comprehensive income and is reduced by distributions to the owners. Because equity is a residual (the net amount of assets less liabilities), equity is affected by all transactions and events that increase or decrease assets without increasing or decreasing liabilities by the same amount. A diagram from SFAC 6 that appears in the Appendix of Chapter 1, Researching GAAP Problems, illustrates this relationship. For example, issuing a bond does not change equity because the increase in the asset (cash) is the same as the increase in the liability (bonds payable). Paying the interest on the bond does change equity. The decrease in the asset (cash) is not offset by a corresponding decrease in the liability (bonds payable).

In practice, the distinction between equity and liabilities may be difficult to ascertain. Securities such as convertible debt and preferred stock may have characteristics of both equity (residual ownership interest) and liabilities (nondiscretionary future sacrifices). For these items, accounting standards are used to ensure that similar transactions are reported in a similar manner by different entities.

Valuation account. A separate item on a balance sheet that reduces or increases the carrying amount of an asset or a liability. It is neither an asset nor a liability in its own right; it is merely part of the related asset or liability. For example, an estimate of uncorrectable amounts reduced the carrying amount of a receivable, and a bond premium increases the carrying amount of a payable.

CONCEPTS, RULES, AND EXAMPLES

Limitations of a Balance Sheet

Although a balance sheet shows an entity's financial position at a point in time, it does not purport to report the entity's value at that point in time. There are several reasons that a balance sheet cannot reflect the entity's value. Many assets and liabilities are recorded in the financial statements under the historical cost principle. Historical exchange prices are used because they are objective and capable of being independently verified. One limitation of the balance sheet is that historical cost does not always reflect current value. When a balance sheet is presented, many assets are reported at historical cost. Many accountants believe that the balance sheet would be more useful if the assets were restated in terms of current values. These current values may be market related or may simply be historical cost adjusted for the changing value of the dollar. Although assets are often stated at historical cost, if market information indicates a permanent and material decline in value, generally accepted accounting principles usually requires immediate recognition of the economic loss.

Another limitation of the balance sheet is that it ignores the effects of the time value of money on its elements. Although certain receivables and payables may be discounted (APB 21), most items are stated at face value regardless of the timing of the cash flows that they will generate. Although recognition of impairments of assets is generally required, recognition of appreciation of value is often recorded only when realized through an arm's-length transaction (sale). Financial standards have been changing to reflect changes in market values in financial statements. SFAS 115, issued in 1993, and SFAS 133, issued in 1998, require debt securities, most equity securities, and derivative financial instruments to be reported at fair value. The FASB is working on a project that could result in reporting certain liabilities at fair value as well.

However, for some assets and liabilities, cost is a close approximation of current value. Monetary assets such as cash, short-term investments, and receivables closely approximate current value. Current liabilities, which are liabilities that require either a current asset or another current liability to liquidate, are payable in a short period and closely approximate current value. If they were discounted, any discount value would be immaterial because of the short time period before payment.

For other assets and liabilities, cost can be significantly different from current value. Productive assets such as property, plant, equipment, and intangibles are reported at cost less any reduction due to depreciation, depletion, or amortization, which may differ from their current value to the entity or others. Long-term liabilities are recorded as the discounted value of future payments to be made under contract. On the date of issuance, the discount rate equals the market rate and current value equals balance sheet cost. However, as time passes and the market rate fluctuates, the recorded cost will not necessarily approximate the current value.

Another limitation of historical cost balance sheets is that estimates are used to determine the carrying/book values of many of the assets. Estimates are used in determining the collectibility of receivables, salability of inventory, and useful life of long-term assets. Estimates are necessary in order to divide and separate economic events occurring between two distinct accounting periods. However, such estimates require informed judgments for which there is little guidance in accounting literature.

A final limitation of the balance sheet is that it ignores items that are of financial value to the firm but that cannot be objectively determined. For example, internally generated goodwill, human resources, and secret processes are of financial value, but since these values are not measurable under current accounting principles and practices, they are not recorded on the balance sheet. Only assets obtained in a market transaction are recorded on the books and records of an entity.

Form of Balance Sheet

The format of a balance sheet is not specified by any authoritative pronouncement. Instead, formats and titles have developed as a matter of tradition and, in some cases, through industry practice.

Two basic formats are used.

1. The balanced format, in which the sum of the amounts for liabilities and equity are added together on the face of the statement to illustrate that assets equal liabilities plus equity

2. The equity format, which shows totals for assets, liabilities, and equity but no sums, illustrating that assets less liabilities equals equity

Those two formats can take one of two forms.

1. The account form, which shows assets on the left-hand side of the page and liabilities and equity on the right-hand side
2. The report form, which is a top-to-bottom or running presentation

The three elements that are displayed in the heading of a balance sheet are

1. The name of the entity whose financial position is being presented
2. The title of the statement
3. The date of the statement

The entity's name should appear as written in the legal document that created it (e.g., the certificate of incorporation, partnership agreement, etc.). The title may also reflect the legal status of the enterprise as a corporation, partnership, sole proprietorship, or divisions of some other entity. Where the entity's name does not disclose its legal status, supplemental information could be added to the title in order to clarify that status. A few examples are as follows:

ABC Company
(a partnership)

ABC Company
(a sole proprietorship)

ABC Company
(a division of DEF, Inc.)

The use of the titles "balance sheet," "statement of financial position," or "statement of financial condition" denotes the use of generally accepted accounting principles. If some other comprehensive basis of accounting, such as income tax or cash, is used, the title of the financial statement must be adjusted to reflect this variation. Titles such as "Statements of Assets and Liabilities—Tax Basis" would be necessary to differentiate the financial statement being presented from a balance sheet.

The last day of the fiscal period should be used as the statement date. Usually, that is a month-end date unless the entity uses a fiscal reporting period always ending on a particular day of the week such as Friday or Sunday. In these cases, the balance sheet would be dated accordingly (i.e., December 26, October 1, etc.).

Balance sheets generally should be uniform in appearance from one period to the next. The form, terminology, captions, and pattern of combining insignificant items should be consistent. If comparative statements are presented, the prior year's information should be restated to conform with the current year's presentation if changes in presentation are made.

Classification of Assets

Assets, liabilities, and stockholders' equity are separated in the balance sheet so that important relationships can be shown and attention can be focused on significant subtotals.

Current assets. Per ARB 43, Chapter 3, current assets are cash and other assets that are reasonably expected to be realized in cash or sold or consumed during the normal operating cycle of the business. When the normal operating cycle is less than one year, a one-year period is used to distinguish current assets from noncurrent assets. However, when the operating cycle exceeds one year, the operating cycle will serve as the proper period for purposes of current asset classification. When the operating cycle is very long, the usefulness of the concept of current assets diminishes. The following items would be classified as current assets:

1. **Cash and cash equivalents** include cash on hand consisting of coins, currency, undeposited checks; money orders and drafts; deposits in banks; and certain short-term, highly liquid investments. Anything accepted by a bank for deposit would be considered as cash. Cash must be available for a demand withdrawal. Cash that is restricted as to withdrawal, such as certificates of deposit, would not be included with cash because of the time restrictions. Also, cash must be available for current use in order to be classified as a current asset. Cash that is restricted in use would not be included in cash unless its restrictions will expire within the operating cycle. Cash restricted for a noncurrent use, such as cash designated for the purchase of property or equipment, would not be included in current assets. Per SFAS 95, cash equivalents include short-term, highly liquid investments that (1) are readily convertible to known amounts of cash and (2) are so near their maturity (maturities of three months or less from the date of purchase by the enterprise) that they present negligible risk of changes in value because of changes in interest rates. Treasury bills, commercial paper, and money market funds are all examples of cash equivalents. Chapter 5, Cash, Receivables, and Prepaid Expenses, discusses cash in more detail.

2. **Short-term investments** are readily marketable securities acquired through the use of temporarily idle cash. To be classified as current assets, management must be willing and able to sell the security to meet current cash needs or the investment must mature within one year (or the operating cycle, if longer). These securities are accounted for under SFAS 115. Securities classified as trading securities under SFAS 115 must be reported as current assets. Securities classified as held-to-maturity or available-for-sale are reported as either current or noncurrent dependent upon management's intended holding period, the security's maturity date (if any), or both. It is not necessary to show the SFAS 115 classification on the face of the balance sheet. Short-term investments can be combined into a single line if the

classification details appear in the notes to the financial statements. The balance sheet presentation might be as follows:

    Marketable securities $xxx

Chapter 6, Short-Term Investments and Financial Instruments, discusses short-term investments in more detail.

3. **Receivables** include accounts and notes receivable, receivables from affiliate companies, and officer and employee receivables. The term "accounts receivable" represents amounts due from customers arising from transactions in the ordinary course of business. Valuation allowances, if any, should be clearly stated. Allowances for uncollectibility may be based on a percentage of sales or based on direct analysis of the receivables. Valuation allowances to reflect the time value of money (discounts) should be reported with the related receivable. If material, the receivables should be broken down into their component parts. Receivables pledged as collateral should be reported as a separate line on the balance sheet or should be disclosed in the notes to financial statements. A receivables section might be presented as follows:

Receivables:	
Accounts	$xxx
Notes	xxx
	xxx
Less allowance for doubtful accounts	(xxx)
	xxx
Affiliate companies	xxx
Officers and employees	xxx
	$xxx

Chapter 5, Cash, Receivables, and Prepaid Expenses, discusses receivables in more detail.

4. **Inventories** are goods on hand and available for sale. The basis of valuation and the method of pricing should be disclosed.

    Inventories—at the lower of cost or market
        (specific identification) $xxx

In the case of a manufacturing concern, raw materials, work in process, and finished goods should be disclosed separately on the balance sheet or in the notes to financial statements.

Inventories:	
Finished goods	$xxx
Work in process	xxx
Raw materials	xxx
	$xxx

Chapter 7, Inventory, discusses inventories in more detail.

5. **Prepaid expenses** are prepayments made to secure the use of assets or the receipt of services at a future date. Prepaid expenses will not be converted to cash, but they are classified as current assets because, if not prepaid, they would have required the use of current assets during the coming year (or operating cycle, if longer). Prepaid rent, prepaid insurance, prepaid interest, and prepaid advertising are examples of prepaid expenses. Chapter 5, Cash, Receivables, and Prepaid Expenses, discusses prepaid expenses in more detail.

Noncurrent assets. Excluded from the classification of current assets are assets that will not be realized in cash during the next year (or operating cycle, if longer). The following assets would be classified as noncurrent assets:

1. **Long-term investments** are investments that are intended to be held for an extended period of time (longer than one operating cycle). The following are the three major types of long-term investments:

    a. **Debt and equity securities** are stocks, bonds, and long-term notes. Securities that are classified as available-for-sale or held-to-maturity investments under SFAS 115 would be included here if management intended to hold them for more than one year. Under SFAS 115, the classifications of these securities need not be reported on the face of the balance sheet if they are reported in the notes.

Long-term investments:		
Investments in A company stock		$xxx
Notes receivable	$ xxx	
Less discount on notes receivable	(xxx)	xxx
Investment in B company bonds		xxx
		$xxx

    b. **Tangible assets** not currently used in operations (e.g., land held for sale).

    c. **Investments held in special funds** (e.g., sinking funds, pension funds, amounts held for plant expansion, and cash surrender values of life insurance policies).

    Chapter 10, Investments, describes investments in more detail.

2. **Property, plant, and equipment** are assets of a durable nature that are to be used in the production or sale of goods, sale of other assets, or rendering of services rather than being held for sale (e.g., machinery and equipment, buildings, furniture and fixtures, natural resources, and land). These should be disclosed with related accumulated depreciation/depletion as follows:

Machinery and equipment	$xxx
Less accumulated depreciation	(xxx)
or	$xxx
Machinery and equipment (net of $xxx accumulated depreciation)	$xxx

Accumulated depreciation may be shown in total or by major classes of depreciable assets. In addition to showing this amount on the balance sheet, the notes to the financial statements should contain balances of major classes of depreciable assets, by nature or function, at the balance sheet date. Assets under capital leases should be separately disclosed in accordance with the above requirements. A general description of the method or methods used in computing depreciation with respect to major classes of depreciable assets (APB 12) should also be included in the notes to financial statements. Chapter 9, Long-Lived Assets, discusses property, plant, and equipment in more detail.

3. **Intangible assets** include rights that are expected to have future economic benefits and purchased goodwill. Goodwill is the reputation of an entity with its customers. Goodwill that is purchased in a business combination is recognized, internally generated goodwill is not. Patents, copyrights, logos, and trademarks are examples of rights that are recognized as intangible assets. Amortization reports the diminishment of the value of intangible assets through use or the passage of time. Generally, the amortization of an intangible asset is credited directly to the asset account, although it is acceptable to use an accumulated amortization account. Chapter 11, Business Combinations and Consolidated Financial Statements, discusses goodwill in more detail. Chapter 9, Long-lived Assets, discusses other intangible assets.

4. **Other assets.** An all-inclusive heading for accounts that do not fit neatly into any of the other asset categories (e.g., long-term prepaid expenses, deferred taxes, bond issue costs, noncurrent receivables, and restricted cash).

Classification of Liabilities

Liabilities are displayed on the balance sheet in the order of payment. The distinction between current and noncurrent assets and liabilities generally rests upon both the ability of the entity and the intent of the entity to liquidate or not to liquidate within the traditional one-year time frame.

Current liabilities. Per ARB 43, Chapter 3, obligations are classified as current if their liquidation is reasonably expected to require the use of existing resources properly classifiable as current assets or to create other current obligations. Obligations that are due on demand or that are callable at any time by the lender are classified as current regardless of the intent of the entity or lender. The following items would be classified as current liabilities:

1. **Accounts payable** are obligations that arise primarily from the acquisition of goods and services entering the operating cycle. Accounts payable includes amounts for trade payables, salaries and wages payable, commissions and bonuses payable.

2. **Notes payable** also are obligations that generally arise from the acquisition of goods and services. They differ from accounts payable because the supplier or vendor finances the purchase on terms longer than the customary period for trade payables. The supplier or vendor generally charges interest for the privilege. If interest is not charged, it is imputed in accordance with APB 21. (Imputation of interest is discussed further in Chapter 13, Long-Term Debt.) Valuation accounts for the resulting discount are shown with the note, as follows:

Notes payable, net of discounts of $xx		$ xxx
or		
Notes payable	$ xxx	
Less discounts	(xxx)	$ xxx

3. **Dividends payable** become a liability of the entity when declared.
4. **Advances and deposits** are collections of cash or other assets in advance to ensure the future delivery of goods or services. Advances and deposits are classified as current liabilities if the goods and services are to be delivered within the next year (or the operating cycle, if longer). Advances and deposits include such items as subscriptions payable, advance rentals, and customer deposits. Certain advances and deposits are sometimes titled unearned revenues.
5. **Agency collections and withholdings** are liabilities that arise because the entity acts as an agent for another. Employee tax withholdings, sales taxes, and wage garnishments are examples of agency collections.
6. **Current portion of long-term debt** is the portion of a long-term obligation that will be settled during the next year (or operating cycle, if longer) by using current assets. Generally, this amount includes only the payments due within the next year under the terms of the underlying agreement. However, if a covenant in a long-term debt agreement has been violated and, as a result, the investor can demand payment, the entire debt amount is classified as current unless the lender waives the right to call the debt for a period in excess of one year (or one operating cycle, if longer). In two cases, obligations to be paid in the next period should not be classified as current liabilities. Debt expected to be refinanced through another long-term issue and debt that will be retired through the use of noncurrent assets, such as a bond sinking fund, are treated as noncurrent liabilities because the liquidation does not require the use of current assets or the creation of other current liabilities.

Chapter 12, Current Liabilities and Contingencies, discusses current liabilities in more detail.

   Noncurrent liabilities. Obligations that are not expected to be liquidated within the current operating cycle are classified as noncurrent. The following items would be classified as noncurrent:

1. **Notes and bonds payable** are obligations that will be paid in more than one year (or one operating cycle, if longer). Most notes and bonds require periodic payments of interests, and some require periodic payments of principal. If the stated rate of interest on a note or bond is different than the market rate on the day the note or bond is issued, the proceeds from issuance will differ from the face amount of the note or bond. If the market rate is higher than the stated rate, the bonds will be issued at a discount, which means that the proceeds were less than the face amount. If the market rate is lower than the stated rate, the bonds will be issued at a premium which means that the proceeds exceed the face amount. Valuation accounts for the resulting discount or premiums are shown with the note, as follows:

Notes payable, including premium of $xx		$xxx
or		
Notes payable	$xxx	
Plus premium	$<u>xxx</u>	$xxx

   Discounts and premiums are amortized using the effective interest rate method, which results in a steady interest rate over the life of the debt. Chapter 13, Long-Term Debt, discusses notes and bonds payable in more detail.

2. **Lease obligations** are debts that arise from obtaining the use of property or equipment via a capital lease contract. Chapter 14, Leases, discusses lease obligations.

3. **Accrued expenses** are long-term obligations that arise out of the normal course of business. Pension obligations, postemployment obligations, and postretirement obligations are long-term obligations to provide future retirement, insurance, or other benefits to employees as a result of their past service. Those obligations are described in more detail in Chapter 16, Pensions. Deferred income taxes are liabilities to pay taxes in the future that result from differences between net income, which is reported in compliance with GAAP, and taxable income, which is reported in compliance with tax law. Chapter 15, Income Taxes, discusses deferred income taxes.

4. **Contingent obligations** are recorded when it is probable that an obligation will occur as the result of a past event. In most cases, a future event will eventually confirm the amount payable, the payee, or the date payable. Examples of contingent obligations are lawsuits that have not been settled, product warranty obligations, guarantees of indebtedness, and agreements to repurchase an asset or make future payments. The classification of a contingent liability as current or noncurrent depends on when the confirming even will occur and how soon afterwards payment must be made. Contingencies are discussed further in Chapter 12, Current Liabilities and Contingencies.

Offsetting Assets and Liabilities

In general, assets and liabilities are not offset against each other. Offsetting in the financial statements is a proper presentation only where the right of setoff exists. FASB Interpretation 39 states that right of setoff exists only when all the following conditions are met:

1. Each of the two parties owes the other determinable amounts (although they may be in different currencies and bear different rates of interest).
2. The entity has the right to set off against the amount owed by the other party.
3. The entity intends to set off.
4. The right of setoff is legally enforceable.

In particular cases, state laws or bankruptcy laws may impose restrictions or prohibitions against the right of setoff. Furthermore, when maturities differ, only the party with the nearest maturity can offset because the party with the later maturity must settle in the manner determined by the party with the earlier maturity.

The offsetting of cash or other assets against a tax liability or other amounts due to governmental bodies is acceptable only under limited circumstances. When it is clear that the purchase of securities is in substance an advance payment of taxes payable in the near future and the securities are acceptable for the payment of taxes, amounts may be offset. Primarily this occurs as an accommodation to governmental bodies that issue tax anticipation notes in order to accelerate the receipt of cash for future taxes.

For forwards, interest rate swaps, currency swaps, options, and other conditional or exchange contracts, the conditions for the right of offset must exist or the fair value of contracts in a loss position cannot be offset against the fair value of contracts in a gain position. Nor can accrued receivable amounts be offset against accrued payable amounts. If, however, there is a master netting arrangement, then fair value amounts recognized for forwards, interest or currency swaps, options, or other such contracts may be offset without respect to the conditions previously specified.

FASB Interpretation 41 permits the offset of amounts recognized as payables in repurchase agreements against amounts recognized as receivables in reverse repurchase agreements with the same counterparty. If certain conditions are met, an entity may, but is not required to, offset the amounts recognized. The additional conditions are

1. The repurchase agreements and the reverse repurchase agreements must have the same explicit settlement date.
2. The repurchase agreements and the reverse repurchase agreements must be executed in accordance within a master netting agreement.
3. The securities underlying the repurchase agreements and the reverse repurchase agreements exist in "book entry" form.

4. The repurchase agreements and the reverse repurchase agreements will be settled on a securities transfer system that transfers ownership of "book entry" securities, and banking arrangements are in place so that the entity must only keep cash on deposit sufficient to cover the net payable.

5. The same account at the clearing bank is used for the cash inflows of the settlement of the reverse repurchase agreements and the cash outflows in the settlement of repurchase agreement.

Classification of Stockholders' Equity

Stockholders' equity is the ownership interest of the stockholders in the assets of the corporation. It is the residual amount after liabilities are subtracted from assets. Stockholders' equity arises from three sources: contributed capital, retained earnings, and other comprehensive income. Stockholders' equity is discussed further in Chapter 17, Stockholders' Equity.

Contributed capital. Contributed capital is the amount of equity invested in the corporation by its owners. It consists of capital stock and additional paid-in capital. Contributed capital arises from issuance of common and preferred stock to investors, from transactions by the corporation in its own stock (for example, treasury stock, stock dividends, conversion of convertible bonds) and from donation of assets or services.

Capital stock. Capital stock is the par or stated value of preferred and common shares. In the past, capital stock was the legal capital of the corporation—the amount that could not be distributed to stockholders so that the interest of creditors would be protected. In recent years, some states have changed laws so that legal capital includes additional paid-in capital (i.e., in those states the distinction between the capital stock and additional paid-in capital is gone). The face of the balance sheet usually provides information about the type of issues, the par or stated value per share, and the number of shares authorized, issued, and outstanding. For preferred stock, the liquidation preferences and features (e.g., whether participating, cumulative, convertible, or callable) are also shown, as follows:

6% cumulative preferred stock, $100 par value, callable at $115, 10,000 shares authorized and outstanding	$xxx
Common stock, $10 par value per share, 2,000,000 shares authorized, 1,500,000 shares issued and outstanding	$xxx

Additional paid-in capital. There are two major categories of additional paid-in capital.

1. Paid-in capital in excess of par/stated value which is the difference between the actual issue price and par/stated value. Amounts in excess should be disclosed separately for common stock and each issue of preferred stock as follows:

Additional paid-in capital—6% preferred stock	$xxx
Additional paid-in capital—common stock	$xxx

2. Paid-in capital from other transactions which includes treasury stock, retirement of stock, stock dividends recorded at market, lapse of stock purchase warrants, conversion of convertible bonds in excess of the par value of the stock, and any other additional capital from the company's own stock transactions.

Donated capital. Donated capital results from gifts of assets or services to the corporation. Transactions that create donated capital are uncommon. If those transaction occur, the amount of donated capital, which is measured at the fair value of the asset or services received, is displayed on the face of the balance sheet, as follows:

Donated capital	$xxx

Retained earnings. Retained earnings is the cumulative earnings of the corporation from the date of inception (or reorganization) to the date of the financial statements less the cumulative distributed to shareholders either directly (dividends or reacquisition of shares) or indirectly (treasury stock).

In the past, some corporations would appropriate (set aside) a portion of retained earnings for a special purpose and indicate on the face of the balance sheet or in the notes to the financial statements that the appropriated amount was unavailable for dividends. That practice is uncommon today.

Accumulated other comprehensive income. Other comprehensive income is the change in equity of a business enterprise during a period that arises from sources other than net income and transactions with owners. Under current accounting standards, its accumulated components include net unrealized holding gains and losses on investments classified as available-for-sale securities (SFAS 115), the excess of minimum pension liability over unrecognized prior service cost, and unrealized gains (losses) on foreign currency translations. The components of accumulated other comprehensive income are shown either in the statement of changes in stockholders' equity or in the stockholders' equity section, as follows:

Accumulated other comprehensive income		
Foreign currency translation adjustments	$xx	
Pension liability adjustment	xx	
Unrealized gains on securities	xx	xx

Treasury stock. Treasury stock is shares of the corporation that have been issued, repurchased by the corporation, and that have not been retired or canceled. These shares have no voting rights and they receive no dividends. Treasury stock is traditionally shown as the last item (a deduction) within the stockholders' equity section. (In very limited circumstances involving employee compensation plans, treasury stock can be shown as an asset.) The number of shares and the method of valuation are generally shown, as follows:

Treasury stock, 1,000 shares at cost	$ xxx

Classification of Partners' Capital

In partnership entities, the balance sheet is the same as all other entities except for the net worth section. In a partnership, this section is usually referred to as partners' capital. In partnership accounting, the net worth section of the balance sheet includes the equity interests of the partners. Although each individual partner's capital need not be displayed, the totals for each class of partner, general or limited, should be shown. Loans to or from partners should be displayed as assets and liabilities of the partnership and not as reductions or additions to partners' capital. Payments to partners of interest on loans are properly classified as expenses on the income statement. Payments to partners of interest on capital or of salaries are considered an allocation of profits and are usually not expensed on the income statement. However, in an attempt to emulate corporate financial reporting, some partnerships, with adequate disclosure, do display such payments as expenses.

Relation to the Other Financial Statements

Financial statements interrelate because they reflect different aspects of the same transactions. For example, an increase in trade receivables (balance sheet) does not occur without an increase in revenue (income statement). A purchase of equipment increases an asset (balance sheet) and decreases cash (statement of cash flows). Likewise, policy decisions generally impact more than one financial statement. A decision to value inventory using the first-in, first-out method determines the amount of cost of goods sold. No single financial statement provides all the information that is necessary when making decisions about investing in or lending money to an entity. Instead, most financial analysis examines relationships between the statements (for example, return on equity, turnover rations, and cash flow per share).

Disclosures

In addition to the measurement accounting principles that guide the values placed on the elements included in the balance sheet, there are disclosure accounting principles which are necessary to make the financial statements not misleading because of their omission.

The following are five techniques of disclosure:

1. Parenthetical explanations
2. Notes to the financial statements
3. Cross-references
4. Valuation accounts
5. Supporting schedules

Parenthetical explanations. Supplemental information is disclosed by means of parenthetical explanations following the appropriate balance sheet items. For example

Common stock ($10 par value, 200,000 shares authorized,
    150,000 issued) $1,500,000

Parenthetical explanations have an advantage over both notes to the financial statements and supporting schedules. Parenthetical explanations place the disclosure in the body of the statement. The supplemental information could be overlooked when it is placed in a note or schedule.

Notes to financial statements. If the additional information cannot be disclosed in a relatively short and concise parenthetical explanation, a note should be used. For example

Inventories (see note 1) $2,550,000

The notes to the financial statements would contain the following:

Note 1: Inventories are stated at the lower of cost or market. Cost is determined on the first-in, first-out method and market is determined on the basis of estimated net realizable value. The market value of the inventory is $2,720,000.

Cross-references. Cross-referencing is used when there is a direct relationship between two accounts on the balance sheet. For example, among the current assets, the following might be shown if $1,500,000 of accounts receivable were required to be pledged as collateral for a $1,200,000 bank loan:

Accounts receivable pledged to bank $1,500,000

Included in the current liabilities would be the following:

Bank loan payable-secured by accounts receivable $1,200,000

Valuation accounts. Valuation accounts are used to reduce or increase the carrying amount of some assets and liabilities found in financial statements. Accumulated depreciation reduces the book value for property, plant, and equipment, and a bond premium (discount) increases (decreases) the face value of a bond payable as shown in the following illustrations:

Equipment	$18,000,000	
Less accumulated depreciation	(1,625,000)	$16,375,000
Bonds payable	$20,000,000	
Less discount on bonds payable	(1,300,000)	$18,700,000
Bonds payable	$20,000,000	
Add premium on bonds payable	1,300,000	$21,300,000

Supporting schedules. A supporting schedule might be used to provide additional detail about an item in the financial statements. For example, consolidating schedules might be included in addition to the basic financial statement or a five-year summary of selected financial data might be included. In general, supporting schedules are not used to provide information required by GAAP because those schedules are not part of the financial statements and are subjected to only limited procedures by auditors.

Accounting policies. There are many different methods of valuing assets, recognizing revenues, and assigning costs. Financial statement users must be aware of the accounting policies used by enterprises so that sound economic decisions can be made. Per APB 22, the disclosures should identify and describe the accounting principles followed by the entity and methods of applying those principles that materially affect the determination of financial position, changes in cash flows, or results of operations. The accounting policies should encompass those accounting principles and methods that involve the following:

1. Selection from acceptable alternatives
2. Principles and methods peculiar to the industry
3. Unique applications of GAAP

The accounting policies disclosure should not duplicate information disclosed elsewhere as part of the financial statements. The accounting policies usually appear in a separate section called "Summary of Significant Accounting Policies" or as the first note of the notes to the financial statements.

Related parties. According to SFAS 57, *Related-Party Disclosures*, financial statements should include disclosure of material related-party transactions other than compensation arrangements, expense allowances, or other similar items in the ordinary course of business.

A related party is essentially any party that controls or can significantly influence the management or operating policies of the company to the extent that the company may be prevented from fully pursuing its own interests. Related parties include affiliates, investees accounted for by the equity method, trusts for the benefit of employees, principal owners, management, and immediate family members of owners or management.

Entities should disclose transactions with related parties even if there is no accounting recognition made for such transactions (e.g., a service is performed without payment). Disclosures should not imply that related-party transactions were on terms essentially equivalent to arm's-length dealings unless those claims can be substantiated. If financial position or the results of operations of the reporting entity could change significantly because of common control or common management, the nature of the ownership or management control should be disclosed, even if there were no transactions between the entities.

The disclosures generally should include

1. Nature of relationship.
2. Description of transactions and effects of such transactions on the financial statements for each period for which an income statement is presented.
3. Dollar amount of transactions for each period for which an income statement is presented and effects of any change in the terms of such transactions as compared to the terms used in prior periods.

4. Amounts due to and from related parties as of the date of each balance sheet presented together with the terms and manner of settlement.

Comparative statements.   In order to increase the usefulness of financial statements, many companies include financial statement for the prior year in their annual reports. Some also include five or ten-year summaries of condensed financial information. These comparative statements allow investment analysts and other interested readers to perform comparative analysis of pertinent information. ARB 43, Chapter 2 states the presentation of comparative financial statements in annual reports enhances the usefulness of such reports and brings out more clearly the nature and trends of current changes affecting the enterprise. That presentation emphasizes the fact that the statements for a series of periods are far more significant than those for a single period and that the accounts for one period are but an installment of what is essentially a continuous history.

Subsequent events.   The balance sheet is dated as of the last day of the fiscal period, but a period of time may elapse before the financial statements are issued. During this period, significant events or transactions may have occurred that materially affect the company's financial position. These events and transactions are called subsequent events. Significant events occurring between the balance sheet date and issue date of the financial statements could make those financial statements misleading if not disclosed.

There are two types of subsequent events (SAS 1, *Subsequent Events*). The first type consists of events that provide additional evidence about conditions that existed at the date of the balance sheet and affect the estimates inherent in the process of preparing financial statements. The second type consists of events that provide evidence with respect to conditions that did not exist at the date of the balance sheet but arose subsequent to that date. The first type results in adjustments of the financial statements. The second type does not require adjustment of the financial statements but may require disclosure in order to keep the financial statements from being misleading. Disclosure can be made in the form of notes, supporting schedules, and pro forma statements.

Examples of subsequent events

1. A loss on an uncollectible trade account receivable that results from a customer's deteriorating financial condition, which led to bankruptcy subsequent to the balance sheet date, would be indicative of conditions existing at the balance sheet date, thereby calling for adjustment of the financial statements before their issuance. On the other hand, a loss on an uncollectible trade account receivable resulting from a customer's major casualty, such as a fire or flood subsequent to the balance sheet date, would not be indicative of conditions existing at the balance sheet date, and the adjustment of the financial statements would not be appropriate. However, if the amount is material, disclosure would be required.

2. A loss arising from the recognition after the balance sheet date that plant and equipment had suffered a material decline in value because of reduced marketability for

the product or service it can produce would be an economic event in process at the balance sheet date and would require adjustment and recognition of the loss.

3. A settlement of a lawsuit would require adjustment of the financial statements if the event that gave rise to the claim occurred prior to the balance sheet date. However, only disclosure is required if the event that gave rise to the claim occurred after the balance sheet date, and then only if the amount involved were material.

4. The second type of events (those not existing at the balance sheet date) that require disclosure but not adjustment include the following:

   a. Sale of a bond or capital stock issue
   b. Purchase of a business
   c. Loss of plant or inventories as a result of fire or flood
   d. Gains or losses on certain marketable securities

Contingencies. A contingency is defined in SFAS 5 as an existing condition, situation, or set of circumstances involving uncertainty as to possible gain or loss. The uncertainty will ultimately be resolved when one or more future events occur or fail to occur. Resolution of the uncertainty may confirm the acquisition of an asset, the reduction of a liability, the loss or impairment of an asset, or the incurrence of a liability.

If it is probable that an asset has been impaired or that a liability has been incurred at the date of the financial statements and the amount of that loss can be reasonably estimated, the loss is accrued by a charge to earnings and the recognition of a liability. Contingencies requiring accrual are discussed more fully in Chapter 12, Current Liabilities and Contingencies.

However, if it is only reasonably possible that a future even will confirm that an asset was impaired or a liability has been incurred at the balance sheet date, an entity should disclose the contingency if the amount involved could have a material effect on the financial statements. The disclosure should include the nature of the contingency and either an estimate of the amount of the loss or the range of possible losses. If an estimate of loss cannot be made, that fact must be disclosed.

If the chance that a loss has been incurred is remote, no disclosure is necessary in most circumstances. However, guarantees of the indebtedness of others, guarantees to repurchase receivables or other assets, and obligations of commercial banks under standby letter of credit are always disclosed. The required disclosure should include the nature and amount of the guarantee. Additionally, if the entity may be able to recover some portion of the loss by proceeding against a third party, that fact might be disclosed.

An estimated gain from a **gain contingency** usually is not reflected in the balance sheet or income statement because doing so might recognize revenue prior to its realization. Adequate disclosure of the gain contingency must be made, but care must be taken to avoid misleading implications as to the likelihood of realization.

Contracts and negotiations. All significant contractual agreements and negotiations should be disclosed in the footnotes to the financial statements. For example, lease contract provisions, pension obligations, requirements contracts, bond indenture convenience, and stock option plans should be clearly disclosed in the notes.

Risks and Uncertainties

AICPA Statement of Position 94-6, *Disclosure of Certain Significant Risks and Uncertainties*, requires disclosure in financial statements about risks and uncertainties existing as of the date of those statements that could significantly affect the amounts reported in the near term. **Near term** is defined as a period of time not to exceed one year from the date of the financial statements. The four areas of disclosure required by SOP 94-6 are risks and uncertainties relating to the entity's **nature of operations, use of estimates in the preparation of financial statements, certain significant estimates,** and **current vulnerability due to certain concentrations.**

Nature of operations. SOP 94-6 requires that entities disclose the major products or services that they sell or provide. In addition, entities must disclose the principal markets that they serve as well as the location of such markets.

If an entity operates in more than one industry, it must disclose all industries it is operating within as well as the relative importance of each industry. The basis for determining the relative importance of each industry (assets, revenue, or earnings) should also be disclosed. Quantification is not required in disclosures about the nature of operations. Comparisons of relative importance for entities operating in more than one business can be conveyed by the use of words such as predominantly, equally, or major and other.

Use of estimates in the preparation of financial statements. Financial statements should disclose as an explanation that the preparation of financial statements in accordance with GAAP requires the use of estimates by management. The purpose of this disclosure is to clearly alert users to the pervasiveness of estimates.

Certain significant estimates. SOP 94-6 requires disclosures regarding estimates used in valuing assets, liabilities, or gain or loss contingencies if **both** of the following conditions are met (SOP 94-6):

1. It is at least **reasonably possible** that the estimate of the effect on the financial statements of a condition, situation, or set of circumstances that existed at the date of the financial statements will change in the **near term** due to one or more future confirming events.
2. The effect of the change would be **material** to the financial statements.

For the purposes of determining materiality, it is not the amount of an estimate that determines whether an item is material and must be disclosed, but rather the effect of using a different estimate that determines materiality.

The disclosure should indicate the nature of the uncertainty and that it is reasonably possible that the estimate will change in the near term. SOP 94-6 is separate from and does not change SFAS 5, *Accounting for Contingencies*. If an estimate is covered under SFAS 5 as a loss contingency, the disclosure should include an estimate of the possible range of loss, or state that an estimate cannot be made. Disclosure of any factors that would make an estimate sensitive to change is encouraged but not required.

Many entities use risk-reduction techniques to mitigate losses. If the effect of a change in the estimate is unlikely to be material because of risk-reduction techniques, the entity is encouraged, but not required, to disclose the uncertainty as well as the relevant risk-reduction techniques.

Examples of items that may be based on estimates that are particularly sensitive to change in the near term (SOP 94-6)

1. Inventory subject to rapid technological obsolescence
2. Specialized equipment subject to technological obsolescence
3. Valuation allowances for deferred tax assets based on future taxable income
4. Capitalized motion picture film production costs
5. Capitalized computer software costs
6. Deferred policy acquisition costs of insurance enterprises
7. Valuation allowances for commercial and real estate loans
8. Environmental remediation-related obligations
9. Litigation-related obligations
10. Contingent liabilities for obligations of other entities
11. Amounts reported for long-term obligations, such as amounts reported for pensions and postemployment benefits
12. Net proceeds recoverable, the provisions for expected loss to be incurred, or both, on disposition of a business or assets
13. Amounts reported for long-term contracts

Current vulnerability due to concentrations. Vulnerability from concentrations occurs when entities fail to diversify in order to mitigate risk. Financial statements must disclose such concentrations if management knows prior to issuance of the financial statements that all of the following conditions are met (SOP 94-6):

1. The concentration exists at the date of the financial statements.
2. The concentration makes the enterprise vulnerable to the risk of a near-term severe impact.
3. It is at least **reasonably possible** that the events that could cause the severe impact will occur in the near term.

Examples of concentrations that require disclosure (SOP 94-6)

1. Concentrations in the volume of business transacted with a particular customer, supplier, lender, grantor, or contributor.
2. Concentrations in revenue from particular products, services, or fundraising events.
3. Concentrations in the available sources of supply of materials, labor, services, or of licenses or other rights used in the entity's operations.
4. Concentrations in the market or geographic area in which an entity conducts its operations.

The potential for severe impact can occur as the result of the total or partial loss of a business relationship, price or demand changes, loss of patent protection, changes in the availability of a resource or right, or the disruption of operations in a market or geographic area. For purposes of SOP 94-6, it is always considered reasonably possible in the near term that any customer, grantor, or contributor will be lost and that operations located outside an entity's home country will be disrupted.

For concentrations of labor subject to collective bargaining agreements and concentrations of operations outside an entity's home country, the following additional disclosures are required (SOP 94-6):

1. For labor subject to collective bargaining agreements, disclosure should include both the percentage of the labor force covered by a collective bargaining agreement and the percentage of the labor force covered by a collectible bargaining agreement that will expire within one year.
2. For operations located outside the entity's home country, disclosure should include the carrying amounts of net assets and the geographic areas in which they are located.

Example of Balance Sheet Classification and Presentation

The classification and presentation of information in a balance sheet may be highly aggregated, highly detailed, or anywhere in between. In general, highly aggregated balance sheets are used in annual reports and other presentations provided to the public. Highly detailed balance sheets are used internally by management. The following highly aggregated balance sheet includes only a few lines items. The additional details required by generally accepted accounting principles are found in the notes to the financial statements.

ABC Corporation
Balance Sheet
December 31, 2002

Assets

Current assets	xxx
Long-term investments	xxx
Plant, property, and equipment, net	xxx
Deferred tax assets	xxx
Intangible and other assets	xxx
Total assets	xxx

Liabilities and Shareholders' Equity

Current liabilities	xxx
Accrued expenses	xxx
Deferred tax liabilities	xxx
Long-term debt	xxx
Total liabilities	xxx

Capital stock	xxx	
Additional paid-in capital	xxx	
Retained earnings	xxx	
Accumulated other comprehensive income	xxx	
Total shareholders' equity	xxx	
Total liabilities and shareholders' equity	xxx	

The following comprehensive balance sheet includes more line items (for details about specific assets and liabilities) than are found in many balance sheets.

ABC Corporation
Balance Sheet
December 31, 2002

Assets
Current assets:

Cash and bank deposits:			
Restricted to current bond maturity	$xxx		
Unrestricted	xxx	$xxx	
Short-term investments:			
Marketable equity securities (trading)		xxx	
Marketable debt securities (available-for-sale)		xxx	
Refundable income taxes		xxx	
Receivables from affiliates		xxx	
Accounts receivable	xxx		
Less allowance for doubtful accounts	(xxx)	xxx	
Notes receivable due in 2003	xxx		
Less discounts on notes receivable	(xxx)	xxx	
Dishonored notes receivable		xxx	
Installment notes due in 2003		xxx	
Interest receivable		xxx	
Creditors' accounts with debit balances		xxx	
Advances to employees		xxx	
Inventories (carried at lower of cost or market by FIFO):			
Finished goods	xxx		
Work in process	xxx		
Raw materials	xxx	xxx	
Prepaid expenses:			
Prepaid rent	xxx		
Prepaid insurance	xxx	xxx	
Total current assets			$xxx

Long-term investments:

Investments in equity securities (available-for-sale)	xxx	
Investments in bonds (held-to-maturity)	xxx	
Investments in equity securities (at cost, plus equity in undistributed net earnings since acquisition)	xxx	
Investments in unused land and facilities	xxx	
Cash surrender value of officers' life insurance policies	xxx	
Sinking fund for bond retirement	xxx	
Plant expansion fund	xxx	
Total long-term investments		$xxx

Property, plant, and equipment:

Land	$xxx	
Buildings	xxx	
Machinery and equipment	xxx	
Furniture and fixtures	xxx	
Leased assets	xxx	
Leasehold improvements	xxx	
Less accumulated depreciation and amortization	(xxx)	
Total property, plant, and equipment		xxx

Intangible assets net of amortization:

Goodwill of acquired businesses	$xxx	
Patents	xxx	
Trademarks	xxx	
Total intangible assets, net		xxx

Other assets:

Installment notes due after 2003	$xxx	
Unamortized bond issue costs	xxx	
Assets to be disposed of	xxx	
Total other noncurrent assets		xxx
Total assets		$xxx

Liabilities and Stockholders' Equity

Current liabilities:

Accounts payable	$xxx	
Commercial paper and other short-term notes	xxx	
Salaries, wages, and commissions payable	xxx	
Taxes withheld from employees	xxx	
Income taxes payable	xxx	
Dividends payable	xxx	
Rent revenue collected in advance	xxx	
Other advances from customers	xxx	
Current portion of long-term debt	xxx	
Current obligations under capital leases	xxx	
Deferred tax liability	xxx	
Short-term portion of accrued warranty	xxx	
Other accrued liabilities	xxx	
Total current liabilities		$xxx

Noncurrent liabilities:

Notes payable due after 2003	$xxx	
Plus unamortized note premium	xxx	$xxx
Long-term bonds:		
10% debentures due 2013	xxx	
9 1/2% collateralized obligations maturing serially to 2006	xxx	
8% convertible subordinated debentures due 2018	xxx	
Less unamortized discounts net of premiums	(xxx)	xxx

Accrued pension cost		xxx	
Obligations under capital leases		xxx	
Deferred tax liability		xxx	
Long-term portion of accrued warranty		xxx	
Total noncurrent liabilities			xxx
Total liabilities			$xxx

Capital stock:

$12.50 convertible preferred stock, $100 stated value, 200,000 shares authorized, 175,000 outstanding	$xxx	
12% cumulative preferred stock, $100 stated value, callable at $115, 100,000 shares authorized and outstanding	xxx	
Common stock, $10 stated value, 500,000 shares authorized, 450,000 issued, 15,000 held in treasury	xxx	
Common stock subscribed 10,000 shares	xxx	
Less: Subscriptions receivable	(xxx)	$xxx

Additional paid-in capital:

From 12% cumulative preferred	xxx	
From common stock	xxx	
From treasury stock transactions	xxx	
From stock dividends	xxx	
From expiration of stock options	xxx	
Warrants outstanding	xxx	xxx

Retained earnings　　　　　　　　　　　　　　　　　xxx

Accumulated other comprehensive income:

Net unrealized loss on available-for-sale securities	(xxx)	
Unrealized loss from foreign currency translation	(xxx)	
Excess of minimum pension liability over unrecognized prior service cost	(xxx)	(xxx)
Less: Treasury stock at cost		(xxx)
Total stockholders' equity		$xxx
Total liabilities and stockholders' equity		$xxx

3 STATEMENTS OF INCOME AND COMPREHENSIVE INCOME

PERSPECTIVE AND ISSUES

The primary focus of financial reporting is to provide information about an entity's performance that is useful to present and potential investors, creditors, and others when they are making financial decisions. In financial reporting, performance is primarily measured by net income and its components, which are provided in the income statement. Although information in the income statement is information about past performance, investors, creditors, and others use that information to predict future performance.

As contrasted to the balance sheet, which provides information about an entity at a point in time, an income statement provides information about a period of time. It reflects information about the transactions and other events occurring within the period. Most of the weaknesses of an income statement are a result of its periodic nature. Entities are continually creating and selling goods and services, and at any single point in time some of those processes will be incomplete. Thus, measurement of net income for a period involves estimates. The degree of completion of inventories, the amounts of inventories that have been manufactured or purchased but ultimately will not be sold, and the amounts of goods and services that have been sold but ultimately will not result in cash receipts are just of few of the many estimates that must be made in order to present an income statement. The entity's ability (or inability) to make these estimates is reflected in the performance measure for the period.

For years, performance was measured only by the income statement. In the last few years, a second performance measure has been added—comprehensive income. Comprehensive income is a broader notion of performance than net income. It includes all recognized changes in equity that occur during a period except those resulting from investments by owners and distributions to owners. Thus, included in comprehensive income but excluded from net income are foreign currency adjustments, unrealized changes in the fair value of available-for-sale securities, and minimum pension liability adjustments. Because comprehensive income includes the effects on an entity of economic events largely outside of its management's control, some have said that net income is a measure of management's performance and comprehensive income is a measure of entity performance.

The requirement to report comprehensive income in addition to net income is another step in the movement toward the capital maintenance concept of income mentioned in Chapter 2, Balance Sheet. Under that concept of income, income is earned only if the amount of an entity's net assets at the end of the period exceed its net assets at the beginning of the period after excluding the effects of transactions with owners. A capital maintenance concept of income is more consistent with investors' expectations that an investment should generate more financial resources than were invested.

Sources of GAAP					
ARB	*APB*	*SFAS*	*TB*	*EITF*	*SOP*
43, Ch. 2	9, 16,	4, 7, 15, 16,	85-6	85-36, 87-4,	98-5
	18, 20, 30	44, 64, 101,		87-24, 90-16,	
		128, 130,142		95-18, 00-9, 00-10	

DEFINITIONS OF TERMS

Comprehensive income. The change in equity of a business enterprise during a period from transactions and other events and circumstances from nonowner sources. It includes all changes in equity during a period, except those resulting from investments by owners and distributions to owners (SFAC 6).

Development stage enterprise. An entity that is devoting substantially all its efforts to establishing itself as a new business and either its principal operations have not commenced or its principal operations have commenced but have not generated a significant amount of revenue.

Disposal date. The date of closing the sale if the disposal is by sale or the date that operations cease if disposal is by abandonment (APB 30).

Distribution to owners. Decreases in net assets of a particular enterprise resulting from transferring assets, rendering services, or incurring liabilities by the enterprise to owners.

Distributions to owners reduce the ownership interest of the receiving owners in the entity and reduce the net assets of the entity by the amount of the distribution. Such transactions are displayed in the statement of changes in equity.

Expenses. Decreases in assets or increases in liabilities during a period resulting from delivery of goods, rendering of services, or other activities constituting the enterprise's central operations (SFAC 6).

Extraordinary item. Events and transactions that are distinguished by their unusual nature and by the infrequency of their occurrence (APB 30).

Gains. Increases in equity (net assets) from peripheral or incidental transactions of an entity and from all other transactions and other events and circumstances affecting the entity during a period except those that result from revenues or investments by owners (SFAC 6).

Investments by owners. Increases in net assets of a particular enterprise resulting from transfers to it of something valuable to obtain or increase ownership interests (or equity) in it.

Investments by owners may be in the form of assets, services, or the payment of entity liabilities. These investments are displayed in the statement of changes in equity. The purchase of an ownership interest from another owner is not a net investment because such a transfer does not increase the net assets of the entity.

Losses. Decreases in equity (net assets) from peripheral or incidental transactions of an entity from all other transactions and other events and circumstances affecting the entity during a period except those that result from expenses or distributions to owners (SFAC 6).

Measurement date. The date on which the management having the authority to approve the action commits itself to a formal plan to dispose of a segment of the business, whether by sale or abandonment (APB 30).

Realization. The process of converting noncash resources and rights into money or, more precisely, the sale of an asset for cash or claims to cash (SFAC 6).

Recognition. The process of formally recording or incorporating an item in the financial statements of an entity (SFAC 6).

Revenues. Increases in assets or decreases in liabilities during a period from delivering goods, rendering services, or other activities constituting the enterprise's central operations (SFAC 6).

Segment of a business. A component of an entity whose activities represent a major line of business or class of customer. A segment may be in the form of a subsidiary, a division, or a department, and in some cases, a joint venture or other nonsubsidiary investee. Its assets, results of operations, and activities can be clearly distinguished, physically and operationally, and for financial reporting purposes, from the other assets, results of operations, and activities of the entity (APB 30).

CONCEPTS, RULES, AND EXAMPLES

Limitations of the Income Statement

Economists have generally adopted a wealth maintenance concept of income. Under this concept, income is the maximum amount that can be consumed during a period and still leave the enterprise with the same amount of wealth at the end of the period as existed at the beginning. Wealth is determined with reference to the current market values of the net productive assets at the beginning and end of the period. Therefore, the economists' definition of income would fully incorporate market value changes (both increases and decreases in wealth) in the determination of periodic income.

Accountants, on the other hand, have generally defined income by reference to specific events that give rise to recognizable elements of revenue and expense during a reporting period. The events that produce reportable items of revenue and expense are a subset of economic events that determine economic income. Many changes in the market values of wealth components are deliberately excluded from the measurement of accounting income, but are included in the measurement of economic income.

The discrepancy between accounting and economic measures of income is primarily the result of accountants' concerns for reliability and measurability. Those concerns prevent revenue and gains from being recognized until an acceptable level of assurance is obtained about the existence and amount of those revenues and gains. In general, accountants do not recognize revenues or gains until they are realizable—convertible into known amounts of cash or claims to cash.

However, some gains are realizable but are still not reported in net income. Holding gains on certain debt and equity investments are readily convertible into known amounts of cash. Those gains are currently excluded from net income for two reasons. First, many consider net income to be a measure of management's performance, and holding gains and losses result from market fluctuations that are outside the control of management. To report holding gains and losses in net income decreases the ability to use that measure to judge management performance. Second, many entities that purchase large amounts of investments finance those investments with liabilities, making money off the spread (the difference between the investment return and the interest expense). Including in net income unrealized holding gains and losses on only the investments, and not the related liabilities, could cause volatility in earnings that is not representative of how those entities are impacted by economic events. However, the FASB is currently working on a project that could lead to reporting certain liabilities at fair value; thus, future changes in accounting standards may eliminate this as a difference between accounting and economic measures of income.

Another reason for the discrepancy between accounting and economic measures of income is the periodic nature of the income statement. Both accountants and economists realize that the earnings process occurs throughout the various stages of production, sales, and final delivery of the product. However, the difficulty in measuring the precise rate at which this earnings process is taking place has led accountants to conclude that income should normally be recognized only when it is fully realized. **Realization** generally implies that the enterprise producing the item has completed all of its obligations relating to the product and that collection of the resulting receivable is assured beyond reasonable doubt. For very sound reasons, accountants have developed a reliable system of income recognition that is based on generally accepted accounting principles applied consistently from period to period.

The economic measure of income would be relatively simple to apply on a life-cycle basis. Economic income would be measured by the difference between its wealth at the termination point versus its wealth at the origination date, plus withdrawals or other distributions and minus additional investments over the course of its life. However, applying the same measurement strategy to discrete fiscal periods, as accountants do, is substantially more difficult. Allocating earnings to individual years, quarters, or months requires both estimates and judgment. Consequently, accountants have concluded that there must be unambiguous guidelines for revenue recognition. These have required recognition only at the completion of the earnings cycle.

Accountants have moved closer to an economic measure of income by introducing the measure "comprehensive income" into the financial statements. Comprehensive income is the change in equity resulting from all sources other than distributions to owners and investments by owners. Thus, definitionally, it is similar to economic income. However, because of the realization and recognition concerns discussed earlier, comprehensive income remains a subset of economic income.

Whether economic income, comprehensive income, net income, or some other measure is the appropriate measure of income is partially dependent upon the perspective of the party doing the measuring. From the perspective of the outside investors taken as a whole, income might be defined as earnings before any payments to those investors, including bondholders and preferred stockholders as well as common shareholders. On the other hand, from the perspective of the common shareholders, income might better be defined as earnings after payments to other investors, including creditors and preferred shareholders. Analysts regularly use earnings before income taxes, depreciation, and amortization. Perhaps the best accounting can do is provide the broadest possible measure (comprehensive income) and include in the financial statements information that allows each reader to compute the measure that is most meaningful to him or her.

Recognition and Measurement

Revenues. Revenues represent actual or expected cash inflows that result from an entity's central operations. Revenues are generally recognized at the culmination of the earnings process—when the entity has substantially completed all it must do to be entitled to future cash inflows (or to retain cash already transferred). Most often, an exchange transaction indicates that revenues have been earned. Merchandise is delivered or services are rendered to a customer, resulting in the receipt of cash or the right to receive cash in the future. Revenues are generally measured by the values of the assets exchanged (or liabilities incurred).

Revenues are different from gains for three reasons. Revenues result from an entity's central operations; gains result from incidental or peripheral activities of the entity. Revenues are usually earned; gains result from nonreciprocal transactions (such as winning a lawsuit or receiving a gift) or other economic events for which there is no earnings process. Revenues are reported gross, gains are reported net.

The existence of an exchange transaction generally is critical to the accounting recognition of revenue. However, an exchange transaction is viewed in a broader sense than the legal concept of a sale. Whenever an exchange of rights and privileges takes place, an exchange transaction is deemed to have occurred. For example, interest revenue and interest expense are earned or incurred ratably over a period without a discrete transaction taking place. Accruals are recorded periodically in order to reflect the interest realized by the passage of time. In a like manner, the percentage-of-completion method recognizes revenue based upon the measure of progress on a long-term construction project. The earnings process is considered to occur simultaneously with the measure of progress (e.g., the incurrence of costs).

The timing of revenue recognition also varies based on the realizability of the future cash flows. For example, the production of certain commodities takes place in an environment in which the ultimate realization of revenue is so assured that revenue can be recognized upon the completion of the production process. At the opposite extreme is the situation in which an exchange transaction has taken place, but significant uncertainty exists as to the ultimate collectibility of the amount. For example, in certain sales of real estate, where the down payment percentage is extremely small and the security for the buyer's notes is minimal, revenue is often not recognized until the time collections are actually received.

Chapter 8, Special Revenue Recognition Areas, provides more information about revenue recognition under special circumstances.

Expenses. Expenses represent actual or expected cash outflows that result from an entity's central operations. Expenses are generally recognized when an asset either is consumed in an entity's central operations or is no longer expected to provide the level of future benefits expected when that asset was recognized.

Expenses are different from losses for three reasons. Expenses result from an entity's central operations; losses result from incidental or peripheral activities of the entity. Expenses are often incurred during the earnings process; losses often result from nonreciprocal transactions (such as thefts or fines) or other economic events unrelated to an earnings process. Expenses are reported gross, losses are reported net.

Although many cash outflows are recognized directly as expenses, that is done for expediency; most expenses are first assets, if only for a moment. Measuring the consumption of assets is done by one of three pervasive measurement principles: associating cause and effect, systematic and rational allocation, or immediate recognition.

Some costs, such as materials and direct labor consumed in the manufacturing process, are relatively easy to identify with the related revenue elements. The matching principle requires that all expenses incurred in the generation of revenue should be recognized in the same accounting period as the related revenues are recognized. Thus, those cost elements are included in inventory and expensed as cost of sales when a product is sold and revenue from the sale is recognized. That process is associating cause and effect.

Other costs are more closely associated with specific accounting periods. In the absence of a cause and effect relationship, the asset's cost should be allocated to the accounting periods benefited in a systematic and rational manner. This form of expense recognition involves assumptions about the expected length of benefit and the relationship between benefit and cost of each period. Depreciation of fixed assets, amortization of intangibles, and allocation of rent and insurance are examples of costs that are recognized by the use of a systematic and rational method.

All other costs are normally expensed in the period in which they are incurred. This includes costs for which no clear-cut future benefits can be identified, costs that were recorded as assets in prior periods but for which no remaining future benefits can be identified, and costs for which no rational allocation scheme can be devised.

The general approach for recognizing expenses is first to attempt to match costs with the related revenues. Next, a method of systematic and rational allocation should be attempted. If neither of those measurement principles is beneficial, the cost should be immediately expensed.

Expenses do not include distributions to owners. Expenses of a corporation are easily identified and separated from distributions to stockholders. In both the sole proprietorship and partnership form of entity, the identification process can be more difficult. Items such as interest or salaries paid to partners or owners may be thought of as distributions of profits rather than expenses. However, many entities adopt the philosophy that financial reporting should be the same regardless of legal form (economic substance takes precedence over legal form). Under the corporate form of business, interest on stockholder loans and salaries paid to stockholders are clearly classified as expenses and not as distributions. Accordingly, these items may be treated as expenses for both partnerships and sole proprietorships. However, full disclosure and consistency of financial reporting treatment would be required. Circumstances may involve treating certain payments, such as guaranteed salaries, as expenses while classifying other "salaries" as profit distributions.

Gains and losses. Gains are increases in equity resulting from transactions and economic events other than those that generate revenues or are investments from owners. Losses are decreases in equity resulting from transactions and economic events other than those that generate expenses or are distributions to owners. Gains and losses result from an entity's peripheral transactions (e.g., sale of used equipment), from economic events outside of the control of management (e.g., holding gains on securities), or from nonreciprocal transactions (e.g., lawsuit settlements, fines, and thefts).

Gains and losses are often described in financial statements by their sources, for example, realized gains (losses) on sale of securities or earthquake loss. They are usually measured at net amounts. For example, gains (losses) from sales of assets are measured by subtracting the unexpired cost of the asset from the proceeds, and holding gains (losses) are measured by subtracting the value at the beginning of the period from the value at the end of the period.

Gains often result from transactions and other events that involve no earnings process; therefore, in terms of recognition, it is more significant that the gain be realized or realizable than earned. Losses are recognized when it becomes evident that future economic benefits of a previously recognized asset have been reduced or eliminated, or that a liability has been incurred without associated economic benefits.

Other comprehensive income. Comprehensive income is the change in equity that results from revenue, expenses, gains, and losses during a period, as well as any other recognized changes in equity that occur for reasons other than investments by owners and distributions to owners.

Other comprehensive income (comprehensive income less net income) is defined in SFAS 130 to include, under current standards, foreign currency items, minimum pension liability adjustments, and unrealized gains and losses on certain investments in debt and equity securities. Other comprehensive income is recognized and measured in accordance with the accounting pronouncement that deems it part of other comprehensive income. Thus, foreign currency adjustments are recognized and measured in accordance with SFAS 52 (Chapter 21, Foreign Currency); additional pension liabilities are recognized and measured in accordance with SFAS 87 (Chapter 16, Pensions); and unrealized gains and losses are recognized and measured in accordance with SFAS 115 (Chapter 10, Investments). In general, those items are recognized and measured whenever a complete set of financial statements is prepared.

Format of Statements of Income and Comprehensive Income

The basic order of presentation of information in an income statement (or statement of income and comprehensive income) is defined by a series of accounting pronouncements, as shown by the diagram on the next page. Other than in the section "income from continuing operations," the display of revenues, expenses, gains, losses, and other comprehensive income is predetermined by authoritative pronouncement. Only within income from continuing operations does tradition and industry practice determine the presentation.

The sections containing information about other comprehensive income and comprehensive income can be presented in a combined statement of income and comprehensive income, as shown in the shaded area on the diagram. Alternatively, that information can be reported in a stand-alone statement of comprehensive income or in an expanded statement of changes in stockholder's equity. In SFAS 130, the FASB encourages the use of either a combined statement in which other comprehensive income appears below net income or a stand-alone statement that begins with net income. Regardless of the reporting location chosen, totals for net income, other comprehensive income, and comprehensive income must appear in the statement, and the statement must be of the same prominence as other financial statements. Information about other comprehensive income cannot be presented only in the notes to financial statements. For ease of reading, this publication uses the term "income statement" to include a combined statement of income and comprehensive income.

Statement of Income and Comprehensive Income	Net of tax?	Reference
Income from continuing operations Sales or service revenues Costs of goods sold Operating expenses Gains and losses Other revenues and expenses Items that are unusual or infrequent, but not both Income tax expense related to continuing operations	No	APB 30
Results from discontinued operations Income (loss) from operations of a discontinued segment Gain (loss) from disposal of a discontinued segment	Yes	APB 30, SFAS 16
Extraordinary items Items that are both unusual and infrequent Gain (loss) on early extinguishment of debt Gains of a debtor in a troubled debt restructuring Disposal of certain assets within two years of a pooling Write-off of operating rights of motor carriers Investor's share of an equity method investee's extraordinary item	Yes	APB 9, APB 16, APB 30, SFAS 4, SFAS 44, SFAS 64, SFAS 101, TB 85-6
Cumulative effect of a change in accounting principle	Yes	APB 20
Net income		
Other comprehensive income Foreign currency adjustments Unrealized gains (losses) on securities Minimum pension liability Income tax related to other comprehensive income (if components are not shown net of tax)	Choice	SFAS 130
Comprehensive income		
Earnings per share information		SFAS 128

NOTE: Alternatively, information in the shaded area can be presented as a separate statement or in a statement of changes in stockholders' equity.

The three items that are shown in the heading of an income statement are

1. The name of the entity whose results of operations is being presented
2. The title of the statement
3. The period of time covered by the statement

The entity's legal name should be used and supplemental information could be added to disclose the entity's legal form as a corporation, partnership, sole proprietorship, or other form if that information is not apparent from the entity's name. The use of the titles "Income Statement," "Statement of Income and Comprehensive Income," "Statement of Operations," or "Statement of Earnings" denotes preparation in accordance with generally accepted accounting principles. If another comprehensive basis of accounting is used, such as the cash or income tax basis, the title of the statement should be modified accordingly. "Statement of Revenue and Expenses—Income Tax Basis" or "Statement of Revenue and Expenses—Modified Cash Basis" are examples of such titles.

The date of an income statement must clearly identify the time period involved, such as "Year Ending March 31, 2002." That dating informs the reader of the length of the period covered by the statement and both the starting and ending dates. Dating such as "The Period Ending March 31, 2002" or "Through March 31, 2002" is not useful because of the lack of precision in those titles. Income statements are rarely presented for periods in excess of one year but are frequently seen for shorter periods such as a month or a quarter. Entities whose operations form a natural cycle may have a reporting period end on a specific day (e.g., the last Friday of the month). These entities should head the income statement "For the 52 Weeks Ended March 28, 2002" (each week containing seven days, beginning on a Saturday and ending on a Friday). Although that fiscal period includes only 364 days, it is still considered an annual reporting period.

Income statements generally should be uniform in appearance from one period to the next. The form, terminology, captions, and pattern of combining insignificant items should be consistent. If comparative statements are presented, the prior year's information should be restated to conform to the current year's presentation if changes in presentation are made.

Aggregation of items should not serve to conceal significant information, such as netting revenues against expenses or combining dissimilar types of resources, expenses, gains, or losses. The category "other or miscellaneous expense" should contain, at maximum, an immaterial total amount of aggregated insignificant items. Once this total approaches 10% of total expenses, some other aggregations with explanatory titles should be selected.

Income from Continuing Operations

The section "income from continuing operations" includes all revenues, expenses, gains, and losses that are not required to be reported in other sections of an income statement.

There are two generally accepted formats for the presentation of income from continuing operations: the single-step and the multiple-step formats.

In the single-step format, items are classified into two groups: revenues and expenses. The operating revenues and other revenues are itemized and summed to determine total revenues. The cost of goods sold, operating expenses, and other expenses are itemized and summed to determine total expenses. The total expenses (including income taxes) are deducted from the total revenues to arrive at income from continuing operations.

Example of single-step format for income from continuing operations

Revenues:		
Sales (net of discounts and returns and allowances)	$xxx	
Gain on sale of equipment	xxx	
Interest income	xxx	
Dividend income	xxx	$xxx
Expenses:		
Cost of goods sold	$xxx	
Selling expenses	xxx	
General and administrative expenses	xxx	
Interest expense	xxx	xxx
Income from continuing operations		xxx

Some believe that a multiple-step format enhances the usefulness of information about an entity's performances by reporting the interrelationships of revenues and expenses, using subtotals to report significant amounts. In a multiple-step format, operating revenues and expenses are separated from nonoperating revenues and expenses to provide more information concerning the firm's primary activities. This format breaks the revenue and expense items into various intermediate income components so that important relationships can be shown and attention can be focused on significant subtotals. Some examples of common intermediate income components are as follows:

1. **Gross profit (margin)**—The difference between net sales and cost of goods sold.
2. **Operating income**—Gross profit less operating expenses.
3. **Income before income taxes**—Operating income plus any other revenue items and less any other expense items.

Example of a multiple-step format for income from continuing operations

Sales:			
Sales			$xxx
Less: Sales discounts		$xxx	
Sales returns and allowances		xxx	(xxx)
Net sales			$xxx
Cost of goods sold			xxx
Gross profit			$xxx

Operating expenses:		
Selling expenses		
Sales salaries	$xxx	
Commissions	xxx	
Advertising expense	xxx	
Delivery expense	xxx	
Selling supplies expense	xxx	
Depreciation of store furniture and equipment	<u>xxx</u>	$xxx
General and administrative expenses		
Officers' salaries	$xxx	
Office salaries	xxx	
Bad debts expense	xxx	
Office supplies expense	xxx	
Depreciation of office furniture and fixtures	xxx	
Depreciation of building	xxx	
Insurance expense	xxx	
Utilities expense	<u>xxx</u>	<u>xxx</u>
Total operating expense		(<u>xxx</u>)
Operating income		$xxx
Other revenues:		
Dividend income	$xxx	
Interest income	<u>xxx</u>	xxx
Other expenses:		
Interest expense		(<u>xxx</u>)
Income from continuing operations		$<u>xxx</u>

The following items of revenue, expense, gains, and losses are included within income from continuing operations:

1. **Sales or service revenues** are charges to customers for the goods and/or services provided during the period. This section should include information about discounts, allowances, and returns in order to determine net sales or net revenues.

2. **Cost of goods sold** is the cost of the inventory items sold during the period. In the case of a merchandising firm, net purchases (purchases less discounts, returns, and allowances plus freight-in) are added to beginning inventory to get cost of goods available for sale. From the cost of goods available for sale amount, the ending inventory is deducted to get cost of goods sold.

Example of calculation of cost of goods sold

ABC Merchandising Company
Schedule of Cost of Goods Sold
For the Year Ended 12/31/02

Beginning inventory		$xxx
Add: Purchases	$xxx	
Freight-in	<u>xxx</u>	
Cost of purchases	xxx	

Less: Purchase discounts	$xx		
Purchase returns and allowances	xx	(xxx)	
Net purchases			xxx
Cost of goods available for sale			xxx
Less: Ending inventory			(xxx)
Cost of goods sold			$xxx

A manufacturing company computes the cost of goods sold in a slightly different way. Cost of goods manufactured would be added to the beginning inventory to arrive at cost of goods available for sale. The ending inventory is then deducted from the cost of goods available for sale to determine the cost of goods sold. Cost of goods manufactured can be computed as follows:

Example of computation of cost of goods manufactured and sold

XYZ Manufacturing Company
Schedule of Cost of Goods Manufactured
For the Year Ended 12/31/02

Direct materials inventory 1/1/02	$xxx	
Purchases of materials (including freight-in and deducting purchase discounts)	xxx	
Total direct materials available	$xxx	
Direct materials inventory 12/31/02	(xxx)	
Direct materials used		$xxx
Direct labor		xxx
Factory overhead:		
Depreciation of factory equipment	$xxx	
Utilities	xxx	
Indirect factory labor	xxx	
Indirect materials	xxx	
Other overhead items	xxx	xxx
Manufacturing cost incurred in 2002		$xxx
Add: Work in process 1/1/02		xxx
Less: Work in process 12/31/02		(xxx)
Cost of goods manufactured		$xxx

XYZ Manufacturing Company
Schedule of Cost of Goods Sold
For the Year Ended 12/31/02

Finished goods inventory 1/1/02	$xxx
Add: Cost of goods manufactured	xxx
Cost of goods available for sale	$xxx
Less: Finished goods inventory 12/31/02	(xxx)
Cost of goods sold	$xxx

3. **Operating expenses** are primary recurring costs associated with central operations (other than cost of goods sold) that are incurred in order to generate sales. Operating expenses are normally reported in the following two categories:

a. Selling expenses
b. General and administrative expenses

Selling expenses are those expenses directly related to the company's efforts to generate sales (e.g., sales salaries, commissions, advertising, delivery expenses, depreciation of store furniture and equipment, and store supplies). General and administrative expenses are expenses related to the general administration of the company's operations (e.g., officers and office salaries, office supplies, depreciation of office furniture and fixtures, telephone, postage, accounting and legal services, and business licenses and fees).

4. **Gains and losses** result from the peripheral transactions of the entity. If immaterial, they are usually combined and shown with the normal, recurring revenues and expenses. If they are individually material, they should be disclosed on a separate line. Examples are write-downs of inventories and receivables, effects of a strike, and gains and losses from exchange or translation of foreign currencies. Holding gains on available-for-sale securities are included in other comprehensive income rather than income from continuing operations.

5. **Other revenues and expenses** are revenues and expenses not related to the central operations of the company (e.g., gains and losses on the disposal of equipment, interest revenues and expenses, and dividend revenues).

6. **Unusual or infrequent** items are items that are either unusual or infrequent, but not both. They should be reported as a separate component of income from continuing operations.

7. **Goodwill impairment losses** will be presented as a separate line item in the income from continuing operations section of the income statement after the effective date of SFAS 142, Goodwill and Other Intangible Assets. SFAS 142 prohibits the amortization of goodwill and instead requires that goodwill be tested for impairment at least annually. If goodwill is found to be impaired, it is to be written down to fair value. The resultant loss will be included in the operations section of the income statement. However, if a goodwill impairment loss is associated with a discontinued operation, the loss would be included (on a net-of-tax basis) within the results of discontinued operations.

8. **Income tax expense** related to continuing operations is that portion of the total income tax expense applicable to continuing operations.

The section ends in a subtotal that varies depending upon the existence of discontinued operations, extraordinary items, and accounting changes. For example, the subtotal is usually titled "income from continuing operations" only when there is a section for discontinued operations in one of the years presented. If there is only a section for extraordinary items, the subtotal is usually titled "income before extraordinary items." If there is only an accounting change, the subtotal is usually titled "income before the cumulative effects of a change in accounting principle." The titles are adjusted accordingly if more than one of the sections are necessary. If there are no discontinued operations, extraordinary items, or accounting changes, the subtotal is titled "net income."

Examples of the format for presentation of various income statement items

Discontinued operations and an extraordinary item

Income (loss) from continuing operations		$ xxx
Discontinued operations		
Income (loss) from operations of Division Z, less applicable income taxes of $xxx	$xxx	
Income (loss) on disposal of Division Z, less applicable income taxes of $xxx	<u>xxx</u>	<u>xxx</u>
Income (loss) before extraordinary item		$ xxx
Extraordinary item, less applicable income taxes of $xxx (Note __)		<u>xxx</u>
Net income		$ <u>xxx</u>
Per share of common stock*		
Income (loss) from continuing operations		$x.xx
Net income		$<u>x.xx</u>

Discontinued operations and a change in accounting principle

Income (loss) from continuing operations		$ xxx
Discontinued operations		
Income (loss) from operations of Division Z, less applicable income taxes of $xxx	$xxx	
Income (loss) on disposal of Division Z, less applicable income taxes of $xxx	<u>xxx</u>	<u>xxx</u>
Income (loss) before cumulative effect		$ xxx
Cumulative effect on prior years (to **date of last year's income statement**) of changing to (change described), less applicable income taxes of $xxx (Note __)		<u>xxx</u>
Net income		$ <u>xxx</u>
Per share of common stock*		
Income (loss) from continuing operations		$x.xx
Net income		$<u>x.xx</u>

Extraordinary item and a change in accounting principle

Income (loss) before extraordinary item and cumulative effect of a change in accounting principle	$ xxx
Extraordinary item, less applicable income taxes of $xxx (Note __)	xxx
Cumulative effect on prior years (to **date of last year's income statement**) of changing to (change described), less applicable income taxes of $xxx (Note __)	<u>xxx</u>
Net income	$ <u>xxx</u>
Per share of common stock*	
Income (loss) before extraordinary item and a change in accounting principle	$x.xx
Net income	$<u>x.xx</u>

* *In these examples, assume per share amounts of discontinued operations, extraordinary items, and cumulative effect of a change in accounting principles are shown in the notes.*

Results from Discontinued Operations

Discontinued operations represent separately identifiable segments (components of a major class of business with separately identifiable assets, liabilities, revenues, and expenses) that are being disposed of. (If long-lived assets and certain intangible assets are to be disposed of but their disposal is not related to the disposal of a segment, the standards in SFAS 121 should be followed [Chapter 9, Long-Lived Assets]. Resulting losses are not included in discontinued operations.) The discontinued operations section of an income statement consists of two components, the "income (loss) from operations" and the "gain (loss) on the disposal." The first component, income (loss) from operations, is disclosed for the current year only if the decision to discontinue operations is made after the beginning of the fiscal year for which the financial statements are being prepared. In the diagram below, the income (loss) from operations component is determined for the time period designated by A—the period from the beginning of the year to the date the decision is made to discontinue a segment's operations (**measurement date**). The second component, gain (loss) on disposal, consists of the following two elements:

1. Income (loss) from operations during the phaseout period (the period between the measurement date and **disposal date**), B in the diagram below
2. Gain (loss) from disposal of segment assets

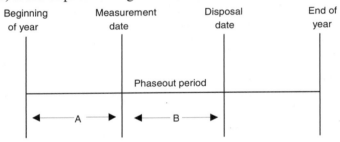

After it has been determined that certain discontinued operations constitute the disposal of a segment in accordance with APB 30, results of the discontinued segment must be segregated from normal, recurring operations. The gain or loss on disposal should include costs and expenses directly associated with the decision to dispose of a segment, such as severance pay, additional pension costs, employee relocation expenses, and future rentals on leases (net of sublease rentals). The gain or loss on disposal should not include adjustments of valuation accounts, costs, and expenses that should have been recognized prior to the measurement date but were not. The allocation of interest to discontinued operations is permitted but not required. The maximum allocation of interest cannot exceed the total of (1) interest on debt of the discontinued operation assumed by the buyer and (2) an allocated share of other interest not directly attributable to other operations of the entity.

If a loss is expected from the proposed sale or abandonment of a segment, the estimated loss should be provided for at the measurement date. If a gain is expected, it should be recognized when realized, which ordinarily is the disposal date. The results of discontinued operations should be disclosed separately as a component of income before extraordinary items and the cumulative effect of accounting changes (if applicable) as shown below.

Example of income statement presentation for discontinued operations

Income from continuing operations before income taxes		$xxxx
Provisions for income taxes		xxx
Income from continuing operations		$xxxx
Discontinued operations (Note __):		
Income (loss) from operations of discontinued Division X (less applicable income taxes of $__)	$xxxx	
Loss on disposal of Division X, including provision of $__ for operating losses during phaseout period (less applicable income taxes of $__)	(xxxx)	xxxx
Net income		$xxxx

There are special rules for situations in which the disposal date occurs in the year after the measurement date. The problem is one of estimating the unrealized gain (loss) on disposal for that part of the phaseout period that is in the following year and comparing it to the actual gain (loss) on disposal that has **already been realized** at the end of the preceding year for which the financial statements are being prepared. The following two rules apply to this situation:

1. A realized loss on disposal may be increased by an estimated loss, or it may be reduced by an estimated gain (but only to zero).
2. A realized gain on disposal may be reduced by an estimated loss but cannot be increased due to an estimated gain.

The diagram below depicts the relationships discussed above.

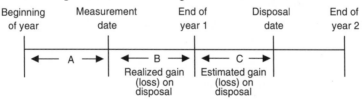

To find the year-end gain (loss), the amounts for periods B and C are compared and adjusted using the rules stated above.

Example of computing the year-end gain (loss) on disposal

Assume the following:

1. Loss from operations from beginning of year to the measurement date, $699, net of taxes of $466
2. Realized loss from operations from measurement date to end of current year, $400, net of taxes of $267
3. Estimated loss from operations from year-end to disposal date, $200, net of taxes of $133

4.   Estimated gain from disposal of assets during next year, $500, net of taxes of $333

The loss from operations of the discontinued segment represents the first component of discontinued operations and is to be shown net of tax. Items 2. and 3. above are to be reported as the second component of discontinued operations: $400 loss realized during phaseout period minus the $300 estimated **net** gain to be realized in the next period (estimated gain on disposal less the estimated loss from operations). The income statement presentation would be as follows:

Income from continuing operations before provision for income taxes	$598	
Provision for income taxes	239	
Income from continuing operations		$359
Discontinued operations:		
Loss from operations of discontinued Division Z (less applicable taxes of $466)	(699)	
Loss on disposal of Division Z including operating losses during phaseout period of $1,000 and gain on disposal of assets of $833, net of applicable taxes of $67	(100)	(799)
Net loss		$(440)

When discontinued operations are disclosed in a comparative income statement, the income statement presented for each previous year must be adjusted retroactively to enhance comparability with the current year's income statement. Accordingly, the revenues, cost of goods sold, and operating expenses (including income taxes) for the discontinued segment are removed from the revenues, cost of goods sold, and operating expenses of continuing operations. These items are netted into one figure [i.e., income (loss) from operations] that is disclosed under the discontinued operations section.

Example of comparative income statement disclosure

Assume the following:

1.   The 2002 information is from the preceding example.
2.   The 2001 information is given as shown.

	2002	2001
Discontinued operations:		
Loss from operations of discontinued Division Z, net of applicable taxes of $466 and $546	$699	$820
Loss on disposal of assets of discontinued Division Z including loss during phaseout period, net of applicable taxes of $67	100	--

Example of computing and presenting income from discontinued operations

Assume the following:

1.   Income from continuing operations is $400,000 in 2002
2.   The following net of tax figures are given where
     A — is the **income** (loss) **from operations** of Discontinued Segment X, net of taxes, in 2002.

B_1 — is the gain (loss) on **disposal of assets** of Discontinued Segment X, net of taxes, excluding **operating** losses or gains during the phaseout period in 2002.

B_2 — is the operating gain (loss) net of taxes, during the phaseout period in 2002.

C_1 — is the expected gain (loss) on **disposal of assets** of Discontinued Segment X, net of taxes, **excluding operating** losses or gains during the phaseout period in 2003.

C_2 — is the expected **operating** gain (loss) during the phaseout period in 2003, net of taxes.

	Case 1	*Case 2*	*Case 3*	*Case 4*	*Case 5*	*Case 6*
A	$ 50,000	$ 50,000	$ 50,000	$ (50,000)	$ (50,000)	$ (50,000)
B_1	100,000	100,000	(100,000)	100,000	(100,000)	(100,000)
B_2	60,000	(110,000)	(60,000)	(40,000)	110,000	90,000
C_1	(80,000)	(80,000)	80,000	80,000	60,000	(10,000)
C_2	10,000	70,000	(70,000)	(70,000)	(80,000)	80,000

The key is to net B_1 with B_2 and C_1 with C_2 before potential netting of the B's with the C's. Then the cases simplify, as follows:

	Case 1	*Case 2*	*Case 3*	*Case 4*	*Case 5*	*Case 6*
A	$ 50,000	$ 50,000	$ 50,000	$(50,000)	$(50,000)	$(50,000)
B	160,000	(10,000)	(160,000)	60,000	10,000	(10,000)
C	(70,000)	(10,000)	10,000	10,000	(20,000)	70,000

Now income statements for 2002 can be readily prepared.

	Case 1	*Case 2*	*Case 3*	*Case 4*	*Case 5*	*Case 6*
Income from continuing operations (net of taxes)	$400,000	$400,000	$ 400,000	$400,000	$400,000	$400,000
Discontinued operations (net of taxes)						
Income (loss) from operations of discontinued Division X	$ 50,000	$ 50,000	$ 50,000	$ (50,000)	$ (50,000)	$ (50,000)
Gain (loss) on disposal of Division X, including provision for operating losses during phase-out period	90,000	(20,000)	(150,000)	60,000	(10,000)	--
Total	$140,000	$ 30,000	$(100,000)	$ 10,000	$ (60,000)	$(50,000)
Net income (or income before extraordinary items and accounting changes) in 2002	$540,000	$430,000	$ 300,000	$410,000	$340,000	$350,000
Income to be reported in 2003	$ --	$ --	$ --	$ 10,000	$ --	$ 60,000

Note that in Case 4, the $10,000 expected gain cannot be recognized since it will not be realized until 2003. The gain was recognized in Case 3 because it offset the actual loss incurred. In Case 6 when the $70,000 anticipated gain is used to offset losses, only $10,000 can be used and $60,000 is delayed until the next year. Future gains can only be recognized to the extent of losses incurred.

When amounts actually realized differ from estimates, differences between estimated and actual amounts are treated as changes in accounting estimates. These are reported net of tax on the appropriate line in the "discontinued operations" section of the income statement in the period recognized. Amounts previously reported are not revised.

In addition to the amounts that should be disclosed in the financial statements, the notes to financial statements for the period encompassing the measurement date should disclose the following:

1. The identity of the **segment of business** that has been or will be discontinued
2. The expected disposal date
3. The expected manner of disposal
4. A description of the remaining assets and liabilities of the segment at the balance sheet date
5. The income or loss from operations and any proceeds from disposal of the segment during the period from the measurement date to the balance sheet date

Financial statements of periods after the measurement date, including the period of disposal, should disclose items 1., 2., 3., and 4. In addition, the later periods should include a comparison of the information required to be disclosed in item 5. to the prior estimates of those amounts.

Shortly, the FASB is expected to issue a Statement on asset impairment and disposal issues. The Statement would amend APB 30 by eliminating "segment of a business" and replacing it with "any component of an entity with separately identifiable operations (including revenues and expenses), assets, and cash flows that either has been disposed of or is classified as held for sale." Thus, the amendment would make APB 30 applicable to a broader class of disposals than in the past. The Statement would also establish standards for the recognition and measurement of obligations associated with disposal. Those obligations include employee termination benefits, costs incurred under existing operating leases, costs of closing plant facilities, and relocating employees. Expected future operating losses would not qualify for recognition as liabilities as they do under APB 30. However, a loss would be recognized if it resulted from a preexisting contractual obligation, such as a contract obligating the entity to provide at a future date goods produced using the assets to be disposed of. For additional information about the proposed changes, see Chapter 9, Long-Lived Assets.

Extraordinary Items

An event or transaction should be presumed to be an ordinary and usual activity (and thus, included in income from continuing operations) unless the event or transaction is both of an unusual nature and infrequent in its occurrence.

Unusual nature. The underlying event or transaction should possess a high degree of abnormality and be of a type clearly unrelated to, or only incidentally related to, the ordinary and typical activities of the entity, taking into account the environment in which the entity operates.

In determining whether an event or transaction is of an unusual nature, the following special characteristics of the entity should be considered:

1. Type and scope of operations
2. Lines of business
3. Operating policies
4. Industry in which the entity operates
5. Geographic location of its operations
6. Nature and extent of government regulation

An event that is of an unusual nature for one entity can be an ordinary and usual activity of another because of the above characteristics. Whether an event or transaction is beyond the control of management is irrelevant in the determination of whether it is of an unusual nature.

Infrequency of occurrence. The underlying event or transaction should be of a type that would not reasonably be expected to recur in the foreseeable future, taking into account the environment in which the entity operates.

Items specifically included or excluded from extraordinary items. In addition, accounting pronouncements have specifically required the following items to be disclosed as extraordinary, even though they may not meet the criteria stated above:

1. Material gains and losses from the extinguishment of debt (SFAS 4). Does not apply, however, to gains and losses from extinguishments of debt made to satisfy sinking-fund requirements that an enterprise must meet within one year of the date of extinguishment (SFAS 64). Chapter 13, Long-Term Debt, provides additional information about extinguishment of debt.
2. Profit or loss resulting from the disposal of a significant part of the assets or a separable segment of previously separate companies, provided the profit or loss is material and the disposal is within two years after a pooling of interest (APB 16).
3. Write-off of operating rights of motor carriers (SFAS 44).
4. The investor's share of an investee's extraordinary item when the investor uses the equity method of accounting for the investee (APB 18).
5. Gains of a debtor related to a troubled debt restructuring (SFAS 15). Chapter 13, Long-Term Debt, provides additional information about troubled debt restructuring.
6. Net effect of adjustments relating to the discontinuation of the application of SFAS 71 (SFAS 101).

The following items are, by definition, not extraordinary items:

1. Write-down or write-off of receivables, inventories, equipment leased to others, or intangible assets

2. Foreign currency gains and losses
3. Gains and losses on the disposal of a segment of a business
4. Gains and losses from sale or abandonment of property, plant, or equipment used in operations
5. Effects of a strike
6. Adjustments of accruals on long-term contracts

Per FASB Technical Bulletin 85-6, neither the cost incurred by a company to defend itself from a takeover attempt nor the cost incurred as part of a "standstill" agreement meet the criteria for extraordinary classifications as discussed in APB 30.

Presentation. Extraordinary items should be segregated from the results of ordinary operations and be shown net of taxes in a separate section of the income statement, following "discontinued operations" and preceding "cumulative effect of a change in accounting principle," if any. If more than one extraordinary item occurs during a period, they should be reported separately or details should be included in the notes to financial statements.

Example of the income statement presentation for extraordinary items

An extraordinary item would be presented as follows:

Income before extraordinary items	$xxx
Extraordinary items (less applicable income taxes of $__) (Note __)	xxx
Net income	$xxx

Accounting Changes

A change in accounting principle results from adoption of a generally accepted accounting principle different from the one previously used for reporting purposes. The term **accounting principle** includes not only accounting principles and practices, but also the methods of applying them. Changes in accounting principles (or the method of applying them) must be justified by those who make the change (the entity's management), unless they are made in order to comply with a FASB position. (See Chapter 20, Accounting Changes and Correction of Errors, for a detailed discussion of accounting changes.)

Example of disclosure for a change in accounting principle

ABC Company
Income Statement
For the Year Ended December 31, 2002

	2002	*2001*
Income before cumulative effect of a change in accounting principle	$xxx	$xxx
Cumulative effect on prior years (to 12/31/01) of changing to (change described) (net of $__ tax)	xxx	___
Net income	$xxx	$xxx
Per share amounts (simple capital structure)		
Income before cumulative effect of a change in accounting principle	$xxx	$xxx
Cumulative effect on prior years (to12/31/01) of changing to (change described)	xxx	___
Earnings per common share	$xxx	$xxx

Pro forma amounts assuming the new (change principle) is applied retroactively:

Net income	$xxx	$xxx
Earnings per share	$xxx	$xxx

Other Comprehensive Income

Under current accounting standards, other comprehensive income includes foreign currency adjustments, unrealized changes in the fair value of available-for-sale securities, and minimum pension liability adjustments. SFAS 130 requires that the components of other comprehensive income along with totals for net income, other comprehensive income, and comprehensive income must appear in a statement of the same prominence as other financial statements. (However, an entity that has no items of other comprehensive income in any period presented is required to report only net income.) Presenting those required amounts in a combined statement of income and comprehensive income is only one of three permissible methods. The other two are discussed later in this chapter.

Some items impact other comprehensive income in one period and then affect net income in the same or a later period. For example, an unrealized holding gain on an available-for-sale security is included in other comprehensive income in the period in which the market fluctuation occurs. Later, perhaps years later, the security is sold and the realized gains are included in net income. An adjustment to the unrealized holding gain component of other comprehensive income is necessary to avoid double counting the gain—once in net income in the current year and also in other comprehensive income in the earlier period. Adjustments of that type are called reclassification adjustments.

Usually, a sale triggers the need for a reclassification adjustment. The sale of an available-for-sale security in the current period triggers the need for an adjustment for the gains (losses) included in other comprehensive income in a prior period. Likewise, the sale of an investment in a foreign entity triggers an adjustment for foreign currency items included in other comprehensive income that are related to that entity. An adjustment is also necessary upon the complete (or substantially complete) liquidation of an investment in a foreign entity. Only minimum pension liabilities will not require reclassification adjustments (because they will not be reported in net income in a future period).

Reclassification adjustments can be presented on the face of the statement with the components of other comprehensive income or can be netted against the related component and the details of the reclassification provided in the notes to financial statements.

The tax effects of items reported in other comprehensive income must also be included in other comprehensive income. The items of other comprehensive income can be reported either net of related tax effects on the face of the statement or gross with the tax effects related to all components reported on a single, separate line. If gross reporting is used, the notes to the financial statements must disclose the tax effects related to each component (if there is more than one component). The following examples illustrate the two presentations.

Example of the "net of tax" presentation

Hypothetical Corporation
Statement of Income and Comprehensive Income
For the Year Ended December 31, 2002
($000 omitted)

Sales		$395,400
(details omitted)		
Net earnings		83,250
Other comprehensive income		
Foreign currency translation adjustment, net of $5,100 tax		11,900
Unrealized gain on securities:		
Unrealized holding gains arising during period, net of $7,500 tax	17,500	
Less: Reclassification adjustment, net of $1,500 tax, for gain included currently in net income	(3,500)	14,000
Minimum pension liability adjustment, net of $1,950 tax		(4,550)
Other comprehensive income		21,350
Comprehensive income		$104,600

Example of the "gross of tax" presentation

Hypothetical Corporation
Statement of Income and Comprehensive Income
For the Year Ended December 31, 2002
($000 omitted)

Sales		$395,400
(details omitted)		
Net earnings		83,250
Other comprehensive income		
Foreign currency translation adjustment		17,000
Unrealized gains on securities:		
Unrealized holding gains arising during period	25,000	
Less: Reclassification adjustment for gain included currently in net income	(5,000)	20,000
Minimum pension liability adjustment		(6,500)
Tax effects of items included in other comprehensive income		(9,150)
Other comprehensive income		21,350
Comprehensive income		$104,600

If the "gross" approach illustrated above were utilized, it would also be necessary to present in the notes to the financial statements details regarding the allocation of the tax effects to the several items included in other comprehensive income. An example of that note disclosure follows.

Note X: Income Taxes

The tax effects of items included in other comprehensive income for the year ended December 31, 2002, are as follows:

	Before-tax amount	Tax expense (benefit)	Net-of-tax amount
Foreign currency translation adjustments	$17,000	$5,100	$11,900
Unrealized gains on securities:			
Unrealized holding gains arising during period	25,000	7,500	17,500
Reclassification adjustment	(5,000)	(1,500)	(3,500)
Net unrealized holding gains	20,000	6,000	14,000
Minimum pension liability adjustment	(6,500)	(1,950)	(4,550)
Other comprehensive income	$30,500	$9,150	$21,350

Earnings Per Share

Earnings per share is often used in evaluating a firm's stock price and in assessing the firm's future earnings and ability to pay dividends. Because of the importance of earnings per share, the profession has concluded that it should be disclosed on the face of the income statement.

Earnings per share is a very compact indicator of a company's performance. In order to assess quality of earnings, SFAS 128 requires presentation of **basic earnings per share** on the face of the income statement for public-market issued common stock or potential common stock (such as options, warrants, convertible securities or contingent stock agreements). Shares outstanding are determined by the weighted-average method. Earnings is defined as both income from continuing operations and net income available to common stockholders. Thus, dividends declared on preferred stock and dividends for the period on cumulative preferred stock, whether or not earned or paid, are deducted from both income from continuing operations and net income before computing per share amounts.

Diluted earnings per share is computed similarly to basic earnings per share but changing the number of shares outstanding to include the number of additional common shares that would be issued if the potentially dilutive shares had been issued.

Entities with simple capital structures, that is, only common stock, should display basic earnings per share for both continuing operations and net income on the face of the income statement. All other entities are required to display both basic and diluted per share amounts for both continuing operations and net income. For discontinued operations, extraordinary items, or cumulative effect of an accounting change, basic and diluted per share amounts may be either reported on the face of the income statement or disclosed in the notes. More details on the per share calculations can be found in Chapter 18, Earnings Per Share.

Example of the presentation and computation of earnings per share

Assume that 100,000 shares were outstanding throughout the year.

ABC Company
Income Statement
For the Year Ended December 31, 2002

Sales		$2,000,000
Cost of goods sold		750,000
Gross profit		$1,250,000
Selling and administrative expenses		500,000
Income from operations		$ 750,000
Other revenues and expense		
Interest income	$40,000	
Interest expense	(30,000)	10,000
Income before unusual or infrequent items and income taxes		$ 760,000
Unusual or infrequent items:		
Loss from permanent impairment of value of manufacturing facilities		(10,000)
Income from continuing operations before income taxes		$ 750,000
Income taxes		300,000
Income from continuing operations		$ 450,000
Discontinued operations:		
Income from operations of Division X, less applicable income taxes of $20,000	$30,000	
Loss on disposal of Division X, less applicable income taxes of $40,000	(60,000)	(30,000)
Income before extraordinary item and cumulative effect of accounting change		$ 420,000
Extraordinary item—loss from earthquake less applicable income taxes of $8,000		(12,000)
Cumulative effect on prior years of retroactive application of new depreciation method, less applicable income taxes of $40,000		(60,000)
Net income		$ 348,000
Basic EPS computation		
Income from continuing operations ($450,000/100,000)		$ 4.50
Extraordinary items* ($12,000/100,000)		(0.12)
Accounting change* ($60,000/100,000)		(0.60)
Discontinued operations* ($30,000/100,000)		(0.30)
Net income available for common stockholders		$ 3.48

* *May be shown in the notes to the financial statements.*

Prior Period Adjustments

SFAS 16 defines a prior period adjustment and clearly states that only the following items shall be excluded from the determination of net income for the current period:

1. The correction of an error in the financial statements of a prior period
2. Adjustments that result from realization of income tax benefits of preacquisition operating loss carryforwards of purchased subsidiaries

APB 9 specifies the recording and presentation of a prior period adjustment. When prior period adjustments are recorded, the resulting effects on the net income of prior periods shall be disclosed in the year in which the adjustments are made. The adjustments are reported at both their gross amount and net of applicable income taxes. If the statements are presented for only a single period, then the beginning balance of retained earnings is restated to reflect the effects of the correction or change. When comparative statements are presented, adjustments should be made of the amounts of net income (and the components thereof) and retained earnings balance (as well as other affected balances) for all of the periods included in the financial statements.

An example of the accounting presentation for a prior period adjustment appears in Chapter 20, Accounting Changes and Correction of Errors.

Statement of Income and Retained Earnings

An acceptable practice is to combine the income statement and the statement of retained earnings into a single statement called the Statement of Income and Retained Earnings. The income statement is prepared in the normal manner. The beginning balance in retained earnings is added to the net income (loss) figure. Declared dividends are deducted to obtain the retained earnings ending balance.

Example of a statement of income and retained earnings

Baker, Inc.
Statement of Income and Retained Earnings
For the Year Ended December 31, 2002

Sales		$2,482
Cost of goods sold		1,489
Gross margin on sales		$ 993
Operating expenses		
Selling expenses	$ 220	
Administrative expenses	255	475
Income from operations		$ 518
Other revenues/gains (expenses/losses)		
Interest revenue (expense)—net	$ (40)	
Gain on sale of investment in ABC Company	100	
Gain on translation of foreign currencies	20	80
Income before unusual or infrequent items		$ 598
Unusual or infrequent items:		
Write-down of property and equipment	$ (20)	
Loss from permanent impairment of value of distributing		
facility	(50)	(70)
Income from continuing operations before provision for income taxes		$ 528
Provision for income taxes		211
Income from continuing operations		$ 317
Discontinued operations:		
Loss from operations of discontinued Division Z (less		
applicable taxes of $466)	$ (699)	
Loss on disposal of Division Z including operating		
losses during phaseout period (less applicable taxes of $67)	(100)	(799)

Loss before extraordinary items and cumulative effect of a change in accounting principle		$ (482)
Extraordinary loss from earthquake (less applicable income taxes of $30)		(45)
Cumulative effect on prior years of retroactive application of new depreciation method (less applicable income taxes of $80)		(120)
Net loss		$ (647)
Retained earnings, January 1, 2002	$1,900	
Prior period adjustment:		
Correction of depreciation error (less applicable income taxes of $28)	(42)	
Adjusted retained earnings, January 1, 2002		1,858
Deduct dividends:		
Preferred stock	$ (40)	
Common stock	(30)	(70)
Retained earnings, December 31, 2002		$1,141
Per share amounts (100 shares)*		
Income from continuing operations		$ 3.17
Net loss		$ (6.47)

* *Assumes other per share amounts are included in notes to financial statements.*

Reporting Comprehensive Income in a Statement other than a Combined Statement of Income and Comprehensive Income

Entities are not required to present information about comprehensive income in a combined statement of income and comprehensive income. Instead, they need only to present the components of other comprehensive income along with totals for net income, other comprehensive income, and comprehensive income in a statement of the same prominence as other financial statements. Thus, two other alternatives are available.

1. In an expanded statement of changes in stockholder's equity, or
2. In a stand-alone statement of comprehensive income

In SFAS 130, the FASB encourages the use of either a combined statement of income and comprehensive income or a stand-alone statement that begins with net income. In practice, the expanded statement of changes in stockholder's equity is also widely used.

Example of presentation of comprehensive income in the statement of changes in stockholders' equity

If comprehensive income is reported in the statement of changes in stockholders' equity, there are several formats that can be employed to accomplish this goal. Each of these modes of presentation is somewhat cumbersome, primarily because one element of comprehensive income (earnings) must be added to retained earnings while another (comprehensive income) is not.

Consider the case of Leisuretime Industries, which has preferred and common shares outstanding, and also has three classes of other comprehensive income. If Leisuretime Industries chooses to report comprehensive income in the statement of changes in stockholders' equity (rather than in either a freestanding statement of comprehensive income or combined statement of earnings and comprehensive income), one of two formats might be selected. These are illustrated below.

Leisuretime Industries
Statement of Changes in Stockholders' Equity
For the Year Ended December 31, 2002
($000 omitted)

	Preferred stock	Common stock	Comprehensive income	Retained earnings	Accumulated other comprehensive income	Total
Balances, January 1, 2002	$500,000	$4,500,000		$715,600	$ (8,450)	$5,707,150
Comprehensive income						
Net income			$66,760	66,760		
Other comprehensive income:						
Foreign currency translation adjustments, net of tax			3,000			
Unrealized gains on securities:						
Unrealized holding gains arising during period, net of tax			23,000			
Less: reclassification adjustment, net of tax, for gain included in net income			(5,500)			
Minimum pension liability adjustment, net of tax			(3,800)			
Other comprehensive income			16,700		16,700	
Comprehensive income			$83,460			83,460
Proceeds from issuance of shares	50,000	200,000				250,000
Dividends paid				(24,825)		(24,825)
Balances, December 31, 2002	$550,000	$4,700,000		$757,535	$ 8,250	$6,015,785

Leisuretime Industries
Statement of Changes in Stockholders' Equity
For the Year Ended December 31, 2002
($000 omitted)

	Preferred stock	Common stock	Retained earnings	Foreign currency translation	Unrealized gains on securities	Minimum pension liability	Total
Balances January 1, 2002	$500,000	$4,500,000	$715,600	$(9,275)	$ 3,325	$(2,500)	$5,707,150
Comprehensive income							
Net income			66,760				66,760
Other comprehensive income:							

Foreign currency translation adjustments, net of tax							3,000	3,000
Unrealized gains on securities:								
Unrealized holding gains arising during period, net of tax							23,000	23,000
Less: reclassification adjustment, net of tax, for gain included in net income							(5,500)	(5,500)
Minimum pension liability adjustment, net of tax							(3,800)	(3,800)
Other comprehensive income								16,700
Comprehensive income								83,460
Proceeds from issuance of shares	50,000	200,000						250,000
Dividends paid			(24,825)					(24,825)
Balances, December 31, 2002	$550,000	$4,700,000	$757,535	$(6,275)	$20,825	$(6,300)		$6,015,785

Development Stage Enterprises

SFAS 7 indicates that **development stage enterprises** should prepare their financial statements in accordance with the same GAAP applicable to established operating entities. SFAS 7 indicated that specialized accounting practices are unacceptable and that accounting treatment should be governed by the nature of the transaction rather than the age of the entity. SFAS 7 also provided that a development stage enterprise should disclose certain additional information that would alert readers to the fact that the company is in the development stage. Disclosure requirements include

1. All disclosures applicable to operating entities
2. Identification of the statements as those of a development stage enterprise
3. Disclosure of the nature of development stage activities

4. A balance sheet that, in the equity section, includes the cumulative net losses since inception
5. An income statement showing current period revenue and expense as well as the cumulative amount from the inception of the entity
6. A statement of cash flows showing cash flows for the period as well as those from inception
7. A statement of stockholders' equity showing the following from the enterprise's inception:

    a. For each issuance, the date and number of equity securities issued for cash or other consideration
    b. For each issuance, the dollar amounts (per share and in total) assigned to the consideration received for equity securities
    c. For each issuance involving noncash consideration, the nature of the consideration and the basis used in assigning the valuation

8. For the first period in which an enterprise is no longer a development stage enterprise, it shall disclose that in prior periods the entity was a development stage enterprise. If comparative statements are presented, the foregoing disclosure presentations (2-7) need not be shown.

FASB Interpretation 7 allows parent or equity method investor companies to capitalize or defer some development stage company costs that would have to be expensed by the development stage company. Costs may be deferred if recoverable within the entire entity.

Reporting on the Costs of Start-up Activities

SOP 98-5 provides guidance on financial reporting of start-up costs and organization costs and requires such costs to be expensed as incurred. Start-up costs are defined as onetime activities related to opening a new facility, introducing a new product or service, conducting activities in a new territory, pursuing a new class of customer, initiating a new process in an existing facility, or some new operation. Those costs are sometimes referred to as preopening costs, preoperating costs, organization costs, and start-up costs. Routine ongoing efforts to improve existing quality of products, services, or facilities are not start-up costs. Other costs, related to specific activities listed below, are excluded from the SOP and should be accounted for in accordance with other existing authoritative literature. These include

1. Costs of acquiring or constructing long-lived assets and getting them ready for their intended uses. (However, the costs of using long-lived assets that are allocated to start-up activities [for example, depreciation of equipment] are within the scope of the SOP.)
2. Costs of acquiring or producing inventory.

3. Costs of acquiring intangible assets. (However, the costs of using intangible assets that are allocated to start-up activities [for example, amortization of a purchased patent] are within the scope of the SOP.)
4. Costs related to internally developed assets (for example, internal-use computer software costs). (However, the costs of using those assets that are allocated to start-up activities are within the scope of the SOP.)
5. Costs that are within the scope of SFAS 2, *Accounting for Research and Development*, and SFAS 71, *Accounting for the Effects of Certain Types of Regulation*.
6. Costs of fund-raising incurred by not-for-profit organizations.
7. Costs of raising capital.
8. Costs of advertising.
9. Costs incurred in connection with existing contracts as stated in SOP 81-1, *Accounting for Performance of Construction-Type and Certain Production-Type Contracts*.
10. Costs of merger or acquisition activities
11. Costs of ongoing customer acquisition, such as policy acquisition costs and loan origination costs

Restructuring Costs

Restructuring costs have been a hot topic with the SEC as part of the "big bath" practice in which companies clean up their balance sheets to ensure future profitability.

Restructuring charges, which have been taken with increasing frequency by companies, typically include costs such as employee benefits, costs associated with product line elimination or relocation, costs for new systems development or acquisitions, retraining costs, and losses on asset impairment and dispositions. Many of these are not addressed by existing accounting standards (some, like severance costs, are already dealt with in the literature, however), and it is not clear when such costs are to be recognized.

Employee termination benefits. EITF 94-3, *Liability Recognition for Certain Employee Termination Benefits and Other Costs to Exit an Activity (Including Certain Costs Incurred in a Restructuring),* applies to benefits to be provided to involuntarily terminated employees. Specifically excluded from consideration were employee termination benefits

1. Associated with a disposal of a segment and accounted for under APB 30
2. Paid pursuant to the terms of an ongoing employee benefit plan, regardless of whether the plan was preexisting or is newly created
3. Paid under the terms on an individual deferred compensation agreement.

A consensus was reached that a liability should be recognized in the period management approves the termination plan if all of the following conditions exist:

1. Prior to the date of the financial statements, management approves and commits to the termination plan and establishes the level of benefits that employees will receive upon termination.
2. Prior to the date of the financial statements, the benefit arrangement is communicated to employees in sufficient detail that employees can determine the type and amount of benefits they will receive if they are terminated.
3. The termination plan specifies the number of employees to be terminated, their job classifications, and their locations.
4. The plan is near enough to implementation that changes to the plan are unlikely.

The liability should be measured at the minimum required termination benefits. Thus, if the termination plan states that an employee will receive $10,000 upon voluntary termination and, if a sufficient number of employees do not volunteer, an employee will receive $6,000 upon involuntary termination, the liability should be initially measured at $6,000 times the number of employees to be terminated. The incremental voluntary benefits should be recognized when employees voluntarily accept the termination offer.

However, if the involuntary termination benefits are only available if the employee works until the day that he or she is involuntarily terminated, then it is necessary to determine if all or some of the benefits are payments for future services. If so, the benefits attributable to future services should be evaluated as a cost to exit an activity rather than as an employee termination benefit.

Costs to exit an activity. EITF 94-3 also concludes that a commitment by an entity's management to execute an exit plan represents an obligating event for exit costs. Exit costs are

1. Costs that are the direct result of the exit plan and did not exist in the entity prior to the commitment date.
2. Costs that will be incurred by the entity under a contractual obligation that existed prior to the commitment date and that will continue after the exit plan is completed without economic benefit to the entity. The cost could be a penalty to cancel the contract.

Costs that relate to activities that will be continued after the exit plan is completed are not exit costs. Those costs and any other costs that do not qualify as exit costs should not be recognized as liabilities. An entity should recognize a liability for exit costs if those costs will not generate revenues after the commitment date and those costs can be reasonably estimated. Expected gains on the sale of assets to be disposed of should not be used to offset the liability for exit costs.

The commitment date for an exit plan occurs when all of the following conditions are met:

1. Prior to the date of the financial statements, management approves and commits to the exit plan.

2. The exit plan specifically identifies all significant actions to be taken to complete the plan, which activities will not be continued, and the expected completion date.

3. The plan is near enough to implementation that changes to the plan are unlikely.

SEC Staff Accounting Bulletin 67. The issue of reporting restructuring costs was also addressed in EITF 87-4, *Restructuring of Operations: Implications of SEC Staff Accounting Bulletin 67.* A consensus was reached that the provisions of SAB 67, which require that restructuring charges be deducted in determining "income from operations" and prohibiting the presentation of "income before restructuring charges," are not required to be followed by nonpublic companies for a fair presentation of the results of operations in accordance with GAAP. The task force notes that nonpublic companies should exercise judgment in selecting the most meaningful presentation for the income statement.

Status. Despite the EITF consensuses, accounting for restructuring costs continues to be controversial. Shortly, the FASB is expected to issue a Statement on asset impairment and disposal issues. The standards in the proposed Statement are expected to nullify the consensus opinions in EITF 94-3. The proposed Statement would amend APB 30 to make it applicable to "any component of an entity with separately identifiable operations (including revenues and expenses), assets, and cash flows that either has been disposed of or is classified as held for sale." The proposed Statement would also establish standards for the recognition and measurement of obligations associated with disposal. Those obligations include employee termination benefits, costs incurred under existing operating leases, costs of closing plant facilities, and costs of relocating employees. Expected future operating losses would not qualify for recognition as liabilities as they do under APB 30. However, a loss would be recognized if it resulted from a preexisting contractual obligation, such as a contract obligating the entity to provide at a future date goods produced using the assets to be disposed of.

EMERGING ISSUES TASK FORCE CONSENSUS SUMMARIES

85-36 Discontinued Operations with Expected Gain and Interim Operating Losses

A consensus was reached that estimated losses from operations during the period between the measurement date and the disposal date should be deferred until the disposal date if there is reasonable assurance there will be a net gain on disposal. This consensus also applies to the sale of a significant portion of a line of business that is not considered a segment.

The Task Force also reached a consensus that a net gain resulting from the disposal of separate segments as part of the same formal plan should be reported net if one segment disposal results in a gain and one results in a loss. The Task Force notes that the net gain treatment would not be appropriate for disposal of a portion of a line of business.

87-24   Allocation of Interest to Discontinued Operations

A consensus was reached that the allocation of interest expense to discontinued operations is permitted but not required. If the corporation decides to allocate, the EITF provides guidance regarding the maximum amount and methods of allocation. Additionally, the Task Force reached a consensus that general corporate overhead may not be allocated to discontinued operations.

90-16   Accounting for Discontinued Operations Subsequently Retained

The Task Force reached consensus on two issues regarding how a company should account for the subsequent decision to retain a business segment if the company had previously decided to dispose of that segment and had accounted for the disposal in accordance with APB 30. The first consensus was that if a company has accrued a loss on the disposal of segment in accordance with APB 30, the remaining estimated accrued loss should be reversed in the period the company subsequently decides to retain the segment. The second consensus was that the financial statements of the prior reporting period should not be restated. However, the prior period results of operations of the business segment should be reclassified from discontinued operations to continuing operations. The SEC Observer agreed with the consensus, noting that this accounting treatment is required, not merely permitted. In addition to the disclosure requirements of APB 30, supplemental disclosures are required when the consensus is applied.

92-13   Accounting for Estimated Payments in Connection with the Coal Industry Retiree Health Benefit Act of 1992

Enterprises that have ongoing operations in the coal industry should account for their obligation under the Act as either participation in a multiemployer plan or as a liability. Enterprises that choose to report a liability and enterprises that do not have ongoing operations in the coal industry should account for the loss under SFAS 5 and report the estimated loss as an extraordinary item.

94-3   Liability Recognition for Certain Employee Termination Benefits and Other Costs to Exit an Activity (Including Certain Costs Incurred in a Restructuring)

See the discussion in this chapter under the heading "Restructuring Costs."

95-3   Recognition of Liabilities in Connection with a Purchase Business Combination

If costs to exit an activity of an acquiree and involuntary termination or relocation costs relative to employees of an acquiree are anticipated at or very shortly after the acquisition, they should be reflected in the allocation of the purchase price, unless the costs are incurred to generate revenue of the combined entity after the acquisition, in which case these would be period costs. (This is analogous to Issue 94-3 and examples in that consensus apply here also.)

95-18　Accounting and Reporting for a Discontinued Business Segment When the Measurement Date Occurs after the Balance Sheet Date but before the Issuance of Financial Statements

A consensus was reached that in accordance with APB 30 a presumption exists that estimated losses from the planned disposal of a segment should be recognized in the still-to-be-issued financial statements for the period prior to the measurement date. Additionally, the segment's operating results should be presented as a component of discontinued operations in the income statement of the still-to-be-released financial statements. Only an unexpected discrete and identifiable event, such as an unsolicited offer after the balance sheet date, can overcome the presumption above. If the presumption is overcome, the estimated loss would be recognized in the period's financial statements that include the measurement date. In situations in which the presumption is overcome or a gain occurs, the still-to-be-issued financial statements should show the segment's results as discontinued operations.

00-9　Classification of a Gain or Loss from a Hedge of Debt That Is Extinguished

The issue is whether a gain or loss from debt extinguishment should be classified as an extraordinary item if the gain or loss results from an adjustment to the carrying amount of the debt as required by the hedge accounting requirements of SFAS 133. If the hedge was a fair value hedge, the component of gain or loss that results from the prior adjustment of the debt's carrying amount (because of the hedge) should be classified in accordance with the requirements of SFAS 4. If the hedge was a cash flow hedge of debt, the reclassification to earnings of the amount in accumulated comprehensive income required by SFAS 133 should be excluded from extinguishment gain or loss (i.e., should not be reported as extraordinary).

00-10　Accounting for Shipping and Handling Fees and Costs

Shipping and handling costs are a major expense for product sellers. The amounts charged to customers for shipping and handling often differ from the amounts the seller pays for delivery. Any and all amounts related to shipping and handling billed to a customer in a sale transaction should be classified as revenue.

4 STATEMENT OF CASH FLOWS

PERSPECTIVE AND ISSUES

SFAS 95, as amended by SFAS 102 and 104, establishes standards for cash flow reporting. A statement of cash flows is a required part of a complete set of financial statements for business enterprises and not-for-profit organizations. Only defined benefit plans, certain other employee benefit plans, and highly liquid investment companies that meet specified conditions are not required to present the statement.

The primary purpose of the statement of cash flows is to provide information about cash receipts and cash payments of an entity during a period. A secondary purpose is to provide information about the investing and financing activities during the period.

Specifically, the statement of cash flows helps investors and creditors assess

1. Ability to generate future positive cash flows
2. Ability to meet obligations and pay dividends
3. Reasons for differences between net income and net cash receipts and payments
4. The cash and noncash aspects of investing and financing transactions on an entity's financial position

SFAC 1 states that "financial reporting should provide information that is useful to present and potential investors, creditors, and other users for making rational investment and credit decisions." Since the ultimate objective of investment and credit decisions is the maximization of net cash inflows, information for assessing the amounts, timing, and uncertainty of prospective cash flows is needed. SFAC 5 concludes that financial statements must show cash flows during the period in order to be complete.

Sources of GAAP		
SFAC	*EITF*	*SFAS*
1, 5	95-13, 00-15	95, 102, 104, 115, 117, 133

DEFINITIONS OF TERMS

Cash equivalents. Short-term, highly liquid investments that (1) are readily convertible to known amounts of cash and (2) are so near their maturity (maturity of three months or less from the date of purchase by the enterprise) that they present negligible risk of changes in value because of changes in interest rates. Treasury bills, commercial paper, and money market funds are all examples of cash equivalents.

Direct method. A method which derives the net cash provided by operating activities from the components of operating cash receipts and payments as opposed to adjusting net income for items not affecting cash.

Financing activities. The transactions a firm engages in to acquire and repay capital (e.g., borrowings, sale of capital stock, repayments, etc.).

Indirect (reconciliation) method. A method which derives the net cash provided by operating activities by adjusting net income for revenue and expense items not resulting from cash transactions.

Investing activities. The transactions the firm engages in which affect their investments in noncurrent assets (e.g., purchase or sale of plant, property, and equipment).

Operating activities. The transactions not classified as financing or investing activities, generally involving producing and delivering goods or providing services.

CONCEPTS, RULES, AND EXAMPLES

Cash Focus

The statement of cash flows includes only inflows and outflows of cash and cash equivalents. Cash equivalents include any short-term highly liquid investments (see definition for criteria) used as a temporary investment of idle cash. The effects of investing and financing activities that do not result in receipts or payments of cash are to be reported in a separate schedule immediately following the statement or in the notes to the financial statements. The reasoning for not including noncash items in the statement of cash flows and placing them in a separate schedule is that it preserves the statement's primary focus on cash flows from operating, investing, and financing activities. Thus, if a transaction is part cash and part noncash, only the cash portion is reported in the statement of cash flows.

Classification

The statement of cash flows requires classification of cash receipts and cash disbursements into three categories.

Investing activities include the acquisition and disposition of (1) long-term productive assets or (2) securities held in available-for-sale or held-to-maturity portfolios that are not considered cash equivalents. Investing activities also include the lending of money and collection on loans.

However, per SFAS 102, as amended by SFAS 115, cash flows are classified as operating cash flows if originating from the purchase or selling of loans, debt, or equity instruments acquired specifically for resale and carried at market value in a trading account.

Financing activities include obtaining resources from and returning resources to the owners. Also included is obtaining resources from creditors on long-term credit and repaying the amount borrowed. The financing activities of not-for-profit organizations also include receiving contributions from donors that require the resources to be used for long-term purposes, such as endowment or the purchase of long-lived assets.

Operating activities include all transactions that are not investing and financing activities. Operating activities include delivering or producing goods for sale and providing services.

The following are examples of the statement of cash flows classification:

	Operating	*Investing*	*Financing*
Cash Inflows	• Receipts from sale of goods or services	• Principal collections from loans and sales of other entities' debt instruments*	• Proceeds from issuing stock
	• Sale of loans, debt, or equity instruments carried in trading portfolio	• Sale of equity instruments* of other enterprises and from returns of investment in those instruments	• Proceeds from issuing debt (short-term or long-term)
	• Returns on loans (interest) • Returns on equity securities (dividends)	• Sale of plant & equipment	• Not-for-profits' donor-restricted cash gifts that are limited to long-term purposes
Cash Outflows	• Payments for inventory	• Loans made and acquisition of other entities' debt instruments*	• Payment of dividends
	• Payments to employees and other suppliers	• Purchase of equity instruments* of other enterprises	• Repurchase of entity's stock
	• Payments of taxes • Payments of interest • Purchase of loans, debt, or equity instruments carried in trading portfolio	• Purchase of plant & equipment	• Repayment of debt principal, including capital lease obligations

* *Held in available-for-sale or held-to-maturity portfolios*

Noncash Investing and Financing Activities

(May be disclosed following statement or in the notes)

- Acquiring an asset through a capital lease or by assuming long-term debt
- Conversion of debt to equity
- Exchange of noncash assets or liabilities for other noncash assets or liabilities
- Issuance of stock to acquire assets
- Obtaining an investment asset or a building by receiving a contribution

Example of a statement of cash flows (without detail of the required operating activities section)

Liquid Corporation
Statement of Cash Flows
For the Year Ended December 31, 2001

Net cash flows from operating activities		$ xxx
Cash flows from investing activities:		
Purchase of property, plant, and equipment	$(xxx)	
Sale of equipment	xx	
Collection of notes receivable	xx	
Net cash **used** in investing activities		(xx)
Cash flows from financing activities:		
Sale of common stock	xxx	
Repayment of long-term debt	(xx)	
Reduction of notes payable	(xx)	
Net cash **provided** by financing activities		xx
Effect of exchange rate changes on cash		xx
Net increase in cash		$ xxx
Cash and cash equivalents at beginning of year		xxx
Cash and cash equivalents at end of year		$xxxx
Schedule of noncash financing and investing activities:		
Conversion of bonds into common stock		$ xxx
Property acquired under capital leases		xxx
		$ xxx

Operating Activities Presentation

Direct vs. indirect. The operating activities section of the statement of cash flows can be presented under the direct or indirect method. However, the FASB has expressed a preference for the direct method of presenting net cash from operating activities.

The **direct method** shows the items that affected cash flow. Cash received and cash paid are presented, as opposed to converting accrual-basis income to cash flow information. At a minimum, entities using the direct method are required to report the following classes of operating cash receipts and payments:

1. Cash collected from customers
2. Interest and dividends received
3. Other operating cash receipts
4. Cash paid to employees and other suppliers

5. Interest and income taxes paid
6. Other operating cash payments

The direct method allows the user to clarify the relationship between the company's net income and its cash flows. For example, payments of expenses are shown as cash disbursements and are deducted from cash receipts. In this way, the user is able to recognize the cash receipts and cash payments for the period. The information needed to prepare the operating activities section using the direct method can often be obtained by converting information already appearing in the balance sheet and income statement. Formulas for conversion of various income statement amounts for the direct method presentation from the accrual basis to the cash basis are summarized below.

Accrual basis	*Additions*	*Deductions*	*Cash basis*
Net sales	+ Beginning AR	− Ending AR AR written off	= Cash received from customers
Cost of goods sold	+ Ending inventory Beginning AP	− Manufacturing depreciation and amortization Beginning inventory Ending AP	= Cash paid to suppliers
Operating expenses	+ Ending prepaid ex- penses Beginning accrued expenses	− Sales and administrative depreciation and amorti- zation Beginning prepaid ex- penses Ending accrued expenses payable Bad debts expense	= Cash paid for operating expenses

When the direct method is used, a separate schedule reconciling net income to net cash flows from operating activities must also be provided. That schedule reports the same information as the operating activities section prepared using the indirect method.

The **indirect method** is the most widely used presentation of cash from operating activities, primarily because it is easier to prepare. It focuses on the differences between net income and cash flows. The indirect format begins with net income, which is obtained directly from the income statement. Revenue and expense items not affecting cash are added or deducted to arrive at net cash provided by operating activities. For example, depreciation and amortization would be added back because they reduce net income without affecting cash.

The statement of cash flows prepared using the indirect method emphasizes changes in the components of most current asset and current liability accounts. Changes in inventory, accounts receivable, and other current accounts are used to determine the cash flow from operating activities. It is important to note that the change in accounts receivable should be calculated using the balances net of the allowance account in order to assure write-offs of uncollectible accounts are treated properly. Other adjustments under the indirect method include changes in the account balances of deferred income taxes and the income (loss) from investments reported using the equity method. However, short-term borrowing used to purchase equipment would be classified as a financing activity.

The following diagram may facilitate understanding of the adjustments to net income necessary for converting accrual-based net income to cash-basis net income when using the indirect method. The diagram is simply an expanded balance sheet equation.

	*Current assets**	−	*Noncurrent assets*	=	*Current liabilities*	+	*Long-term liabilities*	+	*Income*	*Accrual income adjustment to convert to cash flow*
1.	Increase			=					Increase	Decrease
2.	Decrease			=					Decrease	Increase
3.				=	Increase				Decrease	Increase
4.				=	Decrease				Increase	Decrease

* *Other than cash and cash equivalents*

For example, using Row 1, a credit sale would increase accounts receivable and accrual-basis income but would not affect cash. Therefore, its effect must be removed from the accrual income in order to convert to cash income. The last column indicates that the increase in a current asset balance must be deducted from income to obtain cash flow.

Similarly, an increase in a current liability, Row 3, must be added to income to obtain cash flows (e.g., accrued wages are on the income statement as an expense, but they do not require cash; the increase in wages payable must be added back to remove this noncash expense from accrual-basis income).

If the indirect method is chosen, then the amount of interest and income tax paid must be included in the related disclosures.

The major drawback to the indirect method involves the user's difficulty in comprehending the information presented. This method does not show where the cash came from or where the cash went to. Only adjustments to accrual-basis net income are shown. In some cases the adjustments can be confusing. For instance, the sale of equipment resulting in an accrual-basis loss would require that the loss be added to net income to arrive at net cash from operating activities. (The loss was deducted in the computation of net income, but because the sale will be shown as an investing activity, the loss must be added back to net income.)

Although the indirect method is more commonly used in practice, the authors believe that the direct method is preferable. It portrays both the amounts of funds provided by and used in the firm's operations, instead of presenting net income and reconciling items. The direct method reports only the items that affect cash flow (inflows/outflows of cash) and ignores items that do not affect cash flow (depreciation, gains, etc.). Both the direct method and the indirect method are shown below.

Direct method

Cash flows from operating activities:		
Cash received from sale of goods	$xxx	
Cash interest received	xxx	
Cash dividends received	<u>xxx</u>	
Cash provided by operating activities		$xxx
Cash paid to suppliers	(xxx)	
Cash paid for operating expenses	(xxx)	
Cash interest paid	(xxx)	
Cash paid for taxes	<u>(xxx)</u>	
Cash disbursed for operating activities		<u>(xxx)</u>
Net cash flows from operating activities		$<u>xxx</u>

Indirect method

Cash flows from operating activities:	
Net income	$ xx
Add/deduct items not affecting cash:	
Increase in accounts receivable	(xx)
Depreciation expense	xx
Increase in accounts payable	xx
Decrease in inventories	xx
Loss on sale of equipment	<u>xx</u>
Net cash flows from operating activities	$<u>xxx</u>

Other Requirements

Gross vs. net basis. The emphasis in the statement of cash flows is on gross cash receipts and cash payments. For instance, reporting the net change in bonds payable would obscure the financing activities of the entity by not disclosing separately cash inflows from issuing bonds and cash outflows from retiring bonds. In a few circumstances, netting of cash flows is allowed. Items having quick turnovers, large amounts, and short maturities may be presented as net cash flows if the cash receipts and payments pertain to (1) investments (other than cash equivalents), (2) loans receivable, and (3) debts (original maturity of three months or less).

Extraordinary items and discontinued operations. SFAS 95 permits, but does not require, separate disclosure of cash flows related to extraordinary items and discontinued operations. If an entity chooses to disclose this information, disclosure must be consistent for all periods affected.

Cash flow per share. This information shall **not** be reported in the financial statements of an enterprise.

Entities Exempt from Providing a Statement of Cash Flows

Per SFAS 102, a statement of cash flows is not required for a defined benefit pension plan that presents the financial information under the guidelines of SFAS 35. Other employee benefit plans are exempted provided that the financial information presented is similar to the requirements of SFAS 35. Investment enterprises or a common trust fund held for the collective investment and reinvestment of moneys are not required to provide a statement of cash flows if the following conditions are met:

1. Substantially all of the entity's investments are highly liquid.
2. Entity's investments are carried at market value.
3. Entity had little or no debt, based on average debt outstanding during the period, in relation to average total assets.
4. Entity provides a statement of changes in net assets.

Net Reporting by Financial Institutions

Per SFAS 104, banks, savings institutions, and credit unions are allowed to report net cash receipts and payments for the following:

1. Deposits placed with other financial institutions
2. Withdrawals of those deposits
3. Time deposits accepted
4. Repayments of time deposits
5. Loans made to customers
6. Principal collections of loans made to customers

Not-for-Profit Organizations

SFAS 117 requires not-for-profit organizations to include a statement of cash flows in a complete set of financial statements. The statement of cash flows is prepared as it is for business enterprises with the following differences:

1. The indirect method of reporting cash flows from operations (or reconciliation of net income to net cash flows from operations required when the direct method is used) is prepared beginning with the change in net assets.
2. Investing activities also include receiving contributions that are restricted by the donor to the purchase or improvement of long-lived assets or for long-term investment such as permanent or term endowment.
3. Noncash activities include gifts of long-lived assets and gifts of securities held for long-term investment.

Reporting Hedging Transactions

Per SFAS 104, as amended by SFAS 133, providing the accounting method is disclosed, the cash flows resulting from derivative instruments that are accounted for as fair value hedges or cash flow hedges may be classified as the same type of cash flows as the hedged items.

Reporting Foreign Currency Cash Flows

If an entity has foreign currency transactions or foreign operations, it should translate the foreign currency cash flows using exchange rates in effect at the time of the cash flows. A weighted-average exchange rate for the period can be used for the translation if the result is substantially the same. The effect of changes in exchange rates on any cash balances held in foreign currencies should be shown as a separate part of the reconciliation of the change in cash and cash equivalents during the period. An example of reporting the effect of exchange rate changes is shown in the statement of cash flows in the "Classification" section of this chapter.

Noncash exchange gains and losses recognized in net income should be reported as a separate item when reconciling net income and operating activities.

For a more detailed discussion of the exchange rate effects on the statement of cash flows, see Chapter 21, Foreign Currency.

Preparation of the Statement

Under a cash and cash equivalents basis, the changes in the cash account and any cash equivalent account is the "bottom line" figure of the statement of cash flows. Using the 2000 and 2001 balance sheet shown below, an increase of $25,000 can be computed. This is the difference between the totals for cash and treasury bills between 2000 and 2001 ($41,000 – $16,000).

When preparing the statement of cash flows using the direct method, gross cash inflows from revenues and gross cash outflows to suppliers and for expenses are presented in the operating activities section.

In preparing the reconciliation of net income to net cash flow from operating activities (indirect method), changes in all accounts (other than cash and cash equivalents) that are related to operations are additions to or deductions from net income to arrive at net cash provided by operating activities.

A T-account analysis may be helpful when preparing the statement of cash flows. A T-account is set up for each account, and beginning (2000) and ending (2001) balances are taken from the appropriate balance sheet. Additionally, a T-account for cash and cash equivalents from operating activities and a master or summary T-account of cash and cash equivalents should be used.

Example of preparing a statement of cash flows

The financial statements below will be used to prepare the statement of cash flows.

Johnson Company
Balance Sheets
December 31, 2001 and 2000

	2001	*2000*
Assets		
Current assets:		
Cash	$ 37,000	$ 10,000
Treasury bills	4,000	6,000
Accounts receivable—net	9,000	11,000
Inventory	14,000	9,000
Prepaid expenses	10,000	13,000
Total current assets	$ 74,000	$ 49,000
Noncurrent assets:		
Investment in available-for-sale securities	7,500	15,000
Add (less) adjustment for changes in fair value	1,000	(3,000)
Investment in XYZ (35%)	16,000	14,000
Patent	5,000	6,000
Leased asset	5,000	--
Property, plant, and equipment	39,000	37,000
Less accumulated depreciation	(7,000)	(3,000)
Total assets	$140,500	$115,000

	2001	2000
Liabilities		
Current liabilities:		
Accounts payable	$ 2,000	$ 12,000
Notes payable—current	9,000	--
Interest payable	3,000	2,000
Dividends payable	5,000	2,000
Income taxes payable	2,180	1,000
Lease obligation	700	--
Total current liabilities	21,880	17,000
Noncurrent liabilities:		
Deferred tax liability	9,360*	4,920*
Bonds payable	10,000	25,000
Lease obligation	4,300	--
Total liabilities	$ 45,540	$ 46,920
Stockholders' equity		
Common stock, $10 par value	$ 33,000	$ 26,000
Additional paid-in capital	16,000	3,000
Retained earnings	45,320	41,000
Accumulated other comprehensive income		
Net unrealized loss on available-for-sale securities	640	(1,920)
Total stockholders' equity	$ 94,960	$ 68,080
Total liabilities and stockholders' equity	$140,500	$115,000

* *Net of deferred tax asset ($540) and ($1,080) respectively.*

Johnson Company
Statement of Earnings and Comprehensive Income
For the Year Ended December 31, 2001

Sales		$100,000
Other income		8,500
		$108,500
Cost of goods sold, excluding depreciation		60,000
Selling, general, and administrative expenses		12,000
Depreciation		8,000
Amortization of patents		1,000
Interest expense		2,000
		$ 83,000
Income before taxes		$ 25,500
Income taxes:		
Current	$6,180	
Deferred	3,000	9,180
Net income		$ 16,320
Other comprehensive income, net of tax		
Unrealized gains on securities:		
Unrealized holding gains (less applicable income taxes of $900)		1,600
Add reclassification adjustment (less applicable income taxes of $540)		960
Total other comprehensive income		$ 2,560
Comprehensive income		$ 18,880

Additional information (relating to 2001)

1. Equipment costing $6,000 with a book value of $2,000 was sold for $5,000.
2. The company received a $3,000 dividend from its investment in XYZ, accounted for under the equity method and recorded income from the investment of $5,000 which is included in other income.
3. The company issued 200 shares of common stock for $5,000.
4. The company signed a note payable for $9,000.
5. Equipment was purchased for $8,000.
6. The company converted $15,000 bonds payable into 500 shares of common stock. The book value method was used to record the transaction.
7. A dividend of $12,000 was declared.
8. Equipment was leased on December 31, 2001. The principal portion of the first payment due December 31, 2002, is $700.
9. The company sold half of their available-for-sale investments during the year for $8,000. The fair value of the remaining available-for-sale investments was $8,500 on December 31, 2001.
10. The income tax rate is 36%.

Summary of Cash and Cash Equivalents

Inflows	Outflows	
(d) 5,000		
	8,000 (g)	
(h) 5,000	9,000 (i)	
(n) 9,000		
(s) 8,000		
(t) 15,000		
42,000	17,000	
	25,000	Net increase in cash
42,000	42,000	

Cash and Cash Equivalents—Oper. Act.

(a) 16,320		
(b) 8,000		
(c) 1,000	3,000 (d)	
(e) 3,000	5,000 (f)	
(f) 3,000		
(j) 2,000	5,000 (k)	
(l) 3,000	10,000 (m)	
(o) 1,000		
(p) 1,180	500 (s)	
38,500	23,500	
	15,000 (t)	
38,500	38,500	

Accounts Receivable (net)

11,000	
	2,000 (j)
9,000	

Inventory

9,000	
(k) 5,000	
14,000	

Prepaid Expenses

13,000	
	3,000 (l)
10,000	

Investment in AFS Securities

15,000	
	7,500 (s)
7,500	

Adjustment for Changes in FV of AFS Securities

	3,000
(s) 1,500	
(s) 2,500	
1,000	

Investment in XYZ

14,000	
(f) 5,000	3,000 (f)
16,000	

Patent

6,000	
	1,000 (c)
5,000	

Leased Equipment

(r) 5,000	
5,000	

Prop., Plant, & Equip.

Debit	Credit
37,000	6,000 (d)
(g) 8,000	
39,000	

Accumulated Depr.

Debit	Credit
	3,000
	8,000 (b)
(d) 4,000	
	7,000

Accounts Payable

Debit	Credit
	12,000
(m) 10,000	
	2,000

Notes Payable

Debit	Credit
	9,000 (n)
	9,000

Interest Payable

Debit	Credit
	2,000
(o) 1,000	2,000 (o)
	3,000

Dividends Payable

Debit	Credit
	2,000
(i) 9,000	12,000 (i)
	5,000

Income Taxes Payable

Debit	Credit
	1,000
(p) 5,000	6,180 (p)
	2,180

Deferred Tax Liability (Net)

Debit	Credit
	4,920
	3,000 (e)
	540 (s)
	900 (s)
	9,360

Bonds Payable

Debit	Credit
	25,000
(q) 15,000	
	10,000

Lease Obligation

Debit	Credit
	5,000 (r)
	5,000

Common Stock

Debit	Credit
	26,000
	2,000 (h)
	5,000 (q)
	33,000

Addl. Paid-in Capital

Debit	Credit
	3,000
	3,000 (h)
	10,000 (q)
	16,000

Retained Earnings

Debit	Credit
	41,000
	16,320 (a)
(i) 12,000	
	45,320

Unrealized Gain (Loss) on AFS Securities

Debit	Credit
1,920	
960 (s)	
1,600 (s)	
640	

Explanation of entries

a. Cash and Cash Equivalents—Operating activities is debited for $16,320 (net income) and the credit is to Retained Earnings.

b. Depreciation is not a cash flow; however, depreciation expense was deducted to arrive at net income. Therefore, Accumulated Depreciation is credited and Cash and Cash Equivalents—Operating activities is debited.

c. Amortization of patents is another expense not requiring cash; therefore, Cash and Cash Equivalents—Operating activities is debited and Patent is credited.

d. The sale of equipment (additional information, item 1.) resulted in a $3,000 gain. The gain is computed by comparing the book value of $2,000 with the sales price of $5,000. Cash proceeds of $5,000 are an inflow of cash. Since the gain was included in net income, it must be deducted from net income to determine cash provided by operating activities. This is necessary to avoid counting the $3,000 gain both in cash provided by operating activities and in investing activities. The following entry would have been made on the date of sale:

Cash	5,000	
Accumulated depreciation ($6,000 – $2,000)	4,000	
Property, plant, and equipment		6,000
Gain on sale of equipment ($5,000 – $2,000)		3,000

Adjust the T-accounts as follows: debit Summary of Cash and Cash Equivalents for $5,000, debit Accumulated Depreciation for $4,000, credit Property, Plant, and Equipment for $6,000, and credit Cash and Cash Equivalents—Operating activities for $3,000. Note that per SFAS 95, the gross gain, not the net of tax gain, is removed from operating activities. The tax effect on this gain is left in operating activities.

e. The deferred income tax liability account shows an increase of $4,440. The $3,000 increase that pertains to amounts reported in the income statement must be added to income from operations. Although the $3,000 was deducted as part of income tax expense in determining net income, it did not require an outflow of cash. Therefore, debit Cash and Cash Equivalents—Operating activities and credit Deferred Taxes. The other two amounts in the deferred tax liability account are covered under s.

f. Item 2. under the additional information indicates that the investment in XYZ is accounted for under the equity method. The investment in XYZ had a net increase of $2,000, which is the result of the equity in the earnings of XYZ of $5,000 and the receipt of a $3,000 dividend. Dividends received (an inflow of cash) would reduce the investment in XYZ, while the equity in the income of XYZ would increase the investment without affecting cash. The journal entries would have been

Cash (dividend received)	3,000	
Investment in XYZ		3,000
Investment in XYZ	5,000	
Equity in earnings of XYZ		5,000

The dividend received ($3,000) is an inflow of cash, and the equity earnings are not. Debit Investment in XYZ for $5,000, credit Cash and Cash Equivalents—Operating activities for $5,000, debit Cash and Cash Equivalents—Operating activities for $3,000, and credit Investment in XYZ for $3,000.

g. The Property, Plant, and Equipment account increased because of the purchase of $8,000 (additional information, item 5.). The purchase of assets is an outflow of cash. Debit Property, Plant, and Equipment for $8,000 and credit Summary of Cash and Cash Equivalents.

h. The company sold 200 shares of common stock during the year (additional information, item 3.). The entry for the sale of stock was

Cash	5,000	
Common stock (200 shares x $10)		2,000
Additional paid-in capital		3,000

This transaction resulted in an inflow of cash. Debit Summary of Cash and Cash Equivalents $5,000, credit Common Stock $2,000, and credit Additional Paid-in Capital $3,000.

i. Dividends of $12,000 were declared (additional information, item 7.). Only $9,000 was actually paid in cash resulting in an ending balance of $5,000 in the Dividends Payable account. Therefore, the following entries were made during the year:

Retained Earnings	12,000	
Dividends Payable		12,000
Dividends Payable	9,000	
Cash		9,000

These transactions result in an outflow of cash. Debit Retained Earnings $12,000 and credit Dividends Payable $12,000. Additionally, debit Dividends Payable $9,000 and credit Summary of Cash and Cash Equivalents $9,000 to indicate the cash dividends paid during the year.

j.   Accounts Receivable (net) decreased by $2,000. This is added as an adjustment to net income in the computation of cash provided by operating activities. The decrease of $2,000 means that an additional $2,000 cash was collected on account above and beyond the sales reported in the income statement. Debit Cash and Cash Equivalents—Operating activities and credit Accounts Receivable for $2,000.

k.   Inventories increased by $5,000. This is subtracted as an adjustment to net income in the computation of cash provided by operating activities. Although $5,000 additional cash was spent to increase inventories, this expenditure is not reflected in accrual-basis cost of goods sold. Debit Inventory and credit Cash and Cash Equivalents—Operating activities for $5,000.

l.   Prepaid Expenses decreased by $3,000. This is added back to net income in the computation of cash provided by operating activities. The decrease means that no cash was spent when incurring the related expense. The cash was spent when the prepaid assets were purchased, not when they were expensed on the income statement. Debit Cash and Cash Equivalents—Operating activities and credit Prepaid Expenses for $3,000.

m.   Accounts Payable decreased by $10,000. This is subtracted as an adjustment to net income. The decrease of $10,000 means that an additional $10,000 of purchases were paid for in cash; therefore, income was not affected but cash was decreased. Debit Accounts Payable and credit Cash and Cash Equivalents—Operating activities for $10,000.

n.   Notes Payable increased by $9,000 (additional information, item 4.). This is an inflow of cash and would be included in the financing activities. Debit Summary of Cash and Cash Equivalents and credit Notes Payable for $9,000.

o.   Interest Payable increased by $1,000, but interest expense reported on the income statement was $2,000. Therefore, although $2,000 was expensed, only $1,000 cash was paid ($2,000 expense – $1,000 increase in interest payable). Debit Cash and Cash Equivalents—Operating activities for $1,000 for the noncash portion, debit Interest Payable for $1,000 for the cash portion, and credit Interest Payable for $2,000 for the expense.

p.   The following entry was made to record the incurrence of the tax liability:

Income tax expense	9,180	
Income taxes payable		6,180
Deferred tax liability		3,000

Therefore, $9,180 was deducted in arriving at net income. The $3,000 credit to Deferred Income Taxes was accounted for in entry e. above. The $6,180 credit to Taxes Payable does not, however, indicate that $6,180 cash was paid for taxes. Since Taxes Payable increased $1,180, only $5,000 must have been paid and $1,180 remains unpaid. Debit Cash and Cash Equivalents—Operating activities for $1,180, debit Income Taxes Payable for $5,000, and credit Income Taxes Payable for $6,180.

q. Item 6. under the additional information indicates that $15,000 of bonds payable were converted to common stock. This is a **noncash** financing activity and should be reported in a separate schedule. The following entry was made to record the transaction:

Bonds payable	15,000	
Common stock (500 shares x $10 par)		5,000
Additional paid-in capital		10,000

Adjust the T-accounts with a debit to Bonds Payable, $15,000; a credit to Common Stock, $5,000; and a credit to Additional Paid-in Capital, $10,000.

r. Item 8. under the additional information indicates that leased equipment was acquired on the last day of 2001. This is also a noncash financing activity and should be reported in a separate schedule. The following entry was made to record the lease transaction:

Leased asset	5,000	
Lease obligation		5,000

s. The company sold half of its available-for-sale investments during the year for $8,000 (additional information, item 9.). The entry for the sale of the investments was

Cash	8,000	
Investment in available-for-sale securities		7,500
Gain on sale of investments		500

This transaction resulted in an inflow of cash. Debit Summary of Cash and Cash Equivalents $8,000, credit Investment in Available-for-Sale Securities $7,500, and credit Cash and Cash Equivalents—Operating activities $500. The following additional journal entries were made:

Adjustment for changes in FV	1,500	
Other comprehensive income ($1,500 x 64%)		960
Deferred tax liability ($1,500 x 36%)		540

To adjust the allowance account for the sale, one-half of the amounts provided at the end of 2000 must be taken off the books when the related securities are sold.

Adjustment for changes in FV	2,500	
Unrealized gain on available-for-sale securities		
($2,500 x 64%)		1,600
Deferred tax liability ($2,500 x 36%)		900

To adjust for the change in FV of the remaining securities at year-end (additional information, item 9.). The book value of the securities before the adjustment above is $6,000 ($7,500 – $1,500). The fair value of the securities is $8,500. An adjustment of $2,500 is necessary.

t. The cash and cash equivalents from operations ($15,000) is transferred to the Summary of Cash and Cash Equivalents.

All of the changes in the noncash accounts have been accounted for and the balance in the Summary of Cash and Cash Equivalents account of $25,000 is the amount of the year-to-year increase in cash and cash equivalents. The formal statement may now be prepared using the T-account, Summary of Cash and Cash Equivalents. The alphabetic characters in the statement below refer to the entries in that T-account. The following statement of cash flows is prepared under the direct method. The calculations for gross receipts and gross payments needed for the direct method are shown below the statement.

Johnson Company
Statement of Cash Flows
For the Year Ended December 31, 2001

Cash flow from operating activities

Cash received from customers	$102,000		
Dividends received	3,000		
Cash provided by operating activities			$105,000
Cash paid to suppliers	$ 75,000		
Cash paid for expenses	9,000		
Interest paid	1,000		
Income taxes paid	5,000		
Cash paid for operating activities			(90,000)
Net cash flow provided by operating activities		(t)	$ 15,000

Cash flow from investing activities

Sale of equipment	5,000	(d)	
Sale of investments	8,000	(s)	
Purchase of property, plant, and equipment	(8,000)	(g)	
Net cash provided by investing activities			5,000

Cash flow from financing activities

Sale of common stock	$ 5,000	(h)	
Increase in notes payable	9,000	(n)	
Dividends paid	(9,000)	(i)	
Net cash provided by financing activities			5,000
Net increase in cash and cash equivalents			$ 25,000
Cash and cash equivalents at beginning of year			16,000
Cash and cash equivalents at end of year			$ 41,000

Calculation of amounts for operating activities section

    Cash received from customers = Net sales + Beginning AR – Ending AR

      $100,000 + $11,000 – $9,000 = $102,000

    Cash paid to suppliers = Cost of goods sold + Beginning AP – Ending AP + Ending inventory – Beginning inventory

      $60,000 + $12,000 – $2,000 + $14,000 – $9,000 = $75,000

    Cash paid for operating expenses = Operating expenses + Ending prepaid expenses – Beginning prepaid expenses – Depreciation expense (and other noncash operating expenses)

      $12,000 + $8,000 + $1,000 + $10,000 – $13,000 – $8,000 – $1,000 = $9,000

    Interest paid = Interest expense + Beginning interest payable – Ending interest payable

      $2,000 + $2,000 – $3,000 = $1,000

    Taxes paid = Income taxes + Beginning income taxes payable – Ending income taxes payable – Change in deferred income taxes—operating portion

      $9,180 + $1,000 – $2,180 – $3,000 = $5,000

When a statement of cash flows is prepared using the direct method of reporting operating cash flows, the reconciliation of net income to operating cash flows must also be provided. The T-account, Cash and Cash Equivalents—Operating Activities is used to prepare the reconciliation. The alphabetic characters in the reconciliation below refer to the entries in the T-account.

Reconciliation of net income to net cash provided by operating activities

Net income		(a)	$16,320
Add (deduct) items not using (providing) cash:			
Depreciation	8,000	(b)	
Amortization	1,000	(c)	
Gain on sale of equipment	(3,000)	(d)	
Increase in deferred taxes	3,000	(e)	
Equity in XYZ	(2,000)	(f)	
Decrease in accounts receivable	2,000	(j)	
Increase in inventory	(5,000)	(k)	
Decrease in prepaid expenses	3,000	(l)	
Decrease in accounts payable	(10,000)	(m)	
Increase in interest payable	1,000	(o)	
Increase in income taxes payable	1,180	(p)	
Gain on sale of AFS securities	(500)	(s)	(1,320)
Net cash flow provided by operating activities		(t)	$15,000

Schedule of noncash transactions

Conversion of bonds into common stock	(q)	$15,000
Acquisition of leased equipment	(r)	$ 5,000

Disclosure of accounting policy
For purposes of the statement of cash flows, the Company considers all highly liquid debt instruments purchased with original maturities of three months or less to be cash equivalents.

Statement of Cash Flows for Consolidated Entities

A consolidated statement of cash flows must be presented when a complete set of consolidated financial statements is issued. The consolidated statement of cash flows would be the last statement to be prepared as the information to prepare it will come from the other consolidated statements (consolidated balance sheet, income statement, and statement of retained earnings). The preparation of these other consolidated statements is discussed in Chapter 11, Business Combinations and Consolidated Financial Statements.

The preparation of a consolidated statement of cash flows involves the same analysis and procedures as the statement for an individual entity with a few additional items. When the indirect method is used, the additional noncash transactions relating to the business combination such as the differential amortization must also be reversed and all transfers to affiliates must be eliminated, as they do not represent cash inflows or outflows of the consolidated entity.

All unrealized intercompany profits should have been eliminated in preparation of the other statements. Any income or loss allocated to noncontrolling parties would need to be added back, as it would have been eliminated in computing consolidated net income but does not represent a true cash outflow or inflow. Finally, only dividend payments that are not intercompany should be recorded as cash outflows in the financing activities section.

In preparing the operating activities section of the statement by the indirect method following a purchase business combination, the changes in assets and liabilities related to operations since acquisition should be derived by comparing the consolidated balance sheet as of the date of acquisition with the year-end consolidated balance sheet. These changes will be combined with those for the acquiring company up to the date of acquisition as adjustments to net income. The effects due to the acquisition of these assets and liabilities are reported under investing activities. Under the pooling-of-interests method, the combination is treated as having occurred at the beginning of the year. Thus, the changes in assets and liabilities related to operations should be those derived by comparing the beginning of the year balance sheet amounts on a consolidated basis with the end of the year consolidated balance sheet amounts.

EMERGING ISSUES TASK FORCE CONSENSUS SUMMARIES

95-13   Classification of Debt Issue Costs in the Statement of Cash Flows

Cash paid for debt issue costs should be shown as a financing activity in the statement of cash flows.

00-15   Classification in the Statement of Cash Flows of the Income Tax Benefit Received by a Company upon Exercise of a Nonqualified Employee Stock Option

This issue discusses how a company should classify in the statement of cash flows the income tax benefit (reduction of a cash flow) from an employee's exercise of a nonqualified stock option and whether disclosure of the benefit is necessary. The reduction of income taxes paid should be classified as an operating cash flow. Disclosure of a material tax benefit is required if that benefit is not presented as a separate line in the statement of cash flows or the statement of changes in stockholders' equity.

5 CASH, RECEIVABLES, AND PREPAID EXPENSES

PERSPECTIVE AND ISSUES

The asset side of a balance sheet displays the resources available to the entity to support its current and future operations. To provide information about liquidity, the assets are often divided into current and noncurrent assets. Current assets consist of cash and other assets that are reasonably expected to be realized in cash or sold or consumed during the normal operating cycle of the business. When the normal operating cycle is less than one year, a one-year period is used to distinguish current assets from noncurrent assets. If the operating cycle exceeds one year, the operating cycle is the proper period to use for current asset identification. When information about current assets is accompanied by information about current liabilities, readers of the financial statements can assess the working capital of the entity (current assets less current liabilities) and its current ratio (current assets divided by current liabilities). Both of those measures provide useful information about the liquidity of the entity.

Current assets usually include cash, short-term investments, receivables, inventory, and prepaid expenses. This chapter discusses cash, receivables, and prepaids. Chapter 6, Short-Term Investments and Financial Instruments, discusses short-term investments, and Chapter 7, Inventory, discusses inventory. This chapter also discusses the standards in SFAS 140, *Accounting for Transfers and Servicing of Financial Assets and Extinguishments of Liabilities*. SFAS 140 is included in this chapter because it describes the proper accounting for sales of receivables to third parties and the use of receivables as collateral in secured borrowings. This chapter also includes SFAS 140's standards for repurchase agreements and securities lending. Although those two types of transfers usually involve investments, they are discussed in this chapter because the same underlying theory—the financial components approach—is used for those transactions as is used for transfers involving receivables. SFAS 140's standards for extinguishment of debt are set forth in Chapter 13, Long-Term Debt.

Recognition and measurement of cash is generally straightforward. However, it is necessary to inform readers of the financial statements about any limitations on the ability to use cash in current operations.

Trade receivables and other customary trade term receivables that are due in no longer than one year are measured at net realizable value. Net realizable value is the undiscounted amount of cash, or its equivalent, that will be received in the due course of business as payment of the receivable, less the direct costs, if any, necessary to convert the receivable to cash. Because not all receivables are ultimately realized as cash, a valuation allowance (the allowance for uncollectible amounts) reduces the gross amount of the receivables to their net realizable value.

If a receivable is due on terms exceeding one year, the proper valuation is the present value of future payments to be received, computed by using an interest rate commensurate with the risks involved at the date of the receivable's creation. In many situations the interest rate commensurate with the risks involved is the rate stated in the agreement between the payee and the obligor. However, if the receivable is noninterest-bearing or if the rate stated in the agreement is not indicative of the market rate for a debtor of similar creditworthiness under similar terms (the market rate), interest is imputed at the market rate. The resulting discount is amortized as additional interest income over the life of the agreement (APB 21).

Receivables that are pledged or assigned to a lender as collateral for a lending agreement remain under the control of the entity and therefore remain on its balance sheet. It is necessary, however, to inform readers of the financial statements about the pledge or assignment.

Receivables are sometimes sold in order to generate cash before the receivables are due. If the transferor has no continuing involvement with the transferred assets or with the transferee, it is clear that a sale has taken place, and a gain or loss on sale is measured and recognized. However, in many cases, the transferor of the receivables has continuing involvement with the transferred assets because it sells the receivables with recourse for uncollectible amounts, retains an interest in the receivables, or agrees to service the receivables after the sale. The greater the control that the transferor retains over the receivables, the more likely that the transfer will be accounted for as a secured borrowing rather than a sale.

Under the financial components approach used in SFAS 140, a sale is recognized only if control over the transferred assets is surrendered. A determination that control has been surrendered is made if three criteria are met. If control has been surrendered, an entity recognizes the financial and servicing assets it controls, removes from its books the carrying value of any assets surrendered, recognizes any liabilities assumed, and removes from its books any liabilities that are extinguished. The same accounting and the same three criteria are applied to all transfers of financial assets, regardless of their types. Thus, the standards apply to sales of receivables with recourse, sales of receivables with retained interests or servicing, securitizations (the transformation of the receivables into securities that are sold to other investors), repurchase agreements (a "sale" of a security accompanied by an agreement to "repurchase" it at a future date), and securities lending agreements.

If control has not been surrendered, the transfer of financial assets is accounted for as a secured borrowing. The accounting for the collateral by the debtor and the secured party depends on whether the debtor has defaulted and the nature of the rights and obligations that result from the collateral agreement. If the secured party (the lender) has the right to sell or repledge the collateral, then the debtor reports that asset in its balance sheet separately from other assets not so encumbered. If the secured party does in fact sell the collateral, it recognizes the proceeds from the sale and its obligation to return the collateral. Accounting for the sale of the collateral is also subject to the standards set forth by SFAS 140. If the original debtor defaults on the secured borrowing agreement, thereby forfeiting the right to redeem the collateral, the lender will recognize the collateral as its asset, measured at fair value, or, if it has already sold the collateral, derecognize its obligation to return the collateral; concurrently, the debtor will derecognize the collateral, as it no longer has an equitable claim to it.

Sources of GAAP			
ARB	*APB*	*SFAS*	*EITF*
43, Ch. 1A	6, 21	6, 114, 140	86-8, 87-18, 88-11,
43, Ch 3A			88-22, 88-23, 90-18,
			92-2, 97-3, D-51,
			D-52, D-63, D-64, D-65,
			D-66, D-69, D-75

DEFINITIONS OF TERMS

Accounts receivable. Amounts due from customers for goods or services provided in the normal course of business operations.

Aging the accounts. Computation of the adjustment for uncollectibility of accounts receivable outstanding at the end of the period based upon the length of time the accounts have been unpaid.

Assignment. The formal procedure for collateralization of borrowings through the use of accounts receivable. It normally does not involve debtor notification.

Beneficial interests. Rights to receive all or portions of specified cash inflows to a trust or other entity.

Cash. Coins and currency on hand and balances in checking accounts available for immediate withdrawal.

Cash equivalents. Short-term, highly liquid investments that are readily convertible to known amounts of cash and are so near their maturity that they present negligible risk of changes in value due to changes in interest rates. Examples include treasury bills, commercial paper, and money market funds.

Collateral. Personal or real property used to secure the performance of a loan or other obligation. Upon default of the obligation, the collateral may be sold by the lender in order to satisfy the obligation.

Current assets. Those assets that are reasonably expected to be realized in cash or sold or consumed within a year or within the normal operating cycle of the entity.

Factoring. The outright sale of accounts receivable to a third-party financing entity. The sale may be with or without recourse.

Financial asset. Cash, evidence of an ownership interest in an entity, or a contract that conveys to another entity a right to (1) receive cash or a financial instrument from a first entity, or (2) exchange other financial instruments on potentially favorable terms with the first entity.

Financial liability. A contract that imposes on one entity a contractual obligation to (1) deliver cash or a financial instrument to another entity, or (2) exchange other financial instruments on potentially unfavorable terms with another entity.

Interest-only strip. The contractual right to receive some or all of the interest due on a financial instrument without the rights to receive the principal.

Net realizable value. The amount of cash anticipated to be produced in the normal course of business from an asset, net of any direct costs of the conversion into cash.

Operating cycle. The average time between the acquisition of materials or services and the cash realization from the sale of products or services produced using the acquired materials or services.

Percentage-of-sales method. Computing the adjustment for uncollectible accounts receivable based on the historical relationship between bad debts and gross credit sales.

Pledging. Using an asset as collateral for borrowings. It generally refers to borrowings secured by accounts receivable.

Recourse. The right of a transferee (factor) to receive payment from the transferor of receivables for uncollectible accounts, prepayments by the debtors, merchandise returns, or other defects in the eligibility of the receivables.

Securitization. The transformation of receivables into securities that are sold to other investors.

Servicing asset. A contract to service financial assets that provides the servicer with estimated future revenues (e.g., fees, late charges) that more than adequately compensate the servicer for performing the service.

Servicing liability. A contract to service financial assets that provides the servicer with estimated future revenues (e.g., fees, late charges) that are not expected to adequately compensate the servicer for performing the service.

Transfer. Conveyance of noncash financial asset by or to someone other than issuer of financial asset.

CONCEPTS, RULES, AND EXAMPLES

Cash

To be included as cash in the balance sheet, funds must be represented by coins, currency, undeposited checks, money orders, drafts, and demand deposits available without restriction. Cash that is restricted as to use would not be included with cash unless the restrictions on it expire within the year (or the operating cycle, if longer). Thus, cash legally required to be held in a sinking fund should be shown as a current asset if it will be used to retire the current portion of long-term debt. However, if material, it would be reported on a separate line rather than included with cash. Cash in a demand deposit account that is being held for the retirement of long-term debts that do not mature currently should be excluded from current assets and shown as a noncurrent investment. SFAS 6 identifies the intent of management as a key criterion in the classification of cash. To be included in cash, it must be management's intention that the cash be available for current purposes. Thus, cash that is designated for the purchase of property or equipment would be included in noncurrent assets.

It has become more common to see the caption "Cash and Cash Equivalents" in the balance sheet. That caption includes other forms of near-cash as well as demand deposits and liquid, short-term securities. **Cash equivalents** must be available upon demand in order to justify inclusion.

Compensating balances. An entity will often be required to maintain a minimum amount of cash on deposit (compensating balance). The purpose of this balance is to substitute for fees foregone for services offered by the bank (or fees at a rate less than market) or to increase the yield on a loan to the lender. Since most organizations must maintain a certain working balance in their cash accounts simply to handle routine transactions and to cushion against unforeseen variations in the demand for cash, borrowers often will not find compensating balance arrangements objectionable. Nevertheless, the compensating balance is not available for unrestricted use and penalties will result if it is used. If material, the portion of an entity's cash account that is a compensating balance must be segregated and shown as a separate line item on the balance sheet. The line should be shown as a noncurrent asset if related borrowings are noncurrent liabilities. If the borrowings are current liabilities or if the compensating balance reduces fees that would have been incurred in the next year, it is acceptable to show the compensating balance as a **separately captioned** current asset.

Cash in savings accounts subject to a statutory notification requirement and cash in certificates of deposit maturing during the current **operating cycle** or within one year may be included as current assets but, if material, should be separately captioned in the balance sheet to avoid the misleading implication that these funds are available immediately upon demand. Typically, such items will be included in the **short-term investments** caption, but these could be labeled as time deposits or restricted cash deposits.

Petty cash and other imprest cash accounts are usually combined in financial statements with other cash accounts.

Prepaid Expenses

Prepaid expenses are prepayments made to secure the use of assets or the receipt of services at a future date. Prepaid expenses will not be converted to cash, but they are classified as current assets because, if not prepaid, they would have required the use of current assets during the coming year (or operating cycle, if longer). Prepaid rent, prepaid insurance, prepaid interest, and prepaid advertising are examples of prepaid expenses. The balance in the prepaid expense account is amortized to expense on a ratable basis over the period in which the benefits (services) are received. For example, if rent is prepaid for the quarter at the beginning of the quarter, two months of the rent will be included in the prepaid rent account. At the beginning of the second month, the equivalent of one month's rent (half the account balance) would be expensed. At the beginning of the third month, the remaining account balance would be expensed.

Receivables

Accounts receivable, open accounts, or trade accounts are agreements by customers to pay for services received or merchandise obtained. Notes receivable are formalized obligations evidenced by written promissory notes. Other categories of receivables include trade acceptances, third-party instruments, and amounts due from officers, stockholders, employees, or affiliated companies. The latter categories of receivables generally arise from cash advances but could result from sales of merchandise or the provision of services. The nature of amounts due from trade customers is often different from that of balances receivable from related parties, such as employees or stockholders. Thus, generally accepted accounting principles require that the different classes of receivables be separately identified either on the face of the balance sheet or in the notes.

Receivables due within one year (or one operating cycle, if longer) generally should be presented at **net realizable value**. Deductions from face value should be taken for amounts estimated to be uncollectible and also for the estimated returns, allowances, and other discounts to be taken by customers prior to or at the time of payment. In practice, the deductions that would be made for estimated returns, allowances, and trade discounts are usually deemed to be immaterial and such adjustments are rarely made. However, if it is known that sales are recorded for merchandise that is shipped "on approval" and available data suggests that a sizable proportion of such sales are returned by the customers, then the estimated future returns must be accrued. Similarly, material amounts of anticipated discounts and allowances should be recorded in the period of sale.

Valuation allowance for bad debts. The recording of a valuation allowance for anticipated uncollectible amounts is almost always necessary. The direct write-off method, in which a receivable is charged off only when it is clear that it cannot be collected, is unsatisfactory since it overstates assets and results in a mismatching of revenues and expenses. Proper matching can only be achieved if bad debts are recorded in the same fiscal period as the revenues to which they are related. Since the amount of uncollectible accounts is not known with certainty, an estimate must be made.

There are two popular estimation techniques. The **percentage-of-sales** method is principally oriented towards achieving the best possible matching of revenues and expenses. **Aging the accounts** is more oriented toward the presentation of the correct net realizable value of the trade receivables in the balance sheet. Both methods are acceptable and widely employed.

For the percentage-of-sales method, historical data are analyzed to ascertain the relationship between bad debts and credit sales. The derived percentage is then applied to the current period's sales revenues in order to arrive at the appropriate debit to bad debts expense for the year. The offsetting credit is made to Allowance for Uncollectibles. When specific customer accounts are subsequently identified as uncollectible, they are written off against this allowance.

Example of percentage-of-sales method

Total credit sales for year:	$7,500,000
Bad debt ratio from prior years or other data source:	1.75% of credit sales
Computed year-end adjustment for bad debts expense:	$131,250 ($7,500,000 x .0175)

The entry required is

Bad debts expense	131,250	
Allowance for uncollectibles		131,250

Care must be taken to ensure that the bad debt ratio computed will be representative of uncollectibility of the current period's credit sales. A ratio based on historical experience may require an adjustment to reflect the current economic climate. For example, if a large percentage of customers are concentrated in a geographic area that is experiencing an economic downturn, rates of default may increase.

When aging the accounts, an analysis is prepared of the customer receivables at the balance sheet date. Each customer's balance is categorized by the number of days or months the underlying invoices have remained outstanding. Based on the entity's past experience or on other available statistics, historical bad debts percentages are applied to each of these aggregate amounts, with larger percentages being applied to the older accounts. The end result of this process is a computed total dollar amount that is the proper balance in the allowance for uncollectibles at the balance sheet date. The computed amount is compared to the balance in the valuation account, and an adjustment is made for the differences. Thus, the adjustment needed will be an amount other than the amount computed by the aging.

Example of the aging method

	Under 30 days	Age of accounts 30-90 days	Over 90 days	Total
Gross receivables	$1,100,000	$425,000	$360,000	
Bad debt percentage	0.5%	2.5%	15%	
Provision required	$5,500	$10,625	$54,000	$70,125

The credit balance required in the allowance account is $70,125. Assuming that a **debit** balance of $58,250 already exists in the allowance account (from charge-offs during the year that exceeded the credit balance in the allowance account at the previous year-end), the necessary entry is

Bad debts expense	128,375	
Allowance for uncollectibles		128,375

Both of the estimation techniques will produce approximately the same result over the course of a number of years. Nonetheless, these adjustments are based upon estimates and will never be totally accurate. When facts subsequently become available to indicate that the amount provided as an allowance for uncollectible accounts was incorrect, an adjustment classified as a change in estimate is made. For information about impairment of loans receivable and troubled debt restructurings, see Chapter 13, Long-Term Debt.

Valuation allowance for unearned interest. If a receivable is due on terms exceeding one year, the proper valuation is the present value of future payments to be received, determined by using an interest rate commensurate with the risks involved at the date of the receivable's creation. In many situations the interest rate commensurate with the risks involved is the rate stated in the agreement between the payee and the debtor. However, if the receivable is noninterest-bearing or if the rate stated in the agreement is not indicative of the market rate for a debtor of similar creditworthiness under similar terms (the market rate), interest is imputed at the market rate. A valuation allowance is used to adjust the face amount of the receivable to the present value at the market rate. The balance in the valuation allowance is amortized as additional interest income over the life of the agreement.

APB 21 specifies when and how interest is to be imputed when the receivable is noninterest-bearing or the stated rate on the receivable is not reasonable. APB 21 divides receivables into three categories for discussion: notes issued solely for cash, notes issued for cash and a right or privilege, and notes issued in exchange for property, goods, or services.

When a note is issued solely for cash, its present value is necessarily assumed to be equal to the cash proceeds. The interest rate is that rate which equates the cash proceeds received by the borrower to the amounts to be paid in the future. For example, if a borrower agrees to pay $1,060 in one year in exchange for cash today of $1,000, the interest rate implicit in that agreement is 6%. A valuation allowance of $60 is applied to the face amount ($1,060) so that the receivable in included in the balance sheet at its present value ($1,000).

When a note receivable that bears an unrealistic rate of interest is issued in exchange for cash, an additional right or privilege is usually granted. The difference between the present value of the receivable and the cash advanced is the value assigned to the right or privilege. It is an addition to the cost of the products purchased for the purchaser/lender and an additional revenue to the debtor.

Example of accounting for a note issued for both cash and a contractual right

1. Schwartz borrows $10,000 from Weiss via an unsecured five-year note. Simple interest at 2% is due at maturity.
2. Schwartz agrees to sell Weiss a car for $15,000, which is less than its market price.
3. The market rate of interest on a note with similar terms and a borrower of similar creditworthiness is 10%.

The present value factor for an amount due in five years at 10% is .62092. Therefore, the present value of the note is $6,830 [($10,000 principal + $1,000 interest at the stated rate) x .62092]. According to APB 21, the $3,170 ($10,000 – $6,830) difference between the present value of the note and the face value of the note is regarded as part of the cost/purchase price of the car. The following entry would be made by Weiss to record the transaction:

Note receivable	10,000	
Car	18,170	
Cash		25,000
Discount on note receivable		3,170

The discount on note receivable is amortized using the effective interest method, as follows:

	Effective interest (10%)	*Stated interest (2%)*	*Amortization*	*Note and interest receivable*
01/01/01				6,830
01/01/02	683	200	(483)	7,513
01/01/03	751	200	(551)	8,264
01/01/04	826	200	(626)	9,091
01/01/05	909	200	(709)	10,000
01/01/06	1,000	200	(800)	11,000

The entry for the first year would be

Discount on note receivable	483	
Interest receivable	200	
Interest revenue		683

When a note is issued in exchange for property, goods, or services and the transaction is entered into at arm's length, the stated interest rate is presumed to be fair unless (1) no interest rate is stated, (2) the stated rate is unreasonable, (3) the face value of the note receivable is materially different from fair value of the property, goods, or services received, or (4) the face value of the note receivable is materially different from the current market value of the note at the date of the transaction. According to APB 21, when the rate on the note is not fair, the note is to be recorded at the fair market value of the property, goods, or services sold or the market value of the note, whichever is the more clearly determinable. The difference is recorded as a discount or premium and amortized to interest income.

Example of accounting for a note exchanged for goods

1. Green sells Brown inventory that has a fair market value of $8,573.
2. Green receives a two-year noninterest-bearing note having a face value of $10,000.

In this situation, the fair market value of the consideration is readily determinable and, thus, represents the amount at which the note is to be recorded. The following entry would be made by Green:

Notes receivable	10,000	
Discount on notes receivable		1,427
Sales revenue		8,573

The discount will be amortized to interest expense over the two-year period using the interest rate implied in the transaction, which is 8%. The present value factor is .8573 ($8,573/$10,000). Using a present value table for amount due in two years, .8573 is located under the 8% rate.

If neither the fair value of the property, goods, or services sold nor the fair value of the note receivable is determinable, then the present value of the note must be determined using an imputed market interest rate. This rate will then be used to establish the present value of the note by discounting all future payments on the note at that rate. General guidelines for determining the appropriate interest rate, which are provided by APB 21, include the prevailing rates of similar instruments with debtors having similar credit ratings and the rate the debtor could obtain for similar financing from other sources. Other factors to be considered include any collateral or restrictive covenants involved, the current and expected prime rate, and other terms pertaining to the instrument. The objective is to approximate the rate of interest that would have resulted if an independent borrower and lender had negotiated a similar transaction under comparable terms and conditions. This determination is as of the issuance date, and any subsequent changes in market interest rates are irrelevant.

Additional discussion about present value techniques, including additional examples, is found in Chapter 13, Long-Term Debt.

Pledging, assigning, and factoring receivables. An organization can alter the timing of cash flows resulting from sales to its customers by using its accounts receivable as collateral for borrowings or by selling the receivables outright. A wide variety of arrangements can be structured by the borrower and lender, but the most common are pledging, assignment, and factoring.

Pledging is an agreement in which accounts receivable are used as collateral for loans. The customers whose accounts have been pledged are not aware of this event, and their payments are still remitted to the original obligee. The pledged accounts merely serve as security to the lender, giving comfort that sufficient assets exist to generate cash flows adequate in amount and timing to repay the debt. However, the debt is paid by the borrower whether or not the pledged receivables are collected and whether or not the pattern of their collection matches the payments due on the debt.

The only accounting issue relating to pledging is that of adequate disclosure. The accounts receivable, which remain assets of the borrowing entity, continue to be shown as current assets in its financial statements but must be identified as having been pledged. This identification can be accomplished either parenthetically or by note disclosures. Similarly, the related debt should be identified as having been collateralized by the receivables.

Example of disclosure for pledged receivables

Current assets:
Accounts receivable, net of allowance for doubtful accounts of
  $600,000 ($3,500,000 of which has been pledged as collateral for
  bank loans)   8,450,000

Current liabilities:
Bank loans payable (collateralized by pledged accounts receivable)   2,700,000

A more common practice is to include the disclosure in the notes to the financial statements. Since the borrower has not surrendered control of the pledged receivables, it continues to carry the pledged receivables as its assets (SFAS 140).

The assignment of accounts receivable is a more formalized transfer of the receivables to the lending institution. The lender will make an investigation of the specific receivables that are being proposed for assignment and will approve those that it deems worthy as collateral. Usually customers are not aware that their accounts have been assigned and they continue to forward their payments to the original obligee (the borrowing entity). In some cases, the assignment agreement requires that collection proceeds be immediately delivered to the lender. The borrower is, however, the primary obligor of the debt and is required to make timely payment on the debt whether or not the receivables are collected as anticipated. The borrowing is with recourse, and the general credit of the borrower is pledged to the payment of the debt.

Since the lender knows that not all the receivables will be collected on a timely basis by the borrower, only a fraction of the face value of the receivables will be advanced as a loan to the borrower. Typically, this amount ranges from 70 to 90%, depending upon the credit history and collection experience of the borrower.

Assigned accounts receivable remain the assets of the borrower and continue to be presented in its financial statements, with appropriate disclosure of the assignment similar to that illustrated for pledging. Prepaid finance charges would be debited to a prepaid expense account and amortized to expense over the period to which the charges apply.

In the typical case involving the assignment of receivables, the borrower retains control of the receivables, and it is clear that the transaction is a secured borrowing rather than a sale. If it is unclear whether the borrower has retained control of the receivables, a determination must be made as to whether to account for the transfer as a sale or as a secured borrowing. Making that determination is discussed later in this chapter in the section titled "Transfers of Financial Assets under SFAS 140."

Factoring involves the outright sale of receivables to a finance company known as a factor. These arrangements involve (1) notification to the customer to forward future payments to the factor and (2) the transfer of receivables without recourse. The factor assumes the risk of an inability to collect. Thus, once a factoring arrangement is completed, the transferor has no further involvement with the accounts, except for a return of merchandise.

In its simplest form, the receivables are sold and the difference between the cash received and the carrying value is recognized as a gain or loss.

Example of accounting for the factoring of receivables without recourse

Thirsty Corp., on July 1, 2000, enters into an agreement with Rich Company to sell a group of its receivables without recourse. A total face value of $200,000 accounts receivable (against which a 5% allowance had been recorded) are involved. The entries required are as follows:

Cash	180,055	
Allowance for bad debts (200,000 x .05)	10,000	
Loss on sale of receivables	19,945	
Bad debts expense		10,000
Accounts receivable		200,000

The classic variety of factoring provides two financial services to the business: it permits the entity to obtain cash earlier than waiting for customers to pay, and it transfers to the factor the risk of bad debts. The factor is compensated for each of the services. Interest is charged based on the anticipated length of time between the date the factoring is consummated and the expected collection date of the receivables sold. A fee is charged based upon the factor's anticipated bad debt losses.

Example of accounting for the factoring of receivables without recourse

Thirsty Corp., on July 1, 2000, enters into an agreement with Rich Company to sell a group of its receivables without recourse. The receivables have a total face value of $200,000 (against which a 5% allowance had been recorded). The factor will charge 20% interest computed on the weighted-average time to maturity of the receivables of thirty-six days plus a 3% fee.

The entries required are as follows:

Cash	180,055	
Allowance for bad debts (200,000 x .05)	10,000	
Interest expense (or prepaid) (200,000 x .20 x 36/365)	3,945	
Factoring fee (200,000 x .03)	6,000	
Loss on sale of receivables	10,000	
Bad debts expense		10,000
Accounts receivable		200,000

The interest expense, factor's fee and loss can be combined into a $19,945 loss on the sale of receivables.

Some companies factor receivables as a means of transferring the risk of bad debts, but leave the cash on deposit with the factor until the weighted-average due date of the receivables, thereby avoiding interest charges. This arrangement is still referred to as factoring, since the customer receivables have been sold. However, the borrowing entity does not receive cash but creates a new receivable, usually captioned "Due from Factor." This receivable, in contrast to the original customer receivables, is essentially riskless and will be presented in the balance sheet without a deduction for estimated uncollectibles.

Merchandise returns will normally be the responsibility of the transferor, who must then make the appropriate settlement with the factor. To protect against the possibility of merchandise returns that diminish the total of receivables to be collected, a factoring arrangement will frequently advance only a portion of the face amount of the factored receivables (less any interest and factoring fee deductions). The factor will retain a certain fraction of the total proceeds relating to the portion of sales that are anticipated to be returned by customers. This sum is known as the factor's holdback. When merchandise is returned to the transferor, an entry is made offsetting the receivable from the factor. At the end of the return privilege period, any remaining holdback will become due and payable to the transferor.

Example of accounting for the factoring of receivables without recourse

1. Thirsty Corp., on July 1, 2000, enters into an agreement with Rich Company to sell a group of its receivables without recourse. The receivables have a total face value of $200,000 (against which a 5% allowance had been recorded). The factor will charge 20% interest computed on the weighted-average time to maturity of the receivables of thirty-six days plus a 3% fee. A 5% holdback will also be retained.
2. Thirsty's customers return for credit $4,800 of merchandise.
3. The customer return privilege period expires and the remaining holdback is paid to the transferor.

The entries required are as follows:

1.	Cash	180,055	
	Allowance for bad debts (200,000 x .05)	10,000	
	Interest expense (or prepaid) (200,000 x .20 x 36/365)	3,945	
	Factoring fee (200,000 x .03)	6,000	
	Factor's holdback receivable		
	[$10,000/($10,000 + $190,000) x $190,000]	9,500	
	Loss on sale of receivables	500	
	Bad debts expense		10,000
	Accounts receivable		200,000

The interest expense, factor's fee and loss can be combined into a $10,445 charge to loss on the sale of receivables.

2.	Sales returns and allowances	4,800	
	Factor's holdback receivable		4,800
3.	Cash	5,200	
	Factor's holdback receivable		4,700
	Loss on sale of receivables		500

The factor's holdback receivable on the seller's books is required by SFAS 140 to be an allocation of the carrying value of the receivables ($190,000) between the assets sold (the receivables) and the assets retained (the holdback) based on their relative fair values at the date of the factoring agreement. The factor holds back 5% of the face value ($200,000) for a total of $10,000. Upon settlement the loss or gain recorded at the origination of the factoring arrangement needs to be adjusted because the factor pays the remaining holdback of $5,200 ($10,000 holdback – $4,800 returns) in settlement of an asset with a carrying value of $4,700 ($9,500 – $4,800).

Factoring transfers title. Where there is a no recourse provision or other continuing involvement with the receivables, the removal of the receivables from the borrower's balance sheet is clearly warranted.

Another variation is known as factoring with recourse. Accounting for factoring with recourse requires a determination of whether the transfer is a sale or a secured borrowing. That determination is made using the standards in SFAS 140.

Transfers of Financial Assets under SFAS 140

If receivables or other financial assets are transferred to another entity and the transferor has no continuing involvement with the transferred assets or with the transferee, it is clear that a sale has taken place, and a gain or loss on sale is measured and recognized. However, in many cases, the transferor of the receivables has continuing involvement with the transferred assets, either because it sells the receivables with recourse for uncollectible amounts, retains an interest in the receivables, or agrees to service the receivables after the sale. The more control that the transferor retains over the receivables, the more the transfer appears to be in substance a secured borrowing rather than a sale.

SFAS 140 provides standards to determine whether a transfer of financial assets is a sale or a secured borrowing. The standards use a financial components approach in which a single financial asset is viewed as a mix of component assets (controlled economic benefits) and component liabilities (obligations for probable future sacrifices of economic benefits). The focus is on who controls the components and whether that control has changed as a result of a given transfer. If the transferor has surrendered control of the transferred assets, the transfer is a sale. If the transferor retains control of the transferred assets, the transfer is a secured borrowing.

Scope. SFAS 140 covers transfers of noncash financial assets by and to an entity other than the issuer of the financial asset. Thus, a transfer includes selling a receivable, transferring a receivable to a trust, or using a receivable as security for a loan. A transfer does not include the origination of a receivable, the settlement of a receivable, or the restructuring of a receivable in a troubled debt restructuring because those transactions are transfers involving the issuer of the receivable.

Among the types of transfers of financial assets for which SFAS 140 establishes standards are

- Transfers of receivables with recourse (factoring)
- Transfers of undivided partial interests in receivables (retained interests)
- Transfers of receivables with servicing retained
- Securitizations
- Repurchase agreements
- Securities lending
- Transfers of receivables as collateral

Those types of transactions are discussed in this chapter. In addition, SFAS 140 sets standards for extinguishments of liabilities. Those matters are discussed in Chapter 13, Long-Term Debt.

Examples of items **included** in the scope of SFAS 140

1. Beneficial interests in a securitization trust that holds nonfinancial assets such as securitized stranded costs or similar imposed rights (unless a third party must consolidate the trust).
2. A litigation judgment that is enforceable and contractually reduced to a fixed payment schedule.
3. Transfer of an equity method investment unless subject to EITF 98-7 (similar productive assets) or EITF 98-8 (sale of real estate).
4. A forward contract on a financial instrument that may be net settled or physically settled by exchange for cash or some other financial asset.
5. Recognized financial instruments that may be either financial assets or financial liabilities at some point (forward or swap contracts), which must meet the criteria of both paragraphs 9 and 16 to be derecognized.

6. Recognized derivatives that are nonfinancial liabilities (a written commodity option) at the date of transfer because paragraph 16 applies to the extinguishment of all liabilities. Nonfinancial derivative instruments with characteristics of both assets and liabilities (commodity forwards) have to satisfy the conditions of both paragraph 9 and paragraph 16 to qualify for derecognition.
7. Dollar rolls in connection with the transfer of existing securities.
8. Transfers of minimum lease payments under sales-type and direct financing leases and any related guaranteed residual.
9. Transfers of investments in subsidiaries that have not been consolidated either because the control over the subsidiary is temporary or because the parent carries the investment at fair value (e.g., an investment company).

The following items are **excluded** from the scope of SFAS 140:

1. The right to receive the minimum lease payments under an **operating** lease since it is an unrecognized financial asset.
2. Transfers of servicing rights that are contractually separated from the serviced assets because they are nonfinancial assets.
3. Payment of cash or conveyances of noncash financial assets in partial or full settlement of a debt. An origination, settlement, or restructuring of a receivable is not a transfer since it does not involve a conveyance of a noncash financial asset by or to someone other than the issuer.
4. Acquisition of treasury stock by exchanging noncash financial assets, because it is an investment by or a distribution to owners.
5. Desecuritization of securities into loans or other financial assets.
6. Securitized stranded costs of electric utilities (although enforceable rights) are not considered financial assets since they arise from an imposition of tax rather than a contractual agreement.
7. Contingent receivables from litigation before terms are reduced to a contract.
8. Transfer of ownership interest in a consolidated subsidiary if the subsidiary's assets are not all financial assets.
9. Recognized derivatives that are nonfinancial assets (an option to purchase commodities) at the date of transfer.
10. Dollar rolls when the underlying securities do not yet exist or are to be announced (TBA GNMA rolls).
11. Transfers of **unguaranteed** residual values on transfers of sales-type or direct financing lease receivables.

Surrender of control. A transfer of financial assets (or a portion of a financial asset) is a sale if the transferor surrenders control over those assets in exchange for consideration. However, control is not surrendered to the extent that the consideration received is a beneficial interest in the transferred assets. For example, a transferor's exchange of one form of beneficial interests in a trust for an equivalent, but different, form in the same transferred financial assets cannot be accounted for as a sale. If the trust initially issued the beneficial interests, the exchange is not even a transfer under SFAS 140.

Paragraph 9 specifies that control is deemed to have been surrendered by the transferor only if **all** of the following conditions are met:

1. The assets transferred are beyond the reach of the transferor and its affiliates, its creditors, potential bankruptcy trustees or other receivers, except for an affiliate that is a qualifying special-purpose entity.

2. The transferee (or if the transferee is a qualifying special-purpose entity (SPE), each holder of its beneficial interests) has the right to pledge or exchange the assets (or beneficial interests) it received, and no condition both (1) constrains the transferee (or holder) from taking advantage of its right to pledge or exchange and (2) provides more than a trivial benefit to the transferor.

3. The transferor does not maintain effective control over the transferred assets. A transferor maintains effective control if (1) an agreement both entitles and obligates the transferor to repurchase or redeem the assets before their maturity or (2) the transferor has the ability to unilaterally cause the holder to return specific assets. If the transferor can cause the holder to return assets only through a cleanup call, that ability does not indicate effective control. (A cleanup call is an option to purchase the remaining transferred financial assets, or the remaining beneficial interests in a qualifying SPE if the amount of outstanding assets or beneficial interests falls to a prespecified level at which the cost of servicing those assets or beneficial interests becomes burdensome in relation to the benefits of servicing.)

A transferee has control of transferred assets if there is the unconstrained right to both pledge and exchange the assets. It is more difficult to tell if the transferee has control if the transferee can pledge the transferred assets but cannot sell them. The key to a determination of control by a transferee with the right to pledge **or** exchange the assets rests on whether the transferee obtains all or most of the cash inflows that are the primary economic benefits of the pledged or exchanged assets. Generally, the right of first refusal, prohibition of a sale to competitors, and the requirement to obtain transferor permission that won't be unreasonably withheld (judgment is necessary in this case) to sell or pledge won't preclude accounting as a sale. Agreements that constrain the transferee from pledge or exchange are accounted for as secured borrowings.

All available evidence should be assessed to determine if transferred assets would be beyond the reach of the powers of a bankruptcy trustee (or equivalent). The likelihood or remoteness of bankruptcy at date of transfer does not satisfy the requirements. Such determination may require a legal opinion regarding the application of the laws of the relevant jurisdiction.

Maintaining effective control. The criteria in paragraph 9 must be met in order for a transfer to be accounted for as a sale, and the criteria in paragraphs 27-34 and 47-54 (implementation guidance) are an integral part of paragraph 9. If the transferor maintains effective control, the transfer is accounted for as a secured borrowing and not as a sale.

A transferor maintains effective control over the transferred assets if a repurchase or redemption agreement meets all of the following conditions:

1. The assets covered by the agreement must be the same or substantially the same as the transferred assets. In order to meet this condition, the assets transferred and those to be repurchased or redeemed must meet all of the following conditions:

   a. The same primary obligor or, in the case of government-guaranteed instruments, the same guarantor and terms of the guarantee. (If the asset is debt guaranteed by a sovereign government, central bank, government-sponsored enterprise or agency thereof, the guarantor and the terms of the guarantee must be the same.)

   b. Identical form and type providing the same risks and rights

   c. The same maturity, or, in the case of mortgage-backed pass-through or pay-through securities, have similar remaining weighted-average maturities that provide approximately the same market yield

   d. Identical contractual interest rates

   e. Similar collateral

   f. The same aggregate unpaid principal amount or principal amounts that are within accepted "good delivery" standards for the type of security being transferred

2. The transferor is able to repurchase or redeem the assets on substantially the agreed terms even if the transferee were to default. In order to meet this condition, the transferor must, during the entire term of the contract, have obtained cash or other collateral sufficient to fund substantially the entire cost of purchasing replacement assets from others. For example, a contractual provision that terminates a repurchase agreement immediately if the value of the collateral become insufficient to fund substantially all of the cost of purchasing replacement assets would satisfy the requirement, as would a margining provision.

3. The redemption or repurchase agreement is executed concurrently with the transfer of the assets and requires repurchase or redemption prior to maturity at a fixed or determinable price.

Accounting for transfers. Upon any transfer (whether accounted for as a sale or as a secured borrowing), the transferor will allocate, based on relative fair values at the date of transfer, the previous carrying amount between the retained interests, if any, and the assets transferred. Retained interests are interests in the transferred assets over which control has not been given up by the transferor. They include **servicing assets and liabilities**, undivided interests in the transferred assets, and beneficial interests in assets transferred to a qualifying special-purpose entity in a securitization.

If a sale, the transferor (seller) should

1. Derecognize all assets sold
2. Recognize all assets (including cash, options, swaps, etc.) obtained and liabilities (including forward commitments and servicing liabilities) incurred in consideration as proceeds
3. Measure assets controlled and liabilities incurred at fair value initially if they are part of the proceeds of the sale (new assets and liabilities). If it is not practical to estimate the fair value of the assets, the transferor will record those assets at zero. If it is not practical to estimate the fair value of the liabilities, the transferor will not recognize any gain on the transaction and will record liabilities at the greater of

   a. Excess fair value of the assets obtained minus the fair value of the liabilities incurred, over the carrying value of the assets transferred or
   b. The amount to be recorded in conjunction with SFAS 5 and FASB I 14 that represents the minimum amount in an estimated range of a probable liability.

4. Recognize gains or losses in earnings.

All financial asset transfers not meeting the sale criteria are required to be accounted for as secured borrowings with collateral (or other security interest) pledged.

Measuring assets and liabilities after completion of a transfer. SFAS 140 addresses initial recognition and measurement but, except for servicing, does not address subsequent measurement. Existing GAAP must be used for that purpose. For example

1. Interest-only strips, retained interests in securitizations, loans, other receivables, or other financial assets that can contractually be prepaid or otherwise settled in such a way that the holder would not recover substantially all of its recorded investment (except for derivative instruments that are within the scope of SFAS 133) should be subsequently measured like investments in debt securities classified as available-for-sale or trading under SFAS 115.
2. Equity securities that have readily determinable fair values should be subsequently measured in accordance with SFAS 115.
3. Debt securities should be subsequently measured in accordance with SFAS 115, SFAS 65 (mortgage-backed securities) or EITF 99-20 (purchased and retained beneficial interests in securitized financial assets).
4. Derivative financial instruments should be subsequently measured in accordance with SFAS 133.

If it was initially impracticable to measure the fair value of an asset or liability but it later becomes practicable, the transferor does not remeasure the asset or liability (or the gain or loss) under SFAS 140 unless it is a servicing asset or liability. However, adjustment of the carrying value may be required by other standards, such as SFAS 115.

Transfers of receivables with recourse. Some entities have such a poor history of uncollectible accounts that factors are only willing to purchase their accounts if a substantial fee is collected to compensate for the risk. When the company believes that the receivables are of a better quality, a way to avoid excessive factoring fees is to sell these receivables with recourse. This variation of factoring is really an assignment of receivables with notification to the customers.

In a transfer of receivables with recourse, the transferor is obligated to make payments to the transferee or to repurchase receivables sold upon the happening of an uncertain future event. Typically, recourse provisions compensate the transferee for uncollectible accounts, but they can also be written to compensate the transferee for prepayments of the receivables, merchandise returns, or other events that change the anticipated cash flows from the receivables. The effect of a recourse provision on the application of SFAS 140's surrender of control provisions (paragraph 9) may vary by jurisdiction and by the level of recourse provided. For example, in some jurisdictions, full recourse will not place the receivables beyond the reach of the transferor and its creditors but a limited recourse provision may. Thus, some transfers of receivables with recourse will meet the criteria of paragraph 9 and be accounted for as a sale. Others will fail the criteria and be accounted for as a secured borrowing.

In computing the gain or loss to be recognized at the date of a transfer of receivables that meets the criteria of paragraph 9, the borrower (transferor) must take into account the anticipated chargebacks from the transferee for bad debts incurred. This action requires an estimate by the transferor, based on past experience. Adjustments should also be made at the time of sale for the estimated effects of any prepayments by customers (where the receivables are interest-bearing or where cash discounts are available), and for the effects of any defects in the eligibility of the transferred receivables.

Example of accounting for the transfer of receivables with recourse

1. Thirsty Corp., on July 1, 2000, enters into an agreement with Rich Company to sell a group of its receivables with a face value of $200,000 on which a 5% allowance had been recorded. Rich Company (the factor) will charge 20% interest computed on the weighted-average time to maturity of the receivables of thirty-six days and a 3% fee. A 5% holdback will also be retained.
2. Generally, 40% of Thirsty's customers take advantage of a 2% cash discount.
3. The factor accepts the receivables subject to recourse for nonpayment.
4. In this jurisdiction, the transfer qualifies as a sale.

Under SFAS 140, Thirsty must record the recourse liability. It has accepted the obligation for all credit losses and has, in effect, guaranteed the receivables. The recourse obligation is measured as the estimate of uncollectibles (5% of face value).

The entry required to record the sale is

Cash	180,055	
Allowance for bad debts	10,000	
Interest expense (200,000 x .20 x 36/365)	3,945	
Factoring fee (200,000 x .03)	6,000	
Factor's holdback receivable		
[$10,000/($10,000 + $190,000) x $190,000]	9,500	
Loss on sale of receivables	2,100	
Due to factor for discounts (200,000 x .40 x .02)		1,600
Accounts receivable		200,000
Recourse obligation		10,000

Simplified, the entry is

Cash	180,055	
Allowance for bad debts	10,000	
Factor's holdback receivable (9,500 – 1,600)	7,900	
Loss on sale of receivables (3,945 + 6,000 + 2,100)	12,045	
Accounts receivable		200,000
Recourse obligation		10,000

The accounts receivable net of the allowance for bad debts (a valuation account) is removed from the transferor's books as it has been sold. Previously accrued bad debts expense is not reversed, however, as the transferor still expects to incur that expense through the recourse provision of the factoring agreement. (Alternatively, the bad debts expense could have been reversed and the charge to loss on sale increased by $10,000.) The loss on sale of receivables is the sum of the interest charged by the factor ($3,945), the factor's fee ($6,000), the expected chargeback for cash discounts to be taken ($1,600), and the difference between the holdback receivable at face value and at carrying value ($500). The factor's holdback receivable is a retained interest in the receivables transferred, and it is measured by allocating the original carrying amount ($190,000) between the assets sold ($190,000) and the assets retained ($10,000).

If, subsequent to the sale of the receivables, the actual experience relative to the recourse terms differs from the provision made at the time of the sale, a change in an accounting estimate results. It is reflected as an additional gain or loss in the subsequent period. These changes are not corrections of errors or retroactive adjustments.

If the above facts apply, but the transfer does not qualify as a sale, the borrower's entry will be

Cash	180,055	
Interest expense (or prepaid)	3,945	
Factoring fee	6,000	
Factor borrowing payable		190,000

The accounts receivable remain on the borrower's books. Both the accounts receivable and the factor borrowings payable should be cross-referenced on the face of the balance sheet or in the notes to the financial statements. The accounting for the collateral under SFAS 140 depends upon the terms of the collateral agreement. Accounting for collateral is discussed later in this chapter.

Retained interests. Retained interests include undivided interests for which control has not been given up by the transferor, servicing (mortgages, credit card receivables, etc.) assets and liabilities and beneficial interests in assets transferred to a qualifying special-purpose entity in a securitization. In general, the more extensive an interest that the transferor of assets retains, the less likely the transaction will be classified as a sale and the more likely the transaction will be classified as a secured borrowing. The primary reason for this result is that in a true sale, the transferor should no longer bear the risks or reap the rewards associated with the transferred assets. If a determination cannot be made between classification as proceeds of a sale or as retained interests, the asset should be classified as proceeds and should be measured at fair value. Interests in transferred assets that are not a part of the proceeds are considered retained interests that are still under the control of the transferor.

Retained interests are to be measured by allocating the carrying value of the transferred assets before the transfer between the assets sold (if any) and the assets retained based on their fair values on the date of transfer. This allocation is similar to that recommended in EITF 88-11 and must be applied to all transfers that have retained interests, regardless of whether or not they qualify as sales. It should be noted that this fair value allocation may result in a relative change in basis unless the fair values are proportionate to their carrying values. Thus, the gain or loss from any sale component could also be affected.

The retained interests continue to be the transferor's assets since control of these assets has not been transferred. Thus, the retained interest is considered continuing control over a previously owned asset (although the form may have changed). It should not be remeasured at fair value, nor should a gain or loss be recognized on it.

Example: Sale of partial interest in receivables

Facts Given

Receivables' fair value	$16,500
Receivables' book value	15,000

Seller sells 80% of receivables and agrees to service them. The benefits of servicing are just adequate to compensate for the servicing, thus there is no servicing asset or liability.

	FV	*80% FV*	*20% FV*	*Allocated 80% BV**	*Allocated 20% BV**
Receivables sold	$16,500	$13,200		$12,000	
Retained amount (20%)			$3,300		$3,000

* Allocated based on the relative fair values.

Seller's Journal Entry

Cash	13,200	
Receivables		12,000
Gain		1,200

Seller reports retained amount at $3,000.

Example: Sale of loans with various types of retained interests

Facts Given

Loans' fair value and amount of cash proceeds	$16,500
Loans' book value	15,000
Fair value of recourse obligation	(900)
Fair value of call option* on portfolio of $16,500	800
Fair value of interest rate swap on portfolio of $16,500	700

 * *An option that permits the seller/transferor to repurchase the same or similar loans.*

Seller's Journal Entries

1. Sale only

Cash	16,500	
Loans		15,000
Gain		1,500

2. Sale with recourse obligation

Cash	16,500	
Loans		15,000
Recourse obligation		900
Gain		600

3. Sale with recourse obligation and call option to purchase the loans sold or similar loans

Cash	16,500	
Call	800	
Loans		15,000
Recourse obligation		900
Gain		1,400

4. Sale with recourse obligation, call and swap (seller provides floating interest rate return although the underlying loans are at fixed interest rate terms)

Cash	16,500	
Call	800	
Swap	700	
Loans		15,000
Recourse obligation		900
Gain		2,100

5. Partial sale with recourse obligation, call and swap. Seller sells 80% of loans.

	FV	80% FV	20% FV	Allocated 80% BV*	Allocated 20% BV*
Loans	$16,500	$13,200		$11,579	
Call	800	640		561	
Swap	700	560		491	
Recourse obligation	(900)	(720)		(631)	
Retained amount (20%)			$ 3,420		$3,000
	$17,100	$13,680	$ 3,420	$12,000	$3,000

Cash		13,200
Call		640
Swap		560
Loans		12,000
Recourse obligation		720
Gain		1,680

Seller reports retained amount at $3,000.

* *Allocated based on the relative fair values.*

In some transfers of receivables, the transferor provides **credit enhancement** similar to a recourse provision by retaining a beneficial interest that absorbs the credit risk. If there is no liability beyond the transferor's retained subordinated interests, the retained interest is initially measured at allocated carrying value based on relative fair value, and no recourse liability is necessary. The retained interest would be subsequently measured like other retained interests held in the same form.

Cash reserve accounts and subordinated beneficial interests created as credit enhancements are retained interests and are accounted for as such even if the seller collects the proceeds and deposits a portion in the cash reserve account. (New asset credit enhancements such as financial guarantees and credit derivatives are measured at the fair value of the amount to benefit the transferor.) Paragraphs 68-70 provide guidance on estimating fair values and should be used in the case of credit enhancements. One possible method of estimating fair value of a credit enhancement is the cash-out method. Using that method, cash flows are discounted from the date the credit enhancement asset becomes available to the transferor (i.e., when the cash in the credit enhancement account is expected to be paid out to the transferor). The present value can be computed using an expected present value technique with a risk-free rate or a "best estimate" technique with an appropriate discount rate. Among other transferor assumptions, time period of restrictions, reinvestment income, and potential losses due to uncertainties must be included. Pronouncements, other than SFAS 140, should be looked to for guidance concerning subsequent measurement of credit enhancements.

Servicing. Servicing of financial assets can include such activities as

1. Collecting payments (principal, interest, and escrows)
2. Paying taxes and insurance from escrows
3. Monitoring delinquencies
4. Foreclosing
5. Investing funds temporarily prior to their distribution
6. Remitting fees to guarantors, trustees, and service providers
7. Accounting for and remitting distributions to holders of beneficial interests

Although inherent in holding most financial assets, servicing is a distinct asset or liability only when separated contractually from the underlying financial asset. The servicing asset usually results either from separate purchase or assumption of rights or from securitization with retained servicing. The servicer's obligations are specified in the contract.

Adequate compensation for servicing is determined by the marketplace. The concept of adequate compensation is judged by requirements that would be imposed by a new or outside servicer. It includes profit demanded by the marketplace and does not vary with the specific servicing costs of the servicer. Thus, it would not be acceptable to use the servicer's cost plus a profit margin to estimate the fair value of a servicing asset or liability. Adequate compensation does not result in an asset or a liability. A purchaser would not receive or pay to obtain the right to service for a rate just equal to adequate compensation.

Typically, the benefits are more than adequate compensation for the servicing and the servicing contract results in an asset. The benefits include

1. Fees
2. Late charges
3. Float
4. Other income

If the above benefits are not expected to provide adequate compensation, the contract results in a liability. With regard to the sale of assets, a servicing liability would reduce the net proceeds and would affect the gain or loss calculation.

Example: Sale of receivables with servicing liability

Facts Given

Receivables' fair value	$16,500
Receivables' book value	15,000
Servicing liability of $16,500 portfolio	(500)

Partial sale of receivables with servicing liability retained. Seller sells 80% of receivables.

	FV	80% FV	20% FV	Receivables allocated 80% BV*	Receivables allocated 20% BV*
Receivables sold	$16,500	$13,200		$12,000	
Servicing liability**	(500)	(400)			
Retained amount (20%)			$3,200		$3,000
	$16,000	$12,800	$3,200	$12,000	$3,000

*   *Allocated based on the relative fair values.*
**   *Liabilities are initially measured at fair value, if practicable.*

Journal Entry

Cash	13,200	
Servicing liability		400
Receivables		12,000
Gain		800

Seller reports retained receivables at $3,000 and the servicing liability at its fair value of $400.

Every time an entity undertakes a duty to service financial assets, it should recognize either a servicing asset or a servicing liability. There are two exceptions. An entity does not recognize a servicing asset or liability if

1. The benefits of servicing neither exceed nor are less than adequate compensation, that is, there is no asset or liability to record.
2. The transfer is to a qualifying SPE in a guaranteed mortgage securitization and the transferor retains all of the resulting securities and classifies them as held-to-maturity debt securities. In this case, the servicing asset or liability may either be reported together with the asset being serviced or be reported separately. The choice is the election of an accounting policy.

If servicing is retained, any resulting servicing assets are measured at book value allocated based on relative fair value at the date of sale, if practical. Servicing liabilities undertaken, servicing assets purchased, and servicing liabilities assumed are measured at fair value.

Specifically, servicing assets or servicing liabilities from each contract are to be accounted for separately as follows:

1. Assets are to be reported separately from liabilities. They are not netted.
2. Initially measure retained servicing assets at allocated carrying value based on relative fair values at date of sale or securitization.
3. Initially measure at fair value all purchased servicing assets, assumed servicing liabilities, and servicing liabilities undertaken in a sale or securitization.
4. Account separately for interest-only strips (future interest income from serviced assets that exceeds servicing fees).

5. Amortize servicing assets in proportion to and over the period of estimated net servicing income (the excess of servicing revenues over servicing costs).
6. Evaluate and measure impairment of servicing assets as follows:
    a. Stratify recognized servicing assets based on predominant risk (asset size, type, interest rate, term, location, date of organization, etc.)
    b. Individual stratum should have impairment recognized through a valuation allowance in the amount of the excess of carrying value over fair value.
    c. Adjust the valuation allowances to reflect subsequently needed changes. Excess fair value for a stratum should not be recognized.
7. Amortize servicing liabilities in proportion to and over the period of net servicing loss (excess of servicing costs over servicing revenues). In cases where subsequent changes have increased the fair value of the servicing liability above the carrying value, an increased liability and a loss should be recognized.

A servicing asset is remeasured for impairment based on the fair value of the contract and not on the gain or loss from carrying out the terms of the contract. SFAS 140 (paragraph 63) requires that entities separately evaluate and measure impairment of designated strata of servicing assets. Stratification requires that judgment be used when selecting the most important characteristic. SFAS 140 does not require that either the most predominant risk characteristic or more than one predominant risk characteristic be used to stratify the servicing assets for purposes of evaluating and measuring impairment. The stratum selected should be used consistently and a change is accounted for as a change in estimate under APB 20. The change and reasons for the change should be included in the disclosures made in accordance with paragraph 17 of SFAS 140.

Different stratification criteria may be used for SFAS 140 impairment testing and for SFAS 133 grouping of similar assets to be designated as a hedged portfolio in a fair value hedge.

A servicing liability is remeasured for increases in fair value that would be recognized as a loss. Similar to the accounting for changes in a valuation allowance for an impaired asset, increases in the servicing obligation may be recovered, but the obligation cannot be adjusted to less than the amortized measurement of its initially recognized amounts.

The fair value of a servicing asset or liability at date of transfer is best measured by quoted market prices for similar servicing responsibilities. There is the potential for significantly different estimates of fair value when a quoted market price is not available. The transferor should analyze all available information to obtain the best estimate of the fair value of the servicing contract. These include

1. The amount that would result in a current transaction between willing parties other than in a forced or liquidation sale
2. The legitimacy of the offer
3. The third party's specific knowledge about relevant factors
4. The experience of the broker with similar contracts
5. The price of other parties that have demonstrated an interest
6. The right to benefit from cash flows of potential future transactions (late charges, ancillary revenue, etc.)
7. The nature of the assets being serviced

In cases where there are few servicing contracts purchased or sold, present value methods may be used for estimating the fair value of servicing. Paragraph 17 requires disclosure of the methods and significant assumptions followed to determine the estimate of fair value (unless not practicable) of recognized servicing assets and liabilities.

Example: Sale of receivables with servicing asset retained

Facts Given

Receivables' fair value	$16,500
Receivables' book value	15,000
Servicing asset fair value on portfolio of $16,500	700
Recourse obligation on portfolio of $16,500	(900)

1. Servicing asset retained, no recourse obligation

	FV	%	BV allocated
Receivables sold	$16,500	96	$14,400
Servicing asset	700	4	600
	$17,200	100	$15,000

Journal Entry

Cash	16,500	
Servicing asset	600	
Receivables		15,000
Gain		2,100

2. Partial sale of receivables with servicing asset retained and recourse obligation. Seller sells 80% of receivables.

	FV	80% FV	20% FV	Allocated 80% BV*	Allocated 20% BV*
Receivables sold	$16,500	$13,200		$11,512	
Servicing asset	700	560		488	
Recourse obligation	(900)	(720)			
Retained amount (20%)			$3,260		$3,000
	$16,300	$13,040	$3,260	$12,000	$3,000

* *Allocated based on the relative fair values of the assets.*

Journal Entry

Cash	13,200	
Servicing asset	488	
Receivables		12,000
Recourse obligation		720
Gain		968

Seller reports retained receivables at $3,000.

If it is not practicable to measure the fair value of servicing at the date of transfer, the transferor must evaluate whether a liability has been incurred and should not automatically assume that an asset exists. If it is determined that a liability does not exist, then a value of zero should be assigned to the servicing asset that cannot be measured. If it is determined that a liability does exist, a valuation technique using discounted cash flows should be used to estimate its fair value.

Example: Estimate of fair values is not practical

Entity A sells loans with a recourse obligation to repurchase any delinquent loans and retains the servicing, which is expected to provide more than adequate compensation for performance.

	Case I *Asset fair value* *cannot be determined*	Case II *Liability fair value* *cannot be determined*
Loans' fair value	$16,500	$16,500
Loans' book value	15,000	15,000
Fair value of servicing asset	?	700
Fair value of recourse obligation	(900)	?

Proceeds

Cash	$16,500	$16,500
Less: Recourse obligation	(900)	?
Net proceeds	$15,600	$16,500

Allocation of book value based on fair value of assets

	FV	*%*	*BV* *allocated*	*FV*	*%*	*BV* *allocated*
Loans sold	$15,600	100	$15,000	$16,500	96	$14,400
Servicing assets	0	0	0	700	4	600
	$15,600	100	$15,000	$17,200	100	$15,000

Journal Entries

Cash	16,500			16,500	
Servicing asset	0			600	
Loans		15,000			15,000
Recourse obligation		900			2,100
Gain		600			0

In Case I, it is not practicable to measure the fair value of servicing, but it is known that the servicing is expected to provide more than adequate compensation. Thus, servicing is an asset and not a liability. If it is not practicable to measure the fair value of an asset, that asset is measured at zero. In Case II, it is not practicable to measure the fair value of the recourse obligation. If it is not practicable to measure the fair value of a liability, no gain is recorded on the sale. The liability is recorded at the greater of (1) the excess fair value of the assets obtained minus the fair value of the liabilities incurred over the carrying value of the assets transferred or (2) the amount to be recorded in conjunction with SFAS 5 and FASB I 14. In Case II, the liability is recognized at the excess fair value.

Subcontracting the servicing to another entity is not accounted for under SFAS 140 because it does not involve a transfer. It should be accounted for under other existing guidance.

In the unusual case that servicing assets are assumed without a cash payment, the facts and circumstances will determine how the transaction is recorded. For example, the servicing asset may represent consideration for goods or services provided by the transferee to the transferor of the servicing. The servicing assets also might be received in full or partial satisfaction of a receivable from the transferor of the servicing. Another possibility is that the transferor (the party providing servicing) is in substance making a capital contribution to the transferee (the party receiving the servicing) in exchange for an increased ownership interest. Additionally, the possibility that there is an overstatement of the value of the servicing by the transferee must be carefully considered.

The amount to be paid to a replacement servicer under the terms of the servicing contract is not relevant to the determination of adequate compensation. This amount could, however, be relevant for determining the contractually specified servicing fees.

Rights to future income from serviced assets that exceed contractually specified servicing fees should be accounted for as a servicing asset, an interest-only strip, or both, depending on whether the servicer would continue to receive the value of the right to future income if a replacement servicer started servicing the assets. Generally, the value of the right to receive future cash flows from ancillary sources such as late fees is included with the servicing asset if retention of the right depends on servicing being performed satisfactorily. An interest-only strip doesn't depend on satisfactory performance of servicing, and any portion that would continue to be received if servicing were shifted to a replacement servicer would be accounted for separately as a financial asset and subsequently measured as an investment in debt securities classified as available-for-sale or trading under SFAS 115.

Securitizations. Entities that generate a large number of similar receivables, such as mortgages, credit card receivables, or car loans, sometimes securitize those receivables. Securitization is the transformation of the receivables into securities that are sold to other investors. For example, mortgages can be converted into mortgage-backed securities, which entitle the investors to receive specific cash flows generated by the mortgages. With an established market, issuance of the securities can cost less than using the receivables as collateral for a borrowing. Additionally, the resulting securities are more liquid than the underlying receivables. Securitizations are accounted for as sales only if (1) a qualified special-purpose entity is used to buy the assets, (2) each holder of its beneficial interests has the right to pledge or exchange the beneficial interest and there is no condition that both constrains the holder from taking advantage of that right and provides more than a trivial benefit to the transferor, and (3) the transferor does not maintain effective control over the assets.

The transferor (also called issuer or sponsor) forms a securitization mechanism (separate corporation or a trust, referred to as a special-purpose entity [SPE]) to buy the assets and to issue the securities. The securitization mechanism then generates beneficial interests in the assets or resulting cash flows that are sold. The form of the securities chosen depends on such things as the nature of the assets, income tax considerations, and returns to be received.

Payments by the securitization mechanism are usually classified as **pay-through, pass-through** or **revolving-period**. In a **pay-through**, cash flows from the assets pay off the debt securities. The assets are essentially collateral. In a **pass-through**, undivided interests are issued and the investors share in the net cash flows. In a **revolving-period**, undivided interests are issued, but until liquidation, the net cash flows are split between buying additional assets and paying off investors.

A SPE is considered qualified if it meets the criteria of paragraph 35. Those four criteria are

1. The SPE is demonstrably distinct from the transferor. To be demonstrably distinct, the transferor, its affiliates, or its agents cannot unilaterally dissolve the SPE and either

    a. At least 10% of the fair value of its beneficial interests is held by parties other than the transferor, its affiliates, or its agents or

    b. The transfer is a guaranteed mortgage securitization. A guaranteed mortgage securitization is a securitization of mortgage loans that is within the scope of SFAS 65 and includes a substantive guarantee by a third party.

2. The permitted activities of the SPE

    a. Must be significantly limited

    b. Must have been entirely specified in the legal documents that established the SPE or created the beneficial interests in the transferred assets it holds

    c. May be significantly changed only with the approval of a majority of the holders of the beneficial interests not including the transferor, its affiliates, or its agents

3. The SPE may hold only

   a. Financial assets that are passive in nature. A financial asset is passive only if holding the asset requires no decisions of the holder other than decisions inherent in servicing. For example, an equity instrument is not passive if the SPE is permitted to choose how to vote the shares, and an investment accounted for by the equity method is not passive since that method is used when the investor has the ability to exercise significant influence over that investment.

   b. Passive derivative instruments related to beneficial interests issued or sold to parties other than the transferor, its affiliates, or its agents

   c. Financial assets that would reimburse the SPE if the servicer failed to adequately perform or if others failed to pay timely. The financial assets must have been entered into when the SPE was created, when assets were transferred to it, or when it issued beneficial interests.

   d. Servicing rights related to the financial assets it holds

   e. Nonfinancial assets obtained in connection with the collection of financial assets it holds, but only temporarily

   f. Cash collected from financial assets it holds

   g. Investments purchased pending distribution to holders of beneficial interests, provided that those investments are appropriate for that purpose. For example, the investments must be relatively risk-free and have a maturity date no later than the expected distribution date.

4. The SPE can sell or dispose of noncash financial assets only in automatic response to one of the following conditions:

   a. Occurrence of an event that causes the fair value of those financial assets to decline by a specified degree below the fair value of those assets when the SPE obtained them. The occurrence of the event must be outside the control of the transferor, its affiliates, or its agents. The nature of the event must be specified in the legal documents that established the SPE or created the beneficial interests in the transferred assets it holds.

   b. Exercise of a right to put a beneficial interest back to the SPE by a beneficial interest holder other than the transferor, its affiliates, or its agents

   c. Exercise by the transferor of a call or a removal-of-accounts provision, provided that the exercise is specified in the legal documents that established the SPE, transferred assets to the SPE, or created the beneficial interests in the transferred assets it holds

   d. Termination of the SPE or maturity of the beneficial interests in those financial assets on a fixed or determinable date that was specified at the inception

Various financial components arise from securitizations. Examples include servicing contracts, interest-only strips, retained interests, recourse obligations, options, swaps, and forward contracts. All controlled assets and liabilities must be recognized under SFAS 140.

Example: Sale of receivables with servicing retained with interest-only strip receivable

Receivables' fair value	$16,500
Receivables' book value	15,000
Servicing asset fair value	700
Interest-only strip receivable fair value	600

Servicing asset retained with interest-only strip receivable.

	FV	*%*	*BV Allocated*
Receivables sold	$16,500	93	$13,950
Servicing asset	700	4	600
Interest-only strip receivable	600	3	450
	$17,800	100	$15,000

Journal Entry

Cash	16,500	
Servicing asset	600	
Interest-only strip receivable	450	
Receivables		15,000
Gain		2,550

If the interest-only strip was measured as an available-for-sale security, another entry would be

Interest-only strip ($600 FV-$450)	150	
Equity (or other comprehensive income)		150

The credit would be to income if it was classified as a trading security.

Just as it is necessary to distinguish new assets, which are recorded at fair value, from retained interests, which are recorded at allocated carrying value, when accounting for a transfer to another enterprise, it is necessary to do so when accounting for a transfer to an SPE. In certain securitization transactions, more than one transferor contributes assets to a single qualifying SPE. A transferor should treat the beneficial interests it receives in a securitization that commingles assets from more than one transferor as

1. New assets to the extent that the sources of the cash flows to be received by the transferor are assets transferred by another entity
2. Retained interests to the extent that the sources of the cash flows are assets transferred by the transferor
3. New assets to the extent that any derivatives, guarantees, or other contracts were entered into by the qualifying SPE to "transform" the transferred assets. (They are new because they were entered into by the qualifying SPE rather than transferred into the qualifying SPE by another entity.)

After a securitization, the beneficial interests held by the transferor either are in the form of securities that are accounted for under SFAS 115 or are required to be accounted for as available-for-sale securities or trading securities in accordance with paragraph 14 of SFAS 140. Thus, the transferor must classify the beneficial interests into one of the SFAS 115 categories. If beneficial interests held by the transferor after the transfer convey rights to the same cash flows as the transferor was entitled to receive from securities that it transferred to the SPE, the SFAS 115 classification of the beneficial interests should be the same as the securities held before the transfer. For example, if prior to the transfer the debt securities were accounted for as available-for-sale securities in accordance with Statement 115, the beneficial interests should be classified as available-for-sale securities if the transferor receives the cash flows from those securities via its beneficial interest. In contrast, if the transferred assets were not Statement 115 securities prior to the transfer but the beneficial interests were issued in the form of debt securities or in the form of equity securities that have readily determinable fair values, then the transferor has the opportunity to decide the appropriate SFAS 115 classification at the date of the transfer.

Revolving-period securitizations present some unique issues because they contain an implicit forward contract to sell new receivables during the revolving period. The forward contract may become valuable to the transferor or burdensome depending upon how interest rates and market conditions change. The value of the implicit forward contract arises from the difference between the rate promised to the holders of the beneficial interests and the market rate of return on similar investments. For example, if the agreed-upon rate to holders is 5% and the market rate is 7%, the forward contract's value to the transferor is 2% of the amount of the investment for each year remaining in the revolving period after the initially transferred receivables are collected. When receivables are sold to a revolving-period securitization trust, gain or loss recognition is limited to receivables that exist and have been sold. Similarly, servicing assets or liabilities are limited to servicing receivables that exist and have already been transferred. As proceeds from collection of the receivables are used to purchase new receivables for the trusts, the additional transfers can result in recognition of additional servicing assets and liabilities.

SFAS 140 does not address the accounting for desecuritization of securities into loans or other financial assets. EITF Topic D-51, *The Applicability of FASB Statement No. 115 to Desecuritizations of Financial Assets*, addresses that issue.

Repurchase agreements. Repurchase agreements are used to obtain short-term use of funds. Under the terms of a repurchase agreement the transferor transfers a security to a transferee in exchange for cash. Concurrently, the transferor agrees to reacquire the security at a future date for an amount equal to the cash exchanged and an interest factor. Many repurchase agreements are for short terms, often overnight.

It is necessary to determine if the repurchase agreement meets the requirements of paragraph 9 (described in the section, "Surrender of control"). Usually the critical determination is whether the repurchase agreements gives the transferor effective control over the transferred assets. That determination is made by applying the criteria in paragraphs 47-49 (described in the section, "Maintaining effective control"). In most cases, if the repurchase is required prior to the maturity of the security transferred and the cash transferred is sufficient to repurchase the assets if the transferee defaults, the transferor retains effective control and the agreement is accounted for as a secured borrowing. For example, fixed-coupon and dollar-roll repurchase agreements, and other contracts under which the securities to be repurchased need not be the same as the securities sold, qualify as borrowings if the return of substantially the same securities as those transferred is assured. However, if a transferor does not maintain control over the transferred assets and other criteria in SFAS 140 are met, the transfer is accounted for as a sale and a forward commitment.

Securities lending transactions. Broker-dealers and other financial services companies initiate securities lending transactions when they need to obtain specific securities to cover a short sale or a customer's failure to deliver securities sold. The transferor/lender provides the securities to the transferee/borrower in exchange for "collateral," usually in an amount greater than the fair value of the borrowed securities. This collateral is commonly cash but could alternatively be other securities or standby letters of credit.

When the collateral is cash, the transferor/lender invests the cash during the period that the security is loaned. The investment return on the cash collateral is larger than the fees paid by the lender under the agreement (the rebate). Because the cash collateral is usually valued daily and adjusted frequently for changes in the market value of the underlying securities, the transaction has very low credit risk.

In determining whether to account for a securities lending transaction as a sale or a secured borrowing, the same criteria used for other asset transfers are applied. Many securities lending transactions are accompanied by an agreement that entitles and obligates the transferor/lender to repurchase or redeem the transferred assets before their maturity. Thus, the transferor maintains effective control over the securities lent. If that is the case, the transaction is accounted for as a secured borrowing. The following is an example of a securities lending transaction accounted for as a secured borrowing:

Example: Securities lending transaction (30 days)

Fair value of loaned security	$16,500
Book value of loaned security	16,500
Collateral (cash)	16,995
Transferor/lender's return from investing cash	5%
Transferor/lender's rebate to transferee/borrower	4%

Transferor/lender's journal entries

At date of loan:

Securities pledged	16,500	
Securities		16,500
To record transfer of securities as a loan		
Cash	16,995	
Loan agreement payable		16,995
To record receipt of cash collateral		
Money market instrument	16,995	
Cash		16,995
To invest cash collateral		

At end of 30 days:

Cash	17,065	
Interest income		70
Money market instrument		16,995
To transfer cash from money market and record interest earned		
Securities	16,500	
Securities pledged		16,500
To record securities returned by transferee/borrower		
Loan agreement payable	16,995	
Interest rebate	56	
Cash		17,051
To return cash collateral and pay rebate		

Accounting for collateral. Accounting for collateral depends both on whether the secured party has the right to sell or repledge the collateral and on whether the debtor has defaulted. Ordinarily, the transferor should carry the collateral as an asset and the transferee should not record the pledged asset.

The collateral provisions of paragraph 15 of SFAS 140 apply to all transfers (repurchase agreements, dollar-roll, securities lending, etc.) of financial assets pledged as collateral and accounted for as a secured borrowing. The provisions do not apply to the accounting for cash in secured borrowing transactions.

If the secured party (transferee) has the right to sell or repledge the collateral, then the debtor (transferor) reclassifies the asset used as collateral and reports it in the balance sheet separately from other assets not similarly encumbered. That is, the debtor (transferor) continues to hold the collateral assets as its own, and the secured party (transferee) does not recognize the collateral asset. If the secured party (transferee) sells the collateral, it recognizes the proceeds from the sale and the obligation to return the collateral to the debtor (transferor).

Although collateral is required to be reclassified and reported separately by the transferor if the transferee has the right to sell or repledge the collateral, that requirement does not change the transferor's measurement of the collateral. The same measurement principles should be used as before the transfer and the collateral should not be derecognized. The subsequent measurement of transferee's obligation to return the collateral in securities borrowing and resale agreement transactions is not addressed by SFAS 140.

If the transferor defaults and is not entitled to the return of the collateral, it should be derecognized by the transferor. If not already recognized, the transferee should record its asset at fair value.

Financial assets subject to prepayment. Paragraph 14 of SFAS 140 requires interest-only strips, loans, other receivables, or retained interests in securitizations to be measured like investments in debt securities. If they can be contractually prepaid or settled in a way that precludes recovery of substantially all of the recorded investment, they should be classified as available-for-sale or trading under SFAS 115. Only assets meeting all of the SFAS 115 requirements and acquired late enough in life that, even if prepaid, the holder would recover substantially all of its recorded investment may be initially classified as held-to-maturity. The probability of prepayment or settlement is not relevant to the classification under SFAS 115.

Although financial assets that do not meet the securities definition of SFAS 115 must be measured like investments under that Statement, other provisions of that Statement (disclosures, etc.) are not required.

Disclosures. SFAS 140 disclosures include

1. For collateral
    a. If the entity has entered into repurchase agreements or securities lending transactions, its policy for requiring collateral or other security
    b. If the entity has pledged any of its assets as collateral that are not reclassified and separately reported on the balance sheet, the carrying amount and classification of those assets on the date on the most recent balance sheet
    c. If the entity has accepted collateral that it is permitted by contract or custom to sell or repledge, the fair value of that collateral as of the date of each balance sheet, the portion of that collateral that it has sold or repledged, and the sources and uses of that collateral
2. Description of items for which it is not practicable to estimate fair value and reasons why it is not practicable
3. For servicing assets and liabilities
    a. Amounts recognized and amortized during the period
    b. Fair value recognized, method and assumptions used to estimate fair value
    c. Risk characteristics used to stratify recognized servicing assets in order to measure impairments
    d. Valuation allowance and all related activity for each period for which results of operations are reported

4. If the entity has securitized any financial assets during any period presented and accounted for that securitization as a sale, it must disclose the following information for each major asset type (e.g., mortgage loans, auto loans, credit card receivables)

   a. Accounting policies for initially measuring the retained interests
   b. The method used in measuring the fair value of the retained interests and the key assumptions used in that measurement (at a minimum, assumptions about discount rates, expected prepayments, expected weighted-average life of prepayable assets, anticipated credit losses)
   c. A description of the entity's continuing involvement with the assets securitized
   d. The amount of the gain or loss from sale of the assets in the securitization
   e. Cash flows between the SPE and the entity

5. If the entity has retained interests in securitized financial assets at the most recent balance sheet presented, it must disclose the following information for each major asset type (e.g., mortgage loans, auto loans, credit card receivables)

   a. Accounting policy for subsequently measuring the retained interests
   b. The method used in measuring the fair value of the retained interests and the key assumptions used in that measurement (at a minimum, assumptions about discount rates, expected prepayments, expected weighted-average life of prepayable assets, anticipated credit losses, expected static pool losses, if applicable)
   c. A sensitivity analysis or stress test showing the hypothetical effect on the fair value of the retained interests of two or more unfavorable variations from the expected level for each key assumption (computed independently of any other change in the key assumptions) and a description of the objectives, methodology, and limitations of the sensitivity analysis or stress test
   d. For the securitized assets and any other financial assets managed with them, the total principal amount, the portion derecognized, the portion remaining, and delinquencies as of the end of the period, and the credit losses, net of recoveries, during the period. This disclosure should exclude securitized assets that the entity manages but with which the entity does not have any other continuing involvement.
   e. Average balances during the period for the securitized assets and any other financial assets managed with them. (This disclosure is not required but merely encouraged.)

EMERGING ISSUES TASK FORCE CONSENSUS SUMMARIES

86-8   Sale of Bad Debt Recovery Rights

A financial institution sells to a third party the right to an amount of future recoveries from loans previously written off by the financial institution. The buyer is entitled to the purchase price plus a market rate of interest on the unrecovered purchased price. The transaction is a secured borrowing from the seller's perspective. There was no consensus on whether the proceeds should reduce the loan-loss allowance.

87-18   Use of Zero Coupon Bonds in a Troubled Debt Restructuring (affected by SFAS 140)

In connection with a troubled debt restructuring, a debtor, with the creditor's approval, sells the collateral and invests the proceeds in zero coupon bonds that are held as collateral for the restructured loan by the creditor. The bonds mature on a schedule that meets the debt service requirements under the new terms. The fair value of the zero coupon bonds is less than the creditor's net investment in the loan. The creditor should recognize a loss for the difference between the fair value and the net investment.

The debtor is required by SFAS 140 to reclassify the zero coupon bonds to another asset account (such as bonds pledged as collateral) if the creditor can sell or repledge them.

88-11   Allocation of Recorded Investment When a Loan or Part of a Loan Is Sold (affected by SFAS 140)

Relative fair values at acquisition (adjusted for payments and other activity from that date) should be used to allocate the recorded investment between the portion of the loan retained and the portion sold. If it is not practical to determine relative fair values at acquisition, relative fair value on date of sale may be used. Amounts in the allowance for loan losses should be excluded when considering the recorded investment to be allocated. Any gain recognized when selling a portion of the loan should not exceed that which would be recognized if the entire loan was sold. A portion of the recorded investment should be allocated to excess servicing if it is retained.

For transactions after 4/6/89 involving sales with disproportionate credit **and** prepayment risk but with no disproportionate interest rates, the SEC requires the relative fair value method.

When an entire principal balance is sold at a price near par, including transactions where the seller passes through a rate of interest different from the coupon rate, the seller should measure excess servicing (or deficiency in normal servicing) in accordance with SFAS 65. The difference in fees should be calculated using prepayment, default and interest rate assumptions that market participants would use for similar financial instruments and should be discounted using an interest rate that an unrelated purchaser would demand.

88-22 Securitization of Credit Card Portfolios (affected by SFAS 140)

Amounts received from transferring to investors a participating interest in credit card receivables in a trust should be accounted for as a sale if the conditions in paragraph 9 of SFAS 140 are met.

The type of liquidation method specified in the securitization agreement does not affect the determination of whether the transferor would get sale treatment.

Gain on the sale of receivables should be limited to amounts related to receivables that exist at the sale date. The gain generally will not be material. Terms of the agreement should be examined to determine whether a loss should be recognized for expected costs to be incurred for future servicing obligations. Transaction costs relating to the sale may be recognized over the initial and reinvestment period in a rational and systematic manner unless a loss is indicated.

88-23 Lump-Sum Payments under Union Contracts

This EITF consensus relates solely to union contracts and not to individual employment contracts. In negotiating union contracts, lump-sum cash payments made to employees in lieu of all or a portion of a base-wage rate increase may be deferred and amortized. The Task Force's consensus requires that (1) there is no evidence that the payment is related to past services, (2) the payment will benefit a future period in the form of a lower base-wage rate, and (3) the amortization period not extend beyond the contract period. Facts surrounding the contract and negotiations must be reviewed to determine how to account for the payment.

92-2 Measuring Loss Accruals by Transferors for Transfers of Receivables with Recourse (affected by SFAS 140)

All probable credit losses (not only those recognized in accordance with SFAS 5) over the life of the receivables transferred should be included in the recourse obligation recorded at the date of sale. The recourse obligation can be recognized on a present value (PV) basis if the cash flows can be reasonably estimated. If PV is used, the interest rate used in subsequent accruals should be the same rate used in determining the initial obligation.

The recourse obligation is a liability and should not be offset unless a right of setoff exists (see FASB Interpretation 39).

If the seller's recourse obligation is contractually limited to and paid from an escrow account (consisting of excess cash from the coupon interest on the receivables over the interest passed through to the buyer), the escrow is a retained interest that is initially measured at previous carrying value allocated in proportion to relative fair values.

97-3   Accounting for Fees and Costs Associated with Loan Syndications and Loan Participation after the Issuance of FASB Statement No. 140

A consensus was reached that the accounting for financial asset transfers as described in SFAS 140 is applicable to loan participation, including those which are "in-substance loan syndications."

A consensus was also reached that all transactions legally structured as loan syndications including "in-substance loan participation," should be accounted for as loan syndications per SFAS 91.

6 SHORT-TERM INVESTMENTS AND FINANCIAL INSTRUMENTS

PERSPECTIVE AND ISSUES

SFAS 133, *Accounting for Derivative Instruments and Hedging Activities*, was issued in June 1998 and (with the one-year delay mandated by SFAS 137) became effective for all fiscal quarters of fiscal years beginning after June 15, 2000, although earlier application had been encouraged. The standard was not to be applied retroactively. SFAS 133 has been amended by SFAS 138, which has slightly altered several of the provisions of the original standard.

SFAS 133 applies to all entities and requires that all derivative instruments (DI) be recognized as either assets or liabilities on the balance sheet, at their respective fair values. Gains and losses on DI which are not designated as hedges are recognized currently in earnings (or, in the case of a not-for-profit entity, as a change in net assets). Special accounting (effectively, the deferral of gains or losses) for derivatives is permissible only when the instrument has been designated as a hedge. After meeting the conditions specified in the standard, a derivative may be specifically designated as a hedge of fair value changes, of cash flows, or of certain foreign currency exposures.

Hedges of the changes in fair value can be associated with a recognized asset or liability, or of an unrecognized firm commitment. In a fair value hedge, all gains and losses (of both the DI and the hedged item) are recognized in earnings in the period of change. In a perfectly effective hedge, these will offset each period, but in most cases precise offsetting will not be achieved.

Cash flows hedges pertain to forecasted transactions. The effective portion of the hedge is initially reported in other comprehensive income and is reclassified into earnings when the forecasted transaction affects earnings. The ineffective portion of the hedge is reported in earnings immediately.

Hedges of the foreign currency exposure of a net investment in a foreign operation also qualify for special accounting treatment. In a foreign currency net investment hedge, the gain or loss is reported in other comprehensive income as part of the cumulative translation adjustment. In the case of foreign currency hedges of unrecognized firm commitments, the gain or loss is reported the same way as a fair value hedge. A gain or loss on a foreign currency hedge that is associated with an available-for-sale security will also be reported the same way as a fair value hedge. Finally, a gain or loss arising from a hedge relating to a foreign currency denominated forecasted transaction is reported in the same way as a cash flow hedge.

Not-for-profits (NFP) cannot use hedge accounting for forecasted transactions. This is because NFPs do not report other comprehensive income—all such items are included in the statement of activity, which provides an all-inclusive measure of changes in net assets for the period.

A nonderivative financial instrument cannot generally be designated as a hedge. One exception, however, occurs when that instrument is denominated in a foreign currency and is designated as a hedge of a net investment in a foreign operation or an unrecognized firm commitment.

Hedge accounting, where applicable, can only be continued if, and to the extent that, the hedge is judged to be effective, using criteria set forth in SFAS 133. The method used for assessing the effective and ineffective portions of a hedge must be determined at inception and must be consistent with the approach used by the reporting entity for managing risk.

SFAS 133, as further amended by SFAS 138, has superseded SFAS 80, 105, and 119; amended ARB 43 and SFAS 52, 60, 65, 95, 107, 113, 115, 124, 125, and 126, and TB 79-19; and nullified or modified numerous EITF consensuses.

Recently, SFAS 125 had introduced a financial components approach that relied on control to establish standards for the accounting for transfers and servicing of financial assets and extinguishments of liabilities. Due to the desire to make certain rather limited changes to that standard, SFAS 140 was issued in 2000, and entirely supersedes SFAS 125. Under both standards, after a transfer of financial assets, an entity recognizes the financial and servicing assets it controls and the liabilities it has incurred, derecognizes financial assets when control has been surrendered, and derecognizes liabilities when extinguished. Multiple criteria pertaining to surrender of control must all be met for sale treatment to apply. Derivatives and liabilities resulting from a transfer of financial assets are measured at fair value. In-substance defeasance of debt (under which both the debt and the related segregated assets were removed from the obligor's balance sheet) was banned by SFAS 125 and remains prohibited under SFAS 140.

SFAS 115 is GAAP regarding investments in all debt securities and in equity securities that have a readily determinable fair value. It classifies these securities into one of three categories: held-to-maturity, trading, or available-for-sale. The first of these can only be applied to debt securities, which are then to be reported at amortized cost. The trading category can include both debt and equity securities, which are to be reported at fair value. The available-for-sale category is used for those investments that do not fit in either of the other two classifications; these are also reported at fair value in the balance sheet.

SFAS 115 does not change the accounting for financial liabilities and does not apply to DI. In the case of an investment subject to this standard with an embedded derivative, the host instrument is accounted for under SFAS 115 and the embedded derivative is accounted for under SFAS 133.

SFAS 107 requires entities to disclose the fair value of **all** (recognized and unrecognized) financial instruments that it is practicable to estimate, including liabilities. Pertinent descriptive information regarding the instrument is to be disclosed if an estimate of fair value cannot be made without incurring excessive costs. Certain types of financial instruments—including pensions, postretirement benefits, deferred compensation, insurance contracts, lease contracts, and warranty obligations—are excluded from the requirements of this standard. SFAS 107 was amended by SFAS 133 to include the disclosure requirements concerning concentrations of credit risk for **all** financial instruments from now-superseded SFAS 105.

SFAS 126 made SFAS 107 disclosures optional for entities meeting the following criteria:

1. Enterprise is nonpublic.
2. Total enterprise assets are less than $100 million on financial statement date.
3. During the reporting period, enterprise has not held or issued any derivative financial instruments.

As a general principle, the offsetting of assets and liabilities is not permitted. However, when a right of setoff exists—defined as a debtor's legal right to discharge debt owed to another party by applying against the debt an amount the other party owes to the debt—offsetting is allowed. FASB Interpretation 39 makes another exception in the case of multiple forward, swap, and similar contracts executed with the same party under master netting arrangements. The conditions to be met are

1. Each of the two parties owes the other determinable amounts.
2. The reporting party has the right to set off.
3. The reporting party intends to set off.
4. The right of setoff is enforceable at law.

Sources of GAAP				
ARB	*APB*	*SFAS*	*FASB I*	*EITF*
43, Ch. 3A	22	52, 65, 80, 95, 102, 107, 109, 111, 112, 115, 123, 126, 127, 130, 133, 137, 138, 140	39 *FASB TB* 94-1	84-7, 84-14, 85-9, 85-29, 86-24, 86-25, 86-28, 86-34, 86-40, 87-2, 87-12, 87-26, 87-30, 88-8, 89-18, 90-17, 95-5, 96-11, 96-12, 96-13, 96-15, 98-10, D-11, D-39, D-50, D-73, D-75

DEFINITIONS OF TERMS

Accounting loss. Accounting loss refers to the loss that may have to be recognized due to credit and market risk as a direct result of the rights and obligations of a financial instrument.

Bifurcation. Separation of embedded derivative instrument from the host contract so that separate accounting can be applied to the embedded derivative instrument.

Carrying amount (value). The amount at which securities are being carried, net of allowances.

Contractual obligations. All contractual obligations that are financial instruments meet the definition of a liability set forth in SFAC 6, *Elements of Financial Statements.* Some may not be recognized as liabilities in financial statements—may be "off-balance-sheet"—because they fail to meet some other criterion for recognition. For some financial instruments, the obligation is owed to or by a group of entities rather than a single entity.

Contractual rights. All contractual rights that are financial instruments meet the definition of asset set forth in SFAC 6. Some may not be recognized as assets in financial statements—may be "off-balance-sheet"—because they fail to meet some other criterion for recognition. For some financial instruments, the obligation is held by or due from a group of entities rather than a single entity.

Cost (of a security). The original purchase price plus all costs incidental to the acquisition (e.g., brokerage fees and taxes) unless a new cost basis is assigned as a result of a decline in market value which is other than temporary.

Credit risk. Credit risk is the possibility that a loss may occur from the failure of another party to perform according to the terms of a contract.

Derivative. A financial instrument or contract (options, swaps, futures, etc.) whose value is derived from some other financial measure (underlyings, that is, commodity prices, interest rates, exchange rates, indexes of financial items, etc.) and includes payment provisions (notional amounts, that is, cash, commodities, shares of stock, etc.).

Equity instrument. Any evidence of an ownership interest in an entity.

Financial asset. Any asset that is (1) cash, (2) a contractual right to receive cash or another financial asset from another entity, (3) a contractual right to exchange other financial instruments on potentially favorable terms with another entity, or (4) an equity instrument of another entity.

Financial instrument. A financial instrument is cash, evidence of an ownership interest in an entity, or a contract that both

    a.   Imposes on one entity a contractual obligation (1) to deliver cash or another financial instrument to a second entity or (2) to exchange financial instruments on potentially unfavorable terms with the second entity.

    b.   Conveys to that second entity a contractual right (1) to receive cash or another financial instrument from the first entity or (2) to exchange other financial instruments on potentially favorable terms with the first entity.

Financial instrument with off-balance-sheet risk. A financial instrument has off-balance-sheet risk of accounting loss if the risk of accounting loss to the entity may exceed the amount recognized as an asset, if any, or if the ultimate obligation may exceed the amount that is recognized as a liability in the statement of financial position.

Financial liability. Any liability that is a contractual obligation (1) to deliver cash or another financial asset to another entity or (2) to exchange financial instruments on potentially unfavorable terms with another entity.

Firm commitment. An agreement with an unrelated party, binding on both parties and usually legally enforceable. The agreement usually specifies all significant terms (including quantity to be exchanged, fixed price, timing of the transaction) and includes a disincentive for nonperformance that is sufficiently large enough to make performance probable.

Forecasted transaction. A transaction that is expected to occur for which there is no firm commitment. Because no transaction or event has yet occurred, when the transaction or event does occur, it will be at the prevailing market price.

Market risk. Market risk is the possibility that future changes in market prices may make a financial instrument less valuable.

Marketable equity securities. Instruments representing actual ownership interest, or the rights to buy or sell such interests, and which are actively traded or listed on a national securities exchange.

Net realizable value. The amount of cash anticipated to be produced in the normal course of business from an asset, net of any direct costs of the conversion into cash.

Normal purchases and sales. Contracts without a settlement provision and without a market mechanism to facilitate net settlement; or which require delivery of nonfinancial assets that constitute normal purchases or normal sales of the reporting entity.

Notional amount. A number of currency units, shares, bushels, pounds, or other units specified in a derivative instrument.

Other-than-temporary decline. A downward movement in the value of a marketable equity security for which there are known causes. The decline indicates a remote likelihood of a price recovery.

Realized gain (loss). The difference between the cost or adjusted cost of a marketable security and the net selling price realized by the seller which is to be included in the determination of net income in the period of the sale.

Risk of accounting loss. The risk of accounting loss from a financial instrument includes the (1) possibility that a loss may occur from the failure of another party to perform according to the terms of a contract (credit risk), (2) the possibility that future changes in market prices may make a financial instrument less valuable (market risk), and (3) the risk of theft or physical loss. SFAS 105 addresses credit and market risk only.

Short-term investments. Securities or other assets acquired with excess cash, having ready marketability and intended by management to be liquidated, if necessary, within the current operating cycle.

Temporary decline. A downward fluctuation in the value of a marketable equity security that has no known causes that suggest the decline is of a permanent nature.

Unrealized gain (loss). The unrealized difference between the market value of short-term investments and their carrying value which is deemed not to be of a permanent nature.

Valuation allowance. An account used to value marketable equity securities at fair value. The offset is either a gain or loss account (for trading securities) or a contra equity account (for available-for-sale securities).

CONCEPTS, RULES, AND EXAMPLES

Short-Term Investments

Short-term (or temporary) investments usually consist of marketable debt and equity securities. Accordingly, investments that are held for purposes of control of another entity or pursuant to an ongoing business relationship, for example, stock held in a supplier, would be excluded from current assets and would instead be listed as **other assets** or **long-term investments** (see Chapter 10, Investments).

Debt securities and marketable equity securities. SFAS 115 is GAAP governing the accounting for all debt securities and for equity securities that have a readily determinable fair value. FASB TB 94-1 includes restructured loans involving a modification of terms (even if a restructuring took place before the effective date of SFAS 114) under SFAS 115 if such loans meet the definition of a security. Equity securities include not only stock, but also the rights to purchase stock, such as warrants or call options, and the right to sell stock, such as put options. SFAS 115 does not apply to securities accounted for by the equity method. These securities are accounted for in accordance with APB 18 and are discussed in Chapter 10, Investments. This statement also does not apply to specialized industries that account for substantially all debt and equity securities at market or fair value with changes recognized in earnings or in the change in net assets. Not-for-profit organizations are excluded from the provisions of SFAS 115, but the statement does apply to cooperatives and mutual enterprises (including credit unions and mutual insurance companies). In addition, unsecuritized loans are not covered, but mortgage-backed securities are covered. Accounting for financial liabilities is not changed.

The standard requires all debt securities and equity securities with readily determinable fair values to be classified into one of three categories.

Classification of Debt and Equity Securities

Categories	Type	Characteristics	Reported on balance sheet	Effect on income
1. Held-to-maturity	Debt	Positive intent and ability to hold until maturity	Amortized cost	Interest Realized gains and losses
2. Trading	Debt & equity	Bought and held principally to sell short-term	Fair value	Interest and dividends Realized gains and losses Unrealized gains and losses
3. Available-for-sale	Debt & equity	Neither held-to-maturity nor trading securities	Fair value Unrealized gains and losses to accumulated other comprehensive income (component of owners' equity)	Interest and dividends Realized gains and losses

If a classified balance sheet is presented, the debt and equity securities owned by an entity should be grouped into current and noncurrent portfolios. All trading securities are classified as current assets. The determination of current or noncurrent status for individual held-to-maturity and individual available-for-sale securities is made on the basis of whether or not the securities are considered working capital available for current operations (ARB 43, ch 3A).

Fair value. SFAS 115 applies to equity securities if

1. Prices or bid-and-ask quotations are available on SEC registered exchanges or from the NASDAQ or the National Quotation Bureau. Unless qualified for sale within one year, restricted stock does not meet this definition.
2. Traded on a foreign market of comparable breadth and scope as the US markets identified above.
3. Fair value per unit (share) of a mutual fund is determined and published and is the basis for current transactions.

Classification. Classification is to be made at acquisition. The appropriateness of classification should be reassessed at each reporting date.

Held-to-maturity debt securities. If an entity has the **positive intent** and **ability** to hold debt securities to maturity, they are measured at amortized cost. All **transfers** or **sales** of securities in this category must disclose the following in the notes for each period for which the results of operations are presented:

1. Amortized cost
2. Realized or unrealized gain or loss
3. Circumstances leading to the decision to sell or transfer

Isolated, nonrecurring, and unusual events that could not have been reasonably anticipated may cause a sale or transfer without calling intent or ability to hold into question. Other changes in circumstances that are not considered inconsistent include

1. Material deterioration in creditworthiness of the issuer
2. Elimination or reduction of tax-exempt status of interest through a change in tax law
3. Major business disposition or combination
4. Statutory or regulatory changes that materially modify what a permissable investment is or the maximum level of the security to be held
5. Downsizing in response to a regulatory increase in the industry's capital requirements
6. A material increase in risk weights for regulatory risk-based capital purposes

This category does not include securities available for sale in response to a need for liquidity or changes in

1. Market interest rates
2. Foreign currency risk
3. Funding sources and terms
4. Yield and availability of alternative investments
5. Prepayment risk

For asset-liability management purposes, similar or identical securities may be classified differently depending upon intent and ability to hold.

SFAS 125 amended SFAS 115 to preclude held-to-maturity classification for securities that can be prepaid or settled in a manner where the recorded investments could not be substantially recovered, which rule continues under successor standard SFAS 140. These securities, including certain loans, interest-only strips, retained interests in securitizations, and so forth, should be classified as either trading or available-for-sale, as the facts demand.

SFAS 133 specifies that a held-to-maturity debt security denominated in a foreign currency should be accounted for under SFAS 52.

Maturity date. The sale of a security within three months of its maturity meets the requirement to hold to maturity since the interest rate risk is substantially diminished. Likewise, if a call is considered probable, a sale within three months of that date meets the requirement. The sale of a security after collection of at least 85% of the principal outstanding at acquisition (due to prepayments or to scheduled payments of principal and interest in equal installments) also qualifies since the "tail" portion no longer represents an efficient investment due to the economic costs of accounting for the remnants. Scheduled payments are not required to be equal for variable-rate debt.

Example of held-to-maturity debt securities

The 12/31/01 debt security portfolio categorized as held-to-maturity is as follows:

Security	Maturity value	Amortized cost	Assumed fair value
DEF 12% bond, due 12/31/02	$ 10,000	$10,320	$10,200
PQR mortgage-backed debt, due 12/31/04	$100,000	$92,000	$90,000
JKL 8% bond, due 12/31/08	$ 10,000	$ 8,929	$ 9,100

The balance sheet would report all the securities in this category at amortized cost and would classify them as follows:

Security	Maturity date	Balance sheet	Classification
DEF	12/31/02	$10,320	Current
PQR	12/31/04	$92,000	Noncurrent
JKL	12/31/08	$ 8,929	Noncurrent

Interest income, including premium and discount amortization, is included in income. Any realized gains or losses are also included in income.

Trading securities. If an entity has debt and/or equity securities (with readily determinable fair value) that it intends to actively and frequently buy and sell for short-term profits, those securities are classified as trading securities. Unless classified as held-to-maturity securities, SFAS 65 mortgage-backed securities held for sale require classification as trading securities. The securities in this category are required to be carried at fair value on the balance sheet as current assets. All applicable interest and dividends, realized gains and losses, and unrealized gains and losses on changes in fair value are included in income from continuing operations.

Example of accounting for trading securities

The year one current trading securities portfolio is as follows:

Security	Cost	Market	Difference (Market minus cost)
ABC	$1,000	$ 900	$(100)
MNO calls	1,500	1,700	200
STU	2,000	1,400	(600)
XYZ 7% bond	2,500	2,600	100
	$7,000	$6,600	$(400)

A $400 adjustment is required in order to recognize the decline in market value. The entry required is

Unrealized loss on trading securities	400	
Trading securities—MNO calls	200	
Trading securities—XYZ 7% bond	100	
Trading securities—ABC		100
Trading securities—STU		600

The unrealized loss would appear on the income statement as part of other expenses and losses. Dividend income and interest income (including premium and discount amortization) is included in income. Any realized gains or losses from the sale of securities are also included in income.

An alternative to direct write-up and write-down of securities is the use of an asset valuation allowance account to adjust the portfolio totals. In the above example, the entry would be

Unrealized loss on trading securities	400	
Valuation allowance (contra asset)		400

The valuation allowance of $400 would be deducted from historical cost to obtain a fair value of $6,600 for the trading securities on the balance sheet.

All trading securities are classified as current assets and the balance sheet would appear as follows:

Current assets:
Trading securities at fair value (cost = $7,000) $6,600

The year two current trading portfolio is as follows:

Security	New securities cost	Old securities X1 market	X2 market	Difference*
ABC		$ 900	$1,000	$100
DEF Puts	$1,500		1,500	0
STU		1,400	1,800	400
VWX	2,700	____	2,800	100
	$4,200	$2,300	$7,100	$600

* *Difference = X2 market – (Cost or X1 market)*

A $600 adjustment is required in order to recognize the increase in market value. The entry required is

Trading securities—ABC	100	
Trading securities—STU	400	
Trading securities—VWX	100	
Unrealized gain on trading securities		600

The unrealized gain would appear on the income statement as part of other income.

Example of accounting for a realized gain

1. The same information as given in the above example for year one
2. In year two, the MNO calls are sold for $1,600 and the XYZ 7% bonds are sold for $2,700.

The entry required to record the sale is

Cash	4,300	
Realized loss on sale of trading securities	100	
Realized gain on sale of trading securities		100
Trading securities—MNO calls (X1 market)		1,700
Trading securities—XYZ 7% bonds (X1 market)		2,600

Under the valuation allowance method, the current trading portfolio would appear as follows:

Security	Cost	X2 market
ABC	$1,000	$1,000
DEF Puts	1,500	1,500
STU	2,000	1,800
VWX	2,700	2,800
	$7,200	$7,100

The required entries to recognize the increase in market value and the realized gain are

Valuation allowance	300	
Unrealized gain on trading securities		300

To adjust the valuation allowance to reflect the unrealized loss of $100 at the end of year two on the remaining trading portfolio

Cash	4,300	
Trading securities—MNO calls (Cost)		1,500
Trading securities—XYZ 7% bonds (Cost)		2,500
Realized gain on sale of trading securities		300

The balance sheet under both methods would appear as follows:

Current assets:
Trading securities at fair value (cost = $7,200) $7,100

Available-for-sale. Investments in debt securities and in equity securities with a readily determinable fair value that are **not** classified as either trading securities or held-to-maturity are classified as available-for-sale. The securities in this category are required to be carried at fair value on the balance sheet. The determination of current or noncurrent status for individual securities depends on whether the securities are considered working capital (ARB 43, chapter 3A).

Other than the possibility of having some noncurrent securities on the balance sheet, the major difference between trading securities and available-for-sale securities is the handling of unrealized gains and losses. Unlike trading securities, the **unrealized** gains and losses are excluded from net income. Instead, they are reported in other comprehensive income per SFAS 130. All applicable interest (including premium and discount amortization) and any realized gains or losses from the sale of securities are included in income from continuing operations.

Deferred tax effects. The recognition of unrealized gains and losses for financial statement purposes is likely to have deferred tax effects. See the discussion in Chapter 10, Investments, page 410.

Transfers. Fair value is used for transfers between categories. When the security is transferred, any unrealized holding gains and losses are accounted for in the following manner:

1. **From trading**—Already recognized and should not be reversed
2. **Into trading**—Recognize immediately in income
3. **Available-for-sale debt security into held-to-maturity**—Continue to report the unrealized holding gain or loss at the transfer date as other comprehensive income and amortize the gain or loss over the investment's remaining life as an adjustment of yield in the same manner as a premium or discount. The transferred-in security will probably record a premium or discount since fair value is used. Thus, the two amortizations will tend to cancel each other on the income statement.
4. **Held-to-maturity debt security into available-for-sale**—Recognize in other comprehensive income per SFAS 130. Few transfers are expected from the held-to-maturity category.

See examples in Chapter 10, Investments.

Impairment. Other-than-temporary impairment (probable that all contractual amounts due won't be collected) of either the held-to-maturity or available-for-sale securities should be recognized as a realized loss. The cost basis should be written down to fair value and the write-down should be included in net income. The accounting should then proceed as required for the category. Subsequent recoveries will not change the new cost basis.

Cash flow statement. Cash flows resulting from sales, purchases or maturity of securities should be accounted for as follows:

1. Trading   – Operating activity
2. Held-to-maturity   – Investing activity
3. Available-for-sale   – Investing activity

Cash flows from 2 and 3 above are required to be reported gross (cash inflows from gross proceeds separately from outflows for purchase of investments) for each security classification.

Options

Call and put options can be effectively used as valuable hedging instruments or as highly leveraged speculative ventures. One call contract gives the **buyer** the right to **buy** 100 shares of the underlying security at a specific exercise price, regardless of the market price. The **seller** of the call, on the other hand, must **sell** the security to the buyer at that exercise price, regardless of the market price. For example, assume a Disney July 75 call has a quoted market price of $6 (per share or $600 per contract). These facts indicate that a buyer that pays $600 to a seller for a call has the right to purchase 100 shares of Disney at any time until July (typically the end of trading on the third Friday of the month quoted) for $75 per share. The buyer can exercise this right at any time until it expires. The seller of the call must stand ready to deliver 100 shares to the buyer for $75 per share until expiration. Typically, the buyer expects the market price to rise and the seller expects the market price to stay the same or to fall.

A put is the opposite of a call. A put gives the **buyer** the right to **sell** the underlying security at the exercise price regardless of the market price. It gives the **seller** the obligation to **buy** at the exercise price. Typically, the buyer expects the market price to fall and the seller expects the market price to stay the same or to rise. Strips, straps, straddles, and spreads are combinations and/or variations of the basic call and the basic put. These and other compound instruments should be analyzed in terms of their constituent elements, and accounted for accordingly.

Example

Seller D owns 100 shares of Disney at a cost of $75 per share and sells 1 Disney July 75 call to Buyer E at $6. The following positions result if the market price:

		Position	
		Seller (D)	*Buyer (E)*
1.	Stays at 75 and there is no exercise	+$600	–$600

D receives the $600 premium and E pays for the right to call the stock. If the market price doesn't move, the option expires; E is out $600 and D collects it.

2.	Rises to 95 and there is an exercise	+$600	+$1,400
	and immediate sale	(0 + $600)	($2,000 – $600)

If the price rises to $95 per share and the security is called, D sells the security to E at $75 ($0 profit on the shares) and is effectively $600 (the amount of the premium) better off. E, however, buys the security at $75 per share and immediately sells it for $95 per share. E gains $2,000 from the security sale less the $600 premium and is $1,400 better off.

3.	Falls to 55 and there is no exercise	−$1,400 (− $2,000 + $600)	−$600 (0 − $600)

If the market price falls to $55 per share, D incurs an effective $2,000 decrease in value of the shares held, less the $600 premium received. E does not exercise the option and loses the premium paid.

The issue in accounting for options is whether cost or market values—or some combination—should be used in accounting for the option itself and for the associated underlying security. For instance, assume M buys 100 shares of XYZ at $15 per share and the security price immediately moves to $25 per share. At this point, M buys a November 25 put contract at $100 for the contract. M has effectively hedged and guaranteed a minimum profit of $900 [(100 shares x $10) − ($1 x 100 shares)] regardless of market price movement, since XYZ can be sold for $25 per share until the third Friday in November. If the price continues upward, the put will expire unexercised and M will continue to benefit point for point. If the price stays the same, M locks in a profit of $900. If the price falls, M has locked in a profit of $900. The question is whether these facts can be accounted for by applying the cost principle to both option and security, by applying the market principle to both option and security, or by applying some combination of both principles.

Before SFAS 133, SFAS 115 was the only relevant guidance, and it was not really definitive. Theoretically, SFAS 115 only applied to purchased puts and calls, since written options are liabilities, not investments. Likewise, cash settled options and equity indexed options do not represent ownership interests and debt securities options are not covered by SFAS 115. In the absence of formal standards, however, numerous aspects of the issue had been addressed by the EITF. The result was that options were usually carried at market value.

Financial Instruments

SFAS 133, issued in June 1998, had its effective date deferred by one year pursuant to SFAS 137, and ultimately became effective for all fiscal quarters of fiscal years beginning after June 15, 2000, although earlier application had been encouraged. Initial application was to have been only at the beginning of a fiscal quarter, at which time hedging relationships were to be designated and documented. SFAS 138 amended specific provisions of SFAS 133.

SFAS 133 specifies recognition of all derivative instruments (not just derivative **financial** instruments) in the balance sheet as assets or liabilities measured at fair value. Derivatives can be specifically designated as hedges. The standard superseded SFAS 80, 105, and 119, and it also amended numerous other SFAS and nullified or modified numerous EITF consensuses. SFAS 133 carried forward the financial components approach first set forth in SFAS 125, which in turn was superseded by SFAS 140 with, alas, the same basic model.

Derivative financial instruments. The now-superseded SFAS 119 was in effect an interim standard on derivatives which only addressed disclosure requirements, pending the completion of a comprehensive standard, and required issuers and holders of derivative financial instruments (DFI) to disclose information about those instruments. When SFAS 119 was issued, it amended the disclosure requirements of SFAS 105 (which has now also been superseded) as well as SFAS 107 (which was accordingly amended). There was a very pressing need for this standard, since the derivatives market had grown extremely large, with DFI being an important part of the operations of many institutions.

Derivatives are financial instruments that derive their value from changes in a benchmark based on stock prices, interest rates, mortgage rates, currency rates, commodity prices or some other agreed-upon reference. Option contracts and forward contracts are the two basic forms of derivatives, and they can be either publicly or privately traded. Forward contracts have symmetrical gain and loss characteristics—that is, they provide exposure to both losses and gains from market movements, although generally there is no initial premium to be paid. Forward contracts are usually settled on or near the delivery date by paying or receiving cash, rather than by physical delivery. On the other hand, option contracts have asymmetrical loss functions: they provide little or no exposure to losses (beyond the premium paid) from unfavorable market movements, but can provide large benefits from favorable market movements. Both futures and options have legitimate roles to play in hedging programs, if properly understood and managed.

Typical derivative financial instruments include

1. Option contracts	7. Forward contracts
2. Interest rate caps	8. Forward interest rate agreements
3. Interest rate floors	9. Interest rate collars
4. Fixed-rate loan commitments	10. Futures
5. Note issuance facilities	11. Swaps
6. Letters of credit	12. Instruments with similar characteristics

It should be noted that DFI exclude all on-balance-sheet **receivables** and **payables** including

1. Mortgage-backed securities
2. Interest-only obligations
3. Principal-only obligations
4. Indexed debt
5. Other optional characteristics incorporated within those receivables and payables (such as convertible bond conversion or call terms)

In addition, DFI exclude contracts that either

1. Require exchange for a nonfinancial commodity or
2. Permit settlement by delivering a nonfinancial commodity

Thus, most product (petroleum, grain, etc.) futures contracts would be excluded, while swaps (if settled in cash) would be included.

As with other financial instruments, they can be acquired for investment purposes or for speculation. For enterprises which are not in the business of speculation, however, the typical purpose of DFI is to manage risk, such as that associated with stock price movements, interest rate variations, currency fluctuations, and commodity price volatility. The parties involved tend to be brokerage firms, financial institutions, insurance companies, and large corporations, although any two or more entities of any size can hold or issue derivatives.

The DFI are contracts that are supposed to protect or hedge one or more of the parties from adverse movement in the underlying base, which can be a financial instrument position held by the entity or a commitment to acquire same at some future date, among others. Unfortunately, these protections or hedges are rarely perfect and sometimes the hedge, once established, is later modified—such as by disposing of the underlying position—so that the DFI becomes only a speculative position. The DFI themselves can become risky and, if leveraged, small adverse price or interest rate variations can produce significant losses. Thus, instead of providing protection, many DFI have actually generated losses.

Instruments such as interest rate swaps (exchanging variable- or floating-rate debt for fixed-rate debt) and interest rate caps (limiting exposure to rising interest rates) have also resulted in losses along with mortgage-backed bonds and such "exotics" as "kitchen sink" bonds, structured notes, inverse floaters, and interest-only strips. Accounting concerns about these losses arose from the formerly off-balance-sheet nature of many DFI, the amount of capital that should be required for trading DFI, and the suitability of DFI for holders, given the risks of loss that could result. Over the past decade, many users and issuers reassessed their policies regarding DFI and examined and strengthened their internal controls to limit the risk.

Prior to the promulgation of SFAS 133, a preferred method of accounting for DFI had not been established. The accounting for these complex instruments was not standardized and in many cases users of the financial statements were unaware of derivatives positions held by the reporting entities. In many cases, the individual positions were accounted for separately at fair value with the gains or losses reported in operating income or in net income; in other cases, hedge accounting was used with its associated deferral of gains and losses. As a first step, in SFAS 119 the FASB (without specifying the accounting to be used) mandated disclosures in an attempt to require relevant information to be given to interested parties, as an indication of the DFI's risk.

A number of anomalies existed under prior GAAP. For example, options held and certain other DFI were not disclosed under SFAS 105 because they did not represent off-balance-sheet risk of accounting loss. Later, SFAS 119 amended SFAS 105 to replace the term "class of financial instrument" with the term "category of financial instrument," so that the formerly undisclosed instruments then required disclosure—by category of financial instrument—of face, contract, or notional principal amount; the nature and terms including credit risk, market risk, cash requirements; and any leverage features (or multipliers) and their general effects on these matters. As introduced by SFAS 119, category of financial instrument is the class, business activity, risk, or other category consistent with managing these instruments. Whenever class of DFI was not used as the category for the disclosure, the class of financial instruments included in the category had to be described. All DFI were to be classified as (1) "trading" (including dealing and all activities measured at fair value and reported in a trading account) or (2) "other than trading."

For "traded" DFI, the required disclosures established by SFAS 119 included net gains or losses (net trading revenue) reported in income by category of financial instrument and where the net gains or losses are reported and the average fair value of DFI during the period, together with the related value at the end of the period, differentiating assets and liabilities. Disclosure of this information was also encouraged for other types of financial instruments or nonfinancial assets that are traded. For "other than traded" DFI, required disclosures included a description, including the class of DFI used, of the objectives for holding, sufficient context required to understand the objectives, and the strategy employed for achieving the objectives; and a description of how each class of DFI was reported in the statements, including recognition and measurement policies for DFI held or issued, the location of DFI in the balance sheet and where the related gains or losses are reported in income; if held or issued and accounted for as hedges of anticipated transactions, requirements included information about the transaction being hedged and about the time period until occurrence, a description of the classes of DFI used to hedge, amounts of explicitly deferred (i.e., in separate accounts as required by SFAS 52 and the now superseded SFAS 80) hedging gains or losses, and events that would result in recognition in earnings of deferred items.

Interest rate, commodity price, foreign exchange, or other market risk information which was useful for comparing strategic results with objectives of derivatives and which was consistent with the entity's management of risk was encouraged, but not required, to be disclosed under SFAS 119. Different organizations reported this information in different ways, and the development and evolution of effective ways of reporting the above data was being actively encouraged.

SFAS 119 also amended SFAS 107 by requiring that fair value information be presented along with the related carrying value so that it would be clear whether the values represent assets or liabilities. If disclosed in more than one note, a summary table containing the above data was required in one of these notes, with a cross-reference to the location of the other SFAS 107 notes. In addition, the relationship between the carrying amounts and what was reported in the balance sheet was to be disclosed. "Traded" (including dealing and other activities measured at fair value with gains or losses recognized in earnings) financial instruments were to be distinguished from those that were categorized as "other than traded." In disclosing fair value of a DFI, that fair value was not to be aggregated, netted or combined (even if considered related) with either the fair value of a nonderivative financial instrument or other DFI except as permitted by FASB Interpretation 39 (right of offset).

SFAS 119 represented an evolutionary phase in the development of financial reporting of derivative financial instruments. It has now been superseded by SFAS 133, which has incorporated most of the disclosure requirements, as modified necessarily for the new accounting rules regarding the use of fair value accounting and the hedge accounting provisions of the newer standard.

Off-balance-sheet and credit risk. SFAS 105, which has been superseded by SFAS 133, was the first standard to require various disclosures of information (1) about financial instruments with off-balance-sheet risks of accounting loss that exceeded the amounts recorded, if any, in the statement of financial position and (2) about all financial instruments with concentrations of credit risk. It addressed credit and market risks only.

One problem retarding the development of financial reporting standards for financial instruments was the lack of a universally agreed-upon definition. SFAS 105 established the definition of financial instruments to include cash, any ownership interest in an entity, or a contract that both imposes a contractual obligation on one entity (1) to surrender cash or another financial instrument to a second entity or (2) to exchange financial instruments on potentially unfavorable terms with the second entity, and simultaneously conveys a contractual right to the second entity (1) to receive from the first entity cash or another financial instrument or (2) to exchange with the first entity other financial instruments on potentially favorable terms.

A **contractual obligation** whose economic benefit or sacrifice is receipt or delivery of a financial instrument other than cash was to be considered a financial instrument. For example, a note that is payable in US Treasury bonds gives an issuer the contractual obligation to deliver and gives a holder the contractual right to receive bonds, not cash. But because the bonds represent obligations of the US Treasury to pay cash they are considered financial instruments. Therefore, the note is also a financial instrument to both the holder of the note and the issuer of the note.

Another type of financial instrument is one that gives an entity the **contractual right** or obligation to exchange other financial instruments on potentially favorable or unfavorable terms. An example of this type of financial instrument would be a call option to purchase a US Treasury note for $100,000 in six months. The option holder has a contractual right to exchange the financial instrument on potentially favorable terms. Six months later, if the market value of the note exceeds $100,000, the holder will exercise the option because the terms are favorable. The writer of the call option has a contractual obligation to exchange financial instruments on potentially unfavorable terms if the holder exercises the option. The writer is normally compensated for accepting this obligation. A put option to sell a Treasury note has similar but opposite effects. A bank's commitment to lend $100,000 to a customer at a fixed rate of 10% any time during the next six months at the customer's option is also a financial instrument.

An interest rate swap can be explained as a series of forward contracts to exchange, for example, fixed cash payments for variable cash receipts. The cash receipts would be computed by multiplying a floating-rate market index by a notional amount. An interest rate swap is both a contractual right and a contractual obligation to both parties.

Excluded from financial instrument classification under SFAS 105, however, were options and contracts that contain the right or obligation to exchange a financial instrument for a **physical** asset, such as bushels of wheat. For example, two entities enter a sale-purchase contract in which the purchaser agrees to take delivery of wheat or gold six months later and pay the seller $100,000 at the time of delivery. The contract is not considered a financial instrument because it requires the delivery of wheat or gold that are not considered financial instruments.

Also excluded from financial instrument classification are contingent items that may ultimately require the payment of cash but do not as yet arise from contracts. An example would be a contingent liability for tort judgments payable. However, when such an obligation becomes enforceable and is reduced to a fixed payment schedule, it would then be considered a financial instrument.

SFAS 105 required all entities to disclose in the body of the financial statements, or in footnotes, information about financial instruments with off-balance-sheet risk. Disclosures were to be by category of financial instrument, and were to include the face, contract, or notional principal amount; and the nature and terms of the instruments including a discussion of (1) the credit and market risks, (2) the cash requirements, and (3) the related accounting policies (pursuant to APB 22).

For financial instruments with off-balance-sheet credit risk, an entity was to have disclosed in the body of the statement, or in notes to the statement, information about the amount of accounting loss the entity would have incurred if any party to the financial instrument failed completely to perform according to the terms of the contract and if any collateral proved worthless; and the entity's policy for requiring collateral on financial instruments subject to credit risks, information about access to that collateral, and the nature and brief description of collateral supporting financial instruments.

A financial instrument had off-balance-sheet risk of **accounting loss** if there was a risk than an accounting loss to the entity could exceed the amount recognized as an asset or if the ultimate obligation could exceed the amount that was recognized as a liability in the statement of financial position. The risk of accounting loss includes the possibility that the loss may occur from credit risk or from market risk. The issue of off-balance-sheet risk of loss has been effectively made moot by the requirement, under SFAS 133, that all derivative instruments be reported at fair value, coupled with the impact of SFAS 115 requiring fair value reporting (or at least disclosure) of most financial instruments held as investments. SFAS 133, accordingly, superseded SFAS 105 in its entirety.

Fair value disclosures. SFAS 107, amended by SFAS 133 to include the disclosure requirements of credit risk for **all** financial instruments from superseded SFAS 105, requires entities to disclose the fair value of **all** (recognized and unrecognized) financial instruments that it is practicable to estimate, including liabilities. Pertinent descriptive information as to the fair value of the instrument is to be disclosed if an estimate of fair value cannot be made without incurring excessive costs.

Fair value has been defined as the exchange price in a current transaction (other than in a forced or liquidation sale) between willing parties. If a quoted market price is available, it should be used. If there is more than one market price, the one used should be the one from the most active market. The possible effect on market price from the sale of large holdings and/or from thinly traded issues can be disregarded for purposes of this statement.

If quoted market prices are unavailable, management's best estimate of fair value can be used. Some bases from which an estimate may be made include

1. Matrix pricing models
2. Option pricing models
3. Financial instruments with similar characteristics adjusted for risks involved
4. Financial instruments with similar valuation techniques (i.e., present value) adjusted for risks involved

SFAS 107 contains examples of procedures for estimating fair value.

If the **carrying amount** for trade receivables and payables approximates fair value (which is usually the case), no disclosure is required.

If an estimate of fair value cannot be made without incurring excessive costs, disclose the following:

1. Information pertinent to estimating fair value such as carrying amount, effective interest rate, and maturity
2. Reasons why estimating fair values is not practicable

SFAS 107 did not change any other requirements of GAAP in regard to financial instruments. It applies to all entities and to all financial instruments except pensions, postretirement benefits, deferred compensation, defeased debt, insurance contracts, lease contracts, warranty obligations and a limited number of other instruments. Despite possible variations in definitions, amounts computed under GAAP requirements satisfy the requirements of SFAS 107.

Disclosures are required for each year included for comparative purposes and may be in the body of the financial statements or in the notes. Methods and significant assumptions used should be disclosed.

Example

Note 1: Summary of Accounting Policies

The Corporation does not deal or trade financial instruments. Derivatives are limited in use and leveraged swaps and items with embedded terms are not used.

Derivative products and other financial instruments are used for nontrading purposes including the management of foreign currency exposure and interest rate positions. Asset amounts are reported as other assets. Liability amounts are reported as other liabilities. Gains or losses are recognized as other income or expense currently or deferred if qualified as a hedge.

Note X: Financial Instruments Disclosures of Fair Value

The estimates of fair value of financial instruments are summarized as follows (in 000s):

Carrying amounts approximate fair values:

	Carrying amount
Cash	$987
Cash equivalents	876
Trade receivables	765
Trade payables	654

Fair values approximate carrying values because of the short time until realization.

Assets with fair values exceeding carrying amounts:

	Carrying amount	Fair value
Short-term securities	$876	$987
Long-term investments	765	876
Forward foreign exchange contracts	154	165

Estimated fair values are based on available quoted market prices, present value calculations and option pricing models.

Liabilities with carrying amounts exceeding fair values:

	Carrying amount	Fair value
Long-term debt	($543)	($432)

Estimated fair values are based on quoted market prices, present value calculations, and the prices of the same or similar instruments after considering risk, current interest rates, and remaining maturities.

Unrecognized financial instruments:

	Carrying amount	Fair value
Interest rate swap agreements		
Net receivable	$1,012	$1,865
Net payable	(1,753)	(1,543)
Commitments to extend credit	(5,432)	(4,321)
Financial guarantees	(6,543)	(7,654)

Estimated fair values after considering risk, current interest rates, and remaining maturities were based on the following:

Interest rate swaps—Amounts to be received or paid to terminate swap agreements at reporting date.

Credit commitments—Value of the same or similar instruments after considering credit ratings of counterparties.

Financial guarantees—Cost to settle or terminate obligations with counterparties at reporting date.

Fair value not estimated:

	Carrying amount	*Fair value*
Long-term investment	$1,234	Unavailable

Fair value could not be estimated without incurring excessive costs. Investment is carried at original cost and represents an 8% investment in the common stock of a privately held **untraded** company that supplies the corporation. Management considers the risk of loss to be negligible.

Accounting for Derivatives and Hedging Transactions Per SFAS 133: An Overview

Following a lengthy period of development, during which a number of possible sets of rules were debated, SFAS 133 was issued in 1998 and was finally implemented beginning in 2000. This standard, while far more comprehensive than any of the predecessors discussed above, is still not an all-inclusive standard on the accounting for all financial instruments. (A further standard, which is expected to mandate full fair value accounting for all financial instruments, whether assets or liabilities, is anticipated.) SFAS 133 addresses the accounting for derivatives (which formerly presented the most intractable financial reporting problems) and continues, in much modified form, the practice of "special accounting" for hedges, which would not be necessary if a universal fair value financial reporting rule were imposed.

Fair values are defined in SFAS 133 as they were in SFAS 107, discussed above. The new standard will resolve a number of previous inconsistencies and other inadequacies found in previous standards, including

- The effects of derivative instruments were not easily understood, were often not properly displayed in the financial statements, and, sometimes, were not even recognized in the financial statements.
- The available accounting guidance was incomplete. Many derivative instruments were carried off balance sheet.
- The accounting guidance was inconsistent. There was different measurement of various derivative instruments, and different qualifications for alternative types of hedging.
- The guidance that did exist was difficult to apply. There was a variety of sources and no single comprehensive approach.

SFAS 133 requires standardized accounting and reporting for all derivative instruments (including derivatives which are embedded in other instruments) and for hedging activities.

Underlying principles. There are four key principles underlying the new standard.

1. Derivative instruments are assets and liabilities.
2. The fair value of derivative instruments is the only relevant measure to be reported.
3. Only true assets and liabilities should be reported as such. Gains and losses from derivative instruments are not separate liabilities or assets and should not be reported as such.
4. Only designated qualifying items that are effectively offset by changes in fair value or cash flows during the term of the hedge should use the special accounting for hedging.

Derivative instruments represent rights and obligations, and these must be reported as assets and liabilities at fair value (which reflects the current cash equivalent). Gains and losses on derivative instruments not designated as hedges are recognized in earnings (or as a change in net assets, in the case of not-for-profit enterprises). The ability to apply hedge accounting requires that specified criteria be met, because of its elective nature and because of its reliance on management intent. Strategic risk hedges do not meet the qualifying criteria. Thus, hedge accounting is limited to relationships involving derivative instruments and certain foreign currency denominated instruments that are designated as hedges and meet the qualifying criteria.

Terminology

SFAS 133 defines a number of important terms that are used to describe various derivative instruments and hedging relationships. These include the following:

Derivative instruments. In SFAS 133, derivative instruments are defined by their three distinguishing characteristics. Specifically, derivative instruments are financial instruments or other contracts that have

1. One or more underlyings and one or more notional amounts (or payment provisions or both);
2. No initial net investment or a smaller net investment than required for contracts expected to have a similar response to market changes; and
3. Terms that require or permit
   a. Net settlement
   b. Net settlement by means outside the contract
   c. Delivery of an asset that results in a position substantially the same as net settlement

In contrast to superseded standard SFAS 119, this standard defines derivative instruments by reference to specific characteristics rather than in terms of classes or categories of financial instruments. These distinctive features are believed to represent the fundamental nature of derivative instruments like options and futures.

Fair value. Defined as in SFAS 107 as the amount at which the asset or liability could be bought or settled in an arm's-length transaction; measured by reference to market prices or estimated by net present value of future cash flows, options pricing models, or by other techniques.

Financial instrument. Defined as it was in SFAS 105.

Firm commitment. An agreement with an unrelated party, binding on both, usually legally enforceable, specifying all significant terms and including a disincentive for nonperformance sufficient to make performance likely.

Forecasted transaction. A transaction expected to occur for which there is no firm commitment, and thus, which gives the entity no present rights or obligations. Under SFAS 133, forecasted transactions can be hedged and special hedge accounting can be applied.

Initial net investment. A derivative instrument is one where the initial net investment is zero or is less than the notional amount (possibly plus a premium or minus a discount). This characteristic refers to the relative amount of investment. Derivative instruments allow the opportunity to take part in the rate or price change without owning the asset or owing the liability. If an amount approximating the notional amount must be invested or received, it is not a derivative instrument. The two basic forms of derivative instruments are futures contracts and options. The futures contract involves little or no initial net investment. Settlement is usually near the delivery date. Call options, when purchased, require a premium payment that is less than the cost of purchasing the equivalent number of shares. Even though this distinguishing characteristic is the result of only one of the parties, it determines the application for both.

Net settlements. To qualify as a derivative instruments, one of the following settlement criteria must be met:

1. No delivery of an asset equal to the notional amount is required. For example, an interest rate swap does not involve delivery of the instrument in which the notional amount is expressed.

2. Delivery of an asset equal to the notional amount is required of one of the parties, but an exchange (or other market mechanism, institutional arrangement or side agreement) facilitates net settlement. For example, a call option has this attribute.

3. Delivery by one of the parties of an asset equal to the notional amount is required but the asset is either readily convertible to cash (as with a contract for the delivery of a marketable equity security), or is required but that asset is itself a derivative instrument (as is the case for a swaption [an option on a swap]).

This characteristic means that the derivative instrument can be settled by a net delivery of assets (the medium of exchange does not have to be cash). Contract terms based on changes in the price or rate of the notional that implicitly or explicitly require or permit net settlement qualify. Situations where one of the parties can liquidate their net investment or be relieved of the contract rights or obligations without significant transaction costs because of a market arrangement (broadly interpreted) or where the delivered asset can be readily converted to cash also meet the requirements for net settlement. It is assumed that an exchange-traded security is readily converted to cash. Thus, commodity-based contracts for gold, oil, wheat, etc. are now included under this standard. The convertible to cash condition requires an active market and consideration of interchangeability and transaction volume. Determining if delivery of a financial asset or liability equal to the notional amount is a derivative instrument may depend upon whether it is readily convertible into cash. Different accounting will result if the notional is not readily converted to cash. Using the notional as collateral does not necessarily mean it is readily convertible to cash.

Notional amount. The notional amount (or payment provision) is the referenced units of measure associated with the underlying asset or liability, such as shares of stock, principal amount, face value, stated value, basis points, barrels of oil, etc. It may be that amount plus a premium or minus a discount. The interaction of the price or rate (underlying) with the referenced associated asset or liability (notional amount) determines whether settlement is required and, if so, the amount.

Underlyings. An underlying is commonly a specified price or rate such as a stock price, interest rate, currency rate, commodity price, or a related index. However, any variable (financial or physical) with (1) observable changes or (2) objectively verifiable changes such as a credit rating, insurance index, climatic or geological condition (temperature, rainfall) qualifies. Unless it is specifically excluded, a contract based on any qualifying variable is accounted for under SFAS 133 if it has distinguishing characteristics 2. and 3. above.

Contracts Not Subject to SFAS 133

The following contracts are considered exceptions and are not subject to the requirements of SFAS 133:

1. **Regular-way security trades**—Delivery of a security readily convertible to cash within the time period generally established by marketplace regulations or conventions where the trade takes place rather than by the usual procedure of an individual enterprise.

   For example, most trades of equity securities in the US require settlement in three business days. If an individual contract requires settlement in more than three business days (even if this is normal for a particular entity), this exception would not apply. This exception also applies to when-issued and to-be-announced securities, if there is no other way to purchase or sell them and if the trade will settle within the shortest period permitted.

Based on the foregoing, the following may be excluded: forward purchases or sales of to-be-announced securities, and when-issued, as-issued, or if-issued securities.

2. **Normal purchases and normal sales**—Contracts for future delivery of assets (other than derivative instruments or financial instruments) that are readily convertible to cash and for which there is no net settlement provision and no market mechanism to ease net settlement. Terms must be consistent with normal transactions and quantities must be reasonable in relation to needs. All relevant factors are to be considered. An example would include contracts similar to binding purchase orders. However, take or pay contracts that require little or no initial net investment, and that have products readily convertible to cash that do not qualify as normal purchases, would be a derivative instrument, and not an exception.

   The purpose of the "normal purchases and normal sales" definition was to exclude certain routine types of transactions from the required accounting as derivative instruments. SFAS 138 has expanded this exemption to include certain contracts which do contain net settlement or market mechanisms if it is judged probable, at the inception and throughout the duration of such contracts, that they will not in fact settle net and will instead result in physical delivery. Notwithstanding, this more broadly based exemption from the accounting requirements of SFAS 133, certain contracts will not qualify for exemption in any case; these include contracts the price of which are based on an underlying that is not clearly and closely related to the assets being sold or purchased, and those requiring cash settlement for any gains or losses or otherwise settled net on a periodic basis. Documentary evidence is required to support the use of the expanded exemption from the SFAS 133 provisions.

   Counterparties may reach different conclusions as to whether the contracts are a derivative instrument. Asymmetrical results are acceptable (i.e., the exception may apply to one party but not the other).

3. **Certain insurance contracts**—Contracts where the holder is only compensated when an insurable event (other than price or rate change) takes place and (a) the value of the holder's asset or liability is adversely changed or (b) the holder incurs a liability. For example, contracts generally not considered to be derivative instruments include those within the scope of SFAS 60, 97, and 113, traditional life insurance, and traditional property and casualty insurance policies.

   Most traditional insurance contracts will not be derivative instruments. Some, however, can include embedded derivatives that must be accounted for separately. For example, embedded derivatives may be found in indexed annuity contracts, variable life and annuity contracts, and property and casualty contracts involving changes in currency rates.

4. **Certain financial guarantee contracts**—Contracts that call for payments only to reimburse for a loss from debtor failure to pay when due. However, a credit-indexed contract requiring payment for changes in credit ratings (an underlying) would not be an exception.

5. **Certain contracts that are not exchange traded**—Contracts with underlyings based on one of the following:

   a. Climatic, geological or other physical variable: for example, inches of rain or heating-degree days;
   b. Value or price involving a nonfinancial asset not readily converted to cash or a nonfinancial liability that does not require delivery of an asset that is readily converted to cash; or
   c. Specified volumes of revenue of one of the parties: examples are royalty agreements or contingent rentals based on related sales.

   In the case of a mixture of underlyings, some of which are exceptions, the predominant characteristic of the combined variable of the contract is the determinant. If there is a high correlation with the behavior of the excepted variables above, it is an exception and if there is a high correlation with the nonexcepted variables, it is a derivative instrument.

6. **Derivatives that serve as impediments to sales accounting**—A derivative instrument that affects the accounting for the transfer of an asset. For example, a call option on transferred assets under SFAS 140 would prevent accounting for the transfer as a sale. This is necessary, since recognizing the call as a derivative instrument would result in double counting. For instance, a lessor guarantee of the residual value may prevent the accounting for a sales-type lease.

In addition to the foregoing, the following are not considered derivative instruments:

1. Contracts issued or held that are both

   a. Indexed to the enterprise's own stock, and
   b. Classified in shareholders' equity.

   Derivative instruments are assets or liabilities. Items properly accounted for in shareholders' equity are thus excluded from the definition of derivatives. Contracts that can or must be settled through issuance of an equity instrument but that are indexed in part or in full to something other than the enterprise's own stock are considered derivative instruments if they qualify and they are to be classified as assets or liabilities. Some of these kinds of items will be revisited later by the FASB.

2.   Contracts issued in connection with stock-based compensation arrangements as addressed in SFAS 123.

Many instruments under SFAS 123 are classified in shareholder equity. The FASB felt that those properly classified as liabilities have been adequately addressed.

3.   Contracts issued as contingent consideration in a business combination under APB 16, using the purchase method.

Contracts in a business combination that are similar to, but are not accounted for as contingent consideration under APB 16, are subject to this standard as derivative instruments or embedded derivative instruments.

The exceptions for the above three issued contracts are not applicable to the counterparties.

Embedded Derivative Instruments

An enterprise is not allowed to circumvent the requirements of SFAS 133 recognition and measurement by embedding a derivative instrument in another contract. If these embedded derivative instruments would otherwise be subject to this standard, they are included in its scope. However, some common compound instruments that generally have been in existence for some time and that bear a close economic relationship to the host contract are excluded from SFAS 133 for practical reasons.

Embedded derivative instruments are defined as explicit or implicit terms affecting (1) the cash flows or (2) the value of other exchanges required by contract in a way similar to a derivative instrument (one or more underlying can modify the cash flows or exchanges). An embedded derivative instrument is to be separated from the host contract and accounted for separately as a derivative instrument by both parties **if and only if** all of the following three criteria are met:

1.   Risks and economic characteristics are not **clearly and closely related** to those of the host contract;
2.   The hybrid instrument is not required to be measured at fair value under GAAP with changes reported in earnings; and
3.   A separate instrument with the same terms as the embedded derivative instrument would be accounted for as a derivative instrument. For this condition, the initial net investment of the hybrid instrument is not the same as that for the embedded derivative instrument.

These three conditions for the separate accounting for embedded derivatives are explained in the following paragraphs.

Risks and economic characteristics are not clearly and closely related to those of the host contract. If the underlying is an interest rate or interest rate index that changes the net interest payments of an interest-bearing contract, it is considered clearly and closely related **unless** one of the following conditions exist:

1. The hybrid instrument can be settled contractually in a manner that permits any possibility whatsoever that the investor would not recover **substantially all** of the initial recorded investment.
2. The embedded derivative instrument could under any possibility whatsoever (a) at least double the investor's initial rate of return (ROR) on the host contract and (b) could also result in a ROR at least twice the market return for a similar contract (same host contract terms and same debtor credit quality).

The date acquired (or incurred) is the assessment date for the existence of the above conditions. Thus, the issuer and an acquirer in a secondary market could account for the instrument differently because of different points in time.

Example of embedded instruments which are separately accounted for

Assuming that the host contract is a debt instrument, the following are considered not to be clearly and closely related and would normally have to be separated out as embedded derivatives:

1. Interest rate indexes, floors, caps and collars not meeting the criteria for exclusion (see below);
2. Leveraged inflation-indexed interest payments or rentals;
3. Calls and puts that do not accelerate repayment of the principal but require a cash settlement equal to the option price at date of exercise. Subsequently added options that cause one party to be exposed to performance or default risk by different parties for the embedded option than for the host contract;
4. Term extending options where there is no reset of interest rates;
5. Equity-indexed interest payments;
6. Commodity-indexed interest or principal payments;
7. A convertible debt conversion option for the investor if it qualifies as a derivative instrument (readily convertible to cash, etc.); and
8. A convertible preferred stock conversion option if the terms of the preferred stock (not the conversion option) are more similar to debt (a cumulative fixed rate with a mandatory redemption feature) than to equity (cumulative, participating, perpetual).

Example of embedded instruments which are not separately accounted for

Assuming that the host contract is a debt instrument, the following are considered to be clearly and closely related and would not normally have to be separated out as embedded derivative instruments:

1. Interest rate indexes (see below);
2. Interest rate floors, caps and collars, if **at issuance**

   a. The cap is at or above the current market price (or rate) and/or
   b. The floor is at or below the current market price (or rate).

3. Nonleveraged inflation-indexed interest payments or rentals.
4. Credit-sensitive payments (interest rate resets for debtor creditworthiness).

5. "Plain-vanilla" servicing rights not containing a separate embedded derivative instrument.
6. Calls and puts that can accelerate repayment of principal unless
    a. The debt involves substantial premium or discount (zero coupon) and
    b. The call or put is only contingently exercisable (not exercisable unless default occurs) and is indexed only to credit risk or interest rates.
7. Term-extending options if the interest rate is concurrently reset to approximately the current market rate for the extended term and the host contract had no initial significant discount.
8. Contingent rentals based on a variable interest rate.

Based on the foregoing, calls and puts embedded in equity instruments are normally accounted for as follows:

1. **Investor**—Both the call and the put are embedded derivative instruments.
2. **Issuer**—Only the put could be an embedded derivative instrument. The put and the call would not be embedded derivative instruments if they are both
    a. Indexed to their own stock and
    b. Classified in shareholders' equity.

The hybrid instrument is not required to be measured at fair value under GAAP with changes reported in earnings. For example, most unsettled foreign currency transactions are subject to SFAS 52. Gains or losses are recognized in earnings and thus instruments of this nature are not considered embedded derivative instruments. Trading and available-for-sale securities that have cash flows denominated in a foreign currency also are not considered embedded derivative instruments.

A separate instrument with the same terms as the embedded derivative instrument would be accounted for as a derivative instrument. For this condition, the initial net investment of the hybrid instrument is not the same as that for the embedded derivative instrument.

To illustrate, a convertible debt conversion option for the **issuer** would not be an embedded derivative instrument since a separate option with the same terms would not be a derivative instrument because it is indexed to the issuer's own stock and would be classified in shareholders' equity.

Another example would involve convertible preferred stock. A convertible preferred stock conversion option would not be an embedded derivative instrument if the terms of the preferred stock (not the conversion option) are more similar to equity (cumulative, participating, perpetual) than to debt (a cumulative fixed rate with a mandatory redemption feature).

Interest-only strips and principal-only strips are specifically not subject to this standard assuming (1) the original financial instrument did not contain an embedded derivative instrument and (2) they don't incorporate any new terms from the original. In addition, foreign currency derivative instruments are specifically not separated from the host contract if (1) the currency of the primary economic environment is the functional currency of one of the parties or (2) the good or service price is routinely denominated in that currency in international commerce.

If an embedded derivative instrument is separated from the host, the accounting is as follows:

1. The embedded derivative instrument is accounted for based on SFAS 133; and
2. The host contract is accounted for based on GAAP for that instrument, without the embedded derivative instrument.

If the embedded derivative instrument cannot be reliably identified and measured separately, the entire contract must be measured at fair value with the gain or loss recognized in income. In this case, the contract cannot be designated as a hedging instrument.

Gains and losses of derivative instruments not designated as hedges are recognized in earnings or, for a not-for-profit organization, in the change in net assets.

Hedging Activities—General Requirements

Overview. Matters relating to hedging activities constitute the core of the new standard and represent the most difficult accounting issues. While the standard requires that all derivatives be reported at fair value in the balance sheet, the changes in fair value will be reported in different ways depending on the nature and effectiveness of the hedging activities to which they are related, if held for hedging purposes. SFAS 133 identifies changes in the fair values of derivatives as being the result of (1) effective hedging, (2) ineffective hedging, or (3) unrelated to hedging. Furthermore, the hedging itself can be related to the fair value of an existing asset or liability or of a firm commitment, the cash flow associated with forecasted transactions, or foreign currency exposures.

After meeting specified conditions, a qualified derivative may be specifically designated as a total or partial (expressed as a percentage where the risk exposure profile is the same as that in the whole derivative) hedge of

1. Changes in the fair value of

    a. A recognized asset or liability; or
    b. An unrecognized firm commitment.

    In a fair value hedge, all gains and losses (of both the derivative instrument and the hedged item) are recognized in earnings in the period of change.
2. Variable cash flows of a forecasted transaction.

    In a cash flow hedge, the effective portion of the hedge is reported in other comprehensive income and is reclassified into earnings when the forecasted transaction affects earnings.
3. Foreign currency exposure of

   a. A net investment in a foreign operation

      In a foreign currency net investment hedge, the gain or loss is reported in other comprehensive income as part of the cumulative translation adjustment to the extent that it is effective.

   b. An unrecognized firm commitment

      In a foreign currency unrecognized firm commitment hedge, the gain or loss is reported the same way as a fair value hedge (see category 1., above).

   c. An available-for-sale security

      In a foreign currency available-for-sale security hedge, the gain or loss is reported the same way as a fair value hedge (see category 1., above).

   d. A foreign currency denominated forecasted transaction.

      In a foreign currency denominated forecasted transaction hedge, the gain or loss is reported in the same way as a cash flow hedge (see category 2., above).

Hedge portions that are not effective are reported in earnings immediately.

A nonderivative financial instrument cannot generally be designated as a hedge. One exception, however, occurs when that instrument is denominated in a foreign currency and is designated as a hedge under 3a. or 3b. above. Not-for-profit enterprises cannot use hedge accounting for forecasted transactions.

Effectiveness—General observations. The method used for assessing the effective and ineffective portions of a hedge must be defined at the time of designation, must be used throughout the hedge period and must be consistent with the approach used for managing risk. Similar hedges should usually be assessed for effectiveness in a similar manner unless a different method can be justified. If an improved method is identified and is to be applied prospectively to an existing hedge, that hedge must be discontinued. The new method can then be designated and a new hedge relationship can be established.

Factors to be included in the effectiveness assessment must be specified at inception. The effect of all excluded factors and ineffective amounts are to be included in earnings. For example, if an option contract hedge is assessed for effectiveness based on changes in the option's intrinsic value, the change due to the time value of the contract would be excluded from the effectiveness assessment and that amount would be included in earnings. As another example, differences in key terms between the hedged item and the hedging instrument such as notional amounts, maturities, quantities, location or delivery dates would cause ineffectiveness and that amount would be included in earnings.

Fair Value Hedges

The change in the fair value of an entire financial asset or liability for a period is computed as the fair value at the end of the period, adjusted to exclude changes in fair value (1) from payments received or made (partial recoveries or settlements) and (2) from the passage of time, minus the fair value at the beginning of the period.

To qualify as a fair value hedge, both the hedged items and the designated hedging instruments must meet **all** of the following criteria:

1. At the hedge's origin, formal documentation exists of the

    a. Hedging relationship;
    b. Risk management objectives;
    c. Strategy for undertaking the hedge;
    d. Identification of the hedged item, the hedging instrument, the nature of the risk being hedged, the method of assessing effectiveness and the components (if any) that are excluded (such as time value) from the effectiveness assessment; and the
    e. Reasonable method to be used in recognizing in earnings the asset or liability representing the gain or loss in the case of a hedged firm commitment.

2. The hedging relationship is expected to be highly effective in producing offsetting fair value changes throughout the hedge period. This relationship must be assessed at least every three months and each time financial statements or earnings are reported.

3. If hedging with a **written** option, the combination must provide as much potential for gains from positive fair value changes as potential for losses from negative fair value changes. If a net premium is received, a combination of options is considered a written option. The combination of a written option and some other nonoption derivative is also considered a written option.

Unless foreign currency is involved, a nonderivative instrument cannot be designated as a hedging instrument.

According to SFAS 133, an asset or liability will be eligible for designation as a hedged item in a fair value hedge (to which a hedging position will be related, for purposes of reporting gain or loss) if the hedged item is specifically identified as all or a specific portion of a recognized asset or liability, or an unrecognized firm commitment; is exposed to fair value changes that are attributable to the hedged risk such that earnings would be affected; and is not either remeasured at fair value for financial reporting purposes, or an equity method investment, or an equity method or minority interest in a consolidated subsidiary, a firm commitment related to the foregoing, or an equity instrument issued by the entity. Other limitations also apply, affecting held-to-maturity debt securities and nonfinancial assets.

More specifically, to be eligible for designation as a hedged item, an asset or liability must meet **all** of the following criteria:

1. The single item (or portfolio of similar items) must be specifically identified as hedging all or a specific portion.

    a. If similar items are aggregated and hedged, each item has to share the risk exposure that is being hedged (i.e. each individual item must respond in a generally proportionate manner to the change in fair value).

    b. A specific portion must be one of the following:

        (1) A percentage of the total asset, liability, or portfolio;
        (2) One or more selected contractual cash flows: for instance, the present value of the interest payments due in the first two years of a four-year debt instrument;
        (3) An embedded put, call, cap, or floor that does not qualify as an embedded derivative in an existing asset or liability; or
        (4) Residual value in a lessor's net investment in a sales-type or direct financing lease.

2. The item has an exposure to fair value changes that could affect earnings (this does not apply to not-for-profit enterprises).

3. The item is **not**

    a. Remeasured with changes reported currently in earnings; for example, a foreign currency denominated item;
    b. An APB 18 equity method investment or an equity investment in a consolidated subsidiary;
    c. A minority interest;
    d. A firm commitment to enter into a business combination or to acquire or dispose of

        (1) A subsidiary;
        (2) A minority interest; or
        (3) An equity method investee; or

    e. An entity-issued equity interest classified in stockholder's equity.

4. The item is not a held-to-maturity debt security (or similar portfolio) unless the hedged risk is for something other than for fair value changes in market interest rates or foreign exchange rates; examples include hedges of fair value due to changes in the obligor's creditworthiness, and hedges of fair value due to changes in a prepayment option component.

5. If the item is a nonfinancial asset or liability (other than a recognized loan servicing right or a nonfinancial firm commitment with financial components), the designated hedged risk is the fair value change of the total hedged item (at its actual location, if applicable); SFAS 133 stipulates that

the price of a major ingredient cannot be used, and the price of a similar item at a different location cannot be used without adjustment.

6. If the item is a financial asset or liability, a recognized loan servicing right or a nonfinancial firm commitment with financial components, the designated hedge risk is the risk of changes in fair value from fair value changes in

   a. The total hedged item;
   b. Market interest rates;
   c. Related foreign currency rates;
   d. The obligor's creditworthiness; or
   e. Two or more of the above, other than a.

Prepayment risk for a financial asset cannot be hedged, but an option component of a prepayable instrument can be designated as the hedged item in a fair value hedge. Embedded derivatives have to be considered also in designating hedges. For instance, in a hedge of interest rates, the effect of an embedded prepayment option must be considered in the designation of the hedge.

Reporting gains and losses from fair value hedges. The accounting for qualifying fair value hedges' gains and losses is as follows:

- On the hedging instrument, gains and losses are recognized in earnings.
- On the hedged item, gains and losses are recognized in earnings, even if they would normally be included in other comprehensive income if not hedged. For example, gains and losses on an available-for-sale security would be taken into income, if this is being hedged. The carrying amount of the hedged item is adjusted by the gains and losses resulting from the hedged risk.

Differences between the gains and losses on the hedged item and the hedging instrument are either due to amounts excluded from the assessment of hedging effectiveness, or are due to ineffectiveness. These gains and losses are to be recognized currently in earnings.

Example

An available-for-sale security carrying amount is adjusted by the amount resulting from the hedged risk, a fair value hedge.

Hedged item:	Available-for-sale security
Hedging instrument:	Put option
Underlying:	Price of the security
Notional amount:	100 shares of the security

On July 1, X1, Company XYZ purchased 100 shares of Disney at a cost of $15 per share and classified it as an available-for-sale security. On October 1, Company XYZ purchased for $350 an at-the-money put on Disney with an exercise price of $25 and an expiration date of April X2. This put purchase locks in a profit of $650 ($1,000 spread in market price less $350 cost of the put), if the price stays at $25 or goes lower, but allows continued profitability if the price of the Disney stock continues to go up. Company XYZ specifies that only the intrinsic value of the option is to be used to measure effectiveness. Thus, the time value decreases in the fair value of the put will be charged against the income of the period. Company XYZ then documents the hedge's strategy, objectives, hedging relationships, and method of measuring effectiveness. The following table shows the fair value of the hedged item and the hedging instrument.

Case 1

Hedged Item	*10/1/X1*	*12/31/X1*	*3/31/X2*	*4/17/X2*
Disney share price	$ 25	$ 22	$ 20	$ 20
Number of shares	100	100	100	100
Total	$2,500	$2,200	$2,000	$2,000

Hedging Instrument
Put option (100 shares)

Intrinsic value	$ 0	$ 300	$ 500	$ 500
Time value	350	215	53	0
Total	$ 350	$ 515	$ 553	$ 500

Intrinsic Value

Gain (Loss) on Put	$ 0	$ 300	$ 200	$ 0

Entries: Tax Effects and Transaction Costs Are Ignored

Date		Entry	Dr	Cr
7/1/X1	Purchase:	Available-for-sale security	1,500	
		Cash		1,500
9/30/X1	End of Quarter:	Valuation allowance—available-for-sale security	1,000	
		Other comprehensive income		1,000
10/1/X1	Put Purchase:	Put option	350	
		Cash		350
12/31/X1	End of Year:	Put option	300	
		Hedge gain (intrinsic value gain)		300
		Hedge loss	135	
		Put option (time value loss)		135
		Hedge loss	300	
		Valuation allowance—available-for-sale security (market value loss)		300

Partial Balance Sheet
Effect of Hedging Relationships
December 31, X1
Dr (Cr)

Cash	$(1,850)
Available-for-sale securities	1,200
Plus: Valuation allowance	1,000
Put option	515
Other comprehensive income	(1,000)
Retained earnings	135

Entries

			Dr	Cr
3/31/X2	End of Quarter:	Put option	200	
		Hedge gain (intrinsic value changes)		200
		Hedge loss	162	
		Put option (time value loss)		162
		Hedge loss	200	
		Available-for-sale security (market value loss)		200
4/17/X2	Put Expires:	Put option	0	
		Hedge gain (intrinsic value changes)		0
		Hedge loss	53	
		Put option (time value changes)		53
		Hedge loss	0	
		Available-for-sale security (market value changes)		0

Partial Balance Sheet
Effect of Hedging Relationships
April 17, X2 (Expiration of put)
Dr (Cr)

Cash	$(1,850)
Available-for-sale securities	1,500
Plus: Valuation allowance	500
Put option	500
Other comprehensive income	(1,000)
Retained earnings	350

At or before expiration, an in-the-money put must be sold or exercised. Assuming that it is sold, the entry would be

Cash	500	
Put option		500

On the other hand, if the put is exercised, the entry would be

Cash (exercise price)	2,500	
Other comprehensive income	1,000	
Available-for-sale security		1,500
Valuation allowance		500
Put option		500
Gain on sale		1,000

The net effect on retained earnings of the hedge and sale is a net gain of $650 ($1,000 – $350)

Case 2

	10/1/X1	12/31/X1	3/31/X2	4/17/X2
Hedged Item				
Disney share price	$ 25	$ 28	$ 30	$ 31
Number of shares	100	100	100	100
Total	$2,500	$2,800	$3,000	$3,100
Hedging Instrument				
Put option (100 shares)				
Intrinsic value	$ 0	$ 0	$ 0	$ 0
Time value	350	100	25	0
Total	$ 350	$ 100	$ 25	$ 0
Intrinsic Value Gain (Loss) on Put	$ 0	$ 0	$ 0	$ 0

Entries: Tax Effects and Transaction Costs Are Ignored

7/1/X1	Purchase:	Available-for-sale security	1,500	
		Cash		1,500
9/30/X1	End of Quarter:	Valuation allowance—		
		available-for-sale security	1,000	
		Other comprehensive income		1,000
10/1/X1	Put Purchase:	Put option	350	
		Cash		350
12/31/X1	End of Year:	Put option	0	
		Hedge gain (intrinsic value gain)		0
		Hedge loss	250	
		Put option (time value loss)		250
		Valuation allowance—available-for-sale security	300	
		Hedge gain (market value gain)		300

Partial Balance Sheet
Effect of Hedging Relationships
December 31, X1
Dr (Cr)

Cash	$(1,850)
Available-for-sale securities	1,500
Plus: Valuation allowance	1,300
Put option	100
Other comprehensive income	(1,000)
Retained earnings	(50)

Entries

3/31/X2	End of Quarter:	Put option	0	
		Hedge gain (intrinsic value change)		0
		Hedge loss	75	
		Put option (time value loss)		75
		Valuation allowance—available-for-sale security	200	
		Hedge gain (market value gain)		200
4/17/X2	Put Expires:	Put option	0	
		Hedge gain (intrinsic value change)		0
		Hedge loss	25	
		Put option (time value change)		25
		Valuation allowance—available-for-sale security	100	
		Hedge gain (market value change)		100

Effect of Hedging Relationships
April 17, X2 (Expiration of put)
Dr (Cr)

Cash	$(1,850)
Available-for-sale securities	1,500
Plus: Valuation allowance	1,600
Put option	0
Other comprehensive income	(1,000)
Retained earnings	(250)

The put expired unexercised and Company XYZ must decide whether to sell the security. If it continues to hold, normal SFAS 115 accounting would apply. If it continues to hold and a new put is purchased, the above example would be applicable again with the present position as a starting point. If the security is sold, the entry would be

Cash (market value)	3,100	
Other comprehensive income	1,000	
Available-for-sale security		1,500
Valuation allowance		1,600
Gain on sale		1,000

Measuring the effectiveness of fair value hedges. Although there are specific conditions applicable to the hedge type (fair value or cash flow), in general, the assumption of no ineffectiveness in a hedging relationship between an interest bearing financial instrument and an interest rate swap can be assumed if **all** of the following conditions are met:

1. The principal amount and the notional amount of the swap match;
2. The fair value of the swap is zero at origin;
3. The net settlements under the swap are computed the same way on each settlement date;
4. The financial instrument is not prepayable; and
5. The terms are typical for those instruments and don't invalidate the assumption of effectiveness.
6. The maturity date of the instrument and the expiration date of the swap match;
7. No floor or ceiling on the variable interest rate of the swap exists; and
8. The interval (three to six months or less) between repricings is frequent enough to assume the variable rate is a market rate.

The fixed rate on the hedged item is not required to exactly match the fixed rate on the swap. The fixed and variable rates on the swap can be changed by the same amount. As an example, a swap payment based on LIBOR and a swap receipt based on a fixed rate of 5% can be changed to a payment based on LIBOR plus 1% and a receipt based on 6%.

Under SFAS 133, a "shortcut method" is permitted to be used to compute fair value adjustments, which produces the same reporting results as when the method illustrated above has been applied. This shortcut is only appropriate for a fair value hedge of a fixed-rate asset or liability using an interest rate swap and only with the assumption of no ineffectiveness is appropriate (i.e., if the criteria above have been met.[1] The FASB's decision to redefine interest rate risk (by permitting "benchmark rate" hedging in SFAS 138) necessitated that is also address the effect on the short-cut method for fair value hedges and cash flow hedges.

For fair value hedges, an assumption of no ineffectiveness is invalidated when the interest rate index embodied in the variable leg of the interest rate swap is different from the benchmark interest rate being hedged. In situations in which the interest rate index embodied in the variable leg of the swap has greater credit risk than that embodied in the benchmark interest rate, the effect of the change in the swap's credit sector spread over that in the benchmark interest rate would represent hedge ineffectiveness because it relates to an unhedged risk (credit risk) rather than to the hedged risk (interest rate risk).

In situations in which the interest rate index embodied in the variable leg of the swap has less credit risk than that embodied in the benchmark interest rate, the effect of the change in a certain portion of the hedged item's spread over the swap interest rate would also represent hedge ineffectiveness. In order for an entity to comply with an assumption of no ineffectiveness, the index on which the variable leg of the swap is based should match the benchmark interest rate designated as the interest rate risk being hedged for the hedging relationship.

Discontinuance of a fair value hedge. The accounting for a fair value hedge should not continue if any of the events below occur.

1. The criteria are no longer met;
2. The derivative instruments expire or are sold, terminated or exercised; or
3. The designation is removed.

If the fair value hedge is discontinued, a new hedging relationship may be designated with a different hedging instrument and/or a different hedged item, as long as the criteria established in SFAS 133 are met.

Ineffectiveness of a fair value hedge. Unless the shortcut method is applicable, the reporting entity must assess the hedge's effectiveness at the inception of the hedge and at least every three months thereafter. In addition, SFAS 133 requires

---

[1] *The steps in the shortcut method are as follows:*

 a. *Determine the difference between the fixed rate to be received on the swap and the fixed rate to be paid on the bonds.*

 b. *Combine that difference with the variable rate to be paid on the swap.*

 c. *Compute and recognize interest expense using that combined rate and the fixed-rate liability's principal amount. (Amortization of any purchase premium or discount on the liability also must be considered, although that complication is not incorporated in this example.)*

 d. *Determine the fair value of the interest rate swap.*

 e. *Adjust the carrying amount of the swap to its fair value and adjust the carrying amount of the liability by an offsetting amount.*

that at the inception of the hedge the method to be used to assess hedge effectiveness must be identified. To comply, the reporting entity should decide which changes in the derivative's fair value will be considered in assessing the effectiveness of the hedge, and the method to be used to assess hedge effectiveness. Regarding the former, some derivative instruments (options) have two components: intrinsic value and time value. The intrinsic value of a call option is the excess, if any, of the market price over the strike or exercise price; the intrinsic value of an option recognizes that the price of the underlying item may move above the strike price (for a call) or below the strike price (for a put) during the exercise period. The enterprise elects to measure effectiveness either including or excluding time value; it must do so consistently once the designation is made.

Hedge effectiveness must be assessed in two different ways—in **prospective** considerations and in **retrospective** evaluations. SFAS 133 provides flexibility in selecting the method the entity will use in assessing hedge effectiveness, but an entity should assess effectiveness for similar hedges in a similar manner and that the use of different methods for similar hedges should be justified.

Prospectively, the entity must, at both inception and on an ongoing basis, be able to justify an expectation that the relationship will he **highly effective** in achieving offsetting changes in fair value over future periods. That expectation can be based upon regression or other statistical analysis of past changes in fair values or on other relevant information. **Retrospectively**, the entity must, at least quarterly, determine whether the hedging relationship has been **highly effective** in having achieved offsetting changes in fair value through the date of periodic assessment. That assessment can also be based upon regression or other statistical analysis of past changes in fair values, as well as on other relevant information. If at inception the entity elects to use the same regression analysis approach for both prospective and retrospective effectiveness evaluations, then during the term of that hedging relationship those regression analysis calculations should generally incorporate the same number of data points. As an alternative to using regression or other statistical analysis, an entity could use the dollar-offset method to perform the retrospective evaluations of assessing hedge effectiveness.

SFAS 133 does not define **hedging effectiveness** quantitatively. However, it is useful in this regard to contemplate the similar international accounting standard, IAS 39. That standard specifies that a hedge is normally regarded as highly effective if, at inception and throughout the life of the hedge, the enterprise can expect that the change in fair values of the hedging instrument and the hedged item will "almost fully offset." In addition, the standard requires that actual results be within a range of 80 - 125%. Interpretive guidance to that standard suggests that the appropriateness of any method of assessing hedge effectiveness depends on the nature of the risk being hedged and the type of hedging instrument used. Any method of assessing effectiveness must be reasonable and consistent with other similar hedges unless different methods are explicitly justified.

Logic suggest that the approach used under IAS 39 could also be applied under SFAS 133, with a arrange of 80 - 125% being defined as effectiveness for hedge accounting purposes.

Impairment. All assets or liabilities designated as fair value hedges are subject to the normal GAAP requirements for impairment. Those requirements are to be applied, however, only after the carrying amounts have been adjusted for the period's hedge accounting. Since the hedging instrument is a separate asset or liability, its fair value is not considered in applying the impairment criteria to the hedged item.

Cash Flow Hedges

The second major subset of hedging arrangements relate to uncertain future cash flows, as contrasted with hedged items engendering uncertain fair values. A derivative instrument may be designated as a hedge to the exposure of fluctuating expected future cash flows produced by a particular risk. The exposure may be connected with an existing asset or liability or with a forecasted transaction. To qualify as a cash flow hedge, both the hedged items and the designated hedging instruments must meet **all** of the following criteria:

1. At the hedge's origin, formal documentation exists of the

    a. Hedging relationship;
    b. Risk management objectives;
    c. Strategy for undertaking the hedge; and
    d. Identification of the hedged transaction, the hedging instrument, the nature of the hedged risk, the method of assessing effectiveness and the components (if any) that are excluded (such as time value) from the effectiveness assessment.

2. Documentation must include

    a. All relevant details;
    b. The specific nature of any asset or liability involved;
    c. When (date on or period within) a forecasted transaction is expected to occur; and
    d. The expected currency amount (exact amount of foreign currency being hedged) or expected quantity (specific physical quantities such as number of items, weight, etc.) of a forecasted transaction. If a price risk is being hedged in a forecasted sale or purchase, the hedged transaction **cannot**

        (1) Be specified solely in terms of expected currency amounts; or
        (2) Be specified as a percentage of sales or purchases.

The current price of the transaction should be identified and the transaction should be described so that it is evident that a given transaction is or is not the hedged transaction. For instance, a forecasted sale of the first 2,000 units in January is proper, but the forecasted sale of the last 2,000 units is not because they can't be identified when they occur—the month has to end before the last units sold can be identified.

3. The hedging relationship is expected to be highly effective in producing offsetting cash flows throughout the hedge period. This relationship must be assessed at least every three months and each time financial statements or earnings are reported.

4. If hedging with a **written** option, the combination must provide at least as much potential for positive cash flow changes as exposure to negative cash flow changes. A derivative that results from the combination of a written option and another nonoption derivative is also considered a written option.

5. A link must be used to modify interest receipts or payments of a recognized financial asset or liability from one variable rate to another variable rate. It has to be between a designated asset (or group of similar assets) and a designated liability (or group of similar liabilities) and it has to be highly effective. A link occurs when the basis of one leg of an interest rate swap is the same as the basis of the interest rate receipt of a designated asset and the basis of the other leg of the swap is the same as the basis of the interest payments for a designated liability.

A nonderivative instrument cannot be designated as a hedging instrument for a cash flow hedge.

In addition to the above, to be eligible for designation as a cash flow hedge, a forecasted transaction must meet **all** of the following criteria:

1. The single transaction (or group of individual transactions) must be specifically identified. If individual transactions are grouped and hedged, each has to share the same risk exposure that is being hedged (i.e. each individual transaction must respond in a proportionate manner to the change in cash flow). Thus, a forecasted sale and a forecasted purchase cannot both be included in the same group of transactions.

2. The occurrence is probable.

3. It is a transaction with an external party (unless a foreign currency cash flow hedge) and it has an exposure to cash flow changes that could affect earnings.

4. The transaction is **not** to be remeasured under GAAP with changes reported in earnings; for example, foreign currency denominated items would be excluded for this reason. Forecasted sales on credit and forecasted accrual of royalties on probable future sales are not considered the forecasted acquisition of a receivable. Also, if related to a recognized asset or liability, the asset or liability is not remeasured under GAAP with changes in fair value resulting from the hedged risk reported in earnings.

5. The item is not a held-to-maturity debt security (or similar portfolio) unless the hedged risk is for something other than for cash flow changes in market interest rates, as for example, in a hedge of cash flow changes due to an obligor's creditworthiness or default.

6. It does **not** involve

   a. A business combination;
   b. A parent company's interest in consolidated subsidiaries;
   c. A minority interest;
   d. An equity method investment; or
   e. An entity-issued equity interest classified in stockholder's equity.

7. If it involves a purchase or sale of a **nonfinancial** asset, the hedged risk is

   a. The change in the functional-currency-equivalent cash flows resulting from changes in the related foreign currency rates; or
   b. The change in cash flows relating to the total hedged purchase or sales price (at its actual location, if applicable); for example, the price of a similar item at a different location cannot be used.

8. If it involves a purchase or sale of a **financial** asset or liability or the variable cash flow of an existing financial asset or liability, the hedged risk is the risk of changes in cash flow of

   a. The total hedged item;
   b. Market interest rates;
   c. Related foreign currency rates;
   d. Obligor's creditworthiness or default; or
   e. Two or more of the above, other than a.

Prepayment risk for a financial asset cannot be hedged.

Gains and losses from cash flow hedges. The accounting for qualifying cash flow hedges' gains and losses is as follows:

1. The effective portion of the gain or loss on the derivative instrument is reported in other comprehensive income.
2. The ineffective portion of the gain or loss on the derivative instrument is reported in earnings.
3. Any component excluded from the computation of the effectiveness of the derivative instrument is reported in earnings.
4. Accumulated other comprehensive income from the hedged transaction should be adjusted to the lesser (in absolute amounts) of the following:

   a. The cumulative gain or loss on the derivative from the creation of the hedge minus any component excluded from the determination of hedge effectiveness and minus any amounts reclassified from accumulated other comprehensive income into earnings;

b. The portion of the cumulative gain or loss on the derivative needed to offset the cumulative change in expected future cash flow on the transaction from the creation of the hedge minus any amounts reclassified from accumulated other comprehensive income into earnings.

The adjustment of accumulated other comprehensive income should recognize in other comprehensive income either a part or all of the gain or loss on the adjustment of the derivative instrument to fair value.

5. Any remaining gain or loss is reported in earnings.

Reclassifications to earnings. In the period that the hedged forecasted transaction affects earnings, amounts in accumulated other comprehensive income should be reclassified into earnings. If the transaction results in an asset or liability, amounts in accumulated other comprehensive income should be reclassified into earnings when the asset or liability affects earnings through cost of sales, depreciation, interest expense, etc. Any time that a net loss on the combined derivative instrument and the hedged transaction is expected, the amount that isn't expected to be recovered should immediately be reclassified into earnings.

Example of a "plain vanilla" interest rate swap

On July 1, 2002, Abbott Corp. borrows $5 million with a fixed maturity (no prepayment option) of June 30, 2006, carrying interest at prime + 1/2%. Interest only is due semiannually. At the same date, it enters into a "plain vanilla" type swap arrangement, calling for fixed payments at 8% and receipt of prime + 1/2%, on a notional amount of $5 million. At that date prime is 7.5%, and there is no premium due on the swap arrangement.

This swap qualifies as a cash flow hedge under SFAS 133, and it is appropriate to assume no ineffectiveness, since the criteria set forth in that standard are all met.

NOTE: These criteria are that: the notional amount of the swap and the principal amount of the debt are equal; the fair value of the swap at inception is zero; the formula for computing net settlements under the swap is constant during its term; the debt is not prepayable; all interest payments on the debt are designated as being hedged and no payments beyond the term of the swap are so designated; there is no floor or cap on the variable rate of the debt that is not likewise designated for the swap; the repricing dates of the swap match those of the variable rate debt; and the same index is designated for the hedging instrument and the underlying obligation.

Accordingly, as rates change over the term of the debt and of the swap arrangement, changes in the value of the swap are reflected in other comprehensive income, and the swap will appear on the balance sheet as an asset or liability at fair value. As the maturity of the debt approaches, the value of the swap will converge on zero. Periodic interest expense in the income statement will be at the effective rate of 8%.

Assume that the prime rate over the four-year term of the loan, as of each interest payment date, is as follows, along with the fair value of the remaining term of the interest rate swap at those dates:

Date	Prime rate (%)	Fair value of swap*
December 31, 2002	6.5	$ - 150,051
June 30, 2003	6.0	- 196,580
December 31, 2003	6.5	- 111,296
June 30, 2004	7.0	- 45,374
December 31, 2004	7.5	0
June 30, 2005	8.0	23,576
December 31, 2005	8.5	24,038
June 30, 2006	8.0	0

* *Fair values are determined as the present values of future cash flows resulting from expected interest rate differentials, based on current prime rate, discounted at 8%.*

Regarding the fair values presented in the foregoing table, it should be assumed that the market (fair) values are precisely equal to the present value, at each valuation date (assumed to be the interest payment dates), of the differential future cash flows resulting from utilization of the swap. Future variable interest rates (prime + 1/2%) are assumed to be the same as the existing rates at each valuation date (i.e., there is no basis for any expectation of rate changes, and therefore the best estimate is that the current rate will persist over time). The discount rate, 8%, is assumed to be constant over time.

Thus, for example, the fair value of the swap at December 31, 2002, would be the present value of an annuity of seven payments (the number of remaining semiannual interest payments due) of $25,000 each (pay 8%, receive 7%, based on then-existing prime rate of 6.5%) to be made to the swap counterparty, discounted at an annual rate of 8% (using 4% for the semiannual discounting, which is a slight simplification). This computation yields a present value of a stream of seven $25,000 payments to the swap counterparty amounting to $150,051 at December 31, 2002, which is a liability to be reported by the entity at that date. The offset is a debit to other comprehensive income, since the hedge is (presumably) judged to be 100% effective in this case. Semiannual accounting entries will be as follows:

December 31, 2002

Interest expense	175,000	
Accrued interest (or cash)		175,000

To accrue or pay semiannual interest on the debt at the variable rate of prime + 1/2% (7.0%)

Interest expense	25,000	
Accrued interest (or cash)		25,000

To record net settlement on swap arrangement [8.0 - 7.0%]

Other comprehensive income	150,051	
Swap contract		150,051

To record the fair value of the swap contract as of this date (a net liability because fixed rate payable to counterparty of 8% exceeds floating rate receivable from counterparty of 7%)

June 30, 2003

Interest expense	162,500	
Accrued interest (or cash)		162,500

To accrue or pay semiannual interest on the debt at the variable rate of prime + 1/2% (6.5%)

Interest expense	37,500	
Accrued interest (or cash)		37,500

To record net settlement on swap arrangement [8.0 - 6.5%]

Other comprehensive income	46,529	
Swap contract		46,529

To record the fair value of the swap contract as of this date (increase in obligation because of further decline in prime rate)

December 31, 2003

Interest expense	175,000	
Accrued interest (or cash)		175,000

To accrue or pay semiannual interest on the debt at the variable rate of prime + 1/2% (7.0%)

Interest expense	25,000	
Accrued interest (or cash)		25,000

To record net settlement on swap arrangement [8.0 - 7.0%]

Swap contract	85,284	
Other comprehensive income		85,284

To record the fair value of the swap contract as of this date (decrease in obligation due to increase in prime rate)

June 30, 2004

Interest expense	187,500	
Accrued interest (or cash)		187,500

To accrue or pay semiannual interest on the debt at the variable rate of prime + 1/2% (7.5%)

Interest expense	12,500	
Accrued interest (or cash)		12,500

To record net settlement on swap arrangement [8.0 - 7.5%]

Swap contract	65,922	
Other comprehensive income		65,922

To record the fair value of the swap contract as of this date (decrease in obligation due to further increase in prime rate)

December 31, 2004

Interest expense	200,000	
Accrued interest (or cash)		200,000

To accrue or pay semiannual interest on the debt at the variable rate of prime + 1/2% (8.0%)

Interest expense	0	
Accrued interest (or cash)		0

To record net settlement on swap arrangement [8.0 - 8.0%]

Swap contract	45,374	
Other comprehensive income		45,374

To record the fair value of the swap contract as of this date (further increase in prime rate to the original rate of inception of the hedge eliminates fair value of the derivative)

June 30, 2005

Interest expense	212,500	
Accrued interest (or cash)		212,500

To accrue or pay semiannual interest on the debt at the variable rate of prime + 1/2% (8.5%)

Receivable from counterparty (or cash)	12,500	
Interest expense		12,500

To record net settlement on swap arrangement [8.0 - 8.5%], counterparty remits settlement

Swap contract	23,576	
Other comprehensive income		23,576

To record the fair value of the swap contract as of this date (increase in prime rate creates net asset position for derivative)

December 31, 2005

Interest expense	225,000	
Accrued interest (or cash)		225,000

To accrue or pay semiannual interest on the debt at the variable rate of prime + 1/2% (9.0%)

Receivable from counterparty (or cash)	25,000	
Interest expense		25,000

To record net settlement on swap arrangement [8.0 - 9.0%], counterparty remits settlement

Swap contract	462	
Other comprehensive income		462

To record the fair value of the swap contract as of this date (increase in asset value due to further rise in prime rate)

June 30, 2006 (Maturity)

Interest expense	212,500	
Accrued interest (or cash)		212,500

To accrue or pay semiannual interest on the debt at the variable rate of prime + 1/2% (8.5%)

Receivable from counterparty (or cash)	12,500	
Interest expense		12,500

Other comprehensive income	24,038	
Swap contract		24,038

To record the fair value of the swap contract as of this date (value declines to zero as expiration date approaches)

Example of an option on an interest rate swap

The facts of this example are a variation on the previous example. Abbott Corp. anticipates as of June 30, 2002, that as of June 30, 2004, it will become a borrower of $5 million with a fixed maturity four years hence (June 30, 2008). Based on its current credit rating, it expects to be able to borrow at prime + 1/2%. As of June 30, 2002, it is able to purchase, for a single payment of $25,000, a "swaption" (an option on an interest rate swap), calling for fixed pay at 8% and variable receipt at prime + 1/2%, on a notional amount of $5 million, for a term of four years. The option will expire in two years. At June 30, 2002, prime is 7.5%.

NOTE: The interest rate behavior in this example differs somewhat from the prior example, to better illustrate the "one-sidedness" of options, versus the obligation under a swap arrangement or other futures and forwards.

It will be assumed that the time value of the swaption expires ratably over the two years.

This swaption qualifies as a cash flow hedge under SFAS 133. However, while the change in fair value of the contract is an effective hedge of the cash flow variability of the prospective debt issuance, the premium paid is a reflection of the time value of money and is thus to be expensed ratably over the period that the swaption is outstanding.

The table below gives the prime rate at semiannual intervals including the two-year period prior to the debt issuance, plus the four years during which the forecasted debt (and the swap, if the option is exercised) will be outstanding, as well as the fair value of the swaption (and later, the swap itself) at these points in time.

Date	Prime rate (%)	Fair value of swaption/swap*
December 31, 2002	7.5	$ 0
June 30, 2003	8.0	77,925
December 31, 2003	6.5	0
June 30, 2004	7.0	- 84,159
December 31, 2004	7.5	0
June 30, 2005	8.0	65,527
December 31, 2005	8.5	111,296
June 30, 2006	8.0	45,374
December 31, 2006	8.0	34,689
June 30, 2007	7.5	0
December 31, 2007	7.5	0
June 30, 2008	7.0	0

* *Fair value is determined as the present value of future expected interest rate differentials, based on current prime rate, discounted at 8%. An "out of the money" swaption is valued at zero, since the option does not have to be exercised. Since the option is exercised on June 30, 2004, the value at that date is recorded, although negative.*

The value of the swaption contract is only recorded (unless and until exercised, of course, at which point it becomes a contractually binding swap) if it is positive, since if "out of the money" the holder would forego exercise in most instances and thus there is no liability by the holder to be reported. (This example is an illustration of the opposite, however, as despite having a negative value the option holder determines that exercise is advisable.) At June 30, 2003, for example, the swaption is an asset, since the reference variable rate (prime + 1/2% or 8.5%) is greater than the fixed swap rate of 8%, and thus the expectation is that the option will be exercised at expiration. This would, if present rates hold steady, which is the naïve assumption, result in a series of eight semiannual payments from the swap counterparty in the amount of $12,500. Discounting this at a nominal 8%, the present value as of the debt origination date (to be June 30, 2004) would be $84,159, which, when further discounted to June 30, 2003, yields a fair value of $77,925.

Note that the following period (December 31, 2003) prime drops to such an extent that the value of the swaption evaporates entirely (actually goes negative, which will not be reported since the holder is under no obligation to exercise it), and the carrying value is therefore eliminated. At expiration, the holder does (for this example) exercise, notwithstanding a negative fair value, and from that point forward the fair value of the swap will be reported, whether positive (an asset) or negative (a liability).

As noted above, assume that, at the option expiration date, despite the fact that prime + 1/2% is below the fixed pay rate on the swap, the management of Abbott Corp. is convinced that rates will climb over the four-year term of the loan, and thus exercises the swaption at that date. Accounting journal entries over the six years are as follows:

June 30, 2002

Swaption contract	25,000	
Cash		25,000

To record purchase premium on swaption contract

December 31, 2002

Loss on hedging transaction	6,250	
Swaption contract		6,250

To record change in time value of swaption contract—charge premium to income since this represents payment for time value of money, which expires ratably over two-year term

June 30, 2003

Swaption contract	77,925	
Other comprehensive income		77,925

To record the fair value of the swaption contract as of this date

Loss on hedging transaction	6,250	
Swaption contract		6,250

To record change in time value of swaption contract—charge premium to income since this represents payment for time value of money, which expires ratably over two-year term

December 31, 2003

Other comprehensive income	77,925	
Swaption contract		77,925

To record the change in fair value of the swaption contract as of this date; since contract is "out of the money," it is not written down below zero (i.e., a net liability is not reported)

Loss on hedging transaction	6,250	
Swaption contract		6,250

To record change in time value of swaption contract—charge premium to income since this represents payment for time value of money, which expires ratably over two-year term

June 30, 2004

Other comprehensive income	84,159	
Swap contract		84,159

To record the fair value of the swap contract as of this date—a net liability is reported since swap option was exercised

Loss on hedging transaction	6,250	
Swaption contract		6,250

To record change in time value of swaption contract—charge premium to income since this represents payment for time value of money, which expires ratably over two-year term

December 31, 2004

Interest expense	200,000	
Accrued interest (or cash)		200,000

To accrue or pay interest on the debt at the variable rate of prime + 1/2% (8.0%)

Interest expense	0	
Accrued interest (or cash)		0

To record net settlement on swap arrangement [8.0 - 8.0%]

Swap contract	84,159	
Other comprehensive income		84,159

To record the change in the fair value of the swap contract as of this date

June 30, 2005

Interest expense	212,500	
Accrued interest (or cash)		212,500

To accrue or pay interest on the debt at the variable rate of prime + 1/2% (8.5%)

Receivable from counterparty (or cash)	12,500	
Interest expense		12,500

To record net settlement on swap arrangement [8.0 - 8.5%]

Swap contract	65,527	
Other comprehensive income		65,527

To record the fair value of the swap contract as of this date

December 31, 2005

Interest expense	225,000	
Accrued interest (or cash)		225,000

To accrue or pay interest on the debt at the variable rate of prime + 1/2% (9.0%)

Receivable from counterparty (or cash)	25,000	
Interest expense		25,000

To record net settlement on swap arrangement [8.0 - 9.0%]

Swap contract	45,769	
Other comprehensive income		45,769

To record the fair value of the swap contract as of this date

June 30, 2006

Interest expense	212,500	
Accrued interest (or cash)		212,500

To accrue or pay interest on the debt at the variable rate of prime + 1/2% (8.5%)

Receivable from counterparty (or cash)	12,500	
Interest expense		12,500

To record net settlement on swap arrangement [8.0 - 8.5%]

Other comprehensive income	65,922	
Swap contract		65,922

To record the change in the fair value of the swap contract as of this date (declining prime rate causes swap to lose value)

December 31, 2006

Interest expense	212,500	
Accrued interest (or cash)		212,500

To accrue or pay interest on the debt at the variable rate of prime + 1/2% (8.5%)

Receivable from counterparty (or cash)	12,500	
Interest expense		12,500

To record net settlement on swap arrangement [8.0 - 8.5%]

Other comprehensive income	10,685	
Swap contract		10,685

To record the fair value of the swap contract as of this date (decline is due to passage of time, as the prime rate expectations have not changed from the earlier period)

June 30, 2007

Interest expense	200,000	
Accrued interest (or cash)		200,000

To accrue or pay interest on the debt at the variable rate of prime + 1/2% (8.0%)

Receivable from counterparty (or cash)	0	
Interest expense		0

To record net settlement on swap arrangement [8.0 - 8.0%]

Other comprehensive income	34,689	
Swap contract		34,689

To record the decline in the fair value of the swap contract to zero as of this date

December 31, 2007

Interest expense	200,000	
Accrued interest (or cash)		200,000

To accrue or pay interest on the debt at the variable rate of prime + 1/2% (8.0%)

Receivable from counterparty (or cash)	0	
Interest expense		0

To record net settlement on swap arrangement [8.0 - 8.0%]

Swap contract	0	
Other comprehensive income		0

No change to the zero fair value of the swap contract as of this date

June 30, 2008 (Maturity)

Interest expense	187,500	
Accrued interest (or cash)		187,500

To accrue or pay interest on the debt at the variable rate of prime + 1/2% (7.5%)

Interest expense	12,500	
Accrued interest (or cash)		12,500

To record net settlement on swap arrangement [8.0 - 7.5%]

Other comprehensive income	0	
Swap contract		0

No change to the zero fair value of the swap contract, which expires as of this date

Effectiveness of cash flow hedges. The assumption of no ineffectiveness in a cash flow hedge between an interest-bearing financial instrument and an interest rate swap can be assumed if all of the following conditions are met:

1. The principal amount and the notional amount of the swap match;
2. The fair value of the swap is zero at origin;
3. The net settlements under the swap are computed the same way on each settlement date;
4. The financial instrument is not prepayable; and
5. The terms are typical for those instruments and don't invalidate the assumption of effectiveness.
6. All variable rate interest payments or receipts on the instrument during the swap term are designated as hedged and none beyond that term;
7. No floor or cap on the variable rate of the swap exists unless the variable rate instrument has one. If the instrument does, the swap must have a comparable (not necessarily equal) one;
8. Repricing dates match; and
9. The index base for the variable rates match.

The variable rate on the instrument is not required to exactly match the variable rate on the swap. The fixed and variable rates on the swap can be changed by the same amount.

Example of using options to hedge future purchase of inventory

Friendly Chemicals Corp. uses petroleum as a feedstock from which it produces a range of chemicals for sale to producers of synthetic fabrics and other consumer goods. It is concerned about the rising price of oil and decides to hedge a major purchase it plans to make in mid-2002. Oil futures and options are traded on the New York Mercantile exchange and other markets; Friendly decides to use options rather than futures because it is only interested in protecting itself from a price increase; if prices decline, it wishes to reap that benefit rather than suffer the loss which would result from holding a futures contract in a declining market environment.

At December 31, 2001, Friendly projects a need for ten million barrels of crude oil of a defined grade to be purchased by mid-2002; this will suffice for production through mid-2003. The current world price for this grade of crude is $14.50 per barrel, but prices have been rising recently. Management desires to limit its crude oil costs to no higher than $15.75 per barrel, and accordingly purchases, at a cost of $2 million, an option to purchase up to ten million barrels at a cost of $15.55 per barrel (which, when added to the option premium, would make the total cost $15.75 per barrel if the full ten million barrels are acquired), at any time through December 2002.

Management has studied the behavior of option prices and has concluded that changes in option prices which relate to time value are not correlated to price changes and hence are ineffective in hedging price changes. On the other hand, changes in option prices which pertain to pricing changes (intrinsic value changes) are highly effective as hedging vehicles. The table below reports the value of these options, analyzed in terms of time value and intrinsic value, over the period from December 2001 through December 2002.

| | Price of | Fair value of option relating to | |
Date	oil/barrel	Time value*	Intrinsic value
December 31, 2001	$14.50	$2,000,000	$ 0
January 31, 2002	14.90	1,900,000	0
February 28, 2002	15.30	1,800,000	0
March 31, 2002	15.80	1,700,000	2,500,000
April 30, 2002	16.00	1,600,000	4,500,000
May 31, 2002	15.85	1,500,000	3,000,000
June 30, 2002**	16.00	700,000	2,250,000
July 31, 2002	15.60	650,000	250,000
August 31, 2002	15.50	600,000	0
September 30, 2002	15.75	550,000	1,000,000
October 31, 2002	15.80	500,000	1,250,000
November 30, 2002	15.85	450,000	1,500,000
December 31, 2002***	15.90	400,000	1,750,000

*	*This example does not address how the time value of options would be computed in practice.*
**	*Options for five million barrels exercised; remainder held until end of December, then sold.*
***	*Values cited are immediately prior to sale of remaining options.*

At the end of June 2002, Friendly Chemicals exercises options for 5 million barrels, paying $15.55 per barrel for oil selling on the world markets for $16.00 each. It holds the remaining options until December, when it sells these for an aggregate price of $2.1 million, a slight discount to the nominal fair value at that date.

The inventory acquired in mid-2002 is processed and included in goods available for sale. Sales of these goods, in terms of the five million barrels of crude oil which were consumed in their production, are as follows:

Date	Equivalent barrels sold in month	Equivalent barrels on hand at month end
June 30, 2002	300,000	4,700,000
July 31, 2002	250,000	4,450,000
August 31, 2002	400,000	4,050,000
September 30, 2002	350,000	3,700,000
October 31, 2002	550,000	3,150,000
November 30, 2002	500,000	2,650,000
December 31, 2002	650,000	2,000,000

Based on the foregoing facts, the journal entries prepared on a **monthly** basis (for illustrative purposes) for the period December 2001 through December 2002 are as follows:

December 31, 2001

Option contract	2,000,000	
Cash		2,000,000

To record purchase premium on option contract for up to ten million barrels of oil at price of $15.55 per barrel

January 31, 2002

Loss on hedging transaction	100,000	
Option contract		100,000

To record change in time value of option contract—charge premium to income since this represents payment for time value of money, which expires ratably over two-year term and does not qualify for hedge accounting treatment

Option contract	0	
Other comprehensive income		0

To reflect change in intrinsic value of option contracts (no value at this date)

February 28, 2002

Loss on hedging transaction	100,000	
Option contract		100,000

To record change in time value of option contract—charge premium to income since this represents payment for time value of money, which expires ratably over two-year term and does not qualify for hedge accounting treatment

Option contract	0	
Other comprehensive income		0

To reflect change in intrinsic value of option contracts (no value at this date)

March 31, 2002

Loss on hedging transaction	100,000	
Option contract		100,000

To record change in time value of option contract—charge premium to income since this represents payment for time value of money, which expires ratably over two-year term and does not qualify for hedge accounting treatment

Option contract	2,500,000	
Other comprehensive income		2,500,000

To reflect change in intrinsic value of option contracts

April 30, 2002

Loss on hedging transaction	100,000	
Option contract		100,000

To record change in time value of option contract—charge premium to income since this represents payment for time value of money, which expires ratably over two-year term and does not qualify for hedge accounting treatment

Option contract	2,000,000	
Other comprehensive income		2,000,000

To reflect change in intrinsic value of option contracts (further increase in value)

May 31, 2002

Loss on hedging transaction	100,000	
Option contract		100,000

To record change in time value of option contract—charge premium to income since this represents payment for time value of money, which expires ratably over two-year term and does not qualify for hedge accounting treatment

Other comprehensive income	1,500,000	
Option contract		1,500,000

To reflect change in intrinsic value of option contracts (decline in value)

June 30, 2002

Loss on hedging transaction	800,000	
Option contract		800,000

To record change in time value of option contract—charge premium to income since this represents payment for time value of money, which expires ratably over two-year term and does not qualify for hedge accounting treatment; since one-half the options were exercised in June, the remaining unexpensed time value of that portion is also entirely written off at this time

Option contract	1,500,000	
Other comprehensive income		1,500,000

To reflect change in intrinsic value of option contracts (further increase in value) **before** *accounting for exercise of options on five million barrels*

June 30 intrinsic value of options before exercise	4,500,000
Allocation to oil purchased at $15.55	2,250,000
Remaining intrinsic value of option	2,250,000

The allocation to exercised options will be maintained in other comprehensive income until transferred to cost of goods sold as a contra cost, as the five million barrels are sold, at the rate of 45¢ per equivalent barrel ($16.00 – $15.55).

Inventory	77,750,000	
Cash (or accounts payable)		77,750,000

To record purchase of five million barrels of oil at option price of $15.55/barrel

Inventory	2,250,000	
Option contract		2,250,000

To increase the recorded value of the inventory to include the fair value of options given up (exercised) in acquiring the oil (taken together, the cash purchase price and the fair value of options surrendered add to $16 per barrel, the world market price at date of purchase)

Cost of goods sold	4,800,000	
Inventory		4,800,000

To record cost of goods sold (300,000 barrels at $16) before amortizing deferred hedging gain in other comprehensive income

Other comprehensive income	135,000	
Cost of goods sold		135,000

To amortize deferred hedging gain at rate of 45¢ per barrel sold

July 31, 2002

Loss on hedging transaction	50,000	
Option contract		50,000

To record change in time value of option contract—charge premium to income since this represents payment for time value of money, which expires ratably over two-year term, and does not qualify for hedge accounting treatment

Other comprehensive income	2,000,000	
Option contract		2,000,000

To reflect change in intrinsic value of remaining option contracts (decline in value)

Cost of goods sold	4,000,000	
Inventory		4,000,000

To record cost of goods sold (250,000 barrels at $16) before amortizing deferred hedging gain in other comprehensive income

Other comprehensive income	112,500	
Cost of goods sold		112,500

To amortize deferred hedging gain at rate of 45¢ per barrel sold

August 31, 2002

Loss on hedging transaction	50,000	
Option contract		50,000

To record change in time value of option contract—charge premium to income since this represents payment for time value of money, which expires ratably over two-year term, and does not qualify for hedge accounting treatment

Other comprehensive income	250,000	
Option contract		250,000

To reflect change in intrinsic value of remaining option contracts (decline in value to zero)

Cost of goods sold	6,400,000	
Inventory		6,400,000

To record cost of goods sold (400,000 barrels at $16) before amortizing deferred hedging gain in other comprehensive income

Other comprehensive income	180,000	
Cost of goods sold		180,000

To amortize deferred hedging gain at rate of 45¢ per barrel sold

September 30, 2002

Loss on hedging transaction	50,000	
Option contract		50,000

To record change in time value of option contract—charge premium to income since this represents payment for time value of money, which expires ratably over two-year term, and does not qualify for hedge accounting treatment

Option contract	1,000,000	
Other comprehensive income		1,000,000

To reflect change in intrinsic value of remaining option contracts (increase in value)

| Cost of goods sold | 5,600,000 | |
| Inventory | | 5,600,000 |

To record cost of goods sold (350,000 barrels at $16) before amortizing deferred hedging gain in other comprehensive income

| Other comprehensive income | 157,500 | |
| Cost of goods sold | | 157,500 |

To amortize deferred hedging gain at rate of 45¢ per barrel sold

October 31, 2002

| Loss on hedging transaction | 50,000 | |
| Option contract | | 50,000 |

To record change in time value of option contract—charge premium to income since this represents payment for time value of money, which expires ratably over two-year term, and does not qualify for hedge accounting treatment

| Option contract | 250,000 | |
| Other comprehensive income | | 250,000 |

To reflect change in intrinsic value of remaining option contracts (further increase in value)

| Cost of goods sold | 8,800,000 | |
| Inventory | | 8,800,000 |

To record cost of goods sold (550,000 barrels at $16) before amortizing deferred hedging gain in other comprehensive income

| Other comprehensive income | 247,500 | |
| Cost of goods sold | | 247,500 |

To amortize deferred hedging gain at rate of 45¢ per barrel sold

November 30, 2002

| Loss on hedging transaction | 50,000 | |
| Option contract | | 50,000 |

To record change in time value of option contract—charge premium to income since this represents payment for time value of money, which expires ratably over two-year term, and does not qualify for hedge accounting treatment

| Option contract | 250,000 | |
| Other comprehensive income | | 250,000 |

To reflect change in intrinsic value of remaining option contracts (further increase in value)

| Cost of goods sold | 8,000,000 | |
| Inventory | | 8,000,000 |

To record cost of goods sold (500,000 barrels at $16) before amortizing deferred hedging gain in other comprehensive income

| Other comprehensive income | 225,000 | |
| Cost of goods sold | | 225,000 |

To amortize deferred hedging gain at rate of 45¢ per barrel sold

December 31, 2002

| Loss on hedging transaction | 50,000 | |
| Option contract | | 50,000 |

To record change in time value of option contract—charge premium to income since this represents payment for time value of money, which expires ratably over two-year term, and does not qualify for hedge accounting treatment

Option contract	250,000	
Other comprehensive income		250,000

To reflect change in intrinsic value of remaining option contracts (further increase in value) before sale of options

Cost of goods sold	10,400,000	
Inventory		10,400,000

To record cost of goods sold (650,000 barrels at $16) before amortizing deferred hedging gain in other comprehensive income

Other comprehensive income	292,500	
Cost of goods sold		292,500

To amortize deferred hedging gain at rate of 45¢ per barrel sold

Cash	2,100,000	
Loss on sale of options	50,000	
Option contract		2,150,000

Other comprehensive income	1,750,000	
Gain on sale of options		1,750,000

To record sale of remaining option contracts; the cash price was $50,000 lower than carrying value of asset sold (options having unexpired time value of $400,000 plus intrinsic value of $1,750,000), but transfer of other comprehensive income to income recognizes formerly deferred gain; since no further inventory purchases are planned in connection with this hedging activity, the unrealized gain is taken into income

Note that at December 31, 2002, other comprehensive income has a remaining credit balance of $900,000, which represents the deferred gain pertaining to the two million equivalent barrels of oil in inventory. As this is sold, the other comprehensive income will be transferred to cost of goods sold as a reduction of cost of sales.

Discontinuance of a cash flow hedge. The accounting for a cash flow hedge should not continue if any of the events below occur.

1. The criteria are no longer met;
2. The derivative instrument expires or is sold, terminated or exercised; or
3. The designation is removed by management.

The net gain or loss in accumulated other comprehensive income should remain there until it is properly reclassified when the hedged transaction affects earnings. If it is probable that the original forecasted transactions won't occur, the net gain or loss in accumulated other comprehensive income should immediately be reclassified into earnings.

If the cash flow hedge is discontinued, a new hedging relationship may be designated with a different hedging instrument and/or a different hedged item as long as the criteria established in SFAS 133 are met.

Ineffectiveness of a cash flow hedge. In assessing the effectiveness of a cash flow hedge, the time value of money generally will need to be considered, if significant in the circumstances. Doing so becomes especially important if the hedging instrument involves periodic cash settlements. For example, a **tailing strategy** with futures contracts is a situation in which an entity likely would reflect the time value of money. When employing such a strategy, the entity adjusts the size or contract amount of futures contracts used in a hedge so that earnings (or expense) from reinvestment (or funding) of daily settlement gains (or losses) on the futures do not distort the results of the hedge. To assess offset of expected cash flows when a tailing strategy has been used, an entity could reflect the time value of money, possibly comparing the present value of the hedged forecasted cash flow with the results of the hedging instrument.

As with fair value hedges, SFAS 133 does not provide a quantitative definition of **hedging effectiveness** for cash flow hedges. Again, it is useful in this regard to contemplate the similar international accounting standard, IAS 39, which specifies that a hedge is regarded as highly effective if, at inception and throughout the life of the hedge, the enterprise can expect that the change in cash flows of the hedging instrument and the hedged item will "almost fully offset." Actual results within a range of 80 - 125% could reasonably be expected to qualify as effective.

Impairment. All assets or liabilities designated as cash flow hedges are subject to normal GAAP requirements for impairment. Those requirements are to be applied, however, after hedge accounting has been applied for the period. Since the hedging instrument is a separate asset or liability, its expected cash flow or fair value is not considered in applying the impairment criteria to the hedged item. If an impairment loss or recovery on a hedged forecasting asset or liability is recognized, any offsetting amount should be immediately reclassified from accumulated other comprehensive income into earnings.

Expanded application of interest rate hedging. SFAS 138 has amended SFAS 133 to permit the use of hedge accounting where the interest rate being hedged is the "benchmark interest rate." As used in the standard, this rate will be either the risk-free rate (i.e., that applicable to direct Treasury borrowings) or the LIBOR swap rate. LIBOR-based swaps in fact are the most commonly employed interest rate hedging vehicles, and it was the persistence of requests made to the FASB's derivatives implementation group regarding the application of hedge accounting to such swaps that resulted in this amendment.

The FASB has thus concluded that, with respect to the separation of interest rate risk and credit risk, the risk of changes in credit sector spread and any credit spread attributable to a specific borrower should be encompassed in credit risk rather than interest rate risk. Under such an approach, an entity would be permitted to designate the risk of changes in the risk-free rate as the hedged risk, and any spread above that rate would be deemed to reflect credit risk. The Board concluded that considering all the effects of credit risk together was more understandable and more operational than this distinction between interest rate risk and credit risk that was at first set forth in the implementation guidance for SFAS 133.

SFAS 138 requires that all contractual cash flows be used in determining the changes in fair value of the hedged item when benchmark interest rates are being employed. In other words, cash flows pertaining to the portion of interest payments which is related to the entity's credit risk (the risk premium over the benchmark rate) cannot be excluded from the computation.

The accounting for an interest rate hedge using a benchmark rate is very similar to that illustrated beginning on page 192 of this chapter. However, the variable rate used, rather than reflecting the credit riskiness of the party doing the hedging (which was prime + ½% in that illustration), would instead be the benchmark rate (e.g., the rate on Treasury five-year notes). Since changes in the benchmark rate might not exactly track the changes in the underlying instrument (due to changes in the "credit spread" which are a reflection of changes in the underlying party's perceived credit risk), the hedge will likely be imperfect, such that a net gain or loss will be reflected in periodic earnings.

Foreign Currency Hedges

The FASB's basic objectives in hedge accounting for foreign currency exposure are

1. To continue to permit the hedge accounting required under SFAS 52; and
2. To increase the consistency of accounting guidance by broadening the scope of hedges that are eligible for this treatment.

Unlike SFAS 52, this standard allows hedges of forecasted foreign currency transactions, including some intercompany transactions. Hedging foreign currency intercompany cash flows with foreign currency options is a common practice that is allowed under certain conditions by EITF 91-1. SFAS 133 modifies that accounting to permit using other derivative instruments (forward contracts, etc.) because the accounting for all derivative instruments should be the same.

SFAS 133 precluded hedge accounting for an asset or liability that is remeasured for changes in price attributable to the risk being hedged when those changes are reported currently in earnings. It also precluded fair value or cash flow hedge accounting for foreign currency risk associated with any asset or liability that is denominated in a foreign currency and remeasured into the functional currency under SFAS 52. Subsequently, the FASB considered removing the preclusion for any asset or the liability denominated in a foreign currency because, even though the transaction gain or loss on the undesignated asset or liability and the change in fair value of the undesignated derivative were reported currently in earnings, different measurement criteria were used for each instrument, which created volatility in earnings. It eventually decided to permit all recognized foreign-currency-denominated assets and liabilities for which a foreign currency transaction gain or loss is recognized in earnings to be hedged items.

Designated hedging instruments and hedged items qualify for fair value hedge accounting and cash flow hedge accounting under SFAS 138 only if all of the criteria in SFAS 133 for fair value hedge accounting and cash flow hedge accounting are met. The FASB concluded that fair value hedges could be used for all recognized foreign-currency-denominated asset or liability hedging situations and that cash flow hedges could be used for recognized foreign-currency-denominated asset or liability hedging situations in which all of the varability in the functional-currency-equivalent cash flows are eliminated by the effect of the hedge. Remeasurement of the foreign-currency-denominated assets and liabilities will continue to be based on the guidance in SFAS 52, which requires remeasurement based on spot exchange rates, regardless of whether a fair value hedging relationship or a cash flow hedging relationship exists.

Foreign currency net investment hedge. Either a derivative instrument or a nonderivative financial instrument (that can result in a foreign currency transaction gain or loss under SFAS 52) can be designated as a hedge of a foreign currency exposure of a net investment in a foreign operation. The gain or loss from the designated instrument to the extent that it is effective is reported as a translation adjustment. The hedged net investment is accounted for under SFAS 52.

Foreign currency unrecognized firm commitment hedge. Either a derivative instrument or a nonderivative financial instrument (that can result in a foreign currency transaction gain or loss under SFAS 52) can be designated as a fair value hedge of an unrecognized firm commitment (or a specific portion) attributable to foreign currency. If the criteria are met, this hedging relationship is accounted for as a fair value hedge. (An example appears in Chapter 21, Foreign Currency.)

Foreign currency available-for-sale security hedge. Only a derivative instrument can be designated as a fair value hedge of an available-for-sale **debt** security (or a specific portion) attributable to foreign currency. If the criteria are met, this hedging relationship is accounted for as a fair value hedge. For an available-for-sale **equity** security to be accounted for as a fair value hedge, it must meet all of the fair value hedge criteria **and** the following two requirements:

1. The security **cannot** be traded on an exchange (or similar marketplace) denominated in the investor's functional currency; and
2. Dividends (or other cash flows) to the holders must be denominated in the same foreign currency as that expected to be received upon the sale of the security.

If the available-for-sale equity security qualifies as a foreign currency hedge, the change in fair value from foreign exchange risk is reported in earnings and not in other comprehensive income.

Any gain or loss on a designated nonderivative hedging instrument from foreign currency risk is determined under SFAS 52 (as the increase or decrease in functional currency cash flows produced by the change in spot exchange rates) and is reported in earnings along with the change in the carrying amount of the hedged firm commitment.

Foreign currency denominated forecasted transaction. Only a derivative instrument can be designated as a cash flow hedge of a foreign currency denominated forecasted transaction. The parties to this transaction can either be external or intercompany. To qualify for hedge accounting, **all** of the following criteria must be met:

1. An operating unit with foreign currency exposure is a party to the derivative instrument;
2. The transaction is denominated in a currency that is **not** the functional currency;
3. All of the criteria for a cash flow hedge are met (with the possible exception of allowing a qualifying intercompany transaction); and
4. If a group of individual transactions is involved, both an inflow and an outflow of foreign currency cannot be included in the same group.

If the foregoing criteria are met, this hedging relationship is accounted for as a cash flow hedge.

Using certain intercompany derivatives as hedging instruments in cash flow hedges of foreign currency risk in the consolidated financial statements. SFAS 138 has amended SFAS 133 to permit the use of intercompany derivatives as the hedging instruments in cash flow hedges of foreign currency risk in the consolidated financial statements, if those intercompany derivatives are offset by unrelated third-party contracts on a net basis. The new standard defines an "internal derivative" as a foreign currency derivative contract that has been entered into with another member of a consolidated group and which can be a hedging instrument in a foreign currency cash flow hedge of a forecasted borrowing, purchase, or sale or an unrecognized firm commitment in the consolidated financial statements only if the following two conditions are satisfied. First, from the perspective of the member of the consolidated group using the derivative as a hedging instrument, specific criteria for foreign currency cash flow hedge accounting are satisfied. Second, the members of the consolidated group who are not using the derivative as a hedging instrument must either (1) enter into a derivative contract with an unrelated third party to offset the exposure that results from that internal derivative or (2) if certain defined conditions are met, enter into derivative contracts with unrelated third parties that would offset, on a net basis for each foreign currency, the foreign exchange risk arising from multiple internal derivative contracts.

Organizations That Do Not Report Earnings

Not-for-profits or other organizations not reporting earnings should recognize gains or losses on nonhedging derivative instruments and hedging instruments as a change in net assets. Changes in the carrying amount of the hedged items are also recognized as a change in net assets.

Organizations that do not report earnings cannot use cash flow hedges. If the hedging instrument is a foreign currency net investment hedge, it is accounted for in the same manner as described above.

Summary of Accounting for Hedges

		Type of hedge—SFAS 133	
Attribute	*Fair value*	*Cash flow*	*Foreign currency (FC)*
Types of hedging instruments permitted	Derivatives	Derivatives	Derivatives or nonderivatives depending on the type of hedge
Balance sheet valuation of hedging instrument	Fair value	Fair value	Fair value
Recognition of gain or loss on changes in value of hedging instrument	Currently in earnings	Effective portion currently as a component of other comprehensive income (OCI) and reclassified to earnings in future period(s) that forecasted transaction affects earnings Ineffective portion currently in earnings	**FC denominated firm commitment** Currently in earnings **Available-for-sale security (AFS)** Currently in earnings **Forecasted FC transaction** Same as cash flow hedge **Net investment in a foreign operation** OCI as part of the cumulative translation adjustment to the extent it is effective as a hedge
Recognition of gain or loss on changes in the fair value of the hedged item	Currently in earnings	Not applicable; these hedges are not associated with recognized assets or liabilities	**FC denominated firm commitment** Currently in earnings **Available-for-sale security (AFS)** Currently in earnings **Forecasted FC transaction** Not applicable; same as cash flow hedge

Disclosures

SFAS 133 requires certain disclosures for derivative instruments and nonderivative instruments designated and qualifying as hedging instruments. Specifically required are the objectives for holding or issuing the instruments, the context needed to understand the objectives, the strategies for achieving them, the risk management policy and a description of items or transactions which are hedged for each of the following:

1. Fair value hedges;
2. Cash flow hedges;
3. Foreign currency net investment hedges; and
4. All other derivatives.

Derivative instruments not designated as hedges are to have the purpose of their activity disclosed. Qualitative disclosures concerning the use of derivative instruments are encouraged, particularly in a context of overall risk management strategies employed by the entity. The FASB also encourages disclosure of similar quantitative information about other nonderivative financial instruments or nonfinancial assets and liabilities related by activity to derivative instruments.

Hedge disclosures. In addition to the above, for every reporting period for which a complete set of financial statements is issued, there are required disclosures by hedge type.

Fair value hedges. For all designated and qualified instruments and the related hedged items that give rise to foreign currency transaction gains or losses under SFAS 52, disclosure is required of the net gain or loss included in earnings, a description of where it is reported, and the amounts due to

1. Hedge ineffectiveness;
2. Components that were excluded from the assessment of effectiveness; and
3. Hedged firm commitments that no longer qualify as hedges.

Cash flow hedges. For all designated and qualified instruments and the related hedged items in cash flow hedges, the following are disclosed:

1. The net gain or loss in earnings, a description of where it is reported, and the amounts due to

   a. Hedge ineffectiveness; and
   b. Components that were excluded from the assessment of effectiveness;

2. A description of events that will result in reclassification of amounts in accumulated other comprehensive income to earnings and the net amount expected to be reclassified during the next twelve months;
3. The maximum length of time of any cash flow hedges of forecasted transactions (excluding those relating to payment of variable interest on existing financial instruments); and
4. The amount reclassified from accumulated other comprehensive income into earnings because a cash flow hedge was discontinued due to it being probable that the original forecasted transactions wouldn't occur.

Foreign currency net investment hedges. For all such designated and qualified instruments that give rise to foreign currency transaction gains or losses under SFAS 52, the net gain or loss that is included in the cumulative translation adjustment.

Comprehensive income. The net gain or loss from cash flow hedges on derivative instruments reported in other comprehensive income must be shown as a separate classification. Accumulated other comprehensive income disclosures should show separately the following:

1. Beginning and ending accumulated derivative instrument gain or loss;
2. Net change from current period hedging transactions; and
3. Net amount of reclassifications to earnings.

Other Pronouncements Affected by Issuance of SFAS 133

SFAS 133 has superseded SFAS 80, 105, and 119, and has amended ARB 43, and SFAS 52, 60, 65, 95, 107, 113, 115, 124, 125, and 126, as well as FASB TB 79-19. It has nullified or modified a number of EITF consensuses. (SFAS 140 later replaced SFAS 125, although these are very similar in most regards.)

SFAS 107 was amended by SFAS 133 to include the disclosure requirements concerning concentrations of credit risk for all financial instruments from superseded SFAS 105. The disclosure of the fair value of all financial instruments is still required, and SFAS 107 is relied on to provide valuation guidance for measuring fair value in the new standard.

SFAS 133 is broader in scope than the superseded SFAS 119 because its focus includes not only derivative financial instruments but, rather, all derivative instruments. The result is the inclusion of some contracts that are settled by a commodity or nonfinancial asset. In addition, the scope change means that certain contracts that were included under SFAS 119 may now be excluded and certain contracts that were excluded may now be included.

Transition

At initial application, the following is required:

1. All freestanding derivative instruments are recognized as assets or liabilities at fair value. At this date only, a compound derivative instrument composed of a foreign currency derivative and another derivative can be separated into two parts with each accounted for at fair value not to exceed the aggregate the fair value of the compound derivative instrument.
2. Differences between fair value and carrying amounts of derivative instruments are reported as transition adjustments as explained further below.
3. Offsetting gains and losses on hedged assets, liabilities, and firm commitments are recognized by adjusting carrying amounts.
4. Deferred losses or gains on derivative instruments that are reported as assets or liabilities are derecognized and reported as transition adjustments.
5. Gains or losses on derivative instruments reported in other comprehensive income as fair value hedges of available-for-sale securities are reported as transition adjustments.
6. Gains or losses on derivative instruments reported in accumulated other comprehensive income because of cash flow hedges of a forecasted transaction related to available-for-sale securities should remain in accumulated other comprehensive income and are **not** reported as transition adjustments.

7. Gains or losses on derivative instruments that adjusted the carrying amounts of recognized hedged assets or liabilities prior to initial application are not affected and are **not** reported as transition adjustments.

8. With respect to embedded derivatives, SFAS 137 amended SFAS 133 to permit the entity to choose to either (1) recognize as assets or liabilities all embedded derivatives required under SFAS 133 to be separated from their host contracts or (2) select either January 1, 1998, or January 1, 1999, as a transition date for embedded derivatives. If the entity chose option (2), it had to recognize as separate assets and/or liabilities only derivatives embedded in hybrid instruments issued, acquired, or substantively modified by the entity on or after the selected transition date. This election was to be applied on an "all-or-none" basis and was not to be applied selectively to hybrid instruments. If separated, the following should be considered in determining the transition adjustment:

    a. The host contract's carrying amount should be the fair value at date of issue or acquisition adjusted for subsequent activity (cash receipts or payments and/or amortization of premiums or discounts necessitated by the separation of the embedded derivative instrument).

    b. The embedded derivative instrument's carrying amount should be the fair value at initial application.

    c. The transition adjustment is the difference between the sum of the fair values in a. and b. above and the previous carrying amount of the hybrid instrument. A hedging designation is not permitted to be made retroactively even if it could have been made had the embedded derivative been initially separated from the host contract.

The transition adjustments are to be reported in net income or in other comprehensive income as required. It is considered to be a cumulative effect of a change in accounting principle under APB 20. The accounting for the derivative instrument under GAAP before the initial application of SFAS 133 is the determining factor for reporting the transition adjustment in earnings, in other comprehensive income, or in allocating it between both. Specifically, the transition adjustment to a derivative instrument should be reported as follows:

1. If designated as a cash flow hedge of a forecasted transaction, it is reported as a cumulative effect adjustment of accumulated other comprehensive income.

2. If designated as a fair value hedge of an asset, liability, or a firm commitment, it is reported as a cumulative effect adjustment of net income. The gain or loss on the difference between the fair value of the hedged item and its carrying amount is recognized by adjusting the carrying amount at initial application to the extent of the offsetting transition adjustment for the derivative instrument. That adjustment is also reported as a cumulative effect adjustment of net income. In the case of a hedged available-for-sale secu-

rity, the transition adjustment gain or loss on the derivative instrument reported in accumulated other comprehensive income together with the gain or loss on the related security (to the extent of the offset) is reclassified to earnings as a cumulative effect adjustment of both net income and accumulated other comprehensive income.

3. If designated in a multiple hedge of cash flow of a forecasted transaction and fair value of an asset or liability, it is allocated between them as a cumulative effect adjustment of both accumulated other comprehensive income and net income and is reported as in 1. and 2. above. Any gain or loss on the hedged item is reported as in 2. above.

All other transition adjustments are reported as cumulative effect adjustments of net income.

Transition adjustment amounts reported as cumulative effect adjustments of accumulated other comprehensive income are to be subsequently reclassified into earnings in the normal manner under SFAS 133. In the year of initial application, the amounts of gains and losses from the transition adjustment that are being reclassified from accumulated other comprehensive income into earnings during the next twelve months must be disclosed.

At initial application, held-to-maturity securities (including financial assets received or retained in a previous desecuritization) can be transferred to the available-for-sale or trading categories without calling into question the intent to hold other debt securities to maturity in the future. This movement may be desired so that the security or some component (interest rates, fair value, etc.) can be designated as the hedged item. The unrealized holding gain or loss is reported as required by SFAS 115 and is included in the transition adjustment discussed above.

At initial application, available-for-sale securities can be transferred to the trading category. After any related transition adjustment has been recognized, any remaining unrealized holding gain or loss is reclassified into earnings (not as a transition adjustment) as required by SFAS 115. If a derivative instrument was being used as a hedge of cash flows associated with a forecasted transaction related to an available-for-sale security transferred into the trading category upon adoption and the entity had reported a gain or loss in other comprehensive income, the gain or loss should be reclassified into earnings (not as a transition adjustment) upon transfer.

With regard to servicing rights (as set forth in SFAS 140, which supersedes SFAS 125), for contracts in existence before January 1997, the previously recognized servicing rights and "excess servicing" receivables, to the extent these did not exceed the contractually specified servicing fees, were to be combined and reported, net, as a servicing asset or liability. Any excess over the contractually agreed fees is required to be reclassified as an "interest-only strip" and the subsequent remeasurement provisions of SFAS 140 are to be separately applied to the servicing asset and the interest-only strip.

EMERGING ISSUES TASK FORCE CONSENSUS SUMMARIES

Short-Term Investments

85-9   Revenue Recognition of Options to Purchase Stock of Another Entity

If debt is issued with detachable warrants to acquire the stock of **another** entity, no income should be recognized until the warrant is exercised or expires and a liability should be recorded for the value of the warrant. No consensus was reached on the accounting for exchangeable debt. In practice, most accountants follow APB 14. The SEC observer, however, did not believe APB 14 was applicable and thought that separation was required.

86-40   Investments in Open-End Mutual Funds That Invest in US Government Securities

The investment in the mutual fund should be at fair value per SFAS 115.

96-11   Accounting for Forward Contracts and Purchased Options to Acquire Securities Covered by FASB Statement 115

This issue addresses the accounting only when terms require physical settlement. Forward contracts and purchased options with no intrinsic value at acquisition should be designated and accounted for as prescribed in SFAS 115.

96-12   Recognition of Interest Income and Balance Sheet Classification of Structured Notes

When recognizing interest income on structured note securities in an available-for-sale or held-to-maturity portfolio, the retrospective interest method should be used if three conditions are satisfied. These are

1. Either the original investment amount or the maturity amount of the contractual principal is at risk
2. Return of investment on note is subject to volatility arising from
    a. No stated rate or stated rate is not a constant percentage or in same direction as changes in market-based interest rates or interest rate index, or
    b. Fixed or variable coupon rate is lower than that for interest for traditional notes with similar maturity and a portion of potential yield is based on occurrence of future circumstances or events
3. Contractual maturity of bond is based on a specific index or on occurrence of specific events or situations outside the control of contractual parties

96-15 Accounting for the Effects of Changes in Foreign Currency Exchange Rates on Foreign-Currency-Denominated Available-for-Sale Debt Securities (AFS)

Total changes in fair value of foreign-currency-denominated AFS debt securities should be reported in stockholders' equity.

Foreign currency transaction losses and gains arising from a foreign-currency-denominated liability or forward exchange contract should be reported in the SFAS 115 component of stockholders' equity. Then, it would offset the change in market value of a foreign-currency-denominated AFS debt security if the foreign-currency-denominated AFS debt security or forward exchange contract is either identified or does serve as a hedge of the foreign-currency-denominated AFS debt security.

Options

90-17 Hedging Foreign Currency Risks with Purchased Options

SFAS 52 foreign currency risk is risk associated with transactions and commitments in currencies other than the transacting entity's functional currency. Hedge accounting is appropriate for purchased foreign currency options used to hedge an anticipated transaction if the conditions of SFAS 80 are met. Specifically

1. The hedged item must expose the entity to foreign currency risks.
2. The option must be designated as a hedge and must reduce exposure to risk.
3. Expected terms and significant characteristics of the transaction must be identified.
4. It is probable that the transaction will occur.

Consensus was reached that purchased options having little or no intrinsic value at the time designated as a hedge and meeting the high correlation criteria **would** qualify for hedge accounting in the following situations:

1. Hedging foreign export sales
2. Hedging identifiable anticipated transactions with risk

The above options would **not** qualify for hedge accounting in the following situations:

1. Hedging foreign subsidiary sales
2. Hedging anticipated transactions with no enterprise risk
3. Hedging net income
4. Hedging competitive risk

The propriety of hedge accounting for "anticipated sales for several years" depends on the assessment of the transaction using SFAS 80 criteria. The further into the future the transaction is expected, the less likely it will meet the criteria.

Foreign Currency Forwards

86-25   Offsetting Foreign Currency Swaps

The currency swap accrual cannot be netted against the foreign currency debt. They are separate transactions without the right of setoff.

87-2   Net Present Value Method of Valuing Speculative Foreign Exchange Contracts

Discounting is allowed but not required in applying para 19 of SFAS 52.

87-26   Hedging of a Foreign Currency Exposure with a Tandem Currency

A tandem currency may not be used to hedge a net investment in a foreign subsidiary only because it is less expensive. SFAS 52 phrases "practical" or "feasible" refer to the availability of a hedging investment.

Swaps

84-7   Termination of Interest Rate Swaps

If accounted for as a hedge, terminated interest rate swaps should not be recognized immediately in income. Instead, the accounting should follow SFAS 80 and the gain or loss should be deferred until the offsetting gain or loss on the hedged transaction is recognized. No consensus was reached on nonhedge transactions.

88-8   Mortgage Swaps

The notional amount of mortgage-backed securities and the related debt in a mortgage swap are similar to an executory contract and should not be recognized at the inception of the transaction. Except for mortgage swaps that qualify for hedge accounting, it is appropriate to recognize subsequent changes in the market value (at market or the lower of cost or market) of the swap over its term in a manner consistent with the company's accounting for similar investments. Consensus was reached that hedge accounting is appropriate if hedge criteria under GAAP are met. The SEC observer noted that mortgage swap hedges should be accounted for by financial institutions in the trading account and would be recorded at market value.

Other Financial Instruments

84-14   Deferred Interest Rate Setting

If the deferred rate setting agreement is an integral part (i.e., must be with the underwriter of the debt) of the original issuance of debt, any cash receipt or cash payment should be accounted for over the term of the debt as a yield adjustment to interest expense.

86-24 Third-Party Establishment of Collateralized Mortgage Obligations (CMO)

The sale of mortgages to an unrelated third party which then uses them as collateral to issue CMO should be accounted for as a sale. The gain or loss from the sale should be recognized in the period of the transaction and should include the present value of the residual interest if it can be reliably estimated. The recognition phase of the FASB's project on financial instruments will address this issue.

86-28 Accounting Implications of Indexed Debt Instruments

The issuer is required to allocate the proceeds between the investor's right to receive contingent payments and the debt instrument if the right is separable. No consensus was reached regarding a nonseparable right. As the index increases, a liability or an additional liability is required if the issuer must pay a contingent payment at maturity. The balance sheet date index value should be used and future changes should not be anticipated. If there were no proceeds initially allocated, any additional liability is an adjustment of the debt's carrying amount. Settlement by delivering the actual commodity fixes the issuer's cost of settlement. This issue is to be addressed as a part of the FASB's financial instrument project.

86-34 Futures Contracts Used as Hedges of Anticipated Reverse Repurchase Transactions

Gains or losses on futures contracts could qualify for SFAS 80 hedge accounting if they reduce the interest rate risk and if the criteria of para 9 of SFAS 80 is met. All relevant facts and circumstances should be considered.

Upon the sale of fixed-rate assets, if deferral criteria continue to be met, gains should be recognized while futures losses continue to be deferred. The future contracts were designated as hedges of the reverse repurchase liabilities.

If the hedge is terminated prior to the future issuance of short-term debt, the SFAS 80 high correlation requirement is not applicable after discontinuance.

87-12 Foreign Debt-for-Equity Swaps

If the foreign government requires the proceeds to be invested in that country, the difference between the US dollar values of the two transactions should be used, first, to reduce the basis of long-lived assets acquired in compliance with the arrangement and, second, to reduce the basis of existing long-lived assets (starting with the fixed asset with the longest remaining life and following that order to the shortest remaining life) other than goodwill. If all long-lived assets are reduced to zero, the remaining excess is reported as negative goodwill.

87-30 Sale of a Short-Term Loan Made under a Long-Term Credit Commitment

If the long-term credit commitment contains a substantive **subjective** covenant, the transaction should be recorded as a sale. If it contains only **objective** covenants, it is only a sale if those covenants are substantive.

Substantive means that they are specific to the borrower and are expected to be meaningful and relevant. There was also consensus that long-term commitment fees should be recognized in accordance with SFAS 91.

89-18 Divestitures of Certain Investment Securities to an Unregulated Commonly Controlled Entity under FIRREA

The transfer of securities to an affiliate at book value does **not** obviate the need for the savings association to account for the securities at fair value per SFAS 115. The SEC observer noted that gain recognition would not be appropriate when the securities are sold to the affiliate.

95-5 Determination of What Risks and Rewards, if Any, Can Be Retained and Whether Any Unresolved Contingencies May Exist in a Sale of Mortgage Loan Servicing Rights

This consensus supersedes the consensus reached in Issue 89-5. If substantially all risks and rewards of ownership have irrevocably passed to the buyer and any protection provisions retained by the seller are minor and can be reasonably estimated, then sales of rights to service mortgage loans should be recognized at the date title passes. If a sale is recognized and minor protection provisions exist, a liability should be accrued for the estimated obligation associated with those protection provisions. Protection provisions are considered to be minor if (1) the provisions are no more than 10% of the sales price and (2) the risk of prepayment is retained for no longer than 120 days. Additionally, temporary subservicing agreements in which the subservicing will be performed by the seller for a short period of time will not necessarily preclude recognizing a sale at the closing date.

96-13 Accounting for Derivative Financial Instruments Indexed to, and Potentially Settled in, a Company's Own Stock

The consensuses reached in this EITF involve detailed illustrations of models applied to freestanding contracts that are indexed to, and potentially settled in, a company's own stock. Refer to the original consensus for detailed guidance.

98-10 Accounting for Contracts Involved in Energy Trading and Risk Management Activities

Energy trading contracts should be marked to market with any gains or losses included in earnings and separately disclosed in the financial statements or accompanying footnotes. The determination of whether an entity is involved in energy trading activities is a matter of judgment that depends on the relevant facts and circumstances. The factors included in Exhibit 98-10A of this EITF should be used in evaluating whether an operation's energy contracts are entered into for trading purposes. Due to the nature of trading activities, reclassifications into or from the trading category should be rare. Regardless of whether an operation is considered to be involved in trading activities, when an operation enters into complex written options or options in which the operation does not stand ready to deliver energy, such contracts should be treated as energy trading contacts.

99-2   Accounting for Weather Derivatives

The consensus addresses a new but rapidly growing risk management tool, weather derivative contracts. At issue was whether such contracts should be reported under accrual accounting, under settlement accounting, under insurance accounting, marked to fair value through earnings at each reporting date, or under some other method. Also at issue was whether the accounting for these derivatives should vary based on the type of contract. Past practice had been diverse.

SFAS 133 provides that contracts that are not exchange traded are not subject to the requirements of that Statement if settlement is based on a climatic or geological variable or on some other physical variable. Any derivative based on a physical variable that eventually becomes exchange-traded automatically becomes subject to the requirements of SFAS 133.

The Task Force consensus is that an entity that enters into a non-exchange-traded forward-based weather derivative in connection with nontrading activities should account for the contract by applying an "intrinsic value method." The intrinsic value method computes an amount based on the difference between the expected results from an upfront allocation of the cumulative strike and the actual results during a period, multiplied by the contract price (for example, dollars per heating degree day). The use of external statistical sources, such as the National Weather Service, is necessary in applying this technique.

Furthermore, the Task Force concluded that an entity that purchases a non-exchange-traded option-based weather derivative in connection with nontrading activities should amortize to expense the premium paid (or due) and apply the intrinsic value method to measure the contract at each interim balance sheet date. The premium asset should be amortized in a rational and systematic manner.

Also, it was decided that all entities that sell or write a non-exchange-traded option-based weather derivative should initially recognize the premium as a liability and recognize any subsequent changes in fair value currently in earnings (the premium would not be amortized).

The Task Force observed that a purchased or written weather derivative may contain an "embedded" premium or discount when the contract terms are not consistent with current market terms. In those circumstances, the premium or discount should be quantified, removed from the calculated benchmark strike, and accounted for as noted above.

Finally, the Task Force reached a consensus that all weather derivative contracts entered into under trading or speculative activities should be accounted for at their fair value, with subsequent changes in fair value reported currently in earnings.

99-3 Application of Issue No. 96-13 to Derivative Instruments with Multiple Settlement Alternatives

EITF 96-13 established a framework for accounting for freestanding derivative contracts that are indexed to, and potentially settled in, a company's own stock. The initial balance sheet classification generally is based on the concept that contracts that require net cash settlement are assets or liabilities and contracts that require settlement in shares are equity instruments. If the contract provides the issuer with a choice of net cash settlement or settlement in shares, the 96-13 model assumes settlement in shares; if the contract provides the counter party with a choice of net cash settlement or settlement in shares, net cash settlement is assumed. It is unclear, however, how the issuer should account for a contract, indexed to and potentially settled in the issuer's stock, with multiple settlement alternatives if the settlement alternatives differ depending on whether the contract is in a gain or a loss position.

Accordingly, this issue deals with the matter of how certain contracts indexed to, and potentially settled in, a company's own stock, that contain multiple settlement alternatives should be accounted for.

The consensus is that a contract indexed to, and potentially settled in, the issuer's stock, with multiple settlement alternatives that require the issuer to receive net cash when the contract is in a gain position but pay (a) net stock or (b) either net cash or net stock at the issuer's option when the contract is in a loss position should be accounted for as an equity instrument. The consensus does not apply to a contract that is predominantly a purchased option in which the amount of cash that could be received when the contract is in a gain position is significantly larger than the amount that could be paid when the contract is in a loss position because, for example, there is a small contractual limit on the amount of the loss; rather, those contracts should be accounted for as assets or liabilities.

A consensus was also reached that a contract indexed to, and potentially settled in, the issuer's stock, with multiple settlement alternatives that require the issuer to pay net cash when the contract is in a loss position but receive (a) net stock or (b) either net cash or net stock at the issuer's option when the contract is in a gain position should be accounted for as an asset or a liability.

**00-17	Measuring the Fair Value of Energy-Related Contracts in Applying EITF Issue No. 98-10,** *Accounting for Contracts Involved in Energy Trading and Risk Management Activities*

Issue 00-17 provides guidance on measuring the fair value of energy-related contracts (energy transportation, storage, and tolling contracts) and the related energy purchase and sales contracts. Energy contracts, including energy-related contracts, should be reported at fair value on a stand-alone (individual) contract basis, using the best information available in the circumstances. The price at which a contract is exchanged is its initial fair value, although market transactions may provide for recognition of a "dealer's profit." Subsequent changes in fair values should be estimated using current market transactions, if available. If market transactions are not available, valuation techniques, including option-pricing models, should be used.

7 INVENTORY

PERSPECTIVE AND ISSUES

The accounting for inventories is a major consideration for many entities because of its significance to both the income statement (cost of goods sold) and the balance sheet. Inventories are defined in ARB 43, Chapter 4 as

> *...those items of tangible personal property which are held for sale in the ordinary course of business, are in the process of production for such sale, or are to be currently consumed in the production of goods or services to be available for sale.*

The complexity of accounting for inventories arises from several factors.

1. The high volume of activity (or turnover) in the account
2. The various cost flow alternatives
3. The classification of inventories

There are two types of entities for which the accounting for inventories is relevant. The merchandising entity (generally a retailer or wholesaler/distributor) purchases inventory for resale to its customers. The manufacturer buys **raw materials**, and processes those raw materials using labor and machinery into **finished goods** that are then sold to its customers. While the production process is progressing, the costs of the raw materials, salaries and wages paid to the labor force (and related benefits), depreciation of the machinery, and an allocated portion of the manufacturer's overhead are accumulated by the accounting system as **work in process** (WIP). Finished goods inventory is the completed product which is on hand awaiting shipment or sale.

In the case of either type of entity we are concerned with answering the same basic questions.

1. At what point in time should the items be included in inventory (ownership)?
2. What costs incurred should be included in the valuation of inventories?
3. What cost flow assumption should be used?
4. At what value should inventories be reported (LCM)?

ARB 43, Chapter 4 discusses the definition, valuation, and classification of inventory. APB 28 addresses the measurement and classification of inventories during interim periods. Finally, SFAS 48 concerns revenue recognition when the buyer has the right to return the product, and SFAS 49 addresses product financing arrangements.

Sources of GAAP				
ARB	*APB*	*SFAS*	*EITF*	*AICPA PB*
43, Ch. 4; 51	20, 28, 29	48, 49	86-46	2

DEFINITIONS OF TERMS

Absorption (full costing). In accordance with GAAP, this method includes all manufacturing costs (fixed and variable) in the cost of finished goods inventory.

Base stock. Based on the theory that a minimal level of inventory is a permanent investment. This amount is carried on the books at its historical cost.

Ceiling. In lower of cost or market computations, market (replacement cost) cannot be higher than the ceiling (net realizable value). Net realizable value is selling price less selling costs and costs to complete.

Consignments. A marketing method in which the consignor ships goods to the consignee, who acts as an agent for the consignor in selling the goods. The inventory remains the property of the consignor until sold by the consignee.

Direct (variable) costing. This method includes only variable manufacturing costs in the cost of ending finished goods inventory. This method is not acceptable for financial reporting purposes.

Dollar-value LIFO. A variation of conventional LIFO in which layers of inventory are priced in dollars adjusted by price indexes, instead of layers of inventory priced at unit prices.

Double-extension. A method used to compute the conversion price index. The index indicates the relationship between the base-year and current prices in terms of a percentage.

Finished goods. The completed, but unsold, products produced by a manufacturing firm.

First-in, first-out (FIFO). A cost flow assumption; the first goods purchased or produced are assumed to be the first goods sold.

Floor. In lower of cost or market computations, market is limited to net realizable value less a normal profit, called the floor. Market (replacement cost) cannot be below the floor.

Goods in transit. Goods being shipped from seller to buyer at year-end.

Gross profit method. A method used to estimate the amount of ending inventory based on the cost of goods available for sale, sales, and the gross profit percentage.

Inventory. Those items of tangible property which are held for sale in the normal course of business, are in the process of being produced for such purpose, or are to be used in the production of such items.

Inventory layer. Under the LIFO method, an increase in inventory quantity during a period.

Last-in, first-out (LIFO). A cost flow assumption; the last goods purchased are assumed to be the first goods sold.

LIFO conformity rule. An IRS requirement that if the LIFO method is used for tax purposes, it must also be used for financial reporting purposes.

LIFO liquidation. Liquidation of the LIFO base or old inventory layers when inventory quantities decrease. This liquidation can distort income since old costs are matched against current revenues.

LIFO reserve. The difference, at a specified date, between inventory using LIFO and inventory valued using the method the company uses for internal management or reporting purposes.

LIFO retail. An inventory costing method which combines the LIFO cost flow assumption and the retail inventory method.

Link-chain. Method of applying dollar-value LIFO by developing a single cumulative index. This method may be used instead of double-extension only when there are substantial changes in product lines over the years.

Lower of cost or market. Inventories must be valued at lower of cost or market (replacement cost). Market cannot exceed the ceiling (net realizable value) or be less than the floor (net realizable value less a normal markup).

Markdown. A decrease below original retail price. A markdown cancellation is an increase (not above original retail price) in retail price after a markdown.

Markup. An increase above original retail price. A markup cancellation is a decrease (not below original retail price) in retail price after a markup.

Moving average. An inventory costing method used in conjunction with a perpetual inventory system. A weighted-average cost per unit is recomputed after every purchase. Goods sold are costed at the most recent moving average cost.

Parking transaction. An arrangement which attempts to remove inventory and a current liability from the balance sheet. See **Product financing arrangement**.

Periodic. An inventory system where quantities are determined only periodically by physical count.

Perpetual. An inventory system where up-to-date records of inventory quantities are kept.

Product financing arrangement. An arrangement whereby a firm buys inventory for another firm which agrees to purchase the inventory over a certain period at specified prices which include handling and financing costs.

Purchase commitment. A noncancelable commitment to purchase goods. Losses on such commitments are recognized in the accounts.

Raw materials. For a manufacturing firm, materials on hand awaiting entry into the production process.

Replacement cost. The cost to reproduce an inventory item by purchase or manufacture. In lower of cost or market computations, the term market means replacement cost, subject to the ceiling and floor limitations.

Retail method. An inventory costing method which uses a cost ratio to reduce ending inventory (valued at retail) to cost.

Specific identification. An inventory system where the seller identifies which specific items are sold and which remain in ending inventory.

Standard costs. Predetermined unit costs, which are acceptable for financial reporting purposes if adjusted periodically to reflect current conditions.

Weighted-average. A periodic inventory costing method where ending inventory and cost of goods sold are priced at the weighted-average cost of all items available for sale.

Work in process. For a manufacturing firm, the inventory of partially completed products.

CONCEPTS, RULES, AND EXAMPLES

Ownership of Goods

For accounting purposes, it is necessary to determine when title has legally passed in order to obtain an accurate measurement of inventory quantity. The most common error made in this area is to assume that the entity has title only to the goods on hand. This may be incorrect in two ways: (1) the goods on hand may not be owned, and (2) goods that are not on hand may be owned. There are four areas which create a question as to proper ownership: (1) goods in transit,

(2) consignment sales, (3) product financing arrangements, and (4) sales made with the buyer having the right of return.

At year-end, any **goods in transit** from seller to buyer must be included in one of those parties' inventories based on the conditions of the sale. Such goods are included in the inventory of the firm financially responsible for transportation costs. This responsibility may be indicated by shipping terms such as FOB, which is used in overland shipping contracts, and by FAS, CIF, C&F, and ex-ship, which are used in maritime contracts.

The term FOB stands for "free on board." If goods are shipped FOB destination, transportation costs are paid by the seller and title does not pass until the carrier delivers the goods to the buyer. These goods are part of the seller's inventory while in transit. If goods are shipped FOB shipping point, transportation costs are paid by the buyer and title passes when the carrier takes possession. These goods are part of the buyer's inventory while in transit. The terms FOB destination and FOB shipping point often indicate a specific location at which title to the goods is transferred, such as FOB Cleveland. This means that the seller retains title and risk of loss until the goods are delivered to a common carrier in Cleveland who will act as an agent for the buyer.

A seller who ships FAS (free alongside) must bear all expense and risk involved in delivering the goods to the dock next to (alongside) the vessel on which they are to be shipped. The buyer bears the cost of loading and of shipment. Title passes when the carrier takes possession of the goods.

In a CIF (cost, insurance, and freight) contract the buyer agrees to pay in a lump sum the cost of the goods, insurance costs, and freight charges. In a C&F contract, the buyer promises to pay a lump sum that includes the cost of the goods and all freight charges. In either case, the seller must deliver the goods to the carrier and pay the costs of loading. Both title and risk of loss pass to the buyer upon delivery of the goods to the carrier.

A seller who delivers goods ex-ship bears all expense and risk until the goods are unloaded, at which time both title and risk of loss pass to the buyer.

In **consignments,** the consignor ships goods to the consignee who acts as the agent of the consignor in trying to sell the goods. In some consignments, the consignee receives a commission. In other arrangements, the consignee "purchases" the goods simultaneously with the sale of the goods to the customer. Goods out on consignment are included in the inventory of the consignor and are excluded from the inventory of the consignee.

SFAS 49 addresses the issues involved with **product financing arrangements.** A product financing arrangement is a transaction in which an entity sells and agrees to repurchase inventory with the repurchase price equal to the original sales price plus the carrying and financing costs. The purpose of this transaction is to allow the seller (sponsor) to arrange financing of his/her original purchase of the inventory. The substance of the transaction is illustrated by the diagram below.

1. In the initial transaction the sponsor "sells" inventoriable items to the financing entity in return for the remittance of the sales price and at the same time agrees to repurchase the inventory at a specified price (usually the sales price plus carrying and financing costs) over a specified period of time.
2. The financing entity procures the funds remitted to the sponsor by borrowing from a bank (or other financial institution) using the newly purchased inventory as collateral.
3. The financing entity actually remits the funds to the sponsor and the sponsor presumably uses these funds to pay off the debt incurred as a result of the original purchase.
4. The sponsor then repurchases the inventory for the specified price plus costs from the financing entity at a later time when the funds are available.

The FASB ruled that the substance of this transaction is that of a borrowing transaction. That is, the transaction is, in substance, no different from the sponsor obtaining third-party financing to purchase inventory. The FASB, in SFAS 49, ruled that the proper accounting is to record a liability when the funds are received for the initial transfer of the inventory in the amount of the selling price. The sponsor is then to accrue carrying and financing costs in accordance with his/her normal accounting policies. These accruals are eliminated and the liability satisfied when the sponsor repurchases the inventory. The inventory is **not** to be taken off the balance sheet of the sponsor and a sale is not to be recorded. This is logical because the goods do not physically move and this is merely a financing arrangement. Thus, although legal title has passed to the financing entity, for purposes of measuring and valuing inventory, the inventory is considered to be owned by the sponsor.

Another area which requires special consideration is the situation which exists when the buyer is granted a **right of return**, as defined by SFAS 48. Consideration must be given to the propriety of recognizing revenue at the point of sale under such a situation (this topic is discussed in detail in Chapter 8, Special Revenue Recognition Areas). The sale is to be recorded if the future amount of the returns can be reasonably estimated. If the ability to make a reasonable estimate is precluded, then the sale is not to be recorded until the returns are unlikely. This, too, results in a situation where, although legal title has passed to the buyer, the seller must continue to include the goods in its measurement and valuation of inventory.

Accounting for Inventories

A major objective of accounting for inventories is the matching of appropriate costs against revenues in order to arrive at the proper determination of periodic income. The accounting for inventories is done under either a periodic or perpetual system.

In a **periodic** inventory system, the inventory quantity is determined periodically by a physical count. The quantity is then priced in accordance with the cost method used. Cost of goods sold is computed by adding beginning inventory and net purchases (or cost of goods manufactured) and subtracting ending inventory.

Alternatively, a **perpetual** inventory system keeps a running total of the quantity (and possibly the cost) of inventory on hand by recording all sales and purchases as they occur. When inventory is purchased, the inventory account (rather than purchases) is debited. When inventory is sold, the cost of goods sold and reduction of inventory are recorded. Periodic physical counts are necessary only to verify the perpetual records and to satisfy the tax regulations (tax regulations require that a physical inventory be taken, at least annually).

Valuation of Inventories

The primary basis of accounting for inventories is cost. Cost is defined as the sum of the applicable expenditures and charges directly or indirectly incurred in bringing an article to its existing condition and location.

This definition allows for a wide interpretation of the costs to be included in inventory. For **raw materials** and merchandise inventory which are purchased outright, the identification of cost is relatively straightforward. The cost of these purchased inventories will include all expenditures incurred in bringing the goods to the point of sale and putting them in a salable condition. These costs include the purchase price, transportation costs, insurance while in transit, and handling costs.

It is important to note that purchases can be recorded at their gross amount or net of any allowable discount. If recorded at gross, the discounts taken represent a reduction in the purchase cost for purposes of determining cost of goods sold. On the other hand, if they are recorded at net, any lost discounts are treated as a financial expense, **not** part of cost of goods sold. The net method is considered to be theoretically preferable, but the gross method is simpler and, thus, more commonly used. Either method is acceptable under GAAP, provided that it is consistently applied.

The impact of interest costs as they relate to the valuation of inventoriable items (SFAS 34) is discussed in Chapter 9, Long-Lived Assets. Per APB 29, if similar items of inventory are exchanged with another entity, the earnings process is not culminated. The acquired items are recorded at the book value of the items given up.

Full absorption costing—GAAP. The basis for valuing any inventory is cost. The basis for establishing cost in a manufacturing firm is to include both acquisition and production costs. This concept is commonly referred to as absorption or full costing. As a result, the **WIP** and **finished goods** inventory accounts are to include an appropriate portion of direct materials, direct labor, and indirect production costs (both fixed and variable). The difficulty in determining the cost for these manufacturing inventory accounts is in the allocation of indirect costs. Prior to the Tax Reform Act of 1986 (TRA 1986), production costing for GAAP and for income tax purposes was very similar. However, the Act has changed inventory costing for tax purposes by requiring certain additional indirect costs to be capitalized rather than expensed.

Under some circumstances expenses related to an idle facility, excessive spoilage, double freight, and rehandling costs may be abnormal and, therefore, require treatment as period costs. On the other hand, there may be instances in which certain general and administrative expenses are directly related to the production process and, therefore, should be allocated to the WIP and finished goods inventory. Selling costs do not constitute inventory costs. The chart below shows items which would ordinarily be included in inventory to the extent such costs are incident to and necessary for production.

Indirect production costs typically included in inventory under full absorption

- Repairs
- Maintenance
- Utilities
- Rent
- Indirect labor
- Production supervisory wages
- Indirect materials and supplies
- Quality control and inspection
- Small tools not capitalized

Full absorption costing—Income taxes. TRA 1986 requires that manufacturing firms capitalize rather than expense these additional items.

1. Depreciation and amortization in excess of that reported in financial statements.
2. Percentage depletion in excess of cost.
3. Rework labor, scrap, and spoilage costs.
4. Allocable general and administrative costs related to the production function.

For tax purposes, these costs, as well as the indirect production costs listed above for inventory costing under GAAP, are allocated to the WIP and finished goods inventory. Examples of general and administrative costs that must be allocated include payroll department costs, wages of security guards, and the president's salary. The difference between the book and tax inventory carrying values is a temporary difference, which requires interperiod income tax allocation (discussed in Chapter 15, Income Taxes).

Uniform capitalization rules—Tax vs. financial. TRA 1986, which established new uniform capitalization rules for inventory costs for tax purposes, raised new accounting issues. These issues were considered by the Emerging Issues Task

Force (Issue 86-46) and involve whether the costs capitalized for tax purposes should also be capitalized under GAAP and if so, whether the new costing method would be preferable for purposes of justifying a change in accounting principle.

The Task Force reached a consensus that capitalizing a cost for tax purposes does not indicate that it is preferable or appropriate to capitalize the cost for financial reporting purposes. Although the cost may be capitalized for tax purposes, an enterprise must analyze its individual facts and circumstances and determine whether to capitalize for financial reporting purposes based on the nature of its operations and industry practice.

Direct costing. The alternative to absorption costing is direct costing. Direct costing is also referred to as variable costing and requires classifying only direct materials, direct labor, and variable overhead related to production as inventory costs. All fixed costs are accounted for as period costs. The exclusion of all overhead from inventory costs does not constitute an accepted accounting procedure, consequently, direct costing is not allowable for GAAP. Treasury regulations require the allocation of fixed overhead to inventory for tax purposes.

Inventory capitalization for retailers/wholesalers—GAAP and income taxes. Retailers and wholesalers previously recorded their inventory as the invoice price plus the cost of applicable sales tax and freight-in under both GAAP and tax law. TRA 1986 introduced a requirement that additional costs be capitalized. These uniform capitalization rules (Unicap) exempt inventories of retailers/wholesalers whose average annual gross receipts for the preceding three years are $10 million or less.

The costs which must be capitalized have been divided into two categories. The first category is direct costs and includes the inventory invoice price plus transportation. Also included in direct costs is the cost of labor for purchasing, storing, and handling inventory items. The second category is indirect costs and consists of any costs that directly benefit or are incurred because of the performance of a resale activity. The following types of indirect costs must be capitalized:

1. Off-site storage or warehousing
2. Purchasing
3. Handling, processing, assembly, and repackaging
4. Allocable general and administrative costs related to the above three functions

The indirect costs are allocated between inventory and cost of goods sold by using traditional methods (specific identification, standard costing methods, etc.) or one of three simplified methods. Temporary differences require interperiod income tax allocation.

Specific identification. The theoretical basis for valuing inventories and cost of goods sold requires assigning the production and/or acquisition costs to the specific goods to which they relate. This method of inventory valuation is usually referred to as specific identification. Specific identification is generally not practical as the product will generally lose its separate identity as it passes through the production and sales process. Exceptions to this would arise in situations involving small inventory quantities with high unit value and low turnover rate. Because of the limited applicability of specific identification, it is necessary to make certain assumptions regarding the cost flows associated with inventory. These cost flows may or may not reflect the physical flow of inventory.

Cost Flow Assumptions

According to ARB 43, Chapter 4

> *...cost for inventory purposes shall be determined under any one of several assumptions as to the flow of cost factors; the major objective in selecting a method should be to choose the one which, under the circumstances, most clearly reflects periodic income.*

The most common cost flow assumptions used are (1) first-in, first-out (FIFO), (2) last-in, first-out (LIFO), and (3) weighted-average. Additionally, there are variations to each of these assumptions which are commonly used in practice.

In selecting the cost flow assumption to be used, the entity should give thought to a variety of considerations. First, the industry norm should be examined as this will facilitate interfirm comparison. The appropriateness of using a particular cost flow assumption will vary depending on the nature of the industry and the expected economic climate. The method which should be selected in a period of rising prices differs from that which is most appropriate for a period of declining prices. Each of the foregoing assumptions and their relative advantages or disadvantages are discussed below. Examples are provided to enhance the understanding of the application.

First-In, First-Out (FIFO)

The **FIFO method** of inventory valuation assumes that the first goods purchased are the first goods used or sold, regardless of the actual physical flow. This method is thought to most closely parallel the physical flow of the units in most industries. The strength of this cost flow assumption lies in the inventory amount reported on the balance sheet. Because the earliest goods purchased are the first ones removed from the inventory account, the remaining balance is composed of items at the latest cost. This yields results similar to those obtained under current cost accounting on the balance sheet. However, the FIFO method does not necessarily reflect the most accurate income figure as historical costs are being matched against current revenues.

The following example illustrates the basic principles involved in the application of FIFO:

	Units available	Units sold	Actual unit cost	Actual total cost
Beginning inventory	100	--	$2.10	$210
Sale	--	75	--	--
Purchase	150	--	2.80	420
Sale	--	100	--	--
Purchase	50	--	3.00	150
Total	300	175		$780

Given this data, the cost of goods sold and ending inventory balance are determined as follows:

	Units	Unit cost	Total cost
Cost of goods sold	100	$2.10	$210
	75	2.80	210
	175		$420
Ending inventory	50	3.00	$150
	75	2.80	210
	125		$360

Notice that the total of the units in cost of goods sold and ending inventory, as well as the sum of their total costs, is equal to the goods available for sale and their respective total costs.

The FIFO method provides the same results under either the periodic or perpetual system.

Last-In, First-Out (LIFO)

The **LIFO method** of inventory valuation assumes that the last goods purchased are the first goods used or sold. This allows the matching of current costs with current revenue and provides the best measure of periodic income. However, unless costs remain relatively unchanged over time, the LIFO method will usually misstate the ending inventory balance for balance sheet purposes because inventory usually consists of costs from earlier periods. LIFO does not usually follow the physical flow of merchandise or materials. However, the matching of physical flow is not considered to be an objective of accounting for inventories.

The LIFO method is not a promulgated accounting principle. Rather, the basis for LIFO is found in the Internal Revenue Code (the Code) §472 and, as such, is a tax concept. The Treasury regulations indicate that any taxpayer who maintains inventories may select LIFO application for any or all inventoriable items. This election is made with the taxpayer's tax return on Form 970 after the close of any taxable year. Partial adoption of LIFO is allowed for both accounting and tax purposes. (See Appendix B for a further discussion of partial adoption of LIFO for accounting purposes.)

Once elected, the LIFO method must continue to be used in future periods. In order to revert to another method, the taxpayer must apply for a change in accounting method on Form 3115 within the first 180 days of the taxable year during which the change is desired. A change to or from the LIFO method is an accounting change (see Chapter 20, Accounting Changes and Correction of Errors).

LIFO restrictions. In addition, for tax reporting purposes a taxpayer must adhere to the following two significant restrictions for the portions of its inventory valued under LIFO:

1. The inventory is to be valued at cost regardless of market value (i.e., application of the lower of cost or market rule is not allowed).
2. The taxpayer may not use a different inventory method in ascertaining profit or loss of the entity for external financial reports (i.e., if LIFO is elected for tax purposes, it must also be used for accounting purposes). This is known as the **LIFO conformity rule**. (See Appendix A for exceptions to this rule.)

The quantity of ending inventory on hand at the beginning of the year of election is termed the "base layer." This inventory is valued at actual (full absorption) cost, and unit cost is determined by dividing total cost by the quantity on hand. At the end of the initial and subsequent years, increases in the quantity of inventory on hand are referred to as increments, or **LIFO layers**. These increments are valued individually by applying one of the following costing methods to the quantity of inventory representing a layer:

1. The actual cost of the goods most recently purchased or produced.
2. The actual cost of the goods purchased or produced in order of acquisition.
3. An average unit cost of all goods purchased or produced during the current year.
4. A hybrid method which will more clearly reflect income (for tax purposes, this method must meet with the approval of the IRS Commissioner).

Thus, after using the LIFO method for five years, it is possible that an enterprise could have ending inventory consisting of the base layer and five additional layers (or increments) provided that the quantity of ending inventory increased every year.

The single goods (unit) LIFO approach is illustrated in the following example:

XYZ Co. is in its first year of operation and elects to use the periodic LIFO method of inventory valuation. The company sells only one product. XYZ will apply the LIFO method using the order of current year acquisition cost. The following data are given for years 1 through 3:

	Units	Unit cost	Total cost
Year 1			
Purchase	200	$2.00	$400
Sale	100	--	--
Purchase	200	3.00	600
Sale	150	--	--
	Units	Unit cost	Total cost
Year 2			
Purchase	300	$3.20	$960
Sale	200	--	--
Purchase	100	3.30	330
Year 3			
Purchase	100	$3.50	$350
Sale	200	--	--
Sale	100	--	--

In year 1 the following occurred:

1. The total goods available for sale were 400 units.
2. The total sales were 250 units.
3. Therefore, the ending inventory was 150 units.

The ending inventory is valued at the earliest current year acquisition cost of $2.00 per unit. Thus, ending inventory is valued at $300 (150 x $2.00).

Another way to look at this is to analyze both cost of goods sold and ending inventory.

	Units	Unit cost	Total cost
Cost of goods sold	200	$3.00	$600
	50	2.00	100
	250		$700
Ending inventory	150	2.00	$300

Note that the base-year cost is $2.00 and that the base-year level is 150 units. Therefore, if ending inventory in the subsequent period exceeds 150 units, a new layer (or increment) will be created.

Year 2	Units	Unit cost	Total cost	
Cost of goods sold	100	$3.30	$330	
	100	3.20	320	
	200		$650	
Ending inventory	150	2.00	$300	Base-year layer
	200	3.20	640	Year 2 increment
	350		$940	

Now, if ending inventory exceeds 350 units in the next period, a new layer will be created.

Year 3	Units	Unit cost	Total cost	
Cost of goods sold	100	$3.50	$350	
	200	3.20	640	
	300		$990	
Ending inventory	150	2.00	$300	Base-year layer

Notice how the decrement of 200 units in year 3 eliminated the entire year 2 increment. Thus, any year 4 increase in the quantity of inventory would result in a **new** increment which would be valued at year 4 prices.

In situations where the ending inventory decreases from the level established at the close of the preceding year, the enterprise experiences a decrement or **LIFO liquidation**. Decrements will reduce or eliminate previously established LIFO layers. Once any part of a layer has been eliminated, it **cannot** be reinstated after year-end. For example, if in its first year after the election of LIFO an enterprise establishes a layer (increment) of ten units, then in the next year inventory decreases by four units leaving the first layer at six units, the enterprise cannot reestablish the first layer (back up to ten units) in the year that inventory next increases. Rather, it will be forced to create a new layer for the increase. The effect of LIFO liquidations in periods of rising prices is to release costs which are below the current cost being paid into cost of goods sold from ending inventory. Thus, the resultant effect of a LIFO liquidation is to increase income for **both** accounting and tax purposes. Because of this, LIFO is most commonly used by industries in which inventories are maintained or increased.

LIFO liquidations can take two forms, voluntary or involuntary. A voluntary liquidation exists when an enterprise decides, for one reason or another, to let inventory levels drop. Such a liquidation occurs because current prices may be too high, less inventory is needed for efficient production, or maybe because of a transition in the product lines. Involuntary LIFO liquidations stem from reasons beyond the control of the enterprise, such as a strike, shortages, shipping delay, etc. Regardless of the reason, all liquidations result in a corresponding increase in income (assuming rising prices).

To compute the effect of the liquidation, the company must compute the difference between actual cost of sales and what cost of sales would have been had the inventory been reinstated. The Internal Revenue Service has ruled that this hypothetical reinstatement must be computed under the company's normal pricing procedures for valuing its LIFO increments. In the above example the effect of the year 3 LIFO liquidation would be computed as follows:

Inventory reinstatement:

200 units @ $3.50 − $3.20 = $60

Because the 200 units liquidated would have been stated at the year 3 price of $3.50 if there had been an increment, the difference between $3.50 and the actual amount charged to cost of sales for these units ($3.20) measures the effect of the liquidation.

The following is considered acceptable GAAP disclosure in the event of a LIFO liquidation:

During 2002, inventory quantities were reduced. This reduction resulted in a liquidation of LIFO inventory quantities carried at lower costs prevailing in prior years as compared with the cost of 2002 purchases, the effect of which decreased cost of goods sold by approximately $xxx and increased net income by approximately $xx or $x per share.

An inordinate amount of recordkeeping is required in applying the unit LIFO method. The recordkeeping is much greater as the number of products increases. For this reason a "pooling" approach is generally applied to LIFO inventories.

Pooling is the process of grouping items which are naturally related and then treating this group as a single unit in determining the LIFO cost. Because the quantity of ending inventory includes many items, decreases in one item can be made up for by increases in others, whereas under the single goods unit approach a decrease in any one item results in a liquidation of LIFO layers.

The problem in applying the pooling method emanates from the tax regulations, not the practical side of application. The tax regulations state that each type of good in the opening inventory must be compared with a similar type in the closing inventory. These items must be similar as to character, quality, and price. This qualification has generally been interpreted to mean identical. The effect of this statement is to require a separate pool for each item under the unit LIFO method. The need for a simpler, more practical approach to using the LIFO concept and allowing for a greater use of the pooling concept was met by dollar-value LIFO.

Dollar-Value LIFO

Use of dollar-value LIFO may be elected by any taxpayer. The dollar-value LIFO method of inventory valuation determines the cost of inventories by expressing base-year costs in terms of total dollars rather than specific prices of specific units. The dollar-value method also gives rise to an expanded interpretation of the use of pools. Increments and liquidations are treated the same as under the unit LIFO approach but are reflected only in terms of a **net** liquidation or increment for the entire pool.

Identifying pools. Three alternatives exist for determining pools under dollar-value LIFO: (1) the natural business unit, (2) multiple pools, and (3) pools for wholesalers, retailers, jobbers, etc.

The natural business unit is defined by the existence of separate and distinct processing facilities and operations and the maintenance of separate income (loss) records. The concept of the natural business unit is generally dependent upon the type of product, not the various stages of production for that project. Thus, the pool can (and will) contain raw materials, WIP, and finished goods. The three examples below, taken from the treasury regulations, illustrate the application of the natural business unit concept.

Example 1

A corporation manufactures, in one division, automatic clothes washers and dryers of both commercial and domestic grade as well as electric ranges and dishwashers. The corporation manufactures, in another division, radios and television sets. The manufacturing facilities and processes used in manufacturing the radios and television sets are distinct from those used in manufacturing the automatic clothes washers, etc. Under these circumstances, the enterprise would consist of two business units and two pools would be appropriate: one consisting of all of the LIFO inventories involved with the manufacture of clothes washers and dryers, electric ranges and dishwashers and the other consisting of all of the LIFO inventories involved with the production of radios and television sets.

Example 2

A taxpayer produces plastics in one of its plants. Substantial amounts of the production are sold as plastics. The remainder of the production is shipped to a second plant of the taxpayer for the production of plastic toys which are sold to customers. The taxpayer operates its plastics plant and toy plant as separate divisions. Because of the different product lines and the separate divisions, the taxpayer has two natural business units.

Example 3

A taxpayer is engaged in the manufacture of paper. At one stage of processing, uncoated paper is produced. Substantial amounts of uncoated paper are sold at this stage of processing. The remainder of the uncoated paper is transferred to the taxpayer's finishing mill where coated paper is produced and sold. This taxpayer has only one natural business unit since coated and uncoated paper are within the same product line.

The treasury regulations require that a pool shall consist of all items entering into the entire inventory investment of a natural business unit, unless the taxpayer elects to use the multiple-pooling method.

The multiple-pooling method is the grouping of substantially similar items. In determining substantially similar items, consideration should be given to the processing applied, the interchangeability, the similarity of use, and the customary practice of the industry. While the election of multiple pools will necessitate additional recordkeeping, it may result in a better estimation of periodic income.

According to Reg. §1.472-8(c), inventory items of wholesalers, retailers, jobbers, and distributors are to be placed into pools by major lines, types, or classes of goods. The natural business unit method may be used with permission of the Commissioner.

All three methods of pooling allow for a change in the components of inventory. New items which properly fall within the pool may be added, and old items may disappear from the pool, but neither will necessarily effect a change in the total dollar value of the pool.

Computing dollar-value LIFO. The purpose of the dollar-value LIFO method of valuing inventory is to convert inventory which is priced at end-of-year prices to that same inventory priced at base-year (or applicable LIFO layer) prices. The dollar-value method achieves this result through the use of a conversion price index. The inventory at current year cost is divided by the appropriate index to arrive at the base-year cost. The main focus is on the determination of the conversion price index. There are four basic methods that can be used in the computation of the LIFO value of a dollar-value pool: (1) double-extension, (2) link-chain, (3) the index method, and (4) the alternative LIFO method for auto dealers.

Double-extension method. This method was originally developed to compute the conversion price index. It involves extending the entire quantity of ending inventory for the current year at both base-year prices and end-of-year prices to arrive at a total dollar value for each, hence the title of double-extension. The end-of-year dollar total is then divided by the base-year dollar total to arrive at the index, usually referred to as the conversion price index. This index indicates the relationship between the base-year and current prices in terms of a percentage. Each layer (or increment) is valued at its own percentage. Although a representative sample is allowed (meaning that not all of the items need be double-extended; this is discussed in more detail under indexing), the recordkeeping under this method is very burdensome. The base-year price must be kept for each inventory item. Depending upon the number of different items included in the inventory of the company, the necessary records may be too detailed to keep past the first year.

The following example illustrates the double-extension method of computing the LIFO value of inventory. The example presented is relatively simple and does not attempt to incorporate all of the complexities of inventory accounting.

Example

ABC, Inc. uses the dollar-value method of LIFO inventory valuation and computes its price index using the double-extension method. ABC has a single pool which contains two inventory items, A and B. Year 1 is the company's initial year of operations. The following information is given for years 1 through 4:

Year	Ending inventory current prices	Ending quantity (units) and current price			
		A		*B*	
1	$100,000	5,000	$6.00	7,000	$10.00
2	120,300	6,000	6.30	7,500	11.00
3	122,220	5,800	6.40	7,400	11.50
4	133,900	6,200	6.50	7,800	12.00

In year 1 there is no computation of an index; the index is 100%. The LIFO cost is the same as the actual current year cost. This is the base year.

In year 2 the first step is to double-extend the quantity of ending inventory at base-year and current year costs.

Item	Quantity	Base-year cost/unit	Extended	Current year cost/unit	Extended
A	6,000	$ 6.00	$ 36,000	$ 6.30	$ 37,800
B	7,500	10.00	75,000	11.00	82,500
			$111,000		$120,300*

---

* *When using the double-extension method and extending **all** of the inventory items to arrive at the index, this number must equal the ending inventory at current prices. If a sampling method is used (as discussed under indexing), this number **divided by** your ending inventory at current prices will give you the percentage sampled.*

Now we can compute the conversion price index which is

$$\frac{\text{Ending inventory at current year prices}}{\text{Ending inventory at base-year prices}}$$

In this case $\dfrac{120,300}{111,000}$ = 108.4% (rounded)

Next, compute the year 2 layer at the base-year cost by taking the current year-ending inventory at base-year prices (if you only extend a sample of the inventory, this number is arrived at by dividing the ending inventory at current year prices by the conversion price index) of $111,000 and subtracting the base-year cost of $100,000. In year 2 we have an increment (layer) of $11,000 valued at base-year costs.

The year 2 layer of $11,000 at base-year cost must be converted so that the layer is valued at the prices in effect when it came into existence (i.e., at year 2 prices). This is done by multiplying the increment at base-year cost ($11,000) by the rounded conversion price index (1.084). The result is the year 2 layer at LIFO prices.

Base-year layer	$100,000
Year 2 layer ($11,000 x 1.084)	11,924
	$111,924

In year 3 the same basic procedure is followed.

Item	Quantity	Base-year cost/unit	Extended	Current year cost/unit	Extended
A	5,800	$ 6.00	$ 34,800	$ 6.40	$ 37,120
B	7,400	10.00	74,000	11.50	85,100
			$108,800		$122,220

There has been a decrease in the base-year cost of the ending inventory ($111,000 – $108,800 = $2,200) which is referred to as a decrement. A decrement results in the decrease (or elimination) of previously provided layers. In this situation, the computation of the index is not necessary as there is no LIFO layer that requires a valuation. If a sampling approach has been used, the index is needed to arrive at the ending inventory at base-year cost and thus determine if there has been an increment or decrement.

Now the ending inventory at base-year cost is $108,800. The base-year cost layer is still intact at $100,000, so the cumulative increment is $8,800. Since this is less than the $11,000 increment of year 2, no additional increment is established in year 3. The LIFO cost of the inventory is shown below.

Base-year layer	$100,000
Year 2 layer ($8,800 x 1.084)	9,539
	$109,539

The fourth year then follows the same steps.

Items	Quantity	Base-year cost/unit	Extended	Current year cost/unit	Extended
A	6,200	$ 6.00	$ 37,200	$ 6.50	$ 40,300
B	7,800	10.00	78,000	12.00	93,600
			$115,200		$133,900

The conversion price index is 116.2% (133,900/115,200).

A current year increment exists because the ending inventory at base-year prices in year 4 of $115,200 exceeds the year 3 number of $108,800. The current year increment of $6,400 must be valued at year 4 prices. Thus, the LIFO cost of the year 4 inventory is

Base-year layer	$100,000
Year 2 layer ($8,800 x 1.084)	9,539
Year 4 layer ($6,400 x 1.162)	7,437
	$116,976

It is important to point out that once a layer is reduced or eliminated it is never reinstated (as with the year 2 increment) after year-end.

Link-chain method. Since the computations for application become arduous even if only a few items exist in the inventory, consider the problems that arise when there is a constant change in the inventory mix or in situations in which the breadth of the inventory is large. The link-chain method of applying dollar-value LIFO was developed to combat these problems.

Another purpose served by the link-chain method is to eliminate the problem created by a significant turnover in the components of inventory. Under the double-extension or indexing method, the regulations require that any new products added to the inventory be costed at base-year prices. If these are not available, then the earliest cost available after the base year is used. If the item was not in existence in the base year, the taxpayer may reconstruct the base cost, using a reasonable method to determine what the cost would have been if the item had been in existence in the base year. Finally, as a last resort, the purchase price can be used. While this does not appear to be a problem on the surface, imagine a base period which is twenty-five to fifty years in the past. The difficulty involved with finding the base-year cost may require using a more current cost, thus eliminating some of the LIFO benefit. Imagine a situation faced by a company in a "hi-tech" industry where inventory is continually being replaced by newer, more advanced products. The effect of this rapid change under the double-extension method (because the new products didn't exist in the base period) is to use current prices as base-year costs. When inventory has such a rapid turnover, the overall LIFO advantage becomes diluted as current and base-year costs are sometimes synonymous. This situation is the major reason for the development of the link-chain method.

The link-chain method was originally developed for (and limited to) those companies that wanted to use LIFO but, because of a substantial change in product lines over time, were unable to recreate or keep the historical records necessary to make accurate use of the double-extension method. It is important to note that the double-extension and link-chain methods are not selective alternatives for the same situation. For tax purposes, the link-chain election **requires** that substantial change in product line be evident over the years, and it is not electable because of its ease of application. The double-extension and index methods must be demonstrated as impractical in order to elect the link-chain method. However, a company may use different computational techniques for financial reporting and tax purposes. Therefore, the link-chain method could be used for financial reporting purposes even if a different application is used for tax purposes.

The link-chain method is the process of developing a single cumulative index which is applied to the ending inventory amount priced at the beginning-of-the-year costs. Thus, the index computed at the end of each year is "linked" to the index from all previous years. A separate cumulative index is used for each pool regardless of the variations in the components of these pools over the years. Technological change is allowed for by the method used to calculate each current year index. The index is derived by double-extending a representative sample (generally thought to be between 50% and 75% of the dollar value of the pool) at both beginning-of-year prices and end-of-year prices. This annual index is then applied to (multiplied by) the previous period's cumulative index to arrive at the new current year cumulative index.

An example of the link-chain method is shown below. Notice that the end-of-year costs and inventory quantity used are the same as those used in the double-extension example.

Assume the following inventory data for years 1-4. Year 1 is assumed to be the initial year of operation for the company. The LIFO method is elected on the first tax return. Assume that A and B constitute a single pool.

Product	Ending inventory quantity	Cost per unit Beg. of yr.	Cost per unit End of yr.	Extension Beginning	Extension End
Year 1					
A	5,000	N/A	$ 6.00	N/A	$ 30,000
B	7,000	N/A	10.00	N/A	70,000
					$100,000
Year 2					
A	6,000	$ 6.00	6.30	$ 36,000	$ 37,800
B	7,500	10.00	11.00	75,000	82,500
				$111,000	$120,300
Year 3					
A	5,800	6.30	6.40	$ 36,540	$ 37,120
B	7,400	11.00	11.50	81,400	85,100
				$117,940	$122,220
Year 4					
A	6,200	6.40	6.50	$ 39,680	$ 40,300
B	7,800	11.50	12.00	89,700	93,600
				$129,380	$133,900

The initial year (base year) does not require the computation of an index under any LIFO method. The base-year index will always be 1.00.

Thus, the base-year inventory layer is $100,000 (the end-of-year inventory restated at base-year cost).

The second year requires the first index computation. Notice that in year 2 our extended totals are

	Beginning-of-year prices	End-of-year prices
A	$ 36,000	$ 37,800
B	75,000	82,500
	$111,000	$120,300

The year 2 index is 1.084 (120,300/111,000). This is the same as computed under the double-extension method because the beginning-of-the-year prices reflect the base-year price. This will not always be the case, as sometimes new items may be added to the pool, causing a change in the index.

Thus, the cumulative index is the 1.084 current year index multiplied by the preceding year index of 1.00 to arrive at a link-chain index of 1.084.

This index is then used to restate the inventory to base-year cost by dividing the inventory at end-of-year dollars by the cumulative index: $120,300/1.084 = $111,000. The determination of the LIFO increment or decrement is then basically the same as the double-extension method. In year 2 the increment (layer) at base-year cost is $11,000 ($111,000 – 100,000). This layer must be valued at the prices effective when the layer was created, or extended at the cumulative index for that year. This results in an ending inventory at LIFO cost of

	Base-year cost	Index	LIFO cost
Base-year layer	$100,000	1.00	$100,000
Year 2 layer	11,000	1.084	11,924
	$111,000		$111,924

The index for year 3 is computed as follows:

	Beginning-of-year prices	End-of-year prices
A	$ 36,540	$ 37,120
B	81,400	85,100
	$117,940	$122,220

$$122,220/117,940 = 1.036$$

The next step is to determine the cumulative index which is the product of the preceding year's cumulative index and the current year index, or 1.123 (1.084 x 1.036). The new cumulative index is used to restate the inventory at end-of-year dollars to base-year cost. This is accomplished by dividing the end-of-year inventory by the new cumulative index. Thus, current inventory at base-year cost is $108,833 ($122,220 ÷ 1.123). In this instance we have experienced a decrement (a decrease from the prior year's $111,000). The determination of ending inventory is

	Base-year cost	Index	LIFO cost
Base-year layer	$100,000	1.00	$100,000
Year 2 layer	8,833	1.084	9,575
Year 3 layer	--	1.123	--
	$108,833		$109,575

Finally, perform the same steps for the year 4 computation. The current year index is 1.035 (133,900/129,380). The new cumulative index is 1.162 (1.035 x 1.123). The base-year cost of the current inventory is $115,232 (133,900/1.162). Thus, LIFO inventory at the end of year 4 is

	Base-year cost	Index	LIFO cost
Base-year layer	$100,000	1.00	$100,000
Year 2 layer	8,833	1.084	9,575
Year 3 layer	--	1.123	--
Year 4 layer	6,399	1.162	7,435
	$115,232		$117,010

Notice how even though the numbers used were the same as those used in the double-extension example, the results were different (year 4 inventory under double-extension was $116,976), however, not by a significant amount. It is much easier to keep track of beginning-of-the-year prices than it is to keep base-year prices, but perhaps more importantly, it is easier to establish beginning-of-the-year prices for **new items** than to establish their base-year price. This latter reason is why the link-chain method is so much more desirable than the double-extension method. However, before electing or applying this method, a company must be able to establish a sufficient need as defined in the treasury regulations.

Indexing. Indexing methods can basically be broken down into two types: (1) an internal index and (2) an external index.

The internal index is merely a variation of the double-extension method. The regulations allow for a representative sample (or some other statistical method) of the inventory to be double-extended. The representative index computed from the sample is then used to restate the inventory to base-year cost and to value the new layer.

The external index method involves using an index published by the Bureau of Labor Statistics (BLS) and applying this index to the inventory figures. This method was primarily limited to retailers initially. However, regulations issued in 1981 permit these various indices to be used by small businesses (defined as three-year average sales of less than $5 million) to 100% of the change and any other businesses to 80% of the change. The reader is referred to Reg. §1.472-8(e)(3). It should also be noted that application of the 80% method has not yet been addressed by the FASB, but the Accounting Standards Executive Committee (AcSEC) did not support its use for financial reporting purposes. Thus, larger businesses must still use one of the other alternatives in computing the dollar-value index.

Automobile Dealers' Alternative LIFO Method

Beginning in September 1992 a simplified dollar-value method became available for use by retail automobile dealers for valuing inventory of new automobiles and new light-duty trucks. The use of this method and its acceptance for tax purposes is conditioned on the application of several LIFO sub-methods, definitions and special rules. The reader is referred to Rev. Proc. 92-79 for a further discussion of this method.

The GAAP for the application of LIFO has been based upon tax rules rather than on financial accounting pronouncements. LIFO is cited in GAAP as an acceptable inventory method but specific rules regarding its implementation are not provided. The tax regulations, on the other hand, do provide specific rules for the implementation of LIFO and require financial statement conformity. For this reason, tax rules have essentially defined the financial accounting treatment of LIFO inventories. In recognition of the lack of authoritative accounting guidelines in the implementation of LIFO, the AICPA's Accounting Standards Division prepared an Issues Paper on this topic. "Identification and Discussion of Certain Financial Accounting and Reporting Issues Concerning LIFO Inventories," prepared by the Task Force on LIFO Inventory Problems, identifies financial accounting issues resulting from the use of LIFO and includes advisory conclusions for these problems. Issues Papers, however, do not establish standards of financial accounting. This Issues Paper is summarized in an appendix to this chapter.

Interim Treatment of LIFO

Interim reporting issues associated with LIFO are discussed on pages 841-842.

Weighted-Average

Another method of inventory valuation involves averaging and is commonly referred to as the weighted-average method. The cost of goods available for sale (beginning inventory and net purchases) is divided by the units available for sale to obtain a weighted-average unit cost. Ending inventory and cost of goods sold are then priced at this average cost. Assume the following data:

	Units available	Units sold	Actual unit cost	Actual total cost
Beginning inventory	100	--	$2.10	$210
Sale	--	75	--	--
Purchase	150	--	2.80	420
Sale	--	100	--	--
Purchase	50	--	3.00	150
Total	300	175		$780

The weighted-average cost is $780/300, or $2.60. Ending inventory is 125 units (300 – 175) at $2.60, or $325; cost of goods sold is 175 units at $2.60, or $455.

When the weighted-average assumption is applied to a perpetual inventory system, the average cost is recomputed after each purchase. This process is referred to as a moving average. Sales are costed at the most recent average. This combination is called the moving-average method and is applied below to the same data used in the weighted-average example above.

	Units on hand	Purchases in dollars	Cost of sales in dollars	Inventory total cost	Inventory unit cost
Beginning inventory	100	$ --	$ --	$210.00	$2.10
Sale (75 units @ $2.10)	25	--	157.50	52.50	2.10
Purchase (150 units, $420)	175	420.00	--	472.50	2.70
Sale (100 units @ $2.70)	75	--	270.00	202.50	2.70
Purchase (50 units, $150)	125	150.00	--	352.50	2.82

Cost of goods sold is 75 units at $2.10 and 100 units at $2.70, or $427.50.

Comparison of Cost Assumptions

Of the three basic cost flow assumptions, LIFO and FIFO produce the most extreme results, while results from using the weighted-average method generally fall somewhere in between. The selection of one of these methods involves a detailed analysis of the organization's objectives and of the current and expected future economic conditions.

In periods of rising prices the LIFO method is generally thought to best fulfill the objective of providing the clearest measure of periodic income. It does not provide an accurate estimate of the inventory value in an inflationary environment. However, this can usually be overcome by the issuance of supplementary data. In periods of rising prices a prudent business should use the LIFO method because it will result in a decrease in the current tax liability when compared to other alternatives. In a deflationary period, the opposite is true.

FIFO is a balance-sheet-oriented costing method. It gives the most accurate estimate of the current value of the inventory account during periods of changing prices. In periods of rising prices, the FIFO method will result in higher taxes than the other alternatives, while in a deflationary period FIFO provides for a lesser tax burden. However, a major advantage of the FIFO method is that it is not subject to all of the regulations and requirements of the tax code as is LIFO.

The average methods do not provide an estimate of current cost information on either the balance sheet or income statement. The average method will not serve to minimize the tax burden, nor will it result in the highest burden among the various alternatives.

Although price trends and underlying objectives are important in the selection of a cost flow assumption, other considerations are the risk of LIFO liquidations, cash flow, capital maintenance, etc.

Lower of Cost or Market (LCM)

As stated in ARB 43, Chapter 4

> *...a departure from the cost basis of pricing the inventory is required when the utility of the goods is no longer as great as its cost.... Where there is evidence that the utility of goods...will be less than cost...the difference should be recognized as a loss of the current period.*

The term market means current **replacement cost** not to exceed a **ceiling** of net realizable value (selling price less reasonably estimable costs of completion and disposal) nor below a **floor** of net realizable value adjusted for a normal profit margin.

LCM is not applied in conjunction with the LIFO method of inventory valuation for tax purposes. However, it is important to note that LCM/LIFO may be applied for financial reporting purposes. Such application gives rise to a temporary difference in the carrying value of inventory between financial statements and tax returns. Appendix B provides additional guidance on LCM/LIFO for financial reporting.

LCM may be applied to either the entire inventory or to each individual inventory item. The primary objective for selecting between the alternative methods of applying the LCM rule is to select the one which most clearly reflects periodic income. The rule is most commonly applied to the inventory on an item-by-item basis. The reason for this application is twofold.

1. It is required by tax purposes unless it involves practical difficulties, and
2. It provides the most conservative valuation of inventories, because decreases in the value of one item are not offset by increases in the value of another.

The application of these principles is illustrated in the example below. Assume the following information for products A, B, C, D, and E:

Item	Cost	Replacement cost	Est. selling price	Cost to complete	Normal profit percentage	Normal profit amount
A	$2.00	$1.80	$ 2.50	$0.50	24%	$0.60
B	4.00	1.60	4.00	0.80	24%	0.96
C	6.00	6.60	10.00	1.00	18%	1.80
D	5.00	4.75	6.00	2.00	20%	1.20
E	1.00	1.05	1.20	0.25	12.5%	0.15

First, determine the market value and then compare this to historical cost. Market value is equal to the replacement cost, but cannot exceed the net realizable value (NRV) nor be below net realizable value less the normal profit percentage.

Market Determination

Item	Cost	Replacement cost	NRV (ceiling)	NRV less profit (floor)	Market	LCM
A	$2.00	$1.80	$2.00	$1.40	$1.80	$1.80
B	4.00	1.60	3.20	2.24	2.24	2.24
C	6.00	6.60	9.00	7.20	7.20	6.00
D	5.00	4.75	4.00	2.80	4.00	4.00
E	1.00	1.05	0.95	0.80	0.95	0.95

NRV (ceiling) equals selling price less costs of completion (e.g., item A: $2.50 – .50 = $2.00). NRV less profit (floor) is self-descriptive (e.g., $2.50 – .50 –.60 = $1.40). Market is replacement cost unless lower than the floor or higher than the ceiling. Note that market must be designated before LCM is determined. Finally, LCM is the lower of cost or market value

Replacement cost is a valid measure of the future utility of the inventory item since increases or decreases in the purchase price generally foreshadow related increases or decreases in the selling price. The ceiling and the floor provide safeguards against the recognition of either excessive profits or excessive losses in future periods in those instances where the selling price and replacement cost do not move in the same direction in a proportional manner. The ceiling avoids the recognition of additional losses in the future when the selling price is falling faster than replacement cost. Without the ceiling constraint, inventories would be carried at an amount in excess of their net realizable value. The floor avoids the recognition of abnormal profits in the future when replacement cost is falling faster than the selling price. Without the floor, inventories would be carried at a value less than their net realizable value minus a normal profit.

The loss from writing inventories down to LCM is generally reflected on the income statement in cost of goods sold. If material, the loss should be separately disclosed in the income statement. While GAAP is not explicit as to presentation, it would appear that this adjustment could be disclosed as a separately identified charge within cost of goods sold, or as an administrative expense. The write-down is recorded with a debit to a loss account and a credit either to an inventory or an allowance account.

Special Valuation Methods

There are instances in which an accountant must estimate the value of inventories without an actual physical count. Some of the methods used are the retail method, the LIFO retail method, and the gross profit method.

Retail method. The conventional retail method is used by retailers to estimate the cost of their ending inventory. The retailer can either take a physical inventory at retail prices or estimate ending retail inventory and then use the cost-to-retail ratio to convert the ending inventory at retail to its estimated cost. This eliminates the process of going back to original invoices or other documents in order to determine the original cost for each inventoriable item. The retail method can be used under any of the three cost flow assumptions discussed earlier: FIFO, LIFO, or average cost. As with ordinary FIFO or average cost, the LCM rule can also be applied to the retail method when either one of these two cost assumptions is used.

The key to applying the retail method is determining the cost-to-retail ratio. The calculation of this number varies depending upon the cost flow assumption selected. The cost-to-retail ratio provides a relationship between the **cost** of goods available for sale and the **retail** price of these same goods. This ratio is used to convert the ending retail inventory back to cost. The computation of the cost-to-retail ratio for each of the available methods is described below. The use of the LIFO cost flow assumption with this method is discussed in the next section.

1. **FIFO cost**—The concept of FIFO indicates that the ending inventory is made up of the latest purchases. Therefore, beginning inventory is excluded from the computation of the cost-to-retail ratio, and the computation becomes net purchases divided by their retail value adjusted for both net markups and net markdowns.
2. **FIFO (LCM)**—The computation is basically the same as FIFO cost except that markdowns are excluded from the computation of the cost-to-retail ratio.
3. **Average cost**—Average cost assumes that ending inventory consists of all goods available for sale. Therefore, the cost-to-retail ratio is computed by dividing the cost of goods available for sale (Beginning inventory + Net

purchases) by the retail value of these goods adjusted for both net markups and net markdowns.

4. **Average cost (LCM)**—Is computed in the same manner as average cost except that markdowns are excluded for the calculation of the cost-to-retail ratio.

A simple example illustrates the computation of the cost-to-retail ratio under both the FIFO cost and average cost methods in a situation where no markups or markdowns exist.

	FIFO cost		Average cost	
	Cost	*Retail*	*Cost*	*Retail*
Beginning inventory	$100,000	$ 200,000	$100,000	$ 200,000
Net purchases	500,000 (a)	800,000(b)	500,000	800,000
Total goods available for sale	$600,000	1,000,000	$600,000 (c)	1,000,000 (d)
Sales at retail		(800,000)		(800,000)
Ending inventory—retail		$ 200,000		$ 200,000

Cost–to–retail ratio

$$\frac{(a)500,000}{(b)800,000} = 62.5\% \qquad \frac{(c)\ 600,000}{(d)1,000,000} = 60\%$$

Ending inventory—cost
200,000 x 62.5% $ 125,000
200,000 x 60% $ 120,000

Note that the only difference in the two examples is the numbers used to calculate the cost-to-retail ratio.

The lower of cost or market aspect of the retail method is a result of the treatment of net markups and net markdowns. **Net markups** (markups less markup cancellations) are net increases above the original retail price, which are generally caused by changes in supply and demand. **Net markdowns** (markdowns less markdown cancellations) are net decreases below the original retail price. An approximation of lower of cost or market is achieved by including net markups but excluding net markdowns from the cost-to-retail ratio.

To understand this approximation, assume a toy is purchased for $6, and the retail price is set at $10. It is later marked down to $8. A cost-to-retail ratio including markdowns would be $6 divided by $8 or 75%, and ending inventory would be valued at $8 times 75%, or $6 (original cost). A cost-to-retail ratio excluding markdowns would be $6 divided by $10 or 60%, and ending inventory would be valued at $8 times 60%, or $4.80 (LCM). The write-down to $4.80 reflects the loss in utility which is evidenced by the reduced retail price.

The application of the lower of cost or market rule is illustrated for both the FIFO and average cost methods in the example below. Remember, if the markups and markdowns below had been included in the previous example **both** would have been included in the cost-to-retail ratio.

	FIFO cost (LCM)		Average cost (LCM)	
	Cost	Retail	Cost	Retail
Beginning inventory	$100,000	$ 200,000	$100,000	$ 200,000
Net purchases	500,000 (a)	800,000 (b)	500,000	800,000
Net markups	--	250,000 (b)	--	250,000
Total goods available for sale	$600,000	1,250,000	$600,000 (c)	1,250,000 (d)
Net markdowns		(50,000)		(50,000)
Sales at retail		(800,000)		(800,000)
Ending inventory—retail		$ 400,000		$ 400,000

Cost-to-retail ratio $\dfrac{\text{(a) } 500,000}{\text{(b) } 1,050,000} = 47.6\%$ $\dfrac{\text{(c) } 600,000}{\text{(d) } 1,250,000} = 48\%$

Ending inventory—LCM
400,000 x 47.6% $ 190,400
400,000 x 48% $ 192,000

Notice that under the FIFO (LCM) method all of the markups are considered attributable to the current period purchases. While this is not necessarily accurate, it provides the most conservative estimate of the ending inventory.

There are a number of additional inventory topics and issues which affect the computation of the cost-to-retail ratio. Purchase discounts and freight affect only the cost column in this computation. The sales figure which is subtracted from the adjusted cost of goods available for sale in the retail column must be gross sales after adjustment for sales returns. Sales discounts are not included in the computation. If sales are recorded at gross, then deduct the gross sales figure. If sales are recorded at net, then both the recorded sales and sales discount must be deducted to give the same effect as deducting gross sales. Normal spoilage is generally allowed for in the firm's pricing policies, and for this reason it is deducted from the retail column **after** the calculation of the cost-to-retail ratio. Abnormal spoilage, on the other hand, should be deducted from **both** the cost and retail columns **before** the cost-to-retail calculation as it could distort the ratio. It is then generally reported as a separate loss, either within the cost of goods sold section or as an administrative expense. Abnormal spoilage generally arises from a major theft or casualty, while normal spoilage is usually due to shrinkage or breakage. These determinations and their treatments will vary depending upon the firm's policies.

When applying the retail method, separate computations should be made for any departments which experience significantly higher or lower profit margins. Distortions arise in the retail method when a department sells goods with varying margins in a proportion different from that purchased, in which case the cost-to-retail percentage would not be representative of the mix of goods in ending inventory. Also, manipulations of income are possible by planning the timing of markups and markdowns.

The retail method is an acceptable method of valuing inventories for tax purposes. Tax regulations require valuation at lower of cost or market (except for LIFO) and an annual physical inventory.

LIFO retail method. As with other LIFO concepts, treasury regulations are the governing force behind the LIFO retail method. The regulations differentiate between a "variety" store which is required to use an internally computed index and a "department" store which can use a price index published by the Bureau of Labor Statistics. The computation of an internal index was previously discussed in the dollar-value LIFO section. It involves applying the double-extension method to a representative sample of the ending inventory. Selection of a published index is to be in accordance with the regulations set forth by the Treasury.

The steps used in computing the value of ending inventory under the LIFO retail method are listed below and then applied to an example for illustrative purposes.

1. Calculate (or select) the current year conversion price index. Recall that in the base year this index will be 1.00.
2. Calculate the value of the ending inventory at both cost and retail. Remember, as with other LIFO methods, tax regulations **do not** permit the use of LCM, so both markups and markdowns are included in the computation of the cost-to-retail ratio. However, the beginning inventory is excluded from goods available for sale at cost and at retail.
3. Restate the ending inventory at retail to base-year retail. Divide the current ending inventory at retail by the current year index determined in step 1.
4. Layers are then treated as they were for the dollar-value LIFO example presented earlier. If the ending inventory restated to base-year retail exceeds the previous year's amount at base-year retail, a new layer is established.
5. The computation of LIFO cost is the last step and requires multiplying each layer at base-year retail by the appropriate price index and multiplying this product by the cost-to-retail ratio in order to arrive at the LIFO cost for each layer.

The following example illustrates a two-year period to which the LIFO retail method is applied. The first period represents the first year of operations for the organization and is its base year.

Year 1

Step 1 — Because this is the base year, there is no need to compute an index, as it will always be 1.00.

Step 2 —

	Cost	*Retail*
Beginning inventory	$ --	$ --
Purchases	582,400	988,600
Markups	--	164,400
Markdowns	--	(113,000)
Subtotal	$582,400	$1,040,000
Total goods available for sale	$582,400	$1,040,000
Sales—at retail		840,000
Ending year 1 inventory—at retail		$ 200,000

$$\text{Cost-to-retail ratio} \quad \frac{582,400}{1,040,000} = 56\%$$

Ending inventory at cost
$200,000 x 56% $112,000

Step 3 — Because this is the base year, the restatement to base-year cost is not necessary; however, the computation would be
$200,000/1.00 = $200,000.

Steps 4
and 5 — The determination of layers is again unnecessary in the base year; however, the computation would take the following format.

	Ending inventory at base-year retail	*Conversion price index*	*Cost-to-retail ratio*	*LIFO cost*
Base year ($200,000/1.00)	$200,000	1.00	0.56	$112,000

Year 2

Step 1 — We make the assumption that the computation of an internal index yields a result of 1.12 (obtained by double-extending a representative sample).

Step 2 —

	Cost	*Retail*
Beginning inventory	$112,000	$ 200,000
Purchases	716,300	1,168,500
Markups	--	87,500
Markdowns	--	(21,000)
Subtotal	$716,300	$1,235,000
Total goods available for sale		$1,435,000
Sales—at retail		1,171,800
Ending year 2 inventory—at retail		$ 263,200

$$\text{Cost-to-retail ratio} \quad \frac{716,300}{1,235,000} = 58\%$$

Step 3 — The restatement of ending inventory at current year retail to base-year retail is done using the index computed in step 1. In this case it is $263,200/1.12 = $235,000.

Steps 4
and 5 — There is a LIFO layer in year 2 because the $235,000 inventory at base-year retail exceeds the year 1 amount of $200,000.

The computation of the LIFO cost for each layer is shown below.

	Ending inventory at base-year retail	*Conversion price index*	*Cost-to-retail ratio*	*LIFO cost*
Base year ($200,000/1.00)	$200,000	1.00	0.56	$112,000
Year 2 layer	35,000	1.12	0.58	22,736
	$235,000			
Ending year 2 inventory at LIFO cost				$134,736

The treatment of subsequent increments and decrements is the same for this method as it is for the regular dollar-value method.

Gross profit method. The gross profit method is used to estimate ending inventory when a physical count is not possible or feasible. It can also be used to evaluate the reasonableness of a given inventory amount. Assume the following data:

Beginning inventory	$125,000
Net purchases	450,000
Sales	600,000
Estimated gross profit percentage	32%

Ending inventory is estimated as follows:

Beginning inventory	$125,000
Net purchases	450,000
Cost of goods available for sale	575,000
Cost of goods sold [$600,000 – (32% x $600,000)] or (68% x $600,000)	408,000
Estimated ending inventory	$167,000

The gross profit method is used for interim reporting estimates, analyses by auditors, and estimates of inventory lost in fires or other catastrophes. The method is not acceptable for either tax or annual financial reporting purposes. Thus, its major purposes are for internal and interim reporting.

Other Cost Topics

Base stock. The base stock method assumes that a certain level of inventory investment is necessary for normal business activities and is, therefore, permanent. The base stock inventory is carried at historical cost. Decreases in the base stock are considered temporary and are charged to cost of goods sold at replacement cost. Increases are carried at current year costs. The base stock approach is seldom used in practice since it is not allowed for tax purposes, and the LIFO method gives similar results.

Standard costs. Standard costs are predetermined unit costs used by manufacturing firms for planning and control purposes. Standard costs are often incorporated into the accounts, and materials, work in process, and finished goods inventories are all carried at standard costs. The use of standard costs in financial reporting is acceptable if adjustments are made periodically to reflect current conditions and if its use approximates one of the recognized cost flow assumptions.

Relative sales value. Relative sales (or net realizable) values are used to assign costs to inventory items purchased or manufactured in groups. This method is applicable to joint products, subdivided assets such as real estate lots, and basket purchases.

For example, products A and B have the same processes performed on them up to the split-off point. The total cost incurred to this point is $80,000. This cost can be assigned to products A and B using their relative sales value at the split-off point.

If A could be sold for $60,000 and B for $40,000, the total sales value is $100,000. The cost would be assigned on the basis of each product's relative sales value. Thus, A would be assigned a cost of $48,000 (60,000/100,000 x 80,000) and B a cost of $32,000 (40,000/100,000 x 80,000).

Other Inventory Topics

Purchase commitments. Purchase commitments generally are not recognized in the financial statements because they are executory in nature. However, footnote disclosure is required for firm purchase commitments which are material in amount.

If at year-end the contract price on these commitments exceeds the market value, the estimated loss is recognized and reported in the income statement. This results in recognition of loss before the asset is recognized on the books.

Inventories valued at selling price. In exceptional cases, inventories may be reported at sales price less disposal costs. Such treatment is justified when cost is difficult to determine, quoted market prices are available, marketability is assured, and units are interchangeable. Precious metals, certain agricultural products, and meat are examples of inventories valued in this manner. When inventory is valued above cost, revenue is recognized before the point of sale. Full disclosure in the financial statements is required.

Interim reporting. The principles used to determine ending inventory and cost of goods sold in annual reports are also used in interim reports, although four exceptions are allowed (APB 28). These are

1. The gross profit method may be used to estimate cost of goods sold and ending inventory.
2. When LIFO layers are liquidated during the interim period but are expected to be replaced by year-end, cost of goods sold should reflect current costs rather than old LIFO costs.
3. Temporary market declines need not be recognized if substantial evidence exists that market prices will recover. If LCM losses recorded in one interim period are recovered by year-end, the recovery is recognized as a gain.
4. Planned standard cost variances expected to be offset by year-end can be deferred.

EMERGING ISSUES TASK FORCE CONSENSUS SUMMARIES

86-46   Uniform Capitalization Rules for Inventory Under the Tax Reform Act of 1986

The fact that a cost is capitalizable for tax purposes does not, by itself, indicate that it is preferable, or even appropriate, to capitalize that cost for financial reporting purposes. An analysis of the individual facts and circumstances should be performed to determine if costs should be capitalized for financial reporting purposes.

APPENDIX A

LIFO CONFORMITY RULE

As stated earlier in this chapter, Treasury Regulations require that in order to take advantage of LIFO for tax purposes, a company must also use LIFO for determining income, profit, or loss for financial statement purposes. The regulations also cite certain exceptions to this general rule. Among the exceptions allowable under the regulations are the following:

1. The use of an inventory method other than LIFO in presenting information reported as a supplement to or explanation of the taxpayer's primary presentation of income in financial reports to outside parties. [Reg. §1.472-2(e)(1)(i)]

2. The use of an inventory method other than LIFO to determine the value of the taxpayer's inventory for purposes of reporting the value of such inventory as an asset on the balance sheet. [Reg. §1.472-2(e)(1)(ii)]

3. The use of an inventory method other than LIFO for purposes of determining information reported in internal management reports. [Reg. §1.472-2(e)(1)(iii)]

4. The use of an inventory method other than LIFO for financial reports covering a period of less than one year. [Reg. §1.472- 2(e)(1)(iv)]

5. The use of lower of LIFO cost or market to value inventories for financial statements while using LIFO cost for tax purposes. [Reg. §1.472-2(e)(1)(v)]

6. For inventories acquired in a section 351 transaction, the use of the transferor's acquisition dates and costs for book purposes while using redetermined LIFO layers for tax purposes. [Reg. §1.472-2(e)(1)(vii)]

7. The inclusion of certain costs (under full absorption) in inventory for tax purposes, as required by regulations, while not including those same costs in inventory under GAAP, (full absorption) for book purposes. [Reg. §1.472-2(e)(8)(i)]

8. The use of different methods of establishing pools for book purposes and tax purposes. [Reg. §1.472-2(e)(8)(ii)]

9. The use of different determinations of the time sales or purchases are accrued for book purposes and tax purposes. [Reg. §1.472-2(e)(8)(xii)]

10. In the case of a business combination, the use of different methods to allocate basis for book purposes and tax purposes. [Reg. §1.472-2(e)(8)(xiii)]

Another important consideration in applying the LIFO conformity rule is the law concerning related corporations. In accordance with the Tax Reform Act of 1984, all members of the same group of financially related corporations shall be treated as a single taxpayer when applying the conformity rule. Previously, taxpayers were able to circumvent the conformity rule by having a subsidiary on LIFO, while the non-LIFO parent presented combined non-LIFO financial statements. This is a violation of the conformity requirement [Sec. 472(g)].

APPENDIX B

TASK FORCE ON LIFO INVENTORY PROBLEMS

Most of the prescribed rules concerning the implementation of LIFO have their origins in the Internal Revenue Code and Treasury Regulations. Because authoritative financial accounting pronouncements on implementing LIFO are virtually nonexistent, GAAP has followed tax. The AICPA Task Force on LIFO Inventory problems developed an Issues Paper to discuss certain financial accounting issues related to LIFO. Issues Papers constitute generally accepted accounting principles but are not mandatory. The key conclusions from this Issues Paper (entitled "Identification and Discussion of Certain Financial Accounting and Reporting Issues Concerning LIFO Inventories") are described below.

1. **Specific goods vs. dollar-value.** The Task Force believes that either the specific goods approach or dollar-value approach to LIFO is acceptable for financial reporting. They also believe that it is not necessary to disclose whether the specific goods or dollar-value approach is used. TRA 1986 provides an election for qualifying small businesses to account for their inventories using a simplified dollar-value LIFO method.

2. **Pricing current year purchases.** Three approaches to pricing LIFO inventory increments are available under tax regulations—earliest acquisition price, latest acquisition price, and average acquisition price. The Task Force believes that the earliest acquisition price approach is the most compatible with financial reporting objectives, but finds all three to be acceptable for financial reporting.

3. **Quantity to use to determine price.** The Task Force believes that the price used to determine the inventory increment should be based on the cost of the quantity or dollars of the increment rather than on the cost of the quantity or dollars equal to the ending inventory. They also believe that it is not necessary to disclose which approach is used.

4. **Disclosure of LIFO reserve or replacement cost.** The Task Force believes that either the LIFO reserve or replacement cost and its basis for determination should be disclosed for financial reporting.

5. **Partial adoption of LIFO.** The Task Force believes that if a company changes to LIFO, it should do so for all of its inventories. Partial adoption should only be allowed if there exists a valid business reason for not fully adopting LIFO. A planned gradual adoption of LIFO over several time periods is considered acceptable if valid business reasons exist (lessening the income statement effect of adoption in any one year is not a valid business reason). The Task Force also believes that where partial adoption of LIFO has been justified, the extent to which LIFO has been adopted should be disclosed. This can be disclosed by indicating either the portion of the

ending inventory priced on LIFO or the portion of cost of sales resulting from LIFO inventories.

6. **Methods of pooling.** The Task Force addressed several issues related to establishing pools. They believe that an entity should have valid business reasons for establishing its LIFO pools. Additionally, it is believed that the existence of a separate legal entity that has no economic substance is not reason enough to justify separate pools. It also believes that an entity's pooling arrangements need not be disclosed.

7. **New items entering a pool.** The Task Force believes that new items should be added to the pool based on what the items would have cost had they been acquired in the base period (reconstructed cost) rather than based on their current cost. The reconstructed cost should be determined based on the most objective sources available including published vendor price lists, vendor quotes, and general industry indexes. The Task Force believes it is not necessary to disclose the way that new items are priced.

    It also believes that, where necessary, the use of a substitute base year in making the LIFO computation is acceptable.

8. **Dollar-value index.** The required index can be developed using two possible approaches, the unit cost method or the cost component method. The unit cost method measures changes in the index based on the weighted-average increase or decrease in the unit costs of raw materials, work in process, and finished goods inventory. The cost component method, on the other hand, measures changes in the index by the weighted-average increase or decrease in the component costs of material, labor, and overhead that make up ending inventory. The Task Force believes that either of these methods is acceptable.

9. **LIFO liquidations.** The Task Force believes that the effects on income of LIFO inventory liquidations should be disclosed in the notes to the financial statements. A replacement reserve for the liquidation should not be provided. When an involuntary LIFO liquidation occurs, the Task Force does not believe that the income effect of the liquidation should be deferred.

    When a LIFO liquidation occurs, there are three possible ways to measure its effect on income.

    a. The difference between actual cost of sales and what cost of sales would have been had the inventory been reinstated under the entity's normal pricing procedure

    b. The difference between actual cost of sales and what cost of sales would have been had the inventory been reinstated at year-end replacement cost

    c. The amount of the LIFO reserve at the beginning of the year which was credited to income (excluding the increase in the reserve due to current year price changes)

The Task Force supports the first method. It also believes that disclosure of the effect of the liquidation should give effect only to pools with decrements (i.e., there should be no netting against increments in other pools).

10. **Lower of cost or market.** The Task Force believes that the most reasonable approach to applying the lower of cost or market rules to LIFO inventory is to base the determination on groups of inventory rather than on an item-by-item approach. They believe that a pool constitutes a reasonable grouping for this purpose. They also believe, however, that an item-by-item approach is permitted by authoritative accounting literature, particularly for obsolete or discontinued items.

For companies with more than one LIFO pool, it would be permissible to aggregate the pools in applying the lower of cost or market test if the pools are similar. It is believed that where the pools are significantly dissimilar, aggregating the pools is not appropriate.

The Task Force also believes that previous write-downs to market value of the cost of LIFO inventories should be reversed after a company disposes of the physical units of the inventory for which reserves were provided. The reserves at the end of the year should be based on a new computation of cost or market.

11. **LIFO conformity and supplemental disclosures.** The Task Force believes that a company may present supplemental non-LIFO disclosures within the historical cost framework. If nondiscretionary variable expenses (i.e., profit sharing based on earnings) would have been different based on the supplemental information, then the company should give effect to such changes. Additionally, the supplemental disclosure should reflect the same type of tax effects as required by generally accepted accounting principles in the primary financial statements.

The Task Force also believes a company may use different LIFO applications for financial reporting than it uses for income tax purposes. Any such differences should be accounted for as temporary differences with the exception of differences in the allocation of cost to inventory in a business combination. They further believe that any differences between LIFO applications used for financial reporting and those used for income tax purposes need not be disclosed beyond the requirements of APB 11 (subsequently superseded by SFAS 109).

12. **Interim reporting and LIFO.** The Task Force's conclusions on interim reporting of LIFO inventory are discussed on pages 841-842.

13. **Different financial and income tax years.** The Task Force believes that a company which has a year-end for financial reporting different from that for income tax reporting should make a separate LIFO calculation for financial purposes using its financial reporting year as a discrete period for that calculation.

14. **Business combinations accounted for by the purchase method.** Inventory acquired in a business combination accounted for by the purchase method will be recorded at fair market value at the date of the combination. The acquired company may be able to carry over its prior basis for that inventory for tax purposes, causing a difference between book and tax basis. The Task Force believes that an adjustment should be made to the fair value of the inventory only if it is reasonably estimated to be liquidated in the future. The adjustment would be for the income tax effect of the difference between tax and book basis.

    The Task Force further believes that inventory acquired in such a combination should be considered the LIFO base inventory if the inventory is treated by the company as a separate business unit or a separate LIFO pool. If instead the acquired inventory is combined into an existing pool, then the acquired inventory should be considered as part of the current year's purchases.

15. **Changes in LIFO applications.** The Task Force believes that a change in a LIFO application is a change in accounting principle. LIFO applications refer to the approach (i.e., dollar value or specific goods), computational technique, or the numbers or contents of the pools.

    The AICPA Task Force did not include intercompany transfers in the 1984 Issues Paper; however, the AICPA issued Practice Bulletin 2 in 1987 to provide guidance for this complex area.

    The focus of this bulletin is the LIFO liquidation effect caused by transferring inventories which in turn create intercompany profits. This liquidation can occur when (1) two components of the same taxable entity transfer inventory, for example, when a LIFO method component transfers inventory to a non-LIFO component, or (2) when two separate taxable entities that consolidate transfer inventory, even though both use the LIFO method.

    This LIFO liquidation creates profit which must be eliminated along with the other intercompany profits.

8 SPECIAL ACCOUNTING AND REPORTING ISSUES

Few issues are receiving as much attention in the accounting profession as accounting for revenue, especially with respect to the proper timing for its recognition. At first glance, the issue seems fairly simple and straightforward. The FASB eloquently set forth the conceptual basis for revenue recognition in SFAC 5, *Recognition and Measurement in Financial Statements of Business Enterprises.*

Revenues are not recognized until earned. An entity's revenue-earning activities involve delivering or producing goods, rendering services, or other activities that constitute its ongoing major or central operations, and revenues are considered to have been earned when the entity has substantially accomplished what it must do to be entitled to the benefits represented by the revenues.

SFAC 5 states that revenue should be recognized when (1) it is realized or realizable and (2) it has been earned. In practice, this is quite straightforward when applied to a retailer, a wholesaler, or a manufacturer. When the enterprise delivers its goods to its customer who inspects them and accepts them, revenue should be recognized.

Notwithstanding the lack of ambiguity in the conceptual requirements, in practice, abuses in revenue recognition have been common. In March 1999, a report entitled *Fraudulent Financial Reporting 1987-1997: An Analysis of U.S. Public Companies* was issued by the Committee of Sponsoring Organizations of the Treadway Commission (commonly referred to as COSO) that indicated over half of the financial reporting frauds in the study involved overstatement of revenue. While this is not a new phenomenon, it is receiving heightened attention due to several high-profile frauds (and alleged audit failures) that have been given substantial attention in the business press.

This chapter addresses circumstances where the terms of the transaction do not allow for the clear application of the revenue realization principle. These are as follows:

1. Long-term construction contracts
2. Service sales transactions
3. Sales when collection is uncertain
4. Revenue recognition when right of return exists
5. Profit recognition on real estate
6. Real estate operations
7. Franchising
8. Other special accounting and reporting issues

Each of these sections may be read as individual units.

LONG-TERM CONSTRUCTION CONTRACTS

PERSPECTIVE AND ISSUES

Accounting for long-term construction contracts involves questions as to when revenue should be recognized and how to measure the revenue to be recorded. The basic GAAP governing the recognition of long-term contract revenue is contained in ARB 45, *Long-Term Construction-Type Contracts,* AcSEC Statement of Position 81-1, *Accounting for Performance of Construction-Type and Certain Production-Type Contracts* and the AICPA *Audit and Accounting Guide for Construction Contractors.*[1] In accordance with SAS 69, Accounting Research Bulletins (ARB) are "category a" (the highest level) GAAP, and SOP 81-1 and the Audit and Accounting Guide are "category b" GAAP.

The accounting for long-term construction contracts is complicated by the need to rely upon estimates of revenues, costs, and progress toward completion and the principle of recognition of losses when apparent.

Sources of GAAP					
SFAC	*ARB*	*APB*	*SFAS*	*SOP*	*EITF*
5	45	20	109	81-1	91-6, 96-17

---

[1] *The SOP is included as an appendix to the Audit and Accounting Guide.*

DEFINITIONS OF TERMS

Back charges. Billings for work performed or costs incurred by one party (the biller) that, in accordance with the agreement, should have been performed or incurred by the party billed.

Change orders. Modifications of an original contract that effectively change the provisions of the contract without adding new provisions.

Claims. Amounts in excess of the agreed contract price that a contractor seeks to collect from customers for customer-caused delays, errors in specifications and designs, unapproved change orders, or other causes of unanticipated costs. (SOP 81-1)

Combining contracts. Grouping two or more contracts into a single profit center for accounting purposes.

Completed-contract method. A method of accounting that recognizes income only after the contract is complete.

Construction-in-progress (CIP) or Work-in-progress (WIP) An inventory account used to accumulate the construction costs of the contract project.

Cost-to-cost method. A percentage-of-completion method used to determine the extent of progress toward completion on a contract. The ratio of cost incurred to the end of the current period to the total estimated costs of the project is used to recognize income.

Estimated cost to complete. The anticipated additional cost of materials, labor, subcontracting costs, and indirect costs (overhead) required to complete a project at a scheduled time.

Percentage-of-completion method. A method of accounting that recognizes income on a contract as work progresses.

Precontract costs. Costs incurred before a contract has been accepted (e.g., architectural designs, purchase of special equipment, engineering fees, and start-up costs).

Profit center. A unit for the accumulation of revenues and cost for the measurement of income.

Progress billings on long-term contracts. Requests for partial payments sent to the purchaser in accordance with the terms of the contract at intervals as various points in the project are reached.

Segmenting contracts. Dividing a single contract or group of contracts into two or more profit centers for accounting purposes.

Subcontractor. A second-level contractor who enters into a contract with a prime (general) contractor to perform a specific part or phase of a construction project.

Substantial completion. The point at which the major work on a contract is completed and only insignificant costs and potential risks remain.

CONCEPTS, RULES, AND EXAMPLES

Long-term construction contract revenue may be recognized during construction rather than at the completion of the contract. This "as earned" approach to revenue recognition is justified because under most long-term construction contracts both the buyer and the seller (contractor) obtain enforceable rights. The buyer has the legal right to require specific performance from the contractor and, in effect, has ownership claim to the contractor's work in progress. The contractor, under most long-term contracts, has the right to require the buyer to make progress payments during the construction period. The substance of this business activity is that a continuous sale occurs as the work progresses.

ARB 45 describes the two generally accepted methods of accounting for long-term construction contracts.

> The **percentage-of-completion method** *recognizes income as work on a contract (or group of closely related contracts) progresses. The recognition of revenues and profits is generally related to costs incurred in providing the services required under the contract.*

Under this method, the **construction-in-progress (CIP)** account is used to accumulate costs. At any point in time if the cumulative amount billed to date under the contract exceeds the amount of the CIP plus the portion of the contract's estimated gross profit attributable to that CIP, then the contractor recognizes a current liability captioned as "billings in excess of costs and estimated earnings." This liability recognizes the remaining obligation of the contractor to complete additional work prior to recognizing the excess billing as revenue. If the reverse is true, that is, the accumulated CIP and gross profit earned exceed billings to date, then the contractor recognizes a current asset captioned as "costs and estimated earnings in excess of billings." This asset represents the portion of the contractor's revenues under the contract that have been earned but not yet billed under the contract provisions. Where more than one contract exists, these assets and liabilities should be determined on a project-by-project basis, with the accumulated assets and liabilities being separately stated on the balance sheet. Assets and liabilities should not be offset unless a right of offset exists. Thus, the net debit balances for certain contracts should not ordinarily be offset against net credit balances for other contracts. An exception may exist if the balances relate to contracts that meet the criteria for combining described in SOP 81-1.

Under the percentage-of-completion method, income should not be based on cash collections or interim billings. Cash collections and interim billings are based upon contract terms which do not necessarily measure contract performance.

> The **completed-contract method** *recognizes income only when the contract is complete, or substantially complete.*

Under this method, the costs and related billings are accumulated and reported as deferred items on the balance sheet until the project is complete or substantially complete. A contract can be regarded as substantially complete if remaining costs of completion are immaterial. When the accumulated costs (CIP) exceed the related billings, the excess should be shown as a current asset (inventory account). If billings exceed related costs, the difference should be shown as a current liability. This determination should also be made on a project-by-project basis with the accumulated assets and liabilities being separately stated on the balance sheet. An excess of accumulated costs over related billings should be shown as a current asset, and an excess of accumulated billings over related costs should be shown among the liabilities, in most cases as a current liability.

SOP 81-1 deems the percentage-of-completion method to be preferable when estimates are reasonably dependable and the following conditions exist:

1. Contracts executed by the parties normally include provisions that clearly specify the enforceable rights regarding goods or services to be provided and received by the parties, the consideration to be exchanged, and the manner and terms of settlement.
2. The buyer can be expected to satisfy his or her obligations under the contract.
3. The contractor can be expected to perform his or her contractual obligations.

SOP 81-1 presumes that contractors generally have the ability to produce estimates that are sufficiently dependable to justify the use of the percentage-of-completion method of accounting. Persuasive evidence to the contrary is necessary to overcome this presumption.

The principal advantage of the completed-contract method is that it is based on final results, whereas the percentage-of-completion method is dependent upon estimates for unperformed work. The principal disadvantage of the completed-contract method is that when the period of a contract extends into more than one accounting period, there will be an irregular recognition of income.

These two methods should not be used as acceptable alternatives for the same set of circumstances. ARB 45 states that in general, when estimates of costs to complete and extent of progress toward completion of long-term contracts are reasonably dependable, the percentage-of-completion method is preferable. When lack of dependable estimates or inherent hazards cause forecasts to be doubtful, the completed-contract method is preferable.

The completed-contract method may also be acceptable when a contractor has numerous relatively short-term contracts and when results of operations do not vary materially from those that would be reported under the percentage-of-completion method.

Contract Costs

Contract costs are costs identifiable with or allocable to specific contracts. Generally, contract costs would include all direct costs such as direct materials, direct labor, and any indirect costs (overhead) allocable to the contracts. Contract costs can be broken down into two categories: costs incurred to date and estimated costs to complete.

Precontract costs are costs incurred **before** a contract has been entered into, with the expectation of the contract being accepted and thereby recoverable through billings. Precontract costs would include architectural designs, costs of learning a new process, and any other costs which are expected to be recovered if the contract is accepted. SOP 98-5, *Reporting on the Costs of Start-Up Activities,* requires that precontract costs be expensed as incurred, as they are the equivalent of start-up costs in other types of businesses. Consequently, precontract costs are not permitted to be included in CIP. Contract costs incurred after the acceptance of the contract are costs incurred towards the completion of the project and are capitalized in the construction-in-progress (CIP) account.

The company may choose to defer costs related to producing excess goods in anticipation of future orders of the same item. Cost associated with excess production can be treated as inventory if the costs are considered recoverable.

If precontract costs are incurred in connection with a current contract in anticipation of obtaining additional future contracts, those costs should, nevertheless, be accounted for as costs of the current contract. If such costs are not incurred in connection with a current contract, then they must be expensed as incurred. There is no look-back provision in this standard. A contractor may not retroactively record precontract costs as CIP if a contract is subsequently executed.

Estimated costs to complete. These are the **anticipated costs** required to complete a project at a scheduled time. They would be comprised of the same elements as the original total estimated contract costs and would be based on prices expected to be in effect when the costs are incurred.

The latest estimates should be used to determine the progress towards completion. SOP 81-1 provides the practices to be followed when determining estimated costs to complete.

First of all, systematic and consistent procedures should be used. These procedures should be correlated with the cost accounting system and should be able to provide a comparison between actual and estimated costs. Additionally, the determination of estimated total contract costs should identify the significant cost elements.

Another procedure requires that the estimation of the costs to complete should include the same elements of costs included in accumulated costs. Additionally, the estimated costs should reflect any expected price increases. These expected price increases should not be "blanket provisions" for all contract costs, but rather specific provisions for each type of cost. Expected increases in each of the cost elements such as wages, materials, and overhead items should be taken into consideration separately.

Finally, estimates of costs to complete should be reviewed periodically to reflect new information. Estimates of costs should be examined for price fluctuations and also should be reviewed for possible future problems, such as labor strikes or direct material delays.

Accounting for contract costs is similar to accounting for inventory. Costs necessary to ready the asset for sale would be recorded in the construction-in-progress account, as incurred. CIP would include both direct and indirect costs but would usually not include general and administrative expenses or selling expenses since they are not normally identifiable with a particular contract and should therefore be expensed. However, general and administrative expenses **may** be included in contract costs under the completed contract method since a preferable allocation of revenues and costs might take place, especially in years when no contracts were completed.

Subcontractor costs. Since a contractor may not be able to perform all facets of a construction project, one or more subcontractors may be engaged. The amount billed to the contractor for work done by the subcontractor should be included in contract costs. The amount billed is directly traceable to the project and would be included in the CIP account, similar to direct materials and direct labor.

Back charges. Contract costs may have to be adjusted for back charges. Back charges are billings for costs incurred that the contract stipulated should have been performed by another party. These charges are often disputed by the parties involved.

Example of a back charge situation

The subcontract (the contract between the general contractor and the subcontractor) obligates the subcontractor to raze a building and prepare the land for construction of a replacement building. The general contractor had to clear away debris left by the subcontractor before construction could begin. The general contractor expects to be reimbursed for the work since it should have been performed by the subcontractor. The contractor back charges the subcontractor for the costs of debris removal.

The contractor treats the back charge as a receivable from the subcontractor and reduces contract costs by the amount recoverable. If the subcontractor disputes the back charge, the cost becomes a claim. Claims are an amount in excess of the agreed contract price or amounts not included in the original contract price that the contractor seeks to collect. Claims should only be recorded as additional contract revenue if the requirements set forth in SOP 81-1 are met.

The subcontractor should record the back charge as a payable and as additional contract costs if it is probable the amount will be paid. If the amount or validity of the liability is disputed, the subcontractor would have to consider the probable outcome in order to determine the proper accounting treatment.

Types of Contracts

Four types of contracts are distinguished based on their pricing arrangements: (1) fixed-price or lump-sum contracts, (2) time-and-materials contracts, (3) cost-type contracts, and (4) unit-price contracts.

Fixed-price contracts are contracts for which the price is not usually subject to adjustment because of costs incurred by the contractor. The contractor bears the risks of cost overruns.

Time-and-materials contracts are contracts that provide for payments to the contractor based on direct labor hours at fixed rates and cost of materials.

Cost-type contracts provide for reimbursement of allowable or otherwise defined costs incurred plus a fee representing profits. Some variations of cost-plus contracts are (1) cost-without-fee: no provision for a fee, (2) cost-plus-fixed-fee: contractor reimbursed for costs plus provision for a fixed fee, and (3) cost-plus-award-fee: same as (2) plus provision for an award based on performance. The contract price on a cost-type contract is determined by the sum of the reimbursable expenditures and a fee. The fee is the profit margin (revenue less direct expenses) to be earned on the contract.

Unit-price contracts are contracts under which the contractor is paid a specified amount for every unit of work performed.

Contract costs (incurred and estimated to complete) should be used to compute the gross profit or loss recognized. Under the percentage-of-completion method, gross profit or loss would be recognized each period. The revenue recognized would be matched against the contract costs incurred (similar to cost of goods sold) to determine gross profit/loss. Under the completed contract method, the gross profit/loss is determined at the **substantial completion** of the contract, and no revenue or contract costs are recognized until this point.

Additionally, inventoriable costs (accumulated in the CIP account) should never exceed the net realizable value of the contract. When contract costs exceed their NRV, they must be written down, requiring a contract loss to be recognized in the current period (this will be discussed in greater detail later). This is similar to accounting for inventory.

Revenue Measurement

In practice, various methods are used to measure the extent of progress toward completion. The most common methods are the cost-to-cost method, efforts-expended method, units-of-delivery method, and units-of-work-performed method. Each of these methods of measuring progress on a contract can be identified as either an input or output measure. The input measures attempt to identify progress in a contract in terms of the efforts devoted to it. The cost-to-cost and efforts-expended methods are examples of input measures. Under the cost-to-cost method, the percentage of completion would be estimated by comparing total costs incurred to date to total costs expected for the entire job. Output measures are made in terms of results by attempting to identify progress toward completion by physical measures. The units-of-delivery and units-of-work-performed methods are examples of output measures. Under both of these methods, an estimate of completion is made in terms of achievements to date.

Both input and output measures have drawbacks in certain circumstances. A significant problem of input measures is that the relationship between input and productivity is only indirect; inefficiencies and other factors can cause this relationship to change. A particular drawback of the cost-to-cost method is that costs of uninstalled materials and other up-front costs may produce higher estimates of completion costs because of their early incurrence. These costs should be excluded or allocated over the contract life when it appears that a better measure of periodic income will be obtained. A significant problem of output measures is that the cost, time, and effort associated with one unit of output may not be comparable to that of another. For example, because of the cost of the foundation, the costs to complete the first story of a twenty-story office building can be expected to be greater than the costs of the remaining nineteen floors.

Because ARB 45 recommends that "recognized income [should] be that percentage of estimated total income...that incurred costs to date bear to estimated total costs," the **cost-to-cost** method has become one of the most popular measures used to determine the extent of progress toward completion.

Under the cost-to-cost method, the percentage of **revenue** to recognize can be determined by the following formula:

$$\left(\frac{\text{Cost to date}}{\text{Cost to date} + \text{Estimated costs to complete}} \times \frac{\text{Contract}}{\text{price}} \right) - \frac{\text{Revenue}}{\text{previously recognized}} = \frac{\text{Current}}{\text{revenue recognized}}$$

By slightly modifying this formula, current **gross profit** can also be determined.

$$\left(\frac{\text{Cost to date}}{\text{Cost to date} + \text{Estimated costs to complete}} \times \frac{\text{Expected total gross profit}}{} \right) - \frac{\text{Gross profit}}{\text{previously recognized}} = \frac{\text{Current gross}}{\text{profit earned}}$$

Example of percentage-of-completion (cost-to-cost) and completed-contract methods with profitable contract

Assume a $500,000 contract that requires three years to complete and incurs a total cost of $405,000. The following data pertain to the construction period:

	Year 1	*Year 2*	*Year 3*
Costs incurred during the period	$150,000	$210,000	$ 45,000
Cumulative costs incurred to date	150,000	360,000	405,000
Estimated costs yet to be incurred at year-end	300,000	40,000	--
Estimated total costs	450,000	400,000	--
Progress billings made during the year	100,000	370,000	30,000
Cumulative billings to date	100,000	470,000	500,000
Collections of billings	75,000	300,000	125,000

Completed-Contract & Percentage-of-Completion Methods

	Year 1		Year 2		Year 3	
Construction-in-progress	150,000		210,000		45,000	
Cash, payables, etc.		150,000		210,000		45,000
Contract receivables	100,000		370,000		30,000	
Billings on contracts		100,000		370,000		30,000
Cash	75,000		300,000		125,000	
Contract receivables		75,000		300,000		125,000

Completed-Contract Method Only

	Year 1		Year 2		Year 3	
Billings on contracts					500,000	
Cost of revenues earned					405,000	
Contract revenues earned						500,000
Construction-in-progress						405,000

Percentage-of-Completion Method Only

	Year 1		Year 2		Year 3	
Cost of revenues earned	150,000		210,000		45,000	
Construction-in-progress		150,000		210,000		45,000
Costs and estimated earnings in excess of billings on uncompleted contracts	66,667			66,667		
Billings in excess of costs and estimated earnings on uncompleted contracts			20,000		20,000	
Billings on contracts	100,000		370,000		30,000	
Contract revenues earned		166,667		283,333		50,000

Income Statement Presentation

	Year 1	Year 2	Year 3	Total
Percentage-of-completion				
Contract revenues earned	$166,667*	$283,333**	$ 50,000***	$ 500,000
Cost of revenues earned	(150,000)	(210,000)	(45,000)	(405,000)
Gross profit	$ 16,667	$ 73,333	$ 5,000	$ 95,000
Completed-contract				
Contract revenues earned	--	--	$ 500,000	$ 500,000
Cost of revenues completed	--	--	(405,000)	(405,000)
Gross profit	--	--	$ 95,000	$ 95,000

$$* \quad \frac{\$150,000}{450,000} \quad x \quad 500,000 \quad = \quad \$166,667$$

$$** \quad \left(\frac{\$360,000}{400,000} \quad x \; 500,000\right) \; - \; 166,667 \quad = \quad \$283,333$$

$$*** \quad \left(\frac{\$405,000}{405,000} \quad x \; 500,000\right) \; - \; 166,667 \; - \; 283,333 \; = \quad \$50,000$$

<u>*Balance Sheet Presentation*</u>

	Year 1	Year 2	Year 3
Percentage-of-completion			
Current assets:			
Contract receivables	$ 25,000	$ 95,000	*
Costs and estimated earnings in excess of billings on uncompleted contracts	66,667		
Current liabilities:			
Billings in excess of costs and estimated earnings on uncompleted contracts, year 2		20,000	
Completed-contract			
Current assets:			
Contract receivables	$ 25,000	$ 95,000	*
Costs in excess of billings on uncompleted contracts			

Construction-in-progress	150,000			
Less billings on long-term contracts	(100,000)	$ 50,000		

Current liabilities:

Billings in excess of costs on uncompleted contracts, year 2 $110,000
($470,000 – 360,000)

* *Since the contract was completed, there are no balance sheet amounts at the end of year 3.*

Contract Losses

When the current estimate of total contract cost exceeds the current estimate of total contract revenue, a provision for the entire loss on the entire contract should be made. Provisions for losses should be made in the period in which they become evident under either the percentage-of-completion method or the completed-contract method. The loss provision should be computed on the basis of the **total** estimated costs to complete the contract, which would include the contract costs incurred to date plus estimated costs (use same elements as contract costs incurred) to complete. The provision should be shown separately as a current liability on the balance sheet.

In any year when a **percentage-of-completion** contract has an expected loss, the amount of the loss reported in that year can be computed as follows:

Reported loss = Total expected loss + All profit previously recognized

Example of percentage-of-completion and completed-contract methods with loss contract

Using the previous information, if the costs yet to be incurred at the end of year two were $148,000, the total expected loss is $8,000 [$500,000 – (360,000 + 148,000)], and the total loss reported in year two would be $24,667 ($8,000 + 16,667). Under the completed-contract method, the loss recognized is simply the total expected loss, $8,000.

Journal entry at end of year 2	Percentage-of-completion	Completed-contract
Loss on uncompleted long-term contract (expense)	24,667	8,000
Estimated loss on uncompleted contract (liability)	24,667	8,000

Profit or Loss Recognized on Contract
(Percentage-of-Completion Method)

	Year 1	Year 2	Year 3
Contract price	$500,000	$500,000	$500,000
Estimated total costs:			
Costs incurred contract-to-date	$150,000	$360,000	$506,000*
Estimated cost yet to be incurred	300,000	148,000	--
Estimated total costs for the three-year period, actual for year 3	$450,000	$508,000	$506,000
Estimated gross profit (loss), actual for year 3	50,000	(8,000)	(6,000)
Summary of Effect on Results of Operation			
Current end-of-year estimate of gross profit (loss) actual for year 3	--	$ (8,000)	$ (6,000)
Accumulated effect of gross profit (loss) recognized in prior years	--	16,667	(8,000)
Effect on gross profit (loss) recognized in current year	--	$ (24,667)	$ 2,000

* *Assumed*

Profit or Loss Recognized on Contract
(Completed-Contract Method)

	Year 1	Year 2	Year 3
Contract price	$500,000	$500,000	$500,000
Estimated total costs:			
Costs incurred to date	$150,000	$360,000	$506,000*
Estimated cost yet to be incurred	300,000	148,000	--
Estimated total costs for the three-year period, actual for year 3	$ 50,000	$ (8,000)	$ (6,000)
Loss previously recognized	--	--	$ (8,000)
Amount of estimated income (loss) recognized in the current period, actual for year 3	--	$ (8,000)	$ (2,000)

* *Assumed*

Upon completion of the project during year 3, it can be seen that the actual loss was only $6,000 ($500,000 – $506,000); therefore, the estimated loss provision was overstated in previous years by $2,000. However, since this is a change of an estimate, the $2,000 difference must be handled prospectively; consequently, $2,000 of income should be recognized in year 3 ($8,000 loss previously recognized – $6,000 actual loss).

Combining and Segmenting Contracts

The profit center for accounting purposes is usually a single contract, but under some circumstances the profit center may be a combination of two or more contracts, a segment of a contract or of a group of combined contracts. The contracts must meet requirements in SOP 81-1 in order to combine, or segment; otherwise, each individual contract is presumed to be the profit center.

For accounting purposes, a group of contracts may be combined if they are so closely related that they are, in substance, parts of a single project with an overall profit margin. Per SOP 81-1, a group of contracts may be combined if the contracts

a.   *Are negotiated as a package in the same economic environment with an overall profit margin objective.*
b.   *Constitute an agreement to do a single project.*
c.   *Require closely interrelated construction activities.*
d.   *Are performed concurrently or in a continuous sequence under the same project management.*
e.   *Constitute, in substance, an agreement with a single customer.*

Segmenting a contract is a process of breaking up a larger unit into smaller units for accounting purposes. If the project is segmented, revenues can be assigned to the different elements or phases to achieve different rates of profitability based on the relative value of each element or phase to the estimated total contract revenue. According to SOP 81-1, a project may be segmented if all of the following steps were taken and are documented and verifiable:

a.   *The contractor submitted bona fide proposals on the separate components of the project and on the entire project.*
b.   *The customer had the right to accept the proposals on either basis.*
c.   *The aggregate amount of the proposals on the separate components approximated the amount of the proposal on the entire project.*

A project that does not meet the above criteria may still be segmented if all of the following are applicable:

a.   *The terms and scope of the contract or project clearly call for the separable phases or elements.*
b.   *The separable phases or elements of the project are often bid or negotiated separately.*
c.   *The market assigns different gross profit rates to the segments because of factors such as different levels of risk or differences in the relationship of the supply and demand for the services provided in different segments.*
d.   *The contractor has a significant history of providing similar services to other customers under separate contracts for each significant segment to which a profit margin higher than the overall profit margin on the project is ascribed.*

e.   *The significant history with customers who have contracted for services separately is one that is relatively stable in terms of pricing policy rather than one unduly weighted by erratic pricing decisions (responding, for example, to extraordinary economic circumstances or to unique customer-contractor relationships).*

f.   *The excess of the sum of the prices of the separate elements over the price of the total project is clearly attributable to cost savings incident to combined performance of the contract obligations (for example, cost savings in supervision, overhead, or equipment mobilization). Unless this condition is met, segmenting a contract with a price substantially less than the sum of the prices of the separate phases or elements would be inappropriate even if the other conditions are met. Acceptable price variations should be allocated to the separate phases or elements in proportion to the prices ascribed to each. In all other situations a substantial difference in price (whether more or less) between the separate elements and the price of the total project is evidence that the contractor has accepted different profit margins. Accordingly, segmenting is not appropriate, and the contracts should be the profit centers.*

g.   *The similarity of services and prices in the contract segments and services and the prices of such services to other customers contracted separately should be documented and verifiable.*

Note that the criteria for combining and segmenting should be applied consistently to contracts with similar characteristics and in similar circumstances.

Joint Ventures and Shared Contracts

Contracts that are obtained by long-term construction companies are sometimes shared by more than one contractor. When the owner of the contract puts it up for bids, many contractors will form syndicates or joint ventures in order to bid on and successfully obtain a contract that each contractor individually could not perform.

When this transpires, a separate set of books is maintained for the joint venture. If the percentages of interest for each of the venturers are identical in more than one contract, the joint venture might keep its records almost like another construction company. Usually, the joint venture is for a single contract and ends upon completion of that contract.

A joint venture is a form of a partnership, organized for a limited purpose. An agreement of the parties and the terms of the contract successfully bid upon will determine the nature of the accounting records. Income statements are usually cumulative statements showing totals from date of contract inception until reporting date. Each venturer records its share of the amount from the venture's income statement less its previously recorded portion of the venture's income as a single line item similar to the equity method for investments. Similarly, balance sheets of the venturer give rise to a single line asset balance of investment and advances in joint ventures. In most cases, footnote disclosure is similar to the equity method in displaying condensed financial statements of material joint ventures.

Accounting for Change Orders

Change orders are modifications of specifications or provisions of an original contract. Contract revenue and costs should be adjusted to reflect change orders that are approved by the contractor and customer. According to SOP 81-1, the accounting for the change order depends upon the scope and price of the change.

If the scope and price have both been agreed upon by the customer and contractor, contract revenue and cost should be adjusted to reflect the change order.

According to SOP 81-1, accounting for unpriced change orders depends on their characteristics and the circumstances in which they occur. Under the completed-contract method, costs attributable to unpriced change orders should be deferred as contract costs if it is probable that total contract costs, including costs attributable to the change orders, will be recovered from contract revenues. Recovery should be deemed probable if the future event or events are likely to occur.

Per SOP 81-1, the following guidelines should be followed when accounting for unpriced change orders under the percentage-of-completion method:

a. *Costs attributable to unpriced change orders should be treated as costs of contract performance in the period in which the costs are incurred if it is **not** probable that the costs will be recovered through a change in the contract price.*

b. *If it is probable that the costs will be recovered through a change in the contract price, the costs should be deferred (excluded from the cost of contract performance) until the parties have agreed on the change in contract price, or, alternatively, they should be treated as costs of contract performance in the period in which they are incurred, and contract revenue should be recognized to the extent of the costs incurred.*

c. *If it is probable that the contract price will be adjusted by an amount that exceeds the costs attributable to the change order and the amount of the excess can be reliably estimated, the original contract price should also be adjusted for that amount when the costs are recognized as costs of contract performance if its realization is probable. However, since the substantiation of the amount of future revenue is difficult, revenue in excess of the costs attributable to unpriced change orders should only be recorded in circumstances in which realization is assured beyond a reasonable doubt, such as circumstances in which an entity's historical experience provides such assurance or in which an entity has received a bona fide pricing offer from a customer and records only the amount of the offer as revenue.*

Accounting for Contract Options

Per SOP 81-1, an addition or option to an existing contract should be treated as a separate contract if any of the following circumstances exist:

a. *The product or service to be provided differs significantly from the product or service provided under the original contract.*

b. *The price of the new product or service is negotiated without regard to the original contract and involves different economic judgments.*

c. *The products or services to be provided under the exercised option or amendment are similar to those under the original contract, but the contract price and anticipated contract cost relationship are significantly different.*

If the addition or option does not meet the above circumstances, the contracts should be combined. However, if the addition or option does not meet the criteria for combining, they should be treated as change orders.

Accounting for Claims

These represent amounts in excess of the agreed contract price that a contractor seeks to collect from customers for unanticipated additional costs. The recognition of additional contract revenue relating to claims is appropriate if it is probable that the claim will result in additional revenue and if the amount can be reliably estimated. SOP 81-1 specifies that all of the following conditions must exist in order for the probable and estimable requirements to be satisfied:

a. *The contract or other evidence provides a legal basis for the claim; or a legal opinion has been obtained, stating that under the circumstances there is a reasonable basis to support the claim.*

b. *Additional costs are caused by circumstances that were unforeseen at the contract date and are not the result of deficiencies in the contractor's performance.*

c. *Costs associated with the claim are identifiable or otherwise determinable and are reasonable in view of the work performed.*

d. *The evidence supporting the claim is objective and verifiable, not based on management's "feel" for the situation or on unsupported representations.*

When the above requirements are met, revenue from a claim should be recorded only to the extent that contract costs relating to the claim have been incurred.

When the above requirements are not met, SOP 81-1 states that a contingent asset should be disclosed in accordance with SFAS 5.

Accounting Changes

According to APB 20, a change in method of accounting for long-term construction contracts is a special change in principle requiring retroactive treatment and restatement of previous financial statements. (See Chapter 20, Accounting Changes and Correction of Errors, for further discussion.)

Revisions in revenue, cost, and profit estimates or in measurements of the extent of progress toward completion are changes in accounting estimates. Such changes should be accounted for prospectively in order for the financial statements to fully reflect the effects of the latest available estimates.

Deferred Income Taxes

Deferred income taxes resulting from temporary differences should be classified in accordance with SFAS 109, *Accounting for Income Taxes*. Contract-related deferred income taxes result from the use of a method of income recognition for tax purposes different from the method used for financial reporting purposes. (Refer to Chapter 15, Income Taxes, for further discussion of deferred taxes.)

EMERGING ISSUES TASK FORCE CONSENSUS SUMMARIES

91-6   Revenue Recognition of Long-Term Power Sales Contracts

A consensus was reached that Nonutility Generators (NUG) should recognize the lesser of (1) the amount billable under the contract or (2) a formula-based pricing arrangement, as revenue. The formula-based pricing arrangement is determined by the kilowatt-hours (kwhs) made available during the period multiplied by the estimated average revenue per kwh over the term of the contract for the fixed or scheduled price period of the contract. Revenue should not be recognized utilizing the formula-based pricing arrangement if its only purpose is to establish liquidating damages. Additionally, a receivable arises when the amounts billed are less than the amount computed pursuant to the formula-based pricing arrangement and if the contract requires a payment, probable of recovery, to the NUG at the end of the contract term.

96-17   Revenue Recognition under Long-Term Power Sales Contracts That Contain Both Fixed and Variable Pricing Terms

This pronouncement extends the consensus of 91-6. Fixed price arrangements should be handled in accordance with 91-6. Variable price arrangements in which the rate is at least equal to expected costs should recognize revenue as billed, in accordance with the provisions of the contract for that variable price period. A long-term power sales contract should be periodically reviewed to determine whether it is a loss contract, in which case the loss should be recognized immediately. Finally, the Task Force observed that any premium related to a contractual rate in excess of the current market rate should be amortized over the remaining portion of the contract for long-term power sales contracts acquired in a purchase business combination.

SERVICE SALES TRANSACTIONS

PERSPECTIVE AND ISSUES

Service sales transactions represent over half of the US economy's transactions; however, there are no official pronouncements that provide specific accounting standards for them. Accounting for service sales transactions has evolved primarily through industry practice. As a result, different accounting methods have developed to apply the fundamental principles of revenue and cost recognition. In fact, different accounting methods are used by similar entities for practically identical transactions. Because of these wide variations, the FASB and the AICPA combined efforts in an attempt to establish accounting standards for service transactions through their issuance of *Accounting for Certain Service Transactions, FASB Invitation to Comment* (the Invitation). The Invitation contained an AICPA draft Statement of Position that set forth conclusions on the following:

1. The guidelines to apply to transactions in which both services and products are provided
2. The appropriate manner of revenue recognition
3. The classification of costs as initial direct costs, direct costs, and indirect costs and the accounting for each
4. The accounting for initiation and installation fees

This section reflects the conclusions in the AICPA draft Statement of Position. Although no further progress has been made in this area, this section can still provide guidance in service industry issues.

Sources of GAAP		
Other	FASB TB	*EITF*
*	90-1	91-9

* *FASB Invitation to Comment,* **Accounting for Certain Service Transactions**

DEFINITIONS OF TERMS

Collection method. Revenue recognized upon the collection of cash.

Completed performance method. A method that recognizes revenue after the last significant act has been completed.

Direct costs. Costs that are directly related to the performance of services.

Indirect costs. Costs that are not directly related to the negotiation or consummation of service agreements and are not directly related to the performance of services.

Initial direct costs. Costs that are directly associated with the negotiation and consummation of service agreements.

Initiation fee. A onetime, up-front charge that gives the purchaser the privilege of using the service or the use of facilities.

Installation fee. A onetime, up-front charge for the installation of equipment essential to the provision of the service.

Product transaction. A transaction between a seller and a purchaser in which the seller supplies a product to the purchaser.

Proportional performance method. A method that recognizes revenue on the basis of the number of acts performed in relation to the total number of acts to be performed.

Service transaction. A transaction between a seller and a purchaser in which the seller provides a service, or agrees to maintain a readiness to perform a service, for the purchaser.

Specific performance method. A method that recognizes revenue after one specific act has been performed.

CONCEPTS, RULES, AND EXAMPLES

The AICPA has defined service transactions as follows:

> *...transactions between a seller and a purchaser in which, for a mutually agreed price, the seller performs, agrees to perform, agrees to perform at a later date, or agrees to maintain readiness to perform an act or acts, including permitting others to use enterprise resources that do not alone produce a tangible commodity or product as the principal intended result (the Invitation).*

Generally accepted accounting principles require that revenue should generally be recognized when (1) it is **realized or realizable** and (2) it has been **earned**. With respect to service transactions, the AICPA concluded

> *...revenue from service transactions should be based on performance, because performance determines the extent to which the earnings process is complete or virtually complete.*

In practice, performance may involve the execution of a defined act, a set of similar or identical acts, or a set of related but not similar or identical acts. Performance may also occur with the passage of time. Accordingly, one of the following four methods should serve as a guideline for the recognition of revenue from service transactions:

1. The specific performance method
2. The proportional performance method
3. The completed performance method
4. The collection method

Service vs. Product Transactions

Many transactions involve the sale of a tangible product and a service; therefore, for proper accounting treatment, it must be determined whether the transaction is primarily a service transaction accompanied by an incidental product, primarily a product transaction accompanied by an incidental service, or a sale in which both a service transaction and a product transaction occur. The following criteria are applicable:

1. If the seller offers both a service and a product in a single transaction and if the terms of the agreement for the sale of the service are worded in such a manner that the inclusion or exclusion of the product would not change the total transaction price, the product is incidental to the rendering of the service; the transaction is a service transaction that should be accounted for in accordance with one of the four methods presented. For example, fixed-price equipment maintenance contracts that include parts are service transactions.

2. If the seller offers both a service and a product in a single transaction and if the terms of the agreement for the sale of the product are worded in such a manner that the inclusion or exclusion of the service would not change the total transaction price, the rendering of the service is incidental to the sale of the product; the transaction is a product transaction that should be accounted for as such. For example, the sale of a product accompanied by a guarantee or warranty for repair is considered a product transaction.

3. If the seller offers both a product and a service and the agreement states the product and service are separate elements such that the inclusion or exclusion of the service would vary the total transaction price, the transaction consists of two components: a product transaction that should be accounted for separately as such, and a service transaction that should be accounted for in accordance with one of the four accepted methods.

Revenue Recognition Methods

Once the sale has been identified as a service transaction, one of the following four methods should be used to recognize revenue. The method chosen should reflect the nature and extent of the service(s) to be performed.

1. **Specific performance method.** The specific performance method should be used when performance consists of the execution of a single act. Revenue is recognized at the time the act takes place. For example, a stockbroker should record sales commissions as revenue upon the sale of a client's investment.

2. **Proportional performance method.** The proportional performance method should be used when performance consists of a number of identical or similar acts.

   a. If the service transaction involves a **specified number** of **identical** or **similar** acts, an equal amount of revenue should be recorded for each act performed. For example, a refuse disposal company would recognize an equal amount of revenue for each weekly removal of a customer's garbage.

b.   If the service transaction involves a specified number of defined but **not** identical or similar acts, the revenue recognized for each act should be based on the following formula:

$$\frac{\text{Direct cost of individual act}}{\begin{array}{c}\text{Total estimated direct costs}\\\text{of the transaction}\end{array}} \quad \times \quad \begin{array}{c}\text{Total revenues from}\\\text{complete transaction}\end{array}$$

For example, a correspondence school that provides lessons, examinations, and grading should use this method. If the measurements suggested in the preceding equation are impractical or not objectively determinable, revenue should be recognized on a systematic and rational basis that reasonably relates revenue recognition to service performance.

c.   If the service transaction involves an **unspecified** number of acts over a fixed time period for performance, revenue should be recognized over the period during which the acts will be performed by using the straight-line method unless a better method of relating revenue and performance is appropriate. For example, a health club might recognize revenue on a straight-line basis over the life of a member's membership.

3.   **Completed performance method.** The completed performance method should be used when more than one act must be performed and when the final act is so significant to the entire transaction taken as a whole that performance can't be considered to have taken place until the performance of that final act occurs. For example, a moving company packs, loads, and transports merchandise; however, the final act of delivering the merchandise is so significant that revenue should not be recognized until the goods reach their intended destination. If the services are to be performed in an **indeterminable** number of acts over an **indeterminable** period of time and if an objective measure for estimating the degree to which performance has taken place can't be found, the revenue should be recognized under the completed performance method.

4.   **Collection method.** The collection method should be used in circumstances when there is a significant degree of uncertainty surrounding the collection of service revenue. Under this method, revenue should not be recorded until the cash is collected. For example, personal services may be provided to a customer whose ability to pay is uncertain.

Expense Recognition

GAAP, in general, requires that costs should be charged to expense in the period that the revenue with which they are associated is recognized. Costs should be deferred only when they are expected to be recoverable from future revenues. When applying these principles to service transactions, special consideration must be given to the different types of costs that may arise. The three major classifications of costs arising from service transactions are as follows:

1. Initial direct costs
2. Direct costs
3. Indirect costs

The three types of cost classifications arising from service transactions are defined as follows (the Invitation):

1. **Initial direct costs.** Costs that are directly associated with the negotiation and consummation of service agreements. They include, but are not limited to, legal fees, commissions, costs of credit investigations, installment paper processing fees, and the portion of salespersons' and other employees' compensation, other than commissions, that is applicable to the time spent on consummated agreements. They do not include costs allocable to time spent on service transactions that are not consummated or portions of supervisory, administrative, or other indirect costs, such as rent.

2. **Direct costs.** Costs that have a clear, beneficial, or causal relationship to the services or level of services performed. For example, servicemen's labor and repair parts on a fixed-price maintenance contract are considered direct costs.

3. **Indirect costs.** All costs that cannot be classified as either an initial direct cost or a direct cost. They include provisions for uncollectible accounts, general and administrative expenses, advertising expenses, general selling expenses, the portion of salespersons' and other employees' compensation allocable to the time spent in negotiating service transactions that are not consummated, and all allocations of facility costs (depreciation, rent, maintenance, etc.).

Accounting treatment. The accounting treatments for indirect costs, initial direct costs and direct costs, and service transaction losses are discussed below.

1. **Indirect costs.** Regardless of the service revenue recognition method selected, indirect costs should always be charged to expense as incurred.

2. **Initial direct costs and direct costs.**

   a. *Specific performance and completed performance methods.* Under the **specific performance** or **completed performance** methods, all **initial direct costs** and **direct costs** should be recognized as expense at the time the related service revenue is recognized. Thus, any initial direct costs and direct costs incurred prior to the performance of the service should be deferred as prepayments and expensed at the time of service performance (i.e., at the point revenue is recognized).

   b. *Proportional performance method.* When service revenue is recognized under the **proportional performance method, initial direct**

costs should be proportionately charged to expense at the time revenues are recognized. Thus, any initial direct costs incurred prior to performance should be deferred as prepayments and allocated to expense over the length of service performance in proportion to the recognition of service revenue. **Direct costs**, on the other hand, should be charged to expense as incurred because, normally, there is a close correlation between the amount of direct costs incurred and the extent of performance achieved.

   c. *Collection method.* When service revenue is recognized under the collection method (high uncertainty surrounding the realization of revenue), both **initial direct costs** and **direct costs** should be charged to expense as incurred.

3. **Service transaction losses.** A loss on a service transaction should be recognized when initial direct costs plus estimated total direct costs of performance exceed the current estimated realizable revenue. The loss (Initial direct costs + Estimated total direct costs – Estimated realizable revenue) should be first used to reduce any deferred costs. If an estimated loss remains, it should be credited to an estimated liability account.

Initiation and Installation Fees

Many service transactions also involve the charge of a nonrefundable initiation fee with subsequent periodic payments for future services and/or a nonrefundable fee for installation of equipment essential to the provision of future services with subsequent periodic payments for the services. These nonrefundable fees may, in substance, be partly or wholly advance charges for future services.

Initiation fees. If there is an objectively determinable value for the right or privilege granted by the initiation fee, that value should be recognized as revenue on the initiation date. Any related direct costs should be charged as expense on the initiation date. If the value of the right or privilege cannot be objectively determined, the fee should be recorded as a liability for future services and recognized as revenue in accordance with one of the recognition methods.

Installation fees. If the equipment and its installation costs are essential for the service to be provided and if customers cannot normally purchase the equipment in separate transactions, the installation fee should be considered an advance charge for future services. This fee should be recognized as revenue over the estimated service period. The costs of installation and installed equipment should be amortized over the period the installation is expected to provide revenue. If customers can normally purchase the equipment in a separate transaction, the installation fee is then a product transaction that should be accounted for separately as such.

Recommended Disclosures—Not Required by GAAP

1. The revenue recognition method used and its justification

2. Information concerning unearned revenues
3. Information concerning deferred costs
4. Periods over which services are to be performed

EMERGING ISSUES TASK FORCE CONSENSUS SUMMARIES

91-9   Revenue and Expense Recognition for Freight Services in Process

The Task Force discussed the appropriate accounting methods which could be used for recognizing revenue and expense related to a freight service company's freight-in-transit at the end of a reporting period. A consensus was reached that recognition of revenue when freight is received from the shipper or when freight leaves the carrier's terminal with expenses recognized as incurred is no longer acceptable.

FASB TECHNICAL BULLETINS

90-1   Accounting for Separately Priced Extended Warranty and Product Maintenance Contracts

Background: Extended warranties provide additional protection to that of the manufacturer's original warranty or lengthen the period of coverage specified in the manufacturer's original warranty. A product maintenance contract is an agreement for services to maintain a product for a certain length of time.

Question: How should revenue and costs from a separately priced extended warranty or product maintenance contract be recognized?

Response: Revenue from these contracts should be deferred and recognized on a straight-line basis unless evidence exists that costs are incurred on some other basis. If so, allocate revenue to each period in the ratio of the period's cost to estimated total cost. Direct costs of obtaining a contract should be capitalized and expensed in the ratio that revenue recognized each period bears to total anticipated revenue on that contract. Any other costs should be charged to expense as incurred. Losses on these contracts should be recognized if the future costs and remaining direct acquisition costs exceed the related unearned revenue.

SALES WHEN COLLECTION IS UNCERTAIN

PERSPECTIVE AND ISSUES

Under GAAP, revenue recognition customarily does not depend upon the collection of cash. Accrual accounting techniques normally record revenue at the point of a credit sale by establishing a receivable. When uncertainty arises surrounding the collectibility of this amount, the receivable is appropriately adjusted by establishing a contra valuation allowance account. In some cases, however, the collection of the sales price may be so uncertain that an objective measure of ultimate collectibility cannot be established. When such circumstances exist, APB 10 permits the seller to use either the installment method or the cost recovery method to account for installment transactions. Both of these methods allow for a deferral of gross profit until cash has been collected.

An installment transaction occurs when a seller delivers a product or performs a service and the buyer makes periodic payments over an extended period of time. Under the installment method, income recognition is deferred until the period(s) of cash collection. The seller recognizes both revenues and cost of sales at the time of the sale; however, the related gross profit is deferred to those periods in which cash is collected. Under the cost recovery method, both revenues and cost of sales are recognized at the time of the sale, but none of the related gross profit is recognized until all cost of sales has been recovered. Once the seller has recovered all cost of sales, any additional cash receipts are included in income. APB 10 does not specify when one method is preferred over the other. However, the cost recovery method is more conservative than the installment method because gross profit is deferred until all costs have been recovered; therefore, it should be reserved for situations of extreme uncertainty.

Sources of GAAP	
APB	*SFAC*
10	3

DEFINITIONS OF TERMS

Cost recovery method. The method of accounting for an installment basis sale whereby the gross profit is deferred until all cost of sales has been recovered.

Deferred gross profit. The gross profit from an installment basis sale that will be recognized in future periods.

Gross profit rate. The gross profit on the installment sale divided by the revenue from the installment sale.

Installment method. The method of accounting for a sale whereby the gross profit is recognized in the period(s) the cash from the sale is collected.

Installment sale. A sales transaction for which the sales price is collected through the receipt of periodic payments over an extended period of time.

Net realizable value. The fair value of an asset less any estimated costs of disposal.

Realized gross profit. The gross profit recognized in the current period.

Repossessions. Merchandise sold by a seller under an installment arrangement which the seller physically takes back after the buyer defaults on the payments.

CONCEPTS, RULES, AND EXAMPLES

The **installment method** was developed in response to an increasing number of sales contracts that allowed buyers to make payments over several years. As the payment period becomes longer, the risk of loss resulting from uncollectible accounts increases; consequently, circumstances surrounding a receivable may lead to considerable uncertainty as to whether payments will actually be received. Under these circumstances, the uncertainty of cash collection suggests that revenue recognition should be deferred until the actual receipt of cash.

The installment method can be used in most sales transactions for which payment is to be made through periodic installments over an extended period of time and the collectibility of the sales price cannot be reasonably estimated. This method is applicable to the sales of real estate (covered in the last section of this chapter), heavy equipment, home furnishings, and other merchandise sold on an installment basis. Installment method revenue recognition is not in accordance with accrual accounting because revenue recognition should not normally be based upon cash collection; however, its use may be justified on the grounds that accrual accounting may result in "front-end loading" (i.e., all of the revenue from a transaction is recognized at the point of sale with an improper matching of related costs). For example, the application of accrual accounting to transactions that provide for installment payments over periods of ten, twenty, or thirty years may underestimate losses from contract defaults and other future contract costs.

Accounting Treatment

When a seller uses the installment method, both revenue and cost of sales are recognized at the point of sale, but the related gross profit is deferred to those periods over which cash will be collected. As receivables are collected, a portion of the **deferred gross profit** equal to the gross profit rate times the cash collected is recognized as income. When this method is used, the seller must compute each year's **gross profit rate** and also must maintain installment accounts receivable and deferred revenue accounts that are identified by the year of sale. All other general and administrative expenses are normally expensed in the period incurred.

The steps to use in accounting for sales under the installment method are as follows:

1. During the current year, record sales revenue and cost of sales in the regular manner. Record **installment sales** transactions separately from other sales.

Set up installment accounts receivable identified by the year of sale (e.g., Installment Accounts Receivable—2002).

2. Record cash collections from installment accounts receivable. Care must be taken so that the cash receipts are properly identified as to the year in which the receivable arose.

3. At the end of the current year, close out the installment sales revenue and installment cost of sales accounts into a deferred gross profit account that properly identifies the year of sale. Compute the current year's gross profit rate on installment sales as follows:

$$\text{Gross profit rate} \ = \ 1 \ - \ \left(\frac{\text{Cost of installment sales}}{\text{Installment sales revenue}}\right)$$

Alternatively, the gross profit rate can be computed as follows:

$$\text{Gross profit rate} \ = \ \frac{\text{Installment sales revenue} - \text{Cost of installment sales}}{\text{Installment sales revenue}}$$

4. Apply the current year's gross profit rate to the cash collections from the current year's installment sales to compute the realized gross profit from the current year's installment sales.

$$\text{Realized gross profit} \ = \ \frac{\text{Cash collections from the cur-}}{\text{rent year's installment sales}} \ \times \ \frac{\text{Current year's gross}}{\text{profit rate}}$$

5. Apply the previous years' gross profit rates to cash collections from previous years' installment sales to compute the realized gross profit from previous years' installment sales.

$$\text{Realized gross profit} \ = \ \frac{\text{Cash collections from the pre-}}{\text{vious years' installment sales}} \ \times \ \frac{\text{Previous years' gross}}{\text{profit rates}}$$

6. Defer the current year's unrealized gross profit to future years. The deferred gross profit to carry forward to future years can be computed in the following manner:

$$\frac{\text{Deferred gross profit}}{(2002)} \ = \ \frac{\text{Ending balance installment}}{\text{account receivable (2002)}} \ \times \ \frac{\text{Gross profit}}{\text{rate (2002)}}$$

Example of the installment method of accounting

	2002	*2003*	*2004*
Sales on installment	$ 400,000	$ 450,000	$ 600,000
Cost of installment sales	(280,000)	(337,500)	(400,000)
Gross profit on sales	$ 120,000	$ 112,500	$ 200,000
Cash collections:			
2002 sales	$ 150,000	$ 175,000	$ 75,000
2003 sales		$ 200,000	$ 125,000
2004 sales			$ 300,000

Journal entries would be made for steps 1 and 2 above using this data; the following computations are required for steps 3-6:

Wiley GAAP 2002

Step 3 — Compute the current year's gross profit rate.

	2002	2003	2004
Gross profit on sales	$120,000	$112,500	$200,000
Installment sales revenue	$400,000	$450,000	$600,000
Gross profit rate	30%	25%	33 1/3%

Step 4 — Apply the current year's gross profit rate to cash collections from current year's sales.

Year	Cash collections		Gross profit rate		Realized gross profit
2002	$150,000	x	30%	=	$ 45,000
2003	200,000	x	25%	=	50,000
2004	300,000	x	33 1/3%	=	100,000

Step 5 — Apply the previous years' gross profit rates to cash collections from previous years' installment sales.

In Year 2003

From year	Cash collections		Gross profit rate		Realized gross profit
2002	$175,000	x	30%	=	$52,500

In Year 2004

From year	Cash collections		Gross profit rate		Realized gross profit
2002	$ 75,000	x	30%	=	$22,500
2003	125,000	x	25%	=	31,250
					$53,750

Step 6 — Defer the current year's unrealized gross profit to future years.

12/31/02

Deferred gross profit (2002) = ($400,000 − 150,000) x 30% = $ 75,000

12/31/03

Deferred gross profit (2003) = ($450,000 − 200,000) x 25% = $ 62,500
Deferred gross profit (2002) = ($400,000 − 150,000 − 175,000) x 30% = 22,500
  $ 85,000

12/31/04

Deferred gross profit (2004) = ($600,000 − 300,000) x 33 1/3% = $100,000
Deferred gross profit (2003) = ($450,000 − 200,000 − 125,000) x 25% = 31,250
  $131,250

Financial Statement Presentation

If installment sales transactions represent a significant portion of the company's total sales, the following three items of gross profit should, theoretically, be reported on the company's income statement:

1. Total gross profit from current year's sales
2. Realized gross profit from current year's sales
3. Realized gross profit from prior years' sales

An income statement using the previous example would be prepared as follows (assume all sales are accounted for by the installment method):

Jordan Equipment Company
Partial Income Statement
For the Years Ending December 31

	2002	2003	2004
Sales	$400,000	$450,000	$600,000
Cost of sales	(280,000)	(337,500)	(400,000)
Gross profit on current sales	$120,000	$112,500	$200,000
Less deferred gross profit on current sales	(75,000)	(62,500)	(100,000)
Realized gross profit on current sales	$ 45,000	$ 50,000	$100,000
Plus realized gross profit on prior sales	--	52,500	53,750
Total gross profit on sales	$ 45,000	$102,500	$153,750

However, when a company recognizes only a small portion of its sales under the installment basis, the previous method of income reporting may be confusing. Therefore, in practice, some companies simply report the realized gross profit from installment sales by displaying it as a single line item on the income statement as follows:

Stevens Furniture Company
Partial Income Statement
For the Year Ended December 31, 2002

Sales	$ 2,250,000
Cost of sales	(1,350,000)
Gross profit on sales	$ 900,000
Realized gross profit on installment sales	35,000
Total gross profit on sales	$ 935,000

The balance sheet presentation of the installment accounts receivable will depend upon whether the installment sales are part of normal operations. If a company sells most of its products on an installment basis, the installment accounts receivable will be classified as a current asset because the operating cycle of the business is the average period of time covered by an installment contract. If the installment sales are not part of normal operations, installment accounts receivable that are not to be collected for a year or more should not be reported as current assets. In all cases, to avoid any confusion, it is generally desirable to fully disclose the year of maturity next to each set of installment accounts receivable as illustrated by the following example:

Current assets:		
Trade customers	$180,035	
Less allowance for uncollectible accounts	(4,200)	
	$175,835	
Installment accounts—collectible in 2003	26,678	
Installment accounts—collectible in 2004	42,234	$244,747

The accounting for the deferred gross profit account(s) is addressed in SFAC 3 which states that the deferred gross profit account is not a liability. The reason is that the seller company is not obligated to pay cash or provide services to the customer. Rather, the account arose because of the uncertainty surrounding the collectibility of the sales price. SFAC 3 goes on to say, "deferred gross profit on installment sales is conceptually an asset valuation—that is, a reduction of an asset." However, in practice, the deferred gross profit account is generally presented as either an unearned revenue classified as a current liability or a deferred credit displayed between liabilities and equity. Following the guideline given by SFAC 3, the current asset section would be presented as follows (using information from the Jordan Equipment example and assuming a 12/31/04 balance sheet):

Installment accounts receivable	(2003)	$125,000	
Installment accounts receivable	(2004)	300,000	$ 425,000
Less: Deferred gross profit	(2003)	$ 31,250	
Deferred gross profit	(2004)	100,000	(131,250)	$293,750

Interest on Installment Contracts

The previous examples ignored interest, a major component of most installment sales contracts. It is customary for the seller to charge interest to the buyer on the unpaid installment receivable balance. Generally, installment contracts call for equal payments, each with an amount attributable to interest on the unpaid balance and the remainder to the installment receivable balance. As the maturity date nears, a smaller amount of each installment payment is attributable to interest and a larger amount is attributable to principal. Therefore, to determine the amount of gross profit to recognize, the interest must first be deducted from the installment payment and then the difference is multiplied by the gross profit rate as follows:

Realized gross profit = (Installment payment – Interest portion) x Gross profit rate

The interest portion of the installment payment should be recorded as interest revenue at the time of the cash receipt. Appropriate adjusting entries are required to accrue interest revenue when the collection dates do not correspond with the year-end.

To illustrate the accounting for installment sales contracts involving interest, assume that Babich Equipment Company sold a piece of machinery on January 1, 2002, to a customer with a dubious credit history. The equipment had a cost of $3,750 and a sales price of $5,000. Terms of the agreement required that a $1,000 down payment be made on the date of the sale and that the remaining balance ($4,000) plus 10% annual interest be paid in equal installments of $1,261.88 at the end of each of the next four years.

For each cash receipt Babich must determine the amount applicable to interest revenue and the value applicable to the installment account receivable balance because gross profit is recognized only on those amounts applicable to the installment receivable balance. It can be seen in the following schedule that gross profit is recognized on the entire down payment, whereas the annual installment payments are separated into their interest and receivable portions with gross profit only being recognized on the latter portion.

Schedule of Cash Receipts

Date	Cash (debit)	Interest revenue (credit)	Installment accounts receivable (credit)	Installment accounts receivable balance	Realized gross profit
1/1/02				$5,000.00	
1/1/02	$1,000.00	$ --	$1,000.00	4,000.00	$ 250.00[a]
12/31/02	1,261.88	400.00[b]	861.88[c]	3,138.12[d]	215.47[e]
12/31/03	1,261.88	313.81	948.07	2,190.05	237.02
12/31/04	1,261.88	219.01	1,042.87	1,147.18	260.72
12/31/05	1,261.88	114.70	1,147.18	--	286.79
			Total realized gross profit		$1,250.00

Gross profit rate = $1 - (\$3,750/5,000) = 25\%$

[a] $\$1,000 \times 25\% = \$250$

[b] $\$4,000 \times 10\% = \$400$

[c] $\$1,261.88 - 400 = \$861.88$

[d] $\$4,000 - 861.88 = \$3,138.12$

[e] $\$861.88 \times 25\% = \$215.47$

Bad Debts and Repossessions

The standard accounting treatment for uncollectible accounts is to accrue a bad debt loss in the year of sale by estimating the amount that is expected to be uncollectible. This treatment is in line with the accrual concept. However, just as income recognition under the accrual basis is sometimes abandoned for certain installment basis sales, the accrual basis of recognizing bad debts is also often abandoned.

When the installment method is used, it is usually appropriate to recognize bad debts by the direct write-off method (i.e., bad debts are not recognized until the account has been determined to be uncollectible). This practice is acceptable because most installment contracts contain a provision that allows the seller to repossess the merchandise when the buyer defaults on the installment payments. The loss on the account may be eliminated or reduced because the seller has the option of reselling merchandise. When an installment account is written off, the following three things must be accomplished:

1. The installment account receivable and the deferred gross profit must be eliminated.
2. The repossessed merchandise must be recorded at its **net realizable value**. Net realizable value is the resale value less any sales or reconditioning costs. The repossessed asset is recorded at this fair value because any asset acquired should be put on the books at the best approximation of its fair value. Repossessed merchandise is inventory in the seller's hands and, therefore, should be presented in the inventory section of the balance sheet.
3. A bad debt expense, a repossession loss, or a repossession gain should be recognized. The bad debt expense or repossession gain or loss is the difference between the unrecovered cost (Installment account receivable—Deferred gross profit) and the net realizable value of the repossessed merchandise.

To illustrate, assume that the Marcie Company determined that a $3,000 installment receivable is uncollectible. The deferred gross profit ratio on the original sale was 30%; thus, $900 deferred gross profit exists ($3,000 x 30%). If the repossessed equipment has a $1,500 net realizable value, a $600 repossession loss (or bad debt expense) would need to be recorded.

Installment account receivable	$ 3,000
Less deferred gross profit	(900)
Unrecovered cost	$ 2,100
Less net realizable value	(1,500)
Repossession loss	$ 600

Marcie Company would record this loss by making the following entry:

Deferred gross profit	900	
Repossessed merchandise	1,500	
Repossession loss	600	
Installment account receivable		3,000

Cost Recovery

The cost recovery method does not recognize any income on a sale until the cost of the item has been recovered through cash receipts. Once the seller has recovered all costs, any subsequent cash receipts are included in income. The cost recovery method is used when the uncertainty of collection of the sale price is so great that even use of the installment method cannot be justified.

Under the cost recovery method, both revenues and cost of sales are recognized at the point of sale, but the related gross profit is deferred until all costs of sales have been recovered. Each installment must also be divided between principal and interest, but unlike the installment method where a portion of the principal recovers the cost of sales and the remainder is recognized as gross profit, all of the principal is first applied to recover the cost of the asset sold. After all costs of sales have been recovered, any subsequent cash receipts are realized as gross profit. The cost recovery method can be illustrated by using the information from the Babich Company example used in the interest on installment sales contract section. If Babich used the cost recovery method, gross profit would be realized as follows:

Schedule of Cash Receipts

Date	Cash (debit)	Deferred interest revenue (credit)*	Installment accounts receivable (credit)	Installment accounts receivable balance	Unrecovered cost	Realized gross profit	Realized interest revenue
1/1/02				$5,000.00	$3,750.00		
1/1/02	$1,000.00	$ --	$1,000.00	4,000.00	2,750.00	$ --	$ --
12/31/02	1,261.88	400.00	861.88	3,138.12	1,488.12	--	--
12/31/03	1,261.88	313.81	948.07	2,190.05	226.24	--	--
12/31/04	1,261.88	(713.81)	1,042.87	1,147.18	--	102.82	932.82**
12/31/05	1,261.88	--	1,147.18	--	--	1,147.18	114.70
	$6,047.52		$5,000.00			$1,250.00	$1,047.52

*   *Interest received in 2002 and 2003 would be credited to deferred interest revenue since the cost of the asset was not recovered until 2004.*

** *Includes deferred interest revenue received in 2002 and 2003 [$713.81 (2002 and 2003) + $219.01 (2004)].*
    Interest revenue can only be realized after the cost of the asset is recovered (2004, in this example).

REVENUE RECOGNITION WHEN RIGHT OF RETURN EXISTS

PERSPECTIVE AND ISSUES

In some industries it is common practice for customers to be given the right to return a product to the seller for a credit or refund. However, for companies that experience a high ratio of returned merchandise to sales, the recognition of the original sale as revenue is questionable. In fact, certain industries have found it necessary to defer revenue recognition until the return privilege has substantially expired. Sometimes the return privilege expires soon after the sale, as in the newspaper and perishable food industries. In other cases, the return privilege may last over an extended period of time, as in magazine and textbook publishing and equipment manufacturing. The rate of return normally is directly related to the length of the return privilege. An accounting problem arises when the recognition of the revenue occurs in one period while substantial returns occur in later periods.

SFAS 48, *Revenue Recognition When Right of Return Exists,* reduces the diversity in the accounting for revenue recognition when such rights exist.

Sources of GAAP
SFAS
5, 48

DEFINITIONS OF TERMS

Deferred gross profit. The gross profit from a sale that is recognized in future periods because of the uncertainty surrounding the collection of the sales price.

Return privilege. A right granted to a buyer by express agreement with a seller or by practice of the industry that allows the buyer to return merchandise to the seller within a stated period of time.

CONCEPTS, RULES, AND EXAMPLES

SFAS 48 provides criteria for recognizing revenue on a sale in which a product may be returned (as a matter of contract or a matter of industry practice), either by the ultimate consumer or by a party who resells the product to others. Paragraph 6 states the following:

> If an enterprise sells its product but gives the buyer the right to return the product, revenue from the sales transaction shall be recognized at time of sale only if all of the following conditions are met:
>
> a.   The seller's price to the buyer is substantially fixed or determinable at the date of sale.
> b.   The buyer has paid the seller, or the buyer is obligated to pay the seller and the obligation is not contingent on resale of the product.
> c.   The buyer's obligation to the seller would not be changed in the event of theft or physical destruction or damage of the product.
> d.   The buyer acquiring the product for resale has economic substance apart from that provided by the seller.

     *e.   The seller does not have significant obligations for future perform-
         ance to directly bring about the resale of the product by the buyer.*

     *f.   The amount of future returns can be reasonably estimated. For pur-
         poses of this statement "returns" do not include exchanges by ulti-
         mate customers of one item for another of the same kind, quality, and
         price.*

If all of the above conditions are met, the seller should recognize revenue from the sales transaction at the time of the sale and "any costs or losses that may be expected in connection with any returns are to be accrued in accordance with SFAS 5, *Accounting for Contingencies*." SFAS 5 states that estimated losses from contingencies shall be accrued and charged to income when it is probable that an asset has been impaired or a liability incurred and the amount of loss can be reasonably estimated.

The interplay between SFAS 48 and SFAS 5 needs further explanation. Although SFAS 48 requires under condition f. that the amount of the returns be reasonably estimated, it does not reference the standard to the SFAS 5 loss accrual criteria. Accordingly, a strict interpretation of both SFAS 48 and SFAS 5 would indicate that only when the conditions for loss accrual under SFAS 5 are met would the condition f. above under SFAS 48 also be met, and both sales and estimated returns can be recorded. However, a more literal interpretation of SFAS 48 would indicate that, by not cross-referencing SFAS 5, the FASB intended that the sole criterion for return accrual under SFAS 48 be the "reasonably estimated" condition f. Then, whether losses are probable or reasonably possible, they would be accrued under SFAS 48 and the sales could also be recognized. If the likelihood of losses is remote, no footnote would be required under SFAS 5, and condition f. under SFAS 48 would be achieved and sales recorded. Under this theory, only if returns cannot be reasonably estimated, regardless of whether losses are probable or reasonably possible, would accrual of sales under SFAS 48 be precluded.

Example of sale with right of return

    Assume that Lee, Inc. began the sale of its new textbook on computer programming in 2002 with the following results: On December 1, 2002, 2,000 textbooks with a sales price of $45 each and total manufacturing costs of $30 each are delivered to school bookstores on account. The bookstores have the right to return the textbooks within four months of the delivery date. The bookstores remit cash payments when the books are sold. Payment and returns for the initial deliveries are as follows:

	Cash receipts		Returns	
	Units	*Amount*	*Units*	*Amount*
December 2002	600	$27,000	--	--
January 2003	500	22,500	40	$1,800
February 2003	400	18,000	90	4,050
March 2003	300	13,500	30	1,350
	1,800	$81,000	160	$7,200

Lee, Inc. has had similar agreements with the bookstores in the past and has experienced a 15% return rate on similar sales.

Requirements for revenue recognition met. If all six of the requirements were met, the following journal entries would be appropriate:

12/1/02	Accounts receivable	90,000	
	Sales (2,000 units x $45 per unit)		90,000
	To record sale of 2,000 textbooks		
12/3/02	Cash (600 units x $45 per unit)	27,000	
	Accounts receivable		27,000
	To record cash receipts for the month		
	Cost of sales	60,000	
	Inventory (2,000 units x $30 per unit)		60,000
	To record cost of goods sold for the month		
	Sales (15% x 2,000 units x $45 per unit)	13,500	
	Cost of sales (15% x 2,000 units x $30 per unit)		9,000
	Deferred gross profit on estimated returns (15% x 2,000 units x $15 per unit)		4,500
	To record estimate of returns		
1/1/03 to 3/31/03	Cash	54,000	
	Accounts receivable		54,000
	To record cash receipts		
	Inventory (160 units x $30 per unit)	4,800	
	Deferred gross profit on estimated returns	2,400	
	Accounts receivable (160 units x $45 per unit)		7,200
	To record returns		
3/31/03	Cost of sales (140 units x $30 per unit)	4,200	
	Deferred gross profit on estimated returns	2,100	
	Sales (140 units x $45 per unit)		6,300

The revenue and cost of goods sold recognized in 2002 are based on the number of units expected to be returned, 300 (15% x 2,000 units). The net revenue recognized is $76,500 (85% x 2,000 units x $45 per unit) and the cost of goods sold recognized is $51,000 (85% x 2,000 units x $30 per unit). The deferred gross profit balance is carried forward until the textbooks are returned or until the privilege expires.

Requirements for revenue recognition not met. If all six conditions are not met, revenue and cost of sales from the sales transactions must be deferred until either the return privilege has substantially expired or the point when all the conditions are subsequently met, whichever comes first.

In the Lee case, if any one of the six conditions is not met, the following entries would be required. The return privilege is assumed to be lost by the store when the books are sold to final customers.

12/1/02	Accounts receivable	90,000	
	Sales		90,000
	To record sale of 2,000 units		
12/31/02	Cash	27,000	
	Accounts receivable		27,000
	To record cash receipts		
	Cost of sales	60,000	
	Inventory		60,000
	To record cost of goods sold		
	Sales (1,400[2] units x $45 per unit)	63,000	
	Cost of sales (1,400[2] units x $30 per unit)		42,000
	Deferred gross profit		21,000
	To defer revenue recognition on goods for which the right of return expires on 3/31/03		
1/1/03 to 3/31/03	Cash	54,000	
	Accounts receivable (1,200 units x $45 per unit)		54,000
	To record cash receipts		
	Cost of sales (1,200 units x $30 per unit)	36,000	
	Deferred gross profit	18,000	
	Sales (1,200 units x $45 per unit)		54,000
	To recognize revenue and cost of goods sold on cash receipts		
	Inventory (160 units x $30 per unit)	4,800	
	Deferred gross profit	2,400	
	Accounts receivable (160 units x $45 per unit)		7,200
	To record sales returns		
3/31/03	Cost of sales (40[3] units x $30 per unit)	1,200	
	Deferred gross profit	600	
	Sales (40 units x $45 per unit)		1,800
	To record revenue and cost of goods sold on products for which right of return expired		

---

[2] *2,000 units sold – 600 units paid for*

[3] *2,000 units sold – 160 units returned – 1,800 units paid for*

PROFIT RECOGNITION ON REAL ESTATE SALES
PERSPECTIVE AND ISSUES

The substance of a sale of any asset is that the transaction should unconditionally transfer the risks and rewards of ownership to the buyer. However, the economic substance of many real estate sales is that the risks and rewards of ownership have not been clearly transferred. The turbulent environment in the real estate market over the last fifteen years has led to the evolution of many complex methods of financing real estate transactions. For example, in some transactions the seller, rather than an independent third party, finances the buyer, while in others, the seller may be required to guarantee a minimum return to the buyer or operate the property for a specified period of time. In many of these complex transactions, the seller still has some association with the property even after the property has been sold. The question that must be answered in these transactions is: At what point does the seller become disassociated enough from the property that profit may be recognized on the transaction?

Accounting for sales of real estate is governed by SFAS 66. FASB Interpretation 43 clarifies that sales of real estate under SFAS 66 include property that has improvements or integral equipment not movable without incurring significant costs. Due to the complex nature of these real estate transactions, SFAS 66 is very detailed and complex. The purpose of this section is to present the guidelines that need to be considered when analyzing nonretail real estate transactions. SFAS 98 dealing with sales-type real estate leases and sales-leaseback real estate transactions is covered by the lease chapter on pages 593, 611, and 613 respectively.

Sources of GAAP		
SFAS	*FASB I*	*EITF*
66, 98	43	00-13

DEFINITIONS OF TERMS

Continuing investment. Payments that the buyer is contractually required to pay on its total debt for the purchase price of the property.

Cost recovery method. A method which defers the recognition of gross profit on a real estate sale until the seller recovers the cost of the property sold.

Deposit method. A method which records payments by the buyer as deposits rather than a sale. The seller continues to report the asset and related debt on the balance sheet until the contract is canceled or until the sale has been achieved.

First mortgage (primary debt). The senior debt the seller has on the property at the time the buyer purchases the property. A first mortgage lender (mortgagee) has foreclosure rights superior to those of second (or junior) mortgage lenders.

Full accrual method. A method which recognizes all profit from a real estate sale at the time of sale.

Initial investment. The sales value received by the seller at the point of sale. It includes cash down payment, buyer's notes supported by an irrevocable letter of credit and payment by the buyer to third parties to reduce seller indebtedness on the property.

Installment method. A method which recognizes income on the basis of payments made by the buyer on debt owed to the seller and payments by the buyer to the holder of primary debt. Each payment is apportioned between profit and cost recovery.

Lien. A claim or charge a creditor has on property which serves as security for payment of debt by the debtor.

Minimum initial investment. The minimum amount that an initial investment must equal or exceed so that the criterion for full accrual is met.

Partial sale. A sale in which the seller retains an equity interest in the property or has an equity interest in the buyer.

Property improvements. An addition made to real estate, usually consisting of buildings but may also include any permanent structure such as streets, sidewalks, sewers, utilities, etc.

Reduced profit method. A method which recognizes profit at the point of sale, but only a reduced amount. The remaining profit is deferred to future periods.

Release provision. An agreement that provides for the release of property to the buyer. This agreement releases the property to the buyer free of any previous liens.

Sales value. The sales price of the property increased or decreased for other consideration in the sales transaction that are, in substance, additional sales proceeds to the seller.

Subordination. The process by which a person's rights are ranked below the rights of others.

CONCEPTS, RULES, AND EXAMPLES

Real Estate Sales other than Retail Land Sales

SFAS 66 coverage. SFAS 66, *Accounting for Sales of Real Estate*, established standards applicable to all real estate sales for all types of businesses. However, variations in applying this Statement in practice suggested that additional guidance was needed. FASB Interpretation 43 makes it clear that SFAS 66 is consistent with that of the sale-leaseback requirements of SFAS 98, *Accounting for Sales and Leasebacks*.

FASB I 43 explicitly states that real estate sales transactions under SFAS 66 include real estate with property enhancements or integral equipment. This Interpretation defines property improvements and integral equipment as "any physical structure or equipment attached to real estate or other parts thereof, that cannot be removed and used separately without incurring significant cost." Examples include an office building or manufacturing plant.

This interpretation also identifies transactions excluded from the provisions of SFAS 66 as follows:

1. A sale of improvements or integral equipment with no sale or plans for a sale of the land.
2. A sale of stock, net assets of a business, or a segment of a business which contain real estate except in cases in which an "in-substance" real estate sale occurs.
3. Securities accounted for under SFAS 115.

Profit recognition methods. Profit from real estate sales may be recognized in full, provided the following:

1. The profit is determinable (i.e., the collectibility of the sales price is reasonably assured or the amount that will not be collectible can be estimated).
2. The earnings process is virtually complete, that is, the seller is not obliged to perform significant activities after the sale to earn the profit.

When both of these conditions are satisfied, the method used to recognize profits on real estate sales is referred to as the **full accrual method.** If both of these conditions are not satisfied, recognition of all or part of the profit should be postponed.

For real estate sales, the collectibility of the sales price is reasonably assured when the buyer has demonstrated a commitment to pay. This commitment is supported by a substantial **initial investment**, along with **continuing investments** that give the buyer a sufficient stake in the property such that the risk of loss through default motivates the buyer to honor its obligations to the seller. Collectibility of the sales price should also be assessed by examining the conditions surrounding the sale (e.g., credit history of the buyer; age, condition, and location of the property; and history of cash flows generated by the property).

The full accrual method is appropriate and profit shall be recognized in full at the point of sale for real estate transactions when all of the following criteria are met:

1. A sale is consummated.
2. The buyer's initial and continuing investments are adequate to demonstrate a commitment to pay for the property.
3. The seller's receivable is not subject to future **subordination**.
4. The seller has transferred to the buyer the usual risks and rewards of ownership in a transaction that is, in substance, a sale and does not have a substantial continuing involvement in the property.

On sales in which an independent third party provides all of the financing for the buyer, the seller should be most concerned that criterion 1. is met. For such sales, the sale is usually consummated on the closing date. When the seller finances the buyer, the seller must analyze the economic substance of the agreement to ascertain that criteria 2., 3., and 4. are also met (i.e., whether the transaction clearly transfers the risks and rewards of ownership to the buyer).

The FASB Emerging Issues Task Force (EITF) reached a consensus in its Issue 88-24 that provides the following guidelines for a seller of real estate to follow when considering the various forms of financing that may be applicable to the transaction:

1. The SFAS 66 conditions for obtaining sufficient initial and continuing investment by the buyer before full accrual profit recognition is allowed must be applied unless the seller receives as the full sales value of the property

   a. Cash without any seller contingent liability on any debt on the property incurred or assumed by the buyer,
   b. The buyer's assumption of the seller's existing nonrecourse debt on the property,
   c. The buyer's assumption of all recourse debt on the property with the complete release of the seller from those obligations, or
   d. Any combination of such cash and debt assumption.

2. In computing the buyer's initial investment, debt incurred by the buyer that is secured by the property is not considered part of the buyer's initial investment. This is true whether the debt was incurred directly from the seller or other parties or indirectly through assumption. Payments to the seller from the proceeds of such indebtedness is not included as part of the buyer's initial investment.

3. If the transaction does not qualify for full accrual accounting and, consequently, it is being accounted for using installment, cost recovery or reduced profit methods, payments made on debt described in 2. above are not considered to be buyer's cash payments. However, if the profit deferred under the applicable method exceeds the outstanding amount of seller financing and the outstanding amount of buyer's debt secured by the property for which the seller is contingently liable, the seller recognizes the excess in income.

Consummation of a sale. A sale is considered consummated when the following conditions are met:

1. The parties are bound by the terms of a contract.
2. All consideration has been exchanged.
3. Any permanent financing for which the seller is responsible has been arranged.
4. All conditions precedent to closing have been performed.

When a seller is constructing office buildings, condominiums, shopping centers, or similar structures, item 4. may be applied to individual units rather than the entire project. These four conditions are usually met on or after closing, not at the point the agreement to sell is signed or at a preclosing. Closing refers to the final steps of the transaction (i.e., when consideration is paid, the mortgage is secured, and the deed is delivered or placed in escrow). If the consummation criteria **have not** been satisfied, the seller should use the deposit method of accounting until the sale has been consummated.

Adequacy of the buyer's initial investment. Once it has been determined that the sale has been consummated, the next step is to determine whether the buyer's initial investment adequately demonstrates a commitment to pay for the property and the reasonable likelihood that the seller will collect it. This determination is made by comparing the buyer's initial investment to the sales value of the property. SFAS 66 specifically details items that are includable as the initial investment and the minimum percentages that the initial investment must bear to the sales value of the property. In order to make the determination of whether the initial investment is adequate, the sales value of the property must also be computed.

Computation of sales value. The sales value of property in a real estate transaction can be computed by the following formula:

	Stated sales price
+	Proceeds from the issuance of an **exercised** purchase option
+	Other payments that are, in substance, additional sales proceeds (e.g., management fees, points, or prepaid interest or fees required to be maintained in advance of the sale that will be applied against amounts due to the seller at a later point)
−	A discount that reduces the buyer's note to its present value
−	Net present value of services seller agrees to perform without compensation
−	Excess of net present value of services seller performs over compensation that seller will receive
=	Sales value of the property

Composition of the initial investment. Sales transactions are characterized by many different types of payments and commitments made between the seller, buyer, and third parties; however, the buyer's initial investment shall only include the following:

1. Cash paid to the seller as a down payment
2. Buyer's notes given to the seller that are supported by irrevocable letters of credit from independent lending institutions
3. Payments by the buyer to third parties that reduce existing indebtedness the seller has on the property
4. Other amounts paid by the buyer that are part of the sale value
5. Other consideration received by the seller that can be converted to cash without recourse to the seller; for example, other notes of the buyer

SFAS 66 specifically states that the following items should not be included as initial investment:

1. Payments by the buyer to third parties for improvements to the property

2. A permanent loan commitment by an independent third party to replace a loan made by the seller
3. Funds that have been or will be loaned, refunded, or directly or indirectly provided to the buyer by the seller or loans guaranteed or collateralized by the seller for the buyer

Size of initial investment.   Once the initial investment is computed, its size must be compared to the sales value of the property. To qualify as an adequate initial investment, the initial investment should be equal to at least a major part of the difference between usual loan limits established by independent lending institutions and the sales value of the property. The **minimum initial investment** requirements for real estate sales (other than retail land sales) vary depending upon the class of property being sold. The following table from SFAS 66 provides the limits for the various properties:

Type of property	*Minimum initial investment expressed as a percentage of sales value*
Land	
Held for commercial, industrial, or residential development to commence within two years after sale	20
Held for commercial, industrial, or residential development to commence after two years	25
Commercial and Industrial Property	
Office and industrial buildings, shopping centers, and so forth:	
Properties subject to lease on a long-term lease basis to parties with satisfactory credit rating; cash flow currently sufficient to service all indebtedness	10
Single-tenancy properties sold to a buyer with a satisfactory credit rating	15
All other	20
Other income-producing properties (hotels, motels, marinas, mobile home parks, and so forth):	
Cash flow currently sufficient to service all indebtedness	15
Start-up situations or current deficiencies in cash flow	25
Multifamily Residential Property	
Primary residence:	
Cash flow currently sufficient to service all indebtedness	10
Start-up situations or current deficiencies in cash flow	15
Secondary or recreational residence:	
Cash flow currently sufficient to service all indebtedness	15
Start-up situations or current deficiencies in cash flow	25

Single-Family Residential Property (including condominium or cooperative housing)

Primary residence of the buyer	5^a
Secondary or recreational residence	10^a

a *If collectibility of the remaining portion of the sales price cannot be supported by reliable evidence of collection experience, the minimum initial investment shall be at least 60% of the difference between the sales value and the financing available from loans guaranteed by regulatory bodies such as the Federal Housing Authority (FHA) or the Veterans Administration (VA), or from independent, established lending institutions. This 60% test applies when independent first-mortgage financing is not utilized and the seller takes a receivable from the buyer for the difference between the sales value and the initial investment. If independent first mortgage financing is utilized, the adequacy of the initial investment on sales of single-family residential property should be determined in accordance with paragraph 53.*

However, lenders' appraisals of specific properties often differ. Therefore, if the buyer has obtained a permanent loan or firm permanent loan commitment for maximum financing of the property from an independent lending institution, the minimum initial investment should be the greater of the following:

1. The minimum percentage of the sales value of the property specified in the above table
2. The lesser of
   a. The amount of the sales value of the property in excess of 115% of the amount of a newly placed permanent loan or firm loan commitment from a primary lender that is an independent established lending institution
   b. 25% of the sales value

To illustrate the determination of whether an initial investment adequately demonstrates a commitment to pay for property, consider the following example:

Example determining adequacy of initial investment

Krueger, Inc. exercised a $2,000 option for the purchase of an apartment building from Gampfer, Inc. The terms of the sales contract required Krueger to pay $3,000 of delinquent property taxes, pay a $300,000 cash down payment, assume Gampfer's recently issued **first mortgage** of $1,200,000, and give Gampfer a second mortgage of $500,000 at a prevailing interest rate.

Step 1 — Compute the sales value of the property.

Payment of back taxes to reduce Gampfer's liability to local municipality	$ 3,000
Proceeds from exercised option	2,000
Cash down payment	300,000
First mortgage assumed by Krueger	1,200,000
Second mortgage given to Gampfer	500,000
Sales value of the apartment complex	$2,005,000

Step 2 — Compute the initial investment.

Cash down payment	$300,000
Payment of back taxes to reduce Gampfer's liability to local municipality	3,000
Proceeds from exercised option	2,000
	$ 305,000

Step 3 — Compute the minimum initial investment required.

    a.   The minimum percentage of the sales value of the property as specified in the table is $200,500 ($2,005,000 x 10%).

    b.   1.   The amount of the sales value of the property in excess of 115% of the recently placed permanent mortgage is $625,000 (sales value of $2,005,000 – $1,380,000 [115% of $1,200,000]).

            2.   25% of the sales value ($2,005,000) is $501,250.

The lesser of b.1 and b.2 is b.2, $501,250. The greater of a. and b. is b., $501,250. Therefore, to record this transaction under the full accrual method (assuming all other criteria are met), the minimum initial investment must be equal to or greater than $501,250. Since the actual initial investment is only $305,000, all or part of the recognition of profit from the transaction must be postponed.

If the sale has been consummated but the buyer's initial investment does not adequately demonstrate a commitment to pay, the transaction should be accounted for by the **installment method** when the seller is reasonably assured of **recovering the cost** of the property if the buyer defaults. However, if the recovery of the cost of the property is not reasonably assured should the buyer default or if the cost has been recovered and the collection of additional amounts is uncertain, the cost recovery or deposit methods should be used.

Adequacy of the buyer's continuing investments. The collectibility of the buyer's receivable must be reasonably assured; therefore, for full profit recognition under the full accrual method, the buyer must be contractually required to pay each year on its total debt for the purchase price of the property an amount at least equal to the level annual payment that would be needed to pay that debt (both principal and interest) over a specified period. This period is no more than twenty years for land, and no more than the customary amortization term of a first mortgage loan by an independent lender for other types of real estate. For continuing investment purposes, the contractually required payments must be in a form that is acceptable for an initial investment. If the seller provides funds to the buyer, either directly or indirectly, these funds must be subtracted from the buyer's payments in determining whether the continuing investments are adequate.

The indebtedness on the property does not have to be reduced proportionately. A lump-sum (balloon) payment will not affect the amortization of the receivable as long as the level annual payments still meet the minimum annual amortization requirement. For example, a land real estate sale may require the buyer to make level annual payments at the end of each of the first five years and then a balloon payment at the end of the sixth year. The continuing investment criterion is met provided the level annual payment required in each of the first five years is greater than or equal to the level annual payment that would be made if the receivable were amortized over the maximum twenty-year (land's specified term) period.

Continuing investment not qualifying. If the sale has been consummated and the minimum initial investment criteria have been satisfied but the continuing investment by the buyer does not meet the stated criterion, the seller shall recognize profit by the **reduced profit method** at the time of sale if payments by the buyer each year will at least cover both of the following:

1. The interest and principal amortization on the maximum first mortgage loan that could be obtained on the property
2. Interest, at an appropriate rate, on the excess of the aggregate actual debt on the property over such a maximum first mortgage loan

If the payments by the buyer do not cover both of the above, the seller may recognize profit by either the **installment** or **cost recovery** method.

Release provisions. An agreement to sell real estate may provide that part or all of the property sold will be released from liens by payment of an amount sufficient to release the debt or by an assignment of the buyer's payments until release. In order to meet the criteria of an adequate initial investment, the investment must be sufficient both to pay the release on property released and to meet the initial investment requirements on property not released. If not, profit is recognized on each released portion as if a separate sale when a sale has been deemed to have taken place.

Seller's receivable subject to future subordination. The seller's receivable should not be subject to future subordination. Future subordination by a primary lender would permit the lender to obtain a **lien** on the property, giving the seller only a secondary residual claim. This subordination criterion does not apply if either of the following occur:

1. A receivable is subordinate to a first mortgage on the property existing at the time of sale.
2. A future loan, including an existing permanent loan commitment, is provided for by the terms of the sale and the proceeds of the loan will be applied first to the payment of the seller's receivable.

If the seller's receivable is subject to future subordination, profit shall be recognized by the **cost recovery method**. The cost recovery method is justified because the collectibility of the sales price is not reasonably assured in circumstances when the receivable may be subordinated to other creditors.

Seller's continuing involvement. Sometimes sellers continue to be involved with property for periods of time even though the property has been legally sold. The seller's involvement often takes the form of profit participation, management services, financing, guarantees of return, construction, etc. The seller does not have a substantial continuing involvement with property unless the risks and rewards of ownership have been clearly transferred to the buyer.

If the seller has some continuing involvement with the property and does not clearly transfer substantially all of the risks and rewards of ownership, profit shall be recognized by a method other than the full accrual method. The method chosen should be determined by the nature and extent of the seller's continuing involvement. As a general rule, profit should only be recognized at the time of sale if the amount of the seller's loss due to the continued involvement with the property is limited by the terms of the sales contract. In this event, the profit recognized at this time should be reduced by the maximum possible loss from the continued involvement.

Leases involving real estate. SFAS 98 dealing with sales-type real estate leases and sales-leaseback real estate transactions is covered in the lease chapter on pages 611, 621, and 623 respectively.

Profit-sharing, financing, and leasing arrangements. In real estate sales, it is often the case that economic substance takes precedence over legal form. Certain transactions, though possibly called sales, are in substance profit-sharing, financing, or leasing arrangements and should be accounted for as such. These include situations in which

1. The seller has an obligation to repurchase the property, or the terms of the transaction allow the buyer to compel the seller or give an option to the seller to repurchase the property.
2. The seller is a general partner in a limited partnership that acquires an interest in the property sold and holds a receivable from the buyer for a significant part (15% of the maximum first-lien financing) of the sales price.
3. The seller guarantees the return of the buyer's investment or a return on that investment for an **extended** period of time.
4. The seller is required to initiate or support operations, or continue to operate property at its own risk for an **extended** period of time.

Options to purchase real estate property. Often a buyer will buy an option to purchase land from a seller with the hopeful intention of obtaining a zoning change, building permit, or some other contingency specified in the option agreement. Proceeds from the issue of an option by a property owner (seller) should be accounted for by the **deposit method.** If the option is exercised, the seller should include the option proceeds in the computation of the sales value of the property. If the option is not exercised, the seller should recognize the option proceeds as income at the time the option expires.

Partial sales of property. Per SFAS 66, "a sale is a partial sale if the seller retains an equity interest in the property or has an equity interest in the buyer." Profit on a partial sale may be recognized on the date of sale if the following occur:

1. The buyer is independent of the seller.
2. Collection of the sales price is reasonably assured.

3. The seller will not be required to support the operations of the property on its related obligations to an extent greater than its proportionate interest.

If the buyer is not independent of the seller, the seller may not be able to recognize any profit that is measured at the date of sale.

If the seller is not reasonably assured of collecting the sales price, the **cost recovery** or **installment method** should be used to recognize profit on the partial sale.

A seller who separately sells individual units in condominium projects or time-sharing interests should recognize profit by the percentage-of-completion method on the sale of individual units or interests if all of the following criteria are met:

1. Construction is beyond a preliminary stage (i.e., engineering and design work, execution of construction contracts, site clearance and preparation, excavation, and completion of the building foundation have all been completed).
2. The buyer is unable to obtain a refund except for nondelivery of the units or interest.
3. Sufficient units have been sold to assure that the entire property will not revert to rental property.
4. Sales prices are collectible.
5. Aggregate sales proceeds and costs can be reasonably estimated.

The **deposit** method would be appropriate to account for these sales up to the point all the criteria are met for recognition of a sale.

Selection of method. If, however, a loss is apparent (e.g., the carrying value of the property exceeds the sum of the deposit, fair value of unrecorded note receivable, and the debt assumed by the buyer), then immediate recognition is required.

The installment method is appropriate if the full accrual method cannot be used due to an inadequate initial investment by the buyer, provided that recovery of cost is reasonably assured if the buyer defaults. The cost recovery method or the deposit method are appropriate if such cost recovery is not assured.

The reduced profit method is appropriate when the buyer's initial investment is adequate but the continuing investment is not adequate, and payments by the buyer at least cover the sum of the amortization (principal and interest) on the maximum first mortgage that could be obtained on the property and the interest, at an appropriate rate, on the excess of aggregate debt over the maximum first mortgage.

Description of the Methods of Accounting for Real Estate Sales other than Retail Land Sales

Full accrual method. This method of accounting for nonretail sales of real estate is appropriate when all four of the recognition criteria have been satisfied. The full accrual method is simply the application of the revenue recognition principle. A real estate sale is recognized in full when the profit is determinable and the earnings process is virtually complete. The profit is determinable when the first three criteria have been met, the sale is consummated, the buyer has demonstrated a commitment to pay, and the seller's receivable is not subject to future subordination. The earnings process is virtually complete when the fourth criterion has been met, the seller has transferred the risks and rewards of ownership and does not have a substantial continuing involvement with the property. If all of the criteria have not been met, the seller should record the transaction by one of the following methods as indicated by SFAS 66:

1. Deposit
2. Cost recovery
3. Installment
4. Reduced profit
5. Percentage-of-completion (see the section on Long-Term Construction Contracts in this chapter)

Profit under the full accrual method is computed by subtracting the cost basis of the property surrendered from the sales value given by the buyer. Also, the computation of profit on the sale should include all costs incurred that are directly related to the sale, such as accounting and legal fees.

Installment method. Under the installment method, each cash receipt and principal payment by the buyer on debt assumed with recourse to the seller consists of part recovery of cost and part recovery of profit. The apportionment between cost recovery and profit is in the same ratio as total cost and total profit bear to the sales value of the property sold. Therefore, under the installment method, the seller recognizes profit on each payment that the buyer makes to the seller and on each payment the buyer makes to the holder of the primary debt. When a buyer assumes debt that is without recourse to the seller, the seller should recognize profit on each payment made to the seller and on the entire debt assumed by the buyer. The accounting treatment differs because the seller is subject to substantially different levels of risk under the alternative conditions. For debt that is without recourse, the seller recovers a portion, if not all, of the cost of the asset surrendered at the time the buyer assumes the debt.

Example of the installment method

Assume Benson sells to Golden a plot of undeveloped land for $2,000,000. Golden will assume, with recourse, Benson's existing first mortgage of $1,000,000 and also pay Benson a $300,000 cash down payment. Golden will pay the balance of $700,000 by giving Benson a second mortgage payable in equal installments of principal and interest over a ten-year period. The cost of the land to Benson was $1,200,000 and Golden will commence development of the land immediately.

1. Computation of sales value:

Cash down payment	$ 300,000
First mortgage	1,000,000
Second mortgage	700,000
Sales value	$2,000,000

2. Computation of the initial investment:

Cash down payment	$ 300,000

3. Computation of the minimum required initial investment:

   a. $400,000 ($2,000,000 x 20%)
   b. 1. $850,000 [$2,000,000 – (115% x 1,000,000)]
       2. $500,000 ($2,000,000 x 25%)

   The minimum initial investment is $500,000 since b.2. is less than b.1. and b.2. is greater than a.

The initial investment criterion has not been satisfied because the actual initial investment is less than the minimum initial investment. Therefore, assuming the sale has been consummated and Benson is reasonably assured of recovering the cost of the land from Golden, the installment method should be used. The gross profit to be recognized over the installment payment period by Benson would be computed as follows:

Sales value	$ 2,000,000
Cost of land	(1,200,000)
Gross profit	$ 800,000

The gross profit percentage to apply to each payment by Golden to Benson and the primary debt holder is 40% ($800,000/$2,000,000).

If Golden also pays $50,000 of principal on the first mortgage and $70,000 of principal on the second mortgage in the year of sale, Benson would recognize the following profit in the year of sale:

Profit recognized on the down payment ($300,000 x 40%)	$120,000
Profit recognized on the principal payments:	
First mortgage ($50,000 x 40%)	20,000
Second mortgage ($70,000 x 40%)	28,000
Total profit recognized in year of sale	$168,000

Note that Benson recognizes profit only on the **payment** applicable to the first mortgage. This is because Benson may be called upon to satisfy the liability on the first mortgage if Golden defaults.

If Benson's first mortgage was assumed without recourse, Benson would recognize the following profit in the year of sale:

Profit recognized on the down payment ($300,000 x 40%)	$120,000
Profit recognized on Golden's assumption of Benson's first	
mortgage without recourse ($1,000,000 x 40%)	400,000
Profit recognized on the principal payment of the second	
mortgage ($70,000 x 40%)	28,000
Total profit recognized in year of sale	$548,000

The income statement (or related footnotes) for the period of sale should include the sales value received, the gross profit recognized, the gross profit deferred, and the costs of sale. In future periods when further payments are made to the buyer, the seller should realize gross profit on these payments. This amount should be disclosed as a single line item in the revenue section of the income statement.

If, in the future, the transaction meets the requirements for the full accrual method of recognizing profit, the seller may change to that method and recognize the remaining deferred profit as income at that time.

Cost recovery method. When the cost recovery method is used (e.g., when the seller's receivable is subject to subordination or the seller is not reasonably assured of recovering the cost of the property if the buyer defaults), no profit is recognized on the sales transaction until the seller has recovered the cost of the property sold. If the buyer assumes debt that is with recourse to the seller, profit should not be recognized by the seller until the cash payments by the buyer, including both principal and interest on debt due the seller and on debt assumed by the buyer, exceed the seller's cost of the property sold. If the buyer assumes debt that is without recourse to the seller, profit may be recognized by the seller when the cash payments by the buyer, including both principal and interest on debt due the seller, exceed the difference between the seller's cost of the property and the nonrecourse debt assumed by the buyer.

For the cost recovery method, principal collections reduce the seller's related receivable, and interest collections on such receivable increase the deferred gross profit on the balance sheet.

Example of the cost recovery method

Assume that on January 1, 2002, Maher, Inc. purchased undeveloped land with a sales value of $365,000 from Bernard Co. The sales value is represented by a $15,000 cash down payment, Maher assuming Bernard's $200,000 first mortgage (10%, payable in equal annual installments over the next twenty years), and Maher giving Bernard a second mortgage of $150,000 (12%, payable in equal annual installments over the next ten years). The sale has been consummated, but the initial investment is below the minimum required amount and Bernard is not reasonably assured of recovering the cost of the property if Maher defaults. The cost of the land to Bernard was $300,000. The circumstances indicate the cost recovery method is appropriate. The transaction would be recorded by Bernard as follows:

1/1/02	Notes receivable	150,000	
	First mortgage payable	200,000	
	Cash	15,000	
	Revenue from sale of land		365,000
	Revenue from sale of land	365,000	
	Land		300,000
	Deferred gross profit		65,000

Case 1 — The first mortgage was assumed with recourse to Bernard. Immediately after the sale, the unrecovered cost of the land would be computed as follows:

Land	$300,000
Less: Cash down payment	(15,000)
Unrecovered cost	$285,000

The note (second mortgage) would be reported as follows:

Note receivable	$150,000	
Less: Deferred gross profit	(65,000)	$ 85,000

At the end of the year Maher would pay $26,547.64 ($8,547.64 principal and $18,000.00 interest) on the second mortgage note and $23,491.94 ($3,491.94 principal and $20,000.00 interest) on the first mortgage. At 12/31/02 the unrecovered cost of the land would be computed as follows:

Previous unrecovered cost		$285,000.00
Less: Note receivable payment	$26,547.64	
First mortgage payment	23,491.94	(50,039.58)
Unrecovered cost		$234,960.42

The receivable would be reported on the 12/31/02 balance sheet as follows:

Note receivable ($150,000 – 8,547.64)	$141,452.36	
Less: Deferred gross profit ($65,000 + 18,000)	83,000.00	$58,452.36

Case 2 — The first mortgage was assumed without recourse to Bernard. The reporting of the note would be the same as Case 1; however, the unrecovered cost of the property would be different. Immediately after the sale, the unrecovered cost of the property would be computed as follows:

Land	$300,000
Less: Cash down payment	(15,000)
Nonrecourse debt assumed by Maher	(200,000)
Unrecovered cost	$ 85,000

After Maher makes the payments at the end of the year, the unrecovered cost would be computed as follows:

Previous unrecovered cost	$85,000.00
Less: Notes receivable payment	26,547.64
Unrecovered cost	$58,452.36

For the cost recovery method, the income statement for the year the real estate sale occurs should include the sales value received, the cost of the property given up, and the gross profit deferred. In future periods, after the cost of the property has been recovered, the income statement should include the gross profit earned as a separate revenue item.

If, after accounting for the sale by the cost recovery method, circumstances indicate that the criteria for the full accrual method are satisfied, the seller may change to the full accrual method and recognize any remaining deferred gross profit in full.

Deposit method. When the deposit method is used (e.g., when the sale is, in substance, the sale of an option and not real estate), the seller does not recognize any profit, does not record a receivable, continues to report in its financial statements the property and the related existing debt even if the debt has been assumed by the buyer, and discloses that those items are subject to a sales contract. The seller also continues to charge depreciation expense on the property for which the deposits have been received. Cash received from the buyer (initial and continuing investments) is reported as a deposit on the contract. However, some amounts of cash may be received that are not subject to refund, such as interest on the unrecorded principal. These amounts should be used to offset any carrying charges on the property (e.g., property taxes and interest charges on the existing debt). If the interest collected on the unrecorded receivable is refundable, the seller should record this interest as a deposit before the sale is consummated and then include it as a part of the initial investment once the sale is consummated. For contracts that are cancelled, the nonrefundable amounts should be recognized as income and the refundable amounts returned to the depositor at the time of cancellation.

As stated, the seller's balance sheet should continue to present the debt assumed by the buyer (this includes nonrecourse debt) among its other liabilities. However, the seller should report any principal payments on the mortgage debt assumed as additional deposits, while correspondingly reducing the carrying amount of the mortgage debt.

Reduced profit method. The reduced profit method is appropriate when the sale has been consummated and the initial investment is adequate but the continuing investment does not clearly demonstrate the willing commitment to pay the remaining balance of the receivable. For example, a buyer may purchase land under an agreement in which the seller will finance the sale over a thirty-year period. SFAS 66 specifically states twenty years as the maximum amortization period for the purchase of land; therefore, the agreement fails to meet the continuing investment criteria.

Under the reduced profit method, the seller recognizes a portion of the profit at the time of sale with the remaining portion recognized in future periods. The amount of reduced profit to be recognized at the time of sale is determined by discounting the receivable from the buyer to the present value of the lowest level of annual payments required by the sales contract over the maximum period of time specified for that type of real estate property (twenty years for land and the customary term of a first mortgage loan set by an independent lending institution for other types of real estate). The remaining profit is recognized in the periods that lump-sum or other payments are made.

Example of the reduced profit method

Assume Zarembski, Inc. sells a parcel of land to Stees Co. Zarembski receives sales value of $2,000,000. The land cost $1,600,000. Stees gave Zarembski the following consideration:

Cash down payment	$ 500,000
First mortgage note payable to an independent lending institution (payable in equal installments of principal and 12% interest, $133,887 payable at the end of each of the next twenty years)	1,000,000
Second mortgage note payable to Zarembski (payable in equal installments of principal and 10% interest, $53,039 payable at the end of each of the next thirty years)	500,000
Total sales value	$2,000,000

The amortization term of the second mortgage (seller's receivable) exceeds the twenty-year maximum permitted by SFAS 66. It is assumed that the payments by the buyer will cover the interest and principal on the maximum first mortgage loan that could be obtained on the property and interest on the excess aggregate debt on the property over such a maximum first mortgage loan; consequently, the reduced profit method would be appropriate. It is also assumed that the market interest rate on similar agreements is 14%.

The present value of $53,039 per year for twenty years at the market rate of 14% is $351,278 ($53,039 x 6.623).

The gross profit on the sale ($400,000) is reduced by the difference between the face amount of the seller's receivable ($500,000) and the reduced amount ($351,278) or $148,722. The profit recognized at the time of sale is the sales value less the cost of the land less the difference between the face amount of the receivable and the reduced amount. Therefore, the reduced profit recognized on the date of sale is computed as follows:

Sales value	$ 2,000,000
Less: Cost of land	(1,600,000)
Excess	(148,722)
Reduced profit	$ 251,278

Under the reduced profit method, the seller amortizes its receivable at the market rate, not the rate given on the second mortgage. The receivable's carrying balance is zero after the specified term expires (in this case, twenty years). The remaining profit of $148,722 is recognized in the years after the specified term expires as the buyer makes payments on the second mortgage (years 21-30).

Retail Land Sales

Recognition of profit. A single method of recognizing profit is applied to all sales transactions within a project that is consummated.

The full accrual method of accounting is applied if **all** of the following conditions are met and a sale can be recorded:

a. **Expiration of refund period.** The buyer has made the down payment and each required subsequent payment until the period of cancellation with refund has expired. That period is the longest period of those required by local law, established by the seller's policy, or specified in the contract.

b. **Sufficient cumulative payments.** The cumulative payments of principal and interest equal or exceed 10% of the contract sales price.

c. **Collectibility of receivables.** Collection experience for the project in which the sale is made or for the seller's prior projects indicates that at least 90% of the contracts in the project in which the sale is made that are in force six months after sale will be collected in full. The collection experience with the seller's prior projects may be applied to a new project if the prior projects have

    (1) The same characteristics (type of land, environment, clientele, contract terms, sales methods) as the new project

    (2) A sufficiently long collection period to indicate the percentage of current sales of the new project that will be collected to maturity

A down payment of at least 20% is an acceptable indication of collectibility.

d. **Nonsubordination of receivables.** The receivable from the sale is not subject to subordination to new loans on the property except that subordination by an individual lot buyer for home construction purposes is permissible if the collection experience on those contracts is the same as on contracts not subordinated.

e. **Completion of development.** The seller is not obligated to complete improvements of lots sold or to construct amenities or other facilities applicable to lots sold.

Percentage-of-completion. The percentage-of-completion method should be used if criteria a., b., c., and d. above are met, and full accrual criteria are not met (criterion e. is not satisfied). However, additional criteria (f. and g.) must be satisfied.

f. **There has been progress on improvements.** The project's improvements progressed beyond preliminary stages and the work apparently will be completed according to plan. Some indications of progress are

    (1) The expenditure of funds

    (2) Initiation of work

    (3) Existence of engineering plans and work commitments

    (4) Completion of access roads and amenities such as golf courses, clubs, and swimming pools

Additionally, there should be no indication of significant delaying factors, such as the inability to obtain permits, contractors, personnel, or equipment. Finally, estimates of costs to complete and extent of progress toward completion should be reasonably dependable.

g. **Development is practical.** There is an expectation that the land can be developed for the purposes, represented and the properties will be useful for those purposes; restrictions, including environmental restrictions, will not seriously hamper development; and that improvements such as access roads, water supply, and sewage treatment or removal are feasible within a reasonable time period.

Installment. The installment method is appropriate if criteria a. and b. are met, full accrual criteria are not met, and the seller is financially capable, as shown by capital structure, cash flow, or borrowing capacity. If the transaction subsequently meets the requirements for the full accrual method, the seller is permitted to change to that method. This would be a change in accounting estimate. This method may be changed to the percentage-of-completion method when all of the criteria are met.

Other. If a retail land sale transaction does not meet any of the above, the deposit method is appropriate.

EMERGING ISSUES TASK FORCE CONSENSUS SUMMARIES

00-13 Determining Whether Equipment is "Integral Equipment" Subject to FASB Statement No. 66, *Accounting for Sales of Real Estate*, and No. 98, *Accounting for Leases*

Because FASB Interpretation 43, issued in June 1999, states that sales of integral equipment are within the scope of SFAS 66, *Accounting for Sales of Real Estate*, the determination of whether equipment is integral has increased in importance. A determination of whether equipment to be leased is integral is also necessary for proper accounting for sales-type leases by lessors. This issue discusses how the determination should be made.

The determination of whether equipment is integral should be made based on two factors. The first is the significance of the cost to remove the equipment from its existing location (which would include the costs of repairing the damage done to that location by the removal). The second factor is the decrease in value of the equipment that results from its removal (which is, at a minimum, the cost to ship and reinstall the equipment at a new site). The nature of the equipment and whether others can use it should be considered in determining whether there is further diminution in fair value. When the combined total of the cost to remove and any further diminution of value exceeds 10% of the fair value of the equipment (installed), the equipment is integral equipment.

REAL ESTATE OPERATIONS

PERSPECTIVE AND ISSUES

SFAS 67, *Real Estate: Accounting for Costs and Initial Rental Operations of Real Estate Projects,* deals with the accounting for various costs in acquiring and developing real estate projects. It does not apply to

a. Real estate developed by an entity for its own use rather than sale or rental
b. Initial direct costs of leases
c. Costs directly related to manufacturing, merchandising or service activities rather than real estate activities
d. Rental operations in which the predominant rental period is less than a month

The standard does include accounting for costs of real estate whether rented or sold.

Sources of GAAP		
SFAS	*EITF*	*SOP*
67, 121	84-17, 85-27, 86-6,	75-2, 78-9,
	86-7, 87-9, 88-12, 88-24,	92-1
	89-14, 90-20, 91-2,	
	94-2, 95-6, 95-7, 97-11, 98-8	

DEFINITIONS OF TERMS

Amenities. Amenities include golf courses, utility plants, clubhouses, swimming pools, tennis courts, indoor recreational facilities, and parking facilities.

Common costs. Costs that relate to two or more units within a real estate project.

Costs incurred to rent real estate projects. Includes costs of model units and their furnishings, rental facilities, semipermanent signs, rental brochures, advertising, "grand openings," and rental overhead including rental salaries.

Costs incurred to sell real estate projects. Includes costs of model units and their furnishings, sales facilities, sales brochures, legal fees for preparation of prospectuses, semipermanent signs, advertising, "grand openings," and sales overhead including sales salaries.

Fair value. The amount in cash or cash equivalent value of other consideration that a real estate parcel would yield in a current sale between a willing buyer and a willing seller (other than in a forced or liquidation sale). The fair value of a parcel is affected by its physical characteristics, ultimate use, and the time required to make such use of the property considering access, development plans, zoning restrictions, and market absorption factors.

Incidental operations. Revenue-producing activities engaged in during the holding or development period to reduce the cost of developing the property for its intended use, as distinguished from activities designed to generate a profit or a return from the use of the property.

Incremental costs of incidental operations. Costs that would not be incurred except in relation to the conduct of incidental operations. Interest, taxes, insurance, security, and similar costs that would be incurred during the development of a real estate project regardless of whether incidental operations were conducted are not incremental costs.

Incremental revenue from incidental operations. Revenues that would not be produced except in relation to the conduct of incidental operations.

Indirect project costs. Costs incurred after the acquisition of the property, such as construction administration, legal fees, and various office costs, that clearly relate to projects under development or construction.

Net realizable value. The estimated selling price in the ordinary course of business less estimated costs of completion, holding, and disposal.

Phase. A parcel on which units are to be constructed concurrently.

Preacquisition costs. Costs related to a property that are incurred for the express purpose of, but prior to, obtaining that property. Examples may be costs of surveying, zoning or traffic studies, or payments to obtain an option on the property.

Project costs. Costs clearly associated with the acquisition, development, and construction of a real estate project.

Relative fair value before construction. The fair value of each land parcel in a real estate project in relation to the fair value of the other parcels in the project, exclusive of value added by on-site development and construction activities.

CONCEPTS, RULES, AND EXAMPLES

Preacquisition Costs

Payments are generally capitalized if they relate to an option to obtain the real property or if all of the following conditions are met:

a. Costs are directly identified with the property.
b. Costs would be capitalized if the property already were acquired.
c. Acquisition of the option or property is probable. The purchaser wants the property and believes it to be available for sale and has the ability to finance its acquisition.

Once capitalized, these costs are project costs which, if not receivable in the future, or if the property is not acquired should be charged to expense.

Taxes and Insurance

Real estate taxes and insurance are capitalized as property costs only when the property is undergoing activities necessary to get the property ready for its intended use. After the property is substantially complete and ready for its intended use such items are expensed.

Project Costs

Costs that are identifiable and clearly associated with acquisition, development, and construction of a real estate project are capitalized as a cost of the project.

Indirect costs that relate to several projects should be capitalized and allocated to these projects. Indirect costs that do not clearly relate to any project such as general and administrative expenses should be expensed as incurred.

Amenities

Amenities that are to be sold or transferred in connection with the sale of individual units should have the costs in excess of anticipated proceeds treated as **common costs** of the project.

Amenities that are to be sold separately or retained by the developer should have the costs capitalized with those costs in excess of estimated fair value treated as common costs. **Fair value** is determined as of the expected date of substantial physical completion and the amounts allocated to the amenity should not be revised later. The sale of the amenity results in a gain or loss when the selling price differs from the fair value less accumulated depreciation.

Costs of amenities should be allocated among land parcels benefited for which development is probable. Before completion and availability for use, operating income or loss is an adjustment to common costs. After such date, operating income or loss is included in the income statement.

Incidental Operations

Revenue from incidental operations should be combined with the costs of such operations and any excess of incremental revenue over incremental costs should reduce capitalized project costs. If such costs exceed revenues they should be charged to expense as incurred.

Allocation of Costs

Capitalized costs should be allocated by specific identification. If this is not feasible, then for all costs prior to construction, the costs should be allocated by the relative fair value before construction and, for construction costs, allocated by the relative sales value of each unit.

If relative values are impractical then allocation may be square footage or other area method, or other values deemed appropriate.

Revisions of Estimates

Estimates made and cost allocations should be reviewed at least annually until the project is substantially complete and available for sale. Costs should be revised and reallocated as required for changes in current estimates.

Abandonment and Change in Use

Abandonment of a project requires all capitalized costs to be expensed and not reallocated to other components of the project or other projects. Real estate dedicated to governmental units is not deemed abandoned and should have its costs treated as project common costs.

Changes in use require that costs incurred and expected to be incurred that exceed the estimated value of the required project (when substantially complete and ready for intended use) should be charged to expense. If no formal plan for the project exists, then project costs in excess of current net realizable value should be expensed.

Selling Costs

Costs incurred to sell should be capitalized if they are

a. Reasonably expected to be recovered from sale of the project or from incidental operations, and

b. Incurred for tangible assets used directly throughout the selling period to assist the selling process or incurred for services required to obtain regulatory approval of sales.

Other costs may be capitalized as prepaid expenses if directly associated with sales, cost recovery is reasonably expected from sales and the full accrual method of sale cannot be used.

All other costs should be expensed in the period incurred. Capitalized costs are expensed in the period in which the related revenue is earned.

Rental Costs

Costs related to and reasonably expected to be recoverable from future rental operations should be capitalized. This excludes initial direct costs as defined and described in accounting for leases. Costs that cannot be capitalized should be expensed as incurred.

Capitalized costs should be amortized over the term of the lease, if directly related to a specific operating lease, or over the period of expected benefit. Amortization should begin when the project is substantially completed and available for occupancy. Estimated unrecoverable amounts should be expensed when it is probable that the lease will be terminated.

A project is substantially completed and available for occupancy when tenant improvements are completed or after one year from the end of major construction activity. Then normal operations take place with all revenues and costs (including depreciation and other amortized costs) recognized in the income statement. If part of a project is occupied but other parts are not yet complete, completed portions should be considered as separate projects.

Recoverability

Projects held for sale or development cannot be valued in excess of reductions in the carrying amounts of real estate assets prescribed by SFAS 121. Such projects, or parts thereof, that are substantially complete and ready for intended use shall be accounted for at the lower of carrying amount or fair value less cost to sell as described in SFAS 121. The recognition and measurement principles articulated in SFAS 121 apply to real estate held for development and sale as well as property to be developed in the future as well as property undergoing current development. Costs should, however, continue to be capitalized as required by the standards. Recoverability may be determined for each separate project. The determination of which components add up to a separate project may involve issues of homogeneity and other similarities.

Real estate rental projects which are valued in excess of that indicated by rental demand should be assessed in accordance with SFAS 121. This statement also details other events or changes in circumstances that suggest that the recoverability of the carrying amount of an asset should be assessed.

There are issues concerning the methods of applying a write-down to property. Generally, the rule is that impairment is evaluated project by project. Projects are not combined in order to offset a potential future profit on one project against other project losses that are required to be recognized currently. Also, once losses are taken on property, similar to inventory, a new cost basis is adopted and future recoveries in value are not recognized. Furthermore, if a project has identifiable elements with separate cash flows such as residential and commercial or houses and condominiums, then each element should be evaluated separately and not combined for the whole project. The appropriate test is the similarity in nature, amount, and timing of cash flows.

EMERGING ISSUES TASK FORCE CONSENSUS SUMMARIES

84-17   Profit Recognition on Sales of Real Estate with Graduated Payment Mortgages and Insured Mortgages

Discusses the application of SFAS 66 to such mortgages. Graduated payment mortgages for which negative principal amortization is recognized do not meet the continuing investment tests in SFAS 66 and thus full profit should **not** be recognized immediately. No consensus was reached regarding partially or fully insured mortgages. See EITF 87-9 for further discussion of the issue.

85-27   Recognition of Receipts from Made-up Rentals Shortfalls

When a seller of real estate agrees to make up any rental shortfalls for a period of time, the Task Force reached a consensus that payments to and receipts from the seller are adjustments to the cost of the property and will affect future depreciation.

86-6   Antispeculation Clauses in Real Estate Sales Contracts

Land sale agreements may contain an "antispeculation" clause requiring the buyer to develop the land in a specific manner or within a specific period of time or the seller has the right, but not the obligation, to reacquire the property. The Task Force concluded that this option would not preclude recognition of a sale if the probability of the buyer not complying is remote.

86-7   Recognition by Homebuilders of Profit from Sales of Land and Related Construction Contracts

A homebuilder enters into a contract to build a home on its own lot, relinquishing title to both the lot and the home at closing. The Task Force determined that SFAS 66 guidance provides that profit recognition is not appropriate until the conditions specified in that pronouncement are met. Deposit accounting should be used for both the land and building activity until that point.

87-9   Profit Recognition on Sales of Real Estate with Insured Mortgages or Surety Bonds

For sales of real estate, the EITF in 84-17 reached a consensus that a sale with a graduated payment mortgage that does not meet the continuing investment test in SFAS 66 should not result in full immediate profit recognition.

In 87-9, on a related matter, the Task Force reached a consensus that mortgage insurance should not be considered the equivalent of an irrevocable letter of credit in determining whether profit should be recognized. Purchase of such insurance is not in itself a demonstration of commitment by the buyer to honor its obligation to pay for the property. The sole exception to this rule is that for all FHA (Federal Housing Administration) and VA (Veteran's Administration) insured loans, profits may be recognized under the full accrual method.

88-12   Transfer of Ownership Interest as Part of Down Payment under FASB Statement 66

The Task Force reached a consensus that the buyer's ownership interest in a purchased property that is pledged as security for a note cannot be included as part of the buyer's initial investment in determining whether profit can be recognized under SFAS 66.

88-24   Effect of Various Forms of Financing under FASB Statement 66

The EITF reached a consensus that the following guidelines should be used in sales of real estate under SFAS 66:

1. The initial and continuing investment requirements of SFAS 66 for profit recognition are applicable unless the seller has unconditionally received all amounts due and is not at risk related to the financing.

2. Debt incurred by the buyer that is secured by the property, incurred from the seller or other parties or by assumption, is not part of an initial investment. The buyer must pay cash or other forms of investment that qualify under SFAS 66.
3. Payments of debt secured by the property are not to be considered part of the buyer's cash payments.

89-14   Valuation of Repossessed Real Estate

Foreclosed property should be recorded at the lower of the net receivable due to the seller at foreclosure or the fair value of the property. SOP 92-3 provides further guidance and states that, after foreclosure, foreclosed assets should be carried at the lower of fair value (less costs to sell) or cost.

90-20   Impact of an Uncollateralized Irrevocable Letter of Credit on a Real Estate Sale-Leaseback Transaction

The Task Force concluded that an uncollateralized irrevocable letter of credit is not a form of continuing involvement that precludes sale-leaseback accounting under SFAS 98. However, all written contracts between the seller-lessee and the issuer of the letter of credit must be evaluated since the latter may have other forms of collateral (e.g., right of offset of amounts on deposit).

91-2   Debtor's Accounting for Forfeiture of Real Estate Subject to a Nonrecourse Mortgage

The Task Force concluded that SFAS 15 applies when a nonrecourse borrower transfers property to lender in full satisfaction of the lien even though fair value of the property is less than the balance due the lender.

94-2   Treatment of Minority Interests in Certain Real Estate Investment Trusts

A sponsor's interest in an operating partnership should be reported as a minority interest in the REIT's consolidated financial statements. The net equity of the operating partnership (after the contributions of the sponsor and the REIT) multiplied by the sponsor's ownership percentage in the operating partnership represents the amount to be initially reported as the minority interest in the REIT's consolidated financial statements.

95-6   Accounting by a Real Estate Investment Trust for an Investment in a Service Corporation

Regardless of method of accounting by a REIT for its investment in a service corporation, the service corporation should not be considered an independent party. Thus, capitalized lease amounts should not exceed the allowable costs under SFAS 13.

Additionally, this EITF includes a list of factors that indicate that the equity method of accounting should be used.

95-7 Implementation Issues Related to the Treatment of Minority Interests in Certain Real Estate Investment Trusts

This is follow-up to Issue 94-2. If minority interest balance is negative, the related charge in REIT income statement would be greater of minority's share of current earnings or amount of distributions to minority during the year; any excess should be credited to equity directly. Other REIT accounting matters are also addressed; consensus that subsequent acquisitions of sponsor's minority interest should be accounted for consistent with accounting for formation of the partnership.

97-11 Accounting for Internal Costs Relating to Real Estate Property Acquisitions

Internal costs of preacquisition activities incurred in connection with the acquisition of a property that will be classified as nonoperating at the date of acquisition that are directly identifiable with the acquired property and that were incurred subsequent to the time that acquisition of that specific property was considered probable should be capitalized as part of the cost of that acquisition. If the entity later classifies the property as operating at the date of acquisition, such costs should be charged to expense and any additional costs should be expensed as incurred. Internal costs of preacquisition activities incurred in connection with the acquisition of a property that will be classified as operating at the date of acquisition should be expensed as incurred. If the entity subsequently determines that the property will be classified as nonoperating at the date of acquisition, previously expensed costs should not be capitalized as part of the cost of that acquisition.

A property would be considered operating if, at the date of acquisition, major construction activity is substantially completed on the property and it is held available for occupancy upon completion of tenant improvements by the acquirer or it is already income producing. Costs incurred should be allocated between portions under construction and the portions substantially completed and held available for occupancy, per SFAS 67.

98-8 Accounting for Transfers of Investments That Are in Substance Real Estate

A consensus was reached that when investments in the form of financial assets that are in substance real estate are transferred, the accounting should follow SFAS 66. Per the EITF, the implications of this consensus are

1. Transfers of acquisition, development, and construction loans (ADC loans) deemed in substance real estate under Issue 84-4 are subject to this consensus.

2.   Marketable investments in REIT accounted for under SFAS 115 should be accounted for per SFAS 140.

STATEMENTS OF POSITION ON REAL ESTATE

75-2   Accounting Practices of Real Estate Investment Trusts

Interest income should not be recorded when it is not reasonable to expect collection. Commitment fees should be amortized over the combined commitment and loan period. The provisions dealing with loan losses and property valuation have been effectively superseded by SFAS 114 and 121 respectively.

78-9   Accounting for Investments in Real Estate Ventures

Owners of real estate ventures should generally use the equity method of accounting to account for their investments. However, limited partners may have such a minor interest and have no influence or control, in which case, the cost method may be appropriate.

If there are losses in excess of investment, such losses should be recorded regardless of any increase in the estimated fair value of the venture's assets. Losses in excess of investment are a liability. Losses which cannot be borne by certain investors require the remaining investors to use SFAS 5, *Accounting for Contingencies*, to determine their share of any additional loss. Limited partners are not required to record losses in excess of investment. If investors do not recognize losses in excess of investment, the equity method should be resumed only after the investor's share of net income exceeds net losses not recognized previously.

Venture agreements may designate different allocations for profits, losses, cash distributions and cash from liquidation. Accounting for equity in profits and losses requires careful consideration of allocation formulas because the substance over form concept requires equity accounting to follow the ultimate cash allocations.

Contributions of real estate to a venture as capital should be recorded by the investor at cost and should not result in recognition of a gain since a capital contribution is not the culmination of the earning process.

Interest on loans and advances that are in substance capital contributions should be accounted for as distributions and not interest income.

In late 2000, AcSEC issued an Exposure Draft (ED) of a proposed SOP, *Accounting for Investors' Interests in Unconsolidated Real Estate Investments*. If adopted for the fourth quarter of 2001, this would supersede SOP 78-9. Highlights of AcSEC's tentative conclusions are as follows:

In general, investors holding equity investments in an investee would continue to apply the equity method of accounting for that investee when the investor has the ability to exercise significant influence over the investee. Exceptions to this treatment are provided for situations where the investment is in nonvoting common stock or nonredeemable preferred stock that meets the SFAS 115 definition of an equity security having a readily determinable fair value. In those cases, the investor would apply SFAS 115 instead of the equity method.

When the investee is a "specific ownership account" entity (e.g. partnerships and limited liability companies) and the investor does not have the ability to exercise significant influence, the investor would apply SFAS 115 if applicable, or the equity method if SFAS 115 is not applicable.

The application of the equity method under the ED differs from the traditional equity method as set forth in APB 18, which emphasizes the income statement by recording the investor's share of investee earnings. The ED establishes the "hypothetical liquidation at book value" (HLBV) method, which is balance-sheet-focused. Under HLBV, the investor first must determine its "claim on the investee's book value." This is computed as the amount that the investor would either receive or be obligated to pay should the investee liquidate all of its assets at their recorded amounts determined in accordance with GAAP and distribute the cash to creditors and investors in accordance with their respective legal priorities. The difference between the HLBV at the end of the period and at the beginning of the period would be recorded as the investor's share of earnings or losses of the investee for that period.

In computing HLBV, all forms of investor interest in the investee are taken into account including common stock, preferred stock, general or limited partnership interests, debt securities, loans, advances, notes receivable, and other obligations. In some cases, this can cause interaction between application of the provisions of the ED with both SFAS 114 (with respect to receivables, loans, and advances) and SFAS 115 (with respect to debt securities and preferred stock with a readily determinable fair value). The ED provides for application of HLBV prior to applying SFAS 114 and 115. This treatment is consistent with EITF 98-13, Accounting by an Equity Method Investor for Investee Losses When the Investor Has Loans to and Investments in Other Securities of the Investee.

If adopted, the proposed SOP would be effective for fiscal years beginning after December 15, 2001 with early application encouraged. The cumulative effect of the change would be recorded in the period of adoption with retroactive restatement prohibited.

92-1 Accounting for Real Estate Syndication Income

This SOP applies to all income recognition from real estate syndication activities. SFAS 66 applies to profit and loss recognition on sales of real estate by syndicators to partnerships. This SOP requires that the same concepts be applied to syndicators even though they may have never owned the property.

All fees charged by syndicators are includable in determination of sales value as required by SFAS 66 except for syndication fees and fees for which future services must be performed. Syndication fees are recognized as income when the earning process is complete and collectibility is reasonably assured. If fees are unreasonable, they should be adjusted and the sale price of the real estate appropriately adjusted as well. If a partnership interest is received by the syndicator, the value should be included in the test of reasonableness of fees. If it is part of the fee, the syndicators should account for this interest as retained interest from partial sale of real estate in conformity with SFAS 66. Fees for future services should be recognized when the service is rendered.

Fees received from blind pool transactions should be recognized ratably as the syndication partnership invests in property but only to the extent that such fees are nonrefundable. If syndicators may incur future losses from material involvement or from uncertainties regarding collectibility, income should be deferred until the losses can be reasonably estimated. For purposes of determining the SFAS 66 requirement concerning the buyer's initial and continuing investment for profit recognition, cash received by syndicators should first be allocated to unpaid syndication fees and only after such fees are paid in full, then to fees for future services already performed before being allocated to the investment. If syndicators receive or retain partnership interests which are subordinated, these should be accounted for as participations in future profits without risk of loss.

FRANCHISING: ACCOUNTING BY FRANCHISORS

PERSPECTIVE AND ISSUES

Franchising has become a popular growth industry with many businesses seeking to sell franchises as their primary income source and individuals seeking to buy franchises and become an entrepreneur. How to recognize revenue on the individual sale of franchise territories and on the continuing relationship between the franchiser and franchisee are prime issues.

Originally, in 1973, the AICPA published an industry accounting guide, *Accounting for Franchise Fee Revenue* from which the FASB extracted the principles in SFAS 45 with the same title.

Sources of GAAP
SFAS
45

DEFINITIONS OF TERMS

Area franchise. An agreement that transfers franchise rights within a geographical area permitting the opening of a number of franchised outlets. The number of outlets, location, and so forth are decisions usually made by the franchisee.

Bargain purchase. A transaction in which the franchisee is allowed to purchase equipment or supplies for a price that is significantly lower than the fair value of the equipment or supplies.

Continuing franchise fee. Consideration for the continuing rights granted by the franchise agreement and for general or specific services during its life.

Franchise agreement. A written business agreement that meets the following principal criteria:

a. The relation between the franchiser and franchisee is contractual, and an agreement, confirming the rights and responsibilities of each party, is in force for a specified period.

b. The continuing relation has as its purpose the distribution of a product or service, or an entire business concept, within a particular market area.

c. Both the franchiser and the franchisee contribute resources for establishing and maintaining the franchise. The franchiser's contribution may be a trademark, a company reputation, products, procedures, manpower, equipment, or a process. The franchisee usually contributes operating capital as well as the managerial and operational resources required for opening and continuing the franchised outlet.

d. The franchise agreement outlines and describes the specific marketing practices to be followed, specifies the contribution of each party to the operation of the business, and sets forth certain operating procedures that both parties agree to comply with.

e. The establishment of the franchised outlet creates a business entity that will, in most cases, require and support the full-time business activity of the franchisee.

f. Both the franchisee and the franchiser have a common public identity. This identity is achieved most often through the use of common trade names or trademarks and is frequently reinforced through advertising programs designed to promote the recognition and acceptance of the common identity within the franchisee's market area.

Franchisee. The party who has been granted business rights (the franchise) to operate the franchised business.

Franchiser. The party who grants business rights (the franchise) to the party (the franchisee) who will operate the franchised business.

Initial franchise fee. Consideration for establishing the franchise relationship and providing some initial services. Occasionally, the fee includes consideration for initially required equipment and inventory, but those items usually are the subject of separate consideration. The payment of an initial franchise fee or a continuing royalty fee is not a necessary criterion for an agreement to be considered a franchise agreement.

Initial services. Common provision of a franchise agreement in which the franchiser usually will agree to provide a variety of services and advice to the franchisee, such as the following:

a. Assistance in the selection of a site. The assistance may be based on experience with factors such as traffic patterns, residential configurations, and competition.

b. Assistance in obtaining facilities, including related financing and architectural and engineering services. The facilities may be purchased or leased by the franchisee, and lease payments may be guaranteed by the franchiser.

c. Assistance in advertising, either for the individual franchisee or as part of a general program

d. Training of the franchisee's personnel

e. Preparation and distribution of manuals and similar material concerning operations, administration, and recordkeeping

f. Bookkeeping and advisory services, including setting up the franchisee's records and advising the franchisee about income, real estate, and other taxes, or about local regulations affecting the franchisee's business

g. Inspection, testing, and other quality control programs

CONCEPTS AND RULES

Franchise Sales

Franchise operations are generally subject to the same accounting principles as all regular enterprises. However, there are special issues which arise out of **franchise agreements** which require understanding and have special accounting rules.

Revenue should be recognized, with an appropriate provision for bad debts, when the franchiser has substantially performed all material services or conditions. Only when revenue is collected over an extended period of time and collectibility cannot be predicted in advance would the use of the cost recovery or installment methods of revenue recognition be appropriate. Substantial performance means

1. The **franchiser** has no remaining obligation to either refund cash or forgive any unpaid balance due.
2. Substantially all **initial services** required by the agreement have been performed.
3. No material obligations or conditions remain.

Even if the contract does not require initial services, the pattern of performance by the franchiser in other sales will impact the time period of revenue recognition. This can delay such recognition until services are either performed or it can reasonably be assured they will not be performed. The **franchisee** operations will be considered as started when such substantial performance has occurred.

If **initial franchise fees** are large compared to services rendered and **continuing franchise fees** are small compared to services to be rendered, then a portion of the initial fee should be deferred in an amount sufficient to cover the costs of future services and a reasonable profit, after considering the impact of the continuing franchise fee.

Area Franchise Sales

Sometimes franchisers sell territories rather than individual locations. In this event, the franchiser may render services to the area independent of the number of individual franchises to be established. Under this circumstance, revenue recognition for the franchiser is the same as stated above. If, however, substantial services are performed by the franchiser for each individual franchise established, then revenue should be recognized in proportion to mandatory service. The general rule is that when the franchisee has no right to receive a refund, all revenue should be recognized. It may be necessary for revenue recognition to treat a franchise agreement as a divisible contract and allocate revenue among existing and estimated locations. Future amendments to these estimates will require that remaining unrecognized revenue will be recorded in proportion to remaining services to be performed.

Other Relationships

Franchisers may guarantee debt of the franchisee, continue to own a portion of the franchise, or control the franchisee's operations. Revenue should not be recognized until all services, conditions, and obligations have been performed.

In addition, the franchiser may have an option to reacquire the location. Accounting for initial revenue should consider the probability of exercise of the option. If the expectation at the time of the agreement is that the option is likely to be exercised, the entire franchise fee should be deferred and not recognized as income. Upon exercise, the deferral reduces the investment of the franchiser.

An initial fee may cover both franchise rights and property rights, including equipment, signs, and inventory. A portion of the fee applicable to property rights should be recognized to the extent of the fair value of these assets. However, fees relating to different services rendered by franchisers are generally not allocated to these different services because segregating the amounts applicable to each service could not be performed objectively. The rule of revenue recognition when all services are substantially performed is generally upheld. If objectively determinable separate fees are charged for separate services, then recognition of revenue can be determined and recorded for each service performed.

Franchisers may be an agent for the franchise by placing purchase orders for inventory and equipment. These should not be recorded as sales and purchases by the franchiser; instead, receivables and payables should be reported on the balance sheet of the franchiser.

Continuing Franchise and Other Fees

Continuing franchise fees are recognized as revenue as the fees are earned. Related costs are expensed as incurred. Regardless of the purpose of the fees, revenue is recognized when the fee is earned and receivable. The exception is when a portion of the fee is required to be segregated and used for a specific purpose, such as advertising. The franchiser should defer this amount and record it as a liability. This liability is reduced by the cost of the services received.

Sometimes, the franchisee has a period of time where **bargain purchases** of equipment or supplies are granted by the contract. If the bargain price is lower than other customers pay or denies a reasonable profit to the franchiser, a portion of the initial franchise fee should be deferred and accounted for as an adjustment of the selling price when the franchisee makes the purchase. The deferred amount should be either the difference in the selling price among customers and the bargain price or an amount sufficient to provide a reasonable profit to the franchiser.

Costs

Direct and incremental costs related to franchise sales should be deferred and recognized when revenue is recorded. However, deferred costs cannot exceed anticipated future revenue, net of additional expected costs.

Indirect costs are expensed as incurred. These usually are regular and recurring costs that bear no relationship to sales.

Repossessed Franchises

If, for any reason, the franchiser refunds the franchise fee and obtains the location, previously recognized revenue should be reversed in the period of repossession. If a repossession is made without a refund, there is no adjustment of revenue previously recognized. However, any estimated uncollectible amounts should be provided for and any remaining collected funds should be recorded as revenue.

Business Combinations

Business combinations where the franchiser acquires the business of a franchisee should be accounted for in accordance with the rules of APB 16.

If the transaction is deemed a pooling of interests, the financial statements are combined retroactively with franchise fee revenue and other sales eliminated in consolidation.

If the transaction is a purchase, no adjustment of prior revenue is made since the financial statements are not retroactively consolidated. Care must be taken to ensure that the purchase is not a repossession. If the transaction is deemed to be a repossession, it should be accounted for as described in the above section.

OTHER SPECIAL ACCOUNTING AND REPORTING ISSUES

Sources of GAAP
EITF
99-19, 00-8, 00-14

EMERGING ISSUES TASK FORCE CONSENSUS SUMMARIES

99-19   Reporting Revenue Gross as a Principal versus Net as an Agent

This issue provides guidance on whether an entity is an agent for a vendor-manufacturer, and thus should recognize the net retainage (commission) for serving in that capacity, or whether that entity is a seller of goods (principal), and thus should recognize revenue for the gross amount billed to a customer and an expense for the amount paid to the vendor-manufacturer.

The following factors should be considered when determining whether revenue should be reported as the net retainage (hereinafter, "net") or the gross amount billed to a customer ("gross"). None of the indicators are presumptive or determinative, although the relative strength of each indicator should be considered.

- Is the company the primary obligor in the arrangement; that is, is the company responsible for the fulfillment of the order, including the acceptability of the product or service to the customer? If the company, rather than a supplier, is responsible, that fact is a strong indicator that the company should record revenue gross. Responsibility for arranging transportation for the product is not responsibility for fulfillment. If a supplier is responsible for fulfillment, including the acceptability to the customer, that fact indicates that the company should recognize only the net retainage.

- Does the company have general inventory risk? General inventory risk exists if a company takes title to a product before the product is ordered by a customer or will take title to the product if the customer returns it (provided that the customer has a right of return). In considering this indicator, arrangements with a supplier that reduce or mitigate the company's risk level should be considered. Unmitigated general inventory risk is a strong indicator that the company should recognize revenue gross.

- Does the company have physical loss inventory risk? Physical loss inventory risk exists if the title to the product is transferred to the company at the shipping point and then transferred to the customer upon delivery. Physical loss inventory risk also exists if a company takes title to the product after the order is received but before the product is transferred to the shipper. While less persuasive than general inventory risk, this indicator provides some evidence that a company should record revenue gross.

- Does the company establish the selling price? If a company establishes the selling price, that fact may indicate that the company should recognize revenue gross.
- Is the amount earned by the company fixed? If a company earns a fixed amount per transaction or if it earns a percentage of the selling price, that fact may indicate that the company should report revenue net.
- Does the company change the product or perform part of the service? If a company changes the product (beyond packaging) or performs part of the service ordered by the customer such that the selling price is greater as a result of the company's efforts, that fact is indicative that a company should recognize revenue gross. Marketing skills, market coverage, distribution system, or reputation should not be evaluated in determining whether the company changes the product or performs part of the service.
- Does the company have multiple suppliers for the product or service ordered by the customer? If a company has the discretion to select the supplier, that fact may indicate that the company should record revenue gross.
- Is the company involved in determining the nature, type, characteristics or specifications of the product or service by the customer? If so, that fact may indicate that the company should record revenue gross.
- Does the company have credit risk for the amount billed to the customer? Credit risk exists if a company must pay the supplier after the supplier performs, regardless of whether the customer has paid. If the company has credit risk, this fact provides weak evidence that the company should record revenue gross. If the supplier assumes the credit risk, the company should record revenue net.

The EITF consensus includes thirteen examples to assist in its implementation.

00-8 Accounting by a Grantee for an Equity Instrument to Be Received in Conjunction with Providing Goods or Services

In exchange for goods or services, an entity (the grantee) may receive equity instruments that have conversion or exercisability terms that vary based on future events, such as attainment of sales levels or a successful initial public offering. This issue describes the appropriate accounting if SFAS 133 does not apply because the instruments received have underlyings based on either the grantee's or issuer's performance.

The grantee should measure the fair value of the equity instruments received using the stock price and measurement assumptions as of the earlier of two dates. The first date is the date on which the grantee and the issuer reach a mutual understanding of both the terms of the equity-based compensation and the goods to be delivered (or services to be performed). The second date is the date at which the performance necessary to earn the equity is completed by the grantee, that is, the grantee's rights have vested.

If the terms of the equity agreement are dependent on the achievement of a market condition, the fair value of the instrument should include the effects on fair value of the commitment to change the terms if the market condition is met. Pricing models are available to value path-dependent equity instruments.

If the terms of the equity agreement are dependent on the achievement of certain performance goals (beyond those that initially established the goods to be delivered or services to be performed), the fair value of the instrument should be computed without the effects of the commitment to change the terms if the goals are met. If those goals are subsequently met, the fair value should be adjusted to reflect the new terms and the adjustment reported as additional revenue (similar to modification accounting described on page *776).*

00-14 Accounting for Certain Sales Incentives

This Issue discusses the income statement classification of and disclosure requirements for rebates and other discounts, including accounting for free or heavily discounted products. Sales incentives within its scope are offers that can be accepted by a customer as a result of a single exchange transaction. In addition, this Issue discusses the income statement classification of refunds and commitments to provide future service caused by service outages. This Issue does not address coupons, rebates, and other forms of rights for free products or services received in a prior exchange transaction and accounted for as a separate element in that prior transaction.

Appropriate accounting for a sales incentive depends on whether the sales incentive will result in a loss on the sale of the product or service. If the incentive will not result in a loss, a vendor should recognize the cost of the sales incentive at the later of the following dates:

- The date at which the related revenue is recognized, or
- The date at which the sales incentive is offered.

If a sales incentive will result in a loss on the sale of the product or service, a vendor should not recognize a liability for the sales incentive prior to the date at which the related revenue is recognized. Further, offering customers a sales incentive that will result in a loss on sale may indicate an impairment of inventory.

For refunds or rebates, a vendor should recognize a liability (or deferred revenue) for the estimated amount of refunds or rebates that will be claimed by customers. If this amount cannot be estimated, the vendor should recognize the maximum potential amount of the refund or rebate. When recognized, a cash sales incentive should be recognized as a reduction of revenue. For a free product- or service-type incentive, the cost of the free item should be classified as an expense.

SEC registrants should apply the consensus guidance no later than the fourth quarter of the fiscal year beginning after December 15, 1999. Nonregistrants should apply the guidance in the annual financial statements for the fiscal year beginning after December 31, 1999.

9 LONG-LIVED ASSETS

PERSPECTIVE AND ISSUES

Long-lived assets are those which provide an economic benefit to the enterprise for a number of future periods. GAAP regarding long-lived assets involves the determination of the appropriate cost at which to initially record the asset including the cost associated with the eventual retirement of that asset and the cost of interest incurred during its construction, the appropriate method to be used to allocate those costs over the periods benefiting, subsequent increases in cost attributable to changes in the estimate of the retirement cost, the measurement of impairment losses, and the accounting for assets to be disposed of.

These assets are primarily operational assets, and they are broken down into two basic types: tangible and intangible. Tangible assets have physical substance and are categorized as follows:

1. Depreciable
2. Depletable
3. Other tangible assets

Intangible assets have no physical substance. Their value is found in the rights or privileges that they grant to the business enterprise.

Most of the accounting issues associated with long-lived assets involve proper measurement and timing of the transactions. Adequate consideration must be given to the economic substance of the transaction.

All entities are required to review long-lived assets and certain identifiable intangible assets for impairment whenever circumstances and situations change such that there is an indication that the carrying amount may not be recoverable. If, upon review, the undiscounted future cash flows (without interest charges) are less than the carrying amount, the carrying amount is reduced to fair value and an impairment loss is recognized. This fair value is considered the new cost basis that is not subject to subsequent adjustment except for depreciation and further impairment. Thus, there is no restoration of recognized impairment losses.

Long-lived assets and identifiable intangibles to be disposed of (except those associated with discontinued operations) are carried at the lower of carrying value or fair value less the cost to sell. These assets should not be depreciated during the holding period.

With some exceptions, this standard applies to rate-regulated assets. Costs excluded by a regulator from the enterprise's rate base would be recognized as an impairment.

Sources of GAAP					
ARB	*APB*	*SFAS*	*FASB I*	*EITF*	*SOP*
43, Ch. 9; 44	1, 6, 17, 29, 30	2, 34, 42, 58, 62, 68, 109, 121, 141, 142, 143	30, 33	86-29, 87-29, 89-13, 90-8, 91-10, 93-11, 95-23, 96-14, 99-5, 99-9, 99-16, 00-2, D-45	88-1, 92-3, 93-7

Other: Accounting Research Monograph 1

DEFINITIONS OF TERMS

Amortization. The periodic charge to income that results from a systematic and rational allocation of cost over the life of an intangible asset.

Asset retirement obligation. A commitment associated with the eventual permanent removal from service of an asset that is unavoidable as a result of either the acquisition or the normal operation of that asset.

Assets to be disposed of. All long-lived assets and certain identifiable intangibles to be disposed of that are not covered by APB 30 and for which management, having the authority to approve the action, has committed to a plan to dispose of the assets, whether by sale or abandonment, shall be reported at the lower of the fair value less the cost to sell or the carrying amount. Fair value is to be measured as specified in SFAS 121.

Book value. The cost of a long-lived asset less the related accumulated depreciation or amortization to the date of measurement.

Boot. The monetary consideration given or received in an asset exchange.

Component parts of larger groups. As used in SFAS 143, one or more assets within a functional group (see definition below) for which there is a separately identifiable asset retirement obligation.

Depreciation. The periodic charge to income that results from a systematic and rational allocation of cost over the life of a tangible asset.

Dividends-in-kind. Dividends paid to stockholders from assets of the corporation other than cash.

Exchange. A reciprocal transfer between an enterprise and another entity that results in the acquisition of assets or services, or the satisfaction of liabilities through a transfer of assets, services, or obligations.

Fixed assets. Those assets which are used in a productive capacity, have physical substance, are relatively long-lived, and provide future benefit which is readily measurable.

Functional groups. As used in SFAS 143, a functional group is comprised of two or more long-lived assets that are used together and, for operating purposes, are considered to be one asset.

Impairment. If circumstances indicate that the carrying amount of an asset that an entity expects to hold and use may not be recoverable, and if the sum of the expected future cash flows (undiscounted and without interest charges) is less than the carrying amount of the asset, an impairment loss should be recognized in accordance with SFAS 121. The impairment loss is measured as the amount by which the carrying value exceeds the fair value of the asset.

Intangible assets. Those assets which provide future economic benefit but have no physical substance. Examples include goodwill, patents, copyrights, etc.

Monetary assets. Assets whose amounts are fixed in terms of units of currency. Examples are cash, accounts receivable, and notes receivable.

Nonmonetary assets. Assets other than monetary assets. Examples are inventories; investments in common stock; and property, plant, and equipment.

Nonmonetary transactions. Exchanges and nonreciprocal transfers that involve little or no monetary assets or liabilities.

Nonreciprocal transfer. A transfer of assets or services in one direction, either from an enterprise to its owners or another entity, or from owners or another entity to the enterprise. An enterprise's reacquisition of its outstanding stock is a nonreciprocal transfer.

Productive assets. Assets held for or used in the production of goods or services. Productive assets include an investment in another entity if the investment is accounted for by the equity method but exclude an investment not accounted for by that method.

Retirement. The removal from service of a long-lived asset by sale, abandonment, recycling, or other disposal on an other-than-temporary basis. Retirement can occur before or at the end of the asset's useful life. However, retirement does not include the temporary idling of an asset.

Similar productive assets. Productive assets that are of the same general type, that perform the same function, or that are employed in the same line of business.

CONCEPTS, RULES, AND EXAMPLES

Fixed Assets

Fixed assets are tangible property used in a productive capacity that will benefit the enterprise for a period of more than one year.

Three issues in accounting for fixed assets are

1. The cost at which the assets should be recorded
2. The rate at which the cost should be allocated to future periods
3. The recording of the subsequent disposal of the assets

Recorded cost. Any reasonable cost involved in bringing the asset to the buyer and incurred prior to using the asset in actual production is capitalized. Examples include sales taxes, finders' fees, freight costs, installation costs, breaking-in costs, and set-up costs. These costs are **not** to be expensed in the period in which they are incurred.

Costs incurred subsequent to purchase. Costs that occur subsequent to the purchase such as repairs, maintenance, or betterments are treated in one of the following ways:

1. Expensed
2. Capitalized
3. Reduced accumulated depreciation

Ordinary maintenance and repair expenditures are charged to expense.

Extraordinary repairs or maintenance increase the value (utility) of the asset or increase the estimated useful life of the asset. Those costs that increase the value of the asset should increase the recorded asset amount, while those that extend the useful life of the asset should decrease accumulated depreciation.

The chart on the following page summarizes the treatment of expenditures subsequent to acquisition.

Construction of assets for self-use. All direct costs (labor, materials, and variable overhead) of constructing an entity's own fixed assets should be capitalized. However, a controversy exists regarding the proper treatment of fixed overhead. Two different views are

1. Charge the asset with its fair share of fixed overhead (i.e., use the same basis of allocation used for inventory).
2. Charge the fixed asset account with only the identifiable **incremental** amount of fixed overhead.

However, the AICPA has suggested that

> ...*in the absence of compelling evidence to the contrary, overhead costs considered to have "discernible future benefits" for the purposes*

Costs Subsequent to Acquisition of Property, Plant, and Equipment

Type of expenditure	Characteristics	Expense when incurred	Capitalize — Charge to asset	Capitalize — Charge to accum. deprec.	Other
1. Additions	• Extensions, enlargements, or expansions made to an existing asset		x		
2. Repairs and maintenance a. Ordinary	• Recurring, relatively small expenditures				
	1. Maintain normal operating condition	x			
	2. **Do not** add materially to use value	x			
	3. **Do not** extend useful life	x			
b. Extraordinary (major)	• Not recurring, relatively large expenditures				
	1. Primarily increase the use value		x		
	2. Primarily extend the useful life			x	
3. Replacements and betterments	• Major component of asset is removed and replaced with the same type of component with comparable performance capabilities (replacement) or a different type of component having superior performance capabilities (betterment)				• Remove old asset cost and accum. deprec. • Recognize any loss (or gain) on old asset • Charge asset for replacement component
a. Book value of old component is known	1. Primarily increase the use value 2. Primarily extend the useful life		x		
b. Book value of old component is not known				x	
4. Reinstallations and rearrangements	• Provide greater efficiency in production or reduce production costs				
	1. Material costs incurred; benefits extend into future accounting periods		x		
	2. No measurable future benefit	x			

of determining the cost of inventory should be presumed to have "discernible future benefits" for the purpose of determining the cost of a self-constructed depreciable asset.

While this treatment is not binding, it does provide guidance in establishing consistency.

If the total cost of the fixed asset constructed exceeds the fair market value, the asset should be written down to fair market value. The amount of the write-down is included in the determination of net income in the period that construction is completed.

Depreciation of fixed assets. The costs of fixed assets are allocated to the periods they benefit through depreciation. The method of depreciation chosen must result in a systematic and rational allocation of the cost of the asset (less its residual or salvage value) over the asset's expected useful life. The determination of useful life must take a number of factors into consideration, including technological change, normal deterioration, and actual physical usage. The method of depreciation is determined as a function of time (e.g., technological change or normal deterioration) or as a function of actual physical usage.

Depreciation methods based on time.

1. Straight-line—Depreciation expense is incurred evenly over the life of the asset.

$$\frac{\text{Cost less salvage value}}{\text{Estimated useful life}}$$

2. Accelerated methods—Depreciation expense is higher in the early years of the asset's useful life and lower in the later years.

    a. Declining balance—A multiple of the straight-line rate times the book value at the beginning of the year.

    $$\text{Straight-line rate} \ = \ \frac{1}{\text{Estimated useful life}}$$

Example

Double-declining balance depreciation (stop when book value = estimated salvage value)

$$2 \text{ x Straight-line rate x Book value at beginning of year}$$

    b. Sum-of-the-years' digits (SYD) depreciation =
        (Cost less salvage value) x Applicable fraction

$$\text{where applicable fraction} = \frac{\text{number of years of estimated life remaining as of the beginning of the year}}{\text{SYD}}$$

$$\text{and SYD} = \frac{n(n+1)}{2} \ \text{where n = estimated useful life}$$

3. Present value methods—Depreciation expense is lower in the early years and higher in the later years. The rate of return on the investment remains constant over the life of the asset. Time value of money formulas are used.

a. Sinking fund—Uses the future value of an annuity formula.
b. Annuity fund—Uses the present value of an annuity formula.

Partial-year depreciation. When an asset is either acquired or disposed of during the year, the full-year depreciation calculation is prorated between the accounting periods involved.

Example of partial-year depreciation

Ginger Corporation, a calendar-year entity, acquired a machine on June 1, 2002, which cost $40,000 with an estimated useful life of four years and a $2,500 salvage value. The depreciation expense for each full year of the asset's life is calculated as

	Straight-line	Double-declining balance				Sum-of-years' digits			
Year 1	37,500* ÷ 4 = 9,375	50% x	40,000	= 20,000	4/10	x	37,500*	= 15,000
Year 2	9,375	50% x	20,000	= 10,000	3/10	x	37,500	= 11,250
Year 3	9,375	50% x	10,000	= 5,000	2/10	x	37,500	= 7,500
Year 4	9,375	50% x	5,000	= 2,500	1/10	x	37,500	= 3,750

* *(40,000 – 2,500)*

Because the first full year of the asset's life does not coincide with the company's fiscal year, the amounts shown above must be prorated as follows:

	Straight-line	Double-declining balance				Sum-of-years' digits			
2002	7/12 x 9,375 = 5,469	7/12	x 20,000	= 11,667	7/12	x	15,000	= 8,750
2003	9,375	5/12	x 20,000	= 8,333	5/12	x	15,000	= 6,250
		7/12	x 10,000	= 5,833	7/12	x	11,250	= 6,563
				14,166				12,813
2004	9,375	5/12	x 10,000	= 4,167	5/12	x	11,250	= 4,687
		7/12	x 5,000	= 2,917	7/12	x	7,500	= 4,375
				7,084				9,062
2005	9,375	5/12	x 5,000	= 2,083	5/12	x	7,500	= 3,125
		7/12	x 2,500	= 1,458	7/12	x	3,750	= 2,188
				3,541				5,313
2006	5/12 x 9,375 = 3,906	5/12	x 2,500	= 1,042	5/12	x	3,750	= 1,562

As an alternative to proration, an entity may follow any one of several simplified conventions.

1. Record a full year's depreciation in the year of acquisition and none in the year of disposal.
2. Record one-half year's depreciation in the year of acquisition and one-half year's depreciation in the year of disposal.

Depreciation method based on actual physical usage—Units of production.
Depreciation is based upon the number of units produced by the asset in a given year.

$$\text{Depreciation rate} = \frac{\text{Cost less salvage value}}{\text{Estimated number of units to be produced by the asset over its estimated useful life}}$$

$$\text{Units of production depreciation} = \text{Depreciation rate} \times \text{Number of units produced during the current year}$$

Other depreciation methods. In addition to the foregoing, a group (composite) method is sometimes used. This method averages the service lives of a number of assets using a weighted-average of the units and depreciates the group or composite as if it were a single unit. A group consists of similar assets, while a composite is made up of dissimilar assets.

Depreciation rate:

$$\frac{\text{Sum of the straight-line depreciation of individual assets}}{\text{Total asset cost}}$$

Depreciation expense:

$$\text{Depreciation rate} \times \text{Total group (composite) cost}$$

Gains and losses are not recognized on the disposal of an asset but are netted into accumulated depreciation.

Tax method. Assets placed in service prior to 1981 are depreciated based on the asset's useful life and cannot be depreciated below their salvage value. The depreciation method used depends upon the type of property and whether it was new or used when it was placed into service. Assets placed in service between 1981 and 1986 are depreciated under the Accelerated Cost Recovery System (ACRS). ACRS ignores salvage value. Thus, the asset's entire basis is depreciable over the specified recovery period to be used for each asset. Property is placed into classes and the depreciation method for each class is specified. Optional depreciation methods may be elected. In addition, Section 179 allows taxpayers to deduct, subject to limitations, an asset's entire cost in the year of acquisition. Depreciation deductions are calculated by multiplying the asset's unadjusted basis by the specified depreciation percentage for the related time period. The depreciation percentage will depend upon the asset's class, recovery year, depreciation method and convention. For assets placed into service after 1986, tax depreciation is calculated using the Modified Accelerated Cost Recovery System (MACRS) which also ignores salvage value and divides assets into classes. The asset's class and recovery period is specified in Rev. Proc. 87-56. Depreciation deductions are calculated by multiplying the asset's unadjusted basis by the appropriate depreciation percentage. Depreciation percentages are listed in Rev. Proc. 87-57. The percentages are based on the type of property, class life, depreciation method, and convention. Depreciation deductions are limited for certain assets such as listed property (primarily automobiles). Optional depreciation methods or Section 179 may also be elected.

Tax depreciation will differ in amount from financial depreciation because of the difference in treatment of salvage value, recovery methods, recovery periods, and the use of conventions. The difference between tax depreciation and financial depreciation is reported as a Schedule M-1 adjustment on a corporation's tax return.

MACRS is not considered to be in accordance with generally accepted accounting principles. Therefore, any differences between financial and tax depreciation must be used in the calculation of deferred taxes.

Asset retirement obligations. In mid-2001, FASB issued SFAS 143 which establishes standards for measuring the future cost to retire an asset and recognizing it in financial statements as a part of the cost of the asset.

SFAS 143 applies to tangible long-lived assets of all entities as well as lessee capital lease assets and lessor assets that are leased under operating leases. The provisions of the statement apply to **functional groups** of long-lived assets and component parts of larger groups of long-lived assets for which there are separately identifiable asset retirement obligations.

Asset retirement obligations requiring recognition. When an entity acquires, constructs, and operates assets, it often incurs obligations that are unavoidable. Examples include the eventual dismantling and removal of an asset from the location in which it has been constructed or installed, decommissioning of a nuclear power plant, reclamation of a mine, and clean up of a landfill. In the period in which **all** of the following conditions are met, the entity is required to recognize a liability for the asset retirement obligation (ARO) under the new statement.

1. The obligation meets the definition of a liability as set forth in the FASB's conceptual framework (i.e., a probable future sacrifice of economic benefits arising from a present obligation of the entity to transfer assets or provide services to other entities in the future as a result of transactions or events occurring in the past).
2. A future transfer of assets associated with the obligation is probable (i.e., likely to occur).
3. The amount of the liability can be reasonably estimated.

Under the first provision above, a qualifying obligation will arise if an event that has already occurred (the purchase and placing in service of the long-lived asset), that affords the entity little or no discretion to avoid the future transfer or use of its assets, and that involves a present obligation to one or more third parties in connection with the acquisition, construction, or operation of the long-lived asset. For example, in accordance with the terms of a lease, the lessee is obligated to remove its specialized machinery from the leased premises prior to vacating those premises or to compensate the lessor accordingly.

Specifically excluded from the scope of the new statement are

- Obligations related to the ongoing operation of the asset, but not related to the asset's eventual retirement.
- Obligations arising solely from a plan to dispose of a long-lived asset in accordance with SFAS 121.
- Obligations arising from the consequences of improper operation of a long-lived asset including environmental remediation liabilities under AcSEC SOP 96-1; presumably these refer to penalties and fines.

The examples and much of the discussion included in the new statement regarding its application are centered around specialized industry applications such as offshore oil platforms, nuclear power plants, mining operations, landfills, and underground storage tanks. However, in the authors' opinion, the criteria of the statement appear to apply to situations encountered more frequently in practice, such as the purchase, installation, or construction of production machinery which, when its useful life is over, will need to be dismantled and removed from the premises. There are several variations of this scenario that could potentially be covered by the scope of the new statement.

1. The machinery is owned by the entity (or leased under a capital lease) and installed in a factory that it leases (under either an operating or capital lease). The factory lease expires at the end of ten years and contains a provision requiring the lessee to restore the leased premises to their original condition or to compensate the lessor for the costs of doing so.
2. The machinery described in the first scenario is installed in a factory that the entity owns. At the end of the useful life of the machinery, the entity will either incur the costs to dismantle and remove the asset or will leave it idle in place which would adversely affect the fair value of the premises should the entity choose to sell the premises on an "as is" basis. Conceptually, under the new standard, the cost of asset retirement should have been recognized systematically and rationally over the productive life of the asset and not in the period of retirement as either a charge against income or a reduction in the gain on sale of the facilities.

Timing of recognition of liabilities for obligating events. The new standard separates qualifying obligating events into three categories and specifies the timing of recognition for each category.

Incurred during acquisition, construction, or development. Liabilities are recognized concurrently with the original recognition of the cost of the long-lived asset. Passage of time and normal operations of the asset do not change the fact that the obligation exists even though, over time, the estimated amount of the obligation may change.

Incurred during the operating life. Liabilities are recognized over the life of the asset concurrently with the events that create the obligation. Depending on the timing of these events, this approach can result in recognition that is disproportionate in the different stages of the asset's life.

Other obligations. These obligations are incurred during the asset's useful life because of a newly enacted law or statute, because of a change in contract provisions, or because the entity has incurred a new duty or responsibility to one or more entities. Recognition of these obligations as liabilities depends on the timing of the obligating event.

Example of an obligation requiring immediate recognition.

Phyl Corporation owns and operates a chemical company. At its premises, it maintains underground tanks used to store various types of chemicals. The tanks were installed when Phyl Corporation purchased its facilities seven years prior. On February 1, 2002, the governor of the state signed a law passed by the state legislature which requires removal of such tanks at such time as they are no longer being used. The obligating events in this example are the enactment of the law and the installation of the tank in the ground. Upon the enactment of the law, immediate recognition would be required.

Example of an obligation requiring partial recognition.

Joyce Manufacturing Corporation (JMC) operates a factory. As a result of its normal operations it stores production byproducts and used cleaning solvents on site in a reservoir specifically designed for that purpose. The reservoir and surrounding land, all owned by JMC, are contaminated with these chemicals. On February 1, 2002, the governor of the state signed a law passed by the state legislature which requires clean up and disposal of hazardous waste from an already existing production process upon retirement of the facility. The obligating events in this example are the enactment of the law and the contamination of the site. Therefore, upon the enactment of the law, immediate recognition would be required for the obligation associated with the contamination that has already occurred. In addition, liabilities will continue to be recognized over the remaining life of the facility as additional contamination occurs.

Accounting considerations. Implementation of the new standard raises several important accounting issues which require careful consideration.

Recognition and allocation. Upon initial recognition, the entity records an increase to the carrying amount of the related long-lived asset and an offsetting liability. The entity then depreciates the combined cost of the asset and the capitalized asset retirement obligation using a systematic and rational allocation method over the period during which the long-lived asset is expected to provide benefits. Conceptually, this standard is an application of the matching principle in that the total investment in the asset, including its eventual retirement, are charged to expense over the periods benefited. Depending on the pattern and timing of obligating events, an entity could, under this standard, capitalize an amount of asset retirement cost during a period and, in the same period, allocate an equal amount to depreciation expense. It is important to note that the amount added to the carrying amount of the long-lived asset does not constitute an expenditure for the purpose of capitalizing interest under the provisions of SFAS 34.

Impairment. Retirement obligations added to the carrying amounts of long-lived assets are, obviously, to be included in those carrying amounts for the purpose of testing those assets for impairment. In estimating future cash flows under the impairment standard, the cash flows related to settling the liability for an asset retirement obligation are to be excluded from both the undiscounted cash flows used to test the asset for recoverability and the discounted cash flows used to measure the asset's fair value.

Measurement. Asset retirement obligations are initially measured at fair value. Fair value is defined as the amount that the entity would be required to pay in an active market to settle the obligation in a current transaction in circumstances other than a forced or liquidation settlement. From the perspective of the entity, fair value is the amount that would be demanded by a willing third party with a credit standing comparable to that of the entity, to assume all of the duties risks and uncertainties inherent in the entity's obligation. FASB acknowledged that, due to the risks involved, and the number of years expected to elapse between the date that the obligation is incurred and the date that it is expected to be settled, such current settlement may not be available. In addition, some entities may have the internal resources or expertise to discharge the liability by performing the necessary work using their internal workforce rather than contracting with third parties. Nevertheless, the standard requires this "third-party" market-based approach.

Expected present value. In general, active markets do not exist for the settlement of an ARO. Consequently, FASB expects that most entities will use the **expected present value** technique set forth in SFAC 7 to compute fair value (see the discussion in Chapter 1). Under this technique, the entity estimates the range of estimated cash flows associated with settlement of the ARO and computes the sum of these cash flows on a probability-weighted basis. The statement acknowledges the fact that marketplace data may not be available on which to base assumptions regarding future cash flows. The entity is, therefore, permitted to use information and assumptions that are available "without undue cost and effort" based on its own expectations. If, however, data is available regarding assumptions that marketplace participants would make that contradicts the entity's own assumptions, the entity must adjust its assumptions accordingly. For example, if the costs of labor in the marketplace exceed those of the entity, the higher marketplace costs are to be used in the cash flow estimates. Again, even if the entity expects to settle the ARO by use of its own labor force the cash flows to be used in the estimates of the expected present value are those that would be required to contract with third parties to do the work.

Initially applying the expected present value method. The entity begins by estimating a series of cash flows that reflect its marketplace estimates of the cost and timing of performing the required retirement activities. Marketplace amounts are those amounts that would be expended by the entity to hire a third party to perform the work or to pay a third party to fully settle the ARO should a market to do so exist. Explicit assumptions are to be developed and incorporated in the estimates about all of the following matters:

1. The costs that a third party would incur in performing the necessary tasks associated with retiring the asset.
2. Additional amounts that the third party would include in pricing the work (or the settlement) related to such factors as inflation, overhead, equipment charges, profit margins, anticipated technological advances, and offsetting cash inflows, if any.
3. The extent to which the amount of the third party's costs or their timing might differ under various different future scenarios and the relative probabilities of those scenarios actually occurring.
4. The price that third party would demand and could expect to receive for bearing the uncertainties and unforeseeable circumstances inherent in the obligation. This is referred to as **market risk premium**.

The discount rate to be used in the present value calculations is the **credit-adjusted risk-free rate** that adjusts a risk-free rate of interest for the credit standing of the entity. The risk-free interest rate is the market interest rate on monetary assets that are essentially risk-free, and that have maturity dates that coincide with the expected timing of the estimated cash flows required to satisfy the ARO. In the United States, this is the rate available for zero-coupon US Treasury instruments.

In adjusting the risk-free rate for the entity's credit standing, the entity takes into account the effects of all terms, collateral, and existing guarantees that would affect the amount required to settle the liability.

The ARO may be incurred in one or more of the entity's reporting periods. Each period's incremental liability incurred is recognized as a separate liability and is estimated using these principles based on market and interest rate assumptions existing in the period of subsequent recognition.

Accounting in subsequent periods. After the initial period of ARO recognition, the liability will change as a result of either the passage of time or a revision to the original estimate of either the amount of estimated cash flows or their timing. Such changes can arise due to the effects of inflation, changes in the probabilities used in the original estimate, changes in interest rates, changes in laws, regulations, statutes, and contracts.

The entity recognizes these changes to the liability by first adjusting the carrying amount of the liability for changes due to the passage of time and then, if applicable, for changes due to revisions in either amounts or timing of estimated cash flows. Changes due to the passage of time increase the carrying amount of the liability because there are fewer periods remaining from the measurement date until the settlement date and, thus, the present value of the discounted future settlement amount increases. These changes are recorded as a period cost called **accretion**

expense and classified separately from interest expense in the statement of income (or not-for-profit statement of activities). Accretion is computed using an interest method of allocation which results in periodic accretion expense that represents a level effective interest rate applied to the carrying amount of the liability at the beginning of each period The effective interest rate used to calculate accretion is, of course, the credit-adjusted risk-free rate or rates applied when the liability, or portion of the liability (as explained below) was initially measured and recognized. Accretion expense is not considered interest cost for the purpose of applying the interest capitalization criteria of SFAS 34.

Changes in the ARO that result from changes in the estimates of the timing or amount of future cash flows are accounted for using a bifurcated approach. If the expected present value increases, the increase gives rise to a new obligation accounted for separately just as the ARO was originally measured but using current market value assumptions, and the current credit-adjusted risk-free rate. Thus, over time, a particular long-lived asset may have multiple layers of obligations associated with it which are based on different assumptions measured at different dates during the asset's useful life. The incremental obligation is recorded by increasing the recorded ARO and capitalizing the additional cost as a part of the carrying amount of the related long-lived asset. If multiple layers have been recorded and it is not practicable to separately identify the period (or layer) to which subsequent revisions in estimated cash flows relate, the statement permits the use of a **weighted-average credit-adjusted risk-free rate** to measure the change in the liability resulting from that revision.

If, however, the expected present value subsequently decreases, the difference between the remeasured amount and the carrying amount of the liability (after adjustment for inception-to-date accretion) is recorded as a gain in the current period. In this case, the previously recognized layers of liabilities are reduced pro rata so as not to affect the overall effective rate of accretion over the remaining life of the obligation.

For the purposes of measurement in subsequent periods, an entity that originally determined its ARO based on available market prices rather than using the expected present value method, is required to determine the undiscounted cash flows embedded in that market price.

SFAS 143 does not require detailed cash flow estimates every reporting period but rather allows the entity to exercise judgment as to when facts and circumstances indicate that the initial estimate should be updated.

If the increase in carrying amount of the affected long-lived asset resulting from the remeasurement of ARO in a subsequent period impacts only that period, then the increase is fully depreciated in that period. Otherwise, the increase is depreciated in the period of change and future periods as a change in estimate in accordance with APB 20. Depreciation is classified as an operating expense in the statement of income.

Other provisions. Other provisions of the new standard affect the calculation of the credit adjusted rate as well as how it is to be applied by rate-regulated entities.

Funding and assurance provisions. Factors such as laws, regulations, public policy, the entity's creditworthiness, or the sheer magnitude of the future obligation may cause an entity to be required to provide third parties with assurance that the entity will be able to satisfy its ARO in the future. Such assurance is provided using such instruments as surety bonds, insurance policies, letters of credit, guarantees by other entities, establishment of trust funds, or by custodial arrangements segregating other assets dedicated to satisfying the ARO. Although providing such means of assurance does not satisfy the underlying obligation, the credit-adjusted interest rate used in calculating the expected present value should be adjusted for the effect on the entity's credit standing of employing one or more of these techniques.

Rate-regulated entities. Many rate-regulated entities (as defined in SFAS 71 and discussed in Chapter 23) follow current specialized accounting that capitalizes costs not otherwise afforded that treatment under GAAP. These entities recover these additional costs in the rates that they charge their customers. These additional capitalized costs may or may not meet the definition of ARO under SFAS 143. The differences in the amounts and timing of assets and liabilities between GAAP and regulatory accounting used for rate-making purposes give rise to timing differences.

SFAS 143 provides that, if the criteria in SFAS 71 are met, the rate-regulated entity is to recognize a regulatory asset on liability for differences in the timing of recognition of the period costs associated with ARO for financial reporting and rate-making purposes. Accounting for the ARO arising from closed or abandoned long-lived assets of rate-regulated entities is covered by SFAS 90.

Effective date and transition. SFAS 143 is effective for financial statements issued for fiscal years beginning after June 15, 2001 with early application encouraged. The statement is to be initially applied as of the beginning of the entity's fiscal year. If early adoption is elected during an interim period other than the first interim period of the entity's fiscal year, all previous interim periods of that fiscal year are to be restated.

The initial adoption of the statement involves the following steps:

1. Compute the liability related to the ARO for long-lived assets that are in service at the date of adoption using market information, assumptions, and interest rates that are current as of the date of adoption.
2. Compute the accumulated accretion from the date that the liability would have been recognized had SFAS 143 been in effect to the date of initial adoption.
3. Increase the carrying amount of the long-lived asset for the amount computed in step 1.

4. Increase the accumulated depreciation of the long-lived asset for the depreciation that would have been recognized from the date the ARO would have been recognized had SFAS 143 been in effect to the date of initial adoption.

5. The difference remaining is to be reported as the cumulative effect of the initial application of the new statement in accordance with the provisions of APB 20 governing a change in accounting principle.

Disclosures. The following information about ARO is required to be disclosed in the financial statements.

1. A general description of the ARO and the related long-lived assets.

2. A description of how the fair value of the ARO was determined (e.g., by using an expected present value method or some other market-based valuation technique).

3. The funding policy, if any, for ARO.

4. The fair value of assets dedicated to satisfy the liability, if any.

5. A reconciliation of the beginning and ending aggregate carrying amount of the liability showing separately the changes attributable to

   a. The liability incurred in the current period
   b. The liability settled in the current period
   c. Accretion expense, and
   d. Revisions in expected cash flows.

6. An explanation of any significant changes in the ARO not otherwise apparent in other disclosures required by the statement.

7. In the period of adoption, the entity shall, in accordance with APB 20 and the provisions of SFAS 143 disclose

   a. The effect of adopting the new statement on income before extraordinary items and on net income (and, for public companies, the related per share amounts) of the period of the change.
   b. Income before extraordinary items and net income (and, for public companies, the related per share amounts), computed on a pro forma basis, and presented on the face of the income statements for all periods presented as if SFAS 143 had been applied during all periods affected.
   c. The liability for ARO at the beginning of the earliest year presented and the end of all years presented, computed on a pro forma basis, and displayed on the face of the statement of financial position as if SFAS 143 had been applied during all periods affected. As previously explained, the pro forma computation of the ARO liability is to be made using current information, assumptions, and interest rates.

Example—initial measurement and recognition

Gerald Corporation constructs and places into service on January 1, 2002, specialized machinery on premises that it leases under a fifteen-year operating lease. The machinery cost $1,750,000 and has an estimated useful life of ten years. Gerald Corporation is contractually obligated, under the terms of the lease, to remove the machinery from the premises when it is no longer functional. Gerald is unable to obtain current market-related information regarding the costs of settling the liability at inception and, therefore, chooses to estimate the initial fair value of the ARO using an expected present value technique. The significant assumptions used by Gerald in applying this technique are as follows:

1. Labor costs are based on prevailing wage rates in that geographic area that a contractor would pay to hire qualified workers. Gerald assigns probability assessments to the range of cash flow estimates as follows:

Cash flow estimate	Probability assessment	Expected cash flows for labor costs
$40,000	25%	$10,000
60,000	50	30,000
75,000	25	18,750
	100%	$58,750

2. Based on its own experience, which Gerald believes is indicative of local market conditions, Gerald estimates that a contractor will apply a 75% burden rate to labor costs to charge for overhead and equipment usage and that, based on published industry statistics, a contractor would add a markup of 8% to the combined labor, overhead, and equipment costs.

3. Since the eventual dismantlement and removal will be occurring ten years from now, Gerald expects that a contractor would receive a market-risk premium of 5% of the estimated inflation-adjusted cash flows. This premium is to compensate the contractor for assuming the risks and uncertainties of contracting now for a project ten years later.

4. The risk-free rate of interest as evidenced by the price of zero-coupon US Treasury instruments that mature in ten years is 4.5%. Gerald adjusts that rate by 2.5% to reflect the effect of its credit standing. Therefore, the credit-adjusted risk-free rate used to compute the expected present value is 7%.

5. Gerald assumes an average rate of inflation of 3.5% over the ten-year period.

The ARO is initially measured as follows as of January 1, 2002

	Expected cash flows as of January 1, 2002
Expected cash flows for labor costs	$ 58,750
Allocated overhead and equipment charges (75% x $58,750)	44,063
Contractor's markup [8% x ($58,750 + $44,063)]	8,225
Expected cash flows before inflation adjustment	111,038
Average annual compounded inflation rate of 3.5% for 10 years (1.035^{10})	x 1.4106
Inflation-adjusted expected cash flows	156,630
Market-risk premium (5% x $156,630)	7,832
Inflation adjusted expected cash flows adjusted for market risk	164,462
Present value using credit-adjusted risk-free rate of 7% for 10 years, compounded annually	$ 83,604

On January 1, 2002, Gerald would record the initial ARO as follows

Machinery and equipment	83,604	
ARO liability		83,604

Example—accounting in subsequent periods

Assuming the same facts as above, during the ten year life of the machinery, Gerald would record entries to recognize accretion and depreciation as follows (assuming no remeasurement of the ARO is required)

Year	Liability balance as of January 1	Annual accretion	Liability balance as of December 31
2002	$ 83,604	$ 5,852	$ 89,456
2003	89,456	6,262	95,718
2004	95,718	6,700	102,418
2005	102,418	7,169	109,587
2006	109,587	7,671	117,258
2007	117,258	8,208	125,466
2008	125,466	8,783	134,249
2009	134,249	9,397	143,646
2010	143,646	10,055	153,701
2011	153,701	10,761	164,462

Entries to record annual accretion

The accretion for each year presented in the table is recorded as follows

Accretion expense (presented on the income statement as part of other income and expense separately from interest expense)	xx,xxx	
Asset retirement obligation		xx,xxx

Depreciation computations

Acquisition cost of asset	$ 1,750,000
Capitalized ARO	83,604
Adjusted carrying amount of asset	$ 1,833,604
Estimated useful life	÷ 10 years
Annual depreciation expense	$ 183,360

Entry to record annual depreciation

Depreciation expense	183,360	
Accumulated depreciation		183,360

Settlement of ARO

On December 31, 2011, Gerald uses its internal workforce to dismantle and dispose of the machinery and incurred costs as follows

Labor	$ 70,000
Internally allocated overhead and equipment charges (75% of labor)	52,500
Total costs incurred	122,500
ARO liability	164,462
Gain on settlement of ARO obligation	$ 41,962

Depletion. Depletion is the annual charge for the use of natural resources. The depletion base includes all development costs such as exploring, drilling, excavating, and other preparatory costs. The amount of the depletion base charged to income is determined by the following formula:

$$\frac{1}{\text{Total expected recoverable units}} \quad \text{x} \quad \text{Depletion base} \quad \text{x} \quad \text{Units sold}$$

The unit depletion rate is revised frequently due to the uncertainties surrounding the recovery of natural resources. The revision is made prospectively; the remaining undepleted cost is allocated over the remaining expected recoverable units.

Nonmonetary transactions. There are three types of nonmonetary transactions

1. Nonreciprocal transfers with owners
2. Nonreciprocal transfers with other than owners
3. Nonmonetary exchanges

The accounting issue is the determination of the amount to assign to the nonmonetary asset transferred to or from the enterprise.

The general rule is that the accounting for nonmonetary transactions should be based on the fair values of the assets involved. The fair value to be used is that of the asset surrendered unless the fair value of the asset received is "more clearly evident." Fair value is defined as

> ...*the estimated realizable values in cash transactions of the same or similar assets, quoted market prices, independent appraisals, estimated fair values of assets or services received in exchange, and other available evidence.*

While this general rule is considered adequate for most situations, certain modifications should be made under two specific circumstances. First, if the fair value is not reasonably determinable, the recorded amount (i.e., book value) may be the only amount available to measure the transaction. The fair value is to be considered not determinable within reasonable limits if

> ...*major uncertainties exist about the realizability of the value that would be assigned to an asset received in a nonmonetary transaction accounted for at fair value.*

Second, an exception to the rule is also required in the case of an exchange which is not essentially the culmination of the earnings process. The following two types of nonmonetary exchanges do not result in a culmination of the earnings process:

1. An exchange of a product or property held for sale in the ordinary course of business for a product or property to be sold in the same line of business to facilitate sales to customers other than the parties to the exchange.
2. An exchange of a productive asset not held for sale in the ordinary course of business for a similar productive asset or an equivalent interest in the same or similar productive asset in the same line of business.

A product or property held for sale exchanged for a productive asset (even in the same line of business) should be recorded at fair value.

Nonreciprocal transfers. Examples of nonreciprocal transfers with owners would include dividends-in-kind, nonmonetary assets exchanged for common stock, split-ups, and spin-offs. An example of a nonreciprocal transaction with other than the owners is a donation of property either by or to the enterprise.

The valuation of most nonreciprocal transfers should be based upon the fair market value of the asset given (or received if the fair value of the nonmonetary asset is both objectively measurable and would be clearly recognizable). However, nonmonetary assets distributed to owners of an enterprise in a spin-off or other form of reorganization or liquidation should be based on the recorded amount. Where there is no asset given, the valuation of the transaction should be based upon the fair value of the asset received.

Example of accounting for a nonreciprocal transfer

1. Jacobs Corporation donated property with a book value of $10,000 to a charity during the current year.
2. The property had a fair market value of $17,000 at the date of the transfer.

According to the opinion, the transaction is to be valued at the fair market value of the property transferred, and any gain or loss on the transaction is to be recognized. Thus, Jacobs should recognize a gain of $7,000 ($17,000 – $10,000) in the determination of the current period's net income. The entry to record the transaction would be as follows:

Charitable donations	17,000	
Property		10,000
Gain on donation of property		7,000

Nonmonetary exchanges. An exchange of nonmonetary assets can take two basic forms.

1. Dissimilar assets may be involved in the exchange.
2. Similar assets may be involved in the exchange.

The recognition of a gain or loss on the exchange is dependent upon whether or not the gain or loss is deemed to be realized. If an exchange is considered to be the culmination of the earnings process, then the resulting gain or loss will be recognized. If the exchange is not considered to be the culmination of the earnings process, the resulting gain will not be recognized.

Dissimilar assets. An exchange is the culmination of the earnings process when dissimilar assets are involved. The general rule is to value the transaction at the **fair market value** of the asset given up **(unless the fair value of the asset received is more clearly evident)** and to recognize the gain or loss.

Example of an exchange involving dissimilar assets and no boot

1. Brian, Inc. exchanges a forklift with a book value of $2,500 with Emma & Co. for a tooling machine with a fair market value of $3,200.
2. No boot is exchanged in the transaction.
3. The fair value of the forklift is not readily determinable.

In this case, Brian, Inc. has a realized gain of $700 ($3,200 − $2,500) on the exchange. Because the exchange involves dissimilar assets, the earnings process has culminated and the gain should be included in the determination of net income. The entry to record the transaction would be as follows:

Machine	3,200	
Forklift		2,500
Gain on exchange of forklift		700

Similar assets. Similar assets are those that are used for the same general purpose, are of the same general type, and are employed in the same line of business. It is not necessary to exchange identical assets. The treatment described applies to those assets which are exchanged as a result of technological advancement as well as to those which are exchanged as a result of wearing out (trade-ins). The general rule involving the exchange of **similar** assets involving a gain is to value the transaction at the **book value** of the asset given up. In this situation, the gain is deferred over the life of the new asset by allowing a lower amount of annual depreciation.

A single exception to the nonrecognition rule for similar assets occurs when the exchange involves both a monetary and nonmonetary asset being exchanged for a similar nonmonetary asset. The monetary portion of the exchange is termed **boot**. When boot is at least 25% of the fair value of the exchange, it is considered a monetary transaction and both parties should record the exchange at fair value. When boot less than 25% is received in exchange, only the boot portion of the earnings process is considered to have been culminated. The portion of the gain applicable to the boot is considered realized and should be recognized in the determination of net income for the period of the exchange.

The formula for the recognition of the gain in an exchange involving boot of less than 25% of fair value can be generalized as follows:

$$\frac{\text{Boot}}{\text{Boot + Fair value of nonmonetary asset received}} \quad \text{x} \quad \begin{array}{c}\text{Total gain}\\\text{indicated}\end{array} \quad = \quad \begin{array}{c}\text{Gain}\\\text{recognized}\end{array}$$

Example of an exchange involving similar assets and boot

1. Amanda Metals exchanged a casting machine for a technologically newer model. The cost of the old machine was $75,000, and the accumulated depreciation was $5,000.
2. The fair value of the machine received was $90,000.
3. Boot was received in the amount of $10,000.

$$\frac{\$10,000}{\$10,000 + \$90,000} \quad \text{x} \quad \$30,000 \quad = \quad \$3,000$$

A total gain of $30,000 is created by the transaction. This amount is the difference between the fair value of the assets received and the cost of the assets surrendered ($100,000 – $70,000). The amount of the gain to be recognized can be computed as shown below. The entry required to record the transaction is as follows:

Cash	10,000	
New machine	63,000*	
Accumulated depreciation	5,000	
Old machine		75,000
Gain on exchange of machine		3,000

* *The book value of the new machine is the book value of the old machine less the amount of boot received, plus the gain recognized.*

An exchange is the culmination of the earnings process when a loss is created as a result of the exchange of similar assets. While the earnings process is not generally considered complete when dealing with the exchange of similar assets, to record the asset at anything greater than the fair market value would be imprudent.

In an exchange of similar real estate that qualifies as a monetary transaction because boot is at least 25% of the fair value exchanged, the fair value would be allocated between the monetary and nonmonetary components based on relative fair values. The receiver of boot would have a sale under SFAS 66 to the extent of the monetary portion and the nonmonetary portion would be accounted for under APB 29 by adjusting the basis of the property. The payer of boot records the payment as a purchase of real estate and, for the nonmonetary portion, follows APB 29 and adjusts the basis of the property.

Involuntary conversions. Certain conditions may occur which necessitate the involuntary conversion of a nonmonetary asset into a monetary asset. Involuntary conversions of nonmonetary assets to monetary assets are monetary transactions, and the resulting gain or loss shall be recognized in the period of conversion. It makes no difference that the monetary assets received are immediately reinvested in nonmonetary assets. An example of an involuntary conversion would be the condemnation of property.

This rule does not apply to the involuntary conversion of LIFO inventories that are intended to be replaced but have not been replaced by the year-end.

Summary. In some situations, the fair value of the asset cannot be determined. If the fair value is not determinable, the book values of the assets involved are to be used as the valuation measure.

The situations involving the exchange of nonmonetary assets can be summarized in the diagram on the next page.

Deferred taxes. A difference between the amount of gain or loss recognized for book purposes and that recognized for tax purposes constitutes a temporary difference. The difference in the gain or loss will result in a difference between the tax basis and the financial basis of the asset received. The difference in the gain or loss reverses as a result of the annual charge to depreciation. The proper treatment of temporary differences is discussed in Chapter 15, Income Taxes.

ACCOUNTING FOR NONMONETARY EXCHANGES

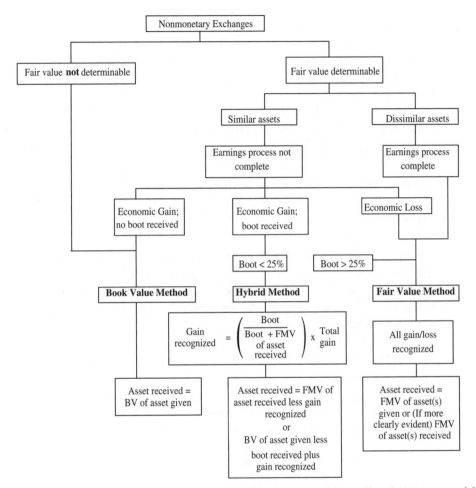

Impairment. The FASB standard on impairment of long-lived assets provides separate rules governing the impairment of assets that the enterprise intends to hold and use versus assets which it plans to dispose of.

Assets to be held and used. Impairment occurs if the book value of fixed assets is determined not to be recoverable. In a **total impairment** the obsolete asset and related depreciation are removed from the accounts and a loss is recognized for the difference. If a **partial impairment** of a depreciable asset results, the asset should be written down to a new cost basis. That cost is then depreciated over the remaining life. The journal entry follows:

Accumulated depreciation	xxx	
Loss due to impairment	xxx	
Asset		xxx

The loss amount would appear in the income statement as a component of income from continuing operations before taxes or in a statement of activities (not-for-profit entity). Entities that present on their income statement a subtotal indicating a measure of operations (income or loss from operations or similar caption) are required to include the impairment loss in that subtotal.

Long-lived assets and certain identifiable intangibles are required to be reviewed for impairment whenever circumstances and situations change such that there is an indication that the carrying amount is not recoverable. Recoverability should be assessed under the following circumstances (among others):

1. The asset market value decreases significantly
2. The use of the asset is significantly changed in extent or manner
3. Legal factors or business climate changes adversely affect asset value
4. Regulator's adverse assessment or action
5. Original expected costs are significantly exceeded
6. A history of cash flow losses and continued asset losses are forecasted

The lowest level at which there are identifiable cash flows independent of cash flows from other groupings should be used to group assets for review. If, upon review, management's best estimate of the undiscounted future cash flows (without interest charges) is less than the carrying amount, the carrying amount is reduced to fair value and an impairment loss is recognized. This fair value is considered a new cost basis that is not subject to subsequent adjustment except for depreciation and further impairment. There is no restoration of recognized impairment losses.

Example of impairment

Price Corporation is a commercial printer. Due to the introduction of new technology in their industry, Price Corporation determined that it must test its equipment and patents for impairment as of January 1, 2002. Data regarding these assets follows

	1/1/02 Book values	Expected future cash flows	1/1/02 Fair value
Printing equipment	$600	$800	$580
Patents	140	120	105

The above analysis shows that there is no impairment loss recognized on the printing equipment because the expected future cash flows ($800) exceed the adjusted carrying value of the equipment ($600) on 1/1/02. This is true even though the fair value of the printing equipment is less than its carrying value.

However, the patent's future cash flows ($120) are less than the carrying amount ($140). The amortization policy was reviewed and found to be satisfactory. The patent's carrying value is adjusted as follows

Impairment loss	35	
Patent		35

The resulting balance of the patent account is amortized over its remaining life. If the fair value of the patent was $140 or above, there would be no impairment loss.

If an impairment loss is recognized, the following disclosures should be made:

1. Description of the impaired assets and the situation surrounding the impairment.
2. Amount of impairment loss and the method of determining fair value.
3. If the impairment losses are not reported separately or parenthetically, the caption where the losses are aggregated.
4. The business segment affected, if applicable.

Impairment applies to all entities. In applying impairment to rate-regulated assets, costs excluded by a regulator from the enterprise's rate base would be recognized as an impairment.

The GAAP rules for measuring and recording impairment of assets are not uniform for all assets or for all specialized industries. The table below distinguishes between those assets subject to the general impairment standard and those for which different, specialized rules apply.

Subject to General Impairment Standard

Cable television plant
Capitalized interest cost
Capitalized motion picture film costs
Development stage enterprises' assets
Real estate
Title plant costs of title insurance and title abstract companies, and title agents

Subject to Specialized Impairment Standard(s)

Assets associated with discontinued operations
Broadcasters' program rights
Computer software to be sold, leased, or otherwise marketed
Deferred tax assets
Equity method investments
Financial institutions' long-term customer relationships (core deposit intangibles, etc.)
Financial instruments
Intangible assets of motor carriers
Loans receivable
Mortgage servicing rights
Recording masters in the recorded music industry

Split between General and Specialized Impairment Standards

Subject to General Impairment Standard	*Subject to Specialized Impairment Standard*
Public utilities and certain other regulated enterprises	Abandoned plants and disallowed plant costs of regulated enterprises
Goodwill identified with acquired long-lived assets and identifiable intangibles acquired after October 31, 1970	Goodwill not identified with acquired long-lived assets
	Goodwill and identifiable intangibles acquired before November 1, 1970 (impairment not permitted)
Lessee capital leases	Lessor direct financing, sales-type, and leveraged leases
Lessor assets subject to operating leases	
Proved properties and wells of oil and gas producing companies with related facilities and equipment	Unproved properties of oil and gas producing companies
All insurance assets except deferred insurance policy acquisition costs	Deferred insurance policy acquisition costs

Resulting impairment losses are reported in the period when the recognition criteria are initially applied.

Assets to be disposed of. Long-lived assets and identifiable intangibles to be disposed of (except those associated with discontinued operations) are carried at the lower of carrying value or fair value less cost to sell. Expected costs to sell beyond one year are discounted to present value. If fair value less cost to sell is used, subsequent revisions in estimates are reported as adjustments to the carrying amount. However, these adjustments cannot exceed the carrying value of the disposed asset (before adjustment) at the date of the decision to dispose. These assets are not depreciated during the holding period.

Disclosures to be made in the case of assets to be disposed of are as follows:

1. The initial loss
2. Gains or losses resulting from subsequent revision in estimates of fair value less cost to sell
3. If they can be identified and to the extent they are included in the entity's operations for the period, the results of operations for the disposed assets
4. If not reported separately or parenthetically, the caption where the gains and losses are aggregated
5. Description of the assets and the situation surrounding the disposal, the carrying amount of the assets and the expected date of disposal
6. The business segment affected (for public companies)

Proposed replacement standard on accounting for impairments. SFAS 121 has been in use for over six years, and has generally been effective in imposing discipline regarding the testing for, and accounting recognition of, impairments of long-lived assets. However, it was clear when the standard was first issued that there were notable inconsistencies among the mandated impairment measurements for assets to be held and used, those to be disposed of, and **business segments** as that term is used in the context of discontinued operations as set forth in APB 30. Shortly after the implementation of SFAS 121, in fact, the FASB added to its technical agenda another project, to deal with implementation questions, the inconsistencies under the various standards, and the development of a uniform approach to impairments.

In a draft standard issued in mid-2000, the FASB proposed to supersede SFAS 121 with a set of requirements that would also replace APB 30's provisions on discontinued operations, and also nullify the guidance in EITF 94-3 pertaining to exit costs. It is expected that a final standard will be forthcoming by late 2001.

The replacement for SFAS 121 was to differ from its predecessor standard by eliminating the "best estimate" approach to future cash flows, as set forth in SFAS 121, and replacing it with the "expected cash flows" methodology that has been embraced by SFAC 7. The effect would have been to give greater formal consideration to the uncertainties surrounding future cash flows, and is consistent with the approach incorporated into the new statement on intangible assets, as explained later in this chapter. However, in its redeliberations, the FASB decided to permit either the **expected cash flows** or the **best estimate** approaches to be used. It will still encourage the use of probabilities whenever a range (such as minimum, most likely, and maximum annual cash flows) is utilized, but this is less strict a requirement than had been proposed earlier.

As under the existing standard, future cash flows would have to be projected; if assets are employed in groups (as is typical), the cash flows for the group could be estimated. Under the proposed standard, cash flows for the remaining useful lives of the assets would need to be projected; if assets are grouped, the projected cash flows would have to cover the useful life of its primary tangible asset or identifiable intangible asset being amortized. If some, but not all, assets of a reporting unit are included in a single group, goodwill should be excluded from the grouping for which cash flows are to be projected. If a loss is recognized for a grouping of assets (or if a formerly recognized loss is reversed), the loss (or recovery) should be allocated to the long-lived assets; no adjustment to fair value should be made to any associated liabilities in the group.

In some instances an asset grouping may include assets currently in use as well as other assets under development. In such cases, projected future cash flows should be based on the existing service potential of those assets already in use, and on the expected service potential of assets under development. For assets in use, the existing service potential would govern; that is, projected incremental cash flows associated with future capital expenditures (overhauls, betterments, etc.) could not be incorporated.

The new standard would set forth a series of criteria to qualify an asset as being held for sale. Groups of assets, and assets plus liabilities, could be evaluated as a single unit in this regard, even if some of the assets or liabilities in the grouping were not to be disposed of. If an asset or liability were to be removed from a grouping previously defined as being held for sale, all the other assets and liabilities of that group would need to be measured individually, unless the plan-of-sale criteria are met for the remaining group, in which case group measurement could continue. The definition of discontinued operations, formerly set forth by APB 30, would be expanded to include all significant components of the reporting entity. This would hopefully end the confusion that universally surrounds decisions regarding the categorization of operations as discontinued.

Costs associated with dispositions (and thus impacting the net cash flows being projected) would be limited to the incremental direct costs necessary to transact the sale. This means that ongoing operating costs of the asset awaiting a sale will not be included. Gains or losses to be reported in connection with the disposal of an asset pertain to a loss recognized to write down the carrying amount to fair value less costs to sell; a gain resulting from a subsequent increase in fair value—limited to the earlier write-down; and a gain realized from selling the asset for an amount in excess of its carrying value.

The standard would also stipulate that liabilities associated with decisions to exit an activity (as discussed currently in EITF 94-3) could only be recognized when the definition of liability is met. This would end the current practice of recognizing liabilities associated with management plans or intentions as evidenced by its commitment to a plan of disposition or exiting an activity.

Fair value, in the absence of observable market prices, will generally be based on present value as set forth in SFAC 7. The new impairment standard, and a possible companion communication from the FASB, will expand on the techniques of applying present value to estimate fair value. Estimates of future cash flows would exclude income taxes, unless unique tax attributes of the asset, such as tax credits, directly affect its fair value.

The scope of the new standard on impairment would exclude goodwill or other identifiable intangibles that are not being amortized (i.e., that have indefinite lives) to be used, as well as goodwill associated with a reporting unit or portion thereof to be disposed of. These matters have been addressed in the new standard on intangibles, which was promulgated in mid-2001.

Capitalization of interest costs. The cost of an asset should include all of the costs necessary to get the asset set up and functioning properly for its intended use including interest.

The principal purposes to be accomplished by the capitalization of interest costs are

1. To obtain a more accurate original asset investment cost
2. To achieve a better matching of costs deferred to future periods with revenues of those future periods

All assets that require a time period to get ready for their intended use should include a capitalized amount of interest costs. However, accomplishing this level of capitalization would usually violate a reasonable cost/benefit test because of the added accounting and administrative costs generated. In many situations, the effect of interest capitalization would be immaterial. Thus, interest costs should only be capitalized as a part of the historical cost of the following qualifying assets when such costs are considered to be material:

1. Assets constructed for an entity's own use or for which deposit or progress payments are made
2. Assets produced as discrete projects that are intended for lease or sale
3. Equity method investments when the investee is using funds to acquire qualifying assets for its principal operations which have not yet begun

Generally, inventories and land that are not undergoing preparation for intended use are not qualifying assets. When land is being developed, it is a qualifying asset. If land is developed for lots, the capitalized interest cost is added to the cost of the **land**. The interest is then matched against revenues when the lots are sold. If, however, the land is developed for a building, then the capitalized interest cost is added to the cost of the **building**. The interest is then matched against revenues as the building is depreciated.

The capitalization of interest costs does not apply to the following situations:

1. When routine inventories are produced in large quantities on a repetitive basis
2. When effects are not material, compared to the effect of expensing interest
3. When qualifying assets are already in use or ready for use
4. When qualifying assets are not being used and are not awaiting activities to get them ready for use
5. When qualifying assets are not included in a consolidated balance sheet
6. When principal operations of an investee accounted for under the equity method have already begun
7. When regulated investees capitalize both the cost of debt and equity capital
8. When assets are acquired with grants and gifts restricted by the donor to the extent that funds are available from those grants and gifts

The amount of interest capitalized. Interest cost includes the following:

1. Interest on debt having explicit interest rates
2. Interest related to capital leases
3. Interest required to be imputed on payables

The most appropriate rate to use as the capitalization rate is that rate which is applicable to specific new debt that resulted from the need to finance the acquired assets. If there was no specific new debt, the capitalization rate should be a weighted-average of the rates of the other borrowings of the entity. This latter case reflects the fact that the previously incurred debt of the entity could be repaid if not for the acquisition of the qualifying asset. Thus, indirectly, the previous debt is financing the acquisition of the new asset and its interest should be part of the cost of the new asset. The selection of borrowings to be used in the calculation of the weighted-average of rates requires judgment. The amount of interest to be capitalized is that portion which could have been avoided if the qualifying asset had not been acquired. Thus, the capitalized amount is the incremental amount of interest cost incurred by the entity to finance the acquired asset.

The base used to multiply the rate by is the average amount of accumulated net capital **expenditures** incurred for qualifying assets during the relevant time frame. Capitalized costs and expenditures are not the same terms. Theoretically, a capitalized cost financed by a trade payable for which no interest is recognized is not a capital expenditure to which the capitalization rate should be applied. Reasonable approximations of net capital expenditures are acceptable, however, and capitalized costs are generally used in place of capital expenditures unless there is a material difference.

If the average capitalized expenditures exceed the specific new borrowings for the time frame involved, then the **excess** expenditures should be multiplied by the weighted-average of rates and not by the rate associated with the specific debt. This requirement more accurately reflects the interest cost incurred by the entity to acquire the fixed asset.

The interest being paid on the debt may be simple or compound. Simple interest is computed on the principal alone, whereas compound interest is computed on principal **and** on any interest that has not been paid. Most fixed assets will be acquired with debt having interest compounded. Compound interest can be computed using compound interest tables or computer software (electronic spreadsheets or specialized software applications that compute the time value of money).

The total amount of interest actually incurred by the entity is the ceiling for the amount of interest cost capitalized. The amount capitalized cannot exceed the amount actually incurred during the period involved. On a consolidated basis, the ceiling is defined as the total of the parent's interest cost plus that of the consolidated subsidiaries. If financial statements are issued separately, the interest cost capitalized should be limited to the amount that the separate entity has incurred, and that amount should include interest on intercompany borrowings. The interest incurred is a gross amount and is not netted against interest earned except in cases involving externally restricted tax-exempt borrowings.

Example of accounting for capitalized interest costs

1. On January 1, 2002, Daniel Corp. contracted with Leo Company to construct a building for $2,000,000 on land that Daniel had purchased years earlier.
2. Daniel Corp. was to make five payments in 2002 with the last payment scheduled for the date of completion, December 31, 2002.

3. Daniel Corp. made the following payments during 2002:

January 1, 2002	$ 200,000
March 31, 2002	400,000
June 30, 2002	610,000
September 30, 2002	440,000
December 31, 2002	350,000
	$2,000,000

4. Daniel Corp. had the following debt outstanding at December 31, 2002:

a. A 12%, three-year note dated 1/1/02 with interest compounded quarterly. Both principal and interest due 12/31/04 (relates specifically to building project). $850,000

b. A 10%, ten-year note dated 12/31/96 with simple interest and interest payable annually on December 31. $600,000

c. A 12%, five-year note dated 12/31/98 with simple interest and interest payable annually on December 31. $700,000

The amount of interest to be capitalized during 2002 is computed as follows:

Average Accumulated Expenditures

Date	*Expenditure*	*Capitalization period**	*Average accumulated expenditures*
1/1/02	$ 200,000	12/12	$200,000
3/31/02	400,000	9/12	300,000
6/30/02	610,000	6/12	305,000
9/30/02	440,000	3/12	110,000
12/31/02	350,000	0/12	
	$2,000,000		$915,000

* *The number of months between the date expenditures were made and the date interest capitalization stops (December 31, 2002).*

Potential Interest Cost to Be Capitalized

($850,000	x 1.12551)*	− $850,000	=	$106,684
65,000	x	.1108**	=	7,202
$915,000				$113,886

* *The principal, $850,000, is multiplied by the factor for the future amount of $1 for four periods at 3% to determine the amount of principal and interest due in 2000.*

** *Weighted-average interest rate:*

	Principal	*Interest*
10%, ten-year note	$ 600,000	$ 60,000
12%, five-year note	700,000	84,000
	$1,300,000	$144,000

$$\frac{Total\ interest}{Total\ principal} = \frac{\$144,000}{\$1,300,000} = \underline{11.08\%}\ weighted\text{-}average\ interest\ rate$$

The actual interest is

12%, three-year note [($850,000 x 1.12551) − $850,000]	=	$106,684
10%, ten-year note ($600,000 x 10%)	=	60,000
12%, five-year note ($700,000 x 12%)	=	84,000
Total interest		$250,684

The interest cost to be capitalized is the lesser of $113,886 (avoidable interest) or $250,684 (actual interest), which is $113,886. The remaining $136,798 ($250,684 − $113,886) would be expensed.

Determining the time period for interest capitalization. Three conditions must be met before the capitalization period begins.

1. Necessary activities are in progress to get the asset ready to function as intended
2. Qualifying asset expenditures have been made
3. Interest costs are being incurred

As long as these conditions continue, interest costs are to be capitalized.

Necessary activities are interpreted in a very **broad** manner. They start with the planning process and continue until the qualifying asset is substantially complete and ready to function. Brief, normal interruptions do not stop the capitalization of interest costs. However, if the entity intentionally suspends or delays the activities for some reason, interest costs should not be capitalized from the point of suspension or delay until substantial activities in regard to the asset resume.

If the asset is completed by parts, the capitalization of interest costs stops for each part as it becomes ready. An asset that must be entirely complete before the parts can be used capitalizes interest costs until the total asset becomes ready.

Interest costs should continue to be capitalized until the asset is ready to function as intended, even in cases where lower of cost or market rules are applicable and market is lower than cost. The required write-down should be increased accordingly.

Capitalization of interest costs incurred on tax-exempt borrowings. If qualifying assets have been financed with the proceeds from tax-exempt, **externally restricted** borrowings and if temporary investments have been purchased with those proceeds, a modification is required. The interest costs incurred from the date of borrowing must be reduced by the interest earned on the temporary investment in order to calculate the ceiling for the capitalization of interest costs. This procedure must be followed until the assets financed in this manner are ready. When the specified assets are functioning as intended, the interest cost of the tax-exempt borrowing becomes available to be capitalized by other qualifying assets of the entity. Portions of the tax-exempt borrowings that are not restricted are eligible for capitalization in the normal manner.

Assets acquired with gifts or grants. Qualifying assets that are acquired with externally restricted gifts or grants are not subject to capitalization of interest. The principal reason for this treatment is the belief that there is no economic cost of financing when a gift or grant is used in the acquisition.

Summary of interest capitalization requirements. The diagram on the following page summarizes the accounting for interest capitalization.

SUMMARY OF ACCOUNTING FOR INTEREST CAPITALIZATION

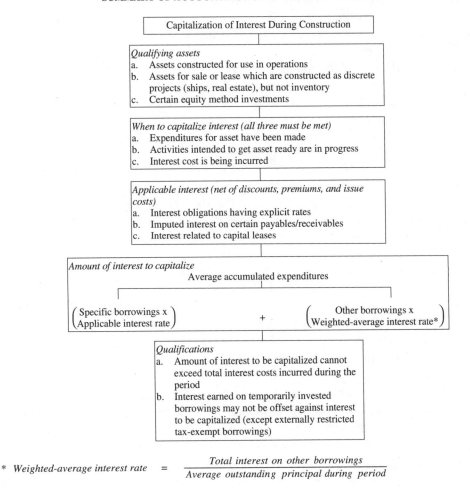

$$* \text{ Weighted-average interest rate} = \frac{\text{Total interest on other borrowings}}{\text{Average outstanding principal during period}}$$

Intangible Assets

Since August 1996, the FASB had been considering changes to the current accounting for business combinations including goodwill and other acquired intangibles. An Exposure Draft of a proposed SFAS was issued September 1999 (1999 ED). The 1999 ED tentatively concluded that the pooling-of-interests method of accounting for a business combination (See Chapter 11 for an in-depth discussion of this issue) should be eliminated. Further, the 1999 ED proposed that goodwill be amortized over its useful economic life, not to exceed twenty years and that other identifiable purchased intangibles be recognized as either having an indefinite life and not be subject to amortization, or be subject to the same twenty-year limitation as goodwill.

Primarily because of the elimination of pooling-of-interests, the proposal met with substantial resistance from FASB constituents in comment letters and at public hearings. A bill was introduced in the US House of Representatives, which, if enacted, would have postponed implementation of a final standard. As a result of this resistance, the FASB redeliberated the 1999 ED. In February 2001, the FASB issued a "limited revision" of the 1999 ED (2001 ED) which reaffirmed its intent to eliminate pooling-of-interests and, perhaps to placate its critics, adopted a different, nonamortization approach to goodwill. The 2001 ED, however left intact the tentative conclusions reached in the 1999 ED regarding intangibles other than goodwill.

Finally, in June 2001, the FASB concurrently issued separate final pronouncements on business combinations (SFAS 141) and intangible assets (SFAS 142), respectively. SFAS 142 supersedes APB 17 and establishes new accounting standards for both identifiable and unidentifiable intangible assets acquired or created, including goodwill. Goodwill is not considered an identifiable intangible asset, and accordingly, under SFAS 142, is accounted for differently from identifiable intangibles.

Intangible assets are defined as both current and noncurrent assets that lack physical substance. Specifically excluded, however, are financial instruments and deferred tax assets. Acquired intangibles are recognized separately from goodwill if they meet either of the following criteria:

1. Control over the future economic benefits of the asset is obtained through contractual or other legal rights irrespective of whether those rights are transferable or separable from other rights and obligations.
2. The asset is capable of being separated or divided and sold, transferred, licensed, rented, or exchanged irrespective of whether the acquirer intends to do so. This criterion is met if the asset can be sold, transferred, licensed, rented or exchanged along with a related contract, asset, or liability.

APB 17 required amortization of all intangible assets over the lesser of their useful economic lives or forty years. Perhaps the most important change from APB 17 is that under the terms of SFAS 142, indefinite life intangibles will again be recognized. Beginning with the promulgation of APB 17, amortization of all intangible assets over a finite life had been a requirement. The new statement, somewhat surprisingly, departs from this longstanding rule. It provides that if an identifiable intangible asset has an indefinite useful economic life that is supported by clearly identifiable cash flows, then it will not be subject to regular periodic amortization. Instead, the carrying amount of the intangible is to be reviewed for impairment under SFAS 121 whenever events or circumstances warrant such a review. An impairment would be recognized if the carrying amount exceeded the fair value. Furthermore, amortization of the asset would commence when evidence suggests that its useful economic life could no longer be deemed indefinite.

The decision to permit the recognition of "infinite-life" intangibles was likely based in part on the growing ubiquity of intellectual assets and the phenomenon of "knowledge-based businesses." The range of intangibles is perhaps more clearly understood today than it was in the past, and there is more pressure to make financial reporting more relevant to changing business conditions. For manufacturing companies the primary assets typically are tangible ones, such as buildings and equipment. For financial institutions the major assets are financial instruments. For high technology, knowledge-based companies, however, the primary assets are intangible ones such as patents and copyrights, and for professional service firms the key assets may be "soft" resources such as knowledge bases and client relationships. Overall, enterprises for which intangible assets constitute a large and growing component of total assets are a rapidly growing part of the economy.

In considering what characteristics of other intangible assets distinguish them from goodwill, APB 17 had described several bases on which intangible assets might be classified: identifiability, manner of acquisition, expected period of benefit, and separability. Goodwill is the preeminent unidentifiable intangible, and this characteristic (i.e., the lack of identifiability) has been determined by the FASB to be the critical element in the definition of goodwill. Accordingly, it was decided that identifiable intangible assets that are reliably measurable should be recognized separately from goodwill.

Many intangible assets are based on rights that are conveyed legally by contract, statute, or similar means. For example, governments grant franchises or similar rights to taxi companies, cable companies, and hydroelectric plants; and companies and other private-sector organizations grant franchises to automobile dealers, fast-food outlets, and professional sports teams. Other rights, such as airport landing rights, are granted by contract. Some of those franchises or similar rights are for finite terms, while others are perpetual. Many of those with finite terms are routinely renewed, absent violations of the terms of the agreement, and the costs incurred for renewal are minimal. Many such assets are also exchangeable, and the prices at which they trade reflect expectations of renewal at minimal cost. However, for others, renewal is not assured, and their renewal may entail substantial cost.

Other similar intangible assets include trademarks, service marks, trade names, copyrights, and patents. Trademarks, service marks, and trade names may be registered with the government for a period of twenty years and are renewable for additional twenty-year periods as long as the trademark, service mark, or trade name is used continuously. (Brand names, often used synonymously with trademarks, are typically not registered and thus the required attribute of control will be absent.) The US government now grants copyrights for the life of the creator plus fifty years. Patents are granted by the government for a period of seventeen years but may be effectively renewed by adding minor modifications that are patented for additional seventeen-year periods. Such assets also are commonly exchangeable.

Furthermore, not all identifiable intangible assets are based on rights that have been conveyed by legal means; some may have been developed internally. Some of those assets may be in the form of knowledge or databases, such as title plant or customer lists. Others may relate to human factors, such as customer relationships and work forces. Some of those assets may be exchangeable while others may not. Title plant and customer lists are examples of intangible assets that are exchangeable, whereas customer relationships and work forces generally are not.

In recognition of the vast diversity of intangible assets and their central role in modern business operations, the FASB concluded that exchangeability is a useful basis for distinguishing different types of intangible assets because those that are capable of being sold or otherwise transferred constitute a potential source of cash flow. It concluded that the guidance offered by APB 17 had been inadequate, as demonstrated by the fact that relatively few intangible assets have been recorded under that standard. Thus, SFAS 142 provides additional needed guidance in the form of a very comprehensive listing of intangibles that the FASB stipulates will generally meet the criteria for recognition separate from goodwill. Some of the major items are noted in the following paragraphs.

Customer- or market-based intangibles include those that relate to customer structure or market factors of the business, such as various lists (advertising, customer, dealer, mailing, subscription); the customer base; depositor or borrower relationships (of financial institutions); customer routes; the delivery system and distribution channels; customer service capability and product or service support; effective advertising programs; trademarked brand names; newspaper mastheads; a presence in specific geographic locations or markets; the value of insurance-in-force and insurance expirations; production backlog; concession stands; airport gates and slots; retail shelf space; and files and records (e.g., credit or medical).

Contract-based assets are intangible assets that have a fixed or definite term, such as many types of agreements (e.g., consulting, income, licensing, manufacturing, royalty, or standstill); contracts (such as those for advertising, construction, consulting, customer, employment, insurance, maintenance, management, marketing, mortgage, purchase, service, and supply); covenants (e.g., not to compete); easements; leases (if containing valuable or favorable terms); permits (such as those for construction); and various rights (e.g., for broadcasting, development, gas allocation, landing, lease, mineral, mortgage servicing, reacquired franchise, servicing, timber cutting, use, or water).

Technology-based assets are those assets that relate to innovations or technological advances within the business. These could include computer software and license, computer programs, information systems, program formats, and Internet domain names and portals; secret formulas and processes, and recipes; technical drawings, technical and procedural manuals, and blueprints; databases and certain types of title plants; manufacturing processes, procedures, and production lines; research and development; and technological know-how.

Statutory-based assets would be those which have statutorily established useful lives. The most traditional of all intangible assets, these include patents, copyrights (e.g., for manuscripts, literary works, and musical compositions), franchises (for cable, radio, and television), and trademarks and trade names.

Identifiable intangible assets, such as franchise rights, customer lists, trademarks, patents and copyrights, and licenses are to be amortized over the expected useful economic life, even if that life exceeds the former forty-year ceiling, with required reviews for impairment when necessitated by SFAS 121. The statement also requires consideration of the intangible's residual value (analogous to salvage value for a tangible asset) in determining the amount of the intangible to amortize. The statement defines residual value as the value of the intangible to the entity at the end of its useful life reduced by any estimated disposition costs.

A broadcast license which, while nominally subject to expiration in five years, might be indefinitely renewable at little additional cost to the broadcaster. If cash flows can be projected indefinitely, and assuming a market exists for the license, no amortization is to be recorded until such time as a finite life is predicted. However, impairment is required to be assessed when events and circumstances warrant such an assessment to ensure that the asset is carried at no more than its fair value.

The foregoing examples all addressed identifiable intangibles, which are given (when purchased or otherwise developed in ways that associates them with costs) separate recognition in the financial statements. There are other intangibles, which are deemed to not be identifiable because they cannot be reliably measured. The statement uses technological know-how and an assembled workforce as examples of such intangible assets. Intangibles that cannot be separately identified must be considered to be integral components of goodwill.

Goodwill is generally afforded special treatment under SFAS 142 due to the fact that it is not separately identifiable or transferable. The statement exempts goodwill arising from combinations between two or more not-for-profit organizations or in an acquisition of a for-profit enterprise by a not-for-profit organization. Also exempted is the special accounting for unidentifiable intangible assets recognized in an acquisition of a bank or thrift institution under SFAS 72.

Initially, goodwill is recognized as the excess of the cost of an acquired entity over the net of the amounts assigned to identifiable assets (including identifiable intangibles) acquired and liabilities assumed.

Under the statement, goodwill is not to be amortized. Goodwill is, however, subject to an impairment test detailed in the statement that is unique to goodwill. Therefore, SFAS 121 will not apply to goodwill and goodwill associated with acquisitions of tangible property and equipment will no longer be tested for impairment in tandem with that property and equipment as originally set forth in SFAS 121.

The goodwill impairment test is to be applied at least annually and, additionally, on an interim basis whenever events or circumstances occur that indicate that impairment **might** exist. If indicators exist that require testing both goodwill and tangible long-lived assets (property and equipment), the goodwill impairment test is to be performed first.

The impairment test for goodwill is performed at the level of the **reporting unit**. The reporting unit is defined as the lowest level of an entity that is a business and that can be distinguished, physically and operationally and for internal reporting purposes, from other activities, operations, and assets of the entity. The enterprise may internally refer to reporting units by such terms as business units, operating units, or divisions. Determination of reporting units is largely dependent on how the business is managed and its structure for reporting and management accountability. The statement indicates that a reporting unit will often be the lowest level of the entity at which operating plans are prepared and operating profitability is measured for assessing management performance. Reporting units should be distinguished from operating segments (segments) as set forth in SFAS 131 (applicable to publicly held companies) as the reporting unit is expected to be at a lower level than the segment. In all cases, however, the reporting unit may not be at a higher level than the segment to which it belongs. The Statement acknowledges that an entity may have only one reporting unit which would, of course, result in the impairment test being performed at the entity level.

On the date of acquisition, all assets and liabilities (net assets) of an acquired entity, including goodwill, must be assigned to the reporting units in which it is management's intent that they will be utilized in operations. The methodology used is to be reasonable and supportable and should be applied similar to how aggregate goodwill is determined in a purchase business combination. Net assets include assets and liabilities that are recognized as "corporate" items if they, in fact, relate to the operations of the reporting unit (e.g., environmental liabilities associated with land owned by a reporting unit, and pension assets and liabilities attributable to employees of a reporting unit). Purchased in-process research and development assets are specifically excluded from assets of a reporting unit. Executory contracts (e.g., operating leases, contracts for purchase or sale, construction contracts) are considered part of net assets only if the amount reflected in the acquirer's financial statements is based on a fair value measurement subsequent to entering into the contract. To illustrate, if an acquiree had a preexisting operating lease on either favorable or unfavorable terms as compared to its fair value on the date of acquisition, the acquirer would recognize, in its purchase price allocations, an asset or liability for the fair value of the favorable or unfavorable terms, respectively. SFAS 142 distinguishes between accounting for this fair value of an otherwise unrecognized executory contract and prepaid rent or rent payable which generally have carrying values that approximate their fair values.

The Statement requires the entity to complete, within six months of the date of adoption, a **benchmark assessment** measured as of the first of the fiscal year as a basis for developing and documenting its process for performing impairment tests should they be required in the future. When goodwill is significant in relation to the carrying amount of other net assets of a reporting unit, benchmark assessments are to be performed within a specified period of time (indicated parenthetically below) after

- A new reporting unit is created (one year)
- The assets of a reporting unit are changed substantially due to an acquisition (one year)
- A reporting unit is significantly modified by a reorganization of an entity's reporting structure (at the date of reorganization)

It is important to note, however, that should management identify events or circumstances that indicate that goodwill **might** be impaired, the benchmark assessment is required to be completed immediately to facilitate the impairment calculation.

Management is required, at the acquisition date, to create and maintain documentation regarding the methods and assumptions to be used in making the benchmark assessment including

- The basis for and method of determining the purchase price of an acquired entity
- Other factors related to the acquisition such as
  - The reasons for making the acquisition
  - Management's expectations related to dilution, synergies and other financial measurements

SFAS 142 contemplates that the benchmark assessment of each reporting unit will be made as follows

1. Identify and document the reporting unit's goodwill and other recognized net assets.
2. Identify and document the key expectations related to the future performance of the reporting unit.
3. Identify and document the model and key assumptions to be used to measure the fair value of the reporting unit as a whole (as distinguished from the individual fair values of the net assets of the reporting unit). Such assumptions would include a description of the model to be used to forecast future cash flows and key interest rate assumptions used to compute the present value of those cash flows.
4. Identify and document the methods and assumptions to be used to measure the recognized assets and liabilities of the reporting unit (excluding goodwill).
5. Measure and document the fair value of the reporting unit as a whole as of the date of acquisition or reorganization that gave rise to the benchmark assessment.

6. Compare the fair value of the reporting unit as a whole to the carrying amount of its net assets (including goodwill). Use this comparison to evaluate the reasonableness of the models and key assumptions used to determine the fair value of the reporting unit and the amount of goodwill assigned by management to that reporting unit.

   a. If the carrying amount of the net assets of the reporting unit (including its goodwill) exceeds fair value, management should reassess the amount of goodwill assigned to the reporting unit, the model used to measure the fair value of the reporting unit, and other assumptions.

   b. If, as a result of the reassessment, any of the information identified and documented in steps 1 through 3 above change, the fair value of the reporting unit as a whole is to be remeasured.

   c. If, after the reassessment and remeasurement, the carrying amount of the net assets of the reporting unit (including goodwill) still exceeds the fair value of the reporting unit as a whole, then the reporting unit's goodwill is to be tested for impairment.

SFAS 142 requires that nonamortizing intangible assets be tested for impairment at least annually and, additionally, on an interim basis if an event of circumstance occurs between annual tests that might reduce the fair value of that asset. The Statement provides examples of events or circumstances that require goodwill of a reporting unit to be tested for impairment.

1. A current period operating or cash flow loss for the reporting unit combined with a history of such operating or cash flow losses or a forecast of continuing losses.

2. A significant adverse change in one or more of the assumptions or expectations used in the most recent determination of the reporting unit's fair value such as

   a. Competitors' introduction of products, services or technologies that causes or is expected to cause a significant reduction in the reporting unit's market share for an existing similar product, technology or service.

   b. Estimates of future reporting unit revenues that are significantly lower than previously estimated due to changes in technology, loss of a customer or group of customers, increased competition or other factors.

   c. Estimates of future reporting unit operating profit or cash flows that are significantly lower than previously estimated due to unplanned increases in costs, the inability to achieve planned cost reduction targets, or other factors.

   d. A product or technology of a reporting unit acquired in a business combination has been or is expected to be replaced significantly earlier than the end of its previously estimated useful economic life, and that product or technology has no alternative use. For the purpose of this indicator, it is assumed that, unlike a patent or trademark, which would be subject to SFAS 121 impairment rules, the fair value of the product or technology does not meet the criteria for recognition as an identifiable intangible separate from goodwill. Thus, its fair value is inherently included in the goodwill of the reporting unit.

   e. Loss of key personnel has or is expected to have a significant adverse impact on the reporting unit's ability to generate revenues or develop new products, services, or technologies as originally planned.

   f. Management decides to change or restructure the operating model of the reporting unit. The change results in a significant departure from the business strategy that was assumed in the most recent determination of the reporting unit's fair value (e.g., a plant closure, product discontinuation, or disposition of assets or a product line).

3. A change in legal factors or a regulator's action or assessment that has had or is expected to have a significant adverse effect on the reporting unit.

4. An expectation that it is more-likely-than-not that a whole or significant portion of the reporting unit will be sold or otherwise disposed of.

5. Application of SFAS 121 to a significant group of the reporting unit's long-lived assets requires testing for impairment of that group of assets.

6. A decline in the market capitalization of the entity (or the reporting unit) below the carrying amount of its net assets (including goodwill) that is judged to be other than temporary.

7. A significant decline in the market price of the common stock of the entity (or the reporting unit) that is judged to be other than temporary.

8. A downgrading in the credit rating of publicly traded debt of the entity (or the reporting unit) below investment grade.

Special considerations apply to examples 7. and 8. above. Management must evaluate if the causes of the decline in market price (and related impact on market capitalization) or the decline in the credit rating of the publicly traded debt are associated with events or circumstances occurring in one or more specific reporting units. If management makes such an association, then the goodwill impairment test is limited to the specifically identified reporting unit or units. If no such association exists, then the goodwill of each of the entity's reporting units is to be tested separately for impairment.

Similar to the list of events in circumstances in SFAS 121, this list is not intended to be all-inclusive and other indicators may come to the attention of management that would indicate that goodwill impairment testing should be performed.

If goodwill impairment testing is indicated, the actual determination of whether goodwill is impaired would be made as follows:

1. Determine the fair value of the reporting unit as a whole.
2. Determine the fair value of the recognized net assets of the reporting unit.
3. Compute the difference between the fair value of the reporting unit's recognized net assets and the fair value of the reporting unit. This difference is referred to as the **implied fair value** of the reporting unit's goodwill.
4. If the carrying amount of the reporting unit's goodwill exceeds its implied value, the goodwill is impaired by the excess and an impairment loss is recognized.

Consistent with long-standing practice in GAAP, upon recognition of an impairment loss, the adjusted carrying amount of goodwill would become its new cost basis, and future restoration of the written down amount is prohibited.

The fair value of an asset (or liability) is the amount at which the asset (or liability) could be bought (or incurred) or sold (or settled) in a current transaction between willing parties other than in a forced or liquidation sale. Quoted market prices in active markets are considered the best evidence of fair value and are to be used if available. If quoted market prices are not available, the estimate of fair value is to be based on the best information available including prices for similar assets and liabilities or the results of applying available valuation techniques. Such techniques include present value of expected cash flows, option pricing models, matrix pricing, option-adjusted spread models, and fundamental analysis. The weight to be given to evidence gathered in the valuation process should be proportional to the ability to objectively verify it. When an estimate is in the form of a range of either the amount or timing of estimated future cash flows, the likelihood of possible outcomes is to be considered (i.e., probability weightings should be assigned in order to estimate the most likely outcome). SFAS 142 retains certain exceptions to this method of determining fair values for certain assets and liabilities to be consistent with APB 16 (e.g., deferred income taxes recorded by the acquiree prior to the acquisition). The Statement acknowledges cost/benefit considerations by providing that "all evidence available without undue cost and effort shall be considered in developing those estimates."

The fair value of the reporting unit is defined as the amount at which the unit as a whole could be bought or sold in a current transaction between willing parties. The determination of the implied value of goodwill is based on the assumption that the fair value of a reporting unit as a whole will almost always differ from the fair value of its net assets. This is the general principle that gives rise to goodwill in the first place. The acquirer assigns additional value to the acquiree (as evidenced by a purchase price that exceeds the collective fair values of the assets and liabilities to be acquired) based on its perceived ability to take advantage of synergies and other benefits that flow from its control over the acquiree. Market capitalization of a publicly traded business unit is computed based on a quoted market price per share that does not consider any advantages that might inure to an acquirer in a situation where control is obtained. For this reason, the Statement cautions that the market capitalization of a reporting unit with publicly traded stock may not be representative of its fair value. The Statement also prescribes that, when a significant portion of a reporting unit is comprised of an acquired entity, the same techniques and assumptions used to determine the purchase price of the acquisition should be used to measure the fair value of the reporting unit unless such techniques and assumptions are not consistent with the objective of measuring fair value.

The measurement techniques and assumptions used to estimate the fair values of the reporting unit's net assets are to be consistent with those used to measure the fair value of the reporting unit as a whole. For example, estimates of the amounts and timing of cash flows used to value the significant assets of the reporting unit should be consistent with those assumptions used to estimate such cash flows at the reporting unit level when a cash flow model is used to estimate the reporting unit's fair value as a whole.

Negative goodwill results from situations (sometimes referred to as "bargain purchases") where the fair values of the net assets acquired in a business combination exceed the purchase price and is discussed in detail in Chapter 11, Business Combinations and Consolidated Financial Statements. SFAS 141 requires that negative goodwill first be allocated pro rata to reduce amounts assigned to the acquired assets with the exception of

- Cash and cash equivalents
- Trade receivables
- Inventory
- Financial instruments required to be stated at fair value
- Assets to be disposed of by sale or as part of discontinued operations
- Deferred tax assets

After applying the negative goodwill to reduce the values assigned to the assets permitted to be adjusted, if negative goodwill still remains, SFAS 141 prescribes that it be recognized as an extraordinary gain in the period in which the business combination is initially recognized. However, two exceptions are provided to this general rule.

- When an extraordinary gain is recognized prior to completion of the purchase price allocations, the subsequent change necessitated by completion of the allocations is also recognized as either an extraordinary gain or loss in the period that the purchase price allocation is finalized.
- If the purchase price includes a provision for contingent consideration (e.g., a subsequent adjustment to the purchase price based on the acquiree attaining certain postacquisition levels of sales or pretax income), the remaining negative goodwill is recorded as a deferred credit until the contingency is resolved. In the period in which the contingency is resolved, any remaining negative goodwill is reclassified from the deferred credit to an extraordinary gain.

Other provisions included in SFAS 142 include

- Equity method goodwill will continue to be recognized under APB 18 and will not be subject to amortization. However, this goodwill would not be tested for impairment under the Statement, but rather, would continue to be tested under APB 18. This test considers whether the fair value of the underlying investment has declined and whether that decline is "other than temporary."
- Goodwill of a reporting unit that is fully disposed of is included in the carrying amount of the net assets to be disposed of in making the determination of gain or loss on disposal.
- When a significant portion of a reporting unit is disposed of, the goodwill of that unit is required to be tested for impairment. In performing the impairment test, only the net assets to be retained after the disposal are to be included in the computation. If, as a result of the test, the carrying amount of goodwill exceeds its implied fair value, the excess carrying amount is allocated to the carrying amount of the net assets to be disposed of in making the determination of gain or loss on disposal and, consequently, would not be considered an impairment loss.

SFAS 142 attempts to increase the transparency of goodwill in financial statements by requiring separate line item treatment.

- On the balance sheet (statement of financial position): The aggregate amount of goodwill included in assets
- On the income statement: The aggregate amount of goodwill impairment losses are to be shown separately in the operating section unless associated with discontinued operations

Disclosures regarding goodwill required under SFAS 142 are as follows:

1. General information about an acquisition in the period in which the business combination is completed including the primary reason for the acquisition, including a description of the factors that contributed to a purchase price that reflects a premium that results in recognition of goodwill or a discount that results in negative goodwill being recognized as an extraordinary gain.
2. If goodwill is significant in relation to the total cost of each significant business combination completed in the current reporting period (or the total of individually insignificant business combinations that, in the aggregate, are significant to the acquirer), the following information determined as of acquisition date
   a. The amount of goodwill acquired
   b. The amount of goodwill acquired related to each segment (for publicly held companies subject to segment reporting under SFAS 131)
   c. The amount of goodwill acquired that is deductible for income tax purposes

3. For each period for which a balance sheet (statement of financial position) is presented, the changes in the carrying amount of goodwill during the period including, where applicable the amount of goodwill

   a. Acquired
   b. Recognized as an impairment loss
   c. Included in gain or loss on disposal of all or a portion of a reporting unit.

4. For entities required to report segment information under SFAS 131, the information in 3. is required to be provided for each segment along with a description of any changes in the allocation of goodwill between segments.

5. For each goodwill impairment loss recognized in the financial statements

   a. The facts and circumstances leading to the impairment
   b. Identification of the affected reporting unit, the adjusted carrying amount of goodwill of that reporting unit and the amount of the impairment loss
   c. If the impairment loss recognized is tentative because an estimate has not yet been finalized, that fact and the reasons that the estimate is still tentative and, in subsequent periods, the nature and amount of any significant adjustments made to the initial estimate
   d. For entities required to report segment information under SFAS 131, identification of the segment with impaired goodwill

6. In periods in which negative goodwill is recognized as an extraordinary item, the disclosures regarding extraordinary items set forth in APB 30.

To follow current developments in this important area and other emerging areas of GAAP between the annual editions of this Publication, we recommend that you monitor the FASB website at http://accounting.Rutgers.edu/raw/fasb/ and the Wiley GAAP Update website at www.wiley.com/GAAP.

Leasehold improvements represent physical enhancements made to property by or on behalf of the property's lessee. By law, when improvements are made to real property and those improvements are permanently affixed to the property, the title to those improvements automatically transfers to the owner of the property. The rationale behind this is that the improvements, when permanently affixed, are inseparable from the real estate.

As a result of this automatic title transfer, the lessee's interest in the improvements is an intangible right to use and benefit from them during the term of the lease. Consequently, the capitalized costs incurred by a lessee in constructing improvements to property that it leases represent an intangible asset analogous to a license to use them. Thus, when allocating the costs of leasehold improvements to the periods benefited, the expense is referred to as amortization (as used in amortization of goodwill, patents and other intangibles) and not depreciation.

A frequently encountered issue with respect to leasehold improvements relates to the period over which they should be amortized. Normally, the cost of long-lived assets is charged to expense over the estimated useful lives of the assets. However, the right to use a leasehold improvement expires when the related lease expires, irrespective of whether the improvement has any remaining useful life. Thus, the appropriate useful life for a leasehold improvement is the **lesser of** the useful life of the improvement or the term of the underlying lease.

Some leases contain a fixed, noncancelable term and additional renewal options. When considering the term of the lease for the purposes of amortizing leasehold improvements, normally only the initial fixed noncancelable term is included. There are exceptions to this general rule that arise out of the application of GAAP, to the lessee's accounting for the lease. If a renewal option is a **bargain renewal option**, then it is probable at the inception of the lease that it will be exercised and, therefore, the option period should be included in the lease term for purposes of determining the amortizable life of the leasehold improvements. Additionally, under the definition of the **lease term** there are other situations where it is probable that an option period would be exercised. These situations would include periods for which failure to renew the lease imposes a penalty on the lessee in such amount that a renewal appears, at the inception of the lease, to be reasonably assured. Another potential situation of this kind would be where an otherwise excludable renewal period precedes a provision for a bargain purchase of the leased asset.

It is important to note that, in deciding whether to include a renewal option in the calculation of the amortizable life of the leasehold improvements, the lessee must be consistent with the interpretation of renewal options included in the minimum lease payment calculations that were made to determine whether the lease should be accounted for as a capital or operating lease.

Example

Marcie Corporation occupies a warehouse under a five-year operating lease commencing January 1, 2001, and expiring December 31, 2005. The lease contains three successive options to renew the lease for additional five-year periods. The options are not bargain renewals as they call for fixed rentals at the prevailing fair market rents that will be in effect at the time of exercise. When the initial calculation was made to determine whether the lease should be accounted for as an operating lease or a capital lease, only the initial noncancelable term of five years was included in the calculation. Consequently, for the purpose of determining the amortizable life of any leasehold improvements, only the initial five-year term would be used. If Marcie Corporation decided, at the beginning of year four of the lease, to make a substantial amount of leasehold improvements to the leased property, it could be argued that it would now be probable that the lessee would exercise one or more of the renewal periods, since not doing so would impose the substantial financial penalty of abandoning expensive leasehold improvements. This would trigger accounting for the lease by treating the period or periods for which it is likely that the lessee will renew as a new agreement and testing to determine whether the lease, prospectively, qualifies as a capital or operating lease.

Research and Development Costs

Research and development (R&D) are defined as follows:

1. Research is the planned search or critical investigation aimed at the discovery of new knowledge with the hope that such knowledge will be useful in developing a new product or service or a new process or technique or in bringing about a significant improvement to an existing product or process.
2. Development is the translation of research findings or other knowledge into a plan or design for a new product or process or for a significant improvement to an existing product or process whether intended for sale or use.

There are three ways in which R&D costs are incurred by a business.

1. Through the purchase of R&D from other entities
2. Through conducting R&D for others under a contractual arrangement
3. Through R&D activities conducted for the benefit of the enterprise

The accounting treatment relative to R&D depends upon the nature of the cost. R&D costs incurred in the ordinary course of operations consist of materials, equipment, facilities, personnel, and indirect costs that can be attributed to research or development activities. These costs are expensed in the period in which they are incurred unless they have alternative future uses.

Examples of such R&D costs include

1. Laboratory research to discover new knowledge
2. Formulation and design of product alternatives

    a. Testing for product alternatives
    b. Modification of products or processes

3. Preproduction prototypes and models

    a. Tools, dies, etc. for new technology
    b. Pilot plants not capable of commercial production

4. Engineering activity until the product is ready for manufacture

Examples of costs that are not considered R&D would include

1. Engineering during an early phase of commercial production
2. Quality control for commercial production
3. Troubleshooting during a commercial production breakdown
4. Routine, ongoing efforts to improve products
5. Adaptation of existing capacity for a specific customer or other requirements
6. Seasonal design changes to products
7. Routine design of tools, dies, etc.
8. Design, construction, startup, etc. of equipment except that used solely for R&D

In many cases, entities will pay other parties to perform R&D activities on their behalf. It is axiomatic that a financial reporting result cannot be obtained indirectly if it would not have been permitted if accomplished directly. Thus, if the cost incurred is in substance for R&D activities that could, hypothetically, have been performed by the reporting entity itself, those costs must be expensed as incurred. On the other hand, if the payment is to acquire intangibles for use in R&D activities, and these assets have other uses, then the expenditure should be capitalized and amortized.

When R&D costs are incurred as a result of contractual arrangements, the nature of the agreement dictates the accounting treatment of the costs involved. The key determinant is the transfer of the risk associated with the R&D expenditures. If the business receives funds from another party to perform R&D and is obligated to repay those funds regardless of the outcome, a liability must be recorded and the R&D costs expensed as incurred. In order to conclude that a liability does not exist, the transfer of the financial risk must be substantive and genuine.

In-process research and development. There has been recent concern that large amounts of acquired R&D are being written off. The result of this action is a reduction of the goodwill recorded and a subsequent reduction of amortization appearing on the income statement. All associated with the preparation of the financial statements should consider the reasonableness of any write-offs and the possibility of a challenge by the SEC.

The FASB has decided that R&D costs should be dealt with in a comprehensive manner in a future project. Until then, immediate write-off of purchased in-process research and development costs is required.

EMERGING ISSUES TASK FORCE CONSENSUS SUMMARIES

86-29 Nonmonetary Transactions: Magnitude of Boot and the Exceptions to the Use of Fair Value

When boot is at least 25% of the fair value of the exchange, it is considered a monetary transaction and both parties should record the exchange at fair value. When boot less than 25% is received in exchange, only the boot portion of the earnings process is considered to have been culminated. The portion of the gain applicable to the boot is considered realized and should be recognized in the determination of net income for the period of the exchange.

The formula for the recognition of the gain in an exchange involving boot of less than 25% of fair value can be generalized as follows:

$$\frac{\text{Boot}}{\text{Boot} + \text{Fair value of nonmonetary asset received}} \times \text{Total gain indicated} = \text{Gain recognized}$$

EITF consensus 86-29 specifies that a product or property held for sale exchanged for a productive asset (even in the same line of business) should be recorded at fair value. (See the interpretive guidance in EITF consensus EITF 00-5 later in this Chapter.)

87-29   Exchange of Real Estate Involving Boot

In an exchange of similar real estate that is a monetary transaction under EITF 86-29 because boot is at least 25% of the fair value exchanged, the fair value would be allocated between the monetary and nonmonetary components based on relative fair values. The receiver of boot would have a sale under SFAS 66 and, for the nonmonetary portion, would account for it under APB 29, adjusting basis of the property.

The payer of boot records the payment as a purchase of real estate and, for the nonmonetary portion, follows APB 29 and adjusts basis of the property.

89-13   Accounting for the Cost of Asbestos Removal

The cost of treating property acquired with a known asbestos problem should be capitalized. In the case of existing property, asbestos-treating costs should be recorded as a betterment. Both capitalizations are subject to an impairment test.

When removal costs incurred due to the anticipation of the sale of property can be recovered from the sale, these costs should be deferred and recognized at the time of sale.

Expensed asbestos costs are not considered extraordinary items. SEC registrants should disclose any significant exposure for asbestos treatment in the MD&A.

90-8   Capitalization of Costs to Treat Environmental Contamination

In general, environmental contamination treatment costs should be charged to expense. Costs may be capitalized if recoverable, but only if one of the following criteria is met:

1. The costs extend the life, increase the capacity, or improve the safety or efficiency of property owned by the company.
2. The costs mitigate or prevent future environmental contamination while also improving the property.
3. The costs are incurred in preparing for sale a property that is currently held for sale.

91-10   Accounting for Special Assessments and Tax Increment Financing Entities

A property owner should recognize an obligation for special assessments levied by a municipality or by a Tax Increment Financing Entity (TIFE) that are for a fixed or determinable amount for a fixed or determinable period. A company may be contingently liable under SFAS 5 if

1. It must satisfy any shortfall in annual debt service
2. It has pledged its assets

3. It provides a letter of credit or other credit enhancements in support of the TIFE's debt.

If constructing facilities for its own use, the presence of these factors creates a presumption that the TIFE debt is a liability.

93-11   Accounting for Barter Transactions Involving Barter Credits

A consensus was reached that APB 29 applies to these kinds of transactions and that the basis for recording should be the fair value of the nonmonetary asset given up. Ordinarily, this fair value measurement should not be higher than its carrying value.

Impairment, if applicable, should be recorded before the exchange. Thus, a new cost basis is established and a loss is recognized on the income statement. If an operating lease is involved, impairment is measured as the amount of remaining lease costs in excess of fair value of the probable sublease rentals for the remaining lease term. SFAS 15 should be helpful in defining fair value.

The value of barter credits should not be used to record fair value unless they can be converted to cash in the short term or there are independent existing market prices available for items to be received for the barter credits.

Impairment after the exchange should be recorded if the carrying amount exceeds the fair value of the barter credits or if the business determines that it will not be able to use the barter credits.

95-23   Treatment of Certain Site Restoration/Environmental Exit Costs When Testing a Long-Lived Asset for Impairment

For purposes of SFAS 121, site restoration/environmental exit costs that **have** been recorded as a liability are to be excluded from the undiscounted expected future cash flows used to test for recoverability. The intent of management determines whether exit costs that **have not** been recorded as a liability are to be excluded or included. In general, if disposition is not expected to incur exit costs or if the exit costs will not result in net cash outflow, the costs are excluded from the test; and if abandonment, sale, or closure are expected to incur exit costs, the costs are included in the test.

96-14   Accounting for the Costs Associated with Modifying Computer Software for the Year 2000

All specifically associated internal and external costs of modifying internal-use software should be expensed.

99-5   Accounting for Preproduction Costs Related to Long-Term Supply Arrangements

Manufacturers often incur costs referred to as preproduction costs, related to products that they will supply to their customers under long-term supply arrangements. The following consensuses were reached with respect to these costs:

1. Design and development costs should be expensed as incurred.
2. Design and development costs for molds, dies, and other tools that a supplier will own and that will be used in producing the products under the long-term supply arrangement should be capitalized as part of the molds, dies, and other tools (subject to a SFAS 121 impairment assessment when one or more of the impairment indicators is present). There is an exception, however, for molds, dies, and other tools involving new technology which should be expensed as incurred as research and development costs under SFAS 2.
3. If the molds, dies, and other tools described in 2. above are **not to be owned** by the supplier, then their costs should be expensed as incurred unless the supply arrangement provides the supplier the noncancelable right (as long as the supplier is performing under the terms of the supply arrangement) to use the molds, dies, and other tools during the supply arrangement.
4. If there is a legally enforceable contractual guarantee for reimbursement of design and development costs that would otherwise be expensed under these consensuses, the costs should be recognized as an asset as incurred. Such a guarantee must contain reimbursement provisions that are objectively measured and verified. The consensus contains examples that illustrate the application of this provision.

Under these consensuses, SEC registrants are expected to disclose

1. Their accounting policy for preproduction design and development costs.
2. The aggregate amounts of
   a. Assets recognized pursuant to agreements providing for contractual reimbursement of preproduction design and development costs.
   b. Assets recognized for molds, dies, and other tools that the supplier owns.
   c. Assets recognized for molds, dies, and other tools that the supplier does not own.

99-9   Effect of Derivative Gains and Losses on the Capitalization of Interest

The interest rate to use in capitalizing interest under SFAS 34 should be the effective yield that takes into account gains and losses on the effective portion of a derivative instrument that qualifies as a fair value hedge of fixed interest rate debt. The amount of interest subject to capitalization could include amortization of the adjustments of the carrying amount of the hedged liability under SFAS 133, if the entity elects to begin amortization of those adjustments during the period in which interest is eligible for capitalization. Any ineffective portion of the fair value hedge should not be reflected in the capitalization rate.

During the EITF's deliberations, the FASB staff expressed a belief that when the variable-rate interest on a specific borrowing is associated with an asset under construction and capitalized as part of the cost of that asset, the amounts in accumulated other comprehensive income related to a cash flow hedge of the variability of that interest should be reclassified into earnings over the depreciable life of the constructed asset, since that depreciable life coincides with the amortization period for the capitalized interest cost on the debt.

99-16 Accounting for Transactions with Elements of Research and Development Arrangements

This issue discusses the accounting for transaction in which a sponsor creates a wholly owned subsidiary with cash and rights to certain technology originally developed by the sponsor, and receives from the newly created subsidiary two classes of stock. The sponsor then distributes one of the classes of stock (e.g., Class A) to its shareholders. This class of stock has voting rights. Under a purchase option, the sponsor has the right, for a specified period of time, to repurchase all the Class A stock distributed to the shareholders for an exercise price approximating the fair value of the Class A shares. The class retained by the sponsor (e.g., Class B) conveys essentially no financial interest to the sponsor and has no voting rights other than certain blocking rights. The certificate of incorporation prohibits the subsidiary from changing its capital structure, from selling any significant portion of its assets, and from liquidating or merging during the term the purchase option is outstanding.

The sponsor and the subsidiary enter into a development contract that requires the subsidiary to spend all the cash contributed by the sponsor for research and development activities mutually agreed upon with the sponsor. The subsidiary has no employees other than its CEO. The subsidiary contracts with the sponsor to perform, on behalf of the subsidiary, all of the research and development activities under the development contract.

The sponsor should account for the research and development contract as follows

- The sponsor should reclassify the cash contributed to the subsidiary as restricted cash when the Class A shares are distributed to its shareholders.
- The distribution of the Class A shares by the sponsor to its shareholders should be accounted for as a dividend based on the fair value of the shares distributed.
- In the financial statements of the sponsor, the Class A shares should be presented similar to a minority interest.
- The sponsor should recognize research and development expense as the research and development activities are conducted.

- The research and development expense recognized by the sponsor should not be allocated to the Class A shares in determining net income or in calculating earnings per share.
- If the Class A purchase option is exercised, the sponsor should account for the purchase as the acquisition of a minority interest.
- If the Class A purchase option is not exercised by its expiration date, the sponsor should reclassify the Class A stock to additional paid-in capital as an adjustment of the original dividend.

The effect of the above guidance is quite similar to what would be achieved by consolidating the subsidiary.

The EITF consensus is effective for arrangements consummated after May 18, 2000, and contains an example of the application of the above guidance.

00-2   Accounting for Website Development Costs

The costs of developing a website, including the costs of developing services that are offered to visitors (e.g., chat rooms, search engines, e-mail, calendars, and so forth), are often quite significant. The SEC staff had expressed the opinion that a large portion of those costs should be accounted for in accordance with AICPA SOP No. 98-1, *Accounting for the Costs of Computer Software Developed or Obtained for Internal Use*, which sets forth certain conditions which must be met before costs may be capitalized.

In this consensus, the EITF held that costs incurred in the planning stage must be expensed as incurred. Cost of software used to operate a website must be accounted for consistent with SOP 98-1, unless a plan exists to market the software externally, in which case SFAS 86 governs. Costs incurred to develop graphics (broadly defined as the "look and feel" of the web page) are included in software costs, and thus accounted for under SOP 98-1 or SFAS 86, as noted in the foregoing. However, the accounting for costs of content development will be addressed as a separate EITF issue. Costs of operating websites should be accounted for in the same manner as other operating costs analogous to repairs and maintenance.

Issue 00-2 includes a detailed exhibit stipulating how a variety of specific costs are to be accounted for consistent with this consensus. The consensus applies to costs incurred for quarters beginning after June 30, 2000.

00-5   Determining Whether a Nonmonetary Transaction is an Exchange of Similar Productive Assets

Accounting for an exchange of productive assets for similar productive assets should be based on the recorded book value of the assets exchanged, rather than at fair value. This issue discusses the circumstances in which an exchange of assets can be considered an exchange of similar productive assets. If the productive assets exchanged are in the same line of business, the assets must be similar in regard to both the nature of the output from the productive asset and the nature of the process used to create the output. An exchange of productive assets that consists of a group should be examined at the group level. The group should not be broken into individual assets to perform the assessment of whether the assets are similar. If the assets are not initially similar, but the company intends to convert them to use as similar productive assets, the activities necessary to convert the asset from one line of business to the other must be initiated by the end of the quarter in which the transaction closes. In addition, the cost to convert cannot exceed 25% of the fair value of the productive assets.

If an entity receives a noncontrolling ownership interest in another entity in exchange for its asset(s) and the fair value of the asset(s) given up is less than its (their) carrying value(s), the difference should be recognized as a loss. If the fair value of the asset(s) given up is greater than its (their) carrying value(s), then a gain should be recognized if the entity accounts for the ownership interest received at cost, or a partial gain should be recognized if the entity accounts for the ownership interest received using the equity method. The partial gain would exclude the portion of the gain represented by the economic interest retained.

This consensus supersedes conflicting guidance in Issues 86-29 and 89-7. It does not apply to transfers between a joint venture and its owners, to transfers of real estate in exchange for an unconsolidated real estate investment or for nonmonetary assets other than real estate, or to transfers of assets used in oil- and gas-producing activities for other assets used in oil- and gas-producing activities.

STATEMENTS OF POSITION

88-1   Accounting for Developmental and Preoperating Costs, Purchases and Exchanges of Take-off and Landing Slots, and Airframe Modifications

The Accounting Standards Division concluded that developmental costs related to the operation of new routes should not be capitalized, whereas preoperating costs related to the integration of new types of aircraft may be capitalized and amortized beginning on the date that the new aircraft is ready for use. In addition, take-off and landing slots purchased by an airline are recorded as identifiable intangible assets in accordance with APB 17, while slots acquired through exchange are nonmonetary assets to be recorded as in APB 29 and amortized according to APB 17. The cost of modifications to an aircraft's interior that increase the usefulness of the craft are capitalized and depreciated over the lesser of the life of the aircraft or of the modifications. The net cost less salvage value of the replaced asset is charged to current income.

92-3   Accounting for Foreclosed Assets

This SOP applies to all reporting entities (except those that account for assets at fair value) and applies to all assets obtained through foreclosure or repossession (except inventories, marketable equity securities and real estate owned by the lender and accounted for under SFAS 67). Foreclosed assets held for sale should be measured on an individual asset basis on the balance sheet at the lower of (1) cost or (2) fair value less estimated selling costs. A valuation account should be used to show an amount less than cost.

If the asset is subject to senior debt, that debt should not be deducted from carrying value but should be reported as a liability. Payments should be deducted from the liability. After foreclosure, accrued interest should be recognized as interest expense.

For foreclosed assets used in the production of income, the accounting should be the same as for any other nonforeclosed acquired asset in their category. If assets that have been foreclosed and classified as held for sale are to be used in the production of income, reclassification of the asset's carrying amount is required. The adjustment should be the amount necessary to get the asset to the value that it would have been if it had been used in the production of income since foreclosure. Selling costs in the valuation account should be reversed and the net effect should be reported in income from continuing operations in the period of reclassification.

If a change in accounting principle results, the nature of the change should be included in income from continuing operations. No restatement or cumulative-effect adjustment is permitted as of the beginning of the year this SOP is first applied.

93-7   Reporting on Advertising Costs

This SOP is an initial step in providing guidance concerning the financial reporting for the cost of activities such as advertising, start-up, and customer acquisition. The existing guidance is inconsistent and, as a result, there has been diversity in the accounting treatment of these costs.

The costs of advertising should be expensed either as incurred or the first time the advertising takes place. However, there are two exceptions: (1) direct-response advertising (a) whose primary purpose is to elicit sales to customers who could be shown to have responded specifically to the advertising and (b) that results in probable future economic benefits; and (2) expenditures for advertising costs that are made subsequent to recognizing revenues related to those costs.

Expenditures for direct-response advertising should be capitalized if both of the conditions listed above are met. The future benefits to be received are the future revenues arising from the advertising. The company is required to provide persuasive evidence that there is a linkage between the direct-response advertising and these future benefits. These costs are then amortized over the period in which the future benefits are to be received. The decision to capitalize direct-response advertising relied on the recognition criteria and the definition of an asset SFAC 5 and 6. On the other hand, the advertising expenditures made subsequent to the recognition of revenue should be accrued and these advertising costs should be expensed when the related revenues are recognized.

10 INVESTMENTS

PERSPECTIVE AND ISSUES

The appropriate accounting for noncurrent (or long-term) investments in equity and debt securities is dependent upon the degree of marketability, management's intentions regarding the holding period, and (in the case of equity investments, only) the investor's ownership percentage.

For "passive" investments in marketable equity securities, generally defined as those circumstances where the investor holds less than a 20% interest in the investee, SFAS 115 requires that the investment be reported at fair market value. Such equity investments must be classified at the acquisition date as being for "trading purposes" or as being "available-for-sale." While what is often called "mark-to-market" accounting is prescribed in either case, only in the "trading purposes" case will the change in fair value be reflected on the income statement in the current period. For investments in equity securities that are considered to be "available-for-sale," unrealized gains and losses are to be carried in an equity account referred to as accumulated other comprehensive income, after being reported as a component of other comprehensive income per SFAS 130. However, if there is a permanent decline in the "available-for-sale" securities, this adjustment will be taken to income in the current period.

When an investor has **significant influence** over an investee, and thus is no longer a passive investor, the equity method must be used to account for the investment. Generally, significant influence is deemed to exist when the investor owns from 20 to 50% of the investee's voting shares, although APB 18 contemplates circumstances where such influence is present with under 20% ownership, or conversely is absent with holdings of 20% or greater. (Over 50%, of course, signals **control**, and under the provisions of SFAS 94, full consolidation of financial statements is mandatory unless one of the few exception conditions stipulated therein is met.) The equity method involves increasing the original cost of the investment by the investor's pro rata share of the investee's earnings, and decreasing it for the investor's share of the investee's losses and for dividends paid. Equity method accounting has been referred to as "one-line consolidation," because the net result of applying APB 18 on reported net earnings and on net worth should be identical to what would have occurred had full consolidation been applied. Thus, to the extent that the cost of acquiring the intercorporate investment exceeds the fair value of the investor's share of the investee's underlying net assets, the excess must be accounted for analogous to goodwill. SFAS 142, the recently issued standard addressing goodwill, also affects application of the equity method of accounting: the portion of the purchase cost identified as goodwill will no longer be subject to amortization, but must be tested, as conditions warrant, for impairment.

This chapter also discusses investments in marketable equity securities and in debt securities, as prescribed by SFAS 115. Under SFAS 115, fair value reporting is embraced to a greater extent than it had been in the past, although there is still the use of the accumulated other comprehensive income account to postpone income statement recognition of some changes in value. Debt securities that are being held to maturity are still accounted for at amortized historical cost. While unrealized gains and losses are still excluded from earnings, as such, they will be given much greater attention in the financial statements than had been the case prior to the promulgation of SFAS 130.

SFAS 115 applies to most industries and supersedes the specialized industry guidance (e.g., for the banking and thrift industries) previously found in AICPA audit and accounting guides. It does not apply to those industries for which fair value reporting is strictly required, such as brokers and dealers in securities. Furthermore, SFAS 115 does not apply to not-for-profits, which are governed by the provisions of recently issued SFAS 124, and which prescribes fair value reporting for all categories of investments, including those debt investments being held to maturity.

The graphic on the following page summarizes the distinctions for financial reporting purposes of varying levels of ownership in an investee entity. These requirements have not changed since the promulgation of SFAS 115; consolidation is still required when the parent owns over 50% of the subsidiary, regardless of actual control exerted. The announced intent to abandon a pure ownership test in favor of a new "control" criterion, which could result in full consolidation with only a minority share of ownership, has now been dropped by FASB. Thus the time-tested approach (under 20% ownership, cost or fair value accounting; 20% or greater, assume significant influence and apply the equity method; over 50%, fully consolidate) continues in effect.

Percentage of Outstanding Voting Stock Acquired

Sources of GAAP				
APB	*ARB*	*SFAS*	*FASB I*	*EITF*
17, 18, 23	43	52, 94, 107,	35	84-5, 85-40, 89-4, 93-18,
		109, 115, 125,		94-4, 96-10, 96-16, 97-7,
		126, 130, 133,		98-7, 98-13, 98-15, 99-8,
				99-10, 99-20, 00-1, 00-6,
				D-11, D-39, D-44, D-46,
				D-68

DEFINITIONS OF TERMS

Available-for-sale securities. Investments (debt or equity) that are not classifiable as held-to-maturity or as trading.

Corporate joint venture. A corporate business owned equally by two or more investor entities; it is typically accounted for by the equity method or, less commonly, by the proportional consolidation method by the investors.

Cost method. A method of accounting for investment whereby the investor recognizes only dividends received from investee as income.

Differential. The difference between the carrying value of common stock investment and book value of underlying net assets of the investee; it should be allocated between excess (deficiency) of fair value over (under) book value of net assets, with any remainder accounted for as goodwill (or negative goodwill), and tested periodically for impairment (if positive goodwill) or allocated against the underlying investee assets and, if necessary, recognized as an extraordinary income item (if negative goodwill).

Equity method. A method which includes recognition of a percentage share of income or loss, dividends, and any changes in the investment percentage in an investee by an investor. This method recognizes the effects of any intercompany transactions between the investor and investee.

Goodwill. The excess of the cost of the acquired enterprise over the sum of the amounts assigned to identifiable assets acquired less liabilities assumed.

Held-to-maturity securities. Investments in debt securities which the entity has the ability and intent to hold to maturity.

Investee. An enterprise that issued voting stock which is held by an investor.

Investee capital transaction. The purchase or sale by the investee of its own common shares, which alters the investor's ownership interest and is accounted for by the investor as if the investee were a consolidated subsidiary.

Investor. A business enterprise that holds an investment in voting stock of another enterprise.

Other comprehensive income. Revenues, expenses, gains and losses that under generally accepted accounting principles are included in comprehensive income but excluded from earnings.

Significant influence. The ability of the investor to affect the financial or operating policies of the investee; it is presumed to exist when there is at least 20% voting common stock ownership by the investor.

Trading securities. Investments (debt or equity) which the entity intends to sell in the near term, and which are usually acquired as part of an established strategy to buy and sell, thereby generating profits based on short-term price movements.

Undistributed investee earnings. The investor's share of investee earnings in excess of dividends paid.

CONCEPTS, RULES, AND EXAMPLES

Accounting for Marketable Equity Securities

The question of how to account for long-term investments in equity securities has been widely debated for many years. Historical cost was traditionally prescribed for investments where the **investor** did not exercise control (i.e., had no more than a 50% voting interest). The threshold for the use of historical cost was later reduced to only those circumstances where **significant influence** was not a factor, generally defined as under a 20% voting interest. The **equity method**, promulgated by APB 18, is the prescribed method of accounting for investments where significant influence over **investee** actions is held by the investor.

More recently, the trend in accounting thought has begun to favor a market (or fair) value approach. There are many reasons why users of financial statements as well as standard setters (including the SEC) have increasingly focused on the fair market value approach, including the enhanced availability of fair market value information, and the concern that the limitations of the historical cost model may have contributed to some of the more widely publicized business failures of recent years, particularly those of financial institutions. The current standard, SFAS 115, is the culmination of several years' study of and debate over these issues.

SFAS 115 is applicable to almost all reporting entities, except those whose specialized accounting practice has already been to account for all investments at market value; it is also inapplicable to not-for-profit enterprises. Under the provisions of SFAS 124, not-for-profits will have to account for all investments in debt and equity securities at fair value, with the changes in value taken into results from operations currently. All marketable equity securities (except those accounted for by the equity method, discussed later in this chapter) are to be classified at acquisition as being either for trading purposes or as available-for-sale. **Trading securities** are those which are bought with the intention of being sold in the near term with the general objective of realizing profits from short-term price movements. While a time criterion is not established, a persistent practice of active and frequent trading would be suggestive of the fact that new acquisitions of marketable equity securities are intended to be traded. If management does not admit an intention to trade, and it cannot be demonstrated that the securities are being held for trading, the investments are to be categorized as being **available-for-sale**.

The distinction between these classifications is important. While equity securities in either category are reported at fair market value (that is, they are marked-to-market), changes in the trading account are recognized in earnings in the current period. Thus, holding gains and losses are accounted for as if realized. The only exceptions will be the relatively few entities, such as securities broker-dealers, for which specialized industry accounting practices have long prescribed a pure mark-to-market approach.

Under SFAS 115, fair value of an equity security is considered to be determinable if it is quoted in an organized trading exchange or, generally, in over-the-counter trading. Restricted stock is, by definition, not traded and hence fair values are not readily determinable, but stock that is subject to "Rule 144" or similar restrictions, which are due to expire within one year, is not deemed to be restricted for purposes of applying SFAS 115. Stock traded only on foreign exchanges is included in the definition if the markets are comparable in breadth and scope to those in the US. Fair values for investments in mutual funds are generally considered to be determinable.

For available-for-sale equity securities, balance sheet presentation is identical to that for trading securities—current fair value. However, unless there has been a permanent impairment to the value of those securities, the change in fair value is excluded from earnings, but rather is reported in a separate stockholders' equity account, with the current period's change in this account being included in other comprehensive income.

SFAS 115 imposed this mode of reporting changes in the fair value of available-for-sale equity securities because of the expectation that most changes in investments intended to be held for an indeterminate period will experience only temporary fluctuations which, over the longer term, may tend to largely be offset. Thus, the belief is that interim fluctuations in value would not necessarily be indicative of the long term economic impact from holding the investments, and accordingly, that including these changes in earnings could be misleading.

While others have argued that the goal of periodic financial reporting should be to report the economic events of the period being presented, without concealing or "smoothing" the results, FASB ultimately agreed with those who favored the longer-term view. Notwithstanding substantial sentiment in favor of adopting a pure mark-to-market approach, with gains and losses on all financial instruments being reported in current period earnings, FASB's deliberations resulted in a standard which preserves many attributes of traditional historical cost concepts. The subsequent adoption of SFAS 130, requiring the display of comprehensive income, somewhat ameliorates the potentially misleading implications of omitting these changes from earnings. However, the defining of accounting for certain transactions based on management intent, rather than on objectively verifiable circumstances, remains a concern for the profession.

Example of accounting for investments in equity securities

Assume that Ralph Corporation purchases the following equity securities for investment purposes during 2002:

Security description	Acquisition cost	Value at year-end
1,000 sh. Bell Steel common	$ 34,500	$ 37,000
2,000 sh. Whammer pfd. "A"	125,000	109,500
1,000 sh. Hilltopper common	74,250	88,750

Assume that, at the respective dates of acquisition, management of Ralph Corporation designated the Bell Steel and Hilltopper investments as being for trading purposes, while the Whammer shares were designated as having been purchased for long term investment purposes. Accordingly, the entries to record the purchases were as follows:

Investment in equity securities—held-for-trading	108,750	
Cash		108,750
Investment in equity securities—available-for-sale	125,000	
Cash		125,000

At year-end, both portfolios are adjusted to fair market value; the decline in Whammer preferred stock, series A, is judged to be a temporary market fluctuation rather than a permanent decline. The entries to adjust the investment accounts at December 31, 2002, are

Investment in equity securities—held-for-trading	17,000	
Gain on holding equity securities		17,000

Unrealized loss on securities—available-for-sale (other comprehensive income)	15,500	
Investment in equity securities—available-for-sale		15,500

Thus, the change in value of the portfolio of trading securities is recognized in earnings, whereas the change in the value of the available-for-sale securities is reflected directly in stockholders' equity, after being reported in other comprehensive income.

Permanent Impairments of Investments Available for Sale

A permanent impairment in value of equity securities classified as available-for-sale must be reflected in earnings. The standard uses the term "other than temporary" rather than permanent to stress that the burden of proof is on those who believe a decline is only temporary. In other words, it is a refutable presumption that a decline in value is permanent in character. Absent an ability to demonstrate that a decline is temporary, the conclusion must be that the loss in value is other than temporary, in which case it must be recognized in income. Declines are measured at the individual security level and thus, losses in one security's value cannot be offset by gains in another's value.

Once a permanent impairment is recognized, the reduced carrying amount becomes the new cost basis from which other increases or decreases in value are measured. Increases or decreases in value that are temporary are recognized in other comprehensive income and then included in stockholders' equity in accumulated other comprehensive income, not in earnings. Further "other than temporary" declines in value are recognized in earnings. Recoveries in value in available-for-sale securities which have previously suffered a decline that was judged to be other than temporary cannot be recognized in earnings until the investment is liquidated. The fact that an equity investment has once suffered an other than temporary decline in value does not prevent a subsequent decline from being judged to be only temporary in character.

Assume now that in January 2003 new information comes to Ralph Corporation management regarding the viability of Whammer Corp. Based on this information, it is determined that the decline in Whammer preferred stock is probably not a temporary one, but rather is "other than temporary" (i.e., the asset is impaired). SFAS 115 prescribes that such a decline be reflected in earnings, and the written down value be treated as the new cost basis. The fair value has remained at the amount last reported, $109,500. Accordingly, the entry to recognize the fact of the investment's permanent impairment is as follows:

Loss on holding equity securities	15,500	
Unrealized loss on securities—available-for-sale (other comprehensive income)		15,500

Any subsequent recovery in this value would not be recognized in earnings unless realized through a sale of the investment to an unrelated entity in an arm's-length transaction, as long as the investment continues to be categorized as "available-for-sale," as distinct from "held-for-trading." However, if there is an increase in value (not limited to just a recovery of the amount of the loss recognized above, of course) the increase will be added to the investment account and shown in a separate account in stockholders' equity, since the asset is to be marked to fair value on the balance sheet.

It should be noted that the issue of permanent impairment does not arise in the context of investments held-for-trading purposes, inasmuch as unrealized holding gains and losses are immediately recognized without limitation. In effect, the distinction between realized and unrealized gains or losses does not exist for trading securities. To illustrate this point, consider now that in March 2003 further information comes to management's attention, which now suggests that the decline in Whammer preferred was indeed only a temporary decline; in fact, the value of Whammer now rises to $112,000. Since the carrying value after the recognition of the impairment was $109,500, which is treated as the cost basis for purposes of measuring further declines or recoveries, the increase to $112,000 will be accounted for as an increase to be reflected in the additional stockholders' equity account, as follows:

Investment in equity securities—available-for-sale	2,500	
Unrealized gain on securities—available-for-sale		
(other comprehensive income)		2,500

Note that this increase in value is not taken into earnings, since the investment is still considered to be available-for-sale, rather than a part of the trading portfolio. Even though the previous decline in Whammer stock was realized in current earnings, because judged at the time to be a permanent impairment in value, the recovery cannot be recognized in earnings. Rather, the change in value will be included in other comprehensive income and then displayed in an additional equity account.

Transfers between Available-for-Sale and Trading Investments

Under SFAS 115, transfers among portfolios are accounted for at fair value as of the date of the transfer. For investments in the trading category being transferred to available-for-sale, there is generally no further recognition of gain or loss at this point, as the investments have been marked to market value already. The only exception is that, if the investment accounts, as a practical matter, have not been updated for fair values since the latest balance sheet date, any changes since that time will need to be recognized at the date the transfer occurs. The fair value at the date of transfer becomes the new "cost" of the equity security to the available-for-sale portfolio.

To illustrate, consider Ralph Corporation's investment in Hilltopper common stock, which was assigned to the trading portfolio and at December 31, 2002, was marked to fair value of $88,750. Assume that in April 2003 management now determines that this investment will not be traded, but rather will continue to be held indefinitely. Under the criterion established by SFAS 115, this investment now belongs in the available-for-sale portfolio. Assume also that the value at the date this decision is made is $92,000, and that no book adjustments have been made since the one that recognized the value increase to $88,750. The entry to record the transfer from the trading to the available-for-sale portfolio is

Investment in equity securities—available-for-sale	92,000	
Investment in equity securities—held-for-trading		88,750
Gain on holding equity securities		3,250

Unrealized gains and losses on trading securities are always recognized in income, and in this example the additional increase in fair value since the last "mark-to-market" adjustment, $3,250, is recognized at the time of the transfer to the available-for-sale portfolio. Further gains after this date, however, will not be recognized in earnings, but rather will be included in other comprehensive income per SFAS 130.

For securities being transferred into the trading category, any unrealized gain or loss (recorded in the accumulated other comprehensive income account, as illustrated above) is deemed to be "realized" at the date of the transfer. Also, any fair value changes since the date of the most recent balance sheet may need to be recognized at this time. To illustrate, consider the investment in Whammer preferred stock, which was held in the available-for-sale portfolio, and which in March 2003 was adjusted to a fair value of $112,000 (as illustrated above). The increase from adjusted cost ($109,500, after a permanent impairment in value had been recognized) was reflected in other comprehensive income, rather than in earnings, given that the security was not at the time being held for trading. Now assume that, in June 2003, a decision is made to try to sell the investment in the short-term. This means that the holding of Whammer stock will be treated as being in the trading portfolio. Further, the value of the shares held, at the date of this decision, is $114,700. The entry to record the transfer from available-for-sale to trading, and the "realization" of the increased value at that date, is as follows:

Investment in equity securities—held-for-trading	114,700	
Unrealized gain on securities—available-for-sale (other comprehensive income)	2,500	
Investment in equity securities—available-for-sale		112,000
Gain on holding equity securities (an income statement account)		5,200

The recognized gain at the time of transfer, in this case, is the sum of the previously unrecognized gain that had been recorded in the additional equity account ($2,500) plus the further gain not yet given any recognition in the investor's financial statements ($2,700). Note that the elimination of the additional equity representing the previously reported unrealized gain will be included in comprehensive income in the current period as a debit, since the additional equity account is being reversed at this time. On the other hand, had there been a decline since the date of the last balance sheet, the gain to be recognized at the date of this transfer would have been the net of the previous, unrecognized gain, and the later loss; if the loss exceeded the earlier gain, a net loss would be recognized at this point. Any further gains or losses after the transfer to the trading portfolio will be handled as earlier described (i.e., recognized in income currently).

Presentation of Investments in Marketable Equity Securities

Investments in equity securities that are held for trading should be presented as current assets in classified balance sheets. Investments that are available for sale may be either current or noncurrent, depending upon the reporting entity's intentions. For purposes of reporting in the statement of cash flows, all purchases and sales of trading securities must be included in the operations section, while those of available-for-sale investments are to be shown as part of investing activities.

SFAS 115 requires specific disclosures of the components of a reporting entity's portfolios of investments. For available-for-sale securities, a classification by type of security is necessary: equity securities will be grouped together in this disclosure, and thus distinguished from debt securities. Furthermore, aggregate fair values, gross unrealized holding gains and gross unrealized holding losses are also to be disclosed as of the date of each balance sheet being presented.

For each income statement presented, proceeds from the sales of available-for-sale securities and gross realized gains and losses must be disclosed. Further, the basis upon which the gains or losses were determined (e.g., average cost, specific identification, etc.) must be disclosed. In addition, the notes must identify gross gains or losses included in earnings resulting from transfers of securities from the available-for-sale to the trading portfolio, and the net change in unrealized gains or losses recognized by an adjustment of the accumulated other comprehensive income account.

Changes in Fair Value after the Balance Sheet Date

Under GAAP, events occurring after the balance sheet date are generally not reflected in the balance sheet. However, disclosure may be necessary if, absent that information, the user of the financial statements would be misled. While not addressed explicitly by SFAS 115, presumably material changes in fair value occurring subsequent to the date of the balance sheet but prior to issuance of the financial statements should be disclosed.

Sometimes changes in value can be indicative of the underlying cause of the price fluctuations. Of most interest here would be declines in value of available-for-sale securities held at the balance sheet date which suggest that an "other than temporary" impairment has occurred. If the decline actually occurred after year-end as evidenced by a bankruptcy filing, then the event would be disclosed but not reflected in the year-end balance sheet. However, in some instances, the subsequent decline would be seen as a "confirming event" which provided evidence that the classification or other treatment of an item on the balance sheet was incorrect. Thus, if a decline in the fair value of available-for-sale securities at the balance sheet date had been accounted for as temporary (and hence reported in other comprehensive income) a further decline after the balance sheet date might suggest that the decline **as of the balance sheet date** had, in fact, been a permanent impairment. Note that any further value decline after year-end would not be recorded in the financial statements; the only question to be addressed is whether the decline that occurred **prior to year-end** should have been treated as a permanent impairment rather than as a temporary market fluctuation.

If it is clear that the impairment at year-end had, in fact, been permanent in nature, then the financial statements should be adjusted to reflect this loss in earnings. Absent sufficient basis to reach this conclusion, the appropriate course of action is to not adjust the statements, but merely to disclose the (material) change in fair value that occurred subsequent to year-end including, if appropriate, a statement to the effect that the later decline was deemed to be a permanent impairment, and will be reflected in the earnings of the next year's financial statements. It should also be made clear that the decline occurring prior to year-end was not considered to be a permanent impairment, at that time.

The FASB staff noted that when an entity has decided to sell a security classified as available-for-sale having a fair value less than cost at year-end, and it does not reasonably expect a recovery in value before the sale is to occur, then a write-down for an other than temporary decline is prescribed. This would most obviously be necessary if the actual sales transaction, anticipated at year-end, occurs prior to the issuance of the financial statements.

Deferred Tax Effects of Changes in Fair Value of Marketable Equity Securities

Unrealized gains or losses on holdings of marketable securities are not recognized for income tax purposes until realized through a sale. Thus, the gains or losses that are included in the financial statements (either in the income statement or in other comprehensive income) are temporary differences as defined by SFAS 109. Under this standard, the tax effects of all temporary differences are recognized in the financial statements as deferred tax benefits or deferred tax liabilities, with an additional requirement that an allowance be provided for deferred tax benefits that are "more likely than not" not going to be realized. Accordingly, adjustments to the carrying value of debt or equity investments included in either the trading or available-for-sale portfolios for changes in fair value will give rise to deferred taxes, as will any recognition of "other than temporary" declines in the value of debt securities being held to maturity.

For gains or losses recognized in connection with holdings of investments classified as trading, since the fair value changes are recognized in earnings currently, the deferred tax effects of those changes will also be presented in the income statement. For example, assume that Odessa Corp. purchased Zeta Company bonds as a short-term speculation, at a cost of $100,000. At year-end, the bonds had a fair value of $75,000. Odessa has a 40% effective tax rate. The entries to record the fair value adjustment and tax effect thereof are

Loss on holding of trading securities	25,000	
Investment in debt securities—trading portfolios		25,000
Deferred tax benefit	10,000	
Provision for income taxes		10,000

On the other hand, if the investment in Zeta Company bonds had been classified (at the date of acquisition, or subsequently if the intentions had been revised) as available-for-sale, the adjustment to fair value would have been reported in other comprehensive income, and not included in earnings. Accordingly, the tax effect of the adjustment would also have been included in other comprehensive income. The entries would have been as follows:

Unrealized loss on securities—available-for-sale	25,000	
Investment in debt securities—available-for-sale		
(other comprehensive income)		25,000
Deferred tax benefit	10,000	
Unrealized loss on securities—available-for-sale		
(other comprehensive income)		10,000

Finally, if the investment in Zeta Company bonds had been made with the intention and ability to hold to maturity, recognition of the decline in value would have depended upon whether it was judged to be temporary or other than temporary in nature. If the former, no recognition would be given to the decline, and hence there would be no deferred tax effect either. If deemed to be other than temporary, the investment would need to be written down, with the loss included in earnings. Accordingly, the tax effect would also be reported in the income statement. The entries would be as follows:

Loss on decline of securities—held-to-maturity	25,000	
Investment in debt securities—held-to-maturity		25,000
Deferred tax benefit	10,000	
Provision for income taxes		10,000

An other than temporary decline in value in securities available for sale would also have been recognized in earnings (not merely in other comprehensive income), and accordingly the tax effect of that loss would have been reported in earnings.

As with all other transactions or events giving rise to deferred tax assets, an evaluation must be made as to whether the entity would be "more likely than not" to ultimately realize the tax benefit so recorded. To the extent that it was concluded that some or all of the deferred tax asset would not be realized, an allowance would be recorded, with the offset being either to the current tax provision (if the tax effect of the timing difference was reported in earnings) or to other comprehensive income (if the tax effect had been reported there).

Deferred taxes will also be recorded in connection with unrealized gains recognized due to changes in the fair value of debt or equity investments. Deferred tax liabilities will be reported in the balance sheet, and the corresponding tax provision will be reported in the income statement (for fair value gains arising from holdings of securities in the trading portfolio) or in other comprehensive income (for value changes relative to available-for-sale investments).

Accounting for Investments in Debt Securities

Historically, accounting for marketable investments in debt securities was not well developed in the professional literature. In fact, the principal guidance concerning long-term investments in debt instruments was found in ARB 43, which stipulated that the amortized **cost method** be used, absent a substantial, other than temporary decline in value. However, in more recent years this topic has become highly controversial, largely due to the problems encountered by financial institutions, and to the popular belief that "gains trading" had widely been abused, permitting entities to manipulate reported earnings almost at will.

Culminating several years of research and discussion, the FASB issued SFAS 115 in mid-1993. This standard applies to both equity and debt instruments held as investments, and prescribes fair market value accounting for all except debt instruments being held to maturity. For that limited category, amortized historical cost is generally preserved as the measurement principle.

SFAS 115 requires that investments in debt securities be classified upon acquisition as belonging to one of three portfolios: trading, available-for-sale, or held-to-maturity. The first of these is characterized by frequent purchase and sale activities, with the general objective of realizing profits from short-term price movements, which in the case of investments in debt instruments will largely be the result of changes in market interest rates but which may also be affected by market perceptions of credit risk. Since intention is the prime criterion applied, even a paucity of sales activity does not necessarily mean that specific debt securities acquired during a period do not belong in the trading portfolio.

The held-to-maturity category is the most restrictive of the three; debt instruments can be so classified only if the reporting entity has the positive intent and the ability to hold the securities for that length of time. A mere intent to hold an investment for an indefinite period is not adequate to permit such a classification. On the other hand, a variety of isolated causes may necessitate transferring an investment in a debt security from the held-to-maturity category without calling into question the investor's general intention to hold other similarly classified investments to maturity. Among these are declines in the creditworthiness of a particular investment's issuer or a change in tax law or regulatory rules. On the other hand, sales of investments that were classified as held-to-maturity for other reasons will call into question the entity's assertions, both in the past and in the future, about its intentions regarding these and other similarly categorized securities. For this reason, transfers from or sales of held-to-maturity securities will be very rare indeed.

If it cannot be established that a particular debt security held as an investment will be held for trading or held to maturity, it must be classed as available-for-sale. Whatever the original classification of the investment, however, transfers among the three portfolios will be made as intentions change.

Accounting for debt securities that are held for trading and those that are available for sale is based on fair value. For balance sheet purposes, increases or decreases in value are reflected by adjustments to the asset account; such adjustments are to be determined on an individual security basis. Changes in the values of debt securities in the trading portfolio are recognized in earnings immediately, while most changes in the values of debt securities in the available-for-sale category are reported in other comprehensive income rather than being included in earnings. The only exception is for declines that are deemed to be other than temporary, in which case the loss is recognized currently in earnings. Once the investment is written down for a decline that is other than temporary, subsequent increases are reported only in changes to the contra equity account; these cannot be accounted for as "recoveries" of previous permanent declines. (See "Permanent Impairments of Investments Available for Sale" in the discussion of equity investments, above, for an example.)

There had been some confusion regarding the applicability of SFAS 115, which has been resolved by the issuance of FASB TB 94-1. The problem arose from the "grandfathering" provision of SFAS 114, permitting debt restructured prior to that standard's effective date to continue to be accounted for consistent with the provisions of SFAS 15, which SFAS 114 superseded. The concern was that this might have suggested that SFAS 115 could not be applied to restructured loans which qualified as debt securities. However, FASB TB 94-1 makes it clear that SFAS 115 applies to all loans which qualify as debt securities, and that the "grandfathering" provision would not be applicable in such circumstances. In other words, the provisions of SFAS 115 take precedence over those of SFAS 114, in situations where SFAS 115 applies.

Presentation in the Financial Statements

Trading securities must always be grouped with current assets in classified balance sheets, and held-to-maturity investments will be noncurrent (unless the maturity date is within one year). Available-for-sale securities may conceivably be classified as either current or noncurrent. Unlike under SFAS 12, classification as current or noncurrent no longer determines whether gains or losses are reported in earnings or are to be recognized at all. Instead, intent and ability to hold are the determinants of accounting and financial reporting treatment.

If declines in value are deemed to meet SFAS 115's definition of other than temporary, then these are to be included in earnings in the current period. However, subsequent recoveries cannot be recognized in earnings. If available-for-sale investments are written down for permanent impairments that later reverse, the recovery is accounted for as an increase in fair value to be reflected in other comprehensive income account on the balance sheet only. If held-to-maturity investments are similarly written down and later recover some or all of the lost value, the fair value increase will not be reported in the balance sheet at all, although disclosure will generally be made in the notes.

For purposes of reporting in the statement of cash flows, all purchases and sales of trading securities must be included in the operations section, while those of available-for-sale and held-to-maturity investments are to be shown as part of investing activities.

SFAS 115 requires specific disclosures of the components of a reporting entity's portfolios of investments. For available-for-sale securities and (separately) for **held-to-maturity securities**, classification by type of security is necessary; categories of issuers, such as US Treasury, other US agencies, state and municipal governmental units, foreign governmental units, corporations, mortgage-backed, and others are suggested. Aggregate fair values, gross unrealized holding gains, and gross unrealized holding losses must also be disclosed, by major security type, as of the date of each balance sheet being presented.

For the available-for-sale and held-to-maturity portfolios, information about contractual maturities must be presented as of the date of the latest balance sheet presented and must be grouped into at least four categories: within one year; one to five years; five to ten years; and, over ten years. Both fair values and amortized cost of debt securities in each maturity category must be presented.

For each income statement presented, proceeds from the sales of available-for-sale securities, and the gross realized gains and losses therefrom, also must be disclosed. Further, the basis upon which the gains or losses were determined, (e.g., average cost, specific identification, etc.) must be disclosed. In addition, the notes must identify gross gains or losses included in earnings resulting from transfers of securities from the available-for-sale to the trading portfolio, and the net change in unrealized gains or losses recognized by an adjustment of the contra equity account.

For sales or transfers from securities categorized as held-to-maturity, the amortized cost amounts, the related gains or losses realized or unrealized, and the circumstances surrounding the decision to sell or to reclassify the investment, are all to be disclosed in the notes to the financial statements for each period for which an income statement is being presented. There is, of course, a presumption that sales or transfers from the held-to-maturity portfolio will be rare occurrences.

Transfers of Debt Securities among Portfolios

Transfers of any given security between classifications is accounted for at fair market value. If the transfer is from the trading portfolio, there is no further income statement effect since the fair market value-based gains or losses have already been reported. If the transfer is to the trading portfolio, the unrealized gain or loss is recognized immediately; depending on whether the transfer is from the available-for-sale or the held-to-maturity category, such unrealized gain or loss would have been included in the accumulated other comprehensive income account on the balance sheet, after having been reported as an element of other comprehensive income, or would not have been reported at all prior to the transfer.

If the debt security is being transferred from held-to-maturity to the available-for-sale portfolio, the unrealized gain or loss, not previously reflected in the investment account, will be added to the appropriate accumulated other comprehensive income account at the date of transfer and reported in other comprehensive income. If a security is being transferred from available-for-sale to held-to-maturity, the unrealized holding gain or loss previously accrued will continue to be maintained in the accumulated other comprehensive income account, but now will be amortized to income over the period until maturity as an adjustment of yield, using the effective interest method. The fair value as of the date of transfer to the held-to-maturity classification, net of any subsequent amortization of the discrepancy between fair value and maturity or par value as of the transfer date, will be the "cost" for purposes of the disclosures required by SFAS 115.

Example of accounting for debt securities

Marcy Corporation purchases the following debt securities as investments in 2002:

Issue	*Face value*	*Price paid**
Dukane Chemical 8% due 2006	$200,000	$190,000
Forwall Pharmaceutical 9.90% due 2018	500,000	575,000
Luckystrike Mining 4% due 2004	100,000	65,000

* *Accrued interest is ignored in these amounts; the normal entries for interest accrual and receipt are assumed.*

Management has informed us that Marcy's objectives differed among the various investments; the Dukane bonds are considered to be suitable as a long-term investment, with the intention that they will be held until maturity. The Luckystrike bonds are a speculation; the significant discount from par value was seen as very attractive, despite the low coupon rate. Management believes the bonds were depressed because mining stocks and bonds have been out of favor, but believes the economic recovery will lead to a surge in market value, at which point the bonds will be sold for a quick profit. The Forwall Pharmaceutical bonds are deemed a good investment, but with a maturity date sixteen years in the future, management is unable to commit to holding these to maturity.

Based on the foregoing, the appropriate accounting for the three investments in bonds would be as follows:

Dukane Chemical 8% due 2006

Account for these as held-to-maturity; maintain at historical cost, with discount ($10,000) to be amortized over term to maturity (assumed to be four years, for an amortization of $2,500 per year).

Forwall Pharmaceutical 9.90% due 2018

Account for these as available-for-sale, since neither the held-for-trading nor held-to-maturity criteria apply. These should be reported at fair market value at each balance sheet date, with any unrealized gain or loss included in the additional/contra equity account, unless an "other than temporary" decline occurs.

Luckystrike Mining 4% due 2004

As an admitted speculation, these should be accounted for as part of the trading portfolio, and also reported at fair market value on the balance sheet. All adjustments to carrying value will be included in earnings each year, whether the fluctuations are temporary or permanent in nature.

Transfers between portfolio categories are to be accounted for at fair market value at the date of the transfer. Consider the following events.

1. Marcy management decides in 2003, when the Forwall bonds have a market (fair) value of $604,500, that the bonds will be disposed of in the short term, hopefully when the price hits $605,000. The bonds are presently carried on the books at $580,000, which was the fair value at the time the year-end 2002 financial statements were being prepared. Based on this description of the decision, the bonds should be transferred to the trading portfolio at a "cost" of $604,500. The entry to record this would be the following:

Investment in debt securities—held-for-trading	604,500	
Unrealized gain on holding debt securities as investment	5,000	
Investment in debt securities—available-for-sale		580,000
Gain on holding debt securities		29,500

The previously unrealized gain (reflected in the write-up of the investment from original cost, $575,000, to the fair market value at year-end 2002, $580,000) is now "realized" for financial reporting purposes, as is the further rise in value from $580,000 to $604,500 at the time the portfolio transfer takes place.

2. Assume that at year-end 2002 the investment in the Forwall bonds is still held, and the fair value has declined to $602,000. Management's intentions regarding this holding have not changed since the decision to transfer to held-for-sale. The year-end adjustment will be

Loss on holding debt securities	2,500	
Investment in debt securities—held-for-trading		2,500

The market decline is reflected in earnings in 2002, since the bonds are in the held-for-trading portfolio.

3. Now, assume that in 2003, management determines that a major investment in plant renewal and expansion will likely be necessary by the year 2019,

based on a detailed capital budget prepared. With this in mind, Marcy Corporation determines that the holding of Forwall Pharmaceutical bonds would be an excellent vehicle to provide for these future cash needs, and accordingly concludes to hold these to maturity. At the time this decision is made, the fair market value of the bonds is quoted at $603,000. The entry to record the transfer from held-for-trading to held-to-maturity is as follows:

Investment in debt securities—held-for-trading	1,000	
Gain on holding debt securities		1,000

The bonds are again transferred at fair market value, which in this case gives rise to a $1,000 recognized gain.

4. In 2003 Marcy management also made a decision about its investment in Dukane Chemical bonds. These bonds, which were originally designated as held-to-maturity, were accounted for at amortized historical cost. Assume the amortization in 2002 was $2,000 (because the bonds were not held for a full year), so that the book value of the investment at year-end 2002 was $192,000. In 2003, at a time when the value of these bonds was $198,000, management concluded that it was no longer certain that they would be held to maturity, and therefore transferred this holding to the available-for-sale portfolio. The entry to record this would be

Investment in debt securities—available-for-sale	198,000	
Unrealized gain on holding debt securities as investment		6,000
Investment in debt securities—held-to-maturity		192,000

The transfer is at fair market value, but since the bonds are being transferred into the available-for-sale category (for which unrealized gains and losses are recorded in an additional or contra equity account), the gain at this date, $6,000, is not recognized in earnings, but rather will be reported in other comprehensive income.

5. In 2004, for the same reason management determined to hold the Forwall Pharmaceuticals bonds to maturity, it also reverses its prior decision regarding the Dukane Chemical bond holding. It now professes an intention to hold these until their maturity, in 2006. At the date this decision is made, the Dukane bonds are quoted at $195,000. Assume that the fair market value at year-end 2003 had been $198,000, so no adjustment was needed at that time to the carrying value of the investment. Again the transfer will be recorded at fair market value.

Investment in debt securities—held-to-maturity	195,000	
Unrealized gain on holding debt securities as investment	3,000	
Investment in debt securities—available-for-sale		198,000

The unrealized gain previously recognized in an equity account is partially eliminated, since fair value at the date of this transfer is less than the previously recorded amount. The change in this equity account must be reported as other comprehensive income for the period in which this portfolio reclassification occurs. The remaining balance in the additional/contra equity account (whether a net debit or credit) is accounted for as **additional** premium or discount, and is amortized over the remaining term to maturity. GAAP mandates that the effective yield method be used, but for this example, assume that the discount will be amortized over the remaining two years on the straight-line basis (if this difference from the effective yield method is not material, it is an acceptable practice). Thus, the actual discount as measured by the spread between the new carrying value, $195,000, and face value to be received at maturity, $200,000, **plus the additional discount** measured by the unrealized gain being reported currently in the equity section of $3,000, gives a total discount amounting to $8,000 to be amortized over the remaining two years. This $8,000, when added to the $2,000 discount amortized in 2003 (when the bonds were in the original held-to-maturity portfolio), equals $10,000, which is the discount between the face value, $200,000 and the price paid by Marcy Corporation ($190,000).

Implications of Accounting for Investments on Reporting of Comprehensive Income

Under the provisions of SFAS 130, there is expanded reporting of the changes in items (other than investments by or distributions to owners) that are reported in the equity section of the balance sheet. Among these items are unrealized gains or losses on securities held in the available-for-sale portfolio, and accordingly **changes** in these gains or losses must be reported in the statement of comprehensive income or via the other allowable reporting mechanisms described in Chapter 3, Statements of Income and Comprehensive Income. These changes may be reported net of tax or gross, with the tax effect separately presented within other comprehensive income.

The major complicating factor arising from reporting changes in the unrealized gains or losses of available-for-sale securities derives from the "recycling" of gains or losses when the underlying securities are later sold or transferred into the trading portfolio; either of these necessitate recognition of the entire gain or loss in earnings, including any unrealized gain or loss that might have previously been reported in other comprehensive income (but not in earnings). To avoid "double counting" the gain or loss, the amount of gain or loss previously reported in other comprehensive income must be reversed simultaneously with the recognition in earnings.

To illustrate the "recycling" problem, consider an investment by Zenobia Co. in $500,000 face amount of Vaught Corp. bonds due July 1, 2012, carrying coupons of 8%. The purchase, for a total of $530,000, occurs on July 1, 2002, and the bonds are deemed available for sale, as defined by SFAS 115. Per that standard, periodic interest income must be computed by the effective yield method based on the acquisition cost (i.e., the face value net of any premium or discount), but the difference, if any, between amortized cost and fair value as of the balance sheet date must be reported as a contra or additional equity account, with changes being taken into other comprehensive income for the period.

The yield to maturity on the Zenobia bonds is approximately 7.15%; for simplicity, the premium will be amortized straight-line ($1,500 per semiannual interest payment period) in this example, rather than by the effective yield method as is actually required.

Assume that the bonds have a fair value of $522,000 as of year-end 2002 and $527,000 as of year-end 2003. As of March 31, 2004, the value of the bonds is $528,000, at which time they are in fact sold.

Given the foregoing, as of December 31, 2002, the amortized cost basis of the investment would be $530,000 – $1,500 = $528,500. Since the fair value at that date is $522,000, an unrealized loss of $528,500 – $522,000 = $6,500 must be recorded in other comprehensive income, before any tax effects (which will be ignored here, again for simplicity). Interest income for the half-year ended December 31, 2000, was $20,000 – $1,500 = $18,500 under the simplifying assumption of straight-line amortization, and this would be included in earnings.

At year-end 2003, the bonds have an amortized cost basis of $528,500 – $3,000 = $525,500 vs. a fair value of $527,000. Interest income for the year ended December 31, 2003, included in earnings, was $40,000 – $3,000 = $37,000. A **positive** adjustment (i.e., income) of $8,000 must be reported in other comprehensive income for 2003 in order to carry the bonds at fair value as of the year-end.

For the three-month period ended March 31, 2004, further premium amortization of $750 must be recorded (along with an interest accrual), which will reduce the bond's amortized cost basis to $525,500 – $750 = $524,750 as of the date of the sale, which is made at the market value of $528,000. For purposes of reporting results of operations for the quarter ended March 31, 2004, a positive other comprehensive income adjustment of $1,750 must be reflected—this is necessary to bring the carrying value of the bonds up to their fair value as of that date. However, since the bonds are sold and a realized gain of $3,250 is to be reported in earnings, a "reclassification adjustment" of the same amount must be included as a **negative** (i.e., expense) item in other comprehensive income for that period, which will thus cause the **net** other comprehensive income item pertaining to the bonds held in the available-for-sale portfolio to be a **negative** $1,500 for the period ended March 31, 2004.

The foregoing can be summarized as shown in the following table (it is assumed that the 2004 transaction is reported at year-end):

Zenobia Co.
Selected Portions of Combined Statements of Earnings and Comprehensive Income
(ignoring tax effects)
December 31, 2002, 2003, and 2004

December 31, 2002

	$ --
Other income and expense:	
Interest income (net of premium amortization, $1,500)	18,500
	--
Net earnings	--
Other comprehensive income:	
Unrealized loss on bonds available for sale	(6,500)
Total other comprehensive income	--
Comprehensive income	$ --

December 31, 2003

	$ --
Other income and expense:	
Interest income (net of premium amortization, $3,000)	37,000
	--
Net earnings	--
Other comprehensive income:	
Unrealized gain on bonds available for sale	8,000
Total other comprehensive income	--
Comprehensive income	$ --

December 31, 2004

		$ --
Other income and expense:		
Interest income (net of premium amortization, $750)		9,250
Gain on sale of bonds		3,250
		--
Net earnings		--
Other comprehensive income:		
Unrealized loss on bonds available for sale	1,750	
Less: Reclassification adjustment for gain		
realized on sale	(3,250)	(1,500)
Total other comprehensive income		--
Comprehensive income		$ --

Disclosure of Fair Value Information

The basic disclosure requirements pertaining to investments in debt and marketable equity securities are set forth in SFAS 107 and 115. SFAS 133 contains certain amendments to SFAS 107, primarily with regard to disclosures of concentrations of credit risk and the optional disclosures that are encouraged concerning market risk. It should be noted that, since under SFAS 115 both trading and available-for-sale investments are marked to fair value, the impact of SFAS 107 is largely felt on investments in the held-to-maturity portfolio; even though these are maintained at amortized historical cost, per SFAS 107 fair value information must also be presented, and this is typically accomplished via the informative notes to the financial statements, although it can also be presented on the face of the financials, parenthetically. (Per SFAS 126, nonpublic entities having under $100 million in total assets are exempted from these extended disclosure requirements, however.)

The Equity Method of Accounting for Investments

The equity method, sometimes referred to as "one-line consolidation," permits an entity (investor) owning a percentage of the common stock of another entity (investee) to incorporate its pro rata share of the investee's operating results into its earnings. However, rather than include its share of each component (e.g., sales, cost of sales, operating expenses, etc.) in its financial statements, the **investor** shall only include its share of the investee's **net** income as a separate line item in its income. Note that there are exceptions to this one-line rule. The investor's share of **investee** extraordinary items and prior period adjustments retain their identities in the investor's income and retained earnings statements and are separately reported if material in relation to the investor's income. It should be noted that the final bottom-line impact on the investor's financial statements is **identical** whether the equity method or full consolidation is employed; only the amount of detail presented within the statements will differ.

The equity method is generally **not** a substitute for consolidation; it is employed where the investor has **significant influence** over the operations of the investee but lacks control. In general, significant influence is inferred when the investor owns between 20% and 50% of the investee's voting common stock. Any ownership percentage over 50% presumably gives the investor actual control, making full consolidation of financial statements necessary. The 20% threshold stipulated in APB 18 is not absolute; circumstances may suggest that significant influence exists even though the investor's level of ownership is less than 20%, or that it is absent despite a level of ownership above 20%. In considering whether significant influence exists, FASB Interpretation 35 identifies the following factors: (1) opposition by the investee, (2) agreements under which the investor surrenders shareholder rights, (3) majority ownership by a small group of shareholders, (4) inability to obtain desired information from the investee, (5) inability to obtain representation on investee board of directors, etc. Whether sufficient contrary evidence exists to negate the presumption of significant influence is a matter of judgment. Judgment requires a careful evaluation of all pertinent facts and circumstances, over an extended period of time in some cases.

Prior to the issuance of SFAS 94, some investors used the equity method in those rare instances in which the investor owned over 50% of the investee's voting common shares but consolidated statements were deemed to be inappropriate (usually because consolidated statements would mask important differences in the financial or operating characteristics of the investor-parent and investee-subsidiary). However, SFAS 94 eliminated this once popular "nonhomogeneity" justification for nonconsolidation. This leaves only temporary control, noncontrol, and foreign exchange restrictions and related reasons as justification for not consolidating majority-owned subsidiaries. The equity method continues to be used in accounting for nonconsolidated majority-owned subsidiaries (see Chapter 11).

Complexities in the use of the equity method arise in two areas. First, the cost of the investment to the investor might not be equal to the fair value of the investor's share of investee net assets; this is analogous to the existence of **goodwill** in a purchase business combination. Or the fair value of the investor's share of the investee's net assets may not be equal to the book value thereof; this situation is analogous to the purchase cost allocation problem in consolidations. Since the ultimate income statement result from the use of equity method accounting must generally be the same as full consolidation, an adjustment must be made for each of these **differentials**.

The second major complexity relates to interperiod income tax allocation. The equity method causes the investor to reflect current earnings based on the investee's operating results; however, for income tax purposes the investor reports only dividends received and gains or losses on disposal of the investment. Thus, temporary differences result, and SFAS 109 provides guidance as to the appropriate method of computing the deferred tax effects of these differences.

In the absence of these complicating factors, the use of the equity method by the investor is straightforward: the original cost of the investment is increased by the investor's share of the investee's earnings and is decreased by its share of investee losses and by dividends received. The basic procedure is illustrated below.

Example of a simple case ignoring deferred taxes

Assume the following information. On January 2, 2002, R Corporation (the investor) acquired 40% of E Company's (the investee) voting common stock on the open market for $100,000. Unless demonstrated otherwise, it is assumed that R Corporation can exercise significant influence over E Company's operating and financing policies. On January 2, E's stockholders' equity consists of the following accounts:

Common stock, par $1, 100,000 shares authorized, 50,000 shares issued and outstanding	$ 50,000
Additional paid-in capital	150,000
Retained earnings	50,000
Total stockholders' equity	$250,000

Note that the cost of E Company common stock was equal to 40% of the book value of E's net assets. Assume also that there is no difference between the book value and the fair value of E Company's assets and liabilities. Accordingly, the balance in the investment account in R's records represents exactly 40% of E's stockholders' equity (net assets). Assume further that E Company reported a 2002 net income of $30,000 and paid cash dividends of $10,000. Its stockholders' equity at year-end would be as follows:

Common stock, par $1, 100,000 shares authorized, 50,000	
shares issued and outstanding	$ 50,000
Additional paid-in capital	150,000
Retained earnings	70,000
Total stockholders' equity	$270,000

R Corporation would record its share of the increase in E Company's net assets during 2002 as follows:

Investment in E Company	12,000	
Equity in E income		12,000
($30,000 x 40%)		
Cash	4,000	
Investment in E Company		4,000
($10,000 x 40%)		

When R's balance sheet is prepared at December 31, 2002, the balance reported in the investment account would be $108,000 ($100,000 + $12,000 – $4,000). This amount represents 40% of the book value of E's net assets at the end of the year (40% x $270,000). Note also that the equity in E income is reported as one amount on R's income statement under the caption "Other income and expense."

In computing the deferred tax effects of income recognized by the equity method, the investor must make an assumption regarding the means by which the **undistributed earnings of the investee** will be realized by the investor. The earnings can be realized either through later dividend receipts or by disposition of the investment at a gain. The former assumption would result in taxes at the investor's marginal tax rate on ordinary income (net of the 80% dividends received deduction permitted by the Internal Revenue Code for intercorporate investments of less than 80% but at least 20%; a lower deduction of 70% applies if ownership is below 20%). The latter option would be treated as a capital gain, which is currently taxed at the full corporate tax rate, since the preferential capital gain rate was eliminated by the 1986 Tax Reform.

Example of a simple case including deferred taxes

Assume the same information as in the example above. In addition, assume that R Corporation has a combined (federal, state, and local) marginal tax rate of 34% on ordinary income and that it anticipates realization of E Company earnings through future dividend receipts. R Corporation's entries at year-end 2002 will be as follows:

1.	Investment in E Company	12,000	
	Equity in E income		12,000
2.	Income tax expense	816	
	Deferred taxes		816

Taxable portion of investee earnings to be received in the future as dividends times marginal tax rate: $12,000 x 20% x 34% = $816

3.	Cash	4,000	
	Investment in E Company		4,000
4.	Deferred taxes	272	
	Taxes payable—current		272

Fraction of investee earnings currently taxed ($4,000/$12,000) x $816 = $272

SFAS 109 is based upon an entirely different concept (the "asset and liability approach") than was its predecessor, APB 11. The deferred tax liability is originally computed with reference to the **projected** tax effect of the "temporary difference reversal." It may be subsequently adjusted for a variety of reasons, including changed tax rates and altered management expectations (see Chapter 15, Income Taxes, for a complete discussion).

Notwithstanding SFAS 109's requirement that deferred taxes be adjusted for changed expectations at each subsequent balance sheet date, the actual tax effect of the temporary difference reversal may still differ from the deferred tax provided. This difference may occur because the actual tax effect is a function of the entity's other current items of income and expense in the year of reversal (while SFAS 109 requires the use of a projected effective tax rate, actual rates may differ). It may also result from a realization of the investee's earnings in a manner other than anticipated (assuming that tax rates on "ordinary" income differ from those on capital gains).

To illustrate this last point, assume that in 2002, before any further earnings or dividends are reported by the investee, the investor sells the entire investment for $115,000. The tax impact is

Selling price	$115,000
Less cost	100,000
Gain	$ 15,000
Capital gain rate (marginal corporate rate)	x 34%
Tax liability	$ 5,100

The entries to record the sale, the tax thereon, and the amortization of previously provided deferred taxes on the undistributed 2002 earnings are as follows:

1.	Cash	115,000	
	Investment in E Company		108,000
	Gain on sale of investment		7,000
2.	Income tax expense	4,556	
	Deferred tax liability	544	
	Taxes payable—current		5,100

The income tax expense of $4,556 is the sum of two factors: (1) the capital gains rate of 34% applied to the actual **book** gain realized ($115,000 selling price less $108,000 carrying value), for a tax of $2,380, and (2) the difference between the capital gains tax rate (34%) and the effective rate on dividend income (20% x 34% = 6.8%) on the undistributed 2002 earnings of E Company previously recognized as ordinary income by R Corporation [$8,000 x (34% − 6.8%) = $2,176].

Note that if the realization through a sale of the investment had been anticipated at the time the 2002 balance sheet was being prepared, the deferred tax liability account would have been adjusted (possibly to reflect the entire $5,100 amount of the ultimate obligation), with the offset included in 2002's ordinary tax expense. The above example explicitly assumes that the sale of the investment was **not** anticipated prior to 2003.

Accounting for a differential between cost and book value. The simple examples presented thus far avoided the major complexity of equity method accounting, the allocation of the **differential** between the cost to the investor and the investor's share in the net equity (net assets at book value) of the investee. Since the net impact of equity method accounting must equal that of full consolidation accounting, this differential must be analyzed into the following components and accounted for accordingly:

1. The difference between the book and fair values of the investee's net assets at the date the investment is made
2. The remaining difference between the fair value of the net assets and the cost of the investment, which is generally attributable to goodwill

According to APB 18, the difference between the book and fair value of the net assets should be identified and allocated to specific asset categories. These differences are then amortized to the income from investee account as appropriate, for example, over the economic lives of fixed assets whose fair values exceeded book values. The difference between fair value and cost will be treated like goodwill and accounted for consistent with the recently promulgated standard superseding APB 17. Under this new standard, an excess of cost over the fair value of identifiable net assets is no longer subject to amortization, but rather is to be tested for possible impairment on an annual basis. In cases where the fair value of the identifiable net assets exceeds the cost of the investment (popularly referred to as creating negative goodwill) is to be allocated to most noncurrent assets (described in Chapter 11), with any remainder being reflected in earnings as an extraordinary gain. Negative goodwill is very unlikely to arise in equity investment situations, because it implies a bargain purchase which normally would result from the acquisition of a majority holding rather than a minority position in an investee, but it is nonetheless possible that this might occur.

In the following examples, the accounting for equity method investments involving both positive goodwill and negative goodwill will be presented.

Example of complex case ignoring deferred taxes—goodwill

Assume again that R Corporation acquired 40% of E Company's shares on January 2, 2002, but that the price paid was $140,000. E Company's assets and liabilities at that date had the following book and fair values:

	Book values	Fair values
Cash	$ 10,000	$ 10,000
Accounts receivable (net)	40,000	40,000
Inventories (FIFO cost)	80,000	90,000
Land	50,000	40,000
Plant and equipment (net of accumulated depreciation)	140,000	220,000
Total assets	$320,000	$400,000
Liabilities	$ (70,000)	$ (70,000)
Net assets (stockholders' equity)	$250,000	$330,000

The first order of business is the calculation of the differential, as follows:

R's cost for 40% of E's common	$140,000
Book value of 40% of E's net assets ($250,000 x 40%)	(100,000)
Total differential	$ 40,000

Next, the $40,000 is allocated to those individual assets and liabilities for which fair value differs from book value. In the example, the differential is allocated to inventories, land, and plant and equipment, as follows:

Item	*Book value*	*Fair value*	*Difference debit (credit)*	*40% of difference debit (credit)*
Inventories	$ 80,000	$ 90,000	$10,000	$ 4,000
Land	50,000	40,000	(10,000)	(4,000)
Plant and equipment	140,000	220,000	80,000	32,000
Differential allocated				$32,000

The difference between the allocated differential of $32,000 and the total differential of $40,000 is goodwill of $8,000. Goodwill, as shown by the following computation, represents the excess of the cost of the investment over the fair value of the net assets acquired.

R's cost for 40% of E's common	$140,000
40% of the fair value of E's net assets ($330,000 x 40%)	(132,000)
Excess of cost over fair value (goodwill)	$ 8,000

It is important to note that the allocation of the differential is not recorded formally by either R Corporation or E Company. Furthermore, R does not remove the differential from the investment account and allocate it to the respective assets, since the use of the equity method (one-line consolidation) does not involve the recording of individual assets and liabilities. R leaves the differential of $40,000 in the investment account, as a part of the balance of $140,000 at January 2, 2002. Accordingly, information pertaining to the allocation of the differential is maintained by the investor, but this information is outside the formal accounting system, which is comprised of journal entries and account balances.

After the differential has been allocated, the amortization pattern is developed. To develop the pattern in this example, assume that E's plant and equipment have ten years of useful life remaining and that E depreciates its fixed assets on a straight-line basis. Under recently promulgated standards, goodwill is no longer subject to amortization, but must be tested annually for impairment. R would prepare the following amortization schedule:

Item	*Differential debit (credit)*	*Useful life*	*Amortization*		
			2002	*2003*	*2004*
Inventories (FIFO)	$ 4,000	Sold in 2002	$4,000	$ --	$ --
Land	(4,000)	Indefinite	--	--	--
Plant and equipment (net)	32,000	10 years	3,200	3,200	3,200
Goodwill	8,000	Not relevant	--	--	--
Totals	$40,000		$7,200	$3,200	$3,200

Note that the entire differential allocated to inventories is amortized in 2002 because the cost flow assumption used by E is FIFO. If E had been using LIFO instead of FIFO, no amortization would take place until E sold some of the inventory that existed at January 2, 2002. Since this sale could be delayed for many years under LIFO, the differential allocated to LIFO inventories would not be amortized until E sold more inventory than it manufactured/purchased. Note, also, that the differential (in this example, a negative valuation amount) allocated to E's land is not amortized, because land is not a depreciable asset. In a complete break with past practice, the goodwill component of the differential will not be amortized, but must be tested for impairment annually, as described further below.

The **amortization** of the differential is recorded formally in the accounting system of R Corporation. Recording the amortization adjusts the equity in E's income that R recorded based upon E's income statement. E's income must be adjusted because it is based upon E's book values, not upon the cost that R incurred to acquire E. R would make the following entries in 2002, assuming that E reported net income of $30,000 and paid cash dividends of $10,000:

1.	Investment in E Company	12,000	
	Equity in E income		12,000
	$30,000 x 40%		
2.	Equity in E income (amortization of differential)	7,200	
	Investment in E Company		7,200
3.	Cash	4,000	
	Investment in E Company		4,000
	$10,000 x 40%		

The balance in the investment account on R's records at the end of 2002 is $140,800 [$140,000 + $12,000 − ($7,200 + $4,000)], and E's stockholders' equity, as shown previously, is $270,000. The investment account balance of $140,800 is not equal to 40% of $270,000. However, this difference can easily be explained, as follows:

Balance in investment account at December 31, 2002		$140,800
40% of E's net assets at December 31, 2002		108,000
Difference at December 31, 2002		$ 32,800
Differential at January 2, 2002	$40,000	
Differential amortized during 2002	(7,200)	
Unamortized differential at December 31, 2002		$ 32,800

With the passing years, the balance in the investment account approaches the amount representing 40% of the book value of E's net assets, as the differential is amortized to equity method income or loss. However, since a part of the differential was allocated to land, which is not depreciating, and to goodwill, which is no longer subject to amortization, the carrying value will most likely never equal the equity in the investee's net assets. However, if the investee disposes of the land, the investor must also eliminate the associated portion of the differential. If the carrying value of the investment becomes impaired, as described below, the goodwill portion of the differential may also be eliminated. Thus, under certain conditions the investor's carrying value may subsequently be adjusted to equal the underlying net asset value, although this outcome is relatively unlikely to occur.

To illustrate how the sale of land would affect equity method procedures, assume that E sold the land in the year 2008 for $80,000. Since E's cost for the land was $50,000, it would report a gain of $30,000, of which $12,000 ($30,000 x 40%) would be recorded by R, when it records its 40% share of E's reported net income, ignoring income taxes. However, from R's viewpoint, the gain on sale of land should have been $40,000 ($80,000 – $40,000) because the cost of the land from R's perspective was $40,000 at January 2, 2002 (since the allocated fair value of the land was below its book value). Therefore, in addition to the $12,000 share of the gain recorded above, R should record an additional $4,000 gain [($40,000 – $30,000) x 40%] by debiting the investment account and crediting the equity in E's income account. This $4,000 debit to the investment account will negate the $4,000 differential allocated to land on January 2, 2002, since the original differential was a credit (the fair market value of the land was $10,000 less than its book value).

Adjustments to the goodwill portion of the differential are somewhat more complex. APB 18 requires that that difference between cost and underlying book value be accounted for as if the investee were a consolidated subsidiary. An investor is therefore required to complete a purchase price allocation, as illustrated above, and this may result in the identification of part of the difference as goodwill (referred to as "equity method goodwill"). Under new goodwill accounting standards, this is no longer to be amortized, but rather to be evaluated for impairment. However, FASB decided that equity method investments should continue to be tested for impairment in accordance with APB 18 (i.e., the equity investment as a whole, not the underlying net assets, should be tested for impairment) and that equity method goodwill will not be treated as being separable from the related investment. Accordingly, goodwill should not be tested for impairment in accordance with the new goodwill and intangible assets standard.

To illustrate, consider the following assumed facts (ignoring income taxes). E Company's reported earnings in 2003 and loss in 2004 are $15,000 and ($12,000), respectively. No dividends are paid by E after 2002. R's carrying value, before considering possible impairment in value, as of year end 2004 is computed as follows:

Carrying value of investment, December 31, 2002	$140,800
R's interest in E's 2003 net income	6,000
Amortization of carrying value	(3,200)
Carrying value, December 31, 2003	143,600
R's interest in E's 2004 net loss	(4,800)
Amortization of carrying value	(3,200)
Carrying value, December 31, 2004, before considering additional charge for impairment	$135,600

If, at December 31, 2004, R determines that the fair value of its investment in E has declined to $130,000, and this decline in value is other than temporary in nature, then it must, per APB 18, recognize a further loss amounting to $5,600 for the year. Notice that this fair value decline is assessed with reference to the fair (presumably, but not necessarily, market) value of the investment in E Company. It would not be determined with specific reference to the value of E's business operations, as goodwill is assessed in connection with purchase business combinations accounted for by the presentation of consolidated financial statements, although the permanent decline in value of the investment would likely be related to the value of E's operations.

While the standard is silent on this issue, it is reasonable that any recognized decline in value be assigned first to the implicit goodwill component of the investment account. In this example, since the value decline, $5,600, is less than the goodwill component of the differential, it will be fully absorbed, and future periods' amortization of the differential assigned to other assets will not be affected. On the other hand, if the value decline had exceeded $8,000, the excess would logically have been allocated to the underlying nonmonetary assets of the investee, such that the remaining differential previously identified with plant and equipment might have been reduced or eliminated, thereby altering future amortization.

Example of complex case including deferred taxes—goodwill

The impact of interperiod income tax allocation in the foregoing example is similar to that demonstrated earlier in the simplified example. Under prior GAAP, a complication arose with regard to the portion of the differential allocated to goodwill, since equity method goodwill is not amortizable for tax purposes and, therefore, represented a permanent (not a temporary) difference that would not give rise to deferred taxes. Under the new goodwill rules, since amortization will no longer be applied to equity method goodwill, there will be no book-tax difference and hence no deferred tax issue to be addressed. The other components of the differential in the foregoing example are all temporary differences, with normal deferred tax implications.

The entries recorded by R Corporation in 2002 would be

1.	Investment in E Company	12,000	
	Equity in E income		12,000
2.	Income tax expense	816	
	Deferred tax liability		816
	$12,000 x 20% x 34%		
3.	Cash	4,000	
	Investment in E Company		4,000
4.	Deferred tax liability	272	
	Taxes payable—current		272
	$4,000/$12,000 x $816		
5.	Equity in E income	7,200	
	Investment in E Company		7,200
6.	Deferred tax liability	490	
	Income tax expense		490
	$7,200 x 20% x 34%		

Example of complex case ignoring deferred taxes—negative goodwill

The facts in this example are similar to the previous case, but in this instance the price paid by the investor, Lucky Corp., is less than the proportionate share of the investee's net assets, at fair value. This is analogous to negative goodwill in a purchase business combination, and the accounting for the negative differential between cost and fair value should follow that mandated for bargain purchases under the business combinations and goodwill standards recently promulgated by FASB.

Assume that Lucky Corp. acquired 40% of Compliant Company's shares on January 2, 2002, for a cash payment of $120,000. Compliant Company's assets and liabilities at that date had the following book and fair values:

	Book values	Fair values
Cash	$ 10,000	$ 10,000
Accounts receivable (net)	40,000	40,000
Inventories (FIFO cost)	80,000	90,000
Land	50,000	40,000
Plant and equipment (net of accumulated depreciation)	140,000	220,000
Total assets	$320,000	$400,000
Liabilities	$ (70,000)	$ (70,000)
Net assets (stockholders' equity)	$250,000	$330,000

The first step is to compute the differential, which is as follows:

Lucky's cost for 40% of Compliant's common	$120,000
Book value of 40% of E's net assets ($250,000 x 40%)	(100,000)
Total differential	$ 20,000

Next, the $20,000 is allocated, on a preliminary basis, to those individual assets and liabilities for which fair value differs from book value. In the example, the differential is initially allocated to inventories, land, and plant and equipment, as follows:

Item	Book value	Fair value	Difference debit (credit)	40% of difference debit (credit)
Inventories	$ 80,000	$ 90,000	$10,000	$ 4,000
Land	50,000	40,000	(10,000)	(4,000)
Plant and equipment	140,000	220,000	80,000	32,000
Differential allocated				$32,000

The difference between the allocated differential of $32,000 and the net differential of $20,000 is negative goodwill of $12,000. Negative goodwill, as shown by the following computation, represents the excess of the fair value of the net assets acquired over the cost of the investment.

Lucky's cost for 40% of Compliant's common	$120,000
40% of the fair value of Compliant's net assets ($330,000 x 40%)	(132,000)
Excess of fair value over cost (negative goodwill)	$ 12,000

Although the topic is not addressed explicitly by the newly promulgated standard on goodwill accounting, the investor's handling of negative goodwill should track how this would be dealt with by a parent company preparing consolidated financial statements following a "bargain purchase" business combination. Under GAAP, the amount preliminarily identified as negative goodwill is to be offset, on a pro rata basis, against all of the acquired assets other than cash and cash equivalents, trade receivables, inventory, financial instruments that are required by U.S. generally accepted accounting principles (GAAP) to be carried on the balance sheet at fair value, assets to be disposed of by sale, and deferred tax assets. In the present example, the assets qualifying for having negative goodwill allocated against their respective fair values are land and plant and equipment. The negative goodwill, $12,000, will therefore be assigned as follows:

Item	Preliminary value assignment	Differential assigned	Proportion of qualified costs	Allocation of negative goodwill	Net differential
Inventories	$ 36,000	$ 4,000	0.0%	0	4,000
Land	16,000	(4,000)	15.4%	(1,848)	(5,848)
Plant and equipment	88,000	32,000	84.6%	(10,152)	21,848
Total	$140,000	$32,000	100.0%	(12,000)	$20,000

It will be noted in the above table that inventories are not qualified to be assigned a portion of the negative goodwill. Both land and plant and equipment, however, will be allocated some of the amount identified, on a preliminary basis, as negative goodwill, notwithstanding that land has already been written down because its fair value was lower than the investee's carrying (i.e., book) value for that asset. The net differential, after offsetting of negative goodwill, is $20,000, which is the excess of the purchase cost, $120,000, over the book value of the underlying net assets of Compliant Company at the date of the transaction.

In this example, the net differential assigned to plant and equipment, $21,848, will be amortized over the next ten years (the average life of that asset group), for a charge of $2,185 per year against the earnings from the investee. Land, of course, is not depreciable and thus the total differential, a negative $5,848, will remain until the investee disposes of the land. The amount assigned to inventory, $4,000, will be taken into earnings in 2003 because of the FIFO costing convention.

Since the entire amount preliminarily identified as negative goodwill has been successfully offset against qualifying assets, no amount remains to be recognized as an extraordinary gain in 2002, the year in which the investment is made. In the (extremely unlikely) event that the bargain purchase was of such a magnitude that even after offsetting the preliminary amount determined to be negative goodwill there remained an unabsorbed balance, that would have to be reported by Lucky Corp. as an extraordinary gain in 2002, in order to conform to the requirements of the new goodwill standard.

Item	Differential debit (credit)	Useful life	Amortization 2002	2003	2004
Inventories (FIFO)	$ 4,000	Sold in 2002	$4,000	$ --	$ --
Land	(5,848)	Indefinite	--	--	--
Plant and equipment (net)	21,848	10 years	2,185	2,185	2,185
Totals	$20,000		$6,185	$2,185	$2,185

Again, the entire differential allocated to inventories is amortized in 2002 because the cost flow assumption used by Compliant is FIFO. If Compliant had been using LIFO instead of FIFO, no amortization would take place until Compliant sold some of the inventory that existed at January 2, 2002. Since this sale could be delayed for many years under LIFO, the differential allocated to LIFO inventories would not be amortized until Compliant sold more inventory than it manufactured/purchased. Note, also, that the differential allocated to Compliant's land is not amortized, because land is not a depreciable asset.

The amortization of the differential is recorded formally in the accounting system of Lucky Corp. Recording the amortization adjusts the equity in Compliant's income that Lucky Corp. recorded based upon Compliant's income statement. Compliant's income must be adjusted because it is based upon Compliant's book values, not upon the cost that Lucky Corp. incurred to acquire Compliant. Lucky Corp. would make the following entries in 2002, assuming that Compliant reported net income of $30,000 and paid cash dividends of $10,000:

1.	Investment in Compliant Company	12,000	
	Equity in Compliant Company's income		12,000
	$30,000 x 40%		
2.	Equity in Compliant Company's income (amortization of differential)	6,185	
	Investment in Compliant Company		6,185
3.	Cash	4,000	
	Investment in Compliant Company		4,000
	$10,000 x 40%		

The balance in the investment account on Lucky's records at the end of 2002 is $121,815 [$120,000 + $12,000 − ($6,185 + $4,000)], and Compliant's stockholders' equity, as shown previously, is $270,000. The investment account balance of $121,815 is not equal to 40% of $270,000. However, this difference can easily be explained, as follows:

Balance in investment account at December 31, 2002	$121,815
40% of E's net assets at December 31, 2002	108,000
Difference at December 31, 2002	$ 13,815
Differential at January 2, 2002	$20,000
Differential amortized during 2002	(6,185)
Unamortized differential at December 31, 2002	$ 13,815

As with the case of positive equity method goodwill, illustrated in the previous example, as the years pass the balance in the investment account will approach that representing 40% of the book value of E's net assets. In this case, the adjustment to land (consisting of both a fair value adjustment and an allocation of negative goodwill) will persist until the land is disposed of. This will be handled as in the prior (positive goodwill) illustration, above.

Example of complex case including deferred taxes—negative goodwill

The impact of interperiod income tax allocation in the foregoing example is similar to that demonstrated earlier in the simplified example.

The entries recorded by Lucky Corp. in 2002 would be

1.	Investment in Compliant Company	12,000	
	Equity in Compliant income		12,000
2.	Income tax expense	816	
	Deferred tax liability		816
	$12,000 x 20% x 34%		
3.	Cash	4,000	
	Investment in Compliant Company		4,000
4.	Deferred tax liability	272	
	Taxes payable--current		272
	$4,000/$12,000 x $816		

5.	Equity in Compliant income	6,185	
	Investment in Compliant Company		6,185
6.	Deferred tax liability	421	
	Income tax expense		421
	$6,185 x 20% x 34%		

Investor share of investee losses in excess of the carrying value of investment. As demonstrated in the foregoing paragraphs, the carrying value of an investment which is accounted for by the equity method is increased by the investor's share of investee earnings and reduced by its share of investee losses and by dividends received from the investee. Sometimes the losses are so large that the carrying value is reduced to zero, and this raises the question of whether the investment account should be allowed to "go negative," or whether losses in excess of the investment account should be recognized in some other manner.

In general, an equity method investment would not be permitted to have a negative (i.e., credit) balance, since this would imply that it represented a liability. In the case of normal corporate investments, the investor would enjoy limited liability and would not be held liable to the investee's creditors should, for instance, the investee become insolvent. For this reason, excess losses of the investee would not be reflected in the financial statements of the investor. The practice is to discontinue application of the equity method when the investment account reaches a zero balance, with adequate disclosure being made of the fact that further investee losses are not being reflected in the investor's earnings. If the investee later returns to profitability, the investor should ignore its share of earnings until the previously ignored losses have been fully offset; thereafter, normal application of the equity method can be resumed.

There are, however, limited circumstances in which further investee losses would be reflected. Often the investor has guaranteed or otherwise committed to indemnify creditors or other investors in the investee entity for losses incurred, or to fund continuing operations of the investee. Having placed itself at risk in the case of the investee's insolvency, continued application of the equity method is deemed to be appropriate, since the net credit balance in the investment account (reportable as a liability entitled "losses in excess of investment made in investee") would indeed represent an obligation of the investor.

The other situation in which investee losses in excess of the investor's actual investment in common stock of the investee are to be reflected is somewhat more complicated. When the investor has investments consisting of both common stock holdings accounted for under APB 18, and other investments in or loans to the investee, such as in its preference shares (including mandatorily redeemable preferred stock) or debt obligations of the investee, there will not only be further application of APB 18, but also possible interaction between the provisions of APB 18 and those of SFAS 114 and/or SFAS 115. In addition, there will be the question of the appropriate proportion of the investee's loss to be recognized by the investor—that is, should the investor's share of further investee losses be computed based only on its common stock ownership interest, or would some other measure of economic interest be more relevant?

The Emerging Issues Task Force (in Issues 98-13 and 99-10) has attempted to address the accounting to be applied under the circumstances described in the foregoing paragraph. A principal concern was that an anomaly could develop if, for example, the common shareholdings were being accounted for by application of the equity method (including a suspension of the method when the carrying value declined to zero due to investee losses) while investments in the same investee's debt or preferred shares were being carried at fair value per SFAS 115 (assuming that the debt was not being carried at amortized cost due to classification as a held-to-maturity investment). A parallel concern invokes the accounting for loans under SFAS 114 when investee debt is being held by the investor.

According to EITF 98-13, the adjusted basis of the other (preferred stock, debt, etc.) investments should be adjusted for the equity method losses, after which the investor should apply SFAS 114 and 115 to the other investments, as applicable. The order in which those equity method losses should be applied to the other investments should be in reverse order of the seniority of the other investments (that is, the respective priority in liquidation). This sequence is logical because it tracks the risk of investor loss: common shareholders' interests are the first to be eliminated, followed by those of the preferred shareholders, and so on—with debt having the highest claim to investee assets in the event of liquidation. If the investee later becomes profitable, equity method income subsequently recorded (if, as described earlier, any unrecognized losses have first been exceeded) should be applied to the adjusted basis of the other investments in reverse order of the application of the equity method losses (i.e., equity method income is applied to the more senior securities first).

In applying this standard, the **cost basis** of the other investments is taken to mean the original cost of those investments adjusted for the effects of other than temporary write-downs, unrealized holding gains and losses on SFAS 115 securities classified as trading, and amortization of any discount or premium on debt securities or loans. The **adjusted basis** is defined as the cost basis adjusted for the SFAS 114 valuation allowance account for an investee loan and the cumulative equity method losses applied to the other investments.

The interaction of APB 18 and SFAS 114 and 115 could mean, for example, that investee losses are recognized via a reduction in carrying value of preferred shares, which might then be immediately upwardly adjusted to recognize fair value as of the balance sheet date in accordance with SFAS 115. In a situation such as this, the equity method downward adjustment would be a loss recognized currently in earnings, while the upward revaluation to fair value would typically be credited to other comprehensive income, and thus excluded from current period earnings (unless defined as being held for trading purposes, which would be unusual).

EITF 98-13 addressed only the situation where the investor had the same percentage interests in common stock and all the other equity or debt securities of the investee. However, a further complication can arise when the investor's share in the common stock of the investee is not mirrored in its investment in the other debt or equity securities of the investee that it also holds. While this is discussed in EITF 99-10, GAAP is not definitive regarding the mechanism by which the investor's share of further losses should be recognized in such situations. What is clear, however, is that merely applying the investor's percentage interest in the investee's common stock to the period's loss would **not** be appropriate in these cases.

Two approaches are deemed to be justifiable. The first is to eliminate the carrying value of first, the common stock and then, the other securities of the investee (including loans made to the investee), in reverse order of seniority, as set forth under EITF 98-13. The percentage of the investee's loss to be absorbed against each class of investment other than common stock would be governed by the proportion of **that investment** held by the investor—**not** its common stock ownership percentage. The logic is that, if the investor entity were to be harmed by the investee's further losses (once the common stock investment were reduced to zero carrying value), the harm would derive from being forced to take a reduced settlement in a liquidation of the investee, at which point the percentage ownership in separate classes of stock or in holdings of classes of debt would determine the amount of the investor's losses.

The second acceptable approach also takes into account the investor's varying percentage interests in the different equity and debt holdings, but rather than being driven by the investee's reported loss for the period, the investor's loss recognition is determined by the period-to-period change in its claim on the net assets of the investee, measured by book value. This approach implicitly assumes that fair values upon a hypothetical liquidation of the investee would equal book values—an assumption which is obviously unlikely to be borne out, but given the enormous difficulty of applying this measurement technique to the fair value of the investee's assets and liabilities, a necessary compromise.

Thus, both methods of computing the excess investee losses to be recognized by an investor having more than just a common stock interest in the investee depend on the varying levels of those other investment vehicles. These two alternative, acceptable approaches are described and illustrated below.

Example of accounting for excess loss of investee when other investments are also held in same entity, when proportions of all investments are identical

Assume the following facts: Dardanelles Corporation owns 25% of the common stock of Bosporus Company. Dardanelles also owns 25% of Bosporus' preferred shares, and 25% of its commercial debt. Bosporus has $50,000 of debt and $100,000 of preferred stock outstanding.

As of 1/1/2002 the carrying (i.e., book) value of Dardanelles' investment in Bosporus common stock was $12,000, after having applied the equity method of accounting in prior periods, per APB 18. In 2002, 2003, and 2004, Bosporus incurs net losses of $140,000, $50,000 and $30,000, respectively.

As of 1/1/2002, the carrying (book) values of Dardanelles' investment in Bosporus' preferred stock and commercial debt were $25,000 and $12,500, respectively. Due to its continuing losses, the market or fair value of Dardanelles' outstanding preferred shares and its commercial debt decline over the years 2002-2004; Bosporus' portion of these values are as follows:

	Fair value of preferred shares, consistent with SFAS 115	*Fair value of commercial debt, consistent with SFAS 114*
1/1/2002	N/A	N/A
12/31/2002	$20,000	$12,000
12/31/2003	9,500	8,000
12/31/2004	2,000	7,000

The following table indicates the adjustments that would be made on the books of Dardanelles to record its share of Bosporus' losses in 2002-2004:

	Common stock (Book value)	*Preferred stock* Book value	Fair value	*Commercial debt* Book value	Fair value
1/1/2002	$ 12,000	$ 25,000	N/A	$ 12,500	N/A
2002 loss (25% x 140,000 = 35,000	(12,000)	(23,000)		--	
		2,000	$20,000	12,500	$12,000
Adjust pfd. stk. to FMV and debt to FV		18,000		(500)	
12/31/2002 values	0	20,000		12,000	
2003 loss (25% x 50,000 = 12,500)		(2,000)		(10,500)	
		18,000	9,500	1,500	8,000
Adjust pfd. stk. to FMV and debt to FV		(8,500)		--	
12/31/2003 values	0	9,500		1,500	
2004 loss (25% x 30,000 = 7,500)		--		(1,500)	
		9,500	2,000	0	7,000
Adjust pfd. stk. to FMV and debt to FV		(7,500)		--	
12/31/2004 values	$ 0	$ 2,000		$ 0	

Actual journal entries and explanations for the foregoing are given as follows:

12/31/02	Investee losses	35,000	
	Investment in Bosporus common stock		12,000
	Investment in Bosporus preferred stock		23,000

To record Dardanelles' share of Bosporus' loss for the year; the excess over the carrying value of the common stock is used to reduce the carrying value of the preferred shares

	Investment in Bosporus preferred stock	18,000	
	Unrealized gain on securities available for sale (other comprehensive income)		18,000

Since the fair market value of the preferred shares is $20,000, per SFAS 115 the carrying value must be upwardly revalued and the adjustment is included in other comprehensive income for the year

	Loss from impairment of loan	500	
	Investment in Bosporus commercial debt		500

As required by SFAS 114, the impairment of the loan to Bosporus must be recognized by a charge against current period earnings

12/31/03	Investee losses	12,500	
	Investment in Bosporus preferred stock		2,000
	Investment in Bosporus commercial debt		10,500

To record Dardanelles' share of Bosporus' loss for the year; the excess over the remaining carrying value of the preferred stock (without consideration of the SFAS 115 adjustment) is used to reduce the carrying value of the commercial debt held

	Unrealized gain on securities available for sale		
	(other comprehensive income)	8,500	
	Investment in Bosporus preferred stock		8,500

Since the fair market value of the preferred shares is not $9,500, the adjustment booked in the prior period must be partially reversed, this adjustment is included in other comprehensive income for the year

12/31/04	Investee losses	1,500	
	Investment in Bosporus commercial debt		1,500

To record Dardanelles' share of Bosporus' loss for the year; the maximum to be recognized is the carrying value of the commercial debt since the carrying value of common and preferred stock investments have already been reduced to zero

	Unrealized gain on securities available for sale		
	(other comprehensive income)	7,500	
	Investment in Bosporus preferred stock		7,500

Since the fair value of the preferred shares are now $2,000, the carrying value must be further reduced, with the adjustment included in other comprehensive income

It should be noted in the foregoing example that in year 2004 there will be $6,000 of unrecognized investee losses, since as of the end of that year the carrying value of all the investor's investments in the investee will have been reduced to zero, except for the fair value of the preferred stock which is presented pursuant to SFAS 115. Also note that the carrying value of the commercial debt is reduced for an impairment in 2002 because the fair value is lower than the cost basis; in later years the fair value exceeds the cost basis, but under SFAS 114 net upward adjustments would not be permitted.

Example of accounting for excess loss of investee when other investments are also held in same entity, when proportions of investments vary—first method: investee's reported loss used as basis for recognition

When the percentage interest in common stock of the investee is not mirrored by the level of ownership in its other securities, the process of recognizing the investor's share of investee losses becomes much more complex. Per EITF 99-10, there are two acceptable approaches, both of which are illustrated here. The first approach is to recognize the investor's share of investee losses by reducing the various investments held in the investee (common and preferred stock and commercial debt, in this example) by the relevant percentages applicable to each class of investment.

In the following, the same facts as in the preceding example are continued, **except** that the percentage of ownership in the equity and debt instruments is as follows:

	Percentage ownership by
	Dardanelles Corporation
Common stock	25%
Preferred stock	50%
Commercial debt	100%

Note that the fair values of the securities held (using the new assumed percentages of ownership of each class) are as follows:

	Fair value of preferred shares, consistent with SFAS 115	*Fair value of commercial debt, consistent with SFAS 114*
1/1/2002	N/A	N/A
12/31/2002	$40,000	$48,000
12/31/2003	19,000	32,000
12/31/2004	4,000	28,000

Given the foregoing, the period-by-period adjustments are summarized in the following table:

	Common stock (Book value)	*Preferred stock* Book value	Fair value	*Commercial debt* Book value	Fair value
1/1/2002	$ 12,000	$ 50,000	N/A	$50,000	N/A
2002 loss = $140,000					
Eliminate @ 25% ratio	(12,000)				
Reduce preferred @ 50% ratio		(46,000)			
		4,000	$40,000		$48,000
Adjust pfd. stk. to FMV and debt to FV		36,000		(2,000)	
12/31/2002 values	0	40,000		48,000	
2003 loss = $50,000					
Eliminate preferred @50% ratio		(4,000)			
Reduce commercial debt @ 100% ratio				(42,000)	
		36,000	19,000	6,000	32,000
Adjust pfd. stk. to FMV and debt to FV		17,000		--	
12/31/2003 values	0	19,000		6,000	
2004 loss = $30,000					
Reduce commercial debt @ 100% ratio				(6,000)	
			4,000	0	7,000
Adjust pfd. stk. to FMV and debt to FV		(15,000)		--	
12/31/2004 values	$ 0	$ 4,000		$ 0	

Journal entries and explanations for the adjustments that would be made consistent with the foregoing fact pattern are as follows:

12/31/02	Investee losses	58,000	
	Investment in Bosporus common stock		12,000
	Investment in Bosporus preferred stock		46,000

To record Dardanelles' share of Bosporus' loss for the year; the excess over the carrying value of the common stock is used to reduce the carrying value of the preferred shares based on Dardanelles' 50% ownership interest in the preferred stock outstanding

	Investment in Bosporus preferred stock	36,000	
	Unrealized gain on securities available for sale		
	(other comprehensive income)		36,000

Since the fair market value of the preferred shares is $40,000, per SFAS 115 the carrying value must be upwardly revalued and the adjustment is included in other comprehensive income for the year

	Loss from impairment of loan	2,000	
	Investment in Bosporus commercial debt		2,000

As required by SFAS 114, the impairment of the loan to Bosporus must be recognized by a charge against current period earnings

12/31/03	Investee losses	46,000	
	Investment in Bosporus preferred stock		4,000
	Investment in Bosporus commercial debt		42,000

To record Dardanelles' share of Bosporus' loss for the year; the excess over the remaining carrying value of the preferred stock (without consideration of the SFAS 115 adjustment) is used to reduce the carrying value of the commercial debt held

	Unrealized gain on securities available for sale		
	(other comprehensive income)	17,000	
	Investment in Bosporus preferred stock		17,000

Since the fair market value of the preferred shares is not $19,000, the adjustment booked in the prior period must be partially reversed, this adjustment is included in other comprehensive income for the year

12/31/04	Investee losses	6,000	
	Investment in Bosporus commercial debt		6,000

To record Dardanelles' share of Bosporus' loss for the year; the maximum to be recognized is the carrying value of the commercial debt since the carrying value of common and preferred stock investments have already been reduced to zero

	Unrealized gain on securities available for sale		
	(other comprehensive income)	15,000	
	Investment in Bosporus preferred stock		15,000

Since the fair value of the preferred shares are now $4,000, the carrying value must be further reduced, with the adjustment included in other comprehensive income

It should be noted in the foregoing example that the limitation on loss recognition each year is given by reference to the investor's percentage interests in the various classes of equity or debt held. The 2002 loss is allocated between the common and preferred interests. A $12,000, 25% interest in the common stock equates to a total of $48,000 of common stock ($12,000 ÷ 25%). Therefore, if the full $140,000 loss were first allocated to reduce the book value of the common stock, $48,000 would have been applied to reduce that book value to zero. That would leave $92,000 of loss ($140,000 – 48,000) that remains to be allocated to the preferred interests. $92,000 x the 50% preferred interest of the investor is $48,000. Since the carrying value of the preferred stock investment is greater than this amount, the full loss is recognized by the investor proportional to its interest.

Similarly, the investee loss of $50,000 in 2003 is first used to eliminate the remaining carrying value (**before** the SFAS 115 adjustment) of the preferred stock investment, at a 50% ratio. The total of the preferred interests is computed by dividing the remaining carrying value of the preferred stock, $4,000, by the 50% interest that it represents. Therefore, the $8,000 of the $50,000 loss would be allocated to the preferred interests, thus leaving $42,000 to allocate to the commercial debt. Since Dardanelles owns all of this debt issue, the limitation on loss recognition would be the lesser of the remaining loss ($42,000) or the carrying value of the debt (**before** the SFAS 114 adjustment) of $48,000.

Finally, note that in year 2004 there will be $24,000 of unrecognized investee losses, since as of the end of that year the carrying value of all the investor's investments in the investee will have been reduced to zero (except for the fair value of the preferred stock which is presented pursuant to SFAS 115).

Example of accounting for excess loss of investee when other investments are also held in same entity, when proportions of investments vary—second method: investee's reported change in net assets used as basis for recognition

The alternative, acceptable approach to investee loss recognition when various equity and debt interests are held in the investee, at varying percentage ownership levels, ignores the investee's reported loss for the period in favor of an indirect approach, making reference to the change in the investor's interest in the investee's reported net assets (net book value). In theory, the results will often be very similar if not identical, but investee capital transactions with other owners (e.g., issuing another series of preferred shares) could impact the loss recognition by the investor under some circumstances. Furthermore, since the investor's cost of its investments in the investee will normally vary from the investee's book value of those investments (e.g., if the investments were acquired in the secondary market), the losses computed by this method may differ from those computed by the first of the two alternative approaches.

To illustrate, again assume all the facts above, including the percentage interests in the immediately preceding example. Also, the condensed balance sheets of Bosporus Corporation as of the relevant dates are given as follows:

	1/1/02	*12/31/02*	*12/31/03*	*12/31/04*
Total assets	$270,000	$135,000	$ 90,000	$ 50,000
Commercial debt	50,000	50,000	50,000	50,000
Other liabilities	20,000	25,000	30,000	20,000
Preferred stock	100,000	100,000	100,000	100,000
Common stock + retained earnings	100,000	(40,000)	(90,000)	(120,000)
Total liabilities and equity	$270,000	$135,000	$ 90,000	$ 50,000

The investor's share of the investee's net assets at these respective dates and the changes to be recognized therein as the investor's share of investee losses for the years 2002–2004 are given below.

	1/1/02	12/31/02	12/31/03	12/31/04
		(At investee's book values)		
Investor's shares of:				
Commercial debt (100%)	$ 50,000	$ 50,000	$ 50,000	$ 30,000
Preferred stock (50%)	50,000	30,000	5,000	0
Common stock + retained earnings (25%)	25,000	0	0	0
Total share of investee's net assets	$125,000	$ 80,000	$ 55,000	$ 30,000
Change in share from prior year (investor's share of investee loss for year)		$(45,000)	$(25,000)	$(25,000)

In terms of how the actual investee losses should be recorded by the investor, the EITF guidance is not explicit, but there is no reason to depart from the approach illustrated above. Thus, the investment in Bosporus common stock would be eliminated first, then the investment in the preferred stock, and finally the investment in the debt securities. The provisions of SFAS 114 and 115 would have to be adhered to as well, again similar to the illustration above.

One part of the foregoing analysis that may need elaboration is the decision, in 2004, to absorb all the excess investee losses against the investor's interest in the commercial debt. In many cases, of course, the commercial debt will be secured or for other reasons have preference over the other liabilities (which would tend to include accruals, trade payables, etc.). In an actual liquidation situation, therefore, the unsecured creditors would eliminated before the commercial debtholders. However, the purpose of this computation—determining how much of the investee's losses should be reported by the investor—is not predicated on an actual liquidation, but rather is based on a going concern assumption and conservatism. Since the investor in this example owns a major position in the common stock, half the preferred stock, and all the debt, presumably if the ongoing losses were indicative of imminent demise the investor would have already put the investee into liquidation or taken other dramatic steps. Since this has not occurred, the appropriate computational strategy, it is believed, is to allocate further losses against the investor's remaining interest, which is in the commercial debt. (If actual liquidation were being contemplated, it would be necessary to consider even a greater write-down of the carrying value of this investment.)

Note that the loss recognized each period differs from that under the previous approach, since the allocation is based on the book values of the various interests on the investee's balance sheet, not the cost basis from the investor's perspective, as detailed below.

	Common stock (Book value)	Preferred stock Book value	Preferred stock Fair value	Commercial debt Book value	Commercial debt Fair value
1/1/2002	$12,000	$50,000	N/A	$ 50,000	N/A
2002 change in investor's share of investee's net book value = –45,000					
Eliminate carrying value of common	(12,000)				
Reduce carrying value of preferred		(33,000)			
		17,000	$40,000		$48,000
Adjust pfd. stk. to FMV and debt to FV		23,000		(2,000)	
12/31/2002 values	0	40,000		48,000	
2003 change in investor's share of investee's net book value = –25,000					
Reduce carrying value of commercial debt		(17,000)		(8,000)	
		23,000	19,000	40,000	32,000
Adjust pfd. stk. to FMV and debt to FV		(4,000)		(8,000)	
12/31/2003 values	0	19,000		32,000	
2004 change in investor's share of investee's net book value = –25,000					
Reduce carrying value of commercial debt				(25,000)	
			4,000	7,000	7,000
Adjust pfd. stk. to FMV and debt to FV		(15,000)		--	
12/31/2004 values	$ 0	$ 4,000		$ 7,000	

Journal entries and explanations for the adjustments that would be made consistent with the foregoing fact pattern would be similar to those shown earlier in this section, and therefore will not be repeated here.

Intercompany transactions between investor and investee. Transactions between the investor and the investee **may** require that the investor make certain adjustments when it records its share of the investee earnings. According to the realization concept, profits can be recognized by an entity only when realized through a sale to outside (unrelated) parties in arm's-length transactions (sales and purchases) between the investor and investee. Similar problems, however, can arise when sales of fixed assets between the parties occur. In all cases, there is **no** need for any adjustment when the transfers are made at book value (i.e., without either party recognizing a profit or loss in its separate accounting records).

In preparing consolidated financial statements, all intercompany (parent-subsidiary) transactions are eliminated. However, when the equity method is used to account for investments, only the **profit component** of intercompany (investor-investee) transactions is eliminated. This is because the equity method does not result in the combining of all income statement accounts (such as sales and cost of sales), and therefore will not cause the financial statements to contain redundancies. In contrast, consolidated statements would include redundancies if the gross amounts of all intercompany transactions were not eliminated.

Another distinction between the consolidation and equity method situations pertains to the percentage of intercompany profit to be eliminated. In the case of consolidated statements, the entire intercompany profit is eliminated, regardless of the percentage ownership of the subsidiary. However, according to Accounting Interpretation 1 of APB 18, only the **investor's pro rata share** of intercompany profit would be eliminated in equity accounting, whether the transaction giving rise to the profit is "downstream" (a sale to the investee) or "upstream" (a sale to the investor). An exception is made when the transaction is not "arm's-length" or if the investee company was created by or for the benefit of the investor. In these cases, 100% profit elimination would be required, unless realized through a sale to a third party before year-end.

Example of accounting for intercompany transactions

Continue with the basic facts set forth in an earlier example and also assume that E Company sold inventory to R Corporation in 2003 for $2,000 above E's cost. Thirty percent of this inventory remains unsold by R at the end of 2003. E's net income for 2003, including the gross profit on the inventory sold to R, is $15,000; E's income tax rate is 34%. R should make the following journal entries for 2003 (ignoring deferred taxes):

1.	Investment in E Company	6,000	
	Equity in E income		6,000
	$15,000 x 40%		
2.	Equity in E income (amortization of differential)	3,200	
	Investment in E Company		3,200
3.	Equity in E income	158	
	Investment in E Company		158
	$2,000 x 30% x 66% x 40%		

The amount in the last entry needs further elaboration. Since 30% of the inventory remains unsold, only $600 of the intercompany profit remains unrealized at year-end. This profit, net of income taxes, is $396. R's share of this profit ($158) is included in the first ($6,000) entry recorded. Accordingly, the third entry is needed to adjust or correct the equity in the reported net income of the investee.

Eliminating entries for intercompany profits in fixed assets are similar to those in the examples above. However, intercompany profit is realized only as the assets are depreciated by the purchasing entity. In other words, if an investor buys or sells fixed assets from or to an investee at a price above book value, the gain would only be realized piecemeal over the asset's remaining depreciable life. Accordingly, in the year of sale the pro rata share (based on the investor's percentage ownership interest in the investee, regardless of whether the sale is upstream or downstream) of the unrealized portion of the intercompany profit would have to be eliminated. In each subsequent year during the asset's life, the pro rata share of the gain realized in the period would be added to income from the investee.

Example of eliminating intercompany profit on fixed assets

Assume that Investor Co., which owns 25% of Investee Co., sold to Investee a fixed asset, having a five-year remaining life, at a gain of $100,000. Investor Co. is in the 34% marginal tax bracket. The sale occurred at the end of 2002; Investee Co. will use straight-line depreciation to amortize the asset over the years 2003 through 2007.

The entries related to the foregoing are

2002

1.	Gain on sale of fixed asset	25,000	
	Deferred gain		25,000
	To defer the unrealized portion of the gain		
2.	Deferred tax benefit	8,500	
	Income tax expense		8,500
	Tax effect of gain deferral		

Alternatively, the 2002 events could have been reported by this single entry.

Equity in investee income	16,500	
Investment in Investee Co.		16,500

2003 through 2007 (each year)

1.	Deferred gain	5,000	
	Gain on sale of fixed assets		5,000
	To amortize deferred gain		
2.	Income tax expense	1,700	
	Deferred tax benefit		1,700
	Tax effect of gain realization		

The alternative treatment would be

Investment in Investee Co.	3,300	
Equity in investee income		3,300

In the above example, the tax currently paid by Investor Co. (34% x $25,000 taxable gain on the transaction) is recorded as a deferred tax benefit in 2002 since taxes will not be due on the book gain recognized in the years 2003 through 2007. Under provisions of SFAS 109, deferred tax benefits are recorded to reflect the tax effects of all deductible temporary differences. Unless Investor Co. could demonstrate that future taxable amounts arising from existing temporary differences exist (or, alternatively, that a NOL carryback could have been elected), this deferred tax benefit will be offset by an equivalent valuation allowance in Investor Co.'s balance sheet at year-end 2002. Thus, the deferred tax benefit might not be recognizable, net of the valuation allowance, for financial reporting purposes unless other temporary differences not specified in the example provided future taxable amounts to offset the net **deductible** effect of the deferred gain.

NOTE: The deferred tax impact of an item of income for book purposes in excess of tax is the same as a deduction for tax purposes in excess of book.

Investee income items separately reportable by investor. In the examples thus far, the investor has reported its share of investee income, and the adjustments to this income, as a single item described as equity in investee income. However, when the investee has extraordinary items and/or prior period adjustments that are material, the investor should report its share of these items separately on its income and retained earnings statements.

Example of accounting for separately reportable items

Assume that both an extraordinary item and a prior period adjustment reported in an investee's income and retained earnings statements are individually considered material from the investor's viewpoint.

Income statement

Income before extraordinary item	$ 80,000
Extraordinary loss from earthquake (net of taxes of $12,000)	(18,000)
Net income	$ 62,000

Retained earnings statement

Retained earnings at January 1, 2002, as originally reported	250,000
Add prior period adjustment—correction of an error made in 2001 (net of taxes of $10,000)	20,000
Retained earnings at January 1, 2002, restated	$270,000

If an investor owned 30% of the voting common stock of this investee, the investor would make the following journal entries in 2002:

1.	Investment in investee company	24,000	
	Equity in investee income before extraordinary item		24,000
	$80,000 x 30%		
2.	Equity in investee extraordinary loss	5,400	
	Investment in investee company		5,400
	$18,000 x 30%		
3.	Investment in investee company	6,000	
	Equity in investee prior period adjustment		6,000
	$20,000 x 30%		

The equity in the investee's prior period adjustment should be reported on the investor's retained earnings statement, and the equity in the extraordinary loss should be reported separately in the appropriate section on the investor's income statement.

Accounting for a partial sale or additional purchase of the equity investment. This section covers the accounting issues that arise when the investor sells some or all of its equity in the investee, or acquires additional equity in the investee.

Example of accounting for a discontinuance of the equity method

Assume that an investor owns 10,000 shares (30%) of XYZ Company common stock for which it paid $250,000 ten years ago. On July 1, 2002, the investor sells 5,000 XYZ shares for $375,000. The balance in the investment in XYZ Company account at January 1, 2000, was $600,000. Assume that all the original differential between cost and book value has been amortized. To calculate the gain (loss) upon this sale of 5,000 shares, it is first necessary to adjust the investment account so that it is current as of the date of sale. Assuming that the investee had net income of $100,000 for the six months ended June 30, 2002, the investor should record the following entries:

1.	Investment in XYZ Company	30,000	
	Equity in XYZ income		30,000
	$100,000 x 30%		
2.	Income tax expense	2,040	
	Deferred tax liability		2,040
	$30,000 x 20% x 34%		

The gain upon sale can now be computed, as follows:

Proceeds upon sale of 5,000 shares	$375,000
Book value of the 5,000 shares ($630,000 x 50%)	315,000
Gain from sale of XYZ common	$ 60,000

Two entries will be needed to reflect the sale: one to record the proceeds, the reduction in the investment account, and the gain (or loss) and the other to record the tax effects thereof. Remember that the investor must have computed the deferred tax effect of the undistributed earnings of the investee that it had recorded each year, on the basis that those earnings either would eventually be paid as dividends or would be realized as capital gains. When those dividends are ultimately received or when the investment is disposed of, the previously recorded deferred tax liability must be amortized.

To illustrate, assume that the investor in this example provided deferred taxes at an effective rate for dividends (considering the 80% exclusion) of 6.8%. The realized capital gain will be taxed at an assumed 34%. For tax purposes, this gain is computed as $375,000 – $125,000 = $250,000, yielding a tax effect of $85,000. For accounting purposes, the deferred taxes already provided are 6.8% x ($315,000 – $125,000), or $12,920. Accordingly, an **additional** tax expense of $72,080 is incurred upon the sale, due to the fact that an additional gain was realized for book purposes ($375,000 – $315,000 = $60,000; tax at 34% = $20,400) **and** that the tax previously provided for at dividend income rates was lower than the real capital gains rate [$190,000 x (34% – 6.8%) = $51,680 extra tax due]. The entries are as follows:

1.	Cash	375,000	
	Investment in XYZ Company		315,000
	Gain on sale of XYZ Company stock		60,000
2.	Deferred tax liability	12,920	
	Income tax expense	72,080	
	Taxes payable—current		85,000

The gains (losses) from sales of investee stock are reported on the investor's income statement in the "Other income and expense" section, assuming that a multistep income statement is presented.

In this example, the sale of investee stock reduced the percentage owned by the investor to 15%. In such a situation, the investor should discontinue use of the equity method. The balance in the investment account on the date the equity method is suspended ($315,000 in the example) will be accounted for on the basis of fair value, under SFAS 115; presumably being reported in the available-for-sale investment portfolio. This accounting principle change does **not** require the computation of a cumulative effect or any retroactive disclosures in the investor's financial statements. In periods subsequent to this principles change, the investor records cash dividends received from the investment as dividend revenue and places the security in its long-term marketable equity securities portfolio where it will be subjected to the lower of aggregate cost or market calculation. Any dividends received in excess of the investor's share of postdisposal earnings of the investee should be credits to the investment account, rather than to income.

The process of discontinuing the use of the equity method and adopting SFAS 115, as necessitated by a reduction in ownership below the significant influence threshold level, does not require a retroactive restatement. However, the opposite situation having the 20% ownership level equaled or exceeded again (or for the first time), is more complex. APB 18 stipulates that this change in accounting principle (**to** the equity method) requires that the investment account, results of operations (all periods being presented, current and prior), and retained earnings of the investor company be retroactively adjusted.

Example of accounting for a return to the equity method of accounting

Continuing the same example, XYZ Company reported earnings for the second half of 2002 and all of 2003 respectively, of $150,000 and $350,000; XYZ paid dividends of $100,000 and $150,000 in December of those years. In January 2004, the investor purchased 10,000 XYZ shares for $700,000, increasing its ownership to 45% and thereby necessitating a return for equity method accounting, including retroactive adjustment. The relevant entries are as follows:

1.	Cash	15,000	
	Income from XYZ dividends		15,000
2.	Income tax expense	1,020	
	Taxes payable—current		1,020

To record dividend income and taxes thereon at current effective tax rate ($15,000 x .068) in 2002

3.	Cash	22,500	
	Income from XYZ dividends		22,500
4.	Income tax expense	1,530	
	Taxes payable—current		1,530

To record dividend income and taxes thereon ($22,500 x .068) in 2003

5.	Investment in XYZ Company	700,000	
	Cash		700,000

To record additional investment in XYZ Company

6.	Investment in XYZ Company	37,500	
	Retained earnings		34,950
	Deferred tax liability		2,550

To adjust investment to reflect equity method accounting

Entry 6. is the cumulative effect adjustment for 15% of XYZ Company's **undistributed** earnings for the second half of 2002 and all of 2003. This adjustment is computed as follows:

Income earned in 2002 subject to equity method	
2002 income ($100,000 + $150,000)	$250,000
Less income earned through June 30 which is reflected in the	
investment account through previous use of equity method	(100,000)
2002 income subject to equity method adjustment	$150,000
Income earned in 2003 subject to equity method	350,000
Total income subject to equity method	$500,000
Less dividends declared in 2002 and 2003	(250,000)
Increase in investee equity since suspension of equity method (un-	
distributed income)	$250,000
Investor's equity during the period July 1, 2002, through Decem-	
ber 31, 2003 (cumulative effect) ($250,000 x 15%)	$ 37,500

Besides showing the cumulative effect as a prior period adjustment on the retained earnings statement, the investor also must retroactively adjust the 2002 and 2003 financial statements to reflect use of the equity method. This means that the dividend income of $15,000 in 2002 and $22,500 in 2003 should be eliminated to reflect the equity method. Accordingly, the term "dividend income" is eliminated and "equity in investee income" is substituted. Since the equity method was used for half of the year 2002 and equity in investee income was accrued through June 30, the term should already appear on 2002's income statement. However, the equity in investee income should be increased by $22,500, the investor's share of the income for the last six months of 2002 ($150,000 x 15%). The net effect on 2002's income **before taxes** is a $7,500 increase ($22,500 increase in equity in investee income less a $15,000 decrease in dividend income). For 2003, the net effect on income before taxes is $30,000. This results from adding equity in investee income of $52,500 ($350,000 x 15%) and eliminating dividend income of $22,500. In addition to the income statement, the balance sheets at December 31, 2002 and 2003, are adjusted as follows (before income tax effects):

1. Add $7,500 to the investment in investee and the retained earnings balances at December 31, 2002.
2. Add $37,500 to the investment in investee and the retained earnings balances at December 31, 2003.

Investor accounting for investee capital transactions. According to APB 18, investee transactions of a capital nature that affect the investor's share of the investee's stockholders' equity shall be accounted for as if the investee were a consolidated subsidiary. These transactions principally include situations where the investee purchases treasury stock from, or sells unissued shares or shares held in the treasury to, outside shareholders. (If the investor participates in these transactions on a pro rata basis, its percentage ownership will not change and no special accounting will be necessary.) Similar results will be obtained when holders of outstanding options or convertible securities acquire investee common shares.

When the investee engages in one of the above capital transactions, the investor's ownership percentage is changed. This gives rise to a gain or loss, depending on whether the price paid (for treasury shares acquired) or received (for shares issued) is greater or lesser than the per share carrying value of the investor's interest in the investee. However, since no gain or loss can be recognized on capital transactions, these purchases or sales will affect paid-in capital and/or retained earnings directly, without being reflected in the investor's income statement. This method is consistent with the treatment that would be accorded to a consolidated subsidiary's capital transaction. An exception is that, under certain circumstances, the SEC will permit income recognition based on the concept that the investor is essentially selling part of its investment.

Example of accounting for an investee capital transaction

Assume R Corp. purchases, on 1/2/02, 25% (2,000 shares) of E Corp.'s outstanding shares for $80,000. The cost is equal to both the book and fair values of R's interest in E's underlying net assets (i.e., there is no differential to be accounted for). One week later, E Corp. buys 1,000 shares of its stock from other shareholders for $50,000. Since the price paid ($50/share) exceeded R Corp.'s per share carrying value of its interest, $40, R Corp. has in fact suffered an economic loss by the transaction. Also, its percentage ownership of E Corp. has increased as the number of shares held by third parties has been reduced.

R Corp.'s new interest in E's net assets is

$$\frac{2,000 \text{ shares held by R}}{7,000 \text{ shares outstanding}} \quad \text{x} \quad \text{E Corp. net assets}$$

$$.2857 \text{ x } (\$320,000 - \$50,000) = \$77,143$$

The interest held by R Corp. has thus been diminished by $80,000 - $77,143 = $2,857.

Therefore, R Corp. should make the following entry:

Paid-in capital (or retained earnings)	2,857	
Investment in E Corp.		2,857

R Corp. should charge the loss against paid-in capital if paid-in capital from past transactions of a similar nature exists; otherwise the debit is to retained earnings. Had the transaction given rise to a gain it would have been credited to paid-in capital only (never to retained earnings) following the prescription in APB 6 that transactions in one's own shares cannot produce earnings.

Note that the amount of the charge to paid-in capital (or retained earnings) in the entry above can be verified as follows: R Corp.'s share of the posttransaction net equity (2/7) times the "excess" price paid ($50 – $40 = $10) times the number of shares purchased = 2/7 x $10 x 1,000 = $2,857.

EMERGING ISSUES TASK FORCE CONSENSUS SUMMARIES

84-5   Sale of Marketable Securities with a Put Option (affected by SFAS 140)

The original consensus held that accounting, as a sale or as secured borrowing, depended upon the assessed probability of the put being exercised by the holder. SFAS 125 replaced this probability assessment with an evaluation of whether the transferor has surrendered control and whether it has received consideration other than a beneficial interest in the asset transferred. If control has been transferred, even a high likelihood of exercise of the put option would not result in secured borrowing accounting treatment. If accounted for as a sale, the gain is determined with reference to all assets received and liabilities incurred by transferor to be recorded at fair value—including the put option liability, which would reflect its likelihood of exercise. SFAS 140 restores the need for probability assessment, but only if transfer qualifies for sale treatment and security is not readily available. The assessment of likelihood of exercise of the put is at transaction date only; SFAS 140 does not address any subsequent reassessment.

85-40   Comprehensive Review of Sales of Marketable Securities with Put Arrangements (affected by SFAS 140)

In general, the existence of put option does not affect accounting for sales of marketable securities, to be accounted for as sales if control is transferred, and as secured borrowings otherwise. However, per SFAS 140, probability of exercise becomes relevant when sale accounting was used and security is not readily obtainable. If a put option is granted to transferee, it is recorded at fair value as a liability by the transferor, thus affecting the computation of gain or loss to be recognized on the sale.

93-18   Impairment Recognition for a Purchased Investment in a Collateralized Mortgage Obligation Instrument or in a Mortgage-Backed Interest-Only Certificate

The EITF agreed that SFAS 115 governs the measurement of impairment of mortgage-backed securities, based on fair value. An earlier consensus, 89-4, had held that impairment of mortgage-backed securities was indicated if the recalculated effective yield of the securities became negative; the new consensus holds that negative yield (using a risk-free discount rate) is presumptive evidence of an impairment which is other than temporary.

94-4   Classification of an Investment in a Mortgage-Backed Interest-Only Certificate as Held-to-Maturity

No consensus had been reached regarding whether interest-only strips could be classified as held-to-maturity under the criteria of SFAS 115. SFAS 140 has led to a resolution of this issue, as it amends SFAS 115 to prohibit the use of the held-to-maturity classification.

96-10 Impact of Certain Transactions on the Held-to-Maturity Classification under FASB Statement No. 115

Transactions involving held to maturity investments that are not accounted for as sales (e.g., wash sales) do not call into question the classification of investments as held-to-maturity. A similar conclusion would result from bond swaps. However, if intent is to not hold new security received until maturity, then intent regarding other bond holdings, etc., is subject to being questioned. Issuance of SFAS 140 had the effect of partially nullifying this consensus: Unless the closing side of the wash sale transaction is a concurrently entered contract, the opening side must be accounted for as a sale, which then would trigger the concern over the classification as held-to-maturity. SFAS 140 does not affect conclusion on desecuritizations, however.

96-16 Investor's Accounting for an Investee When the Investor Has Majority of the Voting Interest but the Majority Shareholder or Shareholders Have Certain Approval or Veto Rights

This consensus deals with situations in which the majority owner of an entity does not exercise control and thus, under SFAS 94, potentially should not consolidate the investee. The situation arises when the minority owners have rights such as approval of management compensation, selection or termination of management, or the establishment of operating and capital policies and procedures. Collectively, these approval or veto powers are referred to as "substantive participating rights," and are contrasted to "protective rights" such as those relating to entering bankruptcy proceedings, or to major acquisitions or dispositions of assets. The EITF concluded that a finding that the majority owner lacks control depends on the facts and circumstances, and that its lack of control is generally related to the minority owner's ability to effectively participate in decisions in the "ordinary course of business." In its view, a minority owner's protective rights would not be sufficient to overcome the presumption of majority control, while substantive participating rights would overcome that presumption.

The Task Force further concluded that a number of other factors must be given consideration in reaching a conclusion on the matter of a possible negating of majority owner control. Among these are the relative size of majority and minority interests (the greater the disparity, the more likely the minority's rights are only protective in nature); the mechanisms of governance (which decisions are reserved to stockholders as opposed to being made by the directors); other possible relationships between the majority and minority owners; and the likelihood of occurrence of decision-making situations in which the minority would have the right to significantly participate.

97-7   Accounting for Hedges of the Foreign Currency Risk Inherent in an Available-for-Sale Marketable Equity Security

This issue relates to some investments, such as those registered on foreign exchanges, which have inherent foreign exchange risk associated with them. If these investments are categorized as available-for-sale, value changes may include the effects of both market and exchange rate changes. In some cases, the entity will enter into foreign exchange hedging to protect against exchange rate risk; the issue then is whether transaction gains or losses on forward contract should be included in contra equity account for available-for-sale securities' unrealized gains or losses. The consensus was in support of this treatment: The gain or loss should be shown in the same account if it is associated with the securities' price change. Foreign exchange risk is inherent only if two conditions are met: securities are not traded on exchange denominated in investor's functional currency; and dividends or other cash flows are all denominated in foreign currency. This consensus has been affected by the later promulgation of SFAS 130 and 133.

98-7   Accounting for Exchanges of Similar Equity Method Investments

A consensus was reached that exchanges of similar equity method investments should be accounted for per APB 29. EITF 86-29 provides guidelines for determining similarity/nonsimilarity of productive assets.

98-13   Accounting by an Equity Method Investor for Investee Losses When the Investor Has Loans to and Investments in Other Securities of the Investee

This considers how the loss recognized under the equity method per APB 18 should be recorded by the investor when the carrying amount of the common stock has already been reduced to zero, and how that interacts with the applicable literature relating to investments in the other securities of the investee (either SFAS 114 or 115). In its consensus, the Task Force found that in situations where (1) an investor is not required to advance additional funds to the investee and (2) previous losses have reduced the common stock investment account to zero, the investor should continue to report its share of equity method losses in its statement of operations to the extent of, and as an adjustment to, the adjusted basis of the other investments in the investee. The order in which those equity method losses should be applied to the other investments should follow the seniority (i.e., priority in liquidation) of the other investments.

The adjusted basis of the other investments should be adjusted for the equity method losses, then the investor should apply SFAS 114 and 115 to the other investments, as applicable. The cost basis of the other investments is the original cost of those investments adjusted for the effects of other than temporary writedowns, unrealized holding gains and losses on SFAS 115 securities classified as trading, and amortization of any discount or premium on debt securities or loans.

The adjusted basis is the cost basis adjusted for the SFAS 114 valuation allowance account for an investee loan and the cumulative equity method losses applied to the other investments. When the investee later becomes profitable, equity method income subsequently recorded should be applied to the adjusted basis of the other investments in reverse order of the application of the equity method losses, that is, equity method income is applied to the more senior securities first.

A detailed example of this standard is set forth in the body of this chapter. Also note that EITF 99-10 (below) further addresses this matter.

98-15 Structured Notes Acquired for a Specified Investment Strategy

Structured notes are debt obligations that are coupled with derivatives, typically related to interest rates or foreign currency exchange rates, such that a prescribed increase or decrease in the reference rate will have a large impact on some defined attribute of the debt obligation, such as its interest rate, maturity value or maturity date. In some instances, two or more such instruments may be acquired, having essentially opposite characteristics, such that, for example, a change in a reference interest rate will cause the fair value on one holding to increase and the other to decrease, by equal amounts. In some instances, this may have been arranged in order to be able to achieve a recognizable loss on the one (losing) investment by selling it, while holding the other (winning) one as an available-for-sale security with unrealized gains reported in other comprehensive income. This consensus effectively ends this practice by requiring that the related investments be accounted for as a unit while held, but if one is sold the (joint) carrying amount must be allocated based on relative fair values as of the date of sale, consistent with guidance in SFAS 140. The result will be that neither gain nor loss, recognized or included in stockholders' equity, will be realized from such transactions.

99-8 Accounting for Transfers of Assets That Are Derivative Instruments but That Are Not Financial Assets

This pertains to certain assets that meet the definition of a derivative instrument under SFAS 133 but that are not financial assets as defined in SFAS 140. The definitions of financial asset and financial liability in SFAS 140 are derived from those in SFAS 105. SFAS 140 applies only to transfers of financial assets even though it is used to account for extinguishments of all liabilities (both financial and nonfinancial). It is unclear how transfers of assets that are derivative instruments but that are not financial assets should be accounted for. The Task Force consensus is that transfers of assets that are derivative instruments and subject to the requirements of SFAS 133, but that are not financial assets, should be accounted for by analogy to SFAS 140. An example would be a transfer to another entity of a derivative instrument, such as a forward contract to purchase gold that requires physical settlement and is or will be subject to the requirements of SFAS 133. This consensus is effective for transfers after September 23, 1999, regardless of whether an entity has yet adopted SFAS 133.

99-10   Percentage Used to Determine the Amount of Equity Method Losses

This expands upon the material presented in Issue 98-13, which addresses the situation where an investor owns common stock and "other investments" in an investee and the investor is not required to advance additional funds to the investee and previous losses have reduced the common stock investment account to zero. The issue is how additional equity method losses should be measured and recognized by the investor in such a circumstance. The consensus is that an investor should not recognize equity method losses based solely on the percentage of investee common stock held by the investor. As to whether an investor should recognize equity method losses based on (1) the ownership level of the particular investee security or loan/advance held by the investor to which the equity method losses are being applied or (2) the change in the investor's claim on the investee's book value, the Task Force was not asked to reach a consensus.

See the body of this chapter for a comprehensive example of how investee losses should be accounted for under these circumstances.

99-20   Recognition of Interest Income and Impairment on Purchased and Retained Beneficial Interests in Securitized Financial Assets

Under SFAS 140 (as under SFAS 125, its predecessor), if an entity sells a portion of an asset that it owns, the portion retained becomes an asset separate from the portion sold and separate from the assets obtained in exchange. This is the situation when financial assets such as loans are securitized, with certain interests being retained. The entity must allocate the previous carrying amount of the assets sold based on the relative fair values of each component at the date of sale. In most cases, the initial carrying amount (allocated cost) of the retained interest will be different from the fair value of the instrument. Furthermore, cash flows from those instruments may be delayed depending on the contractual provisions of the entire structure (for example, cash may be retained in a trust to fund a cash collateral account). The issue for the EITF was how interest income and impairment should be recognized for retained interests in securitizations classified as available-for-sale or as held-to-maturity.

The consensus was that the holder of the beneficial interest should recognize the excess of all cash flows anticipated at the acquisition transaction date over the initial investment as interest income using the effective yield method. The holder should update the estimate of cash flows over the life of the beneficial interest. If the estimated cash flows change (but there is still an excess over the carrying amount), the adjustment should be accounted for as a change in estimate with the amount of the periodic accretion adjusted over the life of the beneficial interest. If the fair value of the beneficial interest declines below its carrying amount, the holder should apply the impairment guidance in SFAS 115. If it is not practicable for a holder/transferor to estimate the fair value of the beneficial interest at the securitization date, interest income should be recognized using the cash basis rather than the effective yield method.

Subsequently, certain revisions were made to clarify that if, based on current information and events that the holder of the beneficial interest anticipates a market participant will use in determining the current fair value of the beneficial interest, there is a change in estimated cash flows, the amount of accretable yield should be recalculated and if the change in estimated cash flows is adverse, an other than temporary impairment should be considered to have occurred. The change in estimated cash flows need not be "probable" as is currently stated (which has led to some confusion in practice).

00-1 Investor Balance Sheet and Income Statement Display under the Equity Method for Investments in Certain Partnerships and Other Unincorporated Noncontrolled Ventures

Under some circumstances, investor-venturers account for undivided interests in assets by means of pro rata consolidation, including a fraction of each asset category of the investee in the investor's balance sheet, typically commingled with the investor's own assets. The issue is whether this method can be used to account for an investment in a partnership or a joint venture, rather than by means of either full consolidation, the equity method, or historical cost. In its consensus, the EITF concluded that the pro rata method of consolidation is not appropriate for an investment in an unincorporated legal entity, except when the investee is in either the construction industry or the extractive industry (where this methodology has long been in use).

00-6 Accounting for Freestanding Derivative Financial Instruments Indexed to, and Potentially Settled in, the Stock of a Consolidated Subsidiary

EITF Issue 96-13 establishes a framework for accounting for freestanding derivative instruments that are indexed to, and potentially settled in, a company's own stock. That consensus did not, however, provide guidance on how to account for free standing derivative instruments that are indexed to, and potentially settled in, a subsidiary's stock. The issue addressed here is how such contracts should be classified and measured in the consolidated financial statements.

A consensus exists that stock of a subsidiary is not equity of the parent; therefore, derivatives indexed to and to be settled in stock of a subsidiary do not meet SFAS 133's exclusion criteria. If derivatives meeting the criteria of SFAS 133 (e.g., for net settlement, etc.), these must be accounted for under the provisions of SFAS 133, and not of Issue 96-13. The consensus also discusses a number of exceptions based on the criteria set forth in SFAS 133.

The EITF reached several consensuses regarding derivatives not within the scope of SFAS 133, while also noting that option or forward strike prices and premiums could be indicative of impairments of the parent's investment in subsidiaries—to be assessed using SFAS 121. A parent's contract to purchase a subsidiary's (minority held) common stock should not be recorded until settled; during the period of the contract, income should continue to be allocated to the minority interest. A contract to sell shares in a subsidiary, likewise, should be recorded when settled; until that time, income would not be allocated to outside interests (counter parties to the derivative). No consensus was reached regarding written options.

11 BUSINESS COMBINATIONS AND CONSOLIDATED FINANCIAL STATEMENTS

PERSPECTIVE AND ISSUES

For over fifty years US generally accepted accounting principles permitted two different and very distinct approaches to the accounting for business combinations—the purchase and pooling methods. In recent years, the pooling method had come under increasing criticism, in part because it promoted a concept—the "marriage of equals"—that was virtually never reflected in the facts of a given business combination. The SEC was reported to have devoted inordinate time to the making of determinations regarding the acceptability of pooling accounting for specific business acquisitions. Furthermore, in the era of growing convergence between various national accounting standards and the International Accounting Standards, U.S. GAAP was by far the most lenient regarding pooling of interest accounting, which had already been effectively banned by a number of major standard setters.

With the recent culmination of its long-standing project to reexamine accounting for business combinations, the FASB has imposed the strictest of such standards. Beginning July 1, 2001, all business combinations, except for those involving not-for-profit entities and combinations of entities under common control (e.g., parent/subsidiary and brother/sister mergers), must be accounted for as purchases. The new standard amends APB 16 by deleting all guidance pertaining to poolings of interest, which is henceforth banned. Among other things, this means that all future business combinations will be presented in a far more comparable manner, making it easier to measure the performance of enterprises which engage in significant business combinations. Poolings completed before the effective date of the new standard do not, however, need to be restated.

The basic accounting for a purchase business combination is straightforward: the purchase price is allocated to tangible and identifiable intangible assets and to liabilities assumed, based on fair values. Excess cost over the fair value of the net assets acquired will be designated as "goodwill." Should the fair value of the net assets acquired exceed the cost of the purchase, the "negative goodwill" is offset against the allocated fair value of certain assets, with any residual now to be taken into earnings immediately (formerly, amortized to earnings over a period of no longer than forty years).

How goodwill is handled **after** the date of the purchase transaction, however, has been entirely altered under the newly imposed standards, beginning January 1, 2002. For more than thirty years, GAAP demanded that goodwill be amortized, on a straight-line basis, over no greater than forty years. Under unusual impairment circumstances, a partial or even complete write-off of the carrying value of goodwill could occur, but as a practical matter, amortization over an extended period of time was virtually the universal practice. Goodwill amortization was a noncash charge to be reported in operating results; the lengthier the amortization period, the less painful the impact on results of operations.

The FASB's original intent, as set forth in its 1999 Exposure Draft, was to both eliminate pooling accounting and continue goodwill amortization—which in fact was to have been constrained to a twenty-year maximum period, down from forty years under APB 17. For a variety of reasons, this proposal was strenuously objected to. The FASB first compromised by proposing that goodwill amortization be reported, net of tax, as a special, "below the line" expense, permitting financial statement preparers and users to focus on a preamortization earnings measure. Subsequently, however, the FASB abandoned even this compromised approach, and embraced what appears to be a diametrically opposite approach: there will be no periodic amortization, but rather, only sporadic write-downs for "impairment."

Under the new standard, then, goodwill (which often represents a very major component of the cost of business combinations) will be recorded and maintained semipermanently as an asset on the balance sheet. The standard does demand that greater efforts be made, henceforth, in separately identifying other intangibles, such as customer lists, which in the past were often included in goodwill, as those assets will generally be amortized, and there is concern to not exaggerate the true goodwill component. Furthermore, there are elaborate requirements to test the goodwill for impairment on a somewhat regular basis; when impairment is detected, goodwill must be written down, with the expense included in operations. However, there are likely to be substantial difficulties in actually implementing the impairment testing rules—not to mention the struggle by independent auditors to enforce this requirement. It is likely that further interpretive guidance will have to be mandated as greater experience is gained with this new approach. APB 17 is superseded by the new standard.

This chapter will address purchase accounting for business combinations in detail, and the accounting for goodwill to a lesser extent. Chapter 9 addresses the accounting for all intangible assets, including goodwill, in greater detail.

When the acquired entity is merged into the acquiring entity or when both entities are consolidated into a new (third) entity, all assets and liabilities are recorded directly on the books of the surviving organization. However, when the acquirer obtains a majority (or all) of the common stock of the acquired entity (which maintains a separate legal existence), the assets and liabilities of the acquired company will not be recorded on the acquirer's books. In this case, GAAP normally requires that consolidated financial statements be prepared (i.e., that an accounting consolidation be effected). In either case, under the newly imposed standard purchase accounting must be applied, which normally will result in the recognition of goodwill. In the case of accounting consolidations, goodwill does not appear on the acquirer's (or acquiree's) books, but will arise from the consolidation entries made to generate the financial statements.

In certain cases combined financial statements of entities under common control (but neither of which is owned by the other) are also prepared. This process is very similar to an accounting consolidation using (the now obsolete) pooling accounting, except that the equity accounts of the combining entities are carried forward intact.

The major accounting issues in business combinations and consolidated or combined financial statement preparation are as follows:

1. The proper accounting basis for the assets and liabilities of the combining entities
2. The accounting for goodwill or negative goodwill, if any exists
3. The elimination of intercompany balances and transactions in the preparation of consolidated or combined statements

Over the years, there has been an evolution in thinking regarding the role and importance of consolidated financial statements. Since the late 1980s it has been required that general-purpose financial statements consolidate all of the reporting entity's majority owned subsidiaries. Beginning in the 1990s, the fact that one enterprise can effectively control another entity without majority ownership has begun to receive greater attention, and the idea that the consolidation requirement should be based on control, rather than majority ownership, has gained currency. In fact, in 1994 the AICPA adopted a standard for not-for-profits (SOP 94-3) which applies the notion of control and can be viewed as a model for the FASB's later efforts.

An initial proposal by the FASB to adopt this concept for all other entities, made in 1995, was vigorously debated, and a revised proposal was exposed in 1999. In early 2001, however, the FASB concluded that a workable majority could not be assembled to support any change in existing practice. Accordingly, consolidation continues to be required when interests of "50% plus one share" is held in another entity's voting stock, and equity method accounting (discussed in Chapter 10) continues to be used when a significant nonmajority interest is held. (The FASB may revisit this issue again, but that would likely be years from now.)

Sources of GAAP				
APB	*ARB*	*SFAS*	*TB*	*EITF*
16, 18,	51	38, 94,	85-5,	84-13, 84-33, 84-35, 85-12, 85-28,
29		125**	85-6	85-45, 86-29, 86-32, 87-11, 87-17,
				87-21, 87-27, 88-16, 89-7, 90-5, 90-
				6, 90-12, 90-13, 90-15, 91-5, 93-7,
				95-3, 95-8, 95-14, 95-19,
				95-21, 96-4, 96-5, 96-7, 96-20,
				97-2, 97-6, 97-8, 97-15, 98-1, 98-2,
				98-3, 98-4, 99-6, 99-12, 99-15,
				D-54, D-58, D-81

** *New standards on consolidations and goodwill, issued July 2001.*

DEFINITIONS OF TERMS

Accounting consolidation. The process of combining the financial statements of a parent company and one or more legally separate and distinct subsidiaries.

Acquisition. One enterprise pays cash, or issues stock or debt, for all or part of the voting stock of another enterprise. The acquired enterprise remains intact as a separate legal entity. The parent-subsidiary relationship is accounted for as a purchase, and it is referred to as an acquisition.

Combination. Any transaction whereby one enterprise obtains control over the assets and properties of another enterprise, regardless of the resulting form of the enterprise emerging from the combination transaction.

Combined financial statements. Financial statements presenting the financial position and/or results of operations of legally separate entities, related by common ownership, as if they were a single entity.

Consolidated financial statements. Consolidated statements present, primarily for the benefit of the shareholders and creditors of the parent company, the results of operations and the financial position of a parent company and its subsidiaries essentially as if the group were a single enterprise with one or more branches or divisions.

Consolidation. A new enterprise is formed to acquire two or more other enterprises through an exchange of voting stock. The acquired enterprises then cease to exist as separate legal entities.

Control. Ownership by one enterprise, directly or indirectly, of more than 50% of the outstanding voting shares of another enterprise.

Entity concept. A method of preparing consolidated financial statements of a parent and majority-owned subsidiary which involves restatement of net assets of the subsidiary to fair value at the date of acquisition for **both** majority and minority interests.

Goodwill. The excess of the cost of an acquisition price over the fair value of acquired net assets which is recorded as an asset and written down only when, and if, impairment is identified and measured, based on future events and conditions.

Merger. One enterprise acquires all of the net assets of one or more other enterprises through an exchange of stock, payment of cash or other property, or the issue of debt instruments.

Minority interest. Any remaining outstanding voting stock of a subsidiary not purchased by the acquiring enterprise.

Negative goodwill. Properly known as the "excess of fair value over cost of acquired net assets." This amount represents the **net** excess of fair value of the net assets of a business acquisition, after allocation as a pro rata reduction of the amounts that otherwise would be assigned to all of the acquired assets other than cash and cash equivalents, trade receivables, inventory, financial instruments that are required to be carried on the balance sheet at fair value, assets to be disposed of by sale, and deferred tax assets. This excess is generally reported as an extraordinary gain in the period in which the business combination is initially recognized, unless the purchase price involves contingent consideration, in which case it is reported as a deferred credit until the contingency is resolved.

Parent company concept. A method of preparing consolidated financial statements of a parent and majority-owned subsidiary which involves restatement of net assets of the subsidiary to fair value at the date of acquisition for **only** the majority interest.

Preacquisition contingencies. Uncertainties existing at the date of an acquisition accounted for by the purchase method which, if resolved within one year of the acquisition, result in a reallocation of the purchase price.

Purchase method. The accounting method used for a business combination which recognizes that one combining entity was acquired by another. It establishes a new basis of accountability for the acquiree.

Purchased preacquisition earnings. An account used to report the earnings of a subsidiary attributable to percentage ownership acquired at the interim date in the current reporting period.

Reverse acquisition. An acquisition when one entity, nominally the acquirer, issues so many shares to the former owners of the target entity that they become the majority owners of the successor entity.

Subsidiary. An enterprise that is controlled, directly or indirectly, by another enterprise.

Unrealized intercompany profit. The excess of the transaction price over the carrying value of an item (usually inventory or plant assets) transferred from (or to) a parent to (or from) the subsidiary (or among subsidiaries) and not sold to an outside entity. For purposes of consolidated financial statements, recognition must be deferred until subsequent realization through a transaction with an unrelated party.

CONCEPTS, RULES, AND EXAMPLES

Purchase Accounting under the New Standards

Any business combination (of whatever legal form) involving unrelated entities (i.e., those not under common control), neither of which are not-for-profit entities, must be treated as a purchase. The long-standing option to treat certain transactions, meeting a series of restrictive criteria, as "poolings of interests" no longer exists. Purchase accounting is an application of the cost principle, whereby assets obtained are accounted for at the price that was paid. A purchase transaction gives rise to a **new basis of accountability** for the purchased assets (and liabilities).

Pooling, which had become subject to growing criticism from the SEC, from some academicians, and to a much lesser extent, from some in the corporate and public accounting realms as well, has finally been banned outright, effective for transactions **initiated** after June 30, 2001. The use of grossly disparate methods of accounting for what could be almost identical economic transactions was no longer seen as being conceptually defensible, despite widespread use not only in the U.S. but in many other nations as well (although, in recent years, the use of pooling had been sharply curtailed by many nations' accounting standards). Despite being defended by some (principally publicly-held entities which generally were able to structure stock-swap acquisitions and which were often very driven by the desire to avert future goodwill amortization charges) all future transactions will be accounted for as purchases.

The new standard embraces the definition of "initiated" found in APB 16: it is the earlier of (1) the date that the major terms of a plan, including the ratio of exchange of stock, are announced publicly or otherwise formally made known to the stockholders of any one of the combining companies, or (2) the date that stockholders of a combining company are notified in writing of an exchange offer. Purchase accounting must be used for acquisitions initiated after June 30, 2001. The other provisions of the new standard (e.g., strengthened rules for identification and separate recognition of intangibles other than goodwill, discussed later in this chapter) are effective for acquisitions **completed** after June 30, 2001; thus these requirements are applicable to transactions that may have been initiated earlier.

The new standard amends APB 16, essentially retaining the guidance in that standard pertaining to purchase business combinations and deleting that which addressed poolings of interests. A companion standard supersedes APB 17 (which itself was a companion to APB 16 when both were promulgated over thirty years ago), and arguably mitigates to a great extent the salutary impact of the pooling ban, by dropping the requirement to amortize goodwill arising from business acquisitions accounted for as purchases. (The goodwill issue is addressed later in this chapter and also in Chapter 9.)

Cost allocation, goodwill, and negative goodwill. The major purchase business combinations accounting issue is how to allocate the purchase cost to the various assets and liabilities acquired. Where the legal form of combination is a merger or a consolidation, the acquirer records all the assets and liabilities purchased at their **fair values** (**not** the acquired entity's book values). If the actual cost exceeds the fair value of the identifiable net assets acquired, this excess is recorded as an intangible asset (**goodwill**). Under newly imposed accounting requirements, goodwill will not be subject to periodic amortization (as it had been under the now-superseded APB 17), but will be subject to periodic evaluation for impairment. It is expected that many, if not most, purchase business combinations will involve the recognition of goodwill.

The new standards for goodwill accounting are vastly different from both previous practice and from the direction the FASB appeared to be headed when it unveiled its original proposal in 1999. Under present standards (APB 17), goodwill must be amortized, straight-line, over no longer than forty years; as a practical matter (particularly when the SEC had critically reviewed a registrant's proposed treatment of goodwill following a major acquisition) this often was over a somewhat shorter time horizon. As proposed by the FASB in 1999, the maximum amortization period was to be cut to twenty years, again applying a straight-line approach. At the time, the Board considered several approaches that would have permitted some or all goodwill to be capitalized and not amortized, but stated that it found that none of those approaches could be operationalized. Because of the subjectivity involved in identifying and measuring the discernible elements of goodwill, particularly those with indefinite lives, as well as what the FASB then perceived to be the inability to adequately review goodwill for impairment (since goodwill has no identifiable direct cash flows), it stated that it was not possible to lift the requirement for mandatory amortization.

The FASB later offered a compromise, of sorts, to those objecting to the "double whammy" of forced purchase accounting and mandatory amortization of goodwill over a shorter time interval. This would have moved amortization expense out of the operating costs section of the income statement, to a new position "below the line," separately set out on a net-of-tax basis. This would have facilitated reporting of an "operating income before goodwill amortization" earnings number and eased the sting of amortization charges arising from acquisitions which formerly would have been given pooling of interests treatment.

In a surprising move, in early 2001 the FASB offered a radically revised draft on goodwill accounting, virtually diametrically opposed to its earlier position. Despite its previously stated objections to capitalization without amortization, the Board now fully embraced that methodology, stating that a (complex and possibly almost unauditable) impairment testing strategy would supersede mandatory amortization. Arguably, a heightened concern over the admittedly highly arbitrary choice of amortization life (twenty years in the earlier draft) was a major reason for this shift in perspective. This was coupled with favorable results of research into impairment testing as a basis for the radically revised approach embodied in the 2001 draft. Obviously, this represented a (possibly necessary) political compromise, in order to achieve the major goal: the elimination of pooling of interests accounting.

With only slight modifications, the 2001 goodwill proposal has now been enacted, effective for fiscal years beginning after December 15, 2001. Not only will goodwill arising from future purchase transactions not be amortized, but also the remaining unamortized balance of goodwill from earlier acquisitions will be "frozen" and not subject to further amortization. No restatements to previous transactions may be made, however.

Far less common than transactions giving rise to goodwill are the "bargain purchases," where the cost of the acquisition is actually less than the fair value of the net assets acquired. Under the newly imposed accounting standards, this deficiency of cost under fair value is first allocated as a pro rata reduction of the amounts that otherwise would be assigned to the acquired assets other than cash and cash equivalents, trade receivables, inventory, financial instruments that are required to be carried on the balance sheet at fair value, assets to be disposed of by sale, and deferred tax assets. (Note: Under prior GAAP, the offset was against all noncurrent assets, other than marketable securities, with any residual being deferred and amortized in the manner of positive goodwill. In practical terms, the new requirement is very close to the superseded one. On the other hand, the FASB's 1999 proposal would have offset negative goodwill first against intangible assets acquired having no observable market; second, against acquired depreciable nonfinancial assets and to any other acquired intangible assets; and finally, any excess would have been recognized immediately as an extraordinary gain.)

If the initially recorded amounts of these acquired assets are entirely eliminated, the excess, commonly called **negative goodwill**, is generally to be recognized immediately as an extraordinary gain item. In cases in which there are contingent consideration issues (discussed below), however, the negative goodwill will be carried as a deferred credit on the balance sheet, until the contingency is resolved.

The logical foundation for gain recognition in bargain purchases is the belief that the very act of consummating the acquisition gives rise to income. This is in contradistinction to the former conception that income results only from the use of assets, not their mere purchase. However, if care is given to accurate measurement of fair values, and the bargain of such a great magnitude (unlikely to occur, in reality) that the allocated fair values of most noncurrent assets is entirely offset by the negative goodwill, with an excess yet remaining, then a gain has probably indeed been achieved by the acquirer. By requiring that this residual gain be categorized as extraordinary, rather than included in operations or in other income, the risk of misleading users of the financial statements is minimized.

Accounting for mergers. If the acquisition form of combination is used, the acquired entity maintains a separate legal and accounting existence and all assets and liabilities remain, in the records of the aquiree, at their premerger book values. However, when an **accounting consolidation** is performed (i.e., when consolidated financial statements are prepared), exactly the same results are obtained as those outlined above (i.e., assets and liabilities are adjusted to fair values, and goodwill is recorded, as noted above). In terms of how the parent-level (i.e., consolidated) financial statements are presented, there is absolutely no difference between acquisition combinations and outright mergers.

When less than 100% of the stock of the acquired entity is owned by the acquirer, a complication arises in the preparation of consolidated statements, and a minority interest (discussed below) must be computed.

When one entity is acquired by another, whether by outright merger or via a stock holding, a distinguishing characteristic of the purchase accounting method is that none of the equity accounts of the acquired entity (including its retained earnings) will appear on the acquirer's books or on the consolidated financial statements. In other words, ownership interests of the acquired entity's shareholders are not continued after the merger, consolidation, or combination (acquisition) takes place.

In some transactions there is a continuity of ownership, as when, for example, shareholders in one entity exchange their shares for stock of the other (acquiring) entity. Under prior rules (APB 16), if a number of restrictive conditions were met, these transactions would be accounted for as poolings of interests, and (with some limitations) the equity of both combining enterprises would be carried forward to the postcombination balance sheets. Despite the appearance of being "mergers of equals," however, the vast preponderance of these transactions were acquisitions of one entity by the other. Under current GAAP, pooling accounting has been eliminated (for transactions after June 30, 2001), and the acquiree's equity accounts cannot be carried forward under any circumstances.

In determining which entity is the acquirer in transactions involving two or more enterprises, the new standard stresses that consideration be given to all pertinent facts, with emphasis on the relative voting rights in the combined enterprise and the composition of the board of directors and the senior management of the combined enterprise. In determining which of the shareholder groups retained or received the larger portion of the voting rights in the combined enterprise, the existence of any major voting blocks, unusual or special voting arrangements, and options, warrants, or convertible securities needs to be considered. If a new enterprise is formed to issue stock to effect a business combination (sometimes referred to as a consolidation), one of the existing combining enterprises must, on the basis of the evidence available, be deemed the acquirer.

Determining fair values. The purchase method requires that a determination be made of the fair value of each of the acquired company's identifiable tangible and intangible assets and for each of its liabilities, as of the date of combination. The determination of these fair values is crucial for proper application of the purchase method. The newly-imposed purchase accounting standard has carried forward the guidance found in APB 16, with some elaboration. The list below indicates how this is to be accomplished for various assets and liabilities.

1. **Marketable securities**—Fair values, which, for trading and available for sale securities, are already reflected in the acquiree's balance sheet
2. **Receivables**—Present values of amounts to be received determined by using current interest rates, less allowances for uncollectible accounts
3. **Inventories**
    a. Finished goods and merchandise inventories—Estimated selling prices less the sum of the costs of disposal and a normal profit
    b. Work in process inventories—Estimated selling prices less the sum of the costs of completion, costs of disposal, and a normal profit
    c. Raw material inventories—Current replacement cost
4. **Plant and equipment**
    a. If expected to be used in operations—Current replacement costs for similar capacity unless the expected future use of the assets indicates a lower value to the acquirer
    b. If expected to be sold—Fair value less cost to sell
5. **Identifiable intangible assets and other assets** (such as land, natural resources, and nonmarketable securities)—Appraised (fair) value
6. **Liabilities** (such as notes and accounts payable, long-term debt, pensions, warranties, claims payable)—Present value of amounts to be paid determined at appropriate current interest rates

In-process research and development. One of the more controversial asset types is "in-process research and development." Under GAAP, research and development expenditures must be expensed as incurred. In many cases, however, an acquirer will purchase another enterprise which has previously incurred, and expensed, substantial sums for research and development; in some instances, much or most of the price paid for the acquisition is for the value of the acquiree's previous R&D efforts. FASB Interpretation 4 is unambiguous in requiring the acquirer to expense that portion of the purchase price; were this to be recorded as an acquired asset, it would create a back door for R&D capitalization which is prohibited by SFAS 2.

While the traditional concern had been that acquiring entities would attempt to capitalize in-process research and development, in more recent years the opposite situation more frequently arose: that is, excessive portions of purchase premiums were attributed to in-process research and development, and then immediately expensed, thereby reducing the allocation to goodwill and averting future amortization charges. With the new "no amortization" requirement, the expectation is that the motivation for exaggerated allocations to in-process research and development will be alleviated. However, the new standard emphasizes again that appropriate allocation of the purchase cost to in-process research and development is required, and that this must be immediately expensed by the acquiring entity.

Identifying all intangibles. Prior to undertaking the purchase price allocation, the acquiring enterprise must review the purchase consideration, if other than cash, to ensure that it has been appropriately valued. It must also be careful to identify **all** of the assets acquired and liabilities assumed, including intangible assets. As the move to the "knowledge-based economy" continues, an increasing share of the purchase cost for business acquisitions will pertain to intangible assets, adding to the challenge as time goes on.

Under the new standards, greater effort is required to identify all intangibles; these cannot expediently be classified as part of goodwill, since the newly prescribed treatment for goodwill is not mirrored in the accounting for other intangibles. An identifiable intangible asset will be recognized separately from goodwill if it meets the asset recognition criteria in SFAC 5 and if either (1) control over the future economic benefits of the asset results from contractual or other legal rights or (2) the intangible asset is capable of being separated or divided and sold, transferred, licensed, rented, or exchanged. Furthermore, even if the intangible asset cannot be sold, transferred, licensed, rented, or exchanged individually, it would meet the criterion for separate recognition if it could be sold, transferred, licensed, rented, or exchanged along with a related contract, asset, or liability.

The new standard sets forth a lengthy listing of intangibles which are to be given separate recognition, along with the terms over which amortization is generally to be applied, with certain exceptions for those intangibles having indefinite lives, such as perpetually renewable broadcast licenses, which are maintained at cost until a finite life can be ascertained, if ever. These intangibles generally fall into one of a set of categories, such as customer- or market-based assets (e.g., customer lists, newspaper mastheads, and trademarked brand names); contract-based assets (e.g., covenants not to compete, broadcast rights); technology-based assets (e.g., title plant, databases, computer software); statutory based assets (e.g., patents, copyrights); workforce based assets (e.g., trained staff, technical expertise); and corporate, organizational and financial assets (e.g., favorable financial arrangements, outstanding credit rating). Under the new standards, except for indefinite life intangibles, the assets must be amortized, generally over the useful economic lives, with a limit of twenty years unless further criteria are met. (See Chapter 9 for a complete discussion.)

The standards demand that all identifiable assets acquired and liabilities assumed in a business combination, **whether or not recorded separately in the financial statements of the acquired enterprise**, are to be assigned a portion of the total cost of the acquisition, based on their respective fair values as of the date of acquisition. Independent appraisals and actuarial or other valuations may be useful in determining those fair values but, interestingly enough, the tax basis of an asset or liability is not to be considered in determining fair value. Given that the residual asset, goodwill, will not be amortized, the emphasis on accurate and complete valuation of all other identifiable intangibles is necessary.

While all assets are to be carefully evaluated, it is equally important to note that assets having no value are to be assigned no allocated cost. A typical example arises when facilities of the acquired entity duplicate those of the acquirer and accordingly are to be disposed of. The cost allocated to these facilities should equal the estimated net salvage value, zero if no salvage is anticipated, and even a negative amount equal to the estimated costs of disposal, if warranted. The EITF has approved the allocation of "holding costs" to assets to be disposed of when debt from the business acquisition is to be paid down from the proceeds of such asset sales. In effect, the value assigned to such assets to be sold is the present value of the estimated selling price; interest incurred on debt used to finance these assets is then charged to the asset rather than to interest expense until the disposition actually occurs. On the other hand, if facilities of the acquired entity duplicate and are superior to facilities of the purchaser, with the intention that the latter will be disposed of, fair value must be allocated to the former. Eventual disposition of the redundant facilities of the acquirer may later result in a recognized gain or loss. This would fall into the general category of indirect costs of acquisition, which are not capitalizable or allocable to assets acquired in the purchase business combination.

The EITF has reached a similar conclusion with regard to entire subsidiaries of acquired entities (EITF 87-11 and 90-6). In such situations, the expected cash flows from the subsidiary's operations, through the expected date of disposition (but not longer than one year from the acquisition date), are considered in the purchase price allocation process. Ideally, operations of the subsidiary, including the cost of borrowed funds, if relevant, will **not** impact the acquirer's income statement, absent changes in estimates or altered plans for its disposition. Failure to achieve the planned disposition within one year, however, will result in all further operating results, including borrowing costs, being reported in the consolidated statement of income for future periods. Any difference between the subsidiary's carrying value at the disposition date and the proceeds of the disposition should be treated as a reallocation of the original purchase price of the business combination. If, however, the difference arises from identifiable events that occur after the merger date, gain or loss would be reported at the disposition date.

Tax accounting implications of purchase business combinations. Accounting for the tax implications of purchase business combinations changed substantially with the issuance of SFAS 109. Prior to that, any existing deferred tax benefits or liabilities of the acquired entity, or any deferred tax effects created by the purchase transaction itself (e.g., due to different tax and book bases of the acquired assets or liabilities), were not recognized **as such** in the postacquisition consolidated balance sheet of the acquirer. Instead, these tax effects were deemed to be components of the valuation process whereby the total purchase cost was allocated to acquired identifiable assets and liabilities and, when necessary, to goodwill or negative goodwill. Accordingly, purchased assets and liabilities were recorded on a net-of-tax basis under APB 16.

Under SFAS 109, the net-of-tax method has been prohibited. Instead, values are assigned "gross," and tax effects, if any, are recorded in deferred tax accounts. Under the SFAS 109 "asset and liability" approach to deferred tax accounting (detailed in Chapter 15), deferred tax liabilities and assets are evaluated and adjusted at the date of each balance sheet. Therefore, any deferred taxes of an acquired entity, or any deferred taxes generated by the acquisition transaction itself, are to be recognized in recording the purchase business combination.

If an acquired entity has unrecorded deferred tax benefits which can be used to offset the acquirer's deferred tax liabilities, these benefits will be recognized in the postacquisition balance sheet. Similarly, under the provisions of SFAS 109, the NOL benefits of an acquired entity will also be recognized in the balance sheet of the acquirer if the acquirer can utilize those benefits under existing tax law. The gross amount of the tax benefits will always be recorded if the benefits are available to the acquirer. An offsetting valuation allowance will also be recorded if it is **more likely than not** that it will not be realized by the reporting entity (for example, if it is estimated that there will not be future taxable income against which to absorb the net operating losses).

The subsequent realization of unrecognized NOL benefits of an acquired entity will affect only goodwill and other noncurrent intangible assets, which are adjusted on a prospective basis when NOL benefits are subsequently recognized. Benefits exceeding recorded goodwill and other intangibles are credited to income tax expense (not, as under earlier GAAP, to extraordinary income) in the period when first recognized. (See Chapter 15 for details.)

The 1993 Tax Reconciliation Act provided for the amortization of goodwill over a fifteen-year period (previously, goodwill amortization was not deductible). If, before the new standard on goodwill was promulgated, the management of an enterprise had selected a longer or shorter amortization period, a temporary difference would have resulted. Under the new standard, there is no amortization of goodwill, but the tax requirement continues as before. This also creates a temporary difference, and thus deferred tax effects must be reported.

Other costs of business combinations. Direct costs of a business acquisition (e.g., finders' fees) are part of the cost to be allocated to tangible and intangible assets, including goodwill. However, stock registration and related expenses are offset against the proceeds (credits) of the stock issuance. Indirect costs are simply expensed in the period when the combination is effected.

In some instances, there are alternative ways to handle certain costs, influencing their treatment as either direct or indirect costs of a business acquisition. For example, if a prospective acquiree company has employee stock options outstanding, and it pays the employees to settle the options prior to the acquisition, then (per APB 25, as later interpreted by the EITF in 84-13 and 85-45) compensation expense must be recognized. On the other hand, if the employees exercise their options and then have their shares purchased by the acquirer (or exchanged for stock in the acquirer), there is no compensation expense but instead an additional cost of the purchase.

Costs related to a takeover defense by a prospective acquiree company are not capitalized, but are expenses of the period incurred. However, the EITF has suggested that if the costs are related to a "going private" transaction, these expenses may be classified as an extraordinary item in the statement of income.

In some takeover defense strategies, a target company will repurchase some of its own shares, generally at a price higher than that being offered by the prospective acquirer. Although generally the cost of repurchased stock is simply charged to the treasury stock account, there is the recognition that excessive repurchase costs are not always related to the "fair value" of the stock. When the price paid explicitly contains consideration for the seller's agreement not to purchase any further shares (a "standstill agreement"), this excess cost must be expensed (per Technical Bulletin 85-6), with only the fair market value of the shares themselves being charged to the treasury stock account. The EITF did not reach a consensus about the treatment of excessive costs of treasury shares absent explicit payment for other services. However, the SEC favors expensing any excess costs. As a general rule, judgment should be applied in evaluating each circumstance.

Example of purchase transaction—goodwill

Accent Corp. acquired all of the common stock of Detroit Boiler Manufacturing Co. on January 2, 2002 at a cost of $32 million, paid $15 million in cash and the balance with a long-term note to former Detroit shareholders. As of January 2, 2002, immediately prior to the transaction, Detroit's balance sheet is as follows, with both book and fair values indicated ($000 omitted):

	Book value	Fair value		Book value	Fair value
Cash	1,000	1,000	Current liabilities	26,200	26,200
Accounts receivable, net	12,200	12,000	Long-term debt	46,000	41,500
Inventory	8,500	9,750	Guarantee of debt	0	75
Other current assets	500	500			
Plant, property and equipment, net	38,500	52,400			
Customer list	0	1,400			
Patents	2,400	3,900			
In-process research and development	0	8,600	Stockholders' equity	(9,100)	21,775
Totals	63,100	89,550		63,100	89,550

The fair value of inventory exceeded the corresponding book value because Detroit had been using LIFO for many years to cost its inventory, and actual replacement cost was therefore somewhat higher than carrying value at the date of the acquisition. The long term debt's fair value was slightly lower than carrying value (cost) because the debt carries a fixed interest rate and the market rates have risen slightly since the debt was incurred, which reduces the economic burden that it represents. Finally, the fair value of Detroit's receivables have also declined from the carrying amount, due both to the higher market rates of interest (which add to the cost of carrying the receivables until collection) and to the greater risk of collectibility because of the change in ownership.

Detroit's customer list has been appraised conservatively at $1.4 million and is a major reason for the company's being acquired by Accent. Having been internally developed over many years, the customer list is not recorded as an asset by Detroit, however. The patents have been amortized down to $2.4 million on Detroit's books, consistent with GAAP, but an appraisal finds that on a fair value (replacement cost) basis the value is somewhat higher.

Similarly, plant, property and equipment has been depreciated down to a book value of $38.5 million, but has been appraised at a sound value (that is, replacement cost new adjusted for the fraction of the useful life already elapsed) of $52.4 million.

A key asset being acquired by Accent, albeit one not formally recognized by Detroit, is the in-process research and development, which pertains to significant process and product improvements made over several years, which has enhanced Detroit's market position and will be captured by the new combined operations. It has been determined that duplicating the benefits of this ongoing R&D work would cost Accent $8.6 million. The strong motivation to make this acquisition, and to pay a substantial premium over book value, is based on Detroit's customer list and its in-process research and development. Detroit has previously expensed all R&D expenditures, as required under GAAP (SFAS 2).

Detroit had guaranteed a $1.5 million bank debt of a former affiliated entity, but this was an "off the books" event. The actual obligation has been appraised as having a fair value (considering both the amount and likelihood of having to honor the commitment) of $75,000.

Thus, although Detroit's balance sheet reflects a deficit stockholders' equity (including paid in capital and retained earnings) of $9.1 million, the value of the acquisition, including the in-process research and development, is much higher. The preliminary computation of goodwill is as follows:

Purchase price		$32,000,000
Net working capital	(2,950,000)	
Plant, property and equipment	52,400,000	
Customer list	1,400,000	
Patents	3,900,000	
In-process research and development	8,600,000	
Guarantee of indebtedness of others	(75,000)	
Long-term debt	(41,500,000)	21,775,000
Goodwill (excess of cost over fair value)		$10,225,000

Under GAAP (FASB Interpretation 4), the fair value allocated to the in-process research and development must be immediately expensed. All other assets and liabilities are recorded by Accent at the allocated fair values, with the excess cost being assigned to goodwill. The entry to record the purchase (for preparation of consolidated financial statements, for example) is as follows:

Cash	1,000,000	
Accounts receivable, net	12,000,000	
Inventory	9,750,000	
Other current assets	500,000	
Plant, property, and equipment	52,400,000	
Customer list	1,400,000	
Patents	3,900,000	
Goodwill	10,225,000	
Research and development expense	8,600,000	
Current liabilities		26,200,000
Guarantee of indebtedness of others		75,000
Long-term debt		41,500,000
Notes payable to former shareholders		17,000,000
Cash		15,000,000

Note that, while the foregoing example is for a stock acquisition, an asset and liability acquisition would be accounted for in the exact same manner. Also, since the debt is recorded at fair value, which will often differ from face (maturity) value, the differential (premium or discount) must be amortized using the effective yield method, and thus there will be differences between actual payments of interest and the amounts recognized in the income statements as interest expense. Finally, note that plant, property, and equipment is recorded "net"—that is, the allocated fair value becomes the "cost" of these assets; accumulated depreciation on the books of the acquired entity does not carry forward to the postacquisition financial statements of the consolidated entity.

Example of purchase transaction—negative goodwill

Desiree Corp. acquires, on March 4, 2002, all the capital stock of Strook Co. for $800,000 in cash. A formerly successful enterprise, Strook had recently suffered from declining sales and demands for repayment of its outstanding bank debt, which were threatening its continued existence. Desiree management perceived an opportunity to make a favorable purchase of a company operating in a related business segment, and accordingly made this modest offer, which was accepted by the acquiree. Strook's balance sheet at the date of acquisition is as follows, with both book and fair values indicated ($000 omitted):

	Book value	Fair value		Book value	Fair value
Cash	800	800	Current liabilities	2,875	2,875
Accounts receivable, net	3,600	3,400	Long-term debt	11,155	11,155
Inventory	1,850	1,800			
Plant, property, and equipment	6,800	7,200			
Net operating loss carryforwards	0	2,400	Stockholders' equity	(980)	1,570
Totals	13,050	15,600		13,050	15,600

Strook had provided a valuation allowance for the deferred tax asset attributable to the net operating loss carryforward benefit, since recurring and increasing losses made it more likely than not that these benefits would not be realized, consistent with GAAP (SFAS 109). Desiree Corp., which is highly profitable, is in the same business segment, and intends to continue Strook's operations, expects to be able to realize these benefits, and therefore will have no valuation allowance against this asset.

Thus, although Strook's balance sheet reflects a deficit stockholders' equity (including paid in capital and retained earnings) of $980,000, the value of the acquisition is much higher, and furthermore the acquirer is able to negotiate a bargain purchase. The preliminary computation of negative goodwill is as follows:

Net working capital	$ 3,125,000	
Plant, property and equipment	7,200,000	
Net operating loss carryforward	2,400,000	
Long-term debt	(11,155,000)	1,570,000
Purchase price		800,000
Negative goodwill (excess of fair value over cost)		$ 770,000

Under GAAP, the negative goodwill is first offset against all of the acquired assets other than cash and cash equivalents, trade receivables, inventory, financial instruments that are required to be carried on the balance sheet at fair value, assets to be disposed of by sale, and deferred tax assets, on a pro rata basis. In the present instance, only the plant, property and equipment is available for this offsetting (the NOL benefits are equivalent to deferred tax assets under SFAS 109; see further discussion in Chapter 15). The entry to record the purchase before allocating negative goodwill is therefore as follows:

Cash	800,000	
Accounts receivable, net	3,400,000	
Inventory	1,800,000	
Plant, property and equipment, net	7,200,000	
Net operating loss carryforward	2,400,000	
Current liabilities		2,875,000
Long-term debt		11,155,000
Cash		800,000
Negative goodwill		770,000

The entry to record the offsetting of the negative goodwill is as follows:

Negative goodwill	770,000	
Plant, property and equipment, net		770,000

Since the negative goodwill is fully absorbed by the plant, property and equipment, there will be no residual to recognize in earnings.

Example of purchase transaction—excess negative goodwill

The facts are similar to the immediately preceeding example, except that Strook Co.'s long term debt amounts to only $3,155,000 (book and fair values) as of the date of the acquisition transaction. This results in such a large amount of negative goodwill that an excess remains after plant, property, and equipment is reduced to zero. This excess negative goodwill is reported in the period in which the transaction occurs as an extraordinary gain.

Strook's balance sheet at the date of acquisition is as follows, with both book and fair values indicated ($000 omitted):

	Book Value	Fair Value		Book Value	Fair Value
Cash	800	800	Current liabilities	2,875	2,875
Accounts receivable, net	3,600	3,400	Long-term debt	3,155	3,155
Inventory	1,850	1,800			
Plant, property and equipment, net	6,800	7,200			
Net operating loss carryforwards	0	2,400	Stockholders' equity	7,020	9,570
Totals	13,050	15,600		13,050	15,600

The preliminary computation of negative goodwill is as follows:

Net working capital	$3,125,000	
Plant, property and equipment	7,200,000	
Net operating loss carryforward	2,400,000	
Long-term debt	(3,155,000)	9,570,000
Purchase price		800,000
Negative goodwill (excess of fair value over cost)		$8,770,000

The entry to record the purchase before allocating negative goodwill is therefore as follows:

Cash	800,000	
Accounts receivable, net	3,400,000	
Inventory	1,800,000	
Plant, property and equipment, net	7,200,000	
Net operating loss carryforward	2,400,000	
Current liabilities		2,875,000
Long-term debt		3,155,000
Cash		800,000
Negative goodwill		8,770,000

The entry to record the offsetting of the negative goodwill is as follows:

Negative goodwill	8,770,000	
Plant, property and equipment, net		7,200,000
Extraordinary item—gain on purchase		1,570,000

Since the negative goodwill is not fully absorbed by the plant, property and equipment, there will be a residual to recognize in earnings. Under GAAP, this is presented as an extraordinary item (net of tax, not computed here) in the income statement.

However, if the transaction provided for a contingent purchase price (e.g., based on meeting earnings targets over the next several years), the excess negative goodwill ($1,570,000 in this example) would be treated as a deferred credit, not subject to amortization, until the contingency was resolved. To the extent an increase in the purchase price resulted, that would reduce (in the extreme, even eliminate) the negative goodwill. Any remaining negative goodwill after the contingent purchase price has been resolved will be reported in that period as an extraordinary gain.

Goodwill

Intangible assets: A new standard. The change to GAAP for the accounting for business combinations, whereby the acceptability of pooling of interests accounting has been ended, has been accompanied by an even more fundamental change in the accounting for goodwill. Goodwill, of course, arises in the GAAP financial reporting sense only in connection with business combinations which are accounted for as purchases. Concurrent with its decision to ban pooling accounting, the FASB undertook a comprehensive reexamination of the concept of goodwill and the proper means of accounting for it. After making a rather remarkable U-turn—first preparing to demand the accelerated amortization of goodwill while precluding impairment testing, then prohibiting any form of amortization in favor of the formerly rejected intermittent testing for impairment—an entirely new methodology has now been promulgated.

The asset commonly known as goodwill, inextricably linked to business combinations, is also a sub-et of the broader topic intangible asset accounting. The standard addresses the accounting for all intangibles, and raises the bar for delineating among different types of intangibles (i.e., distinguishing those having finite lives, those arguably having indefinite lives, and goodwill, which is unique in being "unidentifiable" and having indeterminate life which makes periodic amortization impossible, in the FASB's current view). Chapter 9 discusses intangibles other than goodwill in great detail. Accordingly, this subject will only be addressed in the present chapter to the extent that the recognition and measurement of **identifiable** intangibles acquired in a purchase business combination impacts upon the measurement of goodwill, which is normally seen as being a residual asset following the assignment of purchase cost to all other assets and liabilities.

SFAC 5, *Recognition and Measurement in Financial Statements of Business Enterprises*, states that an asset should be recognized if it meets the definition of assets (found in SFAC 6), has a relevant attribute measurable with sufficient reliability, and the information about it is representationally faithful, verifiable, neutral (i.e., it is reliable), and capable of making a difference in user decisions (i.e., it is relevant). In a business acquisition, any acquired **identifiable** intangible asset (e.g., patents, customer lists, etc.) must be recognized separately from goodwill when it meets these SFAC 5 asset recognition criteria, and additionally meets **either** of the following criteria:

1. Control over the future economic benefits of the asset results from contractual or other legal rights (regardless of whether those rights are transferable or separable from other rights and obligations), or
2. The asset is capable of being separated or divided and sold, transferred, licensed, rented, or exchanged (regardless of whether there is an intent to do so or whether a market currently exists for that asset)—or, if it cannot be individually sold, etc., it is capable of being sold, transferred, licensed, rented or exchanged along with a related contract, asset, or liability.

All intangible assets acquired from other enterprises or individuals, whether singly, in groups, or as part of a business combination, are recognized initially and are measured based on their respective fair values. (Note that initially determined fair value may be reduced in the case of business combinations with which negative goodwill is associated.) Under the provisions of the new standard on intangibles (but, arguably, also under predecessor standard APB 17), serious effort must be directed to identifying the various classes of intangibles acquired, particularly in a bulk purchase such as a business combination.

Reliably measurable identifiable intangible assets, with the exception of those meeting the criteria for nonamortization (explained below), must be amortized over their respective useful economic lives. Under the new standards, the useful economic life of intangible assets is presumed to be twenty years or less. Useful economic life is the period over which the asset is expected to generate future economic benefits, that is, the period over which it will generate identifiable cash flows. Factors to be considered in estimating the useful economic life of an intangible asset include

1. Legal, regulatory, or contractual provisions that may limit the maximum useful life;
2. Legal, regulatory, or contractual provisions that may enable renewal or extension of a specified limit on the asset's legal or contractual life (provided there is evidence to support renewal or extension without substantial cost);
3. The effects of obsolescence, demand, competition, and other economic factors (such as the stability of the industry, the rate of technological change, and expected changes in distribution channels);
4. The expected useful life of assets or groups of assets of the enterprise or of individuals or groups of employees to which the useful life of the asset may parallel (such as mineral rights to depleting assets);
5. The expected use of the intangible asset by the enterprise; and
6. The level of maintenance expenditure required to obtain the expected future economic benefits from the asset.

Typically, the entire amount assigned to an intangible asset will be subject to amortization, although in some instances a residual value may be determined, which reduces the amortizable basis. The residual value should be assumed to be zero unless the useful life to the acquiring enterprise is shorter than the asset's useful economic life, and either (1) the acquiring enterprise has a commitment from a third party to purchase the asset at the end of its useful life, or (2) the residual value can be determined by reference to an observable market for that asset and that market is expected to exist at the end of the asset's useful life. The method of amortization should reflect the pattern in which the economic benefits of the intangible asset are to be consumed; absent the ability to ascertain this, straight-line amortization should be applied. However, if impairment (determined by application of the SFAS 121 criteria) is later detected, the carrying amount will be written down.

The presumption of a maximum life of twenty years may be overcome if the asset generates clearly identifiable cash flows that are expected to continue for more than twenty years, **and** either (1) the asset is exchangeable or (2) control over the future economic benefits of the asset is obtained through contractual or other legal rights that extend for more than twenty years. Clearly identifiable cash flows are cash flows that may be associated with the specific intangible asset or with a group of assets that includes the intangible asset. (This is further discussed in Chapter 9.)

In those instances where an intangible asset meets the criteria for overcoming the twenty-year useful life presumption, is of a type that has an observable market, and is determined to have an indefinite useful economic life that is not otherwise limited, it will not be amortized until its life is determined to be finite. An example of such an asset would be a broadcast license, expiring in five years, but which may be renewed indefinitely at little cost. If the acquirer intends to renew the license indefinitely, and there is evidence to support its ability to do so, the cash flows related to that license are expected to continue indefinitely, and there is an observable market for the intangible asset, then no amortization would be recognized until such time as these criteria are no longer met.

Goodwill—The residual. After completing the purchase price allocation (a process described in APB 16 and unaltered by the new standards), any residual of cost over fair value of the net identifiable assets and liabilities is assigned to the unidentifiable asset, goodwill. Formerly subject to mandatory amortization, this now may not be amortized at all, by **any** allocation scheme and over **any** useful life. Impairment testing, using a methodology at variance with that set forth in SFAS 121 (which, however, continues in effect for all other types of long-lived assets and intangibles other than goodwill), must be applied periodically, and any impairment detected will be expensed in that period's income statement.

The FASB had proposed an elaborate typology of constituent elements that often are incorporated into goodwill, possibly hoping to narrow the definition of that portion of goodwill which would be deemed a nonamortizing asset. This proved to be impractical, in much the way that the conceptual definition of goodwill, as the excess earnings power of the acquiree's operations, has not provided a workable blueprint for measurement. Thus, goodwill will continue to be computed by reference to the residual cost of the purchase transaction. If all other acquired assets have been identified (including, at the moment the transactions occurs, in-process research and development, which is then expensed) and properly valued, the remaining excess of purchase price can be assigned to no asset other than goodwill.

The decision to eliminate the requirement for amortization was based on the recognition that **any** assigned useful life would be quite arbitrary. (Of course, much the same observation can be made about tangible, long-lived assets, and no parallel proposal has been made to end depreciation accounting.) The FASB recognized that not all goodwill declines in value and that any decline in value rarely occurs on a straight-line basis. Furthermore, the FASB found during its field testing of the revised proposal that the estimation (albeit, indirectly) of future cash flows associated with goodwill (which is critical to implementation of an impairment approach) was feasible, contrary to earlier expectations. Finally, elimination of periodic amortization charges against earnings was a political price the FASB was willing to pay in order to secure its primary goal, elimination of the pooling method of accounting for business combinations.

Impairment. With a determination to end amortization, it became necessary to construct a detailed mechanism for the periodic assessment of impairment, so that the carrying amount of the asset does not exceed its recoverable amount, consistent with GAAP for other long-lived assets. A major concern is that any testing for impairment will be confounded by the existence, along with the purchased goodwill, of internally generated goodwill created subsequent to the date of the business combination. Since GAAP did not historically permit recognition of internally generated goodwill, there appeared to be a need to address, and hopefully control, this measurement risk. However, FASB has concluded that it would be impossible to track "acquisition-specific" goodwill for impairment testing purposes and has, accordingly, endorsed a major departure from the traditional prohibition against recognition of any internally generated intangibles.

The impairment testing strategy created under the new standards acknowledges that, as the revised proposal stated, "anomalies that result from the differences in how acquired goodwill and internally generated goodwill are accounted for also justify a departure from the current model of accounting." In effect, as long as the total goodwill identifiable with the "reporting unit" to which acquisition-based goodwill was assigned can be shown to have a fair value exceeding the book value of the goodwill arising from the acquisition (which means apples will be compared to oranges, of course), no impairment will be found. This represents a major departure from longstanding accounting practice.

In its revised (2001) draft, which introduced the idea of impairment testing, the FASB proposed that goodwill be tested at the "reporting unit" level, defined as "the lowest level of an entity that is a business and that can be distinguished physically and operationally and for internal reporting purposes from the other activities, operations, and assets of the entity." The FASB envisioned that a "reporting unit generally would be at a level somewhere between a segment and an asset group (as that term is used in SFAS 121)." It acknowledged that a reporting unit could be the same as a segment for some entities, and could be the entity as a whole in other cases.

As ultimately promulgated, however, **reporting unit** means

> *"the level at which the segment management reviews and assesses the performance of the operating segment. . . (it) would be one level below the operating segment if a component or components of an operating segment (1) is a separate unit that engages in business activities for which discrete financial information is available, (2) has economic characteristics different from the other components of the operating segment, and (3) is the level at which the benefits of goodwill will be realized. Otherwise, a reporting unit would be the same as the operating segment."*

In other words, goodwill will not have to be identified with as low a level of operations as would have been the case under the proposed standard.

The definition of reporting unit, which relates to the definition of operating segment as the term is used in SFAS 131, applies equally to publicly held and private companies. This is true even though nonpublic entities are exempted from reporting segment information. This may necessitate the establishment of an enhanced internal reporting mechanism by some of these enterprises. On the other hand, improved reporting could have salutary effects on the management of those entities.

Measurement procedures. It was recognized at the time of the revised draft that goodwill testing could not be effected by the same mechanical approach as SFAS 121 sets forth for other long-lived assets (and, until terminated by this new standard, for goodwill as well). The reason is that the potentially very long-enduring cash flows emanating from goodwill would obviate the usefulness of SFAS 121's "undiscounted cash flows" threshold test for impairment. In other words, given the very high threshold for declaring **any** impairment under SFAS 121, and the possibility that cash flows associated with goodwill could with little difficulty be projected far into the future, the SFAS 121 approach was seen as futile.

Accordingly, a new impairment testing protocol has been devised for goodwill. The draft standard had envisioned an impairment test that would determine the best estimate of the fair value of goodwill, which would have been compared with its carrying amount to determine whether there had been an impairment. Since direct measurement of the fair value of goodwill would clearly not be possible, measurement of goodwill could have been approached as it is at the date of its acquisition (i.e., as a residual amount). The FASB concluded that a method similar to the method of allocating the purchase price to the net assets acquired in a business combination would need to be used to measure the value of goodwill subsequent to its acquisition date. Thus, it decided that the net assets of a reporting unit should be subtracted from the fair value of that reporting unit to determine the implied fair value of goodwill.

The fair value of the net assets of the reporting unit can be measured in a variety of ways. Direct market observation is certainly the most objective method, but in the absence of that information, other techniques can be substituted. SFAC 7, recently promulgated, sets forth an "expected present value technique" which uses the sum of probability-weighted present values in a range of estimated cash flows adjusted for risk, all discounted using the same interest rate convention. The FASB has indicated that such a technique is a more effective measurement tool than is the traditional present value approach, especially in situations in which the timing or the amount of estimated cash flows is uncertain, as is the case in measuring nonfinancial assets and liabilities.

In order to operationalize an approach that incorporates the values of the recognized assets and liabilities, the FASB concluded that all of the assets and liabilities of an acquired entity (including goodwill) that will be used in the operations of a reporting unit would have to be allocated to that reporting unit as of the acquisition date. For many business enterprises, this will require changes to the internal, management accounting: for example, many entities have not heretofore allocated liabilities such as pension and environmental obligations below the corporate or entity level. To the extent these liabilities relate to one or more reporting unit or units, they must now be included in the determination of the fair value of the recognized net assets of that unit or units.

Under SFAS 131, the standard on segment reporting required of publicly held corporations, "corporate" assets and liabilities are not assigned to any operating segment. Goodwill has often been included in these nonallocated corporate assets. The impairment testing process, however, could not proceed if a similar approach were adhered to, and accordingly under the new goodwill standard goodwill and all other related assets and liabilities are to be assigned to reporting units for purposes of testing goodwill for impairment. The new standard also requires that the amount of goodwill in each segment be disclosed in the notes to the financial statements.

Under the terms of the final standard, goodwill impairment testing will be a two-step process (as is impairment testing under SFAS 121, although these two standards differ fundamentally in their respective approaches). In the first step, the existence of impairment is assessed by comparing the fair value of the "reporting unit" to its carrying (book) value. If fair value of the reporting unit exceeds book value, there is no need for further analysis, since no impairment will be found to have occurred.

If carrying value exceeds fair value, on the other hand, impairment will be indicated. In this second step, the amount of the impairment will be measured as the excess of the recorded goodwill over its fair value, computed in the same manner as when completing a business combination's "purchase price allocation." Thus, the fair value of the reporting unit will be allocated to all the unit's assets and liabilities (including any unrecognized intangibles, according to the standard, even though this raises a question of noncomparability with book value), including, as a residual, goodwill. If the amount thus assigned to goodwill is less than its carrying value, the excess book value must be written off as an impairment expense. No other adjustments are to be made to carrying values of any of the reporting unit's assets or liabilities.

Unlike SFAS 121's impairment measurement requirements, which uses net (i.e., discounted) present values to actually measure the magnitude of any indicated impairment, the new goodwill impairment approach uses the pseudo-purchase price allocation methodology. Implicitly, of course, present value of future cash flows are incorporated, since the overall fair value measure of the reporting unit, and the fair values of some or all of the individual assets and liabilities, may look to discounted cash flows as the bases for value assessments. Nonetheless, this is a new approach and one which has been carefully conceived to address the measurement peculiarities attendant to goodwill.

Initial assessment of goodwill's fair value. In order to facilitate periodic assessments of possible impairment, it is necessary that a "benchmark" assessment be made. This benchmark assessment should be performed in conjunction with most significant acquisitions, regardless of how much goodwill arises from that acquisition. Similarly, a benchmark assessment should be performed in conjunction with a reorganization of an entity's reporting structure.

The **benchmark assessment** involves identifying the valuation model to be used, documenting key assumptions, and measuring the fair value of the reporting unit. While not costless to accomplish, this benchmark assessment is necessary to ensure that the entity has identified and documented all key assumptions and tested the outputs of the selected valuation model for reasonableness prior to actually testing goodwill for impairment. Furthermore, measuring the fair value of the reporting unit as part of the benchmark assessment will provide management with a "reality check" on whether the amount of goodwill assigned to the reporting unit was reasonable, by comparing the fair value of the reporting unit with its carrying (book) value. If the fair value of the reporting unit is found to be less than its carrying amount, the goodwill allocation could be reassessed, and the selected valuation model and the assumptions underpinning the initial valuation could be critically re-examined. In rare cases, should the indicated fair value of the reporting unit still be less than its carrying amount, goodwill would be tested for impairment, and possibly be adjusted.

The change, in moving from the revised proposal to final standard (from requiring impairment assessments on a sporadic "events and circumstances" basis to an annual basis) would seemingly have mitigated the necessity of having the initial benchmark assessment. However, the final standard demands that the first step in the two-step impairment review process (i.e., comparing the fair value of the reporting unit to its carrying amount) be completed **within six months** of adoption of the new standard. An impairment detected during this process will be reflected in the income statement of the first year as part of the charge for a change in accounting principles, which is reported "below the line." Any impairments identified after the first six months will be reported as impairment loss, which is an operating expense.

All goodwill must be allocated to one or more reporting units in order to facilitate impairment testing. However, conceivably goodwill might be assigned to reporting units to which no other acquired assets or liabilities have been assigned; for example, if the purchase gives a division of the acquirer access to a market niche affecting one of its operating units even as all the tangible and other intangible assets are assigned to other parts of the enterprise. Goodwill may also be split among two or more reporting units of the acquirer. Any allocation method should be consistently applied and the logic for doing so should be documented.

At transition, all **existing** assets and liabilities, including goodwill, must be apportioned to reporting units, using the methodology noted in the foregoing paragraphs. For many entities, this will be a demanding exercise. Presumably, if an entity has no goodwill because it never engaged in a purchase acquisition, or because all acquired goodwill has already been amortized and never expects to participate in a business combination in the future, this may be ignored, since no goodwill impairment testing will be needed. For many companies, however, even the mere possibility of a future transaction will underscore the need to make the initial allocation among its reporting units.

Ongoing testing for impairment of goodwill. In the FASB's 2001 revised goodwill proposal, impairment testing on an "events and circumstances" basis was endorsed. Accordingly, the draft included a number of indicators suggesting that impairment might have been experienced. For example, current period and/or continuing operating or cash flow losses, forecasted ongoing losses, loss of key operating personnel, and unplanned obsolescence of key products would all be suggestive of possible impairment. Under the standard that was promulgated in mid-2001, however, annual impairment testing has been mandated, and thus there would seem to be a reduced need for a listing of triggering events.

However, the FASB decided that a requirement for interim goodwill impairment testing should be retained, in the case of an event or circumstance that occurs between annual tests that might reduce the fair value of a reporting unit below its carrying value. Examples would include an adverse change in the business climate or market, a legal factor, an action by regulators, the introduction of new competition, or a loss of key personnel. The FASB has mandated that goodwill should also be tested for impairment on an interim basis when it is "more likely than not" that a reporting unit or a significant portion of a reporting unit will be sold or otherwise disposed of, and, furthermore, when a significant asset group within a reporting unit is tested for recoverability under SFAS 121.

Obviously, annual assessments of impairment would be extended, and possibly expensive, exercises. In recognition of this fact, the FASB decided that under defined circumstances in which the risk of impairment would be quite low, the fair value of each reporting unit would **not** have to be recomputed each year. To qualify for this exception, there must not have been changes to the components of the reporting unit since the previous fair value computation, the fair value amount must have exceeded the carrying amount of the reporting unit by a substantial margin when last measured, and there must be no evidence to suggest that the current fair value of the reporting unit may be less than its current carrying amount.

The annual impairment tests need not be performed at fiscal year-ends. Instead, the fair value measurement for each reporting unit could be performed any time during the fiscal year, as long as that measurement date is used consistently from year to year. Different measurement dates can be used for different reporting units.

Display of goodwill and of goodwill impairment. The aggregate amount of goodwill is to be presented as a separate line item in the statement of financial position (balance sheet). Traditionally, in classified balance sheets, goodwill is an "other" noncurrent asset, distinguished from plant, property, and equipment.

The aggregate amount of goodwill impairment losses is generally to be presented as a separate line item in the operating section of the income statement. The exception to this rule is when the goodwill impairment loss is associated with a discontinued operation, in which case the impairment loss will be included, on a net-of-tax basis, within the results of discontinued operations. The portion of goodwill associated with net assets to be disposed of is recognized as part of the gain or loss on disposal, not as an impairment loss.

Disclosures about business combinations have been expanded under the new standards to include the primary reason for the acquisition, including a description of the factors that contributed to a purchase price that reflects a premium that results in recognition of goodwill or a discount that results in recognition of an extraordinary gain (negative goodwill). If goodwill is material in relation to the total cost of a business acquisition, disclosure is required to be made of the amount of acquired goodwill; the amount of acquired goodwill related to each segment (for only those entities that are required to report segment information); and the amount of acquired goodwill that is deductible for income tax purposes.

For each period for which a balance sheet is presented, the notes to the financial statements must disclose the changes in the carrying amount of goodwill during the period. This must include the amount of goodwill acquired, the amount of impairment loss recognized, and the amount of goodwill included in the gain or loss on disposal of all or a portion of a reporting unit. For publicly held entities, this information has to be provided for each segment, and should disclose any significant changes in the allocation of goodwill by segment.

For each goodwill impairment loss recognized, disclosure must be made of the following information: a description of the facts and circumstances leading to the impairment; a description of the reporting unit for which the impairment loss is recognized, the adjusted carrying amount of goodwill of that reporting unit, and the amount of the impairment loss; if appropriate, the fact that the impairment loss is an estimate that has not yet been finalized, with the reasons therefor and, in subsequent periods, the nature and amount of any significant adjustments made to the initial estimate of the impairment loss; and, when salient, the segment to which the impaired goodwill.

In the period in which an excess over cost related to an acquisition (i.e., negative goodwill) is recognized as an extraordinary gain, it will be shown net of tax, as set forth by APB 30.

Finally, a special disclosure requirement applies during the transition period, from the date the new standard was effective until full implementation is achieved. Upon completion of the first step of the transitional impairment test (i.e., comparing the fair value of the reporting unit to its carrying amount), the reporting entity is to disclose the reporting segment or segments for which an impairment loss might have to be recognized, and the period in which that potential loss will be measured.

Transition rules. The new goodwill accounting requirements are to be initially applied (adopted) at the beginning of the first fiscal quarter that occurs after December 15, 2001 for all entities, including those that do not report on an interim basis. Early adoption is permitted for companies with a fiscal year beginning after March 15, 2001, provided that the first quarter financial statements have not been previously issued. In all cases, the new standard must be adopted as of the beginning of a fiscal year.

Goodwill arising from acquisitions completed before July 1, 2001 (that is, existing goodwill) will no longer be amortized once the new standard is implemented. Goodwill and intangible assets acquired in a transaction completed after June 30, 2001 but before the new standard is initially applied would be accounted for in accordance with the amortization and non amortization provisions of the statement. Thus, for example, if an entity with a December 31, 2001 year-end completes an acquisition on October 15, 2001, it will **not** amortize goodwill acquired in that acquisition. However, previously acquired goodwill would continue to be amortized until January 1, 2002. The impairment provisions of the new standard would be applicable to the recently acquired goodwill beginning January 1, 2002.

If a reporting entity has an unamortized deferred credit related to an excess over cost (that is, negative goodwill) arising from acquisitions completed before the date the new standard is adopted, that balance is to be recognized as an extraordinary gain in the period of adoption. Information about that extraordinary gain is to be disclosed as set forth by APB 30; that is, reported net of tax and apart from income before extraordinary items.

In the period of adoption and thereafter, until all periods presented reflect goodwill accounted for in accordance with the new standard, income before extraordinary items and net income computed on a pro forma basis are to be displayed for all periods presented. Those pro forma amounts are to reflect the reversal of amortization related to goodwill, any deferred credit related to an excess over cost, and equity method goodwill (see Chapter 10). However, goodwill impairment losses recognized in those prior periods, if any, are not to be increased to reflect what the losses might have been if goodwill had not been amortized. The pro forma information can be displayed either on the face of the income statement or in the notes to the financial statements. The notes to the financial statements must also set forth a reconciliation of reported earnings to the pro forma earnings, reflecting adjustments for the amortization of goodwill, any deferred credit, and equity method goodwill. Pro forma earnings per share, where required, can be presented either on the face of the income statement or in the notes thereto.

Special requirements for disposal of segments or other operations containing goodwill. Conducting impairment assessments in the context of asset dispositions has been addressed by FASB, and its guidance evolved very significantly during the interval from the initial draft (late 1999) to the revised draft (early 2001) and then to the promulgation of the final standard (mid-2001). When a significant portion of a reporting unit is disposed of, goodwill should be allocated based on the relative fair values of the portion of the reporting unit being disposed of and the portion of the unit remaining. An impairment test of the goodwill in the remaining (i.e., not disposed of) portion of the reporting unit would be required after the allocation of goodwill to ensure that the reporting unit can support the remaining goodwill.

Goodwill should be allocated to a portion of a reporting unit being disposed of only when that portion constitutes a business. However, the allocation approach should not be used when the business being disposed of is not classified as held-for-sale and was never integrated into the reporting unit. In that scenario, since the operating unit's identity and the original goodwill are still intact, all of the goodwill associated with that business would be included in the determination of the gain or loss on disposal.

The relative fair value allocation approach also should be used to determine how goodwill should be allocated when an entity reorganizes its reporting structure.

Other impairment considerations. SFAS 121 requires that goodwill associated with a long-lived asset be combined with that asset's carrying value when testing that long-lived asset (or group of assets) for impairment. However, under the new standard goodwill is to be tested for impairment at the reporting unit level. If the asset group being tested for impairment is also a reporting unit, goodwill does not need to be tested for impairment with the asset group under SFAS 121, since that would be duplicative with the testing to be performed under the new goodwill standard. In those circumstances, goodwill would be tested for impairment (and any impairment loss recognized) **before** the other long-lived assets are tested for impairment.

In some instances, however, a reporting unit may consist of multiple asset groups, and an event might occur that would necessitate impairment testing of some, but not all, long-lived assets of that reporting unit, per SFAS 121. That same event might or might not require an impairment test of reporting unit goodwill, since the criteria differ between the two pertinent standards. However, under the new requirements, the reporting unit is the unit of account for goodwill, and thus the reporting unit is the lowest level of assets with which goodwill can be associated. Therefore, goodwill cannot be associated with lower-level asset groups, and there is no need to allocate or otherwise associate reporting unit goodwill with asset groups when those assets are tested for impairment. The FASB acknowledges that adjusting cash flow projections for goodwill when testing long-lived assets for recoverability may prove to be challenging in such circumstances.

Goodwill may be an asset of a consolidated subsidiary, and the subsidiary may also prepare and present financial statements on a stand-alone basis (for example, to provide to creditors of, and minority shareholders in, that subsidiary). The subsidiary might represent a constituent part of a reporting unit at the parent company level. Per the new standard, impairment must be tested at the subsidiary level when stand-alone financial reports of the subsidiary are produced, whether the subsidiary is publicly held or private. For consolidated financial reporting purposes, impairment loss at the subsidiary level would not automatically be "pushed up," but testing for impairment at the level of the parent's reporting unit that contains that subsidiary would be called for due to the indicator of possible impairment. Upon testing, however, it might be the case that impairment would be found to **not** exist; this would be the result of the reporting unit's fair value exceeding its carrying value, probably because other component parts of that unit had value appreciation offsetting the diminution in value of the subsidiary.

Minority Interests in Purchase and Pooling Combinations

When a company acquires some, but not all, of the voting stock of another entity, the shares held by third parties represent a **minority interest** in the acquired company. This occurs when the acquisition form is employed. A legal merger or consolidation would give the acquirer a 100% interest in whatever assets it obtained from the selling entity. Under GAAP, if a parent company owns more than half of another entity, the two should be consolidated for financial statement purposes (unless control is temporary or the parent company does not have control over the subsidiary). The minority interest in the assets and earnings of the consolidated entity must also be accounted for.

When consolidated statements are prepared, the full amount of assets and liabilities (in the balance sheet) and income and expenses (in the income statement) of the subsidiary are generally presented. Accordingly, a contra must be shown for the portion of these items that does not belong to the parent company. In the balance sheet this contra is normally a credit item shown between total liabilities and stockholders' equity, representing the minority interest in consolidated net assets equal to the minority's percentage ownership in the net assets of the subsidiary entity. Although less likely, a debit balance in minority interest could result when the subsidiary has a deficit in its stockholders' equity **and** when there is reason to believe that the minority owners will make additional capital contributions to erase that deficit. This situation sometimes occurs where the entities are closely held and the minority owners are related parties having other business relationships with the parent company and/or its stockholders. In most other circumstances, a debit in minority interest would be charged against parent company retained earnings under the concept that the loss will be borne by that company. Although some believe that this debit should be added to goodwill on the consolidated balance sheet instead, it might be difficult to demonstrate that this would not result in an overstatement of total assets.

In the income statement, the minority interest in the income (or loss) of a consolidated subsidiary is shown as a deduction from (or addition to) the consolidated net income account. As above, if the minority interest in the net assets of the subsidiary has already been reduced to zero, and if a net debit minority interest will **not** be recorded (the usual case), then the minority's interest in any further losses should **not** be recorded. (However, this must be explained in the footnotes.) Furthermore, if past minority losses have not been recorded, the minority's interest in current profits will not be recognized until the aggregate of such profits equals the aggregate unrecognized losses. This closely parallels the rule for equity method accounting recognition of profits and losses.

Example of consolidation process involving a minority interest

Assume the following:

Alto Company and Bass Company
Balance Sheets at 1/1/01
(Immediately before combination)

	Alto Company	*Bass Company*
Assets		
Cash	$ 30,900	$ 37,400
Accounts receivable (net)	34,200	9,100
Inventories	22,900	16,100
Equipment	200,000	50,000
Less accumulated depreciation	(21,000)	(10,000)
Patents	--	10,000
Total assets	$267,000	$112,600
Liabilities and stockholders' equity		
Accounts payable	$ 4,000	$ 6,600
Bonds payable, 10%	100,000	--
Common stock, $10 par	100,000	50,000
Additional paid-in capital	15,000	15,000
Retained earnings	48,000	41,000
Total liabilities and stockholders' equity	$267,000	$112,600

Note that the book value of the net assets of Bass Company may be computed by one of the following two methods:

1. Subtract the book value of the liability from the book values of the assets.

$$\$112,600 - \$6,600 = \$106,000$$

2. Add the book values of the components of Bass Company stockholders' equity.

$$\$50,000 + \$15,000 + \$41,000 = \$106,000$$

At the date of combination, the fair values of all the assets and liabilities were determined by appraisal, as follows:

Bass Company Item	Book value (BV)	Fair market value (FMV)	Difference between BV and FMV
Cash	$ 37,400	$ 37,400	$ --
Accounts receivable (net)	9,100	9,100	--
Inventories	16,100	17,100	1,000
Equipment (net)	40,000	48,000	8,000
Patents	10,000	13,000	3,000
Accounts payable	(6,600)	(6,600)	--
Totals	$106,000	$118,000	$12,000

When a minority interest exists, as in this example, the concept employed will determine whether the consolidated balance sheet reflects the **full** excess of fair market values over book values of the subsidiary's net assets, or only the parent company's percentage share thereof. Under the **parent company** concept, only the parent's share of the revaluation is recognized, and minority interest is reported based on the book value of the subsidiary. If the **entity concept** is used, however, the full revaluation from book to fair value is recognized in the consolidated balance sheet, and the minority interest is based on the fair value of the subsidiary's net assets. Both techniques are acceptable.

Assume the following:

1. On January 1, 2001, Alto Company acquires a 90% interest in Bass Company in exchange for 5,400 shares of $10 par stock having a total market value of $120,600.
2. The purchase method of accounting is used for the combination.
3. Any goodwill resulting from the combination will not be amortized.

The workpaper for a consolidated balance sheet at the date of acquisition is presented below. The first two columns are the trial balances from the books of Alto Company and Bass Company immediately following the acquisition.

Alto Company and Bass Company Consolidated Working Papers
For Date of Combination—1/1/01

Purchase accounting
90% interest

	Alto Company	Bass Company	Adjustments and eliminations Debit	Adjustments and eliminations Credit	Minority interest	Consolidated balances
Balance sheet, 1/1/01						
Cash	$ 30,900	$ 37,400				$ 68,300
Accounts receivable	734,200	9,100				43,300
Inventories	22,900	16,100	$ 900[b]			39,900
Equipment	200,000	50,000	9,000[b]			259,000
Accumulated depreciation	(21,000)	(10,000)		$ 1,800[b]		(32,800)
Investment in stock of						
Bass Company	120,600			120,600[a]		
Difference between						
cost and book value			25,200[a]	25,200[b]		
Excess of cost over fair						
value (goodwill)			14,400[b]			14,400
Patents		10,000	2,700[b]			12,700
Total assets	$ 387,600	$112,600				$404,800
Accounts payable	$ 4,000	$ 6,600				$ 10,600
Bonds payable	100,000					100,000
Capital stock	154,000	50,000	45,000[a]		$ 5,000	154,000
Additional paid-in capital	81,600	15,000	13,500[a]		1,500	81,600
Retained earnings	48,000	41,000	36,900[a]		4,100	48,000
Minority interest					$10,600	10,600 MI
Total liabilities and equity	$387,600	$112,600	$147,600	$147,600		$404,800

1. Investment on Alto Company's books

 The entry to record the 90% purchase-acquisition on Alto Company's books was

Investment in stock of Bass Company	120,600	
Capital stock		54,000
Additional paid-in capital		66,600

 To record the issuance of 5,400 shares of $10 par stock to acquire a 90% interest in Bass Company

 Although common stock is used for the consideration in our example, Alto Company could have used debentures, cash, or any other form of consideration acceptable to Bass Company's stockholders to make the **purchase** combination.

2. Difference between investment cost and book value

 The difference between the investment cost and the parent company's equity in the net assets of the subsidiary is computed as follows:

Investment cost		$120,600
Less book value % at date of combination		
Bass Company's		
Capital stock	$ 50,000	
Additional paid-in capital	15,000	
Retained earnings	41,000	
Total	$106,000	
Parent's share of ownership	x 90%	
Parent's share of book value		95,400
Excess of cost over book value		$ 25,200

This difference is due to several undervalued assets and to unrecorded goodwill. The allocation procedure is similar to that for a 100% purchase; however, in this case, the parent company obtained a 90% interest and, thus, will recognize 90% of the difference between the fair market values and book values of the subsidiary's assets, not 100%. The allocation is presented as follows:

Allocation of the Differential

Item	Book value (BV)	Fair market value (FMV)	Difference between BV and (FMV)	Ownership percentage	Percentage share of difference between BV and FMV
Cash	$ 37,400	$ 37,400	$ --		
Accounts receivable (net)	9,100	9,100	--		
Inventories	16,100	17,100	1,000	90%	$ 900
Equipment	50,000	60,000	10,000	90%	9,000
Accumulated depreciation	(10,000)	(12,000)	(2,000)	90%	(1,800)
Patents	10,000	13,000	3,000	90%	2,700
Accounts payable	(6,600)	(6,600)	--		
Total	$106,000	$118,000	$12,000		

Amount of difference between cost and book value share allocated to revaluation of net assets	$10,800
Total differential	25,200
Remainder allocated to goodwill	$14,400

The equipment has a book value of $40,000 ($50,000 less 20% depreciation of $10,000). An appraisal concluded that the equipment's replacement cost was $60,000 less 20% accumulated depreciation of $12,000 resulting in a net fair value of $48,000.

3. Elimination entries on workpaper

The basic reciprocal accounts are the investment in subsidiary account on the parent's books and the subsidiary's stockholders' equity accounts. Only the parent's share of the subsidiary's accounts may be eliminated as reciprocal accounts. The remaining 10% portion is allocated to the minority interest. The entries below include documentation showing the company source for the information. The workpaper entry to eliminate the basic reciprocal accounts is as follows:

Capital stock—Bass Co.	45,000	
Additional paid-in capital—Bass Co.	13,500	
Retained earnings—Bass Co.	36,900*	
Differential	25,200	
Investment in stock of Bass Co.—Alto Co.		120,600

* *($41,000 x 90% = $36,900)*

Note that only 90% of Bass Company's stockholders' equity accounts are eliminated. Also, an account called differential is debited in the workpaper entry. The differential account is a temporary account to record the difference between the cost of the investment in Bass Company from the parent's books and the book value of the parent's interest (90% in our case) from the subsidiary's books.

The next step is to allocate the differential to the specific accounts by making the following workpaper entry:

Inventory	900	
Equipment	9,000	
Patents	2,700	
Goodwill	14,400	
Accumulated depreciation		1,800
Differential		25,200

This entry reflects the allocations prepared in step 2 on the previous page and recognizes the parent's share of the asset revaluations.

The minority interest column is the 10% interest of Bass Company's net assets owned by outside, third parties. Minority interest must be disclosed because 100% of the book values of Bass Company are included in the consolidated statements, although Alto Company controls only 90% of the net assets. An alternative method to prove minority interest is to multiply the net assets of the subsidiary by the minority interest share, as follows:

Stockholders' equity of Bass Company	x	Minority interest %	=	Minority interest
$106,000	x	10%	=	$10,600

The $10,600 would be reported on the credit side of the consolidated balance sheet between liabilities and stockholders' equity.

The **parent company concept** was used above to prepare the consolidated balance sheet. If the **entity concept** had been employed, minority interest would have been as follows:

Total fair market value of net assets of Bass Company	x	Minority percentage	=	Minority interest
$118,000	x	10%	=	$11,800

The example does not include any other intercompany accounts as of the date of combination. If any existed, they would be eliminated to fairly present the consolidated entity. Several examples of other reciprocal accounts will be shown later for the preparation of consolidated financial statements subsequent to the date of acquisition.

If the previous example were accounted for on a push-down basis, Bass would record the following entry on its books:

Inventories	1,000	
Equipment	10,000	
Patents	3,000	
Accumulated depreciation		2,000
Paid-in capital		12,000

As a result, Alto would have an investment of $120,600 in a company whose net equity was $118,000. Then 90% x $118,000 or $106,200 contrasted with the cost of $120,600 would mean the only number unaccounted for by Alto would be goodwill of $14,400. The elimination entry on the worksheet would change only with respect to the paid-in capital of Bass as follows:

Capital stock	45,000	
Paid-in capital	24,300	
Retained earnings	36,900	
Goodwill	14,400	
Investment		120,600

This would leave $5,000 of capital stock, $2,700 of paid-in capital, and $4,100 of retained earnings as minority interest or the same $11,800 as under the entity concept.

Consolidated Statements in Subsequent Periods

The same concepts employed to prepare a consolidated balance sheet at the date of acquisition are applicable to later consolidated statements. Where a minority interest exists, income in subsequent periods must be allocated to it. The exact nature of the worksheet entries depends on whether the parent is maintaining the investment in subsidiary account on the cost, partial equity, or full equity basis (all of which are acceptable since the consolidated financial statements will be identical under any alternative). In practice, the cost and partial equity methods are most likely to be encountered. The partial equity method is used when separate, parent-only statements are expected to be prepared in addition to consolidated statements (which commonly is the case). Using the partial equity method, the parent records its share of the subsidiary's income or loss but does not amortize the differential between cost and book value against equity in the subsidiary's earnings.

In addition to the elimination entries for the parent investment account and subsidiary equity accounts, other eliminations will be needed when there are intercompany balances or transactions resulting from parent-subsidiary loans (advances), sales of inventory items (whether or not these occurred at a profit to the seller), sales of fixed assets at other than net book value, and bond transactions or transactions in stock other than voting common shares. The selected items in the following example will demonstrate the accounting issues applicable to all such intercompany items and the proper handling of these items in the consolidated workpapers.

Example of a consolidation in subsequent periods

The basic facts of the Alto Company-Bass Company case have already been presented; additional information is as follows:

1. Alto Company uses the partial equity method to record changes in the value of the investment account.

2. During 2001, Alto Company sold merchandise to Bass Company that originally cost Alto Company $15,000, and the sale was made for $20,000. On December 31, 2001, Bass Company's inventory included merchandise purchased from Alto Company at a cost to Bass Company of $12,000.

3. Also during 2001, Alto Company acquired $18,000 of merchandise from Bass Company. Bass Company uses a normal markup of 25% above its cost. Alto Company's ending inventory includes $10,000 of the merchandise acquired from Bass Company.

4. Bass Company reduced its intercompany account payable to Alto Company to a balance of $4,000 as of December 31, 2001, by making a payment of $1,000 on December 30. This $1,000 payment was still in transit on December 31, 2001.

5. On January 2, 2001, Bass Company acquired equipment from Alto Company for $7,000. The equipment was originally purchased by Alto Company for $5,000 and had a book value of $4,000 at the date of sale to Bass Company. The equipment had an estimated remaining life of four years as of January 2, 2001.

6. On December 31, 2001, Bass Company purchased for $44,000, 50% of the outstanding bonds issued by Alto Company. The bonds mature on December 31, 2006, and were originally issued at par. The bonds pay interest annually on December 31 of each year, and the interest was paid to the prior investor immediately before Bass Company's purchase of the bonds.

The worksheet for the preparation of consolidated financial statements as of December 31, 2001, is presented below, on the assumption that purchase accounting is used for the business combination.

The investment account balance at the statement date should be reconciled to ensure the parent company made the proper entries under the method of accounting used to account for the investment. Since the partial equity method is used by Alto, the amortizations of the excess of cost over book value will be recognized only on the worksheets.

An analysis of the investment account at December 31, 2001, is as follows:

	Investment in Stock of Bass Company		
Original cost	120,600		
% of Bass Co.'s income ($9,400 x 90%)	8,460	3,600	% of Bass Co.'s dividends declared ($4,000 x 90%)
Balance, 12/31/01	125,460		

Any errors will require correcting entries before the consolidation process is continued. Correcting entries will be posted to the books of the appropriate company; eliminating entries are **not** posted to either company's books.

The difference between the investment cost and the book value of the net assets acquired was determined and allocated in the preparation of the date of combination consolidated statements presented earlier. The same computations are used in preparing financial statements for as long as the investment is owned.

The following adjusting and eliminating entries will be required to prepare consolidated financials as of December 31, 2001. Note that a consolidated income statement is required and, therefore, the nominal accounts are still open. The number or letter in parentheses to the left of the entry corresponds to the key used on the worksheet.

Step 1 —Complete the transaction for any intercompany items in transit at the end of the year.

(1)	Cash	1,000	
	Accounts receivable		1,000

This **adjusting** entry will now properly present the financial positions of both companies, and the consolidation process may be continued.

Step 2 —Prepare the eliminating entries.

(a)	Sales	38,000	
	Cost of goods sold		38,000

Total intercompany sales of $38,000 include $20,000 in a downstream transaction from Alto Company to Bass Company and $18,000 in an upstream transaction from Bass Company to Alto Company.

(b)	Cost of goods sold	5,000	
	Inventory		5,000

The ending inventories are overstated because of the unrealized profit from the intercompany sales. The debit to cost of goods sold is required because a decrease in ending inventory will increase cost of goods sold to be deducted on the income statement. Supporting computations for the entry are as follows:

	In ending inventory of	
	Alto Company	*Bass Company*
Intercompany sales not resold, at selling price	$10,000	$12,000
Cost basis of remaining intercompany merchandise		
From Bass to Alto (÷ 125%)	(8,000)	
From Alto to Bass (÷ 133 1/3%)		(9,000)
Unrealized profit	$ 2,000	$ 3,000

When preparing consolidated workpapers for 2002 (the next fiscal period), an additional eliminating entry will be required if the goods in 2001's ending inventory are sold to outsiders during 2002. The

additional entry will recognize the profit for 2002 that was eliminated as unrealized in 2001. This entry is necessary since the entry
at the end of 2001 was made only on the worksheet. The 2002 entry will be as follows:

Retained earnings—Bass Co., 1/1/02	2,000	
Retained earnings—Alto Co., 1/1/02	3,000	
Cost of goods sold, 2002		5,000

(c)

Accounts payable	4,000	
Accounts receivable		4,000

This entry eliminates the remaining intercompany receivable/
payable owed by Bass Company to Alto Company. This eliminating entry is necessary to avoid overstating the consolidated entity's
balance sheet. The receivable/payable is not extinguished, and Bass
Company must still transfer $4,000 to Alto Company in the future.

(d)

Gain on sale of equipment	3,000	
Equipment		2,000
Accumulated depreciation		250
Depreciation expense		750

This entry eliminates the gain on the intercompany sale of the
equipment, eliminates the overstatement of equipment, and removes
the excess depreciation taken on the gain. Supporting computations
for the entry are as follows:

	Cost	*At date of intercompany sale accum. depr.*	*2001 depr. ex.*	*End-of-period accum. depr.*
Original basis (to seller, Alto Co.)	$5,000	($1,000)	$ 1,000	($2,000)
New basis (to buyer, Bass Co.)	7,000	--	1,750	(1,750)
Difference	($2,000)		($ 750)	$ 250

If the intercompany sale had not occurred, Alto Company would
have depreciated the remaining book value of $4,000 over the esti-
mated remaining life of four years. However, since Bass Company's acquisition price ($7,000) was more than Alto Company's
basis in the asset ($4,000), the depreciation recorded on the books
of Bass Company will include part of the intercompany unrealized
profit. The equipment must be reflected on the consolidated statements at the original cost to the consolidated entity. Therefore, the
write-up of $2,000 in the equipment, the excess depreciation of
$750, and the gain of $3,000 must be eliminated. The ending balance of accumulated depreciation must be shown at what it would
have been if the intercompany equipment transaction had not occurred. In future periods, a retained earnings account will be used
instead of the gain account; however, the other concepts will be extended to include the additional periods.

(e)	Bonds payable	50,000	
	Investment in bonds of Alto Company		44,000
	Gain on extinguishment of debt		6,000

This entry eliminates the book value of Alto Company's debt against the bond investment account of Bass Company. To the consolidated entity, this transaction must be shown as a retirement of debt even though Alto Company has the outstanding intercompany debt to Bass Company. SFAS 4 specifies that gains or losses on debt extinguishment, if material, should be shown as an extraordinary item. In future periods, Bass Company will amortize the discount, thereby bringing the investment account up to par value. A retained earnings account will be used in the eliminating entry instead of the gain account.

(f)	Equity in subsidiary's income—Alto Co.	8,460	
	Dividends declared—Bass Co.		3,600
	Investment in stock of Alto Co.		4,860

This elimination entry adjusts the investment account back to its balance at the beginning of the period and also eliminates the subsidiary income account.

(g)	Capital stock—Bass Co.	45,000	
	Additional paid-in capital—Bass Co	13,500	
	Retained earnings—Bass Co.	36,900	
	Differential	25,200	
	Investment in stock of Bass Company—Alto Co.		120,600

This entry eliminates 90% of Bass Company's stockholders' equity at the beginning of the year, 1/1/01. Note that the changes **during** the year were eliminated in entry (f) above. The differential account reflects the excess of investment cost over the book value of the assets acquired.

(h)	Inventory	900	
	Equipment	9,000	
	Patents	2,700	
	Goodwill	14,400	
	Accumulated depr.		1,800
	Differential		25,200

This entry allocates the differential (excess of investment cost over the book values of the assets acquired). Note that this entry is the same as the allocation entry made to prepare consolidated financial statements for January 1, 2001, the date of acquisition.

(i)	Cost of goods sold	900	
	Depreciation expense	1,800	
	Other operating expenses—patent amortization	270	
	Inventory		900
	Accumulated depr.		1,800
	Patents		270

The elimination entry amortizes the revaluations to fair market value made in entry (h). The inventory has been sold and, therefore, becomes part of cost of goods sold. Under recently promulgated GAAP, goodwill is not to be amortized, but will be reviewed for possible impairment. The remaining revaluations will be amortized as follows:

	Revaluation	*Amortization period*	*Annual amortization*
Equipment (net)	$7,200	4 years	$1,800
Patents	2,700	10 years	270

The amortizations will continue to be made on future worksheets. For example, at the end of the next year (2002), the amortization entry (i) would be as follows:

Differential	2,970	
Depreciation expense	1,800	
Other operating expenses—patent amortization	270	
Inventory		900
Accumulated depr.		3,600
Patents		540

The initial debit of $2,970 to differential is an aggregation of the prior period's charges to income statement accounts ($900 + $1,800 + $270). During subsequent years, some accountants prefer reducing the allocated amounts in entry (h) for prior period's charges. In this case, the amortization entry in future periods would reflect just that period's amortizations.

In adjusting for the minority interest in the consolidated entity's equity and earnings, the following guidelines should be observed:

1. Only the parent's share of the subsidiary's shareholders' equity is eliminated in the basic eliminating entry. The minority interest's share is presented separately.
2. The entire amount of intercompany reciprocal items is eliminated. For example, all receivables/payables and sales/cost of sales with a 90% subsidiary are eliminated.
3. For intercompany transactions in inventory and fixed assets, the possible effect on minority interest depends on whether the original transaction affected the subsidiary's income statement. Minority interest is adjusted only if the subsidiary is the selling entity. In this case, the minority interest is adjusted for its percentage ownership of the common stock of the subsidiary. The minority interest is **not** adjusted for unrealized profits on downstream sales. The effects of downstream transactions are confined solely to the parent's (i.e., controlling) ownership interests.

The minority interest's share of the subsidiary's income is shown as a deduction on the consolidated income statement since 100% of the subsidiary's revenues and expenses are combined, even though the parent company owns less than a

100% interest. For our example, the minority interest deduction on the income statement is computed as follows:

Bass Company's reported income	$9,400
Less unrealized profit on an upstream inventory sale	(2,000)
Bass Company's income for consolidated financial purposes	$7,400
Minority interest share	x 10%
Minority interest on income statement	$ 740

The minority interest's share of the net assets of Bass Company is shown on the consolidated balance sheet between liabilities and controlling interest's equity. The computation for the minority interest shown in the balance sheet for our example is as follows:

Bass Company's capital stock, 12/31/01	$50,000	
Minority interest share	x 10%	$ 5,000
Bass Company's additional paid-in capital, 12/31/01	$15,000	
Minority interest share	x 10%	1,500
Bass Company's retained earnings, 1/1/01	$41,000	
Minority interest share	x 10%	4,100
Bass Company's 2001 income for consolidated purposes	$ 7,400	
Minority interest share	x 10%	740
Bass Company's dividends during 2001	$ 4,000	
Minority interest share	x 10%	(400)
Total minority interest, 12/31/01		$10,940

Alto Company and Bass Company Consolidated Working Papers
Year Ended December 31, 2001

Purchase accounting
90% owned subsidiary
subsequent year, partial equity method

	Alto Company	Bass Company	Adjustments and eliminations Debit	Credit	Minority interest	Consolidated balances
Income statements for year ended 12/31/01						
Sales	$750,000	$420,000	$ 38,000[a]			$1,132,000
Cost of sales	581,000	266,000	5,000[b] 900[i]	$ 38,000[a]		814,900
Gross margin	169,000	154,000				317,100
Depreciation and interest expense	28,400	16,200	1,800[i]	750[d]		45,650
Other operating expenses	117,000	128,400	270[i]			245,670
Net income from operations	23,600	9,400				25,780
Gain on sale of equipment	3,000		3,000[d]			
Gain on bonds				6,000[e]		6,000
Equity in subsidiary's income	8,460		8,460[f]			
Minority income ($7,400 x .10)					$ 740	(740)
Net income	$ 35,060	$ 9,400	$ 57,430	$ 44,750	$ 740	$ 31,040

Statement of retained earnings
for year ended 12/31/01

	Alto	Bass	Debit	Credit	Minority interest	Consolidated
1/1/01 retained earnings						
Alto Company	$ 48,000					$ 48,000
Bass Company		$ 41,000	$ 36,900[g]		$ 4,100	
Add net income (from above)	35,060	9,400	57,430	$ 44,750	740	31,040
Total	83,060	50,400			4,840	79,040
Deduct dividends	15,000	4,000		3,600[f]	400	15,000
Balance, 12/31/01	$ 68,060	$ 46,400	$ 94,330	$ 48,350	$ 4,440	$ 64,040

	Alto Company	Bass Company	Adjustments and eliminations Debit	Credit	Minority interest	Consolidated balances
Balance sheet, 12/31/01						
Cash	$ 45,300	6,400	$ 1,000[1]			$ 52,700
Accounts receivable (net)	43,700	12,100		$ 1,000[1] 4,000[c]		50,800
Inventories	38,300	20,750	900[h]	5,000[b] 900[i]		54,050
Equipment	195,000	57,000	9,000[h]	2,000[d]		259,000
Accumulated depreciation	(35,200)	(18,900)		250[d] 1,800[h] 1,800[i]		(57,950)
Investment in stock of						
Bass Company	125,460			4,860[f] 120,600[g]		
Differential			25,200[g]	25,200[h]		
Goodwill			14,400[h]			14,400
Investment in bonds of						
Alto Company		44,000		44,000[e]		
Patents		9,000	2,700[h]	270[i]		11,430
	$412,560	$130,350				$384,430
Accounts payable	$ 8,900	$ 18,950	4,000[c]			$ 23,850
Bonds payable	100,000		50,000[e]			50,000
Capital stock	154,000	50,000	45,000[g]		$ 5,000	154,000
Additional paid-in capital	81,600	15,000	13,500[g]		1,500	81,600
Retained earnings (from above)	68,060	46,400	94,330	48,350	4,440	64,040
Minority interest					$10,940	10,940
	$412,560	$130,350	$260,030	$260,030		$384,430

The remainder of the consolidation process consists of the following worksheet techniques:

1. Take all income items across horizontally and foot the adjustments, minority interest, and consolidated columns down to the net income line.
2. Take the amounts on the net income line (on income statement) in the adjustments, minority interest, and consolidated balances columns **down to** retained earnings items across the consolidated balances column. Foot and crossfoot the retained earnings statement.
3. Take the amounts of ending retained earnings in each of the four columns down to the ending retained earnings line in the balance sheet. Foot the minority interest column and place its total in the consolidated balances

column. Take all the balance sheet items across to consolidated balances column.

Other Accounting Problems in Business Combinations

Contingent consideration. Many business acquisitions include contingent consideration features, which requires, if specified conditions are later met, that additions to the purchase price must be paid, either in cash or in shares of the acquiring entity. Under prior GAAP, the presence of this feature made it mandatory that the purchase method of accounting for the acquisition be used. Since the pooling of interests method is now prohibited, and the purchase method must be used for every business combination (with minor exceptions, noted earlier in the chapter), contingent consideration no longer is a factor to evaluate in making a determination of how to account for a given transaction.

Nonetheless, the presence of contingent consideration provisions in an acquisition arrangement must be addressed, both at the time of the acquisition and later, if and when contingent consideration is earned and paid.

At the date of the acquisition, contingent consideration is important to the extent that it precludes immediate recognition of an extraordinary gain arising from the excess of "negative goodwill" over the amounts allocable to various assets (all assets other than cash, receivables, inventory, financial instruments carried on the balance sheet at fair value, assets to be disposed of by sale, and deferred tax assets). Under GAAP, if such an excess exists, it is to be classified as a deferred credit, not taken into earnings, until the contingency regarding the purchase price has been resolved. Only a small fraction of business combinations are true "bargain purchases," and of these, it is expected that only a minute portion will result in such a large amount of negative goodwill that an excess will remain after offsetting against the qualified assets. Of those, an even smaller proportion will relate to transactions in which contingent consideration is to be paid, and thus for which the deferral of what otherwise would be immediately recognized as extraordinary gain would be prescribed.

The accounting for the subsequent payment of the added consideration depends upon whether the contingency was related to the earnings of the acquired entity or to the market value of the original consideration package given by the acquirer.

In the former instance, a subsequent payment of added cash, stock, or any other valuable consideration will require a reevaluation of the purchase price. This reevaluation possibly could alter the amounts allocable to certain (mostly noncurrent) assets (where cost in the original purchase transaction was less than fair value acquired (i.e., a "bargain purchase") and the difference was offset against those assets), or could result in an increased amount of goodwill being recognized. The effects of a revaluation are handled prospectively (i.e., the additional depreciation of fixed assets is allocated to the remaining economic lives of those items) without making any adjustment to postacquisition periods' results already reported.

In the latter case, the event triggering the issuance of additional shares is a decline in market value of the original purchase package. Additional shares of the acquirer's stock are paid in order to increase the value of the consideration to the amount intended by the parties at the date of the transaction. According to APB 16, this does not alter the total cost of the transaction for accounting recognition purposes, even though, obviously, further consideration is later transferred to the former owners of the acquiree. The total value of the purchase would **not** be changed and, thus, no alteration of amounts allocated to the various assets and liabilities acquired would be needed. However, the issuance of extra shares of common stock will typically require that the allocation between the common stock and the additional paid-in capital accounts be adjusted.

In rare instances, contingent consideration based on the value of the securities used to effect the acquisition may involve transactions in which common stock was not used. If part of the original purchase price had been paid in bonds or other debt instruments, the reallocation might affect the premium or discount recognized on the debt, which would have an impact on future earnings as these accounts are subsequently amortized.

Net operating loss carryforward of acquired entity. An entity acquired in a purchase business combination may have a tax loss carryforward that will be available for use by the acquiring entity. Prior GAAP (APB 11 and SFAS 96) generally prohibited recognition of the tax benefit of NOL carryforwards, albeit for different reasons. Under APB 11, the subsequent realization of the NOL carryforward necessitated the reallocation of the purchase price. Reallocation was often accompanied by the restatement of the results of operations for the intervening years after the date of the purchase transaction. Under SFAS 96, subsequent realization of tax loss carryforward benefits was accounted for as a limited reallocation of the purchase transaction: only goodwill and other identifiable intangibles were to be restated, with any further tax benefit being reported in current period tax expense.

Essentially this same approach has been adopted by SFAS 109. As discussed more fully in Chapter 15, Income Taxes, recognition **for the first time** of the benefits of NOL carryforwards (acquired in a purchase business combination at a date subsequent to the purchase) is accomplished by reducing recorded goodwill to zero. Next, other identifiable intangible assets acquired in the same transaction are reduced to zero. Any excess is reduced from current period tax expense. Under the provisions of SFAS 109 benefits related to acquired NOL are reported in the acquirer's balance sheet (as are benefits arising from any other deductible temporary differences). A valuation allowance is also recorded if realization is not considered **more likely than not. For the first time** means that the allowance account has been reduced or eliminated, either because the probability of realization has been reassessed or because the tax benefits have, in fact, been realized in the current period.

Preacquisition contingencies. At the time a business combination is consummated, the purchase price must be allocated to acquired assets and assumed liabilities in accordance with their respective fair values, with any excess purchase price being assigned to goodwill (if fair value exceeds cost, the cost deficiency is allocated primarily against noncurrent assets, with any remainder treated as "negative goodwill" and, in general, taken into earnings at the date of the acquisition). In some cases, however, the fair values of certain assets (e.g., those to be disposed of) may not be known with precision, and the amounts of certain estimated or contingent liabilities (such as outstanding litigation claims) may also be subject to uncertainty. Since the promulgation of SFAS 16 (prior period adjustments) ended the earlier practice of restating prior period financial statements unless an "error" could be shown to have occurred, it became necessary to develop a new standard, SFAS 38, to provide for a "look back" to reallocate the purchase price when these contingencies are ultimately resolved. However, under SFAS 38 there is a limited period, usually deemed to be one year, during which a reallocation can be effected; thereafter, resolutions of preacquisition contingencies must be treated as current period events and reported in earnings.

An exception to this rule exists in the case of income tax uncertainties existing at the date of a purchase business combination. Resolution of these must be accounted for in accordance with SFAS 109, which stipulates that such adjustments are to be applied to increase or decrease the remaining balance of goodwill attributable to that business combination; if goodwill is reduced to zero, the remaining amount should be used to first reduce other noncurrent intangible assets from the same acquisition to zero, and any excess beyond that amount is to be taken into income. Thus, the resolution of these specific uncertainties cannot result in a general reallocation of the purchase price, as are other resolutions of preacquisition contingencies.

Changes in majority interest. The parent's ownership interest can change as a result of purchases or sales of the subsidiary's common shares by the parent, or as a consequence of capital transactions of the subsidiary. The latter circumstance is generally handled precisely as demonstrated in the equity method discussion in Chapter 10, Investments (see pages 403-406). If the parent's relative book value interest in the subsidiary has changed, then gains or losses are treated as incurred in an entity's own treasury stock transactions. Gains are credited to paid-in capital; losses are charged to any previously created paid-in capital or to retained earnings. However, the SEC requires that when a subsidiary sells shares to outside interests at a price greater than the parent's carrying amount, the parent company should recognize a gain on the transaction.

When the parent's share of ownership increases through a purchase of additional stock, simply debit investment and credit cash for the cost. A problem occurs with consolidated income statements when the change in ownership takes place in midperiod. Consolidated statements should be prepared based on the ending ownership level.

Example of a consolidation with a change in the majority interest

Assume that Alto Company increased its ownership of Bass Company from 90% to 95% on October 1, 2001. The investment was acquired at book value of $5,452.50 and is determined as follows:

Capital stock at 10/1/01		$50,000
Additional paid-in capital, 10/1/01		15,000
Retained earnings at 10/1/01		
Balance, 1/1/01	$41,000	
Net income for nine months ($9,400 x .75)	7,050*	
Preacquisition dividends	(4,000)	44,050
		$ 109,050
		x 5%
Book value acquired		$5,452.50

* *Assumes income was earned evenly over the year.*

The consolidated net income should reflect a net of

90%	x	$9,400	x	12/12	=	$8,460.00
5%	x	$9,400	x	3/12	=	$ 117.50
95%						$8,577.50

The interim stock purchase will result in a new account being shown on the consolidated income statement. The account is **Purchased preacquisition earnings**, which represents the percentage of the subsidiary's income earned, in this case, on the 5% stock interest from January 1, 2001, to October 1, 2001. The basic eliminating entries would be based on the 95% ownership as follows:

Equity in subsidiary's income—Alto Co.	8,577.50	
Dividends declared—Bass Co.		3,600.00
Investment in stock of Bass Co.		4,977.50
Capital stock—Bass Co.	47,500.00	
Additional paid-in capital—Bass Co.	14,250.00	
Retained earnings—Bass Co.	38,750.00**	
Purchased preacquisition earnings	352.50***	
Differential	25,200.00	
Investment in stock of Bass Co.— Alto Co.		126,052.50

** 95% x $41,000 beginning 2001 balance	$38,950
Less preacquisition dividend of 5% x $4,000	(200)
Retained earnings available, as adjusted	$38,750

*** *5% x $9,400 x 9/12 = $352.50*

Purchased preacquisition earnings is shown as a deduction, along with minority interest, to arrive at consolidated net income. Purchased preacquisition earnings are used only with interim acquisition under the purchase accounting method.

Requirement that all majority-owned subsidiaries be consolidated. GAAP has long held that when one entity is owned outright or controlled by another entity (the parent company), the most meaningful representation of the economic substance of the parent company will be through consolidated financial statements.

This presumption dates from ARB 51, which did not, however, absolutely require that consolidated financial reporting be employed. Over the years since the issuance of ARB 51, a number of popular exceptions to the general rule have arisen, which eventually resulted in a substantial diversity of reporting practices. This lack of comparability led the FASB to reconsider the value of consolidated financial reporting; the issuance of SFAS 94 was the first (and thus far, only) result of the Board's announced three-phase project on the reporting entity, consolidated financial statements, and the equity method.

Varied reasons were given previously for excluding some or all subsidiaries from the parent company's financial statements. Lack of absolute control over the affairs of the subsidiary, whether because of legal restrictions or due to the relationship with minority owners, was often cited as a valid justification for not consolidating the subsidiary entity in the parent's financial statements. In other situations, control was present but expected to be only temporary; to prepare consolidated statements in one reporting period would likely cause comparability problems in later, postdivestment periods.

More controversial than the above were situations where "off-balance-sheet financing" was accomplished through the use of majority or wholly owned leasing, factoring, or other financing subsidiaries that were then excluded from the parent's financial statements. The actual justification given was that consolidation of such "nonhomogeneous" operations would distort the parent's key financial and operating statistics, such as the working capital ratio and gross profit margin. This situation was cited as the rationale for excluding highly leveraged financing subsidiaries.

The flaw in the above-noted argument is that the use of consolidated financial statements as the primary reporting vehicle never precluded the presentation of supplementary financial information, including separate subsidiary financial statements or **consolidating** financial statements if deemed necessary to convey the true essence of a company's operations. Also, since comparability of financial data across entities has always been an important underlying postulate of accounting theory, the lack of a standardized approach by diversified entities was a major hindrance to financial analysis.

SFAS 94 significantly narrows, but does not totally eliminate, the ability of entities to exclude majority owned subsidiaries from parent company financial statements. Most importantly, the "nonhomogeneity" argument cannot be employed any longer to exclude leasing, real estate, financing, insurance, or other subsidiary operations. Henceforth, unless one of the exceptions stated below applies, these operations must be included in consolidated financial statements.

The "consolidate everything" rule of SFAS 94 offers only the following exceptions:

- Control over the subsidiary is expected to be temporary in nature; or
- Control does not reside with the majority owner.

Absence of control is likely to occur only when a domestic subsidiary is in bankruptcy proceedings or when a foreign subsidiary operates in an environment of extreme exchange controls or restrictions on repatriation of earnings.

Separate financial statements of entities that are majority owned by other companies are still permitted. In fact, minority shareholders and other interested parties (creditors, vendors, or customers, as well as regulatory authorities) might receive little useful information from the parent company's consolidated financial statements in most instances. However, if the reporting subsidiary itself had one or more majority owned subsidiaries of its own, these would be consolidated in the financial statements of the first-tier subsidiary.

Majority owned subsidiaries **not** consolidated (because one of the two available exception conditions applies) will generally be accounted for by the equity method. The Board's exposure draft preceding SFAS 94 would have proscribed the use of the equity method (i.e., would have required that the cost method of accounting for those investments be used). However, this requirement was dropped from the final standard. As a result, specific circumstances must determine whether the equity method is appropriate.

Combined Financial Statements

When a group of entities is under common ownership, control, or management, it is often useful to present combined (or combining—showing the separate as well as the combined entities) financial statements. In this situation, the economic substance of the nominally independent entities' operations may be more important to statement users than is the legal form of those enterprises. When consolidated statements are not presented, combined statements may be used to show the financial position, or operating results, of a group of companies that are each subsidiaries of a common parent.

According to ARB 51, the process of preparing combined statements is virtually the same as consolidations employing the pooling-of-interests method. The major exception is that the equity section of the combined balance sheet will incorporate the paid-in capital accounts of each of the combining entities. However, only a single combined retained earnings account need be presented.

Example of a combined financial statement

Adams Corporation and Benbow Company, Inc.
Combined Balance Sheet
December 31, 2001

Stockholders' equity

Capital stock:

Preferred, $100 par, authorized 90,000 shares, issued 5,000 shares	$ 500,000
Common, $50 par, authorized 100,000 shares, issued 60,000 shares	3,000,000
Common, $10 par, authorized 250,000 shares, issued 100,000 shares	1,000,000
Additional paid-in capital	650,000
Retained earnings	3,825,000
	$8,975,000

Combinations of Entities under Common Control

Both APB 16 and its replacement, SFAS 141, explicitly do **not** apply to combinations of entities under common control (parent and subsidiary, brother-sister corporations, etc.). Mergers among such affiliated entities must be accounted for "as if" poolings, per AICPA Interpretation 39. This treatment is consistent with the concept of poolings as combinations of common shareholder interests. Notwithstanding the banning of pooling accounting under the new standards, this prescription still remains in effect.

A question arises, however, when a parent (Company P) transfers ownership in one of its subsidiaries (Company B) to another of its subsidiaries (Company A) in exchange for additional shares of Company A. If P's carrying value of its investment in B differs from B's book value, there appears to be a requirement under Interpretation 39 for A to reflect its new investment in B at B's book value, rather than at P's cost (or equity) basis.

EITF 90-5 resolved this apparent conflict by stating that A's carrying value for the investment in B should be P's basis, not B's book value. Furthermore, if A subsequently retires the interests of minority owners of B, the transaction should be accounted for as a purchase, whether it is effected through a stock issuance by A or by a cash payment to the selling shareholders.

The EITF further concluded (in Issue 90-13) that when a purchase transaction is closely followed by a "sale" of the parent's subsidiary to the newly acquired (target) entity, these two transactions should be viewed as a single transaction. Accordingly, and notwithstanding AICPA Interpretation 39 (above), the parent should recognize gain or loss on the sale of its subsidiary to the target company, to the extent of minority interest in the target entity. As a result, there will be a new basis (step-up) not only for the target company's assets and liabilities, but also for the subsidiary company's net assets. Basis is stepped up to the extent of minority participation in the target entity to which the subsidiary company was transferred.

Accounting for Leveraged Buyouts

Possibly one of the most complex accounting issues to have arisen over the past two decades has been the appropriate accounting for leveraged buyouts (LBO). At the center of this issue is the question of whether a **new basis** of accountability has been created by the LBO transaction. If so, then a step-up in the reported value of assets and/or liabilities is warranted. If not, the carryforward bases of the predecessor entity should continue to be reported in the company's financial statements.

The EITF has addressed leveraged buyouts, first in 86-16, then in 88-16 and 90-12. The task force's conclusion was that partial or complete new basis accounting is appropriate only when the transaction is characterized by a **change in control of voting interest**. Consensus 88-16 established a series of mechanical tests by which this change in interest is to be measured. The EITF identified three groups of interests: shareholders in the newly created company, management, and shareholders in the old company (who may or may not also have an interest in the new company). Depending upon the relative interests of these groups in the old entity (OLDCO) and in the new enterprise (NEWCO), there will be **either**, (1) a finding that the transaction was a purchase (new basis accounting applies) or (2) that it was a re-capitalization or a restructuring (carryforward basis accounting applies).

Among the tests which the EITF decreed to determine proper accounting for any given LBO transaction is the "monetary test." This test requires that at least 80% of the net consideration paid to acquire OLDCO interests must be **monetary**. In this context, monetary means cash, debt, and the fair value of any equity by securities given by NEWCO to selling shareholders of OLDCO. Loan proceeds provided OLDCO to assist in the acquisition of NEWCO shares by NEWCO shareholders are excluded from this definition. If the portion of the purchase that is effected through monetary consideration is less than 80%, but other criteria of EITF 88-16 are satisfied, there will be a step up. This step up will be limited to the percentage of the transaction represented by monetary consideration.

EITF 88-16 presents an extensive series of examples illustrating the circumstances that would and would not meet the purchase accounting criteria to be employed in LBO. These examples should be consulted as needed when addressing an actual LBO transaction accounting issue.

Reverse Acquisitions

Reverse acquisitions occur when one entity (the nominal acquirer) issues so many shares to the former owners of another entity (the nominal acquiree) that they become the majority owners of the resultant combined enterprise. The result of this event is that the legal and accounting treatments of the transaction will diverge, with the nominal acquiree being the acquirer for financial reporting purposes. While often the nominal acquirer will adopt the acquiree's name, thus alerting users of the statements to the nature of the organizational change, this does not necessarily occur, and, in any event, it will be critical that the financial statements contain sufficient disclosure so that users are not misled. This will be important particularly in the periods immediately following the transaction, and especially when comparative financial statements are presented which include some periods prior to the acquisition, since comparability will be affected.

A typical reverse acquisition would occur when a "shell" enterprise, which often is a publicly held but dormant company, merges with an operating company, which often will be nonpublic. The objective is for the operating entity to "go public" without the usual time consuming and expensive registration process. However, reverse acquisitions are not limited to such situations, and there have been many such transactions involving two public or two nonpublic companies, and the nominal acquirer may have substantial operations of its own, although of lesser scope or with lower growth prospects than those of the nominal acquiree.

A number of difficult questions arise in reverse acquisitions, and GAAP does not provide definitive guidance on these important issues. The SEC has provided some direction which, under the hierarchy of GAAP, should be viewed as definitive absent higher level "official" indicators from the profession. Among the matters to be considered, and which will be discussed in the following paragraphs, are these.

1. What circumstances signal a reverse acquisition?
2. How should the consolidated financial statements be presented in the subsequent periods?
3. How should the purchase cost be computed and allocated in a reverse acquisition?
4. What would the shareholders' equity section of the balance sheet be immediately following the reverse acquisition?
5. What would be the impact on computation of earnings per share?
6. How will minority interest be presented in the financial statements?

Reverse acquisitions occur when the former shareholders of the nominal acquiree become the majority owners of the postacquisition consolidated enterprise, and most commonly this will result when a stock-for-stock swap occurs. Under prior rules, if all of the twelve restrictive conditions set forth in APB 16 were met, the transaction would be accounted for as a pooling, thus obviating the concerns noted above. Under recently promulgated GAAP, however, poolings are prohibited and all business combinations will be accounted for as purchases. Unless the combining entities were under common control prior to the transaction (in which case the transaction is accounted for in the manner of a pooling, continuing the exception first established by Interpretation 39 under APB 16), purchase accounting is required for all reverse acquisitions.

If the former owners of the nominal acquiree in a purchase business combination become the majority owners of the consolidated enterprise following the transactions, it will be deemed to have been a reverse acquisition. Following a reverse acquisition, consolidated financial statements will be presented. Although the financial statements will be identified as being those of the nominal acquirer (which will be the legal owner of the nominal acquiree), in substance these will be the financial statements of the acquiree company, with the assets and liabilities, and revenues and expenses, of the nominal acquirer being included effective with the date of the transaction. Put another way, the legal parent company will be deemed to be a continuation of the business of the legal subsidiary, notwithstanding the formal structure of the transaction or the name of the successor enterprise. For this reason, if the legal parent (nominally the acquirer) does not change its name to that of the acquiree, it would be appropriate for the financial statement titles to be captioned in a way that most clearly communicates the substance of the transaction to the readers. For example, the statements may be headed "ABC Company, Inc.—successor to XYZ Corporation."

Given the foregoing, it is clear that the stockholders' equity section of the post-transaction consolidated balance sheet should be that of the acquiree, not the acquirer, with appropriate modification for the new shares issued in the transaction and ancillary adjustments, if any. Comparative financial statements for earlier periods, if presented, should be consistent, meaning that these would be the financial statements of the nominal acquiree. Since in some instances the acquiree's name is different than that shown in the heading, care must be taken to fully communicate with the readers. The fact that the prior period's financial information identified as being that of the legal parent is really that of the nominal acquiree obviously is extremely pertinent to a reader's understanding of these statements.

Consistent with the accounting imposed on other purchase business combinations, the cost of reverse acquisitions should be measured at the fair value of the net assets acquired, or the value of the consideration paid, if more apparent. A special rule is that, if fair market value cannot be determined for the issuer's stock, and the transaction is valued at the fair market value of the issuer's net assets, no goodwill should be recognized in the transaction. In addition, in the special case of a publicly held shell company and a privately held acquiree, the SEC has ruled that no goodwill can be recognized in any event. Clearly, in such instances there is substantial doubt about the true existence of goodwill and unusual difficulty in valuing the transaction, and this prohibition is prudent under the circumstances.

If the fair value of the shares of the nominal acquiree (which becomes the legal subsidiary after the transaction is completed) is used to determine the cost of the purchase, it is suggested that a calculation be made to determine the number of shares that the acquiree would have issued in order to provide the same level of ownership in the combined entity to the shareholders of the nominal acquirer as they have as a consequence of the reverse acquisition. The fair value of the number of shares thus determined is used to value the transaction, as illustrated later in this section.

In some instances, the market price of acquiree shares may not be fairly indicative of the value of the transaction. In such cases, the most feasible alternative would be to use the fair market value of all the outstanding shares of the ostensible acquirer, prior to the transaction, to value the purchase transaction. In some instances, adjustments would have to be made for trading volume, price fluctuations, etc., to most accurately reflect the substance of the acquisition.

In other cases, particularly where the acquirer is a dormant shell entity, market price of its shares may not be meaningful. If possible to determine, utilizing the fair value of the net assets of the acquirer may be a more meaningful technique.

Whatever specific technique is employed under the circumstances, the total purchase cost should be allocated to the net assets of the acquirer (not the acquiree) following the principles set forth in APB 16 (which continue unchanged under the successor standard, SFAS 141). If the purchase cost exceeds the fair value of net identifiable assets, the excess is allocated to goodwill, which will be tested for impairment as explained elsewhere in this chapter, and written down or eliminated when and if impairment is detected. The financial statements of the consolidated enterprise following the reverse acquisition would reflect the assets and liabilities of the nominal acquirer at fair value, and those of the nominal acquiree at historical cost.

Since for financial reporting purposes the nominal acquiree is the parent company, the retained earnings or deficit of the acquiree will be carried forward in the equity section of the successor entity's balance sheet. The retained earnings or deficit of the nominal acquirer will not be presented. The amount shown for paid-in capital would be valued in terms of the issued capital of the nominal acquiree (the new subsidiary), plus the cost of the acquisition as described above and illustrated below. However, in the actual financial statement, which must reflect the legal structure of the transaction, paid-in capital would be expressed in terms of the legal parent company, which was the nominal acquirer. An example of accounting for a reverse acquisition follows.

Assume that Agoura Corp., which is the nominal acquirer that becomes the legal parent company, issues shares in exchange for the outstanding common stock of Belmar Co., Inc., which is the nominal acquiree which becomes the legal subsidiary of Agoura. For accounting purposes, this will be a reverse acquisition such that Belmar is the actual acquirer.

The balance sheets of the two entities at the end of 2001 and as of September 30, 2002, the date of the transaction, are given as follows:

	Agoura Corporation	
	December 31, 2001	*September 30, 2002*
Current assets	$ 800,000	$1,000,000
Plant, property, and equipment, net	2,400,000	2,600,000
	$3,200,000	$3,600,000
Current liabilities	$ 400,000	$ 600,000
Long-term debt	600,000	400,000
Deferred tax liabilities	200,000	200,000
	1,200,000	1,200,000
Stockholders' equity		
8% redeemable preferred stock, 2,000 shs.	200,000	200,000
Common stock, 100,000 shs.	600,000	600,000
Retained earnings	1,200,000	1,600,000
	$3,200,000	$3,600,000

	Belmar Company, Inc	
	December 31, 2001	*September 30, 2002*
Current assets	$2,500,000	$1,750,000
Plant, property and equipment, net	5,000,000	7,500,000
	$7,500,000	$9,250,000
Current liabilities	$1,250,000	$1,500,000
Long-term debt	1,750,000	2,000,000
Deferred tax liabilities	500,000	750,000
	3,500,000	4,250,000
Stockholders' equity		
Common stock, 60,000 shs.	1,500,000	1,500,000
Retained earnings	2,500,000	3,500,000
	$7,500,000	$9,250,000

Agoura had net income of $400,000 for the nine months ended September 30, 2002, while Belmar Co. enjoyed earnings of $1,000,000 for that period. Neither company paid any dividends during this period.

The fair value of each share of Belmar common stock was $100 at the date of the acquisition. Agoura shares were quoted at $24 on the date.

Agoura's identifiable net assets had fair values equal to their respective book values, with the exception of the plant, property and equipment, which were appraised at $3,000,000 at September 30, 2002.

In effecting the acquisition, Agoura issues 150,000 new shares of its common stock to the owners of Belmar in exchange for all outstanding Belmar shares. Thus, former Belmar owners become the owners of a majority of the common stock of Agoura after this transaction.

To compute the cost of the reverse acquisition, the number of shares of the nominal acquiree entity, Belmar, which would have had to have been issued to acquire the nominal acquirer, Agoura, must be computed. This is done as follows:

Actual Agoura shares issued to former Belmar owners	150,000
Agoura shares outstanding prior to transaction	100,000
Total Agoura shares outstanding after transaction	250,000
Fraction held by former Belmar owners (150,000/250,000)	60%
Number of Belmar shares outstanding before transaction	60,000
Number of Belmar shares that could have been issued in transaction if 60% of total would have remained with original Belmar shareholders	40,000

If Belmar had issued 40,000 of its shares to effect the acquisition of Agoura, the cost would have been (given the fair value of Belmar shares at September 30, 2002) $100 x 40,000 = $4,000,000. This purchase cost would have been allocated to Agoura's assets and liabilities as follows:

Current assets		$1,000,000
Plant, property and equipment		3,000,000
		$4,000,000
Current liabilities	$600,000	
Long-term debt	400,000	
Deferred tax liabilities	200,000	1,200,000
		2,800,000
8% redeemable preferred stock, 2,000 shs.		200,000
		2,600,000
Cost of purchase (from above)		4,000,000
Goodwill to be recognized		$1,400,000

From the foregoing, the information needed to construct a consolidated balance sheet as of the date of the transaction, September 30, 2002, can be determined.

Agoura Corporation
Consolidated Balance Sheet
September 30, 2002

Current assets	$ 2,750,000
Plant, property and equipment, net	10,500,000
Goodwill	1,400,000
	$14,650,000
Current liabilities	$ 2,100,000
Long-term debt	2,400,000
Deferred tax liabilities	950,000
	5,450,000
Stockholders' equity	
8% redeemable preferred stock, 2,000 shs.	200,000
Common stock, 100,000 shs.	5,500,000
Retained earnings	3,500,000
	9,200,000
	$14,650,000

Computing earnings per share after a reverse acquisition poses special problems, particularly so in the year in which the transaction occurs and for any subsequent years when comparative financial statements are presented that include pre-transaction periods. For this purpose, the number of shares outstanding for the period from the beginning of the current reporting year until the date of the reverse acquisition should be the number of shares issued by the nominal acquirer (the legal parent company) to the shareholders of the nominal acquiree. For the period after the transaction, the number of shares considered to be outstanding would be actual number of shares of the legal parent company outstanding during that period. The average number of shares outstanding for the full year being reported upon would be computed by averaging these two amounts. Other appropriate adjustments would be made to deal with changes in numbers of shares issued during the period, as is done under other circumstances (as described in Chapter 18, Earnings per Share), if necessary. Under the current standard for computing earnings per share (SFAS 128), the calculation of basic earnings per share (replacing the former measure, primary earnings per share) is simplified for all entities.

Earnings per share for any earlier periods presented for comparative purposes is likewise complicated by the occurrence of a reverse acquisition. The number of shares issued by the legal parent (nominal acquirer) in the reverse acquisition transaction would be used to make this calculation.

Continuing with the Agoura-Belmar acquisition example above, earnings per share can be computed. Assume that consolidated net income for the year ended December 31, 2002, after deducting preferred dividends, equals $1,600,000. This includes Belmar Co., Inc. earnings for the full year 2002, plus Agoura Corp. earnings from the date of acquisition, September 30, 2002, until year-end. Remember that, notwithstanding that the new entity is called Agoura, from an accounting perspective this is Belmar Company.

Earnings per share would thus be computed as follows:

Number of shares outstanding from September 30, 2002   250,000
Number of shares deemed outstanding before September 30—
the number of Agoura shares issued to Belmar   150,000

Average number of shares

$$[(150,000 \times 9) + (250,000 \times 3)] \div 12 = 175,000$$

Earnings per share for 2002

$$\$1,600,000 \div 175,000 = \$9.14 \text{ per share}$$

For 2001, assuming Belmar alone had earnings of $1,400,000 for the year, earnings per share would be

$$\$1,400,000 \div 150,000 = \$9.33 \text{ per share}$$

Finally, there is the question of minority interest. In a reverse acquisition situation, the minority is comprised of the former shareholders of the legal subsidiary who do not exchange their shares for those of the new parent company, but continue on as stockholders in the legal subsidiary entity. Note that this holds even though from the accounting perspective they are shareholders in an entity which acquired another company. In other words, the identity of the minority is determined by the legal structure of the transaction, not the accounting substance. Since the net assets of the legal subsidiary (but substantive parent) are included in the consolidated financial statements at the old book values, minority interest is likewise computed based on the book value of the legal subsidiary's net assets.

For example, in the present case all shareholders of Belmar might not agree to tender their shares in exchange for Agoura stock, and if so they will continue on as minority owners of the legal subsidiary, Belmar, after it is nominally acquired by Agoura Corp. To illustrate, consider these assumed facts.

Agoura offered 2.5 shares for each share of Belmar common stock. In the example above, 150,000 shares of Agoura were exchanged for 60,000 Belmar shares. Now, however, assume that owners of 4,000 Belmar shares decline to participate in this transaction, so Agoura issues only 140,000 shares in exchange for 56,000 Belmar shares. After the exchange, former Belmar owners hold 140,000 of a total of 240,000 Agoura Corp. shares, or 58.33% of the total outstanding; still a majority and thus enough to define this as a reverse acquisition.

The cost of the purchase is computed similar to what was illustrated above. Since the owners of 56,000 Belmar shares participated and the transaction resulted in these owners obtaining a 58.33% interest in the successor entity, the calculation of the number of Belmar shares that hypothetically would have had to have been issued in a "straight" acquisition of Agoura is as follows:

56,000 shares outstanding ÷ .5833 = 96,000 total shares after transaction

96,000 total shares − 56,000 shares outstanding = 40,000 new shares to be issued

Thus, it can be seen that the cost of the purchase, determined in the manner that is necessary when a reverse acquisition takes place, remains 40,000 x $100 = $4,000,000 even given the existence of the minority interest.

The minority interest is 4,000 shares ÷ 60,000 shares = 6.6667%. It consists, as of the acquisition date, of 6.6667% of the book value of Belmar common stock and retained earnings, as follows:

6.6667% x $1,500,000 =		$100,000
6.6667% x $3,500,000 =		233,310
Total minority interest		$333,310

The consolidated balance sheet at acquisition date would differ from that shown above only as follows: a minority interest of $333,310 would be presented (under current GAAP, as a liability, as equity, or in a semiequity account); common stock would be only $5,400,000, comprised of 93.33% (1 – 6.66667%) of Belmar's $1,500,000, plus the $4 million purchase cost); and retained earnings would be only 93.33% or Belmar's pretransaction balance of $3.5 million, or $3,266,655. All other asset and liability account balances would be identical to the presentation above.

Spin-Offs

Occasionally an entity disposes of a wholly or partially owned subsidiary or of an investee by transferring it unilaterally to the entity's shareholders. The proper accounting for such a transaction, generally known as a spin-off, depends upon the percentage of the company that is owned.

If the ownership percentage is relatively minor, 25% for example, the transfer to stockholders would be viewed as a "dividend in kind" and would be accounted for at the fair value of the property (i.e., shares in the investee) transferred.

However, when the entity whose shares are distributed is majority or wholly-owned, the effect is not merely to transfer a passive investment, but to remove the operations from the former parent and to vest them with the parent's shareholders. This transaction is a true spin-off transaction, not merely a property dividend. APB 29 requires that spin-offs and other similar nonreciprocal transfers to owners be accounted for at the recorded book values of the assets and liabilities transferred.

If the operations (or subsidiary) being spun off are distributed during a fiscal period, it may be necessary to estimate the results of operations for the elapsed period prior to spin-off in order to ascertain the net book value as of the date of the transfer. Stated another way, the operating results of the subsidiary to be disposed of should be included in the reported results of the parent through the actual date of the spin-off.

In most instances, the subsidiary being spun off will have a positive net book value. This net worth represents the cost of the nonreciprocal transfer to the owners, and, like a dividend, will be reflected as a charge against the parent's retained earnings at the date of spin-off. In other situations, the operations (or subsidiary) will have a net deficit (negative net book value). Since it is unacceptable to recognize a credit to the parent's retained earnings for other than a culmination of an earnings process, the spin-off should be recorded as a credit to the parent's paid-in capital. In effect, the stockholders (the recipients of the spun-off subsidiary) have made a capital contribution to the parent company by accepting the operations having a negative book value. As with other capital transactions, this would **not** be presented in the income statement, but only in the statement of changes in stockholders' equity (and in the statement of cash flows).

Push-Down Accounting

For years the subject of "push-down" accounting (also known as "new basis accounting") was on the FASB's technical agenda, with no progress being made, notwithstanding that the SEC had long required, under narrowly defined circumstances, that this accounting be applied. In 1996 the topic was removed from the FASB's agenda, but has recently resurfaced as part of the Board's business combinations project. It has reportedly approved the bases of a draft working principle to be utilized in the determination of the appropriateness of recognizing a new basis of accounting, and has decided that the scope of the project should include the issue of gain recognition in the financial statements of the entity that has transferred or lost control over net assets for which a new basis of accounting is recognized. It appears that the earliest issues to be addressed, however, will deal with joint venture accounting and the reporting of contributions made by venture partners to the venture, and not with the application of "push down" accounting to traditional business acquisitions.

The concept of push-down (or new basis) accounting is to reflect a revaluation of the assets and/or liabilities of the acquired company **on its books** based on the price paid for some or all of its shares by the acquirer. Push-down accounting has no impact on the presentation of consolidated financial statements or on the separate financial statements of the parent (investor) company, which would continue to be based on the price paid for the acquisition and not on the acquired entity's book value. However, the use of this accounting technique represents a departure in the way separate financial statements of the acquired entity are presented.

Advocates of push-down accounting point out that in a purchase business combination a new basis of accounting is established. They believe that the new basis should be pushed down to the acquired entity and should be used when presenting its own separate financial statements.

While the push-down treatment has been used by a number of entities it remains controversial and lacks clear authoritative guidance. Although push-down makes some sense in the case where a major block of the investee's shares is acquired in a single free-market transaction, if new basis accounting were to be used in the context of a series of step transactions, continual adjustment of the investee's carrying values for assets and liabilities would be necessary. Furthermore, the price paid for a fractional share of ownership of an investee may not always be meaningfully extrapolated to a value for the investee company as a whole.

While there is no requirement under GAAP to apply the push-down concept, the SEC position is substantial authoritative support and can be referenced even for nonpublic company financial reporting. It would be defensible in any instance where there is a change in control and/or a change in ownership of a majority of the common shares, when separate financial statements of the subsidiary are to be presented. Full disclosure should be made of the circumstances whenever push-down accounting is applied.

Example of push-down accounting

Assume that Pullup Corp. acquires, in an open market, arm's-length transaction, 90% of the common stock of Pushdown Co. for $464.61 million. At that time, Pushdown Co.'s net book value was $274.78 million (for the entire company). Book and fair values of selected assets and liabilities of Pushdown Co. as of the transaction date are summarized as follows ($000,000 omitted):

	Book value		Fair value of	Excess of
	100% of entity	*90% interest*	*90% interest*	*FV over book*
Assets				
Receivables	$ 24.6	$ 22.14	$ 29.75	$ 7.61
Inventory	21.9	19.71	24.80	5.09
Property, plant & equipment, net	434.2	390.78	488.20	97.42
All others	223.4	201.06	201.06	0.00
Add'l goodwill			120.00	120.00
Total assets	$704.1	$633.69	$863.81	$230.12
Liabilities				
Bonds payable	$104.9	$ 94.41	$ 88.65	$ 5.76
All other liabilities	325.0	292.50	310.55	18.05
Total liabilities	429.9	386.91	399.20	12.29
Equity				
Preferred stock	40.0	36.00	36.00	0.00
Common stock	87.4	78.66	78.66	0.00
Revaluation surplus*			217.83	217.83
Retained earnings	146.8	132.12	132.12	0.00
Total equity	274.2	246.88	464.61	217.83
Liabilities + Equity	$704.1	$633.69	$863.81	$230.12

* *Net premium paid over book value by arm's-length of "almost all" common stock*

Assuming that "new basis" accounting is deemed to be acceptable and meaningful, since Pushdown Co. must continue to issue separate financial statements to its creditors and holders of its preferred stock, and also assuming that a revaluation of the share of ownership that did **not** change hands (i.e., the 10% minority interest in this example) should **not** be revalued based on the majority transaction, the entries on the subsidiary's (Pushdown Co.'s) books for purposes only of preparing stand-alone financial statements would be as follows:

Accounts receivable	7,610,000	
Inventory	5,090,000	
Plant, property and equipment (net)	97,420,000	
Goodwill	120,000,000	
Discount on bonds payable	5,760,000	
Other liabillities		18,050,000
Paid-in capital from revaluation		217,830,000

The foregoing entry would only be made for purposes of preparing separate financial statements of Pushdown Co. If consolidated financial statements of Pullup Corp. are also presented, essentially the same result will be obtained. The additional paid-in capital account would be eliminated against the parent's investment account, however, since in the context of the consolidated financial statements this would be a cash transaction rather than a mere accounting revaluation.

There is also a body of opinion that says that the separate financial statements of Pushdown Co. in this example should be "grossed up" for the imputed premium that would have been achieved on the transfer of the remaining 10% ownership interest. This is less appealing, however, given the absence of a "real" transaction involving that last 10% ownership stake, making the price at which it would have traded somewhat speculative.

The foregoing example obviously also ignored the tax effects of the transaction. Since the step-ups in carrying value would not, in all likelihood, alter the corresponding tax bases of the assets and liabilities, deferred tax effects would have also had to be recognized. This would be done following the procedures set forth at SFAS 109, as described fully in Chapter 15, Income Taxes.

Non-Sub Subsidiaries

Another issue that has concerned accountants and the Securities and Exchange Commission is the sudden popularity of what have been called "non-sub subsidiaries." This situation arises when an entity plays a major role in the creation and financing of what is often a start-up or experimental operation, but does not take an equity position at the outset. For example, the parent might finance the entity by means of convertible debt or debt with warrants for the later purchase of common shares. The original equity partner in such arrangements most often will be the creative or managerial talent, which generally exchanges its talents for a stock interest. If the operation prospers, the parent will exercise its rights to a majority voting stock position; if it fails, the parent presumably avoids reflecting the losses in its statements.

While this strategy may seem to avoid the requirements of equity accounting or consolidation, the economic substance clearly suggests that the operating results of the subsidiary should be reflected in the financial statements of the real parent, even absent stock ownership. Until formal requirements are established in this area, an approach akin to the preparation of combined statements would seem reasonable.

Proposed New Criteria for Consolidated Financial Reporting

It had long been recognized that consolidated financial statements provided a more meaningful representation of the financial position and results of operations of controlled or closely related groups of entities, particularly for owners and creditors of the parent enterprise. However, it had been difficult to establish coherent requirements for situations other than for typical, corporate, parent-subsidiary types of relationships. Traditionally (beginning with ARB 51, in 1959), it had been accepted practice that ownership by one company, directly or indirectly, of over 50% of the outstanding voting shares of another company was a condition generally dictating the presentation of consolidated financial statements. Exceptions existed such as the "nonhomogeneity" rule that, for example, permitted industrial companies to exclude wholly owned finance companies from consolidated financial statements, but over time these had been reduced, particularly by SFAS 94, issued in 1987.

Notwithstanding improvements in reporting that had occurred, it was clear that a number of issues remained, such as when effective control was exercised by means other than majority ownership of voting shares. Also, business enterprises and not-for-profit organizations have been conducting increasingly diverse ranges of activities through increasingly complex organization structures, which occasionally have been created explicitly for the purpose of avoiding consolidated financial reporting. There was a widespread sense that a more universal guideline as to when, and how, consolidated financial reporting was to be required was needed.

The FASB's 1995 Exposure Draft, *Consolidated Financial Statements: Policy and Procedures,* would have extended consolidated financial reporting requirements to not-for-profit enterprises and, most significantly, would have adopted the concept of control as the criterion for consolidation, replacing ownership percentage as the principal test. In that draft statement, control was defined as the ability to derive benefits from the use of the individual assets of the controlled entity, in essentially the same way as the controlling entity could direct the use of its own assets. This controversial proposal was superseded by the Board's 1999 draft, essentially carrying forward the concepts of the earlier draft, but expanding the definition of control by changing the focus to the controlling entity's ability to direct the policies and management of the controlled entity so as to derive benefits from its operations. It was expected that a new standard would soon be forthcoming.

However, the FASB announced in early 2001 that it was unable to assemble the requisite majority support for any concrete proposal on this topic, and was therefore suspending this project. Accordingly, for the foreseeable future, consolidated financial reporting will only be required when the parent owns over 50% of the voting stock of the subsidiary entity; when that condition is met, nonconsolidation will be permitted only when the exceptions set forth in SFAS 94 are satisfied.

Disclosure Requirements

In the period in which a material business combination is completed, the notes to the acquirer's financial statements must disclose the following information:

1. The name and a brief description of the acquiree, together with the percentage of voting shares acquired;
2. The period for which the results of the acquiree's operations are included in the income statement of the acquirer;

3. The cost of the transaction and, if applicable, the number of shares of stock issued or issuable, the value assigned to those shares, and the basis for determining that value;

4. Contingent payments, options, or commitments specified in the acquisition agreement and the accounting treatment that will be followed should any such contingency occur;

5. A condensed balance sheet disclosing the following for each major asset and liability caption of the acquiree: (a) the book value as reflected in the acquiree's financial records at the date of acquisition before fair value adjustments and (b) the fair values assigned at the date of acquisition (including, if pertinent, how negative goodwill was allocated to preliminarily determined asset fair values);

6. For any purchase price allocation that has not been finalized, that fact and the reasons therefor and, in subsequent periods, the nature and amount of any material adjustments made to the initial allocation of the purchase price; and

7. If the amount assigned to goodwill or to other intangible assets acquired is significant in relation to the total cost of the acquired enterprise, (a) the amount of acquired goodwill, (b) the amount of acquired goodwill related to each segment (for entities that are required to report segment information in accordance with SFAS 131), and (c) the amount of acquired goodwill that is deductible for income tax purposes.

The notes to the financial statements of the acquirer also must disclose the following information in the period in which individually **immaterial** business combinations have been completed, if material in the aggregate:

1. The number of entities acquired and a brief description of the acquirees;

2. The aggregate cost of the acquisitions, the number of shares of stock issued or issuable, and the value assigned to those shares;

3. The aggregate amount of any contingent payments, options, or commitments and the accounting treatment that will be followed should any such contingency occur (if potentially significant in relation to the aggregate cost of the acquirees); and

4. Information pertaining to recorded goodwill, if the aggregate amount assigned to goodwill or to other intangible assets acquired is significant in relation to the aggregate cost of the acquirees.

Notes to the financial statements also must disclose, for any material business combination completed **after** the balance sheet date but before the financial statements are issued, information similar to that for completed transactions, above.

For each period for which a statement of financial position is presented, the notes to the financial statements also are to disclose the changes in the carrying amount of goodwill during the period. That would include the amount of goodwill acquired, the amount of impairment loss recognized, and the amount of goodwill included in the gain or loss on disposal of all or a portion of a reporting unit. Entities that report segment information in accordance with SFAS 131 are to provide that information for each segment, disclosing any significant changes in the allocation of goodwill by segment.

When goodwill impairment losses are recognized, disclosure is required of

1. The facts and circumstances leading to the impairment;
2. The reporting unit for which the impairment loss is recognized, the adjusted carrying amount of goodwill of that reporting unit, and the amount of the impairment loss;
3. If relevant, the fact that the impairment loss estimate has yet to be finalized, the reasons therefor and, in subsequent periods, the nature and amount of any significant adjustments made to the initial estimate of the impairment loss; and
4. The segment to which the impaired goodwill relates (for entities that are required to report segment information in accordance with SFAS 131).

In the period in which an excess over cost related to an acquisition is recognized as an extraordinary gain, it will be presented net of tax, as required under the provisions of APB 30, with appropriate disclosure in the notes to the financial statements.

EMERGING ISSUES TASK FORCE CONSENSUS SUMMARIES

84-13 Purchase of Stock Options with Stock Appreciation Rights in a Leveraged Buyout

This pronouncement addressed the question of whether options and similar rights which are purchased by a target company before completion of a leveraged buyout, with or without funds advanced by acquirer, should be deemed as compensation or as part of cost of the buyout. The consensus was that GAAP (APB 25) requires that this be accounted for as compensation.

84-33 Acquisition of a Tax Loss Carryforward—Temporary Parent-Subsidiary Relationship

Assume that Company X has a large NOL carryforward while Company Y is profitable. In a highly leveraged purchase combination, Company X acquires 80% of Company Y while giving Y's owners the option to repurchase a 60% interest in Y at a fixed price. The Task Force concurred that in such a situation the companies' financial statements should not be consolidated and that income should be recognized on the equity method only until the carrying amount of the investment equals the probable repurchase price.

85-12 Retention of Specialized Accounting for Investments in Consolidation

A consensus was reached that specialized accounting principles which are appropriately applied at a subsidiary company level should also be used in the consolidated financial statements.

85-28 Consolidation Issues Relating to Collateralized Mortgage Obligations

A special purpose subsidiary, created to originate collateralized mortgage obligations, must be consolidated, if it was formed by a parent company that normally originates mortgages and then transfers them to the subsidiary.

85-45 Business Combinations: Settlement of Stock Options and Awards

This pronouncement extends the consensus of 84-13. If a target company in an LBO (leveraged buyout) settles options voluntarily, the payments must be accounted for as compensation expense in the separate financial statement of the target company. However, no consensus was reached on how the target should account for a reimbursement of costs received from the acquirer.

86-29 Nonmonetary Transactions: Magnitude of Boot and the Exceptions to the Use of Fair Value

This consensus primarily addresses APB 29 issues, but also offers interpretation on exchanges of investments which are accounted for under the provisions of either APB 16 or 18. A consensus was reached that an entity should account for an exchange of securities in which it acquires control of a subsidiary as an acquisition to be accounted for per APB 16. If control is not achieved but the investment will be accounted for by the equity method, the exchange should be treated as a monetary transaction per APB 29. However, this accounting would not apply to the acquisition of a minority interest.

86-32 Early Extinguishment of a Subsidiary's Mandatorily Redeemable Preferred Stock

This extinguishment is a capital stock transaction with no gain or loss recognized. Dividends would be included in minority interest as a charge against income.

87-11 Allocation of Purchase Price to Assets to Be Sold

A consensus was reached that earnings or losses of a division which is to be sold, as well as interest on any incremental debt used to acquire it, and the gain or loss on the ultimate sale of the division, should not be included in income, if the sale is within one year. Under the provisions of SFAS 38, these should be accounted for as reallocations of the purchase price, inasmuch as they effectively are resolutions of preacquisition contingencies.

87-17 The Spin-Offs or Other Distributions of Loans Receivable to Shareholders

A consensus was reached that a transfer of loans receivable to a newly formed subsidiary in consideration for stock of the subsidiary should be recorded at fair market value by the enterprise and the recipient. The transaction would be classified as a dividend-in-kind rather than a spin-off because the subsidiary is not an operating company.

87-21 Change of Accounting Basis in Master Limited Partnership Transactions

This pronouncement addressed the variety of transactions that are used to create master limited partnerships, and specifically was intended to specify when a new basis of accounting should be recognized. The consensus was that a new basis of accounting is not appropriate in "roll-ups" where the general partner was the general partner in all of the predecessors. Similarly, new basis of accounting is not appropriate in a "drop down" in which the sponsor is the corporate parent that maintains effective control after the restructuring. Also, a new basis of accounting is not appropriate in a "rollout" or in a reorganization. Likewise, even if general partner was the general partner in only some of the predecessors, no new basis could be established. Transaction costs incurred in connection with a roll-up should be expensed, not capitalized, in a manner similar to the accounting for poolings under APB 16.

88-16 Basis in Leveraged Buyout Transactions

One of the most complex accounting areas, first addressed in EITF 86-16, this pronouncement stipulates how to compute the new cost basis after an LBO transaction. A consensus was reached that a new basis is to be recognized only when there is a change in the voting control from the former entity to the post-LBO entity; that a "substance over form" rule applies when seeking to determine if there had in fact been a change in control; and that a "monetary test" is established whereby fair value can only be used if at least 80% of the fair value of consideration paid to make the acquisition is monetary in nature.

89-7 Exchange of Assets or Interest in a Subsidiary for a Noncontrolling Equity Interest in a New Entity

The Task Force analyzed two example transactions and reached a consensus that full gain recognition is not appropriate for either transaction. The specific facts of the transactions are described in the EITF. The Task Force did note that because of the many possible variations, the specific facts and circumstances of each transaction would affect gain or loss recognition.

90-5 Exchanges of Ownership Interests between Entities under Common Control

This consensus stipulates that there is no step up in a transfer of a subsidiary from a parent company to another of its subsidiaries, and that the subsidiary's basis in the new subsidiary will be the same as was the parent company's. However, a buyout of minority interests by the subsidiary should be accounted for as a purchase transaction, whether effected by cash or by a stock transaction.

90-6 Accounting for Certain Events Relating to an Acquired Operating Unit to Be Sold

This pronouncement addresses circumstances in which a division of an acquired company is expected to be sold within one year of the acquisition transaction, but the disposition does not occur in a timely manner. The consensus was that a strict interpretation of SFAS 38 should be applied; therefore, after one year, further changes must be included in earnings, and no longer by a reallocation of the purchase price. If the decision to sell is reversed, the accounting to be employed depends upon whether this occurs before or after the one-year time horizon is reached. If before, a reallocation of the purchase price is prescribed, including a cumulative restatement for depreciation, etc. If the decision to sell is reversed after one-year period elapses, then a fair value adjustment is to be made to the assets and liabilities as of the date of the decision: if this is a write-down, it is to be taken to income, while if it is a write-up, the adjustment will be to goodwill and amortization prospectively.

90-12 Allocating Basis to Individual Assets and Liabilities for Transactions within the Scope of EITF 88-16

This consensus prescribes the use of the partial purchase (step acquisition accounting) method, even if retained earnings are eliminated as a consequence.

90-13 Accounting for Simultaneous Common Control Mergers

This consensus addresses situations in which a parent company obtains control of a target, then spins one of its previously owned subsidiaries off to the target in exchange for more shares in the target (i.e., the old subsidiary becomes a "grandson" after the series of transactions). A consensus was reached that this latter step must be viewed as an integral part of the acquisition, not as an "Interpretation 39" transfer among entities under common control. A step-up in basis would be permitted to the extent of a change in control, both upon the acquisition of the target and on the sale of the subsidiary to the new target subsidiary. The accounting for a spin-off of the old subsidiary to the target company is to be accounted for as "reverse acquisition" of the target by the subsidiary, per APB 16.

90-15   Impact of Nonsubstantive Lessors, Residual Value Guarantees, and Other Provisions in Leasing Transactions (as altered by SFAS 140, as it pertains to consolidation of SPE)

This important consensus requires consolidation of a special purpose entity (SPE)/lessor into the financial statements of the lessee when all these conditions are met: substantially all activities of the SPE involve assets leased to single lessee; expected substantive residual risks and substantially all residual rewards of leased assets and obligation imposed by underlying debt of the SPE reside with lessee through such means as terms of lease agreement, residual value guarantee (e.g., assumption of first dollar of loss provisions), guarantee of SPE's debt, or option granting lessee right to purchase leased asset at fixed or defined price other than fair market value, or to receive excess sales proceeds from lessor; and absence of substantive capital infusion by record owner of SPE which remains at risk for entire lease term.

91-5   Nonmonetary Exchanges of Cost-Method Investments

The Task Force reached consensus on three issues regarding how an investor should account for its investment in a company, subsequent to a business combination, if the cost method is used. The first consensus reached was that the cost-method investor in the acquired company would record the transaction at fair value. The second consensus reached was that the cost-method investor in the acquiring company would continue to carry the investment at historical cost. The third consensus was that if an investor in the acquired company also possessed a cost-method investment in the acquiring company, the first two conclusions would still apply.

93-7   Uncertainties Related to Income Taxes in a Purchase Business Combination

The consensus was that all income tax uncertainties (such as uncertainties about the allocation of purchase price to individual assets and liabilities for tax purposes in a taxable business combination, uncertainties about carryforwards in a nontaxable combination, and uncertainties about preacquisition tax returns of the acquired entity) existing at the time of a purchase business combination are to be accounted for under the provisions of SFAS 109, not under the provisions of SFAS 38 (preacquisition contingencies). Any such adjustments are to be applied to increase or decrease the remaining balance of goodwill attributable to that business combination; if goodwill is reduced to zero, the remaining amount should be used to reduce other noncurrent intangible assets from the same acquisition to zero, with any excess taken to income.

95-3   Recognition of Liabilities in Connection with a Purchase Business Combination

If costs to exit an activity of an acquiree and involuntary termination or relocation costs relative to employees of an acquiree are anticipated at or very shortly after the acquisition, they should be reflected in the allocation of the purchase price, unless the costs are incurred to generate revenue of the combined entity after the acquisition, in which case these would be period costs. (This is analogous to Issue 94-3 and examples in that consensus apply here also.) If later settled for amounts are less than accrued, the savings should be used to reduce the purchase price of the entity, which usually means goodwill recorded on the acquisition would be reduced; these adjustments are **not** preacqusition contingencies as defined by SFAS 38, and thus the one-year limit is probably not applicable. Costs not identified timely would be period costs of the postacquisition entity. Costs related to assets or employees of the acquirer are not costs of the acquisition and cannot be part of the purchase price allocation process; these must be reflected in the income statement in all cases. A number of restrictions on the use of accrued liability treatment are prescribed—generally, to avoid a "big bath" by anticipating vague future costs. Costs of activities or employees of the acquirer are not allocable to the purchase price, per FASB TB 85-5. The consensus also identified certain disclosures to be made under these circumstances, including a description of plans to exit activities, possible reallocation of purchase transaction, etc.

95-8   Accounting for Contingent Consideration Paid to the Shareholders of an Acquired Company in a Purchase Business Combination

Whether contingent consideration based on earnings should be accounted for as an adjustment of the purchase price or as compensation for services, for the use of property, or for profit sharing depends on the facts and circumstances of each case. Some of the factors that can assist in making this determination relate to the terms of continuing employment, components of shareholder group, reasons for the contingent payment provisions, the formula used for determining contingent consideration, and other agreements and issues. For example, if compensation other than contingent payments is set at a reasonable level, this supports treatment of the contingent payments as an additional purchase price.

95-14   Recognition of Liabilities in Anticipation of a Business Combination

The issue involves contingency plans for exiting businesses and/or terminating employees if a business combination is consummated. The specific questions are whether the conditions specified in Issue 94-3 will be met only if the combination does occur. The consensus was that the commitment date for exit plan costs, and the recognition date for involuntary termination benefits, cannot occur prior to consummation.

95-19   Determination of the Measurement Date for the Market Price of Securities Issued in a Purchase Business Combination

Where there is conflicting guidance on which market price is to be considered in determining cost of acquisition using stock, the guidance in APB 16 should be relied upon: market price for a reasonable period before and after the event should be considered, although this span is usually brief (i.e., a few days). If number of shares to be exchanged is subsequently changed, this creates a new measurement date for valuation.

95-21   Accounting for Assets to Be Disposed of Acquired in a Purchase Business Combination

This involves the interaction among Issue 87-11 (allocation of purchase cost to assets to be sold), APB 16, SFAS 121, and a proposed standard on consolidation. There was no attempt to reach a consensus, and further consideration at a later date is likely. The key issue is whether expected cash flows from operation of assets to be sold off should be considered, per 87-11, or whether assets should simply be booked at fair value less costs to sell, as suggested by proposed SFAS on consolidations, which builds on the SFAS 121 rule.

96-4   Accounting for Reorganizations Involving a Non-Pro-Rata Split-Off of Certain Nonmonetary Assets to Owners

The EITF's consensus was that the accounting for a non-pro-rata split-off in a corporate plan of organization should be at fair value. With regard to a pro rata basis distribution in the split-off of a targeted business, the distribution to holders of related targeted stock should be at historical cost.

96-5   Recognition of Liabilities for Contractual Termination Benefits or Changing Benefit Plan Assumptions in Anticipation of a Business Combination

Termination costs to be incurred from business combination should not be accrued when business combination is merely deemed probable, but only when it is actually consummated.

96-7   **Accounting for Deferred Taxes on In-Process Research and Development Activities Acquired in a Purchase Business Combination**

Per FASB Interpretation 4, the purchase price allocated in a purchase business combination to research and development costs must be expensed immediately. At issue is whether, under SFAS 109, a deferred tax liability must be allocated to the initial (pre-write-off) basis difference between tax and book bases. The consensus was that since write-off occurs prior to the measurement of deferred taxes, no deferred taxes should be assigned.

97-2   **Application of FASB Statement No. 94 and APB Opinion No. 16 to Physician Practice Management Entities and Certain Other Entities with Contractual Management Arrangements**

A physician practice management can establish a controlling financial interest in physician practices via contractual management agreement, and thus trigger SFAS 94 consolidation requirement, if six criteria are met: life of ten years minimum or remaining life of entity; not terminable by physicians under normal conditions; control over all ongoing, major central operations except for dispensing medical services; control over compensation of professionals, hiring and firing, etc.; financial interest is salable or transferable; and right to receive income based on performance risk and change in fair value.

97-8   **Accounting for Contingent Consideration Issued in a Purchase Business Combination**

This EITF deals with indirect contingent consideration arrangements, such as those that are embedded in a security or are part of a separate financial instrument. At issue was the timing of recognition of the cost of the contingent consideration. The consensus was that the fair value of the instrument should be recognized at the date of acquisition as part of purchase cost to be allocated if the instrument is traded or indexed to an instrument which is traded. Subsequent changes in value are to be ignored. On the other hand, if the instrument is not traded, contingent cost would be measured only when contingency is resolved, per APB 16. Other related accounting issues are addressed in EITF 86-28 and 96-13.

97-15   Accounting for Contingency Arrangements Based on Security Prices in a Purchase Business Combination

This issue relates to "below market" or "above market" guarantees of market value of securities issued in purchase transaction; under APB 16 the normal type of market value guarantee does not get reflected in purchase cost. The consensus is that for below market value guarantee, there would be no purchase cost adjustment, as cost is fair value of unconditional securities given at date of combination only. On the other hand, in an above market contingent issuance (e.g., issue more shares if price three years hence is not at least $x, where $x > $y [price at deal date]), there will be a requirement to issue more shares if the price exceeds some defined threshold, perhaps with a declining number of shares up to price of $z, where $z > $x. In these cases, the cost of the purchase is the maximum number of additional shares times price as of the date of transaction, with no later adjustments to be recognized.

98-1   Valuation of Debt Assumed in a Purchase Business Combination

APB 16 directs cost allocation based on fair values of assets and liabilities, with fair value of liabilities being computed using present value. Issue arises because present value ≠ fair value in some cases, such as when prepayment option affects fair value but present value would often ignore this contingent change in future cash flows. Consensus was to use fair value, even if ≠ present value of cash flows. Since market values may not be available, some use of present value method may be required, but the value of option features, etc. must be included in the calculation.

98-2   Accounting by a Subsidiary for an Investment in Its Parent Company's Stock

This issue relates to the display of an investment by subsidiary in parent's or joint venture partner's stock in separate statements of the subsidiary or the joint venture specifically, how; SFAS 115 rules affect this presentation. Questions to be answered are how to account for initial purchase and subsequent accounting for such investments. Possible answers are to account for the investment as an asset to be accounted for at fair value; a distribution to the parent or joint venture partner (similar to treasury stock); or as an asset measured by the equity method, with an elimination of reciprocal ownership investments. No consensus has been reached on this issue yet.

98-3 Determining Whether a Transaction Is an Exchange of Similar Productive Assets or a Business Combination

APB 29 states that nonmonetary exchanges should generally be reported at fair value, but exchange of productive assets are to be recorded at carrying value or assets relinquished. APB 16, however, uses a fair value approach. Some exchanges (e.g., of radio stations or other groups of operating assets) may be either nonmonetary exchanges or business combinations. No consensus yet achieved on this issue; the SEC favor APB 16 accounting, even for exchanges of entire similar businesses.

98-4 Accounting by a Joint Venture or Businesses Received at Its Formation

Issue is how a joint venture should record, in stand-alone financials, businesses received from venture partner, in situations where either the relationship between joint venturer and venturers has none of the five attributes of a corporate joint venture set forth in APB 18 but there is joint control, or where all five attributes exist and there is joint control. In common practice, the carryforward basis is used. A need for definition of joint control is noted, and this will be further pursued by EITF. SEC supports the APB 16 treatment for contributions to newly formed, jointly controlled entity if entity is not joint venture (presumably means carryforward basis); and also would object to the conclusion that joint control is the only defining characteristic of a joint venture. More discussion of these matters is anticipated.

99-6 Impact of Acceleration Provisions in Grants Made between Initiation and Consummation of a Pooling-of-Interests Business Combination

The issue is whether granting stock options (or restricted stock) that provide for automatic vesting upon a change in control, after initiation of a business combination, violates the change-in-equity-interests condition and thus precludes pooling treatment for that business combination. The consensus is that this would not violate the change-in-equity-interests condition, provided the option grant is consistent with a pattern of past grants made prior to initiation of the business combination, and the change in control provision was not added to the plan in contemplation of the business combination. To the contrary, the removal of such a provision in contemplation of the business combination would be an alteration of equity interests that would preclude pooling-of-interests accounting.

99-12 Accounting for Formula Arrangements under Issue No. 95-19

A consensus on Issue 95-19 stipulated that if the purchase price, including the number of shares, is subsequently changed, a new measurement date is established for valuing the equity securities to be issued. That guidance applies to changes in the number of shares or amount of other consideration when the change is pursuant to a formula in the initial acquisition agreement that could adjust the number of shares or amount of other consideration as a result of changes in the market price of the acquirer's common stock. There is the further issue of which date is to be used as the measurement date to value equity securities issued in a purchase business combination if the number of shares or amount of other consideration to be issued could change pursuant to a formula in the initial acquisition agreement. There is no consensus yet, but the tentative conclusion is that if the number of shares or amount of other consideration could change pursuant to a formula in the initial acquisition agreement, the date on which the number of shares and amount of other consideration become fixed as a result of the final application of the formula is the measurement date.

A further issue is: once a measurement date is determined pursuant to the foregoing, how should the guidance in Issue 95-19 that requires the shares to be valued based on market prices "a few days before and after" the measurement date be applied? The Task Force reached a tentative conclusion that the securities should be valued based on market prices a few days before and after the measurement date determined in the foregoing, provided that the measurement period would not include any dates after the date the business combination is consummated. Appropriate changes will be made to Issue 95-19; this will apply prospectively to purchase business combinations initiated after the date final consensuses are reached.

99-15   Accounting for Decreases in Deferred Tax Asset Valuation Allowances Established in a Purchase Business Combination As a Result of a Change in Tax Regulations

This issue arises as a result of new consolidated tax return regulations issued in 1999, which changed the rules for utilizing certain net operating loss carryovers and carrybacks (NOLC) by eliminating the requirement to apply the limitations on the separate return limitation year losses to situations in which a change in ownership as defined in Section 382 of the Internal Revenue Code has occurred within six months of a target company becoming a member of a consolidated group.

The change in tax regulations requires an entity to reevaluate the need for an existing valuation allowance for deferred tax assets relating to NOLC acquired in a prior purchase business combination. The specific question is whether the effect of the adjustment should be (1) included in operations or (2) applied first to reduce to zero any goodwill related to the acquisition, second to reduce to zero other noncurrent intangible assets related to the acquisition, and third to reduce income tax expense.

The Task Force consensus is that the effect of a change in tax law or regulation that results in a decrease in a valuation allowance that initially was recorded in the allocation of the purchase price in a purchase business combination should be included in income from continuing operations. The consensus applies to any reduction in the valuation allowance that otherwise would not have been recognized except for the change in tax law or regulation, regardless of whether the valuation allowance is reduced in the period of the tax law change or in a subsequent period.

00-4   Majority Owner's Accounting for a Transaction in the Shares of a Consolidated Subsidiary and a Derivative Indexed to the Minority Interest in That Subsidiary

This issue addresses how a majority owner should account for entering into a derivative financial instrument with the minority owner, if the derivative instrument provides the majority owner with substantially all the risks and rewards of the ownership of the minority share. The consensus was that the derivative instrument should be combined with the minority interest and accounted for as a financing. After combination, the derivative will not be subject to the provisions of SFAS 133.

12 CURRENT LIABILITIES AND CONTINGENCIES

PERSPECTIVE AND ISSUES

The division of assets and liabilities into current and noncurrent allows working capital (current assets minus current liabilities) to be calculated. Working capital, which is the relatively liquid portion of total entity capital, can be used to determine the ability of an entity to repay obligations. Working capital assumes a going-concern concept. If the entity is to be liquidated in the near future, classification of assets and liabilities is inappropriate.

ARB 43, Chapter 3, defines current liabilities as those obligations whose liquidation is reasonably expected to require the use of existing resources properly classifiable as current assets or the creation of other current liabilities. This definition excludes from the current liability classification any currently maturing obligations which will be satisfied by using long-term assets and currently maturing obligations expected to be refinanced.

The offsetting of assets and liabilities is generally prohibited under GAAP. However, under certain narrowly defined circumstances, where a right of setoff actually exists, netting for financial reporting purposes can be done, as described in this chapter.

Many current liabilities are measured at settlement value, which is the amount of cash (or its equivalent amount of assets) that will be paid to the creditor to liquidate the obligation during the operating cycle. Accounts payable, dividends payable, salaries payable, and other current obligations are measured at settlement value because they require the entity to pay a determinable amount of cash. Other current liabilities are measured at the proceeds received when the obligation arose. Liabilities that are measured at proceeds generally require the entity to discharge the obligation by providing goods or services rather than paying cash. Subscriptions payable, deposits payable, and deferred revenues are examples of current liabilities measured at proceeds.

Although measurement of current liabilities is generally straightforward, some liabilities are difficult to measure because of uncertainties. Uncertainties regarding whether an obligation exists, how much of an entity's assets will be needed to settle the obligation, and when the settlement will take place can impact whether, when, and for how much an obligation will be recognized in the financial statements. SFAS 5 is the primary standard that describes accounting for potential liabilities in circumstances involving uncertainties. It requires a liability to be recognized if it is (1) probable that an obligation has been incurred because of a transaction or event happening on or before the date of the financial statements and (2) the amount of the obligation can be reasonably estimated. Thus, uncertainties about the existence of an obligation need not be resolved before the liability is recorded. For example, estimated settlement amounts for ongoing lawsuits are recognized prior to a court's decision if it is probable that the outcome will be unfavorable. Further, difficulty in measuring an obligation is not, by itself, a reason for not recording a liability if the amount can be estimated. For example, warranty obligations are commonly recognized as liabilities even though the number of claims and the amount of each claim are unknown at the time of the sale of the warrantied item. Although future events will eventually resolve the uncertainties (the warranty claims will be paid and the lawsuit will be settled), the liabilities are required to be recognized before all of the uncertainties are resolved so that relevant information is provided on a timely basis.

Sources of GAAP						
ARB	*APB*	*SFAS*	*FASB I*	*FASB TB*	*EITF*	*SOP*
43, Ch. 3, 50	6, 10, 21	5, 6, 11, 43, 48, 78, 112	8, 14, 34, 39, 41	79-3	85-20, 86-5, 86-12, 86-15, 86-30, 93-14, 95-22, 00-23, D-77, D-79	96-1

DEFINITIONS OF TERMS

Accumulated benefits. Employee benefits that can be carried over into the next year but that expire upon termination of employment.

Contingency. An existing condition, situation, or set of circumstances involving uncertainty as to possible gain or loss that will ultimately be resolved when one or more future events occur or fail to occur.

Current liabilities. Obligations whose liquidation is reasonably expected to require the use of existing resources properly classified as current assets or the creation of other current liabilities. Obligations that are due on demand or will be due on demand within one year or the operating cycle, if longer, are current liabilities. Long-term obligations callable because of the debtor's violation of a provision of the debt agreement are current liabilities unless specific SFAS 78 conditions are met.

FICA. Social security taxes levied upon both employees and employers.

FUTA. Social security tax levied upon employers to finance the administration of federal unemployment benefit programs.

Indirect guarantee of indebtedness of others. A guarantee under an agreement that obligates one enterprise to transfer funds to a second enterprise upon the occurrence of specified events under conditions whereby (1) the funds are legally available to the creditors of the second enterprise, and (2) those creditors may enforce the second enterprise's claims against the first enterprise.

Operating cycle. The average length of time necessary for an enterprise to convert inventory to receivables to cash.

CONCEPTS, RULES, AND EXAMPLES

ARB 43, Chapter 3, contains several examples of current liabilities. It also contains broad general descriptions of the types of items to be shown as current liabilities. These obligations can be divided into those where

1. Both the amount and the payee are known;
2. The payee is known but the amount may have to be estimated;
3. The payee is unknown and the amount may have to be estimated; and
4. The liability has been incurred due to a loss contingency.

Amount and Payee Known

Accounts payable arise primarily from the acquisition of materials and supplies to be used in the production of goods or in conjunction with the providing of services. APB 21 states that payables that arise from transactions with suppliers in the normal course of business and that are due in customary trade terms not to exceed one year may be stated at their face amount rather than at the present value of the required future cash flows.

Notes payable are more formalized obligations which may arise from the acquisition of materials and supplies used in operations or from the use of short-term credit to purchase capital assets (APB 21 also applies to short-term notes payable).

Dividends payable become a liability of the enterprise when the board of directors declares a cash dividend. Since declared dividends are usually paid within a short period of time after the declaration date, they are classified as **current liabilities**.

Unearned revenues or advances result from customer prepayments for either performance of services or delivery of product. They may be required by the selling enterprise as a condition of the sale or may be made by the buyer as a means of guaranteeing that the seller will perform the desired service or deliver the product. Unearned revenues and advances should be classified as current liabilities at the balance sheet date if the services are to be performed or the products are to be delivered within one year or the **operating cycle**, whichever is longer.

Returnable deposits may be received to cover possible future damage to property. Many utility companies require security deposits. A deposit may be required for the use of a reusable container. Refundable deposits are classified as current liabilities if the firm expects to refund them during the current operating cycle or within one year, whichever is longer.

Accrued liabilities have their origin in the end-of-period adjustment process required by accrual accounting. Commonly accrued liabilities include wages and salaries payable, benefits payable, interest payable, and taxes payable. In addition an employer may have a current obligation for the employer portion of **FICA** tax and **FUTA** (unemployment) tax. Payroll taxes are not legal liabilities until the associated payroll is actually paid.

Agency liabilities result from the legal obligation of the enterprise to act as the collection agent for customer or employee taxes owed to various federal, state, or local government units. Examples of agency liabilities include sales taxes, income taxes withheld from employee paychecks, and employee **FICA** contributions.

Product financing liabilities originate when an entity sells and agrees to repurchase its inventory with the repurchase price equal to the original sales price plus the carrying and financing costs. The purpose of this transaction is to allow the seller to arrange financing on the original purchase of the inventory. The transaction is accounted for as a borrowing rather than as a sale. Chapter 7, Inventory, provides more information about product financing arrangements.

Current maturing portion of long-term debt is shown as a current liability if the obligation is to be liquidated by using assets classified as current. However, if the currently maturing debt is to be liquidated by using other than current assets (i.e., by using a sinking fund that is properly classified as an investment), then these obligations should be classified as long-term liabilities.

Obligations that, by their terms, are due on demand (SFAS 78) or will be due on demand within one year (or operating cycle, if longer) from the balance sheet date, even if liquidation is not expected to occur within that period, are classified as current liabilities.

SFAS 78 also requires that **long-term obligations that contain call provisions** be classified as current liabilities, if as of the balance sheet date one of the following occurs:

1. The debtor is in violation of the agreement and that violation makes the obligation callable.
2. The debtor is in violation of the agreement and that violation, unless cured within the grace period specified in the agreement, makes the obligation callable.

However, if circumstances arise that effectively negate the creditor's right to call the obligation, the obligation may be classified as long-term. Examples are

1. The creditor has waived the right to call the obligation caused by the debtor's violation or the creditor has subsequently lost the right to demand

repayment for more than one year (or operating cycle, if longer) from the balance sheet date.

2. Obligations contain a grace period for remedying the violation, and it is probable that the violation will be cured within the grace period. In these situations, the circumstances must be disclosed.

Long-term obligations that contain subjective acceleration clauses are classified as current liabilities if circumstances (such as recurring losses or liquidity problems) indicate that the clause will be exercised and payment will be due within one year (or one operating cycle). If, instead, the likelihood of the acceleration of the due date were remote, the obligation would be reported as long-term debt. Situations between the two extremes require disclosure (FASB TB 79-3).

Short-term obligations expected to be refinanced may be classified as noncurrent liabilities if the conditions specified in SFAS 6 are met. SFAS 6 states that an enterprise may reclassify currently maturing debt (other than obligations arising from transactions in the normal course of business that are due in customary terms) as long-term, provided that the enterprise intends to refinance the obligation on a long-term basis **and** its intent is supported by **either** of the following:

1. Post-balance-sheet-date issuance of a long-term obligation or equity securities. After the date of the enterprise's balance sheet but before that balance sheet is issued, long-term obligations or equity securities have been issued for the purpose of refinancing the short-term obligations on a long-term basis.
2. Refinancing agreement. Before the balance sheet is issued, the enterprise has entered into a financing agreement that clearly permits the enterprise to refinance the short-term obligation on a long-term basis on terms that are readily determinable.

If reclassification of the maturing debt is based upon the existence of a refinancing agreement, then SFAS 6 requires the following:

1. The refinancing agreement is noncancelable and will not expire within one year or operating cycle of the balance sheet date.
2. The replacement debt will not be callable except for violation of a provision of the refinancing agreement with which compliance is objectively determinable or measurable.
3. The enterprise is not in violation of the terms of the refinancing agreement.
4. The lender or investor is financially capable of honoring the refinancing agreement.

Under the provisions of SFAS 6, the amount of currently maturing debt to be reclassified cannot exceed the amount raised by the replacement debt or equity issuance nor can it exceed the amount specified in the refinancing agreement. If the amount specified in the refinancing agreement can fluctuate, then the maximum amount of debt that can be reclassified is equal to a reasonable estimate of the minimum amount expected to be available on any date from the due date of the maturing obligation to the end of the fiscal year. If no estimate can be made of the minimum amount available under the financing agreement, then none of the maturing debt can be reclassified as long-term. If debt or other agreements limit the ability of the organization to fully utilize the proceeds of the refinancing agreement (for example, a clause in another debt agreement sets a maximum debt-to-equity ratio), then only the amount that can be drawn without violating the limitations expressed in those other agreements can be reclassified to long-term. FASB Interpretation 8 states that if an enterprise uses current assets after the balance sheet date to liquidate a current obligation, and then replaces those current assets by issuing either equity securities or long-term debt before the issuance of the balance sheet, the currently maturing debt must still be classified as a current liability.

Payee Known but Amount May Have to Be Estimated

Taxes payable include federal, state, and local income taxes. The amount of income taxes payable is an estimate because the tax laws and rates in effect when the accrual is determined may differ from the tax laws and rates in effect when the taxes ultimately are paid. Temporary differences in recognition and measurement between accounting standards and tax laws create deferred tax liabilities (and deferred tax assets). The portion deemed currently payable must be classified as a current liability. The remaining amount is classified as a long-term liability.

Property taxes payable represent the unpaid portion of an entity's obligation to a state or other taxing authority that arises from ownership of real property. ARB 43, Chapter 10 indicates that the most acceptable method of accounting for property taxes is a monthly accrual of property tax expense during the fiscal period of the taxing authority for which the taxes are levied. The fiscal period of the taxing authority is the fiscal period which includes the assessment or lien date.

A liability for property taxes payable arises when the fiscal year of the taxing authority and the fiscal year of the entity do not coincide or when the assessment or lien date and the actual payment date do not fall within the same fiscal year. For example, XYZ Corporation is a calendar-year corporation which owns real estate in a state that operates on a June 30 fiscal year. In this state, property taxes are assessed and become a lien against property on July 1, although they are not payable until April 1 and August 1 of the next calendar year. XYZ Corporation would accrue an expense and a liability on a monthly basis beginning on July 1. At year-end (December 31), the firm would have an expense for six months' property tax on their income statement and a current liability for the same amount.

Bonus payments may require estimation since the amount of the bonus may be affected by the entity's net income for the year, by the income taxes currently payable, or by other factors. Additional estimation is necessary if bonus payments are accrued on a monthly basis for purposes of interim financial reporting but are determinable only annually by using a formula whose values are uncertain until shortly before payment.

Compensated absences refer to paid vacation, paid holidays, paid sick leave, and other paid leaves of absence. SFAS 43 states that an employer must accrue a liability for employee's compensation of future absences if all of the following conditions are met:

1. The employee's right to receive compensation for future absences is attributable to employee services already rendered.
2. The right vests or accumulates.
3. Payment of the compensation is probable.
4. The amount of the payment can be reasonably estimated.

If an employer is required to compensate an employee for unused vacation, holidays, or sick days even if employment is terminated, then the employee's right to this compensation is said to vest. Accrual of a liability for nonvesting rights depends on whether the unused rights expire at the end of the year in which earned or accumulate and are carried forward to succeeding years. If the rights expire, a liability for future absences should not be accrued at year-end because the benefits to be paid in subsequent years would not be attributable to employee services rendered in prior years. If unused rights accumulate and increase the benefits otherwise available in subsequent years, a liability should be accrued at year-end to the extent that it is probable that employees will be paid in subsequent years for the increased benefits attributable to the accumulated rights and the amount can be reasonably estimated.

SFAS 43 allows an exception for employee paid sick days that accumulate but do not vest. No accrued liability is required for sick days that only accumulate. However, an accrual may be made. The Board stated that these amounts are rarely material and the low reliability of estimates of future illness coupled with the high cost of developing these estimates indicates that accrual is not necessary. The required accounting should be determined by the employer's actual administration of sick pay benefits. If the employer routinely lets employees take time off when they are not ill and allows that time to be charged as sick pay, then an accrual should be made.

Pay for other employee leaves of absence that represent time off for past services (jury duty, personal days) should be considered compensation subject to accrual. Pay for employee leaves of absence that will provide future benefits and that are not attributable to past services rendered would not be subject to accrual. SFAS 43 does not provide guidance as to whether accruals should be based on current pay rates or expected future rates of pay and does not provide guidance regarding discounting of the accrual amounts.

SFAS 112 uses the four conditions of SFAS 43 to accrue an obligation for postemployment benefits other than pensions. Postemployment benefits other than pensions are benefits paid after termination of employment but before retirement to or on behalf of former or inactive employees, their beneficiaries, and covered dependents. Examples of those benefits are salary, continuation agreements, supplemental unemployment compensation, severance benefits, workers' compensation and other disability-related payments, job training or job placement services and continuation of health care or life insurance benefits after employment. If the four conditions in SFAS 43 are met, a liability is accrued. If one or more of the conditions are not met, the employer should assess whether a liability should be accrued under SFAS 5. If neither SFAS 43 nor SFAS 5 is applicable because the amount is not reasonably estimated, this fact must be disclosed.

Payee Unknown and the Amount May Have to Be Estimated

Premiums are usually offered by an enterprise to increase product sales. They may require the purchaser to return a specified number of box tops, wrappers, or other proofs of purchase. They may or may not require the payment of a cash amount. If the premium offer terminates at the end of the current period but has not been completely accounted for, or if it extends into the next accounting period, a current liability for the estimated number of redemptions expected in the future period will have to be recorded. If the premium offer extends for more than one accounting period, the estimated liability must be divided into a current portion and a long-term portion.

Product warranties providing for repair or replacement of defective products may be sold separately or may be included in the sale price of the product. If the warranty extends into the next accounting period, a current liability for the estimated amount of warranty expense expected in the next period must be recorded. If the warranty spans more than the next period, the estimated liability must be partitioned into a current and long-term portion.

Future product returns are accrued if a buyer has a right to return the product purchased and the sale is recognized in accordance with SFAS 48. If an entity is unable to make a reasonable estimate of the amount of future returns, the sale cannot be recognized until the return privilege has expired or conditions permit the loss to be estimated. Examples of factors that might impair the ability to reasonably estimate a loss are

1. Susceptibility of the product to technological or other obsolescence
2. A lengthy period over which returns are permitted
3. Absence of experience with returns on similar products sold to similar markets
4. Sales are few, significant, and have unique terms (rather than a large number of relatively homogeneous sales of small dollar amounts).

Contingencies

SFAS 5 defines a **contingency** as an existing condition, situation, or set of circumstances involving uncertainty as to possible gain or loss. It will ultimately be resolved when one or more future events occur or fail to occur. SFAS 5 defines the different levels of probability as to whether or not future events will confirm the existence of a loss as follows:

1. **Probable**—The future event or events are likely to occur.
2. **Reasonably possible**—The chance of the future event or events occurring is more than remote but less than likely.
3. **Remote**—The chance of the future event or events occurring is slight.

Professional judgment is required to classify the likelihood of the future events occurring. All relevant information that can be acquired concerning the uncertain set of circumstances needs to be obtained and used to determine the classification.

SFAS 5 states that a loss must be accrued if **both** of the following conditions are met:

1. It is **probable** that an asset has been impaired or a liability has been incurred at the date of the financial statements.
2. The amount of loss can be reasonably estimated.

Loss contingency. Loss contingencies are recognized only if there is an impairment of an asset or the incurrence of a liability as of the balance sheet date. Examples of possible loss contingencies include

1. Collectibility of receivables
2. Warranty liabilities and product defects
3. Loss due to fire, explosion, or other hazards
4. Expropriation of assets
5. Litigation, claims, and assessments
6. Incurred but not reported (IBNR) claims if the entity insures its risk of loss with a claims-made policy.
7. Exposures under multiple-year retrospectively rated insurance contacts
8. Catastrophic losses by insurance and reinsurance entities
9. Guarantees
10. Obligations under standby letters of credit
11. Repurchase agreements
12. Withdrawal from a multiemployer plan

Events which give rise to loss contingencies that occur after the balance sheet date (i.e., bankruptcy or expropriation) but before issuance of the financial statements may require disclosure so that statement users are not misled. Note disclosures or pro forma financial statements may be prepared as supplemental information to show the effect of the loss.

It is not necessary that a single amount be identified. A range of amounts is sufficient to indicate that some amount of loss has been incurred and should be accrued. The amount accrued is the amount within the range that appears to be the best estimate. If there is no best estimate, the minimum amount in the range should be accrued since it is probable that the loss will be at least this amount (FASB Interpretation 14). The maximum amount of loss should be disclosed. If future events indicate that the minimum loss originally accrued is inadequate, an additional loss should be accrued in the period when this fact becomes known. This accrual is a change in estimate, not a prior period adjustment.

When a loss is probable and no estimate is possible, these facts should be disclosed in the current period. The accrual of the loss should be made in the earliest period in which the amount of the loss can be estimated. Accrual of that loss in future periods is a change in estimate. It is not a prior period adjustment.

If the occurrence of the loss is reasonably possible, the facts and circumstances of the possible loss and an estimate of the amount, if determinable, should be disclosed. If the occurrence of the loss is remote, no accrual or disclosure is usually required.

Guarantees. Guarantees of indebtedness (direct or indirect), obligations under standby letters of credit, guarantees to repurchase, and guarantees with similar circumstances should be disclosed even if the possibility of loss is remote.

Unasserted claims or assessments. It is not necessary to disclose loss contingencies for an unasserted claim or assessment where there has been no manifestation of an awareness of possible claim or assessment by a potential claimant unless it is deemed probable that a claim will be asserted and a reasonable possibility of an unfavorable outcome exists. Under the provisions of SFAS 5, general or unspecified business risks are not loss contingencies and, therefore, no accrual is necessary. In addition, no disclosure is required. Appropriations of retained earnings may be used for these risks as long as no charge to income is made to establish the appropriation.

Gain contingency. SFAS 5 leaves unchanged the provisions of ARB 50 which state that gain contingencies should not be recorded before they have been realized but that adequate disclosure of the gain contingency should be made. Such disclosure should not contain misleading implications as to the likelihood of realization.

Estimate vs. contingency. Distinguishing between an estimate and a contingency can be difficult because both involve an uncertainty that will be resolved by future events. However, an estimate exists because of uncertainty about the amount of an event requiring an acknowledged accounting recognition. The event has occurred and the effect is known, but the amount itself is uncertain. For example, depreciation is an estimate, but not a contingency because the actual fact of physical depreciation is acknowledged, although the amount is obtained by an assumed accounting method.

In a contingency, the amount is also usually uncertain, although that is not an essential characteristic. Instead, the uncertainty lies in whether the event has (or will) occur and what the effect, if any, on the enterprise will be. Collectibility of receivables is a contingency because both the amount of loss and the identification of which customer will not pay in the future is unknown. Similar logic would hold for obligations related to product warranties. Both the amount and the customer are currently unknown.

Other contingencies are rarely recognized until specific events confirming their existence occur. Every business risks loss by fire, explosion, government expropriation or guarantees made in the ordinary course of business. To the extent those losses are not (or cannot be) insured, the risks are contingencies. Because those events are often random in their occurrence, uncertainty surrounds whether the future event confirming the loss will or will not take place. The passage of time usually resolves the uncertainty. When both conditions are met, the potential loss is recognized in financial statements.

The most difficult area of contingencies is litigation. Accountants must rely on attorneys' assessments concerning the likelihood of such events. Unless the attorney indicates that the risk of loss is remote or slight, or that the loss if it occurs would be immaterial to the company, disclosure in financial statements is necessary and an accrual may also be necessary. For example, in cases where judgments have been entered against the entity, or where the attorney gives a range of expected losses or other amounts and indicates that an unfavorable outcome is probable, accruals of loss contingencies for at least the minimum point of the range must be made. In most cases, however, an estimate of the contingency is unknown and the contingency is reflected only in footnotes.

Offsetting of Assets and Liabilities

APB 10 states that offsetting of assets and liabilities is improper except where a right of setoff exists. A right of setoff is a debtor's legal right to discharge debt owed to another party by applying against the debt an amount the other party owes to the debtor. FASB Interpretation 39 says that a right of setoff exists if all of the following conditions are met:

1. Each of the two parties owes the other determinable amounts.
2. The reporting party has the right to set off.
3. The reporting party intends to set off.
4. The right of setoff is enforceable at law.

FASB Interpretation 39 permits the offsetting of fair value amounts recognized for multiple swap, forward, option, and other conditional or exchange contracts with a single party executed under a master netting arrangement. FASB Interpretation 41 modifies that interpretation to permit offseting of amounts recognized as payables in repurchase agreements against amounts recognized as receivables in reverse repurchase agreements with the same counterparty. If certain conditions are met, an entity may, but is not required to, offset the amounts recognized. The entity's choice to offset or not must be applied consistently.

EMERGING ISSUES TASK FORCE CONSENSUS SUMMARIES

85-20   Recognition of Fees for Guaranteeing a Loan

A guarantor should perform ongoing assessments of the probability of loss related to the guarantee and recognize a liability if the conditions in SFAS 5 are met.

86-5   Classifying Demand Notes with Repayment Terms

An obligation is considered due on demand even if a debt agreement specifies repayment terms if the creditor can demand payment at any time. For example, for an agreement that says "due in monthly installments of principal and interest. . . or on demand, whichever is earlier," the obligation is a current liability.

86-15   Increasing-Rate Debt

Notes that mature in three months but can be continually extended for up to five years are known as "increasing-rate notes." The outstanding term of the debt should be estimated after considering plans, ability and intent to service the debt. Based upon this term, the borrower's periodic interest rate should be determined by the use of the interest method.

Debt interest costs should be amortized over the estimated outstanding term of the debt. Any excess accrued interest resulting from paying the debt before the estimated maturity date is an adjustment of interest expense. It is not an extraordinary item under SFAS 4.

The classification of the debt as to current or noncurrent should be based on the source of repayment. Thus, this classification need not be consistent with the period used to determine the periodic interest cost. For example, the time frame used for the estimated outstanding term of the debt could be a year or less but, because of a planned long-term refinancing agreement, the noncurrent classification could be used.

86-30   Classification of Obligations When a Violation Is Waived by the Creditor

A borrower violates a covenant of a long-term debt agreement on one of the quarterly or semiannual compliance dates, giving the lender the right to call the debt. If the lender waives that right for a period greater than one year (but retains the requirements to meet the covenant in the future), the borrower should classify the debt as noncurrent unless both (1) a covenant violation has occurred at the balance sheet date or would have occurred absent a loan modification and (2) it is probable that the borrower will be unable to comply with the covenant at measurement dates within the next twelve months.

93-14 Accounting for Multiple-Year Retrospectively Rated Insurance Contracts by Insurance Enterprises and Other Enterprises

An entity that enters into a multiple-year retrospectively rated contract with an insurance company should recognize a liability to the extent that it has an obligation to pay cash (or other consideration) to the insurer that would not have had to be paid if it were not for the experience under the contract. The amount recognized in the current period is the total contract costs as of the reporting date with and without the experience under the contact. The amount recognized should include premium adjustments, settlement adjustments, and impairments of coverage. However, if the insurance policy does not transfer risk, the policy premiums are accounted for as a deposit by the insured. Special provisions apply if the insured could terminate the contract prior to the end of its term and that termination would change the amounts paid.

95-22 Balance Sheet Classification of Borrowings Outstanding under Revolving Credit Agreements That Include Both a Subjective Acceleration Clause and a Lock-Box Agreement

This consensus applies to borrowings outstanding under a revolving credit agreement that includes both a subjective acceleration clause and a requirement to maintain a lock-box into which the borrower's customers send remittances that are then used to reduce the debt outstanding. These borrowings are short-term obligations and are classified as current liabilities unless the entity has the intent and ability to refinance the revolving credit agreement on a long-term basis (i.e., the conditions in SFAS 6 are met).

00-23 Issues Related to the Accounting for Stock Compensation under APB Opinion No. 25 and FASB Interpretation No. 44

If a company grants a stock option to an employee and guarantees that if the option does not have an intrinsic value of at least $X at a future date, the company will pay a bonus equal to the shortfall, the "guaranteed" minimum amount should be recognized as compensation expense and a bonus liability over the period of service. Any amount recognized as a bonus liability that exceeds the amount paid to the employee should be reclassified to equity. The recognized cost should not be reversed unless the employee fails to fulfill his or her service obligation.

If a contingent cash bonus and a stock option award are granted at the same time, but the payment of the cash bonus does not depend upon the exercise of the stock option, the cash bonus should be accounted for as a separate element of compensation. For example, if the cash bonus will be paid only if the stock option vests and the stock price exceeds the exercise price at the vesting date, the cash bonus is a separate element of compensation because the bonus will be paid regardless of whether the option is exercised.

Chapter 17, Stockholders' Equity, provides additional discussion of this EITF Issue.

STATEMENTS OF POSITION

96-1   Environmental Remediation Liabilities

This SOP includes a very detailed description of relevant laws, remediation provisions and other pertinent information, which is useful to auditors as well as to reporting entities. In terms of accounting guidance, the SOP provides that SFAS 5 is the principal standard to be interpreted in the context of environmental obligations (e.g., determining the threshold for accrual of a liability, etc.) and its sets "benchmarks" for liability recognition. The benchmarks for the accrual and evaluation of the estimated liability (i.e., the stages which are deemed to be important to ascertaining the existence and amount of the liability) are

a. The identification and verification of an entity as a potentially responsible party (PRP), since the SOP stipulates that accrual should be based on the premise that expected costs will be borne by only the "participating potentially responsible parties" and that the "recalcitrant, unproven and unidentified" PRP will not contribute to costs of remediation

b. The receipt of a "unilateral administrative order"

c. Participation, as a PRP, in the remedial investigation/feasibility study (RI/FS)

d. Completion of the feasibility study

e. Issuance of the Record of Decision (RoD)

f. The remedial design through operation and maintenance, including post remediation monitoring

The amount of the liability that is to be accrued is affected by the entity's allocable share of liability for a specific site, and by its share of the amounts related to the site that will not be paid by the other PRP or the government. The categories of costs to be included in the accrued liability include incremental direct costs of the remediation effort itself, as well as the costs of compensation and benefits for employees directly involved in the remediation effort. The SOP indicates that costs are to be estimated based on existing laws and technologies, and are not to be discounted to estimated present values unless timing of cash payments is fixed or reliability determinable.

Incremental direct costs will include such items as fees paid to outside law firms for work related to the remediation effort, costs relating to completing the RI/FS, fees to outside consulting and engineering firms for site investigations and development of remedial action plans and remedial actions, costs of contractors performing remedial actions, government oversight costs and past costs, the cost of machinery and equipment dedicated to the remedial actions that do not have an alternative use, assessments by a PRP group covering costs incurred by the group in dealing with a site, and the costs of operation and maintenance of the remedial ac-

546 of 1232 at top

tion, including costs of post remediation monitoring required by remedial action plan.

As was first set forth by EITF 93-5, *Accounting for Environmental Liabilities*, the SOP states that potential recoveries cannot be offset against the estimated liability, and further notes that any recovery recognized as an asset should be reflected at fair value, which implies that only the present value of future recoveries can be recorded. It also stipulates that environmental clean up costs are not unusual in nature, and thus cannot be shown as extraordinary items in the income statement. Furthermore, it is presumed that the costs are operating in nature, and thus cannot normally be included in "other income and expense" category of the income statement, either. Disclosure of accounting policies regarding recognition of liability and of related asset (for recoveries from third parties) are also needed, where pertinent.

13 LONG-TERM DEBT

PERSPECTIVE AND ISSUES

Long-term liabilities are liabilities that will be paid or otherwise settled over a period of more than one year, or if longer, more than one operating cycle. This chapter discusses accounting for bonds and long-term notes payable. Other common types of long-term liabilities are lease obligations (Chapter 14, Leases), deferred income taxes (Chapter 15, Income Taxes), pension and deferred compensation plan obligations (Chapter 16, Pensions), and contingencies (Chapter 12, Current Liabilities and Contingencies).

The appropriate valuation of long-term debt at the date of issuance is the present value of the future payments, using an interest rate commensurate with the risks involved. In many situations the interest rate commensurate with the risks involved is the rate stated in the agreement between the borrower and the creditor. However, if the debt is noninterest-bearing or the rate stated in the agreement is not indicative of the market rate for a borrower of similar creditworthiness under similar terms (the market rate), interest is imputed at the market rate, and the resulting premium or discount is amortized as interest over the life of the agreement (APB 21).

Debt remains on the books of the debtor until it is extinguished. In most cases, a debt is extinguished at maturity, when the required principal and interest payments have been made and the debtor has no further obligation to the creditor. In other cases, the debtor may desire to extinguish the debt before its maturity. For example, if market interest rates are falling, a debtor may chose to issue debt at the new lower rate and use the proceeds to retire older higher-interest-rate debt. SFAS 140 states that a debt is extinguished if either of two conditions is met:

1. The debtor pays the creditor and is relieved of its obligation for the liability.
2. The debtor is legally released from being the primary obligor under the liability, either judicially or by the creditor.

SFAS 140 stopped the practice of removing debt from the balance sheet via an insubstance defeasance of debt. (However, in-substance defeasances recognized prior to the date SFAS 140 became effective were allowed to remain off the balance sheet.)

If a debtor experiences financial difficulties before the debt is paid, a creditor may need to recognize an impairment of the debt. Under SFAS 114, an impairment of the debt is recognized when the present value of the expected future cash flows discounted at the debt's original effective interest rate is less than the recorded investment in the debt. If for economic or legal reasons related to the debtor's financial difficulties, the creditor grants the debtor concessions that would not otherwise have been granted, the debtor must determine how to recognize the effects of the troubled debt restructuring (SFAS 15).

Some debt is issued with terms that allow it to be converted to an equity instrument (common or preferred stock) at a future date. When issued, no value is apportioned to the conversion feature. When the debt is converted, the stock issued is generally valued at the carrying value of the debt (APB 14). In certain situations, a debtor will modify the conversion privileges after issuance of the debt in order to induce prompt conversion of the debt into equity. The debtor must recognize an expense for the consideration given to induce conversion (SFAS 84).

Debt can also be issued with stock warrants, which allow the holder to purchase a stated number of common shares at a certain price within a stated time period. If debt is issued with detachable warrants, the proceeds of issuance are allocated between the two financial instruments (APB 14).

In October 2000, the FASB issued for comment proposed standards that would require a compound instrument, such as convertible debt or debt issued with warrants, to be divided into its liability components and equity components. The components would be separately presented in the balance sheet. The FASB believes that that presentation more faithfully represents the rights and obligations embedded in compound instruments than does presenting the instruments entirely as liabilities or entirely as equity.

Through-put contracts, take-or-pay contracts, and other unconditional purchase obligations are sometimes used instead of debt to finance a capital project or a joint venture. These agreements may or may not be recognized on the balance sheet. Entities are required to disclose information about those types of obligations in the notes to the financial statements (SFAS 47).

Short-term obligations that are expected to be refinanced and therefore classified as long-term debt per SFAS 6 are discussed in Chapter 12, Current Liabilities and Contingencies.

Sources of GAAP				
APB	*SFAS*	*FASB I*	*FASB TB*	*EITF*
14, 21, 26	4, 5, 6, 15, 47, 64, 84, 114, 118, 140	8	79-3, 80-1, 80-2, 81-6	85-17, 85-29, 86-36, 87-19, 88-18, 89-15, 90-19, 94-8, 96-19, 96-22, 98-5, 99-1, 00-27, 01-1, D-10, D-23, D-61

DEFINITIONS OF TERMS

Amortization. The process of allocating an amount to expense over the periods benefited.

Bond. A written agreement whereby a borrower agrees to pay a sum of money at a designated future date plus periodic interest payments at the stated rate.

Bond issue costs. Costs related to issuing a bond (i.e., legal, accounting, underwriting fees, printing, and registration costs).

Book value approach. Recording the stock issued from a bond conversion at the carrying value of the bonds converted.

Callable bond. A bond in which the issuer reserves the right to call and retire the bond prior to its maturity.

Carrying value. The face amount of a debt issue increased or decreased by the applicable unamortized premium or discount plus unamortized issue costs.

Collateral. Asset(s) pledged to settle the obligation to repay a loan.

Convertible debt. Debt that may be converted into common or preferred stock at the holder's option after specific criteria are met.

Covenant. A clause in a debt contract written for the protection of the lender that outlines the rights and actions of the parties involved when certain conditions occur (e.g., when the debtor's current ratio declines beyond a specified level).

Debenture. Long-term debt not secured by collateral.

Discount. Created when a debt instrument is issued for less than face value and occurs when the stated rate on the instrument is less than the market rate at the time of issue.

Effective interest method. Amortizing the discount or premium to interest expense so as to result in a constant rate of interest when applied to the amount of debt outstanding at the beginning of any given period.

Effective rate. See **market rate**.

Face value. The stated amount or principal due on the maturity date.

Imputation. The process of interest rate approximation that is accomplished by examining the circumstances under which the note was issued.

Long-term debt. Probable future sacrifices of economic benefits arising from present obligations that are not currently payable within one year or the operating cycle of the business, whichever is longer.

Market rate. The current rate of interest available for obligations issued under the same terms and conditions by an issuer of similar credit standing.

Market value approach. Recording the stock issued from a bond conversion at the current market price of the bonds converted or the stock issued.

Maturity date. The date on which the face value (principal) of the bond or note becomes due.

Maturity value. See **face value**.

Premium. Created when a debt instrument is issued for more than its face value and occurs when the stated rate on the instrument is greater than the market rate at the time of issue.

Principal. See **face value**.

Secured debt. Debt that has collateral to satisfy the obligation (e.g., a mortgage on specific property) if not repaid.

Serial bond. Debt whose face value matures in installments.

Stated rate. The interest rate written on the face of the debt instrument.

Straight-line method. The method of amortizing the premium or discount to interest expense such that there is an even allocation of interest expense over the life of the debt.

Take-or-pay contract. A contract in which a purchaser of goods agrees to pay specified fixed or minimum amounts periodically in return for products, even if delivery is not taken. It results from a project financing arrangement where the project produces the products.

Through-put agreement. An agreement similar to a take-or-pay contract except a service is provided by the project under the financing arrangement.

Troubled debt restructure. Occurs when the creditor, for economic or legal reasons related to the debtor's financial difficulties, grants a concession to the debtor (deferment or reduction of interest or principal) that it would not otherwise consider.

Unconditional purchase obligation. An obligation to transfer a fixed or minimum amount of funds in the future or to transfer goods or services at fixed or minimum prices.

Yield rate. See **market rate**.

CONCEPTS, RULES, AND EXAMPLES

Notes and Bonds

Notes are a common form of exchange in business transactions for cash, property, goods, and services. Notes represent debt issued to a single investor without intending for the debt to be broken up among many investors. A note's maturity, usually lasting one to seven years, tends to be shorter than that of a bond.

Bonds are primarily used to borrow funds from the general public or institutional investors when a contract for a single amount (a note) is too large for any one lender to supply. Dividing up the amount needed into $1,000 or $10,000 units makes it easier to sell the bonds. Bonds also result from a single agreement.

Notes and bonds share common characteristics. They both are promises to pay a sum of money at a designated maturity date plus periodic interest payments at a stated rate. They include a written agreement stating the amount of the **principal**, the interest rate, when the interest and principal are to be paid, and the restrictive **covenants**, if any, that must be met.

The interest rate is affected by many factors, including the cost of money, the business risk factors, and the inflationary expectations associated with the business.

The **stated rate** on a note or bond often differs from the **market rate** at the time of issuance. When this occurs, the present value of the interest and principal payments will differ from the maturity, or **face value**. If the market rate exceeds the stated rate, the cash proceeds will be less than the face value of the debt because the present value of the total interest and principal payments discounted back to the present yields an amount that is less than the face value. Because an investor is rarely willing to pay more than the present value, the bonds must be issued at a discount. The **discount** is the difference between the issuance price (present value) and the face, or stated, value of the bonds. This discount is then amortized over the life of the bonds to increase the recognized interest expense so that the total amount of the expense represents the actual bond yield. When the stated rate exceeds the market rate, the bond will sell for more than its face value (at a **premium**) to bring the effective rate to the market rate. Amortization of the premium over the life of the bonds will decrease the total interest expense.

When the market and stated rates are equivalent at the time of issuance, no discount or premium exists and the instrument will sell at its face value. Changes in the market rate subsequent to issuance are irrelevant in determining the discount or premium or its **amortization**.

All commitments to pay (and receive) money at a determinable future date are subject to present value techniques and, if necessary, interest imputation with the exception of the following:

1. Normal accounts payable due within one year
2. Amounts to be applied to purchase price of goods or services or that provide security to an agreement (e.g., advances, progress payments, security deposits, and retainages)
3. Transactions between parent and subsidiary
4. Obligations payable at some indeterminable future date (warranties)
5. Lending and depositor savings activities of financial institutions whose primary business is lending money
6. Transactions where interest rates are affected by prescriptions of a governmental agency (e.g., revenue bonds, tax exempt obligations, etc.)

APB 21 specifies when and how interest is to be imputed when a debt is noninterest-bearing or the stated rate is not reasonable. APB 21 divides debt into three categories for discussion. A diagram on the next page illustrates the accounting treatment for the three types of debt.

ACCOUNTING FOR MONETARY ASSETS AND LIABILITIES

Notes issued solely for cash. When a note is issued solely for cash, its present value is assumed to be equal to the cash proceeds. The interest rate is that rate that equates the cash proceeds to the amounts to be paid in the future (i.e., **no** interest rate is to be imputed). For example, a $1,000 note due in three years that sells for $889 has an implicit rate of 4% ($1,000 x .889, where .889 is the present value factor of a lump sum at 4% for three years). This rate is to be used when amortizing the discount.

In most situations, a bond is issued at a price other than its face value. The amount of the cash exchanged is equal to the total of the present value of the interest and principal payments. The difference between the cash proceeds and the face value is recorded as a premium if the cash proceeds are greater than the face value or a discount if they are less. The journal entry to record a bond issued at a discount follows:

Cash	(proceeds)	
Discount on bonds payable	(difference)	
Bonds payable		(face value)

Notes issued for cash and a right or privilege. Often when a note bearing an unrealistic rate of interest is issued in exchange for cash, an additional right or privilege is granted, such as the issuer agreeing to sell merchandise to the purchaser at a reduced rate. The difference between the present value of the receivable and the cash loaned is regarded as an addition to the cost of the products purchased for the purchaser/lender and as unearned revenue to the issuer. This treatment stems from an attempt to match revenue and expense in the proper periods and to differentiate between those factors that affect income from operations and income or expense from nonoperating sources. In the situation above, the discount (difference between the cash loaned and the present value of the note) will be amortized to interest revenue or expense, while the unearned revenue or contractual right is amortized to sales and inventory, respectively. The discount affects income from nonoperational sources, while the unearned revenue or contractual right affects the gross profit computation. Because the discount is amortized on a different basis than the contractual right, net income for the period is also affected.

Example of accounting for a note issued for both cash and a contractual right

1. Miller borrows $10,000 via a noninterest-bearing three-year note from Krueger.
2. Miller agrees to sell $50,000 of merchandise to Krueger at less than the ordinary retail price for the duration of the note.
3. The fair rate of interest on a note with similar payment terms and a borrower of similar creditworthiness is 10%.

According to APB 21, the difference between the present value of the note and the face value of the loan is to be regarded as part of the cost of the products purchased under the agreement. The present value factor for an amount due in three years at 10% is .75132. Therefore, the present value of the note is $7,513 ($10,000 x .75132). The $2,487 ($10,000 – $7,513) difference between the face value and the present value is to be recorded as a discount on the note payable and as unearned revenue on the future purchases by the debtor. The following entries would be made by the debtor (Miller) and the creditor (Krueger) to record the transaction:

Miller			*Krueger*		
Cash	10,000		Note receivable	10,000	
Discount on note payable	2,487		Contract right with supplier	2,487	
Note payable		10,000	Cash		10,000
Unearned revenue		2,487	Discount on note receivable		2,487

The discount on note payable (and note receivable) is to be amortized using the effective interest method, while the unearned revenue account and contract right with supplier account are amortized on a pro rata basis as the right to purchase merchandise is used up. Thus, if Krueger purchased $20,000 of merchandise from Miller in the first year, the following entries would be necessary:

Miller			*Krueger*		
Unearned revenue	995		Inventory (or cost of sales)	995	
[$2,487 x (20,000/50,000)]			Contract right with supplier		995
Sales		995			
Interest expense	751		Discount on note receivable	751	
Discount on note payable			Interest revenue		751
($7,513 x 10%)		751			

The amortization of unearned revenue and contract right with supplier accounts will fluctuate with the amount of purchases made. If there is a balance remaining in the account at the end of the loan term, it is amortized to the appropriate account in that final year.

Noncash transactions. When a note is issued for consideration such as property, goods, or services, and the transaction is entered into at arm's length, the stated interest rate is presumed to be fair unless (1) no interest rate is stated; (2) the stated rate is unreasonable; or (3) the face value of the debt is materially different from the consideration involved or the current market value of the note at the date of the transaction. According to APB 21, when the rate on the note is **not** considered fair, the note is to be recorded at the "fair market value of the property, goods, or services received or at an amount that reasonably approximates the market value of the note, whichever is the more clearly determinable." When this amount differs from the face value of the note, the difference is to be recorded as a discount or premium and amortized to interest expense.

Example of accounting for a note exchanged for property

1. A sells B a machine which has a fair market value of $7,510.
2. A receives a three-year noninterest-bearing note having a face value of $10,000.

In this situation, the fair market value of the consideration is readily determinable and, thus, represents the amount at which the note is to be recorded. The following entry by B is necessary:

Machine	7,510	
Discount on notes payable	2,490	
Notes payable		10,000

The discount will be amortized to interest expense over the three-year period using the interest rate **implied** in the transaction. The interest rate implied is 10%, because the factor for an amount due in three years is .75132, which when applied to the $10,000 face value results in an amount equal to the fair value of the machine.

If the fair market value of the consideration or note is not determinable, then the present value of the note must be determined using an **imputed** interest rate. This rate will then be used to establish the present value of the note by discounting all future payments on the note at this rate. General guidelines for imputing the interest rate, which are provided by APB 21, include the prevailing rates of similar instruments from creditors with similar credit ratings and the rate the debtor could obtain for similar financing from other sources. Other determining factors include any collateral or restrictive covenants involved, the current and expected prime rate, and other terms pertaining to the instrument. The objective is to approximate the rate of interest that would have resulted if an independent borrower and lender had negotiated a similar transaction under comparable terms and conditions. This determination is as of the issuance date, and any subsequent changes in interest rates would be irrelevant.

Example of accounting for a note exchanged to property

1. A sells B a used machine The fair market value is not readily determinable.
2. A receives a three-year noninterest-bearing note having a face value of $20,000. The market value of the note is not known.
3. B could have borrowed the money for the machine's purchase from a bank at a rate of 10%.

In this situation, the fair market value of the consideration is not readily determinable, so the present value of the note is determined using an imputed interest rate. The rate used is the rate at which B could have borrowed the money—10%. The factor for an amount due in three years at 10% is .75132, so the present value of the note is $15,026. The following entry by B is necessary:

Machine	15,026	
Discount on notes payable	4,974	
Notes payable		20,000

Effective Interest Method

The **effective interest method** is the preferred method of accounting for a discount or premium arising from a note or bond. Under the effective interest method, the discount or premium is amortized over the life of the debt in such a way as to result in a constant rate of interest when applied to the amount outstanding at the beginning of any given period. Therefore, interest expense is equal to the market rate of interest at the time of issuance multiplied by this beginning figure. The difference between the interest expense and the cash paid represents the amortization of the discount or premium.

Amortization tables are often created at the time of the bond's issuance to provide figures necessary when recording the entries relating to the debt issue. They also provide a check of accuracy since the final values in the unamortized discount or premium and carrying value columns should be equal to zero and the bond's face value, respectively.

Example of applying the effective interest method

1. A three-year, 12%, $10,000 bond is issued at 1/1/X7, with interest payments semiannually.
2. The market rate is 10%.

The amortization table would appear as follows:

Date	Credit cash	Debit int. exp.	Debit prem.	Unam. prem. bal.	Carrying value
1/1/X7				$507.61	$10,507.61[a]
7/1/X7	$ 600.00[b]	$ 525.38[c]	$ 74.62[d]	432.99[e]	10,432.99[f]
1/1/X8	600.00	521.65	78.35	354.64	10,354.64
7/1/X8	600.00	517.73	82.27	272.37	10,272.37
1/1/X9	600.00	513.62	86.38	185.99	10,185.99
7/1/X9	600.00	509.30	90.70	95.29	10,095.29
1/1/X0	600.00	504.71[g]	95.29	--	10,000.00
	$3,600.00	$3,092.39	$507.61		

(a) PV of principal and interest payments
    at 5% for 6 periods
    $10,000(.74622)   = $ 7,462.20
    $ 600(5.07569)   =   _3,045.41_
                            $10,507.61
(b) $10,000.00 x .12 x one-half year

(c) $10,507.61 x .10 x one-half year
(d) $600.00 – $525.38
(e) $507.61 – $74.62
(f) $10,507.61 – $74.62
    (or $10,000 + $432.99)
(g) Rounding error = $.05

Although the effective interest method is the preferred method of amortizing a discount or premium, the **straight-line method** may be used if the results are not materially different. The amortized portion is equal to the total amount of the discount or premium divided by the life of the debt from issuance in months multiplied by the number of months the debt has been outstanding that year. Interest expense under the straight-line method is equal to the cash interest paid plus the amortized portion of the discount or minus the amortized portion of the premium.

When the **interest date does not coincide with the year-end**, an adjusting entry must be made to recognize the proportional share of interest payable and the amortization of the discount or premium. Within the amortization period, the discount or premium can be amortized using the straight-line method.

If **bonds or notes are issued between interest payment dates**, the interest and the amortization must be computed for the period between the sale date and the next interest date. The purchaser usually pays the issuer for the amount of interest that has accrued since the last payment date. That payment is recorded as a payable by the issuer. At the next interest date, the issuer pays the purchaser as though the bond had been outstanding for the entire interest period. The discount or premium is also amortized for the short period.

Example of note issued between payment dates

On June 1, 20X0, Acme Manufacturing issues a $100,000 7% bond with a three-year life at 104. Interest is payable on July 1 and January 1. The computation of the premium would be

Proceeds	$104,000
Face value	100,000
Premium	$ 4,000

The entry to record the bond issuance and the receipt of interest from the purchaser would be

Cash	106,967	
Bonds payable		100,000
Premium on bonds		4,000
Interest payable		2,967

The bonds would be outstanding for two years and seven months. An effective interest rate must be computed that will equate the present value of the future principal and interest payments to the cash received. Using a spreadsheet facilitates the trial and error process. Alternatively, present value tables can be used to compute the value, as shown below.

First, compute the present value of the interest and principal payments as of 7/1/00 using a guess of 5% annually.

Present value of an annuity due of $3,500 for six periods @ 2.5% = 3,500 x 5.6458 =   19,760
Present value of a single payment of $100,000 in five periods @2.5% =100,000 x .88385 =   88,385
                                                                                        108,145

Then, compute the present value of that result one month earlier (at June 1, 2000) using the same interest rate.

Present value of a single payment of $108,145 in one month = 108,145/[1+(.05/12)] = 107,696

The result is more than the cash received ($106,967), so we know that the interest rate must be higher than 5%. Repeat the calculation at a 6% annual rate:

Present value of an annuity due of $3,500 for six periods @3% = 3,500 x 5.5797 =   19,529
Present value of a single payment of $100,000 in five periods @3% =100,000 x .86261 =   86,261
                                                                                       105,790

Present value of a single payment of $105,790 in one month = 105,790/[1+(.06/12)] = 105,263

The result is less than the cash received ($106,967), so we know the rate is between 5 and 6%. By interpolation, we determine that the rate is 5.3%.

$$\frac{107,696-106,967}{107,696-105,263} \quad x \quad (6\%\text{-}5\%) = .299, \text{ which is added to 5\% to get the effective rate.}$$

The amortization of the $4,000 premium would be as follows:

	Cash paid (received)	Interest at 5.3% annually	Amortization	Interest payable	Bond payable
					104,000
06/01/00	(2,967)			2,967	104,000
07/01/00	3,500	459	74	(2,967)	103,926
01/01/01	3,500	2,754	746		103,180
07/01/01	3,500	2,734	765		102,415
01/01/02	3,500	2,714	786		101,629
07/01/02	3,500	2,693	807		100,822
01/01/03	103,500	2,672	822		100,000

The entry to record the first interest payment would be

Interest payable	2,967	
Interest expense	459	
Premium on bonds	74	
Cash		3,500

Costs may be incurred in connection with issuing bonds. Examples include legal, accounting, and underwriting fees; commissions; and engraving, printing, and registration costs. These costs theoretically should be treated as either an expense in the period incurred or a reduction in the related amount of debt, in much the same manner as a discount (SFAC 6). These costs do not provide any future economic benefit and, therefore, should not be an asset. Since these costs reduce the amount of cash proceeds, they in effect increase the effective interest rate and probably should be accounted for the same as an unamortized discount. However, in practice, issue costs are treated as deferred charges and amortized using the straight-line method.

Extinguishment of Debt

Management may reacquire or retire outstanding debt before its scheduled maturity. This decision is usually caused by changes in present or expected interest rates or in cash flows.

In-substance defeasance (irrevocably placing assets in a trust that is to be used solely to service the remaining debt payments) does not result in the extinguishment of a liability. Except for items excluded by SFAS 140, a liability is removed from the balance sheet only if

1. The creditor is paid and the debtor is relieved of the obligation.
2. The debtor is released legally either by the creditor or judicially from being the primary obligor.

If a debtor becomes secondarily liable, through a third-party assumption and a release by the creditor, the original debtor becomes a guarantor. A guarantee obligation, based on the probability that the third party will pay, is to be recognized and initially measured at fair value. The amount of guarantee obligation increases the loss or reduces the gain recognized on extinguishments.

Gain or loss. According to APB 26, the difference between the net carrying value and the price paid to acquire the debt instruments is to be recorded as a gain or loss. If the acquisition price is greater than the carrying value, a loss exists. A gain is generated if the acquisition price is less than the carrying value. These gains or losses are to be recognized in the period in which the retirement took place.

The unamortized premium or discount and issue costs should be amortized to the acquisition date and recorded prior to the determination of the gain or loss. If the extinguishment of debt does not occur on the interest date, the interest payable accruing between the last interest date and the acquisition date must also be recorded.

Except for any gains and losses resulting from purchasing bonds to satisfy sinking fund requirements that occur within one year of the date of the purchase (SFAS 64), all gains and losses from extinguishment, if material in amount, receive extraordinary item treatment (SFAS 4).

Example of accounting for the extinguishment of debt

1. A 10%, ten-year, $200,000 bond is dated and issued on 1/1/97 at 98, with the interest payable semiannually.
2. Associated bond issue costs of $14,000 are incurred.
3. Four years later, on 1/1/01, the entire bond issue is repurchased at $102 per $100 face value and is retired.
4. At 1/1/01 the unamortized discount using the effective interest rate of 10.325% is $2,858.

The gain or loss on the repurchase is computed as follows:

Reacquisition price [(102/100) x $200,000]		$204,000
Net carrying amount:		
Face value	$200,000	
Unamortized discount	(2,858)	
Unamortized issue costs [14,000 x (6/10)]	(8,400)	188,742
Loss on bond repurchase		$ 15,258

The loss on bond repurchase (debt extinguishment) is treated as an extraordinary item.

Troubled Debt Restructurings

Troubled debt restructurings are defined by SFAS 15 as situations where the creditor, for economic or legal reasons related to the debtor's financial difficulties, grants the debtor a concession that would not otherwise be granted. However, in any of the following four situations, a concession granted by the creditor does not automatically qualify as a restructuring:

1. The fair value of the assets or equity interest accepted by a creditor from a debtor in full satisfaction of its receivable is at least equal to the creditor's recorded investment in the receivable.

2. The fair value of the assets or equity interest transferred by a debtor to a creditor in full settlement of its payable is at least equal to the carrying value of the payable.

3. The creditor reduces the effective interest rate to reflect a decrease in current interest rates or a decrease in the risk, in order to maintain the relationship.

4. The debtor, in exchange for old debt, issues new debt with an interest rate that reflects current market rates.

FASB TB 81-6 notes that SFAS 15 does not apply to debtors in bankruptcy unless the restructuring does not result from a general restatement of the debtor's liabilities in bankruptcy proceedings. That is, SFAS 15 applies only if the debt restructuring is isolated to the creditor.

A troubled debt restructuring can occur one of two ways. The first is a settlement of the debt at less than the carrying amount. The second is a continuation of the debt with a modification of terms (i.e., a reduction in the interest rate, face amount, accrued interest owed, or an extension of the payment date for interest or face amount). Accounting for such restructurings is prescribed for both debtors and creditors. FASB TB 80-2 points out that the debtor and creditor must individually apply SFAS 15 to the specific situation since the tests are not necessarily symmetrical and it is possible for one or the other, but not both, to have a troubled debt restructuring when the debtor's carrying amount and the creditor's recorded investment differ. SFAS 114 as amended by SFAS 118 specifies the accounting by creditors for troubled debt restructurings involving a modification of terms.

Debtors. If the debt is settled by the exchange of assets, an extraordinary gain is recognized in the period of transfer for the difference between the carrying amount of the debt (defined as the face amount of the debt increased or decreased by applicable accrued interest and applicable unamortized premium, discount, or issue costs) and the consideration given to extinguish the debt. A two-step process is used: (1) any noncash assets used to settle the debt are revalued at fair market value and the associated ordinary gain or loss is recognized and (2) the extraordinary debt restructuring gain is determined and recognized. If stock is issued to settle the liability, the stock is recorded at its fair market value (SFAS 15).

Example 1: Settlement of debt by exchange of assets

Assume the debtor company transfers land having a book value of $70,000 and a fair market value of $80,000 in full settlement of its note payable. The note has a remaining life of five years, a principal balance of $90,000, and related accrued interest of $10,000 is recorded. The following entries are required to record the settlement:

	Debtor		
Land		10,000	
Gain on transfer of assets			10,000
Note payable		90,000	
Interest payable		10,000	
Land			80,000
Extraordinary gain on			
settlement of debt			20,000

If the debt is continued with a modification of terms, it is necessary to compare the total future cash flows of the restructured debt (both principal and stated interest) with the carrying value of the original debt. If the total amount of future cash payments is greater than the carrying value, no adjustment is made to the carrying value of the debt. However, a new lower effective interest rate must be computed. This rate makes the present value of the total future cash payments equal to the present carrying value of debt and is used to determine interest expense in future periods. The effective interest method must be used to compute the expense. If the total future cash payments of the restructured debt are less than the present carrying value, the current debt should be reduced to the amount of the future cash flows and an extraordinary gain should be recognized. No interest expense would be recognized in subsequent periods, since only the principal is being repaid. If the existing debt is replaced with new debt with the same creditor at a higher interest rate (but still less than the market rate), the transaction is also accounted for as a modification of terms (EITF 89-15).

According to SFAS 15, a troubled debt restructuring that involves only a modification of terms is accounted for prospectively. Thus, there is no change in the carrying value of the liability **unless** the carrying amount of the original debt exceeds the total future cash payments specified by the new agreement.

If the restructuring consists of part settlement and part modification of payments, the part settlement is accounted for first and then the modification of payments.

Example 2: Restructuring with gain/loss recognized (payments are less than carrying value)

Assume that the note has a principal balance of $90,000, accrued interest of $10,000, an interest rate of 5%, and a remaining life of five years. The interest rate is reduced to 4%, the principal is reduced to $72,500, and the accrued interest at date of restructure is forgiven.

Future cash flows (after restructuring):	
Principal	$ 72,500
Interest (5 years x $72,500 x 4%)	14,500
Total cash to be paid	$ 87,000
Amount prior to restructure	
($90,000 principal + $10,000 accrued interest)	(100,000)
Gain/loss to be recognized	
Debtor gain (extraordinary)	$ 13,000

The following entries need to be recorded to reflect the terms of the agreement:

Debtor

Beginning of Year 1

Interest payable	10,000	
Note payable	3,000	
Extraordinary gain on		
restructure of debt		13,000

End of Years 1-5

Note payable	2,900	
Cash		2,900

NOTE: $14,500 ÷ 5 yrs. = $2,900; No interest expense is recorded in this case.

End of Year 5

Note payable	72,500	
Cash		72,500

Example 3: Restructuring with no gain/loss recognized (payments exceed carrying value)

Modify Example 2 as follows:

Assume the $100,000 owed is reduced to a principal balance of $95,000. The interest rate of 5% is reduced to 4%.

Future cash flows (after restructuring):	
Principal	$ 95,000
Interest (5 years x $95,000 x 4%)	19,000
Total cash to be received	$ 114,000
Amount prior to restructure	
($90,000 principal + $10,000 accrued interest)	(100,000)
Interest expense/revenue over 5 years	$ 14,000

In this example, a new effective interest rate must be computed such that the present value of the future payments equals $100,000. A trial and error approach is used to calculate the effective interest rate that discounts the $95,000 principal and the $3,800 annual interest payments to $100,000, the amount owed prior to restructuring.

Trial and Error Calculation

	(n = 5, i = 2.5%)	(n = 5, i = 3%)
PV of ordinary annuity	4.64583	4.57971
PV of 1	.88385	.86261

2.5%:   (.88385 x $95,000) + (4.64583 x $3,800) = $101,620

3%:   (.86261 x $95,000) + (4.57971 x $3,800) = $ 99,351

Interpolation:

$$\left[\frac{101,620-100,000}{101,620-99,351}\right] \quad x \quad (3\% - 2.5\%) \quad = \quad .357$$

New effective rate = 2.5% + .357% = 2.857%

Interest amortization schedule:

Year	Cash	Interest at effective rate	Reduction in carrying value	Carrying amount
				$100,000
1	$ 3,800(a)	$2,857(b)	$ 943(c)	99,057
2	3,800	2,830	970	98,087
3	3,800	2,802	998	97,089
4	3,800	2,774	1,026	96,063
5	3,800	2,745	1,055	95,000*
	$19,000			

* *Rounded*
(a) *$3,800* = *$95,000 x .04*
(b) *$2,857* = *$100,000 x 2.857%*
(c) *$943* = *$3,800 – $2,857*

The following entries are made to recognize the cash payments in the subsequent periods:

Debtor

End of Year 1

Note payable ($3,800 – $2,857)	943	
Interest expense ($100,000 x 0.2857)	2,857	
Cash		3,800

End of Year 5

Note payable	95,000	
Cash		95,000

When the total future cash payments **may** exceed the carrying amount of the liability, no gain or loss is recognized on the books of the debtor unless the maximum future cash payments are less than the carrying amount of the debt. For example, if the debtor is required to make interest payments at a higher rate if its financial condition improves before the maturity of the debt, the debtor should assume that the larger payments would have to be made. The contingent payments would be included in the total future cash payments for comparison with the carrying amount of the debt. If the future cash payments exceed the carrying amount, a new effective interest rate should be determined. The new rate should be the rate that equates the present value of the future cash payments with the carrying amount of the liability. Interest expense and principal reduction are then recognized as the future cash payments are made.

Example 4: Contingent payments

Modify Example 2 as follows: The new agreement states that if financial condition at maturity improves as specified, an additional principal payment of $15,000 is required and additional 1% of interest must be paid in arrears for years 4 and 5.

Future cash payments:	
Required principal per agreement	$ 72,500
Required interest per agreement (5 years x $72,500 x 4%)	14,500
Contingent principal payment	15,000
Contingent interest payments (2 years x 72,500 x 1%)	1,450
	$103,450
Amount prior to restructure ($90,000 + $10,000)	(100,000)
	$ 3,450

When computing the new effective interest rate, only as many contingent payments as are needed to make the future cash payments exceed the carrying value are included in the calculation. Thus, the contingent principal payment would be included, but the contingent interest would not. The contingent interest payments would be recognized using the same criteria as are used in SFAS 5; that is, the payments are recognized when they are both probable and reasonably estimable.

SFAS 114 creditors. SFAS 114, as amended by SFAS 118, applies to all creditors, to all troubled debt restructurings involving a modification of terms, and to all loans except

1. Groups of similar small balance loans that are collectively evaluated
2. Loans measured at fair value or lower of cost or fair value
3. Leases
4. SFAS 115 debt securities

If it is probable that a creditor will not collect all amounts (principal and interest) owed to the degree specified in the loan agreement, a loan is considered impaired. A delay does not impair the loan if the creditor collects all amounts due (including accrued interest during the delay at the contractual rate).

An impaired loan can be measured on a loan-by-loan basis in any of the following ways:

1. Present value of expected future cash flows using the loan's original effective interest rate (the contractual interest rate adjusted for premium or discount and net deferred loan costs or fees at acquisition or origination)
2. Loans' observable market price
3. Fair value of the collateral if the loan is collateral dependent (repayment expected to be provided by the collateral). If foreclosure is probable, this measurement must be used.

Other measurement considerations include

1. Costs to sell on a discounted basis if they will reduce cash flows to satisfy the loan
2. Creation of or adjustment to a valuation allowance account with the offset to bad-debt expense if the recorded investment is greater than the impaired loan measurement
3. If the contractual interest rate varies based on changes in an independent factor, the creditor can choose between

a. Calculating the effective interest on the factor as it changes over the loan's life, or

b. Calculating the effective interest as fixed at the rate in effect at the date of impairment.

The choice must be consistently applied. Projections of factor changes should not be made.

4. Cash flow estimates should be the creditors' best estimate based on reasonable and supportable assumptions

5. Significant changes occurring in measurement values require recalculation and adjustment of the valuation allowance. Net carrying amount of the loan should not exceed the recorded investment.

After impairment, creditors use existing methods to record, measure, and display interest income. If the existing policy results in a recorded investment less than fair value, no additional impairment is recognized.

Under SFAS 114, the creditor would account for the earlier examples as follows:

SFAS 114 Creditor

Example 1

Land	80,000	
Bad debt expense	20,000	
Note receivable		90,000
Interest receivable		10,000

Example 2

Future cash flows (after restructuring) at the agreement's original effective interest rate

		5% 5 yrs PV Factor
Principal	$ 56,806	($72,500 x .78353)
Interest	12,555	($ 2,900 x 4.32948)
Total present value	$ 69,361	
Amount prior to restructure ($90,000 principal + $10,000 accrued interest)	(100,000)	
Creditor loss	($ 30,639)	

Beginning of Year 1

Bad debt expense	30,639	
Interest receivable		10,000
Valuation allowance		20,639

End of Year 1

Cash	2,900	
Valuation allowance	568	
Bad debt expense (or interest income)		3,468 (69,361 x .05)

End of Year 2

Cash	2,900	
Valuation allowance	596	
Bad debt expense (or interest income)		3,496 [(69,361 + 568) = 69,929 x .05]

End of Year 3

Cash	2,900	
Valuation allowance	626	
Bad debt expense (or interest income)		3,526 [(69,929 + 596) = 70,525 x .05]

End of Year 4

Cash	2,900	
Valuation allowance	658	
Bad debt expense (or interest income)		3,558 [(70,525 + 626) = 71,151 x .05]

End of Year 5

Cash	2,900	
Valuation allowance	691	
Bad debt expense (or interest income)		3,591 [(71,151 + 658) = 71,809 x .05]
Cash	72,500	
Valuation allowance	17,500	
Note receivable		90,000

Example 3

Future cash flows (after restructuring) at the agreement's original effective interest rate

		5% 5 yrs PV Factor
Principal	$ 74,435	($95,000 x .78353)
Interest	16,452	($ 3,800 x 4.32948)
Total present value	$ 90,887	
Amount prior to restructure ($90,000 principal + $10,000 accrued interest)	(100,000)	
Creditor loss	$(9,113)	

Beginning of Year 1

Bad debt expense	9,113	
Note receivable—new	95,000	
Note receivable—old		90,000
Interest receivable		10,000
Valuation allowance		4,113

End of Year 1

Cash	3,800	
Valuation allowance	744	
Bad debt expense (or interest income)		4,544 (90,887 x .05)

End of Year 2

Cash	3,800	
Valuation allowance	781	
Bad debt expense (or		4,581 [(90,887 + 744) =
interest income)		91,631 x .05]

End of Year 3

Cash	3,800	
Valuation allowance	821	
Bad debt expense (or		4,621 [(91,631 + 781) =
interest income)		92,412 x .05]

End of Year 4

Cash	3,800	
Valuation allowance	862	
Bad debt expense (or		4,662 [(92,412 + 821) =
interest income)		93,233 x .05]

End of Year 5

Cash	3,800	
Valuation allowance	905	
Bad debt expense (or		4,705 [(93,233 + 862) =
interest income)		94,095 x .05]
Cash	95,000	
Note receivable		95,000

Convertible Debt

Bonds are frequently issued with the right to convert them into common stock of the company at the holder's option. **Convertible debt** is used for two reasons. First, when a specific amount of funds is needed, convertible debt often allows a lesser number of shares to be issued (assuming conversion) than if the funds were raised by directly issuing the shares. Thus, less dilution occurs. Second, the conversion feature allows debt to be issued at a lower interest rate and with fewer restrictive covenants than if the debt was issued without it.

This dual nature of debt and equity, however, creates a question as to whether the equity element should receive separate recognition. Support for separate treatment is based on the assumption that this equity element has economic value. Since the convertible feature tends to lower the rate of interest, a portion of the proceeds should be allocated to this equity feature. The FASB agrees with that view, and in October 2000 it issued proposed standards that would require convertible debt to be divided into its liability components and equity components. Those components would be separately presented in the balance sheet. If issued, those standards would replace the current standards of APB 14, which require that the instrument be reported as either all debt or all equity.

Features of convertible debt typically include (1) a conversion price 15-20% greater than the market value of the stock when the debt is issued; (2) conversion features (price and number of shares) which protect against dilution from stock dividends, splits, etc.; and (3) a callable feature at the issuer's option, which is usually exercised once the conversion price is reached (thus forcing conversion or redemption).

Convertible debt also has its disadvantages. If the stock price increases significantly after the debt is issued, the issuer would have been better off by simply issuing the stock. Additionally, if the price of the stock does not reach the conversion price, the debt will never be converted (a condition known as overhanging debt).

When convertible debt is issued, no value is apportioned to the conversion feature when recording the issue (APB 14). The debt and its interest is reported as if it were a nonconvertible debt. Upon conversion, the stock may be valued at either the book value or the market value of the bonds.

If the **book value approach** is used, the new stock is valued at the carrying value of the converted bonds. This method is widely used since no gain or loss is recognized upon conversion, and the conversion represents the transformation of contingent shareholders into shareholders. It does not represent the culmination of an earnings cycle. The primary weakness of this method is that the total value attributed to the equity security by the investors is not given accounting recognition.

Example of book value method

Assume that a $1,000 bond with an unamortized discount of $50 and a market value of $970 is converted into 10 shares of $10 par common stock whose market value is $97 per share. Conversion using the book value method is recorded as follows:

Bonds payable	1,000	
Discount on bonds payable		50
Common stock		100
Additional paid-in capital		850

The **market value approach** assumes the new stock issued is valued at its cost (i.e., the market price of the stock issued or the market price of the bonds converted, whichever is more easily determinable). A gain (loss) occurs when the market value of the stocks or bonds is less (greater) than the carrying value of the bond.

Example of the market value method

Assume the same facts as the example above. The entry to record the conversion is

Bonds payable	1,000	
Loss on redemption (ordinary)	20	
Discount on bonds payable		50
Common stock		100
Additional paid-in capital		870

Since conversion is initiated by the bondholder and not the firm, the loss does not qualify as an extinguishment and is therefore considered ordinary.

The weakness of this method is that a gain or loss can be reported as a result of an equity transaction. Only the existing shareholders are affected, as their equity will increase or decrease, but the firm as a whole is unaffected. For this reason, the market value approach is not widely used.

When convertible debt is retired, the transaction is handled in the same manner as nonconvertible debt: the difference between the acquisition price and the carrying value of the bond is reported currently as a gain or loss. If material, the gain or loss is considered extraordinary.

Induced Conversion of Debt

A special situation exists in which the conversion privileges of convertible debt are modified after issuance. These modifications may take the form of reduced conversion prices or additional consideration paid to the convertible debt holder. The debtor offers these modifications or "sweeteners" to induce prompt conversion of the outstanding debt.

SFAS 84 specifies the accounting method used in these situations and only applies when the convertible debt is converted into equity securities. Upon conversion, the debtor must recognize an expense for the excess of the fair value of all the securities and other consideration given over the fair value of the securities specified in the original conversion terms. The reported expense should not be classified as an extraordinary item.

Example of induced conversion expense

1. January 1, 1996, XYZ Company issued ten 8% convertible bonds at $1,000 par value without a discount or premium, maturing December 31, 2006.
2. The bonds are initially convertible into no par common stock of XYZ at a conversion price of $25.
3. On July 1, 2001, the convertible bonds have a market value of $600 each.
4. To induce the convertible bondholders to quickly convert their bonds, XYZ reduces the conversion price to $20 for bondholders who convert before July 21, 2001 (within twenty days).
5. The market price of XYZ Company's common stock on the date of conversion is $15 per share.

The fair value of the incremental consideration paid by XYZ upon conversion is calculated for each bond converted before July 21, 2001.

Value of securities issued to debt holders:

Face amount	$1,000	per bond
÷ New conversion price	÷ $20	per share
Number of common shares issued upon conversion	50	shares
x Price per common share	x $15	per share
Value of securities issued	$ 750	(a)
Face amount	$1,000	per bond
÷ Original conversion price	÷ $25	per share
Number of common shares issuable pursuant to original conversion privilege	40	shares
x Price per share	x $15	per share
Value of securities issuable pursuant to original conversion privileges	$ 600	(b)

Value of securities issued	$ 750	(a)
Value of securities issuable pursuant to the original conversion privileges	600	(b)
Fair value of incremental consideration	$ 150	

The entry to record the debt conversion for each bond is

Convertible debt	1,000	
Debt conversion expense	150	
Common stock—no par		1,150

Debt Issued with Stock Warrants

Warrants are certificates enabling the holder to purchase a stated number of shares of stock at a certain price within a certain time period. They are often issued with bonds to enhance the marketability of the bonds and to lower the bond's interest rate.

When bonds with detachable warrants are issued, the purchase price must be allocated between the debt and the stock warrants based on relative market values (APB 14). Since two separate instruments are involved, a market value must be determined for each. However, if one value cannot be determined, the market value of the other should be deducted from the total value to determine the unknown value.

Example of accounting for a bond with a detachable warrant

1. A $1,000 bond with a detachable warrant to buy 10 shares of $10 par common stock at $50 per share is issued for $1,025.
2. Immediately after the issuance the bonds trade at $980 and the warrants at $60.
3. The market value of the stock is $54.

The relative market value of the bonds is 94% [980/(980 + 60)] and the warrant is 6% [60/(980 + 60)]. Thus, $62 (6% x $1,025) of the issuance price is assigned to the warrants. The journal entry to record the issuance is

Cash	1,025	
Discount on bonds payable	37	
Bonds payable		1,000
Paid-in capital—warrants		
(or "Stock options outstanding")		62

The discount is the difference between the purchase price assigned to the bond, $963 (94% x $1,025), and its face value, $1,000. The debt itself is accounted for in the normal fashion.

The entry to record the subsequent future exercise of the warrant would be

Cash	500	
Paid-in capital—warrants	62	
Common stock	100	
Paid-in capital	462	(difference)

Assuming the warrants are not exercised, the journal entry is

Paid-in capital—warrants	62	
Paid-in capital—expired warrants		62

Through-Put and Take-or-Pay Contracts

Through-put and take-or-pay contracts are sometimes used to help a supplier pay for new facilities, machines, or other expenditures. They are negotiated as a way of arranging financing for the facilities that will produce the goods or provide the services desired by a purchaser. A through-put contract is an agreement between the owner of a transportation facility or manufacturing facility (such as a pipeline) and a purchaser (such as an oil processor) that requires the purchaser to pay specified amounts at future dates to the owner in return for the transportation or manufacture of a product. A take-or-pay contract is similar. It is an agreement between a purchaser and a supplier that requires the purchaser to pay specified amounts at future dates in return for products or services. In both types of contracts, the purchaser is required to make the specified payments even if it does not receive goods or services.

Some of these contracts are reported on the balance sheet as an asset and a liability. Others are not reported. Other than standards relating to recognition of losses on unconditional purchase obligations (ARB 43, chap. 4), there are no standards that require the contracts to be recognized on the balance sheet. However, SFAS 47 requires certain disclosures to be made.

EMERGING ISSUES TASK FORCE CONSENSUS SUMMARIES

85-17 Accrued Interest upon Conversion of Convertible Debt

If terms of the debt instrument provide that any accrued interest at the date of conversion is forfeited by the former debt holder, the accrued interest (net of income tax) from the last payment date to the conversion date should be charged to interest expense and credited to capital as a part of the cost of the securities issued.

85-29 Convertible Bonds with a "Premium Put"

A liability for the put premium should be accrued over the period from the date of issuance to the initial put date. Accrual should continue regardless of market value changes. If the put expires unexercised and if the market value of the common stock exceeds the put price at expiration date, the put premium should be credited to additional paid-in capital. If the put expires, unexercised and if the put price exceeds the market value of the common stock, the put premium should be amortized as a yield adjustment over the remaining term of the debt.

86-36 Invasion of a Defeasance Trust

Removal of assets from a defeasance trust does not affect the entity's prior recognition of the extinguishment of debt if at the same time a proportional amount of the outstanding bonds are purchased in the marketplace. Any resulting gain or loss would not be classified as extraordinary.

NOTE: Although SFAS 140 does not permit in-substance defeasance of debt, it allowed those already recognized to remain off the balance sheet. Thus, this opinion applies to those pre-existing defeasance trusts.

87-19   Substituted Debtors in a Troubled Debt Restructuring

Given the sale of real estate collateral (present value less than the net investment) with the requirement for the purchaser to make direct payment to the creditor, the creditor is still required to recognize a loss in the amount by which the net investment in the loan exceeds the fair value of the payments to be received. The fair value of the payments should be recorded as an asset.

88-18   Sales of Future Revenue

Classification of the proceeds from an investor to obtain a right to a specified amount of revenues or a measure of income in the future would be classified as either debt or deferred income by the investee, based upon the specific facts and circumstances of the transaction. This EITF lists six factors that would cause the amounts to be recorded as debt.

Amounts recorded as debt should be amortized under the interest method and amounts recorded as deferred income should be amortized under the units-of-revenue method. Classification of proceeds as debt would not result in foreign exchange gains and losses if three criteria are met. If not met, the debt is a foreign currency transaction and SFAS 52 translation gains or losses are recognized. Classification of the proceeds as deferred income would be a nonmonetary liability. Thus, no foreign exchange gains or losses would arise under SFAS 52. The Task Force did not address any situations when immediate income recognition would be appropriate.

89-15   Accounting for a Modification of Debt Terms When the Debtor Is Experiencing Financial Difficulties

An exchange of existing debt for new debt with the same creditor and with a higher interest rate (but with the new rate less than the market rate for a company with a similar credit rating) does not result in a recognized gain or loss. In this circumstance, the terms of the exchange are not representative of and are less favorable to the creditor than prevailing terms for new borrowings by companies with similar credit ratings. The result is a concession by the creditor and should be accounted for by debtors as a modification of existing obligation under SFAS 15.

90-19   Convertible Bonds with Issuer Option to Settle for Cash upon Conversion

Combined accounting for the debt obligation and the conversion feature is appropriate.

Accounting similar to indexed debt obligations should be used if the issuer must satisfy the obligation entirely in cash or if the issuer must satisfy the accreted value of the obligation in cash and may satisfy the conversion spread in either cash or stock. The carrying value should be adjusted in each reporting period to reflect the current stock price, but not below the accreted value. These adjustments are included currently in income.

If the issuer may satisfy the entire obligation in either stock or cash, it should be accounted for as conventional convertible debt. If the holder exercises the conversion and the issuer pays cash, the debt is extinguished and the issuer should account for the transaction in accordance with APB 26. Gain or loss should be classified in accordance with SFAS 4.

If the issuer must satisfy the obligation entirely with cash, the only EPS effect is the charge to income for the conversion spread. If the entire obligation may be satisfied in either stock or cash, the bond should be considered a common stock equivalent. If the issuer must satisfy the accreted value of the obligation in cash and may satisfy the conversion spread in either cash or stock, the only primary EPS effect is the charge to income for the conversion spread. This accounting is consistent with that of an indexed debt obligation.

94-8   Accounting for Conversion of a Loan into a Debt Security in a Debt Restructuring

The initial cost basis of a debt security of the original debtor received as part of a debt restructuring should be the security's fair value at the date of the restructuring. Any excess fair value of the security over the net carrying amount of the loan should be recorded as a recovery on the loan. Any excess net carrying value amount of the loan over the fair value of the security should be recorded as a charge-off to the allowance for credit losses. Additionally, securities received in a restructuring for only past-due interest on a loan should be measured at the date of the restructuring and accounted for with the entity's policy for recognizing cash received for past-due interest. After the restructuring, the securities should be accounted for according to the provisions of SFAS 115.

96-19   Debtor's Accounting for a Modification or Exchange of Debt Instruments

The Task Force reached a consensus that an exchange of debt instruments with substantially different terms is a debt extinguishment and should be accounted for in accordance with SFAS 140. The Task Force also reached consensus that any substantial modification in the terms of an existing debt, other than for a troubled debt restructuring, should similarly be reported as a debt extinguishment. As the gain or loss recognized from an exchange or modification is to be reported in the same manner as an extinguishment, any gain or loss recognized should be classified as extraordinary.

An exchange or modification is considered substantial when the present value of cash flows under the new debt instrument is at least 10% different from the present value of the remaining cash flows under the terms of the original instrument. For the purpose of the 10% test, the effective interest rate of the original debt instrument is used as the discount rate.

Cash flows can be affected by changes in principal amounts, interest rates, maturity, or by fees exchanged to effect changes in

1. Recourse or nonrecourse features
2. Priority of the obligation
3. Collateralized or noncollateralized features
4. Debt covenants and/or waivers
5. The guarantor
6. Option features

Assuming the 10% test is met and the debt instrument are deemed to be substantially different, the new investment should be initially recorded at fair value and that amount should be used to determine debt extinguishment gain or loss to be recognized, as well as the effective rate of the new instrument. Fees paid by the debtor to the creditor or received by the debtor from the creditor should be included in determining debt extinguishment gain or loss. Additionally, any costs incurred with third parties should be amortized using the interest method in a manner similar to that used for debt issue costs.

Assuming the 10% test is not met and the debt instruments are not deemed to be substantially different, then the new effective interest is to be determined based on the carrying amount of the original instrument and the revised cash flows. Fees paid by the debtor to the creditor or received by the debtor from the creditor should be amortized as an adjustment to interest expense over the remaining term of the modified debt instrument using the interest method. Additionally, any costs incurred with third parties should be expensed as incurred.

96-22 Applicability of the Disclosures Required by FASB Statement 114 When a Loan Is Restructured in a Troubled Debt Restructuring into Two (or More) Loans

Since they are legally distinct from the original loan, restructuring loans should be considered separately in years after restructuring when addressing the applicability of disclosures. The measure of loan impairment would continue to be based on the terms of the original agreement. For SEC purposes, the impact of multiple loan structures on the disclosure of impaired loans should be made clear to users.

98-5   Accounting for Convertible Securities with Beneficial Conversion Features or Contingently Adjustable Conversion Ratios

This consensus applies to convertible securities (debt or preferred stock) that are convertible to common stock (or other securities) via a nondetachable conversion right that is in the money at the date that the investor is committed to purchase the convertible securities. That type of conversion feature is called an "embedded beneficial conversion feature." The securities may be converted at a fixed price, a fixed discount to the market price at date of conversion, a variable discount to the market price at conversion, or the conversion price may be dependent upon future events. In addition, the conversion feature can be exercisable at issuance, at a stated date in the future, or upon the happening of a future event (such as an IPO).

Embedded beneficial conversion features are valued separately at issuance. The feature is recognized as additional paid-in capital by allocating a portion of the proceeds equal to the intrinsic value of the feature. The intrinsic value is computed at the commitment date as (1) the difference between the conversion price and the fair value of the common stock (or other securities) into which the security is convertible, multiplied by (2) the number of shares into which the security is convertible.

For convertible debt securities, a discount on the debt may result from the allocation of a portion of the proceeds to the conversion feature. That discount should be expensed as interest expense if the securities are convertible upon issuance or should be recognized as a discount and amortized over the period to the earliest conversion date. For convertible preferred securities, any "discount" on issuance is analogous to a dividend to the preferred shareholder and should be recognized using the effective interest method through the date of the earliest conversion.

If the conversion feature has multiple steps, the computation of the intrinsic value is made using the conversion terms most beneficial to the investor. Any resulting discount should be amortized over the period to the earliest date at which that most beneficial price can be obtained. For example, if the security was convertible at market price after three months and at a 25% discount to market price after one year, the 25% discount terms would be used to measure the intrinsic value and any resulting discount would be amortized over one year. However, at any financial statement date, the cumulative amortization recorded must be the greater of (1) the amount computed using the effective interest method of amortization or (2) the amount of the benefit the investor would receive if the securities were converted at that date. If the securities are converted prior to the full amortization of the discount, the unamortized discount is included in the amount transferred to equity upon conversion.

If the security becomes convertible only upon occurrence (or failure to occur) of a future event outside the control of the investor or if the conversion terms change based on the occurrence (or failure to occur) of a future event, the value of the contingent beneficial conversion feature should be measured as of the commitment date, but it is not recognized in the financial statements until the contingency is resolved.

If a convertible debt security is extinguished prior to conversion, a portion of the reacquisition price of the debt security is allocated to the beneficial conversion feature. That portion is measured as the intrinsic value of the conversion feature at the extinguishment date. Any residual would be allocated to the debt security, and a gain or loss on extinguishment would be recorded in accordance with SFAS 4.

99-1   Accounting for Debt Convertible into the Stock of a Consolidated Subsidiary

In the consolidated financial statements, (1) debt issued by a consolidated subsidiary that is convertible into that subsidiary's stock and (2) debt issued by a parent company that is convertible into the stock of a consolidated subsidiary should be accounted for in accordance with Opinion 14. That is, no portion of the proceeds from the issuance of the debt should be accounted for as attributable to the conversion feature. This Issue does not apply to convertible debt instruments that require a cash settlement by the issuer of an in-the-money conversion feature, that provide the holder an option to receive cash for an in-the-money conversion feature, or that have a beneficial conversion feature.

00-27   Application for EITF Issue No. 98-5, "Accounting for Convertible Securities with Beneficial Conversion Features or Contingently Adjustable Conversion Rations" to Certain Convertible Instruments

This consensus addresses a number of issues about the application of Issue 98-5 in specific situations.

If an instrument includes both detachable instruments and an embedded beneficial conversion option, the proceeds of issuance should first be allocated among the convertible instrument and the other detachable instruments based on their relative fair values. Then, the Issue 98-5 model should be applied to the amount allocated to the convertible instrument to determine if the embedded conversion option has an intrinsic value.

If the conversion price could change upon the occurrence of a future event, assume that there are no changes to the current circumstances except the passage of time. Use the most favorable price that would be in effect if nothing were changed at the conversion date to measure the intrinsic value of an embedded conversion option. Changes to the conversion terms that are caused by future events not controlled by the issuer are recognized if and when the trigger event occurs.

If there is no intrinsic value to a conversion clause at issuance, but the conversion price resets after the commitment date and, upon reset, the conversion price is greater than the fair market value of the underlying stock, the beneficial conversion amount is recognized when the reset occurs. The beneficial conversion amount is measured by the number of shares that will be issued upon conversion multiplied by the decrease in price between the original conversion price and the reset price.

The definition of commitment date for purposes of applying Issue 98-5 is the same as the definition of a firm commitment in SFAS 133. If an instrument includes both detachable instruments and an embedded beneficial conversion option, the commitment date should also be used when determining the relative fair values of all the instruments issued.

If a convertible instrument has a stated redemption date, a discount resulting from recording a beneficial conversion option should be amortized from the date of issuance to the stated redemption date, regardless of when the earliest conversion occurs.

If the terms of a contingent conversion option do not permit an issuer to compute the number of shares that the holder would receive upon conversion, the issuer should wait until the contingent event occurs and then compute the number of shares that would be received. The number of shares that would be received is compared to the number of shares that would have been received if the contingent event had not occurred to determine the excess number of shares. The number of excess shares multiplied by the stock price as of the commitment date equals the incremental intrinsic value that should be recognized.

If interest or dividends are paid in kind, the commitment date for the paid-in-kind securities is the commitment date for the original instrument if the payment in kind is not discretionary. The payment is not discretionary if (1) neither the issuer nor the holder can elect other forms of payment for the interest or dividends and (2) if the original instrument were converted before dividends are declared or interest is accrued, the holder will receive the number of shares as if the accumulated dividends or interest have been paid in kind. If the payment in kind is discretionary, the commitment date for the paid-in-kind securities is the date that the interest is accrued or the dividends are declared.

If an issuer issues a convertible instrument as repayment of a nonconvertible instrument, the fair value of the newly issued convertible instrument equals the redemption amount owed at the maturity date of the old debt. That is, the carrying amount of the old debt is the proceeds received for applying Issue 98-5 to the new debt.

This Issue describes several other situations on which the EITF has not yet reached consensus.

01-1   Accounting for a Convertible Instrument Granted or Issued to a Non-employee for Goods or Services or a Combination of Goods or Services and Cash

This issue describes the accounting for a convertible instrument that is used to pay a nonemployee for goods or services if that instrument contains a nondetachable conversion option. The measurement date under Issue 96-18 should be used to measure the intrinsic value of the conversion option rather than the commitment date. The proceeds from issuing the instrument for purposes of determining whether a beneficial conversion option exists is the fair value of the instrument or the fair value of the goods and services received, whichever is more reliably measured. The fair value of the convertible instrument can be measured by applying SFAS 123, as interpreted by Issue 96-18. (For details, see Chapter 17, Stockholders' Equity.) Once the convertible instrument is issued, distributions paid or payable are financing costs rather than adjustments of the cost of the goods or services received.

If a purchaser of a convertible instrument that contains an embedded beneficial conversion option provides goods or services to the issuer under a separate contract, the contracts should be considered separately unless the separately stated pricing is not equal to fair value. If not equal to fair value, the terms of the respective transactions should be adjusted. The convertible instrument should be recognized at its fair value with a corresponding increase or decrease to the purchase price of the goods or services.

14 LEASES

PERSPECTIVE AND ISSUES

Lease transactions have grown in popularity over the years as businesses look for new ways to finance their fixed asset additions. A lease agreement involves at least two parties, a lessor and a lessee, and an asset that is to be leased. The lessor, who owns the asset, agrees to allow the lessee to use it for a specified period of time in return for periodic rent payments.

There are several economic reasons why the lease transaction is considered. They are as follows:

1. The lessee (borrower) is able to obtain 100% financing

2. Tax benefits available to one or both of the parties
3. The lessor receives the equivalent of interest as well as an asset with some remaining value at the end of the lease term

The lease transaction derives its accounting complexity from the number of alternatives available to the parties involved. Leases can be structured to allow manipulation of the tax benefits associated with the leased asset. They can be used to transfer ownership of the leased asset, and they can be used to transfer the risks and rewards of ownership. In any event, the substance of the transaction dictates the accounting treatment. The lease transaction is probably the best example of the accounting profession's substance over form argument. If the transaction effectively transfers ownership to the lessee, then the substance of the transaction is that of a sale and should be recognized as such even though the transaction is structured as a lease.

SFAS 13 sets forth the GAAP for lease accounting. Numerous pronouncements have followed which expand upon the base set by SFAS 13. As a result of the extensive additions to the principles related to lease accounting, and the number and extent of changes made to the original pronouncement, it is cumbersome, if not impossible, to research a lease accounting issue by attempting to use the original pronouncements and the amendments thereto. Therefore, we recommend using the codified discussion of leases contained in the FASB Current Text (Section L10) as the basis for such research.

Sources of GAAP			
SFAS	*FASB I*	*FASB TB*	*EITF*
13, 22, 23,	19, 21, 23,	79-10, 79-12,	85-16, 86-17, 86-33,
27, 28, 29,	24, 26, 27,	79-13, 79-14,	87-7, 88-10, 88-21,
66, 77, 91,	43	79-15, 79-16,	89-16, 89-20, 90-14,
98, 125		82-1, 86-2,	90-15, 90-20, 92-1,
		88-1	93-8, 95-1, 95-4,
			95-17, 96-21, 97-1,
			97-10, 98-9, 99-13,
			99-14, 00-13, D-8, D-24

DEFINITIONS OF TERMS

Bargain purchase option. A provision allowing the lessee the option of purchasing the leased property for an amount, exclusive of lease payments, which is sufficiently lower than the expected fair value of the property at the date the option becomes exercisable. Exercise of the option must appear reasonably assured at the inception of the lease. GAAP does not offer additional guidance defining "sufficiently lower," in which many factors such as time value of money, usage, and technological changes influence whether the option fulfills the criteria for a bargain.

Bargain renewal option. A provision allowing the lessee the option to renew the lease agreement for a rental payment sufficiently lower than the expected fair rental of the property at the date the option becomes exercisable. Exercise of the option must appear reasonably assured at the inception of the lease.

Contingent rentals. Rentals that represent the increases or decreases in lease payments that result from changes in the factors on which the lease payments are based occurring subsequent to the inception of the lease. However, changes due to the pass-through of increases in the construction or acquisition cost of the leased property or for increases in some measure of cost during the construction or pre-construction period should be excluded from contingent rentals. Also, provisions that are dependent only upon the passage of time should be excluded from contingent rentals. A lease payment that is based upon an existing index or rate, such as the consumer price index or the prime rate, is a contingent payment, and the computation of the minimum lease payments should be based upon the index or rate applicable at the inception of the lease.

Estimated economic life of leased property. The estimated remaining time that the property is expected to be economically usable by one or more users, with normal maintenance and repairs, for its intended purpose at the inception of the lease. The economic life may be determined by such factors as technological changes, normal deterioration, and physical usage. Judgment on these matters may be influenced by knowledge gained through previous experience. This estimated time period should not be limited by the lease term.

Estimated residual value of leased property. The estimated fair value of the leased property at the end of the lease term.

Executory costs. Those costs such as insurance, maintenance, and taxes incurred for leased property, whether paid by the lessor or lessee. Amounts paid by a lessee in consideration for a guarantee from an unrelated third party of the residual value are also executory costs. If executory costs are paid by the lessor, any lessor's profit on those costs is considered the same as executory costs.

Fair value of leased property. The property's selling price in an arm's-length transaction between unrelated parties.

When the lessor is a **manufacturer or dealer**, the fair value of the property at the inception of the lease will ordinarily be its normal selling price net of volume or trade discounts. In some cases, due to market conditions, fair value may be less than the normal selling price or even the cost of the property.

When the lessor is **not a manufacturer or dealer**, the fair value of the property at the inception of the lease will ordinarily be its costs net of volume or trade discounts. However, if a significant amount of time has lapsed between the acquisition of the property by the lessor and the inception of the lease, fair value should be determined in light of market conditions prevailing at the inception of the lease. Thus, fair value may be greater or less than the cost or carrying amount of the property.

Implicit interest rate. The discount rate that, when applied to the minimum lease payments, excluding that portion of the payments representing executory costs to be paid by the lessor, together with any profit thereon, and the unguaranteed residual value accruing to the benefit of the lessor, causes the aggregate present value at the beginning of the lease term to be equal to the fair value of the leased property to the lessor at the inception of the lease, minus any investment tax credit retained and expected to be realized by the lessor (and plus initial direct costs in the case of direct financing leases).

Inception of the lease. The date of the written lease agreement or commitment (if earlier) wherein all principal provisions are fixed and no principal provisions remain to be negotiated.

Incremental borrowing rate. The rate that, at the inception of the lease, the lessee would have incurred to borrow over a similar term (i.e., a loan term equal to the lease term) the funds necessary to purchase the leased asset.

Initial direct costs.[1] Only those costs incurred by the lessor that are (1) costs to originate a lease incurred in transactions with independent third parties that (a) result directly from and are essential to acquire that lease and (b) would not have been incurred had that leasing transaction not occurred and (2) certain costs directly related to specified activities performed by the lessor for that lease. Those activities are: evaluating the prospective lessee's financial condition; evaluating and recording guarantees, collateral, and other security arrangements; negotiating lease terms; preparing and processing lease documents; and closing the transaction. The costs directly related to those activities shall include only that portion of the employees' total compensation and payroll-related fringe benefits directly related to time spent performing those activities for that lease and other costs related to those activities that would not have been incurred but for that lease. Initial direct costs shall not include costs related to activities performed by the lessor for advertising, soliciting potential lessees, servicing existing leases, and other ancillary activities related to establishing and monitoring credit policies, supervision, and administration. Initial direct costs shall not include administrative costs, rent, depreciation, any other occupancy and equipment costs and employees' compensation and fringe benefits related to activities described in the previous sentence, unsuccessful origination efforts, and idle time.

Lease. An agreement conveying the right to use property, plant, or equipment (land or depreciable assets or both) usually for a stated period of time.

Lease term. The fixed noncancelable term of the lease plus the following:

1. Periods covered by bargain renewal options

---

[1] *Initial direct costs shall be offset by nonrefundable fees that are yield adjustments as prescribed in SFAS 91, **Accounting for Nonrefundable Fees and Costs Associated with Originating or Acquiring Loans and Initial Direct Costs of Leases**.*

2. Periods for which failure to renew the lease imposes a penalty on the lessee in an amount such that renewal appears, at the inception of the lease, to be reasonably assured

3. Periods covered by ordinary renewal options during which a guarantee by the lessee of the lessor's debt directly or indirectly related to the leased property is expected to be in effect or a loan from the lessee to the lessor directly or indirectly related to the leased property is expected to be outstanding

4. Periods covered by ordinary renewal options preceding the date that a bargain purchase option is exercisable

5. Periods representing renewals or extensions of the lease at the lessor's option

However, the lease term shall not extend beyond the date a bargain purchase option becomes exercisable or beyond the useful life of the leased asset.

Minimum lease payments. For the **lessee**: The payments that the lessee is or can be required to make in connection with the leased property. Contingent rental guarantees by the lessee of the lessor's debt, and the lessee's obligation to pay executory costs are excluded from minimum lease payments. Additionally, if a portion of the minimum lease payments representing executory costs is not determinable from the provisions of the lease, an estimate of executory costs shall be excluded from the calculation of the minimum lease payments. If the lease contains a bargain purchase option, only the minimum rental payments over the lease term and the payment called for in the bargain purchase option are included in minimum lease payments. Otherwise, minimum lease payments include the following:

1. The **minimum rental payments** called for by the lease over the lease term

2. Any **guarantee of residual value** at the expiration of the lease term made by the lessee (or any party related to the lessee), whether or not the guarantee payment constitutes a purchase of the leased property. When the lessor has the right to require the lessee to purchase the property at termination of the lease for a certain or determinable amount, that amount shall be considered a lessee guarantee. When the lessee agrees to make up any deficiency below a stated amount in the lessor's realization of the residual value, the guarantee to be included in the MLP is the stated amount rather than an estimate of the deficiency to be made up.

3. Any payment that the lessee must or can be required to make upon **failure to renew or extend** the lease at the expiration of the lease term, whether or not the payment would constitute a purchase of the leased property

For the **lessor**: The payments described above plus any guarantee of the residual value or of the rental payments beyond the lease term by a third party unrelated to either the lessee or lessor (provided the third party is financially capable of discharging the guaranteed obligation).

Noncancelable in this context is a lease that is cancelable only upon one of the following conditions:

1. The occurrence of some remote contingency
2. The permission of the lessor
3. The lessee enters into a new lease with the same lessor
4. Payment by the lessee of a penalty in an amount such that continuation of the lease appears, at inception, reasonably assured

Nonrecourse financing. Lending or borrowing activities in which the creditor does not have general recourse to the debtor but rather has recourse only to the property used for collateral in the transaction or other specific property.

Penalty. Any requirement that is imposed or can be imposed on the lessee by the lease agreement or by factors outside the lease agreement to pay cash, incur or assume a liability, perform services, surrender or transfer an asset or rights to an asset or otherwise forego an economic benefit, or suffer an economic detriment.

Related parties. Entities that are in a relationship where one party has the ability to exercise significant influence over the operating and financial policies of the related party. Examples include the following:

1. A parent company and its subsidiaries
2. An owner company and its joint ventures and partnerships
3. An investor and its investees

The ability to exercise significant influence must be present before the parties can be considered related. Significant influence may also be exercised through guarantees of indebtedness, extensions of credit, or through ownership of debt obligations, warrants, or other securities. If two or more entities are subject to the significant influence of a parent, owner, investor, or common officers or directors, then those entities are considered related to each other.

Renewal or extension of a lease. The continuation of a lease agreement beyond the original lease term, including a new lease where the lessee continues to use the same property.

Sale-leaseback accounting. A method of accounting for a sale-leaseback transaction in which the seller-lessee records the sale, removes all property and related liabilities from its balance sheet, recognizes gain or loss from the sale, and classifies the leaseback in accordance with this section.

Sales recognition. Any method that is described as a method to record a transaction involving real estate, other than the deposit method, or the methods to record transactions accounted for as financing, leasing, or profit-sharing arrangements. Profit recognition methods commonly used to record transactions involving real estate include, but are not limited to, the full accrual method, the installment method, the cost recovery method, and the reduced profit method.

Unrelated parties. All parties that are not related parties as defined above.

Unguaranteed residual value. The estimated residual value of the leased property exclusive of any portion guaranteed by the lessee, by any party related to the lessee, or any party unrelated to the lessee. If the guarantor is related to the lessor, the residual value shall be considered as unguaranteed.

CONCEPTS, RULES, AND EXAMPLES

Classification of Leases—Lessee

For accounting and reporting purposes the lessee has two alternatives in classifying a lease.

1. Operating
2. Capital

The proper classification of a **lease** is determined by the circumstances surrounding the transaction. According to SFAS 13, if substantially all of the benefits and risks of ownership have been transferred to the lessee, the lease should be recorded as a capital lease. Substantially all of the risks or benefits of ownership are deemed to have been transferred if **any one** of the following criteria has been met:

1. The lease transfers ownership to the lessee by the end of the **lease term**
2. The lease contains a **bargain purchase option**
3. The lease term is equal to 75% or more of the **estimated economic life** of the leased property, and the beginning of the lease term does not fall within the last 25% of the total economic life of the leased property
4. The present value (PV) of the minimum lease payments at the beginning of the lease term is 90% or more of the fair value to the lessor less any investment credit retained by the lessor. This requirement cannot be used if the lease's inception is in the last 25% of the useful economic life of the leased asset. The interest rate, used to compute the PV, should be the **incremental borrowing rate** of the lessee unless the **implicit rate** is available and lower.

If a lease agreement meets none of the four criteria set forth above, it is to be classified as an operating lease by the lessee.

Classification of Leases—Lessor

The four alternatives a lessor has in classifying a lease are as follows:

1. Operating
2. Sales-type
3. Direct financing
4. Leveraged

The conditions surrounding the origination of the lease determine its classification on the books of the lessor. If the lease meets **any one** of the four criteria specified above for lessees and **both** of the qualifications set forth below, the lease is classified as either a sales-type lease, direct financing lease, or leveraged lease depending upon the conditions present at the inception of the lease.

1. Collectibility of the minimum lease payments is reasonably predictable
2. No important uncertainties surround the amount of unreimbursable costs yet to be incurred by the lessor under the lease

If a lease transaction does not meet the criteria for classification as a sales-type lease, a direct financing lease, or a leveraged lease as specified above, it is to be classified by the lessor as an operating lease. This classification process must take place prior to considering the proper accounting treatment.

Distinction between Sales-Type, Direct Financing, and Leveraged Leases

A lease is classified as a sales-type lease when the criteria set forth above have been met and the lease transaction is structured in such a way that the lessor (generally a **manufacturer or dealer**) recognizes a profit or loss on the transaction in addition to interest revenue. In order for this to occur, the **fair value of the property (FV)** must be different from the cost (carrying value). The essential substance of this transaction is that of a sale, and thus its name. Common examples of sales-type leases: (1) when an automobile dealership opts to lease a car to its customers in lieu of making an actual sale, and (2) the re-lease of equipment coming off of an expiring lease. However, it should be noted that a lease involving real estate must transfer title (i.e., criterion 1 above) by the end of the lease term for the lessor to classify the lease as a sales-type lease of real estate.

A direct financing lease differs from a sales-type lease in that the lessor does not realize a profit or loss on the transaction other than interest revenue. In a direct financing lease, the fair value of the property at the inception of the lease is equal to the cost (carrying value). This type of lease transaction most often involves entities engaged in financing operations. The lessor (a bank, or other financial institution) purchases the asset and then leases the asset to the lessee. This transaction merely replaces the conventional lending transaction where the borrower uses the borrowed funds to purchase the asset. There are many economic reasons why the lease transaction is considered. They are as follows:

1. The lessee (borrower) is able to obtain 100% financing
2. Flexibility of use for the tax benefits
3. The lessor receives the equivalent of interest as well as an asset with some remaining value at the end of the lease term

In summary it may help to visualize the following chart when considering the classification of a lease from the lessor's standpoint:

One form of a direct financing lease is a leveraged lease. This type is mentioned separately because it receives a different accounting treatment by a lessor. A leveraged lease meets all the definitional criteria of a direct financing lease, but differs because it involves at least three parties: a lessee, a long-term creditor, and a lessor (commonly referred to as the equity participant). Other characteristics of a leveraged lease are as follows:

1. The financing provided by the long-term creditor must be without recourse as to the general credit of the lessor, although the creditor may hold recourse with respect to the leased property. The amount of the financing must provide the lessor with substantial "leverage" in the transaction.
2. The lessor's net investment declines during the early years and rises during the later years of the lease term before its elimination (See Appendix).

Accounting for Leases—Lessee

As discussed in the preceding section, there are two classifications that apply to a lease transaction on the books of the lessee. They are as follows:

1. Operating
2. Capital

Operating leases. The accounting treatment accorded an operating lease is relatively simple; the rental payment shall be charged to expense as the payments are made or become payable. This assumes that the lease payments are being made on a straight-line basis (i.e., an equal payment per period over the lease term). If the lease agreement calls for either an alternative payment schedule or a scheduled rent increase over the lease term, the lease expense should still be recognized on a straight-line basis unless another systematic and rational basis is a better representation of the actual physical usage of the leased property. In such an instance it will be necessary to create either a prepaid asset or a liability depending upon the structure of the payment schedule. If the scheduled increase(s) is due to additional leased property, recognition should be proportional to the leased property with the increased rents recognized over the years that the lessee has control over the use of the additional leased property.

Notice that in the case of an operating lease there is no balance sheet recognition of the leased asset because the substance of the lease is merely that of a rental. There is no reason to expect that the lessee will derive any future economic benefit from the leased asset beyond the lease term.

Capital leases. Recall that the classification of a lease must be determined prior to the consideration of the accounting treatment. Therefore, it is necessary to first examine the lease transaction against the four criteria (transfer of title, bargain purchase option, 75% of useful life, or 90% of net FV). Assuming that the lease agreement satisfies one of these, it must be accounted for as a capital lease.

The lessee records a capital lease as an asset and an obligation (liability) at an amount equal to the present value of the **minimum lease payments** at the beginning of the lease term. The asset should be recorded at the lower of the present value of the minimum lease payments or the fair market value of the asset. When the fair value of the leased asset is less than the present value of the minimum lease payments, the interest rate used to amortize the lease obligation will differ from the interest rate used in the 90% test as determined by the lessor. The interest rate used in the amortization will be the same as that used in the 90% test when the fair value is greater than or equal to the present value of the minimum lease payments. For purposes of this computation, the minimum lease payments are considered to be the payments that the lessee is obligated to make or can be required to make excluding **executory costs** such as insurance, maintenance, and taxes. The minimum lease payments generally include the **minimum rental payments**, any **guarantee of the residual value** made by the lessee, and the **penalty** for **failure to renew** the lease, if applicable. If the lease includes a bargain purchase option (BPO), the amount required to be paid under the BPO is also included in the minimum lease payments. The present value shall be computed using the incremental borrowing rate of the lessee **unless** it is practicable for the lessee to determine the implicit rate computed by the lessor, **and** the implicit rate is less than the incremental borrowing rate. The lease term used in this present value computation is the fixed, **noncancelable** term of the lease plus the following:

1. All periods covered by **bargain renewal options**
2. All periods for which failure to renew imposes a penalty on the lessee
3. All periods covered by ordinary renewal options during which the lessee guarantees the lessor's debt on the leased property
4. All periods covered by ordinary renewals or extensions up to the date a BPO is exercisable
5. All periods representing renewals or extensions of the lease at the lessor's option

Remember, if the amount computed as the present value of the minimum lease payments exceeds the fair value of the leased property at the **inception of the lease**, the amount recorded should be that of the fair value.

The amortization of the leased asset will depend upon how the lease qualified as a capital lease. If the lease transaction met the criteria as either transferring ownership, or containing a bargain purchase option, then the asset arising from the transaction is to be amortized over the estimated useful life of the leased property. If the transaction qualifies as a capital lease because it met either the 75% of useful life or 90% of FV criteria, the asset must be amortized over the lease term. The conceptual rationale for this differentiated treatment arises because of the substance of the transaction. Under the first two criteria, the asset actually becomes the property of the lessee at the end of the lease term (or upon exercise of the BPO). In the latter situations, the title to the property remains with the lessor.

The leased asset is to be amortized (depreciated) over the lease term if title does not transfer to the lessee, while the asset is depreciated in a manner consistent with the lessee's normal depreciation policy if the title is to eventually transfer to the lessee. This latter situation can be interpreted to mean that the asset is depreciated over the useful economic life of the leased asset. The treatment and method used to amortize (depreciate) the leased asset is very similar to that used for any other asset. The amortization entry requires a debit to the lease expense and a credit to an accumulated amortization account. The leased asset shall not be amortized below the estimated residual value.

In some instances when the property is to revert back to the lessor, there may be a guaranteed residual value. This is an amount that the lessee guarantees to the lessor. If the FV of the asset at the end of the lease term is greater than or equal to the guaranteed residual amount, the lessee incurs no additional obligation. On the other hand, if the FV of the leased asset is less than the guaranteed residual value, then the lessee must make up the difference, usually with a cash payment. The guaranteed residual value is often used as a tool to reduce the periodic payments by substituting the lump-sum amount at the end of the term that results from the guarantee. In any event the amortization must still take place based on the **estimated residual value**. This results in a rational and systematic allocation of the expense through the periods and avoids a large loss (or expense) in the last period as a result of the guarantee.

The annual (periodic) rent payments made during the lease term are to be allocated between a reduction in the obligation and interest expense in a manner such that the interest expense represents a constant periodic rate of interest on the remaining balance of the lease obligation. This is commonly referred to as the effective interest method and was described in APB 21.

The following examples illustrate the treatment described in the foregoing paragraphs:

Example of accounting for a capital lease—Asset returned to lessor

1. The lease is initiated on 1/1/02 for equipment with an expected useful life of three years. The equipment reverts back to the lessor upon expiration of the lease agreement.

2. The FV of the equipment is $135,000.
3. Three payments are due to the lessor in the amount of $50,000 per year beginning 12/31/02. An additional sum of $1,000 is to be paid annually by the lessee for insurance.
4. Lessee **guarantees** a $10,000 residual value on 12/31/04 to the lessor.
5. Irrespective of the $10,000 residual value guarantee, the leased asset is expected to have only a $1,000 salvage value on 12/31/04.
6. The lessee's incremental borrowing rate is 10%. (Lessor's implicit rate is unknown.)
7. The present value of the lease obligation is as follows:

PV of guaranteed residual value	=	$10,000	x	.7513 *	=	$ 7,513
PV of annual payments	=	$50,000	x	2.4869 **	=	124,345
						$131,858

* *The present value of an amount of $1 due in three periods at 10% is .7513.*
** *The present value of an ordinary annuity of $1 for three periods at 10% is 2.4869.*

The first step in dealing with any lease transaction is to classify the lease. In this case, the lease term is for three years which is equal to 100% of the expected useful life of the asset. Notice that the 90% test is also fulfilled as the PV of the minimum lease payments ($131,858) is greater than 90% of the FV ($121,500). Thus, the lease is accounted for as a capital lease.

In number 7. (above) the present value of the lease obligation is computed. Note that the executory costs (insurance) are not included in the minimum lease payments and that the incremental borrowing rate of the lessee was used to determine the present value. This rate was used because the implicit rate was not determinable.

NOTE: In order to have used the implicit rate it would have to have been less than the incremental borrowing rate.

The entry necessary to record the lease on 1/1/02 is:

Leased equipment	131,858	
Lease obligation		131,858

Note that the lease is recorded at the present value of the minimum lease payments that, in this case, is less than the FV. If the present value of the minimum lease payments had exceeded the FV, the lease would be recorded at FV.

The next step is to determine the proper allocation between interest and a reduction in the lease obligation for each lease payment. This is done using the effective interest method as illustrated below.

Year	Cash payment	Interest expense	Reduction in lease obligation	Balance of lease obligation
Inception of lease				$131,858
1	$50,000	$13,186	$36,814	95,044
2	50,000	9,504	40,496	54,548
3	50,000	5,452	44,548	10,000

The interest is calculated at 10% (the incremental borrowing rate) of the balance of the lease obligation for each period, and the remainder of the $50,000 payment is allocated to a reduction in the lease obligation. The lessee is also required to pay $1,000 for insurance on an annual basis. The entries necessary to record all payments relative to the lease for each of the three years are shown below.

	12/31/02	*12/31/03*	*12/31/042*
Insurance expense	1,000	1,000	1,000
Interest expense	13,186	9,504	5,452
Lease obligation	36,814	40,496	44,548
Cash	51,000	51,000	51,000

The lease equipment recorded as an asset must also be amortized (depreciated). The balance of this account is $131,858; however, as with any other asset it cannot be amortized below the estimated residual value of $1,000 (note that it is amortized down to the actual estimated residual value, **not** the guaranteed residual value). In this case, the straight-line amortization method is applied over a period of three years. This three-year period represents the lease term, **not** the life of the asset, because the asset reverts back to the lessor at the end of the lease term. Therefore, the following entry will be made at the end of each year:

Amortization expense	43,619	
Accumulated amortization		43,619 [($131,858 – 1,000) ÷ 3]

Finally, on 12/31/04 we must recognize the fact that ownership of the property has reverted back to the owner (lessor). The lessee made a guarantee that the residual value would be $10,000 on 12/31/04; as a result, the lessee must make up the difference between the guaranteed residual value and the actual residual value with a cash payment to the lessor. The following entry illustrates the removal of the leased asset and obligation from the books of the lessee:

Lease obligation	10,000	
Accumulated amortization	130,858	
Cash		9,000
Leased equipment		131,858

The foregoing example illustrated a situation where the asset was to be returned to the lessor. Another situation exists (under BPO or transfer of title) where the asset is expected to remain with the lessee. Remember that leased assets are amortized over their useful life when title transfers or a bargain purchase option exists. At the end of the lease, the balance of the lease obligation should equal the guaranteed residual value, the bargain purchase option price, or a termination penalty.

Example of accounting for a capital lease—Asset ownership transferred to lessee

1. A three-year lease is initiated on 1/1/02 for equipment with an expected useful life of five years.
2. Three annual lease payments of $52,000 are required beginning on 1/1/02 (note that the payment at the beginning of the year changes the PV computation). The lessee pays $2,000 per year for insurance on the equipment and this amount is included in the annual payments.
3. The lessee can exercise a bargain purchase option on 12/31/04 for $10,000. The expected residual value at 12/31/04 is $18,000.
4. The lessee's incremental borrowing rate is 10% (lessor's implicit rate is unknown).

5.   The fair value of the leased property is $140,000.

Once again, the classification of the lease must take place prior to the accounting for it. This lease is classified as a capital lease because it contains a BPO. In this case, the 90% test is also fulfilled.

The PV of the lease obligation is computed as follows:

PV of bargain purchase option =	$10,000 x		.7513*	= $ 7,513
PV of annual payments	= ($52,000 – $2,000) x		2.7355**	= 136,755
				$144,268

* .7513 is the PV of an amount due in three periods at 10%.
** 2.7355 is the PV of an **annuity due** for three periods at 10%.

Notice that the present value of the lease obligation is greater than the FV of the asset. Since the lessee pays $2,000 a year for insurance, this payment is treated as executory costs and excluded from the calculation of the present value of annual payments. Because of this, the lease obligation must be recorded at the FV of the asset leased.

1/1/02 Leased equipment	140,000	
Obligation under capital lease		140,000

According to SFAS 13, the allocation between interest and principal is to be such that interest recognized reflects the use of a constant periodic rate of interest applied to the remaining balance of the obligation. If the FV of the leased asset is greater than or equal to the PV of the lease obligation, the interest rate used would be the same as that used to compute the PV (i.e., the incremental borrowing rate or the implicit rate). In cases such as this when the PV exceeds the FV of the leased asset, a new rate must be computed through a series of trial and error calculations. In this situation the interest rate used was 13.265%. The amortization of the lease takes place as follows:

Date	Cash payment	Interest expense	Reduction in lease obligation	Balance of lease obligation
Inception of lease				$140,000
1/1/02	$50,000	$ --	$50,000	90,000
1/1/03	50,000	11,939	38,061	51,939
1/1/04	50,000	6,890	43,110	8,829
12/31/04	10,000	1,171	8,829	--

The following entries are required in years 2002 through 2004 to recognize the payment and amortization.

		2002		2003		2004	
1/1	Operating expense	2,000		2,000		2,000	
	Obligation under capital lease	50,000		38,061		43,110	
	Accrued interest payable			11,939		6,890	
	Cash		52,000		52,000		52,000
12/31	Interest expense	11,939		6,890		1,171	
	Accrued interest payable		11,939		6,890		1,171
12/31	Amortization expense	27,800		27,800		27,800	
	Accumulated amortization		27,800		27,800		27,800
	($139,000 ÷ 5 years)						
12/31	Obligation under capital lease					10,000	
	Cash						10,000

Accounting for Leases—Lessor

As illustrated above, there are four classifications of leases with which a lessor must be concerned. They are as follows:

1. Operating
2. Sales-type
3. Direct financing
4. Leveraged

Operating lease. As in the case of the lessee, the operating lease requires a less complex accounting treatment. The payments received by the lessor are to be recorded as rent revenues in the period in which the payment is received or becomes receivable. As with the lessee, if either the rentals vary from a straight-line basis or the lease agreement contains a scheduled rent increase over the lease term, the revenue is to be recorded on a straight-line basis unless an alternative basis of systematic and rational allocation is more representative of the time pattern of physical usage of the leased property. If the scheduled increase(s) is due to additional leased property, recognition should be proportional to the leased property with the increased rents recognized over the years that the lessee has control over the use of the additional leased property.

The lessor shall show the leased property on the balance sheet under the caption "Investment in leased property." This account should be shown with or near the fixed assets of the lessor, and depreciated in the same manner as the rest of the lessor's fixed assets.

Any **initial direct costs** are to be amortized over the lease term as the revenue is recognized (i.e., on a straight-line basis unless another method is more representative). However, these costs may be charged to expense as they are incurred if the effect is not materially different from what would have occurred if the above method had not been used.

Any incentives made by the lessor to the lessee are to be treated as reductions of rent and recognized on a straight-line basis over the term of the lease.

If, at the inception of the lease, the fair value of the property in an operating lease involving real estate that would have been classified as a sales-type lease except that it did not transfer title is less than its carrying amount, then the lessor must recognize a loss equal to that difference at the inception of the lease.

Sales-type lease. In the accounting for a sales-type lease, it is necessary for the lessor to determine the following amounts:

1. Gross investment
2. Fair value of the leased asset
3. Cost

From these amounts, the remainder of the computations necessary to record and account for the lease transaction can be made. The first objective is to determine the numbers necessary to complete the following entry:

Lease receivable	xx	
Cost of goods sold	xx	
Sales		xx
Inventory		xx
Unearned interest		xx

The gross investment (lease receivable) of the lessor is equal to the sum of the minimum lease payments (excluding executory costs) plus the **un**guaranteed residual value. The difference between the gross investment and the present value of the two components of gross investment (minimum lease payments and unguaranteed residual value) is recorded as the unearned interest revenue. The present value is to be computed using the lease term and implicit interest rate (both of which were discussed earlier). The lease term used in this computation includes any renewal options exercisable at the discretion of the lessor. The resulting unearned interest revenue is to be amortized into income using the effective interest method. This will result in a constant periodic rate of return on the net investment (the net investment is the gross investment less the unearned income).

Recall from our earlier discussion that the fair value (FV) of the leased property is, by definition, equal to the normal selling price of the asset adjusted by any residual amount retained (this amount retained can be exemplified by an unguaranteed residual value, investment credit, etc.). The adjusted selling price to be used for a sales-type lease is equal to the present value of the minimum lease payments. Thus, we can say that the normal selling price less the residual amount retained is equal to the PV of the minimum lease payments.

The cost of goods sold to be charged against income in the period of the sale is computed as the historic cost or carrying value of the asset (most likely inventory) plus any initial direct costs, less the present value of the unguaranteed residual value. The difference between the adjusted selling price and the amount computed as the cost of goods sold is the gross profit recognized by the lessor at the inception of the lease (sale). Thus, a sales-type lease generates two types of revenue for the lessor.

1. The gross profit on the sale
2. The interest earned on the lease receivable

It should be noted that if the sales-type lease involves real estate, the lessor must account for the transaction under the provisions of SFAS 66 in the same manner as a seller of the same property.

The application of these points is illustrated in the example below.

Example of accounting for a sales-type lease

XYZ Inc. is a manufacturer of specialized equipment. Many of its customers do not have the necessary funds or financing available for outright purchase. Because of this, XYZ offers a leasing alternative. The data relative to a typical lease are as follows:

1. The noncancelable fixed portion of the lease term is five years. The lessor has the option to renew the lease for an additional three years at the same rental. The estimated useful life of the asset is ten years.
2. The lessor is to receive equal annual payments over the term of the lease. The leased property reverts back to the lessor upon termination of the lease.
3. The lease is initiated on 1/1/02. Payments are due on 12/31 for the duration of the lease term.
4. The cost of the equipment to XYZ Inc. is $100,000. The lessor incurs cost associated with the inception of the lease in the amount of $2,500.
5. The selling price of the equipment for an outright purchase is $150,000.
6. The equipment is expected to have a residual value of $15,000 at the end of five years and $10,000 at the end of eight years.
7. The lessor desires a return of 12% (the implicit rate).

The first step is to calculate the annual payment due to the lessor. Recall that present value (PV) of the minimum lease payments is equal to the selling price adjusted for the present value of the residual amount. The present value is to be computed using the implicit interest rate and the lease term. In this case, the implicit rate is given as 12% and the lease term is eight years (the fixed noncancelable portion plus the renewal period). Thus, the structure of the computation would be as follows:

Normal selling price – PV of residual value = PV of minimum lease payment

Or, in this case,

$$\$150,000 - (.40388^* \times \$10,000) = 4.96764^{**} \times \text{Minimum lease payment}$$

$$\frac{\$145,961.20}{4.96764} = \text{Minimum lease payment}$$

$$\$29,382.40 = \text{Minimum lease payment}$$

* *.40388 is the present value of an amount of $1 due in eight periods at a 12% interest rate.*
** *4.96764 is the present value of an annuity of $1 for eight periods at a 12% interest rate.*

Prior to examining the accounting implications of a lease, we must first determine the lease classification. Assume that there are no uncertainties regarding the lessor's costs, and the collectibility of the lease payments is reasonably assured. In this example, the lease term is eight years (discussed above) while the estimated useful life of the asset is ten years; thus, this lease qualifies as something other than an operating lease. [Note that it also meets the 90% of FV criterion because the PV of the minimum lease payments of $145,961.20 is greater than 90% of the FV that is $135,000, .90($150,000)]. Now it must be determined if this is a sales-type, direct financing, or leveraged lease. To do this, examine the FV or selling price of the asset and compare it to the cost. Because the two are not equal, this is a sales-type lease.

Next, obtain the figures necessary to record the entry on the books of the lessor. The gross investment is the total minimum lease payments plus the unguaranteed residual value or

$$(\$29,382.40 \times 8) + \$10,000 = \$245,059.20$$

The cost of goods sold is the historical cost of the inventory ($100,000) plus any initial direct costs ($2,500) less the PV of the unguaranteed residual value ($10,000 x .40388). Thus, the cost of goods sold amount is $98,461.20 ($100,000 + $2,500 – $4,038.80). Note that the initial direct costs will require a credit entry to some account, usually accounts payable or cash. The inventory account is credited for the carrying value of the asset, in this case $100,000.

The adjusted selling price is equal to the PV of the minimum payments, or $145,961.20. Finally, the unearned interest revenue is equal to the gross investment (i.e., lease receivable) less the present value of the components making up the gross investment (the minimum lease payments of $29,382.40 and the unguaranteed residual of $10,000). The present value of these items is $150,000 [($29,382.40 x 4.96764) + ($10,000 x .40388)]. Therefore, the entry necessary to record the lease is

Lease receivable	245,059.20	
Cost of goods sold	98,461.20	
Inventory		100,000.00
Sales		145,961.20
Unearned interest		95,059.20
Accounts payable (initial direct costs)		2,500.00

The next step in accounting for a sales-type lease is to determine the proper handling of each payment. Both principal and interest are included in each payment. Interest is recognized on a basis such that an equal rate is earned over the term of the lease. This will require setting up an amortization schedule as illustrated below.

Year	Cash payment	Interest	Reduction in principal	Balance of net investment
Inception of lease				$150,000.00
1	$ 29,382.40	$18,000.00	$ 11,382.40	138,617.00
2	29,382.40	16,634.11	12,748.29	125,869.31
3	29,382.40	15,104.32	14,278.08	111,591.23
4	29,382.40	13,390.95	15,991.45	95,599.78
5	29,382.40	11,471.97	17,910.43	77,689.35
6	29,382.40	9,322.72	20,059.68	57,629.67
7	29,382.40	6,915.56	22,466.84	35,162.83
8	29,382.40	4,219.57	25,162.83	10,000.00
	$235,059.20	$95,059.20	$140,000.00	

A few of the columns need to be elaborated upon. First, the net investment is the gross investment (lease receivable) less the unearned interest. Notice that at the end of the lease term, the net investment is equal to the estimated residual value. Also note that the total interest earned over the lease term is equal to the unearned interest at the beginning of the lease term.

The entries below illustrate the proper treatment to record the receipt of the lease payment and the amortization of the unearned interest in the first year.

Cash	29,382.40	
Lease receivable		29,382.40
Unearned interest	18,000.00	
Interest revenue		18,000.00

Notice that there is no entry to recognize the principal reduction. This is done automatically when the net investment is reduced by decreasing the lease receivable (gross investment) by $29,382.40 and the unearned interest account by only $18,000. The $18,000 is 12% (implicit rate) of the net investment. These entries are to be made over the life of the lease.

At the end of the lease term the asset is returned to the lessor and the following entry is required:

Asset	10,000	
Lease receivable		10,000

If the estimated residual value has changed during the lease term, then the accounting computations would have changed also to reflect this.

Direct financing lease. The accounting for a direct financing lease holds many similarities to that for a sales-type lease. Of particular importance is that the terminology used is much the same; however, the treatment accorded these items varies greatly. Again, it is best to preface our discussion by determining our objectives in the accounting for a direct financing lease. Once the lease has been classified, it must be recorded. In order to do this, the following numbers must be obtained:

1. Gross investment
2. Cost
3. Residual value

As mentioned earlier, a direct financing lease generally involves a leasing company or other financial institution and results in only interest revenue being earned by the lessor. This is because the FV (selling price) and the cost are equal and, therefore, no profit is recognized on the actual lease transaction. Note how this is different from a sales-type lease that involves both a profit on the transaction and interest revenue over the lease term. The reason for this difference is derived from the conceptual nature underlying the purpose of the lease transaction. In a sales-type lease, **the manufacturer** (distributor, dealer) is seeking an alternative means to finance the sale of the product, whereas a direct financing lease is a result of the consumer's need to finance an equipment purchase. Because the consumer is unable to obtain conventional financing, he or she turns to a leasing company that will purchase the desired asset and then lease it to the consumer. Here the profit on the transaction remains with the manufacturer while the interest revenue is earned by the leasing company.

Like a sales-type lease, the first objective is to determine the amounts necessary to complete the following entry:

Lease receivable	xxx	
Asset		xxx
Unearned interest		xx

The gross investment is still defined as the minimum amount of lease payments exclusive of any executory costs plus the unguaranteed residual value. The difference between the gross investment as determined above and the cost (carrying value) of the asset is to be recorded as the unearned interest revenue because there is no manufacturer's/dealer's profit earned on the transaction. The following entry would be made to record initial direct costs:

Initial direct costs	xx	
Cash (or accounts payable)		xx

Net investment in the lease is defined as the gross investment less the unearned income plus the unamortized initial direct costs related to the lease. Initial direct costs are defined in the same way that they were for purposes of the sales-type lease; however, the accounting treatment is different. For a direct financing lease, the unearned lease (interest) income and the initial direct costs are to be amortized to income over the lease term so that a constant periodic rate is earned on the net investment. Thus, the effect of the initial direct costs is to reduce the implicit interest rate, or yield, to the lessor over the life of the lease.

An example follows that illustrates the preceding principles.

Example of accounting for a direct financing lease

XYZ needs new equipment to expand its manufacturing operation; however, it does not have sufficient capital to purchase the asset at this time. Because of this, XYZ has employed ABC Leasing to purchase the asset. In turn, XYZ will lease the asset from ABC. The following information applies to the terms of the lease:

Lease information

1. A three-year lease is initiated on 1/1/02 for equipment costing $131,858 with an expected useful life of five years. FV at 1/1/02 of the equipment is $131,858.
2. Three annual payments are due to the lessor beginning 12/31/02. The property reverts back to the lessor upon termination of the lease.
3. The unguaranteed residual value at the end of year three is estimated to be $10,000.
4. The annual payments are calculated to give the lessor a 10% return (implicit rate).
5. The lease payments and unguaranteed residual value have a PV equal to $131,858 (FMV of asset) at the stipulated discount rate.

6. The annual payment to the lessor is computed as follows:

PV of residual value   = $10,000 x .7513* = \$7,513$

PV of lease payments   =   Selling price – PV of residual value

                                       = $131,858 – 7,513 = \$124,345$

Annual payment   = $\dfrac{\$124,345}{PV_3, 10\%} = \dfrac{\$124,345}{2.4869^{**}} = \$50,000$

* .7513 is the PV of an amount due in three periods at 10%.

** 2.4869 is the PV of an annuity of $1 for three periods at a 10% interest rate.

7. Initial direct costs of $7,500 are incurred by ABC in the lease transaction.

As with any lease transaction, the first step must be to appropriately classify the lease. In this case, the PV of the lease payments ($124,345) exceeds 90% of the FV (90% x $131,858). Assume that the lease payments are reasonably assured and that there are no uncertainties surrounding the costs yet to be incurred by the lessor.

Next, determine the unearned interest and the net investment in the lease.

Gross investment in lease	
[(3 x $50,000) + $10,000]	$160,000
Cost of leased property	131,858
Unearned interest	$ 28,142

The unamortized initial direct costs are to be added to the gross investment in the lease and the unearned interest income is to be deducted to arrive at the net investment in the lease. The net investment in the lease for this example is determined as follows:

Gross investment in lease	$160,000
Add: Unamortized initial direct costs	7,500
	$167,500
Less: Unearned interest income	28,142
Net investment in lease	$139,358

The net investment in the lease (Gross investment – Unearned revenue) has been increased by the amount of initial direct costs. Therefore, **the implicit rate is no longer 10%**. We must recompute the implicit rate. The implicit rate is really the result of an internal rate of return calculation. We know that the lease payments are to be $50,000 per annum and that a residual value of $10,000 is available at the end of the lease term. In return for these payments (inflows) we are giving up equipment (outflow) and incurring initial direct costs (outflows) with a net investment of $139,358 ($131,858 + $7,500). The only way to obtain the new implicit rate is through a trial and error calculation as set up below.

$$\frac{50,000}{(1+i)}\,1 \;+\; \frac{50,000}{(1+i)}\,2 \;+\; \frac{50,000}{(1+i)}\,3 \;+\; \frac{10,000}{(1+i)}\,3 \;=\; \$139,358$$

Where i = implicit rate of interest

In this case, the implicit rate is equal to 7.008%. Thus, the amortization table would be set up as follows:

(a)	(b) Reduction in un- earned interest	(c) PV x implicit rate (7.008%)	(d) Reduction in initial direct costs (b-c)	(e) Reduction in PVI net invest. (a-b + d)	(f) PVI net invest. in lease $(f)_{(n+1)} = (f)_n - (e)$
Lease payments					
0					$139,358
1	$ 50,000	$13,186 (1)	$ 9,766	$3,420	$ 40,234	99,124
2	50,000	9,504 (2)	6,947	2,557	43,053	56,071
3	50,000	5,455 (3)	3,929	1,526	46,071	10,000
	$150,000	$28,145*	$20,642	$7,503	$129,358	

* Rounded

(b.1) $131,858	x 10%	= $13,186	
(b.2) [$131,858	− ($50,000 − 13,186)]	x 10% =	$9,504
(b.3) [$ 95,044	− ($50,000 − 9,504)]	x 10% =	$5,455

Here the interest is computed as 7.008% of the net investment. Note again that the net investment at the end of the lease term is equal to the estimated residual value.

The entry made to initially record the lease is as follows:

Lease receivable* [($50,000 x 3) + 10,000]	160,000	
Asset acquired for leasing		131,858
Unearned interest		28,142

* Also the "gross investment in lease."

When the payment (or obligation to pay) of the initial direct costs occurs, the following entry must be made:

Initial direct costs	7,500	
Cash (or accounts payable)		7,500

Using the schedule above, the following entries would be made during each of the indicated years:

	2002		2003		2004	
Cash	50,000		50,000		50,000	
Lease receivable*		50,000		50,000		50,000
Unearned interest	13,186		9,504		5,455	
Initial direct costs		3,420		2,557		1,526
Interest revenue		9,766		6,947		3,929

* Also the "gross investment in lease."

Finally, when the asset is returned to the lessor at the end of the lease term, it must be recorded on the books. The necessary entry is as follows:

Used asset	10,000	
Lease receivable*		10,000

* Also the "gross investment in lease."

Leveraged leases. Leveraged leases are discussed in detail in the Appendix of this chapter because of the complexity involved in the accounting treatment.

Special Situations

Change in residual value. For any of the foregoing types of leases, the lessor is to review the estimated residual value on at least an annual basis. If there is a decline in the estimated residual value, the lessor must make a determination as to whether this decline is temporary or permanent. If temporary, no adjustment is required; however, if the decline is other than temporary, then the estimated residual value must be revised in line with the changed estimate. The loss that arises in the net investment is to be recognized in the period of decline. Under no circumstance is the estimated residual value to be adjusted to reflect an increase in the estimate.

Change in the provisions of a lease. Accounting issues arise when the lessee and lessor agree, subsequent to its inception, to change the provisions of the lease (other than by a renewal or term extension that are discussed later). If, from the standpoint of the lessee, the revised lease terms would have, at the inception of the original lease, resulted in a different lease classification (e.g., operating lease versus capital lease or vice versa), the revised agreement is considered to be a new agreement.

If the original lease was accounted for as a capital lease and the revised lease is an operating lease, then on the date of the revision, the lessee eliminates the recorded asset and obligation and recognizes a gain or loss for the difference. For the remaining term of the revised lease, it is accounted for as an operating lease.

If the original lease was accounted for as an operating lease and the revised lease is a capital lease, then on the date of the revision, the lessee will record an asset and an obligation based on the present value of the remaining lease payments (or the fair value of the leased property, if less).

Finally, if the original and revised leases are both capital leases, then the lessee adjusts the recorded asset and obligation by an amount equal to the difference between the present value of the future minimum lease payments under the revised agreement and the recorded balance of the obligation. For the purposes of this calculation, the rate of interest to be used is the rate that was used to record the lease initially. The adjustment would be recognized as a gain or loss in the period of the adjustment.

In the case of either a sales-type or direct financing lease where there is a change in the provisions of a lease, the lease shall be accounted for as discussed below (by the lessor).

We are basically concerned with changes in the provisions that affect the amount of the remaining minimum lease payments. When a change such as this occurs, one of the following three things can happen:

1. The change does not give rise to a new agreement. A new agreement is defined as a change that, if in effect at the inception of the lease, would have resulted in a different classification.
2. The change does give rise to a new agreement that would be classified as a direct financing lease
3. The change gives rise to a new agreement classified as an operating lease

If either 1. or 2. occurs, the balance of the minimum lease payments receivable and the estimated residual value (if affected) shall be adjusted to reflect the effect of the change. The net adjustment is to be charged (or credited) to the unearned income account, and the accounting for the lease over its remaining term adjusted to reflect the change.

If the new agreement is an operating lease, then the remaining net investment (lease receivable less unearned income) is to be removed from the books and the leased asset shall be recorded by the lessor at the lower of its cost, present fair value, or carrying value. The net adjustment resulting from these entries shall be charged (or credited) to the income of the period. Thereafter, the new lease shall be accounted for as any other operating lease.

Termination of a lease. The lessor shall remove the remaining net investment from his/her books and record the leased equipment as an asset at the lower of its original cost, present fair value, or current carrying value. The net adjustment shall be reflected in the income of the current period.

The lessee is also affected by the terminated agreement because s/he has been relieved of the obligation. If the lease is a capital lease, then the lessee should remove both the obligation and the asset from his/her accounts and charge any adjustment to the current period income. If accounted for as an operating lease, there is no accounting adjustment required.

Renewal or extension of an existing lease. The renewal or extension of an existing lease agreement affects the accounting of both the lessee and the lessor. There are two basic situations in this regard: (1) the renewal occurs and makes a residual guarantee or penalty provision inoperative or (2) the renewal agreement does not do the foregoing and the renewal is to be treated as a new agreement. The accounting treatment prescribed under the latter situation for a lessee is as follows:

1. If the renewal or extension is classified as a capital lease, then the (present) current balances of the asset and related obligation should be adjusted by an amount equal to the difference between the present value of the future minimum lease payments under the revised agreement and the (present) current balance of the obligation. The present value of the minimum lease payments under the revised agreement should be computed using the interest rate that was in effect at the inception of the original lease.

2. If the renewal or extension is classified as an operating lease, then the current balances in the asset and liability accounts shall be removed from the books and a gain (loss) recognized for the difference. The new lease agreement resulting from a renewal or extension shall be accounted for in the same manner as other operating leases.

Under the same circumstances, the following treatment is to be followed by the lessor:

1. If the renewal or extension is classified as a direct financing lease, then the existing balances of the lease receivable and the estimated residual value

accounts should be adjusted for the changes resulting from the revised agreement.

NOTE: Remember that an upward adjustment to the estimated residual value is not allowed.

The net adjustment should be charged or credited to an unearned income account.

2. If the renewal or extension is classified as an operating lease, then the remaining net investment under the existing sales-type lease or direct financing lease shall be removed from the books and the leased asset shall be recorded as an asset at the lower of its original cost, present fair value, or current carrying amount. The difference between the net investment and the amount recorded for the leased asset shall be charged to income of the period. The renewal or extension should then be accounted for as any other operating lease.

3. If the renewal or extension is classified as a sales-type lease **and** it occurs at or near the end of the existing lease term, then the renewal or extension should be accounted for as a sales-type lease.

NOTE: A renewal or extension that occurs in the last few months of an existing lease is considered to have occurred at or near the end of the existing lease term.

If the renewal or extension causes the guarantee or penalty provision to be inoperative, the **lessee** shall adjust the current balance of the leased asset and the lease obligation **to** the present value of the future minimum lease payments (according to SFAS 13 "by an amount equal to the difference between the PV of future minimum lease payments under the revised agreement and the present balance of the obligation"). The PV of the future minimum lease payments shall be computed using the implicit rate used in the original lease agreement.

Given the same circumstances, the **lessor** shall adjust the existing balance of the lease receivable and estimated residual value accounts to reflect the changes of the revised agreement (remember, no upward adjustments to the residual value). The net adjustment shall be charged (or credited) to unearned income.

Leases between related parties. Leases between related parties shall be classified and accounted for as though the parties are unrelated, except in cases where it is certain that the terms and conditions of the agreement have been influenced significantly by the fact that the lessor and lessee are related. When this is the case, the classification and/or accounting shall be modified to reflect the true economic substance of the transaction rather than the legal form.

If a subsidiary's principal business activity is leasing property to its parent or other affiliated companies, consolidated financial statements shall be presented.

SFAS 57 requires that the nature and extent of leasing activities between related parties be disclosed.

Accounting for leases in a business combination. A business combination, in and of itself, has no effect upon the classification of a lease. However, if, in connection with a business combination, the lease agreement is modified to change the original classification of the lease, it should be considered a new agreement and reclassified according to the revised provisions.

In most cases, a business combination that is accounted for by the pooling-of-interest method or by the purchase method will not affect the previous classification of a lease unless the provisions have been modified as indicated in the preceding paragraph.

The acquiring company shall apply the following procedures to account for a leveraged lease in a business combination accounted for by the purchase method:

1. The classification of leveraged lease should be kept.
2. The net investment in the leveraged lease should be given a fair market value (present value, net of tax) based upon the remaining future cash flows. Also, the estimated tax effects of the cash flows should be given recognition.
3. The net investment shall then be broken down into three components: net rentals receivable, estimated residual value, and unearned income.
4. Thereafter, the leveraged lease should be accounted for as described in the Appendix.

In a business combination where a lease is acquired that does not conform to SFAS 13 (pre-1979), the acquiring company should account for the lease by retroactively applying SFAS 13 at the date of combination.

Accounting for changes in lease agreements resulting from refunding of tax-exempt debt. If, during the lease term, a change in the lease results from a refunding by the lessor of tax-exempt debt (including an advance refunding) and (1) the lessee receives the economic advantages of the refunding and (2) the revised agreement can be classified as a capital lease by the lessee and a direct financing lease by the lessor, the change should be accounted for as follows:

1. If the change is accounted for as an extinguishment of debt

   a. Lessee accounting. The lessee should adjust the lease obligation to the present value of the future minimum lease payments under the revised agreement. The present value of the minimum lease payments should be computed by using the interest rate applicable to the revised agreement. Any gain or loss should be recognized currently as a gain or loss on the extinguishment of debt in accordance with the provisions of SFAS 4.

   b. Lessor accounting. The lessor should adjust the balance of the lease receivable and the estimated residual value, if affected, for the difference in present values between the old and revised agreements. Any resulting gain or loss should be recognized currently.

2. If the change is not accounted for as an extinguishment of debt

    a. Lessee accounting. The lessee should accrue any costs in connection with the debt refunding that are obligated to be reimbursed to the lessor. These costs should be amortized by the interest method over the period from the date of refunding to the call date of the debt to be refunded.

    b. Lessor accounting. The lessor should recognize any reimbursements to be received from the lessee, for costs paid in relation to the debt refunding, as revenue. This revenue should be recognized in a systematic manner over the period from the date of refunding to the call date of the debt to be refunded.

Sale or assignment to third parties; nonrecourse financing. The sale or assignment of a lease or of property subject to a lease that was originally accounted for as a sales-type lease or a direct financing lease will not affect the original accounting treatment of the lease. Any profit or loss on the sale or assignment should be recognized at the time of transaction except under the following two circumstances:

1. When the sale or assignment is between related parties, apply substance versus form provisions presented above under "leases between related parties"
2. When the sale or assignment is with recourse, it shall be accounted for using the provisions of SFAS 77 or 140

The sale of property subject to an operating lease shall not be treated as a sale if the seller (or any related party to the seller) retains "substantial risks of ownership" in the leased property. A seller may retain "substantial risks of ownership" by various arrangements. For example, if the lessee defaults upon the lease agreement or if the lease terminates, the seller may arrange to do one of the following:

1. Acquire the property or the lease
2. Substitute an existing lease
3. Secure a replacement lessee or a buyer for the property under a remarketing agreement

A seller will **not** retain substantial risks of ownership by arrangements where one of the following occurs:

1. A remarketing agreement includes a reasonable fee to be paid to the seller
2. The seller is not required to give priority to the releasing or disposition of the property owned by the third party over similar property owned by the seller

When the sale of property subject to an operating lease is not accounted for as a sale because the substantial risk factor is present, it should be accounted for as a borrowing. The proceeds should be recorded as an obligation on the seller's books.

Rental payments made by the lessee under the operating lease should be recorded as revenue by the seller even if the payments are paid to the third-party purchaser. The seller shall account for each rental payment by allocating a portion to interest expense (to be imputed in accordance with the provisions of APB 21), and the remainder will reduce the existing obligation. Other normal accounting procedures for operating leases should be applied except that the depreciation term for the leased asset is limited to the amortization period of the obligation.

The sale or assignment of lease payments under an operating lease by the lessor should be accounted for as a borrowing as described above.

Nonrecourse financing is a common occurrence in the leasing industry, whereby the stream of lease payments on a lease is discounted on a nonrecourse basis at a financial institution with the lease payments collateralizing the debt. The proceeds are then used to finance future leasing transactions. Even though the discounting is on a nonrecourse basis, FASB TB 86-2 prohibits the offsetting of the debt against the related lease receivable unless a legal right of offset exists or the lease qualified as a leveraged lease at its inception. The SEC in a Staff Accounting Bulletin has also affirmed this position.

Money-over-money lease transactions. In cases where a lessor obtains nonrecourse financing in excess of the leased asset's cost, FASB TB 88-1 states that the borrowing and leasing are separate transactions and should not be offset against each other unless a right of offset exists. Only dealer profit in sales-type leases may be recognized at the beginning of the lease term.

Transfers of residual value (SFAS 140 and FASB TB 86-2). Recently, there has been an increase in the acquisition of interests in residual values of leased assets by companies whose primary business is other than leasing or financing. This generally occurs through the outright purchase of the right to own the leased asset or the right to receive the proceeds from the sale of a leased asset at the end of its lease term.

In instances such as these, the rights should be recorded by the purchaser at the fair value of the assets surrendered. Recognition of increases in the value of the interest in the residual (i.e., residual value accretion) to the end of the lease term are permitted for guaranteed residual values because they are financial assets. However, recognition of such increases are prohibited for unguaranteed residual values. A nontemporary write-down of a residual value interest (guaranteed/unguaranteed) should be recognized as a loss and is not permitted to be subsequently restored. This guidance also applies to lessors who sell the related minimum lease payments but retain the interest in the residual value. Guaranteed residual values also have no effect on this guidance.

Leases involving government units. Leases that involve government units (i.e., airport facilities, bus terminal space, etc.) usually contain special provisions that prevent the agreements from being classified as anything but operating leases. These special provisions, referred to as fiscal funding clauses, include the governmental body's authority to abandon a facility at any time during the lease term, thus making its economic life indeterminable. These leases also do not contain a BPO or transfer ownership. The fair value is generally indeterminable because neither the leased property nor similar property is available for sale.

However, leases involving government units are subject to the same classification criteria as nongovernment units, except when the following six criteria are met:

NOTE: If all six conditions are met, the agreement shall be classified as an operating lease by both lessee and lessor.

1. A government unit or authority owns the leased property
2. The leased property is part of a larger facility operated by or on behalf of the lessor
3. The leased property is a permanent structure or part of a permanent structure that normally cannot be moved to another location
4. The lessor, or a higher governmental authority, has the right to terminate the lease at any time under the lease agreement or existing statutes or regulations
5. The lease neither transfers ownership nor allows the lessee to purchase or acquire the leased property
6. The leased property or similar property in the same area cannot be purchased or leased from anyone else

If any of the six conditions that qualify the lease for automatic operating lease treatment is not met, then the lease must be evaluated to determine the likelihood of future cancellation. Using the loss contingency criteria from SFAS 5, if it is remote (i.e., the chances are slight) that the lease will be canceled, then the lease agreement would qualify as a noncancelable lease and would be classified the same as any other such lease with a nongovernmental lessee. Otherwise, the lease would be considered to be cancelable and would be accounted for as an operating lease.

Accounting for a sublease. A sublease is used to describe the situation where the original lessee re-leases the leased property to a third party (the sublessee), and the original lessee acts as a sublessor. Normally, the nature of a sublease agreement does not affect the original lease agreement, and the original lessee/sublessor retains primary liability.

The original lease remains in effect, and the original lessor continues to account for the lease as before. The original lessee/sublessor shall account for the lease as follows:

1. If the original lease agreement transfers ownership or contains a BPO and if the new lease meets any one of the four specified criteria (i.e., transfers ownership, BPO, 75% test, or 90% test) and both the collectibility and uncertainties criteria, then the sublessor shall classify the new lease as a sales-type or direct financing lease; otherwise as an operating lease. In either

situation, the original lessee/sublessor should continue accounting for the original lease obligation as before.

2. If the original lease agreement does not transfer ownership or contain a BPO, but it still qualified as a capital lease, then the original lessee/ sublessor should (with one exception) apply the usual criteria in classifying the new agreement as a capital or operating lease. If the new lease qualifies for capital treatment, the original lessee/sublessor should account for it as a direct financing lease, with the unamortized balance of the asset under the original lease being treated as the cost of the leased property. The one exception arises when the circumstances surrounding the sublease suggest that the sublease agreement was an important part of a predetermined plan in which the original lessee played only an intermediate role between the original lessor and the sublessee. In this situation, the sublease shall be classified by the 75% and 90% criteria as well as collectibility and uncertainties criteria. In applying the 90% criterion, the fair value for the leased property will be the fair value to the original lessor at the inception of the original lease. Under all circumstances, the original lessee should continue accounting for the original lease obligation as before. If the new lease agreement (sublease) does not meet the capitalization requirements imposed for subleases, then the new lease should be accounted for as an operating lease.

3. If the original lease is an operating lease, the original lessee/sublessor should account for the new lease as an operating lease and account for the original operating lease as before.

Sale-Leaseback Transactions

Sale-leaseback describes a transaction where the owner of property (seller-lessee) sells the property, and then immediately leases all or part of it back from the new owner (buyer-lessor). These transactions may occur when the seller-lessee is experiencing cash flow or financing problems or because the tax advantages are beneficial. The important consideration in this type of transaction is the recognition of two separate and distinct economic transactions. However, it is important to note that there is not a physical transfer of property. First, there is a sale of property, and second, there is a lease agreement for the same property in which the original seller is the lessee and the original buyer is the lessor. This is illustrated below.

If an entity owns property and is also a lessee in it (e.g., entity invests in a partnership that owns this property), and sells the property while remaining a lessee, the transaction should be accounted for as a sale-leaseback, if the existing lease terms are modified.

A sale-leaseback transaction is usually structured such that the sales price of the asset is greater than or equal to the current market value. The result of this higher sales price is a higher periodic rental payment over the lease term. The transaction is attractive usually because of the tax benefits associated with it. The seller-lessee benefits from the higher price because of the increased gain on the sale of the property and the deductibility of the lease payments that are usually larger than the depreciation that was previously being taken. The buyer-lessor benefits from both the higher rental payments and the larger depreciable basis.

The accounting treatment from the seller-lessee's point of view will depend upon the degree of rights to use that it retains. The degree of rights to use retained may be categorized as follows:

1. Substantially all
2. Minor
3. More than minor but less than substantially all

The guideline for the determination of substantially all is based upon the classification criteria presented for the lease transaction. For example, a test based upon the 90% recovery criterion seems appropriate. That is, if the present value of fair rental payments is equal to 90% or more of the fair value of the sold asset, the seller-lessee is presumed to have retained **substantially all** of the rights to use the sold property. The test for retaining **minor** rights would be to substitute 10% or less for 90% or more in the preceding sentence.

If substantially all the rights to use the property are retained by the seller-lessee, and the agreement meets at least one of the criteria for capital lease treatment, the seller-lessee should account for the leaseback as a capital lease and any profit on the sale should be deferred and amortized in proportion to amortization of the leased asset. If the leaseback is classified as an operating lease, it should be accounted for as such, and any profit on the sale should be deferred and amortized over the lease term in proportion to gross rental charges. Any loss on the sale would also be deferred unless the loss were perceived to be a real economic loss, in which case the loss would be immediately recognized and not deferred.

If only a **minor portion** of the rights to use are retained by the seller-lessee, the sale and the leaseback should be accounted for separately. However, if the rental payments appear unreasonable based upon the existing market conditions at the inception of the lease, the profit or loss should be adjusted so the rentals are at a reasonable amount. The amount created by the adjustment should be deferred and amortized over the life of the property if a capital lease is involved or over the lease term if an operating lease is involved.

If the seller-lessee retains **more than a minor portion but less than substantially all** the rights to use the property, any excess profit on the sale should be recognized on the date of the sale. For purposes of this paragraph, excess profit is derived as follows:

1. If the leaseback is classified as an operating lease, the excess profit is the profit that exceeds the present value of the minimum lease payments over the lease term. The seller-lessee should use its incremental borrowing rate to compute the present value of the minimum lease payments. If the implicit rate of interest in the lease is known and lower, it should be used to compute the present value of the minimum lease payments.
2. If the leaseback is classified as a capital lease, the excess profit is the amount greater than the recorded amount of the leased asset.

When the fair value of the property at the time of the leaseback is less than its undepreciated cost, the seller-lessee should immediately recognize a loss for the difference. In the example below, the sales price is less than the book value of the property. However, there is no economic loss because the FV is greater than the book value.

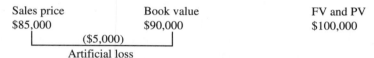

Sales price	Book value	FV and PV
$85,000	$90,000	$100,000

($5,000)
Artificial loss

The artificial loss must be deferred and amortized as an addition to depreciation.

The diagram below summarizes the accounting.

In the above circumstances, when the leased asset is land only, any amortization should be on a straight-line basis over the lease term, regardless of whether the lease is classified as a capital or operating lease.

Executory costs are not to be included in the calculation of profit to be deferred in a sale-leaseback transaction.

The buyer-lessor should account for the transaction as a purchase and a direct financing lease if the agreement meets the criteria of **either** a direct financing lease **or** a sales-type lease. Otherwise, the agreement should be accounted for as a purchase and an operating lease.

Sale-leaseback involving real estate. Three requirements are necessary for a sale-leaseback involving real estate (including real estate with equipment) to qualify for sale-leaseback accounting treatment. Those sale-leaseback transactions not meeting the three requirements should be accounted for as a deposit (see Chapter 8, Special Revenue Recognition Areas) or as a financing. The three requirements are

1. The lease must be a normal leaseback (explained below)
2. Payment terms and provisions must adequately demonstrate the buyer-lessor's initial and continuing investment in the property
3. Payment terms and provisions must transfer all the risks and rewards of ownership as demonstrated by a lack of continuing involvement by the seller-lessee

A normal leaseback involves active use of the leased property in the seller-lessee's trade or business during the lease term.

The buyer-lessor's initial investment is adequate if it demonstrates the buyer-lessor's commitment to pay for the property and indicates a reasonable likelihood that the seller-lessee will collect any receivable related to the leased property. The buyer-lessor's continuing investment is adequate if the buyer is contractually obligated to pay an annual amount at least equal to the level of annual payment needed to pay that debt and interest over no more than (1) twenty years for land, and (2) the customary term of a first mortgage for other real estate.

Any continuing involvement by the seller-lessee other than normal leaseback disqualifies the lease from sale-leaseback accounting treatment. Some examples of continuing involvement other than normal leaseback include

1. The seller-lessee has an obligation or option (excluding the right of first refusal) to repurchase the property
2. The seller-lessee (or party related to the seller-lessee) guarantees the buyer-lessor's investment or debt related to that investment or a return on that investment
3. The seller-lessee is required to reimburse the buyer-lessor for a decline in the fair value of the property below estimated residual value at the end of the lease term based on other than excess wear and tear
4. The seller-lessee remains liable for an existing debt related to the property
5. The seller-lessee's rental payments are contingent on some predetermined level of future operations of the buyer-lessor
6. The seller-lessee provides collateral on behalf of the buyer-lessor other than the property directly involved in the sale-leaseback

7. The seller-lessee provides nonrecourse financing to the buyer-lessor for any portion of the sales proceeds or provides recourse financing in which the only recourse is the leased asset
8. The seller-lessee enters into a sale-leaseback involving property improvements or integral equipment without leasing the underlying land to the buyer-lessor
9. The buyer-lessor is obligated to share any portion of the appreciation of the property with the seller-lessee
10. Any other provision or circumstance that allows the seller-lessee to participate in any future profits of the buyer-lessor or the appreciation of the leased property

Example of accounting for a sale-leaseback transaction

To illustrate the accounting treatment in a sale-leaseback transaction, suppose that Lessee Corporation sells equipment that has a book value of $80,000 and a fair value of $100,000 to Lessor Corporation, and then immediately leases it back under the following conditions:

1. The sale date is January 1, 2002, and the equipment has a fair value of $100,000 on that date and an estimated remaining useful life of fifteen years.
2. The lease term is fifteen years, noncancelable, and requires equal rental payments of $13,109 at the beginning of each year.
3. Lessee Corp. has the option to annually renew the lease at the same rental payments upon expiration of the original lease.
4. Lessee Corp. has the obligation to pay all executory costs.
5. The annual rental payments provide the lessor with a 12% return on investment.
6. The incremental borrowing rate of Lessee Corp. is 12%.
7. Lessee Corp. depreciates similar equipment on a straight-line basis.

Lessee Corp. should classify the agreement as a capital lease since the lease term exceeds 75% of the estimated remaining economic life of the equipment, and because the present value of the lease payments is greater than 90% of the fair value of the equipment. Assuming that collectibility of the lease payments is reasonably predictable and that no important uncertainties exist concerning the amount of unreimbursable costs yet to be incurred by the lessor, Lessor Corp. should classify the transaction as a direct financing lease because the present value of the minimum lease payments is equal to the fair value of $100,000 ($13,109 x 7.62817[2]).

Lessee Corp. and Lessor Corp. would normally make the following journal entries during the first year:

---

[2] *7.62817 is the present value of an annuity due for fifteen periods at a 12% interest rate.*

Upon Sale of Equipment on January 1, 2002

Lessee Corp.			_Lessor Corp._		
Cash	100,000		Equipment	100,000	
Equipment*		80,000	Cash		100,000
Unearned profit on					
sale-leaseback		20,000			
Leased equipment	100,000		Lease receivable		
Lease obligations		100,000	($13,109 x 15)	196,635	
			Equipment		100,000
			Unearned interest		96,635

* *Assumes new equipment; for used equipment the accumulated depreciation would also be debited to remove it.*

To Record First Payment on January 1, 2002

Lessee Corp.			_Lessor Corp._		
Lease obligations	13,109		Cash	13,109	
Cash		13,109	Lease receivable		13,109

To Record Incurrence and Payment of Executory Costs

Lessee Corp.			_Lessor Corp._
			(No entry)
Insurance, taxes, etc.	xxx		
Cash (or accounts payable)		xxx	

To Record Amortization Expense on the Equipment, December 31, 2002

Lessee Corp.			_Lessor Corp._
			(No entry)
Amortization expense	6,667		
Accum. amort.— capital			
leases ($100,000 ÷ 15)		6,667	

To Amortize Profit on Sale-Leaseback by Lessee Corp., December 31, 2002

Lessee Corp.			_Lessor Corp._
			(No entry)
Unearned profit on sale-			
leaseback	1,333		
Amortization expense			
($20,000 ÷ 15)		1,333	

To Record Interest for 2000, December 31, 2002

Lessee Corp.			_Lessor Corp._		
Interest expense	10,427		Unearned interest	10,427	
Accrued interest payable		10,427	Interest income		10,427

Partial Lease Amortization Schedule

Date	_Cash payment_	_Interest expense_	_Reduction of obligation_	_Lease obligation_
Inception of lease				$100,000
1/1/02	$13,109	$ --	$13,109	86,891
1/1/03	13,109	10,427	2,682	84,209

LEASES INVOLVING REAL ESTATE

Leases involving real estate can be divided into the following four categories:

1. Leases involving land only
2. Leases involving land and building(s)
3. Leases involving real estate and equipment
4. Leases involving only part of a building

Leases Involving Land Only

Lessee accounting. If the lease agreement transfers ownership or contains a bargain purchase option, the lessee should account for the lease as a capital lease, and record an asset and related liability in an amount equal to the present value of the minimum lease payments. If the lease agreement does not transfer ownership or contain a bargain purchase option, the lessee should account for the lease as an operating lease.

Lessor accounting. If the lease gives rise to dealer's profit (or loss) and transfers ownership (i.e., title), the lease is to be classified as a sales-type lease and accounted for under the provisions of SFAS 66 in the same manner as a seller of the same property. If the lease transfers ownership, both the collectibility and no material uncertainties criteria are met, but does not give rise to dealer's profit (or loss), the lease should be accounted for as a direct financing or leveraged lease as appropriate. If the lease contains a bargain purchase option and both the collectibility and no material uncertainties criteria are met, the lease should be accounted for as a direct financing, leveraged, or operating lease as appropriate. If the lease does not meet the collectibility and/or no material uncertainties criteria, the lease should be accounted for as an operating lease.

Leases Involving Land and Building

Lessee accounting. If the agreement transfers title or contains a bargain purchase option, the lessee should account for the agreement by separating the land and building components and capitalize each separately. The land and building elements should be allocated on the basis of their relative fair values measured at the inception of the lease. The land and building components are separately accounted for because the lessee is expected to own the real estate by the end of the lease term. The building should be amortized over its estimated useful life without regard to the lease term.

When the lease agreement neither transfers title nor contains a bargain purchase option, the fair value of the land must be determined in relation to the fair value of the aggregate property included in the lease agreement. If the fair value of the land is less than 25% of the fair value of the leased property in aggregate, then the land is considered immaterial. Conversely, if the fair value of the land is 25% or greater of the fair value of the leased property in aggregate, then the land is considered material.

When the land component of the lease agreement is considered immaterial (FV land < 25% total FV), the lease should be accounted for as a single lease unit. The lessee should capitalize the lease if one of the following occurs:

1. The term of the lease is 75% or more of the economic useful life of the building

2. The present value of the minimum lease payments equals 90% or more of the fair value of the leased real estate less any lessor investment tax credit

If neither of the above two criteria is met, the lessee should account for the lease agreement as a single operating lease.

When the land component of the lease agreement is considered material (FV land $\geq$ 25% total FV), the land and building components should be separated. By applying the lessee's incremental borrowing rate to the fair value of the land, the annual minimum lease payment attributed to land is computed. The remaining payments are attributed to the building. The division of minimum lease payments between land and building is essential for both the lessee and lessor. The portion of the lease involving the land should **always** be accounted for as an operating lease. The lease involving the building(s) must meet either the 75% or 90% test to be treated as a capital lease. If neither of the two criteria is met, the building(s) will also be accounted for as an operating lease.

Lessor accounting. The lessor's accounting depends on whether the lease transfers ownership, contains a bargain purchase option, or does neither of the two.

If the lease transfers ownership and gives rise to dealer's profit (or loss), the lessor classifies the lease as a sales-types lease and accounts for the lease as a single unit under the provisions of SFAS 66 in the same manner as a seller of the same property. If the lease transfers ownership, meets both the collectibility and no important uncertainties criteria, but does not give rise to dealer's profit (or loss), the lease should be accounted for as a direct financing or leveraged lease as appropriate.

If the lease contains a bargain purchase option and gives rise to dealer's profit (or loss), the lease should be classified as an operating lease. If the lease contains a bargain purchase option, meets both the collectibility and no material uncertainties criteria, but does not give rise to dealer's profit (or loss), the lease should be accounted for as a direct financing lease or a leveraged lease as appropriate.

If the lease agreement neither transfers ownership nor contains a bargain purchase option, the lessor should follow the same rules as the lessee in accounting for real estate leases involving land and building(s).

However, the collectibility and the no material uncertainties criteria must be met before the lessor can account for the agreement as a direct financing lease, and in no such case may the lease be classified as a sales-type lease (i.e., ownership must be transferred).

The treatment of a lease involving both land and building can be illustrated in the following examples.

Example of lessee accounting for land and building lease containing transfer of title

1. The lessee enters into a ten-year noncancelable lease for a parcel of land and a building for use in its operations. The building has an estimated useful life of twelve years.
2. The FV of the land is $75,000, while the FV of the building is $310,000.

3. A payment of $50,000 is due to the lessor at the beginning of each of the ten years of the lease.
4. The lessee's incremental borrowing rate is 10%. (Lessor's implicit rate is unknown.)
5. Ownership will transfer to the lessee at the end of the lease.

The present value of the minimum lease payments is $337,951 ($50,000 x 6.75902[3]). The portion of the present value of the minimum lease payments that should be capitalized for each of the two components of the lease is computed as follows:

FV of land				$ 75,000
FV of building				310,000
Total FV of leased property				$385,000
Portion of PV allocated to land	$337,951	x	$\dfrac{75,000}{385,000}$	= $ 65,835
Portion of PV allocated to building	$337,951	x	$\dfrac{310,000}{385,000}$	= 272,116
Total PV to be capitalized				$337,951

The entry made to initially record the lease is as follows:

Leased land	65,835	
Leased building	272,116	
Lease obligation		337,951

Subsequently, the obligation will be decreased in accordance with the effective interest method. The leased building will be amortized over its expected useful life.

Example of lessee accounting for land and building lease without transfer of title or bargain purchase option

Assume the same facts as the previous example except that title does not transfer at the end of the lease.

The lease is still a capital lease because the lease term is more than 75% of the useful life of the building. Since the FV of the land is less than 25% of the leased property in aggregate, (75,000/385,000 = 19%), the land component is considered immaterial and the lease will be accounted for as a single lease. The entry to record the lease is as follows:

Leased property	337,951	
Lease obligation		337,951

Assume the same facts as the previous example except that the FV of the land is $110,000 and the FV of the building is $275,000. Once again title does not transfer.

Because the FV of the land exceeds 25% of the leased properties in aggregate (110,000/385,000 = 28%), the land component is considered material and the lease would be separated into two components. The annual minimum lease payment attributed to the land is computed as follows:

$$\begin{array}{l} \text{FV of land} \\ \text{PV factor} \end{array} \quad \dfrac{\$110,000}{6.75902^3} = \$16,275$$

---

[3] *6.75902 is the PV of an annuity due for ten periods at 10%.*

The remaining portion of the annual payment is attributed to the building.

Annual payment	$ 50,000
Less amount attributed to land	(16,275)
Annual payment attributed to building	$33,725

The present value of the minimum annual lease payments attributed to the building is then computed as follows:

Minimum annual lease payment attributed to building	$ 33,725
PV factor	x 6.75902[4]
PV of minimum annual lease payments attributed to building	$227,948

The entry to record the capital portion of the lease is as follows:

Leased building	227,948	
Lease obligation		227,948

There would be no computation of the present value of the minimum annual lease payment attributed to the land since the land component of the lease will be treated as an operating lease. For this reason, each year $16,275 of the $50,000 lease payment will be recorded as land rental expense. The remainder of the annual payment ($33,725) will be applied against the lease obligation using the effective interest method.

Leases Involving Real Estate and Equipment

When real estate leases also involve equipment or machinery, the equipment component should be separated and accounted for as a separate lease agreement by both lessees and lessors. "The portion of the minimum lease payments applicable to the equipment element of the lease shall be estimated by whatever means are appropriate in the circumstances." The lessee and lessor should apply the capitalization requirements to the equipment lease independently of accounting for the real estate lease(s). The real estate leases should be handled as discussed in the preceding two sections. In a sale-leaseback transaction involving real estate with equipment, the equipment and land are not separated.

Refer to the Profit Recognition on Real Estate Sales section of Chapter 8 for a discussion of FASB Interpretation 43, *Real Estate Sales*.

Leases Involving Only Part of a Building

It is common to find lease agreements that involve only part of a building as, for example, when a floor of an office building is leased, or when a store in a shopping mall is leased. A difficulty that arises in this situation is that the cost and/or fair value of the leased portion of the whole may not be objectively determinable.

Lessee accounting. If the fair value of the leased property is objectively determinable, then the lessee should follow the rules and account for the lease as described in "Leases involving land and building." If the fair value of the leased property cannot be objectively determined, consider whether the agreement satisfies

---

[4] *6.75902 is the PV of an annuity due for ten periods at 10%.*

the 75% test. This calculation is made using the estimated remaining economic life of the building in which the leased premises are located. If the test is met (i.e. the term of the lease is 75% or more of the estimated remaining economic life of the building), the lease should be accounted for as a capital lease. If the test is not met, the lease should be accounted for as an operating lease.

Lessor accounting. From the lessor's position, **both the cost and fair value** of the leased property must be objectively determinable before the procedures described under "Leases involving land and building" will apply. If either the cost or the fair value cannot be determined objectively, the lessor should account for the agreement as an operating lease.

Special Situations

Wrap lease transactions. A wrap lease transaction occurs when the lessor of an asset obtains nonrecourse financing using the lease rentals and asset as collateral, sells the underlying asset and nonrecourse debt and then leases the asset back while remaining the substantive lessor under the original lease. When this occurs and the asset is real estate, the specialized rules with respect to sale-leaseback of real estate apply, otherwise the transaction is treated as a sales-leaseback with the lease to the end user treated as a sublease.

Summary of Accounting for Selected Items (See following page)

Reporting of Current and Noncurrent Lease Receivable (Lessor) and Lease Obligations (Lessee)

The balance of lease payments receivable (lessor) and lease obligation (lessee) must be broken down between the current and noncurrent portions. First, the current portion is computed at the date of the financial statements as the present value of the lease payments/receipts to be received within twelve months of the balance sheet date. The noncurrent portion is computed as the difference between the current portion determined and the balance of the lease obligation at the end of the period. The conceptual justification for such treatment can be found in the fact that the total lease obligation is equal to the present value of the future minimum lease payments. Therefore, it follows that the current portion should be the present value of the lease payments due within one year while the noncurrent portion should be the present value of all other remaining lease payments.

TREATMENT OF SELECTED ITEMS IN ACCOUNTING FOR LEASES

	Lessor		Lessee	
	Operating	*Direct financing and sales-type*	*Operating*	*Capital*
Initial direct costs	Capitalize and amortize over lease term in proportion to rent revenue recognized (normally SL basis)	Direct financing: Record in separate account; Add to net investment in lease; Compute new effective rate that equates gross amt. of min. lease payments and unguar. residual value with net invest.; Amortize so as to produce constant rate of return over lease term. Sales-type: Expense in period incurred	N/A	N/A
Investment tax credit retained by lessor	N/A	Reduces FV of leased asset for 90% test	N/A	Reduces FV of leased asset for 90% test
Bargain purchase option	N/A	Include in: Minimum lease payments; 90% test	N/A	Include in: Minimum lease payments; 90% test
Guaranteed residual value	N/A	Include in: Minimum lease payments; 90% test. Sales-type: Include PV in sales revenues	N/A	Include in: Minimum lease payments; 90% test
Unguaranteed residual value	N/A	Include in: "Gross investment in lease". Not included in: 90% test. Sales-type: Exclude from sales revenue; Deduct PV from cost of sales	N/A	Include in: Minimum lease payments; 90% test
Contingent rentals	Revenue in period earned	Not part of minimum lease payments; revenue in period earned	Expense in period incurred	Not part of minimum lease payments; expense in period incurred
Amortization period	Amortize down to estimated residual value over estimated economic life of asset	N/A	N/A	Amortize down to estimated residual value over lease term or estimated economic life[b]
Revenue (expense)[a]	Rent revenue (normally SL basis); Amortization (depreciation expense)	Direct financing: Interest revenue on net investment in lease (gross investment less unearned interest income). Sales-type: Dealer profit in period of sale (sales revenue less cost of leased asset); Interest revenue on net investment in lease	Rent expense (normally SL basis)[c]	Interest expense and depreciation expense

a Elements of revenue (expense) listed for the above items are not repeated here (e.g., treatment of initial direct costs).

b If lease has automatic passage of title or bargain purchase option, use estimated economic life; otherwise, use the lease term.

c If payments are not on a SL basis, recognize rent expense on a SL basis unless another systematic and rational method is more representative of use or benefit obtained from the property, in which case, the other method should be used.

EMERGING ISSUES TASK FORCE CONSENSUS SUMMARIES

85-16 Leveraged Leases

- Real estate leases and sale-leaseback transaction
- Delayed equity contributions by lessors

Under the provisions of SFAS 13, real estate leases can be accounted for as a leveraged lease if the requirements discussed in the appendix to this chapter are met. Furthermore, the Task Force reached a consensus that recourse debt originating from the delayed equity investment can be accounted for as a leveraged lease if the other requirements for such treatment are fulfilled. Finally, the lessor's related obligation should be accounted for as a liability at its present value at the inception of the lease.

86-17 Deferred Profit on Sale-Leaseback with Lessee Guarantee of Residual Value

A consensus was reached that the profit equal to the present value of periodic rents plus the gross amount of the guaranteed residual value should be deferred for sale-leaseback transactions classified as involving more than minor but less than substantially all the use of the property. The present value of the rents should be amortized over the lease term while the guaranteed residual should be deferred until resolution at the end of the lease term. The use of sale-leaseback accounting is limited to transactions in which all risks and rewards of ownership, other than the leaseback, are transferred to the buyer-lessor. SFAS 98 lists examples of continuing involvement by the seller-lessee that indicate the risks and rewards of ownership have not been transferred.

86-33 Tax Indemnification in Lease Agreements

A consensus was reached that tax indemnification payments do not meet the definition of contingent rentals. These payments should be allocated by lessors to: (1) amount resulting from any lost investment tax credit (ITC) and (2) amount linked to all other tax effects.

Amounts associated with lost ITC[5] are accounted for based on the lessor's normal accounting policy for accounting for ITC (the flow-through or deferral methods).

Amounts associated with other tax effects are to be accounted for in accordance with the classification of the underlying lease. Consequently, lessors would adjust their recorded investment in a sales-type or direct financing lease or amortize the payment ratably over the term of an operating lease. Lessees would adjust the

---

[5] *ITC was a tax credit afforded business under the Internal Revenue Code prior to 1986 as an economic incentive to purchase qualifying productive equipment. The incentive was designed to stimulate business expansion and economic growth.*

basis in the leased asset under a capital lease or recognize on a straight-line basis over the remaining lease term under an operating lease.

87-7 Sale of an Asset Subject to a Lease and Nonrecourse Financing: "Wrap-Lease Transactions"

A consensus was reached that the original lessor should separate revenue directly associated with future remarketing rights and defer recognition of income until the remarketing services are performed. A consensus was also reached that the original lessor should record any retained interest in the residual value of the leased asset as an asset in their financial statements. No consensus was reached on how to account for the proceeds other than the revenue from the remarketing rights.

88-10 Costs Associated with Lease Modification or Termination

A consensus was reached regarding situations where a lessee enters into a new lease for replacement property prior to the expiration of a preexisting property lease. If the preexisting lease is terminated, all costs related to the preexisting lease should be expensed when the leased property has no future benefit to the lessee. When the lease is not terminated, the expense should be reduced by any actual or probable sublease income. In addition if the preexisting lease is assumed by the new lessor, any payments to the lessee or assumption of loss by the lessor should be considered incentives. These incentives should be amortized on a straight-line basis to rent expense or rent revenue over the life of the new lease. The amount of the incentive should be determined separately by the lessee and lessor. No consensus was reached on the issue of deferring the costs of moving from one lease to another (moving) however; generally moving costs must be expensed as incurred.

88-21 Accounting for the Sale of Property Subject to the Seller's Preexisting Lease

A consensus was reached regarding situations where an entity sells property in which it has an ownership interest, and continues to lease the property under a preexisting operating lease. The consensus requires recognition of the transaction as a sale-leaseback if the preexisting lease is modified in connection with the sale. If no changes are made or changes are insignificant, profit should be deferred and recognized in accordance with SFAS 28, 66, or 98 as appropriate. Any deferred profit should not be affected by the seller-lessee's prior ownership. In addition, exercise of renewal options or sublease provisions contained in the preexisting lease should not affect the accounting for the transaction. SFAS 98 only applies to renewal options not contained in the original lease term. Finally, leases between parties under common control are not considered preexisting leases and SFAS 98 should apply unless one of the parties is a regulated enterprise.

89-16   Consideration of Executory Costs in Sale-Leaseback Transactions

A consensus was reached that executory costs in the calculation of deferred profit in a sale-leaseback transaction should be excluded from the calculation of deferred profit.

89-20   Accounting for Cross-Border Tax Benefit Leases

A consensus was reached regarding the recognition of income for cash received by the US enterprise for the foreign investor's tax benefits in situations where a US enterprise gives ownership interest in an asset to a foreign investor to allow the foreign investor tax benefits. In exchange, the US enterprise receives cash for the fair value of the ownership interest plus consideration for the tax benefit. The US enterprise may agree to indemnify the foreign investor for future loss of the tax benefit. The income may be recognized immediately or deferred unless there is more than a remote possibility of loss of the cash consideration due to indemnification or other contingencies. In this case, income must be deferred.

90-14   Unsecured Guarantee by Parent of Subsidiary's Lease Payments in a Sale-Leaseback Transaction

The Task Force reached a consensus that when one member of a consolidated group provides an unsecured guarantee of lease payments for another member of the consolidated group, such additional collateral does not reduce the buyer-lessor's risk of loss, except in the event of the seller-lessee's bankruptcy. The unsecured guarantee would, therefore, not constitute a form of continuing involvement. Thus, sale-leaseback accounting would be permitted in the **consolidated financial statements**.

The Task Force reached a different consensus with respect to treatment of the guarantee in the **separate financial statements** of the seller-lessee. Since the guarantee was from a party, albeit related, outside the reporting entity, it would be deemed to represent additional collateral that reduces the risk of loss to the buyer-lessor. Therefore, in the separate financial statements, sale-leaseback accounting would be prohibited due to the "continuing involvement" rules.

90-15   Impact of Nonsubstantive Lessors, Residual Value Guarantees, and Other Provisions in Leasing Transactions

The terms of leases are often deliberately structured to qualify as operating leases in the financial statements of the lessee. The lessee may desire this treatment for a variety of reasons such as to comply with restrictive covenants in loan agreements that limit capital expenditures or simply to avoid the added complexity of capital lease accounting. Although many such leases are true operating leases in both letter and spirit, others have characteristics that make such a classification questionable.

A common technique used to obtain the desired accounting treatment is for the property to be owned and leased by a Special Purpose Entity (SPE). The SPE lacks economic substance because all of the following conditions exist:

1. Substantially all of its activities involve assets leased to a single lessee.
2. The owner or owners of the SPE have not made a substantive equity capital investment that is at risk during the entire term of the lease.
3. The lessee is obligated with substantially all of the risks and will benefit from substantially all of the rewards from the leased property.

The Task Force reached a consensus that when all of the preceding conditions exist, the lessee is required to consolidate the SPE lessor in its financial statements. This consolidation has the same effect as treating the lease as a capital lease since the consolidated financial statements will present the leased asset, related accumulated depreciation and depreciation expense, the underlying third-party debt used to finance the leased asset and interest expense thereon.

The consensus also provides interpretive guidance on whether the risks and rewards reside in the lessee and, accordingly whether an lessor is considered to be an SPE.

90-20 Impact of an Uncollateralized Irrevocable Letter of Credit on a Real Estate Sale-Leaseback Transaction

A consensus was reached that an uncollateralized, irrevocable letter of credit is not considered a form of continuing involvement that would preclude sale-leaseback accounting unless a contract exists between the seller-lessee and third-party guarantor that would create collateral. The existence of collateral relating to the letter of credit is a form of continuing involvement that precludes sale-leaseback accounting.

92-1 Allocation of Residual Value or First-Loss Guarantee to Minimum Lease Payments in Leases Involving Land and Building(s)

A consensus was reached that for both the lessor and lessee the portion of the minimum lease payments attributable to the land is the land's fair market value times the lessee's incremental borrowing rate. Therefore, the remaining part of the minimum lease payments, including the total guaranteed amount are assigned to the building.

93-8 Accounting for the Sale and Leaseback of an Asset That Is Leased to Another Party

A consensus was reached that when a leaseback involves an asset that is personal property falling outside coverage of SFAS 98 and (1) subject to an operating lease or (2) subleased or intended to be subleased to another entity under an operating lease, SFAS 28 should be followed.

95-1   Revenue Recognition on Sales with a Guaranteed Minimum Resale Value

Transactions containing guarantees of resale value of equipment by a manufacturer should be accounted for as leases and not as sales. Minimum lease payments used to determine if criteria have been met for sales-type lease accounting equal the difference between proceeds from transfer of equipment and the amount of the residual value guarantee. Additionally, guidance is provided for those transfers that are accounted for as operating leases.

95-4   Revenue Recognition on Equipment Sold and Subsequently Repurchased Subject to an Operating Lease

This consensus determined that a manufacturer can recognize a sale at the time its product is transferred to a dealer for subsequent sale to a third-party customer even if this ultimate customer enters into an operating lease agreement with the same manufacturer or a finance affiliate thereof if four conditions exist:

1. The dealer must be an independent entity that conducts business separately with manufacturers and customers
2. The passage of the product from the manufacturer to the dealer fully transfers ownership
3. The manufacturer (or finance affiliate) has no obligation to provide a lease arrangement for the customer of the dealer
4. The customer is in control in selecting which of the many financing options available will be used.

95-17   Accounting for Modifications to an Operating Lease That Do Not Change the Lease Classification

A consensus was reached that when the lessee and the lessor agree to shorten the lease term and increase the lease payments over the lease period, the nature of the modification is a matter of judgment that depends on the relevant facts and circumstances. If the modification is deemed to be only a change in future lease payments, the increase should be amortized over the remaining term of the modified lease. On the other hand, the modification deemed a termination penalty should be recognized in the period of modification. Termination penalties should be calculated as the excess of the modified lease payments over the original lease payments that would have been required during the shortened lease term. To determine if the modification is a termination penalty, consider: (1) the length of the modified lease period compared to the remaining term of the original lease, and (2) the difference between the modified lease payments and comparable market rents.

96-21   Implementation Issues in Accounting for Leasing Transactions Involving Special Purpose Entities (SPE)

This is a follow-up to EITF 90-15, this time dealing with the criteria concerning lessors with single lessees, and the failure of the owner of record of the SPE to have made a substantial initial investment in the entity. Consensuses were reached on a number of matters involving, among others, multitiered SPE structures, multiple leases within a single SPE, payments by the lessee prior to the beginning of the lease term, fees paid to owners of record of an SPE, and sources of initial investment in the SPE. This last item is a commonly encountered problem in related entity lessors. This consensus should be reviewed carefully, since it is widely applicable.

97-1   Implementations Issues in Accounting for Lease Transactions, Including Those Involving Special Purpose Entities (SPE)

Yet another follow-up to Issue 90-15; this one is a follow-up to certain responses in Issue 96-21, and focuses on environmental risk indemnifications by lessees, nonperformance-related default covenants, and depreciation. Consensuses were reached on these, which impact upon determining whether consolidation of the SPE would be required under various circumstances.

97-10   The Effect of Lessee Involvement in Asset Construction

The Task Force reached a consensus that a lessee should be considered the owner of a real estate project during its construction period if the lessee has substantially all of the construction period risks. The test to be used in determining if a lessee has substantially all of the construction period risks is virtually the same as the 90% recovery-of-investment test for determining if a lease should be classified as a capital lease by a lessee. Beginning with the earlier of the date of the inception of the lease or the date that the construction terms are agreed to, if at any time during the construction period the documents governing the construction project could require, under any circumstance, that the lessee pay 90% or more of the total project costs, excluding land acquisition costs, then the lessee should be considered to be the owner of the real estate project during its construction period.

The lessee's maximum guarantee includes any payments the lessee could be required to make in connection with a construction project. The lessee's maximum guarantee should include, but is not limited to

1. Lease payments that must be made regardless of when or whether the project is complete
2. Guarantees of the construction financing
3. Equity investments made in the owner-lessor or any party related to the owner-lessor
4. Loans or advances made to the owner-lessor or any party related to the owner-lessor

5. Payments made by the lessee in the capacity of a developer, a general contractor, or a construction manager/agent that are reimbursed less frequently than is normal or customary

6. Primary or secondary obligations to pay project costs under construction contracts

7. Obligations that could arise from being the developer or general contractor

8. An obligation to purchase the real estate project under any circumstances

9. An obligation to fund construction cost overruns

10. Rent or fees of any kind, such as transaction costs, to be paid to or on behalf of the lessor by the lessee during the construction period

11. Payments that might be made with respect to providing indemnities or guarantees to the owner-lessor

Six examples exist for which a lessee should be considered the owner of a real estate project despite the present value of the lessee's maximum guarantee being less than 90% of total project costs (listed in EITF 97-10).

98-9   Accounting for Contingent Rent

The issues are

1. A lessor's appropriate accounting for contingent rental revenue that is based on future specified targets.

2. A lessee's appropriate accounting for contingent rental expense that is based on future specified targets.

A consensus was reached that contingent rentals based on achievement of specified targets should be recognized by the lessee during interim periods if it is probable that the target will be reached by the end of the fiscal year. If the specified target is not met, previously recorded expense should be reversed at the time it becomes probable that the target will not be met. A consensus was reached that lessors should defer recognition of contingent rental income until specified targets have been met.

99-13   Application of Issue No. 97-10 and FASB Interpretation No. 23 to Entities That Enter into Leases with Governmental Entities

A consensus was reached that a government-owned property that is being constructed and is subject to a future lease of the completed improvements is included in the scope of EITF Issue 97-10. If, under Issue 97-10, the lessee is deemed to have substantially all of the construction period risks, then the lessee is considered the owner of the property for accounting purposes. Under that scenario, the transaction is accounted for under the sale-leaseback rules discussed previously in this chapter. The consensus apples to construction projects committed to after

September 23, 1999, and also to those projects that were committed to on or before September 23, 1999, if construction did not commence by March 31, 2000.

99-14 Recognition of Losses on Firmly Committed Executory Contracts

During the term of a lease, the fair value of the leased asset may decline because the underlying asset becomes impaired. As a result of this impairment, the fair value of the remaining contractual rights that will benefit the lessee may be less than the remaining costs that will be expensed under the lease. The same concept applies to other types of executory contracts (e.g., a contract or license to use a trade name, or to future advertising). When such a "loss contract" exists, the "remaining contractual right asset" may or may not be recognized as an asset on the balance sheet depending on the timing of the payment stream. The issue is when, if ever, the holder of the remaining contractual right asset should recognize an impairment of that asset and how that loss should be measured if the purchaser continues to use the asset. A majority of the Task Force members indicated that they believed that impairment should be recognized irrespective of whether an asset has been recognized.

The issue is still under discussion by the EITF and no consensus has been reached.

00-13 Determing Whether Equipment is "Integral Equipment" Subject to FASB Statement No. 66, *Accounting for Sales of Real Estate*, and No. 98, *Accounting for Leases*

Because FASB Interpretation 43, issued in June 1999, states that sales of integral equipment are within the scope of SFAS 66, *Accounting for Sales of Real Estate*, the determination of whether equipment is integral has increased in importance. A determination of whether equipment to be leased is integral is also necessary for proper accounting for sales-type leases by lessors. This issue discusses how the determination should be made.

The determination of whether equipment is integral should be made based on two factors. The first is the significance of the cost to remove the equipment from its existing location (which would include the costs of repairing the damage done to that location by the removal). The second factor is the decrease in value of the equipment that results from its removal (which is, at a minimum, the cost to ship and reinstall the equipment at the new site). The nature of the equipment and whether others can use it should be considered in determining whether there is further diminution in fair value. When the combined total of the cost to remove and any further diminution of value exceeds 10% of the fair value of the equipment (installed), the equipment is integral equipment.

FASB TECHNICAL BULLETINS

79-10 Fiscal Funding Clauses in Lease Agreements

Question: The effect a fiscal funding clause present in a lease agreement has on the classification of the lease under SFAS 13.

Background: Fiscal funding clauses are common in lease agreements with governmental units under which the lease is contingent upon fund appropriations.

Response: If the likelihood of a fiscal funding clause being exercised is remote, the lease agreement is considered noncancelable. Otherwise, the lease is considered cancelable and should be classified as an operating lease.

79-12 Interest Rate Used in Calculating the Present Value of Minimum Lease Payments

Question: The allowability of the use of the secured borrowing rate by a lessee in computing the present value of minimum lease payments.

Background: SFAS 13 requires the lessee to use its incremental borrowing rate or the lessor's implicit rate if it is lower and known by the lessee.

Response: The lessee may use its secured borrowing rate as its incremental borrowing rate if that rate appears reasonable.

79-13 Applicability of FASB Statement No. 13 to Current Value Financial Statements

Question: Applicability of SFAS 13 to current value financial statements.

Response: The provisions of SFAS 13 apply to current value financial statements.

79-14 Upward Adjustment of Guaranteed Residual Values

Question: Allowability of upward adjustments resulting from renegotiations of guaranteed residual values.

Background: Upward adjustments of residual values are prohibited by SFAS 13.

Response: Upward adjustments of guaranteed residual values in lease agreements are not allowed.

79-15 Accounting for Loss on a Sublease Not Involving the Disposal of a Segment

Question: How to determine and whether to recognize a loss on a sublease.

Response: The general principles for recognition of losses should be followed with respect to expected losses on subleases.

79-16   Effect of a Change in Income Tax Rate on the Accounting for Leveraged Leases

Question: The effect of a change in income tax rate on the accounting for leveraged leases.

Background: CT L10.148 requires that rate of return and allocation of income be recalculated from the date of inception of a lease and a gain or loss recognized when an important assumption is changed.

Response: The income effect on a leveraged lease of a change in the income tax rate should be recognized as a gain or loss in the accounting period in which the rate changes. Deferred taxes relating to the change should be recognized in accordance with SFAS 109.

82-1   Disclosure of the Sale or Purchase of Tax Benefits through Tax Leases

Question: Required disclosures for the sale or purchase of tax benefits through tax leases.

Background: Disclosure is required for transactions involving solely the sale or purchase of tax benefits through tax leases.

Response: Information regarding the accounting policies followed for such transactions is to be disclosed. The disclosure should include the method of recognizing revenue and allocating the income tax benefits and asset costs to current and future periods. In addition, in conformity with the disclosure requirements of SFAS 109, these transactions may result in significant reconciling items between income taxes computed at the domestic federal statutory tax rate and income taxes computed at the effective tax rate applied to pretax income from continuing operations. If such transactions are considered unusual or infrequent to the enterprise, they may warrant separate line-item treatment on the face of the income statement or disclosure in the accompanying notes. Finally, the necessity of disclosure of any loss contingencies associated with the transaction would be evaluated under SFAS 5.

86-2   Accounting for an Interest in the Residual Value of a Leased Asset:

- **Acquired by a Third Party or**
- **Retained by a Lessor That Sells the Related Minimum Rental Payments**

Questions: Various questions concerning the accounting for and valuation of an interest in the residual value of a leased asset acquired by a third party or retained by a lessor that sells the related minimum lease payments.

Response: An interest in the residual value of a leased asset should be recorded as an asset at the amount of cash disbursed, the fair value of other consideration given, and the present value of liabilities assumed at the date the right is acquired, unless the fair value of the interest in the residual value is more clearly evident. A lessor retaining an interest in the residual value of the leased asset should not recognize increases in value, but should recognize other than temporary declines in value. (SFAS 140, which superseded only this provision of FASB TB 86-2, permits recognition of such increases for guaranteed residual values, but not for unguaranteed residual values.)

88-1   Issues Relating to Accounting for Leases

Provides guidance on five issues relating to leases.

1. Question: How to account for escalated rents when the physical use of the property changes under an operating lease.

Response: When a lessee controls the use of the leased property, recognition of rental expense or rental revenue should not be affected by the extent to which the lessee utilizes that property. Escalated rents under agreements giving the lessee the right to control the use of the entire leased property at the beginning of the lease term should be included in the minimum lease payments and recognized on a straight-line basis over the term of the lease.

2. Question: How to account for lease incentives in an operating lease.

Response: Incentives paid to or incurred on behalf of the lessee by the lessor are an inseparable part of the new lease agreement. These costs must be recognized as reductions to rental expense or rental revenue on a straight-line basis over the term of a new lease.

3. Question: The applicability of leveraged lease accounting to existing assets of the lessor.

Response: At the inception of a lease, the cost or carrying value and the fair value of an asset must be the same for the lease to be classified as a direct financing lease which is a necessary condition for leveraged lease treatment. The carrying amount of an existing asset before any write-down must equal its fair value in order for the lease to be classified as a leveraged lease.

4. Question: Whether to recognize income on a money-over-money lease transaction.

Response: If an enterprise manufactures or purchases an asset, leases the asset to a lessee and obtains nonrecourse financing in excess of the asset's cost using the leased asset and the future lease rentals as collateral (a money-over-money lease transaction), a lease broker may recognize income at the beginning of the lease term for the cash received in excess of the carrying amount of the leased asset provided four criteria are met. Some modification of the presentation of the nonrecourse debt and lease receivable is appropriate for leasing transactions meeting all of the criteria for leveraged leases.

5. *Question:* How to account for wrap-lease transactions.

Response: If an enterprise purchases an asset, leases the asset to a lessee, obtains nonrecourse financing using the lease rentals or the lease rentals and the asset as collateral, sells the asset subject to the lease and the nonrecourse debt to a third-party investor, and leases the asset back while remaining the substantive principal lessor under the original lease, the transaction should be accounted for as a sale-leaseback transaction. The subleased asset and the related nonrecourse debt should not be offset in the statement of financial position unless a right of setoff exists.

APPENDIX

LEVERAGED LEASES

One of the more complex accounting subjects regarding leases is the accounting for a leveraged lease. Once again, as with both the sales-type and direct financing, the classification of the lease by the lessor has no impact on the accounting treatment accorded the lease by the lessee. The lessee simply treats it as any other lease and, thus, is only interested in whether the lease qualifies as an operating or capital lease. The lessor's accounting problem is substantially more complex than that of the lessee.

In order to qualify as a leveraged lease, a lease agreement must meet the following requirements, and the lessor must account for the investment tax credit (when in effect) in the manner described below.

NOTE: Failure to do so will result in the lease being classified as a direct financing lease.

1. The lease must meet the definition of a direct financing lease (the 90% of FV criterion does not apply).[6]
2. The lease must involve at least three parties.

   a. An owner-lessor (equity participant)
   b. A lessee
   c. A long-term creditor (debt participant)

3. The financing provided by the creditor is nonrecourse as to the general credit of the lessor and is sufficient to provide the lessor with substantial leverage.
4. The lessor's net investment (defined below) decreases in the early years and increases in the later years until it is eliminated.

This last characteristic poses the accounting issue.

The leveraged lease arose as a result of an effort to maximize the tax benefits associated with a lease transaction. In order to accomplish this, it was necessary to involve a third party to the lease transaction (in addition to the lessor and lessee); a long-term creditor. The following diagram illustrates the existing relationships in a leveraged lease agreement:

The leveraged lease arrangement[7]

---

[6] *A direct financing lease must have its cost or carrying value equal to the fair value of the asset at the lease's inception. So even if the amounts are not significantly different, leveraged lease accounting shall not be used.*

[7] *Adapted from "A Straightforward Approach to Leveraged Leasing" by Pierce R. Smith,* **The Journal of Commercial Bank Lending**, *July 1973, pp. 40-47.*

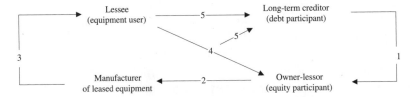

1. The owner-lessor obtains long-term financing from the creditor, generally in excess of 50% of the purchase price. SFAS 13 indicates that the lessor must be provided with sufficient leverage in the transaction, therefore the 50%.
2. The owner then uses this financing along with his/her own funds to purchase the asset from the manufacturer
3. The manufacturer delivers the asset to the lessee
4. The lessee remits the periodic rent to the lessor
5. The debt is guaranteed by either using the equipment as collateral, the assignment of the lease payments, or both, depending on the demands established by the creditor

The FASB concluded that the entire lease agreement be accounted for as a single transaction and not a direct financing lease plus a debt transaction. The feeling was that the latter did not readily convey the lessor's net investment in the lease to the user of the financial statements. Thus, the lessor records the investment as a net amount. The gross investment is calculated as a combination of the following amounts:

1. The rentals receivable from the lessee, net of the principal and interest payments due to the long-term creditor
2. A receivable for the amount of the investment tax credit (ITC) to be realized on the transaction[8]
3. The estimated residual value of the leased asset
4. The unearned and deferred income consisting of

    a. The estimated pretax lease income (or loss), after deducting initial direct costs, remaining to be allocated to income
    b. The ITC remaining to be allocated to income over the remaining term of the lease[8]

The first three amounts described above are readily obtainable; however, the last amount, the unearned and deferred income, requires additional computations. In order to compute this amount, it is necessary to create a cash flow (income) analysis by year for the entire lease term. As described in 4. above, the unearned

---

[8] *The investment tax credit was repealed, effective January 1, 1986. ITC is relevant only for property placed in service prior to this date. We continue to discuss these concepts because Congress has historically reinstated this credit during economic downturns.*

and deferred income consists of the pretax lease income (Gross lease rentals – Depreciation – Loan interest) and the unamortized investment tax credit. The total of these two amounts for all of the periods in the lease term represents the unearned and deferred income at the inception of the lease.

The amount computed as the gross investment in the lease (foregoing paragraphs) less the deferred taxes relative to the difference between pretax lease income and taxable lease income is the net investment for purposes of computing the net income for the period. In order to compute the periodic net income, another schedule must be completed that uses the cash flows derived in the first schedule and allocates them between income and a reduction in the net investment.

The amount of income is first determined by applying a rate to the net investment. The rate to be used is the rate that will allocate the entire amount of cash flow (income) when applied in the years in which the net investment is positive. In other words, the rate is derived in much the same way as the implicit rate (trial and error), except that only the years in which there is a positive net investment are considered. Thus, income is recognized only in the years in which there is a positive net investment.

The income recognized is divided among the following three elements:

1. Pretax accounting income
2. Amortization of investment tax credit
3. The tax effect of the pretax accounting income

The first two shall be allocated in proportionate amounts from the unearned and deferred income included in the calculation of the net investment. In other words, the unearned and deferred income consists of pretax lease accounting income and ITC. Each of these is recognized during the period in the proportion that the current period's allocated income is to the total income (cash flow). The last item, the tax effect, is recognized in the tax expense for the year. The tax effect of any difference between pretax lease accounting income and taxable lease income is charged (or credited) to deferred taxes.

When tax rates change, all components of a leveraged lease must be recalculated from the inception of the lease using the revised after-tax cash flows arising from the revised tax rates.

If, in any case, the projected cash receipts (income) are less than the initial investment, the deficiency is to be recognized as a loss at the inception of the lease. Similarly, if at any time during the lease period the aforementioned method of recognizing income would result in a future period loss, the loss is to be recognized immediately.

This situation may arise as a result of the circumstances surrounding the lease changing. Therefore, any estimated residual value and other important assumptions must be reviewed on a periodic basis (at least annually). Any change is to be incorporated into the income computations; however, there is to be no upward revision of the estimated residual value.

The following example illustrates the application of these principles to a leveraged lease:

Example of simplified leveraged lease

1. A lessor acquires an asset for $100,000 with an estimated useful life of three years in exchange for a $25,000 down payment and a $75,000 three-year note with equal payments due on 12/31 each year. The interest rate is 18%.
2. The asset has no residual value.
3. The PV of an ordinary annuity of $1 for three years at 18% is 2.17427.
4. The asset is leased for three years with annual payments due to the lessor on 12/31 in the amount of $45,000.
5. The lessor uses the ACRS method of depreciation (150% declining balance with a half-year convention in the year placed in service) for tax purposes and elects to reduce the ITC rate to 4% as opposed to reducing the depreciable basis.
6. Assume a constant tax rate throughout the life of the lease of 40%.

Chart 1 analyzes the cash flows generated by the leveraged leasing activities. Chart 2 allocates the cash flows between the investment in leveraged leased assets and income from leveraged leasing activities. The allocation requires finding that rate of return, which when applied to the investment balance at the beginning of each year that the investment amount is positive, will allocate the net cash flow fully to net income over the term of the lease. This rate can be found only by a computer program or by an iterative trial and error process. The example that follows has a positive investment value in each of the three years, and thus the allocation takes place in each time period. Leveraged leases usually have periods where the investment account turns negative and is below zero.

Allocating principal and interest on the loan payments is as follows:

($75,000 ÷ 2.17427 = $34,494)

Year	*Payment*	*Interest 18%*	*Principal*	*Balance*
Inception of lease	$ --	$ --	$ --	$75,000
1	34,494	13,500	20,994	54,006
2	34,494	9,721	24,773	29,233
3	34,494	5,261	29,233	--

Chart 1

	A	B	C	D	E	F	G	H	I
				Taxable	*Income tax payable*	*Loan*		*Cash flow*	*Cumulative*
			Interest	*income (loss)*	*(rcvbl.)*	*principal*		*(A+G-C*	*cash*
	Rent	*Depr.*	*on loan*	*(A-B-C)*	*Dx40%*	*payments*	*ITC*	*-E-F)*	*flow*
Initial	$ --	$ --	$ --	$ --	$ --	$ --	$ --	$(25,000)	$(25,000)
Year 1	45,000	25,000	13,500	6,500	2,600	20,994	4,000	11,906	(13,094)
Year 2	45,000	38,000	9,721	(2,721)	(1,088)	24,773	--	11,594	(1,500)
Year 3	45,000	37,000	5,261	2,739	1,096	29,233	--	9,410	7,910
Total	$135,000	$100,000	$28,482	$ 6,518	$ 2,608	$75,000	$4,000	$ 7,910	

The chart below allocates the cash flows determined above between the net investment in the lease and income. Recall that the income is then allocated between pretax accounting income and the amortization of the investment credit. The income tax expense for the period is a result of applying the tax rate to the current periodic pretax accounting income.

The amount to be allocated in total in each period is the net cash flow determined in column H above. The investment at the beginning of year one is the initial down payment of $25,000. This investment is then reduced on an annual basis by the amount of the cash flow not allocated to income.

Chart 2

	1	2	3	4	5	6	7
		Cash Flow Assumption				*Income Analysis*	
	Investment		*Allocated*	*Allocated*		*Income*	*Investment*
	beginning	*Cash*	*to*	*to*	*Pretax*	*tax*	*tax*
	of year	*flow*	*investment*	*income*	*income*	*expense*	*credit*
Year 1	$25,000	$11,906	$ 7,964	$3,942	$3,248	$1,300	$1,994
Year 2	17,036	11,594	8,908	2,686	2,213	885	1,358
Year 3	8,128	9,410	8,128	1,282	1,057	423	648
		$32,910	$25,000	$7,910	$6,518	$2,608	$4,000

Rate of return = 15.77%

1. Column 2 is the net cash flow after the initial investment, and columns 3 and 4 are the allocation based upon the 15.77% rate of return. The total of column 4 is the same as the total of column H in Chart 1.
2. Column 5 allocates column D in Chart 1 based upon the allocations in column 4. Column 6 allocates column E in Chart 1, (and, of course, is computed as 40% of column 5) and column 7 allocates column G in Chart 1 on the same basis.

The journal entries below illustrate the proper recording and accounting for the leveraged lease transaction. The initial entry represents the cash down payment, investment tax credit receivable, the unearned and deferred revenue, and the net cash to be received over the term of the lease.

The remaining journal entries recognize the annual transactions which include the net receipt of cash and the amortization of income.

	Year 1		*Year 2*		*Year 3*	
Rents receivable [Chart 1 (A-C-F)]	31,518					
Investment tax credit receivable	4,000					
Cash		25,000				
Unearned and deferred income		10,518				
Initial investment, Chart 2 (5+7) totals						
Cash	10,506		10,506		10,506	
Rent receivable		10,506		10,506		10,506
Net for all cash transactions, Chart 1 (A-C-F) line by line for each year						
Income tax receivable (cash)	4,000					
Investment tax credit receivable		4,000				
Unearned and deferred income	5,242		3,571		1,705	
Income from leveraged leases		5,242		3,571		1,705
Amortization of unearned income, Chart 2 (5+7) line by line for each year						

The following schedules illustrate the computation of deferred income tax amount. The annual amount is a result of the temporary difference created due to the difference in the timing of the recognition of income for book and tax purposes. The income for tax purposes can be found in column D in Chart 1, while the income for book purposes is found in column 5 of Chart 2. The actual amount of deferred tax is the difference between the tax computed with the temporary difference and the tax computed without the temporary difference. These amounts are represented by the income tax payable or receivable as shown in column E of Chart 1 and the income tax expense as shown in column 6 of Chart 2. A check of this figure is provided by multiplying the difference between book and tax income by the annual rate.

Year 1

Income tax payable	$ 2,600	
Income tax expense	(1,300)	
Deferred income tax (Dr)		$1,300
Taxable income	$ 6,500	
Pretax accounting income	(3,248)	
Difference	$ 3,252	

$3,252 x 40% = $1,300

Year 2

Income tax receivable	$ 1,088	
Income tax expense	885	
Deferred income tax (Cr)		$1,973
Taxable loss	$ 2,721	
Pretax accounting income	2,213	
Difference	$ 4,934	

$4,934 x 40% = $1,973

Year 3

Income tax payable	$ 1,096	
Income tax expense	(423)	
Deferred income tax (Dr)		$ 673
Taxable income	$ 2,739	
Pretax accounting income	(1,057)	
Difference	$ 1,682	

$1,682 x 40% = $673

15 INCOME TAXES

PERSPECTIVE AND ISSUES

Because periodic income determination for tax reporting purposes and generally accepted accounting principles do not coincide, an entity's income tax liability for a period will not equal the tax provision under GAAP. The difference in periodic income tax expense, which is referred to as the deferred tax provision, has been reportable under GAAP since the 1960s. Originally, given the income statement orientation that was the dominant theme of GAAP at the time, the tax provision was determined to achieve the best matching of pretax earnings and income tax expense. Later, after SFAC 6 was adopted, with its greater emphasis on the measurement of assets and liabilities, a new approach to deferred tax accounting was embraced, first under the ill-fated SFAS 96 (1987) and then under SFAS 109 (1992), which continues as the standard today.

Discounting of deferred taxes has never been permitted under GAAP, even though the ultimate realization of deferred tax assets and liabilities is often far in the future. The recent promulgation of SFAC 7 dealing with present value in accounting measurements, will not change the status of discounting for deferred taxes. As a practical matter, the inability to predict accurately the timing of deferred tax benefits or payments would make discounting very difficult to apply.

SFAS 109 made fundamental changes to the determination of deferred income taxes, and hence to the computation of periodic tax expense. One major change pertained to business combinations. Whereas previously the tax attributes of acquired assets and liabilities were deemed integral to the purchase price allocation process, such that they were to be recorded "net of tax," the new rules require that assets and liabilities be recorded "gross of tax" and that any deferred taxes be recorded separately and reported the same as any other tax effects of temporary differences in the financial statements. Another change is that SFAS 109 makes no distinction between the tax effects of operating losses and other deductible temporary differences, with all being subject to the same recognition and measurement requirements. Also, the former requirement that the tax effects of previously unrecognized operating losses be classed as extraordinary in the income statement, upon realization, has been rescinded.

Deferred tax assets, which were either not reported at all or strictly constrained under earlier GAAP, are now given full recognition. However, deferred tax assets are subject to the provision of an allowance for the portion that is not expected to be realized, using a "more likely than not" criterion, which effectively has been defined as slightly over a 50% probability of occurrence. While there are still certain complexities to be addressed in determining, in any given situation, whether the likelihood of realization is over 50%, these are substantially eased from what the preceding standard, SFAS 96, mandated.

The actual computation of deferred taxes under SFAS 109 has also been facilitated by the FASB's decision to measure them at the average effective tax rate, rather than using the marginal rates as first proposed, or by the actual bracket rates as under the predecessor standard. Changes in expected rates are reflected in earnings as they occur, so that the deferred tax asset and liability accounts are stated at their currently anticipated amounts. Classification as current or noncurrent is generally based on classification of the related asset or liability giving rise to the temporary difference; if that connection cannot be made, SFAS 37, which suggests classification according to timing of expected reversals, provides guidance.

		Sources of GAAP		
APB	*SFAS*	*FASB I*	*FASB TB*	*EITF*
11, 16, 17, 20,	5, 6, 12,	18	83-1	86-9, 86-43, 86-44,
23, 24, 28	37, 52, 96,			88-4, 93-12, 93-13,
	109			93-16, 93-17, 94-10,
				95-10, 95-20, 96-7,
				98-11, 99-15, D-30,
				D-31, D-32, D-33

DEFINITIONS OF TERMS

Deductible temporary differences. Temporary differences that result in future tax deductions; these give rise to deferred tax assets.

Deferred tax asset. The deferred tax consequences of temporary differences that will result in net tax deductions in future years.

Deferred tax liability. The deferred tax consequences of temporary differences that will result in net taxable amounts in future years.

Gains and losses included in comprehensive income but excluded from net income. Certain items which, under GAAP, are events occurring currently but that are reported directly in equity, such as changes in market values of noncurrent portfolios of marketable equity securities.

Interperiod tax allocation. The process of apportioning income tax expense among reporting periods without regard to the timing of the actual cash payments for taxes. The objective is to reflect fully the tax consequences of all economic events reported in current or prior financial statements and, in particular, to report the expected tax effects of the reversals of temporary differences existing at the reporting date.

Intraperiod tax allocation. The process of apportioning income tax expense applicable to a given period between income before extraordinary items and those items required to be shown net of tax such as extraordinary items and prior period adjustments.

Operating loss carryback or carryforward. The excess of tax deductions over taxable income. To the extent that this results in a carryforward, the tax effect thereof is included in the entity's deferred tax asset.

Permanent differences. Differences between pretax accounting income and taxable income as a result of the treatment accorded certain transactions by the income tax regulations that differ from the accounting treatment. Permanent differences will not reverse in subsequent periods.

Pretax accounting income. Income or loss for the accounting period as determined in accordance with GAAP without regard to the income tax expense for the period.

Taxable income. The difference between the revenue and expenses as defined by the Internal Revenue Code for a taxable period without regard to the special deductions (e.g., net operating loss or contribution carrybacks and carryforwards).

Taxable temporary differences. Temporary differences that result in future taxable amounts; these give rise to deferred tax liabilities.

Tax credits. Reductions in the tax liability as a result of certain expenditures accorded special treatment under the Internal Revenue Code. Examples of such credits are: the Investment Tax Credit, investment in certain depreciable property; the Jobs Credit, payment of wages to targeted groups; the Research and Development Credit, an increase in qualifying R&D expenditures; and others.

Tax planning strategy. A representation by management of a planned transaction or series of transactions that would affect the particular future years in which temporary differences will result in taxable or deductible amounts.

Temporary differences. In general, differences between tax and financial reporting bases of assets and liabilities that will result in taxable or deductible amounts in future periods. Temporary differences include "timing differences" as defined by prior GAAP as well as certain other differences, such as those arising from business combinations. Some temporary differences cannot be associated with particular assets or liabilities, but nonetheless do result from events that received financial statement recognition and will have tax effects in future periods.

Unrecognized tax benefits. Deferred tax benefits against which a valuation allowance had been provided as of the date of the financial statements.

Valuation allowance. The contra asset which is to be reflected to the extent that it is "more likely than not" that the deferred tax asset will not be realized.

CONCEPTS, RULES, AND EXAMPLES

Evolution of Accounting for Income Taxes

The differences in the timing of recognition of certain expenses and revenues for tax reporting purposes versus under GAAP had always raised issues for financial reporting. Some argued that only the amount of tax currently owed should be reported as periodic tax expense, on the grounds that potential changes in tax law and the vagaries of the entity's future financial performance would make any projection to future periods speculative. Others held that the matching principle, which is fundamental to GAAP, demanded that reported periodic tax expense be related to pretax accounting income, whether or not that corresponded to the amount of taxes actually payable currently. Yet others took a middle ground approach, acknowledging the need for some deferred tax provision, but only when actual future tax payments or benefits could be accurately foretold. In the US, this debate (among proponents of no interperiod tax allocation, comprehensive allocation, and partial allocation, respectively) was settled long ago, with comprehensive allocation being the victor.

In the 1960s, accounting theory tended to stress the paramount importance of the income statement, with the balance sheet being of substantially lesser interest. The debate over the means of computing periodic deferred tax provisions was, accordingly, won by those who held that compliance with the matching principle was most critical, which resulted in the prescription under APB 11 that the "deferred method" be employed. The annual tax provision (consisting of current and deferred portions) was calculated so that it would bear the expected relationship to pretax accounting income; any excess or deficiency was taken to the deferred tax account on the balance sheet. This account represented a net deferred debit or a deferred credit, which did not necessarily mean that an asset or liability, as defined under GAAP, actually existed in the reported amount.

By the late 1970s, accounting theory (and especially the FASB's financial accounting concepts project) was placing financial reporting priority on the statement of financial position, and specifically on the accurate measurement of assets and liabilities. SFAC 6's definitions of assets and liabilities clearly would not include deferred tax benefits or obligations as these were then being measured. Determination of deferred taxes consistent with a balance sheet orientation makes use of the "liability method," which essentially ascertains, as of each balance sheet date, the amount of future tax benefits or obligations that are associated with the reporting entity's assets and liabilities as of that date. The adjustment necessary to bring the deferred taxes up or down to the correct balance, plus or minus the amount of taxes due currently, determines that periodic tax provision to be reported in the income statement.

The transition to a balance-sheet-oriented measurement approach began with the issuance of SFAS 96, which added a number of complexities to the computation of deferred taxes, while embracing the inherently more straightforward liability approach. SFAS 96 proved to be unwieldy in practice; the effective date of this standard had to be postponed several times, and it was never universally implemented. Chief among the complaints was the need to precisely schedule out the future reversals of temporary differences, which was necessitated by SFAS 96's insistence that deferred tax assets only be recognized to the extent it could be demonstrated that the related reversals of deductible items would be offset by other reversals of taxable items for tax purposes. As a practical matter, this scheduling requirement was very difficult, if not actually unworkable.

SFAS 109 was the replacement for SFAS 96; it was promulgated before most enterprises had ever adopted SFAS 96. SFAS 109 also embraces the balance-sheet-oriented liability method, but takes a diametrically opposite stance concerning deferred tax assets. Under this standard, all deferred tax assets (arising from deductible temporary differences or from operating losses or tax credit carryforwards—no distinctions are made) are given full recognition. However, it is necessary (as with all assets) to assess the possible existence of an impairment; this is done by means of a "more-likely-than-not" criterion which results, when necessary, in the provision of a reserve or allowance account to offset some or all of the deferred tax asset. While the determination of the amount of such allowance may make use of the scheduling of reversals, similar to that required by SFAS 96, other methods may also be employed and, in general, this is a less rigorous, more flexible standard in regard to the financial statement presentation of tax assets.

In summary, interperiod income tax allocation under GAAP is now based on the liability method, using comprehensive allocation. While the basic principle is straightforward, however, there are a number of computational complexities to be addressed. These will be presented in the remainder of this chapter.

An example of application of the liability method of deferred income tax accounting follows.

Simplified example of interperiod allocation using the liability method

Gries International has no permanent differences in either years 2002 or 2003. The company has only two temporary differences, depreciation and prepaid rent. No consideration is given to the nature of the deferred tax account (i.e., current or long-term) as it is not considered necessary for purposes of this example. Gries has a credit balance in its deferred tax account at the beginning of 2002 in the amount of $180,000. This balance consists of $228,000 ($475,000 depreciation temporary difference x 48% tax rate) of deferred taxable amounts and $48,000 ($100,000 prepaid rent temporary difference x 48% tax rate) of deferred deductible amounts.

For purposes of this example, it is assumed that there was a constant 48% tax rate in all of the prior periods. The pretax accounting income and the temporary differences originating and reversing in 2002 and 2003 are as follows:

Gries International

	2002		2003	
Pretax accounting income		$800,000		$1,200,000
Timing differences:				
Depreciation—originating	$(180,000)		$(160,000)	
reversing	60,000	(120,000)	100,000	(60,000)
Prepaid rental income—originating	75,000		80,000	
reversing	(25,000)	50,000	(40,000)	40,000
Taxable income		$730,000		$1,180,000

The tax rates for years four and five are 46% and 38%, respectively. These rates are assumed to be independent of one another and the 2003 change in the rate was not known until it took place in 2003.

Computation of tax provision—2002

Balance of deferred tax account, 1/1/02	
Depreciation ($475,000 x 48%)	$228,000
Prepaid rental income ($100,000 x 48%)	(48,000)
	$180,000

Aggregate temporary differences, 12/31/02
Depreciation ($475,000 + 120,000)	$595,000	
Prepaid rental income ($100,000 + 50,000)	(150,000)	
	$445,000	
Expected future rate (2002 rate)	x 46%	
Balance required in the deferred tax account, 12/31/02		204,700
Required addition to the deferred tax account		$ 24,700
Income taxes currently payable ($730,000 x 46%)		335,800
Total tax provision		$360,500

Computation of tax provision—2003

Balance of deferred tax account, 1/1/03
Depreciation ($595,000 x 46%)		$273,700
Prepaid rental income ($150,000 x 46%)		(69,000)
		$204,700

Aggregate timing differences, 12/31/03
Depreciation ($595,000 + 60,000)	$655,000	
Prepaid rental income ($150,000 + 40,000)	(190,000)	
	$465,000	
Expected future rate (2003 rate)	x 38%	
Balance required in the deferred tax account, 12/31/03		176,700
Required reduction in the deferred tax account		$(28,000)
Income taxes currently payable ($1,180,000 x 38%)		448,400
Total tax provision		$420,400

SFAS 109 in Greater Detail

While conceptually the liability method is rather straightforward, in practice there are a number of complexities to be addressed. SFAS 109 presents fewer of these difficulties than existed under its predecessor, SFAS 96, yet this subject still remains one of the more difficult areas of accounting practice. In the following pages, these measurement and reporting issues will be discussed in greater detail.

1. The nature of temporary differences
2. Treatment of operating loss carryforwards
3. The measurement of deferred tax assets and liabilities
4. The valuation allowance for deferred tax assets which are "more likely than not" to be not realizable
5. The effect of tax law changes on previously recorded deferred tax assets and liabilities
6. The effect of tax status changes on previously incurred deferred tax assets and liabilities
7. Tax effects of business combinations
8. Intercorporate income tax allocation
9. Exceptions to the general rules of SFAS 109

Detailed examples of deferred income tax accounting under SFAS 109 are presented throughout the following discussion of these issues.

The Nature of Temporary Differences

Many or most typical business transactions will be accounted for identically for tax and financial reporting purposes. Thus, most items of revenue and expense reportable in a fiscal period will also be taxable or deductible in that same tax year. Some transactions and events, however, will be subject to disparate tax and accounting treatments, leading to reporting in different periods. Under the prior standard, APB 11, these differences were referred to as "timing differences" and were said to originate in one period and to reverse in a later period. Common timing differences were those deriving from depreciation methods, deferred compensation plans, percentage-of-completion accounting for long-term construction contracts, and cash basis vs. accrual accounting.

The idea of timing differences was replaced by the more comprehensive concept of temporary differences, first as incorporated in SFAS 96 and then in SFAS 109. Temporary differences include all differences between the tax and financial reporting bases of assets and liabilities, if those differences will result in taxable or deductible amounts in future years. Consistent with the underlying objective of the liability method, the key characteristic of a temporary difference is the existence of a balance sheet asset or liability which has a differential measure for tax and book purposes, as contrasted with the earlier reliance on the occurrence of an income statement event to identify an originating timing difference.

Historically, the most common example of an item which did **not** represent a temporary difference had been goodwill, since traditionally this asset, mandatorily amortizable under GAAP, would never become tax deductible. However, this changed with the 1993 tax law, which required that goodwill be amortized over fifteen years. Deferred taxes are to be provided for all temporary differences, but for no permanent differences.

Temporary differences under SFAS 109 that were also timing differences under APB 11 include the following:

Revenue recognized for financial reporting purposes before being recognized for tax purposes. Revenue accounted for by the installment method for tax purposes, but reflected in income currently; certain construction-related revenue recognized on a completed-contract method for tax purposes, but on a percentage-of-completion basis for financial reporting; earnings from investees recognized by the equity method for accounting purposes but taxed only when later distributed as dividends to the investor. These are taxable temporary differences that give rise to deferred tax liabilities.

Revenue recognized for tax purposes prior to recognition in the financial statements. Certain revenue received in advance, such as prepaid rental income and service contract revenue. These are deductible temporary differences in the terminology of SFAS 109, and give rise to deferred tax assets.

Expenses which are deductible for tax purposes prior to recognition in the financial statements. Accelerated depreciation methods or shorter useful lives used for tax purposes, while straight-line depreciation or longer useful economic lives are used for financial reporting; certain preoperating costs and certain capitalized interest costs which are currently tax deductible. These items are taxable temporary differences, and give rise to deferred tax liabilities.

Expenses which are reported in the financial statements prior to becoming deductible for tax purposes. Certain estimated expenses, such as warranty costs, as well as such contingent losses as accruals of litigation expenses, are not tax deductible until the obligation becomes fixed. These are deductible temporary differences, and accordingly give rise to deferred tax assets.

In addition to these familiar and well-understood timing differences, temporary differences include a number of other categories that also involve differences between the tax and financial reporting bases of assets or liabilities. These are

Reductions in tax deductible asset bases arising in connection with tax credits. Under the provisions of the 1982 tax act, taxpayers were permitted a choice of either full ACRS depreciation coupled with a reduced investment tax credit, or a full investment tax credit coupled with reduced depreciation allowances. If the taxpayer chose the latter option, the asset basis was reduced for tax depreciation, but was still fully depreciable for financial reporting purposes. Accordingly, this election was accounted for as a taxable timing difference, and gave rise to a deferred tax liability. This particular accounting treatment was first prescribed by FASB TB 83-1, and was later incorporated in SFAS 96. It has now been included in SFAS 109 as well.

Investment tax credits accounted for by the deferral method. Under GAAP, investment tax credits could be accounted for by either the "flow through" method (by far the most common method in practice), or by the "deferral" method. Under the latter method, the tax credit was reflected in income over the useful lives of the assets giving rise to the credit, although the benefit of the credit was fully received in the years the assets were placed in service. Thus, a deductible temporary difference existed, with which a deferred tax asset would be associated.

The two categories discussed immediately above are no longer of much interest since the investment tax credit was eliminated under current tax law. Of course, there remains the possibility that the ITC could be revived under a future revision of the income tax laws.

Increases in the tax bases of assets resulting from the indexing of asset costs for the effects of inflation. Occasionally proposed but never enacted, such a tax law provision would allow taxpaying entities to finance the replacement of depreciable assets through depreciation based on current costs, as computed by the application of indices to the historical costs of the assets being remeasured. This reevaluation of asset costs would give rise to deductible temporary differences that would be associated with deferred tax benefits.

Certain business combinations accounted for by the purchase method. Under certain circumstances, the costs assignable to assets or liabilities acquired in purchase business combinations will differ from their tax bases. Such differences may be either taxable or deductible and, accordingly, may give rise to deferred tax liabilities or assets. These differences now are explicitly recognized by the reporting of deferred taxes in the consolidated financial statements of the acquiring entity.

Note that these differences are no longer allocable to the financial reporting bases of the underlying assets or liabilities themselves, as was the case under APB 11's **net of tax** method.

A financial reporting situation in which deferred taxes may or may not be appropriate would include life insurance (such as keyman insurance) under which the reporting entity is the beneficiary. Since proceeds of life insurance are not subject to income tax under present law, the excess of cash surrender values over the sum of premiums paid will **not** be a temporary difference under the provisions of SFAS 109, if the intention is to hold the policy until death benefits are received. On the other hand, if the entity intends to cash in the policy at some point (i.e., it is holding the insurance contract as an investment), which would be a taxable event, then the excess surrender value is in fact a temporary difference, and deferred taxes should be provided thereon.

Treatment of Operating Loss Carryforwards

The recognition and measurement of the tax effects of net operating loss carryforwards under SFAS 109 differs materially from earlier standards. Under APB 11, the presumption was that operating losses would generally not be realizable; accordingly, no provision for the tax effects of carryforwards would be made in the financial statements until such time as the benefits were in fact realized for tax purposes. That is, the provision for income taxes in the loss year would generally not reflect benefits of the pretax accounting loss in excess of the amount available as a carryback. (A further amount, up to the existing deferred tax liabilities, could also be recognized to the extent the timing differences related thereto were scheduled to reverse during the statutory carryforward period, thus assuring the entity of realization of the tax benefits of the NOL.) Under that standard, the balance sheet could not display a deferred tax benefit relating to the tax loss carryforward.

This treatment was justified on the basis that assets are not to be reported at amounts greater than net realizable value. In exceptional cases, when realization of the future benefits was deemed to be assured beyond a reasonable doubt (usually justifiable only when losses were highly unusual and recurring annual profits were fairly predictable), recognition in the loss period was permitted.

SFAS 96, the short-lived standard that replaced APB 11, was even more strict with regard to operating losses. The presentation of net deferred tax debits was prohibited, to the extent that they exceeded amounts that would be recoverable through operating loss carrybacks as of the date of the balance sheet. This proscription was based on the view that the display of deferred tax benefits would have been tantamount to anticipating future income. Even the narrow "assured beyond a reasonable doubt" exception provided under APB 11 was foreclosed by SFAS 96.

Under SFAS 109, however, all temporary differences are given identical status, and the tax effects thereof are to be given equal recognition in the balance sheet. Specifically, the tax effects of net operating loss carryforwards are equal to the tax effects of other deductible temporary differences, and the once important distinction between the two has been eliminated. The deferred tax effects of operating losses should be computed and provided for—although, as with all other deferred tax assets, the need for a valuation allowance must also be assessed (as discussed below). The tax effects of credit carryforwards are handled in precisely the same manner as are the tax effects of operating losses.

The reporting of the tax benefit of operating losses has also been changed by the current standard. SFAS 109 provides that the tax benefits of operating loss carrybacks and carryforwards, with limited exceptions (discussed below), are to be reported in the same manner as the source of either income or loss in the current year. As used in the standard, the phrase **in the same manner** refers to the classification of the tax benefit in the income statement (i.e., as taxes on income from continuing operations, discontinued operations, extraordinary items, etc.) or as the tax effect of gains included in comprehensive income but excluded from the income statement. The tax benefits are **not** reported in the same manner as the source of the loss carryforward or taxes paid in a prior year, or as the source of the expected future income that will permit the realization of the carryforward.

For example, if the tax benefit of a loss which arose in a prior year in connection with an extraordinary item is first given recognition in the current year, the benefit would be allocated to taxes on income from continuing operations if the benefit offsets taxes on income from continuing operations in the current year. The expression **first given recognition** means that the **net** deferred tax asset, after deducting the valuation allowance, reflects the tax effect of the loss carryforward for the first time.

Under SFAS 109, of course, the **gross** deferred tax asset will always reflect all deductible temporary differences, including loss carryforwards, in the periods they arise. Thus, **first given recognition** means that the valuation allowance is eliminated for the first time. If it offsets taxes on extraordinary income in the current year, then the benefits would be reported in extraordinary items. As another example, the tax benefit arising from the entity's loss from continuing operations in the current year would be allocated to continuing operations, regardless of whether it might be realized as a carryback against taxes paid on extraordinary items in prior years. The benefit would also be allocated to continuing operations in cases where it is anticipated that the benefit will be realized through the reduction of taxes to be due on extraordinary gains in future years.

Thus, the general rule is that the reporting of tax effects of operating losses are driven by the source of the tax benefits in the current period. There are only two exceptions to the foregoing rule. The first exception relates to existing deductible temporary differences, including operating loss carryforwards which arise in connection with purchase business combinations and for which tax benefits are first recognized. This exception will be discussed below (see tax effects of business combinations).   As in the preceding paragraph, **first recognized** means that a valuation allowance provided previously is being eliminated for the first time.

A second exception to the aforementioned general rule is that certain tax benefits allocable to stockholders' equity are **not** to be reflected in the income statement. Specifically, tax benefits arising in connection with contributed capital, employee stock options, dividends paid on unallocated ESOP shares, or temporary differences existing at the date of a quasi reorganization are reported in the stockholders' equity section and are not included in results of operations.

Measurement of Deferred Tax Assets and Liabilities

SFAS 109 eliminates the need to schedule reversals mandated by SFAS 96 in all but the most exceptional circumstances.   To eliminate the scheduling requirement, it was necessary to endorse the use of the expected average (i.e., effective) income tax rate to measure the deferred tax assets and liabilities, and to omit the more precise measure of marginal tax effects prescribed by the prior standard. Since the greatest objection to SFAS 96 was over its scheduling requirement, this simplification was accepted.

Scheduling will now be encountered primarily when tax rate changes are to be phased in, as well as in a few other situations in which the reporting entity must identify particular years of temporary difference reversals in order to meaningfully calculate their expected tax effects.   There may, however, also be a need to engage in scheduling in order to determine the amount of valuation allowance needed (as discussed in the following section of this chapter).

Reporting entities traditionally having taxable income over $335,000 will face an expected tax rate equal to the 34% marginal rate, since the effect of the surtax exemption has phased out at that level, effectively resulting in a flat tax. Thus, the computation of deferred taxes can be accomplished simply by applying the top marginal rate to all temporary differences outstanding as of the balance sheet date. This technique would be applied both to taxable temporary differences (producing deferred tax liabilities), and to deductible temporary differences (giving rise to deferred tax assets). The deferred tax **assets** computed must still be evaluated for impairment; some, or all, of the projected tax benefits may fail the "more-likely-than-not" test and consequently may need to be offset by a valuation allowance account.

On the other hand, reporting entities which have historically been taxed at an effective federal rate lower than the top marginal rate will compute their deferred tax provisions with reference to their expected, or **effective**, income tax rates. Consistent with the goal of simplifying the process of calculating deferred taxes, entities are permitted to apply a single, long-term expected tax rate, without attempting to differentiate among the years when temporary difference reversals are expected to occur. In any event, the inherent imprecision of forecasting future income levels and the patterns of temporary difference reversals makes it unlikely that a more sophisticated computational effort would produce better financial statements. Therefore, absent such factors as the phasing in of new tax rates, it will not be necessary to consider whether the reporting entity's effective tax rate will vary from year to year.

The effective tax rate convention also facilitated the elimination of one of the least popular features of SFAS 96: the requirement that alternative minimum tax (AMT) be calculated each year for which reversals of temporary differences were scheduled. Application of the AMT was necessary because SFAS 96 applied low statutory rates to at least some, and possibly even all, of the taxable temporary differences. As a consequence, the AMT would have often applied and the reporting entity would have been obliged to pay the higher AMT rather than the lesser regular tax. The result was that reporting entities needed to compute both regular and alternative minimum taxes for each future year; the higher of these would then be used as the necessary deferred tax provision for that future year. AMT credits were then carried forward to be utilized in later years, if any, when regular tax would exceed alternative minimum tax. Under SFAS 109, no attention need be paid to the AMT in computing deferred taxes. By employing the expected tax rate, the number of computations is reduced to as few as one, compared to computations numbering twice the future years over which temporary differences were expected to reverse.

The procedure to compute the gross deferred tax provision (i.e., before addressing the possible need for a valuation allowance) is as follows:

1. Identify all temporary differences existing as of the reporting date.
2. Segregate the temporary differences into those that are taxable and those that are deductible. This step is necessary because a valuation allowance may be provided against the tax effects of the deductible temporary differences, but not against the tax effects of the taxable temporary differences.
3. Accumulate information about the deductible temporary differences, particularly the net operating loss and credit carryforwards that have expiration dates or other types of limitations.
4. Measure the tax effect of aggregate taxable temporary differences by applying the appropriate expected tax rates (federal plus any state, local, and foreign rates that are applicable under the circumstances).
5. Similarly, measure the tax effects of deductible temporary differences, including net operating loss carryforwards.

Separate computations should be made for each tax jurisdiction, since in assessing the need for valuation allowances it is necessary to consider the entity's ability to absorb deferred tax benefits against tax liabilities. Inasmuch as benefits in one tax jurisdiction will not reduce taxes payable in another jurisdiction, these separate calculations will be needed. Also, for purposes of balance sheet presentation (discussed below), offsetting of deferred tax assets and liabilities are only permissible within jurisdictions. Separate computations should be made for each taxpaying component of the business: if a parent company and its subsidiaries are consolidated for financial reporting purposes but file separate tax returns, the reporting entity comprises a number of components, and the tax benefits of any one will be unavailable to reduce the tax obligations of the others.

The principles set forth above are illustrated by the following examples:

Computation of deferred tax liability and asset—Basic example

Assume that Northern Company has pretax financial income of $250,000 in 2002, a total of $28,000 of taxable temporary differences, and a total of $8,000 of deductible temporary differences. There are no operating loss or tax credit carryforwards. The tax rate is a flat (i.e., not graduated) 40%. Also assume that there were no deferred tax liabilities or assets in prior years. Taxable income is computed as follows:

Pretax financial income	$250,000
Taxable temporary differences	(28,000)
Deductible temporary differences	8,000
Taxable income	$230,000

The journal entry to record required amounts is

Current income tax expense	92,000	
Deferred tax asset	3,200	
Income tax expense—deferred	8,000	
Deferred tax liability		11,200
Income taxes currently payable		92,000

Current income tax expense and income taxes currently payable are each computed as taxable income times the current rate ($230,000 x 40%). The deferred tax asset of $3,200 represents 40% of deductible temporary differences of $8,000. The deferred tax liability of $11,200 is calculated as 40% of taxable temporary differences of $28,000. The deferred tax expense of $8,000 is the **net** of the deferred tax liability of $11,200 and the deferred tax asset of $3,200.

In 2003, Northern Company has pretax financial income of $450,000, aggregate taxable and deductible temporary differences are $75,000 and $36,000, respectively, and the tax rate remains a flat 40%.

Taxable income is $411,000, computed as pretax financial income of $450,000 minus taxable differences of $75,000 plus deductible differences of $36,000. Current income tax expense and income taxes currently payable each are $164,400 ($411,000 x 40%).

Deferred amounts are calculated as follows:

	Deferred tax liability	*Deferred tax asset*	*Income tax expense—deferred*
Required balance at 12/31/03			
$75,000 x 40%	$30,000		--
$36,000 x 40%		$14,400	--
Balances at 12/31/02	11,200	3,200	--
Adjustment required	$18,800	$11,200	$7,600

The journal entry to record the deferred amounts is

Deferred tax asset	11,200	
Income tax expense—deferred	7,600	
Deferred tax liability		18,800

Because the **increase** in the liability in 2003 is larger (by $7,600) than the increase in the asset for that year, the result is a deferred tax **expense** for 2003.

The Valuation Allowance for Deferred Tax Assets Which Are More Likely Than Not to Be *Not* Realizable

Prior to SFAS 109, the presentation of deferred tax assets in the balance sheet was constrained or prohibited entirely. SFAS 109 requires that all deferred tax assets be given full recognition, subject to possible offsetting when it is determined that the asset has been impaired. This approach (providing full recognition on a gross basis, but also providing for a valuation or allowance account to reduce the net reported benefit to the unimpaired amount) conveys the greatest amount of useful information to the users of the financial statements.

To ascertain the extent of impairment to the deferred tax asset, the Board could have relied upon the longstanding guidance of SFAS 5, defining the threshold for recognition of the net benefit as the amount of benefit "probable" of realization. The Board rejected the notion of applying that standard to this measurement situation, however. Instead, it developed a new measure, the "more-likely-than-not" criterion, which has thus far been applied exclusively to this situation. The Board has ruled that a valuation allowance is to be provided for that fraction of the computed year-end balances of the deferred tax assets for which it has been determined that it is more likely than not that the reported asset amount will not be realized.

As used in this context, "more likely than not" represents a probability of just over 50%. Since it is widely agreed that the term probable, as used in SFAS 5, denotes a much higher probability (possibly a likelihood as high as 85% to 90%), the threshold for reflecting an asset impairment in the case of deferred tax assets is much lower than is the corresponding threshold for recognition of impairments of other assets.

One reason for the Board's action in developing this new criterion was the concern over whether the threshold test would be applied to the deferred tax asset recognition decision or to the derecognition decision. If to the former, then a criterion such as "assured beyond a reasonable doubt" (such as was applied for the recognition of the benefits of net operating losses under APB 11) could be seen as being too high a threshold; tax benefits which in fact are likely to be realized would be precluded from recognition by such a test. If the threshold criterion were to be applied to the derecognition decision (i.e., for provision of an allowance account), as would a strict application of the SFAS 5 test, then some tax benefits which were **not** likely to have been realizable would still have been reported, since they would fail the high threshold test of probable impairment.

Thus, the concern was whether the threshold test would be utilized as a criterion for recognition of the deferred tax asset, or as a criterion for the recognition of the contra asset (allowance) account, which would thus imply the test was for the derecognition of the asset, not its recognition. To avoid the possibility of ambiguity and of very different results being obtained in essentially identical circumstances, the Board's solution was to devise a threshold test that would produce essentially the same result whether applied to the recognition or to the derecognition decision. Since the more-likely-than-not criterion implies a probability of very close to 50%, the same **net** deferred tax asset would result whether the approach taken was to record only those deferred tax assets which are more likely than not to be realized, or whether the measurement approach was to derecognize (that is, to reserve against) the asset to the extent that it was more likely than not that it would not be realized.

Establishment of a valuation allowance

Assume that Zebra Corporation has a deductible temporary difference of $60,000 at December 31, 2002. The tax rate is a flat 40%. Based on available evidence, management of Zebra Corporation concludes that it is more likely than not that all sources will not result in future taxable income sufficient to realize a tax benefit of more than $15,000 (25% of deductible temporary differences). Also assume that there were no deferred tax assets in previous years and that prior years' taxable income was inconsequential.

At 12/31/02 Zebra Corporation records a deferred tax asset in the amount of $24,000 ($60,000 x 40%) and a valuation allowance of $18,000 (40% of the difference between the $60,000 of deductible temporary differences and the $15,000 of expected future taxable income to absorb a portion of the tax benefit).

The journal entry at 12/31/02 is

Deferred tax asset	24,000	
Valuation allowance		18,000
Income tax benefit—deferred		6,000

The deferred income tax benefit of $6,000 represents that portion of the deferred tax asset (25%) that is more likely than not to be realized.

In 2000 assume that Zebra Corporation's results are

Pretax financial loss	$(32,000)
Reversing deductible differences from 2002	(10,000)
Loss carryforward for tax purposes:	$(42,000)

The total of the loss carryforward (computed above) plus the amount of deductible temporary differences from 2002 not reversing in 2003 ($50,000) is $92,000. A deferred tax asset of $36,800 ($92,000 x 40%) is recognized at the end of 2002. Also assume that management of Zebra Corporation concludes that it is more likely than not that $25,000 of the tax asset will **not** be realized. Thus, a valuation allowance in that amount is required, and the balance in the allowance account of $18,000 must be increased by $7,000 ($25,000 – $18,000).

The journal entry at 12/31/02 is

Deferred tax asset	12,800	
Valuation allowance		7,000
Income tax benefit—deferred		5,800

The deferred tax asset is debited $12,800 to increase it from $24,000 at the end of 2002 to its required balance of $36,800 at the end of 2003. Deferred tax **benefit** of $5,800 represents the **net** of the $12,800 increase in the deferred tax asset and the $7,000 increase in the valuation allowance account.

While the meaning of the **more-likely-than-not** criterion is clear, the practical difficulty of assessing whether or not this threshold test is met in a given situation remains. A number of positive and negative factors need to be evaluated in reaching a conclusion as to whether a valuation allowance is needed. Positive factors (those suggesting that a reserve is not necessary) include

1. Evidence of sufficient future taxable income, exclusive of reversing temporary differences and carryforwards, to realize the benefit of the deferred tax asset
2. Evidence of sufficient future taxable income arising from the reversals of existing taxable temporary differences (deferred tax liabilities) to realize the benefit of the tax asset
3. Evidence of sufficient taxable income in prior year(s) available for realization of an operating loss carryback under existing statutory limitations.
4. Evidence of the existence of prudent, feasible **tax planning strategies** under management control that, if implemented, would permit the realization of the tax asset
5. An excess of appreciated asset values over their tax bases, in an amount sufficient to realize the deferred tax asset
6. A strong earnings history exclusive of the loss that created the deferred tax asset

While the foregoing may suggest that the reporting entity will be able to realize the benefits of the deductible temporary differences outstanding as of the balance sheet date, certain negative factors must also be considered in determining whether a valuation allowance should be established against deferred tax assets. These factors include

1. A cumulative recent history of losses
2. A history of operating losses, or of tax operating loss or credit carryforwards which have expired unused
3. Losses which are anticipated in the near future years, despite a history of profitable operations

Thus, the process of evaluating whether a valuation allowance is needed involves the weighing of both positive and negative factors to determine whether, based on the preponderance of available evidence, it is more likely than not that the deferred tax assets will be realized.

To illustrate the computation of the valuation allowance required in a specific situation, assume the following facts:

1. Mary-lynn Corporation reports on a calendar year, and adopted SFAS 109 in 2000.

2. As of the December 31, 2002 balance sheet, it has taxable temporary differences of $85,000 relating to depreciation; deductible temporary differences of $12,000 relating to deferred compensation arrangements; a net operating loss carryforward (which arose in 1999) of $40,000; and a capital loss carryover of $10,000.

3. Mary-lynn's expected tax rate for future years is 40% for ordinary income, and 25% for net long-term capital gains. Capital losses cannot be offset against ordinary income.

The first steps are to compute the required balances of the deferred tax asset and liability accounts, without consideration of the possible need for a valuation allowance. The computations would proceed as follows:

Deferred tax liability:

Taxable temporary difference (depreciation)	$85,000
Effective tax rate	x 40%
Required balance	$34,000

Deferred tax asset:

Deductible temporary differences:	
Deferred compensation	$12,000
Net operating loss	40,000
	$52,000
Effective tax rate	x 40%
Required balance (a)	$20,800
Capital loss	$10,000
Effective tax rate	x 25%
Required balance (b)	$ 2,500

Total deferred tax asset:

Ordinary	$20,800
Capital	2,500
Total required balance	$23,300

The next step would be to consider the need for a valuation allowance to partially or completely offset the deferred tax asset, based on an assessment that is more likely than not that the asset is not going to be realized. Mary-lynn management must evaluate both positive and negative evidence to determine the need for a valuation allowance, if any. Assume now that management identifies the following factors that may affect this need:

1. Before the net operating loss deduction, Mary-lynn reported taxable income of $5,000 in 2002. Management believes that taxable income in future years, apart from NOL deductions, should continue at approximately the same level experienced in 2002.

2. The taxable temporary differences are not expected to reverse in the foreseeable future.

3. The capital loss arose in connection with a transaction of a type that is unlikely to recur. The company does not generally engage in activities that have the potential to result in capital gains or losses.

4. Management estimates that certain productive assets have a fair value exceeding their respective tax bases by about $30,000. The entire gain, if realized for tax purposes, would be a recapture of depreciation previously taken. Since the current plans call for a substantial upgrading of the company's plant assets, management feels it could easily accelerate those actions in order to realize taxable gains, should it be desirable to do so for tax planning purposes.

Based on the foregoing information, Mary-lynn Corporation management concludes that a $2,500 valuation allowance is required. The reasoning is as follows:

1. There will be some taxable operating income generated in future years ($5,000 annually, based on the earnings experienced in 2002), which will absorb a modest portion of the reversal of the deductible temporary difference ($12,000) and net operating loss carryforward ($40,000) existing at year-end 2002.

2. More importantly, the feasible tax planning strategy of accelerating the taxable gain relating to appreciated assets ($30,000) would certainly be sufficient, in conjunction with operating income over several years, to permit Mary-lynn to realize the tax benefits of the deductible temporary difference and NOL carryover.

3. However, since capital loss carryovers are only usable to offset future capital gains, and Mary-lynn management is unable to project future realization of capital gains, the associated tax benefit accrued ($2,500) will more likely than not be realized, and thus must be reserved against.

Based on this analysis, an allowance for unrealizable deferred tax benefits in the amount of $2,500 should be established by a charge against the current (2002) tax provision.

Of the various positive and negative factors to be considered, perhaps the most difficult to fully grasp is the role to be played by available tax planning strategies. Under the provisions of SFAS 96, tax planning strategies were an important consideration in determining whether the tax benefits of deductible temporary differences would be available to be absorbed against taxes owed pursuant to taxable timing differences. SFAS 96 prohibited the "use" (for computation purposes) of any tax planning strategy that would have involved the incurrence of significant costs. This stance was logical in the framework of SFAS 96's requirement to not anticipate any future events that were not inherently assumed in the financial statements.

The role of tax planning strategies in SFAS 109 differs markedly from that in SFAS 96, however. Since SFAS 109 requires that all available evidence be assessed to determine the need for a valuation allowance, there is less concern about the cost of implementing those strategies. In fact, there is no limitation as there was under the prior standard regarding strategies that may involve significant costs of implementation. However, any costs of implementation must be netted against the benefits to be derived from such implementation in arriving at the measurement of the amount of valuation allowance needed. For example, if a gross deferred tax benefit of $50,000 is recorded, and certain strategies have been identified by management to protect realization of the future deductible item associated with the computed tax benefit at an implementation cost of $10,000, then the net amount of tax benefit which is more likely than not to be realizable would not be $50,000. Rather, it may be only $43,500, which is the gross benefit less the after-tax cost of implementation, assuming a 35% tax rate ($50,000 − [$10,000 x (1 − .35)]). Accordingly, a valuation allowance of $6,500 should be established in this example.

Impact of a qualifying tax strategy

Assume that Kruse Company has a $180,000 operating loss carryforward as of 12/31/02, scheduled to expire at the end of next year. Taxable temporary differences of $240,000 exist that are expected to reverse in approximately equal amounts of $80,000 in 2003, 2004, and 2005. Kruse Company estimates that taxable income for 2003 (exclusive of the reversal of existing temporary differences and the operating loss carryforward) will be $20,000. Kruse Company expects to implement a qualifying tax planning strategy that will accelerate the total of $240,000 of taxable temporary differences to 2003. Expenses to implement the strategy are estimated to approximate $30,000. The tax rate is 40%.

In the absence of the tax planning strategy, $100,000 of the operating loss carryforward could be realized in 2003 based on estimated taxable income of $20,000 plus $80,000 of the reversal of taxable temporary differences. Thus, $80,000 would expire unused at the end of 2003 and the net amount of the deferred tax asset at 12/31/02 would be recognized at $40,000, computed as $72,000 ($180,000 x 40%) minus the valuation allowance of $32,000 ($80,000 x 40%).

However, by implementing the tax planning strategy, the deferred tax asset is calculated as follows:

Taxable income for 2003:	
Expected amount without reversal of taxable temporary differences	$ 20,000
Reversal of taxable temporary differences due to tax-planning strategy, net of costs	210,000
	230,000
Operating loss to be carried forward	(180,000)
Operating loss expiring unused at 12/31/03	$____ --

The gross deferred tax asset thus can be recorded at the full benefit amount of $72,000 ($180,000 x 40%). However, a valuation allowance is required for $18,000, representing the net-of-tax effect of the $30,000 in anticipated expenses related to implementation of the strategy. The **net** deferred tax asset at 12/31/02 is $54,000 ($72,000 − $18,000). Kruse Company will also recognize a deferred tax liability of $96,000 at the end of 2002 (40% of the taxable temporary differences of $240,000).

The adequacy of the valuation allowance must be assessed as of each balance sheet date. Adjustments of the amount of this valuation allowance are effected by a charge against, or a credit to, current earnings, via the current period tax provision. Thus, even if the gross amount of the deductible temporary differences has remained constant during a year, tax expense for that year might be increased or decreased as a consequence of reassessing the valuation allowance account at year-end. It is important that these two computational steps be separately addressed: **first** the computation of the gross deferred tax benefits (the product of the expected tax rate and the total amount of deductible temporary differences) must be made; **then** the amount of the valuation allowance to be provided against the deferred tax asset must be assessed (using the criteria set forth above). Although changes in both the deferred tax asset and valuation allowance accounts affect current period tax expense, the process of measuring these two accounts is quite distinct. Furthermore, SFAS 109 requires disclosure of both the gross deferred tax asset (and also the gross deferred tax liability) and the change in the valuation allowance account for the year. These disclosure requirements underline the need to separately measure these items.

The Effect of Tax Law Changes on Previously Recorded Deferred Tax Assets and Liabilities

As with predecessor standard SFAS 96, the balance-sheet-oriented measurement approach of SFAS 109 makes it necessary to reevaluate the deferred tax asset and liability balances at each year-end. If changes to tax rates or other provisions of the tax law (e.g., deductibility of items) have been enacted, the effect of these changes must be reflected in the deferred tax accounts so that the assets and liabilities will be fairly presented on the balance sheet. Any offsetting adjustments are to be made through the current period's tax provision, that is, the current tax provision will reflect the tax effect of current transactions **and** the revision of previously provided tax effects for transactions which have yet to reverse.

It might have been argued that the change in the deferred tax balances should be recognized when first anticipated (as when tax rate changes are proposed in Congress), the Board concluded that it would be more meaningful to report the effects of such changes in the period when the changes are enacted into law. This provides a more reliable measure of the impact of such changes and is more consistent with the informational needs of financial statement users. Enactment is defined as it is by the taxing jurisdictions; thus for example, federal laws are enacted when the president signs the legislation into law.

When tax rates are revised, this may impact not only the unreversed effects of items which were originally reported in the continuing operations section of the income statement, but also the unreversed effects of items first presented as discontinued operations, extraordinary items, or in other income statement captions. Furthermore, the impact of changes in tax rates on the accumulated balance of deferred tax benefits or obligations which arose through charges or credits to other comprehensive income (under SFAS 130) will be included in tax expense associated with continuing operations.

For example, if an entity has unrealized gains on holding available-for-sale securities at a time when relevant income tax rates (presumably, the capital gains rates) are lowered, the reduction in the tax obligation associated with these unrealized gains will reduce current period tax expense associated with continuing operations, despite the fact that the tax provision was originally reported in an additional equity account (and included in other comprehensive income, not earnings).

When tax law changes occur during an interim reporting period, its effects are to be reported in the interim period in which enactment occurs. The effects of the changes are included in continuing operations, whatever the source of the temporary differences being impacted. For example, if in the first fiscal quarter of a year an entity accrued a loss relating to discontinued operations, which is not tax deductible until realized, the tax effect would be shown in the discontinued operations section of the income statement for that quarter. If tax rates are changed in the third quarter of the same year, the deferred tax benefit recognized in connection with the discontinued operations would now need to be adjusted upward or downward, based on the newly enacted tax rate schedule. The income statement effect of this adjustment would be included with the tax provision pertaining to income from continuing operations in the third quarter.

Computation of a deferred tax asset with a change in rates

Assume the Fantasy Company has $80,000 of deductible temporary differences at the end of 2002, which are expected to result in tax deductions of approximately $40,000 each on tax returns for 2003-2005. Enacted tax rates are 50% for years 2000-2002, and 40% for 2003 and thereafter.

The deferred tax asset is computed at 12/31/02 under each of the following independent assumptions:

1. If Fantasy Company expects to offset the deductible temporary differences against taxable income in years 2003-2005, the deferred tax asset is $32,000 ($80,000 x 40%).
2. If Fantasy Company expects to realize a tax benefit for the deductible temporary differences by loss carryback refund, the deferred tax asset is $40,000 ($80,000 x 50%).

Assume that Fantasy Company expects to realize a tax asset of $32,000 at the end of 2002. Also assume that taxes payable in **each** of the years 2000-2002 were $8,000 (or 50% of taxable income). Realization of $24,000 of the $32,000 deferred tax asset is assured through carryback refunds even if no taxable income is earned in years 2003-2005. Whether a valuation allowance for the remaining $8,000 is needed depends on Fantasy Company's assessment of the levels of future taxable earnings.

The foregoing estimate of the **certain** tax benefit, based on a loss carryback to periods of higher tax rates than are statutorily in effect for future periods, should only be utilized when future losses (for tax purposes) are expected. This restriction applies since the benefit thus recognized (net of the allowance) exceeds benefits which would be available in future periods, when tax rates will be lower.

Reporting the Effect of Tax Status Changes

Reporting changes in the tax status of the entity is done in a manner which is entirely analogous to the reporting of enacted tax rate changes. When the tax status change becomes effective, the effect of any consequent adjustments to deferred tax assets and liabilities is reported in current tax expense, as part of the tax provision relating to continuing operations. These typically arise from a change from (or to) taxable status to (or from) "flow through" or nontaxable status.

When a previously taxable corporation (a C corporation) becomes a flow through entity (an S corporation), the stockholders become personally liable for taxes on the company's earnings, whether the earnings are distributed to them or not (similar to the relationship between a partnership and its partners). Under prior practice, this event was accounted for in a variety of more or less justifiable ways, including the reclassification of deferred tax liabilities as paid-in capital, an approach which was rationalized on the basis that the shareholders were, by assuming personally what was formerly a corporate obligation, making a contribution to the company's equity. Others reported a direct charge or credit to retained earnings, such as might occur if recording a correction of an error.

Post-APB 11, these disparate approaches are no longer permitted. Deferred taxes are to be eliminated by reversal through current period tax expense. Thus, if an entity having a net deferred tax liability elects S corporation status, it will report a tax benefit in its current provision.

Similarly, if an S corporation becomes a C corporation, the effect is to assume a net tax benefit or obligation for unreversed temporary differences existing at the date the change becomes effective. Accordingly, the financial statements for the period of such a change will report the effects of the event in the current tax provision. If the entity had at that date many taxable temporary differences as yet unreversed, it would report a large tax expense in that period. Conversely, if it had a large quantity of unreversed deductible temporary differences, a substantial deferred tax benefit (subject to the more-likely-than-not criterion) would need to be recorded, with a concomitant credit to the current period's tax provision in the income statement.

Whether eliminating an existing deferred tax balance or recording an initial deferred tax asset or liability, the income tax footnote to the financial statements will need to fully explain the nature of the events which had transpired.

Since S corporation elections are automatically effective when filed, if a reporting entity makes an election before the end of the current fiscal year, it is logical that the effects be reported in current year income to become effective at the start of the following period. For example, an election filed in December 2002 would be reported in the 2002 financial statements to become effective at the beginning of the company's next fiscal year, January 1, 2003. No deferred tax assets or liabilities would appear on the December 31, 2002 balance sheet, and the tax provision for the year then ended would include the effects of any reversals that had been previously recorded.

Under existing tax law, a C corporation electing to become an S corporation may be found to have "built-in gains" which will result in a future tax liability, under defined circumstances. Temporary differences are defined as differences in the tax and financial reporting bases of assets and liabilities. Accordingly, in such cases, the entity, notwithstanding the fact that it has become an S corporation, will continue to report a deferred tax liability related to this built-in gain. All other deferred taxes would be eliminated upon election to be taxed as an S corporation, however.

Reporting the Effect of Accounting Changes for Tax Purposes

Occasionally an entity will initiate or be required to adopt changes in accounting which affect income tax reporting, but which will not impact financial statement reporting. Examples from the recent past have included the change to the direct write-off method of bad debt recognition (mandated by a change in the tax law, while the reserve method required by GAAP continued in effect for financial reporting); and the adoption of "full costing" for computing inventory valuations for tax purposes, while continuing to expense currently certain administrative costs not inventoriable under GAAP for financial reporting.

Generally, these mandated changes really involve two distinct temporary differences. The first of these is the onetime, catch-up adjustment which either immediately or over a prescribed time period impacts the tax basis of the asset or liability in question (net receivables or inventory, in the examples above), and which then reverses as these assets or liabilities are later realized or settled and are eliminated from the balance sheet. The second change is the ongoing differential in the amount of newly acquired assets or incurred liabilities being recognized for tax and accounting purposes; these differences also eventually reverse, when the inventory is ultimately depleted or the receivables are ultimately collected. This second type of change is the normal temporary difference that has already been discussed. It is the first type of change which differs from those previously discussed in this chapter, and which will now be explained.

As an example, consider that Leopold Corporation has, at December 31, 2002, gross receivables of $12,000,000 and an allowance for bad debts in the amount of $600,000. Also assume that expected future taxes will be at a 40% rate and that, effective January 1, 2003, the tax law is revised to eliminate deductions for accrued bad debts, with existing allowances to be taken into income ratably over four years (a four-year spread). A balance sheet of Leopold Corporation prepared on January 1, 2003, would report a deferred tax **benefit** in the amount of $240,000 (i.e., $600,000 x 40%, which is the tax effect of future deductions to be taken when specific receivables are written off and bad debts are incurred for tax purposes); a current tax liability of $60,000 (one-fourth of the tax obligation); and a noncurrent tax liability of $180,000 (three-fourths of the tax obligation).

The deferred tax benefit is **not** deemed to be identified with the contra asset allowance for doubtful accounts (if it were, it would all be reported as a current asset), but rather with the future specific bad debts expected to be incurred. Accordingly, the deferred tax benefit should be categorized as current and noncurrent according to Leopold Corporation's best estimate of the timing of those future bad debts (much or most of which will, in all likelihood, occur within one year).

Tax Effects of Dividends Paid on Shares Held by Employee Stock Ownership Plans (ESOP)

SFAS 109 has changed the way the tax benefits arising in connection with dividends paid on ESOP-held shares are recognized. Under APB 11, tax benefits relating to both allocated and unallocated shares were reported in the equity section (i.e., in retained earnings). SFAS 96 took the opposite approach, reporting such tax benefits in income.

Under SOP 93-6, dividends paid on unallocated shares are not considered to be dividends for financial reporting purposes. If used to pay down ESOP debt, these are reported as reductions of debt or of accrued interest; if paid to participants, such dividends would be reported as compensation cost. The tax benefits from dividends paid on **unallocated** shares should be consistent with the reporting of the dividends. Thus, if the dividends were included in compensation cost, the tax benefit would be included in the tax provision associated with continuing operations.

Dividends paid on **allocated** shares are treated as normal dividends for financial reporting purposes. However, per SOP 93-6, any tax benefits resulting from these dividend payments are also to be credited to the tax provision reported in continuing operations.

The Board's decision regarding ESOP dividends was based on its recognition that ESOP and other stock compensation plans are fully analogous. Given that both plans sometimes result in tax deductions for amounts not recognized under GAAP as compensation expense, the accounting treatment of the resulting tax benefits should be the same.

On the other hand, tax deductible dividends for **other** than unallocated ESOP-held shares represents, in the Board's view, an exemption from tax of an equivalent amount of the payor's earnings. For that reason, it concluded that the tax effects should be reported in continuing operations.

Accounting for Income Taxes: Business Combinations

Accounting for the tax effects of business combinations reported as purchases under APB 16 is one of the more complex aspects of interperiod income tax accounting. (Under new standards promulgated in 2001, virtually all business combinations must be accounted for as purchases, essentially as prescribed under APB 16.) The principal complexity relates to the recognition, at the date of the purchase, of the deferred tax effects of the differences between the tax and financial reporting bases of assets and liabilities acquired. Further difficulties arise in connection with the recognition of goodwill and of negative goodwill. In some instances, the reporting entity expects that the ultimate tax allocation will differ from the initial one (such as when disallowance by the tax authorities of an allocation made to identifiable intangibles is anticipated by the taxpayer), and this creates yet another complex accounting matter to be dealt with.

The major distinction between the current approach to interperiod income tax allocation and that espoused by APB 11, as effectively amended by APB 16 (business combinations), is that APB 16 required the "net of tax" method of allocation of purchase cost to identifiable assets and liabilities, which is no longer permitted. The net of tax method considered the differences between tax and financial reporting bases of assets and liabilities to be attributes implicit in the valuations of the assets and liabilities themselves. The net of tax method was prescribed for use only in the context of purchase business combinations (APB 11 required the deferred method for all other applications).

If a given asset had an income tax basis higher than its financial reporting basis, that difference would represent an excess future tax deduction that would enhance the value of the asset. For example: If an asset had a tax basis of $1,000, and a book basis (before considering the tax effect of the basis difference), of $800, and if the tax rates were a flat 30%, then the reportable amount of the asset would be $860 under the net of tax method [$800 + .30($200)]. In another departure from normal APB 11 deferred tax accounting, the tax effects applied to the valuation of acquired assets and liabilities were also to have been discounted to present value, which of course required that the timings of reversals needed to be ascertained.

In actual practice, it appears that the process of allocating purchase cost to assets and liabilities acquired, including consideration of the effects of tax-book basis differences, was not always properly executed. Often the tax effects were imprecisely measured, sometimes rationalized as an indirect attempt to address the discounting issue: Since the tax-book differences were to "reverse" over an extended time period, the present values of the related tax benefits or obligations were likely to be judged immaterial, and thus not in need of measurement.

For example, LIFO inventories acquired in a purchase business combination would often have different tax and financial reporting bases; however, receipt or settlement of the related tax benefit or obligation would likely take place only upon liquidation of the company or of its inventories. Since these events were often assumed to be in the far off, indefinite future, the tax effects, discounted to present value, would only alter slightly the inventories reportable in the financial statements.

Under SFAS 109, assets and liabilities acquired in purchase business combinations should be reported gross of tax effects. The tax effects of any differences in tax and financial reporting bases are to be reflected from the date of the purchase as deferred tax assets and liabilities in their own right.

Purchase business combinations can be either taxable or nontaxable in nature. In a taxable business combination, the total purchase price paid is allocated to assets and liabilities for both tax and financial reporting purposes, although under some circumstances these allocations may differ. In a nontaxable business combination, the predecessor entity's tax bases for the various assets and liabilities are carried forward, while for financial reporting the purchase price is allocated to the assets and liabilities acquired. Thus, in most cases, there will be some possibly significant differences between the tax and financial reporting bases. Accordingly, both taxable and nontaxable purchase business combinations can involve the application of deferred income tax accounting.

Accounting for Purchase Business Combinations at Acquisition Date

SFAS 109 requires that the tax effects of the tax-book basis differences of all assets and liabilities generally be presented as deferred tax assets and liabilities as of the acquisition date. In general, this "grossing up" of the balance sheet is a straightforward matter. An example, in the context of a nontaxable purchase business combination, follows:

Facts:
1. The income tax rate is a flat 40%.
2. The acquisition of a business is effected at a cost of $500,000.
3. The fair values of assets acquired total $750,000.
4. The carryforward tax bases of assets acquired total $600,000.
5. The fair and carryforward tax bases of the liabilities assumed in the purchase are $250,000.
6. The difference between the tax and fair values of the assets acquired, $150,000, consists of taxable temporary differences of $200,000 and deductible temporary differences of $50,000.
7. There is no doubt as to the realizability of the deductible temporary differences in this case.

Based on the foregoing facts, the allocation of the purchase price is as follows:

Gross purchase price	$500,000
Allocation to identifiable assets and (liabilities):	
Assets, other than goodwill and deferred tax benefits	750,000
Deferred tax benefits	20,000
Liabilities, other than deferred tax obligations	(250,000)
Deferred tax obligations	(80,000)
Net of the above allocations	440,000
Allocation to goodwill	$ 60,000

Goodwill should not be "grossed up" in the balance sheet for two reasons. First, at the date on which the business combination is consummated, the tax and book bases of goodwill should generally be the same, inasmuch as amortization for tax purposes has yet to begin. Second, recognition of deferred taxes in connection with goodwill would have the effect of increasing the amount of goodwill to be reported in the financial statements in most cases, and this is not generally seen as being a desirable outcome.

Goodwill and negative goodwill. Goodwill arises when a portion of the price paid in a business combination accounted for as a purchase cannot be allocated to identifiable assets. This excess cost is deemed to relate to the intangible asset that pertains to excess earnings power, which is called goodwill. Historically (since the late 1960s), goodwill was subject to mandatory amortization for GAAP financial reporting, but until relatively recently, it was not deductible for tax purposes. Since 1993, goodwill has been tax-deductible, with a mandatory fifteen-year amortization period. In 2001, the FASB promulgated new business combinations and goodwill accounting requirements, mandating that goodwill no longer be amortized for financial reporting purposes, but rather be subject to periodic impairment testing. (See Chapters 9 and 11 for complete discussions.)

Prior to the 1993 tax law change, goodwill was generally considered to embody a permanent difference, rather than a timing difference (under APB 11), for which deferred tax was not to be provided. When goodwill became statutorily amortizable over fifteen years, the tax-book difference was deemed to be a timing difference, with deferred tax effects to be reported for financial reporting under GAAP. Under recently established GAAP, the pre-1993 situation has, effectively, been completely reversed, with goodwill now to be deductible (over the fifteen-year amortization period) for tax purposes, but not for GAAP basis financial reporting, apart from possible sporadic write-downs for impairment.

Since, under SFAS 109, temporary differences are defined as arising from differences between the tax and book bases of assets and liabilities, deferred tax effects should be measured and reported for goodwill. In general, deductible tax amortization of goodwill will create a deferred tax liability in the financial statements, much as the use of accelerated tax depreciation does. If, in later years, book goodwill is reduced for impairments, a portion of the deferred tax obligation will be reversed. Unless the goodwill is eventually written off entirely due to impairments, some part of the deferred tax obligation will remain on the balance sheet until the goodwill is ultimately eliminated, potentially not until the reporting unit is disposed of or shut down.

In some purchase business combination situations, "negative goodwill" results from what are often referred to as bargain purchases. These are those situations in which the fair value of the net identifiable assets acquired exceeds the price paid for the purchase business combination. Under newly established GAAP (2001), this excess should first be allocated on a pro rata basis to all acquired assets, other than cash and cash equivalents, trade receivables, inventory, financial instruments that are required to be carried on the balance sheet at fair value, assets to be disposed of by sale, and deferred tax assets. This will tend to affect the carrying value of long-lived, mostly depreciable, assets, which will reduce future depreciation charges, over the respective lives of those assets. (Under prior GAAP, the offset was to all noncurrent assets other than marketable securities, which had much the same impact.) Any excess negative goodwill will now be immediately recognized as an extraordinary gain, as distinct from the earlier requirement that this be amortized over up to forty years.

For tax purposes, negative goodwill is handled very much like the new accounting standards require—by offsetting against nonmonetary long lived assets, and with immediate taxability of any excess. (Generally, such excess is presumed to relate to inventory and receivables, the turnover of which are normally rapid, thus justifying the immediate taxability of that component of the negative goodwill.) Thus, a temporary difference will probably no longer arise from the accounting treatment applied to negative goodwill for tax and book purposes. In the past, temporary differences arose from the differential treatments (immediate taxability versus amortization for financial reporting) creating prepaid taxes (deferred tax assets) in many instances.

The accounting for a taxable purchase business combination is essentially similar to that for a nontaxable one. However, unlike the previous example, in which there were numerous assets with different tax and financial reporting bases, there are likely to be only a few differences in the case of taxable purchases. Previously, because goodwill was not deductible, attempts were often made for tax purposes to allocate excess purchase cost to other intangibles, such as covenants not to compete. Since the 1993 tax act makes all such intangibles, including goodwill, amortizable over fifteen years, this motive should no longer be encountered. Accordingly, tax-book differences in taxable business combinations are likely to be less common.

Accounting for Purchase Business Combinations after the Acquisition

As discussed earlier in this chapter, one of the attributes which distinguishes SFAS 109 from its predecessors is that net deferred tax benefits are now fully recognized, subject to the possible need for a valuation allowance. This requirement has a major impact on the accounting for business combinations.

In the example presented above, it was stated that all deductible temporary differences were assumed to be fully realizable, and therefore the deferred tax benefits associated with those temporary differences were recorded as of the acquisition date, with no need for an offsetting valuation account. However, in other situations, it may be that there is substantial doubt concerning realizability (i.e., it may be more likely than not that the benefits will **not** be realized) and accordingly that a valuation allowance would be recognized at the date of the purchase business combination. In such an instance, the allocation of the purchase price should reflect this fact, which would have the result of allocating a greater share of the purchase cost to goodwill than would otherwise be the case. Under current GAAP (as of mid-2001), goodwill cannot be amortized for financial reporting purposes, and the disparity in accounting for goodwill under GAAP and tax reporting rules will add to the deferred tax implications of the business combination.

If, at a date subsequent to the business combination transaction, it is determined that the valuations account should be reduced or eliminated, SFAS 109 stipulates that the effect of such reduction is applied first to eliminate any goodwill recorded in connection with that business combination. Once goodwill has been reduced to zero, the excess is applied to eliminate any identifiable intangible acquired in that business combination, and any further excess is reflected in the current period tax provision. Thus, in this situation the general rule—that changes in the allowance are mated to debits or credits in current period tax expenses from continuing operations—is not followed.

Subsequent realization of a deferred tax asset in a purchase business combination

Assume that Michael Company acquired another entity on January 1, 2002, for $2,000,000. There was no goodwill in the transaction. The tax basis of the net assets is $6,000,000 (i.e., deductible temporary differences equal $4,000,000). The tax rate is 30% and the tax law restricts use of the acquired company's deductible temporary differences and carryforwards to future taxable income of the acquired entity itself. Pretax losses have been incurred in the past three years, and results for the acquired company in 2002 are also expected to be a deficit. Thus, Michael Company concludes that a valuation allowance for the full amount of the deferred tax asset is required. However, at the end of 2003, Michael Company decides that a valuation allowance is no longer necessary. Actual results for years 2002 and 2003 are as follows:

	2002	*2003*
Pretax financial income	$ 1,500,000	$ 1,000,000
Reversal of acquired deductible temporary differences	(1,500,000)	(1,000,000)
Taxable income	$ --	$ --

At the date of acquisition the deferred tax asset is recorded at $1,200,000 ($4,000,000 x 30%) but with a corresponding valuation allowance for the same amount. At the end of 2002, the deferred tax asset is $750,000 computed as 30% of $2,500,000 ($4,000,000 – $1,500,000), again with a corresponding valuation allowance. At the end of 2003, when management determines that a valuation allowance is no longer necessary, elimination of the valuation allowance results in a deferred tax benefit or in a reduction of deferred income tax expense. (Note that had goodwill arisen in the acquisition, the tax benefit would have first been applied to reduce goodwill to zero and then to reduce acquired intangible assets to zero.)

Thus, journal entries related to deferred taxes are

At 1-1-02 (date of acquisition)

Net assets	2,000,000	
Deferred tax asset	1,200,000	
Cash		2,000,000
Valuation allowance		1,200,000

At 12-31-02

Valuation allowance	450,000	
Deferred tax asset		450,000

At 12-31-03

Valuation allowance	750,000	
Deferred tax asset		300,000
Income tax benefit—deferred		450,000

Under SFAS 109, the tax benefits of net operating losses are not distinguished from those arising from temporary differences. Accordingly, the treatments set forth above hold here as well. If the benefits are recognized for the first time at a date after the acquisition (by reducing or eliminating the valuation allowance), then goodwill arising from the business combination is eliminated, other purchased intangibles are reduced to zero, and current tax expense is reduced. Negative goodwill is neither created nor increased in such circumstances, however.

Precisely the same approach is employed in connection with income tax credits which may have existed at the date of the business combination, but which may not have been given recognition due to doubtful realizability. While under APB 11 the treatments accorded net operating losses and tax credit carryforwards were dissimilar, under SFAS 109 they are identical. Under APB 11, recognition of benefits for operating loss carryforwards was possible under limited circumstances, while recognition of tax credit carryforwards was strictly prohibited.

In some instances, entities having unrecognized tax benefits of operating losses or tax credits arising in connection with a purchase business combination may generate other similar tax benefits after the date of the merger. A question in such a circumstance relates to whether a "FIFO" convention should be adopted to guide the recognition of these benefits. While in some instances tax law may determine the order in which the benefits are actually realized, in other cases the law may not do so. SFAS 109 provides that in those latter situations, the benefits realized should be apportioned, for financial reporting purposes, between pre- and postacquisition tax benefits. The former should be accounted for as above, and the latter reported as reductions of current period tax expense, consistent with the general rules of SFAS 109.

Poolings of Interests

In poolings of interests, which are no longer permitted under GAAP, the combining entities generally do not adjust carrying values of assets and liabilities. Reissued or comparative financial statements of periods before the effective date of the combination are restated on a combined basis. However, notwithstanding the general principle of not revising asset or liability carrying amounts, a special rule applies to deferred tax benefits which had been partially or completely reserved against under the more-likely-than-not criterion of SFAS 109.

The standard stipulates that, if one of the combining entities had an unrecognized net deferred tax benefit (i.e., there was a deferred tax benefit recognized, gross, which was offset by a valuation allowance), the restated financials may or may not reflect the net tax benefits as an asset. That is, the valuation allowance **may** be eliminated on a retrospective basis. This treatment depends upon whether the combined entity will be able, under provisions of the tax laws, to utilize the operating loss and tax credit carryforwards of the merged companies. If it can do so, then the deferred tax benefits should be recognized in any restated prior period financial statements. If, under the law, the benefits cannot be utilized in a consolidated tax return or if a consolidated return is not expected to be filed, then the tax benefits would not be recognized in financial statements restated for the pooling of interests.

Thus, the need for a valuation (allowance) account is subject to a revised analysis, but only the ability to utilize the tax benefits in a consolidated return is to be considered; other changes in circumstances are handled as described earlier in this chapter (by adjusting the allowance through current period tax expense). This is strictly consistent with the concept of a pooling of interests, in which financials are presented for current and prior periods as if the entities had always been combined; had they been combined and had the tax benefits been available for use in a consolidated return, the allowance would never have been provided.

Under some circumstances, poolings of interests are taxable, meaning that for tax purposes there will be a step-up of the net assets of one of the merged entities. The differences between the new, stepped-up tax bases and the carryforward book values utilized for financial reporting purposes are temporary differences giving rise to deferred tax benefits. Whether these benefits are given recognition is dependent upon whether the more-likely-than-not criterion is met. If the test is not met, a valuation allowance must be established for some or all of the gross benefits recorded. If a valuation allowance is established, and it is later reduced or eliminated when the likelihood of ultimate realization exceeds the 50% probability threshold, the effect of eliminating the valuation allowance will be reflected in tax expense for the current period.

Tax Allocation for Business Investments

As noted in Chapter 10, Investments, there are two basic methods for accounting for investments in the common stock of other corporations: (1) the fair value method as set forth in SFAS 115, and (2) the equity method, as prescribed by APB 18. The cost method, previously employed for intercorporate investments lacking the attribute "significant influence" by the investor, is no longer appropriate, except for the exceedingly rare situation when fair value information is absolutely unavailable. If the cost method is used, however, there will be no interperiod tax allocation issues, since this conforms to the method prescribed for tax reporting.

The fair value method is used in instances where the investor is not considered to have significant influence over the investee. The ownership threshold generally used to denote significant influence is 20% of ownership; this level of ownership is not considered an absolute (FASB Interpretation 35), but it will be used to identify the break between application of the fair value and equity methods in the illustrations which follow. In practice, the 20% ownership interest defines the point at which there is a rebuttable presumption that the investor has significant influence, and it is often noted that publicly held companies will establish investment ownership percentages very slightly over or under 20%, presumably to support their desires and decisions to use, or not use, the equity method of accounting for those investments.

Under both the cost and fair value methods, ordinary income is recognized as dividends are declared by the investee, and capital gains (losses) are recognized upon the disposal of the investment. For tax purposes, no provision is made during the holding period for the allocable undistributed earnings of the investee. There is no deferred tax computation necessary when using the cost method because there is no temporary difference. Tax allocation issues pertaining to the use of the fair value method are discussed in Chapter 10, Investments.

The equity method is generally to be used whenever an investor owns more than 20% of an investee or has significant influence over the investee's operations with a lower ownership interest. The equity method calls for recording the investment at cost and then increasing this carrying amount by the allocable portion of the investee's earnings. The allocable portion of the investee's earnings is then included in pretax accounting income of the investor. Dividend payments are no longer included in pretax accounting income but are considered to be a reduction in the carrying amount of the investment. However, for tax purposes, dividends are the only revenue realized. As a result, the investor must recognize deferred income tax expense on the undistributed earnings of the investee that will be taxed in the future. The current promulgated GAAP in this area consists of APB 23 and SFAS 109, which superseded APB 24 but continues the principles set forth therein. These standards are discussed below.

GAAP distinguishes between an investee and a subsidiary and prescribes different accounting treatments for each. An investee is considered to be a corporation whose stock is owned by an investor that holds more than 20% but no greater than 50% of the outstanding stock. An investee situation occurs when the investor has significant influence but not control over the corporation invested in. A subsidiary, on the other hand, exists when more than 50% of the stock of a corporation is owned by another. This results in direct control over the corporation invested in. APB 23, as amended by SFAS 109, is the promulgated GAAP regarding the tax effects relating to the ownership of subsidiaries. APB 24 was the promulgated GAAP on the tax effects of investments in common stock of entities other than subsidiaries and corporate joint ventures which are accounted for by the equity method, until being superseded by SFAS 109.

Undistributed earnings of a subsidiary. According to APB 23, the inclusion of undistributed earnings of a subsidiary in the pretax accounting income of a parent company by means of full consolidation or application of equity method reporting (or some combination of the two) would result in a temporary timing difference, although the difference may not reverse until some indefinite future periods. It is presumed nonetheless that eventually all of the undistributed earnings of a subsidiary will be transferred to the parent. As such, tax effects on the temporary difference must be recognized, measured with reference to the tax rates expected to be applicable to either dividends or capital gains.

Prior GAAP did permit one to overcome the presumption that all undistributed income would eventually be transferred (and taxed) to the parent. Under APB 23, if sufficient evidence could be presented that the subsidiary would invest the undistributed earnings indefinitely or that the earnings would be distributed in a tax-free liquidation, deferred taxes would not be needed. Examples of such evidence would be the past experience of the companies involved or specific future plans of indefinite postponement. In such an instance, the opinion required that the following disclosures be made in the notes to the financial statements:

1. A declaration of an intention to reinvest the undistributed earnings of a subsidiary to support the contention that the distribution of those earnings has been indefinitely postponed or that the earnings will be distributed in the form of a tax-free liquidation.
2. The cumulative amount of undistributed earnings on which the parent company has not recognized taxes.

APB 23 provided that when a change occurred in the expectations regarding distributions of subsidiary earnings, the tax effects of the changed expectations were to be reflected in tax expense in the period the new information became available. In other words, the character of the change was that of an accounting estimate; it was not appropriate to treat it as either an extraordinary item or a correction of prior periods.

APB 11's first successor, SFAS 96, left APB 23 in place, with only minor amendments. The most important alteration was that changes in expected future tax effects (due to changes in tax rates, etc.) were to be recognized in the current tax provision, in contrast to APB 11's requirement that, once provided, deferred taxes were not subsequently revised for such items. In permitting the main provisions of APB 23 to remain in force, the Board emphasized (1) the purported complexity of measuring deferred tax liabilities for foreign undistributed earnings, (2) a perceived need to compromise the principles of SFAS 96 to gain its acceptance, and (3) the prohibition against discounting.

In SFAS 109, however, the Board has explicitly recognized that the timing (now temporary) differences addressed by APB 23 do in fact give rise to recognizable deferred tax liabilities. In the current view, while management may control the timing and circumstances of the recognition of earnings of nonconsolidated subsidiaries for tax purposes, their ultimate occurrence is a certainty. The same logic also applies to the recognition of deferred tax assets (an issue that was not addressed earlier because of SFAS 96's prohibition against recognition of net deferred tax assets arising from any sources). In short, the concept of "indefinite reversal" has been debunked.

Nonetheless, SFAS 109 does incorporate a compromise approach to the adoption of comprehensive tax allocation, effectively "grandfathering" certain existing temporary differences for which deferred taxes were not provided. Thus, deferred taxes are **not** to be provided for undistributed earnings of domestic subsidiaries or corporate joint ventures if they are essentially permanent in nature and arose in fiscal years beginning on or prior to December 15, 1992. The procedures of SFAS 109 are to be applied prospectively, but no adjustment needs to be made for temporary differences arising from ownership of subsidiaries prior to the effective date of the new standard.

The amount of tax to be provided depends upon specific application of the tax laws and management intent. If the law provides a mechanism under which the parent company can recover its investment tax-free, no deferred taxes need to be provided. For example, an entity can elect to determine taxable gain or loss on the liquidation of an 80%-or-more-owned subsidiary based on the tax basis of the subsidiary's net assets, rather than by reference to the parent's basis in its investment in the subsidiary. Also, under specified circumstances a parent company can effect a statutory merger, under which no gain or loss is recognized for tax purposes.

In other cases, options to minimize or avoid taxes are available only if the parent company owns a stipulated share of the subsidiary's stock. A parent company owning less than this threshold level may express its intent to utilize a tax planning strategy to acquire the necessary additional shares to realize this benefit. In evaluating this strategy, the cost of acquiring the additional shares must be considered and the benefits to be recognized (reduced deferred tax liability) must be offset by the cost of implementing the strategy.

Undistributed earnings of an investee. APB 24 established GAAP for interperiod tax allocation for situations where an entity exercised significant influence but not control. It was the difference between these two degrees of power, control vs. significant influence, that was the catalyst for APB 24. The fact that an investor has significant influence over the operations of an investee would not be enough to conclude that distribution of the investee's earnings could be postponed indefinitely; hence the principle espoused in APB 23 would not be applicable to such situations. As a result, the inclusion of undistributed earnings of an investee corporation in the pretax accounting income of the parent corporation will always result in a temporary difference although, once again, the facts and circumstances involved in each situation will be the final determinant of whether the temporary difference is assumed to be a future dividend or a capital gain for deferred tax calculation purposes.

SFAS 109 has continued the approach set forth originally in APB 24, although of course the deferred tax provision is now computed by the liability method and no longer is determined by the "with and without" calculation of APB 11.

To illustrate the application of these concepts, assume Parent Company owns 30% of the outstanding common stock of Investee Company and 70% of the outstanding common stock of Subsidiary company. Additional data for Subsidiary and Investee companies for the year 2000 are as follows:

	Investee Company	*Subsidiary Company*
Net income	$50,000	$100,000
Dividends paid	20,000	60,000

The following sections illustrate how the foregoing data are used to recognize the tax effects of the stated events.

Income Tax Effects from Investee Company

The pretax accounting income of Parent Company will include equity in investee income equal to $15,000 ($50,000 x 30%). Parent's taxable income, however, will include dividend income of $6,000 ($20,000 x 30%), and a credit of 80% of the $6,000, or $4,800, will also be allowed for the dividends received. This 80% dividends received deduction is a permanent difference between pretax accounting and taxable income and is allowed for dividends received from domestic corporations in which the ownership is less than 80% but at least 20%; a lower dividend received deduction of 70% is permitted when the ownership is less than 20%. A 100% credit (dividends received deduction) is allowed for dividends received from domestic corporations in which the ownership is 80% to 100%. As discussed in APB 24, the originating temporary difference results from Parent's equity ($9,000) in Investee's undistributed income of $30,000. The amount of the deferred tax credit in 1999 depends upon the expectations of Parent Company as to the manner in which the $9,000 of undistributed income will be received. If the expectation of receipt is via dividends, then the temporary difference is 20% of $9,000, or $1,800, and the deferred tax credit for this originating temporary difference in 2000 is the current tax rate times $1,800. However, if the expectation is that receipt will be through future sale of the investment, then the temporary difference is $9,000 and the deferred tax credit is the current capital gains rate times the $9,000.

The entries below illustrate these alternatives. A tax rate of 34% is used for both ordinary income and for capital gains. Note that the amounts in the entries below relate only to Investee Company's incremental impact upon Parent Company's tax accounts.

	Expectations for undistributed income	
	Dividends	*Capital gains*
Income tax expense	1,020	3,468
Deferred tax liability	612[b]	3,060[c]
Income taxes payable	408[a]	408[a]

[a]Computation of income taxes payable:

Dividend income—30% x ($20,000)	$6,000
Less 80% dividends received deduction	(4,800)
Amount included in Parent's taxable income	$1,200
Tax liability—34% x ($1,200)	$ 408

[b]Computation of deferred tax liability (dividend assumption):
Originating temporary difference:

Parent's share of undistributed income—30% x ($30,000)	$9,000
Less 80% dividends received deduction	(7,200)
Originating temporary difference	$1,800
Deferred tax liability—34% x ($1,800)	$ 612

[c]Computation of deferred tax liability (capital gain assumption):
Originating temporary difference:

Parent's share of undistributed income—30% x ($30,000)	$9,000
Deferred tax liability—34% x ($9,000)	$3,060

Although APB 24 has been superseded by SFAS 109, the accounting procedures prescribed therein are continued essentially unchanged. The one difference, of course, is that under SFAS 109 the tax effect of this (and all other) temporary difference is measured by the tax impact of the future reversal of the difference, and **not** by the "with and without" method of APB 11. The example above therefore assumes that future taxes will continue at current rates.

Income Tax Effects from Subsidiary Company

The pretax accounting income of Parent Company will also include equity in Subsidiary income of $70,000 (70% x $100,000). This $70,000 will be included in pretax consolidated income if Parent and Subsidiary issue consolidated financial statements. For tax purposes, Parent and Subsidiary cannot file a consolidated tax return because the minimum level of control (i.e., 80%) is not present. Consequently, the taxable income of Parent will include dividend income of $42,000 (70% x $60,000), and there will be an 80% dividends received deduction of $33,600. The originating temporary difference discussed in APB 23 results from Parent's equity ($28,000) in the Subsidiary's undistributed earnings of $40,000. The amount of the deferred tax credit in 2000 depends upon the expectations of Parent Company as to the manner in which this $28,000 of undistributed income will be received. The same expectations can exist as previously discussed, for Parent's equity in Investee's undistributed earnings (i.e., through future dividend distributions or capital gains). In addition, however, under APB 23 if Parent could have demonstrated that its share of Subsidiary Company's earnings would have been permanently reinvested by Subsidiary, then APB 23 stated that no timing difference exists and, therefore, no deferred tax credits arose. This treatment was not available for stock investments between 20% and 50%. SFAS 109 rejects the "indefinite reversal" concept, and requires, on a **prospective** basis, that deferred taxes be provided in such circumstances.

The entries below illustrate these alternatives. A marginal tax rate of 34% is assumed. The amounts in the entries below relate only to Subsidiary Company's incremental impact upon Parent Company's tax accounts.

| | *Expectations for undistributed income* | |
	Dividends	*Capital gains*
Income tax expense	4,760	12,376
Deferred tax liability	1,904[b]	9,520[c]
Income taxes payable	2,856[a]	2,856[a]

[a]Computation of income taxes payable:

Dividend income—70% x ($60,000)	$42,000
Less 80% dividends received deduction	(33,600)
Amount included in Parent's taxable income	$ 8,400
Tax liability—34% x ($8,400)	$ 2,856

[b]Computation of deferred tax liability (dividend assumption):
Originating temporary difference:

Parent's share of undistributed income—70% x ($40,000)	$28,000
Less 80% dividends received deduction	(22,400)
Originating temporary difference	$ 5,600
Deferred tax liability—34% x ($5,600)	$ 1,904

[c]Computation of deferred tax liability (capital gain assumption):
Originating temporary difference:

Parent's share of undistributed income—70% x ($40,000)	$28,000
Deferred tax liability—34% x ($28,000)	$ 9,520

If a parent company owns 80% or more of the voting stock of a subsidiary and the parent consolidates the subsidiary for both financial and tax reports, then no temporary differences exist between pretax consolidated income and taxable income. If, in the circumstances noted above, consolidated financial statements are prepared but a consolidated tax return is not, then it should be noted that a dividends received deduction of 100% is allowed. Accordingly, the temporary difference between pretax consolidated income and taxable income is zero if the parent assumes the undistributed income will be realized in dividends.

Summary of Temporary Differences of Investees and Subsidiaries

Level of Ownership Interest

| 0% | <20% | 50% | >80% | 100% |

Accounting for Income Taxes: Intraperiod Tax Allocation

While SFAS 109 is predominantly concerned with the requirements of **inter**period income tax allocation (deferred tax accounting), it also addresses the questions of **intra**period tax allocation. Intraperiod tax allocation relates to the matching in the income (or other financial) statement of various categories of comprehensive income or expense (continuing operations, extraordinary items, corrections of errors, etc.) with the tax effects of those items. Also, the introduction of the requirement to report on other comprehensive income adds a further need for intraperiod income tax allocation, as discussed later in this section. The general principle is that tax effects should follow the items to which they relate; in this regard, SFAS 109 follows the logical precedents of APB 11 and SFAS 96. A "with and without" series of computations is applied under each of these standards, in order to identify the marginal, or incremental, effects of items other than those arising from continuing operations. However, there are some significant differences in the most recent approach, as described in the following paragraphs.

Under APB 11, the "with and without" technique was applied in a step-by-step fashion proceeding down the face of the income statement. For example, an entity having continuing operations, discontinued operations, and extraordinary items would calculate tax expense as follows: (1) Tax would be computed for the aggregate results and for continuing operations. The difference between the two amounts would be allocated to the total of discontinued operations and extraordinary items. (2) Tax expense would be computed on discontinued operations. The residual amount (i.e., the difference between tax on the discontinued operations and the tax on the total of discontinued operations and extraordinary items) would then be allocated to extraordinary items. Thus, under the provisions of APB 11, the amount of tax expense allocated to any given classification in the statement of income (and the other financial statements, if relevant) was partially a function of the location in which the item was traditionally presented in the income and retained earnings statements.

SFAS 96 also utilized an incremental calculation of tax expense to be allocated to classifications other than continuing operations; however, rather than applying successive allocations on the "with and without" basis to determine tax provisions applicable to succeeding income and retained earnings statement captions, the tax effects of all items **other** than continuing operations were allocated pro rata. That is, once the tax provision allocable to continuing operations was determined, the residual tax expense or benefit was apportioned to all the other classifications (discontinued operations, et al.) in the ratios that those other items, on a pretax basis, bore to the total of all such items.

SFAS 109 adopts an approach essentially similar to that described above. Total income tax expense or benefit for the period is allocated among continuing operations, discontinued operations, extraordinary items, and stockholders' equity. However, as defined in SFAS 109, tax provisions on income from continuing operations include not only taxes on the income earned from continuing operations, as expected, but also the following items:

1. The impact of changes in tax laws and rates, which includes the effects of such changes on items which were previously reflected directly in stockholders' equity, as described more fully below
2. The impact of changes in tax status
3. Changes in estimates about whether the tax benefits of deductible temporary differences or net operating loss or credit carryforwards are more likely than not to be realizable (i.e., an adjustment to the valuation allowance account for such items)
4. The tax effects of tax-deductible dividends paid to stockholders, as discussed elsewhere in this chapter

Under SFAS 109, stockholders' equity is charged or credited with the initial tax effects of items that are reported directly in stockholders' equity. These items include the following:

1. Corrections of the effects of accounting errors of previous periods
2. Gains and losses which are defined under GAAP as being part of comprehensive income but are not reported in the income statement, such as translation adjustments under SFAS 52, and the fair value adjustments applicable to available-for-sale portfolios of debt and marketable equity securities held as investments. As a result of amendments to SFAS 109 made by SFAS 130, *Reporting Comprehensive Income*, the tax effects of these types of items will be reported in the same statement where other comprehensive income items are reported. As discussed more fully in Chapter 3, Statements of Income and Comprehensive Income, these items may be reported either in a stand-alone statement of comprehensive income, a combined statement of earnings and other comprehensive income, or in an expanded version of the statement of changes in stockholders' equity.

3. Taxable or deductible increases or decreases in contributed capital, such as offering costs reported under GAAP as reductions of the proceeds of a capital stock offering, but which are either immediately deductible or amortizable for tax purposes

4. Increases in the tax bases of assets acquired in a taxable business combination accounted for as a pooling of interests under GAAP, if a tax benefit is recognized at the date of the business combination (i.e., if the tax effects of existing deductible temporary differences are not fully offset by a valuation account at that date)

5. Expenses incurred in connection with stock issued under provisions of compensatory option plans, which are recognized for tax purposes but are reported for accounting purposes in stockholders' equity under the provisions of APB 25

6. Dividends paid on unallocated shares held in an ESOP, and that are charged against retained earnings

7. Deductible temporary differences and operating loss and credit carryforwards that existed at the date of a quasi reorganization

The effects of tax rate or other tax law changes on items for which the tax effects were originally reported directly in stockholders' equity are reported in continuing operations, if they occur in any period after the original event. For example, assume the reporting entity recognized a tax benefit related to an employee stock option program amounting to $34,000 in 2002, based on the estimated future tax deduction it would receive at the then-current and anticipated future tax rate of 34%. If the statutory tax rate is lowered to 25% in 2004 before the temporary difference reverses, the adjustment to the deferred tax asset account ($34,000 − $25,000 = $9,000) will be reported in the tax provision applicable to income from continuing operations in 2004.

A comprehensive example of the intraperiod tax allocation process prescribed under SFAS 109 is presented below. (This example does not include items that will, under provisions of SFAS 130, be reported in other comprehensive income; the accounting of those is illustrated in Chapter 3, Statements of Income and Comprehensive Income.) Assume there was $50,000 in deductible temporary differences at 12/31/01; these remain unchanged during the current year, 2002.

	2002
Income from continuing operations	$400,000
Loss from discontinued operations	(120,000)
Extraordinary gain on involuntary conversion	60,000
Correction of error: understatement of depreciation in 2001	(20,000)
Tax credits	5,000

Tax rates are: 15% on first $100,000 of taxable income; 20% on next $100,000; 25% on next $100,000; 30% thereafter.

Expected future tax rates were 20% at December 31, 2001, but are judged to be 28% at December 31, 2002.

Retained earnings at December 31, 2001, totaled $650,000.

Intraperiod tax allocation proceeds as follows:

Step 1 — Tax on total taxable income of $320,000 ($400,000 – $120,000 + $60,000 – $20,000) is **$61,000** ($66,000 based on rate structure, less tax credit of $5,000).

Step 2 — Tax on income from continuing operations of $400,000 is **$85,000**, net of tax credit.

Step 3 — The difference, $24,000, is allocated pro rata to discontinued operations, extraordinary gain, and correction of the error in prior year depreciation.

Step 4 — The adjustment of the deferred tax asset, amounting to a $4,000 increase due to an effective tax rate estimate change [$50,000 x (.28 – .20)] is allocated to continuing operations, regardless of the source of the temporary difference.

A summary combined income and retained earnings statement for 2002 is presented below.

Income from continuing operations, before income taxes		$400,000
Income taxes on income from continuing operations:		
Current	$90,000	
Deferred	(4,000)	
Tax credits	(5,000)	81,000
Income from continuing operations, net		319,000
Loss from discontinued operations, net of tax benefit of $36,000		(84,000)
Extraordinary gain, net of tax of $18,000		42,000
Net income		277,000
Retained earnings, January 1, 2002		650,000
Correction of accounting error, net of tax effects of $6,000		(14,000)
Retained earnings, December 31, 2002		$913,000

Classification of Deferred Taxes

An enterprise that presents a classified balance sheet will classify its deferred tax liabilities and assets as either current or noncurrent consistent with the classification of the related asset or liability. A deferred tax asset or liability that is not related to an asset or liability for financial reporting purposes, such as the deferred tax consequences related to an operating loss or tax credit carryforward, is classified based on the expected reversal or utilization date. These classifications must be made for each separate tax-paying component within each taxing jurisdiction. This approach is identical to that employed under APB 11 (as amended by SFAS 37), but differs from that under SFAS 96. The latter standard required that all deferred tax assets and liabilities be classified according to expected reversal or utilization date. Since SFAS 109 has dispensed with the detailed scheduling requirement or its predecessor, however, such a classification strategy would have been unworkable. Accordingly, the formerly employed approach has been reinstated.

Within each of the separate components, the current asset and liability are offset and presented as a single amount, with similar treatment for the noncurrent items. Understandably, offsetting is not permitted for different tax-paying components or for different tax jurisdictions. Thus, a balance sheet may present current and noncurrent deferred tax assets, along with current and noncurrent deferred tax liabilities, under certain circumstances.

If the enterprise has a valuation allowance, it must prorate the allowance between current and noncurrent according to the relative size of the gross deferred tax asset in each classification. The FASB mandated this approach to avoid the necessity of having to determine exactly which deferred tax assets would not be recovered.

Balance Sheet Disclosures

A reporting entity is required to disclose the components of the net deferred tax liability or asset recognized in the statement of financial position as follows:

1. Total of all deferred tax liabilities
2. Total of all deferred tax assets
3. Total valuation allowance
4. Net change in the valuation allowance for the year
5. Types of temporary differences and carryforwards that cause significant portions of deferred tax assets and liabilities. Disclosure of the approximate total tax effect (not the separate tax effect for each tax jurisdiction) of each of these is required only for publicly held companies.

When deferred tax liabilities are not recognized because of the exceptions provided under APB 23 the following information is to be provided:

1. The types of temporary differences and the events that would cause those temporary differences to become taxable
2. The cumulative amount of each type
3. The amount of unrecognized deferred tax liability for any undistributed foreign earnings, or a statement that such a determination is not practicable
4. The amount of unrecognized deferred tax liability for other temporary differences that arose prior to the period for which application of this statement is first required for each of those particular differences

Income Statement Disclosures

SFAS 109 places primary emphasis upon the income tax expense or benefit allocated to continuing operations. The following information must be disclosed about amounts allocated to continuing operations for each year for which an income statement is presented:

1. Current tax expense or benefit
2. Deferred tax expense or benefit (exclusive of the effects of other components listed below)
3. Investment tax credits

4. Government grants (to the extent recognized as a reduction of income tax expense)
5. The benefits of operating loss carryforwards
6. Tax expense that results either from allocating certain tax benefits directly to contributed capital or from allocating them to reduce goodwill or other noncurrent intangible assets of an acquired entity
7. Adjustments to the deferred tax liability or asset for enacted changes in tax laws or rates or a change in the tax status of the enterprise
8. Adjustments to the beginning of year balance of the valuation allowance because of a change in circumstances that causes a change in judgment about the realizability of the related deferred tax asset in future years

SFAS 109 also requires disclosure of the following:

1. The amounts of income tax expense or benefit allocated to financial statement elements other than continuing operations (e.g., discontinued operations, extraordinary items, and retained earnings)
2. The amounts and expiration dates of operating loss and tax credit carryforwards for tax purposes
3. The amount of the valuation allowance for which subsequently recognized tax benefits will reduce goodwill or other noncurrent intangible assets of an acquired entity, or will be allocated to the equity accounts
4. A reconciliation using percentages or dollar amounts of income tax expense or benefit attributable to continuing operations with the amount that would have resulted from applying regular federal statutory tax rates to pretax income from continuing operations is required for publicly held companies only. Other entities must, however, disclose the nature of significant reconciling items.

EMERGING ISSUES TASK FORCE CONSENSUS SUMMARIES

NOTE: Many other consensuses are deemed to have been made obsolete by the adoption of SFAS 109, and accordingly have been deleted from this listing.

86-9   IRC 338 and Push-Down Accounting

The EITF addressed a number of issues concerning whether the use of a step-up in the tax basis of an acquired entity, as permitted by the 1982 tax law, mandated the use of push-down accounting; also the necessary allocation of the tax provision between parent and subsidiaries if a step-up was not elected. There was a consensus that push-down is not required for non-SEC registrants. In addition, a consensus was reached that three different methods of tax allocation were acceptable: allocation to acquiree on preacquisition basis; crediting the tax benefit of tax basis step-up to acquirer's capital surplus upon realization; and crediting the benefit to income of acquirer.

86-43   Effect of a Change in Tax Law or Rates on Leveraged Leases

All components of a leveraged lease must be recalculated from the inception of the lease based upon revised cash flows, resulting from change in the tax law, etc. Differences from original computation are included in income in the year in which the tax law changes are enacted. Later, EITF 87-8 stipulated that assumptions regarding the effect of alternative minimum tax must be included in lease computations.

86-44   Effect of a Change in Tax Law on Investments in Safe Harbor Leases

Related to proposed FASB Statements issued in 1981 and 1982, which were never finalized, concerning accounting for tax leases. Guidance is still valid, however, since it stipulates how recomputations are made analogously to leveraged leases case.

88-4   Classification of Payment Made to IRS to Retain Fiscal Year

There was a consensus that a tax payment is an asset (deposit), which is adjusted annually, and will be ultimately realized when entity liquidates (or law changes), income declines to zero, or conversion to calendar year takes place.

93-12   Recognition and Measurement of the Tax Benefit of Excess Tax-Deductible Goodwill Resulting from a Retroactive Change in Tax Law

Companies have the option of retroactively applying the goodwill amortization provisions of the 1993 tax act to business combinations that occurred after July 25, 1991. The consensus was that the benefit related to tax-deductible goodwill in excess of goodwill for financial reporting purposes is to be included in income from continuing operations in the period of enactment, **if** the entity expects to elect to retroactively amortize goodwill for tax purposes. A current tax benefit relates to the effect of retroactive amortization deducted from the combination date to the enactment date; a deferred tax benefit is related to the tax-deductible goodwill (less retroactive amortization to the enactment date) in excess of the reported amount of goodwill as of the enactment date.

93-13   Effect of a Retroactive Change in Tax Rates That Is Included in Income from Continuing Operations

The tax effect of a retroactive change in rates on current and deferred tax assets and liabilities should be determined at the enactment date (August 10, 1993), using temporary differences and currently taxable income existing as of the date of enactment. The cumulative tax effect is to be included in income from continuing operations. Furthermore, the tax effect of items not included in income from continuing operations (e.g., from discontinued operations) that arose during the current fiscal year and prior to enactment should be measured based on the enacted rate at the time the transaction was recognized for financial reporting purposes; the tax effect of a retroactive change in rates on current or deferred tax assets or liabilities is included in income from continuing operations.

93-16 Application of FASB Statement 109 to Basis Differences within Foreign Subsidiaries That Meet the Indefinite Reversal Criterion of APB Opinion 23

The Task Force concluded that the APB 23 indefinite reversal criterion applies only to "outside basis differences," and not to "inside basis differences" arising in connection with ownership of foreign subsidiaries. Furthermore, if deferred taxes had not previously been provided for the "inside basis differences," under SFAS 109 entities would be required to provide them for differences arising after December 15, 1992, but could elect not to provide them for temporary differences arising earlier, if this had not been done when SFAS 109 was adopted.

93-17 Recognition of Deferred Tax Asset on Discontinued Operations

This consensus relates to the disposal of the stock of a subsidiary which is accounted for as a discontinued operation under APB 30. Notwithstanding the rule in APB 30 that gain recognition at the measurement date is limited to the amount of the loss expected to be realized from the disposal, if the reporting entity has excess tax basis in the subsidiary, the gain recognition limitations under the standard should be applied on a pretax basis, and the deferred tax asset on the "outside basis difference" should be recognized as provided under SFAS 109 at the measurement date. This would only apply, of course, if the deferred tax asset is deemed more likely than not to be realized.

94-10 Accounting for the Income Tax Effect of Transactions between (and With) Stockholders That Have Tax Effects for the Company

Certain transactions among stockholders, but outside the company, can affect the status of deferred taxes. The most commonly encountered of these is the change in ownership of over 50% of the company's stock, which limits or obviates the ability to utilize tax loss carryforwards, and accordingly will necessitate a write-off of deferred tax benefits previously recognized under SFAS 109. Changes in deferred taxes caused by transactions among stockholders are to be included in current period income tax expense in the income statement, since these are analogous to changes in expectations resulting from other external events (e.g., changes in tax rates). However, the tax effects of changes in the tax bases of assets or liabilities caused by transactions among stockholders would be included in equity, not in the income statement, although subsequent period changes in the valuation account, if any, would be reflected in income.

95-10 Accounting for Tax Credits Related to Dividend Payments in Accordance with FASB Statement No. 109

The accounting for a tax credit in the separate financials of the entity paying the dividend should be as a reduction of tax expense.

95-20 Measurement in the Consolidated Financial Statements of a Parent of the Tax Effects Related to the Operations of a Foreign Subsidiary That Receives Tax Credits Related to Dividend Payments

In consolidated statements of a parent company, a future tax credit related to dividends to be paid and related deferred taxes should be recognized based on the distributed rate if the parent is not invoking the indefinite reversal criteria of APB 23. However, the undistributed rate should be used if the parent has not provided deferred taxes.

96-7 Accounting for Deferred Taxes on In-Process Research and Development Activities Acquired in a Purchase Business Combination

In-process R&D acquired in a purchase business combination should be written off before the measurement of deferred taxes. Thus, no deferred taxes are provided on differences in initial bases for tax and financial reporting.

98-11 Accounting for Acquired Temporary Differences in Certain Purchase Transactions That Are Not Accounted for as Business Combinations

SFAS 109 established the principle that the tax effects of temporary differences related to purchase business combinations are to be "grossed up," in contrast to the older, "net of tax" method which had been prescribed by APB 11. However, SFAS 109 did not address the accounting for acquisitions of individual assets having different tax and accounting bases. This consensus holds that the tax attributes of such an acquisition are to be recorded in a manner similar to the accounting for the tax effects of negative goodwill under SFAS 109. Computationally, this involves the use of simultaneous equations or trial and error.

99-15 Accounting for Decreases in Deferred Tax Asset Valuation Allowances Established in a Purchase Business Combination as a Result of a Change in Tax Regulations

In mid-1999 new consolidated tax return regulations were issued that eliminated the requirement to apply the limitations on the separate return limitation year losses to situations in which a change in ownership as defined in Section 382 of the Internal Revenue Code has occurred within six months of a target company becoming a member of a consolidated group. As a result, only the loss limitation of Section 382 applies in those circumstances. The change in tax regulations requires an entity to reevaluate the need for an existing valuation allowance for deferred tax assets relating to NOLCs acquired in a prior purchase business combination.

The issue was whether, in the event that the valuation allowance is reduced or eliminated, the effect of the adjustment should be (1) included in operations or (2) applied first to reduce to zero any goodwill related to the acquisition, second to reduce to zero other noncurrent intangible assets related to the acquisition, and third to reduce income tax expense. Support for both approaches can be found in SFAS 109.

The consensus is that the effect of a change in tax law or regulation that results in a decrease in a valuation allowance that initially was recorded in the allocation of the purchase price in a purchase business combination should be included in income from continuing operations. This applies to any reduction in the valuation allowance that otherwise would not have been recognized except for the change in tax law or regulation, whether the valuation allowance is reduced in the period of the tax law change or in a subsequent period.

APPENDIX A

ACCOUNTING FOR INCOME TAXES IN INTERIM PERIODS

Interim Reporting

SFAS 109 essentially left unchanged the principles applicable to accounting for income taxes in financial statements covering interim periods, the accounting for which was established by APB 28 and FASB Interpretation 18. As set forth in those standards, the appropriate perspective for interim period reporting is to view the interim period as an integral part of the year, rather than as a discrete period. This objective is usually achieved by projecting income for the full annual period, computing the tax thereon, and applying the "effective rate" to the interim period income or loss, with quarterly (or monthly) revisions to the expected annual results and the tax effects thereof, as necessary.

While the Board chose to not comprehensively address interim reporting when promulgating SFAS 109, there were certain clear contradictions between APB 28 and the principles of SFAS 109, which the Board did address. As discussed in more detail below, these issues were (1) recognizing the tax benefits of losses based on expected earnings of later interim or annual periods, (2) reporting the benefits of net operating loss carryforwards in interim periods, and (3) reporting the effects of tax law changes in interim periods. Other matters requiring interpretation, which were left to the user to address without official guidance, included the classification of deferred taxes on interim balance sheets and allocation of interim period tax provisions between current and deferred expense.

While SFAS 109 is silent on the point, it would appear that the "with and without" methodology set forth in APB 28 and FASB Interpretation 18 (based on the now superseded APB 11) is no longer appropriate. The annual computation of tax expense is based upon the current tax provision as indicated in the tax return, plus or minus the adjustment necessary to bring the deferred tax asset and liability accounts to the proper balances as of the balance sheet date, thus a "with and without" approach focusing on the income statement is incorrect. Instead, the computation of interim period tax expense should be consistent with the asset and liability method set forth in SFAS 109.

Below is a relatively simple example that illustrates the basic principles of the opinion.

Basic example of interim period accounting for income taxes

Hartig, Inc. estimates that pretax accounting income for the full fiscal year ending June 30, 2002, will be $400,000. The company expects amortization of goodwill for the year to be $30,000, the annual premium on an officer's life insurance policy is $12,000, and dividend income (from a less than 20% ownership interest) is expected to be $100,000. The company recognized income of $75,000 in the first quarter of the year. The deferred tax liability arises solely in connection with depreciation temporary differences; these differences totaled $150,000 at the beginning of the year and are projected to equal $280,000 at year-end. The effective rate expected to apply to the reversal at both year beginning and year-end is 34%. The change in the taxable temporary difference during the current interim period is $30,000.

Hartig must first calculate its estimated effective income tax rate for the year. This rate is computed using all of the tax planning alternatives available to the company (e.g., tax credits, foreign rates, capital gains rates, etc.).

Estimated pretax accounting income		$ 400,000
Permanent differences:		
Add: Nondeductible officers' life insurance premium	$ 12,000	
Nondeductible amortization of organization costs	30,000	42,000
		442,000
Less: Dividends received deduction ($100,000 x 70%)		(70,000)
Estimated "book" taxable income		372,000
Less: Change in taxable temporary difference		(130,000)
Estimated taxable income for the year		$ 242,000
Tax on estimated taxable income (see below)		$ 70,530
Effective tax rate for **current** tax provision		
[$70,530/(400,000 – 130,000)]		26.1%

Tax rate schedule			Taxable	
At least	*Not more than*	*Rate*	*income*	*Tax*
$ --	$ 50,000	15%	$ 50,000	$ 7,500
50,000	75,000	25%	25,000	6,250
75,000	--	34%	167,000	56,780
				$70,530

The deferred tax provision for the interim period should be based on the actual change in the temporary difference (depreciation, in this example) during the interim period. In this case, the depreciation temporary difference grew by $30,000 during the period, and the expected tax rate that will apply to the reversal, in future years, is the marginal rate of 34%. Accordingly, the tax provision for the period is as follows:

"Ordinary" income for the interim period	$75,000
Less: Change in temporary difference	30,000
Net "ordinary" income	45,000
Applicable tax rate	26.1%
Current tax provision	$11,755
Tax effect of temporary difference ($30,000 x 34%)	10,200
Total provision	$21,955

Therefore, the entry necessary to record the income tax expense at the end of the first quarter is as follows:

Income tax expense	21,955	
Income taxes payable—current		11,755
Deferred tax liability		10,200

The financial statement presentation would remain the same as has been illustrated in prior examples.

In the second quarter, Hartig, Inc. revises its estimate of income for the full fiscal year. It now anticipates only $210,000 of book income, including only $75,000 of dividend income, because of dramatic changes in the national economy. Other permanent differences are still expected to total $42,000.

Estimated pretax accounting income		$210,000
Permanent differences:		
Add: Nondeductible officers' life insurance premium	$12,000	
Nondeductible amortization of organization costs	30,000	42,000
		252,000
Less: Dividends received deduction ($75,000 x 70%)		(52,500)
Estimated "book" taxable income		199,500
Less: Change in taxable temporary difference		(130,000)
Estimated taxable income for the year		$ 69,500
Tax on estimated taxable income (see below)		$ 12,375
Effective tax rate for **current** tax provision		15.5%
[$12,375/($210,000 − $130,000)]		

Tax rate schedule			Taxable	
At least	Not more than	Rate	income	Tax
$ --	$ 50,000	15%	$ 50,000	$ 7,500
50,000	75,000	25%	19,500	4,875
				$12,375

The actual earnings for the second quarter were $22,000, and the change in the temporary difference was only $10,000. The tax provision for the second quarter is computed as follows:

"Ordinary" income for the half year	$97,000
Less: Change in temporary difference	40,000
Net "ordinary" income	57,000
Applicable tax rate	15.5%
Current tax provision	$ 8,835
Tax effect of temporary difference ($40,000 x 34%)	13,600
Total provision	$22,435

Under APB 28, and also under the general principle that changes in estimate are reported prospectively (as stipulated by APB 20), the results of prior quarters are not restated for changes in the estimated effective annual tax rate. Given the provision for current and deferred income taxes that was made in the first interim period, shown above, the following entry is required to record the income taxes as of the end of the second quarter:

Income tax expense	480	
Income taxes payable—current	2,920	
Deferred tax liability		3,400

The foregoing illustrates the basic problems encountered in applying the promulgated GAAP to interim reporting. In the following paragraphs, we will provide a discussion relative to some of the items requiring modifications to the approach described above.

Net Operating Losses in Interim Periods

FASB Interpretation 18 set forth the appropriate accounting when losses were incurred in interim periods or when loss carryforward benefits were realized during an interim reporting period. Given that NOL benefits realized are no longer treated as extraordinary items under SFAS 109, and given that tax benefits of operating losses are fully recognized in the period of loss, subject to the possible need for a valuation allowance, the prescriptions set forth by FASB Interpretation 18 have been revised. The changes affect (1) the calculation of the expected annual tax rate for purposes of interim period income tax provisions, and (2) the recognition of an asset for the tax effects of a loss carryforward.

Carryforward from prior years. Loss carryforward benefits from prior years first given recognition (i.e., by reduction or elimination of a previously provided valuation allowance) in interim periods are now included in the ordinary tax provision, rather than as extraordinary gains. FASB Interpretation 18 provided that an expected annual effective tax rate on **ordinary** income was to be calculated at each interim reporting date, and that this rate be used to provide income taxes on **ordinary** income on a cumulative basis at each interim date. The tax effects of extraordinary items, discontinued operations, and other nonoperating categories were excluded from this computation; those tax effects were separately determined on a "with and without" basis as explained later in this Appendix. Since, under APB 11, NOL benefit realization was not part of operating income, it was excluded from the estimation of the annual effective tax rate.

SFAS 109 amends FASB Interpretation 18 to require that recognition of a previously unrecognized tax benefit be included in the tax provision of the interim period when the reduction or elimination of the valuation allowance is the result of a reevaluation of the likelihood of future tax benefits being realized. An increase in the valuation account resulting from a revised judgment that the benefits are more likely than not going to be unrealizable would cause a catch-up adjustment to be included in the current interim period's ordinary tax provision. In either situation, the effect is **not** prorated to future interim periods by means of the effective tax rate estimate.

To illustrate, consider the following example:

Dillard Corporation has a previously unrecognized $50,000 net operating loss carryforward; a flat 40% tax rate for current and future periods is assumed. Income for the full year (before NOL) is projected to be $80,000; in the first quarter a pretax loss of $10,000 will be reported.

Projected annual income	$ 80,000
x Tax rate	40%
Projected tax liability	$ 32,000

Accordingly, in the income statement for the first fiscal quarter, the pretax operating loss of $10,000 will give rise to a tax **benefit** of $10,000 x 40% = $4,000.

In addition, a tax benefit of $20,000 ($50,000 loss carryforward x 40%) is given recognition, and is included in the current interim period tax provision relating to continuing operations. Thus, total tax benefit for the first fiscal quarter will be $24,000 ($4,000 + $20,000).

If Dillard's second quarter results in a pretax operating income of $30,000, and the expectation for the full year remains unchanged (i.e., operating income of $80,000), the second quarter tax provision is $12,000 ($30,000 x 40%).

The tax provision for the fiscal first half-year will be a **benefit** of $12,000, as follows:

Cumulative pretax income through second quarter ($30,000 – $10,000)	$20,000
x Effective rate	40%
Tax provision before recognition of NOL carryforward benefit	$ 8,000
Benefit of NOL carryforward first recognized in first quarter	(20,000)
Total tax provision (benefit)	$(12,000)

The foregoing example assumes that during the first quarter Dillard's judgment changed as to the full realizability of the previously unrecognized benefit of the $50,000 loss carryforward. Were this **not** the case, however, the benefit would have been recognized only as actual tax liabilities were incurred (through current period earnings) in amounts to offset the NOL benefit.

To illustrate this latter situation, assume the same facts about earnings for the first two quarters, and assume now that Dillard's judgment about realizability of prior period NOL does **not** change. Tax provisions for the first quarter and first half are as follows:

	First quarter	*First half-year*
Pretax income (loss)	$(10,000)	$ 20,000
x Effective rate	40%	40%
Tax provision before recognition of NOL carryforward benefit	$(4,000)	$ 8,000
Benefit of NOL carryforward recognized	--	(8,000)
Tax provision (benefit)	$(4,000)	--

Notice that recognition of a tax benefit of $4,000 in the first quarter is based on the expectation of at least a breakeven full year's results. That is, the benefit of the first quarter's loss was deemed **more likely than not**. Otherwise, no tax benefit would have been reported in the first quarter.

Estimated loss for the year. When the full year is expected to be profitable, it will be irrelevant that one or more interim periods results in a loss, and the expected effective rate for the full year should be used to record interim period tax benefits, as illustrated above. However, when the full year is expected to produce a loss, the computation of the expected annual tax benefit rate must logically take into account the extent to which a net deferred tax asset (i.e., the asset less any related valuation allowance) will be recordable at year-end. For the first set of examples, below, assume that the realization of tax benefits related to operating loss carryforwards are **not entirely** more likely than not. That is, the full benefits will be recognized but will be offset partially or completely by the provision of the valuation allowance.

For each of the following examples we will assume that the Lori Corporation is anticipating a loss of $150,000 for the fiscal year. A deferred tax liability of $30,000 is currently recorded on the company's books; all of the credits will reverse in the fifteen-year carryforward period. Assume future taxes will be at a 40% rate.

Example 1

Assume that the company can carry back the entire $150,000 to the preceding three years. The tax potentially refundable by the carryback would (remember this is only an estimate until year-end) amount to $48,000 (an assumed amount). The effective rate is then 32% ($48,000/150,000).

| | Ordinary income (loss) | | | Tax (benefit) expense | | |
| | | | | | Less | |
Reporting period	Reporting period	Year-to date	Year-to-date	previously provided	Reporting period
1st qtr.	$ (50,000)	$ (50,000)	$(16,000)	$ --	$(16,000)
2nd qtr.	20,000	(30,000)	(9,600)	(16,000)	6,400
3rd qtr.	(70,000)	(100,000)	(32,000)	(9,600)	(22,400)
4th qtr.	(50,000)	(150,000)	(48,000)	(32,000)	(16,000)
Fiscal year	$(150,000)				$(48,000)

Note that both the income tax expense (2nd quarter) and benefit are computed using the estimated annual effective rate. This rate is applied to the year-to-date numbers just as in the previous examples, with any adjustment being made and realized in the current reporting period. This treatment is appropriate because the accrual of tax benefits in the first, third and fourth quarters is consistent with the effective rate estimated at the beginning of the year; in contrast to those circumstances in which a change in estimate is made in a quarter relating to the realizability of tax benefits not previously provided (or benefits which had been partially or fully reserved against).

Example 2

In this case assume that Lori Corporation can carry back only $50,000 of the loss and that the remainder must be carried forward. Realization of income to offset the loss is not deemed to be more likely than not. The estimated carryback of $50,000 would generate a tax refund of $12,000 (again assumed). The company is assumed to be in the 40% tax bracket (a flat rate is used to simplify the example). Although the benefit of the operating loss carryforward is recognized, a valuation allowance must be provided to the extent that it is more likely than not that the benefit will not be realized. In this example, management has concluded that only one-fourth of the gross benefit will be realized in future years. Accordingly, a valuation allowance of $30,000 must be established, leaving a net of $10,000 as an estimated recordable tax benefit related to the carryforward of the projected loss. Considered in conjunction with the carryback of $12,000, the company will obtain a $22,000 tax benefit relating to the projected current year loss, for an effective tax benefit rate of 14.7%. The calculation of the estimated annual effective rate is as follows:

Expected net loss					$150,000
Tax benefit from carryback			$12,000		
Benefit of carryforward					
($100,000 x 40%)	$40,000				
Valuation allowance	(30,000)		10,000		
Total recognized benefit					$22,000
Estimated annual effective rate					
($22,000 ÷ $150,000)					14.7%

	Ordinary income (loss)			Tax (benefit) expense		
			Year-to-date		Less	
Reporting	Reporting	Year-to-		Limited	previously	Reporting
period	period	date	Computed	to	provided	period
1st qtr.	$ 10,000	$ 10,000	$ 1,470	$ --	$ --	$ 1,470
2nd qtr.	(80,000)	(70,000)	(11,733)	--	1,470	(10,263)
3rd qtr.	(100,000)	(170,000)	(14,667)	(22,000)	(10,263)	(4,404)
4th qtr.	20,000	(150,000)	(22,000)	--	(22,000)	--
Fiscal year	$(150,000)					$(22,000)

In the foregoing, the tax expense (benefit) is computed by multiplying the year-to-date income or loss by the estimated annual effective rate, and then subtracting the amount of tax liability or benefit already provided in prior interim periods. It makes no difference if the current period indicates an income or a loss, assuming of course that the full-year estimated results are not being revised. However, if the cumulative loss for the interim periods to date exceeds the projected loss for the full year upon which the effective tax benefit rate had been based, then no further tax benefits can be recorded, as is illustrated above in the provision for the third quarter.

The foregoing examples cover most of the situations encountered in practice. The reader is referred to paragraphs 49-55 in Appendix C of FASB Interpretation 18 for additional examples.

Operating loss occurring during an interim period. An instance may occur in which the company expects net income for the year and incurs a net loss during one of the reporting periods. In this situation, the estimated annual effective rate, which was calculated based upon the expected net income figure, is applied to the year-to-date income or loss to arrive at a total year-to-date tax provision. The amount previously provided is subtracted from the year-to-date figure to arrive at the provision for the current reporting period. If the current period operations resulted in a loss, then the tax provision for the period will reflect a tax benefit.

Tax Provision Applicable to Significant Unusual or Infrequently Occurring Items, Discontinued Operations, or Extraordinary Items Occurring in Interim Periods

Unusual, infrequent, or extraordinary items. The financial statement presentation of these items and their related tax effects are prescribed by SFAS 109. Extraordinary items and discontinued operations are to be shown net of their related tax effects. Unusual or infrequently occurring items that are part of continuing operations and will be separately disclosed in the fiscal year financial statements shall be separately disclosed as a component of pretax income, and the tax or benefit should be included in the tax provision for continuing operations.

The interim treatment accorded these items does not differ from the fiscal year-end reporting required by GAAP. However, according to APB 28, these items **are not** to be included in the computation of the estimated annual tax rate. The opinion also requires that these items be recognized in the interim period in which they occur. Examples of the treatment promulgated by the opinion follow later in this section.

Recognition of the tax effects of a loss due to any of the aforementioned situations is permitted if the benefits are expected to be realized during the year or if they will be recognizable as a deferred tax asset at year-end under the provisions of SFAS 109.

If a situation arises where realization is not more likely than not in the period of occurrence but becomes assured in a subsequent period in the same fiscal year, the previously unrecognized tax benefit should be reported in income from continuing operations until it reduces the tax provision to zero, with any excess reported in other categories of income (e.g., discontinued operations) which provided a means of realization for the tax benefit.

The following examples illustrate the treatment required for reporting unusual, infrequently occurring, and extraordinary items. Again, these items are **not** to be used in calculating the estimated annual tax rate. For income statement presentation, the tax provision relating to unusual or infrequently occurring items is to be included with the tax provision for ordinary income. Extraordinary items are shown net of their applicable tax provision.

The following data apply to the next two examples:

1. Dynamix Company expects fiscal year ending June 30, 2002 income to be $96,000 and net permanent differences to reduce taxable income by $25,500.
2. Dynamix Company also incurred a $30,000 extraordinary loss in the second quarter of the year.

Example 1

In this case, assume that the loss can be carried back to prior periods and, therefore, the realization of any tax benefit is assured. Based on the information given earlier, the estimated annual effective tax rate can be calculated as follows:

Expected pretax accounting income	$96,000
Anticipated permanent differences	(25,500)
Expected taxable income	$70,500

Tax Calculation "Excluding" Extraordinary Item

$50,000	x	.15	=	$ 7,500
20,500	x	.25	=	5,125
$70,500				$12,625

Effective annual rate = 13.15% ($12,625 ÷ 96,000)

No adjustment in the estimated annual effective rate is required when the extraordinary, unusual, or infrequent item occurs. The tax (benefit) applicable to the item is computed using the estimated fiscal year ordinary income and an analysis of the incremental impact of the extraordinary item. The method illustrated below is applicable when the company anticipates operating income for the year. When a loss is anticipated but realization of benefits of loss carryforwards is **not** more likely than not, the company computes its estimated annual effective rate based on the amount of tax to be refunded from prior years. The tax (benefit) applicable to the extraordinary, unusual, or infrequent item is then the decrease (increase) in the refund to be received.

Computation of the tax applicable to the extraordinary, unusual, or infrequent item is as follows:

Estimated pretax accounting income	$96,000
Permanent differences	(25,500)
Extraordinary item	(30,000)
Expected taxable income	$40,500

Tax Calculation "Including" Extraordinary Item

$$\$40,500 \ \times \ .15 = \$6,075$$

Tax "excluding" extraordinary item	$12,625
Tax "including" extraordinary item	6,075
Tax benefit applicable to extraordinary, unusual, or infrequent item	$ 6,550

			Tax (benefit) applicable to				
		Unusual, in-	Ordinary		Unusual, infrequent,		
	Ordinary	frequent, or	income (loss)		or extraordinary item		
Reporting period	income (loss)	extraordinary item	Reporting period	Year-to-date	Year-to-date	Previously provided	Reporting period
1st qtr.	$10,000	$ --	$ 1,315	$ 1,315	$ --	$ --	$ --
2nd qtr.	(20,000)	(30,000)	(2,630)	(1,315)	(6,550)	--	(6,550)
3rd qtr.	40,000	--	5,260	3,945	(6,550)	(6,550)	--
4th qtr.	66,000	--	8,680	12,625	(6,550)	(6,550)	--
Fiscal year	$96,000	$(30,000)	$12,625				$ (6,550)

Example 2

Again, assume that Dynamix Company estimates net income of $96,000 for the year with permanent differences of $25,500 which reduce taxable income. The extraordinary loss of $30,000 cannot be carried back and the ability to carry it forward is not **more likely than not**. Because no deferred tax credits exist, the only way that the loss can be deemed to be realizable is to the extent that current year ordinary income offsets the effect of the loss. As a result, realization of the loss is assured only as, and to the extent that, there is ordinary income for the year.

Reporting period	Ordinary income (loss)	Unusual, infrequent, or extraordinary item	Tax (benefit) applicable to				
			Ordinary income (loss)		Unusual, infrequent, or extraordinary item		
			Reporting period	Year-to-date	Year-to-date	Previously provided	Reporting period
1st qtr.	$ 5,000	$ --	$ 658	$ 658	$ --	$ --	$ --
2nd qtr	20,000	(30,000)	2,630	3,288	(3,288)a	--	(3,288)
3rd qtr.	(10,000)	--	(1,315)	1,973	(1,973)a	(3,288)	1,315
4th qtr.	81,000	--	10,652	12,625	(6,550)a	(1,973)	(4,577)
Fiscal year	$96,000	$(30,000)	$12,625				$(6,550)

a *The recognition of the tax benefit to be realized relative to the unusual, infrequent, or extraordinary item is limited to the lesser of the total tax benefit applicable to the item or the amount available to be realized. Because realization is based upon the amount of tax applicable to ordinary income during the period, the year-to-date figures for the tax benefit fluctuate as the year-to-date tax expense relative to ordinary income fluctuates. Note that at no point does the amount of the tax benefit exceed what was calculated above as being applicable to the unusual, infrequent, or extraordinary item.*

Discontinued operations in interim periods. Discontinued operations, according to APB 28, are included as significant, unusual, or extraordinary items. Therefore, the computations described for unusual, infrequent, or extraordinary items will also apply to the income (loss) from the discontinued segment, including any provisions for operating gains (losses) subsequent to the measurement date.

If the decision to dispose of operations occurs in any interim period other than the first interim period, the operating income (loss) applicable to the discontinued segment has already been used in computing the estimated annual effective tax rate. Therefore, a recomputation of the **total tax** is not required. However, the total tax is to be divided into two components.

1. That tax applicable to ordinary income (loss)
2. That tax applicable to the income (loss) from the discontinued segment

This division is accomplished as follows: a revised estimated annual effective rate is calculated for the income (loss) from ordinary operations. This recomputation is then applied to the ordinary income (loss) from the preceding periods. The total tax applicable to the discontinued segment is then composed of two items.

1. The difference between the total tax originally computed and the tax recomputed on remaining ordinary income
2. The tax computed on unusual, infrequent, or extraordinary items as described above

Example

Realtime Corporation anticipates net income of $150,000 during the fiscal year. The net permanent differences for the year will be $10,000. The company also anticipates tax credits of $10,000 during the fiscal year. For purposes of this example, we will assume a flat statutory rate of 50%. The estimated annual effective rate is then calculated as follows:

Estimated pretax income	$150,000
Net permanent differences	(10,000)
Taxable income	140,000
Statutory rate	50%
Tax	70,000
Anticipated credits	(10,000)
Total estimated tax	$ 60,000
Estimated effective rate ($60,000 ÷ 150,000)	40%

The first two quarters of operations were as follows:

	Ordinary income (loss)			Tax provision	
Reporting period	*Reporting period*	*Year-to-date*	*Year-to-date*	*Less previously provided*	*Reporting period*
1st qtr.	$30,000	$30,000	$12,000	$ --	$12,000
2nd qtr.	25,000	55,000	22,000	12,000	10,000

In the third quarter, Realtime made the decision to dispose of Division X. During the third quarter, the company earned a total of $60,000. The company expects the disposal to result in a onetime charge to income of $50,000 and estimates that operating losses subsequent to the disposal will be $25,000. The company estimates revised ordinary income in the fourth quarter to be $35,000. The two components of pretax accounting income (discontinued operations and revised ordinary income) are shown below.

		Division X	
Reporting period	*Revised ordinary income*	*Loss from operations*	*Provision for loss on disposal*
1st qtr.	$ 40,000	$(10,000)	$ --
2nd qtr.	40,000	(15,000)	--
3rd qtr.	80,000	(20,000)	(75,000)
4th qtr.	35,000	--	--
Fiscal year	$195,000	$(45,000)	$(75,000)

Realtime must now recompute the estimated annual tax rate. Assume that all the permanent differences are related to the revised continuing operations. However, $3,300 of the tax credits were applicable to machinery used in Division X. Because of the discontinuance of operations, the credit on this machinery would not be allowed. Any recapture of prior period credits must be used as a reduction in the tax benefit from either operations or the loss on disposal. Assume that the company must recapture $2,000 of investment tax credit which is related to Division X.

The recomputed estimated annual rate for continuing operations is as follows:

Estimated (revised) ordinary income	$195,000
Less net permanent differences	(10,000)
	$185,000
Tax at statutory rate of 50%	$ 92,500
Less anticipated credits from continuing operations	(6,700)
Tax provision	$ 85,800
Estimated annual effective tax rate ($85,800 ÷ 195,000)	44%

The next step is to then apply the revised rate to the quarterly income from continuing operations as illustrated below.

	Ordinary income			*Tax provision*		
			Estimated		*Less*	
			annual		*previously*	
Reporting	*Reporting*	*Year-to-*	*effective*	*Year-to-*	*previously*	*Reporting*
period	*period*	*date*	*rate*	*date*	*provided*	*period*
1st qtr.	$ 40,000	$ 40,000	44%	$17,600	$ --	$17,600
2nd qtr.	40,000	80,000	44%	35,200	17,600	17,600
3rd qtr.	80,000	160,000	44%	70,400	35,200	35,200
4th qtr.	35,000	195,000	44%	85,800	70,400	15,400
Fiscal year	$195,000					$85,800

The tax benefit applicable to the operating loss from discontinued operations and the loss from the disposal must now be calculated. The first two quarters are calculated on a differential basis as shown below.

	Tax applicable to		*Tax (benefit)*
	ordinary income		*expense*
Reporting	*Previously*	*Recomputed*	*applicable to*
period	*reported*	*(above)*	*Division X*
1st qtr.	$12,000	$17,600	$ (5,600)
2nd qtr.	10,000	17,600	(7,600)
			$(13,200)

The only calculation remaining applies to the third quarter tax benefit pertaining to the operating loss and the loss on disposal of the discontinued segment. The calculation of this amount is made based on the revised estimate of annual ordinary income both including and excluding the effects of the Division X losses. This is shown below.

	Loss from operations of Division X	*Provision for loss on disposal*
Estimated annual income from continuing operations	$195,000	$195,000
Net permanent differences	(10,000)	(10,000)
Loss from Division X operations	(45,000)	--
Provision for loss on disposal of Division X	--	(75,000)
Total	$140,000	$110,000
Tax at the statutory rate of 50%	$ 70,000	$ 55,000
Anticipated credits (from continuing operations)	(6,700)	(6,700)
Recapture of previously recognized tax credits as a result of disposal	--	2,000
Taxes after effect of Division X losses	63,300	50,300
Taxes computed on estimated income before the effect of Division X losses	85,800	85,800
Tax benefit applicable to Division X	(22,500)	(35,500)
Amounts recognized in quarters one and two ($5,600 + $7,600)	(13,200)	--
Tax benefit to be recognized in the third quarter	$ (9,300)	$(35,500)

The quarterly tax provisions can be summarized as follows:

Reporting period	Pretax income (loss) Continuing operations	Operations of Division X	Provision for loss on disposal	Tax (benefit) applicable to Continuing operations	Operations of Division X	Provision for loss on disposal
1st qtr.	$ 40,000	$(10,000)	$ --	$17,600	$ (5,600)	$ --
2nd qtr.	40,000	(15,000)	--	17,600	(7,600)	--
3rd qtr.	80,000	(20,000)	(75,000)	35,200	(9,300)	(35,500)
4th qtr.	35,000	--	--	15,400	--	--
Fiscal year	$195,000	$(45,000)	$(75,000)	$85,800	$(22,500)	$(35,500)

The following income statement shows the proper financial statement presentation of these unusual and infrequent items. The notes to the statement indicate which items are to be included in the calculation of the annual estimated rate.

Income Statement
(FASB Interpretation 18, Appendix D)

Net sales*		$xxxx
Other income*		xxx
		xxxx
Costs and expenses		
Cost of sales*	$xxxx	
Selling, general, and administrative expenses*	xxx	
Interest expense*	xx	
Other deductions*	xx	
Unusual items*	xxx	
Infrequently occurring items*	xxx	xxxx
Income (loss) from continuing operations before income taxes and other items listed below		xxxx
Provision for income taxes (benefit)**		xxx
Income (loss) from continuing operations before items listed below		xxxx
Discontinued operations:		
Income (loss) from operations of discontinued Division X (less applicable income taxes of $xxxx)	xxxx	
Income (loss) on disposal of Division X, including provision of $xxxx for operating losses during phase-out period (less applicable taxes of $xxxx)	xxxx	xxxx
Income (loss) before extraordinary items and cumulative effect of a change in accounting principle		xxxx
Extraordinary items (less applicable income taxes of $xxxx)		xxxx
Cumulative effect on prior years of a change in accounting principle (less applicable income taxes of $xxxx)***		xxxx
Net income (loss)		$xxxx

*   *Components of ordinary income (loss).*

**   *Consists of total income taxes (benefit) applicable to ordinary income (loss), unusual items and infrequent items.*

*** *This amount is shown net of income taxes. Although the income taxes are generally disclosed (as illustrated), this is not required.*

APPENDIX B

SCHEDULE OF COMMON PERMANENT AND TEMPORARY DIFFERENCES

Permanent Differences

Dividends received deduction. Depending on ownership interest, a percentage of the dividends received by a corporation are nontaxable. Different rules apply to subsidiaries. See section in chapter.

Municipal interest income. 100% exclusion is permitted for investment in qualified municipal securities. Note that the capital gains applicable to these securities **are** taxable.

Officer's life insurance premiums. Premiums paid on an officer's life insurance policy on which the company is the beneficiary are not allowed as a taxable deduction, nor are any proceeds taxable.

Organization and start-up costs. Certain organization and start-up costs are not allowed amortization under the tax code. The most clearly defined are those expenditures relating to the cost of raising capital.

Fines and penalties. Any fine or penalty arising as a result of violation of the law is not allowed as a taxable deduction.

Percentage depletion. The excess of percentage depletion over cost depletion is allowable as a deduction for tax purposes.

The portion of wages or salaries used in computing the jobs credit is not allowed as a deduction for tax purposes.

Temporary Differences

Installment sale method. Use of the installment sale method for tax purposes generally results in a timing difference because that method is not used in accordance with GAAP.

Long-term construction contracts. A temporary difference will arise if different methods (e.g., completed-contract or percentage-of-completion) are used for book and tax purposes.

Depreciation. A temporary difference will occur unless the modified ACRS method is used for financial reporting.

Goodwill. For tax purposes, amortization over fifteen years is mandatory. Amortization of goodwill is no longer permitted under GAAP, but periodic write-downs for impairment may occur, with any remainder of goodwill being expensed when the reporting unit to which it pertains is ultimately disposed of.

Estimated costs (e.g., warranty expense). Estimates or provisions of this nature are not included in the determination of taxable income until the period in which they actually occur.

Accounting for investments. Use of the equity method for financial reporting while using the cost method for tax purposes.

Prepaid income (e.g., prepaid rent). Prepaid income of this nature is includable in taxable income in the period in which it is received, while for financial purposes, it is considered a liability until the revenue is earned.

Net capital loss. The loss is recognized currently for financial reporting purposes but is carried forward to be offset against future capital gains for tax purposes.

Accrued contingent liabilities. These cannot be deducted for tax purposes until the liability becomes fixed and determinable.

Excess charitable contributions. These can be carried over to future years for tax purposes.

Mandatory change from cash to accrual. Generally one-fourth of this adjustment is recognized for tax purposes each year.

Uniform cost capitalization adjustment to beginning inventories. This also is recognized over a four-year period, with exceptions, for tax purposes.

Cash basis versus accrual basis. Use of the cash method of accounting for tax purposes and the accrual method for financial reporting is a temporary difference.

Deferred compensation. The present value of deferred compensation agreements must be accrued over the employee's remaining employment period, but cannot be deducted for tax purposes until actually paid.

16 PENSIONS AND OTHER POSTRETIREMENT BENEFITS

PERSPECTIVE AND ISSUES

A convergence of economic and political factors in the US has had a profound impact on the tools and techniques used by businesses and their employees to plan for and fund retirees' postemployment income.

Consider the demographics of the aging "Baby Boom" generation, the resulting financial uncertainties surrounding the financial health of the Social Security retirement system, the low savings rate, and the standard of living they currently enjoy. These conditions have necessitated the establishment of a private, supplemental system for providing pension and postretirement health benefits for retirees. The growth of this system has been promoted by the generous income tax benefits available to enterprises that provide employees with such benefits and to employees for voluntarily contributing portions of their earnings to individual retirement accounts or to employer retirement plans that accept such contributions.

This chapter focuses on accounting for postretirement benefits including single-employer and multiemployer plans, defined benefit pension plans, defined contribution pension plans, and postretirement plans other than pensions that help fund retiree costs of health care benefits.

SFAS 87 specifies the accrual basis of accounting for pension costs. This standard is considered evolutionary and transitional in nature. However, it continues three primary characteristics of APB 8.

1. Delayed recognition (changes are not recognized immediately but are subsequently recognized in a gradual and systematic way)
2. Reporting net cost (aggregates of various items are reported as one net amount)
3. Offsetting assets and liabilities (assets and liabilities are sometimes shown net)

Estimates and averages may be used as long as material differences do not result. Explicit assumptions and estimates of future events must be used for each specified variable included in pension costs and disclosed in the notes to the financial statements.

SFAS 87 focuses directly on the terms of the plan to assist in the recognition of compensation cost over the service period of the employees. It results in recognition of significant liabilities and it recognizes a minimum liability in the case of plans that are underfunded by a material amount.

The principal emphasis of SFAS 87 is the present value of the pension obligation, and the fair value of plan assets. The main accounting issues revolve around the expense to recognize on the income statement and the liability to be accrued on the balance sheet.

SFAS 88 is closely related to SFAS 87. It establishes standards to be followed by employers of defined benefit pension plans when obligations are settled, plans are curtailed, or benefits are terminated.

Although there are some major differences in terminology and measurement, other postretirement benefits (OPEB) accounting basically follows the fundamental framework established for pension accounting and applies to all forms of postretirement benefits. However, in most cases, the main focus will be on postretirement health care benefits. SFAS 106 considers OPEB to be a form of deferred compensation and requires accrual accounting. The terms of the individual contract will govern the accrual of the employer's obligation for deferred compensation and the cost should be attributed over the employee service periods until full eligibility is attained. The employer's obligation for OPEB should be fully accrued when the employee attains full eligibility for all expected benefits.

SFAS 132, entitled *Employers' Disclosures About Pensions and Other Postretirement Benefits*, revised and standardized these disclosures by using a separate but parallel format, eliminating less useful information, requiring some additional data deemed useful by analysts, and allowing some aggregation of presentation. Recognition and measurement aspects were not addressed. It amended only the disclosure requirements for SFAS 87, 88, and 106.

Sources of GAAP		
APB	*SFAS*	*EITF*
12, 16, 30	5, 87, 88, 106,	88-1, 88-5, 90-3,
	112, 130, 132	91-7, 92-13, 93-3, D-36

DEFINITIONS OF TERMS

Accrued pension cost. Cumulative net pension cost accrued in excess of the employer's contributions.

Accumulated benefit obligation. Actuarial present value of benefits (whether vested or nonvested) attributed by the pension benefit formula to employee service rendered before a specified date and based on employee service and compensation (if applicable) prior to that date. The accumulated benefit obligation differs from the projected benefit obligation in that it includes no assumption about future compensation levels. For plans with flat-benefit or no-pay-related pension benefit formulas, the accumulated benefit obligation and the projected benefit obligation are the same.

Accumulated postretirement benefit obligation. The actuarial present value of benefits attributed to employee service rendered to a particular date. Prior to an employee's full eligibility date, the accumulated postretirement benefit obligation as of a particular date for an employee is the portion of the expected postretirement benefit obligation attributed to that employee's service rendered to that date. On and after the full eligibility date, the accumulated and expected postretirement benefit obligations for an employee are the same.

Actual return on plan assets component (of net periodic pension cost). Difference between fair value of plan assets at the end of the period and the fair value at the beginning of the period, adjusted for employer contributions and payments of benefits during the period.

Actuarial present value. Value, as of a specified date, of an amount or series of amounts payable or receivable thereafter, with each amount adjusted to reflect (1) the time value of money (through discounts for interest) and (2) the probability of payment (by means of decrements for events such as death, disability, withdrawal, or retirement) between the specified date and the expected date of payment.

Amortization. Usually refers to the process of reducing a recognized liability systematically by recognizing revenues or reducing a recognized asset systematically by recognizing expenses or costs. In pension accounting, amortization is also used to refer to the systematic recognition in net pension cost over several periods of previously **unrecognized** amounts, including unrecognized prior service cost and unrecognized net gain or loss.

Annuity contract. Irrevocable contract in which an insurance company[1] unconditionally undertakes a legal obligation to provide specified benefits to specific individuals in return for a fixed consideration or premium. It involves the transfer of significant risk from the employer to the insurance company. Participating annuity contracts provide that the purchaser (either the plan or the employer) may participate in the experience of the insurance company. The insurance company ordinarily pays dividends to the purchaser. If the substance of a participating annuity contract is such that the employer remains subject to all or most of the risks and rewards associated with the benefit obligation covered or the assets transferred to the insurance company, the purchase of the contract does not constitute a settlement.

Assumptions. Estimates of the occurrence of future events affecting pension costs, such as mortality, withdrawal, disablement and retirement, changes in compensation and national pension benefits, and discount rates to reflect the time value of money.

Attribution. Process of assigning pension benefits or cost to periods of employee service.

Attribution period. The period of an employee's service to which the expected postretirement benefit obligation for that employee is assigned. The beginning of the attribution period is the employee's date of hire unless the plan's benefit formula grants credit only for service from a later date, in which case the beginning of the attribution period is generally the beginning of that credited service period. The end of the attribution period is the full eligibility date. Within the attribution period, an equal amount of the expected postretirement benefit obligation is attributed to each year of service unless the plan's benefit formula attributes a disproportionate share of the expected postretirement benefit obligation to employees' early years of service. In that case, benefits are attributed in accordance with the plan's benefit formula.

Career-average-pay formula. Benefit formula that bases benefits on the employee's compensation over the entire period of service with the employer. A career-average-pay plan is a plan with such a formula.

Contributory plan. Pension plan under which employees contribute part of the cost. In some contributory plans, employees wishing to be covered must contribute. In other contributory plans, employee contributions result in increased benefits.

Curtailment. Event that significantly reduces the expected years of future service of present employees or eliminates for a significant number of employees the accrual of defined benefits for some or all of their future services. Curtailments include (1) termination of employee's services earlier than expected, which may or may not involve closing a facility or discontinuing a segment of a business and

---

[1] *If the insurance company is controlled by the employer or there is any reasonable doubt that the insurance company will meet its obligation under the contract, the purchase of the contract does not constitute a settlement for purposes of this chapter.*

(2) termination or suspension of a plan so that employees do not earn additional defined benefits for future services. In the latter situation, future service may be counted toward vesting of benefits accumulated based on past services.

Defined benefit pension plan. Pension plan that defines an amount of pension benefit to be provided, usually as a function of one or more factors such as age, years of service, or compensation. Any pension plan that is not a defined contribution pension plan is, for purposes of SFAS 87, a defined benefit pension plan.

Defined contribution pension plan. Plan that provides pension benefits in return for services rendered, provides an individual account for each participant, and specifies how contributions to the individual's account are to be determined instead of specifying the amount of benefits the individual is to receive. Under a defined contribution pension plan, the benefits a participant will receive depend solely on the amount contributed to the participant's account, the returns earned on investments of those contributions, and forfeitures of other participants' benefits that may be allocated to such participant's account.

Expected long-term rate of return on plan assets. Assumption as to the rate of return on plan assets reflecting the average rate of earnings expected on the funds invested or to be invested to provide for the benefits included in the projected benefit obligation.

Expected postretirement benefit obligation. The actuarial present value as of a particular date of the benefits expected to be paid to or for an employee, the employee's beneficiaries, and any covered dependents pursuant to the terms of the postretirement benefit plan.

Expected return on plan assets. Amount calculated as a basis for determining the extent of delayed recognition of the effects of changes in the fair value of assets. The expected return on plan assets is determined based on the expected long-term rate of return on plan assets and the market-related value of plan assets.

Explicit approach to assumptions. Approach under which each significant assumption used reflects the best estimate of the plan's future experience solely with respect to that assumption.

Fair value. Amount that a pension plan could reasonably expect to receive for an investment in a current sale between a willing buyer and a willing seller (i.e., in other than a forced or liquidation sale).

Final-pay formula. Benefit formula that bases benefits on the employee's compensation over a specified number of years near the end of the employee's service period or on the employee's highest compensation periods. For example, a plan might provide annual pension benefits equal to 1% of the employee's average salary for the last five years (or the highest consecutive five years) for each year of service. A final-pay plan is a plan with such a formula.

Flat-benefit formula. Benefit formula that bases benefits on a fixed amount per year of service, such as $20 of monthly retirement income for each year of credited service. A flat-benefit plan is a plan with such a formula.

Full eligibility (for benefits). The status of an employee having reached the employee's full eligibility date. Full eligibility for benefits is achieved by meeting specified age, service, or age and service requirements of the postretirement benefit plan.

Full eligibility date. The date at which an employee has rendered all of the service necessary to have earned the right to receive all of the benefits expected to be received by that employee (including any beneficiaries and dependents expected to receive benefits). Determination of the full eligibility date is affected by plan terms that provide incremental benefits expected to be received by or on behalf of an employee for additional years of service, unless those incremental benefits are trivial. Determination of the full eligibility date is **not** affected by plan terms that define when benefit payments commence or by an employee's current dependency status.

Fund. Used as a verb, to pay over to a funding agency (as to fund future pension benefits or to fund pension cost). Used as a noun, assets accumulated in the hands of a funding agency for the purpose of meeting pension benefits when they become due.

Funding policy. Program regarding the amounts and timing of contributions by the employer(s), participants, and any other sources (for example, state subsidies or federal grants) to provide the benefits a pension plan specifies.

Gain or loss. Change in the value of either the projected benefit obligation or the plan assets resulting from experience different from that assumed or from a change in an actuarial assumption. See also **Unrecognized net gain or loss**.

Gain or loss component (of net periodic pension cost). Sum of (1) the difference between the actual return on plan assets and the expected return on plan assets and (2) the amortization of the unrecognized net gain or loss from previous periods. The gain or loss component is the net effect of delayed recognition of gains and losses (the net change in the unrecognized net gain or loss) except that it does not include changes in the projected benefit obligation occurring during the period and deferred for later recognition.

Interest cost component (of net periodic pension cost). Increase in the projected benefit obligation due to passage of time.

Market-related value of plan assets. Balance used to calculate the expected return on plan assets. Market-related value can be either fair market value or a calculated value that recognizes changes in fair value in a systematic and rational manner over not more than five years. Different ways of calculating market-related value may be used for different classes of assets, but the manner of determining market-related value shall be applied consistently from year to year for each asset class.

Measurement date. Date as of which plan assets and obligations are measured.

Mortality rate. Proportion of the number of deaths in a specified group to the number living at the beginning of the period in which the deaths occur. Actuaries use mortality tables, which show death rates for each age, in estimating the amount of pension benefits that will become payable.

Net periodic pension cost. Amount recognized in an employer's financial statements as the cost of a pension plan for a period. Components of net periodic pension cost are service cost, interest cost, actual return on plan assets, gain or loss, amortization of unrecognized prior service cost, and amortization of the unrecognized net obligation or asset existing at the date of initial application of SFAS 87. The term **net periodic pension cost** is used instead of **net pension expense** because part of the cost recognized in a period may be capitalized as part of an asset such as inventory.

Plan amendment. Change in terms of an existing plan or the initiation of a new plan. A plan amendment may increase benefits, including those attributed to years of service already rendered. See also **Retroactive benefits**.

Postemployment benefits. Benefits provided to former and inactive employees after employment but before retirement. Postemployment benefits include, but are not limited to, salary continuation, supplemental unemployment benefits, severance benefits, disability-related benefits (including workers' compensation), job training and counseling, and continuation of benefits such as health care benefits and life insurance coverage.

Postretirement benefits. All forms of benefits, other than retirement income, provided by an employer to retirees. Those benefits may be defined in terms of specified benefits, such as health care, tuition assistance, or legal services, that are provided to retirees as the need for those benefits arises or they may be defined in terms of monetary amounts that become payable on the occurrence of a specified event, such as life insurance benefits.

Prepaid pension cost. Cumulative employer contributions in excess of accrued net pension cost.

Prior service cost. Cost of retroactive benefits granted in a plan amendment. See also **Unrecognized prior service cost**.

Projected benefit obligation. Actuarial present value as of a date of all benefits attributed by the pension benefit formula to employee service rendered prior to that date. The projected benefit obligation is measured using assumptions as to future compensation levels if the pension benefit formula is based on those future compensation levels (pay-related, final-pay, final-average-pay, or career-average-pay plans).

Retroactive benefits. Benefits granted in a plan amendment (or initiation) that are attributed by the pension benefit formula to employee services rendered in periods prior to the amendment. The cost of the retroactive benefits is referred to as prior service cost.

Service. Employment taken into consideration under a pension plan. Years of employment before the inception of a plan constitute an employee's past service. Years thereafter are classified in relation to the particular actuarial valuation being made or discussed. Years of employment (including past service) prior to the date of a particular valuation constitute prior service.

Service cost component (of net periodic pension cost). Actuarial present value of benefits attributed by the pension benefit formula to services rendered by employees during the period. The service cost component is a portion of the projected benefit obligation and is unaffected by the funded status of the plan.

Settlement. Transaction that (1) is an irrevocable action, (2) relieves the employer (or the plan) of primary responsibility for a pension benefit obligation, and (3) eliminates significant risks related to the obligation and the assets used to effect the settlement. Examples include making lump-sum cash payments to plan participants in exchange for their rights to receive specified pension benefits and purchasing nonparticipating annuity contracts to cover vested benefits. A transaction must meet all of the above three criteria to constitute a settlement.

Substantive plan. The terms of the postretirement benefit plan as understood by an employer that provides postretirement benefits and the employees who render services in exchange for those benefits. The substantive plan is the basis for the accounting for that exchange transaction. In some situations an employer's cost-sharing policy, as evidenced by past practice or by communication of intended changes to a plan's cost-sharing provisions, or a past practice of regular increases in certain monetary benefits may indicate that the substantive plan differs from the existing written plan.

Transition obligation. The unrecognized amount, as of the date SFAS 106 is initially applied, of (1) the accumulated postretirement benefit obligation in excess of (2) the fair value of plan assets plus any recognized accrued postretirement benefit cost or less any recognized prepaid postretirement benefit cost.

Unfunded accumulated benefit obligation. Excess of the accumulated benefit obligation over plan assets.

Unfunded accumulated postretirement benefit obligation. The accumulated postretirement benefit obligation in excess of the fair value of plan assets.

Unrecognized net gain or loss. Cumulative net gain (loss) that has not been recognized as a part of net periodic pension cost. See **Gain or loss.**

Unrecognized prior service cost. Portion of prior service cost that has not been recognized as a part of net periodic pension cost.

CONCEPTS, RULES, AND EXAMPLES

The principal objective of SFAS 87 is to measure the compensation cost associated with employees' benefits and to recognize that cost over the employees' service period. This statement is concerned only with the accounting aspects of pension costs. The **funding** (amount set aside to meet future payment obligations) of the benefits is not covered and is considered to be a financial management matter.

When an entity provides benefits that can be estimated in advance to its retired employees and their beneficiaries, the arrangement is a pension plan. The typical plan is written and the amount of benefits can be determined by reference to the associated documents. The plan and its provisions can also be implied, however, from unwritten but established past practices. The accounting for most types of retirement plans is covered by SFAS 87 and 88. These plans include unfunded, insured, trust fund, **defined contribution** and **defined benefit plans**, and deferred compensation contracts, if equivalent. Independent deferred profit sharing plans and pension payments to selected employees on a case-by-case basis are not considered pension plans.

The establishment of a pension plan represents a commitment to employees that is of a long-term nature. Although some corporations manage their own plans, this commitment usually takes the form of contributions to an independent trustee. These contributions are used by the trustee to obtain plan assets of various kinds (treasury bonds, treasury bills, certificates of deposit, annuities, marketable securities, corporate bonds, etc.). The plan assets are used to generate a return generally in the form of interest, dividends, and/or appreciation in asset value. The return on the plan assets (and occasionally their liquidation) provides the trustee with cash to pay the benefits to which the employees are entitled. These benefits, in turn, are defined by the plan's benefit formula. The benefit formula incorporates many factors including employee compensation, employee service longevity, employee age, etc. and is considered to provide the best indication of pension obligations and costs. It is used as the basis for determining the pension cost recognized each fiscal year.

Net Periodic Pension Cost

It is assumed that a company will continue to provide retirement benefits well into the future. The accounting for the plan's costs should be reflected in the financial statements and these amounts should not be discretionary. All pension costs incurred should be charged against income. No amounts should be charged directly to retained earnings.

By their very nature, a sponsor's pension obligations are long-term liabilities. Short-term fluctuations in interest rates, market prices of plan investments, and other factors could, if recognized as incurred, cause material swings in net periodic pension cost in the company's financial statements. Such swings often would be offset by reversals in subsequent periods. As illustrated in the subsequent discussion, the FASB permitted the use of smoothing techniques to recognize certain of these changes in a systematic and rational manner by amortizing them instead of recognizing them immediately. This practice was adopted to soften the effects of such short-term fluctuations on reported earnings.

The benefits earned and costs recognized over the employees' service periods must be computed by reference to the pension plan's benefit formula. **Net periodic pension cost** consists of the sum of the following six components:

1. Service cost
2. Interest cost on projected benefit obligation
3. Actual return on plan assets
4. Gain or loss
5. Amortization of unrecognized prior service cost
6. Amortization of unrecognized net assets or net obligation existing at date of initial application of SFAS 87

In order to compute net periodic pension cost, the **accumulated benefit obligation (ABO)** and the **projected benefit obligation (PBO)** must be computed. Both of these obligations are actuarially determined using the actuarial present value of benefits earned that are attributable to services rendered by the employee to the date of the computation. The ABO is computed by reference to the present compensation level of the employee. It does not consider expected compensation increases that normally occur during the remaining time that the employee is expected to work prior to retirement. The PBO adjusts the accumulated benefit obligation for expected future compensation increases. Under the provisions of most pension plans, this provides a more relevant measure of the estimated cost of the benefits to be paid upon retirement. This is because the benefit formula set forth in the plan normally results in increases in future pension benefits based on increases in the employee's compensation.

Pay-related, **final-pay**, or **career-average-pay** plans are examples of plans based on future compensation levels. These plans measure benefits based on **service** to date but include **assumptions** as to compensation increases, turnover, etc. In non-pay-related or **flat-benefit plans**, both obligations are the same.

Example

	January 1, 2002
Accumulated benefit obligation	$(1,500)
Progression of salary and wages	(400)
Projected benefit obligation	$(1,900)

The expected progression of salary and wages is added to the accumulated benefit obligation to arrive at the projected benefit obligation. These amounts are provided by the actuary in a pension plan report.

Computation of the amounts to be shown on the balance sheet requires the determination of plan assets. Plan assets include contributions made by the employer that sponsors the pension plan (sponsor) plus the net earnings on the plan's investment (dividends, interest, and asset appreciation, less asset depreciation), less benefits paid to retired participants.

Example

Plan assets, January 1, 2002	$1,000
Investment earnings during 2002	200
Sponsor's contributions during 2002	400
Benefits paid to retired participants	(100)
Plan assets, December 31, 2002	$1,500

Service costs. This component of net periodic pension cost is the actuarial present value of benefits attributed during the current period. Under SFAS 87, the plan's benefit formula is the key to attributing benefits to employee service periods. In most cases, this **attribution** is straightforward.

If the benefit formula is ambiguous, the accounting for pension service costs must be based on the **substantive plan**. In some cases, this means that if an employer has committed to make future **amendments** to provide benefits greater than those written in the plan, that commitment shall be the basis for the accounting. The relevant facts regarding that commitment shall be disclosed.

Employers use pensions as a compensation tool to aid in the long-term retention of employees. In order to provide incentives for employees to continue their employment with the company over time, plan participants' rights to receive present or future pension benefits are often conditioned on continued employment with the employer/plan sponsor for a specified period. As the conditions are satisfied, the employee is said to "vest" in that portion of the future benefits that become unconditional. This can result in a disproportionate share of plan benefits being attributed to later years. In this situation, instead of the benefit formula, proportions or ratios need to be used to accumulate the total projected benefit in a manner that more equitably reflects the substance of the earning of the employee benefits. If the benefit formula does not specify a relationship between services and benefits, the following applies:

1. **Includable** in vested benefits (e.g., supplemental early retirement benefit)

$$\text{Benefit accumulation} = \frac{\text{Number of completed years of service}}{\substack{\text{Number of years when benefit} \\ \text{first fully vests}}}$$

2. **Not includable** in vested benefits (e.g., death or disability benefit)

$$\text{Benefit accumulation} = \frac{\text{Number of completed years of service}}{\text{Total projected years of service}}$$

SFAS 87 actuarial assumptions must reflect plan continuation, must be consistent as to future economic expectations, and must be the best estimate in regard to each individual assumption. It is not acceptable to determine that the aggregate assumptions are reasonable.

The discount rate used in the calculation of service costs should be the rate at which benefits could be settled. Examples include those rates in current **annuity contracts**, those published by Pension Benefit Guaranty Corporation (PBGC), and those that reflect returns on high-quality, fixed-income investments.

Future compensation is considered in the calculation of the service cost component to the extent specified by the benefit formula. To the degree considered, future compensation would include changes due to advancement, longevity, inflation, etc. Indirect effects, such as predictable bonuses based on compensation levels, and automatic increases specified by the plan also need to be considered. The effect of **retroactive amendments** are included in the calculation when the employer has contractually agreed to them. Service costs attributed during the period increase the ABO and PBO since they result in additional benefits to be payable in the future.

Example

	January 1, 2002	*2002 Service cost*
Accumulated benefit obligation	$(1,500)	$ (90)
Progression of salary and wages	(400)	(24)
Projected benefit obligation	$(1,900)	$(114) (a)*

*Component of net periodic pension cost

The current period service cost component is found in the actuarial report.

Interest cost on projected benefit obligation. The PBO is a discounted amount. It represents the discounted actuarial present value at the date of the valuation of all benefits attributed under the plan's formula to employee service rendered prior to that date. Each year, when the actuary calculates the end-of-year PBO, it is one year closer to the year in which the benefits attributed in prior years will be paid to participants. Consequently, the present value of those previously attributed benefits will have increased to take into account the time value of money. This annual increase, computed by multiplying the assumed settlement discount rate times the PBO as of the start of the year, increases net periodic pension cost and PBO. Since this "interest" cost is accounted for as part of pension cost it is not treated as interest for the purposes of computing capitalized interest under SFAS 34.

Example

	January 1, 2002	2002 Service cost	2002 Interest cost
Accumulated benefit obligation	$(1,500)	$ (90)	$(120)
Progression of salary and wages	(400)	(24)	(32)
Projected benefit obligation	$(1,900)	$(114) (a)	$(152) (b)*

* *Component of net periodic pension cost*

The **interest cost component** is calculated by multiplying the start of the year obligation balances by an assumed 8% settlement rate. This amount is found in the actuarial report.

Benefits paid to retirees are deducted from the above to arrive at the end of the year balance sheet figures for the accumulated benefit obligation and the projected benefit obligation.

Example

	January 1, 2002	2002 Service cost	2002 Interest cost	2002 Benefits paid	December 31, 2002
Accumulated benefit obligation	$(1,500)	$ (90)	$(120)	$160	$(1,550)
Progression of salary and wages	(400)	(24)	(32)	--	(456)
Projected benefit obligation	$(1,900)	$(114) (a)	$(152) (b)	$160	$(2,006)

Benefits of $160 were paid to retirees during the current year. This amount is found in the report of the pension plan trustee.

Actual return on plan assets. This component is the difference between the **fair value** of plan assets at the end of the period and the fair value of the plan assets at the beginning of the period adjusted for contributions and payments during the period. Another way to express the result is that it is the net (realized and unrealized) appreciation and depreciation of plan assets plus earnings from the plan assets.

Example

	January 1, 2002	2002 Actual return on plan assets	2002 Sponsor funding	2002 Benefits paid	December 31, 2002
Plan assets	$1,400	$158 (c)*	$145	$(160)	$1,543

* *Component of net periodic pension cost*

The actual return on plan assets of $158, cash deposited with the trustee of $145, and benefits paid ($160) are amounts found in the report of the pension plan trustee. These items increase the plan assets to $1,543 at the end of the year. The actual return on plan assets is adjusted, however, to the expected long-term rate (9% assumed) of return on plan assets ($1,400 x 9% = $126). The difference, $32, is a return on asset adjustment and is deferred as a gain (loss). The return on asset adjustment is a component of net periodic pension cost and is discussed in the following section.

Gain or loss. Gains (losses) result from (1) changes in plan assumptions, (2) changes in the amount of plan assets, and (3) changes in the amount of the projected benefit obligation. As discussed previously, immediate recognition of these gains (losses) is not acceptable under SFAS 87. Also, SFAS 87 does not require that they be matched through recognition in net pension cost in the period of occurrence. Instead, to provide "smoothing" of the effects of short-term fluctuations, **unrecognized net gain (loss)** is **amortized** if it meets certain criteria specified below.

Since actuarial cost methods are based on numerous assumptions (employee compensation, mortality, turnover, earnings of the pension plan, etc.), it is not unusual for one or more of these assumptions to be invalidated by changes over time. Adjustments will probably be necessary in order to bring prior estimates back in line with actual events. These adjustments are known as actuarial gains (losses). The accounting issue regarding the recognition of actuarial adjustments is their timing. All pension costs must be charged to income. Thus, actuarial gains (losses) are not considered prior period adjustments but are considered changes in an estimate that should be recognized in current and future periods.

Plan asset gains (losses) result from both realized and unrealized amounts. They represent periodic differences between the actual return on assets and the expected return. The expected return is generated by multiplying the **expected long-term rate of return** and the **market-related value** of plan assets. Market-related value is a concept unique to pension accounting. It results from the previously discussed smoothing techniques employed by the actuary under SFAS 87. Market-related value consists of two components. The first component is the fair market value of the plan assets. The second component is an adjustment for the unrecognized portion of previous years' market gains or losses that are being amortized over a period of five years or less using a consistently applied method. Consistently applied means from year to year for each asset class (i.e., bonds, equities), since different classes of assets may have their market-related value calculated in a different manner (i.e., fair value in one case, moving average in another case). Thus, the market-related value may be fair value, but it also may be other than fair value if all or a portion results from calculation.

Plan asset gains (losses) include both (1) changes in the market-related value of assets (regardless of definition) from one period to another **and** (2) any changes that are not yet reflected in market-related value (i.e., the difference between the actual fair values of assets and the calculated market-related values). Only the former changes are recognized and amortized. The latter changes will be recognized over time through the calculated market-related values. Differences in the experienced amount of PBO from that assumed will also result in gain (loss).

Irrespective of the income smoothing techniques used, if this unrecognized net gain (loss), however, exceeds a "corridor" of 10% of the greater of the beginning balances of the market-related value of plan assets or the projected benefit obligation, a minimum amortization is required. The **excess** over 10% should be divided by the average remaining service period of active employees and included as a component of net pension costs. Average remaining life expectancies of inactive employees may be used if that is a better measure.

Net pension costs include only **expected return on plan assets**. Any difference that results between actual and expected is deferred through the **gain (loss) component of net pension cost**. If actual returns are greater than expected returns, net pension cost is adjusted. This adjustment results in a **decrease** in net pension cost to adjust the actual return to the expected return. If expected returns are greater than actual returns, the adjustment results in an **increase** to net pension cost to adjust the actual return to the expected return. If the unrecognized net gain (loss) is large enough, it is amortized. Over the long term, the expected return should be a fairly good indicator of performance, although in any given year an unusual or infrequent result may occur.

The expected long-term rate of return used to calculate the expected return on plan assets should be the average rate of return expected to provide for pension benefits. Present rates of return and expected future reinvestment rates of return should be considered in arriving at the rate to be used.

To summarize, the net periodic pension cost includes a gain (loss) component consisting of **both** of the following:

1. As a minimum, the portion of the unrecognized net gain (loss) from previous periods that exceeds the **greater** of 10% of the beginning balances of the market-related value of plan assets **or** the PBO, usually amortized over the average remaining service period of active employees expected to receive benefits.

2. The difference between the expected return and the actual return on plan assets.

An accelerated method of amortization of unrecognized net gain (loss) is acceptable if it is applied consistently to both gains (losses) and if the method is disclosed. In all cases, at least the minimum amount discussed above must be amortized.

Example

	January 1, 2002	2002 Return on asset adjustment	2002 Amortization	December 31, 2002
Unamortized actuarial gain (loss)	$(210)	$32 (d)*	$2(d)*	$(176)

* *Components of net periodic pension cost*

The return on asset adjustment of $32 is the difference between the actual return of $158 and the expected return of $126 on plan assets. The actuarial loss at the start of the year ($210 assumed) is amortized if it **exceeds** a "corridor" of the larger of 10% of the projected benefit obligation ($1,900) or 10% of the fair value of plan assets ($1,400). In this example, $20 ($210 − $190) is amortized by dividing the years of average remaining service (twelve years assumed), with a result rounded to $2. The straight-line method was used, and it was assumed that market-related value was fair value.

Amortization of unrecognized prior service cost. Prior service costs result from plan amendments that result in increases in plan benefits attributable to services rendered by plan participants in the past. These costs are accounted for as a change in estimate. Prior service costs are measured at the amendment date by the increase in the projected benefit obligation. The service period of every active employee expected to receive benefits is to be determined, and then an equal amount of prior service cost should be assigned to each period. Consistent use of an accelerated amortization method is acceptable and must be disclosed if used.

If most of the plan's participants are inactive, remaining life expectancy should be used as a basis for amortization instead of remaining service life. If economic benefits will be realized over a shorter period than remaining service life, amortization of costs should be accelerated to recognize the costs in the periods benefited. If an amendment **reduces** the projected benefit obligation, unrecognized prior service costs should be reduced to the extent that they exist and any excess should be amortized as indicated above for benefit increases.

Example

	January 1, 2002	*2002 Amortization*	*December 31, 2002*
Unamortized prior service cost	$320	$(27) (e)*	$293

* *Component of net periodic pension cost*

Unamortized prior service cost ($320) is amortized over the years of average remaining service (twelve years assumed) at the amendment date with a result rounded to $27. The straight-line method was used. These amounts are found in the actuarial report.

Amortization of unrecognized amount at date of initial SFAS 87 application. Any difference between the projected benefit obligation and the fair value of plan assets minus recognized prepaid or plus accrued pension cost at the beginning of the fiscal year of the initial SFAS 87 application is to be amortized. The amortization is to be on a straight-line basis over the average remaining active employee service period. If the average remaining service period is less than fifteen years, the employer may elect to use a fifteen-year period. If all or almost all of a plan's participants are inactive, the employer shall use the inactive participants' average remaining expectancy period.

Example

	January 1, 2002	*2002 Amortization*	*December 31, 2002*
Unamortized net obligation (asset) existing at SFAS 87 application	$(30)	$3 (f)*	$(27)

* *Component of net periodic pension cost*

The unamortized net asset ($30) existing at SFAS 87 application is amortized over the average service remaining at date of application (twelve years assumed) with a result rounded to $3. The straight-line method was used. These amounts are found in the actuarial report.

Summary of Net Periodic Pension Costs

The components that were identified in the above examples are summed to determine the one amount known as net periodic pension cost as follows:

		2002
Service cost	(a)	$114
Interest cost	(b)	152
Actual return on assets	(c)	(158)
Gain (loss)	(d)	34
Amortization of unrecognized prior service cost	(e)	27
Amortization of unrecognized net obligation (asset) existing at SFAS 87 application	(f)	(3)
Total net periodic pension cost		$166

One possible source of confusion is the return on plan assets ($158) and the unrecognized gain of $34 that total $124. The actual return on plan assets reduces pension cost. This is because, to the extent that plan assets generate earnings, those earnings are helping the plan sponsor subsidize the cost of providing the benefits. Thus, the plan sponsor will not have to fund benefits as they become due, to the extent that plan earnings provide the plan with cash to pay those benefits. This reduction, however, is adjusted by increasing pension cost by the difference between actual and expected return of $32 and the amortization of the excess actuarial loss of $2 for a total of $34. The net result is to include the **expected** return of $126 ($158 − $32) less the amortization of the excess of $2 for a total of $124 ($158 − $34). In recognizing the components of net periodic pension costs, SFAS 132 requires the **disclosure** of this expected return of $126 and the loss of $2.

Employer's Liabilities and Assets

Upon initial adoption of SFAS 87, full implementation of accrual-basis recognition rules would have caused, in FASB's judgment, unacceptably large adjustments to the financial statements of companies whose plans were materially underfunded. Such adjustments would have been necessary to recognize previously unrecognized assets or liabilities representing the differences between PBO and the fair value of plan assets. To ease the perceived burden on these plan sponsors, FASB developed a compromise **minimum liability** approach. This minimum liability is computed by reference to the excess of the ABO (which is a smaller obligation than the PBO since it does not recognize projected future compensation increases) over the fair value of the plan assets. For the purpose of this calculation, the fair value of the assets is used, not the market-related value used to calculate the expected return on plan assets. To the extent that there is a pension liability already recorded, the sponsor need only recognize the additional amount necessary to increase the recorded liability to the amount of the minimum liability.

The theory behind using the ABO is the fact that, if the pension plan were terminated at the balance sheet date, the future compensation increases would never occur and the pension obligation could be settled for the smaller amount.

Fair value is determined as of the financial statement date (or not more than three months prior to that date if used consistently), and in the amount that would result from negotiations between a willing buyer and seller not in a liquidation sale. Fair value is measured in preferred order by market price, selling price of similar investments, or discounted cash flows at a rate indicative of the risk involved.

In SFAS 87, the additional minimum liability is recognized by an offsetting entry to recognize an intangible asset up to the amount of unrecognized prior service cost. Any additional debit needed is considered a loss and is shown net of tax benefits (subject to the restrictions on recognition of deferred tax assets per SFAS 109) in other comprehensive income.

Several points need to be remembered in regard to the additional minimum liability. First, an asset is **not** recorded if the fair value of the plan assets exceeds the accumulated benefit obligation. Second, the calculation of the minimum liability requires consideration of any already recorded prepaid or accrued pension cost. The net liability must be at least equal to the **unfunded accumulated benefit obligation** irrespective of the starting point. A **prepaid pension cost** will increase the amount of the recognized additional liability. An **accrued pension cost** will decrease it. Third, the intangible asset is **not** amortized. Fourth, at the time of the next calculation, the amounts are either added to or reversed out with no effect on the income statement. These balance sheet entries are entirely independent of the income statement and do not affect the calculation of net pension costs. Fifth, unless a significant event occurs or measures of obligations and assets as of a more current date become available, interim financials will show the year-end additional minimum liability adjusted for subsequent contributions and accruals. In this case, previous year-end assumptions regarding net pension cost would also carry over to the interim financials.

A schedule showing the variables of the above example in accordance with SFAS 132 reconciling the balance sheet amounts with the funded status of the plan is shown below.

Required Footnote Disclosure

	2001	*2002*
Change in benefit obligation		
Benefit obligation at beginning of year	$1,800	$1,900
Service cost	111	114
Interest cost	144	152
Amendment (prior service cost)	--	--
Actuarial loss (gain)	--	--
Benefits paid	(155)	(160)
Benefit obligation at end of year	$1,900	$2,006

Change in plan assets

Fair value of plan assets at beginning of year	$1,265	$1,400
Actual return (loss) on plan assets	150	158
Employer contribution	140	145
Benefits paid	(155)	(160)
Fair value of plan assets at end of year	$1,400	$1,543
Funded status	$ (500)	$ (463)
Unrecognized net actuarial loss on assets	210	176
Unrecognized prior service cost	320	293
Unamortized net obligation	(30)	(27)
Asset existing at SFAS 87 application (accrued)/prepaid pension cost	$ 0	$ (21)

Amounts recognized in the statement of financial position (balance sheet) consist of

Accrued benefit liability	$ (100)	$ (21)
Intangible asset	100	0
Accumulated other comprehensive income	0	0
Net amount recognized	$ 0	$ (21)

The difference between the projected benefit obligation and the plan assets indicates that the plan in this example is underfunded by **$500** at the beginning of 2002. Net actuarial losses, prior service costs, and the net asset existing when SFAS 87 was first applied are the remaining reconciling items to the zero amount shown on the balance sheet. **Conceptually**, the zero balance sheet amount is a journal entry netting of the following elements that would be recognized on the employer's books at the end of 2001, if accounting under SFAS 87 mirrored the pension plan's financial statements:

Investments	1,400	
Deferred actuarial loss	210	
Deferred prior service cost	320	
Deferred asset existing at SFAS 87 application		30
Projected benefit obligation		1,900

Only the additional minimum liability in the case of seriously underfunded plans will be required on the balance sheet. This amount is the difference between the accumulated benefit obligation ($1,500) and the plan assets ($1,400) plus prepaid pension cost ($0) or minus accrued pension cost ($0). In the above example, the result is $100 and the journal entry follows:

Intangible asset	100	
Pension liability		100

This journal entry is entirely independent of the calculation of pension cost and has no effect on that calculation. It only affects the balance sheet and remains until adjusted at the end of the next year. At that time, it will be decreased or increased to the extent required.

If the result of the minimum liability calculation exceeds the unamortized prior service cost, SFAS 130 requires the excess to be treated as other comprehensive income. For instance, assume that the required minimum liability in the above example is $350. In this case, the intangible asset would be recorded at the amount of the unamortized prior service cost and the **excess** would be recorded as other comprehensive income. The required journal entry would be

Other comprehensive income	30	
Intangible asset	320	
Pension liability		350

If not needed at the end of the next year, this entry would then be reversed.

Employer contributions of $145, net periodic pension costs of $166, and benefit payments of $160 are used in order to arrive at the end of the year balance sheet amounts. An accrued pension cost of $21 ($166 – $145) is required. This difference results from the employer funding $21 less than pension cost. **Conceptually**, this accrued amount is the netting of the following:

Investment	$1,543	
Deferred actuarial loss	176	
Deferred prior service cost	293	
Deferred assets existing at SFAS 87 application		$ 27
Projected benefit obligation		2,006
Totals	$2,012	$2,033

The excess credit is shown as an accrued pension liability of $21. Note that the additional minimum liability is no longer required since the accumulated benefit obligation ($1,550) and the plan assets ($1,543) differ by only $7 and there is already a pension liability on the balance sheet of $21. Thus, the additional minimum liability balances at the start of the year are reversed through the following journal entry:

Pension liability	100	
Intangible asset		100

This entry does not affect pension cost.

In summary, the only journal entries that are ordinarily required, if applicable, involve (1) the recording of net periodic pension cost and the associated accrued (or prepaid) pension cost, (2) the recording of the payment (funding) of the accrued (or prepaid) pension costs, and (3) the recording of any additional minimum liability and the associated intangible asset (and possible other comprehensive income entry). All of the other information used to determine these amounts are provided by the actuary or worksheet entries and do not appear on the books. Thus, accounts that reflect such things as the actuarial loss and prior service costs will usually not be found in the employer's general ledger.

Other Pension Considerations

If an entity has more than one plan, SFAS 87 provisions should be separately applied to each plan. Offsets or eliminations are not allowed unless there clearly is the right to use the assets in one plan to pay the benefits of another plan.

If annuity contracts and other insurance contracts that are equivalent in substance are valid and irrevocable, if they transfer significant risks to an unrelated insurance company (not a captive insurer), and if there is no reasonable doubt as to their payment, they should be excluded from plan assets and their benefits should be excluded from the accumulated benefit obligation and from the projected benefit obligation. Most other contracts are not considered annuities for SFAS 87 purposes. If a plan's benefit formula specifies coverage by **nonparticipating** annuity contracts, the service component of net pension costs is the cost of those contracts. In the case of a **participating** annuity contract, the cost of the participation right is to be recognized as an asset and measured annually at its fair value. If fair value is inestimable, the cost should be systematically amortized and carried at amortized cost (not to exceed net realizable value). Benefits provided by the formula beyond those provided by annuities should be accounted for in the usual SFAS 87 manner. All other insurance contracts are considered investments and are usually measured at cash surrender value, conversion value, contract value, or some equivalent.

In the typical defined contribution plan, the contribution is either discretionary or derived from a formula, and that amount should be the expense for that year. Benefits are generally paid from the pool of accumulated contributions. If, however, the defined contribution plan has defined benefits, the provision is calculated in the usual manner.

Participation in a multiemployer plan (two or more unrelated employers contribute such as in collectively bargained union-sponsored plans) requires that the contribution for the period be recognized as net pension cost and that any contributions due and unpaid be recognized as a liability. Assets in this type of plan are usually commingled and are not segregated or restricted. A Board of Trustees usually administers these plans. If there is a withdrawal from this type of plan and if an arising obligation is either probable or reasonably possible, SFAS 5 applies.

Some plans are, in substance, a pooling or aggregation of single employer plans and are ordinarily without collective-bargaining agreements. Contributions are usually based on a selected benefit formula. These plans are not considered multiemployer, and the accounting is based on the respective interest in the plan.

Non-US pension arrangements. The terms and conditions that define the amount of benefits and the nature of the obligation determine the substance of a non-US pension arrangement. If they are, in substance, similar to pension plans, SFAS 87 and 88 apply.

Business combinations. When an entity that sponsors a single-employer defined benefit plan is purchased, the purchaser must assign part of the purchase price to an asset if plan assets exceed the projected benefit obligation, or to a liability if the projected benefit obligation exceeds plan assets. The projected benefit obligation should include the effect of any expected plan curtailment or termination. This assignment eliminates any existing unrecognized components, and any future differences between contributions and net pension cost will affect the asset or liability recognized when the purchase took place.

SFAS 88

This statement is meant to be applied within the framework of SFAS 87. It describes the accounting to be followed by obligors when all or part of defined benefit pension plans have been settled or curtailed. It establishes employer accounting procedures in the case of benefits offered when employment is terminated.

Settlements include both the purchase of nonparticipating annuity contracts and lump-sum cash payments. The following three criteria must all be met in order to constitute a pension obligation settlement:

1. Must be irrevocable
2. Must relieve the obligor of primary responsibility for the obligaiton
3. Must eliminate significant risks associated with the obligation and the assets used to effect it

Transactions that do not meet these three criteria do not qualify for treatment as a settlement under SFAS 88. For example, an obligor could invest in a portfolio of high-quality fixed-income securities that would provide cash flows of interest and return-of-principal payments on dates that approximate the dates on which settlement payments are expected to become due. This would not meet the above criteria, however, because the employer is still primarily liable for the pension obligation and the investment is not irrevocable. Such a defeasance strategy does not constitute a settlement.

Under an annuity contract settlement, an unrelated insurance company unconditionally accepts an obligation to provide the required benefits. The following criteria must be met for this type of settlement:

1. Must be irrevocable
2. Must involve transfer of material risk to the insurance company

There can be no reasonable doubt as to the ability of the insurance company to meet its contractual obligation. The substance of any **participating** annuity contract must relieve the employer of most of the risks and rewards or it does not meet the criteria.

Curtailments include early discontinuance of employee services or cessation or suspension of a plan. Additional benefits may not be earned, although future service time may be counted towards vesting. Curtailments must meet the following criteria:

1. Must materially diminish present employees' future service or
2. Must stop or materially diminish the accumulation of benefits by a significant number of employees

A curtailment and a settlement can occur separately or together.

Settlements. If the entire projected benefit obligation is settled, any SFAS 87 unrecognized net gain (loss) plus any remaining unrecognized net asset existing when SFAS 87 was initially applied is immediately recognized. A pro rata portion is used in the case of partial settlement. If the obligation is settled by purchasing **participating** annuities, the cost of the right of participation is deducted from the gain (but not from the loss) before recognition.

If the total of the interest cost and service cost components of the SFAS 87 periodic pension cost is greater than or equal to the settlement costs during a given year, the recognition of the above gain (loss) is not required, but is permitted. However, a consistent policy must be followed in this regard. The settlement cost is generally the cash paid, or the cost of **nonparticipating** annuities purchased, or the cost of **participating** annuities reduced by the cost of the right of participation.

Curtailments. A curtailment results in the elimination of future years of service. The pro rata portions of any (1) unrecognized cost of retroactive plan amendments and (2) remaining unrecognized net obligation existing when SFAS 87 was initially applied that is associated with the eliminated years of service are immediately recognized as a loss.

If curtailment results in a decrease in the projected benefit obligation, a gain is indicated. An increase in the projected benefit obligation (excluding termination benefits) indicates a loss. This indicated gain (loss) is then netted against the loss from unrecognized prior service cost recognized in accordance with the preceding paragraph. The net result is the **curtailment gain** or **curtailment loss**. This gain (loss) is accounted for as provided in SFAS 5. A gain is recognized upon actual employee termination or plan suspension. A loss is recognized when both the curtailment is probable and the effects are reasonably estimable.

After the curtailment gain (loss) is calculated, any remaining unrecognized net asset existing when SFAS 87 was initially applied is transferred from that category and combined with the gain (loss) arising after SFAS 87 application. It is subsequently treated as a component of the new gain (loss) category.

Termination benefits. Termination benefits are accounted for in accordance with SFAS 5. Special short time period benefits require that a loss and a liability be recognized when the offer is accepted and the amount can be reasonably estimated. Contractual termination benefits require that a loss and a liability be recognized when it is probable that employees will receive the benefits and the amount can be reasonably estimated. The cost of these benefits is the cash paid at termination and the present value of future payments. Termination benefits and curtailments can occur together.

Segment disposal. Gains (losses), as calculated above, that result because of a disposal of a business segment should be recognized according to the provisions of APB 30.

Postretirement Benefits other than Pensions (OPEB)

SFAS 106 establishes the standard for employers' accounting for **other** (than pension) **postretirement employee benefits** (OPEB). This standard prescribes a single method for measuring and recognizing an employer's **accumulated postre-**

tirement benefit obligation (APBO). It applies to all forms of postretirement benefits, although the most material benefit is usually postretirement health care. It uses the fundamental framework established by SFAS 87 and 88. To the extent that the promised benefits are similar, the accounting provisions are similar. Only when there is a compelling reason, is the accounting different.

SFAS 106 requires accrual accounting and adopts the three primary characteristics of pension accounting as follows:

1. Delayed recognition (changes are not recognized immediately but are subsequently recognized in a gradual and systematic way)
2. Reporting net cost (aggregates of various items are reported as one net amount)
3. Offsetting assets and liabilities (assets and liabilities are sometimes shown net)

SFAS 106 distinguishes between the **substantive** plan and the **written** plan. Although generally the same, the **substantive plan** (the one understood as evidenced by past practice or by communication of intended changes) is the basis for the accounting if it differs from the written plan.

SFAS 106 focuses on accounting for a single-employer plan that defines the postretirement benefits to be provided. A defined benefit postretirement plan defines benefits in terms of (1) monetary amounts or (2) benefit coverage to be provided. Postretirement benefits include tuition assistance, legal services, day care, housing subsidies, health care (probably the most significant), and other benefits. The amount of benefits usually depends on a benefit formula. OPEB may be provided to current employees, former employees, beneficiaries and covered dependents. This standard applies to **settlement** of the APBO and to **curtailment** of a plan as part of a **special termination** benefit offer. It also applies to deferred compensation contracts with individuals. Taken together, these contracts are **equivalent** to an OPEB plan. SFAS 106 does not apply to benefits provided through a pension plan. If part of a larger plan with active employees, the OPEB shall be segregated and accounted for in accordance with this standard. If not materially different, estimates, averages, and computational shortcuts may be used.

The basic tenet of SFAS 106 is that accrual accounting is better than cash basis accounting. Recognition and measurement of the obligation to provide OPEB is required in order to provide relevant information to financial statement users. Although funding and cash flow information is incorporated into the statement, the overall liability is the primary focus.

The standard attempts, in accordance with the terms of the substantive plan, to account for the exchange transaction that takes place between the employer, who is ultimately responsible for providing OPEB, and the employee who provides services, in part at least, to obtain those OPEB. SFAS 106 accounting requires that the liability for OPEB be fully accrued when the employee is **fully eligible** for all of the expected benefits. The fact that the employee may continue to work beyond this date is not relevant since the employee has already provided the services in order to earn the OPEB.

OPEB are considered to be deferred compensation earned in an exchange transaction during the time periods that the employee provides services. The expected cost generally should be attributed in equal amounts (unless the plan attributes a disproportionate share of benefits to early years) over the periods from the employee's hiring date (unless credit for the service is only granted from a later date) to the date that the employee attains full eligibility for all benefits expected to be received. This accrual should be followed even if the employee provides service beyond the **date of full eligibility**.

Accounting for Postretirement Benefits

The **expected postretirement benefit obligation** (EPBO) is the actuarial present value (APV) as of a specific date of the benefits expected to be paid to the employee, beneficiaries and covered dependents. This term is not used in SFAS 87. Measurement of the EPBO is based on the following:

1. Expected amount and timing of future benefits
2. Expected future costs
3. Extent of cost sharing (contributions, deductibles, coinsurance provisions, etc.) between employer, employee and others (i.e., government). The APV of employee contributions reduces the APV of the EPBO. Obligations to return employee contributions, plus interest if applicable, should be recognized as a component of EPBO.

The EPBO includes an assumed salary progression for a pay-related plan. Future compensation levels should be the best estimate after considering the individual employees involved, general price levels, seniority, productivity, promotions, indirect effects, etc.

The APBO is the APV as of a specific date of all future benefits attributable to service by an employee to that date. It represents the portion of the EPBO earned to date. After full eligibility is attained, the APBO equals the EPBO.

The APBO also includes an assumed salary progression for a pay-related plan. Thus, this term is more comparable to the projected benefit obligation (PBO) under SFAS 87. The accumulated benefit obligation in SFAS 87 has no counterpart in SFAS 106.

Net periodic postretirement benefit costs include the following components:

1. Service cost—APV of benefits attributable to the current period (i.e., the portion of the EPBO earned this period)
2. Interest cost—Interest on the APBO
3. Actual return on plan assets
4. Gain or loss
5. Amortization of unrecognized prior service cost
6. Amortization of the transition asset or obligation

The **transition obligation**, under SFAS 106, is the unrecognized and **unfunded APBO** for all of the participants in the plan. This obligation can either (1) be recognized immediately as the effect of an accounting change, subject to certain limitations, or (2) be recognized on a delayed basis over future service periods with disclosure of the unrecognized amount. The delayed recognition has to result in, at least, as rapid a recognition as would have been recognized on a pay-as-you-go basis.

Service costs and interest costs are defined and measured in the same manner by SFAS 106 and 87. However, under SFAS 106, interest increases the APBO while under SFAS 87, interest increases the PBO.

Under SFAS 106, a single method is required to be followed in measuring and recognizing the net periodic cost and the liability involved. That method attributes the EPBO to employee service rendered to the full eligibility date.

Assumptions

SFAS 106 requires the use of explicit assumptions. Each should be the best estimate available of the plan's future experience, solely with regard to the individual assumption under consideration. Plan continuity can be presumed, unless there is evidence to the contrary. Principal actuarial assumptions include: discount rates, present value factors, retirement age, participation rates (**contributory plans**), salary progression (pay-related plans) and probability of payment (turnover, dependency status, mortality). Present value factors for health care OPEB include cost trend rates, medicare reimbursement rates and per capita claims cost by age.

Current interest rates, as of the **measurement date**, should be used for discount rates in present value calculations. Examples include high-quality, fixed-income investments with similar amounts and timing and interest rates at which the postretirement benefit obligations could be settled. The EPBO, APBO, service cost and interest cost components use assumed discount rates.

The expected long-term rate of return on plan assets should be the average rate of earnings on contributions during the period and on qualifying existing plan assets. Current returns on plan assets and reinvestment returns should be given consideration in arriving at the rate to be used. Related income taxes, if applicable, should reduce the rate. Expected return on plan assets and the market-related value of plan assets use this rate in their calculation.

Example

A sample illustration of the basic accounting for OPEB as established by SFAS 106 follows. Firstime Accrual Co. plans to adopt accrual accounting for OPEB as of January 1, 2002. All employees were hired at age 30 and are fully eligible for benefits at age 60. There are no plan assets. This first calculation determines the unrecognized transition obligation (UTO).

Firstime Accrual
December 31, 2001

Employee	Age	Years of service	Total years when fully eligible	Expected retirement age	Remaining service to retirement	EPBO	APBO
A	35	5	30	60	25	$ 14,000	$ 2,333
B	40	10	30	60	20	22,000	7,333
C	45	15	30	60	15	30,000	15,000
D	50	20	30	60	10	38,000	25,333
E	55	25	30	65	10	46,000	38,333
F	60	30	30	65	5	54,000	54,000
G	65	RET	--		--	46,000	46,000
H	70	RET	--		--	38,000	38,000
					85	$288,000	$226,332

Explanations

1. EPBO (expected postretirement benefit obligation) is usually determined by an actuary, although it can be calculated if complete data is available.
2. APBO is calculated using the EPBO. Specifically, it is EPBO x (Years of service/Total years when fully eligible)
3. The unrecognized transition obligation (UTO) is the APBO at 12/31/01 since there are no plan assets to be deducted. The $226,332 can be amortized over the average remaining service to retirement of 14.17 (85/6) years or an optional period of 20 years, if longer. Firstime Accrual selected the 20-year period of amortization.
4. Note that Employee F has attained full eligibility for benefits and yet plans to continue working.
5. Note that the above 2001 table is used in the calculation of the 2002 components of OPEB cost that follows.

After the establishment of the UTO, the next step is to determine the benefit cost for the year ended December 31, 2002. This calculation follows the framework established by SFAS 87. The discount rate is assumed to be 10%.

Firstime Accrual
OPEB Cost
December 31, 2002

1.	Service cost	$ 5,500
2.	Interest cost	22,633
3.	Actual return on plan assets	
4.	Gain or loss	
5.	Amortization of unrecognized prior service cost	
6.	Amortization of UTO	11,317
	Total OPEB Cost	$39,450

Explanations

1. Service cost calculation uses only employees not yet fully eligible for benefits.

Employee	12/31/01 EPBO	Total years when fully eligible	Service cost
A	$14,000	30	$ 467
B	22,000	30	733
C	30,000	30	1,000
D	38,000	30	1,267
E	46,000	30	1,533
			$5,000
	Interest for 2002 ($5,000 x 10%)		500
	Total service cost		$5,500

2. Interest cost is the 12/31/01 APBO of $226,332 x 10% = $22,633.
3. There are no plan assets so there is no return.
4. There is no gain (loss) since there are no changes yet.
5. There is no unrecognized prior service cost initially.
6. Amortization of UTO is the 12/31/01 UTO of $226,332/20-year optional election = $11,317.

After calculation of the 2002 benefit cost, the next step is to project the EPBO and APBO for December 31, 2002. Assuming no changes, it is based on the December 31, 2001 actuarial measurement and it is calculated as shown earlier in the determination of the UTO.

Firstime Accrual
December 31, 2002

Employee	Age	Years of service	Total years when fully eligible	EPBO	APBO
A	36	6	30	$ 15,400	$ 3,080
B	41	11	30	24,200	8,873
C	46	16	30	33,000	17,600
D	51	21	30	41,800	29,260
E	56	26	30	50,600	43,853
F	61	31	--	59,400	59,400
G	66	RET	--	44,620	44,620
H	71	RET	--	36,860	36,860
				$305,880	$243,546

Changes in experience or assumptions will result in gains (losses). The gain (loss) is measured by the difference resulting in the APBO or the plan assets from that projected. However, except for the effects of a decision to temporarily deviate from the substantive plan, these gains or losses have no impact in the year of occurrence. They are deferred and amortized as in SFAS 87. Amortization of unrecognized net gain (loss) is included as a component of net postretirement cost for a year if, as of the beginning of the year, it exceeds 10% of the **greater** of the APBO or the market-related value of plan assets. The minimum amortization is the **excess** divided by the remaining average service period of active plan participants. A systematic method of amortization that amortizes a greater amount, is applied consistently to both gains and losses and is disclosed may also be used. If gains (losses) are recognized immediately, special rules of offsetting may be required.

Other postemployment benefits. SFAS 112 uses the conditions of SFAS 43 to accrue an obligation for postemployment benefits other than pensions if services have been performed by employees, employees' rights accumulate or vest, payment is probable, and the amount can be reasonably estimable. If these benefits do not vest or accumulate, SFAS 5 applies. If neither SFAS 43 nor SFAS 5 is applicable because the amount is not reasonably estimable, this fact must be disclosed.

Deferred compensation contracts. If the aggregate deferred compensation contracts with individual employees are equivalent to a pension plan, the contracts should be accounted for according to SFAS 87 and 88. All other deferred compensation contracts should be accounted for according to APB 12.

SFAS 106 states that the terms of the individual contract will govern the accrual of the employee's obligation for deferred compensation and the cost should be attributed over the employee service period until full eligibility is attained.

Per APB 12, the amount to be accrued should not be less than the present value of the estimated payments to be made. This estimated amount should be accrued in a systematic and rational manner. When elements of both current and future employment are present, only the portion attributable to the current services should be accrued. All requirements of the contract, such as the continued employment for a specified period and availability for consulting services and agreements not to compete after retirement, need to be met in order for the employee to receive future payments. Finally, the total amount should be amortized to expense over the period from the date the contract is signed to the point when the employee is fully eligible to receive the deferred payments.

One benefit that may be found in a deferred compensation contract is for periodic payments to employees or their beneficiaries for life, with provisions for a minimum lump-sum settlement in the event of early death of one or all of the beneficiaries. The estimated amount to be accrued should be based on the life expectancy of each individual concerned or on the estimated cost of an annuity contract, not on the minimum amount payable in the event of early death.

1974 Employee Retirement Income Security Act. Congress passed the Employee Retirement Income Security Act (ERISA) in 1974. The principal objectives of ERISA were to provide statutory law for pension plan requirements, to strengthen the financial soundness of private pension plans, to safeguard employees' pension rights, and to create the Pension Benefit Guaranty Corporation (PBGC).

Prior to ERISA, the Internal Revenue Code was the principal source of law for governing and managing pension plans. Unfortunately, the thrust of the Code was with tax considerations, and the important nontax aspects of pension plans, such as vesting, funding, and employee participation, were not addressed. ERISA filled the void by mandating minimum vesting, funding, employee participation, and other requirements. Virtually every private pension plan is affected by the provisions of ERISA.

ERISA, as subsequently amended by Congress and interpreted by IRS regulations, provides minimum vesting periods for participants. Amounts contributed by employees must, at all times, be 100% vested. Benefits derived from employer contributions must become nonforfeitable when the employee reaches normal retirement age. Normal retirement age is the earlier of the time a participant attains normal retirement age under the plan or the later of: (1) attainment of age 65, or (2) the 5th anniversary of the individual's participation in the plan.

Plans must meet one of two alternative minimum vesting standards for benefits to be derived from employer contributions prior to normal retirement age: (1) a five-year cliff schedule requiring full vesting after five years of service, or (2) a three-to-seven-year graded schedule requiring 20% vesting after three years of service and 20% additional vesting in each of the following years (IRC § 1.411(a)-3T). For plans that are determined, under a formula to provide a disproportionate share of benefits to highly compensated individuals (top-heavy plans), the minimum vesting is required to be even faster.

In addition, ERISA requires a minimum funding, in accordance with an acceptable actuarial method, for private pension plans. ERISA also established standards for employee participation and has made defined contribution plans more popular.

All of the above requirements strengthen the financial soundness of employee pension funds. To further ensure the ability of a plan to pay pension obligations and to safeguard employee rights, ERISA amended the Internal Revenue Code of 1954 to allow for the assessment of fines and the denial of tax deductions. The Act also requires that pension plans submit annual reports, provide a description of the plan, and make a full disclosure through the submission of various statements and schedules.

Prior to the enactment of ERISA, some employees lost pension benefits when plans were terminated because of bankruptcy or other reasons. In order to protect employee rights under these circumstances, ERISA created PBGC. The function of this agency is to guarantee employees, if the employer cannot pay, at least a minimum amount of benefits for their years of service. This guarantee is financed by an insurance premium charge that is levied on all employers with defined benefit plans. PBGC also has the right to administer terminated plans, to impose liens on employers' assets, and to take over employers' assets under certain specified circumstances.

EMERGING ISSUES TASK FORCE CONSENSUS SUMMARIES

88-1   Determination of Vested Benefit Obligation for a Defined Benefit Pension Plan

In situations not specifically addressed by SFAS 87, the vested benefit obligation can be (1) the actuarial present value of the vested benefits that the employee is entitled to if the employee separates immediately, or (2) the actuarial present value of the vested benefits to which the employee is currently entitled but based on the employee's expected date of separation or retirement. The FASB staff favored (1) but several task force members thought (2) was more consistent with SFAS 87. This issue is usually applicable to foreign defined benefit pension plans.

88-5 Recognition of Insurance Death Benefits

It is **not** appropriate for the purchaser of life insurance to recognize income from death benefits on an actuarially expected basis.

90-3 Accounting for Employers' Obligations for Future Contributions to a Multiemployer Pension Plan

Based on SFAS 87, the existence of an executed agreement does not require a liability beyond currently due and unpaid contributions.

91-7 Accounting for Pension Benefits Paid by Employers after Insurance Companies Fail to Provide Annuity Benefits

A consensus was reached that a loss should be recognized by the employer at the time the employer assumes the benefit obligation payments to retirees for an insolvent insurance company that held these pension obligations. The loss would be recognized as the lesser of any gain recognized in the original contract with the insurance company or the amount of benefit obligation payments assumed by the company. Any additional loss not recognized should be recorded as a plan amendment in accordance with SFAS 87.

92-13 Accounting for Estimated Payments in Connection with the Coal Industry Retiree Health Benefit Act of 1992

If the company is currently operating in the coal industry, it may account for this obligation as either part of its multiemployer plan participation or as a contingent extraordinary loss in accordance with SFAS 5. If the company is no longer operating in the coal industry, the entire obligation would be recorded as an extraordinary loss under SFAS 5.

93-3 Plan Assets under FASB Statement No. 106

A trust established to pay postretirement benefits does not necessarily have to be "bankruptcy proof," or insulated completely from the claims of general creditors, in order to qualify as plan assets in accordance with SFAS 106. Plan assets held in a trust that explicitly makes them available to the general creditors in bankruptcy do not qualify as plan assets under SFAS 106.

17 STOCKHOLDERS' EQUITY

PERSPECTIVE AND ISSUES

SFAC 6 defines stockholders' equity as the residual interest in the assets of an entity after deducting its liabilities. Stockholders' equity is comprised of all capital contributed to the entity plus its accumulated earnings less any distributions that have been made. There are three major categories within the equity section: paid-in capital represents equity contributed by owners; retained earnings represents the sum of all earnings less that not retained in the business (i.e., dividends); and other comprehensive income represents changes in net assets, other than by means of transactions with owners, which have not been reported in earnings under applicable GAAP rules (e.g., accumulated translation gains or losses). (Comprehensive income was discussed in Chapter 3, Statements of Income and Comprehensive Income, and is not addressed in this chapter.)

It is clear, in most instances, that liabilities differ from equity interests, as the former represent claims against the assets of the entity while the latter are only residual claims to net assets. However, there are an increasing variety of instruments that have attributes of both liabilities and equity, and GAAP has not kept pace with these developments. The FASB has made intermittent efforts to address this topic since the mid-1980s, and recently has concluded that separate balance sheet presentation of the liability and equity components of compound instruments would be more representationally faithful. This means that proceeds from the issuance of compound instruments would have to be allocated among its constituent elements, with certain instruments categorized under present GAAP as equity being partially (or entirely) reclassified as liabilities. As of mid-2001 FASB was conducting field tests of the proposed methodology for making these allocations, using the relative fair value approach, with the intent being to issue a new standard to be effective for fiscal years beginning in mid-2002. The FASB proposal is detailed later in this chapter.

Earnings are not generated by transactions in an entity's own equity (e.g., by the issuance, reacquisition, or reissuance of its common or preferred shares). Depending on the laws of the jurisdiction of incorporation, distributions to shareholders may be subject to various limitations, such as to the amount of retained (accounting basis) earnings.

A major objective of the accounting for stockholders' equity is the adequate disclosure of the **sources** from which the capital was derived. For this reason, a number of different paid-in capital accounts may be presented in the balance sheet. The rights of each class of shareholder must also be disclosed. Where shares are reserved for future issuance, such as under the terms of stock option plans, this fact must also be made known.

Accounting for stock compensation has long been controversial, and GAAP has historically been supportive of the fiction that such plans generally impose no costs on the issuing company (the employer). An effort was made in the mid-1990s to conform financial reporting to economic reality, but the bitterly opposed new standard, SFAS 123, ultimately only recommended, but did not require, that the new **fair value** measurement model be adopted. However, under GAAP, rather extensive footnote disclosures are mandatory when the previous standard, APB 25, continues to be applied for purposes of basic financial statement measurement. For the vast majority of companies utilizing stock compensation programs, which eschewed the new measurement approach, this means that two entirely separate sets of computations are required to record and to disclose the impact of their stock compensation plans.

With APB 25 remaining in effect, as a result of the political compromise that led to the issuance of SFAS 123, the FASB found it necessary to address a large number of unresolved issues that were expected to be made moot. FASB Interpretation 44, issued in 2000, and EITF Issue 00-23, released in early 2001, resolve a great many of these matters, which are explained in this chapter in some detail.

SOP 93-6 revised the accounting for employers' contributions to employee stock ownership plans (ESOP). The new standard does optionally permit "grandfathering" shares acquired prior to 1993. The major changes from the prior rules relate to the measurement of compensation cost, which must now be gauged by the fair value of the shares contributed, not their historical cost to the employer. Also, dividends on unallocated shares are now deemed to be part of compensation cost, and thus are reported on the income statement rather than being shown in equity.

				Sources of GAAP			
ARB	*APB*	*SFAS*	*FASB I*	*FASB TB*	*EITF*		*SOP*
43, Ch. 1A,	6,	5, 52,	28, 31,	85-6,	84-18, 84-40, 85-1,		90-7,
1B, 7A,	12, 15,	87, 115,	38, 44	97-1	85-2, 85-46, 86-32,		93-6
7B, 13B;	25, 29	123,			87-6, 87-23, 87-33		
46		129, 130			88-6, 88-9, 89-11,		
					90-7, 90-9, 94-6, 95-16,		
					96-13, 96-18, 97-14,		
					98-2, 99-7, 00-6, 00-16,		
					00-19, 00-23, D-18, D-43, D-60		

DEFINITIONS OF TERMS

Additional paid-in capital. Amounts received at issuance in excess of the par or stated value of capital stock and amounts received from other transactions involving the entity's stock and/or stockholders. It is classified by source.

Allocated shares. ESOP shares assigned to individual participants. These shares are usually based on length of service, compensation or a combination of both.

Appropriation (of retained earnings). A segregation of retained earnings to communicate the unavailability of a portion for dividend distributions.

Authorized shares. The maximum number of shares permitted to be issued by a corporation's charter and bylaws.

Callable. An optional characteristic of preferred stock allowing the corporation to redeem the stock at specified future dates and at specific prices. The call price is usually at or above the original issuance price.

Cliff vesting. A condition of an option or other stock award plan which provides that the employee becomes fully vested at a single point in time.

Combination plans. Awards consisting of two or more separate components, such as options and stock appreciation rights, each of which can be exercised. Each component is actually a separate plan and is accounted for as such.

Committed-to-be-released shares. ESOP shares that will be allocated to employees for service performed currently. They are usually released by payment of debt service.

Compensatory plan. A stock option or similar plan including elements of compensation which are recognized over the service period.

Comprehensive income. The change in equity of a business enterprise during a period from transactions and other events and circumstances from nonowner sources. It includes all changes in equity during a period, except those resulting from investments by and distributions to owners.

Constructive retirement method. Method of accounting for treasury shares which treats the shares as having been retired. The shares revert to authorized but unissued status. The stock and additional paid-in capital accounts are reduced, with a debit to retained earnings or a credit to a paid-in capital account for the excess or deficiency of the purchase cost over or under the original issuance proceeds.

Contributed capital. The amount of equity contributed by the corporation's shareholders. It consists of capital stock plus additional paid-in capital.

Convertible. An optional characteristic of preferred stock allowing the stockholders to exchange their preferred shares for common shares at a specified ratio.

Cost method. Method of accounting for treasury shares which presents aggregate cost of reacquired shares as a deduction from the total of paid-in capital and retained earnings.

Cumulative. An optional characteristic of preferred stock. Any dividends of prior years not paid to the preferred shareholders must be paid before any dividends can be distributed to the common shareholders.

Date of declaration. The date on which the board of directors votes that a dividend shall be paid. A legal liability (usually current) is created on this date in the case of cash, property, and scrip dividends.

Date of grant. The date on which the board of directors awards the stock to the employees in stock option plans.

Date of payment. The date on which the shareholders are paid the declared dividends.

Date of record. The date on which ownership of the shares is determined. Those owning stock on this date will be paid the declared dividends.

Deficit. A debit balance in the retained earnings account. Dividends may not generally be paid when this condition exists. Formally known as accumulated deficit.

Discount on capital stock. Occurs when the stock of a corporation is originally issued at a price below par value. The original purchasers become contingently liable to creditors for this difference.

Employee stock ownership plan (ESOP). A form of defined contribution employee benefit plan, whereby the employer facilitates the purchase of shares of stock in the company for the benefit of the employees, generally by a trust established by the company. The plan may be leveraged by borrowings either from the employer-sponsor or from third-party lenders.

Fair value. An estimate of the value of a stock option which takes into account exercise price, expected term, current stock price, expected volatility, expected dividend yield, and risk-free interest rate during expected term; used to measure compensation under SFAS 123.

Fixed options. Options that grant the holder the rights to a specified numbers of shares at fixed prices. They are not dependent upon achievement of performance targets.

Graded vesting. A vesting process whereby the employee becomes entitled to a stock-based award fractionally over a period of years.

Intrinsic value. The excess of the market price of an underlying stock over the exercise price of a related stock option; used to measure compensation under APB 25.

Issued stock. The number of shares issued by the firm and owned by the shareholders and the corporation. It is the sum of outstanding shares plus treasury shares.

Junior stock. Shares with certain limitations, often as to voting rights, which are granted to employees pursuant to a performance compensation program. Such shares are generally convertible to ordinary shares upon achievement of defined goals.

Legal capital. The aggregate par or stated value of stock. It represents the amount of owners' equity that cannot be distributed to shareholders. It serves to protect the claims of the creditors.

Liquidating dividend. A dividend distribution that is not based on earnings. It represents a return of contributed capital.

Measurement date. The date on which the price that enters into the computation of the fair value of an equity instrument granted as compensation is fixed.

Minimum value. As used in SFAS 123, a computed option value that does not take into account the effect of expected volatility of the price of the underlying stock.

Noncompensatory stock options. Options which do not include an element of compensation. Under APB 25, many stock option plans meet the prescribed criteria and thus are deemed noncompensatory; under SFAS 123 most stock plans will include an element of compensation to be measured and allocated over the service periods of the employees or to be disclosed as such in the notes to the financial statements.

No-par stock. Stock that has no par value. Sometimes a stated value is determined by the board of directors. In this case, the stated value is accorded the same treatment as par value stock.

Outstanding stock. Stock issued by a corporation and held by shareholders (i.e., issued shares that are not held in the treasury).

Par value method. A method of accounting for treasury shares which charges the treasury stock account for the aggregate par or stated value of the shares acquired and charges the excess of the purchase cost over the par value to paid-in capital and/or retained earnings. A deficiency of purchase cost is credited to paid-in capital.

Participating. An optional characteristic of preferred stock whereby preferred shareholders may share ratably with the common shareholders in any profit distributions in excess of a predetermined rate. Participation may be limited to a maximum rate or may be unlimited (full).

Performance-based options. Options that are granted to employees conditional on the achievement of defined goals, such as market price of the underlying stock or earnings of the entity.

Phantom stock plan. A type of stock compensation arrangement that gives employees the right to participate in the increase in value of the company's shares (book value or market value, as stipulated in the plan), without being required to actually purchase the shares initially.

Quasi reorganization. A procedure that reclassifies amounts from contributed capital to retained earnings to eliminate a deficit in that account. All the assets and liabilities are first revalued to their current values. It represents an alternative to a legal reorganization in bankruptcy proceedings.

Retained earnings. The undistributed earnings of a firm.

Service period. The period over which a stock-based compensation award is earned by the recipient. If not otherwise defined in the plan, it is the vesting period. Under SFAS 123, if performance conditions affect either exercise price or date, then the service period must be consistent with the related assumption used in estimating fair value.

Stock-based compensation. Compensation arrangements under which employees receive shares of stock, stock options, or other equity instruments, or under which the employer incurs obligations to the employees based on the price of the company's shares.

Stock options. Enable officers and employees of a corporation to purchase shares in the corporation at a predetermined price for a defined period of time.

Stock rights. Enables present shareholders to purchase additional shares of stock of the corporation. It is commonly used if a preemptive right is granted to common shareholders by some state corporation laws.

Suspense shares. ESOP shares that usually collaterize ESOP debt. They have not been allocated or committed to be released.

Tandem plans. Compensation plans under which employees receive two or more components, such as options and stock appreciation rights, whereby the exercise of one component cancels the other(s). The accounting is based on the component that is more likely to be exercised.

Treasury stock. Shares of a corporation that have been repurchased by the corporation. This stock has no voting rights and receives no cash dividends. Some states do not recognize treasury stock. In such cases, reacquired shares are treated as having been retired.

Vesting. The process whereby the recipient of a stock-based compensation award earns the right to control or exercise the award.

CONCEPTS, RULES, AND EXAMPLES

Legal Capital and Capital Stock

Legal capital typically relates to that portion of the stockholders' investment in a corporation that is permanent in nature and represents assets that will continue to be available for the satisfaction of creditor's claims. Traditionally, legal capital was comprised of the aggregate par or stated value of common and preferred shares issued. In recent years, however, many states have eliminated the requirement that corporate shares have a designated par or stated value. Also, some states have adopted provisions of the Model Business Corporation Act that eliminated the distinction between par value and the amount contributed in excess of par.

The specific requirements regarding the preservation of legal capital are a function of the business corporation laws in the state in which a particular entity is incorporated. Accordingly, any action by the corporation that could affect the amount of legal capital (e.g., the payment of dividends in excess of retained earnings) must be considered in the context of the relevant laws of the state where the company is chartered.

Ownership interest in a corporation is made up of common, and optionally, preferred shares. The common shares represent the residual risk-taking ownership of the corporation after the satisfaction of all claims of creditors and senior classes of equity.

Preferred stock. Preferred shareholders are owners who have certain rights superior to those of common shareholders. Preferences as to earnings exist when the preferred shareholders have a stipulated dividend rate (expressed either as a dollar amount or as a percentage of the preferred stock's par or stated value). Preferences as to assets exist when the preferred shares have a stipulated liquidation value. If a corporation were to liquidate, these preferred holders would be paid a specific amount before the common shareholders would have a right to participate in any of the proceeds.

In practice, preferred shares are more likely to have preferences as to earnings than as to assets. Although unusual, preferred shares may have both preferential rights. Preferred shares may also have the following optional features: **participation** in earnings beyond the stipulated dividend rate; the **cumulative** feature, ensuring that dividends in arrears, if any, will be fully satisfied before the common shareholders participate in any earnings distribution; and **convertibility** or **callability** by the corporation. Preferences must be disclosed adequately in the financial statements, either on the face of the balance sheet or in the notes thereto.

In exchange for the preferences, the preferred shareholders' other rights or privileges are often limited. For instance, the right to vote may be restricted to common shareholders. The most important right denied to the preferred shareholders, however, is the right to participate without limitation in the earnings of the corporation. Thus, if the corporation has exceedingly large earnings for a particular period, most of these earnings would accrue to the benefit of the common shareholders. This statement is true even if the preferred stock is participating (a fairly uncommon feature) because participating preferred stock usually has some upper limitation placed upon its degree of participation.

Occasionally, several classes of stock will be categorized as common (e.g., Class A common, Class B common, etc.). Since there can be only one class of shares that represents the true residual risk-taking ownership in a corporation, it is clear that the other classes, even though described as common shareholders, must in fact have some preferential status. Typically, these preferences relate to voting rights. An example of this situation arises when a formerly closely held corporation sells shares to the public but gives the publicly held shares a disproportionately small capacity to exercise influence over the entity, thereby keeping control in the hands of the former majority owners even as they are reduced to the status of minority owners. The rights and responsibilities of each class of shareholder, even if described as common, must be fully disclosed in the financial statements.

Issuance of shares. The accounting for the sale of shares by a corporation depends upon whether the stock has a par or stated value. If there is a par or stated value, the amount of the proceeds representing the aggregate par or stated value is credited to the common or preferred stock account. The aggregate par or stated value is generally defined as legal capital not subject to distribution to shareholders. Proceeds in excess of par or stated value are credited to an additional paid-in capital account. The **additional paid-in capital** represents the amount in excess of the legal capital that may, under certain defined conditions, be distributed to shareholders.

A corporation selling stock below par value credits the capital stock account for the par value and debits an offsetting **discount account** for the difference between par value and the amount actually received. If the discount is on original issue capital stock, it serves to notify the actual and potential creditors of the contingent liability of those investors. As a practical matter, corporations avoided this problem by reducing par values to an arbitrarily low amount. This reduction in par eliminated the chance that shares would be sold for amounts below par.

Where the Model Business Corporation Act has been adopted or where corporation laws have embraced some of the attributes of that Act, there is often no distinction made between par value and amounts in excess of par. In those jurisdictions, the entire proceeds from the sale of stock may be credited to the common stock account without distinction between the stock and the additional paid-in capital accounts. The following entries illustrate these concepts:

Facts: A corporation sells 100,000 shares of $5 par common stock for $8 per share cash.

Cash	800,000	
Common stock		500,000
Additional paid-in capital		300,000

Facts: A corporation sells 100,000 shares of no-par common stock for $8 per share cash.

Cash	800,000	
Common stock		800,000

Preferred stock will often be assigned a par value because in many cases the preferential dividend rate is defined as a percentage of par value (e.g., 10%, $25 par value preferred stock will have a required annual dividend of $2.50).

If the shares in a corporation are issued in exchange for services or property rather than for cash, the transaction should be reflected at the fair value of the property or services received. If this information is not readily available, then the transaction should be recorded at the fair value of the shares that were issued. Where necessary, appraisals should be obtained in order to properly reflect the transaction. As a final resort, a valuation by the board of directors of the stock issued can be utilized (APB 29). Stock issued to employees as compensation for services rendered should be accounted for at the fair value of the services performed, if determinable, or the value of the shares issued. If shares are given by a major shareholder directly to an employee for services performed for the entity, this exchange should be accounted for as a capital contribution to the company by the major shareholder and as compensation expense incurred by the company. Only when accounted for in this manner will there be conformity with the general principle that all costs incurred by an entity, including compensation, should be reflected in its financial statements.

In certain instances, common and preferred shares may be issued to investors as a unit (e.g., a unit of one share of preferred and two shares of common can be sold as a package). Where both of the classes of stock are publicly traded, the proceeds from a unit offering should be allocated in proportion to the relative market values of the securities. If only one of the securities is publicly traded, then the proceeds should be allocated to the one that is publicly traded based on its known market value. Any excess is allocated to the other. Where the market value of neither security is known, appraisal information might be used. The imputed fair value of one class of security, particularly the preferred shares, can be based upon the stipulated dividend rate. In this case, the amount of proceeds remaining after the imputing of a value of the preferred shares would be allocated to the common stock.

The foregoing procedures would also apply if a unit offering were made of an equity and a nonequity security such as convertible debentures. Under proposed FASB guidelines, proceeds would be apportioned on the basis of relative fair values. (See the detailed discussion later in this chapter.)

Stock Subscriptions

Occasionally, particularly in the case of a newly organized corporation, a contract is entered into between the corporation and prospective investors, whereby the latter agree to purchase specified numbers of shares to be paid for over some installment period. These stock subscriptions are not the same as actual stock issuances and the accounting differs.

The amount of stock subscriptions receivable by a corporation is sometimes treated as an asset on the balance sheet and is categorized as current or noncurrent in accordance with the terms of payment. However, in accordance with SEC requirements, most subscriptions receivable are shown as a reduction of stockholders' equity in the same manner as treasury stock. Since subscribed shares do not have the rights and responsibilities of actual outstanding stock, the credit is made to a stock subscribed account instead of to the capital stock accounts.

If the common stock has par or stated value, the common stock subscribed account is credited for the aggregate par or stated value of the shares subscribed. The excess over this amount is credited to additional paid-in capital. No distinction is made between additional paid-in capital relating to shares already issued and shares subscribed for. This treatment follows from the distinction between legal capital and additional paid-in capital. Where there is no par or stated value, the entire amount of the common stock subscribed is credited to the stock subscribed account.

As the amount due from the prospective shareholders is collected, the stock subscriptions receivable account is credited and the proceeds are debited to the cash account. Actual issuance of the shares, however, must await the complete payment of the stock subscription. Accordingly, the debit to common stock subscribed is not made until the subscribed shares are fully paid for and the stock is issued.

The following journal entries illustrate these concepts:

1. 10,000 shares of $50 par preferred are subscribed at a price of $65 each; a 10% down payment is received.

Cash	65,000	
Stock subscriptions receivable	585,000	
Preferred stock subscribed		500,000
Additional paid-in capital		150,000

2. 2,000 shares of no-par common shares are subscribed at a price of $85 each, with one-half received in cash.

Cash	85,000	
Stock subscriptions receivable	85,000	
Common stock subscribed		170,000

3. All preferred subscriptions are paid, and one-half of the **remaining** common subscriptions are collected in full and subscribed shares are issued.

Cash [$585,000 + ($85,000 x .50)]	627,500	
Stock subscriptions receivable		627,500
Preferred stock subscribed	500,000	
Preferred stock		500,000
Common stock subscribed	127,500	
Common stock ($170,000 x .75)		127,500

When a subscriber defaults on an obligation under a stock subscription agreement, the accounting will follow the provisions of the state in which the corporation is chartered. In some jurisdictions, the subscriber is entitled to a proportionate number of shares based upon the amount already paid on the subscriptions, sometimes reduced by the cost incurred by the corporation in selling the remaining defaulted shares to other stockholders. In other jurisdictions, the subscriber forfeits the entire investment upon default. In this case, the amount already received is credited to an additional paid-in capital account that describes its source.

Additional Paid-in Capital

Additional paid-in capital represents all capital contributed to a corporation other than that defined as par, stated value, no-par stock, or donated capital. Additional paid-in capital can arise from proceeds received from the sale of common and preferred shares in excess of their par or stated values. It can also arise from transactions relating to the following:

1. Sale of shares previously issued and subsequently reacquired by the corporation (treasury stock)
2. Retirement of previously outstanding shares
3. Payment of stock dividends in a manner that justifies the dividend being recorded at the market value of the shares distributed
4. Lapse of stock purchase warrants or the forfeiture of stock subscriptions, if these result in the retaining by the corporation of any partial proceeds received prior to forfeiture
5. Warrants which are detachable from bonds
6. Conversion of convertible bonds
7. Other "gains" on the company's own stock, such as that which results from certain stock option plans

When the amounts are material, the sources of additional paid-in capital should be described in the financial statements.

Donated Capital

Donated capital can result from an outright gift to the corporation (e.g., a major shareholder donates land or other assets to the company in a nonreciprocal transfer) or may result when services are provided to the corporation. Under SFAS 116, such nonreciprocal transactions will be recognized as revenue in the period the contribution is received. Donated capital should be adequately disclosed in the financial statements.

In these situations, historical cost is not adequate to properly reflect the substance of the transaction, since the historical cost to the corporation would be zero. Accordingly, these events should be reflected at fair market value (APB 29). If long-lived assets are donated to the corporation, they should be recorded at their fair value at the date of donation, and the amount so recorded should be depreciated over the normal useful economic life of such assets. If donations are conditional in nature, they should not be reflected formally in the accounts until the appropriate conditions have been satisfied. However, disclosure might still be required in the financial statements of both the assets donated and the conditions required to be met.

Retained Earnings

Legal capital, additional paid-in capital, and donated capital collectively represent the contributed capital of the corporation. The other major source of capital is retained earnings, which represents the accumulated amount of earnings of the corporation from the date of inception (or from the date of reorganization) less the cumulative amount of distributions made to shareholders and other charges to retained earnings (e.g., from treasury stock transactions). The distributions to shareholders generally take the form of dividend payments but may take other forms as well, such as the reacquisition of shares for amounts in excess of the original issuance proceeds.

Retained earnings are also affected by action taken by the corporation's board of directors. **Appropriation** serves disclosure purposes and to restrict dividend payments, but does nothing to provide any resources for the satisfaction of the contingent loss or other underlying purpose for which the appropriation has been made. Any appropriation made from retained earnings must eventually be returned to the retained earnings account. It is not permissible to charge losses against the appropriation account nor to credit any realized gain to that account. The use of appropriated retained earnings has diminished significantly over the years.

An important rule relating to retained earnings is that transactions in a corporation's own stock can result in a reduction of retained earnings (i.e., a deficiency on such transactions can be charged to retained earnings) but cannot result in an increase in retained earnings (any excesses on such transactions are credited to paid-in capital, never to retained earnings).

If a series of operating losses have been incurred or distributions to shareholders in excess of accumulated earnings have been made and if there is a debit balance in retained earnings, the account is generally referred to as **accumulated deficit**.

Dividends

Dividends are the pro rata distribution of earnings to the owners of the corporation. The amount and the allocation between the preferred and common shareholders is a function of the stipulated preferential dividend rate; the presence or absence of (1) a participation feature, (2) a cumulative feature, and (3) arrearages on the preferred stock; and the wishes of the board of directors. Dividends, even preferred stock dividends, where a cumulative feature exists, do not accrue. Dividends only become a liability of the corporation when they are declared by the board of directors.

Traditionally, corporations were not allowed to declare dividends in excess of the amount of retained earnings. Alternatively, a corporation could pay dividends out of retained earnings **and** additional paid-in capital but could not exceed the total of these categories (i.e., they could not impair legal capital by the payment of dividends). States that have adopted the Model Business Corporation Act grant more latitude to the directors. Corporations can now, in certain jurisdictions, declare and pay dividends in excess of the book amount of retained earnings if the directors conclude that, after the payment of such dividends, the fair value of the corporation's net assets will still be a positive amount. Thus, directors can declare dividends out of unrealized appreciation that, in certain industries, can be a significant source of dividends beyond the realized and recognized accumulated earnings of the corporation. This action, however, represents a major departure from traditional practice and demands both careful consideration and adequate disclosure.

Three important dividend dates are

1. The **declaration** date
2. The **record** date
3. The **payment** date

The declaration date governs the incurrence of a legal liability by the corporation. The record date refers to that point in time when a determination is made as to which specific registered stockholders will receive dividends and in what amounts. Finally, the payment date relates to the date when the distribution of the dividend takes place. These concepts are illustrated in the following example:

On May 1, 2000, the directors of River Corp. declared a $.75 per share quarterly dividend on River Corp.'s 650,000 outstanding common shares. The dividend is payable May 25 to holders of record May 15.

May 1	Retained earnings (or dividends)	487,500	
	Dividends payable		487,500
May 15	No entry		
May 25	Dividends payable	487,500	
	Cash		487,500

If a dividends account is used, it is closed to retained earnings at year-end.

Dividends may be made in the form of cash, property, or scrip. Cash dividends are either a given dollar amount per share or a percentage of par or stated value. Property dividends consist of the distribution of any assets other than cash (e.g., inventory or equipment). Finally, scrip dividends are promissory notes due at some time in the future, sometimes bearing interest until final payment is made.

Occasionally, what appear to be disproportionate dividend distributions are paid to some, but not all, of the owners of closely held corporations. Such transactions need to be carefully analyzed. In some cases these may actually represent compensation paid to the recipients. In other instances, these may be a true dividend paid to all shareholders on a pro rata basis, to which certain shareholders have waived their rights. If the former, the distribution should not be accounted for as a dividend, but rather as compensation or some other expense category and included on the income statement. If the latter, the dividend should be "grossed up" to reflect payment on a proportional basis to all the shareholders, with an offsetting capital contribution to the company recognized as having been effectively made by those to whom payments were not made.

Property dividends. If property dividends are declared, the paying corporation may incur a gain or loss. Since the dividend should be reflected at the fair value of the assets distributed, the difference between fair value and book value is recorded at the time the dividend is declared and charged or credited to a loss or gain account.

Scrip dividends. If a corporation declares a dividend payable in scrip that is interest bearing, the interest is accrued over time as a periodic expense. The interest is **not** a part of the dividend itself.

Liquidating dividends. Liquidating dividends are not distributions of earnings, but rather a return of capital to the investing shareholders. A liquidating dividend is normally recorded by the declarer through charging additional paid-in capital rather than retained earnings. The exact accounting for a liquidating dividend is affected by the laws where the business is incorporated, and these laws vary from state to state.

Stock dividends. Stock dividends represent neither an actual distribution of the assets of the corporation nor a promise to distribute those assets. For this reason, a stock dividend is not considered a legal liability or a taxable transaction.

Despite the recognition that a stock dividend is not a distribution of earnings, the accounting treatment of relatively insignificant stock dividends (defined as being less than 20% to 25% of the outstanding shares prior to declaration) is consistent with it being a real dividend. Accordingly, retained earnings are debited for the fair market value of the shares to be paid as a dividend, and the capital stock and additional paid-in capital accounts are credited for the appropriate amounts based upon the par or stated value of the shares, if any. A stock dividend declared but not yet paid is classified as such in the stockholders' equity section of the balance sheet. Since such a dividend never reduces assets, it cannot be a liability.

The selection of 20% to 25% as the threshold for recognizing a stock dividend as an earnings distribution is arbitrary, but it is based somewhat on the empirical evidence that small stock dividends tend not to result in a reduced market price per share for outstanding shares. The aggregate value of the outstanding shares should not change, but the greater number of shares outstanding after the stock dividend should necessitate a lower per share price. As noted, however, the declaration of small stock dividends tends not to have this impact, and this phenomenon supports the accounting treatment.

On the other hand, when stock dividends are larger in magnitude, it is observed that per share market value declines after the declaration of the dividend. In such situations, it would not be valid to treat the stock dividend as an earnings distribution. Rather, it should be accounted for as a split. The precise treatment depends upon the legal requirements of the state of incorporation and upon whether the existing par value or stated value is reduced concurrent with the stock split.

If the par value is not reduced for a large stock dividend and if state law requires that earnings be capitalized in an amount equal to the aggregate of the par value of the stock dividend declared, the event should be described as a stock split effected in the form of a dividend, with a charge to retained earnings and a credit to the common stock account for the aggregate par or stated value. When the par or stated value is reduced in recognition of the split and state laws do not require treatment as a dividend, there is no formal entry to record the split but merely a notation that the number of shares outstanding has increased and the per share par or stated value has decreased accordingly.

Treasury Stock

Treasury stock consists of a corporation's own stock which has been issued, subsequently reacquired by the firm, and not yet reissued or canceled. Treasury stock does not reduce the number of shares issued but does reduce the number of shares outstanding, as well as total stockholders' equity. These shares are not eligible to receive cash dividends. Treasury stock is **not** an asset although, in some circumstances, it may be presented as an asset if adequately disclosed (ARB 43, ch 1A). Reacquired stock that is awaiting delivery to satisfy a liability created by the firm's compensation plan or reacquired stock held in a profit-sharing trust is still considered outstanding and would not be considered treasury stock. In each case, the stock would be presented as an asset with the accompanying footnote disclosure. Accounting for excesses and deficiencies on treasury stock transactions is governed by ARB 43, ch 1B, and APB 6.

Three approaches exist for the treatment of treasury stock: the **cost, par value,** and **constructive retirement** methods.

Cost method. Under the cost method, the gross cost of the shares reacquired is charged to a contra equity account (treasury stock). The equity accounts that were credited for the original share issuance (common stock, paid-in capital in excess of par, etc.) remain intact. When the treasury shares are reissued, proceeds in excess of **cost** are credited to a paid-in capital account. Any deficiency is charged to retained earnings (unless paid-in capital from previous treasury share transactions exists, in which case the deficiency is charged to that account, with any excess charged to retained earnings). If many treasury stock purchases are made, a cost flow assumption (e.g., FIFO or specific identification) should be adopted to compute excesses and deficiencies upon subsequent share reissuances. The advantage of the cost method is that it avoids identifying and accounting for amounts related to the original issuance of the shares and is, therefore, the simpler, more frequently used method.

The cost method is most consistent with the one-transaction concept. This concept takes the view that the classification of stockholders' equity should not be affected simply because the corporation was the middle "person" in an exchange of shares from one stockholder to another. In substance, there is only a transfer of shares between two stockholders. Since the original balances in the equity accounts are left undisturbed, its use is most acceptable when the firm acquires its stock for reasons other than its retirement, or when its ultimate disposition has not yet been decided.

Par value method. Under the par value method, the treasury stock account is charged only for the aggregate par (or stated) value of the shares reacquired. Other paid-in capital accounts (excess over par value, etc.) are relieved in proportion to the amounts recognized upon the original issuance of the shares. The treasury share acquisition is treated almost as a retirement. However, the common (or preferred) stock account continues at the original amount, thereby preserving the distinction between an actual retirement and a treasury share transaction.

When the treasury shares accounted for by the par value method are subsequently resold, the excess of the sale price over par value is credited to paid-in capital. A reissuance for a price **below** par value does not create a contingent liability for the purchaser. It is only the original purchaser who risks this obligation to the entity's creditors.

Constructive retirement method. The constructive retirement method is similar to the par value method, except that the aggregate par (or stated) value of the reacquired shares is charged to the stock account rather than to the treasury stock account. This method is superior when (1) it is management's intention not to reissue the shares within a reasonable time period or (2) the state of incorporation defines reacquired shares as having been retired. In the latter case, the constructive retirement method is probably the only method of accounting for treasury shares that is **not** inconsistent with the state Business Corporation Act, although the state law does not necessarily dictate such accounting. Certain states require that treasury stock be accounted for by this method.

The two-transaction concept is most consistent with the par value and constructive retirement methods. First, the reacquisition of the firm's shares is viewed as constituting a contraction of its capital structure. Second, the reissuance of the shares is the same as issuing new shares. There is little difference between the purchase and subsequent reissuance of treasury shares and the acquisition and retirement of previously issued shares and the issuance of new shares.

Treasury shares originally accounted for by the cost method can subsequently be restated to conform to the constructive retirement method. If shares were acquired with the intention that they would be reissued and it is later determined that such reissuance is unlikely (due, for example, to the expiration of stock options without their exercise), then it is proper to restate the transaction.

Example of accounting for treasury stock

1. 100 shares ($50 par value) that were originally sold for $60 per share are later reacquired for $70 each.
2. All 100 shares are subsequently resold for a total of $7,500.

To record the acquisition, the entry is

Cost method			*Par value method*			*Constructive retirement method*		
Treasury stock	7,000		Treasury stock	5,000		Common stock	5,000	
Cash		7,000	Additional paid-in			Additional paid-in		
			capital—			capital—		
			common stock	1,000		common stock	1,000	
			Retained earnings	1,000		Retained earnings	1,000	
			Cash		7,000	Cash		7,000

To record the resale, the entry is

Cost method			*Par value method*			*Constructive retirement method*		
Cash	7,500		Cash	7,500		Cash	7,500	
Treasury stock		7,000	Treasury stock		5,000	Common stock		5,000
Additional paid-			Additional paid-			Additional paid-		
in capital—			in capital—			in capital—		
treasury stock		500	common stock		2,500	common stock		2,500

If the shares had been resold for $6,500, the entry is

Cost method			*Par value method*			*Constructive retirement method*		
Cash	6,500		Cash	6,500		Cash	6,500	
Retained earnings*	500		Treasury stock		5,000	Common stock		5,000
Treasury stock		7,000	Additional paid-			Additional paid-		
			in capital—			in capital—		
			common stock		1,500	common stock		1,500

* *"Additional paid-in capital—treasury stock" or "Additional paid-in capital—retired stock" of that issue would be debited first to the extent it exists.*

Alternatively, under the par or constructive retirement methods, any portion of or the **entire** deficiency on the treasury stock acquisition may be debited to retained earnings without allocation to paid-in capital. Any excesses would always be credited to an "Additional paid-in capital—retired stock" account.

The laws of some states govern the circumstances under which a corporation may acquire treasury stock and they may prescribe the accounting for the stock. For example, a charge to retained earnings may be required in an amount equal to the treasury stock's total cost. In such cases, the accounting per the state law prevails. Also, some states (including those that have adopted the Model Business Corporation Act) define excess purchase cost of reacquired (i.e., treasury) shares as being "distributions" to shareholders that are no different in nature than dividends. In such cases, the financial statement presentation should adequately disclose the substance of these transactions (e.g., by presenting both dividends and excess reacquisition costs together in the retained earnings statement).

When a firm decides to formally retire the treasury stock, the journal entry is dependent on the method used to account for the stock. Using the original sale and reacquisition data from the illustration above, the following entries would be made if the cost and par value methods, respectively, were employed:

Cost method			*Par value method*		
Common stock	5,000		Common stock	5,000	
Additional paid-in			Treasury stock		5,000
capital—common stock	1,000				
Retained earnings*	1,000				
Treasury stock		7,000			

* *"Additional paid-in capital—treasury stock" may be debited to the extent it exists.*

If the constructive retirement method were used to record the treasury stock purchase, no additional entry would be necessary upon the formal retirement of the shares.

After the entry is made, the pro rata portion of all paid-in capital existing for that issue (i.e., capital stock and additional paid-in capital) will have been eliminated. If stock is purchased for immediate retirement (i.e., not put into the treasury) the entry to record the retirement is the same as that made under the constructive retirement method.

In some circumstances, shares held by current stockholders may be donated back to the enterprise, possibly to facilitate a resale to new owners who will infuse needed capital into the business. In accounting for donated treasury stock, the intentions of management regarding these reacquired shares is key; if these are to simply be retired, the common stock account should be debited for the par or stated value (if par or stated value stock) or the original proceeds received (if no-par, no-stated-value stock). The current fair value of the shares should be credited to the "donated capital" account, and the difference should be debited or credited to a suitably titled paid-in capital account, such as "additional paid-in capital from share donations."

If the donated shares are to be sold (the normal scenario), variations on the par and cost methods of treasury stock accounting can be employed, with "donated capital" being debited and credited, respectively, when shares are received and later reissued, instead of the "treasury stock" account employed in the above illustrations. Note, however, that if the cost method is used, the debit to the donated capital account should be for the fair value of the shares, not the cost (a seeming contradiction). If the constructive retirement method is utilized instead, only a memorandum entry will be recorded when the shares are received; when reissued, the entire proceeds should be credited to "donated capital."

Other Equity Accounts

In principle, modern financial reporting in conformity with GAAP subscribes to what was once known as the "all inclusive" or "clean surplus" concept, which means that all items of income, expense, gain or loss (other than transactions with owners) should flow through the income statement. In fact, of course, there are a number of important exceptions which have been imposed by specific GAAP standards, beginning with the market value declines recognized under the now superseded SFAS 12 on noncurrent portfolios of marketable equity securities, and reported directly in shareholder equity. Later standards added translation gains or losses (SFAS 52), certain adjustments for minimum pension obligations (SFAS 87), and unrealized gains and losses on available-for-sale portfolios of debt or equity investments (SFAS 115) to the litany of recognized economic events which escaped reporting in the income statement. As explained in Chapter 3, Statements of Income and Comprehensive Income, the FASB concepts project had foreseen the need for a flow statement, analogous to the income statement, to report all such changes for the reporting period, and the recent promulgation of SFAS 130 mandates that comprehensive income (the term which now denotes normal earnings plus the change in these other equity accounts) be reported, either in a combined statement with the income statement, as a stand-alone statement, or in an expanded statement of changes in stockholders' equity.

In the balance sheet, the various elements of other comprehensive income (i.e., the current balances of such items as translation gains and losses and unrealized gains and losses from available-for-sale securities holdings) can be aggregated into a single caption, with details reserved to the notes, or the separate items can be grouped into a subsection of the equity section. Since items of other comprehensive income are neither paid-in capital nor retained earnings, this constitutes a third major classification within the equity section of the balance sheet, although many entities will have only minor amounts of such items or none at all.

Refer to Chapter 3, Statements of Income and Comprehensive Income, for a complete discussion of other comprehensive income.

Accounting for Stock Options and Similar Compensation Arrangements

Although it is evident that highly prized and sought-after employee or executive stock options convey economic value, GAAP had traditionally provided a mechanism whereby this component of compensation cost was often not given financial statement recognition. Financial statement preparers were understandably anxious to avoid expense recognition, and APB 25, using the "intrinsic value" method, had rationalized that treatment to the extent that option exercise prices were equal to or greater than the market values of the underlying shares as of the respective dates of the grants. The growing popularity of these compensation arrangements, arguably encouraged by the favorable accounting (and favorable tax) treatment, made the standard setters and financial statement user community increasingly uncomfortable with the fiction that no expense was incurred by employer entities offering such programs. Eventually, FASB undertook a comprehensive reexamination of the subject, with the intent of conforming financial reporting with economic reality.

However, FASB's efforts were strenuously and effectively opposed, particularly by the "high technology" sector, which argued that it would be competitively harmed in its ability to command top talent if it was impeded in its ability to offer sizable option awards to executives while disguising their true cost. Incredibly, this argument was advanced in tandem with the claim that options were in fact without value, and hence without cost. In any event, this organized opposition forced the FASB to accept a deeply flawed compromise, SFAS 123 (explained later in this chapter), which permitted continued application of APB 25 coupled with supplemental (footnote) disclosure of the impact of the new measurement regime. Virtually all publicly held entities have opted for this hybrid approach, even though it necessitates use of two very different and complex measures.

SFAS 123 has been designated as the preferable GAAP for purposes of applying the provisions of APB 20. Thus, if an enterprise adopts SFAS 123, it cannot later revert to APB 25 for financial reporting purposes. An entity must employ only one set of rules, APB 25 or SFAS 123, for all stock compensation programs and plans in effect. It cannot use different rules to measure the impact of different plans. However, as noted, it can utilize APB 25 for the basic financial statements, relegating SFAS 123 for use in preparing footnote disclosures.

APB 25 versus SFAS 123 in brief. APB 25 measures compensation associated with the issuance of stock options by the **intrinsic value** method, under which that cost is limited to the excess of the quoted market price of the stock at the measurement date (generally, grant date) over the option exercise price. Options are categorized, under tax law, as "incentive stock option" (sometimes referred to as qualified options), which do not result in either taxable income to the holder or tax deductions to the issuing corporation upon either grant or exercise, and "nonqualified" options, which will result in taxable income to the recipient and a tax deduction for the issuer upon exercise. The conditions for treatment as incentive stock options are very strict (e.g., limitations on length of exercise period and on maximum amount of annual exercise by each employee), and most plans are therefore nonqualified. However, nonqualified plans can also be structured to be noncompensatory (defined below), meaning that the grantees incur no taxable income at the date of the grant.

Under SFAS 123, on the other hand, a **fair value** approach is prescribed for employee stock options and similar equity instruments. This gives recognition to the fact that the value of options is comprised of three elements: intrinsic value (identical to that identified under APB 25), plus the time value of money and the time value associated with the underlying stock's volatility. Thus, even if intrinsic value were zero (i.e., the option price is equal to or greater than market price at the measurement date), the sum of the other two components would nonetheless most often result in compensation being attributed to grants of fixed options.

Under the standards which apply when APB 25 is being adhered to, variable or performance-based options are accounted for differently than fixed options. FASB Interpretations 28 and 38 address the accounting for such plans, including junior stock plans. Compensation is recognized under these rules, and continues to be recognized under the requirements set forth in SFAS 123. However, the pattern of expense recognition must potentially differ between these two alternative sets of standards. Entities that continue to adhere to APB 25 for fixed option plans will use the related literature (FASB Interpretations 28 and 38) as well. Those that adopt SFAS 123 will be guided by it in accounting for all stock compensation arrangements.

In the following sections, the methodologies of both the old set of requirements (APB 25 et al.) and the new rules (SFAS 123) will be discussed and illustrated.

Accounting for Employee Stock Options under APB 25

Under the provisions of APB 25, there are two types of stock option plans: compensatory and noncompensatory. To be classified as noncompensatory, the plan must meet all of the following four tests:

1. Substantially all full-time employees meeting limited employment qualifications must be eligible to participate;
2. Shares must be offered equally or proportionate to wages earned;
3. Time to exercise must be limited; and
4. There must be no more than a reasonable discount from market price, such as that which would be granted in a typical "rights offering."

Failing to meet even one of these criteria causes the stock option plan to be categorized as compensatory in nature. However, this does not necessarily mean that compensation expense will be recognized.

Any stock option program conveys to the recipients something of value, namely, the time to decide whether or not to purchase the shares of stock at a price that was fixed at the date of the grant. However, because of the strong sentiment against the recognition of compensation, APB 25 continued the practice earlier established by ARB 43, which essentially eliminated compensation recognition from fixed stock option plans. This result had been accomplished by defining compensation as the excess of the quoted market (or fair) value of the shares optioned over the amount to be paid by the employee, determined in most cases as of the grant date. That is, if the option price was equal to or greater than the market (or fair) value as of the date the option was granted, no compensation was to be recognized, regardless of the value later achieved by the shares. Since exercise price typically was fixed at or above the market price as of the grant date, compensation was rarely to be recognized under terms of the most common fixed option plans, regardless of whatever valuable attributes the options carried.

The measurement date stipulated by APB 25 is the earliest date on which both the number of shares to which an individual employee is entitled is known, and the option price is fixed. For most fixed option plans, both of these data are known on the grant date. Note that the measurement date will be the grant date even if the employee must meet certain other conditions, such as continued employment for a specified period, before the options can be exercised. This later date, the vesting date, is used for purposes of allocating compensation, if any, but is not used to compute the amount of such compensation.

If an option plan is compensatory (because one or more of the four conditions are not met), compensation cost is measured by the difference between the **market price** (or the fair market value, for a nontraded stock) and the option price. The **cost** of the shares to the issuing corporation is not the relevant comparison, except in the very limited situation where the shares are specifically acquired to meet the requirements of the stock option plan and are delivered to option holders shortly after acquisition.

Furthermore, even if no compensation cost is deemed to have been incurred at the measurement date (usually the grant date), certain subsequent events may give rise to the recognition of compensation. The most important of these are

1. The renewal or extension of an option, in which case a new measurement date occurs, and if the market price or fair value at that date exceeds the option price, compensation cost will be recognized; and

2. The payment of cash to an employee to settle a previously made stock award or option grant, for which payment will be deemed compensation expense.

If a given option plan involves the payment of compensation to the employees, such compensation cost should be recognized in the period(s) in which the services being compensated are performed. If the grant is unconditional, which means it effectively is in recognition of past services rendered by the employees, then compensation is reported in the period of the grant. If the stock options are granted before some or all of the required services are performed, compensation cost should be recognized over the periods in which the performance is scheduled to occur. Whether compensation cost is recognized ratably over the periods or not is a function of the vesting provisions of the plan. If the plan provides for **cliff vesting**, compensation will be accrued on an essentially straight-line basis, while if it provides for **graded vesting** the pattern of recognition will be more complex.

Example of accounting for stock options—Measurement and grant date the same

Options are granted to corporate officers to purchase 10,000 shares of $1 par stock at a price of $52 per share, when the market price is $58. The options may not be exercised until five years from the grant date. The company has no reason to expect that any of the options will be forfeited by the employees to whom they are granted. The entry to record the granting of the options is

Deferred compensation expense	60,000	
Stock options outstanding		60,000

While deferred taxes are ignored for purposes of this example, in general the recognition of expense for tax purposes would be in a later period, necessitating the recording of a deferred tax benefit. Deferred compensation expense is subtracted from stock options outstanding in the paid-in capital section of owner's equity to indicate the amount of net contributed services on any date [i.e., on the grant date nothing has yet been contributed by the option holders ($60,000 − $60,000 = $0)]. As the employees provide services to earn the options, entries are made assigning compensation expense to years one through five.

Compensation expense	12,000	($60,000 ÷ 5 years)
Deferred compensation expense		12,000

When the option is exercised, cash is received and the stock is issued. The following entry is made (assume exercise after the five-year period):

Cash	520,000	(option price)
Stock options outstanding	60,000	
Common stock		10,000 (par)
Additional paid-in capital		570,000 (excess)

If options are forfeited as a result of an employee failing to fulfill an obligation (e.g., staying with the company), under the provisions of APB 25 compensation expense is credited in the year of forfeiture. The amount credited reflects the total compensation expense previously charged to the income statement for the employee who forfeited the options. Assume that one officer, who was granted options for 1,000 shares, leaves the company in year three, two years before the options can be exercised. The result is handled as a change in an accounting estimate and the following entry is made in year three:

Stock options outstanding	6,000	
Deferred compensation expense		3,600
Compensation expense		2,400

If the measurement date follows the grant date, it is necessary to assume compensation expense based on the market values of the common stock that exist at the end of each period until the measurement date is reached. Per FASB Interpretation 28, changes in the market value of stock between the date of grant and the measurement date are adjustments to compensation expense in **the period the market value of the stock changes**. The effect of such changes is **not** spread over future periods.

Example of accounting for stock options—Measurement and grant date the same, with graded vesting

Assume the same facts as the previous example, except that rights to 2,000 shares vest each year (i.e., the officers can exercise options for a total of 2,000 shares after one year, a total of 4,000 shares after two years, etc.). Where the option program provides for such graded vesting (as contrasted with the cliff vesting of the prior example), the allocation of compensation expense to the period until full vesting has occurred (the end of year five in this example) is to be done in a manner proportional to the number of shares to which rights to exercise the option have vested. As explained in FASB Interpretation 28, the service period is determined separately for each portion of the option. Thus, the 20% which vests in the first year is deemed attributable to services performed in the first year only, while the 20% which vests in the second year is attributed to services performed in years one and two, etc. The effect of this requirement is to heavily front-load the total compensation cost, as follows:

Fraction of options	Allocation to years of service				
	First	*Second*	*Third*	*Fourth*	*Fifth*
1st 20%	20%	--	--	--	--
2nd 20%	10%	10%	--	--	--
3rd 20%	6.67%	6.67%	6.66%	--	--
4th 20%	5%	5%	5%	5%	--
5th 20%	4%	4%	4%	4%	4%
Total allocation	45.67%	25.67%	15.66%	9%	4%

Accordingly, the entries to record compensation in years one and two, respectively, are

Compensation expense	27,402		($60,000 x .4567)
Deferred compensation expense		27,402	
Compensation expense	15,402		($60,000 x .2567)
Deferred compensation expense		15,402	

Example of accounting for stock options—Measurement and grant date different

1. On 1/1/02, a company grants an option to purchase 100 shares of common stock at 90% of the market price at 12/31/2004 and that the compensation period is **four years**. The total compensation amount per share is represented by the difference between the current market price and the estimated purchase price granted by the option (90% x Market price) or simply 10% of the current market price.

2. At 1/1/02, the number of shares is determinable, but the option price is unknown.

3. The market values of the common stock are as follows:

12/31/2002	$10
12/31/2003	13
12/31/2004	15

The following entries for compensation expense are recorded:

	2002	*2003*	*2004*	*2005*
Compensation expense	25	40	47.50	37.50
Stock options outstanding		25	40	47.50	37.50

2002: ($10 x 10% x 100 shares x 1/4) = $<u>25</u>
2003: ($13 x 10% x 100 shares x 2/4) – expense recognized to date = $<u>40</u>
2004: ($15 x 10% x 100 shares x 3/4) – expense recognized to date = $<u>47.50</u>
2005: ($15 x 10% x 100 shares x 4/4) – expense recognized to date = $<u>37.50</u>

The expense recorded from 2003 and 2004 results from a change in estimate. Note that the market value of the stock at the end of 2002 and 2003 is used as the estimate of the market price of the stock at 12/31/2004 and that the total amount of compensation expense previously accrued is subtracted from the latest estimate of cumulative expense.

A time line depicting the actual and estimated compensation expense would appear as follows:

Interpretations of APB 25

APB 25, enacted in 1972, contains certain ambiguities which led to confusion regarding its application. While the FASB pursued the project which was intended to supersede APB 25, little attention was paid to correcting APB 25's deficiencies. After SFAS 123 was promulgated, and it became clear that virtually all companies would continue to report under APB 25, several efforts were initiated to resolve the problems with the older standard. These efforts resulted in the promulgation of FASB Interpretation 44, in early 2000, and EITF Issue 00-23, in early 2001. Taken together, these address many of the areas of ambiguity in APB 25. The more broadly applicable of these matters are addressed in this section.

Much of the new guidance relates to "fixed" awards. Consistency of representation (e.g., to the IRS) is required in the categorization of stock award recipients, which means that independent contractors cannot be treated as employees for purposes of applying APB 25. (SFAS 123 makes it clear, furthermore, that fair value is the appropriate measure of equity instruments issued to nonemployees.) However, the FASB has elected to provide an exception in the case of independent members of an entity's board of directors; awards issued as compensation for their duties **as directors** can be accounted for under APB 25. Awards made as compensation for services as consultants, et al. however, will not qualify for this exception.

Also, while the general rule is that only stock of the employer can be issued to the employee if APB 25 is to be applied, stock of a parent corporation can be issued to employees of its subsidiaries because in consolidated financial statements the parent company is effectively the employer. To avert an inconsistency in reporting, this same position applies even in the case of stand-alone financial statements of the subsidiary.

If a recipient of stock options undergoes a change in status (e.g., from independent contractor to employee) during the vesting period, a new measurement date is required and only the portion of compensation cost applicable to the period of employee status is to be accounted for under APB 25; compensation recognized under the fair value method is not adjusted.

Some stock option plans incorporate "look-back" provisions, which adjust purchase price downward if the market price at the exercise date is lower than at the grant date. Since the Internal Revenue Code permits "look-back" options in qualified employee stock option plans, and since APB 25 defines noncompensatory plans in terms of what is permissible under the IRC, the interpretation is that such options are allowable.

Interpretation 44 states also that a new measurement date is required only for the following modifications to the terms of fixed options and awards: (1) a reduction in the exercise price to zero, or the exchange of a stock option award for a restricted stock award; (2) a direct extension of the award's term or one that occurs upon a future separation event beyond the maximum contractual term, provided the employee could potentially receive the term extension; and (3) an extension of the term that occurs upon a future separation event, but not beyond the award's maximum contractual term, in which case incremental compensation cost is measured at the modification date and recognized if and when the future separation event occurs.

An acceleration of the vesting date pursuant to the original terms of the award does not give rise to a new measurement date determination. Compensation expense will only be recognized if the acceleration of vesting occurs and the award is effectively reinstated as a result of the acceleration (e.g., when an award would have otherwise expired unvested without the modification).

In some cases, cash is given to the employee to settle an earlier award or to repurchase the shares after exercise. The interpretation requires that compensation cost be recognized if cash is paid to settle an earlier grant, or an option or award, or to repurchase shares shortly after exercise or issuance, based on the original intrinsic value of the option plus any cash paid in excess of that original intrinsic value, for the current intrinsic value of the award plus any excess of the current intrinsic value of the award at the settlement date.

Other interpretations would impact on "variable" awards. If the exercise price or the number of shares to be issued in what had been a "fixed" award is changed, a variable award is created. The cancellation of one fixed award, the grant of what is denoted as another fixed award to the same individual(s) shortly thereafter, is to be treated effectively as a modification and as the creation of a variable award, to be accounted for consistent with Interpretation 28, meaning that compensation (and possibly negative compensation) will be recognized over the vesting period.

If a stock award plan features a call privilege and it is expected that the stock will be repurchased by the issuer shortly after exercise, this must be accounted for as a variable award; the repurchase must be separately accounted for. However, for nonpublic companies variable award accounting is not required if certain conditions are present (repurchase price is equal to fair value and repurchase is not expected to occur shortly after exercise or issuance, or if for other than fair value the employee still bears risks and rewards of ownership for a reasonable period). Also, repurchase to effect tax withholding rules will not trigger variable award accounting.

In poolings of interests, exchanges of fixed stock options will not normally trigger a new measurement date, if the aggregate intrinsic value of the new awards do not exceed that of the old immediately prior to the exchange, and the ratio of exercise to market price per share is not reduced. Other modifications, if not *de minimis*, would result in a new measurement date. In purchase business combinations, exchanges involving vested options are deemed part of the purchase transaction and are to be valued as part of the purchase cost, using fair value accounting. Exchanges involving nonvested options would continue to be accounted for per APB 25, however.

The interpretation also addresses minor matters concerned with determination of grant date, accounting for related deferred tax assets, and compound cash bonus and stock-based plans. With regard to cash bonuses, those that are not fixed and that are contingent upon exercise of options result in combined variable accounting; fixed bonuses contingent upon exercise of options results in combined fixed accounting with the bonus reducing the options' stated exercise prices; and fixed or variable cash bonuses that are contingent upon vesting of awards are to be accounted for as a separate compensation element.

Most recently, the EITF has reached consensuses on a number of issues relating to stock compensation under APB 25 and the aforementioned Interpretation 44. As is typical with EITF consensuses, these address rather narrow specialized concerns, and technically are clarifications of existing GAAP (APB 25 and Interpretation 44), not setting new standards, which the EITF, lacking due process, is not empowered to do. In the following paragraphs, the major provisions of EITF 00-23 will be discussed.

Modifications to the terms of outstanding options are sometimes made, for a range of reasons, the most common of which is that the options are "underwater" due to a significant decline in the market price of the underlying shares. The general rule is that modifications in the terms of options triggers a new measurement date; this was narrowed somewhat by Interpretation 44, as discussed above. In EITF 00-23, the conclusion reached was that if the intrinsic value is increased in connection with an exchange of options in one entity for options in another within the same consolidated group, when not part of an equity restructuring, variable accounting for the modified awards will be required. For all other exchanges, such modifications result in a new measurement date.

In some instances, employers lend money to employees in association with a grant of options, with the loan to be forgiven (e.g., if the value of the options do not appreciate by some amount over a defined time horizon). The EITF has decreed that the options and the loan are to be accounted for jointly, with compensation being measured by reference to the guaranteed amount, usually the amount of the loan. This is to be ratably recognized over the service period.

Several of the consensuses in EITF 00-23 pertain to exchanges of options pursuant to business combinations accounted for as poolings of interests. Since pooling accounting is being banned effective mid-2001, these will no longer be of concern. Many other positions pertained to purchase business combinations, however, and these remain relevant. For example, the EITF found that a subsequent repurchase of options issued as consideration in a purchase business combination and were fully vested at that time will be deemed a treasury stock transaction, except that if the settlement exceeds the fair value of the vested awards, the excess will be deemed additional compensation cost. If the options were unvested at the business combination date, a portion equal to the proportion of the vesting period not expired governs the amount of compensation expense to be recognized; the balance is a treasury stock transaction, subject to the caveat that if the settlement price exceeds fair value, further compensation is to be recognized, similar to the case of vested options, above. In no case would any adjustment be made to the purchase transaction from which the option grants arose, since the business combination and the later settlement are deemed separate transactions.

A further purchase business combination question pertains to a subsequent modification of fixed options granted as consideration for the exchange of options in the acquired entity. EITF 00-23 states, tentatively, that if the acquiree options were vested when exchanged, they are treated as canceled or expired, and the new options are a new grant to be accounted for under APB 25 based on the terms as of the modification date. If the exchange involves a reduction in the effective exercise price, only a new measurement date results; but any later exercise price reduction will trigger variable accounting for the awards.

Another tentative finding is that for awards unvested as of the date of the business combination, any modification representing the unexpired percentage of the vesting period will be accounted for as a modification of the compensation arrangement. If this involves a reduction of the exercise price, variable accounting will be triggered for the calculated portion of the awards, from the modification date.

When employees forfeit awards prior to vesting because they fail to fulfill defined obligations, where the options were granted as compensation in a purchase business combination, compensation is reversed in the forfeiture period. Any unearned compensation (the amount not already recognized as expense since the grant date) is reversed through equity. The purchase transaction is not to be remeasured.

EITF 00-23 contains additional guidance with regard to accounting for options granted in purchase transactions, including some which address swaps involving subsidiary shares.

Several of the consensuses in EITF 00-23 pertain to changes in the status of the grantee (e.g., from employee to nonemployee) concurrent with changes to the terms of the grant. The conclusions are that the accounting should follow the grantee's status during the time the status existed. Merely temporary changes in status, reversed shortly afterward, would not precipitate such a result, however.

Under certain circumstances, option plans give grantees the right to demand that the issuer repurchase the options or shares (a put option), and in other cases the issuer may have the right to make this repurchase (a call option). The repurchase feature may either be part of the option arrangement or may be contained in a side agreement between the employees and the employer. The EITF has determined that, with regard to these "immature shares" (i.e., unexercised options, unvested shares, stock purchased with a nonrecourse loan which has yet to be fully repaid, and stock obtained by means of option exercise over the past six months), a fair value repurchase feature triggers variable accounting unless management represents that it has a positive intent to **not** call the shares within the following six months, and this intent is corroborated by other facts and circumstances, such as past history regarding the calling of immature shares.

If the right to call immature shares is contingent on some event, which is assessed as being unlikely to occur and is not under the grantor's control, this condition will not necessitate variable accounting for the options. Likewise, if the grantee has the right to put the immature shares back to the grantor, and such right is contingent on some event, if the likelihood of occurrence is not probable, and the grantee does not control the event, then variable accounting is not prescribed. If the grantor, in the case of the call provision, or the grantee, in the case of the put, controls the contingent event, then variable accounting for the stock compensation is mandatory. EITF 00-23 also contains guidance on a number of other variations on the themes of put or call rights potentially resulting in the repurchase of immature shares.

If "in the money" options are granted subsequent to the cancellation of a previous award, there will be the presumption that there had been an agreement or promise to make adjustment for possible market price increases after the cancellation; this makes variable accounting required, unless sufficient facts and circumstances exist to support the position that the new grant was unrelated to the former one. However, if the new options have an exercise price equal to or greater than the fair value at grant date, there is no requirement for variable accounting.

Under Interpretation 44, a modification reducing the exercise price, or increasing the number of shares, under a fixed option plan generally triggers variable plan accounting. In EITF 00-23, a consensus was reached that, under such circumstances, whether a new measurement date or variable accounting is the consequence of the change is a function of all the facts and circumstances. For example, in some cases changes to terms are made to conform to regulatory mandates or to achieve tax objectives for the grantee. In such cases, fixed award accounting would still be valid, but a new measurement date would be specified.

The EITF also decreed that deferred tax benefits cannot be recognized at the time of a purchase business combination when nonqualified options were issued in a nontaxable merger and were fully vested at the date the combination was consummated. Although the entity will realize tax benefits later, that should be accounted for when realized by adjusting the purchase price allocation (generally, this will be by reducing goodwill recorded in the purchase transaction) to the extent that the deduction for tax purposes does not exceed the fair value of the awards recognized as part of the purchase price; any excess over that would be credited to paid-in capital. Examples of journal entries to be made are included in this consensus.

Finally, if short-term inducements are given to encourage exercise of options, this causes the options to be accounted for as variable awards thereafter, even if the inducements expire unused.

Stock Appreciation Rights under APB 25

The previous section dealt with stock option plans, under which the employees are given the right to purchase shares either at advantageous (i.e., below market) prices or at the market price as of the date of the grant. Another type of stock-based compensation program gives the employees the opportunity to participate in any increase in value of the company's stock without having to incur the cost of actually purchasing the shares. Such plans may be referred to as phantom stock plans, stock appreciation rights, or variable stock award programs. A wide variety of such plans is found in practice: Some provide for the payment of cash to the employees, while others reward participants with shares of the sponsor's stock. Often such plans are granted together with compensatory stock option plans as either combination or tandem plans: The former give the employees the rights to both the options and the phantom stock, while the latter require the employees to choose which they will exercise (simultaneously forfeiting the other).

Accounting for stock appreciation rights (SAR) and similar plans is prescribed by FASB Interpretation 28. There are significant distinctions between APB 25 and Interpretation 28, the most important of which is the method of computing the compensation cost to be allocated to the periods over which services are provided by the employees. Under APB 25, compensation cost (if any) is determined as of the measurement date (usually the grant date), and is not affected by changes in market price thereafter. By contrast, under Interpretation 28, compensation cost incurred in connection with stock appreciation rights or other variable awards is determined prospectively until full vesting is achieved, with future increases or decreases in market price resulting in charges or credits to periodic compensation expense.

Under both standards, however, total compensation cost is allocated ratably (if cliff vesting is provided by the plan) or proportionally (if graded vesting is provided). Likewise, both standards provide that when an employee forfeits options or rights for which compensation had previously been accrued, the accrual is to be reversed against compensation expense in the period of the forfeiture.

Accounting for compensation cost under SAR that provide graded vesting involves particularly complex allocations under the provisions of Interpretation 28. (If an enterprise adopts SFAS 123, the complexity of this computation is relaxed somewhat, but if the entity uses APB 25 for fixed option plans it must continue to apply Interpretations 28 and 38 as well, for variable plans.)

Performance-based stock compensation plans often provide for payment in shares, instead of cash. For example, a stock appreciation rights plan may contain a provision that the increase in value will be distributed to the participant in the form of sufficient shares of the sponsor's stock to have an aggregate fair market value equal to the amount of the award. If the plan provides only for payment in shares (a plan which most often is referred to as a phantom stock plan), the offset to the periodic charge for compensation cost should be to paid-in capital accounts. If the award is payable at the participant's choice in either cash or stock, a liability should be accrued, since the sponsor cannot control the means by which the obligation will be settled. If the payment will be made in cash or stock at the option of the company, the offset to compensation should be either to a liability account or to equity accounts, based on the best available information concerning the sponsor's intentions. As these intentions change from one period to another, the amounts should be reclassified as necessary.

Example of accounting for SAR under Interpretation 28

1. A company grants 100 SAR, payable in cash, to an employee on 1/1/02.
2. The predetermined amount for the SAR plan is $50 per right, and the market value of the stock is $55 on 12/31/02, $53 on 12/31/03, and $61 on 12/31/04.

Compensation expense recorded in each year would be

			Total expense		*Expense previously accrued*		*Current expense*
2002	100 ($55 – $50)	=	$ 500	-	$ 0	=	$ 500
2003	100 ($53 – $50)	=	$ 300	-	$500	=	$(200)
2004	100 ($61 – $50)	=	$1,100	-	$300	=	$ 800

The total expense recognized over the three-year period is $1,100 [100 x ($61 – $50)]. The required journal entries would be as follows:

2002

Compensation expense	500	
Liability under SAR plan		500

2003

Liability under SAR plan	200	
Compensation expense		200

2004

Compensation expense	800	
Liability under SAR plan		800

If the SAR were to be redeemed in common stock, "Stock rights outstanding" (a paid-in capital account) would replace the liability account in the above entries.

The example assumes no service or vesting period, which is the period of time until the SAR become exercisable. If the above plan had a two-year service period, 50% of the total expense would be recognized at the end of the first year and 100% at the end of the second year and thereafter until exercise. The compensation would be accrued as follows:

```
2002:   ($  500 x  50%) = $  250  –  $  0    = $250
2003:   ($  300 x 100%) = $  300  –  $250    = $ 50
2004:   ($1,100 x 100%) = $1,100  –  $300    = $800
```

Often stock option plans and SAR are joined in tandem plans, under the terms of which the exercise of one automatically cancels the other. This feature makes accounting for these types of arrangements more complex. Per FASB Interpretation 28, on the basis of the available facts each period, a determination must be made as to which one of the compensation plans has the higher likelihood of exercise. Once determined, this is the plan accounted for with the other plan being ignored. In the absence of evidence to the contrary, however, the presumption is that the SAR, not the options, will be exercised.

Example of accounting for a combined stock option and stock appreciation rights

To illustrate the accounting for a combined SAR and stock option plan, consider the following facts:

1/1/02　Plan adopted; base price is $100, option price is $95; 1,000 shares exercisable on 1/1/05 **or** 1,000 SAR payable in cash on 1/1/06 on increase over 1/1/02 market value.

Market prices are as follows:

12/31/02	$ 98
12/31/03	110
12/31/04	108
12/31/05	125

Two cases are presented simultaneously, representing two alternative fact situations.

Case 1:　It is assumed that only SAR will be exercised.

Case 2:　It is assumed that 1/2 SAR, 1/2 options will be exercised.

The appropriate journal entries are as follows:

	Case 1		
12/31/02	No entry		

	Case 2		
Compensation expense		625	
Deferred compensation		1,875	
Stock options outstanding			
(500 shares x $5)			2,500

Compensation expense is 1/4 of projected four-year total relating to expected option exercise in Case 2.

No SAR liability is accrued since the market price is below the base price. The compensatory part of the stock options, determined under the rules of APB 25, is $5 per share, which is allocated over the four-year vesting period on a straight-line basis.

	Case 1		
12/31/03	Compensation expense	10,000	
	Liability under SAR plan		
	($10 x 1,000 SAR)		10,000

Case 2		
Compensation expense	5,625	
Deferred compensation		625
Liability under SAR plan		
($10 x 500 SAR)		5,000

Deferred compensation relating to options amortized ratably over option period ($2,500 x 1/4).

SAR liability recognized for difference between year-end market value and base price for number of expected SAR exercisable.

12/31/04	Liability under SAR plan	2,000	
	Compensation expense		2,000

Liability under SAR plan	1,000	
Compensation expense		375
Deferred compensation		625

12/31/05	Compensation expense	17,000	
	Liability under SAR Plan		17,000

Compensation expense	9,125	
Deferred compensation		625
Liability under SAR plan		
($12,500 - $5,000 + $1,000)		8,500

The option holders may exercise either the options or the SAR in ratios other than those presumed as the basis for the accounting. Assume that either (a) holders elect 100% SAR; (b) holders elect 50% SAR, 50% stock; or (c) they elect to exercise only the stock options. For each of the cases above, the entries under each assumed exercise ratio are as follows:

	Case 1		
(a)	Liability under SAR plan	25,000	
(all cash)	Cash		25,000

Case 2		
Liability under SAR plan	12,500	
Stock options outstanding	2,500	
Compensation expense	10,000	
Cash		25,000

(b)	Liability under SAR plan	25,000	
(½ cash,	Cash ($47,500 – $12,500)	35,000	
½ stock)	Common stock—$20 par		10,000
	Additional paid-in capital		50,000

Liability under SAR plan	12,500	
Stock options outstanding	2,500	
Cash	35,000	
Common stock—$20 par		10,000
Additional paid-in capital		40,000

(c)	Liability under SAR plan	25,000	
(all	Cash	95,000	
stock)			
	Common stock—$20 par		20,000
	Additional paid-in capital		100,000

Liability under SAR plan	12,500	
Stock options outstanding	2,500	
Cash	95,000	
Common stock—$20 par		20,000
Additional paid-in capital		90,000

Notice that the proceeds of the stock issuance vary. When stock options are exercised but SAR were accrued, the cost of the shares includes the accrued SAR liability. On the other hand, when the expectation was that options would be exercised but SAR are exercised instead, additional compensation expense will be recorded (as in Case 2a). Since this is due to a change in estimate and not an accounting error, no prior period adjustment can be recorded.

An additional complication arises when there is not **cliff vesting**, as assumed here, but is graded over the years of the option/SAR plans. In such cases, the amount of compensation expense and/or liability under the SAR plan is based on the fraction of vesting at each reporting period. This has the effect of deferring much of the cost to later periods, as was illustrated earlier in the chapter for stock options with graded vesting provisions.

Essentially the same accounting procedures are employed for interim financial reporting. If in subsequent periods the presumed ratio of SAR exercise to stock option exercise in combination (or tandem) plans changes, compensation expense accrued in connection with the anticipated SAR exercise is **not** reduced even though the expected number of SAR to be exercised is diminished. On the other hand, a reduced expectation of stock option exercise may result in a reversal of compensation expense.

Accounting for Employee Stock Options under SFAS 123

The failed effort to end the use of the "implicit value" approach of APB 25 has already been described. SFAS 123, albeit not mandatory, at least does require the pro forma disclosure of net income and earning per share as if SFAS 123 were being utilized for financial reporting purposes. Unlike APB 25, the accounting under SFAS 123 for both fixed and variable awards is consistent, and almost without exception compensation cost, at least equal to a defined "minimum value," will be recognized for both types of plans, over the corresponding service period. SFAS 123 measures compensation with reference to "fair value," which equals the sum of three elements—intrinsic value, time value of money, and time value associated with the stock's volatility.

As under APB 25, intrinsic value is the amount of advantage, if any, that the holder of an option can realize by exercising the option rather than buying the underlying stock directly. The intrinsic value component equals the difference between the market price of the underlying stock and the option's exercise price. For options "at" or "out of the money" when granted, there is no intrinsic value.

The time value of money, as is well understood, arises because the holder of an option does not pay the exercise price until the exercise date. Instead, the holder can invest funds elsewhere while waiting to exercise the option. The time value of money component is determined by reference to the rate of return available on risk-free securities. If the stock pays a dividend, or is expected to pay a dividend during the life of the option, the value to the holder of the option from delaying payment of the exercise price is only the excess (if any) of the return available on a risk-free security over the return available from exercising the option today and owning the shares. The time value of money component for a dividend-paying stock equals the discounted present value of the expected interest income that could be earned less the discounted present value of the expected dividends to be forgone during the expected life of the option.

The time value associated with volatility represents the ability of the holder to profit from appreciation of the underlying stock while being exposed to the loss of only the option premium, not the full current value of the stock. A more volatile stock has a higher probability of big increases or decreases in price, compared with one having lower volatility. As a result, an option on a highly volatile stock has a higher probability of a big payoff than an option on a less volatile stock and so has a higher time value relating to volatility fair value component.

Volatility is the measure of the amount by which a stock's price fluctuates during a period. It is expressed as a percentage because it looks at stock price fluctuations during a period relative to the stock's price at the beginning of the period. Expected annualized volatility is the predicted amount which is the input to the option pricing model. This is calculated largely from the stock's historical price fluctuations.

To illustrate this basic concept, assume that the present market price of underlying stock is $20 per share, and the option plan grants the recipient the right to purchase shares at today's market price at any time during the next five years. If a risk-free rate, such as that available on Treasury notes having maturities of five years is 5%, then the present value of the future payment of $20 is $15.67 [$50 ÷ $(1.05)^5$], which suggests that the option has a value of $20 − $15.67 = $4.33 per share, before considering the value of lost dividends. If the stock is expected to pay a dividend of $.40 per share per year, the present value of the dividend stream that the option holder will forego until exercise five years hence is about $1.64, discounting again at 5%. Therefore, the **net** value of the option being granted, assuming it is expected to be held to the expiration date before being exercised, is $4.33 − $1.64 = $2.69 per share. (Although the foregoing computation was based on the full five-year life of the option, the actual requirement is to use the **expected term** of the option, which may be shorter.)

SFAS 123 in Greater Detail

With one exception (see below), SFAS 123 applies to all stock-based compensation plans, however described, and whether the employees receive stock or cash based on the price of the stock. Included are all stock purchase plans, fixed and variable option arrangements, restricted stock, and stock appreciation rights. SFAS 123 also applies to transactions in which stock is exchanged for goods and services in the normal course of business (e.g., for inventory), but the accounting for such transaction, using fair values, is essentially similar to what has long been considered GAAP.

The fair value of the equity instruments granted is used to measure each of these compensation arrangements. Fair value for publicly traded entities is to be measured by one of the recognized options pricing models, of which the Black-Scholes and binomial models are the universally recognized alternatives. These models take into consideration the term of the option (the longer the term, the greater will be the value of the right, all other factors remaining constant); the market price at grant date and the option exercise price (the greater the excess of the former over the latter, the greater will be the option value); the risk free interest rate, measured by the rate on zero coupon Treasury debt with a term equal to the expected life of the option); the expected dividends to be paid on the stock (the option value is inversely related to expected dividends); and the expected volatility of the stock (the greater the expected volatility, the more valuable the option).

For nonpublicly traded companies, essentially the same approach is to be used, except that the measure of volatility, which would be difficult to assess, or even meaningless, in the absence of an active market for the shares, is dispensed with. This truncated measure is referred to as the **minimum value** model. A full option pricing model approach including a factor for volatility can be used, however, if there is a desire to do so and a means of estimating it.

Exception under SFAS 123 for stock purchase plans. SFAS 123 does provide an exemption for stock purchase plans that meet all of a set of defined conditions. If the plan does this, it will not be deemed to be a compensatory plan. The conditions are as follows:

1. The plan contains no option features **other** than permitting employees a very limited time, no longer than thirty-one days, to enroll in the plan after the purchase price has been fixed, or permitting employees to cancel participation in a program offering stock at the market price on the purchase date and obtaining a refund of moneys already withheld or paid.

2. Any discount from market price is limited to the greater of

   a. That which would be reasonable in a recurring offer to existing shareholders or others or

   b. Stock issuance costs saved by not having a public offering. A 5% discount is assumed defensible; higher discounts would have to be justified.

3. Substantially all full-time employees, subject only to limited qualifications, are permitted to participate on an equitable basis.

With the sole exception of plans that comply with these restrictions, stock option and related programs are compensatory and subject to the measurement and disclosure requirements of SFAS 123. Thus, the new standard is far more restrictive than APB 25. For example, any program which offers employees the right to a lower price at exercise date based on the then-existing market value would be compensatory, as would be one which provided for a purchase price determined as of grant date but gave participants the right to cancel before the exercise.

Measuring volatility. The volatility measure is the most difficult aspect of the option pricing model. SFAS 123 addresses this at great length, and should be consulted by those attempting to apply the Black-Scholes or binomial models. In general, volatility is a measure of the variation in prices of the security over a relevant period, projected to the future period that equals the expected term of the employee options. SFAS 123 stipulates that this is to be computed by reference to the annualized standard deviation of the differences in the natural logarithms of the possible future stock prices. Since future prices cannot be known, the standard suggests that historical volatility be used to forecast future volatility. In general, this will be achieved by using stock prices over a historical period of time equal to the expected life of the options being granted (e.g., for four year options, volatility would be assessed by reference to the prior four years' stock price behavior).

If the stock is expected to pay dividends (again, this can be anticipated based on historical experience, taking into account the frequency with which dividend rates have been adjusted and the amounts of such adjustments, modified to reflect future expectations), the volatility measure will also be affected. This is because the market price of the stock reflects the declaration of dividends, and this would distort the actual price volatility unless explicitly dealt with. The market price will reflect this event on the **ex-dividend** date, which is the last date on which a seller of the shares will still have claim to the dividend. After this date, the buyer will own the dividend, therefore the price of the stock will typically drop by the per share amount of the dividend on this date.

A simple way of thinking about volatility is to relate it to the well understood concept of the "normal distribution." The expected annualized volatility is effectively the standard deviation of the expected price of the stock. One standard deviation plus or minus from the present price, adjusted for the expected (or average) change in price over the period, will have about a 67% probability of including the actual price at the end of the term of the option. For example, if the price per share is $40 currently, and the expected return (based on past price changes) is 10% and the computed volatility measure is 25%, the price of the stock one year hence which is determined at a 67% probability is from $34.43 to $56.76. This is computed as follows: The rate of return over one year, at 67% probability (i.e., one standard deviation plus or minus), is from $-15\% = (10\% - 25\%)$ to $+35\% = (10\% + 25\%)$. The natural logarithms $e^{-.15}$ and $e^{.35}$ equate to .8607 and 1.4191, respectively. Thus, the likely stock price one year hence ranges from $34.43 ($40 x .8607) to $56.76 ($40 x 1.4191).

The discount rate. SFAS 123 specifies the use of a risk-free rate. The risk-free rate of return is easily ascertained as the rate on treasury bills or notes having a remaining term to maturity equal to the expected life of the options being computed. Reasonable approximations would be acceptable (e.g., it would be valid to interpolate a discount rate from published data).

The expected term of the options. The objective of SFAS 123 is to allocate compensation cost to the periods in which services are provided to the entity granting the options. If the award is for past services, as indicated when the options are immediately exercisable by the holders, compensation cost must be fully expensed at the date of the grant. More typically, however, the options will not be exercisable until some later date, called the vesting date, which often will be a few years after the grant date. In such a case, the compensation element is really intended to apply to some or all of the intervening period from grant to vesting dates, and should be accrued over that time, based either on an estimate of the number of options expected to vest or on an estimate of the number of options expected to be exercised.

In some instances there is a performance condition stipulated in the option agreement, and the options will not be exercisable until the condition is met. A variation of this has the number of options dependent upon the extent to which performance is achieved. Compensation cost associated with such option arrangements is to be accrued over the expected period until the conditions will be satisfied.

In the case of either service period-based or performance-based options, provision for forfeitures may be made either at inception or as forfeitures actually occur. The former method requires that compensation cost be accrued based on the number of options that are expected to vest less those which vest but are not, for whatever reason, subsequently exercised by the holders. For example, it may be estimated based on past behavior that of 100 options granted, only 85 will vest (due to employee turnover, failure to meet performance conditions, etc.) and only 78 will be exercised; compensation cost would be based on 78 options in such a case. The latter method would have compensation determined based on the 85 options expected to vest, with compensation cost adjusted if and when some of the 7 (85-78) options are forfeited.

If the former method, basing compensation on the number of options expected to be exercised, is utilized, then changes in that expectation during the period in which compensation is being accrued is to be accounted for as a change in an accounting estimate as defined in APB 20; the effect is reported in the period in which the change occurs. Under the alternative method, the effect of forfeitures is reported in compensation as they individually occur.

Payments in lieu of dividends on options. Normally dividends are not paid on shares that have not been issued; thus, unexercised options do not gain the benefit of any dividends declared on the underlying stock. However, an entity can choose to pay dividend equivalents on options. Under the provisions of SFAS 123, such dividends or dividend equivalents on options which vest are to be accounted for as other dividends, that is, charged against retained earnings. Those paid on options that do not vest are deemed to be compensation expense. The reporting entity can either estimate what fraction of options will vest, and allocate such dividend equivalents between retained earnings and compensation expense accordingly, or else can charge all to retained earnings and account for forfeitures as they occur, by reversing the charge from retained earnings to compensation cost.

Settlements of awards. Sometimes an entity that grants options to employees will repurchase the resulting shares after they are issued, or will purchase and cancel the options, by making a payment to the option holders. To the extent that shares are purchased for market value, the transaction is similar to any other treasury stock transaction, and equity accounts will be charged with the purchase price. If, however, the purchase price exceeds the market or fair value, the excess is deemed to be additional compensation expense. If the payment is made to cancel options which have not yet vested, the remaining unrecognized compensation cost must be expensed, as the options have effectively vested at that point in time. The additional compensation element, if any, is measured by the difference between the price paid and the value of the option repurchased, as computed using the methods prescribed by SFAS 123 (i.e., by the fair value method).

Examples of accounting for options under SFAS 123

Example where calculation of compensation expense does not consider expected forfeitures. Assume the same facts as were presented earlier in this section when APB 25 was being explained.

Options are granted to corporate officers to purchase 10,000 shares of $1 par stock at a price of $52 per share, when the market price is $58. The options may not be exercised until five years from the grant date. The company has no reason to expect that any of the options will be forfeited by the employees to whom they are granted. If the risk-free interest rate is 8% and the stock is expected to pay dividends of $2 annually, the minimum value as prescribed under SFAS 123 is as follows:

Current market	$58.00
Less: Present value of exercise price ($52 x .681)	35.39
Present value of expected dividends ($2 x 3.993)	7.99
	$14.62

Thus the 10,000 options have a value of $146,200 (10,000 x $14.62), to be recognized over five years, or $29,240 per year before considering forfeitures.

The entry to record the granting of the options is

Deferred compensation expense	146,200	
Stock options outstanding		146,200

As was the case under APB 25, deferred compensation expense is subtracted from stock options outstanding in the paid-in capital section of owner's equity to indicate the amount of net contributed services on any date [i.e., on the grant date nothing has yet been contributed by the option holders ($146,200 – $146,200 = $0)]. As the employees provide services to earn the options, entries are made assigning compensation expense to years one to five.

Compensation expense	29,240 ($146,200 ÷ 5 years)	
Deferred compensation expense		29,240

When the option is exercised, cash is received and the stock is issued. The following entry is made (assume exercise after the five-year period):

Cash	520,000	(option price)
Stock options outstanding	146,200	
Common stock	10,000	(par)
Additional paid-in capital	656,200	(excess)

If options are forfeited as a result of an employee failing to fulfill an obligation (e.g., staying with the company), under the provisions of SFAS 123 compensation expense is credited in the year of forfeiture. (This is assuming that compensation expense had not been based on the **net** number of options that were expected to be exercised, which is the alternative, acceptable method under this standard.) The amount credited reflects the total compensation expense previously charged to the income statement for the employee who forfeited the options. Assume that one officer, who was granted options for 1,000 shares, leaves the company in year three, two years before the options can be exercised. The result is handled as a change in an accounting estimate and the following entry is made in year three:

Stock options outstanding	14,620	
Deferred compensation expense		8,772
Compensation expense		5,848

Next consider the case of an option plan which features graded vesting, that is, where instead of having all options vest after five years, 20% of the options granted will vest each year. Under FASB Interpretation 28, which applies to entities that continue to adhere to APB 25, a rather complicated allocation pattern must be employed. These are not freely selectable alternatives, however, if fair value is determined based on different expected lives for options that vest in different years, then the Interpretation 28 method is required. Entities that adopt SFAS 123 can either continue the Interpretation 28 method, illustrated earlier in this section, or can recognize compensation on a straight-line basis. Straight-line compensation recognition can be used only if the expected lives of the award are determined in another manner. If the straight-line method is used, the compensation cost recognized to date must be at least equal to the value of the vested portion of the award at that date. SFAS 123 includes illustrations of the accounting required under such circumstances.

Accounting under SFAS 123 using expected number of options to be exercised. Assume most of the same facts as the example presented immediately above. The company's stock is not publicly traded, and therefore there will be no attempt to address volatility. The risk-free interest rate is now given as 6%. Based on past experience, the company estimates that 2% of the eligible officers will leave each year, thus forfeiting their options. SFAS 123 permits the computation of fair value based on the expected number of options that will vest (i.e., net of expected forfeitures). As noted above, the standard also permits accounting for forfeitures when they occur. With an annual forfeiture rate of 2%, the number of options expected to vest is given as

$$10,000 \times .98 \times .98 \times .98 \times .98 \times .98 = 9,039 \text{ options}$$

The fair value can be determined with reference to either the Black-Scholes option pricing model or a binomial model, or the minimum value model can be used. In the present example, assuming no dividends are expected to be paid on the underlying stock, and given the risk-free rate of 6%, the minimum value model would value each option as follows:

$$\$58 - (\$52 \div 1.06^5) = \$58 - \$38.86 = \$19.14 \text{ per option}$$

Accordingly, the total value of $173,006 (9,039 options x $19.14) will be recognized as compensation expense over the five years on a ratable basis. If the forfeiture rate changes, that would be treated as a change in an accounting estimate, and reflected in income on a prospective basis. The entry to record the granting of the options is

Deferred compensation expense	173,006	
Stock options outstanding		173,006

Stock options outstanding is an additional paid-in capital account. Deferred compensation expense is subtracted from stock options outstanding in the paid-in capital section of owners' equity to indicate the amount of net contributed services on any date [i.e., on the grant date nothing has yet been contributed by the option holders ($173,006 – $173,006 = $0)]. As the employees provide services to earn the options, entries are made assigning compensation expense to years one to five.

Compensation expense	34,601	(173,006 ÷ 5 years)
Deferred compensation expense		34,601

When the option is exercised, cash is received and the stock is issued. The following entry is made (assume exercise after the five-year period, and that the number of forfeitures exactly equals the amount predicted):

Cash	470,028	(option price)
Stock options outstanding	173,006	
Common stock		9,039 (par)
Additional paid-in capital		633,995 (excess)

Note that under this method the effect of forfeitures is reflected in income; that is, compensation cost is reduced on a prospective basis. If the assumption regarding the number of forfeitures changed during the service period, compensation cost attributable to prior periods is effectively adjusted in the current period by making a "catch up" adjustment as illustrated in the following paragraph.

Assume that in year three of the preceding example the holders of 5% of the remaining options leave the company (the forfeiture rate in years one and two having equaled the expected 2%). Management believes that the rate in year three was unusually high, but now expects that the forfeiture rate over the full five-year period will average 3%. Given this new insight, the number of options that it believes will eventually vest will be as follows:

$$10,000 \times .97 \times .97 \times .97 \times .97 \times .97 = 8,587 \text{ options}$$

The total compensation cost over five years, given this revised estimate, will be $164,355 (8,587 options x $19.14). Since aggregate compensation cost of $69,202 ($34,601 x 2) has already been recognized in years one and two, and total compensation cost for years one through three under the revised assumption should be $98,613 (3/5 x $164,355), the difference of $29,411 should be allocated to compensation expense in year three. The entry in year three is

Compensation expense	29,411	
Deferred compensation expense		29,411

The entries in years four and five, assuming no other changes in the forfeiture rate, are

Compensation expense ($164,355 ÷ 5 yrs)	32,871	
Deferred compensation expense		32,871

Also, there should be an adjustment to reduce the amounts in the deferred compensation expense and stock options outstanding accounts, based on the new expected totals, as follows:

Stock options outstanding		
($173,006 – $164,355)	8,651	
Deferred compensation expense		8,651

Assuming that the average forfeiture rate does indeed equal 3% over the vesting period, and that all options are exercised at the vesting date, the entry to be made at the end of year five will be

Cash	446,524 (option price)	
Stock options outstanding	164,355	
Common stock		8,587 (par)
Additional paid-in capital		602,292 (excess)

On the other hand, if the options are not forfeited, but instead expire unexercised after first vesting with the grantees, then the accounting treatment under SFAS 123 would be different. The standard provides that previously recognized compensation cost is not to be reversed if vested options expire unexercised. Thus, in such a circumstance, the stock options outstanding would be closed to another paid-in capital account, such as "capital from unexercised options."

Given the facts in the immediately preceding discussion, assume now that at the time the options vest, only 8,000 are exercised, and that, per the terms of the option agreement, the remaining 587 expire one year later, unexercised. The entries would be as follows:

For the exercise:

Cash	416,000 (option price)	
Stock options outstanding	153,120	
Common stock		8,000 (par)
Additional paid-in capital		561,120 (excess)

For the expiration one year later:

Stock options outstanding	11,235	
Additional paid-in capital from unexercised options		11,235

Accounting for stock appreciation rights (SAR) under SFAS 123. One of the motivating reasons for developing SFAS 123 was to eliminate the disparate treatment applied to fixed options, variable (or performance) options and other stock-based compensation schemes. Thus, under the new standard the measurement principles applicable to SAR are the same as for stock options.

One distinction that may arise in connection with SAR, however, is that the holder may have the ability to elect to receive cash in settlement of the award. In the case of such plans, the accrual of compensation expense will result in the recognition of a liability. (In some such plans, however, the settlement can only be made in shares of stock; in such cases, the accrual will be offset by paid-in capital.)

Accounting for tandem plans under SFAS 123. Accounting for tandem plans has been explained earlier in this chapter for situations where APB 25 and related standards are still being utilized. The concepts are the same for tandem plans by entities that adopt SFAS 123, but the accounting will be somewhat different, for several reasons. First, SFAS 123 requires that when an entity incurs a substantive liability, it must be reported as such. Further, it states that when the employee has the right to receive payment in cash, a liability has been created. Only if the company can choose to settle tandem plans in stock, and past experience suggests that indeed it does choose to do so, will the compensation be based on the stock option part of the plan and will the offset to compensation expense be paid-in capital.

Second, cash SAR are measured with reference to the intrinsic value as of the exercise date, which differs from the fair value approach to measuring stock options under SFAS 123. Note that time value, which is typically a major component of total value assigned to options under this standard, is not measured as part of intrinsic value as applied to SAR. For that reason, compensation cost as determined in the context of tandem plans may be significantly less than would be the case for the option portion of the plan on its own.

To illustrate, consider again the facts presented in the example of tandem plans earlier in this chapter when APB 25 was being discussed.

1/1/02   Plan adopted; base price is $100, option price is $95; 1,000 shares exercisable on 1/1/05 **or** 1,000 SAR payable in cash on 1/1/06 an increase over 1/1/02 market value.

Market prices are as follows:

12/31/02	$ 98
12/31/03	110
12/31/04	108
12/31/05	125

Assuming now a 6% risk-free rate and no dividend yield on the stock, the fair value of the options alone using the minimum value model is $100 − ($95 x .792) =

$24.75 x 1,000 = $24,750. Were these options freestanding and not part of a tandem plan, compensation cost of $6,187.50 would be accrued each year.

However, since the holders have the right to choose cash payments, under SFAS 123 it must be assumed that they will do this, and that the company has incurred a liability (not an equity instrument). Accordingly, compensation cost is debited or credited as the market price varies from the rights price ($100), with the limitation that the cumulative compensation cost cannot be negative (as the employees obviously have no obligation to pay the company if the market declines from the $100 per share level). Therefore the entries will be as follows:

12/31/02   No entry

No SAR liability is accrued since the market price is below the base price. The compensatory stock options are ignored since the holders have the right to demand a cash settlement.

12/31/03	Compensation expense	10,000	
	Liability under SAR plan ($10 x 1,000 SAR)		10,000

SAR liability recognized for difference between year-end market value and base price for number of expected SAR exercisable.

12/31/04	Liability under SAR plan	2,000	
	Compensation expense		2,000
12/31/05	Compensation expense	17,000	
	Liability under SAR plan		17,000

Recall that the option holders may exercise either the options or the SAR, although the accrual under SFAS 123 was based on the presumption that 100% exercise of the SAR would occur. Assume that (a) holders elect 100% SAR; (b) holders elect 50% SAR, 50% stock; or (c) they elect to exercise only the stock options. For each of the cases above, the entries under each assumed exercise ratio are as follows:

(a)	Liability under SAR plan	25,000	
(all cash)	Cash		25,000
(b)	Liability under SAR plan	25,000	
(1/2 cash,	Cash ($47,500 – $12,500)	35,000	
1/2 stock)	Common stock—$20 par		10,000
	Additional paid-in capital		50,000
(c)	Liability under SAR plan	25,000	
(all stock)	Cash	95,000	
	Common stock—$20 par		20,000
	Additional paid-in capital		100,000

Reload options and other plan features. Some option arrangements permit the exercise price to be paid for by delivering shares already held by the grantee (these shares are referred to as "mature shares"), rather than with cash. These shares are valued at the market price as of the date of the exercise. Furthermore, there may be a reload feature, which provides that the holder will be granted another option equal to the number of mature shares used in the exercise, and that the exercise price for the reload option will be equal to the market at the time of exercise of the original option. This feature obviously has value, and in a fair value approach as is adopted under SFAS 123 this feature should be considered in computing compensation cost. However, there are a number of subjective elements that would need to be addressed, including the expected market value at exercise and reload date and the number of options that would be exercised in this fashion. Due to this and the fact that valuation models dealing with reload features are not yet widely understood, SFAS 123 has stipulated that there be no additional value assigned for such options. Rather, if and when a reload option is granted (when mature shares are used to exercise the original option), it is to be accounted for as a new option.

Other modifications of options are accounted for prospectively as exchanges of the old options for a new equity instrument. Fair value is used to account for such transactions. For example, modification of the terms of an outstanding option would be accounted for based on a comparison of the fair value of the modified option at the date it is granted and at the date of the old option that is effectively repurchased, based on the shorter of (1) the remaining initially estimated expected life or (2) the expected life of the modified option. If the fair value of the modified option exceeds that of the option that is replaced, additional compensation cost must be recognized.

Other SFAS 123 Matters

The Board issued FASB TB 97-1 that deals with "look-back options" in the context of SFAS 123. Plans with this feature permit exercise at a price that is the lower of the market price at the grant date or at the date of exercise. This technical bulletin is applicable to stock-based awards with this feature that are granted, renewed, or modified after 1/1/98.

Disclosure requirements under SFAS 123. SFAS 123 significantly expands the disclosures that are required by entities having stock compensation arrangements, and this expansion applies as well, for the most part, to those companies which continue to employ APB 25 for financial statement purposes. Disclosures are set forth in the Disclosure Checklist included at the end of this book.

In addition to the disclosures identified in the checklist, SFAS 123 requires that for options outstanding as of the date of the latest balance sheet, the range of exercise prices, weighted-average exercise price, and weighted-average remaining contractual life must be presented. If the range is wide, exercise prices should be grouped into ranges that are more meaningful for assessing the number and timing of additional share issuances and the cash that may be received as a result of such exercises (SFAS 123 suggests that the range is wide if the highest exercise price exceeds about 150% of the lowest). For each such range the following disclosures are required:

1. The number, weighted-average exercise price, and weighted-average remaining contractual life of options outstanding.
2. The number and weighted-average exercise price of options currently exercisable.

Furthermore, if the company grants options under a number of plans (e.g., fixed and variable plans), the income statement oriented disclosures should be appropriately segregated.

For entities that continue to apply APB 25, the company must also disclose for each year for which an income statement is provided the pro forma net income (and earnings per share, if required under SFAS 128) as if fair value based measurements had been used. Thus, **all** entities will have to apply the Black-Scholes or binomial model (if publicly owned) or the minimum value model (if privately owned), whether SFAS 123 is adopted or not. It should be noted that, in determining the pro forma disclosures, the tax effect of compensation differences will also have to be considered, as discussed below. This particular pro forma disclosure cannot be merged with any other pro forma calculation; it must be possible for financial statement readers to understand the impact on earnings of the choice of accounting method for stock-based compensation alone.

Finally, enterprises that use equity instruments to acquire goods or services other than employee services must also provide disclosures similar to those above (e.g., number of shares, weighted-average prices, etc.).

Accounting for Equity Instruments Issued to other than Employees

While SFAS 123 makes it very clear that stock issuances to persons or entities other than employees (e.g., vendors providing goods or services to the enterprise) are to be measured at fair value (defined by either the value of the goods or services received or the value of the equity instruments delivered in exchange, whichever is subject to more reliable measurement), it offers no specific guidance regarding measurement. The Emerging Issues Task Force has supplemented this basic directive, however, with its consensuses on Issue 96-18, dealing exclusively with those situations in which the fair value of the equity instruments delivered is more objectively ascertainable than is the value of goods or services received. Issue 96-18 is the foundation for the discussion that follows in this section.

Measurement date. For purposes of ascertaining the amounts to be assigned for these transactions, the key concern is the determination of the measurement date. Essentially, the amount of expense or the value of the asset acquired through the issuance of equity instruments is fixed as of the measurement date, although, under certain of the circumstances explained below, some subsequent adjustments may need to be made.

Per the consensus on Issue 96-18, the measurement date will be the **earlier** of the date at which a commitment for performance is made or when the performance is actually completed. Whether or not there has been a "performance commitment" by the party providing the goods or services is a question of fact and must be determined from the surrounding circumstances, but in general will be deemed to exist if there is a "sufficiently large disincentive for nonperformance" to make performance probable. This disincentive must derive from the relationship between the equity instrument issuer/recipient of the goods or services and its counterparty. Mere risk of forfeiture is not enough to qualify as a disincentive, nor is the risk of being sued for nonperformance. When a sufficiently large disincentive exists, however, the measurement date will precede the completion of performance and, accordingly, when accrual of the related expense or recognition of the asset would otherwise be required under GAAP, it will be necessary to include the value of the equity instruments in such cost.

For example, if the agreed-upon price for the construction of a new power plant includes options on the utility company's stock, subject to a completion date of no longer than three years hence, **and** the contract also contains substantial financial disincentives to late completion, such as a provision for liquidated damages, then it would be concluded that there was a "performance commitment" within the meaning of EITF 96-18. On the other hand, if the price agreed to were to be fully payable even in the event of late delivery, there would be no "performance commitment" as that term is used.

In many situations in which the compensation includes significant equity instrument components, there will still be no finding of a performance commitment because the payment arrangement provides for phases of work, with payment in full for work as it is completed. For example, if a contractor agrees to build a multiplicity of sales kiosks in various air terminals for a retailing chain, with payment to be made in cash and the retailer's stock upon the completion of each kiosk, the contractor could terminate the arrangement after any intermediate completion date without significant penalty. In such cases, the measurement date would be, for each subproject, the date on which the work is completed.

When to recognize the fair value of the equity instruments. In general, the normal rules of GAAP would apply in circumstances in which stock or other equity instruments were being granted as part, or all, of the consideration for the transaction. Thus, if the services provided represented an expense of the enterprise, the expense should be recognized when incurred, which could well precede the date on which the payment was ultimately to be made.

No specific guidance has been offered regarding timing or manner of recognition. However, an EITF consensus was reached that once recognized, an asset or expense would not later be reversed if a stock option issued as consideration were to expire unexercised. This is consistent with SFAS 123's treatment of expirations of options granted to employees. (It is, however, in contrast to the accounting prescribed for forfeitures under both APB 25 and SFAS 123, which mandate that compensation be reversed under such circumstances.) Thus, an expense or asset measurement is made with the best information available at that time, and there is no "look back" based on subsequent events; the value assigned to the option would be credited to an appropriate paid-in capital account (e.g., "capital from expired options") if this becomes necessary.

Accounting prior to measurement date. If, under GAAP, it is necessary for the entity to recognize an expense or an asset related to the transaction involving the issuance of equity for goods or services prior to the measurement date, the then-current fair values of the equity instruments must be utilized to determine these amounts. If fair values change later, these variations are attributed to those later periods, consistent with Interpretation 28, discussed earlier in this chapter. Thus, for a transaction which calls primarily for cash payment but also, to a lesser extent, for the issuance of stock, a decline in the value of the equity portion in a later interim period would reduce the cost (or asset value) to be recognized in that period; if the stock portion is a significant component, a decline could largely eliminate the cost otherwise to be accrued or even, conceivably, cause it to become negative in a later reporting period. Of course, overall, the aggregate cost would be positive upon ultimate completion (at worst it could be zero, if the transaction were predicated only on the issuance of equity instruments, and these became worthless—an obviously unlikely scenario).

Measurement of fair value of the equity instrument portion of the transaction when certain terms are not known at inception. In some circumstances where there is a performance commitment there will also be a material uncertainty regarding the valuation of the equity instruments, either because of some question regarding the number of instruments to be delivered, the value of such instruments, or some factor dependent upon the performance of the party providing the service. For example, the arrangement may include a guarantee of the value of the instrument extending for some period subsequent to completion of performance that unless the underlying shares maintain a market price of $15 or greater for one year following delivery, or else a defined number of additional shares will be granted. This type of arrangement is referred to as a "market condition." In other circumstances there may be a condition based on the counterparty's performance, for example, when options are granted to a tax accountant structuring a tax shelter, in which the number of options ultimately deliverable depends upon successfully surviving an IRS audit. Situations such as this are denoted "counterparty performance conditions."

Where the arrangement contains market conditions, measurement of the equity instrument portion of the contracted price should be based on two elements: the first is the fair value of the basic equity instrument; the second is the fair value of the contingent commitment, such as the afore-noted promise to grant a specified number of extra shares if the market price falls below $15 during the one-year period. In practice, the valuation of these contingencies might prove to be challenging, but clearly any such promise has some positive value, and the standard requires that this be assessed. Changes in the value of the second (contingent) element subsequent to the performance commitment date would **not** be recognized since, per EITF 96-13, a derivative financial instrument to be settled in a company's own shares (as contrasted to a settlement in cash) is not to be remeasured.

Compared to market conditions, measurement when there are counterparty performance conditions is more complicated. At the measurement date, the equity instruments are valued at the lowest of the defined alternative amounts. For example, if the value of the option award to the tax accountant noted above is $20,000 (at the performance commitment date) assuming survival against IRS challenge, but only $5,000 if the IRS ultimately prevails, then the measurement of the value of the service would be based on the $5,000 amount. However, later, when the outcome of the performance condition is known, an additional cost would have to be recognized if a more favorable outcome occurred (in this example, successful defense of the tax shelter). The added cost would be based not on the values as of the performance commitment date, but rather as of the date of resolution of the condition. If the value of the options under the "success" outcome is $28,000 at that date, and the value of the "failure" outcome is $19,000, then an added cost of ($28,000 − 19,000) $9,000 would be recognized.

Where a given transaction involves both market and counterparty performance conditions, the accounting specified for situations involving only counterparty performance conditions is to be applied.

Reporting prior to the measurement date when certain terms are not known. When market conditions (e.g., the value of the stock underlying the options two years hence) are not known, and expenses must be accrued or assets recorded prior to the measurement date, the then-current fair values of the equity instruments at such dates should be used, with subsequent adjustments as necessary. When there are counterparty performance conditions, either alone or in conjunction with market conditions, then interim measurements should be based on the lowest of the alternative values as of each date, with subsequent changes in this same measure assigned to later periods.

Reporting after the measurement date when certain terms are not known. When market conditions (e.g., the value of the stock underlying the options two years hence) are not known, **after** the measurement date the principles of EITF 96-13 are to be applied, which generally would mean that changes in value would not be recognized. On the other hand, when there are counterparty performance conditions, with or without market conditions also being present, the principles of SFAS 123, specifically the "modification accounting" procedures, are to be utilized. This results in reporting an adjustment in subsequent periods determined with reference to the difference between the then-current fair value of the revised equity instruments and that of the old instruments immediately prior to the recognition event. In all cases, the "then-current" values are to be determined with reference to the lowest aggregate fair values under the alternative outcomes specified by the contractual arrangement.

Accounting for the Tax Effects of Options and SAR

Generally, amounts reported as compensation expense in connection with stock option and appreciation rights plans are deductible for tax purposes, but the timing and amounts of tax deductions may differ from the amounts reportable as expenses under GAAP. (An exception: incentive stock options provide no deduction for the grantor, and only tax at the capital gains rate for the employee, when shares acquired via option exercises are ultimately sold.) Thus, both temporary and permanent differences may occur, which are accounted for differently under GAAP (SFAS 109).

Timing differences occur because, for tax purposes, the company will be entitled to a deduction in the period in which the employee reports the compensation as ordinary income, whereas for financial reporting purposes the tax must be associated with any compensation expense accrued in the period(s) in which the services are provided. If APB 25 is being used, there probably will be no compensation recognized in any period in connection with the options granted; for this reason, the tax benefit flowing from the deductibility of compensation is not reported in the income statement (a result of applying the matching concept), but instead will be credited to paid-in capital.

If SFAS 123 is being used, on the other hand, compensation expense is recognized, and the tax effect thereof will be included in the income statement. The ultimate amount of the tax deduction depends on the spread between exercise price and fair market value on exercise date; this will differ from the aggregate compensation recognized over the service period, which is keyed to fair value at the grant date, and not to the ultimate market price upon exercise. Accordingly, there will usually be some portion of the tax benefit that will be credited to paid-in capital (similar to that under APB 25), even if most of the tax benefits impact the income statements over the service period.

Since, for compensatory arrangements under APB 25, and for all plans if accounted for under SFAS 123, the actual tax deduction occurs in a period subsequent to the service provision periods, a deferred tax benefit will be recognizable by the sponsoring corporation as compensation is expensed for GAAP reporting purposes. Under current GAAP (SFAS 109), such benefits are to be recorded in every case, although when it is deemed "more likely than not" that the benefit will **not** ultimately be received by the reporting entity, an offsetting valuation account must also be recorded. (See Chapter 15.)

Example of accounting for the tax ramifications of stock options

Assume an option to purchase ten shares at $80 per share is granted to a key employee when the market price is $100 per share, exercisable over four years. The company is continuing to use APB 25 to account for such transactions. This would be deemed a compensatory option; the following entry is made to record the deferred compensation at the grant date:

Deferred compensation expense	200	[= 10 x ($100 – $80)]
Stock options outstanding		200

Compensation, in the total amount $200, is associated with employee service in years one through four. The **annual** entry to recognize the expense is

Compensation expense	50	
Deferred compensation expense		50

Assume the tax rate remains constant at 40% and that the enterprise has been and is expected to continue to be profitable (and that hence there is no need for a reserve against the deferred tax asset). The compensation expense is not deductible for tax purposes until the option is exercised, and the amount of the ultimate deduction depends on the market price on the exercise date. The entry to record the tax effects for each of the years one to four is:

Deferred tax asset	20	(= $50 x .40)
Tax expense (benefit)		20

In year five, the options are exercised at the option price of $80 per share, at a time when the market price per share is $115. Thus, the compensation expense deductible for tax purposes in year five is $350 [= 10 shares x ($115 – $80)], having a tax effect (reducing taxes otherwise payable) of $140. No additional compensation expense is allowed as a deduction in the determination of net income. The result is a permanent difference of $150 (= $350 – $200). The journal entry to reflect the reversal of the previously deferred tax benefit as follows:

Taxes payable	140	($350 x .40)
Paid-in capital	60	(= $150 x .40)
Deferred tax asset	80	(= $20 x 4 yrs.)

The same approach is followed by an entity that has adopted SFAS 123; however the measure of compensation cost will differ, and thus will the measure of the deferred taxes related thereto. It should be noted that the treatment illustrated above applies only to the benefit of the income tax deduction for a specific stock option award that exceeds the compensation expense recognized for that award for financial reporting purposes. Payroll taxes, even though directly related to the appreciation of stock options, are operating expenses and should be reflected as such in the statement of operations.

Finally, note that in the more typical situation found under APB 25, where the stock option plan is noncompensatory in nature, there will be no deferred taxes and only the tax effect of the exercise will be reported. In such cases, the entire tax benefit of the deductible amount (the excess of market value at exercise date over the exercise price) will be credited to paid-in capital.

Convertible Preferred Stock

The treatment of convertible preferred stock at its issuance is no different than that of nonconvertible preferred. When it is converted, the book value approach is used to account for the conversion. Use of the market value approach would entail a gain or loss for which there is no theoretical justification since the total amount of contributed capital does not change when the stock is converted. When the preferred stock is converted, the "Preferred stock" and related "Additional paid-in capital—preferred stock" accounts are debited for their original values when purchased, and "Common stock" and "Additional paid-in capital—common stock" (if an excess over par or stated value exists) are credited. If the book value of the preferred stock is less than the total par value of the common stock being issued, retained earnings is charged for the difference. This charge is supported by the rationale that the preferred shareholders are offered an additional return to facilitate their conversion to common stock. Many states require that this excess instead reduce additional paid-in capital from other sources.

Preferred Stock with Mandatory Redemption

A mandatory redemption clause requires the preferred stock to be redeemed (retired) at a specified date(s). This feature is in contrast to callable preferred stock, which is redeemed at the issuing corporation's option.

The mandatory redemption feature, when combined with a cumulative dividend preference, causes the preferred stock to have the characteristics of debt, especially when the stock is to be redeemed in five to ten years. The dividend payments represent interest and redemption is the repayment of principal. However, there is one important difference. The dividend payments do not receive the same tax treatment as interest payments. They are not deductible in determining taxable income.

Notwithstanding the fact that mandatorily redeemable preferred stock has most of the characteristics of debt, under presently effective GAAP this would be presented as equity in the balance sheet of the issuer. However, if the FASB adopts a new standard on distinguishing liabilities from equity instruments (discussed later in this chapter), mandatorily redeemable preferred stock will become reportable as debt, rather than equity.

It should be noted that even under present GAAP, expanded disclosure of mandatorily redeemable preferred stock is required. This is pursuant to SFAS 129, which supersedes a virtually identical requirement established by SFAS 47. Specifically, the redemption requirements for each of the next five years must be set forth in the notes to the financial statements prepared in accordance with GAAP, if the amounts are either fixed or determinable on fixed or determinable dates. Thus readers can interpret the cash requirements on the reporting entity, in a manner similar to the drawing of inferences about other fixed commitments, such as maturities of long-term debt and lease obligations.

The SEC, conversely, does recognize the debt characteristics of mandatory redeemable preferred stock. According to SAR 268, the stock may not be presented under the heading "Stockholders' Equity." Rather, the amounts pertaining to this type of stock may be presented either as long-term debt or between long-term debt and stockholders' equity.

Book Value Stock Plans

A book value plan is intended also to be a compensation program for participating employees although there are important secondary motives in many such plans, such as the desires to generate capital and to tie the employees to the employer. Under the terms of typical book value plans, employees (or those attaining some defined level, such as manager) are given the opportunity or, in some cases, they are required to purchase shares in the company, which then must be sold back to the company upon termination of employment. EITF 87-23 and 88-6 addressed different aspects of such plans.

In 87-23, a consensus was reached that, if the employees participating in a nonpublic company's book value stock plan have substantive investments in the company that are at risk, then the increases in book value during the period of ownership are not to be treated as compensation. However, if the employees are granted options to purchase shares at book value, compensation is to be recognized for value increases, presumably because under the latter scenario the employee has no investment at risk and is only being given an "upside" opportunity. This interpretation is also applicable to book value options granted to employees of publicly held companies.

For accounting purposes, shares issued at book value to employees are simply recorded as a normal stock sale. To the extent that book value exceeds par or stated value, additional paid-in capital accounts may also be credited.

EITF 88-6 addresses the related question of book value stock plans of publicly held companies. In this consensus, the Task Force concluded that the plan was a performance plan akin to a SAR, and accordingly results in compensation expense recognition. This conclusion was reached at least in part due to SEC pressure, which arose largely in the context of initial public offerings (IPO).

Junior Stock

Another category of stock-based compensation program involves junior stock. Typically, such shares are subordinate to normal shares of common stock with respect to voting rights, dividend rate, or other attributes, and are convertible into regular common shares if and when stipulated performance goals are achieved. Like stock appreciation rights, grants of junior stock represent a performance-based program, in contrast to fixed stock options.

FASB Interpretation 38 specifies that compensation cost incurred in connection with grants of junior stock is generally to be accrued in accordance with the provisions of Interpretation 28. However, compensation is only to be recognized when it is deemed to be probable, as that term is defined by SFAS 5, that the performance goals will be achieved. It may be that achievement is not deemed probable at the time the junior stock is issued, but it later becomes clear that such achievement is indeed likely. In other circumstances, the ability to convert junior stock to regular stock is dependent upon the achievement of more than a single performance goal, and it is not probable that all such goals can be achieved, although some of them are deemed probable of achievement. In both scenarios, full accrual of compensation cost may be delayed until the estimated likelihood of achievement improves.

Interpretation 38 specifies that the measure of compensation is derived from the comparison of the market price of ordinary common stock with the price to be paid, if any, for the junior stock. Since the junior stock will be convertible to ordinary common stock if the defined performance goals are achieved, the compensation to be received by the employees participating in the plan is linked to the value of unrestricted common shares.

Put Warrant

A detachable put warrant can either be put back to the debt issuer for cash or can be exercised to acquire common stock. EITF 88-9 concluded that these instruments should be accounted for in the same manner as mandatory redeemable preferred stock. The proceeds applicable to the put warrant ordinarily are to be classified as equity and should be presented between the liability and equity sections in accordance with SEC SAR 268.

In the case of a warrant with a put price substantially higher than the value assigned to the warrant at issuance, however, the proceeds should be classified as a liability since it is likely that the warrant will be put back to the company.

The original **classification** should not be changed because of subsequent economic changes in the value of the put. The value assigned to the put warrant at issuance, however, should be adjusted to its highest redemption price, starting with the date of issuance until the earliest date of the warrants. Changes in the redemption price before the earliest put dates are changes in accounting estimates and changes after the earliest put dates should be recognized in income. If the put is classified as equity, the adjustment should be reported as a charge to retained earnings, and if the put is classified as a liability the adjustment is reported as interest expense.

Regardless of how the put is classified on the balance sheet, the primary and fully diluted EPS should be calculated on both an equity basis (warrants will be exercised) and on a debt basis (put will be exercised) and the more dilutive of the two methods should be used.

Accounting for Stock Issued to Employee Stock Ownership Plans

Increasingly, corporations have been availing themselves of favorable tax regulations that encourage the establishment of employee stock ownership plans (ESOP). The accounting for ESOP was first set forth in AICPA Statement of Position (SOP) 76-3, which has been superseded by SOP 93-6. However, employers may continue their current accounting methods for shares purchased prior to December 31, 1992.

Employee stock ownership plans (ESOP) are defined contribution plans in which shares of the sponsoring entity are given to employees as additional compensation. Subsequent to the inception of these types of plans some forty years ago, these plans have grown enormously in popularity. SOP 93-6 made significant changes to the employers' accounting for the costs associated with such plans.

In brief, ESOP are created by a sponsoring corporation which either funds the plan directly (unleveraged ESOP) or, as is more often the case, facilitates the borrowing of money either directly from an outside lender (directly leveraged ESOP) or from the employer, who in turn will borrow from an outside lender (indirectly leveraged ESOP). Borrowings from outside lenders may or may not be guaranteed by the sponsor. Since effectively the only source of funds for debt repayment are future contributions by the sponsor, GAAP requires that the ESOP's debt be considered debt of the sponsor. Depending on the reasons underlying the creation of the ESOP (estate planning by the controlling shareholder, expanding the capital base of the entity, rewarding and motivating the work force, etc.), the sponsor's shares may be contributed to the plan in annual installments, in a block of shares from the sponsor, or shares from an existing shareholder may be purchased by the plan.

Direct or indirect borrowings by the ESOP must be reported as debt in the sponsor's balance sheet. An offset to a contra equity account, not to an asset, is also reported since the plan represents a commitment (morally if not always legally) to make future contributions to the plan and **not** a claim to resources. This results in a "double hit" to the sponsor's balance sheet (i.e., the recording of a liability **and** the reduction of net stockholders' equity) which is often an unanticipated and unpleasant surprise. This contra equity account is now referred to as "unearned ESOP shares" under SOP 93-6. If the sponsor lends funds to the ESOP without a "mirror" loan from an outside lender, this loan should not be reported in the employer's balance sheet as debt, although the debit should still be reported as a contra equity account.

As the ESOP services the debt, using contributions made by the sponsor and/or dividends received on sponsor shares held by the plan, the sponsor reflects the reduction of the obligation by reducing the debt and the contra equity account on its balance sheet. Simultaneously, income and thus retained earnings will be impacted as the contributions to the plan are reported in the sponsor's current results of operations. Thus, the "double hit" is eliminated, but net worth continues to reflect the economic fact that compensation costs have been incurred. The interest cost component must be separated from the remaining compensation expense, that is, the sponsor's income statement should reflect the true character of the expenses being incurred, rather than aggregating the entire amount into a category such as "ESOP contribution."

In a leveraged ESOP, shares held serve as collateral for the debt and are not allocated to employee until the debt is retired. In general, shares must be allocated by the end of the year in which the debt is repaid. However, in order to satisfy the tax laws, the allocation of shares may take place at a faster pace than the retirement of the principal portion of the debt.

Under SOP 93-6, the cost of ESOP shares allocated is measured (for purposes of reporting compensation expense in the sponsor's income statements) based upon the fair value on the release date, in contrast to the actual historical cost of the shares to the plan. Second, dividends paid on unallocated shares (i.e., shares held by the ESOP) are no longer treated as dividends (that is, as charges against retained earnings), but rather must be reported in the sponsor's income statement as compensation cost and/or as interest expense. Of less significance to nonpublic companies is the fact that under the new rules only common shares released and committed to be released are treated as being outstanding, and thus are to be considered in both primary and fully diluted EPS calculations.

Prospective application of the rules is not required (but is permitted) for shares acquired by ESOP after December 31, 1992, but not previously committed to be released as of the beginning of the year of adoption. Thus, if it so desired, an entity could preserve the historical acquisition cost of these "grandfathered" shares as the measure of compensation cost in future years, until the supply of these pre-1993 shares was depleted.

Example of accounting for ESOP transactions under the new standard

Assume that Intrepid Corp. establishes an ESOP, which then borrows $500,000 from Second Interstate Bank. The ESOP then purchases 50,000 shares of Intrepid no-par shares from the company; none of these shares are allocated to individual participants. Under SOP 93-6, the entries would be

Cash	500,000	
Bank loan payable		500,000
Unearned ESOP shares (contra equity)	500,000	
Common stock		500,000

The ESOP then borrows an additional $250,000 from the sponsor, Intrepid, and uses the cash to purchase a further 25,000 shares, all of which are allocated to participants.

Compensation	250,000	
Common stock		250,000

Intrepid Corp. contributes $50,000 to the plan, which the plan uses to service its bank debt, consisting of $40,000 principal reduction and $10,000 interest cost. The debt reduction causes 4,000 shares to be allocated to participants at a time when the average market value had been $12 per share.

Interest expense	10,000	
Bank loan payable	40,000	
Cash		50,000
Compensation	48,000	
Additional paid-in capital		8,000
Unearned ESOP shares		40,000

Dividends of $.10 per share are declared (only the ESOP shares are represented in the following entry, but dividends are paid equally on all outstanding shares)

Retained earnings (on 29,000 shares)	2,900	
Compensation (on 46,000 shares)	4,600	
Dividends payable		7,500

Note that in all the foregoing illustrations the effect of income taxes is ignored. Since the difference between the cost and fair values of shares committed to be released is analogous to differences in the expense recognized for tax and accounting purposes with regard to stock options, the same treatment should be applied. That is, the tax effect should be reported directly in stockholders' equity, rather than in earnings.

Disclosure Requirements

Under SFAS 129, which consolidates requirements previously set forth in APB 10 and 15, and SFAS 47, certain disclosures of an entity's capital structure are required. Under this standard, the financial statements will be required to explain, in summary form, the pertinent rights and privileges of the various equity securities outstanding, including dividend and liquidation preferences, participation rights, call prices and dates, conversion and exercise prices or rates along with pertinent dates, sinking fund requirements, unusual voting rights, and significant terms of any contractual obligations to issue additional shares.

Furthermore, the number of shares issued upon conversion, exercise, or satisfaction of required conditions, during at least the most recent annual reporting period and any subsequent interim period that is presented, must be disclosed. If preference shares have a liquidation preference considerably in excess of par or stated value in the event of involuntary liquidation, the aggregate amount must be disclosed. The amount that would be paid upon exercise of call privileges applicable to preferred shares must be disclosed also, but in this case either per share or aggregate data can be given. Any dividend arrearages on cumulative preferred shares must be stated, this on **both** per share and aggregate bases. Finally, if redeemable preferred shares are outstanding, the amount of redemption requirements for each of the subsequent five years must be given, if fixed or determinable on fixed or determinable dates; if there are several series of such shares, this can be given in the aggregate.

Corporate Bankruptcy and Reorganizations

Entities operating under and emerging from protection of the bankruptcy laws. The going concern assumption is one of the basic postulates underlying generally accepted accounting principles and is responsible for, among other things, the historical cost convention in financial reporting. For entities that have entered bankruptcy proceedings, however, the going concern assumption will no longer be of central importance.

Traditionally, the basic financial statements (balance sheet, income statement, and statement of cash flows) presented by going concerns were seen as less useful for entities undergoing reorganization. Instead, the **statement of affairs,** reporting assets at estimated realizable values and liabilities at estimated liquidation amounts, was recommended for use by such organizations. In more recent years, use of the statement of affairs has not been frequently encountered in practice. In late 1990, the AICPA's Accounting Standards Executive Committee promulgated SOP 90-7, setting forth certain financial reporting standards for entities undergoing, and emerging from, reorganization under the bankruptcy laws.

Under provisions of this SOP, assets are presented at estimated realizable values. Liabilities are set forth at the estimated amounts to be allowed in the balance sheet and liabilities subject to compromise are to be distinguished from those that are not. Furthermore, the SOP requires that in both the statements of income and cash flows, normal transactions be differentiated from those which have occurred as a consequence of the entity's being in reorganization. While certain allocations to the latter category are rather obvious, such as legal and accounting fees incurred, others are less clear. For example, the standard suggests that if the entity in reorganization earns interest income on funds which would normally have been used to settle obligations owed to creditors, such income will be deemed to be income arising as a consequence of the bankruptcy action.

Another interesting aspect of this standard is the accounting to be made for the emergence from reorganization (known as *confirmation of the plan of reorganization*). SOP 90-7 provides for **fresh start** financial reporting in such instances. This accounting is similar to that applied to purchase business combinations under APB 16, with the total confirmed value of the entity upon its emergence from reorganization being analogous to the purchase price in an acquisition. In both cases, this total value is to be allocated to the identifiable assets and liabilities of the entity, with any excess being allocated to goodwill. In the case of entities emerging from bankruptcy, goodwill (reorganization value in excess of amounts allocable to identifiable assets) is measured as the **excess** of liabilities existing at the plan confirmation date, computed at present value of future amounts to be paid, over the reorganization value of assets. Reorganization value is calculated with reference to a number of factors, including forecasted operating results and cash flows of the new entity.

SOP 90-7 applies only to entities undergoing formal reorganization under the Bankruptcy Code. Less formal procedures may still be accounted for under pre-existing **quasi reorganization** accounting procedures.

Quasi reorganization. Generally, this procedure is applicable during a period of declining price levels. It is termed "quasi" since the accumulated deficit is eliminated at a lower cost and with less difficulty than a legal reorganization.

Per ARB 43, Ch. 7A, the procedures in a quasi reorganization involve the

1. Proper authorization from stockholders and creditors where required
2. Revaluation of assets to their current values. All losses are charged to retained earnings, thus increasing any deficit.
3. Elimination of any deficit by charging paid-in capital

   a. First, additional paid-in capital to the extent it exists
   b. Second, capital stock when additional paid-in capital is insufficient. The par value of the stock is reduced, creating the extra additional paid-in capital to which the remaining deficit is charged.

No retained earnings may be created by a reorganization. Any excess created by the reduction of par value is credited to "Paid-in capital from quasi reorganization."

ARB 46 requires that retained earnings be dated for ten years (less than ten years may be justified under exceptional circumstances) after a quasi reorganization takes place. Disclosure similar to "since quasi reorganization of June 30, 19XX" is appropriate.

Reporting by Limited Liability Companies and Partnerships

Accounting theory and practice have overwhelmingly developed within the context of businesses organized as normal corporations. Accordingly, there is little official guidance to entities organized as partnerships or other forms of business, which is generally not a serious concern given that most transactions entered into by such entities do not differ generically from those conducted by corporations. The primary differences relate to equity transactions and to the display of the equity section of the balance sheet.

AICPA Practice Bulletin 14 addresses certain issues pertaining to accounting and reporting by limited liability companies and partnerships. This pronouncement establishes that, when an entity restructures itself as a limited liability company or a limited liability partnership, the basis of all assets and liabilities from its predecessor entity are carried forward. Also, as suggested by SFAS 109, if the new entity is not a taxable one, any deferred tax assets or liabilities existing previously are to be written off at the time the change in tax status becomes effective; with the elimination of any debit or credit balance being effected by a charge or credit to current period tax expense.

With regard to financial statement display issues, the practice bulletin establishes that the headings of each statement identify the entity as being a limited liability company or a limited liability partnership, similar to the common practice of identifying partnership entities. The apparent logic is that this alerts the user to certain anomalies, such as (most commonly) an absence of income tax expense and a related liability, and the use of somewhat distinctive captions in the equity section of the balance sheet. In the case of limited liability companies and partnerships, the term "members' equity" has been prescribed, and the changes in members' equity is to be communicated either in a separate financial statement, in a combined statement of operations and changes in members' equity, or in the notes to the financial statements.

The bulletin recommends that, where there are several classes of members' equity, these be set forth separately in the equity section of the balance sheet, although this is not a firm requirement. If not set forth in the balance sheet, however, the notes must provide adequate disclosure about the different classes of equity outstanding. This is entirely analogous to the existing GAAP requirements concerning disclosure about common and preferred stock of typical corporations, which has been analogized further to apply to classes of partnership equity in limited partnerships.

A deficit, if one exists, should be reported in the members' equity account(s), even if there is limited liability for the members. This is consistent with the "going concern" assumption that underlies GAAP. It is not required to disaggregate members' equity into separate components (undistributed earnings, unallocated capital, etc.) on the face of the balance sheet or in the notes, although this is of course permissible.

Amounts due from members for capital contributions, if any remain unpaid at the balance sheet date, should be shown as deductions from members' equity. This is entirely consistent with practice for unpaid stock subscriptions receivable.

GAAP presumes that comparative financial statements are more useful than those for a single period, and accordingly that comparative statements should normally be presented. However, for such financial statements to be meaningful, the information for the earlier period must be truly comparable to that of the more recent period. If the formation of the limited liability company or the limited liability partnership results in a new reporting entity being created, the guidance of APB 20 dealing with changes in accounting entities should be consulted.

Practice Bulletin 14 sets forth certain disclosures to be made in the financial statements of limited liability companies or limited liability partnerships. There should be a description of any limitations on members' equity and of the different classes of members' interests and the respective rights, preferences, and privileges of each class and amounts thereof. If the entity will cease to exist at a stipulated date, this must be disclosed. As suggested above, any change in tax status, and the impact of eliminating any tax liability or benefit from the entity's balance sheet, must be adequately explained in the notes to the financial statements in the period the change in status occurs.

In the period in which a limited liability company or a limited liability partnership is formed by combining entities under common control, or by conversion from another type of entity, the bulletin requires disclosures about the assets and liabilities previously held by the predecessor entity or entities. Entities created by combining predecessors under common control are encouraged, but not required, to make disclosures set forth by APB 16 applicable to poolings.

FASB Proposal: Distinguishing between Liabilities and Equity

In many instances, complex financial instruments, exhibiting characteristics of both liabilities and equity, are issued by companies. Under present GAAP, the accounting for such instruments may sometimes be unclear, although some specific items, such as convertible debentures, are explicitly addressed by existing standards. The FASB undertook a project on distinguishing between liabilities and equity instruments in 1986, resulting in the publication of a discussion memorandum in 1990, which promoted the "fundamental financial instruments" approach to classification of, and accounting for, such instruments. The project was, however, later placed on inactive status for several years, to be given renewed attention beginning in 1997. This culminated with the issuance of a proposed SFAS in 2000, which is expected to be finalized in 2001, for initial application in mid-2002. A companion amendment to SFAC 6, to alter the definition of liabilities to accommodate the proposed standard on distinguishing between liabilities and equity, including certain obligations that can or must be settled by issuance of the entity's shares under the liabilities umbrella, was also proposed, and would be effective when the new SFAS is to be implemented.

Under the approach expected to be adopted, a component would not be classified as equity unless it conveys to the holder certain of the risks and rewards of ownership of the issuer/obligor. Classification as equity would occur only if **either** of the two conditions below are met.

1. The component does **not** embody an obligation on the part of the issuer and does **not** convey to the issuer a contractual right to receive cash or another financial instrument from the holder, or to exchange other financial instruments on potentially favorable terms with the holder; **or**
2. The component embodies an obligation under which the holder has the possibility of receiving the issuer's equity shares upon settlement and the obligation exposes the holder to certain of the risks and rewards of ownership—namely, those associated with changes in the fair value of the issuer's equity shares.

The FASB has concluded that as an ownership interest in an entity, owners are exposed to the risks and rewards of changes in the fair value of those equity shares. The value of such holdings increases if the fair value of the equity shares increases, and conversely, the value decreases if the fair value of the equity shares decreases. In determining whether a financial instrument component establishes a relationship that is essentially an ownership interest, whether the holder of the component is exposed to similar changes in fair value will be determinative. A component that requires or permits the issuer to satisfy the obligation by issuing its own equity shares would **not** be classified as equity **unless** changes in the amount of value that must be conveyed to the holder to settle the obligation upon its maturity (the monetary value) are equal to, and in the same direction as, the change in fair value of a fixed number of the issuer's equity shares. Thus, if changes in the component's monetary value (1) differ from changes in the fair value of a fixed number of the issuer's equity shares or (2) equal changes in the fair value of a fixed number of the issuer's equity shares but are in the opposite direction of changes in the fair value of a fixed number of the issuer's equity shares, the component would be classified as a liability, not as equity.

Criteria for applying that concept have been developed. In order for an obligation to be classified as equity **either** the first or the second of the following criteria must be met:

1. The obligation requires (or permits at the issuer's discretion) settlement by issuance of a fixed number of equity shares; **or**
2. The obligation requires (or permits at the issuer's discretion) settlement by issuance of a variable number of equity shares; **and both**
   a. The obligation's monetary value is equal to the change in the fair value of a fixed number of shares; **and**
   b. The monetary value of the obligation changes in the same direction as the change in value of the underlying equity shares.

In other words, if one of those two criteria is met, the holder of the underlying obligation would be considered to be exposed to risks and rewards similar to those of a holder of an equivalent number of outstanding equity shares. Accordingly, the components would be classified as equity under such circumstances. If at least one of the conditions is not met, the component would be reported as a liability.

In some cases settlement in the issuer's shares is optional. In order to meet either one of the foregoing criteria, the possibility of settlement in the issuer's equity shares must be at the issuer's discretion, if not fixed. That is, it cannot be at the option of the holder. If the type of performance required of the issuer to satisfy the obligation is conditioned upon the occurrence (or nonoccurrence) of a specified future event that is beyond the control of the issuer, that obligation would not be eligible for equity classification even if changes in its monetary value are equal to, and in the same direction as, the issuer's equity shares.

In the case of compound financial instruments that includes both liability and equity components, initial proceeds would be allocated to separately classified liability and equity components using the relative-fair-value method, unless it were impracticable to do so. An exception, however, would be for financial instruments that contain liability components that would qualify as derivatives under SFAS 133; in such cases, a "with-and-without" method would be used, with the residual value, after the liability components were recorded at fair value, being allocated to the equity components.

A special consideration will apply upon a repayment of convertible debt. The consideration paid would be allocated to the liability components and the equity components using the relative fair-value approach, with a gain or loss being recognized for the difference between the carrying amount of the liability component and its relative fair value. (Of course, if retired at maturity, presumably the carrying amount of the debt would equal its face value, since any effective premium or discount would have been fully amortized.) Any difference between the consideration paid allocated to the equity component and the amount that had been allocated to equity at the outset of the convertible debt issuance would remain in equity (i.e., would not be a reportable gain or loss).

The standard is expected to also require that upon conversion of the convertible debt pursuant to original terms, a gain or loss should be recognized for the difference between the carrying amount and the fair value of the liability component.

Other special procedures might also be established for financial instruments comprising three or more components, at least two of which are options that convey counteracting rights to the counterparties. For example, in the case of convertible debt that is callable by the issuer, the value of the call option would not be separately recognized as an asset, but would be accounted for by allocating the proceeds from issuance based on the relative fair values of a callable nonconvertible debt component and a callable conversion option. In the absence of an obtainable fair value for a callable conversion option, an issuer would be required to apply the with-and-without method. In those situations, the proceeds would be allocated as follows: an amount equal to otherwise comparable callable nonconvertible debt would be allocated to the liability component, and the residual amount would be allocated to the conversion option.

Given the criteria described above, the following components would be classified as liabilities:

- All unconditional financial obligations, satisfaction of which require the issuer to transfer assets, including obligations to perform that, in the absence of the holder's exercise of a written option, require a transfer of assets. This would include components such as (1) the obligation to transfer cash to settle convertible debt if the holder does not exercise its option to convert that debt into equity shares and (2) mandatorily redeemable equity shares.
- All unconditional financial obligations that require the issuer to satisfy the obligation by issuing its own equity shares, unless changes in the monetary value of the obligation are equal to, and in the same direction as, changes in the fair value of a fixed number of the issuer's equity shares. Accordingly,

obligations whose monetary values change in a direct relationship to (1) the issuer's net income (or some other measure of profitability) and (2) an index for which the fair value of the issuer's equity shares comprises some portion of the index would be classified as liabilities.

- All written options that, if exercised by the holder, require the issuer to satisfy an obligation by a transfer of assets. Examples include the put option component of puttable stock, and written put options that require physical settlement as described under EITF 96-13, *Accounting for Derivative Financial Instruments Indexed to, and Potentially Settled in, a Company's Own Stock*, which would be a change from the accounting for those options presently required under that consensus.

- All written options that, if exercised by the holder, require the issuer to satisfy an obligation by the issuance of the issuer's equity shares, **unless** changes in the monetary value of the option are equal to, and in the same direction as, changes in the fair value of a fixed number of the issuer's equity shares. Examples include the written option component of convertible debt, that would be classified as a liability if the monetary value of the option remains constant, and written put options that require net share settlement, which would be classified as liabilities because, even though settlement would require issuance of equity shares, the monetary value of the obligation changes in the opposite direction of the change in the fair value of the issuer's equity shares.

- All other financial obligations that provide the issuer with the option to determine how it will satisfy the obligation, **unless** changes in the monetary value of the obligation are equal to, and in the same direction as, changes in the fair value of a fixed number of the issuer's equity shares.

- All financial obligations for which the type of performance required of the issuer to satisfy the obligation is conditioned upon the occurrence (or nonoccurrence) of a specified future event (including the exercise by the holder of a written option) that is beyond the control of the issuer.

The following components would be classified as equity under the new standard:

- All unconditional financial obligations that (1) require (or permit at the issuer's discretion) the issuer to satisfy the obligation by issuing its own equity shares and (2) whose monetary value changes by an equal amount, and in the same direction as, changes in the fair value of a fixed number of the issuer's equity shares.

- All written options that, if exercised by the holder, require the issuer to satisfy the obligation by issuing its own equity shares and whose monetary value changes by an equal amount, and in the same direction as, changes in the fair value of a fixed number of the issuer's equity shares. For example, the written option component of convertible debt would be classified as equity if the monetary value of that component changes by an equal amount, and in the same direction as, the fair value of a fixed number of the issuer's equity shares.

- Financial instrument components that do not embody an obligation on the part of the issuer to perform and do not meet the definition of an asset. This would include all other forms of equity that do not require performance on the part of the issuer.

The likely standard will also provide that equity shares of any entity whose financial statements are consolidated into those of the reporting entity would be considered equity shares of the issuer for purposes of applying the components approach. Noncontrolling interests would be separately presented in the equity section of the reporting entity's consolidated balance sheet and net income attributable to noncontrolling interests would not be recognized as a deduction in arriving at consolidated net income.

Interest, dividends, gains, and losses relating to financial instrument components classified as liabilities will be reported in earnings. Similar items related to components classified as equity should be reported directly in equity.

Existing disclosure requirements for financial instruments classified in their entirety as liabilities or as equity would equally apply to components of financial instruments that are separately classified as liabilities or equity. Issuers of compound financial instruments that have one or more components classified as liabilities and one or more classified as equity would be required to make certain disclosures in the year of issuance. The Board agreed to five specific disclosures in the year of issuance, as follows:

1. The nature of the financial instrument
2. A description of the components into which the financial instrument was separated
3. The proceeds of issuance and the amount allocated to each component
4. A description of the methodology used to allocate the proceeds to the components that includes assumptions used
5. If the methodology used to allocate the proceeds to the components is not the relative-fair-value method, an explanation of why the relative-fair-value method was not used

Application of the FASB's Proposed Classification Approach

Example 1:   Obligations that require net share settlement—monetary value changes in the same direction as the fair value of the issuer's equity shares

Algernon Corp. grants 10,000 stock appreciation rights that entitle the holder to receive a number of equity shares to be determined based on the change in the fair value of Algernon's equity shares. At the date of the grant, the fair value of Algernon's equity shares is $25 per share. Subsequently, the fair value of Algernon's equity shares increases to $28 per share. Algernon is thus required to issue shares worth $30,000 [($28 - $25) x 10,000], or 1,072 shares.

This financial instrument contains an obligation to issue a number of equity shares with a value equal to the appreciation of 10,000 equity shares. The number of shares to be issued, therefore, is not fixed. Classification will depend on whether the monetary value changes in the same direction as changes as the fair value of the equity shares. In this example, the monetary value does change in the same direction as changes as the fair value of the equity shares.

Note that the increase in fair value of the equity shares from $25 to $28 resulted in an increase in the monetary value of the obligation from $0 to $30,000. If the fair value of the equity shares increases further, for example to $30 per share, the monetary value of the obligation increases as well to $50,000 [($30 - $25) x 10,000]. If the fair value of the equity shares then decreases, for example from $30 to $27, the monetary value of the obligation decreases to $20,000 [($27 - $25) x 10,000]. Because the monetary value of the obligation changes in the same direction as the change in the fair value of the issuer's equity shares, the equity classification criteria are met.

Example 2:   Obligations that require net share settlement—monetary value changes in opposite direction as the fair value of the issuer's equity shares

Bocephus Corp. issues equity shares to Middleboro Co. for $5 million (1 million shares at $5 each). Simultaneously, Bocephus enters into a financial instrument with Middleboro, under the terms of which, if the per-share value of Bocephus' shares is greater than $5 on a specified date, Middleboro will transfer shares of Bocephus with a value of [(Share price – $5) x 1,000,000] to Bocephus. If the per share value is less than $5 on a specified date, Bocephus transfers shares of its own equity with a value of [($5 - Share price) x 1,000,000] to Middleboro.

The 1,000,000 shares issued to Middleboro do not embody an obligation. They also do not convey to the issuer the right to receive cash or another financial instrument from the holder, or to exchange other financial instruments on potentially favorable terms with the holder. Therefore, the equity classification criterion are met and the component is classified as equity.

The financial instrument issued to Middleboro contains an obligation to issue a variable number of equity shares if the fair value of Bocephus' equity shares is less than $5 on a certain date. As a result, the classification will depend upon whether the monetary value is equal to the change in fair value of a fixed number of equity shares, and changes in the same direction as the fair value of the equity shares.

The first criterion is met because the monetary value of the obligation is equal to the appreciation of a fixed number (1,000,000) of the issuer's equity shares. However, the monetary value of the obligation changes in a direction opposite to the changes in the fair value of the issuer's equity shares. If the fair value of the equity shares increases, the monetary value of the obligation decreases (and may in fact be reduced to zero or result in a receivable). If the fair value of the equity shares decreases, the monetary value of the obligation increases. Because the monetary value of the obligation does not change in the same direction as the fair value of the equity shares, criterion (b) is not met; therefore, the obligation is not classified as equity.

Example 3: Written put options that require physical settlement

Calabassa Corp. writes a put option that allows the holder, Yetta Co., to put 200 shares of Calabassa stock to Calabassa for $33 per share on a specified date. The put option requires physical settlement (delivery of the shares and payment therefor). Because the put option requires Calabassa to transfer assets (cash) to settle the obligation, the component is classified as a liability. This differs from the result obtained from the application of EITF 96-13 (the current standard), which would result in equity classification for the put option.

Example 4: Written put options that require net share settlement

Delmarva Corp. writes a put option that allows the holder, Zitti Corp., to put 200 shares of Delmarva stock to Delmarva for $44 a share on a specified date. The put requires net share settlement (i.e., shares having a value equal to the spread between the option price and fair value must be delivered in settlement). Assume the fair value of the shares at the date the put is issued is $44. The monetary value of the obligation at that time is therefore zero.

Subsequently, the fair value of Delmarva's equity shares decreases to $36 and the put option is exercised. At this point, the monetary value of the obligation is $1,600 [200 shares x ($44 – $36)]. Delmarva would be required to issue about 45 shares ($1,600 divided by $36). The monetary value of the obligation increased because of a decrease in the fair value of Delmarva's equity shares. Because changes in the monetary value of the obligation are not in the same direction as changes in the fair value of Delmarva's equity shares, the component is not classified as equity, but rather as a liability.

EMERGING ISSUES TASK FORCE CONSENSUS SUMMARIES

84-18   Stock Option Pyramiding

In cases in which an employee exercises a stock option by exchanging shares held instead of cash, some holding period of shares exchanged is necessary to avoid treating the exercise as a SAR. A majority of task force members agreed that it should be at least six months. This EITF only applies to APB 25.

84-40   Long-Term Debt Repayable by a Capital Stock Transaction

The Task Force was unable to reach a consensus on the issue of whether debt issued by a trust created by a subsidiary should be presented as debt or equity, when the proceeds of the debt were used to acquire parent company convertible preferred stock. The SEC's position, however, is that this should be treated as debt, not equity. In addition, there was a consensus that the trust should be consolidated in the parent's financial statements.

85-1   Classifying Notes Received for Capital Stock

A consensus was reached regarding the classification of a contribution to a company's equity in the form of a note receivable. These notes should generally not be reported as an asset unless circumstances indicate both the ability and intent to pay in a short period of time. The Task Force noted that the most widespread practice is to report these notes as a reduction of equity. However, if the cash is received prior to the issuance of the financial statements, the note may be reported as an asset.

86-32 Early Extinguishment of a Subsidiary's Mandatorily Redeemable Preferred Stock

The consensus was that when a parent entity acquires, for early retirement, the mandatorily redeemable preferred stock of a subsidiary, the transaction is to be accounted for as a capital transaction in the consolidated financial statements. No gain or loss is to be recognized in the statement of income.

87-6 Adjustments Relating to Stock Compensation Plans

A. Changes to Stock Option Plans Arising from the Tax Reform Act of 1986

As a result of tax law changes, a company may receive a significant tax deduction by disqualifying outstanding incentive stock options (ISO). The discussion focused on whether these changes to the option plan created a new measurement date for accounting purposes. A consensus was reached that minor technical changes, because of the tax reforms, would not create a new measurement date if the total effect on the value of the option is minimal from the perspective of the employee.

B. Stock Option Plan with Tax-Offset Cash Bonus

The issue was how to account for the cash bonus paid to reimburse employees for the tax liability they incur after exercising their options. The consensus was reached that split accounting treatment, in which the measurement date for the option is the date of grant and for the cash bonus is the date of exercise, should be applied **only** to grants outstanding as of April 4, 1987. The discussion also lists additional characteristics and restrictions that apply to the cash bonus. If these are not met, the plan would be accounted for as a variable plan, compensation measured at the date of exercise.

C. Use of Stock Option Shares to Cover Tax Withholdings

A consensus was reached that such an option plan would be considered a fixed plan if it meets all the other requirements of APB 25. No compensation expense would need to be recorded for the shares used to meet the tax withholding requirements.

D. "Phantom" Stock-for-Stock Exercise

Instead of paying cash to exercise the price of an option, some individuals may exchange shares already owned. The issue in this "phantom" stock-for-stock issue is how to account for this arrangement. A consensus was reached that the plan remains a fixed plan, compensation measured from date of grant, if employee meets the necessary holding period for the shares owned.

87-33   Stock Compensation Issues Related to Market Decline

A number of technical issues arising in the context of the October 1987 market crash were addressed here. There was a consensus that if existing options are repriced downward or are cancelled and replaced with less costly options, none of the previous compensation recognized should be reversed. Any remaining unamortized or unaccrued compensation should be amortized or accrued, and any additional compensation should be measured using current market and exercise prices. The added compensation should be amortized over the remaining service period. In addition, a consensus was reached that APB 25 (recognition of additional compensation when cash is paid to settle an earlier option) would not apply to a buy-back consummated pursuant to a reissuance of options. This interpretation applies equally to restricted stock awards. Another issue addressed by 87-33 related to tandem fixed awards involving a further grant of options, which was interpreted as a conversion to a variable plan, since the employee has the option to exercise either the old or new options, which will cancel the ones not exercised. The consensus was to use the standard approach to measure compensation prospectively, based on the new grant, until the market price increases sufficiently to make exercise of the old options more attractive.

88-6   Book Value Stock Plans in an Initial Public Offering

This consensus extends that set forth in 87-23. For publicly held companies, a book value stock purchase plan is a performance plan akin to stock appreciation rights, and thus gives rise to compensation expense. For book value options outstanding during an initial public offering (IPO), any value change resulting from the IPO is deemed to be compensation expense, as are further value changes after the IPO. However, for book value options that are converted to fair market value option plans during an IPO, compensation is recognized only during the IPO. Book value shares that convert to market value stock issued at or within one year of IPO also give rise to compensation in the amount of any increase in value; however, no further compensation is recognized after the IPO takes place. Book value stock that remains book value stock does not result in compensation during the IPO, but if issued in contemplation of the IPO, then book value increase would be attributable to compensation. Pure market value plans are covered under the provisions of APB 25, and are not affected by this pronouncement.

88-9   Put Warrants

Put warrants consist of both warrants for the purchase of (common, usually) stock and a put feature which allows the holder to redeem the warrants for cash, sometimes in conjunction with the warrant exercise, sometimes as an alternative to it. Put warrants are typically issued in connection with a debt offering, and APB 14 stipulates that the proceeds of the offering must be allocated between the debt and the warrants. The Task Force concluded that the proceeds allocated to the warrants should generally be included in equity; however, a later consensus on Issue 96-13 holds that for public companies, this should be classified as a liability since the holder is given the right to elect whether or not to receive cash. If the put price is adjustable, the adjustments from issuance date until the earliest put date should be made consistent with the balance sheet classification of the put warrant: if equity, the adjustment would be by a charge to retained earnings; if as debt, then the charge would be similar to interest expense. The impact on the earnings per share computation is also addressed.

89-11 Sponsor's Balance Sheet Classification of Capital Stock with a Put Option Held by an Employee Stock Ownership Plan

This pronouncement deals with those circumstances in which an employee participant in an ESOP has a put option (i.e., a right to demand redemption by the sponsoring company). While the ESOP can substitute for the sponsor as the purchaser of the employee's shares, the sponsor cannot legally require the plan to do so; therefore, the employer is obligated to repurchase shares. The issue was: If the sponsor's shares are shown outside of the equity section as a consequence, can the contra equity (unearned compensation) also be presented there? The consensus was that the contra equity should follow the capital stock account.

90-7 Accounting for a Reload Stock Option

A reload stock option should be accounted for as a fixed plan if (1) each reload grant is for exercise at the market price on the reload grant date and (2) shares tendered satisfy the holding period in EITF 84-18.

90-9 Changes to Fixed Employee Stock Option Plans as a Result of Restructuring

A new measurement date does not occur for determining compensation expense (and no additional compensation expense should be recognized) as a result of spin-offs or recapitalization in the form of special, large and nonrecurring dividends if the following criteria are met:

1. Cash or other consideration (excluding additional options) given.

    If given to restore the option holder's economic position, the amount should be recognized as compensation expense once the employer agrees to provide them.

2. No cash or other consideration given.

    Changes to outstanding fixed stock option grants to restore the option holder's economic position if the criteria below are met.

    a. The aggregate intrinsic value of the options immediately after the change is not greater than immediately before.

    b. The rates of exercise price per option to market value per share is not reduced.

      c.   The vesting provisions and option period of the original grant remain the same.

The change in market value should exclude independent, determinable and verifiable effects of other events than the equity restructuring.

Compensation expense should be recognized and measured in accordance with the provisions of APB 25 if changes to outstanding fixed stock options do not meet all of the above criteria. The additional expense would not include the amount that the current market price exceeds the original exercise price per option if that excess was measured as compensation expense at the original measurement date. Any compensation expense unamortized from the original measurement date should continue to be amortized and should not be reversed.

The above consensus applies whether or not the original fixed option grant provided for adjustments to the option terms in case of equity restructuring.

94-6   Accounting for the Buyout of Compensatory Stock Options

The issue addressed was how to measure compensation when stock options granted below current market value are later reacquired by the issuing company before being exercised. In its consensus, the task force concluded that compensation should be measured by the sum of the compensation cost amortized to the buy back date, plus the intrinsic value of the options at the buy back date in excess of that previously recognized, plus any payment to the holder in excess of the intrinsic value. This would not, however, apply if replacement options were granted at or near the time of the buy back. Another consensus, Issue 87-33, would apply if this consensus is not appropriate to the fact pattern.

95-16   Accounting for Stock Compensation Arrangements with Employer Loan Features under APB Opinion No. 25

This issue relates to the situation in which an employee exercises a stock option by issuing a nonrecourse note to the employer, secured by the stock itself. The question is whether, when the terms of the note include either a variable interest rate or fixed interest with a prepayment option, this in effect results in the granting of a new option. The consensus was that the exercise of the option is, in substance, the issuance of a new option having a new measurement date, unless certain conditions are met. Those conditions might include a term in the original option that permitted exercise by issuance of nonrecourse debt having a specified term, or a proviso that implies that such an exercise does not extend the original option period even where the original agreement did not address exercise with a nonrecourse note. Otherwise, there will be another measurement of the compensation implicit in the arrangement. The consensus also stated that if the terms of the original arrangement provided for exercise through the issuance of the note and the interest is determined to be part of the exercise price, then the original grant should be accounted for as a variable plan, since the exercise price is not known at grant date. Furthermore, this may cause a fixed option to be converted into a variable option at the exercise, as when interest on the note is nonrecourse and thus must be deemed part of the exercise price. Lastly, dividends paid during the term of the nonrecourse note are to be treated as additional compensation; and interest received which is deemed part of the exercise price will be accounted for as payment for the shares, not as interest income.

96-13 Accounting for Derivative Financial Instruments Indexed to, and Potentially Settled in, a Company's Own Stock

A company may enter into contracts that are indexed to, and sometimes settled in, its own stock. Examples of these contracts include written put options, written call options (and warrants), purchased put options, purchased call options, forward sale contracts, and forward purchase contracts. These contracts may be settled using a variety of settlement methods, or the issuing company or counterparty may have a choice of settlement methods. These methods include physical settlement (where the party designated in the contract as the buyer delivers the full stated amount of cash to the seller, and the seller delivers the full stated number of shares to the buyer), net share settlement (where the party with a loss delivers to the party with a gain shares with a current fair value equal to the gain), and net cash settlement (where the party with a loss delivers to the party with a gain a cash payment equal to the gain, and no shares are exchanged).

With regard to freestanding derivative financial instruments, the issue is how these contracts that are indexed to, and potentially settled in, a company's own stock should be classified and measured.

As to initial balance sheet classification, if the contract provides the company with a choice of net cash settlement or settlement in shares, settlement in shares is to be assumed; if the contract provides the counterparty with a choice of net cash settlement or settlement in shares, net cash settlement is to be assumed. However, this approach is not applicable when settlement alternatives do not have the same economic value attached to them or when one of the settlement alternatives is fixed or contains caps or floors. In those situations, the accounting for the underlying instrument or combination of instruments should be based on the economic substance of the transaction.

The presumption is that all instruments be initially measured at fair value and subsequently accounted for based on the initial classification and the assumed or required settlement method above. Contracts that are initially classified as equity are accounted for in permanent equity. If physical settlement was assumed or required and the company is obligated to deliver cash as part of the physical settlement, then public companies should refer to SAR 268, which provides guidance by analogy for those transactions.

Contracts that require that the company deliver shares as part of a physical settlement or a net share settlement should be initially measured at fair value and reported in permanent equity. Subsequent changes in fair value should not be recognized.

Contracts pertaining to permanent equity that give the company a choice of (1) net cash settlement or settlement in shares (including net share settlement, or physical settlement that requires that the company deliver shares) or (2) either net share settlement or physical settlement that requires that the company deliver cash should be initially measured at fair value and reported in permanent equity. Subsequent changes in fair value should not be recognized. If such contracts are ultimately settled in a manner that requires that the company deliver cash, the amount of cash paid or received should be reported as a reduction of, or an addition to, contributed capital.

Regarding contracts involving temporary equity, contracts that (1) require that the company deliver cash as part of a physical settlement, (2) give the company a choice of either net cash settlement or physical settlement that requires that the company deliver cash, or (3) give the counterparty a choice of either net share settlement or physical settlement that requires that the company deliver cash should be initially measured at fair value and reported in permanent equity, and an amount equal to the cash redemption amount under the physical settlement should be transferred to temporary equity.

Contracts that are initially classified as assets or liabilities should be measured at fair value, with changes in fair value reported in earnings and disclosed in the financial statements. If contracts initially classified as assets or liabilities are ultimately settled in shares, any gains or losses on those contracts should continue to be included in earnings.

The EITF consensus addresses the accounting for a variety of instruments. Included are written put options and forward purchase contracts; forward sale contracts, written call options or warrants, and purchased put options; purchased call options; detachable stock purchase warrants; and put warrants. The consensus also addressed the impact of these instruments on earnings per share calculations, but this has been superseded by SFAS 128. Related matters are addressed in EITF 96-23, 98-12, and 99-1.

96-18   Accounting for Equity Instruments That Are Issued to other than Employees for Acquiring, or in Conjunction with Selling, Goods or Services

SFAS 123 established the measurement principles for transactions in which equity instruments are issued in exchange for the receipt of goods or services. These are to be measured at the fair value of the consideration received or the fair value of the equity instruments issued, whichever is more reliably measurable. The measurement date was not stipulated, nor was guidance on recognition of the cost of those transactions provided by the standard. Such transactions could involve a contemporaneous exchange of the equity instruments for goods or services, or may involve an exchange that spans several financial reporting periods. Furthermore, the quantity and terms of the equity instruments to be issued may be known or only known within a range when the transaction arrangement is established.

This consensus addresses the measurement date and recognition approach for any of these transactions, if the counterparty to the transaction is other than an employee, superseding the guidance in EITF 96-3. It does not, however, address the accounting for equity instruments either issued to a lender or investor who provides financing to the issuer or issued in a business combination.

The transactions covered are those in which (1) the fair value of the equity instruments is more reliably measurable than the fair value of the goods or services received and (2) the counterparty receives shares of stock, stock options, or other equity instruments in settlement of the entire transaction or, if the transaction is part cash and part equity instruments, in settlement of the portion of the transaction for which the equity instruments constitute the consideration.

A consensus was reached that the issuer should measure the fair value of the equity instruments using the stock price and other measurement assumptions as of the earlier of either of the following: (1) the date at which a commitment for performance by the counterparty to earn the equity instruments is reached (a performance commitment) or (2) the date at which the counterparty's performance is complete. This is referred to as the measurement date.

Furthermore, a consensus was reached that an asset, expense, or sales discount would be recognized (or previous recognition reversed) in the same period(s) and in the same manner (i.e., capitalize versus expense) as if the enterprise had paid cash for the goods or services or used cash rebates as a sales discount instead of paying with or using the equity instruments. Also, a recognized asset, expense, or sales discount should not be reversed if a stock option that the counterparty has the right to exercise expires unexercised.

When it is appropriate under generally accepted accounting principles for the issuer to recognize any cost of the transaction during financial reporting periods prior to the measurement date, for purposes of recognition of costs during those periods the equity instruments should be measured at their then-current fair values at each of those interim financial reporting dates. Changes in those fair values between those interim reporting dates should be attributed in accordance with the methods illustrated in FASB Interpretation 28

If, on the measurement date, the quantity or any of the terms of the equity instruments are dependent on the achievement of market conditions, then the issuer should use the fair value of the equity instruments for recognition purposes. That fair value would be calculated as the fair value of the equity instruments without regard to the market condition plus the fair value of the issuer's commitment to change the quantity or terms of the equity instruments based on whether the market condition is met.

If, on the measurement date, the quantity or any of the terms of the equity instruments are dependent on the achievement of counterparty performance conditions that, based on the different possible outcomes, result in a range of aggregate fair values for the equity instruments as of that date, then the issuer should utilize the lowest aggregate (i.e., the variable terms times the applicable number of equity instruments) amount within that range for recognition purposes, which could be zero.

For transactions that involve both market conditions and counterparty performance conditions, the consensus was that the guidance above (i.e., to use lowest aggregate fair value) also applies. For transactions in which the quantity or any of the terms are not known up front, the accounting prior to the measurement date, which involves only market conditions, the then-current fair value also applies. For transactions that involve only counterparty performance conditions, when it is appropriate under generally accepted accounting principles for the issuer to recognize any cost of the transaction in reporting periods prior to the measurement date, the equity instruments should be measured at their then-current lowest aggregate fair value at each of those interim reporting dates. Changes in those lowest aggregate fair values between those interim reporting dates should be attributed in accordance with the methods illustrated in FASB Interpretation 28.

In the case of transactions that involve both market conditions and counterparty performance conditions, the then-current lowest aggregate fair value also applies. For transactions in which the quantity or any of the terms are not known up front, the accounting after the measurement date, for transactions that involve only market conditions, the issuer should, to the extent necessary, recognize and classify future changes in the fair value of this commitment in accordance with any relevant accounting literature on financial instruments, such as EITF 96-13. For transactions that involve only counterparty performance conditions, the consensus is that as each quantity and term becomes known and until all the quantities and terms that stem from the counterparty's performance become known, the "lowest aggregate" fair value measure would be used to reflect additional cost of the transaction, using the "modification accounting" methodology.

In the case of transactions that involve both market conditions and counterparty performance conditions, the consensus was that through the date the last performance-related condition is resolved, the issuer should apply "modification accounting" for the resolution of both counterparty performance conditions and market conditions. If, at the time the last counterparty performance-related condition is resolved, one or more market conditions remain, then the issuer should measure the then-current fair value of the issuer's commitment to issue additional equity instruments or change the terms of the equity instruments based on whether the market condition is met.

After the issuer measures the then-current fair value of the issuer's commitment related to the market condition, the issuer should, to the extent necessary, recognize and classify future changes in the fair value of this commitment in accordance with any relevant accounting literature on financial instruments, such as EITF 96-13.

97-14 Accounting for Deferred Compensation Arrangements Where Amounts Earned Are Held in a Rabbi Trust and Invested

Assets are placed in a grantor trust representing deferred compensation, invested either in employer securities or diversified; assets in a "rabbi trust" are available to a grantor/employer's creditors in the event of bankruptcy. The tentative conclusion by the EITF is that assets of the trust should be consolidated with employer's financial statements; any employer's stock held would be treated as treasury stock. Also, before diversification of trust assets, amount of deferred compensation would be adjusted through earnings to reflect fair value of amount owed to employee.

98-2 Accounting by a Subsidiary for an Investment in Its Parent Company's Stock

The issue relates to the display of an investment by a subsidiary in the parent's or joint venture partner's stock in separate statements of the subsidiary or the joint venture; specifically, how the SFAS 115 rules affect this presentation. Questions to be answered are how to account for the investment as an asset to be accounted for at fair value; a distribution to the parent or joint venture partner (similar to treasury stock); or as an asset measured by the equity method, with an elimination of reciprocal ownership investments. No consensus has been reached yet.

99-7 Accounting for an Accelerated Share Repurchase Program

The issue pertains to accelerated share repurchase programs, which are combinations of transactions that permit an entity to purchase a targeted number of shares immediately, with the final purchase price determined by an average market price over fixed periods of time. Such programs are intended to combine the immediate share retirement benefits (boosting earnings-per-share, etc.) of tender offers with the market impacts and pricing benefits of disciplined open market stock repurchase programs. At issue were the implications of accelerated share repurchase programs on EPS calculations and entities' abilities to account for business combinations as poolings of interests.

The consensus was that an entity should account for an accelerated share repurchase program as two separate transactions: first, as shares of common stock acquired in a treasury stock transaction recorded on the acquisition date, and second, as a forward contract indexed to its own common stock. Pursuant to Issue 99-3, *Application of Issue No. 96-13 to Derivative Instruments with Multiple Settlement Alternatives*, an entity would classify the forward contract in the above example as an equity instrument because the entity will receive cash when the contract is in a gain position but pay cash or stock when the contract is in a loss position. Changes in the fair value of the forward contract would not be recorded, and the settlement of the forward contract would be recorded in equity.

The treasury stock transaction would result in an immediate reduction of the outstanding shares used to calculate the weighted-average common shares outstanding for both basic and diluted EPS. The effect of the forward contract on diluted EPS would be calculated in accordance with SFAS 128, as interpreted by EITF Topic D-72.

Regarding the impact of accelerated share repurchase programs on the ability to account for a business combination as a pooling of interests, the entity should consider the share repurchase date or, with respect to postconsummation repurchases, the date on which the intent to repurchase shares is formulated to determine whether the treasury stock acquisition results in a violation of APB 16, as interpreted by the SEC's SAB 96. Any resulting preconsummation tainted treasury shares could be "cured" by issuing the same amount of common stock between the purchase date and the date of consummation of the business combination.

The issue of the possible effects of the forward contract in the accelerated share repurchase program on an entity's ability to account for a business combination as a pooling of interests was not resolved, but may be addressed later. The impact of derivative financial instruments indexed to, and potentially settled in, a company's own stock on pooling-of-interests transactions will also be addressed later.

00-6   Accounting for Freestanding Derivative Financial Instruments Indexed to, and Potentially Settled in, the Stock of a Consolidated Subsidiary

EITF Issue 96-13, *Accounting for Derivative Financial Instruments Indexed to, and Potentially Settled in, a Company's Own Stock*, establishes a framework for accounting for freestanding derivative instruments that are indexed to, and potentially settled in, a company's own stock. That consensus did not, however, provide guidance on how to account for freestanding derivative instruments that are indexed to, and potentially settled in, a subsidiary's stock. The issue addressed here is how such contracts should be classified and measured in the consolidated financial statements.

A consensus exists that stock of a subsidiary is not equity of the parent; therefore, derivatives indexed to and to be settled in stock of a subsidiary do not meet SFAS 133's exclusion criteria. If derivatives meeting the criteria of SFAS 133 (e.g., for net settlement, etc.), these must be accounted for under the provisions of SFAS 133, and not of Issue 96-13. The consensus also discusses a number of exceptions based on the criteria set forth in SFAS 133.

The EITF reached several consensuses regarding derivatives not within the scope of SFAS 133, while also noting that option or forward strike prices and premiums could be indicative of impairments of the parent's investment in subsidiaries, to be assessed using SFAS 121. A parent's contract to purchase a subsidiary's (minority held) common stock should not be recorded until settled; during the period of the contract, income should continue to be allocated to the minority interest. A contract to sell shares in a subsidiary, likewise, should be recorded when settled; until that time, income would not be allocated to outside interests (counter parties to the derivative). No consensus was reached regarding written options.

00-16 Recognition and Measurement of Employer Payroll Taxes on Employee Stock-Based Compensation

This issue discusses (1) when a liability for employer payroll taxes on employee stock compensation should be recognized in the employer's financial statements and (2) how that liability should be measured. The consensus was that a liability for employee payroll taxes on stock compensation should be recognized and measured on the date of the event triggering the measurement and payment of the tax to the taxing authority (which would generally be the exercise date).

00-19 Accounting for Derivative Financial Instruments Indexed to, and Potentially Settled in, a Company's Own Stock

This consensus restates a number of earlier, related issues and codifies the EITF's position on this entire subject area. It applies to freestanding derivatives only—similar embedded derivatives are not covered. Also not covered are derivatives which issued to compensate employees or to acquire goods and services from nonemployees, when performance has yet to occur. It does apply, however, to derivatives issued to acquire goods and services from nonemployees, when performance has occurred.

The issue for the EITF was how certain equity derivative contracts indexed to, and potentially settled in, a company's own stock should be accounted for. Such contracts could include written puts, written calls and warrants, purchased puts, purchased calls, forward sale contracts, and forward purchase contracts.

In its consensus, the EITF reached a number of conclusions. These are summarized as follows.

1. Initial balance sheet classification is to be guided by the principle that contracts which require net cash settlements are assets or liabilities, and those that require settlement in shares are equity instruments. If the reporting entity has the choice of settlement modes, settlement in shares is to be assumed; if the counter party has the option, net cash settlement is presumed. An exception occurs if the two settlement alternatives are not of equal value, in which case the economic substance should govern.

2. Initial measurement should be at fair value. Contracts classed as equity are accounted for in permanent equity, with value changes being ig-

nored, unless settlement expectations change. For publicly held companies, under defined circumstances, guidance is provided by analogy from ASR 268. All other contracts would be classified as assets or liabilities, to be measured continuously at fair value. If settlement in shares ultimately occurs, already recognized gains or losses are left in earnings, not reclassified or reversed.

3. Events may necessitate reclassification of contracts from assets/liabilities to equity. If a contract first classed as equity is later reclassed to assets/liabilities, any value change to the date of reclassification will be included in equity, not earnings. Thereafter, value changes will be reported in earnings. If partial net share settlement is permitted, the portion that can be so settled remains in equity. Appropriate disclosure under APB 22 may be required, if more than one contract exists and different methods are applied to them.

4. All the following conditions must be satisfied in order to classify a contract in equity:

   a. The contract permits settlement in unregistered shares (the assumption being that the issuer cannot effectively control the conditions for registration, making cash settlement likely unless unregistered shares can be delivered);

   b. There are sufficient authorized, unissued shares to settle the contact, after considering all other outstanding commitments;

   c. The contract contains an explicit limit on the number of shares to be issued;

   d. There are no required cash payments to the counter party based on the issuer's failure to make timely SEC filings;

   e. There are no "make whole" provisions to compensate the holder after he sells the shares issued in the market at a price below some defined threshold value;

   f. Requirements for net cash settlement are accompanied by similar requirements for existing shareholders;

   g. There are no provisions that indicate that the counter parties have rights greater than those of the actual shareholders; and

   h. There is no requirement for any collateral posting for any reason.

5. Contracts which are subject to this consensus cannot qualify for hedge accounting (this is based on the SEC's position on this matter).

6. Contracts offering multiple settlement alternatives which require the company to receive cash when the contract is in a gain position but pay either stock or cash at the company's option when in a loss position are to be accounted for as equity. Also, such contracts requiring payment of cash when in a loss position but receipt of either cash or stock at the

company's option when in a gain position must be accounted for as assets/liabilities.

7. For EPS computation purposes, for those contracts which provide the company with a choice of settlement methods, settlement in shares is to be assumed, although this can be overcome based on past experience or stated policy. If the counterparty controls the choice, however, the more dilutive assumption must be made, irrespective of past experience or policy.

The consensus is effective for contracts entered into after September 30, 2000; for contracts in existence on that date, the requirements of the consensus are to be applied on June 30, 2001, using a cumulative effect-type presentation. The consensus includes detailed guidance for a number of specific types of contracts.

00-23 Issues Related to the Accounting for Stock Compensation under APB Opinion No. 25 and FASB Interpretation No. 44

A number of practical issues had arisen pertaining to application of APB No. 25 and FASB Interpretation No. 44, which were brought to the EITF's attention by the SEC. A number of these were resolved with consensus positions by the EITF. These include the following (many others also exist; see the consensus for details):

1. When options on the stock of one entity in a consolidated group are exchanged for options in another entity in the group, variable accounting will be required if the effect is to reduce the exercise price, as discussed in Question 11 of Interpretation 44. Otherwise, the exchange results in a new measurement date.

2. Indirect guarantees of the value of stock option grants necessitate recognition of compensation over the service period equal to the "guaranteed" minimum.

3. Fair value repurchase features, in the case of nonpublic issuers, do not trigger variable accounting, if the repurchase is not within six months of exercise.

4. In the case of business combinations accounted for as poolings, the accounting attributes of the combining entity's awards carry forward to the awards issued or granted by the issuer in the business combination. If the combination is a purchase, however, the attributes do not carry forward to acquirer awards issued or granted in the combination.

5. Subsequent repurchase of awards fully vested as of the date of a business combination is the equivalent of reacquisition of residual equity interests, to be accounted for similar to treasury stock, unless the settlement is above fair value, in which case the excess is compensation. Several variations on this issue are also addressed in the consensus.

6. When one entity in a controlled group issues options in its shares to employees in a "sister" entity, the value should be measured at the grant date and recognize that amount as a dividend to the controlling entity. The employer entity should recognize compensation cost and a credit to paid in capital (a contribution by or on behalf of the parent or controlling entity).

Examples are presented in the consensus; other issues will be subsequently addressed. Most of the foregoing consensuses are effective in late 2000.

FASB TECHNICAL BULLETINS

85-6   Accounting for a Purchase of Treasury Shares at a Price Significantly in Excess of the Current Market Price of the Shares and the Income Statement Classification of Costs Incurred in Defending against a Takeover Attempt

Purchase of shares from a party attempting a takeover at an above-market price (sometimes referred to as "greenmail") in order to avert takeover may involve an element of cost that is not properly allocated to treasury stock. Such costs are to be expensed (but not to be reported as extraordinary) and not included in the treasury stock account.

97-1   Accounting under Statement 123 for Certain Employee Stock Purchase Plans with a Look-Back Option

This bulletin provides guidance for accounting for certain employee stock purchase plans that have a look-back option, which is a provision that sets the exercise price equal to the lesser of the market price at the grant date or the exercise date.

APPENDIX

FINANCIAL STATEMENT PRESENTATION

This appendix provides an illustration of the various financial statements that may be required to be presented and are related to the stockholders' equity section of the balance sheet.

Stockholders' Equity Section of a Balance Sheet

Capital stock:

Preferred stock, $100 par, 7% cumulative, 30,000 shares authorized, issued, and outstanding		$ 3,000,000
Common stock, no par, stated value $10 per share, 500,000 shares authorized, 415,000 shares issued		4,150,000
Total capital stock		$ 7,150,000
Additional paid-in capital:		
Issued price in excess of par value—preferred	$ 150,000	
Issued price in excess of stated value—common	845,000	995,000
Total paid-in capital		$ 8,145,000
Donated capital		100,000
Retained earnings:		
Appropriated for plant expansion	$2,100,000	
Unappropriated	2,110,000	4,210,000
Accumulated other comprehensive income		165,000
Total capital, retained earnings, and accumulated other comprehensive income		$12,620,000
Less 10,000 common shares held in treasury, at cost		(120,000)
Total stockholders' equity		$12,500,000

Retained Earnings Statement

Balance at beginning of year, as reported	$ 3,800,000
Prior period adjustment—correction of an error in method of depreciation (less tax effect of $77,000)	115,000
Balance at beginning of year, restated	$ 3,915,000
Net income for the year	583,000
Cash dividends declared during the year	
Preferred stock	(210,000)
Common stock	(78,000)
Balance at end of year	$ 4,210,000

Statement of Changes in Stockholders' Equity

	Preferred stock		Common stock		Additional paid-in capital	Donated capital	Retained earnings	Accumulated other comprehesive income*	Treasury stock (common)	Total stockholders' equity
	Shares	Amount	Shares	Amount						
Balance, 12/31/00, as reported	--	--	400,000	$4,000,000	$840,000	$100,000	$3,800,000	$ 56,000	$(120,000)	$ 8,676,000
Correction of an error in method of depr.	--	--	--	--	--	--	115,000			115,000
Balance, 12/31/00, restated	--	--	400,000	$4,000,000	$840,000	$100,000	$3,915,000		$(120,000)	$ 8,791,000
Preferred stock issued in public offering	30,000	$3,000,000	--	--	150,000	--	--		--	3,150,000
Stock options exercised	--	--	15,000	150,000	5,000	--	--		--	155,000
Net income	--	--	--	--	--	--	583,000		--	583,000
Cash dividends declared:										
Preferred, $7.00 per share	--	--	--	--	--	--	(210,000)		--	(210,000)
Common, $.20 per share	--	--	--	--	--	--	(78,000)		--	(78,000)
Unrealized holding gains on available-for-sale securities arising during period								85,000		
Less: Reclassification for adjustment of gains included in net income								(12,000)		
Foreign currency translation adjustments								36,000		
Total other comprehensive income								109,000		
Balance, 12/31/01	30,000	$3,000,000	415,000	$4,150,000	$995,000	$100,000	$4,210,000	$165,000	$(120,000)	$12,500,000

* Comprehensive income for the period:

Net income	$748,000
Other comprehensive income	109,000
	$857,000

18 EARNINGS PER SHARE

PERSPECTIVE AND ISSUES

Earnings per share (EPS) is an indicator which is widely used by both actual and prospective investors to gauge the profitability of a corporation. Its purpose is to indicate how effective an enterprise has been in using the resources provided by common shareholders. In its simplest form, EPS is net income (loss) divided by the number of shares of outstanding common stock. The EPS computation becomes more complex with the existence of securities that are not common stock but have the potential of causing additional shares of common stock to be issued (e.g., convertible preferred stock or convertible debt, and options or warrants). The computation of an EPS number that ignores these potentially dilutive securities can be very misleading. In addition, a lack of standardization in the way in which these securities are included in an EPS computation would make comparisons among corporations extremely difficult.

In an effort to integrate with international reporting standards and to simplify reporting practices on EPS, the FASB issued SFAS 128 in February 1997. It superseded APB 15. SFAS 128 establishes standards for computing and presenting EPS for public companies. If a nonpublic company chooses to disclose EPS it must do so in accordance with SFAS 128. This statement provides standards that are more comparable to international EPS standards. According to the FASB's statement, publicly traded corporations with a complex capital structure would be obligated to report basic EPS and diluted EPS. The dual presentation is required on the face of the corporation's income statement even if both of these computations result in the same EPS amount. In addition, it also requires a reconciliation of the numerator and the denominator of the basic EPS computation to the numerator and denominator of the diluted EPS computation.

Basic EPS, which includes no dilution, is computed by dividing income available to common shareholders by the weighted-average number of shares outstanding for that particular period. In contrast, diluted EPS considers the potential dilution that could occur from other financial instruments that would increase the total number of outstanding shares of common stock. Under this statement, the calculation of diluted EPS has only minor changes from its method of calculation under APB 15. SFAS 128 requires restatement of all prior period EPS data presented.

In February 1997, the FASB also released SFAS 129 that establishes standards for disclosing information about an entity's capital structure. This statement continues previous disclosure requirements found in APB 10 and 15 and SFAS 47; however, it isolates the standards related to the disclosure of information about an entity's capital structure to one pronouncement. This pronouncement applies to all entities, public and nonpublic. Companies are required to disclose the rights and privileges of each type of security outstanding. Examples of disclosures include company policies on participation rights, on the liquidation of preferred stock, and on redeemable stock.

Sources of GAAP				
APB	*SFAS*	*FASB I*	*FASB TB*	*EITF*
30	128, 129	28	79-8	92-3, 00-19, D-42, D-53, D-62, D-72

DEFINITIONS OF TERMS

There are a number of terms used in discussion of earnings per share that have special meanings in that context. When used, they are intended to have the meanings given in the following definitions.

Antidilution (antidilutive). An increase in earnings per share or reduction in net loss per share resulting from the conversion, exercise, or contingent issuance of certain securities.

Basic earnings per share (basic EPS). The amount of earnings for the period available to each share of common stock outstanding during the reporting period.

Call option. A contract that allows the holder to buy a specified quantity of stock from the writer of the contract at a fixed price for a given period. Refer to **option** and **purchased call option**.

Call price. The amount at which a security may be redeemed by the issuer at the issuer's option.

Common stock. A stock that is subordinate to all other stock of the issuer.

Contingent issuance. A possible issuance of shares of common stock that is dependent upon the exercise of conversion rights, options or warrants, the satisfaction of certain conditions, or similar arrangements.

Contingent stock agreement. An agreement to issue common stock (usually in connection with a business combination accounted for by the purchase method) that is dependent on the satisfaction of certain conditions.

Contingently issuable shares (contingently issuable stock). Shares issuable for little or no cash consideration upon the satisfaction of certain conditions pursuant to a contingent stock agreement.

Conversion price. The price that determines the number of shares of common stock into which a security is convertible. For example, $100 face value of debt convertible into five shares of common stock would be stated to have a conversion price of $20.

Conversion rate. The ratio of (1) the number of common shares issuable upon conversion to (2) a unit of convertible security. For example, a preferred stock may be convertible at the rate of three shares of common stock for each share of preferred stock.

Convertible security. A security that is convertible into another security based on a conversion rate; for example, convertible preferred stock that is convertible into common stock on a two-for-one basis (two shares of common for each share of preferred).

Conversion value. The current market value of the common shares obtainable upon conversion of a convertible security, after deducting any cash payment required upon conversion.

Diluted earnings per share (diluted EPS or DEPS). The amount of earnings for the period available to each share of common stock outstanding during the reporting period and to each share that would have been outstanding assuming the issuance of common shares for all dilutive potential common shares outstanding during the reporting period.

Dilution (Dilutive). A reduction in earnings per share or an increase in net loss per share resulting from the assumption that convertible securities have been converted or that options and warrants have been exercised or other shares have been issued upon the fulfillment of certain conditions.

Dual presentation. The presentation with equal prominence of two types of earnings per share amounts on the face of the income statement: one is basic earnings per share, the other is diluted earnings per share.

Earnings per (common) share (EPS). The amount of earnings attributable to each share of common stock. For convenience, the term is used in SFAS 128 to refer to either net income (earnings) per share or net loss per share. It should be used without qualifying language only when no potentially dilutive convertible securities, options, warrants, or other agreements providing for contingent issuances of common stock are outstanding.

Exercise price. The amount that must be paid for a share of common stock upon exercise of a stock option or warrant.

If-converted method. A method of computing earnings per share data that assumes conversion of convertible securities as of the beginning of the earliest period reported (or at time of issuance, if later).

Income available to common stockholders. Income (or loss) from continuing operations or net income (or net loss) adjusted for preferred stock dividends.

Option. Unless otherwise stated in SFAS 128, a call option that gives the holder the right to purchase shares of common stock in accordance with an agreement upon payment of a specified amount, including, but not limited to, options granted to and stock purchase agreements entered into with employees. Options are considered "securities" in SFAS 128. Refer to **Call option**.

Potential common stock. A security or other contact that may entitle its holder to obtain common stock during the reporting period or after the end of the reporting period.

Preferred stock. A security that has rights to receive distributions that are preferential to common stock.

Purchased call option. A contract that allows the reporting entity to buy a specified quantity of its own stock from the writer of the contract at a fixed price for a given period. Refer to **Call option**.

Put option. A contract that allows the holder to sell a specified quantity of stock to the writer of the contract at a fixed price during a given period.

Redemption price. The amount at which a security is required to be redeemed at maturity or under a sinking fund arrangement.

Reverse treasury stock method. A method of recognizing the dilutive effect on earnings per share of satisfying a put obligation. It assumes that the proceeds used to buy back common stock (pursuant to the terms of a put option) will be raised from issuing shares at the average market price during the period. Refer to **Put option.**

Rights issue. An offer to existing shareholders to purchase additional shares of common stock in accordance with an agreement for a specified amount (which is generally substantially less than the fair value of the shares) for a given period.

Security. The evidence of a debt or ownership or related right. For purposes of SFAS 128, it includes stock options and warrants, as well as debt and stock.

Treasury stock method. A method of recognizing the use of proceeds that would be obtained upon exercise of options and warrants in computing diluted earnings per share. It assumes that any proceeds would be used to purchase common stock at average market prices during the period.

Two-class method. A method employed for securities that are not convertible into common stock and thus cannot use the if-converted method. This method computes earnings per share by treating participating securities (nonconvertible) as though they were common stocks with different dividend rates from that of the other common stock.

Warrant. A security giving the holder the right to purchase shares of common stock in accordance with the terms of the instrument, usually upon payment of a specified amount.

Weighted-average number of shares. The number of shares determined by relating (1) the portion of time within a reporting period that a particular number of shares of a certain security has been outstanding to (2) the total time in that period. For example, if 100 shares of a certain security were outstanding during the first quarter of a fiscal year and 300 shares were outstanding during the balance of the year, the weighted-average number of outstanding shares would be 250 [(100 x 1/4) + (300 x 3/4)]. In computing diluted EPS, equivalent common shares are considered for all dilutive potential common shares.

CONCEPTS, RULES, AND EXAMPLES

Simple Capital Structure

Simple capital structures are those having no potential common shares (options, warrants, etc.). These entities will simply present basic EPS. All other entities are considered to have a complex capital structure. Entities with a complex capital structure will have **potential common stock** in the form of potentially dilutive **securities, options, warrants,** or other rights that upon conversion or exercise could, in the aggregate, dilute **earnings per common share. Dilutive** securities have the potential upon their issuance to reduce the earnings per share.

Computational guidelines. The basic EPS calculation is **income available to common stockholders** (the numerator) divided by the **weighted-average number of common shares outstanding** (the denominator) during the period. The objective of the basic EPS calculation is to measure the performance of an entity over the reporting period. Complexities arise because net income does not necessarily represent the earnings available to the common shareholder, and a simple weighted-average of common shares outstanding does not necessarily reflect the true nature of the situation.

Numerator. The income available to common stockholders figure used as the numerator in any of the EPS computations must be reduced by any preferential claims against it by other securities. The justification for this reduction is that the preferential claims of the other securities must be satisfied before any income is available to the common shareholder. These other securities are usually in the form of **preferred stock,** and the deduction from income is the amount of the dividend declared (whether or not paid) during the year on the preferred stock. If the preferred stock is cumulative, the dividend is to be deducted from income (added to the loss) whether or not declared. Dividends in arrears do not affect the calculation of EPS in the current period; such dividends have been included in prior periods'

EPS computations. However, the amount in arrears should be disclosed, as should all of the effects of the rights given to preferential securities on the EPS calculation.

Denominator. The weighted-average number of common stock shares outstanding is "an arithmetical mean average of shares outstanding and assumed to be outstanding for EPS computations" (SFAS 128). The difficulty in computing the weighted-average exists because of the effect that various transactions have on the computation of common shares outstanding. While it is impossible to analyze all the possibilities, SFAS 128 provides discussion of some of the more common transactions affecting the number of common shares outstanding. The theoretical model set forth in these relatively simple examples can be followed in all situations that are not explicitly discussed.

If a company reacquires its stock (treasury stock), the number of shares reacquired should be excluded from EPS calculations as of the date of acquisition. The same theory holds for the issuance of common stock during the period. The number of shares newly issued is included in the computation only for the period after their issuance date. The logic for this treatment is that the consideration for the shares was not available to generate earnings until the shares were issued. This same logic applies to the reacquired shares because the consideration relative to those shares was no longer available to generate earnings after the acquisition date.

A **stock dividend or split** does not generate additional consideration, but it does increase the number of shares outstanding. SFAS 128 states that the increase in shares as a result of a stock split or dividend, or decrease in shares as a result of a reverse split, should be given retroactive recognition as an appropriate equivalent charge for all periods presented. Thus, even if a stock dividend or split occurs at the end of the period, it is considered outstanding for the entire period of **each** period presented. The reasoning is that a stock dividend or split has no effect on the ownership percentage of the common stockholder. As such, to show a dilution in the EPS reported would erroneously give the impression of a decline in profitability when in fact it was merely an increase in the shares outstanding due to the stock dividend or split. SFAS 128 carries this one step further by requiring the retroactive adjustment of outstanding shares for stock dividends or splits occurring after the end of the period, but before the release of the financial statements. The reason given is that the primary interest of the financial statement user is considered to be the current capitalization. If this situation occurs, disclosure of both the end-of-year outstanding shares and those used to compute EPS is required.

Complications also arise when a **business combination** occurs during the period. The treatment of the additional shares depends upon the nature of the combination. If the business combination is recorded as a pooling of interests, then the additional shares are assumed to have been issued at the beginning of the year, regardless of when the combination occurred. Conversely, if the combination is accounted for as a purchase, the shares are considered issued and outstanding as of the date of acquisition. The reason for this varied treatment lies in the income statement treatment accorded a pooling and a purchase. In a pooling, the income of the acquired company is included in the statements for the entire year, whereas in a purchase, the income is included only for the period after acquisition.

Weighted-Average (WA) Computation	
Transaction	*Effect on WA computation*
• Common stock outstanding at the beginning of the period	• Increase number of shares outstanding by the number of shares
• Issuance of common stock during the period	• Increase number of shares outstanding by the number of shares issued times the portion of the year outstanding
• Conversion into common stock	• Increase number of shares outstanding by the number of shares converted times the portion of the year outstanding
• Company reacquires its stock	• Decrease number of shares outstanding by number of shares reacquired times portion of the year since acquisition
• Stock dividend or split	• Increase number of shares outstanding by number of shares issued for the dividend or resulting from the split
• Reverse split	• Decrease number of shares outstanding by decrease in shares
• Pooling of interests	• Increase number of shares outstanding by number of shares issued
• Purchase	• Increase number of shares outstanding by number of shares issued times portion of year since acquisition

These do not characterize all of the possible complexities arising in the EPS computation; however, most of the others occur under a complex structure. The complications arising under a complex capital structure are discussed in detail later in this chapter. The illustration below applies some of the foregoing concepts to a simple capital structure.

Example of EPS computation—Simple capital structure

Assume the following information:

Numerator information			*Denominator information*	
a.	Income from continuing operations before extraordinary items	$130,000	a. Common shares outstanding 1/1/02	100,000
b.	Extraordinary loss (net of tax)	30,000	b. Shares issued for cash 4/1/02	20,000
c.	Net income	100,000	c. Shares issued in 10% stock dividend declared in July 2002	12,000
d.	6% cumulative preferred stock, $100 par, 1,000 shrs. issued and outstanding	100,000	d. Shares of treasury stock purchased 10/1/02	10,000

When calculating the numerator, the claims related to the preferred stock should be deducted to arrive at the income available to the common shareholders. In this example, the preferred stock is cumulative. Thus, regardless of whether or not the board of directors declares a preferred dividend, holders of the preferred stock have a claim of $6,000 (1,000 shares x $100 x 6%) against 2002 earnings. Therefore, $6,000 must be deducted from the numerator to arrive at the income available to common shareholders. Note that any cumulative preferred dividends in arrears are ignored in computing this period's EPS since they would have been incorporated into previous periods' EPS calculations. Also note that this $6,000 would have been deducted for **non**cumulative preferred only if a dividend of this amount had been declared during the period.

The EPS calculations follow:

Earnings per common share:

On income from continuing operations before extraordinary item	$\dfrac{\$130,000 - \$6,000}{\text{Common stock outstanding}}$
On net income	$\dfrac{\$100,000 - \$6,000}{\text{Common shares outstanding}}$

The computation of the denominator is based upon the weighted-average number of common shares outstanding. A simple weighted-average is not considered appropriate because of the various complexities. The table below illustrates one way of computing the weighted-average number of shares outstanding.

Table 1

Item	*Number of shares deemed outstanding*	*Fraction of the year outstanding*	*Shares times fraction of the year*
Number of shares as of beginning of the year 1/1/02	110,000 [100,000 + 10%(100,000)]	12/12	110,000
Shares issued 4/1/02	22,000 [20,000 + 10%(20,000)]	9/12	16,500
Treasury shares purchased 10/1/02	(10,000)	3/12	(2,500)
Weighted-average number of common shares outstanding			124,000

The stock dividend declared in July is considered to be retroactive to the beginning of the year. Thus, for the period 1/1 through 4/1, 110,000 shares are considered to be outstanding. When shares are issued, they are included in the weighted-average beginning with the date of issuance. The stock dividend applicable to these newly issued shares is also assumed to have existed for the same period. Thus, we can see that of the 12,000-share dividend, 10,000 shares relate to the beginning balance and 2,000 shares to the new issuance (10% of 100,000 and 20,000, respectively). The purchase of the treasury stock requires that these shares be excluded from the calculation for the remainder of the period after their acquisition date. The figure is subtracted from the calculation because the shares were purchased from those outstanding prior to acquisition.

To complete the example, we divided the previously derived numerator by the weighted-average number of common shares outstanding to arrive at EPS.

Earnings per common share:

On income from continuing operations before extraordinary item

$$\frac{\$130,000 - \$6,000}{124,000 \text{ common shares}} = \$1.00$$

On net income

$$\frac{\$100,000 - \$6,000}{124,000 \text{ common shares}} = \$\ .76$$

The numbers computed above are required presentations on the face of the income statement. Reporting a $.24 loss per share ($30,000 ÷ 124,000) due to the extraordinary item is required either on the face of the income statement or in the notes to the financial statements.

Preferred stock dividends payable in common shares. All dividends represent distributions of accumulated earnings, and accordingly, are not expenses to be reported on the income statement under GAAP. However, as illustrated above, for purposes of computing earnings per share, preferred dividends must be deducted in order to ascertain how much income is available for common shareholders. In some cases, preferred dividends are payable not in cash, but rather in common shares (based on market value as of the date of declaration, typically). In certain cases, the dividends maybe payable in common shares or cash at the issuer's option.

SFAS 128 defines income available to common stockholders as "income (or loss) from continuing operations or net income (or net loss) adjusted for preferred stock dividends." Logic suggests that this adjustment should be made for all preferred stock dividends, regardless of the form of payment. This adjustment in computing income available to common stockholders is consistent with the treatment of common stock issued for goods or services.

Complex Capital Structure

The computation of EPS under a complex capital structure involves all of the complexities discussed under the simple structure and many more. A complex capital structure is one that has securities that have the potential to be exercised and **reduce** EPS (dilutive securities). Any **antidilutive** securities (those that increase EPS) would not be included in the computation of EPS. Note that a complex structure requires **dual presentation** of both basic EPS and diluted EPS (DEPS). The common stock outstanding and all other dilutive securities are used to compute DEPS.

Diluted earnings per share (DEPS). DEPS has been identified as the earnings attributable to each share of common stock after giving effect to all potential common shares which were outstanding during the period and dilutive. The computation of DEPS requires that the following steps be performed:

1. Identify all potentially dilutive securities.
2. Compute the effect (dilution) of the other dilutive securities on net income and common shares outstanding.

Identification of potentially dilutive securities. Dilutive securities are those that have the potential of being exercised and reducing the EPS figure. Some examples of dilutive securities identified by SFAS 128 are convertible debt, convertible preferred stock, options, warrants, participating securities, two-class common stocks, and contingent shares.

Convertible securities. A **convertible security** is one type of potentially dilutive security. A security of this type has an inherent dual nature. Convertibles are comprised of two distinct elements: the right to receive dividends or interest, **and** the right to potentially participate in earnings by becoming a common shareholder. Due to the later right, this security is included in the DEPS computation.

Options and warrants. Options, warrants, and their equivalents generally derive their entire value from the right to obtain common stock at specified prices over an extended period of time.

Participating securities and two-class common stocks. The capital structure of some entities includes securities that may participate in dividends with common stocks according to a predetermined formula, or a class of common stock with different dividend rates from those of another class of common stock but without prior or senior rights. The **if-converted method** is used for those securities that are convertible into common stock if the effect is dilutive. For those securities that are not convertible into a class of common stock, the **two-class method** of computing earnings per share is used.

The two-class method. The two-class method is an earnings allocation formula that determines earnings per share for each class of common stock and participating security according to dividends declared (or accumulated) and participation rights in undistributed earnings. Under this method, income from continuing operations (or net income) is reduced by the amount of dividends declared in the current period for each class of stock and by the contractual amount of dividends that must be paid for the current period. The remaining earnings are allocated to common stock and participating securities to the extent that each security may share in earnings if all of the earnings for the period had been distributed. The total earnings allocated to each security are determined by adding together the amount allocated for dividends and the amount allocated for a participation feature. The total earnings allocated to each security shall be divided by the number of outstanding shares of the security to which the earnings are allocated to determine the earnings per share for the security.

Contingent issuances of common stock. Another consideration is **contingent issuances** of common stock (e.g., stock subscriptions). If shares are to be issued in the future with no restrictions on issuance other than the passage of time, they are to be considered issued and treated as outstanding in the computation of DEPS. Other issuances that are dependent upon certain conditions being met are to be evaluated in a different respect. SFAS 128 uses as examples the maintenance of current earnings levels and the attainment of specified earnings increases. If the contingency is to merely maintain the earnings levels currently being attained, then the shares are considered outstanding for the entire period and considered in the computation of DEPS if the effect is dilutive. If the requirement is to increase earnings over a period of time, the DEPS computation includes those shares that would be issued based on the assumption that the current amount of earnings will remain unchanged if the effect is dilutive. Previously reported DEPS should not be restated to give recognition to shares issued as a result of the earnings level attainment. If a contingent issuance is based upon the lapsing of time **and** the market price of the stock (generally affects the number of shares issued), both conditions must be met to include the contingently issuable shares in the DEPS computation. The Board prohibits restatement of DEPS data should fluctuations in the market price occur in future periods.

Computation of DEPS. The second step in the process is the actual computation of DEPS. There are basically two methods used to incorporate the effects of other dilutive securities and EPS (excluding participating and two-class common securities):

1. The treasury stock method, and
2. The if-converted method

The treasury stock method. The treasury stock method which is used for the exercise of most warrants or options requires that DEPS be computed as if the options or warrants were exercised at the beginning of the period (or date of issuance, if later), and that the funds obtained from the exercise were used to purchase common stock at the **average market price** for the period. For example, if a corporation has warrants outstanding for 1,000 shares of common stock exercisable at $10 per share and the average market price of the common stock is $16 per share, the following would occur: the company would receive $10,000 (1,000 x $10) and issue 1,000 shares from the exercise of the warrants which would enable it to repurchase 625 shares ($10,000 ÷ $16) in the open market. The net increase in the denominator (which effects a dilution in EPS) is 375 shares (1,000 issued less 625 repurchased). If the **exercise price** is greater than the average market price, the exercise should not be assumed since the result of this would be antidilutive. In this case, DEPS of prior periods presented in comparative form should **not** be restated to reflect a change in market price.

Treasury Stock Method
Denominator must be increased by net dilution, as follows:
Net dilution = Shares issued – Shares repurchased
where
Shares issued = Proceeds received ÷ Exercise price
Shares repurchased = Proceeds received ÷ Average market price per share

The if-converted method. The if-converted method is used for those securities that are currently sharing in the earnings of the company through the receipt of interest or dividends as preferential securities, but that have the **potential** for sharing in the earnings as common stock. The if-converted method logically recognizes that the convertible security can only share in the earnings of the company as one or the other, not both. Thus, the dividends or interest less tax effects applicable to the convertible security as a preferential security are not recognized in the income available to common stockholders figure used to compute DEPS, and the weighted-average number of shares is adjusted to reflect the assumed conversion as of the beginning of the year (or date of issuance, if later).

If-Converted Method

Numerator

Income available to common stockholders recomputed to reflect conversion

- Add back interest expense less tax effects
- Convertible preferred dividends no longer subtracted
- Add back other expenses attributable to convertible issues

- -

Denominator

Common stock outstanding if convertible securities were assumed converted at beginning or date of issuance, if later

---

Exceptions. Generally, the if-converted method is used for convertible securities, while the treasury stock method is used for options and warrants. There are some situations specified by SFAS 128 for which this does not hold true.

1. When options or warrants contain provisions which permit or require that debt or other securities of the issuer be tendered for all or a portion of the exercise price, the if-converted method should be used.
2. If the terms of the options or warrants require that the proceeds from the exercise are to be used to retire existing debt, the if-converted method should be used.
3. For convertible securities that require cash payment upon conversion, and are, therefore, considered equivalent to warrants, the treasury stock method should be used.

Dual presentation of earnings per share. DEPS is a pro forma presentation which reflects the dilution of EPS that would have occurred if **all** contingent issuances of common stock that would individually reduce EPS had taken place at the beginning of the period (or the date issued, if later). The concept of the dual earnings per share presentation distinguishes between no dilution and potential dilution, providing the users with the most factually supportable range of EPS possibilities. DEPS assumes that all issuances that have the legal right to become common stock exercise that right (unless such exercise would be antidilutive), and therefore anticipates and measures all **potential** dilution. The **dual presentation** of both basic

EPS and DEPS is to be prominently disclosed on the face of the income statements. The underlying basis for the computation is that of conservatism. The DEPS considers all other potentially dilutive securities but only uses those securities which are dilutive. Thus, in most cases, the DEPS is less than the basic EPS. The DEPS can never be greater than the basic EPS, but it could possibly be the same if all of the convertible securities were antidilutive.

NOTE: The FASB concluded that an entity that reports a discontinued operation, an extraordinary item, or the cumulative effect of an accounting change in a period shall use **income from continuing operations** *as the "control number" for determining whether including potential common shares in the diluted EPS computation would be dilutive or antidilutive. Income from continuing operations (or a similar line item above net income if it appears on the income statement) would be adjusted for preferred dividends. If necessary, refer to SFAS 128, footnote 8 for an example.*

Examples of EPS Computation—Complex Capital Structure

Each of the following independent examples is presented to illustrate the foregoing principles. The procedural guidelines are detailed so as to allow the reader to understand the computation without referring back to the preceding explanatory text.

Example of the treasury stock method

Assume that the net income is $50,000 and the weighted-average number of common shares outstanding has been computed as 10,000. Additional information regarding the capital structure is given as

1. 4% nonconvertible, cumulative preferred stock, par $100, 1,000 shares issued and outstanding the entire year
2. Options and warrants to purchase 1,000 shares of common stock at $8 per share were outstanding all year. The average market price of common stock during the year was $10.

The first step in the solution of this problem is the determination of basic EPS. This calculation appears as follows:

$$\frac{\text{Net income} - \text{Preferred dividends}}{\text{Weighted-average number of common shares outstanding}} = \frac{\$50,000 - \$4,000}{10,000 \text{ shares}} = \$4.60$$

The second step is the calculation of DEPS which is based upon outstanding common stock and other dilutive securities. The options and warrants are the only potentially dilutive securities in the example. However, remember that only dilutive options (Market price > Exercise price) are included in the computation. The treasury stock method used to compute the number of shares to be added to the denominator is illustrated below.

Proceeds from assumed exercise of options and warrants (1,000 shares x $8)	$8,000
Number of shares issued	1,000
Number of shares reacquired ($8,000 ÷ $10)	800
Number of shares assumed issued and not reacquired	200*

* *An alternative approach that can be used to calculate this number for DEPS is demonstrated below.*

$$\frac{\text{Average market price} - \text{Exercise price}}{\text{Average market price}} \quad x \quad \begin{array}{c}\text{Number of shares under}\\\text{options/warrants}\end{array} \quad = \quad \begin{array}{c}\text{Shares not}\\\text{reacquired}\end{array}$$

$$\frac{\$10 - \$8}{\$10} \text{ x } 1,000 \text{ shares} = 200 \text{ shares}$$

DEPS can now be calculated as follows, including the effects of applying the treasury stock method:

$$\frac{\text{Net income} - \text{Preferred dividends}}{\begin{array}{c}\text{Weighted-average number of common}\\\text{shares outstanding} + \text{Number of}\\\text{shares not reacquired with}\\\text{proceeds from options and warrants}\end{array}} = \frac{\$50,000 - \$4,000}{10,200 \text{ shares}} = \$4.51$$

Note also that the options and warrants are dilutive, as EPS is reduced from $4.60 to $4.51.

Table 2
Computations of Basic and Diluted Earnings Per Share

Items	EPS on outstanding common stock (Basic EPS)		DEPS	
	Numerator	*Denominator*	*Numerator*	*Denominator*
Net income	$50,000b		$50,000	
Preferred dividends	(4,000)		(4,000)	
Common shs. outstanding		10,000 shs		10,000 shs
Options and warrants				200
Totals	$46,000 ÷	10,000 shs	$46,000 ÷	10,200 shs
EPS		$4.60		$4.51

Example of the if-converted method

Assume a net income of $50,000 and a weighted-average number of common shares outstanding of 10,000. The following information is provided regarding the capital structure:

1. 7% convertible debt, 200 bonds each convertible into forty common shares. The bonds were outstanding the entire year. The income tax rate is 40%. The bonds were issued at par ($1,000 per bond). No bonds were converted during the year.

2. 4% convertible, cumulative preferred stock, par $100, 1,000 shares issued and outstanding. Each preferred share is convertible into two common shares. The preferred stock that was issued at par was outstanding the entire year. No shares were converted during the year.

The first step is to compute basic EPS. As with the previous example, this figure is $4.60. The next step is the computation of DEPS. The convertible bonds are assumed to have been converted at the beginning of the year. The effects of the assumption are twofold. One, if the bonds are converted, there will be no interest expense of $14,000 (7% x $200,000 face value); and two, there will be an additional 8,000 shares (200 bonds x 40 shares) of common stock outstanding during the year. The effect of not having $14,000 of interest expense will increase income, but it will also increase tax expense. Consequently, the net effect of not having interest expense of $14,000 is $8,400 [(1 − .40) x $14,000]. DEPS is computed as follows:

$$\frac{\text{Net income} - \text{Preferred dividends} + \text{Interest expense (net of tax)}}{\begin{array}{c}\text{Weighted-average number of common shares}\\ \text{outstanding} + \text{Shares issued upon}\\ \text{conversion of bonds}\end{array}} = \frac{\$50,000 - \$4,000 + \$8,400}{10,000 + 8,000 \text{ shares}} = \$3.02$$

The convertible debt is dilutive, as it reduces EPS from \$4.60 to \$3.02.

To determine the dilutive effect of the preferred stock, an assumption is made that all of the preferred stock is converted at January 1. The effects of this assumption are twofold. One, if the preferred stock is converted, there will be no preferred dividends of \$4,000 for the year; and two, there will be an additional 2,000 shares of common stock outstanding during the year (the **conversion rate** is 2 for 1 on 1,000 shares of preferred). DEPS considering the preferred stock is computed, as follows, reflecting these two assumptions:

$$\frac{\text{Net income} + \text{Interest expense (net of tax)}}{\begin{array}{c}\text{Weighted-average number of common shares}\\ \text{outstanding} + \text{Shares issued upon conversion}\\ \text{of bonds and conversion of preferred stock}\end{array}} = \frac{\$50,000 + \$8,400}{10,000 + 8,000 + 2,000 \text{ shares}} = \$2.92$$

The convertible preferred stock is also dilutive because it reduced DEPS from \$3.02 to \$2.92.

Together the convertible bonds and preferred stock both reduced EPS from \$4.60 to \$2.92. For a complete explanation of the sequencing process of including multiple dilutive securities in the computations of DEPS, see the comprehensive example in Appendix A. In this example the convertible bonds must first be considered prior to the inclusion of the convertible preferred stock. Table 3 summarizes the computations made for this example.

Table 3
Computations of Basic and Diluted Earnings per Share

	EPS on outstanding common stock (Basic EPS)		DEPS	
Items	*Numerator*	*Denominator*	*Numerator*	*Denominator*
Net income	\$50,000		\$50,000	
Preferred dividend	(4,000)			
Common shs. outstanding		10,000 shs.		10,000 shs.
Conversion of preferred				2,000
Conversion of bonds			8,400	8,000
Totals	\$46,000 ÷	10,000 shs.	\$58,400	20,000 shs.
EPS		\$4.60		\$2.92

In the preceding example all of the potentially dilutive securities were outstanding the entire year and no conversions or exercises were made during the year. If a potentially dilutive security was not outstanding the entire year, then the numerator and denominator effects would have to be "time-weighted." For instance, suppose the convertible bonds in the above example were issued during the current year on July 1. If all other facts remain unchanged, DEPS would be computed as follows:

$$\frac{\text{Net income} + \text{Interest expense (net of tax)}}{\begin{array}{c}\text{Weighted-average number of common shares outstanding} +\\ \text{Shares issued upon conversion of preferred stock}\\ \text{and conversion of bonds}\end{array}} = \frac{\$50,000 + 1/2(8,400)}{10,000 + 2,000 + 1/2(8,000)} = \$3.39$$

In this case, the convertible debt is dilutive whether or not it is outstanding the entire year.

If actual conversions or exercises take place during a period, the common shares issued will be outstanding from their date of issuance, and therefore, will be included in the computation of the weighted-average number of common shares outstanding. These shares are then weighted from their respective times of issuance. Assume that all the bonds in the above example are converted on July 1 into 8,000 common shares; the following effects should be noted:

1. For basic EPS, the weighted-average of common shares outstanding will be increased by (8,000)(.5) or 4,000. Income will increase $4,200 net of tax, because the bonds are no longer outstanding.
2. For DEPS, the if-converted method is applied to the period January 1 to July 1 because it was during this period that the bonds were potentially dilutive. The interest expense, net of tax, of $4,200 is added to the net income in the numerator, and 4,000 shares (.5 of 8,000) are added to the denominator.
3. Interestingly, the net effect of items 1. and 2. is the same for the period whether these dilutive bonds were outstanding the entire period or converted during the period.

Inclusions/Exclusions from Computation of DEPS

The computation of DEPS should include written put options, forward purchase contracts, and other contracts that require the reporting entity to repurchase its own stock if the effect of including such items is dilutive. If during the reporting period the exercise price exceeds the average market price for that period, the potential dilutive effect of the contract on EPS should be computed using the **reverse treasury stock method**. Under this method

1. Issuance of sufficient common shares shall be assumed at the beginning of the period (at the average market price during the period) to raise enough proceeds to satisfy the contract.
2. Assume the proceeds from issuance are used to satisfy the contract (i.e., to buy back shares).
3. The denominator of the DEPS calculation should include the incremental shares (the difference between the number of shares assumed issued and the number of shares received from satisfying the contract).

The computation of DEPS should **not** include contracts such as purchased put options and purchased call options (options held by the entity on its own stock). The inclusion of such contracts would be antidilutive.

Sometimes entities issue contracts that may be settled in common stock or in cash at the election of either the entity or the holder. The determination of whether that contract shall be reflected in the computation of DEPS shall be based on the facts available each period. It shall be presumed that the contract will be settled in common stock and the resulting common shares included in DEPS if the effect is dilutive. This presumption may be overcome if past experience or a stated policy provides a reasonable basis to believe that the contract will be paid partially or wholly in cash.

Consolidated DEPS

When computing consolidated DEPS by entities with subsidiaries that have issued common stock or potential common shares to parties other than the parent company, the following general guidelines should be used:

1. Securities issued by a subsidiary that enable their holders to obtain the subsidiary's common stock shall be included in computing the subsidiary's EPS data. Per share earnings of the subsidiary should be included in the consolidated EPS calculations based on the consolidated group's holding of the subsidiary's securities.
2. For the purpose of computing consolidated DEPS, securities of a subsidiary that are convertible into its parent company's common stock, along with subsidiary's options or warrants to purchase common stock of the parent company, shall all be considered among the potential common shares of the parent company.

Partially Paid Shares

If an entity has common shares issued in a partially paid form and the shares are entitled to dividends in proportion to the amount paid, the common-share equivalent of those partially paid shares shall be included in the computation of basic EPS to the extent that they were entitled to participate in dividends. Partially paid stock subscriptions that do not share in dividends until paid in full are considered the equivalent of warrants and should be included in the calculation of DEPS using the treasury stock method.

Presentation

The reason for the differentiation between simple and complex capital structures is that SFAS 128 requires different financial statement presentation for each. SFAS 128 mandates that EPS be shown on the face of the income statement for each of the following items (when applicable):

1. Income from continuing operations.
2. Net income.

An entity which reports a discontinued operation, an extraordinary item, or the cumulative effect of a change in accounting principle shall present basic and diluted EPS amounts for these line items either on the face of the income statement or in the notes to the financial statements. These requirements must be fulfilled regardless of whether the structure is simple or complex. The difference in the two structures is that a simple capital structure requires presentation of only a single EPS number for each item, while a complex structure requires the dual presentation of both basic EPS and DEPS for each item.

Earnings per share data should be presented for all periods for which an income statement or summary of earnings is presented. If DEPS is reported for at least one period, it should be reported for all periods presented, regardless of whether or not DEPS is different from basic EPS. However, if basic and diluted EPS are the same amount for all periods presented, dual presentation can be accomplished in one line on the income statement.

Rights issue. A **rights issue** whose exercise price at issuance is below the fair value of the stock contains a bonus element. If a rights issue contains a bonus element (somewhat similar to a stock dividend) and is offered to all existing stockholders, basic and diluted EPS should be adjusted retroactively for the bonus element for all periods presented. However, if the ability to exercise the rights issue is contingent on some event other than the passage of time, this retroactive adjustment does not apply until the contingency is resolved.

Restated EPS. When a restatement of the results of operations of a prior period is required to be included in the income statement, EPS data for the prior period(s) should be restated. The effect of the restatement, expressed in per share terms, shall be disclosed in the period of restatement. Restated EPS data should be computed as if the restated income (loss) had been reported in the prior period(s).

Year-to-date DEPS. If an entity has year-to-date income from continuing operations (Topic D-62 in EITF Abstracts) that includes losses in one or more quarters, the calculation of year-to-date DEPS should include dilutive potential shares for all quarters on a quarterly weighted-average basis. Thus, options that are in the money in a quarter(s) in which a net loss(es) occur(s) should be included in the year-to-date denominator in the DEPS calculation. Likewise, contingent shares excluded because of a loss from continuing operations in a quarter(s) should be included in year-to-date DEPS.

Other Disclosure Requirements

The following additional items shall be disclosed by an entity for each period an income statement is presented:

1. A reconciliation of the numerators and the denominators of the basic and diluted EPS computations for income from continuing operations. The reconciliation should include the effects of all securities that affect EPS.
2. The effect of preferred dividends in arriving at income available for common stockholders in computing basic EPS.
3. Securities which could potentially dilute basic EPS in future periods but which were not included in DEPS for the period(s) presented since the results were antidilutive.

In addition for the latest period for which an income statement is presented, a description is required for transactions occurring after the balance sheet date that result in a material change in the number of shares outstanding at the balance sheet date.

EMERGING ISSUES TASK FORCE CONSENSUS SUMMARIES

92-3 EPS Treatment of Tax Benefits for Dividends on Unallocated Stock Held by an Employee Stock Ownership Plan

Under SFAS 109, the tax benefits related to dividends paid on unallocated ESOP common stock held by an ESOP that are charged to retained earnings should not be a deduction to net income when calculating DEPS. Also note, this consensus applies to convertible ESOP preferred stock when calculating the if-converted DEPS. However, under SOP 93-6, dividends paid on unallocated shares are not charged to retained earnings. Since the employers control the use of dividends on unallocated shares, these dividends are not considered dividends for financial reporting purposes. Consequently, the dividends do not affect the DEPS computation. The transition provisions of SOP 93-6 do, however, allow employers to continue their current accounting methods for ESOP shares acquired on or prior to December 31, 1992.

00-19 Accounting for Derivative Financial Instruments Indexed to, and Potentially Settled in, a Company's Own Stock

This consensus, covered in detail in Chapter 17, Stockholders' Equity, provides criteria to apply in determining the initial balance sheet classification of certain derivative financial instruments as debt or equity as well as circumstances that would require their reclassification.

For EPS computation purposes, for those contracts that provide the company with a choice of either cash settlement or settlement in shares, settlement in shares is assumed, although this can be overcome based on past experience or stated policy. If the counter party controls the choice, however, the more dilutive assumption must be made, irrespective of past experience or policy.

The consensus is effective for contracts entered into after September 30, 2000; for contracts in existence on that date, the requirements of the consensus are to be applied on June 30, 2001, using a cumulative-effect-type presentation. The consensus includes detailed guidance for a number of specific types of contracts.

APPENDIX

COMPREHENSIVE EXAMPLE

The examples within the text used a simplified approach for determining whether or not options, warrants, convertible preferred stock, or convertible bonds have a dilutive effect on DEPS. If the DEPS number computed was lower than the basic EPS, the security was considered dilutive. This approach is adequate so long as the firm has only **one** potentially dilutive security. If the firm has more than one potentially dilutive security, a more complex ranking procedure must be employed (SFAS 128).

For example, assume the following facts concerning the capital structure of a firm:

1. Income from continuing operations and net income are both $50,000. Income from continuing operations is not displayed on the firm's income statement.
2. Weighted-average number of common shares outstanding is 10,000 shares.
3. Tax rate is 40%.
4. Options to purchase 1,000 shares of common stock at $8 per share were outstanding all year.
5. Options to purchase 2,000 shares of common stock at $13 per share were outstanding all year.
6. The average market price of common stock during the year was $10.
7. 7% convertible bonds, 200 bonds each convertible into 40 common shares were outstanding the entire year. The bonds were issued at par ($1,000 per bond) and no bonds were converted during the year.
8. 4% convertible, **cumulative** preferred stock, par $100, 1,000 shares issued and outstanding the entire year. Each preferred share is convertible into one common share. The preferred stock was issued at par and no shares were converted during the year.

Note that reference is made below to some of the tables included in the body of the chapter because the facts above represent a combination of the facts used for the examples in the chapter.

In order to determine both basic EPS and DEPS, the following procedures must be performed:

1. Calculate a basic EPS as if the capital structure were simple.
2. Identify other potentially dilutive securities.
3. Calculate the per share effects of assuming issuance or conversion of each potentially dilutive security on an individual basis.
4. Rank the per share effects from smallest to largest.

5. Recalculate EPS (step 1 above) adding the potentially dilutive securities one at a time in order, beginning with the security with the **smallest** per share effect.

6. Continue adding potentially dilutive securities until all have been added or until the addition of a security increases EPS (antidilution) from its previous level.

Applying these procedures to the facts above:

1. Basic EPS:

$$\frac{\text{Net income} - \text{Preferred dividends}}{\substack{\text{Weighted-average number of} \\ \text{common shares outstanding}}} = \frac{\$50,000 - \$4,000}{10,000} = \$4.60$$

2. Identification of other potentially dilutive securities:

    a. Options (two types).
    b. 7% convertible bonds.
    c. 4% convertible cumulative preferred stock.

Diluted EPS (DEPS)

3. Per share effects of conversion or issuance of other potentially dilutive securities:

    a. Options—Only the options to purchase 1,000 shares at $8.00 per share are potentially dilutive. The options to purchase 2,000 shares of common stock are antidilutive because the exercise price is greater than the average market price. Thus, they are not included.

       Proceeds if options exercised:

1,000 shares x $8	=	$8,000
Shares that could be acquired:		
$8,000 ÷ $10	=	800
Dilutive shares: 1,000 – 800	=	200

       $$\frac{\text{Increase/decrease in net income}}{\substack{\text{Increase in weighted-average number of} \\ \text{common shares outstanding}}} = \frac{\$0}{200 \text{ shs.}} = \$0$$

    b. 4% convertible cumulative preferred stock—The outstanding common shares increase by 1,000 when all shares are converted. This results in total dividends of $4,000 not being paid.

       $$\frac{\text{Increase/decrease in net income}}{\substack{\text{Increase in weighted-average number} \\ \text{of common shares outstanding}}} = \frac{\$4,000}{1,000 \text{ shs.}} = \$4.00$$

    c. 7% convertible bonds (see Table 3).

       $$\frac{\text{Increase/decrease in net income}}{\substack{\text{Increase in weighted-average number} \\ \text{of common shares outstanding}}} = \frac{\$8,400}{8,000 \text{ shs.}} = \$1.05$$

4. Rank the per share effects:

    a. Options $ 0
    b. 7% convertible bonds   1.05
    c. 4% convertible cumulative preferred stock   4.00

5. Recalculate the EPS adding in rank order one potentially dilutive security at a time:

    a. DEPS—options added

$$\frac{\text{Net income} - \text{Preferred dividends}}{\substack{\text{Weighted-average number of common} \\ \text{shares outstanding} + \text{Shares not} \\ \text{acquired with proceeds of options}}} = \frac{\$50,000 - \$4,000}{10,000 + 200 \text{ shs.}} = \$4.51$$

    b. DEPS—options and 7% convertible bonds added

$$\frac{\substack{\text{Net income} - \text{Preferred dividends} \\ + \text{Interest expense (net of tax)}}}{\substack{\text{Weighted-average number of common} \\ \text{shares outstanding} + \text{Shares not} \\ \text{acquired with proceeds of options} + \text{Shares} \\ \text{issued upon conversion of bonds}}} = \frac{\$50,000 - \$4,000 + \$8,400}{10,000 + 200 + 8,000 \text{ shs.}} = \$2.99$$

    c. DEPS—options, 7% convertible bonds and 4% convertible cumulative preferred stock added

$$\frac{\substack{\text{Net income} + \text{Interest} \\ \text{expense (net of tax)}}}{\substack{\text{Weighted-average number of common} \\ \text{shares outstanding} + \text{Shares not} \\ \text{acquired with proceeds of options} \\ + \text{Shares issued upon conversion of} \\ \text{bonds and preferred stock}}} = \frac{\$50,000 + 8,400}{10,000 + 200 + 8,000 + 1,000 \text{ shs.}} = \$3.04$$

DEPS = $2.99

Since the addition of the 4% convertible cumulative preferred stock raises DEPS from $2.99 to $3.04, it is antidilutive and is therefore excluded from the DEPS.

A dual presentation of basic EPS and DEPS is required. The dual presentation on the face of the income statement would appear as follows:

Net income	$50,000
Earnings per common share* (Note X)	$4.60
Earnings per common share, assuming dilution*(Note X)	$2.99

* *Basic earnings per share and diluted earnings per share may be substituted, respectively.*

Note X: Earnings Per Share

Earnings per common share were computed by dividing income available to common stockholders by the weighted-average number of common shares outstanding during the year.

Diluted earnings per share were computed assuming the conversion of all options and the 7% convertible bonds. Consequently, the income available to common stockholders figure is adjusted to reflect the preferred dividend and the interest expense (net of tax) related to the convertible bonds. The number of common shares issuable assuming conversion of the convertible bonds and complete exercise of the options as of the beginning of the year were added to the number of common shares outstanding.

19 INTERIM AND SEGMENT REPORTING

INTERIM REPORTING

PERSPECTIVE AND ISSUES

Interim reporting is financial reporting for periods of less than a year. Today, interim reporting generally takes the form of quarterly earnings reports.

For over sixty years, the New York Stock Exchange has required quarterly financial reporting in its listing agreement. Since 1970, the SEC has required companies subject to its periodic reporting requirements to file quarterly financial information on a form 10-Q. Until 1973, however, there was no promulgated GAAP for publicly held companies issuing interim reports to their stockholders. The general guidelines are now set forth in APB 28, SFAS 3, and FASB Interpretation 18.

The basic objective of interim reporting is to provide frequent and timely assessments of enterprise performance. However, interim reporting has inherent limitations. As the reporting period is shortened, the effects of errors in estimation and allocation are magnified. The proper allocation of annual operating expenses is a significant concern. Because, in the US, progressive tax rates are applied to total annual income and various tax credits may arise, the determination of quarterly income tax expense is often difficult. Other annual operating expenses are often concentrated in one interim period, yet benefit the entire year's operations. Examples include advertising expenses and major repairs or maintenance of equipment. The effects of seasonal fluctuations and temporary market conditions further limit the reliability, comparability, and predictive value of interim reports. Because of this reporting environment, the issue of independent auditor association with interim financial reports is subject to continuing controversy.

Two distinct views of interim reporting have developed. Under the first view, the interim period is considered to be an **integral** part of the annual accounting period. Annual operating expenses are estimated and then allocated to the interim periods based on forecasted annual activity levels such as sales volume. The results of subsequent interim periods must be adjusted to reflect estimation errors. The APB in APB 28 indicated a preference for the integral approach. Under the second view, the interim period is considered to be a **discrete** accounting period. Thus, there are no estimations or allocations different from those used for annual reporting. The same expense recognition rules apply as under annual reporting, and no special interim accruals or deferrals are applied. Annual operating expenses are recognized in the interim period incurred, irrespective of the number of interim periods benefited.

Proponents of the **integral view** argue that the unique expense recognition procedures are necessary to avoid misleading fluctuations in period-to-period results. Using the integral view results in interim earnings which are indicative of annual earnings and, thus, useful for predictive purposes. Proponents of the **discrete view** argue that the smoothing of interim results for purposes of forecasting annual earnings has undesirable effects. For example, a turning point during the year in an earnings trend may be obscured.

In response to inconsistencies in interim reporting practices and problems in implementing interim reporting GAAP, the FASB undertook a comprehensive study of the issue. In 1978, the FASB Discussion Memorandum, *Interim Financial Accounting and Reporting*, was issued. A fundamental objective of this project was to resolve the **integral/discrete** debate. However, the FASB has made no recommendations and removed the project from its agenda.

Sources of GAAP				
APB	*SFAS*	*FASB I*	*FASB TB*	*EITF*
28	3, 16,	18	79-9	86-13,
	69, 95, 109,			98-9,
	128, 130, 131			D-70

DEFINITIONS OF TERMS

Discrete view. An approach to measuring interim period income by viewing each interim period separately without regard to the annual period to which it relates.

Estimated annual effective tax rate. An expected annual tax rate which reflects estimates of annual earnings, tax rates, tax credits, etc.

Integral view. An approach to measuring interim period income by viewing each interim period as an integral part of the annual period. Expenses are recognized in proportion to revenues earned through the use of special accruals and deferrals.

Interim reporting. Financial reporting for a period of less than a year, generally for a period of three months.

Last-twelve-months reports. Financial reporting for the twelve-month period which ends on a given interim date.

Liquidation of LIFO inventories. Occurs when quarterly unit sales exceed purchases and base-period costs are released into cost of goods sold.

Seasonality. The normal, expected occurrence of a major portion of revenues or costs in one or two interim periods.

Year-to-date reports. Financial reporting for the period which begins on the first day of the fiscal year and ends on a given interim date.

CONCEPTS, RULES, AND EXAMPLES

Revenues

Revenues are to be recognized as earned during an interim period using the same basis followed in annual reports. This rule applies to both product sales and service revenues. For example, product sales cutoff procedures should be applied at the end of each quarter in the same manner that they are applied at year-end, and revenue from long-term construction contracts should be recognized at interim dates using the same method used at year-end.

Product Costs and Direct Costs

Product costs (and costs directly associated with service revenues) should be treated in interim reports as they are in annual reports (the discrete approach). However, APB 28 provides for four integral view exceptions, described below.

1. The gross profit method may be used to estimate cost of goods sold and ending inventory for interim periods.
2. When inventory consisting of LIFO layers and a portion of the base period is liquidated at an interim date, but is expected to be replaced by year-end, cost of sales should include the expected cost of replacing the liquidated inventory.

3. An inventory market decline reasonably expected to be restored by year-end (i.e., a decline deemed to be **temporary** in nature) need not be recognized in the interim period. The Emerging Issues Task Force (Issue 86-13) has reached a consensus that situations not requiring a write-down are generally limited to seasonal price fluctuations. If an inventory loss from a market decline that is recognized in one period is followed by a market price recovery, such reversal should be recognized as a gain. Recognition of this gain in the later interim period is limited to the extent of loss previously recognized.

4. Firms using standard cost accounting systems ordinarily should report purchase price, wage rate, and usage or efficiency variances in the same manner as used at year-end. Planned purchase price and volume variances should be deferred if expected to be absorbed by year-end.

The first exception above eliminates the need for a physical inventory count at the interim date. The other three exceptions attempt to synchronize the quarterly statements with the annual report. For example, consider the LIFO liquidation exception. Without this exception, interim cost of goods sold could include low base-period costs, while annual cost of goods sold would include only current year costs.

Several additional problems are encountered when using LIFO for interim reporting.

1. What is the best approach to estimating interim LIFO cost of sales?
2. As noted above, when an interim liquidation occurs that is expected to be replaced by year-end, cost of sales should include the expected cost of replacement. How should this adjustment be treated on the interim balance sheet?
3. How should an interim liquidation that is **not** expected to be replaced by year-end be recorded?

These problems are not addressed in APB 28. The only literature related to these problems is the AICPA Task Force Issues Paper, *Identification and Discussion of Certain Financial Accounting and Reporting Issues Concerning LIFO Inventories.*

The Issues Paper describes two acceptable approaches to measuring the interim LIFO cost of sales. The first approach makes specific quarterly computations of the LIFO effect based on year-to-date amounts. This is accomplished by reviewing quarterly price level changes and inventory levels. The second approach projects the expected **annual** LIFO effect and then allocates that projection to the quarters. The allocation can be made equally to each quarter or can be made in relation to certain operating criteria per quarter.

The Issues Paper also describes two acceptable approaches to treating the interim liquidation replacement on the balance sheet. The first approach is to record the adjustment for the pretax income effect of the replacement as a deferred credit in the current liabilities section. The second approach is to instead record the adjustment as a credit to inventory.

When an interim LIFO liquidation occurs that is not expected to be reinstated by year-end, the Task Force believes that a company should recognize the effect of the liquidation in the period in which it occurs to the extent that this can reasonably be determined. They also believe, however, that a company using dollar-value LIFO may allocate the expected effect of the liquidation to the quarters.

Other Costs and Expenses

Most other costs and expenses are recognized in interim periods as incurred. However, an expenditure that **clearly benefits** more than one interim period (e.g., annual repairs or property taxes) may be allocated among the periods benefited. The allocation is to be based on estimates of time expired, benefit received, or activity related to the periods. Such allocation procedures should be consistent with those used by the firm at year-end reporting dates. However, if cost or expense cannot be readily associated with other interim periods, such costs should not be arbitrarily assigned to those periods. Application of these interim reporting expense principles is illustrated in the examples below.

1. Costs expensed at year-end dates that benefit two or more interim periods (e.g., annual major repairs) should be assigned to interim periods through use of deferrals or accruals.
2. Quantity discounts given customers based on annual sales volume should be apportioned to interim periods on the basis of sales to customers during the interim period relative to estimated annual sales.
3. Property taxes (and like costs) may be deferred or accrued at a year-end date to reflect a full year's charge to operations. Charges to interim periods should follow similar procedures.
4. Advertising costs may be deferred to subsequent interim periods within the same fiscal year if such costs clearly benefit the later interim periods. Advertising costs may be accrued and charged to interim periods preceding the time the service is received if there is an advertising program clearly implicit in the sales arrangement.

Costs and expenses subject to year-end adjustment, such as bad debts expense and discretionary bonuses, should be estimated and assigned to interim periods in a reasonable manner.

Income Taxes

At each interim date, the company should make its best **estimate of the effective tax rate** expected for the full fiscal year. This estimate should reflect expected federal and state tax rates, tax credits, and other tax planning techniques. However, changes in tax legislation are reflected in interim periods only after the enactment date of the legislation.

The accounting for income taxes in interim periods is discussed extensively in Appendix A to Chapter 15, Income Taxes.

Discontinued Operations and Extraordinary Items

Extraordinary items and the effects of disposal of a segment should be reported separately in the interim period in which they occur. The same treatment is given to other unusual or infrequently occurring events. No attempt should be made to allocate such items over the entire fiscal year. Materiality is determined by relating the item to the annual results of operations.

Accounting Changes

Retroactive changes in accounting principle are handled on the same basis as in annual reports. Previously issued interim financial statements are retroactively restated.

When a cumulative effect type change occurs in the first quarter, the cumulative effect is included in the first quarter's net income. However, if the cumulative effect change occurs in later quarters, it is treated as if it occurred in the first quarter (to conform with the annual treatment). Therefore, previous quarters' financial statements are restated to reflect the change, and the cumulative effect as of the beginning of the year is included in the first quarter's net income.

The treatment of accounting changes in interim reports is covered extensively in the Appendix to Chapter 20, Accounting Changes and Correction of Errors.

Earnings Per Share

The same procedures used at year-end are used for earnings per share computations and disclosures in interim reports. Note that annual earnings per share generally will not equal the sum of the interim earnings per share amounts, due to such factors as stock issuances during the year and market price changes.

Contingent Items

In general, contingencies at an interim date should be accrued or disclosed in the same manner required for annual reports. The materiality of the contingency is to be evaluated in relation to the expected annual results.

Certain items which are adjustments related to prior interim periods, such as a settlement of litigation or an income tax dispute, are accorded special treatment in interim reports. If such items are material, directly related to prior interim periods of the current fiscal year, and become reasonably estimable in the current interim period, they should be reported as follows:

1. The portion directly related to the current interim period is included in that period's income.
2. Prior interim periods are restated to reflect the portions directly related to those periods.
3. The portion directly related to **prior years** is recognized in the restated first quarter income of the current year.

Seasonality

The operations of many businesses are subject to material seasonal variations. Such businesses should disclose the seasonality of their activities to avoid the possibility of misleading interim reports. APB 28 also suggests that such businesses supplement their disclosures with information for twelve-month periods ending at the interim date of the current and preceding year.

Fourth Quarter Adjustments

When the fourth quarter results are not separately reported, material year-end adjustments as well as disposals of segments, extraordinary items, and unusual or infrequently occurring items for the quarter should be disclosed in a footnote to the annual report.

EMERGING ISSUES TASK FORCE CONSENSUS SUMMARIES

86-13   Recognition of Inventory Market Declines at Interim Reporting Dates

A consensus was reached that, in accordance with APB 28, inventory should be written down to the lower of cost or market unless substantial evidence is available that the market value will recover before the inventory is sold, or, when LIFO is used, that the inventory level will be restored by year-end. Task Force members noted that generally a write-down is required unless the decline is due to seasonal price fluctuations.

98-9   Accounting for Contingent Rent in Interim Financial Periods

A consensus was reached that lessors should not recognize contingent rental income until the target that causes the contingent rental income is reached.

A consensus was also reached that lessees should recognize contingent rental expense in the period that the cause of contingent rental income is probable before the end of the fiscal year. Previously recognized rental expense should be reversed if an assessment deemed probable changes during the year.

SEGMENT REPORTING

PERSPECTIVE AND ISSUES

Segment reporting, the disclosure of information about different components of an enterprise's operations as well as information related to the enterprise's products and services, its geographic areas, and its major customers, is a relatively recent development in financial reporting.

The primary benefit of segment reporting is the release of "hidden data" from consolidated financial information. Different operating segments may possess different levels of profitability, risk, and growth. This important information is merged in the consolidated amounts. Assessing future cash flows and their associated risks can be aided by segmental data. For example, knowledge of the level of enterprise operations in a growing or declining product line can help cash flow predictions, while knowledge of the level of enterprise operations in an unstable geographic area can help assess risk. In general, information about the nature and relative size of an enterprise's various businesses is considered useful.

Still, several arguments, listed below, have been offered against segment reporting.

1. Comparison of segment data between companies is misleading due to the wide variety of measurement techniques in use.
2. Lack of user knowledge could render segment information meaningless or misleading.
3. Disclosure of such information to competitors, labor unions, etc. could harm the enterprise.
4. Such disclosure may discourage management from taking reasonable business risks to avoid reporting unsatisfactory segment data.
5. The investor invests in the entire company and has no right to expect segment information.
6. Accounting classification and allocation problems may be inherent in segment reporting.
7. Information overload—Financial reports have become too detailed and complex for the average user.

Despite the potential disadvantages listed above, segment reporting has become more important as the number and size of conglomerates increase, as foreign operations increase, and as companies continue to diversify. In addition, over the years financial analysts have consistently requested that financial statement data be more disaggregated.

SFAS 131, *Disclosures about Segments of an Enterprise and Related Information*, governs the way public businesses are required to report disaggregated information in financial reports to shareholders, including interim reports. The statement defines operating segments as distinct revenue-producing components of the enterprise about which separate financial information is produced internally, and whose operating results are regularly reviewed by the enterprise. The approach used in SFAS 131 is a "management approach," meaning it is based on the way management organizes segments internally to make operating decisions and assess performance. The management approach will facilitate consistent descriptions of an enterprise for both internal and external reporting and, in general, provides that external financial reporting will more closely conform to internal reporting.

Practitioners of public companies can segment their financial information by products or services, by geography, by legal entity, or by type of customer. The statement requires that each of these operating segments report on segment profit or loss, on certain specific revenue and expense items, and on segment assets, among other items. The entity is required to reconcile segment information with its general-purpose financial statements.

In addition, the statement requires that all public enterprises report information about revenues for each product and service, about countries in which the enterprise earns revenues and holds assets, and about major customers, even if this information is not used by the enterprise in making operating decisions.

The statement does not restrict segment reporting to purely financial information. The statement also requires a description of the company's rationale or methods employed in determining the composition of the operating segments. This description includes the products or services produced by the segment, differences in measurement practices between a segment and the complete entity, and differences in measurement practices in a segment between periods.

Sources of GAAP		
SFAS	*FASB TB*	*EITF*
131	79-4, 79-5	D-70

DEFINITIONS OF TERMS

Assets test. One of the three 10% tests; used to determine reportability of operating segments.

Chief operating decision maker. A person whose general function (not specific title) is to allocate resources to, and assess the performance of, the segments of an enterprise.

Common costs. Operating expenses incurred by the enterprise for the benefit of more than one segment.

Corporate assets. Assets maintained for general corporate purposes and not used in the operations of any segment.

Expenditures for segment assets. Additions to a segment's long-lived assets; generally, property, plant, and equipment.

Financial report. Includes any compilation of information that includes one or more complete sets of financial statements, such as in an annual report to stockholders or in a filing with the Securities and Exchange Commission.

Foreign operations. Operations located outside of the enterprise's home country that generate either unaffiliated or intraenterprise revenues.

General corporate expenses. Expenses incurred for the benefit of the corporation as a whole, which cannot be reasonably allocated to any segment.

Geographic area. An individual country (domestic or foreign).

Intersegment sales. Transfers of products or services, similar to those sold to unaffiliated customers, between operating segments.

Major customer. A customer responsible for at least 10% of an enterprise's revenues.

Management approach. The method chosen by the FASB to determine what information should be reported; it is based on the way that management organizes the segments internally for making operating decisions and assessing performance.

Nonpublic enterprise. An enterprise other than one (1) whose debt or equity securities trade in a public market on a foreign or domestic stock exchange or in the over-the-counter market (including securities quoted only locally or regionally) or (2) that is required to file financial statements with the Securities and Exchange Commission. An enterprise is no longer considered a nonpublic enterprise when its financial statements are issued in preparation for the sale of any class of securities in a public market. Nonpublic enterprises include certain mutual associations, cooperatives, nonbusiness organizations, and partnerships that often make their financial statements available to a broad class, such as insurance policyholders, depositors, members, contributors, or partners.

Operating profit and loss test. One of the three 10% tests; used to determine reportability of operating segments.

Operating segment. A component of an enterprise which may earn revenues and incur expenses, about which separate financial information is available that is evaluated regularly by the chief operating decision maker in deciding how to allocate resources and in assessing performance.

Profit center. Those components of an enterprise that sell primarily to outside markets and for which information about revenue and profitability is accumulated. They are the smallest units of activity for which revenue and expense information is accumulated for internal planning and control purposes.

Reportable segments. Segments considered to be significant to an enterprise's operations; a segment that has passed one of three 10% tests or has been identified as being reportable through other criteria (e.g., aggregation, etc.).

Revenues test. One of three 10% tests; used to determine reportability of operating segments and major customers.

Segment assets. Those tangible and intangible assets directly associable or used by a segment, including any allocated portion of assets used jointly by more than one segment.

Segment operating profit or loss. All of a segment's revenue minus all operating expenses, including any allocated revenues or expenses (e.g., common costs).

Segment reporting. Disclosure of information about different components of an enterprise's operations as well as information related to the enterprise's products and services, its geographic areas, and its major customers.

Segment revenue. Revenue from sales to unaffiliated customers and from Intersegment sales or transfers.

75% test. A test used to determine whether the reportable segments of an enterprise represent a substantial portion of the enterprise's total operations.

Transfer pricing. The pricing of products or services between industry segments or geographic areas.

CONCEPTS, RULES, AND EXAMPLES

Applicability of SFAS 131

SFAS 131 applies to public business enterprises. The statement does not apply to not-for-profit organizations or to **nonpublic enterprises**. However, entities other than public business enterprises are encouraged to provide the disclosures described in SFAS 131.

Operating Segments

In SFAS 131, an **operating segment** is defined as

> *A component of an enterprise engaged in business activity for which it may earn revenues and incur expenses, about which separate financial information is available that is evaluated regularly by the **chief operating decision makers** in deciding how to allocate resources and in assessing performance.*

This general definition leaves it up to management's judgment to determine operating segment classifications. However, the FASB believes meaningful segment information will be provided in external **financial reports** because the externally reported segment information must conform with the segment information that is used internally. The FASB does provide standards to assist enterprises in determining which operating segments are reportable segments.

Reportable Segments

A segment is considered to be reportable if it is significant to the enterprise as a whole. A segment is to be regarded as significant if it satisfies **one** of the three quantitative **10% tests** described below.

Revenues test. Segment revenue (unaffiliated and intersegment) is at least 10% of the combined revenue (unaffiliated and intersegment) of all reported operating segments.

Operating profit and loss test. Segment operating profit (loss) is revenues minus operating expenses. Both revenues and operating expenses consist of unaffiliated and intersegment components. The absolute amount of segment operating profit or loss is at least 10% of the **greater**, in absolute amount, of

1. Combined operating **profits** of all operating segments reporting a profit.
2. Combined operating **losses** of all operating segments reporting a loss.

Assets test. Segment assets are at least 10% of combined assets of all operating segments. **Segment assets** are those assets used exclusively by the segment and any allocated portion of assets shared by two or more segments. Assets held for general corporate purposes are not assigned to segments.

Interperiod comparability must be considered in conjunction with the results of the 10% tests. If a segment fails to meet the tests, but has satisfied the tests in the past and is expected to in the future, it should be considered reportable in the current year for the sake of comparability. Similarly, if a segment which rarely passes the tests does so in the current year as the result of an unusual event, that segment may be excluded to preserve comparability.

After the 10% tests are completed, a **75% test** must be performed. The combined **unaffiliated** revenue of all **reportable** segments must be at least 75% of the combined unaffiliated revenue of all operating segments. If the 75% test is not satisfied, additional segments must be designated as reportable until the test is satisfied. The purpose of this test is to ensure that reportable segments account for a substantial portion of the entity's operations.

The following example illustrates the three 10% tests and the 75% test.

Segment	Unaffiliated revenue	Intersegment revenue	Total revenue	Operating profit (loss)	Assets
A	$ 90	$ 90	$ 180	$ 20	$ 70
B	120	0	120	10	50
C	110	20	130	(40)	90
D	200	0	200	0	140
E	330	110	440	(100)	230
F	380	0	380	60	260
Total	$1,230	$220	$1,450	$ (50)	$840

Revenues test: (10%)($1,450) = $145

Reportable segments: A, D, E, F

Operating profit or loss test: (10%)($140) = $14

Reportable segments: A, C, E, F

NOTE: Total operating loss ($140) is greater than total operating profit ($90).

Assets test: (10%)($840) = $84

Reportable segments: C, D, E, F

Reportable segments are those that pass **at least one** of the 10% tests.

Segments A, C, D, E, and F are reportable in this example.

75% test: (75%)($1,230) = $922.50

Segments A, C, D, E, and F have total unaffiliated revenue of $1,110, which is greater than $922.50. The 75% test is satisfied; no additional segments need be reported.

Certain other factors must be considered when identifying reportable segments. An enterprise may consider aggregating two or more operating segments if they have similar economic characteristics and if the segments are similar in each of the following areas:

1. The nature of the products and services
2. The nature of the production processes
3. The type of customer for their products and services
4. The methods used to distribute their products or provide their services
5. The nature of the regulatory environment (SFAS 131)

This aggregation can occur prior to performing the 10% tests if the enterprise desires.

Additionally, the enterprise may combine information on operating segments that do not meet any of the 10% tests to produce a reportable segment, but only if the segments meet a majority of the aggregation criteria discussed above. It should be noted that information about operating segments that do not meet any of the 10% thresholds may still be disclosed separately. By utilizing the aggregation criteria and quantitative thresholds (10% tests) for determining reportable segments, the statement uses a modified **management approach**.

However, the number of reportable segments should not be so great as to decrease the usefulness of segment reporting. As a rule of thumb, the FASB suggests that if the number of reportable segments exceeds ten, segment information may become too detailed. In this situation, the most closely related operating segments should be combined into broader reportable segments.

Accounting Issues

Since segment revenue as defined by SFAS 131 includes **intersegment sales**, **transfer pricing** becomes an issue. Rather than establishing a basis for setting transfer prices, the FASB requires companies to use the same transfer prices for segment reporting purposes as those used internally. Since most segments are organizational **profit centers**, internal transfer prices would generally reflect market prices.

Another issue in determining operating profit or loss is the allocation of **common costs.** Common costs are operating expenses incurred by the enterprise for the benefit of more than one operating segment. These costs should only be allocated to a segment for external reporting purposes if they are included in the measure of the segment's profit or loss that is used internally by the chief operating decision maker.

A problem can arise in distinguishing common costs from **general corporate expenses.** General corporate expenses are not operating expenses from the point of view of any operating segment; they are incurred for the benefit of the corporation as a whole and cannot be reasonably allocated to any operating segment.

Similarly, only those assets that are included internally in the measure of the segment's assets used to make operating decisions shall be reported as assets of the segment in external financial reports. If management does allocate amounts to segment profit or assets internally and those amounts are used by the chief operating decision maker, then those amounts shall be allocated on a reasonable basis and disclosed.

Segment Disclosures

SFAS 131 requires several disclosures regarding the enterprise's reportable segments. They include

1. **General information**—An explanation of how management identified the enterprise's reportable segments, including whether operating segments have been aggregated. Additionally, a description of the types of products and services from which each reportable segment derives its revenues.
2. **Certain information about reported segment profit and loss, segment assets and the basis of measurement**—This will include certain revenue and expense items included in segment profit and loss, as well as certain amounts related to the determination of segment assets. Also, the basis of measurement for these items must be disclosed.
3. **Reconciliations**—The enterprise will need to reconcile the segment amounts disclosed to the corresponding enterprise amounts.
4. **Interim period information**—Although the interim disclosures are not as extensive as in the annual financial report, certain segment disclosures are required in interim financial reports (SFAS 131).

See Appendix for an illustrative example of the disclosures required for segment reporting. Additionally, SFAS 131 provides an illustrative example.

Restatement of Previously Reported Segment Information

Segment reporting is required on a comparative basis. Therefore, the information must be restated to preserve comparability whenever the enterprise has changed the structure of its internal organization in a manner that causes a change to its reportable segments. The enterprise must explicitly disclose that it has restated the segment information of earlier periods.

Enterprise-Wide Disclosures about Products and Services, Geographic Areas, and Major Customers

The enterprise-wide disclosures are required for all enterprises subject to SFAS 131, even those that have a single reportable segment.

Products and services. Revenue from external customers for each product and service or each group of similar products and services shall be reported by the enterprise unless impracticable. If impracticable, that fact is to be disclosed. If the company's reportable segments have been organized around products and services, then this disclosure will generally not be required.

Geographic areas. An enterprise shall report revenues from external customers and long-lived assets attributable to its domestic operations and **foreign operations**. If the company's reportable segments have been organized around geographic areas, then these disclosures will generally not be required.

An enterprise's domestic operations are those operations located in the enterprise's home country that generate either unaffiliated or intra-enterprise revenues. The enterprise's foreign operations are similar operations located outside of the enterprise's home country.

If the enterprise functions in two or more foreign **geographic areas**, to the extent revenues or assets of an individual foreign geographic area are material, then these amounts should be separately disclosed. In addition, the enterprise's basis for attributing revenue to different geographic areas shall be disclosed. A geographic area is defined as an individual country. If providing this information is impracticable, that fact is to be disclosed.

Information about major customers. If an enterprise earns 10% or more of its revenue on sales to a single external customer, that fact and the amount of revenue from each such customer must be disclosed. Also, the segment making these sales must be disclosed. This disclosure provides information on concentrations of risk.

A group of customers under common control, such as subsidiaries of a parent, is regarded as a single customer. Similarly the various agencies of a government are considered to be a single customer. An insuring entity (such as Blue Cross) should not be considered the customer unless that entity (rather than the patient) controls the decision as to the doctor, type of service, etc.

EMERGING ISSUES TASK FORCE TOPIC SUMMARIES

Topic D-70   Questions Related to the Implementation of FASB Statement 131

The FASB staff addressed the following inquiries regarding the implementation of SFAS 131:

1. Depreciation and amortization expense is required to be disclosed for each reportable segment even if the chief operating decision maker uses earnings prior to taxes, depreciation, and amortization (EBITDA) to evaluate segment performance and receives reports that include each segment's depreciation and amortization separately from EBITDA.

2. Sometimes, in practice, the chief operating decision maker uses different measures of performance to evaluate different segments. The example is given that some segments may be evaluated based on operating income and others based on net income. In applying the 10% of operating profit test, a consistent method should be applied to all segments in making the deter-

mination of which are reportable segments. The FASB Staff pointed out, however, that the disclosures are still required to include the actual measure of profit or loss that the chief operating decision maker uses to evaluate the performance of each reportable segment.

FASB TECHNICAL BULLETINS

79-4 Segment Reporting of Puerto Rican Operations

Puerto Rican operations of U.S. enterprises are not considered to be foreign operations subject to the disclosure requirements of SFAS 131. However, such additional disclosures are not prohibited.

APPENDIX

COMPREHENSIVE ILLUSTRATION

The following illustration is provided for a hypothetical company called Resources Unlimited. The illustration provides segment disclosures by legal entity.

NOTE: An illustration in SFAS 131 provides segment disclosures by product line.

Description of the types of products and services from which each reportable segment derives its revenues

Resources Unlimited has four reportable segments: Wholesale Corporation, Retail Stores Corporation, Library Corporation, and Software Corporation. The Wholesale Corporation buys and resells used elementary and college textbooks. The Retail Stores Corporation operates 200 college book stores selling both new and used college textbooks, trade books, sports apparel, and other sundries. The Library Corporation sells library books primarily to elementary school libraries. Software Corporation develops and sells library system application software.

Measurement of segment profit or loss and segment assets

The accounting policies of the segments are the same as those described in the summary of significant accounting policies except the first-in-first-out (FIFO) method of inventory valuation is used. In addition, for segment reporting, Resources Unlimited allocates interest expense to each segment based on the segment's average borrowings from the corporate office. However, the related debt is not allocated to the segments and remains on the corporate books. Resources Unlimited evaluates performance based on profit or loss before income taxes not including nonrecurring gains and losses.

Resources Unlimited accounts for intersegment sales and transfers as if the sales or transfers were to third parties (i.e., at current market prices).

Factors management used to identify the enterprise's reportable segments

Resources Unlimited's business is conducted through four separate legal entities. At the company's inception, each entity was established by a different Resources Unlimited stockholder/family member. Each corporation is still managed separately, as each business has a distinct customer base and requires different strategic and marketing efforts.

Information about profit and loss and assets

The amounts in the illustration are assumed to be the amounts in reports used by the chief operating decision maker. Resources Unlimited does allocate interest expense to the segments, however income taxes and other unusual items are not allocated.

(Table in thousands)

	Wholesale Corporation	Retail Stores Corporation	Library Corporation	Software Corporation	Totals
Revenues from external customers	$197,500	$263,000	$182,300	$102,200	$745,000
Intersegment revenues	23,000	--	--	--	23,000
Interest revenue	250	150	--	--	400
Interest expense	1,570	2,150	1,390	2,700	7,810
Depreciation & amortization	8,600	13,100	7,180	6,070	34,950
Segment profit	12,100	13,500	9,900	5,100	40,600
Segment assets	121,200	153,350	100,600	85,000	460,150
Expenditures for segment assets	7,200	12,700	5,600	6,700	32,200

Reconciliations

Illustrations of reconciliations for revenues, profit and loss, assets, and other significant items are shown below. In general, this illustration assumes that there are no unreported operating segments, but there is a corporate headquarters, thus most reconciling items relate to corporate profit and loss accounts.

As discussed previously, the company recognizes and measures inventory based on FIFO valuation for segment reporting. The company's financials are assumed not to include discontinued operations or the cumulative effect of a change in accounting principle.

Revenue

Total revenues for reportable segments	$768,000
Elimination of intersegment revenue	(23,000)
Total consolidated revenue	$745,000

Profit and loss

Total profit and loss for reportable segments	$40,600
Elimination of intersegment profits	(6,100)
Unallocated amounts relating to corporate headquarters:	
Interest revenue	500
Interest expense	(800)
Depreciation and amortization	(1,900)
Unrealized gain on trading securities	1,865
Income before income taxes and extraordinary items	$34,165

Assets

Total assets for reportable segments	$460,150
Corporate short-term investments, land and building	25,100
Adjustment for LIFO reserve in consolidation	(9,200)
	$476,050

Other significant items

	Segment totals	Adjustments	Consolidated totals
Expenditures for segment assets	$32,200	800	$33,000

The reconciling adjustment is the amount of expenditures incurred for additions to the corporate headquarters building, which is not included in the segment information.

Products and services

Used textbooks	$296,125
New textbooks	72,150
Trade books	45,700
Sports Apparel	41,325
Sundries	5,200
Library books	182,300
Library software	102,200
Total consolidated revenue	$745,000

Geographic information

	Revenues*	Long-lived assets
United States	$687,400	$253,200
Foreign countries	57,600	18,800
Total	$745,000	$272,000

* *Revenues are attributed to countries based on the shopping location of customer*

Major customers

An illustration of the required disclosures is not provided in this example as Resources Unlimited has no major customers.

20 ACCOUNTING CHANGES AND CORRECTION OF ERRORS

PERSPECTIVE AND ISSUES

Financial statements are the results of choices among different accounting principles and methodologies. Companies select those principles and methods that they believe depict, in their financial statements, the economic reality of their financial position, results of operations, and cash flows. Changes take place because of changes in the assumptions and estimates underlying the application of these principles and methods, changes in the acceptable principles by a standards-setting authority, or other types of changes.

Accounting for and reporting of these changes is a problem that has faced the accounting profession for years. Much financial analysis is based on the consistency and comparability of annual financial statements. Any type of accounting change creates an inconsistency. Thus, a primary focus of management in making the decision to change should be to consider its effect on financial statement comparability. APB 20 was issued so accounting changes could be reported and disclosed in a manner that would improve analysis and understanding of the financial statements.

In APB 20 the Board defined an accounting change as being a change in

1. Accounting principle
2. Accounting estimate
3. Reporting entity

Even though the correction of an error in previously issued financial statements is not considered an accounting change, it is discussed in the opinion.

The Board concluded that in the preparation of the financial statements there is an underlying presumption that an accounting principle, once adopted, should not be changed in accounting for events and transactions of a similar type. This consistent use of accounting principles was believed to enhance the utility of the financial statements. The presumption that an entity should not change an accounting principle may be overcome only if the enterprise justifies the use of an alternative acceptable accounting principle on the basis that it is preferable.

APB 20 contained no definition of preferability or criteria by which to make such assessments. Because there was no universally agreed-upon set of objectives for external financial reporting, what was preferable to one industry or company was not necessarily considered preferable to another. This led to some of the same consistency problems in reporting that existed prior to the issuance of APB 20.

SAS 69 (discussed in Chapter 1, Researching GAAP Problems) requires an entity to adopt the accounting principles in pronouncements whose effective date is after March 15, 1992. An entity initially applying an accounting principle after that date (including those making an accounting change) must follow the applicable hierarchy set forth in SAS 69. An entity following an established accounting principle that was effective as of March 15, 1992, need not change its accounting until a new pronouncement is issued.

According to SFAS 111, an entity making a change in accounting principle to conform with the recommendations of a statement of position, a practice bulletin, or an EITF consensus should report the change as specified in the pronouncement. In the event the pronouncement does not specify a reporting manner, the entity should report the change in accounting principle according to the rules outlined in this chapter. However, EITF consensuses may be applied prospectively to future transactions unless otherwise stated.

Sources of GAAP		
APB	*SFAS*	*FASB I*
20, 28	3, 16, 111	1, 20

DEFINITIONS OF TERMS

Accounting change. Includes a change in (1) an accounting principle, (2) an accounting estimate, and (3) the reporting enterprise's corrections of errors in previously issued financial statements designated as a change in accounting principles.

Accounting principle. Encompasses not only accounting principles and practices but also methods of applying them.

Change in accounting estimate. A revision of an accounting measurement based on new events, additional experience, subsequent developments, better insight, and improved judgment. Such revisions are an inherent part of the accounting process.

Change in accounting principle. A switch from one generally accepted accounting principle to another generally accepted accounting principle, including the methods of applying these principles. This does not include selection of an accounting principle to account for events occurring for the first time.

Change in reporting entity. A special type of change in accounting principle that results in financial statements that, in effect, are those of a different reporting entity. Financial statements are prepared for an entity that is different from the one reported on in previous financial statements.

Comparability. The quality of information that enables users to identify similarities in and differences between two sets of economic phenomena. Normally, comparability is a quantitative assessment of a common characteristic.

Consistency. Conformity from period to period with unchanging policies and procedures. Enhances the utility of financial statements to users by facilitating analysis and understanding of comparative accounting data.

Cumulative effect. The difference between the beginning retained earnings balance of the year in which the change is reported and the beginning retained earnings balance that would have been reported if the new principle had been applied retroactively for all prior periods which would have been affected.

Error. Results from mathematical mistakes, mistakes in applying accounting principles, oversight or misuse of available facts, and use of unacceptable GAAP.

Pro forma. "As if" basis. Disclosure of the required numbers computed on the assumption that certain events have transpired.

Restatement of financial reports. The recasting of a previously determined and published balance sheet or operating statement and its republication where there has been a substantial change in accounting principles or policies.

CONCEPTS, RULES, AND EXAMPLES

APB 20 describes three ways of reporting accounting changes and the type of change for which each should be used. These are

1. Retroactively
2. Currently
3. Prospectively

Retroactive treatment requires an adjustment to all current and prior period financial statements for the effect of the accounting change. Prior period financial statements presented currently are to be restated on a basis consistent with the newly adopted principle.

Current treatment requires reporting the cumulative effect of the accounting change in the current year's income statement as a special item. Prior period financial statements are **not** restated.

Prospective treatment of accounting changes requires **no** restatement of prior financial statements and **no** computing or reporting of the accounting change's cumulative effect in the current period's income statement. Only current and/or future periods' financial statement data will reflect the accounting change.

Each of the types of accounting changes and the proper treatment prescribed for them is discussed in detail in the following sections.

Change in Accounting Principle

According to APB 20 the term "accounting principle" includes the accounting principles and practices used as well as the methods of applying them. FASB Interpretation 1 sets a base for the application of this statement by ruling that a change in the components used to cost a firm's inventory is a change in accounting principle. The Interpretation also stated that the preferability assessment must be made from the perspective of financial reporting and not from the income tax perspective. The Opinion indicates that changes in accounting principles should be accounted for currently using the cumulative effect method; however, there are a few specific exceptions to this general rule. One of these occurs when an authoritative body issues a new standard. The adoption of the standard will require accounting for the change as prescribed by the new pronouncement. Each new SFAS has its own transition rules. However, APB 20 requires that the cumulative effect method be used for most changes in accounting principles, and no restatement is to occur in the prior period financial statements.

The **cumulative effect** method is applied as follows:

1. Previously issued financial statements are **not** restated.
2. The cumulative effect of changing to the new accounting principle on the amount of retained earnings at the beginning of the period in which the change occurs should be included in the net income of the period of the change.
3. The effect of adopting the new principle on income before extraordinary items and net income, including per share amounts of the period of change, should be disclosed in the notes to the statements.
4. Income before extraordinary items and net income computed on a pro forma basis (defined below) should be shown on the face of the income statements for all periods presented as if the newly adopted principle had been applied during all periods affected. The nature of and justification for the change is to be disclosed in the financial statements in which the change is made.

According to the Board's conclusions, **income for the period of the change is to be computed using the newly adopted principle** while all other periods are to be presented as they originally appeared (step 1). **Restatement will occur only in the disclosures and the pro forma calculations.**

The cumulative effect of a change in accounting principle is to appear as a single amount on the income statement between extraordinary items and net income (step 2). The amount shown should be the difference between

1. The amount of retained earnings at the beginning of the period, and
2. The amount of retained earnings that would have been reported at that date if the new accounting principle had been applied retroactively to all prior periods affected.

The cumulative effect is generally determined by first calculating income before taxes for both the new principle and the old principle for all prior periods affected. Second, the difference between the two incomes for each prior period is determined. Third, these differences are adjusted for tax effects. Finally, the net of tax differences for each prior period are totaled. This total represents the cumulative effect adjustment at the beginning of the current period. The cumulative effect will either be an addition to or a subtraction from current income depending on how the change to the new principle affects income. Generally, only the direct effects of the change and the related income tax effect should be included in the cumulative effect calculation (i.e., if the company changes its method of computing depreciation, only the effects of the change in depreciation expense, net of tax, are considered to be direct effects). Indirect effects, such as the effect on a profit sharing contribution or bonus payments that would have occurred as a result of the change in net income, are not included in the cumulative effect computation unless these are to be recorded by the firm (i.e., the expense is actually incurred).

Step 3 requires that the effects of the change on income before extraordinary items and net income be disclosed for the year of the change. This is the difference between the old principle and the new principle on an after tax basis. The amount shall be disclosed for both the total effect and the per share amounts (for public companies). In addition, the nature of and justification for the change must be disclosed, clearly indicating why the newly adopted principle is preferable.

The computation of income on a pro forma basis must be made for each period currently presented. The objective is to present income before extraordinary items and net income as if the new principle were being applied. This is achieved by adjusting each period's income before extraordinary items as previously reported (i.e., applying the old principle). The adjustment is made by adding or subtracting the difference in income net of tax for the period to income before extraordinary items as previously reported. The difference, net of tax, is the change in income that occurs when the new principle is applied instead of the old principle. This results in an income before extraordinary items figure that reflects the application of the new principle. Net income is then calculated as normally done from the adjusted income before extraordinary items. The per share amounts required are based upon the pro forma income before extraordinary items and net income amounts.

The pro forma calculation required by step 4 differs from that of the cumulative effect. It is to include both the direct effects of the change and the "nondiscretionary" adjustments of items **based** on income before taxes or net income. Examples of nondiscretionary items would be profit sharing expense or certain royalties. Both of these expenses are in some way based on net income, generally as a specified percentage. The related tax effects should be recognized for **both** the direct and nondiscretionary adjustments. The pro forma calculation is to be shown on the face of the financial statements for income before extraordinary items and net income. The earnings per share amounts (both basic and diluted as defined in SFAS

128) for both should also be computed and shown for public companies. According to SFAS 128, if space is not available on the face of the financial statements, the pro forma information may be disclosed prominently in the notes to the financial statements.

The following example illustrates the computations and disclosures necessary when applying the cumulative effect method. This particular example is adapted from the one that is included in Appendix A of APB 20.

Example of cumulative effect

ABC Co. decides in 2002 to adopt the straight-line method of depreciation for plant equipment. The straight-line method will be used for all new acquisitions as well as for previously acquired plant equipment for which depreciation had been provided on an accelerated method.

The following assumptions are being made:

1. The direct effect of the change is limited to the change in accumulated depreciation.
2. The tax rate is a constant 40%.
3. The executive incentive bonus is the only nondiscretionary item affected by the change. It is 10% of the pretax accounting income.
4. There are 1,000,000 shares of common stock outstanding throughout the entire period affected by the change.
5. An additional 100,000 shares would be issued if all the outstanding bonds were converted. Annual interest on this bond obligation is $25,000 (net of tax).
6. For 2001 and 2002 the income before extraordinary item is given as $1,100,000 and $1,200,000 respectively. There is an extraordinary item in each year amounting to $100,000 for 2001 and ($35,000) for 2002. The extraordinary items are included to illustrate the proper positioning of the cumulative effect adjustment on the income statement.

Year	Excess of accelerated depreciation over straight-line depreciation	Direct effects of change, net of tax	Nondiscretionary item, net of tax	Adjustment to obtain pro forma amounts
Prior to 1998	$ 20,000	$ 12,000	$ 1,200	$ 10,800
1998	80,000	48,000	4,800	43,200
1999	70,000	42,000	4,200	37,800
2000	50,000	30,000	3,000	27,000
2001	30,000	18,000	1,800	16,200
Total at beg. of 2002	$250,000	$150,000	$15,000	$135,000

The following narrative provides assistance in grasping the computational aspects of the information given above. The "excess of...depreciation" is given in this example. It is generally determined by recomputing the depreciation under the new method and obtaining the difference between the two methods. The "direct...tax" represents the effect of the actual change (i.e., depreciation) upon income before extraordinary items adjusted for the tax effects. For example, in the years prior to 1998 the change in depreciation methods (from accelerated **to** straight-line) resulted in a $20,000 reduction in depreciation expense (or an increase in income). The net of tax number is $12,000 because the $20,000 increase in income is reduced by an $8,000 (40% x $20,000) increase in income tax expense.

The "nondiscretionary item, net of tax" represents the income statement items affected indirectly as a result of the change. In this case, it was given that the executive incentive bonus equal to 10% of pretax accounting income was the only "nondiscretionary item" affected. Thus, in years prior to 1998, when pretax accounting income increased by $20,000, the bonus expense would have been $2,000 higher ($20,000 x 10%). APB 20 indicates that this should also be computed net of tax, and because the expense would have increased by $2,000, the taxes would have decreased by $800 ($2,000 x 40%). The net of tax increase in expense is $1,200. The **pro forma** amounts are to include both the direct and indirect effects of the change. The computation for years prior to 1998 in this example is as follows:

	Increase (decrease) in net income
Reduction in depreciation expense	$20,000
Increase in taxes (depreciation)	(8,000)
Increase in compensation expense	(2,000)
Reduction in taxes (compensation)	800
	$10,800

The pro forma amount is needed for disclosure purposes so that 2001 income can be shown on a comparative basis with 2002 net income (i.e., adding the 2001 income before the change. The pro forma increase or decrease will result in an income figure that reflects the same accounting principles as the 2002 income figure).

Below are the necessary disclosures required by APB 20 for the aforementioned situation.

On the Face of the Income Statement

	2002	2001
Income before extraordinary item and cumulative effect of a change in accounting principle	$1,200,000	$1,100,000
Extraordinary item (description), net of tax	(35,000)	100,000
Cumulative effect on prior years (to December 31, 2001) of changing to a different depreciation method, net of tax	150,000	--
Net income	$1,315,000	$1,200,000
Per share amounts:		
Earnings per common share—assuming no dilution:		
Income before extraordinary item and cumulative effect of a change in accounting principle	$1.20	$1.10
Extraordinary item	(0.04)	0.10
Cumulative effect on prior years (to December 31, 2001) of changing to a different depreciation method	0.15	--
Net income	$1.31	$1.20

	2002	*2001*
Earnings per common share—assuming dilution:		
Income before extraordinary item and cumulative		
effect of a change in accounting principle	$1.11	$1.02
Extraordinary item	(0.03)	0.09
Cumulative effect on prior years (to December 31,		
2001) of changing to a different depreciation method	0.14	--
Net income	$1.22	$1.11
Pro forma amounts assuming the new depreciation method		
is applied retroactively:		
Income before extraordinary item and cumulative effect		
of a change in accounting principle	$1,200,000	$1,116,200
Earnings per common share—assuming no dilution	$1.20	$1.12
Earnings per common share—assuming dilution	$1.11	$1.01
Net income	$1,165,000	$1,216,200
Earnings per common share—assuming no dilution	$1.17	$1.22
Earnings per common share—assuming dilution	$1.08	$1.11

In the Notes to the Financial Statements

Note A: Change in Depreciation Method for Plant Equipment

During 2002 the company decided to change its method of computing depreciation on plant equipment from sum-of-the-years' digits (SYD) to the straight-line method. The company made the change because the straight-line method better matches revenues and cost amortization and, therefore, is a preferable accounting principle. The new method has been applied retroactively to equipment acquisitions of prior years. The effect of the change in 2002 was to increase income before extraordinary items by approximately $10,000 (or $.01 per share). The adjustment of $150,000 (net of $100,000 in taxes) included in 2002 income is the cumulative effect of applying the new method retroactively. The pro forma amounts shown on the income statement have been adjusted for the effect of the retroactive application of the new depreciation method, the change in the provisions for incentive compensation which would have been made had the new method been used, and the related income taxes for both.

If the company elected to disclose the pro forma amounts in notes to the financial statements and not on the face of the income statement, the following disclosure would have been included as part of Note A.

The following pro forma amounts show the effect of the retroactive application of the change from the SYD to straight-line method of depreciation.

	Actual	*Pro forma*
2002		
Income before extraordinary items	$1,200,000	$1,200,000
Basic earnings per share[*]	$1.20	$1.20
Diluted earnings per share[*]	$1.11	$1.11
Net income	$1,315,000	$1,165,000
Basic earnings per share	$1.31	$1.17
Diluted earnings per share	$1.22	$1.08

[*]*SFAS 128 uses these captions but allows for alternatives such as those above.*

2001

Income before extraordinary items	$1,100,000	$1,116,200
Basic earnings per share	$1.10	$1.12
Diluted earnings per share	$1.02	$1.01
Net income	$1,200,000	$1,216,200
Basic earnings per share	$1.20	$1.22
Diluted earnings per share	$1.11	$1.11

Notice how in the above example the four steps provided in APB 20 are followed:

Step 1 — No restatement takes place on the face of the income statements. The 2001 figures provided for comparative purposes are the same as those originally reported.

Step 2 — The cumulative effect of the change is included on the face of the income statement as a single amount. The $150,000 shown in 2002 represents the total direct effect net of tax for all years prior to 2002. The effect of the change in 2002 is included in the computation of operating income for 2002.

Step 3 — The required disclosure of the 2002 effects of the change, both in total and the per share amounts, is usually done in the notes to the financial statements. This is assumed to be $10,000 in the example above or $.01 per share.

Step 4 — The pro forma amounts are used to make the statements from the two years comparable. 2001 income before extraordinary items is increased by $16,200 to $1,116,200. This $16,200 is the amount found in the original table across from 2001. Notice also how the 2002 net income figure no longer contains a cumulative effect adjustment. This is because 2002 and 2001 earnings, under the pro forma computations, are derived using the same accounting principles.

As was mentioned earlier, there are several cases for which the APB (FASB) has determined that a change in accounting principle should be accounted for retroactively in the financial statements. There are five instances that require retroactive treatment.

1. Change from LIFO to another inventory method
2. A change in the method of accounting for long-term contracts
3. A change to or from the full cost method of accounting for exploration costs in the extractive industries
4. Any change made by a company first issuing financial statements for the purpose of obtaining additional equity capital, effecting a business combination, or registering securities
5. Any changes mandated by authoritative pronouncements (while this case is not specified by APB 20, the promulgating bodies have, in most instances, thus far required that the change be made retroactively). FASB Interpreta-

tion 20 has also indicated that an AICPA SOP may mandate the treatment given the change.

The process of restating the financial statements in these situations was favored because it did not require that the cumulative effect of the change be included in net income. Rather, each of the years presented is adjusted to reflect the new accounting principle. The cumulative effect is calculated in the same manner shown earlier for accounting changes receiving nonretroactive treatment. **The cumulative effect of all periods prior to such period presented is treated as an adjustment to beginning retained earnings of the period.** The net income of each period presented is recomputed applying the new principle. Thus, the adjustment to beginning retained earnings includes all income effects prior to each period presented, and the recomputed net income includes the effect of the new principle on income for each period presented. Together these two adjustments restate the retained earnings ending balance for each period presented to the amount it would have been had the new principle always been applied. This restatement process is consistently followed for all periods presented. According to APB 20, the nature of and justification for the change must be disclosed in the year that the change is made. In addition, the effect of the change on income before extraordinary items, net income, and the related per share amounts should be disclosed for all periods presented. Subsequent financial statements do not need to repeat the disclosures.

The restatement need only reflect the direct effects of the change in accounting principle. The exception to this statement arises if the direct effect results in a change in a nondiscretionary item that will be recorded on the books. For example, assume that profit-sharing expense is based on net income. The company changes its method of accounting for long-term construction contracts that results in an increase in income in all of the prior years. This increase in income would have changed the amount of the profit-sharing expense required during the applicable years. However, the expense would only be changed for the purpose of the restatement if it is to be paid. If the profit-sharing agreement does not require an adjustment to the actual contribution, the increase in profit-sharing expense would not be recognized on the restated financial statements.

The following illustration is an adaptation of Appendix B in APB 20 and illustrates the proper restatement in a situation where the company changes its method of accounting for long-term construction contracts. As mentioned above, this is one of the five situations for which APB 20 requires retroactive treatment.

Example of retroactive treatment

During 2002 XYZ Company decided to adopt the percentage-of-completion method in accounting for all of its long-term construction contracts. The company had used the completed contract method in previous years and had maintained records that were adequate to retroactively apply the percentage-of-completion method.

The following assumptions are made for this example:

1. A constant tax rate of 40%.

2. There are 1,000,000 common shares outstanding in all periods affected by the change.
3. An additional 100,000 shares would be issued if all of the outstanding bonds were converted. The annual interest on this bond obligation is $15,000 (net of tax).

| | Pretax accounting income | | Difference in income | |
| | Percentage-of-completion method | Completed-contract method | Direct | Net of tax effect |
Year				
Prior to 1998	$1,800,000	$1,300,000	$500,000	$300,000
1998	900,000	800,000	100,000	60,000
1999	700,000	1,000,000	(300,000)	(180,000)
2000	800,000	600,000	200,000	120,000
2001	1,000,000	1,100,000	(100,000)	(60,000)
Total at beg. of 2002	$5,200,000	$4,800,000	$400,000	$240,000
2002	1,100,000	900,000	200,000	120,000
Total	$6,300,000	$5,700,000	$600,000	$360,000

Following is the proper method of disclosing this type of change as prescribed by APB 20.

On the Face of the Income Statement

	2002	As adjusted see Note A 2001
Income before extraordinary item	$ 660,000	$ 600,000
Extraordinary item (description), net of tax	--	80,000)
Net income	$ 660,000	$ 520,000
Per share amounts:		
Basic earnings per common share:		
Income before extraordinary item	$.66	$.60
Extraordinary item	--	(.08)
Net income	$.66	$.52
Diluted earnings per common share:		
Income before extraordinary item	$.61	$.56
Extraordinary item	--	(.07)
Net income	$.61	$.49

On the Statement of Retained Earnings

	2002	As adjusted see Note A 2001
Balance at beginning of year, as previously reported		$17,330,000
Add adjustment for the cumulative effect on prior years of applying retroactively the new method of accounting for long-term contracts (Note A)		300,000*
Balance at beginning of year, as restated	$18,150,000	$17,630,000
Net income	660,000	520,000
Balance at end of year	$18,810,000	$18,150,000

* *This is the resultant amount of the change less the tax effect through 2000.*

In the Notes to the Financial Statements

Note A: Change in Method of Accounting for Long-term Construction Contracts

In 2002 the company changed its method of accounting for long-term construction contracts from the completed contract method to the percentage-of-completion method. The change was made because management believes that the new method results in a more accurate recognition of revenue and a better matching of revenue and costs. The financial statements of prior periods have been restated to apply the new method retroactively. The company will continue to use the completed contract method for income tax purposes. The effect of the accounting change in income of 2002 and on income previously reported for 2001 is

	Increase (decrease)	
	2002	*2001*
Effect on:		
Income before extraordinary item and net income	$120,000	$(60,000)
Basic earnings per common share	.12	(.06)
Diluted earnings per common share	.11	(.05)

The balance of beginning retained earnings at January 1, 2001, has been adjusted for the effect (net of income taxes) of retroactively applying the new method of accounting to years prior to 2001.

Notice that the income statement does not highlight the change. This lack of disclosure has been the major argument surrounding the use of this method. While both periods reflect the change in income resulting from the change, it is assumed that the average user of the financial statements may not refer to the notes in order to understand the change.

The only change shown "on" the financial statements is the cumulative effect adjustment that is part of the Statement of Retained Earnings. This amount is determined by totaling the effect of the change for all periods prior to the period presented in the financial statements and is reflected as an adjustment to the beginning balance of retained earnings.

The notes to the financial statements must disclose the nature of and reason for the change. In addition, the effect of the change on income before extraordinary items and net income including the related per share amounts (for public companies) should be disclosed for all of the years presented. In this case, the change for 2002 and 2001 is to increase (decrease) net income by $120,000 and ($60,000), respectively.

Cumulative effect not determinable. The Board also realized that there would be certain circumstances in which the pro forma amounts or the cumulative effect amount would not be available. If the pro forma amounts cannot be determined or reasonably estimated for the individual prior periods, the cumulative effect should be shown on the income statement and the reason for not showing the pro forma amounts disclosed in the notes to the financial statements. In an instance where the cumulative effect cannot be determined disclosure will be limited to showing the effect of the change on the results of operations for the period of the change (including per share data) and to explaining the reason for omitting accounting for the cumulative effect and disclosure of pro forma results. The Board specified the change from the FIFO to LIFO method of inventory pricing as one circumstance under which it would be impossible to determine the cumulative effect.

Example of change from FIFO to LIFO

During 2002 Ramirez, Inc. decided to change the method used for pricing its inventories from FIFO to LIFO. The inventory values are as listed below for both FIFO and LIFO cost. Sales for the year amounted to $15,000,000 and the company's total purchases were $11,000,000. Other expenses amounted to $1,200,000 for the year. The company had 1,000,000 shares of common stock outstanding throughout the year.

Inventory values

	FIFO	*LIFO*	*Difference*
12/31/01	$ 2,000,000	$2,000,000	$ --
12/31/02	4,000,000	1,800,000	2,200,000
Variation	$(2,000,000)	$ 200,000	(2,200,000)

The computations for 2002 would be as follows:

		FIFO	*LIFO*	*Difference*
Net income:				
	Sales	$15,000,000	$15,000,000	$ --
Less:	Cost of goods sold	9,000,000	11,200,000	(2,200,000)
	Gross margin	$ 6,000,000	$ 3,800,000	2,200,000
	Other expenses	1,200,000	1,200,000	--
	Net income	$ 4,800,000	$ 2,600,000	$2,200,000

The following footnote would be an example of the required disclosure in this circumstance:

Note A: Change in Method of Accounting for Inventories

During 2002, the company changed its method of accounting for all of its inventories from first-in, first-out (FIFO) to last-in, first-out (LIFO). The change was made because management believes that the LIFO method provides a better matching of costs and revenues. In addition, the adoption of LIFO conforms the company's inventory pricing policy to the one that is predominant in the industry. The change and its effect on net earnings ($000 omitted except for per share) and earnings per share for 2002 are as follows:

	Net earnings	*Earnings per share*
Net earnings before the change	$4,800	$4.80
Reduction of earnings by the change	2,200	2.20
Net earnings	$2,600	$2.60

There is no cumulative effect of the change on prior years because beginning inventory on January 1, 2002, at LIFO is the same as that which was reported on a FIFO basis at December 31, 2001. As a result of this change, the current period's financial statements are not comparable with those of any prior periods.

The current cost of inventories valued at LIFO exceeds the carrying amount by $2,200,000 at December 31, 2002.

Change in amortization method. Another special case in accounting for a change in principle takes place when a company chooses to change the systematic pattern of depreciating the costs of long-lived assets to expense. When a company adopts a new method of depreciation for newly acquired identifiable long-lived assets and uses that method for all new assets of the same class without changing the method used previously for existing assets of the same class, a change in accounting principle has not occurred. Obviously, there is no adjustment required to the financial statements or any cumulative-type adjustment. In these special cases, a description of the nature of the method changed and the effect on net income, income before extraordinary items, and related per share amounts (for public companies) should be disclosed in the period of the change. Should the new method be adopted for all assets, both old and new, then the change in accounting principle would be the usual one and would require a cumulative effect adjustment.

Reclassifications

Occasionally, a company will choose to change the way it applies an accounting principle that results in a change in the way that a particular financial statement caption is displayed or the individual accounts that comprise a caption. These **reclassifications** may occur for a variety of reasons that include

1. In management's judgment, the revised methodology more accurately reflects the economics of a type or class of transaction.
2. An amount that was immaterial in previous periods and combined with another number has become material and warrants presentation as a separate line item.
3. Due to changes in the business or the manner in which the financial statements are used to make decisions, management deems a different form of presentation to be preferable.

In order to maintain comparability of financial statements when such changes are made, the financial statements of all periods presented must be reclassified to conform to the new presentation.

Such reclassifications, which usually affect only the statement of income, do not affect reported net income or retained earnings for any period since they result in simply recasting amounts that were previously reported. Normally a reclassification will result in an increase in one or more reported numbers with a corresponding decrease in one or more other numbers. In addition, these changes reflect changes in the application of accounting principles either for which there are multiple alternative treatments, or for which GAAP is silent and thus management has discretion in presentation.

Reclassifications are not explicitly dealt with in GAAP but nevertheless occur in practice. The following examples are adapted from actual notes that appeared in the summary of significant accounting policies of publicly held companies:

Example 1

Beginning in 2002, amortization of goodwill, which was previously included as a component of cost of goods sold, is included in general and administrative expenses in the consolidated statement of income. Amounts reported for prior years have been reclassified to conform to the 2002 presentation.

Example 2

Effective January 1, 2002, management has elected to reclassify certain expenses in its consolidated statements of income. Costs of the order entry function and certain accounting and information services have been reclassified from cost of sales to selling, general, and administrative expense. Costs related to order fulfillment have been reclassified from selling, general, and administrative expense to cost of sales. These reclassifications resulted in a decrease to cost of sales and an increase to selling, general, and administrative expense of $31.8 million, and $36.2 million for the years ended December 31, 2001 and 2000, respectively.

Change in Accounting Estimate

The preparation of financial statements requires frequent use of estimates for such items as asset service lives, salvage values, collectibility of accounts receivable, warranty costs, pension costs, etc. These future conditions and events and their effects cannot be estimated with certainty. Therefore, changes in estimates will be inevitable as new information and more experience is obtained. APB 20 requires that changes in estimates be handled currently and prospectively. "The effect of the change in accounting estimate should be accounted for in (1) the period of change if the change affects that period only or (2) the period of change and future periods if the change affects both." For example, on January 1, 2002, a machine purchased for $10,000 was originally estimated to have a ten-year life and no salvage value. On January 1, 2007 (five years later), the asset is expected to last another ten years. As a result, both the current period and the subsequent periods are affected by the change. The annual depreciation charge over the remaining life would be computed as follows:

$$\frac{\text{Book value of asset} - \text{Salvage value}}{\text{Remaining useful life}} = \frac{\$5,000 - 0}{10 \text{ yrs}} = \$500/\text{yr.}$$

A permanent impairment affecting the cost recovery of an asset should not be handled as a change in accounting estimate but should be treated as a loss of the period. (See the discussion in Chapter 9, Long-Lived Assets.)

The Board concluded that a change in accounting estimate that is in essence effected by a change in accounting principle should be reported as a change in accounting estimate. The rationale is that the effect of the change in accounting principle is inseparable from the effect of the change in estimate. For example, a company may change from deferring and amortizing a cost to recording it as an expense when incurred because the future benefits of the cost have become doubtful. In this instance, the company is changing its accounting principle (from deferral to immediate recognition) because of its change in the estimate of the future value of a particular cost. The amount of the cumulative effect would be the same as that attributable to the current or future periods. Because the two are indistinguishable, changes of this type are to be considered changes in estimates according to APB 20. However, the change must be clearly indistinguishable to be combined. The ability to compute each element independently would preclude combining them as a single change. Also, under generally accepted auditing standards such a change is deemed a change in accounting principle for purposes of applying the consistency standard.

Change in Reporting Entity

An accounting change which results in financial statements that are, in effect, the statements of a different reporting entity should be reported by restating the financial statements of all prior periods presented in order to show financial information for the new reporting entity for all periods. The following qualify as changes in reporting entity:

1. Consolidated or combined statements in place of individual statements
2. Change in group of subsidiaries for which consolidated statements are prepared
3. Change in companies included in combined statements
4. Business combination accounted for as a pooling of interests

Correction of an Error

APB 20 and SFAS 16 govern the accounting for error corrections. APB 20 identifies examples of some errors and indicates that they are to be treated as prior period adjustments. SFAS 16 reiterates this treatment for accounting errors and provides guidance for the disclosing of prior period adjustments.

APB 20, identifies examples of errors as resulting from mathematical mistakes, mistakes in the application of accounting principles, or the oversight or misuse of facts known to the accountant at the time the financial statements were prepared. APB 20 also states that the change from an unacceptable (or incorrect) accounting principle to a correct principle **is** considered a correction of an error, not a change in accounting principle. This should not be confused with the preferability dilemma discussed earlier that involves two or more acceptable principles. While errors occur that affect both current and future periods, we are primarily concerned with the reporting of the correction of an error occurring in previously issued financial statements. Errors affecting current and future periods require correction but do not require disclosure as they are presumed to be discovered prior to the issuance of financial statements. According to APB 20, the correction of an error in the financial statements of a prior period discovered subsequent to their issuance should be reported as a prior period adjustment. The essential distinction between a change in estimate and the correction of an error depends upon the availability of information. An estimate requires correction because by its nature it is based upon incomplete information. Later data will either confirm or contradict the estimate and any contradiction will require correction. An error **misuses** existing information available at the time of the decision and is discovered at a later date. However, this discovery is not a result of additional information.

The required disclosure regarding the correction of an error is set forth by APB 20 and includes the nature of the error and the effect of its correction on income before extraordinary items, net income, and the related per share amounts (for public companies) in the period in which the error was discovered and corrected. This disclosure does not need to be repeated in subsequent periods.

The major criterion for determining whether or not to report the correction of the error is the materiality of the correction. According to APB 20, there are many factors to be considered in determining the materiality of the error correction. Materiality should be considered for each correction individually, as well as for all corrections in total. If the correction is determined to have a material effect on income before extraordinary items, net income, or the trend of earnings, it should be disclosed in accordance with the requirements set forth in the preceding paragraph.

Thus, the prior period adjustment should be presented in the financial statements as follows:

Retained earnings, 1/1/02, as previously reported	xxx
Correction of error (description) in prior period(s) (net of $___ tax)	xxx
Adjusted balance of retained earnings at 1/1/02	xxx
Net income	xxx
Retained earnings, 12/31/02	xxx

In comparative statements, prior period adjustments should also be shown as adjustments to the beginning balances in the retained earnings statements. The amount of the adjustment on the earliest statement shall be the cumulative effect of the error on periods prior to the earliest period presented.

Example of prior period adjustment

Assume that ABC Company had overstated its depreciation expense by $50,000 in 2001 and $40,000 in 2002, both due to mathematical mistakes. The errors that affected both the income statement and the tax return in 2001 and 2002 are found in 2003.

ABC Company's financial statements for 2003 and 2002 prior to any adjustments to reflect the correction of these errors were presented as follows:

	2003	2002
Retained earnings 1/1	$305,000	$250,000
Net income	90,000	80,000
	395,000	330,000
Dividends	45,000	25,000
Retained earnings, 12/31	$350,000	$305,000

The following prior period adjustment would be required in 2003 to correct the financial statements (assuming a 40% tax rate and ignoring the accrual of tax penalties and interest that would be due when amending the prior years' tax returns):

Accumulated depreciation	90,000	
Income taxes payable		36,000
Retained earnings		54,000

Assuming that we are presenting two-year comparative statements, the comparative statement of retained earnings would appear as follows (all figures other than corrections are assumed):

	2003	2002 Restated
Retained earnings, 1/1 (as previously reported)		$250,000
Adjustments (See Note 1)		30,000
Restated as of 1/1	$359,000	$280,000
Net income	90,000	104,000
	$449,000	$384,000
Dividends	45,000	25,000
Retained earnings, 12/31	$404,000	$359,000

Note 1: The balance of retained earnings at the beginning of 2002 has been restated from the balance previously reported to reflect an adjustment of $30,000 ($50,000 net of $20,000 tax) for an overstatement of depreciation expense in 2001. In addition, 2002 depreciation, as originally reported, was overstated by an additional $24,000 ($40,000 net of $16,000 tax). Consequently, net income for 2002 has been restated to reflect this $24,000 increase. The aggregate effect of the correction of both errors results in an increase of $54,000 ($90,000 net of $36,000 tax) to ending retained earnings at December 31, 2002.

Summary of Accounting for Accounting Changes and Error Correction

(See the following page.)

SUMMARY OF ACCOUNTING FOR ACCOUNTING CHANGES AND ERROR CORRECTION

	Reporting on financial statements						Recording in books	
	Footnote disclosures				Statement disclosures			
			Effect on income before x-items, NI, EPS					
Accounting Changes	Nature of item	Justification*	Current yr. only	All periods presented	Retroactive treatment; previous financial statements restated	Cumulative effect treatment: pro formas shown for all years	Direct dr./cr. to retained earnings	Cumulative tive effect account
In Principle								
General—change in principle or method of application from one acceptable GAAP to another. (Change from unacceptable GAAP is correction of error.)	x	x	x			x		x
Special								
• LIFO to another method	x	x		x	x		x	
• Change in method of accounting for long-term construction contracts.								
• Change to or from "full cost" method of accounting in the extractive industries.								
Special Exemptions for closely held corporation when it changes principles before its initial public offering.	x	x			x		x	
FASB Mandated	x			x	x		x	
Examples: equity method, R&D costs								
In Estimate**								
Natural occurrences because judgment is used in preparation of statements. New events, more experience, and additional information affect earlier good-faith estimates.	x			x***				
In Reporting Entity***								
Includes consolidated or combined statements in place of individual statements, change in group of subsidiaries for which consolidated statements are prepared, change in companies included in combined statements, and business combination accounted for as a pooling of interests.	x	x		x	x			
Reclassifications								
Changes in the method of displaying or aggregating amounts in the statement of income. No effect on net income.	x							
Error Correction								
Mathematical mistakes, mistakes in applying principles, oversight or misuse of available facts, change from unacceptable to acceptable GAAP.	x			x	x		x	

*Should clearly explain why the newly adopted accounting principle is preferable.

**Change in estimate effected by a change in principle is accounted for as a change in estimate.

***For **material** changes affecting more than just the current year.

APPENDIX
ACCOUNTING CHANGES IN INTERIM PERIODS

The relevant GAAP governing the treatment of accounting changes in interim periods is contained in APB 20, 28, and SFAS 3 (which provides clarification and examples). Of particular concern in SFAS 3 is the treatment to be accorded cumulative-effect-type accounting changes (including a change to LIFO for which no cumulative effect can be determined) and accounting changes made in the fourth quarter by publicly traded companies.

The treatment of a cumulative effect change in an interim period depends upon the quarter in which the change is made. If the cumulative-effect-type accounting change is made in the first quarter, then the cumulative effect on the beginning balance of retained earnings should be included in the net income of the first quarter. Again, the income for the first quarter of the current period is computed using the newly adopted method, and the cumulative effect of the change shall be shown on the income statement after extraordinary items and before net income. In accordance with APB 20, the comparative periods are not to be restated.

If the cumulative-effect-type accounting change is made in a period other than the first quarter, then no cumulative effect of the accounting change should be included in the net income of the period. Rather, the prechange interim periods of the year in which the change is made should be restated to reflect the newly adopted accounting principle. The cumulative effect on the beginning balance of retained earnings is then shown in the first interim period of the year in which the change is made. This includes any year-to-date or other financial statements that include the first interim period.

SFAS 3 requires that the following disclosures be made regarding a cumulative-effect-type accounting change in an interim period in addition to the treatment described above for the actual amount of the cumulative effect:

1. In the financial statements for the period in which the change is made, the nature and justification of the change
2. Disclosure of the effect of the change on income from continuing operations, net income, and related per share amounts for the interim period in which the change is made. If the change is made in other than the first interim period, then the disclosures should include the effect of the change on income from continuing operations, net income, and related per share amounts for each prechange interim period, and income from continuing operations, net income, and related per share amounts for each prechange interim period restated.
3. In the period in which the change is made, the pro forma amounts for income from continuing operations, net income, and the related per share amounts should be disclosed for

    a. The interim period in which the change is made

    b. Any interim periods of prior years for which financial information is presented

If no prior fiscal year information is presented, then disclosure should be made, in the period of the change, of the actual and pro forma amounts of income from continuing operations, net income, and related per share amounts for the interim period of the immediately preceding fiscal year that corresponds to the interim period in which the change is made. The pro forma amounts are to be calculated in accordance with APB 20 (discussed earlier).

4. The same disclosures described in 1. and 2. above shall be made regarding any year-to-date or last-twelve-months financial statements that include the period of the change.

5. For a postchange interim period (same fiscal year), disclosure shall be made of the effect of the change on income from continuing operations, net income, and the related per share amounts for the postchange period.

As mentioned earlier, a change to the LIFO method of pricing inventories generally results in a situation where the cumulative effect is not determinable. If such a change occurs in the first interim period, then the same disclosures described above for the cumulative-effect-type accounting change are required, with the exception of the pro forma amounts. If the change is made in a period other than the first interim period, the disclosures should include those mentioned above **and** restatement of the financial information presented for prechange interim periods of that year reflecting the adoption of the new accounting principle.

The following examples will illustrate the foregoing principles relative to a cumulative-effect-type accounting change made in both the first interim period and other than the first period. The same facts and assumptions are used for both examples.

Example of accounting change in first interim period

In 2002, ABC Company decided to adopt the straight-line method of depreciation for plant equipment. The new method was to be used for both new acquisitions and previously acquired plant equipment. In prior periods, the company had used an accelerated method of computing depreciation on plant equipment. The following assumptions are made:

1. The effects of the change are limited to the direct effect on depreciation and the indirect effect on the incentive compensation, as well as the related tax effects.
2. The incentive compensation is 10% of pretax accounting income.
3. There is a constant tax rate of 50%.
4. There were 1,000,000 shares of common stock issued and outstanding throughout the periods covered, with no potential for dilution.
5. The company presents comparative interim statements.
6. Assume that the following information is given for years 2001 and 2002:

	Net income on the basis of old accounting principle (accelerated depreciation)	Gross effect of change to straight-line depreciation	Gross effect less income taxes	Net effect after incentive compensation and related income taxes
Prior to first qtr. 2001		$ 20,000	$ 10,000	$ 9,000
First quarter 2001	$1,000,000	30,000	15,000	13,500
Second quarter 2001	1,200,000	70,000	35,000	31,500
Third quarter 2001	1,100,000	50,000	25,000	22,500
First nine months, 2001	3,300,000	150,000	75,000	67,500
Fourth quarter 2001	1,100,000	80,000	40,000	36,000
Total at beg. of 2002	$4,400,000	$250,000	$125,000	$112,500
First quarter 2002	$1,059,500*	$ 90,000	$ 45,000	$ 40,500*
Second quarter 2002	1,255,000	100,000	50,000	45,000
Third quarter 2002	1,150,500	110,000	55,000	49,500
First nine months, 2002	3,465,000	300,000	150,000	135,000
Fourth quarter 2002	1,146,000	120,000	60,000	54,000
	$4,611,000	$420,000	$210,000	$189,000

*The net income for 2002 has been broken down into income based on the old accounting principle and the effect of the change. These numbers are unrealistic in the sense that the 2002 income figure would be computed based on the new principle (e.g., the first quarter net income is $1,100,000, which is $1,059,500 + 40,500).

The first example applies the SFAS 3 criteria applicable to a change made in the first quarter. In interim reporting the same principles are followed that apply to annual financial reporting. The cumulative effect is considered to be a change in the beginning balance of retained earnings and, therefore, effective at the beginning of the year. To include the cumulative effect in any interim period other than the first, or year-to-date including the first, would be misleading. In this case we are dealing with the first period, and the $125,000, representing the direct effects net of tax, is presented on the face of the income statement. As with the annual reporting, the pro forma amounts reflecting the direct and indirect effects of the change are also presented. In this case the 2002 number already reflects the change, and from the given information we can see that the total effect on the first quarter of 2001 was to increase net income by $13,500.

The notes, as required, state the nature and justification of the change. Also included in the notes are the total cumulative effect, the effect on the earnings of the first quarter of the year in which the change is made (this disclosure makes allowable a comparison between statements), and the nature of the pro forma amounts. Essentially, if the change is made in the first quarter, the reporting and disclosure requirements are very similar to those in the annual financial statements.

The following quarterly financial statements and note illustrate the foregoing principles:

	Three months ended March 31,	
	2002	2001
Income before cumulative effect of a change in accounting principle	$1,100,000	$1,000,000
Cumulative effect on prior years (to December 31, 2001) of changing to a different depreciation method (Note A)	125,000	--
Net income	$1,225,000	$1,000,000
Amounts per common share:		
Income before cumulative effect of a change in accounting principle	$1.10	$1.00
Cumulative effect on prior years (to December 31, 2001) of changing to a different depreciation method (Note A)	0.13	--
Net income	$1.23	$1.00
Pro forma amounts assuming the new depreciation method is applied retroactively (Note A):		
Net income	$1,100,000	$1,013,500
Net income per common share	$1.10	$1.01

Note A: Change in Depreciation Method for Plant Equipment

During the first quarter of 2002, the company decided to change the method of computing depreciation on plant assets from the accelerated method used in previous periods to the straight-line method. The change was made to better match the depreciated cost of the asset to the revenue produced by it. The retroactive application of the new method resulted in a cumulative effect of $125,000 (net of $125,000 in income taxes) that is included in the income for the first quarter of 2002. The effect of the change on the first quarter of 2002 was to increase income before cumulative effect of a change in accounting principle by $40,500 ($.04 per share) and net income by $165,500* ($.17 per share). The pro forma amounts reflect the effect of retroactive application on depreciation, the change in provisions for incentive compensation that would have been made in 2001 had the new method been in effect, and the related income taxes.

The sum of the first quarter effect of $40,500 and the cumulative effect of $125,000.

Example of accounting change in other than first interim period

In this case, the change is made in the third quarter of the year and the company is presenting comparative financial information for both the current quarter and year-to-date. The cumulative effect is not presented in the period of the change because it relates to the beginning of the year. Thus, in the illustration below the three months ended September 30 do not include an amount for the cumulative effect; however, the nine-month statements do. The presentation of the three-month statements reflects the effect of the accounting change for 2002 and does not reflect this change for 2001. The 2001 statement is the same as it was presented in the prior year. The pro forma amounts and the disclosure in the notes provide the information necessary to make these two interim periods comparable.

The nine-month statement for 2002 reflects the effect of the change for the entire nine-month period. Thus, the results of the six-month period for 2002 added to the three-month results would not equal the amounts shown in the nine-month statement. This is because the prior statement for the six-month period would not have reflected the new principle that the three-month and nine-month figures do. Again, the 2001 numbers are presented as they were in the previous year. The remainder of the example is really no different from the disclosure required by another accounting change, with one exception. The exception is that the effect of the change on the preceding interim periods must also be disclosed. Note that the cumulative effect is included in the first period. The total of the three individual quarters will now equal the total income shown in the nine-month statement.

	Three months ended September 30,		Nine months ended September 30,	
	2002	*2001*	*2002*	*2001*
Income before cumulative effect of a change in accounting principle	$1,200,000*	$1,100,000	$3,600,000**	$3,300,000
Cumulative effect on prior years (to December 31, 2001) of changing to a different depreciation method (Note A)	--	--	125,000	--
Net income	$1,200,000	$1,100,000	$3,725,000	$3,300,000
Amounts per common share:				
Income before cumulative effect of a change in accounting principle	$1.20	$1.10	$3.60	$3.30
Cumulative effect on prior years (to December 31, 2001) of changing to a different depreciation method (Note A)	--	--	0.13	--
Net income	$1.20	$1.10	$3.73	$3.30
Pro forma amounts assuming the new depreciation method is applied retroactively (Note A):				
Net income	$1,200,000	$1,122,500	$3,600,000	$3,367,500
Net income per common share	$1.20	$1.12	$3.60	$3.37

*Computed as the $1,150,500 net income based on the old accounting principle plus the $49,500 net effect of the change after incentive compensation and related income taxes.

**Computed as the $3,465,000 net income based on the old accounting principle plus the $135,000 net effect of the change after incentive compensation and related income taxes.

Note A: Change in Depreciation Method for Plant Equipment

During the third quarter of 2002, the company decided to change the method of computing depreciation on plant assets from the accelerated method used in previous periods to the straight-line method. The change was made to better match the depreciated cost of the asset to the revenue produced by it. The retroactive application of the new method resulted in a cumulative effect of $125,000 (net of $125,000 in income taxes) which is included in the income for the nine months ended September 30, 2002. The effect of the change on the three months ended September 30, 2002, was to increase net income by $49,500 ($.05 per share); the effect of the change on the nine months ended September 30, 2002, was to increase income before cumulative effect of a change in accounting principle by $135,000 ($.14 per share) and net income by $260,000 ($.26 per share).*** The pro forma amounts reflect the effect of retroactive application on depreciation, the change in the provisions for incentive pay that would have been made in 2001 had the new method been in effect, and the related income taxes.

***The sum of the $125,000 cumulative effect and the $135,000 nine months' effect.

The effect of the change on the first and second quarters of 2002 is as follows:

	Three months ended	
	March 31, 2002	*June 30, 2002*
Net income as originally reported	$1,059,500	$1,255,000
Effect of change in depreciation method	40,500	45,000
Income before cumulative effect of a change in accounting principle	1,100,000	1,300,000
Cumulative effect on prior years (to December 31, 2001) of changing to a different depreciation method	125,000	--
Net income as restated	$1,255,000	$1,300,000
Per share amounts:		
Net income as originally reported	$1.06	$1.26
Effect of change in depreciation method	0.04	0.04
Income before cumulative effect of a change in accounting principle	1.10	1.30
Cumulative effect on prior years (to December 31, 2001) of changing to a different depreciation method	0.13	--
Net income as restated	$1.23	$1.30

21 FOREIGN CURRENCY

PERSPECTIVE AND ISSUES

Since World War II, international activity by US corporations has increased significantly. Not only are transactions consummated with independent foreign entities, but also with foreign subsidiaries of US firms. In order for the users of these firms' financial statements to properly analyze the foreign involvement, the transactions entered into must be expressed in terms the users can understand (i.e., US dollars). The generally accepted accounting principles governing the translation of foreign currency financial statements and foreign currency transactions into US dollars are found primarily in SFAS 52. Additional guidance in this area is provided by FASB Interpretation 37. These principles apply to the translation of

1. Foreign currency transactions (e.g., exports, imports, and loans) which are denominated in other than a company's functional currency
2. Foreign currency financial statements of branches, divisions, subsidiaries, and other investees which are incorporated in the financial statements of a US company by combination, consolidation, or the equity method

The objectives of translation are to provide

1. Information relative to the expected economic effects of rate changes on an enterprise's cash flows and equity
2. Information in consolidated statements relative to the financial results and relationships of each individual foreign consolidated entity as reflected by the functional currency of each reporting entity

Companies use hedging strategies to attempt to manage their risk and minimize their exposure to fluctuations in the exchange rates of foreign currencies. Hedge accounting under SFAS 133 is covered at the end of this chapter.

Sources of GAAP		
SFAS	*FASB I*	*EITF*
52, 133	37	91-1, 92-4, 92-8, 93-9, 95-2,
		D-12, D-16, D-55, D-56, D-71

DEFINITIONS OF TERMS

Conversion. The exchange of one currency for another.

Current exchange rate. The rate at which one unit of a currency can be exchanged for (converted into) another currency. For purposes of translation of financial statements referred to in SFAS 52, the current exchange rate is the rate as of the end of the period covered by the financial statements or as of the dates of recognition in those statements in the case of revenues, expenses, gains, and losses.

Discount or premium on a forward contract. The foreign currency amount of the contract multiplied by the difference between the contracted forward rate and the spot rate at the date of inception of the contract.

Foreign currency. A currency other than the functional currency of the entity being referred to (for example, the dollar could be a foreign currency for a foreign entity). Composites of currencies, such as the Special Drawing Rights on the International Monetary Fund (SDR), used to set prices or denominate amounts of loans, etc., have the characteristics of foreign currency for purposes of applying SFAS 52.

Foreign currency statements. Financial statements that employ as the unit of measure a functional currency that is not the reporting currency of the enterprise.

Foreign currency transactions. Transactions whose terms are denominated in a currency other than the entity's functional currency. Foreign currency transactions arise when an enterprise (1) buys or sells goods or services on credit whose prices are denominated in foreign currency, (2) borrows or lends funds and the amounts payable or receivable are denominated in foreign currency, (3) is a party to an unperformed forward exchange contract, or (4) for other reasons, acquires or disposes of assets or incurs or settles liabilities denominated in foreign currency.

Foreign currency translation. The process of expressing in the reporting currency of the enterprise those amounts that are denominated or measured in a different currency.

Forward exchange contract. An agreement to exchange at a specified future date currencies of different countries at a specified rate (forward rate).

Functional currency. The currency of the primary economic environment in which the entity operates; normally, that is the currency of the environment in which an entity primarily generates and expends cash.

Local currency. The currency of a particular country being referred to.

Monetary items. Cash, claims to receive a fixed amount of cash, and obligations to pay a fixed amount of cash.

Nonmonetary items. All balance sheet items other than cash, claims to cash, and cash obligations.

Remeasurement. If an entity's books and records are not kept in its functional currency, remeasurement into the functional currency is required. Monetary balances are translated by using the current exchange rate, and nonmonetary balances are translated by using historical exchange rates.

Reporting currency. The currency in which an enterprise prepares its financial statements.

Reporting enterprise. An entity or group of entities whose financial statements are being referred to. For the purposes of this discussion, those financial statements reflect (1) the financial statements of one or more foreign operations by combination, consolidation, or equity method accounting; (2) foreign currency transactions; or (3) both of the foregoing.

Spot rate. The exchange rate for immediate delivery of currencies exchanged.

Transaction date. The date at which a transaction (for example, a sale or purchase of merchandise or services) is recorded in accounting records in conformity with generally accepted accounting principles. A long-term commitment may have more than one transaction date (for example, the due date of each progress payment under a construction contract is an anticipated transaction date).

Transaction gain or loss. Transaction gains or losses result from a change in exchange rates between the functional currency and the currency in which a foreign currency transaction is denominated. They represent an increase or decrease in (1) the actual functional currency cash flows realized upon settlement of foreign currency transactions and (2) the expected functional currency cash flows on unsettled foreign currency transactions.

Translation adjustments. Translation adjustments result from the process of translating financial statements from the entity's functional currency into the reporting currency.

CONCEPTS, RULES, AND EXAMPLES

Translation of Foreign Currency Financial Statements

Selection of the functional currency. Before the financial statements of a foreign branch, division, or subsidiary are translated into US dollars, the management of the US company must make a decision as to which currency is the **functional currency** of the foreign entity. Once chosen, the functional currency cannot be changed unless it is clear that economic facts and circumstances have changed. Additionally, previously issued financial statements are not restated for any changes in the functional currency. The functional currency decision is crucial because different translation methods are applied which may have a material effect on the US company's financial statements.

The Financial Accounting Standards Board defines functional currency but does not list definitive criteria that, if satisfied, would result in the selection of an entity's functional currency. Rather, realizing that such criteria did not exist, the Board listed various factors that were intended to give management guidance in making the functional currency decision. These factors include

1. Cash flows (Do the foreign entity's cash flows directly affect the parent's cash flows and are they immediately available for remittance to the parent?)
2. Sales prices (Are the foreign entity's sales prices responsive to exchange rate changes and to international competition?)
3. Sales markets (Is the foreign entity's sales market the parent's country or are sales denominated in the parent's currency?)
4. Expenses (Are the foreign entity's expenses incurred primarily in the parent's country?)
5. Financing (Is the foreign entity's financing primarily from the parent or is it denominated in the parent's currency?)
6. Intercompany transactions (Is there a high volume of intercompany transactions between the parent and the foreign entity?)

If the answers to the questions above are predominantly yes, the functional currency is the **reporting currency** of the parent company (i.e., the US dollar). If the answers are predominantly no, the functional currency would most likely be the **local currency** of the foreign entity, although it is possible for a foreign currency other than the local currency to be the functional currency.

Translation methods. The Board chose the following two methods to translate a company's foreign subsidiary's accounts into US dollars. The primary distinction between the methods was the classification of assets and liabilities (and their corresponding income statement amounts) that would be translated at either the current or historical exchange rate.

The first method is known as the **current rate method** and is the approach mandated by SFAS 52 when the functional currency is the **foreign currency**. All assets and liabilities are translated at the current rate. The stockholders''equity accounts are translated at the appropriate historical rate. And those revenues and expenses that occur evenly over the year may be translated at the weighted-average rate for the year. The basis of this method is the "net investment concept" wherein the foreign entity is viewed as a separate entity in which the parent invested, rather than it being considered as part of the parent's operations. The Board's reasoning was that users can benefit most when the information provided about the foreign entity retains the relationships and results created in the environment (economic, legal, and political) in which the entity operates.

Under this approach, the reasoning follows that foreign-denominated debt is used to purchase assets that create foreign-denominated revenues. These assets act as a hedge against changes in the settlement amount of the debt due to changes in the exchange rate. The excess (net) assets will, however, be affected by this foreign exchange risk, and this is the effect which is recognized by the parent.

The second method is the **remeasurement method**, which is sometimes referred to as the **monetary/nonmonetary method**. This is the approach required by SFAS 52 when the foreign entity's books and records are not maintained in the functional currency (e.g., when the US dollar is designated as the functional currency for a Brazilian subsidiary). This method translates monetary assets (cash and other assets and liabilities that will be settled in cash) at the current rate. Nonmonetary assets, liabilities, and stockholders' equity are translated at the appropriate historical rate. The appropriate historical rate would be the exchange rate at the date the transaction in the nonmonetary account originated. Also, the income statement amounts related to nonmonetary assets and liabilities, such as cost of goods sold (inventory), depreciation (property, plant, and equipment), and goodwill amortization (goodwill), are translated at the same rate as used for the balance sheet translation. Other revenues and expenses occurring evenly over the year may be translated at the weighted-average exchange rate for the period.

If the foreign entity's local currency is the functional currency, the Board requires the current rate method when translating the foreign entity's financial statements. If, on the other hand, the US dollar is the functional currency, the Board requires the remeasurement method when translating the foreign entity's financial statements. Both of these methods will be illustrated below. All amounts in the following two illustrations, other than exchange rates, are in thousands, but the trailing zeros have been dropped in order to focus on the concepts.

Application of the Current Rate Method

Assume that a US company has a 100% owned subsidiary in Germany that commenced operations in 2001. The subsidiary's operations consist of leasing space in an office building. This building, which cost 500 deutsche marks (DM), was financed primarily by German banks. All revenues and cash expenses are received and paid in deutsche marks. The subsidiary also maintains its books and records in DM. As a result, management of the US company has decided that the DM is the functional currency of the subsidiary.

The subsidiary's balance sheet at December 31, 2001, and its combined statement of income and retained earnings for the year ended December 31, 2001, are presented below in DM.

German Company
Balance Sheet
At December 31, 2001

Assets			*Liabilities and Stockholders' Equity*		
Cash	DM	50	Accounts payable	DM	30
Accounts receivable		20	Unearned rent		10
Land		100	Mortgage payable		400
Building		500	Common stock		40
Accumulated depreciation		(10)	Additional paid-in capital		160
			Retained earnings		20
			Total liabilities and		
Total assets	DM	660	stockholders' equity	DM	660

German Company
Statement of Income and Retained Earnings
For the Year Ended December 31, 2001

Revenues		DM 200
Operating expenses (including depreciation expense of DM 10)		170
Net income		DM 30
Add retained earnings, January 1, 2001		--
Deduct dividends declared		(10)
Retained earnings, December 31, 2001		DM 20

Various exchange rates for 2001 are as follows:

DM 1 = $.40 at the beginning of 2001 (when the common stock was issued and the land and building were financed through the mortgage)

DM 1 = $.43 weighted-average for 2001

DM 1 = $.42 at the date the dividends were declared and the unearned rent was received

DM 1 = $.45 at the end of 2001

Since the DM is the functional currency, the German Company's financial statements must be translated into US dollars by the **current rate method**. This translation process is illustrated below.

German Company
Balance Sheet Translation
(DM is the functional currency)
At December 31, 2001

Assets	*DM*	*Exchange rate*	*US dollars*
Cash	DM 50	.45	$ 22.50
Accounts receivable	20	.45	9.00
Land	100	.45	45.00
Building (net)	490	.45	220.50
Total assets	DM 660		$297.00
Liabilities and Stockholders' Equity			
Accounts payable	DM 30	.45	$ 13.50
Unearned rent	10	.45	4.50
Mortgage payable	400	.45	180.00
Common stock	40	.40	16.00
Additional paid-in capital	160	.40	64.00
Retained earnings	20	See income statement	8.70
Translation adjustments	--		--
Total liabilities and stockholders' equity	DM 660		$297.00

German Company
Statement of Income and Retained Earnings
Statement Translation
For the Year Ended December 31, 2001

	DM	*Exchange rate*	*US dollars*
Revenues	DM 200	.43	$86.00
Expenses (including DM 10 depreciation expense)	170	.43	73.10
Net income	DM 30	.43	$12.90
Add retained earnings, January 1	--	--	--
Deduct dividends declared	(10)	.42	(4.20)
Retained earnings, December 31	DM 20		$ 8.70

German Company
Statement of Cash Flows
For the Year Ended December 31, 2001

	DM	*Exchange rate*	*US dollars*
Operating activities			
Net income	DM 30	.43	$ 12.90
Adjustments to reconcile net income to net cash provided by operating activities:			
Depreciation	10	.43	4.30
Increase in accounts receivable	(20)	.43	(8.60)
Increase in accounts payable	30	.43	12.90
Increase in unearned rent	10	.42	4.20
Net cash provided by operating activities	DM 60		$ 25.70
Investing activities			
Purchase of land	(100)	.40	(40.00)
Purchase of building	(500)	.40	(200.00)
Net cash used by investing activities	DM (600)		$(240.00)
Financing activities			
Common stock issue	200	.40	80.00
Mortgage payable	400	.40	160.00
Dividends	(10)	.42	(4.20)
Net cash provided by financing activities	DM 590		$ 235.80
Effect of exchange rate changes on cash	N/A		1.00
Increase in cash and equivalents	DM 50		$ 22.50
Cash at beginning of year	0		0
Cash at end of year	DM 50	.45	$ 22.50

The following points should be noted concerning the current rate method:

1. All **assets and liabilities** are translated using the **current exchange rate** at the balance sheet date (DM 1 = $.45). All revenues and expenses should be translated at the rates in effect when these items are recognized during the period. Due to practical considerations, however, weighted-average rates can be used to translate revenues and expenses (DM 1 = $.43).

2. **Stockholders' equity** accounts are translated by using historical exchange rates. Common stock was issued at the beginning of 2001 when the exchange rate was DM 1 = $.40. The translated balance of retained earnings is the result of the weighted-average rate applied to revenues and expenses and the specific rate in effect when the dividends were declared (DM 1 = $.42).

3. **Translation adjustments** result from translating all assets and liabilities at the current rate, while stockholders' equity is translated by using historical and weighted-average rates. The adjustments have no direct effect on cash flows. Also, the translation adjustment is due to the net investment rather than the subsidiary's operations. For these reasons, the cumulative translation adjustments balance is reported as a component of accumulated other comprehensive income (AOCI) in the stockholders' equity section of the US parent company's consolidated balance sheet. This balance essentially equates the total debits of the subsidiary (now expressed in US dollars) with the total credits (also in dollars). It also may be determined directly, as shown next, to verify the translation process.

4. The translation adjustments credit of $10.30 is calculated as follows for the differences between the exchange rate of $.45 at the end of the year and the applicable exchange rate at the time of the change in net assets:

Net assets at the beginning of 2001 (after common stock was issued and the land and building were acquired through mortgage financing)	DM 200 ($.45 – $.40) =	$10.00 credit
Net income	DM 30 ($.45 – $.43) =	.60 credit
Dividends declared	DM 10 ($.45 – $.42) =	.30 debit
Translation adjustment		$10.30 credit

5. The translation adjustments balance that appears as a component of AOCI in the stockholders' equity section is cumulative in nature. Consequently, the change in this balance during the year should be disclosed as a component of other comprehensive income (OCI) for the period. In the illustration, this balance went from zero to $10.30 at the end of 2001. The financial statement presentation of other comprehensive income is covered in Chapter 3, Statements of Income and Comprehensive Income. In addition, assume the following occurred during 2002:

German Company
Balance Sheet
At December 31

Assets	*2002*		*2001*		*Increase/(Decrease)*	
Cash	DM	100	DM	50	DM	50
Accounts receivable		--		20		(20)
Land		150		100		50
Building (net)		480		490		(10)
Total assets	DM	730	DM	660	DM	70

Liabilities and Stockholders' Equity

Accounts payable	DM	50	DM	30	DM	20
Unearned rent		0		10		(10)
Mortgage payable		450		400		50
Common stock		40		40		0
Additional paid-in capital		160		160		0
Retained earnings		30		20		10
Total liabilities and stockholders' equity	DM	730	DM	660	DM	70

German Company
Statement of Income and Retained Earnings
For the Year Ended December 31, 2002

Revenues	DM	220
Operating expenses (including depreciation exp. of DM 10)		170
Net income	DM	50
Add: Retained earnings, Jan. 1, 2002		20
Less: Dividends declared		(40)
Retained earnings, Dec. 31, 2002	DM	30

Exchange rates were:

DM 1 = $.45 at the beginning of 2002
DM 1 = $.48 weighted-average for 2002
DM 1 = $.50 at the end of 2002
DM 1 = $.49 when dividends were declared in 2002 and additional land bought by incurring mortgage

The translation process for 2002 is illustrated below.

German Company
Balance Sheet Translation
(DM is the functional currency)
At December 31, 2002

Assets	*DM*		*Exchange rate*	*US dollars*
Cash	DM	100	.50	$ 50.00
Land		150	.50	75.00
Building		480	.50	240.00
Total assets	DM	730		$365.00
Liabilities and Stockholders' Equity				
Accounts payable	DM	50	.50	$ 25.00
Mortgage payable		450	.50	225.00
Common stock		40	.40	16.00
Addl. paid-in capital		160	.40	64.00
Retained earnings		30	(see income statement)	13.10
Translation adjustments		--		21.90
Total liabilities and stockholders' equity	DM	730		$365.00

German Company
Statement of Income and Retained Earnings
Statement Translation
For the Year Ended December 31, 2002

	DM	Exchange rate	US dollars
Revenues	DM 220	.48	$105.60
Operating expenses (including depreciation of DM 10)	170	.48	81.60
Net income	DM 50	.48	$ 24.00
Add: Retained earnings, 1/1/01	20	--	8.70
Less: Dividends declared	(40)	.49	(19.60)
Retained earnings, 12/31/01	DM 30		$ 13.10

German Company
Statement of Cash Flows
For the Year Ended December 31, 2002

	DM	Exchange rate	US dollars
Operating activities			
Net income	DM 50	.48	$24.00
Adjustments to reconcile net income to net cash provided by operating activities:			
Depreciation	10	.48	4.80
Decrease in accounts receivable	20	.48	9.60
Increase in accounts payable	20	.48	9.60
Decrease in unearned rent	(10)	.48	(4.80)
Net cash provided by operating activities	DM 90		$43.20
Investing activities			
Purchase of land	(50)	.49	(24.50)
Net cash used by investing activities	(50)		(24.50)
Financing activities			
Mortgage payable	50	.49	24.50
Dividends	(40)	.49	(19.60)
Net cash provided by financing activities	10		4.90
Effect of exchange rate changes on cash	NA		3.90
Increase in cash and equivalents	DM 50		$27.50
Cash at beginning of year	50		22.50
Cash at end of year	DM 100	.50	$50.00

Using the analysis that was presented before, the change in the translation adjustment attributable to 2002 would be computed as follows:

Net assets at January 1, 2002	DM 220 ($.50 – $.45) =	$ 11.00 credit
Net income for 2002	DM 50 ($.50 – $.48) =	1.00 credit
Dividends for 2002	DM 40 ($.50 – $.49) =	.40 debit
Total		$11.60 credit

The balance in the cumulative translation adjustment account at the end of 2002 would be $21.90. ($10.30 from 2001 and $11.60 from 2002.)

6. The use of the equity method by the US company in accounting for the subsidiary would result in the following journal entries (in 000s), based upon the information presented above:

	2001		2002	
Original investment				
Investment in German subsidiary	80*		--	
Cash		80		--
* $.40 x common stock of DM 40 plus additional paid-in capital of DM 160				
Earnings pickup				
Investment in German subsidiary	12.90		24**	
Equity in subsidiary income		12.90		24
** $.48 x net income of DM 50				
Dividends received				
Cash	4.20		19.60	
Investment in German subsidiary		4.20		19.60
Translation adjustments				
Investment in German subsidiary	10.30		11.60	
OCI—Translation adjustments		10.30		11.60

Note that the stockholders' equity of the US parent company should be the same whether or not the German subsidiary is consolidated. Since the subsidiary does not report the translation adjustments on its financial statements, care should be exercised so that it is not forgotten in the application of the equity method.

7. If the US company disposes of its investment in the German subsidiary, the cumulative translation adjustments balance becomes part of the gain or loss that results from the transaction and must be eliminated. For example, assume that on January 2, 2003, the US company sells its entire investment for DM 300. The exchange rate at this date is DM 1 = $.50. The balance in the investment account at December 31, 2002, is $115 as a result of the entries made previously.

	Investment in German Subsidiary	
1/1/01	80.00	
	12.90	4.20
	10.30	
1/1/02 balance	99.00	
	24.00	
	11.60	19.60
12/31/02 balance	115.00	

The following entries would be made by the US parent company to reflect the sale of the investment:

Cash (DM 300 x $.50)	150	
Investment in German subsidiary		115
Gain from sale of subsidiary		35
AOCI—Translation adjustments	21.90	
Gain from sale of subsidiary		21.90

If the US company had sold a portion of its investment in the German subsidiary, only a pro rata portion of the accumulated translation adjustments balance would have become part of the gain or loss from the transaction. To illustrate, if 80% of the German subsidiary was sold for DM 250 on January 2, 2003, the following journal entries would be made:

Cash (DM 250 x $.50)	125	
Investment in German subsidiary (.8 x $115)		92
Gain from sale of subsidiary		33
AOCI—Translation adjustments (.8 x $21.90)	17.52	
Gain from sale of subsidiary		17.52

Application of the Remeasurement Method

In the previous situation, the DM was the functional currency because the German subsidiary's cash flows were primarily in DM. Assume, however, that the financing of the land and building was in US dollars instead of DM and that the mortgage payable is denominated in US dollars (i.e., must be paid in US dollars). Although the rents collected and the majority of the cash flows for expenses are in DM, management has decided that, due to the manner of financing, the US dollar is the functional currency. The books and records, however, are maintained in DM.

The remeasurement of the German financial statements is accomplished by use of the **remeasurement method** (also known as the monetary/nonmonetary method). This method is illustrated below using the same information that was presented before for the German subsidiary.

German Company
Balance Sheet (Remeasurement)
(US dollar is the functional currency)
At December 31, 2001

Assets	*DM*	*Exchange rate*	*US dollars*
Cash	DM 50	.45	$ 22.50
Accounts receivable	20	.45	9.00
Land	100	.40	40.00
Building (net)	490	.40	196.00
Total assets	DM 660		$267.50
Liabilities and Stockholders' Equity			
Accounts payable	DM 30	.45	$ 13.50
Unearned rent	10	.42	4.20
Mortgage payable	400	.45	180.00
Common stock	40	.40	16.00
Additional paid-in capital	160	.40	64.00
Retained earnings	20	See income statement	(10.20)
Total liabilities and stockholders' equity	DM 660		$267.50

German Company
Income and Retained Earnings Statement Remeasurement
(US dollar is the functional currency)
For the Year Ended December 31, 2001

	DM	Exchange rate	US dollars
Revenues	DM 200	.43	$ 86.00
Expenses (not including depreciation)	(160)	.43	(68.80)
Depreciation expense	(10)	.40	(4.00)
Remeasurement loss	--	See analysis below	(19.20)
Net income (loss)	DM 30	--	$ (6.00)
Retained earnings, January 1	--	--	--
Dividends declared	(10)	.42	(4.20)
Retained earnings, December 31	DM 20		$(10.20)

German Company
Remeasurement Loss
For the Year Ended December 31, 2001

	DM		Exchange rate	US dollars	
	Debit	Credit		Debit	Credit
Cash	DM 50		.45	$22.50	
Accounts receivable	20		.45	9.00	
Land	100		.40	40.00	
Building (net)	490		.40	196.00	
Accounts payable		DM 30	.45		$ 13.50
Unearned rent		10	.42		4.20
Mortgage payable		400	.45		180.00
Common stock		40	.40		16.00
Additional paid-in capital		160	.40		64.00
Retained earnings		--	--		--
Dividends declared	10		.42	4.20	
Revenues		200	.43		86.00
Operating expenses	160		.43	68.80	
Depreciation expenses	10		.40	4.00	
Totals	DM 840	DM 840		$344.50	$363.70
Remeasurement loss				19.20	
Totals				$363.70	$363.70

The following observations should be noted about the remeasurement method:

1. **Assets and liabilities** which have historical cost balances (nonmonetary assets and liabilities) are remeasured by using historical exchange rates (i.e., the rates in effect when the transactions occurred). Monetary assets and monetary liabilities, cash and those items that will be settled in cash, are remeasured by using the current exchange rate at the balance sheet date. In 2002, the unearned rent from 2001 of DM 10 would be remeasured at the rate of DM 1 = $.42. The unearned rent at the end of 2001 is not considered a monetary liability. Therefore, the $.42 historical exchange rate should be used for all applicable future years. See the appendix at the end of this chapter for a listing of accounts that are remeasured using historical exchange rates.

2. **Revenues and expenses** that occur frequently during a period are remeasured, for practical purposes, by using the weighted-average exchange rate for the period. Revenues and expenses that represent allocations of historical balances (e.g., depreciation, cost of goods sold, and amortization of any intangibles) are remeasured by using historical exchange rates. Note that this is a different treatment as compared to the current rate method.

3. If the functional currency is the US dollar rather than the local foreign currency, the amounts of specific line items presented in the reconciliation of net income to net cash flow from operating activities will be different for nonmonetary items (e.g., depreciation). Note, however, that the **net** cash flow from operating activities will be the same in the reporting currency regardless of the applicable functional currency.

4. The calculation of the remeasurement gain (loss), in a purely mechanical sense, is the amount needed to make the dollar debits equal the dollar credits in the German company's trial balance.

5. The remeasurement loss of $19.20 is reported on the US company's consolidated income statement because the US dollar is the functional currency. When the reporting currency is the functional currency, as it is in this example, it is assumed that all of the foreign entity's transactions occurred in US dollars. Accordingly, remeasurement gains and losses are taken immediately to the income statement in the year in which they occur as they can be expected to have direct cash flow effects. They are not deferred as a translation adjustments component of AOCI as they were when the functional currency was the DM (current rate method).

6. The use of the equity method of accounting for the subsidiary would result in the following entries by the US parent company during 2001:

Original investment

Investment in German subsidiary	80	
Cash		80

Earnings (loss) pickup

Equity in subsidiary loss	6	
Investment in German subsidiary		6

Dividends received

Cash	4.20	
Investment in German subsidiary		4.20

Note that remeasurement gains and losses are included in the subsidiary's net income (net loss) as determined in US dollars before the equity pickup is made by the US company.

7. In highly inflationary economies, those in which cumulative inflation is greater than 100% over a three-year period, the FASB requires that the functional currency be the reporting currency, that is, the US dollar. The remeasurement method must be used in this situation even though the fac-

tors indicate the local currency is the functional currency. The Board made this decision in order to prevent the evaporation of the foreign entity's fixed assets, a result that would occur if the local currency was the functional currency.

Summary of Current Rate and Remeasurement Methods

1. Before **foreign currency financial statements** can be translated into US dollars, management of the US entity must select the functional currency for the foreign entity whose financial statements will be incorporated into theirs by consolidation, combination, or the equity method. As the example illustrated, this decision is important because it may have a material effect upon the financial statements of the US company.

2. If the functional currency is the local currency of the foreign entity, the current rate method is used to translate foreign currency financial statements into US dollars. All assets and liabilities are translated by using the current exchange rate at the balance sheet date. This method insures that all financial relationships remain the same in both local currency and US dollars. Owners' equity is translated by using historical rates, while revenues (gains) and expenses (losses) are translated at the rates in existence during the period when the transactions occurred. A weighted-average rate can be used for items occurring numerous times throughout the period. The translation adjustments (debit or credit) which result from the application of these rules are reported in other comprehensive income and then accumulated and reported as a separate component in stockholders' equity of the US company's consolidated balance sheet (or parent-only balance sheet if consolidation was not deemed appropriate).

3. If the functional currency is the reporting currency (the US dollar), the foreign currency financial statements are remeasured into US dollars. All foreign currency balances are restated to US dollars using both historical and current exchange rates. Foreign currency balances which reflect prices from past transactions are remeasured by using historical rates, while foreign currency balances which reflect prices from current transactions are remeasured by using the current exchange rate. Remeasurement gains/ losses that result from the remeasurement process applied to foreign subsidiaries that are consolidated are reported on the US company's consolidated income statement.

The above summary can be arranged in tabular form as shown below.

Functional currency	Functional currency determinants	Translation method	Reporting
Local currency of foreign company	a. Operations not integrated with parent's operations b. Buying and selling activities primarily in local currency c. Cash flows not immediately available for remittance to parent d. Financing denominated in local currency	Current rate (all assets/ liabilities translated using current exchange rate; revenues/ expenses use weighted-average rate; equity accounts use historical rates)	Accumulated translation adjustments are reported in equity section of the US company's consolidated balance sheet as part of AOCI. Changes in accumulated translation adjustments reported as a component of other comprehensive income (OCI).
US dollar	a. Operations integrated with parent's operations b. Buying and selling activities primarily in the US and/or US dollars c. Cash flows immediately available for remittance to parent d. Financing denominated in US dollars	Remeasurement (monetary assets/ liabilities use current exchange rate; historical cost balances use historical rates; revenues/expenses use weighted-average rates and historical rates, the latter for allocations like depr. exp.).	Remeasurement gain/ loss is reported on the US company's consolidated income statement.

Foreign Operations in the US

With the world economy as interconnected as it is, entities in the US are sometimes the subsidiaries of parent companies domiciled elsewhere in the world. The financial statements of the US company may be presented separately in the US or may be combined as part of the financial statements in the foreign country.

In general, financial statements of US companies are prepared in accordance with US generally accepted accounting principles. However, adjustments may have to be made to these statements in order to conform them to the accounting principles where they will be combined or consolidated into non-US companies.

Translation of Foreign Currency Transactions

According to SFAS 52, a **foreign currency transaction** is a transaction " ... denominated in a currency other than the entity's functional currency." Denominated means that the amount to be received or paid is fixed in terms of the number of units of a particular foreign currency regardless of changes in the exchange rate. From the viewpoint of a US company, a foreign currency transaction results when it imports or exports goods or services to or from a foreign entity or makes a loan involving a foreign entity and agrees to settle the transaction in currency other than the US dollar (the functional currency of the US company). In these situations, the US company has "crossed currencies" and directly assumes the risk of fluctuating exchange rates of the foreign currency in which the transaction is denominated. This risk may lead to recognition of foreign exchange **transaction gains or losses** in the income statement of the US company. Note that transaction gains or losses can result only when the foreign currency transactions are denominated in a foreign currency. When a US company imports or exports goods or services and the transaction is to be settled in US dollars, the US company will incur neither gain nor loss because it bears no risk due to exchange rate fluctuations.

The following example will illustrate the terminology and procedures applicable to the translation of foreign currency transactions. Assume that US Company, an exporter, sells merchandise to a customer in Germany on December 1, 2001, for DM 10,000. Receipt is due on January 31, 2002, and US Company prepares financial statements on December 31, 2001. At the transaction date (December 1, 2001), the spot rate for immediate exchange of foreign currencies indicates that DM 1 is equivalent to $.50. To find the US dollar equivalent of this transaction, the foreign currency amount, DM 10,000, is multiplied by $.50 to get $5,000. At December 1, 2001, the foreign currency transaction should be recorded by US Company in the following manner:

Accounts receivable—Germany (DM)	5,000	
Sales		5,000

The accounts receivable and sales are measured in US dollars at the **transaction date** using the spot rate at the time of the transaction. While the accounts receivable is measured and reported in US dollars, the receivable is denominated or fixed in DM. This characteristic may result in foreign exchange transaction gains or losses if the spot rate for DM changes between the transaction date and the date the transaction is settled (January 31, 2002).

If financial statements are prepared between the transaction date and the settlement date, all receivables and liabilities which are denominated in a currency other than the functional currency (the US dollar) must be restated to reflect the spot rates in existence at the balance sheet date. Assume that, on December 31, 2001, the spot rate for DM is DM 1 = $.52. This means that the DM 10,000 are now worth $5,200 and that the accounts receivable denominated in DM should be increased by $200. The following adjusting journal entry would be recorded as of December 31, 2001:

Accounts receivable—Germany (DM)	200	
Foreign currency transaction gain		200

Note that the sales account, which was credited on the transaction date for $5,000, is not affected by changes in the spot rate. This treatment exemplifies the two-transaction viewpoint adopted by the FASB. In other words, making the sale is the result of an operating decision, while bearing the risk of fluctuating spot rates is the result of a financing decision. Therefore, the amount determined as sales revenue at the transaction date should not be altered because of a financing decision to wait until January 31, 2002, for payment of the account. The risk of a foreign exchange transaction loss can be avoided either by demanding immediate payment on

December 1 or by entering into a **forward exchange contract** to hedge the exposed asset (accounts receivable). The fact that US Company, in the example, did not act in either of these two ways is reflected by requiring the recognition of foreign currency transaction gains or losses in its income statement (reported as financial or nonoperating items) in the period during which the exchange rates changed. This treatment has been criticized, however, because both the unrealized gain and/or loss are recognized in the financial statements, a practice which is at variance with traditional GAAP. Furthermore, earnings will fluctuate because of changes in exchange rates and not because of changes in the economic activities of the enterprise.

On the settlement date (January 31, 2002), assume the **spot rate** is DM 1 = \$.51. The receipt of DM 10,000 and their conversion into US dollars would be journalized in the following manner:

Foreign currency (DM)	5,100	
Foreign currency transaction loss	100	
Accounts receivable—Germany (DM)		5,200
Cash	5,100	
Foreign currency (DM)		5,100

The net effect of this foreign currency transaction was to receive \$5,100 from a sale that was measured originally at \$5,000. This realized net foreign currency transaction gain of \$100 is reported on two income statements—a \$200 gain in 2000 and a \$100 loss in 2002. The reporting of the gain in two income statements causes a temporary difference between pretax accounting and taxable income. This results because the transaction gain of \$100 is not taxable until 2002, the year the transaction was completed or settled. Accordingly, interperiod tax allocation is required for foreign currency transaction gains or losses.

Intercompany Transactions and Elimination of Intercompany Profits

Gains or losses from intercompany transactions should be reported on the US company's consolidated income statement unless settlement of the transaction is not planned or anticipated in the foreseeable future. In that case, which is atypical, gains and losses arising from intercompany transactions should be reflected in the accumulated translations adjustments component of the US entity's stockholders' equity. In the typical situation (i.e., gains and losses reported on the US entity's income statement) note that gains and losses result whether the functional currency is the US dollar or the foreign entity's local currency. When the US dollar is the functional currency, foreign currency transaction gains and losses result because of one of the two situations below.

1. The intercompany foreign currency transaction is denominated in US dollars. In this case, the foreign subsidiary has a payable or receivable denominated in US dollars. This may result in a foreign currency transaction gain or loss that would appear on the foreign subsidiary's income statement.

This gain or loss would be translated into US dollars and would appear on the US entity's consolidated income statement.

2. The intercompany foreign currency transaction is denominated in the foreign subsidiary's local currency. In this situation, the US entity has a payable or receivable denominated in a foreign currency. Such a situation may result in a foreign currency transaction gain or loss that should be reported on the US entity's income statement.

The above two cases can be easily altered to reflect what happens when the foreign entity's local currency is the functional currency. The gain or loss from each of these scenarios would be reflected on the other entity's financial statements first (i.e., the subsidiary's rather than the parent's and vice versa).

The elimination of intercompany profits due to sales and other transfers between related entities should be based upon exchange rates in effect when the sale or transfer occurred. Reasonable approximations and averages are allowed to be used if intercompany transactions occur frequently during the year.

Foreign Currency Hedges

Foreign currency denominated assets/liabilities that arise in the normal course of business are often hedged with offsetting forward exchange contracts. This process, in effect, creates a natural hedge. Normal accounting rules (i.e., SFAS 52) apply, and the FASB decided not to change this accounting treatment in the implementation of SFAS 133. SFAS 133 does specify hedge accounting in four areas related to foreign currency hedges. The application of hedge accounting is generally more restrictive under SFAS 133 than it was under SFAS 52. The four foreign currency hedges under SFAS 133 are discussed below. (See Chapter 6, Short-Term Investments and Financial Instruments, for a complete discussion of derivatives and hedging.)

1. **Unrecognized firm commitment.** Either a derivative instrument or a nonderivative financial instrument (such as a receivable in a foreign currency) can be designated as a hedge of an unrecognized firm commitment attributable to changes in foreign currency exchange rates. If the requirements for a fair value hedge are met, then this hedging arrangement can be accounted for as a **fair value hedge**.

2. **Available-for-sale securities.** Prior to SFAS 133, a firm commitment to purchase a trading security and several transactions related to held-to-maturity securities were permitted to use hedging accounting under certain conditions. SFAS 133 has eliminated the use of hedge accounting for both trading and held-to-maturity securities (in many cases hedge accounting wasn't required anyway) and limited the use of hedge accounting to transactions for securities designated as available-for-sale. Derivative instruments can be used to hedge debt or equity available-for-sale securities. However, equity securities must meet two additional criteria.

a. They cannot be traded on an exchange denominated in the investor's functional currency.

b. Dividends must be denominated in the same foreign currency as is expected to be received on the sale of the security.

If the above criteria are met, hedging instruments related to available-for-sale securities can be accounted for as **fair value hedges**.

3. **Foreign currency denominated forecasted transactions.** This is an expansion in SFAS 133 for the permitted use of hedge accounting. Only derivative instruments can be designated as hedges of foreign currency denominated forecasted transactions. A forecasted export sale with the price denominated in a foreign currency might qualify for this type of hedge treatment. Forecasted transactions are distinguished from firm commitments (discussed in 1. above) because the timing of the cash flows remains uncertain. This additional complexity results in hedging instruments related to foreign currency denominated forecasted transactions being accounted for as cash flow hedges. Hedge accounting is permissible for transactions between unrelated parties, and under special circumstances (not discussed here) for intercompany transactions.

4. **Net investments in foreign operations.** The accounting for net investments in foreign operations has not changed from the SFAS 52 rules, except that the hedging instrument has to meet the new "effective" criterion. The change in the fair value of the hedging derivative is recorded in other comprehensive income which increases or decreases accumulated other comprehensive income in the equity section of the balance sheet.

Forward Exchange Contracts

It was stated previously that foreign currency transaction gains and losses on assets and liabilities that are denominated in a currency other than the functional currency can be hedged if a US company enters into a forward exchange contract. The following example shows how a forward exchange contract can be used as a hedge, first against a firm commitment and then, following delivery date, as a hedge against a recognized liability.

SFAS 133 states a general rule for estimating the fair value of forward exchange rates is to use the changes in the forward exchange rates, and discount those estimated future cash flows to a present-value basis. An entity will need to consider the time value of money if significant in the circumstances for these contracts. The following example does not apply discounting of the future cash flows from the forward contracts in order to focus on the relationships between the forward contract and the foreign currency denominated payable.

Example

Baker Simon, Inc. enters into a firm commitment with Dempsey Ing., Inc. of Germany, on October 1, 2001, to purchase a computerized robotic system for

DM 6,000,000. The system will be delivered on March 1, 2002, with payment due sixty days after delivery (April 30, 2002). Baker Simon, Inc. decides to hedge this foreign currency firm commitment and enters into a forward exchange contract on the firm commitment date to receive DM 6,000,000 on the payment date. The applicable exchange rates are shown in the table below.

Date	Spot rates	Forward rates for April 30, 2002
October 1, 2001	DM 1 = $.55	DM 1 = $ .57
December 31, 2001	DM 1 = $.58	DM 1 = $.589
March 1, 2002	DM 1 = $.58	DM 1 = $.585
April 30, 2002	DM 1 = $.60	

The example on the following pages separately presents both the forward contract receivable and the dollars payable liability in order to show all aspects of the forward contract. For financial reporting purposes, most companies present just the net fair value of the forward contract that would be the difference between the current value of the forward contract receivable and the dollars payable accounts. It should be noted that the foreign currency hedges in the illustration are **not** perfectly effective. However, for this example, the degree of ineffectiveness is not deemed to be sufficient to trigger income statement recognition per SFAS 133. (Hedge effectiveness is discussed in Chapter 6, Short-Term Investments and Financial Instruments.)

The transactions that reflect the forward exchange contract, the firm commitment and the acquisition of the asset and retirement of the related liability appear below. The net fair value of the forward contract is shown below each set of entries for the forward exchange contract.

In the case of using a forward exchange contract to speculate in a specific foreign currency, the general rule to estimate the fair value of the forward contract is to use the forward exchange rate for the remainder of the term of the forward contract.

EMERGING ISSUES TASK FORCE CONSENSUS SUMMARIES

91-1   Hedging Intercompany Foreign Currency Risks

Transactions between members of a consolidated group with different functional currencies can present foreign currency risks that may be hedged. All formal exchange contracts and similar agreements are subject to the hedge accounting provisions of SFAS 52. An intercompany foreign currency commitment is considered firm if there is a commitment to a third party or, lacking that, if performance is probable because of sufficiently large disincentives (fiduciary responsibilities, existing laws, or significant economic penalties) for nonperformance. In the latter case, the facts and circumstances of the intercompany transaction must be examined closely. The provisions of EITF 90-17 are also applicable to intercompany transactions.

Forward contract entries

(1) 10/1/01 (forward rate for 4/30/02 DM 1 = $.57)

    Forward contract receivable   3,420,000
        Dollars payable   3,420,000

This entry recognizes the existence of the forward exchange contract using the gross method. Under the net method, this entry would not appear at all, since the fair value of the forward contract is zero when the contract is initiated. The amount is calculated using the 10/1/01 forward rate for 4/30/02 (DM 6,000,000 x $.57 = $3,420,000).

Net fair value of the forward contract = $0

Note that the net fair value of the forward exchange contact on 10/1/01 is zero because there is an exact amount offset of the forward contract receivable of $3,420,000 with the dollars payable liability of $3,420,000. Many firms present only the net fair value of the forward contract in their balance sheets, and therefore, these firms would have no net amount reported in their balance sheets for the forward contract at the time of the inception of the forward contract.

(2) 12/31/01 (forward rate for 4/30/02 DM 1 = $.589)

    Forward contract receivable   114,000
        Gain on hedge activity   114,000

The dollar values for this entry reflect, among other things, the change in the forward rate from 10/1/01 to 12/31/01. However, the actual amount recorded as gain or loss (gain in this case) will be determined by all market factors.

Net fair value of the forward contract = $114,000

The net fair value of the forward exchange contract on 12/31/01 is $114,000 for the difference between the $3,534,000 ($3,420,000 plus $114,000) in the forward contract receivable and the $3,420,000 for the dollars payable liability. Many firms present only the net fair value in their balance sheet, in this case as an asset. And, this $114,000 is the amount that would be discounted to present value, if interest is significant, to recognize the time value of the future cash flow due to the forward contract.

(4) 3/1/02 (forward rate for 4/30/02 DM 1 = $.585)

    Loss on hedge activity   24,000
        Forward contract receivable   24,000

These entries again will be driven by market factors, and they are calculated the same way as entries (2) and (3) above. Notice that the decline in the forward rate from 12/31/01 to 3/1/02 resulted in a loss against the forward contract receivable and a gain against the firm commitment.

(3) 12/31/01

    Loss on hedge activity   114,000
        Firm commitment   114,000

The dollar values for this entry are identical to those in entry (2), reflecting the fact that the hedge is highly effective (100%) and also the fact that the market recognizes the same factors in this transaction as for entry (2). This entry reflects the first use of the firm commitment account, a temporary liability account pending the receipt of the asset against which the firm commitment has been hedged.

(5) 3/1/02

    Firm commitment   24,000
        Gain on hedge activity   24,000

Forward contract entries

Net fair value of the forward contract = $90,000

The net fair value of the forward exchange contract on 3/1/02 is $90,000 for the difference between the $3,510,000 ($3,534,000 minus $24,000) in the forward contract receivable and the $3,420,000 for the dollars payable liability. Another way of computing the net fair value is to determine the change in the forward contract rate from the initial date of the contract, 10/1/01, which is $.585 – $.57 = $.015 x DM 6,000,000 = $90,000. Also note that the amount in the firm commitment temporary liability account is equal to the net fair value of the forward contract on the date the equipment is received.

(7) 4/30/02 (spot rate DM 1 = $.60))

Forward contract receivable	90,000	
Gain on forward contract		90,000

The gain or loss (gain in this case) on the forward contract is calculated using the change in the forward to the spot rate from 3/1/02 to 4/30/02 [DM 6,000,000 x ($.60 – $.585) = $90,000]

Net fair value of the forward contract = $180,000

The net fair value of the forward exchange contract on 4/20/02 is $180,000 for the difference between the $3,600,000 ($3,510,000 plus $90,000) in the forward contract receivable and the $3,420,000 for the dollars payable liability. The net fair value of the forward contract at its terminal date of 4/30/02 is based on the difference between the contract forward rate of DM 1 = $.57 and the spot rate on 4/30/02 of DM 1 = $.60. The forward contract receivable has reached its maturity and the contract is completed on this date at the forward rate of DM 1 = $.57 as contracted on 10/1/01. If the entity recognizes an interest factor in the forward contract over the life of the contract, then interest will be recognized at this time on the forward contract, but no separate accrual of interest is required for the accounts payable in DM.

(9) 4/30/02

Dollars payable	3,420,000	
Foreign currency units (DM)	3,600,000	
Cash		3,420,000
Forward contract receivable		3,600,000

This entry reflects the settlement of the forward contract at the 10/1/01 contracted forward rate (DM 6,000,000 x $.57 = $3,420,000) and the receipt of foreign currency units valued at the spot rate (DM 6,000,000 x $.60 = $3,600,000).

Hedge against a recognized liability entries

(6) 3/1/02 (spot rate DM 1 = $.58)

Equipment	3,390,000	
Firm commitment	90,000	
Accounts payable (DM)		3,480,000

This entry records the receipt of the equipment, the elimination of the temporary liability account (firm commitment), and the recognition of the payable, calculated using the spot rate on the date of receipt (DM 6,000,000 x $.58 = $3,480,000).

(8) 4/30/02

Transaction loss	120,000	
Accounts payable (DM)		120,000

The transaction loss related to the accounts payable reflects only the change in the spot rates and ignores the accrual of interest. [DM 6,000,000 x ($.60 – $.58) = $120,000]

(10)

Accounts payable (DM)	3,600,000	
Foreign currency units (DM)		3,600,000

This entry reflects the use of the foreign currency units to retire the account payable.

92-4 Accounting for a Change in Functional Currency When an Economy Ceases to Be Considered Highly Inflationary

When a foreign subsidiary's economy is no longer considered highly inflationary, the entity should convert the reporting currency values into the local currency at the exchange rates on the date of change, in which these values become the new functional currency accounting bases for nonmonetary assets and liabilities.

92-8 Accounting for the Income Tax Effects under FASB Statement 109 of a Change in Functional Currency When an Economy Ceases to Be Considered Highly Inflationary

The Task Force reached a consensus that, deferred taxes on the temporary differences that arise as a result of a change in the functional currency are treated as an adjustment to the cumulative translation adjustments portion of stockholders' equity (accumulated other comprehensive income).

93-9 Application of FASB Statement 109 in Foreign Financial Statements Restated for Price-Level-Adjusted Financial Statements

Accounting Principles Board Statement 3 states that price-level-adjusted financial statements are preferred for foreign currency financial statements of entities operating in highly inflationary economies when they are intended for readers in the United States. The result is that the tax bases of the assets and liabilities in these financial statements are often restated for inflation. This statement provides guidance on the asset-and-liability approach of SFAS 109 as it relates to these financial statements. A consensus was reached on the following issues: (1) how temporary differences should be computed under SFAS 109 and (2) how deferred income tax expense or benefit for the year should be determined. With regard to the first issue, temporary differences are the difference between the indexed tax basis amount and the related price-level restated amount of the asset or liability. The consensus reached on the second issue is that the deferred income tax expense or benefit is the difference between the deferred tax assets and liabilities reported at the end of the current year and those reported at the end of the prior year. The deferred tax assets and liabilities of the prior year should be recalculated in units of the current year-end purchasing power.

95-2 Determination of What Constitutes a Firm Commitment for Foreign Currency Transactions Not Involving a Third Party

The Task Force reached a consensus in defining significant economic penalty as it appears in Issue 91-1 with respect to consolidated entities. Such penalty exists only when the penalty imposed by an unrelated party provides a compelling disincentive for nonperformance such that performance of the intercompany foreign currency commitment is probable, even if the anticipated transactions do not occur. If this penalty exists, a foreign currency commitment is considered a firm commitment as defined in Issue 91-1.

APPENDIX

ACCOUNTS TO BE REMEASURED USING HISTORICAL EXCHANGE RATES

1. Inventories carried at cost
2. Prepaid expenses such as insurance, advertising, and rent
3. Property, plant, and equipment
4. Accumulated depreciation on property, plant, and equipment
5. Patents, trademarks, licenses, and formulas
6. Goodwill
7. Other intangible assets
8. Deferred charges and credits, except policy acquisition costs for life insurance companies
9. Deferred income
10. Common stock
11. Preferred stock carried at issuance price
12. Revenues and expenses related to nonmonetary items

    a. Cost of goods sold
    b. Depreciation of property, plant, and equipment
    c. Amortization of intangible items such as goodwill, patents, licenses, etc.
    d. Amortization of deferred charges or credits, except policy acquisition costs for life insurance companies

Source: SFAS 52.

22 PERSONAL FINANCIAL STATEMENTS

PERSPECTIVE AND ISSUES

AICPA Statement of Position (SOP) 82-1, *Personal Financial Statements,* addresses the preparation and presentation of personal financial statements, or, more specifically, financial statements of individuals or groups of related individuals (i.e., families). Personal financial statements are generally prepared to organize and plan an individual's financial affairs on a more formal basis. Specific purposes that might require the preparation of personal financial statements include the obtaining of credit, income tax planning, retirement planning, gift and estate planning, or the public disclosure of financial affairs. The aforementioned purposes allow the users of personal financial statements to determine whether to grant credit, in assessing the financial activities of individuals, in assessing the financial affairs of public officials and candidates for public office, and for similar purposes. Estimated current values of assets and liabilities are used in the preparation of personal financial statements as this information has more value than historical cost data to the users of such statements.

Sources of GAAP
SOP
82-1

DEFINITIONS OF TERMS

Estimated current value of an asset. The amount for which an item could be exchanged between a buyer and a seller, each of whom is well informed and willing, and neither of whom is compelled to buy or sell.

Estimated current amount of liabilities. Payables and other liabilities should be presented at the discounted amounts of cash to be paid. The discount rate should be the rate implicit in the transaction in which the debt was incurred. If, however, the debtor is able to discharge the debt currently at a lower amount, the debt should be presented at the lower amount.

Net worth. The difference between total assets and total liabilities, after deducting estimated income taxes on the differences between the estimated current values of assets and the estimated current amounts of liabilities and their tax bases.

CONCEPTS, RULES, AND EXAMPLES

Personal financial statements may be prepared for an individual, husband, wife, or family. An individual may elect to have a personal financial statement prepared for himself/herself without including his/her spouse. If property is held in joint tenancy, as community property, or through a similar joint ownership arrangement, the individual's ownership interest may not be evident. If such is the case, the individual may require the advice of an attorney to determine, under state law, what interest in the property should be included among the individual's assets.

Personal financial statements consist of

1. **Statement of financial condition**—The only required financial statement, the statement of financial condition presents the estimated current values of assets, the estimated current amounts of liabilities, estimated income taxes on the differences between the estimated current values of assets and liabilities and respective tax bases, and net worth at a specified date.
2. **Statement of changes in net worth**—An optional statement, this statement presents the primary sources of increases and decreases in net worth.
3. **Comparative financial statements**—Optional statements, the inclusion of a comparison of the current period's financial statements with one or more previous period's financial statements is often desired.

The accrual basis, rather than the cash basis of accounting, should be used in preparing personal financial statements. The presentation of personal financial statements does not require the classification of assets and liabilities as current and noncurrent. Instead, assets and liabilities are presented in order of liquidity and maturity.

In personal financial statements, **assets** should be presented at their **estimated current value**. This is an amount at which the item could be exchanged assuming both parties are well-informed, neither party is compelled to buy or sell, and material disposal costs are deducted to arrive at current values. A specialist may have to be consulted in the determination of the current value of certain types of assets (e.g., works of art, jewelry, restricted securities, investments in closely held businesses, and real estate). **Liabilities** should be presented at the lesser of the discounted amount of cash to be paid or the current cash settlement amount. The use of recent transactions involving similar types of assets and liabilities, in similar circumstances, constitutes a satisfactory means of determining the estimated current value of an asset and the **estimated current amount of a liability**. If recent information cannot be obtained, other methods can be used (e.g., capitalization of past or prospective earnings, the use of liquidation values, the adjustment of historical cost based on changes in a specific price index, the use of appraisals, and the use of the discounted amounts of projected cash receipts and payments). The methods used should be followed consistently from period to period unless the facts and circumstances dictate a change to different methods. Income taxes payable should include unpaid income taxes for completed tax years and the estimated amount for the elapsed portion of the current tax year. Additionally, personal financial statements should include the estimated income tax on the difference between the current value (amount) of assets (liabilities) and their respective tax bases as if they had been realized or liquidated. The table below summarizes the methods of determining "estimated current values" for assets and "estimated current amounts" for liabilities.

Assets and liabilities	*Discounted cash flow*	*Market price*	*Appraised value*	*Other*
• Receivables	x			
• Marketable securities		x		If traded on valuation day: closing price. If not traded: valuation must fall in range (bid and asked price)
• Options—securities		x		Difference between exercise price and current value of asset; if material, discount the difference
• Options—other assets*				
• Investment in life insurance				Cash value less outstanding loans
• Investment in closely held business	x		x	Liquidation value, multiple of earnings, reproduction value, adjustment of book value or cost
• Real estate	x		x	Sales of similar property
• Intangible assets	x			Net proceeds from current sale or discounted cash flows from asset; otherwise, may use cost of asset
• Future interests (nonforfeitable rights)**	x			
• Payables and other liabilities	x			Discharge amount if lower than discounted amount
• Noncancelable commitments***	x			
• Income taxes payable				Unpaid income tax for completed tax years and estimated income tax for elapsed portion of current tax year to date of financial statements
• Estimated income tax on difference between current values of assets and current amounts of liabilities and their respective tax bases				Computed as if current value of assets and liabilities had been respectively realized or liquidated considering applicable tax laws and regulations, recapture provisions and carryovers.
• Uncertain obligations*				Not covered by SOP 82-1; follow SFAS 5

  * *Taken from: "Personal Financial Statements," Michael D. Kinsman and Bruce Samuelson,* **Journal of Accounting**, *September 1987, pp. 138-148.*
 ** *Rights have all of the following attributes: (1) are for fixed or determinable amounts; (2) are not contingent on holder's life expectancy or occurrence of a particular event (e.g., disability/death), and (3) do not require future performance of service by holder.*
*** *Commitments have all of the following attributes: (1) are for fixed or determinable amounts; (2) are not contingent on others' life expectancies or occurrence of a particular event (e.g., disability/death); and (3) do not require future performance of service by others.*

Business interests that comprise a large portion of a person's total assets should be shown separately from other investments. An investment in a separate entity that is marketable as a going concern (e.g., closely held corporation) should be presented as one amount. If the investment is a limited business activity, not conducted in a separate business entity, separate asset and liability amounts should be shown (e.g., investment in real estate and related mortgage; of course, only the person's beneficial interest in the investment is included in his/her personal financial statements).

The CPA must decide whether to valuate the net investment him/herself or to defer valuation to a specialist. Because of the risk of litigation and the liability coverage limitations on valuation functions, many CPAs prefer using a specialist. If the CPA does the valuation, s/he must ensure that s/he has attained a sufficient level of competence to perform the engagement. The possible valuation methods available are discounted cash flow, appraised value, liquidation value, multiple of earnings, reproduction value, adjustment of book value (e.g., equity method), or cost.

The following disclosures are typically made in either the body of the financial statements or in the accompanying notes. (This list is not all-inclusive.) Source: SOP 90-1.

1. A clear indication of the individuals covered by the financial statements
2. That assets are presented at their estimated current values and liabilities are presented at their estimated current amounts
3. The methods used in determining the estimated current values of major assets and the estimated current amounts of major liabilities or major categories of assets and liabilities, and changes in methods from one period to the next
4. If assets held jointly by the person and by others are included in the statements, the nature of the joint ownership
5. If the person's investment portfolio is material in relation to his or her other assets and is concentrated in one or a few companies or industries, the names of the companies or industries and the estimated current values of the securities
6. If the person has a material investment in a closely held business, the person's ownership percentage as well as the name, nature of, and summarized financial information for the business
7. Description of intangible assets and their estimated useful lives
8. The face amount of life insurance the individual owns
9. Certain nonforfeitable rights, such as pensions based on life expectancy
10. The methods and assumptions used to calculate the estimated income taxes on the differences between the estimated current values of assets and the estimated current amounts of liabilities and their tax bases as well as a statement that the provision will probably differ from the amounts eventu-

ally paid as the timing and method of disposal as well as changes in the tax laws and regulations will affect the actual taxes to be paid

11. Unused operating loss and capital loss carryforwards and any other unused deductions or credits

12. The differences between the estimated current values of major assets and the estimated current amounts of major liabilities or categories of assets and liabilities and their tax bases

13. Maturities, interest rates, collateral, and other pertinent details relating to receivables and debt

14. Certain noncancellable commitments such as operating leases

APPENDIX

HYPOTHETICAL SET OF PERSONAL FINANCIAL STATEMENTS

Marcus and Kelly Imrich
Statements of Financial Condition
December 31, 2002 and 2001

	2002	2001
Assets		
Cash	$ 381,437	$ 207,621
Securities		
Marketable (Note 2)	128,787	260,485
Tax-exempt bonds (Note 3)	1,890,222	986,278
Certificate of deposit	20,000	10,000
Loans receivable (Note 4)	262,877	362,877
Partnership and venture interests (Note 5)	935,000	938,000
Real estate interests (Note 6)	890,000	2,500,000
David Corporation (Note 7)	2,750,687	2,600,277
Cash surrender value of life insurance (Note 8)	388,000	265,000
Personal residences (Note 9)	2,387,229	2,380,229
Deferred losses from partnerships	68,570	60,830
Vested interest in David Corporation benefit plan	545,960	530,960
Personal jewelry and furnishings (Note 10)	513,000	6,700
Total assets	$11,161,769	$11,109,257
Liabilities		
Mortgage payable (Note 11)	$ 254,000	$ 267,000
Security deposits—rentals	--	5,700
Income taxes payable—current year balance	9,800	10,680
Total liabilities	263,800	283,380
Estimated income taxes on difference between estimated current values of assets and estimated current amounts of liabilities and their tax bases (Note 12)	555,400	731,000
Net Worth	10,342,569	10,094,877
Total liabilities and net worth	$11,161,769	$11,109,257

Marcus and Kelly Imrich
Statement of Changes in Net Worth
For the Years Ended December 31, 2002 and 2001

	Year ended December 31,	
	2002	2001
Realized increases in net worth		
Salary and bonus	$ 200,000	$ 175,000
Dividends and interest income	184,260	85,000
Distribution from limited partnerships	280,000	260,000
Gain on sales of marketable securities	58,240	142,800
	722,500	662,800
Realized decreases in net worth		
Income taxes	180,000	140,000
Interest expense	25,000	26,000
Real estate taxes	21,000	18,000
Personal expenditures	242,536	400,000
	468,536	584,000
Net realized increase in net worth	253,964	78,800

Unrealized increases in net worth

Marketable securities (net of realized gains on securities sold)	37,460	30,270
Benefit plan—David Corporation	15,000	14,000
Personal jewelry and furnishings	20,000	18,000
	72,460	62,270

Unrealized decreases in net worth

Estimated income taxes on the difference between the estimated current values of assets and the estimated current amounts of liabilities and their tax bases	78,732	64,118
Net unrealized decrease in net worth	(6,272)	(1,848)
Net increase in net worth	247,692	76,952
Net worth at the beginning of year	10,094,877	10,017,925
Net worth at the end of year	$10,342,569	$10,094,877

Marcus and Kelly Imrich
Notes to Financial Statements

Note 1: The accompanying financial statements include the assets and liabilities of Marcus and Kelly Imrich. Assets are stated at their estimated current values, and liabilities at their estimated current amounts.

Note 2: The estimated current values of marketable securities are either (1) their quoted closing prices or (2) for securities not traded on the financial statement date, amounts that fall within the range of quoted bid and asked prices.

Marketable securities consist of the following:

	December 31, 2002		December 31, 2001	
	Number of	*Estimated current*	*Number of*	*Estimated current*
Stocks	*shares*	*values*	*shares*	*values*
Susan Schultz, Inc.			1,000	$122,000
Ripley Robotics Corp.	500	$ 51,927	1,000	120,485
L.A.W. Corporation	300	20,700	100	5,000
Jay & Kelly Corp.	300	20,700	200	5,000
J.A.Z. Corporation	200	35,460	200	8,000
		$128,787		$260,485

Note 3: The interest income from state and municipal bonds is not subject to federal income taxes but is, except in certain cases, subject to state income tax.

Note 4: The loan receivable from Carol Parker, Inc. matures January 2009 and bears interest at the prime rate.

Note 5: Partnership and venture interests consist of the following:

	Percent owned	*Cost*	*Estimated current value 12/31/2002*	*Estimated current value 12/31/2001*
East Third Partnership	50.0%	$ 50,000	100,000	100,000
631 Lucinda Venture	20.0	10,000	35,000	38,000
27 Wright Partnership	22.5	10,000	40,000	50,000
Eannarino Partnership	10.0	40,000	60,000	50,000
Sweeney Venture	30.0	100,000	600,000	600,000
Kelly Parker Group	20.0	20,000	100,000	100,000
707 Lucinda Venture	50.0	(11,000)	--	--
			$935,000	$938,000

Note 6: Mr. and Mrs. Imrich own a one-half interest in an apartment building in DeKalb, Illinois. The estimated fair market value was determined by Mr. and Mrs. Imrich. Their basis in the apartment building was $1,000,000 for both 2002 and 2001.

Note 7: Kelly Imrich owns 75% of the common stock of the David Corporation. A condensed statement of assets, liabilities, and stockholders' equity (income tax basis) of David Corporation as of December 31, 2002 and 2001 is summarized below.

	2002	*2001*
Current assets	$2,975,000	$3,147,000
Investments	200,000	200,000
Property and equipment (net)	145,000	165,000
Loans receivable	110,000	120,000
Total assets	$3,430,000	$3,632,000
Current liabilities	$2,030,000	$2,157,000
Other liabilities	450,000	400,000
Total liabilities	2,480,000	2,557,000
Stockholders' equity	950,000	1,075,000
Total liabilities and stockholders' equity	$3,430,000	$3,632,000

Note 8: At December 31, 2002 and 2001, Marcus Imrich owned a $1,000,000 whole life insurance policy.

Note 9: The estimated current values of the personal residences are their purchase prices plus their cost of improvements. Both residences were purchased in 2000.

Note 10: The estimated current values of personal effects and jewelry are the appraised values of those assets, determined by an independent appraiser for insurance purposes.

Note 11: The mortgage (collateralized by the residence) is payable in monthly installments of $1,083 a month, including interest at 10% a year through 2018.

Note 12: The estimated current amounts of liabilities at December 31, 2002, and December 31, 2001, equaled their tax bases. Estimated income taxes have been provided on the excess of the estimated current values of assets over their tax bases as if the estimated current values of the assets had been realized on the statement date, using applicable tax laws and regulations. The provision will probably differ from the amounts of income taxes that eventually might be paid because those amounts are determined by the timing and the method of disposal or realization and the tax laws and regulations in effect at the time of disposal or realization.

The estimated current values of assets exceeded their tax bases by $1,850,000 at December 31, 2002, and by $1,770,300 at December 31, 2001. The excess of estimated current values of major assets over their tax bases are

	December 31,	
	2002	*2001*
Investment in David Corporation	$1,400,000	$1,350,000
Vested interest in benefit plan	350,000	300,000
Investment in marketable securities	100,000	120,300

23 SPECIALIZED INDUSTRY GAAP

BANKING AND THRIFT INDUSTRIES

PERSPECTIVE AND ISSUES

The materials referenced below have been incorporated into the most recent edition of the AICPA's Audit and Accounting Guide, *Banks and Savings Institutions* (1999), and will be continued in the new Guide, expected by 2002, which for the first time will unify guidance for **all** financial institutions.

While at one time regulator-imposed rules (regulatory accounting principles, or RAP) were mandated for official filings and were also often adhered to for general purpose financial reporting, these have been repealed. Today, financial reporting by banks and thrifts is governed by the same GAAP as that of entities in other industries. Nonetheless, the unique characteristics of financial service industries does mean that certain aspects of GAAP require more elaboration and interpretation than do these same principles when applied to less specialized entities. These are the key areas of accounting and financial reporting summarized below.

The 1980s and early 1990s were, of course, difficult times for the thrift and (to a lesser degree) banking industries. In an attempt to stave off the pending insolvency of the thrift insurance fund (FSLIC) and even that for the banks (FDIC), a number of mergers were encouraged, by which the net liabilities of insolvent institutions were assumed by stronger ones, with the net deficit being treated as an asset, known as **supervisory goodwill**. The accounting profession objected to this, but eventually was forced to acquiesce, and issued SFAS 72 stipulating how this goodwill should be amortized (which only dictated general purpose financial reporting and differed, in many cases, from that agreed to for regulatory reporting purposes).

The passage of new laws in the late 1980s and early 1990s eliminated supervisory goodwill, and it no longer appears on bank or thrift balance sheets. Goodwill, as generally understood under GAAP, may be found on balance sheets of financial institutions which have engaged in purchase business combinations, however. Under new standards imposed in mid-2001, goodwill will no longer be amortized, but will be tested for impairment under defined circumstances (see discussions in Chapters 9 and 11).

Banks and savings institutions are exempted from the need to present certain cash flow information by SFAS 104. Specifically, gross amounts for such high-volume transaction categories as deposits and withdrawals need not be disclosed. They are not exempt from presenting cash flow statements, however.

Lenders often incur a sizable number of costs directly related to the origination or purchase of loans, and normally receive different nonrefundable fees at the inception of the loans.

In practice, disparate accounting procedures emerged for the accounting for these costs and fees. The FASB responded with the issuance of SFAS 91, *Accounting for Nonrefundable Fees and Costs Associated with Originating or Acquiring Loans and Initial Direct Costs of Leases*. The standard points out various examples of these costs and fees, and the different accounting for each of them.

SFAS 114, effective in 1995, imposed a more rational set of requirements for accounting for impaired loans than did its predecessor standard, SFAS 15. Under the earlier standard, many actual impairments escaped accounting recognition. The current standard mandates loss recognition whenever loans are restructured, unless these involve only an extended payment schedule with full contractual rates of interest being applied to the new due dates. Apart from loan restructurings, however, the issue of when loss reserves are to be provided, and how these are to be determined, continues to receive a good deal of attention from accounting standard setters and regulatory authorities. The banking regulators and the SEC have indicated that heightened scrutiny is to be applied to loan loss provisions, and interpretative guidance has been offered on the interplay between SFAS 5 and 114.

The AICPA proposed a Statement of Position several years ago to address the accounting for differences between contractual and expected future cash flows from an investor's initial investment in certain loans and debt securities acquired in a transfer when such differences are attributable, at least in part, to credit quality. This occurs when nonoriginated loans are acquired at a discount due to the deteriorated credit quality of the debtor. Unlike normal discount (relating to time value of money), the predominant view is that only the portion of the discount pertaining to interest should be subject to accretion, and that the balance of the discount, which is associated with credit quality should be neither accreted nor disclosed.

This proposed SOP would limit the yield that may be accreted (accretable yield) to the excess of the investor's estimate of undiscounted expected future principal and interest cash flows (expected future cash flows) over the investor's initial investment in the loan. It would require that the excess of contractual cash flows over expected future cash flows (nonaccretable difference) not be recognized as an adjustment of yield, loss accrual, or valuation allowance. It would also prohibit investors from displaying accretable yield and nonaccretable difference in the balance sheet. The proposed SOP would establish the investor's estimate of undiscounted expected future principal and interest cash flows as a benchmark for yield and impairment measurements. Subsequent increases in expected future cash flows would be recognized prospectively through adjustment of the loan's yield over its remaining life. If issued, the standard would supersede AICPA Practice Bulletin 6. Issuance is dependent upon resolving certain matters objected to by the FASB, from which clearance must be obtained before the SOP can be issued.

The AICPA is also planning to issue an SOP that will reconcile the specialized accounting and financial reporting guidance established in the existing Guides *Banks and Savings Institutions*, *Audits of Credit Unions*, and *Audits of Finance Companies*. The final provisions would be incorporated in a final combined Guide, *Financial Institutions: Banks, Credit Unions, Finance Companies, and Savings Institutions*. This will eliminate differences in accounting and disclosure established by the respective Guides and carry forward accounting guidance for transactions determined to be unique to certain financial institutions. Major changes are expected to include

- Mortgage companies and corporate credit unions will be explicitly included in the scope of the combined Guide.
- Regulatory capital disclosures will be required for mortgage companies, credit unions, banks, and thrifts.
- Credit unions report amounts placed in their deposit insurance fund as an asset if such amounts are fully refundable, due to unique legal and operational aspects of the credit union share insurance fund. Banks and thrifts expense

payments to their deposit insurance fund as incurred. Under the SOP, both practices are expected to be preserved because of differences in how the funds operate.

- Finance companies record purchases and sales of securities on the settlement date, whereas banks, thrifts, and credit unions follow trade date accounting. Under the SOP, finance companies will follow trade date accounting.
- SFAS 114, *Accounting by Creditors for Impairment of a Loan*, and 118, *Accounting by Creditors for Impairment of a Loan—Income Recognition and Disclosures*, address loan impairment measurement and disclosure requirements, but they do not specify how to recognize income on impaired loans. The Guide for finance companies gives specific guidance on the recognition of interest income on impaired loans. Under the SOP, such guidance for finance companies will be eliminated.
- Certain disclosures for credit unions will be eliminated. These disclosures include, for example, additional information about repurchase agreements, servicing assets, and deposit liabilities.

Sources of GAAP

APB	SFAS	FASB I	FASB TB	EITF
23	72, 91, 104, 109, 114, 115, 118, 134, 140	9	85-1, 87-3	84-4, 84-9, 84-19, 84-20, 84-21, 84-22, 84-31, 85-7, 85-8, 85-13, 85-18, 85-20, 85-24, 85-26, 85-31, 85-41, 85-42, 85-44, 86-21, 86-31, 86-38, 87-22, 87-34, 88-17, 88-19, 88-20, 88-25, 89-3, 89-19, 90-18, 90-21, 92-5, 93-1, D-2, D-4, D-21, D-34, D-35, D-47, D-49, D-54, D-57, D-67, D-74, D-78, D-80

DEFINITIONS OF TERMS

Carrying amount. The face amount of the interest-bearing asset plus (or minus) the unamortized premium (or discount).

Commitment fees. Fees charged for entering into an agreement that obligates the enterprise to make or acquire a loan or to satisfy an obligation of the other party under a specified condition. For purposes of this Statement, the term **commitment fees** includes fees for letters of credit and obligations to purchase a loan or group of loans and pass-through certificates.

General reserve. Used in the context of the special meaning this term has in regulatory pronouncements and in the US Internal Revenue Code.

Incremental direct costs. Costs to originate a loan that (1) result directly from and are essential to the lending transaction and (2) would not have been incurred by the lender had that lending transaction not occurred.

Long-term interest-bearing assets. For purposes of this section, these are interest-bearing assets with a remaining term to maturity of more than one year.

Net-spread method. Under this method, the acquisition of a savings and loan association is viewed as the acquisition of a leveraged whole rather than the acquisition of the separate assets and liabilities of the association.

Origination fees. Fees charged to the borrower in connection with the process of originating, refinancing, or restructuring a loan. This term includes, but is not limited to, points, management, arrangement, placement, application, underwriting, and other fees pursuant to a lending or leasing transaction and also includes syndication and participation fees to the extent they are associated with the portion of the loan retained by the lender.

Pretax accounting income. Represents income or loss for a period, exclusive of related income tax expense, determined in conformity with generally accepted accounting principles.

Reserve for bad debts. Term is used in the context of the special meaning this term has in regulatory pronouncements and in the US Internal Revenue Code.

Separate-valuation method. Under this method, each of the identifiable assets and liabilities (assumed) of the acquired savings and loan association is accounted for in the consolidated financial statements at an amount based on fair value at the date of acquisition, either individually or by types of assets and types of liabilities.

Taxable income. Represents pretax accounting income (1) adjusted for reversal of provisions of estimated losses on loans and property acquired in settlement of loans, gains or losses on the sales of such property, and adjusted for permanent differences and (2) after giving effect to the bad debt deduction allowable by the US Internal Revenue Code assuming the applicable tax return were to be prepared based on such adjusted pretax accounting income.

CONCEPTS, RULES, AND EXAMPLES

Justifying a Change in Accounting Principle

The following sources are preferred for banking and thrift industries that must justify a change in accounting principle:

1. Audit and Accounting Guide, *Banks and Savings Institutions* (1999)
2. Statement of Position 83-1, *Reporting by Banks of Investment Securities Gains or Losses*

Acquisition of a Banking or Thrift Institution

The following discussion applies not only to the acquisition of a savings and loan association, but also to acquisition of savings and loan holding companies, commercial banks, mutual savings banks, credit unions, and other depository institutions with assets and liabilities of the same type.

Purchase method. In accounting for the acquisition of a banking and thrift institution, the fair value of the assets and liabilities acquired must be determined using the **separate-valuation method**. Under this method, each of the identifiable assets and liabilities acquired are accounted for individually, or by type, at its fair value at the date of acquisition. The total amount is reported in the consolidated financial statements.

Note that use of the **net-spread method** is **not** considered appropriate for this type of business combination. The net-spread method, which views acquisition of the institution as a leveraged whole, does not appropriately recognize the fair value of individual, or types of, assets and liabilities.

Liabilities acquired are accounted for at their present value at the date of acquisition. The present value of savings deposits due on demand equals the face amount plus interest accrued or accruable at the acquisition date. The present value of other liabilities assumed is calculated by using interest rates for similar liabilities in effect at the date of acquisition.

While in the past some bank and thrift mergers may have been accounted for as poolings, the promulgation of new accounting standards in mid-2001 mean that henceforth all mergers will be accounted for as purchases. Goodwill will no longer be subject to amortization, but will be tested for impairment. (See Chapters 9 and 11.)

Identified intangible assets. The purchase price of a banking or thrift institution may include intangible benefits from the purchase, such as the capacity of acquired assets to generate new business. Intangible assets that can be separately identified at a determinable fair value should be assigned a portion of the total purchase price and should be amortized over their estimated lives. Any portion of the purchase price that cannot be identified with specific tangible and intangible assets (less liabilities assumed) should be assigned to goodwill. Under prior GAAP, goodwill was to be amortized; under current standards (effective 2002), amortization is to cease, with impairment testing being substituted.

Unidentifiable intangible asset. An unidentifiable intangible asset arises when the fair value of liabilities assumed exceeds the fair value of tangible and identified intangible assets acquired. This asset is amortized over a period no greater than the estimated remaining life of any **long-term interest-bearing assets** acquired. Amortization is applied to the **carrying amount** of the interest-bearing assets expected to be outstanding at the beginning of each subsequent period. If, however, the assets acquired do **not** include a significant portion of long-term interest-bearing assets, the unidentifiable intangible asset is amortized over a period not exceeding the estimated average remaining life of the existing customer base acquired. Amortization in any case shall not exceed forty years.

In the sale or liquidation of a large segment, or separable group, of the operating assets of an acquired banking or thrift institution, the portion of the unidentifiable intangible asset identified with that segment, or separable group, shall be included in the cost of the assets sold. If the sale or liquidation of a large portion of the interest-bearing assets significantly reduces the benefits of the unidentifiable intangible asset, any reduction shall be recognized as a charge to income.

Regulatory-assisted combinations. A regulatory authority may grant financial assistance to either party involved in the acquisition of a banking or thrift institution. The amount of assistance should be accounted for as part of the combination if receipt of the assistance is probable and the amount to be received is reasonably estimable. Otherwise, assistance should be reported as a reduction of the unidentifiable intangible asset with any excess reported in income. Note that assets and liabilities transferred to or assumed by a regulatory authority are **not** recognized in the acquisition. Any agreement by the grantee to repay all or a portion of the assistance shall require recognition of a liability and a charge to income by the grantee. Any assistance received by an enterprise shall be disclosed in the financial statements.

Another form of "assistance" offered to regulatory authorities during the "thrift crisis" of the mid-1980s was the right to treat as an asset (**supervisory goodwill**), for computing regulatory capital, the excess of acquired liabilities over acquired assets, both measured at fair value at acquisition date. Banking reform legislation (FIRREA in 1989, followed by FDICIA in 1991) banished supervisory goodwill, which resulted in litigation continuing to this day. While the ultimate outcomes of most of these proceedings are not yet clear, from a financial reporting perspective one important question is how the recoveries should be accounted for.

The FASB has indicated (in Topic D-78, *Accounting for Supervisory Goodwill Litigation Awards or Settlements*) that any settlements received should not be accounted for as governmental financial assistance (as described in SFAS 72), but rather as any other litigation awards would normally be reported. These are not to be deemed extraordinary gains, but rather are to be included in operating income, with adequate disclosure made to avoid the drawing of misleading inferences regarding possible recurrence. Unsettled claims should be accounted for as only contingent gains (i.e., these should be disclosed if material, but may not be accrued until and unless realized).

Bad-Debt Reserves

Both stock and mutual savings and loan associations are required by regulatory authorities to place a portion of their earnings into a **general reserve** as protection for depositors. Savings and loan associations are allowed by the IRS to maintain a **bad-debt reserve** and to deduct any additions to their reserve in determining taxable income. Since this method differs from the method for determining bad debt expense, **pretax accounting income** and **taxable income** will differ. Savings and loan associations, however, are not allowed to recognize deferred tax on this difference in tax years beginning before December 31, 1987. This restriction occurs because associations could manipulate their bad-debt reserve, thus controlling events leading to the tax consequence.

Accounting by Creditors for Impairment of a Loan

A persistent practice problem has been in the proper determination of loan loss provisions. Since such reserves are necessarily matters of judgment, the possibility of manipulation (by either understatement or overstatement) in order to manage reported earnings or otherwise bias perceptions about the thrift's or bank's performance has always existed. In more recent years, this has received greater attention, first by the issuance of a detailed standard on accounting for impaired loans (SFAS 114), and later by several FASB, SEC and banking regulatory authority policy announcements.

Under SFAS 114, loans are deemed impaired when it is probable that a creditor will be unable to collect all amounts contractually due, including both principal and interest. This determination is made by applying normal loan review procedures. Once impairment has been identified, the creditor institution must compute the present value of all the estimated future cash flows, using the loan's effective interest rate as the discount factor. The effective rate is defined as the loan's contractual rate as adjusted for any deferred loan fees, premiums, or discounts. It is this effective rate, and not the market rate at the time of determination of impairment, which must be used to compute the loss provision.

If the computed present value of the expected future cash flows is less than the carrying amount of the loan, an impairment will be recognized and recorded in a valuation allowance. Significant changes in the amount and/or timing of future estimated cash flows require that the creditor recalculate the amount of the loan's impairment. Adjustments, subject to the LCM criteria, will be reflected through changes in the valuation allowance.

In the event of a formal loan restructuring through a troubled debt restructuring, the loan is remeasured at the fair market value at the date of the restructuring. This treatment differs from an impairment because it is assumed that a new, formally restructured loan reflects current market conditions; therefore, no impairment is deemed to exist.

The standard, as amended, provides that impairment losses be recognized as bad debts when measured; however, no guidance is provided on the recognition and measurement of amounts later recovered.

Recently, new attention has been given to the relationship between SFAS 5 and 114 as definitive guidance for the provision of loss reserves. In several articles and a recent EITF Topic (D-80, *Application of FASB Statements No. 5 and No. 114 to a Loan Portfolio*), the FASB has indicated that loss provisions must be based only on **probable** losses which have occurred as of the balance sheet date, even if the individual loan which may have been impaired cannot be identified. Predictions of likely future losses to be incurred, even if such predictions have been historically highly accurate, cannot be used to anticipate losses that have not yet occurred. The SEC and banking regulatory agencies have lately expressed great interest in this matter (principally, it is assumed, due to a concern with the possibility of earnings management), and have essentially promised to enforce this informal FASB guidance as if it were part of the promulgated standards. Among other things, all loss provisions must be supported by appropriate documentation.

In fact, there is no conflict between SFAS 5 (in force since 1975) and SFAS 114 (effective 1995): losses are to be provided when it is probable that the asset has been impaired and the amount is subject to reasonable estimation. SFAS 114 is more specific than SFAS 5 in that it requires certain methods of measurement for loans that are individually considered impaired, but it does not fundamentally change the recognition criteria for loan losses. SFAS 114 provides guidance on measurement and disclosure for loans that are identified for evaluation and that are individually deemed to be impaired (because it is probable that the creditor will be unable to collect all the contractual interest and principal payments as scheduled in the loan agreement). It also includes all loans that are restructured in a troubled debt restructuring involving a modification of terms, except for those loans that are excluded from the scope of the standard.

In determining the existence and extent of impairment, "environmental" factors such as existing industry, geographical, economic, and political factors, should be given consideration. Obviously, the distinction between existing environmental factors and forecasts of changes in these factors over the near-term horizon is a subtle one, but it is one which must be maintained, since the latter cannot be used to justify current period loan loss provisions. For example, even if the consensus economic forecast is for a recession (which normally results in greater loan losses being experienced as current debtors face financial difficulties) if that downturn is not being experienced at the balance sheet date, loss reserves cannot be boosted to anticipate loan quality deterioration that has not yet occurred.

FASB has noted that some loans that are specifically identified for evaluation may be individually impaired, while other loans that are not impaired individually pursuant to SFAS 114 may have specific characteristics that indicate that there would be probable loss in a group of loans with those characteristics. Loans in the first category must be accounted for under SFAS 114, and loans in the second category should be accounted for under SFAS 5. Under SFAS 5, a loss is accrued if characteristics of a loan indicate that it is probable that a group of similar loans includes some losses even though the loss could not be identified with a specific loan. Characteristics or risk factors must be specifically identified to support an accrual for losses that have been incurred but that have not yet reached the point where it is probable that amounts will not be collected on a specific individual loan. A creditor should not ignore factors and information obtained in the evaluation of the loan's collectibility.

For example, if an individual loan specifically identified for evaluation is fully collateralized with risk-free assets, then consideration of that loan as sharing characteristics with a group of uncollateralized loans is inappropriate. Under SFAS 5, a loss is recognized if characteristics of a loan indicate that it is probable that a group of similar loans includes some losses even though the loss could not be identified to a specific loan. However, a loss would be recognized only if it is probable that the loss has been incurred at the date of the financial statements and the amount of loss can be reasonably estimated.

If a creditor concludes that an individual loan specifically identified for evaluation is impaired, an allowance in addition to one measured under SFAS 114 may **not** be established. That is, the SFAS 114 allowance should be the sole measure of impairment for that loan. This is equally true if the measurement of impairment under SFAS 114 results in no allowance. For example, a creditor might conclude that a given collateral-dependent loan is impaired, because it is probable that the creditor will be unable to collect all the contractual interest and principal payments as scheduled in the loan agreement. The creditor might, however, measure the impairment using the fair value of the collateral, which could result in no allowance if the fair value of the collateral is greater than the recorded investment in the loan. Further consideration of the need for a loss reserve by applying SFAS 5 to these facts would not be legitimate.

Particularly objectionable is the practice of increasing (or not decreasing) the allowance for loan losses in "good" economic times to provide for losses expected to occur in the future. This income smoothing technique is invalid under all circumstances, and cannot be rationalized by citing the historical cyclicality of the economy and the reasonable likelihood that higher losses will follow periods having lower loss experience. Reporting entities can anticipate that these practices will be closely scrutinized by the SEC and other regulatory authorities.

Nonrefundable Loan Fees and Costs

Loan origination fees. These fees should be **deferred** and recognized over the life of the loan as an adjustment of interest income. If there are any related direct loan origination costs, the **origination fees** and origination costs should be **netted**, and only the net amount should be deferred and amortized via the interest method. Origination costs include those **incremental costs** such as credit checks and security arrangements, among others, pertaining to a specific loan.

The only exception to the foregoing rule would be in the instance of certain loans that also qualify as debt instruments under SFAS 115. For those carried in the "trading securities" portfolio, related loan origination fees should be charged to expense when incurred; the requirement that these be carried at fair value would make adding these costs to the asset carrying amounts a useless exercise.

Example 1

Debtor Corp. wishes to take out a loan with Klein Bank for the purchase of new machinery. The fair market value of the machinery is $614,457. The loan is for ten years, designed to give Klein an implicit return of 10% on the loan. The annual payment is calculated as follows:

$$\text{Annual payment} = \frac{\$614,457}{PV_{10},10\%} = \frac{614,457}{6.14457} = \$100,000$$

Unearned interest on the loan would be $385,543 [(10 x $100,000) – $614,457].

Klein also is to receive a "nonrefundable origination fee" of $50,000. Klein incurred $20,000 of direct origination costs (for credit checks, etc.). Thus, Klein has **net** nonrefundable origination fees of $30,000. The new net investment in the loan is calculated below.

Gross investment in loan (10 x $100,000)	$1,000,000
Less: Unamortized net nonrefundable origination fees	(30,000)
	970,000
Less: Unearned interest income (from above)	385,543
Net investment in loan	$ 584,457

The new net investment in the loan can be used to find the new implicit interest rate.

$$\frac{100,000}{(1+i)^1} + \frac{100,000}{(1+i)^2} + \ldots + \frac{100,000}{(1+i)^{10}} = \$584,457$$

where i = implicit rate

Thus, the implicit interest rate is 11.002%. The amortization table for the first three years is set up as follows:

(a)	(b)	(c)	(d)	(e)	(f)
			Reduction	*Reduction*	
	Reduction	*Interest revenue*	*in net*	*in PV of*	*PV of*
Loan	*in unearned*	*(PV x implicit*	*orig. fees*	*net invest*	*net loan*
payments	*interest*	*rate of 11.002%)*	*(c-b)*	*(a-c)*	*investment*
					$584,457
$100,000	$61,446*	$64,302	$2,856	$35,689	548,759
100,000	57,590**	60,374	2,784	39,626	509,133
100,000	53,349***	56,015	2,666	43,985	465,148

```
   * ($614,457 x 10%) = $61,446
  ** [$614,457 – ($100,000 – $61,446)] x 10% = $57,590
 *** [$575,900 – ($100,000 – $57,590)] x 10% = $53,349
```

Commitment fees and costs. Often fees are received in advance in exchange for a **commitment** to originate or purchase a loan. These fees should be deferred and recognized upon exercise of the commitment as an adjustment of interest income over the life of the loan, as in Example 1 for origination costs and fees. If a commitment expires unexercised, the fees should be recognized as income upon expiration.

As with loan origination fees and costs, if **both** commitment fees are received and commitment costs are incurred relating to a commitment to originate or purchase a loan, the **net** amount of fees or costs should be deferred and recognized over the life of the loan.

If there is a **remote** possibility of exercise, the commitment fees may be recognized on a straight-line basis over the commitment period as "service fee income."

If there is a subsequent exercise, the unamortized fees at the date of exercise shall be recognized over the life of the loan as an adjustment of interest income, as in Example 1.

In certain cases, commitment fees are determined retroactively as a percentage of available lines of credit. If the commitment fee percentage is nominal in relation to the stated rate on the related borrowing, with the borrowing earning the market rate of interest, the fees shall be recognized in income as of the determination date.

Example 2

Glass Corp. has a $2 million, 10% line of credit outstanding with Ritter Bank. Ritter charges its annual commitment fee as 0.1% of any available balance as of the end of the prior period. Ritter will report $2,000 ($2 million x 0.1%) as service fee income in its current income statement.

Fees and costs in refinancing or restructurings. (Assume not a troubled-debt restructuring.) When the terms of a refinanced/restructured loan are as favorable to the lender as the terms for loans to customers with similar risks who are not in a restructuring, the refinanced loan is treated as a **new** loan, and all prior fees of the old loan are recognized in interest income when the new loan is made.

When the above situation is not satisfied, the fees or costs from the old loan become part of the net investment in the new loan.

Example 3

Jeffrey Bank refinanced a loan receivable to $1,000,000, at 10% interest, with annual interest receipts for ten years. Jeffrey's "normal" loan in its portfolio to debtors with similar risks is for $500,000 at 9% interest for five years. Jeffrey had loan origination fees from the original loan of $20,000. These fees are recognized in income **immediately** because the terms of the restructuring are as favorable to Jeffrey as a loan to another debtor with similar risks.

Example 4

Assume the same facts as in Example 3 except that the refinanced terms are $500,000 principal, 7% interest for three years. Since the terms of the restructuring are **not** as favorable to Jeffrey as a loan to another debtor with similar risks, the $20,000 origination fees become part of the new investment in the loan and recognized in interest income over the life of the new loan, as in Example 1.

Purchase of a loan or group of loans. Fees paid or fees received when purchasing a loan or group of loans should normally be considered part of the initial investment; to be recognized in income over the lives of the loans. However, if the loans qualify as debt securities under SFAS 115 and are held in the lender's "trading securities" portfolio, these fees should be reported in income when paid or received, and not added to the cost of the loans.

Special arrangements. Often lenders provide demand loans (loans with no scheduled payment terms). In this case, any net fees or costs should be recognized on a straight-line basis over a period determined by mutual agreement of the parties, usually over the estimated length of the loan.

Under a revolving line of credit, any net fees or costs are recognized in income on a straight-line basis over the period that the line of credit is active. If the line of credit is terminated due to the borrower's full payment, any unamortized net fees or costs are recognized in income.

Example 5

Green Bank received $50,000 as a nonrefundable origination fee on a $2 million demand loan. Green's loan dictates that any fees are to be amortized over a period of ten years. Therefore, $5,000 ($50,000 x 1/10) of origination fees will be recognized as an addition to interest income each year for the next ten years.

Financial statement presentation. The unamortized balance of origination, commitment, and other fees/costs that are recognized as an adjustment of interest income shall be reported on the balance sheet as part of the loan balance to which they relate. Except for any special cases as noted in the above paragraphs, the amount of net fees/costs recognized each period as an adjustment will be reported in the income statement as part of interest income.

Cash Flow Statement

Banks, savings institutions, and credit unions are **not** required to report gross cash receipts and payments for the following:

1. Deposits placed with other financial institutions
2. Withdrawals of deposits
3. Time deposits accepted
4. Repayments of deposits
5. Loans made to customers
6. Principal collections of loans

If an enterprise is part of a consolidated enterprise, net cash receipts and payments of the enterprise should be reported separate from the gross cash receipts and payments of the consolidated enterprise.

EMERGING ISSUES TASK FORCE CONSENSUS SUMMARIES

84-4   Acquisition, Development, and Construction Loans

The Task Force discussed the treatment of ADC loans as loans, investments, or interests in a joint venture and the accounting for a partial sale of the arrangement. These issues were resolved by the issuance of the AICPA Notice to Practitioners, ADC Arrangements, which covers ADC arrangements in which the lender expects to participate in residual profit and gives guidance on accounting and reporting concerns.

84-9   Deposit Float of Banks

The Task Force agreed that to allow banks to delay recording assets and liabilities for checks deposited until collection is made from the drawee bank would constitute an accounting change. However, a consensus was reached that the change would be difficult to justify because this approach is conceptually flawed.

84-19   Mortgage Loan Payment Modifications

The Task Force discussed agreements in which the lender allows the borrower to make larger payments for some period (at least twelve payments) and is then relieved of his remaining obligation. A consensus was reached that the loss related to the forgiven portion should be accrued over the period of the larger payments.

84-20   GNMA Dollar Rolls

A consensus was reached on the treatment of only one of the four types of GNMA rolls. The Task Force agreed that forward commitment dollar rolls should be marked to market. The remaining issues were resolved by SOP 85-2, which was subsequently amended by SOP 90-3.

84-21   Sale of a Loan with a Partial Participation Retained

In some instances, an enterprise may sell a loan but retain a share in the interest income as well as servicing rights. The Task Force debated whether the present value of the future interest inflows should be recognized immediately or over the life of the loan and agreed that the accounting treatment specified in the AICPA Audit and Accounting Guide, *Savings and Loan Associations*, should be followed.

84-22   Prior Years' Earnings Per Share Following a Savings and Loan Association Conversion and Pooling

The Task Force agreed that when a mutual savings and loan association converts to stock ownership and pools with another S&L, its EPS should be excluded from the restated combined EPS for years before the date of conversion. The method of presentation must be disclosed.

84-31   Equity Certificates of Deposit

The Task Force concluded that contingent interest expense resulting from equity certificates of deposit is recognized concurrently with gains relating to the assets upon which the equity is given.

85-7   Federal Home Loan Mortgage Corporation Stock

The Task Force debated the proper accounting for the new class of nonvoting, participating preferred stock issued on December 6, 1984, to members of the Federal Home Loan Banking System. A consensus was not reached, although the majority opinion was that the stock is a nonmonetary asset that should be accounted for at fair value in accordance with APB 29. The issue was subsequently resolved by FASB TB 85-1, which concurred with the Task Force and further stated that the resulting income is extraordinary.

85-8 Amortization of Thrift Intangibles

When a banking or thrift institution is acquired, the excess of the fair value of liabilities over the fair value of assets should be amortized to expense in accordance with SFAS 72. Any other goodwill resulting from the combination should be amortized according to APB 17.

85-13 Sale of Mortgage Service Rights on Mortgages Owned by Others

The Task Force agreed that a gain should be recognized upon the sale of mortgage service rights that include participation in the future interest stream of the loans.

85-18 Earnings Per Share Effect of Equity Commitment Notes

The Task Force concluded that neither equity commitment notes nor equity contract notes should be included in earnings per share computations.

85-20 Recognition of Fees for Guaranteeing a Loan

A consensus was reached that a guarantor should recognize loan guarantee fees as revenue over the term of the guarantee. Any direct costs related to the guarantee must be recognized in the same manner. If material, footnote disclosure is required, and the probability of loss should be continually assessed.

85-24 Distribution Fees by Distributors of Mutual Funds That Do Not Have a Front-End Sales Charge

The Task Force concluded that the currently used cost deferral method should be maintained. Under this method, fees expected to be received over some future period should be recognized upon receipt. Deferred incremental direct costs are amortized while indirect costs are expensed as incurred.

85-26 Measurement of Servicing Fees under FASB Statement 65 When a Loan Is Sold with Servicing Retained

The Task Force debated whether mortgage bankers should consider servicing fee rates set by secondary market makers (GNMA, FHLMC, FNMA) to be the minimum for a normal servicing fee rate. A consensus was not reached, but the issue was subsequently resolved by FASB TB 87-3, which states that these rates should be considered normal for transactions with those agencies.

85-31 Comptroller of the Currency's Rule on Deferred Tax Debits

The Task Force reached a consensus that the Comptroller's Banking Circular 202, which limits the net deferred tax debits allowable on a bank's statement of condition, applies only for regulatory purposes and does not affect GAAP financial statements.

85-41 Accounting for Savings and Loan Associations under FSLIC Management Consignment Program

When a troubled thrift is closed under the Management Consignment Program (MCP), its assets (tangible and identifiable intangible) and liabilities are transferred at fair value to a newly chartered federal mutual association. FV constitutes the new cost basis, which should not be adjusted to market on a continuing basis but instead maintained according to GAAP. Any excess of liabilities over assets is recorded as deficit equity. The proper accounting is the same for both stock and mutual institutions, and the transfer does not constitute a business combination.

85-42 Amortization of Goodwill Resulting from Recording Time Savings Deposits at Fair Values

When a financial institution is acquired by purchase, the excess of the fair value of liabilities over the fair value of assets (SFAS 72 goodwill) should be amortized over a period up to the remaining life of the long-term interest-bearing assets acquired. Any other goodwill resulting from the combination should be amortized according to APB 17.

85-44 Differences between Loan Loss Allowances for GAAP and RAP

The Task Force reached a consensus that loan loss allowances recorded by S&Ls may differ under regulatory accounting principles (RAP) and GAAP. However, auditors must make certain that any differences are justifiable.

86-21 Application of the AICPA Notice to Practitioners Regarding Acquisition, Development, and Construction Arrangements to Acquisition of an Operating Property

The Task Force concluded that AICPA Notice to Practitioners, *ADC Arrangements*, which deals with real estate ADC arrangements of financial institutions, should also be considered in relation to ADC arrangements transacted by nonfinancial institutions, shared appreciation mortgages, and loans on operating real estate. The Task Force also reached consensus that paras 3-5 of that Notice should be consulted in determining the nature of expected residual profit on the arrangement.

86-31 Reporting the Tax Implications of a Pooling of a Bank and a Savings and Loan Association

A consensus was reached regarding the tax effects of a required reduction in bad-debt reserves (for tax purposes) in a merger of a savings and loan association and a banking, insurance, or other financial institution. The tax effects should be accounted for as an expense in the current period's combined financial statements of the merged entity.

The Task Force also reached a consensus that after the bad-debt reserves are adjusted for the merger transaction, deferred taxes should be recorded for the difference between bad-debt reserves for tax and financial purposes.

86-38 Implications of Mortgage Prepayments on Amortization of Servicing Rights

An excess service fee receivable (resulting from a higher than normal servicing fee) must be written down to the present value of the remaining future excess service fee revenue discounted with the same factor used to calculate the original receivable.

87-22 Prepayment to the Secondary Reserve of the FSLIC

The secondary reserve of the FSLIC was eliminated as of December 31, 1986, although member institutions were not notified until May 1987. The Task Force agreed that this represents a subsequent event and that the related amounts should be written off as a loss against 1987 operating income.

87-34 Sale of Mortgage Servicing Rights with a Subservicing Agreement

The Task Force discussed events in which a mortgage loan servicer (transferor) transfers the servicing rights and related risks to an unaffiliated enterprise (transferee), which then makes a subservicing agreement whereby the transferor services the loans for a fixed fee. A consensus was reached that income recognition should be deferred and that treatment as a sale or a financing depends on the circumstances surrounding the transaction. However, this consensus does not apply to temporary subservicing agreements. In addition, a loss should be recognized currently if loan prepayments may result in future servicing losses.

88-17 Accounting for Fees and Costs Associated with Loan Syndications and Loan Participations

The Task Force agreed that there are no material differences between loan syndications and some loan participations and thus both should receive the same accounting treatment. In addition, a transaction structured legally as a participation which actually constitutes an in-substance syndication should be accounted for as a syndication. A transaction structured legally as a syndication must also meet certain criteria to be accounted for as such by the lead syndicator.

88-19 FSLIC-Assisted Acquisitions of Thrifts

The Task Force reached a consensus on several issues, which are listed below.

1. In a tax-sharing agreement, the Thrift acts as a conduit for tax benefits accruing to the FSLIC and records only its net benefit in accordance with GAAP.
2. In applying SFAS 72, assets covered by yield maintenance assistance are considered interest-bearing, even if they are not.
3. When allocating the purchase price, the stated interest rate is considered the market rate and is used to determine the fair value of the acquired assets.
4. The basis of an asset covered by yield maintenance assistance is carried over to any new covered asset to which it is converted.
5. Contingency losses related to the acquisition are recorded net of reimbursements under indemnification provisions of the assistance agreement.
6. If the assistance includes a note receivable from the FSLIC and the sale of equity securities to the FSLIC, the note should be offset against that equity.
7. If issue 6 applies, then the Thrift should net divided payments made to the FSLIC against cash received from the FSLIC as interest on the note. This net amount is recorded as regulatory assistance.

SFAS 109 and SEC Staff Accounting Bulletin provide additional guidance.

88-20 Difference between Initial Investment and Principal Amount of Loans in a Purchased Credit Card Portfolio

The Task Force agreed that the excess of the purchase price of a credit card portfolio including cardholder relationships over the amounts due should be allocated between the credit card loans acquired and the cardholder relationships acquired. The premium related to cardholder relationships is an identifiable intangible asset and is amortized over the period of benefit. The premium related to the loans is amortized over the life of the loans.

88-25 Ongoing Accounting and Reporting for a Newly Created Liquidating Bank

The Task Force concluded that the assets and liabilities of liquidating banks should be reported at fair value as of the date of the financial statements, with subsequent increases and decreases in fair value included in the results of each period. The initial valuation method should be used to determine fair value each period. SEC Staff Accounting Bulletin 82 provides additional guidance.

89-3 Balance Sheet Presentation of Savings Accounts in Financial Statements of Credit Unions

The Task Force agreed that the savings accounts deposited in a credit union must be unequivocally listed as a liability if the financial statements of the credit union are to comply with the AICPA Credit Union Guide. The statement of financial condition must present savings accounts either as the first item in the liabilities and equity section or as a separate subtotal before total liabilities.

89-19 Accounting for a Change in Goodwill Amortization for Business Combinations Initiated prior to the Effective Date of FASB Statement 72

A consensus was reached that an enterprise can adopt the provisions of SFAS 72 to account for goodwill obtained in a purchase-type business combination occurring prior to the effective date of the statement. As the adoption of SFAS 72 results in a change in accounting principle, it should be recorded as a cumulative effect adjustment.

The Task Force noted that this consensus applies specifically to SFAS 72 and should not be applied to other situations.

Additionally, the consensus on this issue does not prevent an enterprise from applying the special exemption for an initial public distribution.

90-18 Effect of a "Removal of Accounts" Provision on the Accounting for a Credit Card Securitization

The Task Force concluded that credit card securitizations with "removal of accounts" provisions should be recognized as sales transactions under SFAS 77 as long as the removal meets any specified terms, doesn't reduce the interests of the investor in the pool, and doesn't reduce the seller's percentage interest below a contractually specified level.

90-21 Balance Sheet Treatment of a Sale of Mortgage Servicing Rights with a Subservicing Agreement

The Task Force agreed that such transactions (discussed in Issue 87-34) should be accounted for as a sale if substantially all the risks and rewards of ownership have been transferred to the buyer. If substantially all the risks and rewards have **not** been transferred, then the transaction must be accounted for as a financing.

92-5 Amortization Period for Net Deferred Credit Card Origination Fees

A consensus was reached that credit card origination costs that qualify for deferral in accordance with SFAS 91 should be netted against the credit card fee charged, if any, and the net amount should be amortized on a straight-line basis over the term of the credit card or one year, depending on the significance of the fee.

Additionally, for both purchased and originated credit cards, the accounting policies, the net amount capitalized, and the amortization period should be disclosed.

93-1 Accounting for Individual Credit Card Acquisitions

A consensus was reached that credit card accounts acquired individually should be accounted for as originations under SFAS 91 and EITF Issue 92-5.

FASB TECHNICAL BULLETINS

87-3 Accounting for Mortgage Servicing Fees and Rights

Normal servicing fee rates for mortgage loans are those set by federally sponsored secondary market makers (GNMA, FHLMC, FNMA). For transactions with those agencies or for mortgage loans sold to private sector investors where the seller retains servicing rights, normal servicing rates should be considered. In the latter case, a stated servicing fee rate that differs from the normal rate requires adjustment to the sales price to yield the normal rate. In either case, a loss should be accrued if expected servicing costs exceed anticipated fees based on the stated servicing fee rate. If the servicer refinances a mortgage loan and actual prepayments differ from any anticipated prepayments, then the servicing asset must be adjusted.

BENEFIT PLANS, INCLUDING PENSION FUNDS
PERSPECTIVE AND ISSUES

Employee benefit plans have become increasingly important and diverse. Using assets that are segregated from the plan sponsor, they provide benefits to employees and former employees in accordance with a plan agreement. The provisions of the plan agreement deal with such matters as eligibility, entitlement to benefits, funding, plan amendments, operation and administration, allocation of responsibilities among the fiduciaries, and fiduciaries' ability to delegate duties. A few examples of employee benefit plans are pension plans, profit-sharing plans, stock bonus plans, 401(k) plans, 403(b) plans, disability plans, health care plans, life insurance plans, unemployment benefit plans, tuition assistance plans, dependent care plans, and cafeteria plans. For accounting and reporting purposes, the plans are divided into three major types: defined benefit pension plans, defined contribution pension plans, and health and welfare benefit plans.

Employee benefit plans that are sponsored by and provide benefits to the employees of state and local governmental entities[1] are outside of the scope of this publication. Readers instead should refer to the Wiley publication, *GAAP for Governments*.

All authoritative pronouncements in the GAAP hierarchy apply to employee benefits plans unless the pronouncement specifically excludes employee benefit plans from its scope. Certain authoritative pronouncements apply specifically to employee benefit plans. Because those pronouncements are particularly relevant to the transactions of employee benefit plans, they are discussed in this chapter.

SFAS 35 is the principal standard involving the accounting and reporting of employee plans. Although SFAS 35's provisions apply only to defined pension benefit plans, the AICPA Audit and Accounting Guide, *Audits of Employee Benefit Plans,* requires defined contribution plans and employee health and welfare benefit plans to apply specialized accounting principles and practices that are similar to those of SFAS 35. SFAS 35 applies only to ongoing plans, not to ones that are terminated or expected to be terminated. The Statement describes the objectives of plan financial statements and the necessary components of a complete set of plan financial statements.

SFAS 102 exempts defined benefit pension plans and certain other employee benefit plans from SFAS 95's requirement to present a statement of cash flows.

SFAS 110 requires defined benefit pension plans to report all investment contracts, including guaranteed investment contracts issued by insurance companies, at fair value. Only contracts that incorporate mortality or morbidity risk (insurance contracts) may be reported at contract value.

---

[1] *See Chapter 1, Researching GAAP Problems, for a definition of "governmental entity."*

The Audit Guide mentioned above is the primary AICPA pronouncement that sets standards for employee benefit plans. In addition to providing accounting and reporting guidance for the plans, it provides summaries of statutory rules and regulations applicable to employee benefit plans and illustrations of financial statements.

SOP 92-6 establishes standards for health and welfare benefit plans. It divides the diverse universe of plans into two major types: defined benefit health and welfare plans and defined contribution health and welfare plans. It requires defined benefit health and welfare plans to use certain provisions of SFAS 106, *Employer's Accounting for Postretirement Benefits other than Pensions,* to measure benefit obligations. In addition, SOP 92-6 applies many of the measurement and disclosure provisions of SFAS 35 to health and welfare plans.

SOP 94-4 requires defined contribution plans and health and welfare benefit plans to report insurance and investment contracts in a manner similar to the requirements of SFAS 110.

SOP 99-2 specifies the accounting for and disclosure of 401(h) features of defined benefit pension plans that offer medical benefits to retirees in addition to the normal retirement benefits.

SOP 99-3 amends the Audit Guide and SOP 94-4 to simplify the required disclosures about investments. It also supersedes Practice Bulletin 12, which required information about net assets and significant components of the changes in net assets for each investment fund option of a defined contribution pension plan.

SOP 01-2 amends the Audit Guide and SOP 96-2 to modify the presentation requirements for information about benefit obligations, to clarify the measurement date for benefit obligations, to establish standards for postemployment benefit plans, and to add three new disclosures.

This section presents a highly summarized discussion of accounting and reporting standards by employee benefit plans. Readers who desire a more in-depth discussion should refer to the Wiley publication, *GAAP for Employee Benefit Plans.*

This chapter does not describe an employer's requirements for reporting information about employee benefit plans. That information is described in Chapter 16, Pensions.

Sources of GAAP		
SFAS	*AICPA Guides*	*SOP*
35, 102, 110	*Audits of Employee Benefit Plans*	92-6, 94-4, 99-2, 99-3, 01-2

DEFINITIONS OF TERMS

Accumulated plan benefits or **benefit obligations.** Benefits that are attributable to services rendered by employees before the date as of which the actuarial present value of the plan obligation is computed.

Defined benefit pension plan. A plan that promises stated or otherwise determinable pension benefits to participants based on factors such as compensation, years of service, and age.

Defined contribution pension plan. A plan in which benefits are based on amounts contributed, investment experience, and allocated forfeitures, net of administrative expenses. Each participant's benefits are computed based on his or her individual account.

Health and welfare benefit plan. Plans that provide benefits such as medical, dental, visual, or other health care, insurance, disability, vacation, education, or dependent care.

Net assets. The residual interest in the assets of an employee benefit plan that remains after deducting its liabilities. The liabilities of a plan do not include its accumulated plan benefits (defined benefit pension plans) or its benefit obligation (defined benefit health and welfare plans).

Plan sponsor. The company, association, employee group, or other group of representatives that established or maintains the plan.

CONCEPTS, RULES, AND EXAMPLES

In addition to varying by basic type (defined benefit pension plan, defined contribution pension plan, and health and welfare benefit plan), employee benefit plans vary by operating and administrative characteristics. Plans can be established by one employer or a group of controlled corporations, in that case they are referred to as single employer plans. Alternatively, they can include the employees of many employers who are related in some way, often by a collective-bargaining agreement. Those plans are referred to as multiemployer plans. A plan can be either contributory or noncontributory. A contributory plan requires both the employer and the participants to fund (contribute to) the cost of the future benefits. In a noncontributory plan, the participants do not fund any part of the cost of the future benefits. Insured plans are funded through insurance contracts. Self-funded plans are funded through contributions and investment return. Split-funded plans are funded by a combination of insurance contracts, contributions, and investment return.

Complete Set of Financial Statements

The primary objective of a plan's financial statements is to provide the information necessary to assessing the plan's ability to pay benefits when due. Thus, financial statements should include information about the plan's resources, the results of transactions and events that changed the plan's resources, the stewardship of management over the plan's resources, and any other facts necessary to understand the information provided.

A complete set of financial statements should include a statement of net assets available for benefits as of the end of the plan year (balance sheet equivalent), a statement of changes in net assets available for benefits for the plan year ended (an income statement equivalent), and notes to financial statements. In addition, defined benefit plans must include information about the actuarial present value of accumulated benefits and changes in the accumulated benefits. That information can appear either as additional financial statements or in the notes to financial statements.

SFAS 102 exempted defined benefit pension plans from the requirement that a statement of cash flows be provided. Other employee benefit plans were also exempted if they report similar to defined benefit pension plans, including SFAS 35's requirement to report plan investments at fair value. Although not required, presentation of a statement of cash flows is encouraged if it would provide useful information about the plan's ability to pay future liabilities, as would be the case if the plan either holds illiquid investments or purchases investments using borrowed funds.

SFAS 130, *Reporting Comprehensive Income,* requires that changes in equity other than transactions with owners be reported in financial statements in the period in which they are recognized. The statement of changes in net assets available for benefits is a comprehensive income statement because all changes in net assets available for benefits are reflected in that statement. Thus, although it does not specifically exempt employee benefit plans from its provisions, SFAS 130 does not change the reporting for employee benefit plans.

Statement of Net Assets Available for Benefits

Most investments of the plan are reported at fair value. If there is an active market, quoted market prices should be used. If market quotations are not available, investments should be valued "in good faith" by the plan's trustees and administrator. The selling price of similar investments or discounted cash flows could be useful in estimating fair value. The use of an independent expert may be necessary for the valuation of certain investments. Investment contracts with an insurance company, bank, or other financial institution are reported at fair value. Only insurance contracts—contracts that incorporate mortality or morbidity risk (defined benefit pension plans) or that are fully benefit-responsive (defined contribution plans and health and welfare plans)—may be reported at contract value, and then only if the plan reports at contract value in its annual report filed with government agencies. The financial statements should identify plan investments by type of investment and should indicate how fair value was determined. It is not necessary to disclose the original cost of investments. Plans should disclose in the notes to the financial statements any investments representing 5% or more of the net assets available for benefits as of the end of the year.

Contributions receivable include those due as of the reporting date from participants, employers, withdrawing employers of a multiemployer plan, and other sources (such as a state or federal government in the case of a grant or subsidy).

Receivables arise from formal commitments of an employer, legal requirements, or contractual requirements. The receivables should include an allowance for uncollectible amounts if warranted.

Long-lived assets (such as buildings, equipment, furniture and fixtures, and leasehold improvements) that are used in the plan's operations are presented at cost less accumulated depreciation or amortization.

Statement of Changes in Net Assets Available for Benefits

The statement of changes in net assets available for benefits is a comprehensive income statement that includes all recognized transactions and events that change the net assets available for benefits. At a minimum, the statement should include separate amounts for

1. Contributions from

    a. Employer(s)—separating cash from noncash contributions
    b. Participants, including those transmitted by the plan sponsor
    c. Other identified sources

2. Net appreciation or depreciation (realized and unrealized amounts may be combined) in fair value for each significant class of investment, presented by

    a. Investments measured by quoted market prices
    b. Investments measured by some other means

3. Investment income (not including appreciation or depreciation in fair value)
4. Payments to plan participants for benefits, excluding amounts paid by insurance contracts that are not included in plan assets
5. Payments to insurance companies to purchase contracts that are excluded from plan assets
6. Administrative expenses
7. Other changes, if necessary, with appropriate description(s)

Transactions with Related Parties (SFAS 57)

Transactions between a plan sponsor and its employee benefit plans are subject to the disclosure requirements of SFAS 57, *Related-Party Disclosures*. The required disclosures include

1. The nature of the relationship
2. A description of the transactions for each of the periods in which a statement of changes in net assets available for benefits is presented
3. The dollar amounts of transactions for each of the period in which a statement of changes in net assets available for benefits is presented
4. The effects of any change from the prior period in the method of establishing terms of the transaction

5. The amounts due from related parties at the date of each statement of net assets available for benefits

The disclosures should not represent that transactions were made at arm's length unless such representations can be substantiated.

Risks and Uncertainties

Employee benefit plans must disclose the information required by SOP 94-6, *Disclosures of Certain Significant Risks and Uncertainties.* Risks that are unique to employee benefit plans include

1. A significant industry downturn that could cause employees retire early in order to avoid being laid off, especially if the plan's participants are concentrated within a particular industry or with a single employer
2. Likelihood that an employer will significantly increase pension or health and welfare benefits in order to avoid a union walkout
3. A planned downsizing that is expected to offer early retirement to employees
4. Investments in the stock of the employer

Defined Benefit Pension Plans

In addition to the statement of net assets available for benefits and the statement of changes in net assets available for benefits, defined benefit pension plans must provide information about the actuarial present value of accumulated plan benefits and changes in the actuarial present value of accumulated plan benefits. The information can be included as separate financial statements or as schedules in the notes to the financial statements.

Accumulated plan benefits include the present value of future benefits to retired or terminated employees or their beneficiaries, to beneficiaries of deceased employees, and to present employees or their beneficiaries. Whenever possible, plan provisions should govern the measurement of accumulated plan benefits. If the benefits earned in each year are not determinable from the plan's provisions, a formula for measurement is provided in SFAS 35. When calculating accumulated plan benefits, an ongoing plan should be assumed. Thus, interest rates used for discounting expected future payments should be based on rates of return on investments for the benefit deferral period, and employee turnover and employee mortality should be considered.

At a minimum, the information provided in the financial statements for accumulated plan benefits should include

1. Vested benefits of participants currently collecting benefits
2. Other vested benefits
3. Nonvested benefits
4. Accumulated contributions of active employees in contributory plans, if applicable

Either a reconciliation or a narrative description should identify significant factors changing the accumulated plan benefits from the beginning of the year to the end. The information should include

1. Effects of plan amendments
2. Changes in the nature of the plan, such as a merger or a spin-off
3. Changes in actuarial assumptions
4. Benefits accumulated during the year
5. Benefits paid during the year
6. Interest component (from amortizing the discount)
7. Other changes

The last four items can be combined into a single "other changes" category.

Defined Contribution Pension Plans

The three general types of defined contribution plans are profit-sharing plans, money purchase pension plans, and stock bonus plans. A profit-sharing plan is a plan that is neither a pension plan, as defined in the Internal Revenue Code, nor a stock bonus plan. Employer contributions to a profit-sharing plan are either discretionary or based on a fixed formula. Although the plan is called a profit-sharing plan, the contributions need not be made from the profits of the plan sponsor. A money purchase plan is a pension plan that bases employer contributions on a fixed formula that is unrelated to profits. A stock bonus plan is a plan that makes its distributions to participants in the stock of the employer unless the participant chooses otherwise. Within these three categories of plans are more specialized plans, such as 401(k) plans, 403(b) plans, savings plans, employee stock ownership plans, target benefit plans, and Keogh plans.

The three primary differences between defined contribution plans and defined benefit plans are

1. Employer contributions are determined at the discretion of the employer or according to a contractual formula, rather than being actuarially determined.
2. Individual accounts are maintained for each plan participant, rather than a single account in which all participants partake.
3. Benefits are determined based on the amount accumulated in a participant's account at the time he or she retires or withdraws from the plan, rather than being defined in the plan agreement. If vested, the account's value is either paid to the participant or used to purchase an annuity for the participant.

The liabilities of a defined contribution plan should include accounts payable, amounts owed for securities purchases, borrowings, and income taxes payable. The liabilities should not include amounts that have not been paid to withdrawing participants. Those amounts should be included in net assets available for benefits and should be disclosed in the financial statements. Because those amounts are liabilities for regulatory purposes, a note to reconcile the financial statements to the Form 5500 may be necessary to comply with ERISA.

Employee Health and Welfare Plans

Defined benefit health and welfare plans stipulate a determinable benefit amount, which may take the form of a payment directly to the participant or a payment to a third party (such as a service provider or an insurance company) on the participant's behalf. Factors such as length of employment, age, and salary level determine the level of benefits to be provided. The contributions from the employer may be determined actuarially, by actual claims paid, or by a formula established by the plan sponsor. Regardless of the manner in which the plan is funded, the plan is a defined benefit health and welfare plan if its purpose if to provide a defined benefit.

Like defined benefit pension plans, defined benefit health and welfare plans must include information in their financial statements about the actuarial present value of benefit obligations earned by past service. A benefit obligation exists if all of the following conditions are met:

1. The participants' rights to receive benefits are attributable to services already rendered.
2. The participants' benefits vest or accumulate.
3. Payment of benefits is probable.
4. The amount can be reasonably estimated.

If conditions 1. and 2. are not met, the obligation exists if the event that gives rise to the liability has already occurred and the amount can be reasonably estimated. The benefit obligations should be reported as of the end of the plan year and should include the actuarial present value of

1. Claims payable currently to active or retired participants
2. Claims of active participants that were incurred but are not yet reported (IBNR)
3. Insurance premiums due
4. Accumulated eligibility credits and postemployment benefits, net of amounts currently payable
5. Postretirement benefits for retired participants and their beneficiaries, other plan participants who are eligible to receive benefits, and active participants who are not yet eligible to receive benefits.

Benefit obligations of defined benefit health and welfare plans, similar to accumulated plan benefits of defined benefit pension plans, do not appear as liabilities on the statement of net assets available for benefits. Instead, they are presented either as a separate financial statement, on the face of another financial statement, such as the statement of net assets available for benefits, or in the notes to the financial statements. Regardless of the location selected, the information about benefit obligations should be presented in its entirety in the same location.

A reconciliation, presented as a separate statement, on the face of another financial statement, or in the notes to the financial statements, should identify significant factors changing the benefit obligation from the beginning of the year to the end. The changes should be classified into at least three categories: (1) amounts currently payable, which includes claims payable, claims IBNR, and premiums due insurance companies, (2) accumulated eligibility credits and postemployment benefits, net of amounts currently payable, and (3) postretirement benefit obligations. The information for each category should include

1. Effects of plan amendments
2. Changes in the nature of the plan, such as a merger or a spin-off
3. Changes in actuarial assumptions
4. Benefits accumulated during the year
5. Benefits paid during the year
6. Interest component (from amortizing the discount)
7. Other changes

The last four items can be combined into a single "other changes" line.

Defined contribution health and welfare plans, like other defined contribution plans, maintain an account for each participant that determines the amount of benefits that the participant will eventually receive. The terms of a defined contribution health and welfare plan agreement determine the contribution that will be made by the employer or participant into each account. Defined contribution health and welfare plans do not report information about benefit obligations because a plan's obligation is limited to the amounts accumulated in the participants' accounts.

Government Regulations

Through ERISA, the federal government oversees the operating and reporting practices of employee benefit plans. ERISA establishes minimum standards for participation, vesting, and funding. It defines the responsibilities of plan fiduciaries and standards for their conduct. It requires plans to annually report summarized plan information to plan participants.

The Department of Labor (DOL) and the Internal Revenue Service (IRS) are authorized to issue regulations establishing reporting and disclosure requirements for employee benefit plans that are subject to ERISA. Each year, plans are required to report certain information to the DOL, the IRS, and the Pension Benefit Guaranty Corporation (if applicable). For many plans, the information is reported to the IRS using Form 5500, which includes financial statements prepared in conformity with GAAP and additional financial schedules.

Various provisions of the Internal Revenue Code apply to employee benefit plans. If an employee benefit plan qualifies under Section 401(a) of the Code, certain favorable tax treatments apply. For example, if a plan is qualified, the plan sponsor receives current deductions for contributions to the plan, and the plan participants do not pay income taxes until benefits are distributed to them. In addition, plan participants may receive favorable tax treatment on the distributions. Qualified plans are exempt from income taxes, except for taxes on unrelated business income. Unqualified plans, which generally provide benefits only to a few key employees, are not entitled to those favorable treatments.

Terminating Plans

If a decision has been made to terminate a plan, the plan is a terminating plan, even if another plan will replace the terminated plan. A terminating plan may continue to operate for as long as is necessary to pay accrued benefits. Prominent disclosure of the relevant circumstances is necessary in all financial statements issued by the plan after the decision to terminate is made. Financial statements of a terminating plan are prepared on the liquidation basis of accounting for plan years ending after the termination decision. For plan assets, the change to the liquidation basis may have little or no effect, since many assets are already reported at current market value. However, the liquidation basis for accumulated plan benefits (defined benefit pension plans) and benefit obligations (defined benefit health and welfare plans) may differ from the actuarial present value of benefits for an ongoing plan. For example, certain or all benefits may become vested upon termination.

STATEMENTS OF POSITION

92-6   Accounting and Reporting by Health and Welfare Plans

SOP 92-6 divides health and welfare plans into two major types: defined benefit health and welfare plans and defined contribution health and welfare plans. The SOP requires many of the measurement and disclosure provisions of SFAS 35 to be used in reporting health and welfare plans. For example, it requires defined benefit health and welfare plans to provide information about benefit obligations, including postretirement benefit obligations. It also requires defined benefit health and welfare plans to use certain provisions of SFAS 106, *Employer's Accounting for Postretirement Benefits other than Pensions,* to measure benefit obligations.

SOP 92-6 also provides guidance for recognizing claims incurred but not reported (IBNR) and accumulated eligibility credits. For self-funded plans, the cost of IBNR includes the present value of the estimated cost of settling the claims, even if the costs will be incurred after the financial statement date. For insured plans, the cost of IBNR that will be paid by an insurance company should be excluded from the benefit obligations of the plan. The calculation of the obligation for accumulated eligibility credits should consider mortality rates and the expected employee turnover.

94-4 Reporting of Investment Contracts Held by Health and Welfare Benefit Plans and Defined Contribution Pension Plans

SOP 94-4 requires health and welfare benefit plans and defined contribution pension plans to report investment contracts with fully benefit-responsive features at contract value. Other investment contracts should be reported at fair value. Benefit responsiveness is the extent to which the terms of the investment contract permit and require withdrawals by the participant. To be fully benefit-responsive, a contact must provide participants access to their account at contract value for all transactions permitted by the plan, without limitations other than administrative provisions designed to control the costs of the plan. Insurance contracts, as defined by SFAS 60, *Accounting and Reporting by Insurance Enterprises,* must be presented using the same valuation method (either fair value or contract value) as used in the annual report filed by the plan with certain governmental agencies pursuant to ERISA. Plans not subject to ERISA present insurance contracts as if the plans were subject to the reporting requirements of ERISA.

99-2 Accounting for and Reporting of Postretirement Medical Benefit 401(h) Features of Defined Benefit Pension Plans

This statement specifies the accounting for and disclosure of 401(h) features of defined benefit pension plans. Defined benefit pension plans are required to record the aggregate amount of net assets held in a 401(h) account related to health and welfare obligations as both assets and liabilities on the face of the statement of net assets available for pension benefits. They are required to disclose the fact that the 401(h) account assets are available only to pay retirees' health benefits. The financial statements of the related health and welfare benefit plan must include the 401(h) account assets used to fund health benefits and the changes in those assets. The health and welfare benefit plans must disclose in the notes to its financial statements that retiree health benefits are funded through a 401(h) account of the defined benefit pension plan.

99-3 Accounting for and Reporting of Certain Defined Contribution Plan Investments and Other Disclosure Matters

SOP 99-3 amends the Audit Guide and SOP 94-4 to simplify the required disclosures about investments. For defined contribution plans, it removes the requirement to provide information about participant-directed investment programs in a separate fund (column) of the financial statements. It also supersedes Practice Bulletin 12, *Reporting Separate Investment Fund Option Information of Defined Contribution Pension Plans.* Instead, it requires defined contribution plans that provide both participant-directed and non-participant-directed programs to disclose information about the net assets available for benefits and changes in those net assets for the nonparticipant programs. The information provided should be in sufficient detail to identify the types of investments and the changes in them. If any investment has a value equal to 5% or more of the net assets available for benefits and is also non-participant-directed, that fact must be disclosed in the financial statements. In addition, SOP 99-3 amends SOP 94-4 to remove the requirements to provide necessary disclosures for benefit-responsive investment contracts "by investment option." SOP 99-3 is effective for financial statements for plan years ending after December 15, 1999.

01-2   Accounting and Reporting by Health and Welfare Benefit Plans

SOP 01-2 amends the Audit Guide and SOP 92-6 to modify the presentation requirements for information about benefit obligations, to clarify the measurement date for benefit obligations, to establish standards for postemployment benefit plans, and to add three new disclosures. It permits information about benefit obligations and changes in benefit obligations to be presented in notes to the financial statements. It clarifies that the measurement date of benefit obligation information is as of the fiscal year-end; however, that requirement does not preclude the plan from using the most recent obligation valuation and rolling it forward to account for subsequent events, such as employee service, benefit payments, and changes in the discount rate. SOP 01-2 requires postemployment benefit plan obligations to be recognized using criteria similar to those used in SFAS 106, *Employer's Accounting for Postretirement Benefits other than Pensions*. The SOP requires that a plan disclose (1) the weighted-average assumed discount rate used to measure the plan's obligation for postemployment benefits, (2) investments representing 5% or more of the net assets available for benefits as of the end of the plan year, and (3) the portion of a plan's estimated cost of providing postretirement benefits that is funded by retiree contributions.

BROADCASTING INDUSTRY

PERSPECTIVE AND ISSUES

SFAS 63 sets forth accounting and reporting standards for the broadcasting industry. A broadcaster is an enterprise or an affiliated group of enterprises that transmits radio or television program material. Broadcasters acquire program exhibition rights through license agreements. A typical license agreement for program material (e.g., features, specials, series, or cartoons) covers several programs (a package) and grants a television station, group of stations, network, pay television, or cable television system (licensee) the right to broadcast either a specified number or an unlimited number of showings over a maximum period of time (license period) for a specified fee. Ordinarily, the fee is paid in installments over a period generally shorter than the license period. The agreement usually contains a separate license for each program in the package. The license expires at the earlier of the last allowed telecast or the end of the license period. The licensee pays the required fee whether or not the rights are exercised. If the licensee does not exercise the contractual rights, the rights revert to the licensor with no refund to the licensee. The license period is not intended to provide unlimited use of the program material throughout that period but rather to define a reasonable period of time within which the licensee can exercise the limited rights to use the program material for a specified number of broadcasts.

Sources of GAAP
SFAS
63

DEFINITIONS OF TERMS

Barter. The exchange of unsold advertising time for products or services. The broadcaster benefits (providing the exchange does not interfere with its cash sales) by exchanging otherwise unsold time for such things as programs, fixed assets, merchandise, other media advertising privileges, travel and hotel arrangements, entertainment, and other services or products.

Broadcaster. An enterprise or an affiliated group of enterprises that transmits radio or television program material.

Daypart. An aggregation of programs broadcast during a particular time of day (e.g., daytime, evening, late night) or programs of a similar type (e.g., sports, news, children's shows). Broadcasters generally sell access to viewing audiences to advertisers on a daypart basis.

License agreement for program material. A typical license agreement for program material (e.g., features, specials, series, or cartoons) covers several programs (a package) and grants a television station, group of stations, network, pay television, or cable television system (licensee) the right to broadcast either a specified number or an unlimited number of showings over a maximum period of time (license period) for a specified fee. Ordinarily, the fee is paid in installments over a period generally shorter than the license period. The agreement usually contains a separate license for each program in the package. The license expires at the earlier of the last allowed telecast or the end of the license period. The licensee pays the required fee whether or not the rights are exercised. If the licensee does not exercise the contractual rights, the rights revert to the licensor with no refund to the licensee. The license period is not intended to provide continued use of the program material throughout that period but rather to define a reasonable period of time within which the licensee can exercise the limited rights to use the program material.

Network affiliation agreement. A broadcaster may be affiliated with a network under a network affiliation agreement. Under the agreement the station receives compensation for the network programming that it carries based on a formula designed to compensate the station for advertising sold on a network basis and included in network programming. Program costs, a major expense of television stations, are generally lower for a network affiliate than for an independent station because an affiliate does not incur program costs for network programs.

CONCEPTS, RULES, AND EXAMPLES

Accounting for License Agreements

A broadcaster should account for a license agreement for program material as a purchase of rights. Thus, an asset and a liability for the program rights purchased and the liability assumed should be reported when the license period begins and the broadcaster

1. Knows or can reasonably determine the cost of each program
2. Has accepted the program material according to the license agreement
3. Has access to the program for the first telecast (unless an agreement with another licensor prevents the telecast)

The asset may be capitalized and the liability reported at the gross amount of the liability for program rights. Alternatively, the broadcaster may choose to record the asset and liability at the present value of the liability, which should be calculated using an imputed rate of interest. In this case, the difference between the gross and net amounts is reported as interest. Under either method, the capitalized costs are allocated to each program within a package based on the relative value of each program to the broadcaster.

The asset recorded should be separated into current and noncurrent portions based on expected time of program usage. The liability should likewise be segregated according to the terms of payment.

Amortizing Capitalized Costs

The capitalized costs should be amortized to expense as the program rights are used; generally according to the estimated number of program telecasts. However, licenses granting the right to unlimited broadcasts of programs such as cartoons should be amortized over the license period, since the number of telecasts may be indeterminable.

Feature programs and program series require specific treatment. Feature programs should be amortized program-by-program, unless amortization as a package produces approximately the same result. Syndicated programs should be amortized as a series. If the broadcaster considers the first showing to be more valuable than reruns, the series should be amortized using an accelerated method. If each showing is equally valuable, straight-line amortization should be used.

Accounting for Network Affiliation Agreements

A broadcaster may be affiliated with a network under a network affiliation agreement. Under the agreement, the station receives compensation for the network programming that it carries based on a formula designed to compensate the station for advertising sold on a network basis and included in network programming. Program costs, a major expense of television stations, are generally lower for a network affiliate than for an independent station because an affiliate does not incur program costs for network programs.

Upon termination of a network affiliation agreement, immediate replacement or an agreement to replace the affiliation will allow the broadcaster to recognize a loss measured by the unamortized cost of the previous affiliation less the fair value of the new affiliation. No gain is recognized if the fair value exceeds the unamortized cost. If the terminated affiliation is not replaced, its unamortized cost should be charged to expense.

Accounting for Barter Transactions

Broadcasters may exchange unsold advertising time for products or services. The broadcaster benefits (providing the exchange does not interfere with its cash sales) by exchanging otherwise unsold time for such things as programs, fixed assets, merchandise, other media advertising privileges, travel and hotel arrangements, entertainment, and other services or products. Such transactions should be reported at the fair value of the services or products (except when advertising time is exchanged for programs).

Barter revenue is recognized as the commercials are broadcast. The products or services received in exchange are reported when received or used. A liability results if products or services are received before the commercial is aired, and a receivable results if the commercial is aired first.

Reporting and Disclosure

The capitalized cost of program rights is reported in the balance sheet at the lower of unamortized cost or net realizable value. Net realizable value is estimated on a package, series, program-by-program, or daypart basis. Daypart is an aggregation of programs broadcast during a particular time of day (e.g., daytime, evening, late night) or programs of a similar type (e.g., sports, news, children's shows). Broadcasters generally sell access to viewing audiences to advertisers on a daypart basis. If the broadcaster expects the usefulness of a program to diminish, the program may have to be written down from unamortized cost to estimated net realizable value. This establishes a new cost basis for the program.

Network affiliations agreements are reported in the balance sheet as intangible assets.

Example of accounting for program license agreements

On July 31, 2002, Lakie Media Company executed a license agreement for three movies, which it plans to televise on its local television station. The agreement allows the broadcast of each movie twice during the license period. Lakie is a calendar year-end company. The appropriate rate for imputing interest is 12%. Additional facts and assumptions are as follows:

| | License Period | | First telecast | | | Second telecast | |
| | From | To | Film availability date | Date | % of Total revenue | Date | % of Total revenue |
Film							
A	10/1/02	9/30/04	9/1/02	3/1/03	60%	6/1/04	40%
B	10/1/02	9/30/04	9/1/02	5/1/03	70%	7/1/04	30%
C	11/1/02	8/31/04	10/1/02	6/1/03	75%	6/1/04	25%

Payment terms and discounted present value data are as follows (Films A and B were acquired as a package):

| | Payment | | Discount period* | | | |
Film(s)	Date	Amount	From	To	PV factor	Discounted present value
A & B	7/31/02	$1,000			1.0000	$ 1,000
	1/1/03	6,000	10/1/02	1/1/03	.9707	5,824
	1/1/04	6,000	10/1/02	1/1/04	.8693	5,216
		$13,000				$12,040
C	1/1/04	$3,750	11/1/02	1/1/04	.8771	$3,289

* *Discounted from the first day of the license period to the date of payment.*

Based on management's estimates of expected advertising revenues, Film A represents 70% and Film B 30% of the total package A and B.

Present value approach. When each film's license period begins, an asset and a liability are recorded at the present value of the liability. Since the first three payments apply to the package of films A and B, the $12,040 must be allocated to these films according to the 70%/30% assumption stated above.

Film	Asset and liability recognized	
A	$ 8,428	($12,040 x 70%)
B	3,612	($12,040 x 30%)
	12,040	
C	3,289	

In this case, all costs are capitalized in 2002 because all of the films' licensing periods begin in that year (assuming the three conditions are met).

The amount capitalized as an asset is amortized according to the percentage of revenues to be earned each year from each film. Interest is accrued on the unpaid balance of the liability for each film. Note that for films A and B, the unpaid balance at December 31, 2002, is $11,040 ($12,040 – $1,000).

Film		2002		*Year of expense recognition* 2003		2004	
A	Accrued interest	$232	(a)	$ 439	(d)		
	Amortization			5,057	(1)	$3,371	(4)
B	Accrued interest	100	(b)	189	(e)		
	Amortization			2,528	(2)	1,084	(5)
C	Accrued interest	67	(c)	394	(f)		
	Amortization			2,467	(3)	822	(6)
		$399		$11,374		$5,277	

Interest calculations
(a) $11,040 x 12% x 3/12 x 70%
(b) $11,040 x 12% x 3/12 x 30%
(c) $3,289 x 12% x 2/12
(d) $5,216 x 12% x 70%
(e) $5,216 x 12% x 30%
(f) $3,289 x 12%

Amortization calculations
(1) $8,428 x 60%
(2) $3,612 x 70%
(3) $3,289 x 75%
(4) $8,428 x 40%
(5) $3,612 x 30%
(6) $3,289 x 25%

Note that interest expense equals the difference between the gross amount of the payments minus the present value (films A and B: $13,000 – $12,040 = $960; film C: $3,750 – $3,289 = $461).

Gross method. Costs are capitalized at the gross amount of the liability.

Film	Asset and liability recognized	
A	$ 9,100	($13,000 x 70%)
B	3,900	($13,000 x 30%)
C	3,750	

Again, since the license period for all the films begins in 2002, the assets and liabilities are recognized in that year.

Under the gross approach, no interest is accrued on the unpaid liability. Thus the only expense recognized is the amortization of the program cost.

Film	*Year of expense recognition* 2003		2004	
A	$5,460	(1)	$3,640	(4)
B	2,730	(2)	1,170	(5)
C	2,813	(3)	937	(6)
	$11,003		$5,747	

(1) $9,100 x 60%
(2) $3,900 x 70%
(3) $3,750 x 75%

(4) $9,100 x 40%
(5) $3,900 x 30%
(6) $3,750 x 25%

CABLE TELEVISION INDUSTRY

PERSPECTIVE AND ISSUES

SFAS 51 sets forth accounting and reporting standards for the cable television industry. These standards apply to cable television systems in the prematurity period. During the prematurity period, the cable television system is partially under construction and partially in service. The prematurity period begins with the first earned subscriber revenue. Its end will vary with circumstances of the system but will be determined based on plans for completion of the first major construction period or achievement of a specified predetermined subscriber level at which no additional investment will be required for other than cable television plants. The length of the prematurity period varies with the franchise development and construction plans. Except in the smallest systems, programming is usually delivered to portions of the system, and some revenues are obtained before construction of the entire system is complete. Thus, virtually every cable television system experiences a prematurity period during which it is receiving some revenue while continuing to incur substantial costs related to the establishment of the total system.

Sources of GAAP
SFAS
51, 121

DEFINITIONS OF TERMS

Cable television plant. The cable television plant required to render service to the subscriber includes the following equipment:

Head-end. This includes the equipment used to receive signals of distant television or radio stations, whether directly from the transmitter or from a microwave relay system. It also includes the studio facilities required for operator-originated programming, if any.

Cable. This consists of cable and amplifiers (which maintain the quality of the signal) covering the subscriber area, either on utility poles or underground.

Drops. These consist of the hardware that provides access to the main cable, the short length of cable that brings the signal from the main cable to the subscriber's television set, and other associated hardware, which may include a trap to block particular channels.

Converters and descramblers. These devices are attached to the subscriber's television sets when more than twelve channels are provided or when special services are provided, such as "pay cable" or two-way communication.

Direct selling costs. Direct selling costs include commissions, the portion of a salesperson's compensation other than commissions for obtaining new subscribers, local advertising targeted for acquisition of new subscribers, and costs of processing documents related to new subscribers acquired. Direct selling costs do not include supervisory and administrative expenses or indirect expenses, such as rent and costs of facilities.

Subscriber-related costs. These are costs incurred to obtain and retain subscribers to the cable television system and include costs of billing and collection, bad debts, and mailings; repairs and maintenance of taps and connections; franchise fees related to revenues or number of subscribers; general and administrative system costs, such as salary of the system manager and office rent; programming costs for additional channels used in the marketing effort or costs related to revenues from, or number of subscribers to, per channel or per program service; and direct selling costs.

CONCEPTS, RULES, AND EXAMPLES

Accounting during the Prematurity Period

Before the first subscriber revenue is earned by the cable company, the beginning and end of the prematurity period must be established by management. This period generally will not exceed two years. Once the prematurity period has been established, it may not be changed except in extraordinary circumstances.

Separate accounting is required for any portion[2] of a cable television system that is in the prematurity period and that is distinct from the rest of the system. This distinction may be made if the portion is characterized by a majority of the following differences:

- Accountability (e.g., separate forecasts, budgets, etc.)
- Investment decisions (e.g., separate ROI, breakeven, etc.)
- Geographical (e.g., separate franchise area)
- Mechanical (e.g., separate equipment)
- Timing (e.g., separate inception of construction or marketing)

If the portion meets these requirements, it will be charged costs of the entire system only if these costs are directly traceable to that portion. Separate projections should also be developed for that portion.

During the prematurity period, costs incurred by the plant should be capitalized as usual. General and administrative expenses and subscriber-related costs are considered period costs. Subscriber-related costs are costs incurred to obtain and retain subscribers to the cable television system.

System costs that will benefit the cable system upon completion (e.g., programming costs), and that will remain fairly constant despite changes in the number of subscribers, should be separated into current and noncurrent portions. A fraction is calculated each month and multiplied by the total of these costs for the month to determine the amount of current cost. The fraction is computed as follows:

---

[2] *The word "segment" has been used by some television enterprises. However, since SFAS 131 uses segment in a different context, the FASB uses the word "portion" instead of "segment" to refer to the part of a cable television system that is still in the prematurity period.*

Current portion of system costs benefiting future periods	Greatest of a) Average # of subscribers expected that month as estimated at beginning of prematurity period, b) Average # of subscribers assuming straight-line progress towards estimated subscribers at end of prematurity period, or c) Average # of actual subscribers
	Total # of subscribers expected at end of prematurity period

During the prematurity period, interest cost is capitalized using an interest capitalization rate as described in SFAS 34. The amount of interest cost to be capitalized is determined as follows:

$$\text{Interest cost capitalized} = \text{Interest capitalization rate} \times \text{Average amount of qualifying assets during the period}$$

SFAS 34 defines qualifying assets. The amount of capitalized interest cost may not exceed actual interest cost for the period.

Depreciation and amortization during the prematurity period are determined as follows:

$$\text{Depr. and amort. expense} = \text{Monthly depr. and amort. expected after prematurity period (using depr. method to be used then)} \times \text{Fraction used to determine current portion of system costs benefiting future periods}$$

Amortizing Capitalized Costs

Capitalization based on timing differences. Costs that have been capitalized for a portion of a cable television system that is in the prematurity period and that are clearly distinguishable on the basis of timing differences should be amortized over the same depreciation period used by the main cable plant.

Installation revenues and costs. A cable television system recognizes initial hookup revenue to the extent of the direct selling costs associated with that revenue. The deferred portion is amortized to income over the average expected period that subscribers will continue to receive cable service.

Initial installation costs are capitalized and depreciated over a period that does not exceed the period used to depreciate the cable plant. After the initial installation, any costs incurred to disconnect or reconnect subscribers are charged to expense.

Franchise applications. A cable television franchise is a right granted by a municipality to provide service to its residents. The treatment of franchise costs depends upon whether or not the franchise is successful. If successful, the costs are capitalized and amortized as intangible assets. If unsuccessful or abandoned, all costs are charged to expense.

Recoverability of capitalized costs. Capitalized plant and certain identifiable intangible assets are subject to the impairment provisions outlined in SFAS 121. A separate evaluation should be made for the portion of the cable television system that is in the prematurity period. If total capitalized cost reaches the maximum recoverable amount, capitalization should continue. However, the provision to reduce capitalized costs to recoverable value is increased.

COMPUTER SOFTWARE COSTS AND REVENUES

PERSPECTIVE AND ISSUES

As technology has come to play a more important role in businesses, increasing levels of activity have been devoted to the development of computer software. From the cost perspective, this involves a number of undertakings.

- Software acquired from others for internal use
- Software acquired from others for resale in the normal course of business (either on a stand-alone basis or as part of a larger product)
- Software developed internally for sale to others
- Software developed internally for the developer's use

Software can be licensed, purchased, or leased and can reside on the user's hardware or be "hosted" by an application service provider (ASP) and leased to the user for remote use over the Internet. A growing set of accounting standards deal with some, but not all, of these issues.

The accounting for the cost of software developed internally for sale (or lease, etc.) to others is addressed by SFAS 86; it holds that costs incurred prior to the point at which technological feasibility has been demonstrated are to be expensed as research and development costs, but subsequently incurred costs are capitalized, and later amortized or expensed (e.g., as cost of sales) as appropriate.

The cost of software acquired from others for resale in the normal course of business is not separately addressed by GAAP, but would be handled as are any other inventory costs. The usual inventory costing methods (LIFO, FIFO, etc.) and financial reporting concerns (lower of cost or market, etc.) would be applicable to such situations.

SOP 98-1 addresses accounting for the costs of software acquired from others, or developed internally, for internal use. This standard establishes the conditions that must be met before internal use software costs may be capitalized. To qualify for capitalization, costs must have been incurred **subsequent** to the completion of the conceptual formulation, design and testing of possible project alternatives (including the process of vendor selection for purchased software). In addition, management at the appropriate level of authority must have authorized funding for the development project and conclude that it is probable that the project will be completed and the software will be used to perform the intended functions. This prerequisite is roughly analogous to the "technological feasibility" threshold prescribed by SFAS 86 for software to be sold or leased to customers. Costs that are eventually capitalized under SOP 98-1 will be amortized over the period of expected economic benefit, as is the case with all other long-lived assets used in the business.

The increasingly central role of technology has received the attention of accounting standard setters in another arena as well. For enterprises that sell computer software and associated goods and services (program upgrades, maintenance agreements, etc.), complicated issues of revenue recognition arise. AcSEC has responded by issuing a series of Statements of Position to provide guidance regarding the recognition of revenue on software sales including multiple-element arrangements that can include the cost of the software bundled with elements of training, upgrades, and postcontract customer support (PCS).

Due to the great complexity of the issues involved in software revenue recognition, this topic will be given a rather detailed exposition in the following pages. The recent growth in e-commerce, the transacting of business over the Internet, has driven many traditional "bricks and mortar" companies to establish new channels of sales and distribution by designing and deploying transaction-enabled websites. The EITF has provided guidance as to how to account for the costs of website development.

Sources of GAAP		
SFAS	*EITF*	*SOP*
2, 86	97-13, 00-2, 00-3	97-2, 98-1, 98-4, 98-9

DEFINITIONS OF TERMS

Coding. Generating detailed instructions in a computer language to carry out the requirements described in the detail program design. The coding of a computer software product may begin prior to, concurrent with, or subsequent to the completion of the detail program design.

Customer support. Services performed by an enterprise to assist customers in their use of software products. Those services include any installation assistance, training classes, telephone question and answer services, newsletters, on-site visits, and software or data modifications.

Detail program design. The detail design of a computer software product that takes product function, feature, and technical requirements to their most detailed, logical form and is ready for coding.

Maintenance. Activities undertaken after the product is available for general release to customers to correct errors (bugs) or keep the product updated with current information. Those activities include routine changes and additions.

Product design. A logical representation of all product functions in sufficient detail to serve as product specifications.

Product enhancement. Improvements to an existing product that are intended to extend the life or improve significantly the marketability of the original product. Enhancements normally require a product design and may require a redesign of all or part of the existing product.

Product masters. A completed version, ready for copying, of the computer software product, the documentation, and the training materials that are to be sold, leased, or otherwise marketed.

Testing. Performing the steps necessary to determine whether the coded computer software product meets function, feature, and technical performance requirements set forth in the product design.

Working model. An operative version of the computer software product that is completed in the same software language as the product to be ultimately marketed, performs all the major functions planned for the product, and is ready for initial customer testing (usually identified as **beta testing**).

CONCEPTS, RULES, AND EXAMPLES

Software Developed for Internal Use

SOP 98-1 provides guidance on accounting for the costs of internally developed software. Software must meet two criteria to be accounted for as internally developed software. First, the software's specifications must be designed or modified to meet the reporting entity's internal needs, including costs to customize purchased software. Second, during the period in which the software is being developed, there can be no plan or intent to market the software externally, although development of the software can be jointly funded by several entities that each plan to use the software internally.

In order to justify capitalization of related costs, it is necessary for management to conclude that it is probable that the project will be completed and that the software will be used as intended. Absent that level of expectation, costs must be expensed currently as research and development costs are required to be. Entities which historically were engaged in both research and development of software for internal use and for sale to others would have to carefully identify costs with one or the other activity, since the former would (if all conditions are met) be subject to capitalization, while the latter might be expensed as research and development costs until technological feasibility had been demonstrated, per SFAS 86.

Costs Subject to Capitalization

Cost capitalization commences when an entity has completed the conceptual formulation, design, and testing of possible project alternatives, including the process of vendor selection for purchased software, if any. These early-phase costs (referred to as "preliminary project stage" in SOP 98-1) are analogous to research and development costs and must be expensed as incurred. These cannot be later restored to an asset account if the development proves to be successful.

Costs incurred subsequent to the preliminary project stage that meet the criteria under GAAP as long-lived assets can be capitalized and amortized over the asset's expected economic life. Capitalization of costs will begin when both of two conditions are met. First, management having the relevant authority authorizes and commits to funding the project and believes that it is probable that it will be completed and that the resulting software will be used as intended. Second, the conceptual formulation, design, and testing of possible software project alternatives (i.e., the preliminary project stage) have been completed.

Costs to be capitalized include those of the "program instructions stage" and the "implementation stage" of the software development process. These include coding and testing activities and various implementation costs. In particular, the SOP notes that such costs will be limited to (1) external direct costs of materials and services consumed in developing or obtaining internal-use computer software; (2) payroll and payroll-related costs for employees who are directly associated with and who devote time to the internal-use computer software project to the extent of the time spent directly on the project; and (3) interest costs incurred while developing internal-use computer software, consistent with the provisions of SFAS 34.

As expected, the standard requires that general and administrative costs, overhead costs, and training costs not be capitalized. Even though these may be costs which are associated with the internal development or acquisition of software for internal use, under GAAP those costs relate to the period in which incurred. The issue of training costs is particularly important, since internal-use computer software purchased from third parties often includes, as part of the purchase price, training for the software (and often maintenance fees for routine maintenance as well). Per the SOP, when the amount of training or maintenance fees is not specified in the contract, entities are required to allocate the cost among training, maintenance, and amounts representing the capitalizable cost of computer software. Training costs must be recognized in expense as incurred. (Maintenance fees will be recognized in expense over the maintenance period.)

The SOP provides examples of when computer software is acquired or developed for internal use. Some of these are: when modifications are made to software controlling robots acquired for use in the manufacturing process; software is developed for cash management, payroll processing, or accounts payable system purposes; a bank develops an on-line account status inquiry system for customers to utilize; a travel agency invests in software to give it access to an airline reservation system; a communications provider develops computerized systems to manage customer services such as voice mail; or when a publisher invests in computerized systems to produce a product which is then sold to customers.

On the other hand, software which does not qualify under the standard as being for internal use includes software sold by a robot manufacturer to purchasers of its products; the cost of developing programs for microchips used in automobile electronic systems; software developed for both sale to customers and internal use; computer programs written for use in research and development efforts; and costs of developing software under contract with another entity.

Impairment

The SOP makes it clear that, consistent with the treatment of other long-lived assets, possible impairment of capitalized internal use software will need to be recognized and measured in accordance with the provisions of SFAS 121. Circumstances which might suggest that an impairment has occurred include (1) a realization that the internal-use computer software is not expected to provide substantive service potential; (2) there has been a significant change in the extent or manner in which the software is used; (3) a significant change has been made or is being anticipated to the software program; or (4) the costs of developing or modifying the internal-use computer software significantly exceed the amount originally expected. These conditions are analogous to those generically provided in SFAS 121.

In some instances, ongoing software development projects will become troubled before being aborted. The SOP provides that management needs to assess the likelihood of successful completion of projects in process. When it becomes no longer probable that the computer software being developed will be completed and placed in service, the asset should be written down to the lower of the carrying amount or fair value, if any, less costs to sell. Importantly, it is a rebuttable presumption that any uncompleted software has a zero fair value. The SOP suggests indications that the software is no longer expected to be completed and placed in service. These include (1) a lack of expenditures budgeted or incurred for the project; (2) programming difficulties that cannot be resolved on a timely basis; (3) significant cost overruns; (4) information indicating that the costs of internally developed software will significantly exceed the cost of comparable third-party software or software products, suggesting that management intends to obtain the third-party software instead of completing the internal development effort; (5) the introduction of new technologies which increase the likelihood that management will elect to obtain third-party software instead of completing the internal project; and (6) a lack of profitability of the business segment or unit to which the software relates or actual or potential discontinuation of that segment.

Amortization of Capitalized Costs of Software for Internal Use

As for other long-lived assets, the costs of computer software developed or obtained for internal use should be amortized in a systematic and rational manner over its estimated useful life. The nature of the asset exacerbates the difficulty of developing a meaningful estimate, however. Among the factors to be weighed are the effects of obsolescence, technology, and competition. Entities would especially need to consider if rapid changes are occurring in the development of software products, software operating systems, or computer hardware, and whether management had intentions to replace any technologically obsolete software or hardware.

Amortization of each module or component of a software project should commence when the computer software is ready for its intended use, without regard to whether the software is to be placed in service in planned stages that might extend beyond a single reporting period. The SOP stipulates that computer software is to be deemed ready for its intended use after substantially all testing has been completed.

Other Matters

In some cases internal use software is later sold or licensed to third parties, notwithstanding the original intention of management that the software was acquired or developed solely for internal use. In such cases, the SOP provides that any proceeds received would be applied against the carrying amount of that software. No profit is recognized until the aggregate proceeds from sales exceed the carrying amount of the software. After the carrying value is fully recovered, any subsequent proceeds would be recognized in revenue as earned.

This standard does not add any new disclosure requirements. Relevant standards addressing disclosures include APB 12 and 22, SFAS 121, and SOP 94-6.

Software Development Costs Developed Internally for Sale or Lease

A separate set of accounting issues arise in connection with the costs of computer software developed internally for leasing or sale to others. The principal issue relates to the point in the development process at which efforts are no longer characterized as research and development (and thus expensed currently), but rather may be deferred (i.e., inventoried) and later classified as cost of sales as the finished products are disposed of.

SFAS 86 established the concept of **technological feasibility** to demarcate the point at which it is proper to begin to defer costs. According to this standard, all costs of development are considered to be research and development costs until technological feasibility has been established. This point is reached when all the necessary planning, designing, **coding**, and testing activities have been completed, to the extent these activities are necessary to establish that the product in question can meet its design specifications. Design specifications, in turn, may include such product aspects as functions, features, and technical performance requirements.

If the process of creating the software involves **detail program design**, evidence of having achieved technological feasibility includes having performed these steps

1. The product design (the logical representation of the product) and detailed program design have been completed. This step includes having demonstrated that the necessary skills, hardware, and software technologies are accessible to the entity for it to complete the product development effort.
2. The detailed program design has been documented and traced to product specifications, thus demonstrating completeness and consistency.
3. The detailed program design has been reviewed for any high risk elements, such as unproven functions or product innovations, and any such high risk elements have been resolved through coding and testing.

If the software development effort does **not** involve detailed program design, then the following steps would need to have been completed to demonstrate technological feasibility:

1. A product design and a working model of the software have been completed.
2. The completeness of the working model and its consistency with the product design have been confirmed by testing.

If all the foregoing steps in either of the above listings have been completed as applicable, then technological feasibility has been shown, and costs incurred thereafter are to be capitalized. Such costs could include, but are not limited to, additional product development and the costs of producing product masters (which may include not only the master copy of the software itself but also related training materials and other such items). Capitalization of software costs is to cease, however, once the product is available for general release to customers of the entity. Period costs, such as maintenance and ongoing **customer support** efforts, are to be expensed as incurred in all cases.

The deferred computer software development costs must be amortized, beginning when the product is first available for general release to customers. Amortization is to be computed on a product-by-product basis, which means that costs related to development of earlier products cannot be "rolled forward" into the costs of newer products, thereby delaying expense recognition. Periodic amortization must be the greater of (1) an amount determined with reference to total estimated revenues to be generated by the product, or (2) an amount computed on a straight-line basis with reference to the product's expected life cycle.

Example of amortization of deferred computer software development costs

Assume total costs of $340,000 have been deferred at the point product sales begin. Management estimates that the product will eventually generate revenues of $5,100,000 over a period of four years. For the current period (½ of a year), revenues of $600,000 have been realized. Deferred costs of $42,500 must be amortized, which is the greater of the pro rata amount based on estimated total revenues to be derived from product sales [($600,000 ÷ $5,100,000) x $340,000 = $40,000] or the amount determined on a straight-line basis ($340,000 ÷ 4 x ½ = $42,500).

Other costs, such as product duplication and training material publication costs, are to be capitalized and expensed on a unit-specific basis as sales of product occur. All deferred costs are subject to an annual evaluation for net realizable value; if inventoried costs are adjusted for this reason at any reporting date, such amount becomes the cost basis for further amortization purposes, as well as for comparison to net realizable value in the following period.

Software Revenue Recognition

The basic principles underlying SOP 97-2 are set forth in the following paragraphs.

Licensing vs. sales. AcSEC was concerned that transfers of rights to software by licenses rather than by outright sales (a technique widely employed to protect vendors from the unauthorized duplication of their products) were being accounted for differently. It concluded that any legal distinction between a license and a sale should not cause revenue recognition to differ.

Product may not equate with delivery of software. AcSEC observed that arrangements to deliver software, whether alone or in conjunction with other products, often include services. Services to be provided in such contexts commonly involve significant production, modification, or customization of the software. AcSEC therefore concluded that in such circumstances the software, even if physically delivered, might not constitute the **delivery** of the product contracted for, absent those alterations. This resulted in the new requirement that such arrangements be accounted for as construction-type or production-type contracts, to be accounted for in conformity with ARB 45 and SOP 81-1. However, if the services do not entail significant production, modification, or customization of software, the service element should be accounted for as a separate element.

Delivery is the key threshold issue for revenue recognition. Consistent with the principles set forth in SFAC 5, *Recognition and Measurement in Financial Statements of Business Enterprises*, which states that "An entity's revenue-earning activities involve delivering or producing goods, rendering services, or other activities that constitute its ongoing major or central operations, and revenues are considered to have been earned when the entity has substantially accomplished what it must do to be entitled to the benefits represented by the revenues. . . [t]he two conditions (being realized or realizable and being earned) are usually met by the time the product or merchandise is delivered. . . to customers, and revenues. . .are commonly recognized at time of sale (usually meaning delivery)."

Revenue must be allocated to all elements of the sales arrangement, with recognition dependent upon meeting the criteria on an element-by-element basis. Under prior GAAP, the accounting for vendor obligations remaining after delivery of software was dependent upon whether or not the obligation was deemed to be significant. Under SOP 97-2, however, all obligations are to be accounted for and the revenue from an arrangement should be allocated to each element of the arrangement, based on vendor-specific objective evidence of the fair values of the elements. Revenue associated with a particular element is not to be recognized until the revenue-recognition conditions established by the SOP are met, as the earnings process related to that element will not be considered complete until that time.

Fair values for revenue allocation purposes must be vendor-specific. When there are multiple elements of an arrangement, revenue is generally recognized on an element-by-element basis as individual elements are delivered. Revenue is to be allocated to the various elements in proportion to relative fair values. Under SOP 97-2, this allocation process requires that vendor-specific objective evidence of fair value be employed, regardless of any separate prices stated in the contract for each element, since prices stated in a contract may not represent fair value and, accordingly, might result in an unreasonable allocation of revenue. AcSEC concluded that this approach would be consistent with the accounting for commingled revenue as set forth in the current standard on accounting for franchise fee revenue. The use of surrogate prices, such as those published by the competitors or industry averages, was rejected because of the wide differences in products and services offered by vendors. Separate transaction prices for the elements comprising the arrangement, if they are also being sold on that basis, would be the best such evidence, although under some circumstances (such as when prices in the arrangement are based on multiple users rather than the single user pricing of the element on a stand-alone basis) even that information could conceivably be invalid for revenue allocation purposes. Relative sales prices of the elements as included in the arrangement should be used whenever possible.

The earnings process is not complete if fees are subject to forfeiture. Even when the product has been delivered, if fees allocated to those products are subject to forfeiture, refund, or other concession if the vendor does not fulfill its delivery responsibilities relative to other parts of the arrangement, those fees should not be treated as having been earned. The potential concessions indicate the customer would not have licensed the delivered products without also licensing the undelivered products. For that reason, there must be persuasive evidence that fees allocated to delivered products are not subject to forfeiture, refund, or other concessions before revenue recognition can be justified. Thus, for example, in determining the persuasiveness of the evidence, the vendor's history of making concessions that were not required by the provisions of an arrangement is more persuasive than are terms included in the arrangement that indicate that no concessions are required.

Operational Rules Established by SOP 97-2

1. If an arrangement to deliver software or a software system, either alone or together with other products or services, requires significant production, modification, or customization of software, the entire arrangement should be accounted for in conformity with ARB 45, *Long-Term Construction-Type Contracts*, and SOP 81-1, *Accounting for Performance of Construction-Type and Certain Production-Type Contracts*.

2. If the arrangement does not require significant production, modification, or customization of software, revenue should be recognized when **all** of the following criteria are met:

   a. Persuasive evidence of an arrangement exists;
   b. Delivery has occurred;
   c. The vendor's fee is fixed or determinable; and
   d. Collectibility is probable.

3. For software arrangements that provide licenses for multiple software deliverables (multiple elements), some of which may be deliverable only on a when-and-if-available basis, these deliverables should be considered in determining whether an arrangement includes multiple elements. The requirements with respect to arrangements that consist of multiple elements should be applied to all additional products and services specified in the arrangement, including those described as being deliverable only on a when-and-if-available basis.

4. For arrangements having multiple elements, the fee should be allocated to the various elements based on vendor-specific objective evidence of fair value, regardless of any separate prices stated for each element within the contract. Vendor-specific objective evidence of fair value is limited to the following:

   a. The price charged when the same element is sold separately; or
   b. For an element not yet being sold separately, the price established by management, if it is probable that the price, once established, will not change before the separate introduction of the element into the marketplace.

The revenue allocated to undelivered elements cannot later be adjusted. However, as is traditional under GAAP, if it becomes probable that the amount allocated to an undelivered element will result in a loss on that element of the arrangement, the loss must be recognized. When a vendor's pricing is based on multiple factors such as the number of products and the number of users, the amount allocated to the same elements when sold separately must consider all the salient factors of the vendor's pricing structure. The foregoing limitation on what can be considered valid vendor-specific evidence of fair value was postponed, first by SOP 98-4, then by SOP 98-9, so it did not need to be applied until fiscal years beginning after March 15, 1999.

SOP 98-9 amended the guidance of SOP 97-2 with regard to multiple-element arrangements not accounted for as long-term construction contracts when (1) there is vendor-specific objective evidence of the fair values of all **undelivered** elements, (2) vendor-specific evidence does not exist for one or more of the delivered elements, and (3) all other revenue recognition criteria have been satisfied. In such cases, the newly defined "residual" method of allocation of selling price is to be utilized. This results in deferral of the aggregate fair value of the undelivered elements of the arrangement (to be recognized later as delivery occurs), with the excess of the total arrangement fee over the deferred portion being recognized in connection with the delivered components. This change was made to accommodate the common situation of software which is always sold with one "free" year of support, where additional years of support are also marketed at fixed fees; in this case, the fair value of the "free" support is deferred (and amortized over the year), while the software itself is assigned a revenue amount which is the difference between the package price and the known price of one year's service.

5. If a discount is offered in a multiple-element arrangement, a proportionate amount thereof should be applied to each element included in the arrangement, based on each element's fair value without regard to the discount.

However, no portion of the discount should be allocated to any upgrade rights.

6. If sufficient vendor-specific objective evidence does not exist for the allocation of revenue to the various elements of the arrangement, all revenue from the arrangement should be deferred until the earlier of the point at which (1) such sufficient vendor-specific objective evidence does exist, or (2) all elements of the arrangement have been delivered. The exceptions to this guidance, provided in SOP 97-2, are as follows:

   a. If the only undelivered element is postcontract customer support (PCS), the entire fee should be recognized ratably.

   b. If the only undelivered element is services that do not involve significant production, modification, or customization of software (e.g., training or installation), the entire fee should be recognized over the period during which the services are expected to be performed.

   c. If the arrangement is in substance a subscription, the entire fee should be recognized ratably.

   d. If the fee is based on the number of copies, how the arrangement should be accounted for depends on whether the total fee is fixed, and on whether the buyer can alter the composition of the copies to be received, as follows:

      (1) If the arrangement provides customers with the right to reproduce or obtain copies of two or more software products at a specified price per copy (**not** per product) up to the total amount of the fixed fee, an allocation of the fee to the individual products generally cannot be made, because the total revenue allocable to each software product is unknown and depends on the choices to be made by the customer and, sometimes, on future vendor development activity. Nevertheless, certain arrangements that include products that are not deliverable at the inception impose a maximum number of copies of the undeliverable product(s) to which the customer is entitled. In such arrangements, a portion of the arrangement fee should be allocated to the undeliverable product(s). This allocation should be made assuming that the customer will elect to receive the maximum number of copies of the undeliverable product(s).

      (2) In arrangements in which no allocation can be made until the first copy or product master of each product covered by the arrangement has been delivered to the customer, and assuming the four conditions set forth above are met, revenue should be recognized as copies of delivered products are either (a) reproduced by the customer, or (b) furnished to the customer if the vendor is duplicating the software. Once the vendor has delivered the product master or the first copy of all products covered by the arrangement, any licensing

fees not previously recognized should be recognized, since only duplication of the software is required to satisfy the vendor's delivery requirement and such duplication is incidental to the arrangement, so that delivery is deemed to have occurred upon delivery of the product master or first copy. When the arrangement terminates, the vendor should recognize any licensing fees not previously recognized. Revenue should not be recognized fully until at least one of the following conditions is met: either (a) delivery is complete for all products covered by the arrangement, or (b) the aggregate revenue attributable to all copies of the software products delivered is equal to the fixed fee, provided that the vendor is not obligated to deliver additional software products under the arrangement.

(3) If the arrangement includes products that are not deliverable at inception and it imposes a maximum number of copies of the undeliverable product(s) to which the customer is entitled, then a portion of the arrangement fee should be allocated to the undeliverable product(s). This allocation should be made assuming that the customer will elect to receive the maximum number of copies of the undeliverable product(s).

(4) The revenue allocated to the delivered products should be recognized when the product master or first copy is delivered. If, during the term of the arrangement, the customer reproduces or receives enough copies of these delivered products so that revenue allocable to the delivered products exceeds the revenue previously recognized, such additional revenue should be recognized as the copies are reproduced or delivered. The revenue allocated to the undeliverable product(s) should be reduced by a corresponding amount.

7. The portion of the fee allocated to a contract element should be recognized when the four revenue recognition criteria are met with respect to the element. In applying those criteria, the delivery of an element is considered not to have occurred if there are undelivered elements that are essential to the functionality of the delivered element, because functionality of the delivered element would be impaired.

8. No portion of the fee can be deemed to be collectible if the portion of the fee allocable to delivered elements is subject to forfeiture, refund, or other concession if any of the undelivered elements are not delivered. If management represents that it will not provide refunds or concessions that are not required under the provisions of the arrangement, this assertion must be supported by reference to all available evidence. This evidence may include the following:

a. Acknowledgment in the arrangement regarding products not currently available or not to be delivered currently;

    b. Separate prices stipulated in the arrangement for each deliverable element;

    c. Default and damage provisions as defined in the arrangement;

    d. Enforceable payment obligations and due dates for the delivered elements that are not dependent on the delivery of future deliverable elements, coupled with the intent of the vendor to enforce rights of payment;

    e. Installation and use of the delivered software; and

    f. Support services, such as telephone support, related to the delivered software being provided currently by the vendor.

EMERGING ISSUES TASK FORCE CONSENSUS SUMMARIES

97-13 Accounting for Costs Incurred in Connection with a Consulting Contract or an Internal Project That Combines Business Process Reengineering and Information Technology Transformation

A consensus was reached that all expenditures incurred for business process reengineering activities (either by insiders or outsiders) should be expensed immediately. Guidance also applies when business process reengineering activities are part of development or implementation of internal-use software. Finally, the accounting for internal-use software development and acquisition of property, plant, and equipment are not affected by this consensus.

Another consensus was reached that in cases where a third party is engaged for a business process reengineering project, the entire consulting contract price should be allocated to each activity on the basis of the relative fair values of the separate components.

00-2 Accounting for Website Development Costs

The costs of developing a website, including the costs of developing services that are offered to visitors (e.g., chat rooms, search engines, e-mail, calendars, and so forth) are often quite significant. The SEC staff had expressed the opinion that a large portion of those costs should be accounted for in accordance with AICPA SOP No. 98-1, *Accounting for the Costs of Computer Software Developed or Obtained for Internal Use*, which sets forth certain conditions which must be met before costs may be capitalized.

In this consensus, the EITF held that costs incurred in the planning stage are to be expensed as incurred. Costs of software used to operate a website are accounted for in accordance with SOP 98-1, unless a plan exists to market the software externally, in which case SFAS 86 governs. Costs incurred to develop graphics (broadly defined as the "look and feel" of the web page) are included in software costs, and thus accounted for under SOP 98-1 or SFAS 86, as noted in the foregoing. However, the accounting for costs of content development will be addressed as a separate EITF issue. Costs of operating websites are accounted for in the same manner as other operating costs analogous to repairs and maintenance of tangible long-lived assets.

Issue 00-2 includes a detailed exhibit stipulating how varieties of specific costs are to be accounted for consistent with this consensus.

00-3   Application of AICPA SOP 97-2, Software Revenue Recognition, to Arrangements That Include the Right to Use Software Stored on Another Entity's Hardware

Some software users do not actually receive and load the software on their computers, but instead merely access and use it via the Internet, on the vendor's or a third party's server, on an as-needed basis.   (Commonly, the applications are "hosted" by companies known as application service providers, or ASPs.) In such arrangements, the customer is paying for two elements—the right to use the software and the storage of the software (and sometimes, the customer's proprietary data) on the provider's hardware.

When a vendor provides hosting, several revenue recognition issues may arise. First, the relationship between the customer and the ASP may be structured in the form of a service agreement providing Internet access to the specified site, without a corresponding software license. In such instances, it has not been clear how to apply SOP 97-2. Second, when the transaction is structured as a software license with a service element, it was not clear how to evaluate the delivery requirement of SOP 97-2.

In the consensus on this issue, the EITF found that SOP 97-2 only applies if the customer has the right to take possession of the software at any time during the hosting period, without significant penalty, and install it on its own hardware or contract with another service provider to host it. Most, if not all, ASP arrangements would not provide this option to the customer and therefore SOP 97-2 would not apply. The EITF notes that hosting arrangements might involve multiple elements to be accounted for in a possible variety of ways.

For those few hosting arrangements meeting the foregoing criteria, and thus subject to SOP 97-2, software delivery is deemed to have occurred when the customer first has the option of taking possession. The criteria of SOP 97-2 must be met in order for the ASP to recognize revenue allocable to the software element; revenue relating to the hosting element will be recognized as that service is provided.

FINANCE COMPANIES

PERSPECTIVE AND ISSUES

Until such time as the proposed new Audit and Accounting Guide, which will for the first time unify guidance for all types of financial institutions, GAAP for this industry is largely to be found in *Audits of Finance Companies* (Audit and Accounting Guide, 1999) and SOP 92-3, *Accounting for Foreclosed Assets.* These represent preferable accounting principles for purposes of justifying a change of accounting principles.

Finance companies provide lending and financing services to consumers (consumer financing) and to business enterprises (commercial financing). Some financing companies engage solely in consumer or commercial financing activities; others engage in both types.

Manufacturers, retailers, wholesalers and other business enterprises may provide financing to encourage customers to buy their products or services. Such financing is known as captive financing activity, and may be provided by those companies or affiliated companies. Although most companies originally financed only their own products and services, many have expanded their financing activities to include a wide variety of products and services sold by unaffiliated businesses.

Consumer financing activities include direct consumer loans, retail sales contracts, and insurance services.

Commercial financing enterprises often provide a wide range of services, including factoring arrangements, revolving loans, installment and term loans, floor plan loans, and lease financing.

AcSEC is presently nearing completion of a project to produce an SOP, *Accounting by Certain Entities (Including Entities with Trade Receivables) That Lend to or Finance the Activities of Others*, which would serve to conform the accounting by various institutions such as banks, thrifts, credit unions, finance companies, corporate credit unions, and mortgage companies. It would also apply to manufacturers, retailers, wholesalers, and other business enterprises that provide financing for products and services, and thus would have very wide applicability. The intention is that, once this SOP has been issued, the currently separate Audit and Accounting Guides, including *Audits of Finance Companies*, would be superseded by a universal Guide to all financial institutions.

The proposed SOP would eliminate differences in accounting and disclosure established by the respective Guides and will carry forward accounting guidance for transactions determined to be unique to certain financial institutions. It is not intended to create new accounting guidance. Clearance of the SOP by FASB, as is required, is anticipated for late 2001.

Among the more relevant features of the proposed Guide are the following:

- Mortgage companies and corporate credit unions will be explicitly included in the scope of the combined Guide.
- Regulatory capital disclosures will be required for mortgage companies, credit unions, banks, and thrifts.
- Credit unions report amounts placed in their deposit insurance fund as an asset if such amounts are fully refundable, due to unique legal and operational aspects of the credit union share insurance fund. Banks and thrifts expense payments to their deposit insurance fund as incurred. Under the SOP, both practices are expected to be preserved because of differences in how the funds operate.
- Finance companies record purchases and sales of securities on the settlement date, whereas banks, thrifts, and credit unions follow trade date accounting. Under the SOP, finance companies will follow trade date accounting.
- SFAS 114, *Accounting by Creditors for Impairment of a Loan,* and 118, *Accounting by Creditors for Impairment of a Loan—Income Recognition and Disclosures,* address loan impairment measurement and disclosure requirements, but they do not specify how to recognize income on impaired loans. The Guide for finance companies gives specific guidance on the recognition of interest income on impaired loans. Under the SOP, such guidance for finance companies will be eliminated.
- Certain disclosures for credit unions will be eliminated. These disclosures include, for example, additional information about repurchase agreements, servicing assets, and deposit liabilities.

Sources of GAAP			
SFAS	*FASB I*	*SOP*	*EITF*
91, 124, 127, 140	41, 42	92-3, 96-1	95-22

DEFINITIONS OF TERMS

Accounts receivable loan. A loan collateralized by the accounts receivable of the borrower.

Dealer reserves. Finance company liabilities for dealers' shares of finance charges on retail contracts purchased from dealers.

Direct consumer loan. A two-party transaction in which the finance company lends funds directly to the borrower; such a loan may or may not be collateralized.

Discount. Amount deducted from the face value in advance as a charge for the loan or a deduction for interest at the time of the loan or any charge for credit that is precomputed and included in the face of the instrument.

Discount loan. A loan that is written with the interest or finance charges included in the face amount of the note. Discount loans are also called **precompute** or **add-on loans.**

Effective interest rate. The implicit rate of interest based on the amount advanced and the amount and timing of the specified repayments over the period of the contract.

Factor. A company that engages primarily in factoring.

Factoring. Purchase, usually without recourse, of individual accounts receivable arising in the client's ordinary course of business. Under a factoring agreement, the finance company also provides credit checking, collection, and record-keeping services.

Floor plan checking. Physical inspection of dealer's inventories that are collateral for advances to the dealer to be repaid from the proceeds from sale of specific items. Sometimes referred to as floor plan auditing.

Floor planning. Financing of dealers' inventories, particularly automobiles and other consumer goods, sometimes referred to as **wholesaling**. The dealers are obliged to repay the supplier or manufacturer from proceeds of sale of specific items, or after an elapsed period even though inventory is not sold.

Interest-bearing loan. A loan that is written at the principal amount advanced to the borrower and bearing interest computed monthly on the unpaid balance.

Interest method. A method of computing income under which interest income on a fixed-rate obligation is accrued over the life of the loan based on a constant rate (percent) of interest applied to the outstanding loan balance. As a result, the amount of income recognized at a given time is directly proportional to the outstanding loan balance. Also called the **actuarial method**.

Inventory loan. A loan collateralized by inventory of the borrower.

Nonrefundable fee. Any charge made in connection with a loan that does not have to be refunded to the borrower when the loan is prepaid.

Origination fee. An amount charged by finance companies for originating, refinancing, or restructuring a loan. The amount may be intended to cover costs such as underwriting, loan application processing, and reviewing legal title to property involved.

Overadvance (in factoring). An amount advanced to a client in excess of the amount of uncollected receivables purchased by the factor.

Points. Amounts, generally expressed as a percent of the loan, charged for granting loans, that primarily are adjustments of yield but also may be intended to cover costs such as underwriting, loan application processing, and reviewing title to collateral.

CONCEPTS, RULES, AND EXAMPLES

Finance Receivables

Finance receivables include both interest-bearing and discount loans. The face amount of an interest-bearing or simple interest loan is equal to the amount of cash loaned; unearned interest is not computed. Conversely, for discount loans the amount of cash loaned is less than the face value of the loan. This difference represents unearned interest income to the borrower, and as such, is recognized by the lender over the life of the loan.

Allowance for Loan Losses

A finance company should maintain an allowance for loan losses that is adequate to cover estimated losses. The allowance for loan losses decreases the carrying amount of loans receivable to net realizable value. SFAS 5 and 114 provide guidance for the recognition of estimated losses from the uncollectibility of receivables. SFAS 5 requires that an allowance for loan losses be established when it is probable that a loan has been impaired and the amount can be reasonably estimated. SFAS 114 requires that impairment of a loan be based on the present value of expected future cash flows discounted at the loan's effective interest rate or at the loan's market price or at the fair value of the collateral of the loan if applicable.

Interest Income and Nonrefundable Loan Fees

The interest method should be used to account for interest income in accordance with SFAS 91, *Accounting for Nonrefundable Fees and Costs Associated with Originating or Acquiring Loans and Initial Direct Costs of Leases.* Under this method, often called the actuarial method, interest on installment loans is computed and accrued over the lives of the loans to arrive at constant interest rates throughout the loans' lives. Use of this method produces loans that are carried at amounts equal to future receipts discounted at original implicit interest rates. The accounting for nonrefundable loan fees is also covered in SFAS 91. (See the treatment of this area under the section on Banking and Thrift Industries.)

Other Items

Factoring commissions. The amount a finance company charges as a factoring commission is dependent on such variables as sales volume, number of invoices issued, collection activities, and patterns of returns and chargebacks. Finance companies should recognize factoring commissions over the periods in which services are rendered. A finance company is considered as rendering services from the time a customer's credit is approved until the customer's account is settled.

Advances and overadvances to factoring clients. Finance companies generally do not treat advances to clients as receivables. Instead, advances are applied against amounts owed to clients from the purchase of the client's receivables. Finance companies generally limit advances to percentages of the unpaid amounts of factored receivables. Overadvances, which are amounts in excess of outstanding receivables purchased, should be recorded as loans receivable.

Repossessed assets acquired in liquidation of receivables. Finance companies may repossess goods or other property that collateralize loans when they foreclose on uncollectible loans. Repossessed assets are typically sold as soon as possible to minimize losses from defaulted loans. Certain types of collateral, such as automobiles, may be readily salable in wholesale or other markets. Repossessions of such collateral are fairly common. Repossessions on commercial loans can result in significant losses because of the bargain prices associated with reselling inventories, plant, property, and equipment.

Terms of recourse arrangements include the following:

1. Full recourse—The dealer is required to pay off the uncollected receivable balance to the finance company at the date of repossession.
2. Partial or limited recourse—The dealer is liable for repossession losses up to an agreed amount.
3. Nonrecourse—Loss is borne entirely by the finance company.

Dealer reserves and holdbacks. Finance companies account for dealer reserves and holdbacks as liabilities. Dealer reserve accounts are credited for the dealers' share of the finance charges. Dealer reserve accounts may be charged as the result of customers paying off contracts early, losses on full or partial recourse contracts, and from payments to dealers in excess of minimum requirements.

Sales of receivables. A finance company may decide to sell a portfolio of receivables to another finance company or financial institution. SFAS 140, *Accounting for Transfers and Servicing of Financial Assets and Extinguishment of Liabilities*, controls whether such transactions should be accounted for as sales of receivables or as loans collateralized by receivables. Generally, a transfer is treated as a sale if the transferor surrenders control of the receivables.

GOVERNMENT CONTRACTS

PERSPECTIVE AND ISSUES

ARB 43 covers the accounting and income recognition problems concerning cost-plus-fixed-fee and fixed-price supply contracts. The fees under government cost-plus-fixed-fee contracts may be recognized as income on the basis of partial performance if there is reasonable assurance of realization. Fees may also be accrued as they are billable unless this accrual is not reasonably related to the proportionate performance of total work to be performed.

This pronouncement also covers renegotiation (refunds of excessive profits) and contracts terminated for the convenience of the government.

Sources of GAAP
ARB
43, 11

DEFINITIONS OF TERMS

Contractors. Include prime contractors and subcontractors.

Contracts. Refer to prime contracts and subcontracts.

Cost-plus-fixed-fee contracts. Provide for contractors to receive a specified fixed fee and to be reimbursed for their allowable costs. Because title passes to the government and the contractor obtains an unconditional right to partial payment prior to delivery, delivery of the finished product is not necessarily evidence of performance.

Disposal credits. Deductions from the termination claim receivable for approved retention or sale of inventory previously included in the claim.

No-cost settlements. Settlements in which the contractor waives the right to make a claim. No sale should be recorded and applicable costs should retain their usual classification

Service contracts. Contracts in which the contractor acts only as an agent.

Supply contracts. Contract in which the contractor's services extend beyond that of an agent. Contracts include services such as the use of the contractor's own facilities and responsibility to creditors for material and services, and to employees for salaries.

Subcontractor's claims. Claims made in conjunction with a terminated contract resulting from costs incurred under the terminated contract that did not result in the transfer of billable materials or services to the contractor before termination.

CONCEPTS, RULES, AND EXAMPLES

Cost-plus-fixed-fee contracts (CPFFC) are used for the manufacture and delivery of products, the construction of plants and other facilities, and for management and other services. The amount of the flat-fee payment is usually determined by the ratio of the actual expenditures to the total estimated expenditures. Because

CPFFC may be cancelled and terminated by the government, if this occurs the **contractor** is entitled to reimbursement for expenditures and an appropriate portion of the fixed fee.

Normally, profits are recognized when the right to full payment is unconditional. However, revenues can be accrued and profits recognized for partial performance when total profit can be reasonably estimated and realization is reasonably assured. The fees are usually accrued as they become billable. Because risk is minimal and there is no credit problem, billable amounts are indicative of realization. The contractor's fee is considered earned when it is billable and when the costs are incurred or paid. Accrual based on billable amounts is an application of the percentage-of-completion method, rather than a deviation from the accrual method. The fee is considered billable when approved by the government. An alternative date should be used when a determination is made that estimated and final costs are significantly different. Accrual of the fee upon delivery or based on percentage of completion would be more appropriate when excess costs are extensive.

For **supply contracts**, reimbursable costs and fees should be included in sales. For **service contracts**, only fees should be included in sales. Unbilled amounts should be included in the balance sheet as a receivable, but should be distinguished from billed items. Advances in CPFFC should be offset against **contract** receivables only when there is an expectation that the advances will be applied against those specific charges. Such offsets should be disclosed.

Renegotiation

Renegotiation typically addresses a refund of "excessive" profits. In reality, it is more of an adjustment of the selling price. The financial statements should disclose situations when a substantial portion of a contractor's business consists of contracts that are subject to renegotiation. When a reasonable estimate of renegotiation refunds can be made, a provision should be shown as a deduction from sales in the income statement and as a current liability on the balance sheet. Taxes should be adjusted accordingly. When a reasonable estimate cannot be made, disclosure is required along with the reasons for the inability to make an estimate. Footnote disclosure may also be required regarding material uncertainties and their significance, and regarding the basis for determining the renegotiation provision.

Terminated Defense Contracts

These contracts are contracts terminated for the convenience of the government. Profits accrue as of the effective date of termination and should be included in financial statements after the termination. Disclosure should be made of all material facts and circumstances. Termination claims should be recorded in one account and classified as current assets unless there is an indication of extended delay, such as a serious disagreement indicative of probable litigation. They should be disclosed separately. Pretermination contract advances must be shown as a deduction from claims receivable, and adequately explained. Termination loans are classified as current liabilities.

Termination claims should be accounted for as sales with separate disclosure, if material. When inventory is reacquired, after including it in a termination claim, it should be recorded as a purchase. The credit is to be applied against the termination claim receivable.

INSURANCE INDUSTRY TRANSACTIONS

PERSPECTIVE AND ISSUES

The two major types of insurance companies are life and property and casualty. Each category is further subdivided into stock companies and mutual associations. Due to the regulated nature of the insurance industry, financial reporting may be in conformity to **statutory accounting principles (SAP)** or GAAP. Furthermore, publicly held companies subject to SEC accounting rules will account for certain transactions and events in other manners dictated by those requirements. While accounting principles under GAAP are broadly applicable to all types of insurance companies (including those dealing in such specialized products as mortgage insurance, title insurance, and reinsurance), the nature of the estimation process (such as for claims liabilities) differs substantially depending upon the character of the risks assumed.

The main contrasts between SAP and GAAP arise from the more conservative nature of SAP, which is a reflection of the insurance regulatory agencies' concern with protection of the policyholders' interests, and hence with the liquidity and solvency of the insurance companies. Accordingly, under SAP certain costs, such as policy acquisition expenses, are written off as incurred; certain nonliquid assets, such as property and furniture, are not recognized; and claims liabilities are very conservatively estimated. In contrast to this essentially short-term perspective, financial statements prepared on the GAAP basis are more concerned with the value of the companies' investments and net worth on a going concern basis.

The primary source of insurance industry GAAP is SFAS 60. Although mutual insurance companies and certain other organizations had not been required to apply this standard, SFAS 120 later extended its requirements to these enterprises. Insurance contracts are categorized as short duration (which includes most property and liability insurance) or long duration (which includes most life, mortgage, and title insurance). Nominal insurance contracts that are effectively investment contracts, however, are not accounted for as insurance. The Audit and Accounting Guide, *Audits of Property and Liability Insurance Companies*, was issued in June 1998.

A new Audit and Accounting Guide, *Life and Health Insurance Entities*, was promulgated in 2000, superseding the former AICPA Industry Audit Guide *Audits of Stock Life Insurance Companies* (which was issued in 1972 and updated only for conforming changes subsequently). The new Guide discusses those aspects of accounting and auditing unique to life and health insurance entities, and contains significant discussions of statutory accounting practices (SAP), which comprise laws, regulations, and administrative rulings adopted by various states that govern the operations and reporting requirements of life insurance entities. It does not reflect SAP under the National Association of Insurance Commissioners (NAIC) codification project. It also is not intended to establish any new accounting standards or interpret any existing accounting standards, except for the inclusion of an SEC staff announcement regarding the effects of SFAS 115, *Accounting for Certain Investments in Debt and Equity Securities.*

AcSEC did, however, form a task force to review the necessary changes to SOPs related to the completion of the NAIC Codification of statutory accounting practices for certain insurance enterprises. This resulted in a new proposed SOP that combines an amendment to accounting SOP 94-5, *Disclosures of Certain Matters in the Financial Statements of Insurance Enterprises,* and auditing guidance that has also been updated as a result of the completion of the NAIC Codification. If adopted (which is possible before year-end 2001), the SOP would require insurance enterprises to disclose, at the date of each balance sheet presented, beginning with financial statements for fiscal years beginning on or after January 1, 2001, a description of the prescribed or permitted statutory accounting practice and the related monetary effect on statutory surplus of using an accounting practice that differs from either state-prescribed statutory accounting practices or NAIC statutory accounting practices. Retroactive application would not be permitted.

AcSEC is also in the early stage of a project to address the classification and valuation of liabilities, as well as disclosures for nontraditional annuity and life insurance contracts issued by insurance enterprises. Several conclusions have been reached as discussed later in this section.

Also of some significance, AcSEC issued SOP 00-3, *Accounting by Insurance Enterprises for Demutualizations and Formations of Mutual Insurance Holding Companies and for Certain Long-Duration Participating Contracts,* in late 2000. This provides guidance on accounting by insurance enterprises for demutualizations and the formation of mutual insurance holding companies (MIHCs). The SOP also applies to stock life insurance enterprises that apply SOP 95-1, *Accounting for Certain Insurance Activities of Mutual Life Insurance Enterprises,* to account for participating policies that meet criteria set forth in SOP 95-1. It applies to past and future demutualizations or formations of an MIHC, with specific transition provisions as described in the SOP. Entities must apply the SOP to financial statements no later than the end of the fiscal year that begins after December 15, 2000.

Sources of GAAP			
SFAS	*FASB I*	*SOP*	*EITF*
5, 60, 91, 97, 109, 113,	40	92-5, 94-5, 95-1,	92-9, 93-6,
114, 115, 120, 124		97-3, 98-7, 00-3	93-14, 99-4

CONCEPTS, RULES, AND EXAMPLES

Premium Income

Premium income is recognized differently for short and long duration contracts. For short duration contracts, premium income is recognized over the contract term in proportion to the amount of insurance provided. In the case of long duration contracts, revenue is accrued as the premiums become due from policyholders, except for contracts that provide benefits over a term longer than the premium payment term (such as twenty-year life policies), in which case income is recognized over the longer period during which benefits may be provided.

Claim Cost Recognition

Costs of benefits are recognized when insured events such as property damage occur. Estimated costs are accrued for as claims incurred but not yet reported. For long duration contracts, the present values of estimated future benefits are accrued, net of the present values of future net premiums to be collected. Accrual of these benefit obligations generally involves actuarial determinations. Accountants may be dependent on the services of specialists in such cases, as they are in computing costs related to defined benefit pension plans. Recognition of other expenses is governed by the matching concept. For example, costs that vary with acquisition activity are capitalized and amortized over the period during which premium income is earned. Catastrophic losses (as from natural disasters such as hurricanes) are accrued under the guidelines of SFAS 5: when impairment of the asset or incurring of a liability is probable and the amount is reasonably estimable.

Investments

The other major concern of GAAP for insurance enterprises relates to the presentation of investments held. Prior GAAP (SFAS 60) has been revised by the issuance of SFAS 115, which establishes the accounting requirements for investments in debt and marketable equity securities. Briefly, those investments must be categorized as being either held-for-trading, available-for-sale, or held-to-maturity. Investments falling within the first two categories should be reported at fair value, with value changes affecting the trading securities portfolio being reflected in income, while changes in the available-for-sale portfolio are reported in a separate equity account. Securities to be held to maturity are accounted for at amortized historical cost, absent a permanent decline in value. Equity securities that do not meet the definition of "marketable" are also to be reported at fair value, with gains or losses reported in stockholders' equity.

Deferred Income Taxes

GAAP requires that deferred income taxes be provided for temporary differences. An exception was previously provided under the "indefinite reversal criterion," for stock life insurance companies only, for differences designated as policyholders' surplus. However, SFAS 109 provides that, for such differences arising after 1992, deferred taxes must be provided, consistent with the accounting prescribed for all other temporary differences. Furthermore, if changed circumstances suggest that pre-1993 differences are in fact differences that are likely to reverse, deferred taxes are to be provided, with the provision reflected in current period tax expense.

Other Matters

Reinsurance. Another specialized topic area pertinent to insurance companies is that of reinsurance. After a lengthy period of development and discussion, a new standard, SFAS 113, was promulgated. This standard, which amends SFAS 60, eliminates the former practice of reporting assets and liabilities net of the effects of reinsurance. It requires that reinsurance receivables, including amounts related to claims incurred but not reported, be reported as assets, consistent with the manner in which liabilities relating to the underlying reinsured contracts are accounted for. The standard also establishes criteria for recognition as reinsurance, and sets forth detailed accounting for long and short duration contracts, as well as new disclosure requirements. The Board also ended another long-standing controversy by releasing FASB Interpretation 40, which clarifies that GAAP applies essentially equally to mutual insurance companies as it does to stock companies, unless explicit exceptions were established. Regulatory reporting can no longer, therefore, be deemed to be in accordance with GAAP.

Loss reserves. The AICPA has also been actively reviewing insurance company accounting practices and auditing issues. SOP 92-4 addressed matters relating to estimation of loss reserves, and a number of auditing concerns relating to reserves, reinsurance, loss adjustment expenses, and other topics. SOP 92-5 concerns accounting for foreign property and liability reinsurance, and concludes that except for special circumstances, only the periodic method is acceptable in accounting for foreign reinsurance premiums. SOP 94-5 requires disclosures where permission was received from the National Association of Insurance Commissioners to use different accounting practices. SOP 95-1 covers capitalization and amortization costs and several other matters for mutual life insurance companies. SFAS 120 requires that the provision of this SOP be applied to assessment enterprises, fraternal benefit societies, and stock life insurance companies.

Guaranty funds. A recently issued SOP addresses matters pertaining to guaranty funds and certain other insurance-related assessments. Existing practice has been quite diverse, but the new SOP essentially applies the criteria of SFAS 5, *Accounting for Contingencies*, to these matters, with the exception that practice can be substantially conformed. The key elements of SOP 97-3 are discussed in the following paragraphs.

Under the new standard, guaranty fund and similar assessments would be recognized when (1) it has been imposed or is deemed probable of being imposed, (2) the event obligating an entity to pay the assessment has occurred, and (3) the amount of the assessment can be reasonably estimated. All three conditions would have to be fulfilled before a liability could be accrued. Discounting to present value will be permitted. The SOP offers specific guidance regarding the ability to reasonably estimate the liability for assessments.

Guaranty funds are essentially state-mandated insurance funds used to settle claims against insolvent insurers and, typically, all licensed insurers are assessed premiums based on the volume of defined lines of business they conduct in the given state. A variety of methods have been applied in determining the amounts of guaranty fund assessments (e.g., retrospectively, based on premiums written over the past two years; or prospectively, based on business written over the next several years following an insolvency of a failed insurer), with the result that entities upon which assessments are being levied have been inclined to use different methods of recognizing the cost and related obligation. In general, to warrant accrual under SOP 97-3, an insolvency of another insurer would have to have occurred, since the presumption would be that the assessments would become probable (the threshold criterion) when there has been a formal determination of another entity's insolvency. An example of an exception would be when the state uses prospective premium-based guaranty fund assessments; if the reporting entity **cannot** avoid the obligation by ceasing to write policies, the obligating event would be the determination of insolvency, but if it **could** avoid the assessment, the obligating event is the writing of premiums **after** the insolvency.

Surplus notes. A recent AICPA practice bulletin affects accounting by certain insurance companies that issue a security known as surplus notes. Practice Bulletin 15, *Accounting by the Issuer of Surplus Notes*, requires that these instruments be accounted for as debt and included in the liabilities caption of the balance sheet. Furthermore, interest must be accrued over the term of the notes, whether or not payment of interest and/or principal has been approved by an insurance company. However, disclosure is required as to the status of the request for approval.

A project to produce an industry accounting guide for insurance agents and brokers, was dropped after several years of development, when the intended beneficiaries could not agree on a number of key matters.

Deposit accounting. In 1998 the AICPA completed its project on deposit accounting. Prior to the issuance of SOP 98-7, guidance on how to apply the deposit method has not been available in the professional literature.

The new standard applies to entities entering into short duration insurance and reinsurance contracts that do **not** transfer insurance risk, or multiple year contracts that either do not transfer insurance risk or for which insurance risk transfer is not determinable. Insurance risk is comprised of timing risk and underwriting risk, and one or both of these may not be transferred to the insurer (assuming entity in the case of reinsurance) under certain circumstances. For example, many workers' compensation policies provide for "experience adjustments" which have the effect of keeping the underwriting risk with the insured, rather than transferring it to the insurer; in such instances, deposit accounting would be prescribed.

Under the provisions of SOP 98-7, for contracts that transfer only significant timing risk, or that transfer neither significant timing nor underwriting risk, a deposit asset (from the insured's or ceding entity's perspective, respectively, for insurance and reinsurance arrangements) or liability (from the insurer's or assuming entity's perspective, respectively, for insurance and reinsurance arrangements) should be recognized at inception. The deposit asset or liability should be remeasured at subsequent financial reporting dates by calculating the effective yield on the deposit to reflect actual payments to date and expected future payments. Yield is to be determined as set forth in SFAS 91, using the estimated amounts and timings of cash flows. The deposit is to be adjusted to that which would have existed at the balance sheet date had the new effective yield been applied since inception of the contract; thus, expense or income for a period will be determined by first calculating the necessary amount in the related balance sheet account.

For contracts that transfer only significant underwriting risk, a deposit asset or liability is also established at inception. However, subsequent remeasurement of the deposit does not occur until such time as a loss is incurred that will be reimbursed under the contract; instead, the deposit is reported at its amortized amount. Once the loss occurs, the deposit should be remeasured by the present value of expected future cash flows arising from the contract, plus the remaining unexpired portion of the coverage. Changes in the deposit arising from the present value measure are to be reported in the insured's income statement as an offset against the loss to be reimbursed; in the insurer's income statement, the adjustment should be reported as an incurred loss. The reduction due to amortization of the deposit is reported as an adjustment to incurred losses by the insurer. The discount rate used to compute the present value is to be the rate on government obligations with similar cash flow characteristics, adjusted for differences in default risk, which is based on the insurer's credit rating. Rates are determined at the loss date(s) and not revised later, absent further losses.

For insurance contracts with indeterminate risk, the procedures set forth in SOP 92-5 (the open-year method) should be applied. This involves balance sheet segregation of amounts that have not been adjusted due to lack of sufficient loss or other data. When sufficient information becomes available, the deposit asset or liability is adjusted, which is to be reported as an accounting change per APB 20.

The AICPA has been contemplating issuing either an SOP or an industry audit and accounting guide on mass tort exposure of insurance enterprises. This would include guidance on accounting issues that arise in connection with such mass tort exposures as asbestos and environmental claims and address how the various components of such liabilities are to be measured. Further, it would deal with application of present value concepts to mass tort liabilities and consider the methods used to estimate these obligations. Disclosure requirements would also be established.

An SOP is being developed to deal with the growing matter of **nontraditional long-duration insurance contracts**. The SOP will address the classification and valuation of liabilities as well as disclosures for nontraditional annuity and life insurance contracts issued by insurance enterprises. Among the tentative conclusions are

1. Sales inducements that are earned by the customer immediately, such as "day-one bonuses," should be expensed immediately, whereas sales in-

ducements that are earned over a period of time, such as persistency bonuses or enhanced yields, should be expensed over time;

2. Separate accounts should be recorded in the financial statements of the insurance enterprise that owns them, and should be reported as single line items on the respective sides of the balance sheet (one-line presentation) if all of the following criteria are met

   a. Assets reside in a legally recognized separate account
   b. The separate account is bankruptcy remote from the insurance enterprise
   c. The policyholder directs allocation of investments
   d. All investment performance (net of contract fees) is passed through to the policyholder (including contracts with minimum guarantees, but excluding contracts with caps or ceilings)

3. The guaranteed portion of separate accounts with minimum guarantees should be recorded as a liability in the general account, consistent with the bifurcation approach for embedded derivatives in SFAS 133, *Accounting for Derivative Instruments and Hedging Activities.* Seed money and other insurance company funds invested in separate accounts should be classified and valued as any other general account asset.

Demutualizations. Recent SOP 00-3 has addressed the increasingly common phenomenon of **demutualizations** (whereby formerly mutually owned insurers issue stock), as well as the formation of insurance holding companies (MIHC). A key concern is the accounting for the "closed block" of assets and liabilities, and of earnings allocable to the closed block. This pertains to mechanisms designed to protect the adjustable policy features and dividend expectations of **participating** life insurance policyholders from the competing interests of stockholders. Typically, the plan of demutualization describes how the closed block will operate. The closed block assets and cash returns on those assets will not inure to the stockholders of the demutualized company; instead, all cash flows from these assets will be used to benefit the closed block policyholders. The insurance enterprise remains obligated to provide for minimum guarantees under the participating policy, and it is consequently possible under certain circumstances that additional "stockholder" funds will have to be used to meet the contractual benefits of the closed block policyholders. The assets designated to the closed block are subject to the same liabilities, with the same priority in the case of insolvency or in liquidation, as assets outside the closed block. In many situations, commissions and other expenses (including management expenses) of operating and administering the closed block will not be charged to the closed block. Unless the state insurance department consents to an earlier termination, the closed block will continue in effect until the date on which none of the policies in the closed block remains in force.

Alternatives to the closed block have arisen in practice encompassing, for a number of types of contracts, various mechanisms believed by the insurance enterprise and state insurance regulators to be appropriate in the specific circumstances. Closed block alternative mechanisms have been used in lieu of closed blocks for certain participating life contracts to commit to the insurance regulator that the insurance company will continue to follow its established dividend practices. Closed block alternative mechanisms also have been used to protect nonguaranteed elements of participating and nonparticipating insurance contracts such as interest credits on deferred annuities and adjustable premiums on adjustable premium term business. In some instances, the methodology and limitations defined in the agreements with the state insurance regulators have considered only specific profit components, such as mortality experience on a block of term insurance or investment spreads on a block of annuities, and in other instances have considered virtually all components of product profitability. Where there is a limitation on the profits that may inure to the stockholders, there generally is a formal agreement between the insurance company and the insurance regulators that defines (1) the contracts covered by the limitation, (2) the profit limitation calculation, and (3) the timing and manner (for example, as policy dividends, reduced premiums, or additional benefits) in which amounts that may not be distributed to stockholders are to be distributed to policyholders.

Some of the more important conclusions reached by AcSEC were as follows:

1. The classification of expenses related to a demutualization and the formation of an MIHC should be considered an other than extraordinary expense.
2. Closed block assets and liabilities from the closed block should be included with the corresponding financial statement items of the insurance enterprise.
3. AcSEC has concluded that SOP 95-1, *Accounting for Certain Insurance Activities of Mutual Life Insurance Enterprises*, should continue to be applied after conversion to a stock company. However, provisions of SFAS 60, *Accounting and Reporting by Insurance Enterprises*, relating to dividends on participating contracts should apply to such contracts sold before the date of demutualization or date of formation of the MIHC.
4. The maximum future contribution of the closed block to the earnings of the company is typically the excess of the GAAP liabilities over the GAAP assets at the date of demutualization. Under SFAS 60, a dividend liability should be established for current earnings that will be paid to policyholders through future benefits. From a shareholder perspective, excess earnings of the closed block that will never inure to the shareholders should be set up as a liability. AcSEC decided upon establishment of a dividend liability for excess earnings due to policyholders that cannot inure to shareholders.
5. For a "distribution-form" demutualization, an insurance enterprise should reclassify all of its retained earnings as of the date of demutualization to

capital stock and additional paid-in capital accounts. A "subscription-form" demutualization should not, in and of itself, result in reclassification of retained earnings. AcSEC concluded that the equity accounts of the MIHC at the date of formation should be determined using the principles for transactions of companies under common control with the amount of retained earnings of the demutualized insurance enterprise, before reclassification to the capital accounts, being reported as retained earnings of the MIHC.

EMERGING ISSUES TASK FORCE CONSENSUS SUMMARIES

92-9 Accounting for the Present Value of Future Profits Resulting from the Acquisition of a Life Insurance Company

The Task Force noted that industry practice is to amortize the present value of future profits (PVP) using an interest method with accrual of interest added to the unamortized balance. In the past, there has been some diversity in the application of this method in practice, and so the EITF has worked to standardize this practice. The first consensus reached was that the interest rate used to amortize PVP should be the liability or contract rate. The second consensus was that changes in estimates of future gross profits on SFAS 97 contracts should be accounted for as a catch-up adjustment. And finally, PVP and any related liability should be subject to the premium deficiency test required in SFAS 60 and 97.

93-6 Accounting for Multiple-Year Retrospectively-Rated Contracts by Ceding and Assuming Enterprises

A number of issues involving retrospective rating provisions contained in reinsurance contracts were resolved in this set of consensuses. These address criteria for the recognition and amounts of assets and liabilities by the assuming and ceding enterprises, respectively, and accounting for changes in coverage during the reinsurance period. A number of conditions were identified, satisfaction of which are necessary for a contract to be treated as reinsurance, and in their absence such contracts are to be accounted for by the deposit method.

93-14 Accounting for Multiple-Year Retrospectively-Rated Insurance Contracts by Insurance Enterprises and Other Enterprises

This EITF addresses how enterprises other than insurance companies should account for contracts with insurance companies covering various types of risks such as product and environmental liability risks. This EITF also addresses "pooled risk" contracts and reinsurance contracts entered into by a captive insurer. A consensus was reached that in order for a contract to be considered insurance it must indemnify the insured party as this would result in a transfer of risk. If no transfer of risk exists (SFAS 5), then the contract is not considered insurance, and the balance of the premium less any amount to be retained by the insurer should be accounted for as a deposit. Other consensuses follow those reached in EITF Issue 93-6.

99-4   Accounting for Stock Received from the Demutualization of a Mutual Insurance Company

This offers guidance on the accounting for those formerly mutual insurance companies have undergone demutualization transactions and converted to stock enterprises. In order to effect a demutualization, a company may be required to issue consideration, often in the form of stock, to existing participating policyholders in exchange for their current membership interests. The receipt of such stock has no direct effect on the policyholders' contractual interests of their insurance policies (for example, it does not alter the cash surrender value of their life insurance policies). However, the governance of the mutual insurance company and, in particular, the participating policyholders' interest in that governance are modified. The EITF's consensus was that stock received from a demutualization should be accounted for at fair value with a gain recognized in income from continuing operations.

STATEMENTS OF POSITION

92-5   Accounting for Foreign Property and Liability Reinsurance

This addressed the lack of uniformity of practices among foreign reinsurers, and in particular how US insurers were to account for property and liability reinsurance assumed from foreign companies.

94-5   Disclosures of Certain Matters in the Financial Statements of Insurance Enterprises

Supplements the disclosure requirements in other FASB and SEC pronouncements. Required disclosures are set forth for insurance enterprises that have received permission by the insurance department in their domiciliary states to use accounting practices other than those prescribed by state laws, regulations, and rules and by the National Association of Insurance Commissioners (NAIC). This statement also defines liability for unpaid claims and claims adjustment expenses and lists the related disclosures required.

95-1   Accounting for Certain Insurance Activities of Mutual Life Insurance Enterprises

Provides guidance on applying SFAS 60, 97, and 113 in accounting for mutual life insurance contracts. Capitalization and amortization of acquisition costs is discussed. Premiums are to be reported as revenue when due from policyholders. Death and surrender benefits are reported as expenses, and annual dividends are reported separately as expenses. The calculation of estimated gross margin and liability for future policy benefits is described.

97-3   Accounting by Insurance and Other Entities for Insurance-Related Assessments

In order to address the diversity in practice of accounting for assessments made by government agencies against insurance activities such as workers' compensation second injury funds, this SOP imposed accrual accounting requirements and set forth the conditions that must be met before a liability may be recognized.

98-7   Deposit Accounting: Accounting for Insurance and Reinsurance Contracts That Do Not Transfer Insurance Risk

This provides guidance on how to account for insurance and reinsurance contracts that do not have the effect of transferring insurance risk. It applies to all entities and all types of insurance or reinsurance contracts, other than long-duration life and health insurance contracts. The method prescribed by this SOP is "deposit accounting."

00-3   Accounting by Insurance Enterprises for Demutualizations and Formations of Mutual Insurance Holding Companies and for Certain Long-Duration Participating Contracts

This SOP provides necessary guidance to the proper accounting for demutualization transactions and also for the formation of mutual insurance holding companies. It also provides guidance to stock insurers that choose to apply SOP 95-1 to account for participating policies within the scope of that SOP.

INVESTMENT COMPANIES

PERSPECTIVE AND ISSUES

An investment company pools shareholders' funds to provide shareholders with professional investment management. Investment companies' activities include selling capital shares to the public, investing the proceeds in securities, and distributing net income and net realized gains to its shareholders.

AcSEC issued, in late 2000, a completely revised Audit and Accounting Guide, *Audits of Investment Companies*. This Guide replaced the AICPA Audit and Accounting Guide *Audits of Investment Companies* (1987), which has been updated only for conforming changes. The Guide discusses those aspects of accounting and auditing unique to investment companies, and will provide new guidance on accounting for offering costs, amortization of premium or discount on bonds, liabilities for excess expense plans, reporting complex capital structures, payments by affiliates, and financial statement presentation and disclosures for investment companies and nonpublic investment partnerships. The proposed revised Guide is effective for fiscal years beginning after December 15, 2000.

To address FASB concerns regarding the scope of the Guide, AcSEC has undertaken a project to address whether more specific attributes of an investment company can be identified to determine if an entity is within the scope of the Guide. Until this project is finalized, an entity should consistently follow its current accounting policies for determining whether the provisions of the Guide apply to investees of the entity or to subsidiaries that are controlled by the entity. Tentative conclusions of this project are summarized below. An Exposure Draft is expected before year-end 2001.

Sources of GAAP	
SFAS	*SOP*
102, 126	93-1, 93-2, 93-4, 95-2, 95-3

DEFINITIONS OF TERMS

Closed-end fund. An investment company having a fixed number of shares outstanding, which it does not stand ready to redeem. Its shares are traded similarly to those of other public corporations.

Closed-up fund. An open-ended investment company that no longer offers its shares for sale to the general public but still stands ready to redeem its outstanding shares.

Equalization. An accounting method used to prevent a dilution of the continuing shareholders' per share equity in undistributed net investment income caused by the continuous sales and redemptions of capital shares.

Ex-dividend or ex-distribution. Synonym for **shares being traded without dividend or without capital gains distribution**. The buyer of a stock selling ex-dividend does not acquire a right to receive a previously declared but not-yet-paid dividend. Dividends are payable on a fixed date to shareholders recorded on the stock transfer books of the disbursing company as of a previous date of record. For example, a dividend may be declared as payable to holders of record on the books of the disbursing company on a given Friday. Because five business days are allowed for delivery of the security in regular-way transactions on a stock exchange or over-the-counter, the exchange or the National Association of Securities Dealers (NASD) declares the stock ex-dividend as of the opening of the market on the preceding Monday or on one business day earlier for each intervening nontrading day. Therefore, anyone buying the stock on and after Monday is not entitled to the dividend. In the case of nontraded shares of mutual funds, the ex-dividend date is the same as the record date.

Open-end investment company. A mutual fund that is ready to redeem its shares at any time and that usually offers its shares for sale to the public continuously.

CONCEPTS, RULES, AND EXAMPLES

Several types of investment companies exist: management investment companies, unit investment trusts, collectible trust funds, investment partnerships, certain separate accounts of life insurance companies, and offshore funds. Management investment companies include open-end funds (mutual funds), closed-end funds, special purpose funds, venture capital investment companies, small business investment companies, and business development companies.

All of the investment companies mentioned have the following characteristics:

1. Investment activity—Investing in assets, usually in securities of other entities, for current income, appreciation, or both.
2. Unit ownership—Ownership in the investment company is represented by stock or other units of ownership, to which proportionate shares of net assets can be attributed.
3. Pooling of funds—The funds of the investment company owners are pooled together to take advantage of professional investment management.
4. Reporting entity—The investment company is the primary reporting entity.

Accounting Policies

The accounting policies for an investment company result from the company's role as a vehicle through which investors can invest as a group. These policies are largely governed by the SEC, Small Business Administration, and specific provisions of the Internal Revenue Code relating to investment companies.

Investment companies report all investment securities at market value, or if quoted market values are not available, at fair values as determined by management. Along with other industry groups for which specialized GAAP already existed, calling for presentation of all investments at market value (a group that includes broker-dealers and defined benefit pension plans), investment companies were exempted from the provisions of SFAS 115.

Security purchases and sales are generally recorded at the trade date; therefore, the effects of all securities trades entered into by the investment company to the date of the financial statements are included in the financial report.

Investment companies record dividend income on the ex-dividend date, not on the later record or payable date. The rationale for this treatment is that the market price of market securities may be affected by the exclusion of the declared dividend. Additionally, investment companies record a liability for dividends payable on the ex-dividend date because mutual fund shares are purchased and redeemed at prices equal to or based on net asset value. If investors purchase shares between the declaration and ex-dividend dates they are entitled to receive dividends; however, investors purchasing shares after the ex-dividend date are not entitled to receive dividends.

Open-end investment companies often employ the practice of equalization. This theory states that the net asset value of each share of capital stock sold comprises the par value of the stock, undistributed income, and paid-in capital and other surplus. When shares are sold or repurchased, the investment company calculates the amount of undistributed income available for distribution to its shareholders. Based on the number of shares outstanding, the investment company determines the per share amount; this amount is credited to an equalization account when shares are sold. Conversely, the equalization account is charged when shares are repurchased.

Accounting for High-Yield Debt Securities

The accounting by creditors for investments in "step interest" and "PIK" debt securities, if these qualify as "high-yield" securities, is addressed by the Guide. Step interest bonds are generally unsecured debentures that pay no interest for a specified period after issuance, then pay a stipulated rate for a period, then a higher rate for another period, etc., until maturity. Thus, they combine some of the characteristics of zero-coupon bonds with some features of current interest bonds. PIK (payment in kind) bonds pay some or all interest in the form of other debt instruments ("baby" or "bunny" bonds), which in turn may also pay interest in the form of baby bonds. All babies mature at the due date of the parent bond.

The Guide, as amended, requires that the effective interest method should be used for step interest bonds; to the extent that interest income is not expected to be realized, a reserve against the income should be established. A previously employed technique, the bifurcation method, is no longer acceptable. For PIK bonds, the effective interest method is also required; the market value method, which was widely used in the past, can no longer be employed.

Exemptions from the Requirement to Provide a Statement of Cash Flows

The following conditions must be met for an investment company to be exempted from providing a statement of cash flows:

1. Substantially all of the entity's investments were highly liquid.
2. The entity's investments are carried at market value.
3. The entity had little or no debt, based on average debt outstanding during the period, in relation to average total assets.
4. The entity provides a statement of changes in net assets.

Taxes

Investment companies that distribute all taxable income and taxable realized gains qualifying under Subchapter M of the Internal Revenue Code are not required to record a provision for federal income taxes. If the investment company does not distribute all taxable income and taxable realized gains, a liability should be recorded at the end of the last day of the taxable year. The rationale for recording on the last day of the year is that only shareholders of record at that date are entitled to credit for taxes paid.

Clarification of the Scope of the Investment Companies Guide

AcSEC, in responding to concerns raised by FASB, has undertaken a project to clarify the scope of the investment companies Audit and Accounting Guide issued in 2000. This would take the form of a SOP. Some of the tentative conclusions reached to date are

- For purposes of the separate financial statements of an entity, the Guide would be applicable to entities that are regulated as investment companies and other entities whose primary business activity involves investing for current income, capital appreciation, or both. The SOP would identify conditions that should be evaluated to determine whether the entity's primary business activity is investment activity, including whether investees function as separate autonomous businesses. Entities that meet the conditions and would be required to apply the provisions of the Guide in presenting their financial statements. Entities not meeting those conditions would be prohibited from applying the provisions of the Guide.
- The SOP would also set forth conditions to be evaluated in determining whether the specialized industry accounting principles of the Guide applied by a subsidiary (or equity method investee) should be retained in the financial statements of the parent company (or an investor that applies the equity method of accounting to its investments in the entity). Those conditions are intended to evaluate relationships between the parent company or equity method investor and investees that may indicate that investees are not separate autonomous businesses from the parent company or equity method in-

vestor. If those conditions are not met, the specialized industry accounting principles of the Guide would not be retained in the financial statements of the parent company or equity method investor. In that case, the financial information of the investment company would be adjusted to reflect the accounting principles that would apply to the entity assuming it did not qualify as an investment company within the scope of the Guide.

An Exposure Draft of the scope-clarifying SOP is expected to be issued in the third quarter of 2001.

STATEMENTS OF POSITION

93-1 Financial Accounting and Reporting for High-Yield Debt Securities by Investment Companies

The Division concluded that for PIK and step bonds, (1) the effective-interest method should be used to determine interest income; (2) a reserve against income should be established for interest income not expected to be realized; (3) the cost plus any discount should not exceed undiscounted future cash collections; (4) SEC yield-formula calculations must be made; and (5) all high-yield and restricted debt securities whose values were estimated should be indicated in the portfolio. For defaulted debt securities, any interest receivable written off that had been recognized as income constitutes a reduction of income. Write-offs of purchased interest increase the cost basis and represent an unrealized loss until the security is sold. "Capital infusions" are accounted for as an addition to the cost basis, while related "workout expenditures" are recorded as unrealized losses. Any ongoing expenditures to protect the value of the investment are recorded as operating expenses. Auditors should consider additional pricing valuation audit procedures.

93-2 Determination, Disclosure, and Financial Statement Presentation of Income, Capital Gain, and Return of Capital Distributions by Investment Companies

This statement was developed to clarify the reporting of shareholder distributions that exceed the tax-basis current and accumulated earnings and profits in GAAP financial statements. The statement recommends that the caption "tax return of capital" be used to report such distributions.

93-4 Foreign Currency Accounting and Financial Statement Presentation for Investment Companies

Transactions denominated in a foreign currency must originally be measured in that currency. Reporting exchange rate gains and losses separately from any gain/loss on the investment due to changes in market price is allowable but not required.

95-2   Financial Reporting by Nonpublic Investment Partnerships

This statement pertains to investment partnerships that are exempt from SEC registration under the Investment Company Act of 1940. Specifically, the statement requires that the financial statements include a condensed schedule of securities that categorizes investments by type, country or geographic region, and industry; discloses pertinent information concerning investments comprising greater than 5% of net assets; and aggregates any securities holdings less than the 5% of net assets threshold. The statement of operations for nonpublic investment companies shall be presented in conformity with requirements for public investment companies per the *Audit Guide* so as to reflect their comparable operations. The financial statements shall also present management fees and disclose their computation.

95-3   Accounting for Certain Distribution Costs of Investment Companies

This statement requires investment companies with enhanced 12b-1 plans or board-contingent plans for which the board has committed to pay costs to recognize a liability and the related expense, for the amount of excess costs. This liability should be discounted at an appropriate current rate if the amount and timing of cash flows are reliably determinable and if distribution costs are not subject to a reasonable interest charge. Excess costs are recorded as a liability as the fund has assumed an obligation to pay the 12b-1 fee after the termination of the plan to the extent that the distributor has excess costs.

MORTGAGE BANKING ACTIVITIES

PERSPECTIVE AND ISSUES

Mortgage banking comprises two activities.

1. The origination or purchase of mortgage loans and subsequent sale to **permanent investors**, and
2. Long-term **servicing** of the mortgage loan.

Mortgage loans and mortgage-backed securities held for sale, origination costs, premiums paid to acquire mortgage loans, loan origination fees, and other fees are accounted for in accordance with SFAS 65, 91, 134, and FASB TB 87-3. These pronouncements also apply to other companies that conduct operations similar to the operations of a mortgage banking entity. However, these pronouncements do not apply to the normal lending activities of those other enterprises. Mortgage loans held for sale are valued at lower of cost or market. Mortgage-backed securities are reported under SFAS 115 as held-to-maturity, trading, or available-for-sale, depending on the entity's intent and ability to hold the securities. Loan origination fees and related direct costs for loans held for sale are capitalized as part of the related loan and are not to be amortized. Fees and costs for loans held for investment are deferred and recognized as an adjustment to the yield.

AcSEC has issued an Exposure Draft (ED) of a proposed Statement of Position, *Accounting by Certain Financial Institutions and Entities That Lend to or Finance the Activities of Others*. If adopted, the ED would provide uniform and consistent guidance for the accounting and reporting practices for similar transactions currently contained in the separate AICPA Audit and Accounting Guides for Banks and Savings Institutions, Credit Unions, and Finance Companies. The ED would include in its scope, corporate credit unions and mortgage companies. AcSEC expects to issue a final Statement of Position (SOP) in the third quarter of 2001. If the SOP adopts the provisions of the ED it would require mortgage companies to make new capital disclosure requirements including at a minimum

1. A description of the minimum net worth requirements related to (1) secondary market investors, and (2) state-imposed regulatory mandates.
2. The actual or possible material effects of noncompliance with those requirements.
3. Whether the entity is in compliance with the regulatory capital requirements including, as of the date of each balance sheet presented, the following measures:

   a. The entity's required and actual net worth
   b. Factors that may significantly affect adequacy of net worth such as potentially volatile components of capital, qualitative factors, or regulatory mandates

4. If the entity is not in compliance with capital adequacy requirements as of the most recent balance sheet date, the possible material effects of that condition on amounts and disclosures in the financial statements.

The ED points out that noncompliance with minimum net worth requirements may trigger substantial doubt about the entity's ability to continue as a going concern. The reader is encouraged to monitor developments in this area by visiting the websites of AcSEC at http://www.aicpa.org/members/div/acctstd/status/index.htm and John Wiley & Sons, Inc. at www.wiley.com/gaap.

Sources of GAAP		
SFAS	*FASB TB*	*SOP*
65, 91, 134, 140	87-3	97-1

DEFINITIONS OF TERMS

Affiliated enterprise. An enterprise that directly or indirectly controls, is controlled by, or is under common control with another enterprise; also, a party with which the enterprise may deal if one party has the ability to exercise significant influence over the other's operating and financial policies.

Current (normal) servicing fee rate. A servicing fee rate that is representative of servicing fee rates most commonly used in comparable servicing agreements covering similar types of mortgage loans.

Federal Home Loan Mortgage Corporation (FHLMC). Often referred to as "Freddie Mac," FHLMC is a private corporation authorized by Congress to assist in the development and maintenance of a secondary market in conventional residential mortgages. FHLMC purchases and sells mortgages principally through mortgage participation certificates (PC) representing an undivided interest in a group of conventional mortgages. FHLMC guarantees the timely payment of interest and the collection of principal on the PC.

Federal National Mortgage Association (FNMA). Often referred to as "Fannie Mae," FNMA is an investor-owned corporation established by Congress to support the secondary mortgage loan market by purchasing mortgage loans when other investor funds are limited and selling mortgage loans when other investor funds are available.

Gap commitment. A commitment to provide interim financing while the borrower is in the process of satisfying provisions of a permanent loan agreement, such as obtaining a designated occupancy level on an apartment project. The interim loan ordinarily finances the difference between the floor loan (the portion of a mortgage loan commitment that is less than the full amount of the commitment) and the maximum permanent loan.

Government National Mortgage Association (GNMA). Often referred to as "Ginnie Mae," GNMA is a US governmental agency that guarantees certain types of securities (mortgage-backed securities) and provides funds for and administers certain types of low-income housing assistance programs.

Internal reserve method. A method for making payments to investors for collections of principal and interest on mortgage loans by issuers of GNMA securities. An issuer electing the internal reserve method is required to deposit in a custodial account an amount equal to one month's interest on the mortgage loans that collateralize the GNMA security issued.

Mortgage-backed securities. Securities issued by a governmental agency or corporation (e.g., GNMA or FHLMC) or by private issuers (e.g., FNMA, banks, and mortgage banking enterprises). Mortgage-backed securities generally are referred to as **mortgage participation certificates** or **pass-through certificates** (PC). A PC represents an undivided interest in a pool of specific mortgage loans. Periodic payments on GNMA PC are backed by the US government. Periodic payments on FHLMC and FNMA PC are guaranteed by those corporations, but are not backed by the US government.

Mortgage banking enterprise. An enterprise that is engaged primarily in originating, marketing, and servicing real estate mortgage loans for other than its own account. Mortgage banking enterprises, as local representatives of institutional lenders, act as correspondents between lenders and borrowers.

Permanent investor. An enterprise that invests in mortgage loans for its own account, for example, an insurance enterprise, commercial or mutual savings bank, savings and loan association, pension plan, real estate investment trust, or FNMA.

Securitization. The transformation of financial assets into securities (asset-backed securities).

Servicing. Mortgage loan servicing includes collecting monthly mortgagor payments, forwarding payments and related accounting reports to investors, collecting escrow deposits for the payment of mortgagor property taxes and insurance, and paying taxes and insurance from escrow funds when due.

Standby commitment. A commitment to lend money with the understanding that the loan probably will not be made unless permanent financing cannot be obtained from another source. Standby commitments ordinarily are used to enable the borrower to obtain construction financing on the assumption that permanent financing will be available on more favorable terms when construction is completed. Standby commitments normally provide for an interest rate substantially above the market rate in effect when the commitment is issued.

CONCEPTS, RULES, AND EXAMPLES

Mortgage Loans and Mortgage-Backed Securities

Valuation. Mortgage loans held for sale are reported at the lower of cost or market as of the balance sheet date. Any excess of cost over market should be accounted for as a valuation allowance, changes in which are to be included in income currently. During the period such loans are held for sale, any related purchase discounts may not be amortized as interest revenue.

Mortgage-backed securities are to be accounted for as held-to-maturity, trading, or available-for-sale depending on the entity's intent and ability to hold the securities as specified by SFAS 115 as amended by SFAS 134. However, if a mortgage banking enterprise commits to sell a mortgage-backed security before or during the **securitization** process, the entity must classify the security as trading. The securitization of mortgage loans held for sale should be accounted for as a sale of the mortgage loans and the purchase of mortgage-backed securities. Not-for-profit organizations holding mortgage-backed securities shall report at fair value using the guidance of SFAS 124.

The market value of mortgage loans and mortgage-backed securities held for sale is to be determined by type of loan; at a minimum, separate determinations must be made for residential and commercial loans. Either an aggregate or individual loan basis may be used in determining the lower of cost or market for each type. Market values for loans subject to investor purchase commitments (committed loans) and loans held for speculative purposes (uncommitted loans) must be determined separately.

For committed loans and mortgage-backed securities, market value is defined by the commitment prices. For committed mortgage-backed securities, if the fair value exceeds the commitment price, the implicit loss must be recognized. If the commitment price for committed loans provides for servicing fee rates materially different from current fee rates, the price must be adjusted as described under "Servicing fees," below.

Fair value for uncommitted mortgage-backed securities collateralized by the entity's own loans ordinarily should be based on the market value of the securities. If the trust holding the loans may be terminated and the loans sold directly, fair value for the securities should be based on the market value of the loans or the securities, depending on the entity's intentions. Fair value for other uncommitted mortgage-backed securities should be based on published yield data.

The capitalized costs of servicing rights are excluded from loan cost in calculating lower of cost or market values.

A mortgage loan or mortgage-backed security may not be reported as a long-term investment unless the mortgage banker is both able to and intends to hold the loan or security to maturity or at least into the foreseeable future. These assets are transferred to a long-term investment classification at the lower of cost or market on the date of transfer. If the carrying amount differs from the outstanding principal balance, then the yield is adjusted by the interest method.

Uncollectibility. If full recovery of the carrying amount of a mortgage loan or mortgage-backed security held as a long-term investment is permanently impaired, then the carrying amount should be written down to its expected recoverable amount. This amount becomes the new cost basis and the amount of the write-down is a period loss. Any recovery from the new basis may be reported as a gain **only** upon the maturity or disposition of the loan or security.

Repurchase agreements. Mortgage loans or mortgage-backed securities held for sale may be temporarily transferred by a mortgage banker to another financial institution under a formal or informal agreement which serves as a means of financing these assets. Loans and securities transferred under such agreements are accounted for as collateralized financing arrangements and are still reported as held for sale.

A formal repurchase agreement specifies that the mortgage banker retains control over future economic benefits and also the risk of loss relating to the loans or securities transferred. These assets are subsequently reacquired from the financial institution upon the sale of the assets by the mortgage banking enterprise to permanent investors.

An informal repurchase agreement exists when no formal agreement has been made but loans or securities are transferred by a mortgage banking enterprise that does **all** of the following:

1. Is the sole marketer of the assets
2. Retains any interest spread on the assets
3. Retains risk of loss in market value
4. Reacquires uncollectible loans
5. Regularly reacquires most or all of the assets and sells them to permanent investors

When mortgage loans held for sale are transferred under a repurchase arrangement, they should continue to be reported by the transferor as loans held for sale. Mortgage-backed securities sold under agreements to repurchase should be reported as trading securities as defined in SFAS 115.

Servicing Mortgage Loans

Rights to service mortgage loans for others must be recognized as separate assets by mortgage banking enterprises. If the enterprise acquires such rights through purchase or origination of mortgage loans and retains them upon sale or securitization, the total cost of the mortgage loans must be allocated between the rights and the loans (sans the rights) based on their relative fair values. If it is impossible to determine the fair value of the mortgage servicing rights apart from the mortgage, the transferor shall record the mortgage servicing rights at zero value (SFAS 140). Mortgage servicing rights are capitalized at their fair value and recognized as a net asset if the benefits of servicing the mortgage are expected to be more than adequate compensation to the servicer for performing the duties. If the benefits of servicing the mortgage are not expected to adequately compensate the servicer, then the servicer recognizes a liability. The asset Mortgage Servicing Contract Rights is initially measured at its fair value and subsequently impaired in the following manner:

1. The mortgage servicing assets are stratified based on predominant risk characteristics.
2. Impairment is recognized through a valuation allowance for an individual stratum. The amount of impairment equals the carrying amount for a particular stratum minus its fair value.
3. The valuation allowance is adjusted to reflect changes in the measurement of impairment after the initial measurement of impairment.

Servicing fees. Servicing fees are usually based on a percentage of the outstanding principal balance of the mortgage loan. When a mortgage loan is sold with servicing rights retained, the sales price must be adjusted if the stated rate is materially different from the **current (normal) servicing fee rate** so that the gain or loss on the sale may be determined. The adjustment is

$$\text{Adjustment} = \begin{matrix} \text{Actual} \\ \text{Sales} \\ \text{Price} \end{matrix} - \begin{matrix} \text{Estimated sales price} \\ \text{obtainable if normal} \\ \text{servicing fee rate had} \\ \text{been used} \end{matrix}$$

This adjustment allows for recognition of normal servicing fees in subsequent years.

The adjustment and any recognized gain or loss are determined as of the sale date. If estimated normal servicing fees are less than total expected servicing costs, then this loss is to be accrued on the sale date as well.

Sales to Affiliated Enterprises

When mortgage loans or mortgage-backed securities are sold to an **affiliated enterprise**, the carrying amount of the assets must be adjusted to lower of cost or market as of the date that management decides that the sale will occur. This date is evidenced by formal approval by a representative of the affiliated enterprise (purchaser), issuance of a purchase commitment, and acceptance of the purchase commitment by the seller. Any adjustment is charged to income.

If a group of (or all) mortgage loans are originated specifically for an affiliate, then the originator is an agent of the affiliated enterprise. In this case, the loans are transferred at the originator's cost of acquisition. This treatment does not apply to "right of first refusal" or similar contracts in which the originator retains all risks of ownership.

Issuance of GNMA

An issuer of **GNMA** securities who elects the **internal reserve method** must pay one month's interest cost to a trustee. This cost is capitalized (at no greater than the present value of net future servicing income) and amortized.

Loan and Commitment Fees and Costs

Mortgage bankers may pay or receive loan and commitment fees as compensation for various loan administration services. These fees and costs are accounted for as described in the following paragraphs.

Loan origination. Loan origination fees and direct costs must be deferred. If the loan is later held for resale, these fees and costs are recognized upon sale of the loan. If the loan is held for investment, loan origination fees and costs are recognized as an adjustment of yield using the effective interest method.

Services rendered. Fees for specific services rendered by third parties as part of a loan origination (e.g., appraisal fees) are recognized when the services are performed.

Loans held for sale. Residential or commercial loan commitment fees paid to permanent investors are recognized as expense when the loans are sold or when it is determined that the commitment will not be used. Since residential loan commitment fees typically cover groups of loans, the amount of fees recognized as revenue or expense relating to an individual transaction is calculated as

$$\begin{array}{l}\text{Revenue or} \\ \text{expense recog-} \\ \text{nized on} \\ \text{individual} \\ \text{transaction}\end{array} = \begin{array}{l}\text{Total} \\ \text{residential} \\ \text{loan commit-} \\ \text{ment fee}\end{array} \times \frac{\text{Amount of individual loan}}{\text{Total commitment amount}}$$

Loan placement fees (fees for arranging a commitment directly between investor and borrower) are recognized as revenue once all significant services have been performed. In some cases, a mortgage banker secures a commitment from a permanent investor before or at the same time as a commitment is made to a borrower and the latter commitment requires

1. Simultaneous assignment to the investor, and
2. Simultaneous transfer to the borrower of amounts paid by the investor.

The fees related to such transactions are also accounted for as loan placement fees.

Expired commitments or early repayment of loans. At the time that a loan commitment expires unused or is repaid before repayment is due, any related fees that had been deferred are recognized as revenue or expense.

Reporting

Mortgage banking enterprises must, on the balance sheet, distinguish between mortgage loans and mortgage-backed securities that are held for sale and those that are held for long-term investment.

STATEMENTS OF POSITION

97-1   Accounting by Participating Mortgage Loan Borrowers

Establishes the borrower's accounting for a participating mortgage loan if the lender participates in increases in the market value of the mortgaged real estate project, the results of operations of that mortgaged real estate project, or both. It requires that certain disclosures be made in the financial statements. In addition, this SOP requires the following: (1) At origination, if the lender is entitled to participate in appreciation in the market value of the mortgaged real estate project, the borrower should determine the fair value of the participation feature and should recognize a participation liability for that amount. A corresponding debit should then be recorded to a debt-discount account. The debt discount should be amortized by the interest method, using the effective interest rate. (2) At the end of each reporting period, the balance of the participation liability should be adjusted if necessary, so that the liability equals the fair value of the participation feature at that point in time. The corresponding debit or credit should be adjusted to the related debt-discount account. The revised debt discount should then be amortized prospectively.

MOTION PICTURE INDUSTRY

PERSPECTIVE AND ISSUES

SFAS 53, *Financial Reporting by Producers and Distributors of Motion Picture Films,* had long served as GAAP for the motion picture industry. During the period when the FASB expressed the intent to become the standard setter for all specialized industries, it issued this standard as an endorsement of an early AICPA industry guideline. However, the FASB has since apparently decided not to carry that particular burden itself, but rather to again defer to the AICPA's AcSEC for specialized industry guidance.

Many new developments (e.g., the widespread distribution of videos and DVDs) have occurred since the original motion picture accounting standard was promulgated, and hence this was a good candidate for a thoroughgoing revision. In June 2000, the FASB issued SFAS 139 that rescinded SFAS 53. Concurrently AcSEC issued SOP 00-2, *Accounting by Producers or Distributors of Films.* These new pronouncements were effective for fiscal years beginning after December 15, 2000, and have shifted the standards-setting responsibility for the industry back to AcSEC.

Sources of GAAP	
SOP	*EITF*
00-2	87-10

DEFINITIONS OF TERMS

Cross-collateralized. A contractual arrangement granting distribution rights to multiple films, territories and/or markets to a licensee. In this type of arrangement, the exploitation results of the entire package are aggregated by the licensee in determining amounts payable to the licensor.

Distributor. The owner or holder of the rights to distribute films. Excluded from this definition, for the purposes of applying SOP 00-2, are entities that function solely as broadcasters, retailers (such as video stores), or movie theaters.

Exploitation costs. All direct costs incurred in connection with the film's distribution. Examples include marketing, advertising, publicity, promotion, and other distribution expenses.

Film costs. Film costs include all direct negative costs incurred in the physical production of a film, including allocations of production overhead and interest capitalized in accordance with SFAS 34. Examples of direct negative costs include costs of story and scenario; compensation of cast members, extras, directors, producers, and miscellaneous staff; costs of set construction and operations, wardrobe and accessories; costs of sound synchronization; rental facilities on location; and postproduction costs such as music, special effects, and editing.

Film prints. The materials containing the completed audio and video elements of a film which are distributed to a theater to exhibit the film to its customers.

Firm commitment. An agreement with a third party that is binding on both parties. The agreement specifies all significant terms, including items to be exchanged, consideration, and timing of the transaction. The agreement includes a disincentive for nonperformance that is sufficiently large to ensure the expected performance. With respect to an episodic television series, a firm commitment for future production should include only episodes to be delivered within one year from the date of the estimate of ultimate revenue.

Market. A distribution channel located within a certain geographic territory for a certain type of media, exhibition, or related product. Examples include theatrical exhibition, home video (laser disc, videotape, DVD), pay television, free television, and the licensing of film-related merchandise.

Nonrefundable minimum guarantee. Amount to be paid by a customer in a variable fee arrangement that guarantees an entity a minimum fee on that arrangement. This amount applies to payments paid at inception, as well as to legally binding commitments to pay amounts over the license period.

Overall deal. An arrangement whereby an entity compensates a creative individual (e.g. producer, actor, or director) for the exclusive or preferential use of that party's creative services.

Participation costs. Frequently, persons involved in the production of a film are compensated, in part or in full, with a participation in the financial results of the film. Determination of the amount of compensation payable to the participant is usually based on formulas (participations) and by contingent amounts due under provisions of collective bargaining agreements (residuals). The recipients of this compensation are referred to as participants and the costs are referred to as participation costs. Participations may be paid to creative talent (e.g. actors or writers), or to entities from whom distribution rights are licensed.

Producer. An individual or enterprise that produces and has a financial interest in films for exhibition in movie theaters, on television, or elsewhere.

Revenue. Amounts earned by an entity from its direct distribution, exploitation, or licensing of a film, before deduction for any of the entity's direct costs of distribution. In markets and territories where the entity's fully or jointly owned films are distributed by third-party distributors, revenue is the net amount payable to the entity by the distributor. Revenue is reduced by appropriate allowances, estimated returns, price concessions, or similar adjustments, as applicable.

Sale. The transfer of control of the master copy of a film and all of the associated rights that accompany it.

Set for production. A film qualifies as being set for production when all of the following conditions have been met: (1) management with relevant authority authorizes (implicitly or explicitly) and commits to funding the film's production; (2) active preproduction has begun; and (3) the start of principal photography is expected to begin within six months.

Territory. A geographic area in which a film is exploited, usually a country. In some cases, however, a territory may be contractually defined as countries with a common language.

CONCEPTS, RULES, AND EXAMPLES

SOP 00-2, *Accounting by Producers or Distributors of Films,* provides the authoritative guidance with respect to accounting for arrangements for the sale, licensing, or exhibition of films. The term "film" is generic and includes intellectual property produced on traditional celluloid film as well as videotape, digital, or other video-recording format. The content or format of films includes (1) feature films, (2) television series, (3) television specials, and (4) similar products (including animated films and television programming). The guidance in the SOP applies to producers and distributors who own or hold rights to distribute or **exploit** films. The SOP **does not** apply to the following specialized industries or applications that have their own specialized GAAP:

1. The recording industry (SFAS 50)
2. Cable television (SFAS 51)
3. Broadcasters (SFAS 63)
4. Computer software to be sold, leased, or otherwise marketed (SFAS 86)
5. Software revenue recognition (SOP 97-2)
6. Entertainment and educational software products (EITF 96-6)

There are many varieties of contractual sales or licensing arrangements governing the rights or group of rights to a single or multiple films. The film's producer (referred to in the SOP and in this discussion as "the entity") may license it to distributors, theaters, exhibitors, or other licensees (referred to in the SOP and in this discussion as "customers") on an exclusive or nonexclusive basis in a particular market or territory. The terms of the license may be for a fixed (or flat) fee or the fee may be variable based on a percentage of the customer's revenue. If the arrangement is variable, it may include a **nonrefundable minimum guarantee** payable either in advance or over the licensing period.

Revenue Recognition

An entity is to recognize revenue from a sale or licensing arrangement only when **all** of the following conditions are met:

1. Persuasive evidence of a sale or licensing arrangement with a customer exists.
2. The film is complete and, in accordance with the terms of the arrangement, has been delivered or is available for immediate and unconditional delivery.
3. The license period for the arrangement has started and the customer can begin its exploitation, exhibition, or sale.
4. The arrangement fee is fixed or determinable.
5. Collection of the arrangement fee is reasonably assured.

If any of the above conditions has not been met, the entity should defer recognizing revenue until all of the conditions are met. If the entity recognizes a receivable on its balance sheet for advances under an arrangement for which all of the above conditions have not been met, a liability for deferred revenue of the same amount is to be recognized until such time as all of the conditions have been met.

Persuasive evidence of an arrangement. This condition is met solely by documentary evidence that sets forth, at a minimum, the following terms: (1) the license period, (2) the film or films covered by the agreement, (3) a description of the rights transferred, and (4) the consideration to be exchanged. If the agreement is ambiguous regarding the parties' rights and obligations, or if there is significant doubt as to the ability of either party to perform under the agreement, revenue is not to be recognized. Acceptable documentary evidence must be verifiable (e.g., a contract, a purchase order, or an on-line authorization).

Delivery. The delivery condition may be satisfied by an arrangement providing the customer with immediate and unconditional access to a film print held by the entity. The customer may also receive a **lab access letter** that authorizes it to order a film laboratory to make the film immediately and unconditionally available for its use. Under these conditions, the delivery condition is satisfied if the film is complete and available for immediate delivery.

Some licensing arrangements require the entity to make **significant changes** to the film after it becomes initially available. Significant changes are changes that are additive to the film and that result from the entity creating additional content after the film becomes initially available. The changes can consist of the reshooting of selected scenes or adding additional special effects. When such changes are required to be made to the film, the arrangement does not meet the delivery condition. The costs incurred for these significant changes are added to **film costs** and subsequently recorded as expense when the related revenue is recognized.

Changes that are not considered to be significant changes include insertion or addition of preexisting film footage, addition of dubbing or subtitles to existing footage, removal of offensive language, reformatting to fit a broadcaster's screen dimensions, or adjustments to allow for the insertion of commercials. Such insignificant changes do not alter the film's qualification for the delivery condition. The costs of these insignificant changes should be accrued and charged directly to expense by the entity at the time that revenue recognition commences even if they have not yet been incurred.

Commencement of exploitation. Some arrangements impose on the customer a release date or **street date** before which the film may not be exhibited or sold. Such a date defines the commencement date of the exploitation rights. The entity should not begin to recognize revenue on the arrangement until this restriction has expired.

Fixed or determinable arrangement fee. When there is a **flat fee** that covers a **single film**, the amount of the fee is, of course, considered fixed and determinable and the entity recognizes the entire license fee as revenue when all of the conditions set forth above have been satisfied.

If the flat fee applies to **multiple films**, some of which have not been produced or completed, an entity should allocate the fee to each individual film by market or territory based on relative fair values of the rights to exploit each film under the licensing arrangement. The entity should base the allocations to a film or films not yet produced or completed on the amounts that would be refundable if the entity does not ultimately complete and deliver the films to the customer. The entity should allocate the remaining flat fee to completed films based on the relative fair values of the exploitation rights to those films under the arrangement. These allocations may not be adjusted subsequently even if better information becomes available. After making the allocations described above, the entity recognizes revenue for each film when all of the above conditions are met with respect to that film by market and territory. If the entity is not able to determine relative fair values for the exploitation rights, then the fee is not fixed or determinable and the entity may not recognize revenue until such a determination can be made and it meets all five of the conditions.

An entity's arrangement fees may be **variable** based on a percentage of the customer's revenue from exploitation of the film. When all five conditions have been met, the entity should commence revenue recognition as the customer exploits or exhibits the film.

Certain variable fee arrangements include a **nonrefundable minimum guarantee** whereby the customer guarantees to pay the entity a nonrefundable minimum amount that is applied against the variable fees on a film or group of films that are not **cross-collateralized**. In applying the revenue recognition conditions, the amount of the nonrefundable minimum guarantee is considered to be fixed and determinable and should be recognized as revenue when all of the other conditions have been met. If the nonrefundable minimum guarantee is applied against variable fees from a group of films on a cross-collateralized basis, the amount of the minimum guarantee attributable to each individual film cannot be objectively determined. In this situation, the entity only recognizes revenue when all five of the conditions have been met as the customer exhibits or exploits the film. Under this scenario, if there is a remaining portion of the nonrefundable minimum guarantee that is unearned at the end of the license period, the entity recognizes the remaining guarantee as revenue by allocating it to the individual films based on their relative performance under the arrangement.

Returns and price concessions can affect whether the arrangement fee meets the condition of being fixed and determinable. The factors to consider include the provisions of the arrangement between the entity and its customer and the entity's policies and past actions related to granting concessions or accepting product returns. If the arrangement includes a right-of-return provision or if its past practices allow for such rights, the entity must meet all of the conditions in SFAS 48, in order for it to recognize revenue. Among those conditions is a requirement that the entity be able to reasonably estimate the amount of future returns.

Barter revenue. If an entity licenses programming to television stations in exchange for a specified amount of advertising time on those stations, the exchange should be accounted for as a nonmonetary exchange in accordance with APB 29 as interpreted by EITF 93-11. See the discussion of nonmonetary transactions in Chapter 9, Long-Lived Assets.

Modifications of arrangements. If, during the term of a licensing arrangement, the entity and its customer agree to **extend an existing arrangement** for which all of the revenue recognition conditions have been met, the accounting follows the same rules cited above for flat-fee arrangements, variable fee arrangements, and variable fee arrangements with minimum guarantees.

For modifications that are not extensions of an existing arrangement, the modification is accounted for as a new arrangement. At the time the former arrangement is terminated, the entity should accrue and expense all costs associated with the arrangement or reverse reported revenue for refunds and concessions. In addition, the entity should adjust accumulated film cost amortization and accrued participation costs attributable to the excess revenue.

Product licensing. Any revenue from licensing arrangements to market film-related products is to be deferred until the release date of the film.

Present value. Revenue that an entity recognizes in connection with licensing arrangements is to be recorded at the present value of the license fee computed in accordance with APB 21 as of the date that the entity first recognizes the revenue.

Costs and Expenses—Components

Costs associated with the production and bringing to market of a film can be categorized as one of the following:

1. Film costs
2. Participation costs
3. Exploitation costs
4. Manufacturing costs

Film costs. **Film costs** are recorded separately on the entity's balance sheet. They consist of direct negative costs, production overhead, and production period interest capitalized in accordance with SFAS 34. **Direct negative costs** include costs to acquire the property (e.g., film rights to books or stage plays, or original screenplays); the cost of adaptation or development of the property; compensation of the cast, directors, producers, extras, and other staff members; costs of set construction and operations, wardrobe and accessories; costs of sound synchronization; on-location rental facilities; and postproduction costs such as music, special effects, and editing. **Production overhead** includes allocation of costs of individuals or departments with exclusive or significant responsibility for the production of films. However, production overhead does not include general and administrative expenses, the costs of certain **overall deals**, or charges for losses on properties sold or abandoned. If the entity presents a classified balance sheet, unamortized film costs are presented as a noncurrent asset. The amortization of film costs is explained later in this section.

Participation costs. Participation costs are contingent compensation paid to creative talent such as actors or writers, or to entities from whom the distribution rights are licensed (these recipients are referred to as participants). The costs are computed (accrued) based on contractual formulas (participations) and by contingent amounts due under provisions of collectively bargained union agreements (residuals). The accrual of these costs is discussed later in this section.

Exploitation costs. Exploitation costs are the direct costs associated with the film's distribution. The advertising cost component of exploitation costs is accounted for in accordance with SOP 93-7 which is discussed in Chapter 9, Long-Lived Assets. All other exploitation costs, including marketing costs, publicity, promotion, and other distribution expenses, are to be expensed as incurred.

Manufacturing costs. The cost of making theatrical **film prints** is charged to expense over the period benefited. The cost of manufacturing and/or duplication costs of products to be held for sale such as videocassettes and digital video discs is charged to expense on a unit-specific basis when the related product revenue is recognized. Unsold inventories are to be evaluated at each balance sheet date, for net realizable value and obsolescence.

Costs and Expenses—Amortization of Film Costs and Accrual of Participation Costs

Amortization of capitalized film costs and accrual (expensing) of participation costs commences when the film is released and the entity begins to recognize revenue from the film. The method used to compute the amortization of film costs and the accrual of participation costs is called the **individual-film-forecast-computation method**. This method amortizes film costs using the following formula:

$$\frac{\text{Current period actual revenue}}{\substack{\text{Estimated remaining} \\ \text{unrecognized ultimate revenue as} \\ \text{of the beginning of the fiscal year}}} \quad \text{x} \quad \substack{\text{Unamortized film} \\ \text{costs at the} \\ \text{beginning of the} \\ \text{fiscal year}} \quad = \quad \substack{\text{Film cost} \\ \text{amortization for the} \\ \text{fiscal year}}$$

Similarly, participation costs are accrued and expensed using the following formula:

$$\frac{\text{Current period actual revenue}}{\substack{\text{Estimated remaining} \\ \text{unrecognized ultimate revenue as} \\ \text{of the beginning of the fiscal year}}} \quad \text{x} \quad \substack{\text{Unaccrued} \\ \text{ultimate} \\ \text{participation costs} \\ \text{at the beginning} \\ \text{of the fiscal year}} \quad = \quad \substack{\text{Amount of} \\ \text{participation costs} \\ \text{to be accrued} \\ \text{(expensed) for the} \\ \text{fiscal year}}$$

Irrespective of the above calculation, participation costs are subject to special rules. The liability should only be accrued if it is probable that there will be a sacrifice of assets to settle the entity's obligation under the participation agreement. In addition, at each balance sheet date, accrued participation costs should not be less than the amounts that the entity is obligated to pay at that date.

Using this formulaic approach, if the actual results from the exploitation of the film are realized as originally estimated, the entity would earn a constant rate of profit over the ultimate period for each film before considering exploitation costs, manufacturing costs and other period costs.

It is, of course, likely that the actual results will vary from the estimates and that the estimates will need to be reviewed and refined. At each reporting date, the entity should review and revise estimates of ultimate revenue and participation costs to reflect the most current information available to it. As a result of this review, the denominator should be revised to include only the remaining ultimate revenue at the beginning of the fiscal year of change. In this way, such changes in estimate are accounted for prospectively as of the beginning of the fiscal year of the change. The numerator is unaffected by the change since it is based on actual results. The entity should use this revised denominator in the fraction applied to the net unamortized film costs and to the film's unaccrued ultimate participation costs. The difference between expenses determined using the new estimates and any amounts previously recorded as expense during that fiscal year should be charged (or credited) to the income statement in the period (e.g., quarter) during which the estimates are revised.

Ultimate revenue. In general, the ultimate revenue to be included in the denominator of the fraction should include estimates of revenue to be recognized by the entity from the exploitation, exhibition, and sale of a film in all markets and territories. There are, however, certain limitations that apply to the determination of ultimate revenue.

1. The period over which ultimate revenue for a film may be estimated is limited to ten years following the date of the film's initial release.
2. For previously released films acquired as part of a film library, the period over which ultimate revenue may be estimated is limited to twenty years from the date of acquisition of the library. A film must have been initially released at least three years prior to the acquisition date of the film library in order to be categorized as part of the library for the purposes of applying this limitation.
3. Ultimate revenue should include estimates of revenue for a market or territory only if persuasive evidence exists that such revenue will be earned, or if an entity can demonstrate a history of earning such revenue in that market or territory. Ultimate revenue should include estimates of revenue from newly developing territories only if an existing arrangement provides persuasive evidence that the entity will realize such amounts.
4. Ultimate revenue should include estimates of revenue from licensing arrangements with third parties to market film-related products only if there is persuasive evidence that such revenue from that arrangement will occur for

that particular film (e.g., a signed contract to receive a nonrefundable minimum guarantee or nonrefundable advance) or if an entity can demonstrate a history of earning such revenue from that form of arrangement.

5. Ultimate revenue should include estimates of the portion of the wholesale or retail revenue from an entity's sale of peripheral items (such as toys and apparel) attributable to the exploitation of themes, characters, or other contents related to a particular film only if the entity can demonstrate a history of earning such revenue from that form of exploitation in similar kinds of films. Under this limitation, the amount of such revenue to be included in ultimate revenue is an estimate of the amount that would be earned by the entity if rights for such a form of exploitation had been granted under licensing arrangements with third parties. Thus, the entity's estimate of ultimate revenue should not include the entire gross wholesale or retail revenue from the sale of peripheral items, but rather, the amount that it would realize in net license fees from such sales.

6. Ultimate revenue should exclude estimates of revenue from unproven or undeveloped technologies.

7. Ultimate revenue should exclude estimates of wholesale promotion or advertising reimbursements to be received from third parties. These reimbursements should be accounted for as an offset against exploitation costs.

8. Ultimate revenue should exclude estimates of amounts related to the sale of film rights for periods after those identified in 1. and 2. above.

With respect to episodic television series, the following rules apply:

1. The period over which ultimate revenue for an episodic television series may be estimated is limited to ten years from the date of delivery of the first episode or, if the series is still in production, five years from the date of delivery of the most recent episode, if later.

2. Ultimate revenue should include estimates of secondary market revenue (revenue from syndication of the series to markets other than the initial market) for produced episodes only if the entity can demonstrate through its experience or industry norms that the number of episodes already produced, plus those for which a firm commitment exists and the entity expects to deliver, can be licensed successfully in the secondary market.

3. Ultimate revenue should exclude estimates of amounts related to the sale of rights for periods after those identified in 1. above.

Ultimate revenue should be a gross undiscounted amount and is not to include amounts representing projections of future inflation. The portion of ultimate revenue that is expected to be received in a foreign currency is to be valued at current spot rates.

Ultimate participation costs. The determination of unaccrued ultimate participation costs to be used in the individual-film-forecast-computation method should be determined using assumptions consistent with the entity's estimates of film costs, exploitation costs, and ultimate revenue subject to the limitations set forth above. If, at any balance sheet date, the recognized participation costs liability exceeds the estimated unpaid ultimate participation costs for an individual film, the excess liability should first be applied to reduce unamortized film costs with any remaining excess credited to income. If the entity continues to incur participation costs after the film costs have been fully amortized, the participation costs should be accrued and expensed as the related revenues are recognized.

Valuation of Unamortized Film Costs

Consistent with the rules for recognizing impairment of long-lived assets in SFAS 121, the SOP sets forth examples of events or changes in circumstances that indicate that the entity must assess whether the fair value of the film (whether it has been completed or is still in production) is less than the carrying amount of its unamortized film costs.

1. An adverse change in the expected performance of the film prior to its release
2. Actual costs substantially in excess of budgeted costs
3. Substantial delays in completion or release schedules
4. Changes in release plans, such as a reduction in the initial release pattern
5. Insufficient funding or resources to complete the film and to market it effectively
6. Actual performance subsequent to release fails to meet that which had been expected prior to release

Upon making the comparison between the film's fair value and its unamortized costs, any excess of the unamortized costs over the fair value is to be written off as a charge to the income statement. Amounts written off may not be subsequently restored.

The fair value of a film is often estimated using a traditional discounted cash flow model. The limits regarding the number of years of revenue to include in the determination of ultimate revenue do not apply to the estimation of future cash flows associated with the film for the purpose of determining the film's fair value. Factors that management of the entity should consider in estimating future cash inflows for a film include

1. The film's performance in prior markets, if previously released
2. The public's perception (the popularity and market appeal) of the film's story, cast, director, or producer
3. Historical results of similar films
4. Historical results of the cast, director, or producer on prior films
5. The running time of the film

In addition to estimating the film's cash inflows, management must estimate future costs to complete the film (if any), future exploitation and participation costs, and other necessary cash outflows necessary to achieve the estimated cash inflows.

When using the traditional discounted cash flow method to estimate fair value, the estimates of future cash inflows and outflows should represent management's best estimates of the most likely cash flows. The discount rate to be used should be adjusted to consider the level of risk inherent in investing in a project of this nature.

When using the expected cash flow approach to estimate fair value, all possible relevant future cash inflows and outflows should be probability-weighted by period and the estimated average for each period should be used. In employing this method, the discount rate is risk-adjusted as described above only if the probable expected cash flows have not already been risk-adjusted. Guidance for applying these two estimation techniques is contained in SFAC 7.

Subsequent events. When evidence of the possible need for a write-down of unamortized film costs arises after the date of the balance sheet but before the entity issues its financial statements, a rebuttable presumption exists that the conditions leading to the write-off existed at the balance sheet date. When this situation arises, whether the film was released before or after the balance sheet date, the entity should use this subsequent evidence to compute the adjustment necessary to record a change in estimate in its financial statements. If management is able to demonstrate that the conditions leading to the write-down did not exist at the balance sheet date, the rebuttable presumption can be overcome, and the recognition of the effects of the change in estimate can be postponed until the subsequent period.

EMERGING ISSUES TASK FORCE CONSENSUS SUMMARIES

87-10 Revenue Recognition by Television "Barter" Syndicators

A consensus was reached that revenue from the sale of advertising time acquired from a barter would be recognized when the criteria of SFAS 53 are met and either a noncancelable contract is signed by both parties or the advertisement has been aired. The reference to SFAS 53 will undoubtedly be changed to SOP 00-2, but the consensus will most likely remain unchanged.

NOT-FOR-PROFIT ORGANIZATIONS

PERSPECTIVE AND ISSUES

Not-for-profit organizations have several characteristics that distinguish them from business enterprises. First, and perhaps foremost, not-for-profit organizations exist to provide goods and services without the objective of generating a profit. Rather than obtaining resources by conducting exchange transactions at a profit or from capital infusions from owners, a not-for-profit organization obtains most resources from others that share its desire to serve a chosen mission—an educational, scientific, charitable, or religious goal. Although not-for-profit organizations can be "owned" or controlled by another, the ownership interest is unlike that of business enterprises because the "owner" cannot remove resources from the entity for personal use or gain; the resources must be used for a mission-related purpose. Examples of not-for-profit organizations are: churches and religious organizations, colleges and universities, healthcare organizations, libraries, museums, performing arts organizations, civic or fraternal organizations, federated fund-raising organizations, professional and trade associations, social clubs, research organizations, cemeteries, arboretums, and zoos.

Specifically excluded from the list of not-for-profit organizations are organizations that exist to provide dividends, lower costs, or other economic benefits directly and proportionately to their members, participants, or owners, such as mutual insurance companies, credit unions, farm or utility cooperatives, and employee benefit plans. Further, some not-for-profit organizations are governmental[3] and are required to follow the standards of the Governmental Accounting Standards Board (GASB). Governmental organizations are outside of the scope of this publication. Readers instead should refer to the Wiley publication, *GAAP for Governments.*

All authoritative pronouncements in the GAAP hierarchy, including EITF consensus opinions, apply to not-for-profit organizations unless the pronouncement specifically excludes not-for-profit organizations from its scope. Certain authoritative pronouncements apply specifically to not-for-profit organizations. Because those pronouncements are particularly relevant to the transactions of not-for-profit organizations they are discussed in this chapter.

SFAS 93, issued in 1987, was the first standard issued by the FASB that applied specifically to not-for-profit organizations. It requires not-for-profit organizations to depreciate their long-lived assets and to disclose balances for the major classes of assets, depreciation for the period, accumulated depreciation, and the organization's policy for computing depreciation.

SFAS 116 establishes standards for recognition and display of contributions received and contributions made. It requires all contributions received and made to be measured at fair value and recognized in the period the gift is made. It applies to

---

[3] *See Chapter 1, Researching GAAP Problems, for a definition of "governmental entity."*

any contribution of assets, including contributions of cash, securities, supplies, long-lived assets, use of facilities or utilities, services, intangible assets, or unconditional promises to give those items in the future.

SFAS 117 establishes standards for the general-purpose financial statements issued by not-for-profit organizations. It defines a complete set of financial statements for most organizations as a statement of financial position, a statement of activities, a statement of cash flows, and accompanying notes. It requires an organization's net assets and its revenues, expenses, gains, and losses to be classified based on the existence or absence of restrictions imposed by donors.

SFAS 124 establishes standards for investments held by not-for-profit organizations. It requires equity securities with readily determinable fair values and debt securities to be reported at fair value with the resulting holding gains and losses reported in the statement of activities. It also establishes standards for reporting investment return, including losses on donor-restricted endowment funds.

SFAS 136 establishes standards for transfers of assets to a not-for-profit organization or a charitable trust that raises or holds contributions for others. Although it primarily affects federated fund-raising organizations, community foundations, and institutionally related foundations, all organizations are subject to its standards because they can be the beneficiaries of the contributions raised by those organizations.

The FASB is currently working on a project that will establish standards for accounting and reporting of mergers, acquisitions, and other combinations of not-for-profit organizations. The project is not expected to result in new standards until 2002 or later. Progress of the project can be monitored at the FASB website, www.fasb.org.

Two AICPA Audit and Accounting Guides provide standards for not-for-profit organizations. *Health Care Organizations* applies to providers of health care services, including hospitals, nursing homes, medical clinics, continuing care retirement communities, health maintenance organizations, home health agencies, and rehabilitation facilities. *Not-for-Profit Organizations* applies to all other nongovernmental not-for-profit organizations. Both Guides discuss the aspects of financial statement preparation and audit particularly relevant to their organizations. In addition, each provides a helpful listing of all category (A) GAAP pronouncements and their applicability to not-for-profit organizations.

SOP 94-3 establishes standards for consolidation by not-for-profit organizations of investments in for-profit entities and not-for-profit organizations. It also describes the type of disclosures required when related entities are not consolidated because the relationship does not meet the criteria of control and economic benefit.

SOP 98-2 establishes standards for the functional classification of expenses incurred in activities that combine program or management and general components with fund-raising. It requires that all costs of the combined activity be classified as fund-raising expenses unless three criteria—purpose, audience, and content—are met.

This chapter contains a highly summarized discussion of accounting and reporting standards for not-for-profit organizations. Readers who desire a more in-depth discussion should refer to the Wiley publication, *Not-for-Profit GAAP*.

Sources of GAAP		
SFAS	*AICPA Guides*	*SOP*
93, 116, 117, 124, 136	*Not-for-Profit Organizations, Health Care Organizations*	94-3, 98-2

DEFINITION OF TERMS

Agent. An entity that acts for and on behalf of another. For example, a not-for-profit organization acts as an agent for and on behalf of a donor if it receives resources from the donor and agrees to transfer the resources or the return generated by investing those resources to another entity named by the donor. Similarly, a not-for-profit organization acts for and on behalf of a beneficiary if it agrees to solicit contributions in the name of the beneficiary and distribute any contributions thereby received to the beneficiary.

Collections. Works of art, historical treasures, or similar assets that meet the following three criteria: (1) they are held for public exhibition, education, or research in service to the public rather than for financial gain; (2) they are protected, kept unencumbered, cared for, and preserved; (3) they are subject to a policy that requires that the organization use the proceeds from the sale of an item to acquire another item for the collection.

Contribution. A voluntary and unconditional transfer of assets to an entity (the donee) from another entity that does not expect to receive value in exchange and does not act as an owner (the donor). A contribution can also take the form of a settlement or cancellation of the donee's liabilities.

Donor-imposed restriction. A donor stipulation that specifies a use for contributed resources that is narrower than the limitations that result from the nature of the organization, the environment in which it operates, and the purposes specified in its articles of incorporation, bylaws, or similar documents. A restriction may be temporary or permanent. A **temporary restriction** is a restriction that will expire (be satisfied) either by an action of the organization (such as spending the resources for the purpose described by the donor) or by the passage of time. A **permanent restriction** never expires. Instead, it requires that the contributed resources be maintained permanently, although it allows the organization to spend the income or to use the other economic benefits generated by the resources.

Donor-imposed condition. A donor stipulation that specifies a future and uncertain event whose occurrence (or failure to occur) gives the donor the right of return of resources it has transferred or releases the donor from the obligation to transfer assets in the future. For example, "I will contribute one dollar for each dollar raised during the month of July in excess of $10,000," includes a donor-imposed condition. If only $9,000 is raised, the donor has no obligation to transfer assets.

Endowment fund. A fund of cash, securities, or other assets held to provide income for the support of a not-for-profit organization. A **donor-restricted endowment fund** is a fund established by a donor that specifies that the gift must be invested permanently to generate support (a permanent endowment fund) or invested for a specified period of time (a term endowment fund). A **quasi endowment fund** is a fund established by an organization's governing board to provide income for a long, but usually unspecified, period of time. A quasi endowment fund may be created from unrestricted resources or from resources that are for a restricted purpose but not required by the donor to be invested.

Intermediary. An organization that acts as a facilitator for the transfer of resources between two or more other parties. An intermediary generally does not take possession of the assets transferred.

Net assets. The residual interest in the assets of a not-for-profit organization that remains after deducting its liabilities. Net assets are divided into three classes—permanently restricted, temporarily restricted, and unrestricted—based on the nature and existence of donor-imposed restrictions. **Permanently restricted net assets** is the portion of net assets that result from contributions and other inflows of resources that are subject to permanent donor-imposed restrictions. Permanently restricted net assets cannot be expended or used up. **Temporarily restricted net assets** is the portion of net assets that result from contributions and other inflows of resources that are subject to temporary donor-imposed restrictions. They can be expended or used up as long as their use is consistent with the limitations placed by the donor. **Unrestricted net assets** is the portion of net assets that is neither permanently nor temporarily restricted by donors. The use of unrestricted net assets is subject only to the limitations placed by the nature of the organization, its articles of incorporation or bylaws, and the environment in which it operates.

Promise to give. A written or oral agreement to contribute resources to another entity at a future date. A promise to give can be either conditional or unconditional. A **conditional promise to give** depends on the occurrence (or failure to occur) of a donor-imposed condition to obligate the donor. An **unconditional promise to give** depends only on the passage of time or demand by the donee for payment of the promised assets.

Trustee. An entity that holds and manages assets for the benefit of a specified beneficiary in accordance with a charitable trust agreement.

Voluntary health and welfare organization. An organization formed for the purpose of attempting to prevent or solve health and welfare problems of society, and in many cases, of particular individuals.

CONCEPTS, RULES, AND EXAMPLES

Complete Set of Financial Statements

Financial statements should help donors, creditors, and others who provide resources to a not-for-profit organization assess the services provided by the not-for-profit organization and its ability to continue to provide those services. The statements should also help them assess whether management has properly discharged its stewardship responsibilities and whether it has performed satisfactorily in its other management duties.

SFAS 117, *Financial Statements of Not-for-Profit Organizations,* requires all not-for-profit organizations to present a statement of financial position, a statement of activities, a statement of cash flows, and notes to the financial statements any time it purports to present a complete set of financial statements. In addition, voluntary health and welfare organizations are required to present a statement of functional expenses. In most ways, the content and format of those financial statements are similar to the statements prepared by business enterprises.

However, three major differences between not-for-profit organizations and business enterprises cause differences in the content and format of financial statements of not-for-profit organizations. First, there is no profit motive in the nonprofit sector, and thus no single indicator of performance comparable to a business enterprise's bottom line. In fact, the best indicators of the performance of a not-for-profit organization are generally not measurable in dollar amounts. Nevertheless, dollars are the language of financial reporting. Information to help assess performance is provided in financial statements (1) by reporting revenues and expenses gross rather than net and (2) by classifying expenses based on the mission-related programs and supporting activities they sustain, rather than by their natural classifications (salaries, utilities, depreciation, etc.).

Second, because the bottom line of a not-for-profit organization's statement of activities is not a performance measure, but simply a change in net assets for the reporting period, there is no need for not-for-profit organizations to distinguish between components of comprehensive income as business enterprises do. All revenues, expenses, gains, and losses are reported in a single statement rather than being divided between an income statement and a statement of comprehensive income.

Third, not-for-profit organizations receive contributions, a type of transaction that is without counterpart in business enterprises. Those contributions often have donor-imposed restrictions which can affect the types and levels of service that a not-for-profit organization can offer. Because donor-imposed restrictions are prevalent, recurring, and, in some cases, permanent, financial reporting by not-for-profit organizations needs to reflect the nature and extent of donor-imposed restrictions and changes in them.

Net Assets and Changes in Net Assets

The nature and extent of donor-imposed restrictions are reported in the statement of financial position by distinguishing between the portions of net assets that are permanently restricted, temporarily restricted, and unrestricted. Separate line items on the face of that statement or details in the notes to financial statements are used to meet the requirement to disclose the amounts for different types of permanent and temporary restrictions.

Changes in donor-imposed restrictions are reported in the statement of activities. The organization's revenues, expenses, gains, and losses for the period are classified into the three classes of net assets so that the statement of activities reports amounts for the change in permanently restricted net assets, the change in temporarily restricted net assets, and the change in unrestricted net assets, as well as the change in net assets in total. Transactions and events that do not change the net assets of the organization as a whole, but only their classification, are reported separately as reclassifications. Reclassifications are events that simultaneously increase one class of net assets and decrease another. For example, unrestricted net assets increase and temporarily restricted net assets decrease when the purchase of a long-lived asset fulfills a donor-imposed restriction to acquire long-lived assets with the gift (sometimes referred to as a release of restrictions).

Not-for-profit organizations often use fund accounting as a tool for tracking compliance with donor-imposed restrictions and internal designations. Fund accounting is a system of recording resources whose use is limited either by donors, granting agencies, governing boards, law, or legal covenants. A separate fund (a self-balancing group of accounts composed of assets, liabilities, and net assets) is maintained for each purpose limitation. For external reporting, a fund may be classified entirely in one net asset class or it may need to be allocated among two or three classes. (For an example of the allocations necessary to restate a fund balance to net asset classes, see the discussion of endowment funds in "Investments" in this section.)

Reporting Revenues

Revenues are reported in the statement of activities as increases in unrestricted net assets unless the use of the resources received is subject to a donor-imposed restriction. Thus, contribution revenues increase unrestricted net assets, temporarily restricted net assets, or permanently restricted net assets, depending on the existence and nature of donors' restrictions. Revenues from most exchange transactions (such as sales of goods or services) are classified as unrestricted.

Revenues from exchange transactions only increase restricted net asset classes if a preexisting donor-imposed restriction limits the use of the resources received. For example, if a donor contributes a car to the local library and requires that the proceeds from the sale of the car be used to purchase children's books, the proceeds from the sale of the car (an exchange transaction) increase temporarily restricted net assets. Investment income and gains (also exchange transactions) increase unrestricted net assets unless a donor required that the gift be invested and the investment return used for a restricted purpose. For example, assume a donor contributes securities worth $85,000 to a zoo, requires that all dividends and gains be retained and reinvested until the accumulated value is $100,000, and states that the $100,000 must be maintained as a permanent endowment fund, the income of which is for the purchase of animals. In the early years of the endowment, before the accumulated value reaches $100,000, investment income and gains increase permanently restricted net assets. Investment income and gains earned after the accumulated value of the fund reaches $100,000 increase temporarily restricted net assets.

SFAS 116, *Accounting for Contributions Received and Contributions Made*, requires contributions to be recognized as revenue at the time of the gift and measured at the fair value of the contributed assets regardless of the form of the assets contributed. Donor-imposed restrictions do not change the timing of recognition of a contribution. Donor-imposed restrictions, or the absence of them, affect only a contribution's classification as an increase in permanently restricted net assets, temporarily restricted net assets, or unrestricted net assets. Donor-imposed conditions, however, affect the timing of recognition. Because a contribution is an unconditional transfer, a transfer of assets subject to donor-imposed conditions is not a contribution yet, although it may become one at a future date. Conditional transfers are not recognized as contribution revenues until the conditions are substantially met. Thus, the distinction between donor-imposed restrictions and donor-imposed conditions is very important to the timing of recognition. If a donor's stipulations do not clearly state whether a gift depends on meeting a stated stipulation and the ambiguity cannot be resolved by talking with the donor or by examining the circumstances surrounding the gift, a transfer should be presumed to be conditional.

Unconditional promises to give cash or other assets are recognized in financial statements when the promise is made and received, provided that there is sufficient evidence in the form of verifiable documentation (written, audio, or video). If payments of the promises are due in future periods, the promise has an implied time restriction that expires on the date the payment is due. Thus, unless circumstances surrounding the receipt of the promise indicate that the donor intended the gift to support the current period's activities, unconditional promises increase restricted net assets. The present value of estimated future cash flows is used to measure unconditional promises to give, although short-term promises (due in less than one year) may be reported at net realizable value. Conditional promises are not recognized as revenue until the conditions are substantially met; however, they are required to be disclosed in notes to financial statements.

In a manner similar to recognizing promises to give, a beneficiary recognizes contributions held on its behalf by an agent, trustee, or intermediary. For example, if the assets held by the agent were transferred subject to a condition that is not yet met, the beneficiary does not recognize its potential rights to the assets held by the agent. If a beneficiary has an unconditional right to receive cash flows from a charitable trust or other pool of assets, the beneficiary recognizes its rights when the beneficial interest is created and measures the rights using the present value of the estimated expected cash flows. However, if the beneficiary and the agent, trustee, or intermediary are financially interrelated organizations, the beneficiary reports its rights to the assets held using a method similar to the equity method of accounting for investments. (For further discussion, see "Transfers received as an agent, trustee, or intermediary" in this section.)

Volunteer services are recognized in certain circumstances. Contributed services that create or improve a nonfinancial asset (such as building a shed or replacing a roof) are recognized as revenue either by valuing the hours of service received or by measuring the change in the fair value of the nonfinancial asset created or improved. Other contributed services are recognized only if they meet all three of the following criteria: (1) they require specialized skills, (2) they are provided by persons possessing those skills, and (3) they would typically need to be purchased if not provided by donation. If volunteer services neither meet those three criteria nor create or improve nonfinancial assets, they cannot be recognized in financial statements. However, organizations are required to describe the programs or activities for which contributed services are used, the nature and extent of services received for the period (regardless of whether those services are recognized), and disclose the amount recognized as revenues.

An organization that maintains its works of art, historical treasures, and similar assets in collections, as defined, does not recognize gifts of items that are added to its collections unless it also capitalizes its collections. However, gifts that are not added to collections or items given to organizations that do not maintain collections in accordance with the definition are recognized as revenues and measured at the fair value of the assets received.

Reporting Expenses

Expenses are recognized in the statement of activities as decreases in unrestricted net assets. Financing an expense with donor-restricted resources does not make the expense restricted; instead, it releases the restriction on the restricted resources, causing a reclassification to be reported in the statement of activities.

Expenses must be reported by functional classifications either on the face of the statement of activities or in the notes to financial statements. The functional classifications describe the major classes of program services and supporting activities of an organization. Program services are the mission-related activities of the organization that result in goods and services being distributed to clients, customers, or members. They are the activities that are the major purpose of and the major output of the organization. For example, a not-for-profit organization with the mission of enhancing the lives of the community's senior citizens might have senior center, home visits, transportation services, and home maintenance as its program expense classifications. Supporting activities are all activities of a not-for-profit organization other than program services. Fund raising expenses and management and general are two common supporting activity classifications.

SFAS 117 encourages, but does not require, most not-for-profit organizations to provide an analysis of expenses by natural classification. Information about expenses by natural classifications (salaries, benefits, rent, depreciation, and so forth) can help readers of the financial statements understand the mix of fixed and discretionary costs incurred by the organization. Only voluntary health and welfare organizations are required to report information about expenses by both functional and natural classification. Those organizations must provide that information in a matrix format in a statement of functional expenses.

SFAS 93, *Recognition of Depreciation by Not-for-Profit Organizations,* requires the depreciation of land, buildings, and equipment used by not-for-profit organizations. An exception to that requirement is provided for certain works of art, historical treasures, and similar assets. If a not-for-profit organization can demonstrate both (1) that an asset individually has cultural, historical, or aesthetic value worth maintaining in perpetuity and (2) that the organization has the ability to protect and preserve that value essentially undiminished and is doing so, depreciation need not be recognized. Depreciation expense is a natural expense classification that must be allocated to programs and supporting activities when expenses are reported by functional classification.

Transfers Received as an Agent, Trustee, or Intermediary

SFAS 136, *Transfers of Assets to a Not-for-Profit Organization or Charitable Trust That Raises or Holds Contributions for Others,* establishes standards for transactions in which a donor makes a contribution by using an agent, trustee, or intermediary. (Agents, trustees, and intermediaries are referred to as recipient organizations.) The donor transfers assets to the recipient organization. The recipient organization accepts the assets from the donor and agrees to use the assets on behalf of or transfer the assets, their investment return, or both to another entity—the beneficiary—named by the donor. SFAS 136 also establishes standards for transactions that take place in a similar manner but are not contributions because the transactions are revocable, repayable, or reciprocal. SFAS 136 does not set standards for recipient organizations that are trustees.

In general, a recipient organization reports a liability if it accepts assets from a donor and agrees to use those assets on behalf of or transfer those assets to another organization or individual specified by the donor. When it subsequently spends the assets on behalf of the beneficiary or transfers the assets, their return, or both to the beneficiary, the nonprofit organization reduces the liability it recorded earlier. If the assets received from the donor are donated materials, supplies, or other nonfinancial assets, the recipient organization may choose either to (1) report the receipt of the assets as liability to the beneficiary concurrent with recognition of the assets received or (2) not to report the transaction at all. The choice is an accounting policy that must be applied consistently from period to period and disclosed in the notes to the financial statements.

If the donor explicitly grants the recipient organization variance power, the recipient organization, rather than the beneficiary, recognizes contribution revenue. Variance power is the unilateral power to direct the transferred assets to an entity other than the specified beneficiary. Unilateral power means that the recipient organization does not have to contact the donor, the beneficiary, or any other interested party in order to substitute a different beneficiary. Variance power must be granted in the instrument transferring the assets.

If the recipient organization and the specified beneficiary are financially interrelated organizations, the recipient organization reports contribution revenue and the specified beneficiary recognizes its interest in the net assets of the recipient organization using a method similar to the equity method of accounting for investments in common stock. Organizations are financially interrelated if the relationship between them has both of the following characteristics: (1) one organization has the ability to influence the operating and financial decisions of the other and (2) one organization has an ongoing economic interest in the net assets of the other. The ability to influence the operating and financial decisions of the other can be demonstrated in several ways: (1) the organizations are affiliates as defined in SFAS 57, (2) one organization has considerable representation on the governing board of the other, (3) the charter or bylaws of one organization limit its activities to those that are beneficial to the other, or (4) an agreement between the organizations allows one organization to actively participate in the policymaking processes of the other. An ongoing economic interest in the net assets of another is a residual right to the other organization's net assets that results from an ongoing relationship. A common example of financially interrelated organizations is a foundation that exists to raise, hold, and invest assets for a specific beneficiary and that specific beneficiary it supports.

In addition to establishing standards for contributions transferred to beneficiaries via agents, trustees, and intermediaries, SFAS 136 sets standards for transfers that take place in a similar manner but are not contributions because the terms of the transfer or the relationships between the parties make the transfer revocable, repayable, or reciprocal. Transfers are recognized by the recipient organization as liabilities if one or more of the following terms is present: (1) the transfer is subject to the transferor's right to redirect the transferred assets to another beneficiary, (2) the transfer is accompanied by the transferor's conditional promise to give, (3) the transferor controls the recipient organization and specifies an unaffiliated beneficiary, or (4) the transferor specifies itself or its affiliate as the beneficiary of a transfer that is not an equity transaction. An equity transaction is a transfer that has all of the following terms: (1) the transferor specifies itself or its affiliate as beneficiary, (2) the transferor and the recipient organization are financially interrelated organizations, and (3) neither the transferor nor its affiliate expects payment of the transferred assets (although payment of investment return is allowable). Equity transactions are reported by the recipient organization as a separate line item in the statement of activities.

Investments and Endowment Funds

SFAS 124, *Accounting for Certain Investments Held by Not-for-Profit Organizations,* requires investments in equity securities with readily determinable fair values and all debt securities to be reported at fair value. Although the standard applies to the same securities that SFAS 115 covers for business enterprises, accounting for the resulting gains and losses is different than that standard. Gains and losses (both realized and unrealized) are reported in a not-for-profit organization's statement of activities.

The Audit Guide establishes standards for reporting other investments. The appropriate standards to apply depend on whether the not-for-profit organization is a college or university, a voluntary health and welfare organization, a health care organization, or another type of not-for-profit organization. Most organizations have the option of reporting their other investments at either cost or the lower of cost or market.

Many of the investments held by not-for-profit organizations are held as the investments of endowment funds. Endowment funds generally are established by gifts from donors who desire to provide support for the organization permanently (a permanently restricted endowment fund) or for a specified period of time (a term endowment fund). In addition, a governing board may determine that certain resources be invested and that only the return generated be spent by the organization. These board-designated amounts are referred to as quasi endowment funds or funds functioning as endowment. The net assets of an endowment fund are classified in accordance with the restrictions placed on the resources by donors, if any. Because a donor can place different restrictions on each source of the net assets (original gift, investment gains and losses, and investment income), each source must be examined separately to achieve the proper classification.

Each source is unrestricted unless its use is temporarily or permanently restricted by the donor or by a law that extends the donor's restriction to the source. Thus, the net assets of an endowment fund created by the governing board from a large unrestricted bequest (or from unrestricted net assets) are classified as unrestricted because no donor was involved in the transaction and all amounts are free of donor-imposed restrictions.

In contrast, assume that a donor contributes $50,000 to a museum and stipulates that the gift be invested in perpetuity and the investment income be used to purchase works of art. The donor further stipulates that any gains on the investment be added to the original gift and invested in perpetuity. The donor's original gift ($50,000) increases permanently restricted net assets because of the stipulation that the gift be invested in perpetuity. The income earned by the investment of the gift increases temporarily restricted net assets. When works of art are purchased, the restriction on net assets resulting from the income is fulfilled and the net assets are reclassified to unrestricted net assets. The realized and unrealized gains from investment of the gift increase permanently restricted net assets because the donor required that those gains also be reinvested in perpetuity.

In most cases, the classification of the original gift and the investment income is straightforward because donors explicitly state the time and purpose restrictions on them. Classification of gains and losses on the investments is not as clearly determinable unless the donor explicitly states how gains should be used and whether losses must be restored immediately from other sources, from future gains on the investments, or not at all. However, donors are often silent in their agreements about those matters.

In the absence of explicit donor restrictions, the law in most states provides some direction about the restrictions on investment gains of donor-restricted endowment funds. The Uniform Management of Institutional Funds Act (UMIFA) extends certain donor restrictions to the net appreciation (accumulated net gains) of donor-restricted endowment funds. In states that have adopted UMIFA, net appreciation is expendable unless the donor states that it could not be spent. UMIFA provides that the net appreciation can be spent for the uses and purposes for which the endowment fund was established. Thus, unless the donor specifies otherwise, gains increase unrestricted net assets if the endowment's income is not restricted by the donor, and gains increase temporarily restricted net assets if the endowment's income is temporarily restricted by the donor. Assume in the earlier example of the $50,000 gift to the museum that the donor was silent about the use of gains earned by investing the original gift. In a state that has adopted UMIFA, the accumulated gains on the endowment fund would be restricted to the purchase of artwork because the law requires that the donor's restriction be extended to those gains. The restrictions on those temporarily restricted net assets expire when the museum purchases works of art even if the money to purchase the work of art is not withdrawn from the fund. Thus, this single endowment fund can be composed of permanently restricted net assets (the original $50,000 gift), temporarily restricted net assets (the gains on which restrictions have not yet been met), and unrestricted net assets (the gains on which restrictions were met).

SFAS 124 requires that losses on the investments of an endowment fund reduce temporarily restricted net assets to the extent that temporary restrictions on net appreciation have not yet been met before the loss occurs. The remainder of the loss, if any, reduces unrestricted net assets. If the losses reduce the value of the fund below the level required by the donor or by law, future gains that restore the value to the required level are classified as unrestricted net assets.

Expanding on our previous example, assume that several years after the fund was established, the assets of the fund have increased in value to $65,000. Assume also that the classification of the net assets in the fund is: $50,000 permanently restricted (the original gift), $10,000 temporarily restricted (accumulated gains on which the restrictions have not been met), and $5,000 unrestricted (gains on which the restriction was met by purchasing a work of art with unrestricted funds in years after the inception of the fund). A market correction causes the value of the investments to fall to $58,000. The $7,000 loss decreases temporarily restricted net assets. Assume that a further market correction reduces the value of the investments to $49,000. The $9,000 loss reduces temporarily restricted net assets by $3,000 (the amount remaining after the $7,000 loss decreased the $10,000) and reduces unrestricted net assets by $6,000. After recording the loss, the classification of the $49,000 value of the endowment fund would be: $50,000 permanently restricted (the original gift) and ($1,000) deficit in unrestricted net assets. A not-for-profit is required to disclose the amount by which the value of the endowment fund is less than the level required by the donor.

Continuing the example, assume that the next year the value of the investments increases to $53,000. The $4,000 gain increases unrestricted net assets by $1,000 (the restoration of the deficit) and increases temporarily restricted net assets by $3,000. After the gain, the net assets of the endowment fund are $50,000 permanently restricted (the original gift) and $3,000 temporarily restricted for the purchase of works of art.

Collections

Not-for-profit organizations are allowed an exception to the normal requirement to capitalize purchases of plant, property, and equipment. If a not-for-profit organization maintains collections of works of art, historical treasures, or similar assets in the manner defined in SFAS 116, it can choose whether it will capitalize and report those collections in its statement of financial position. To qualify for the exception, an organization must (1) hold the items for public exhibition, education, or research in service to the public rather than for financial gain, (2) protect the items, keep them unencumbered, care for them, and preserve them, and (3) use the proceeds from the sale of any items to acquire other items for the collection. If an organization meets those criteria, it can choose one of the following policies: (1) capitalize its collections, (2) capitalize only collection items acquired after the adoption of SFAS 116, or (3) not capitalize any collections. An organization cannot selectively choose to capitalize only certain collections.

If an organization does not capitalize its collections, transactions involving collection items must be separately reported on the face of its statement of activities. Similarly, if an organization chose to capitalize its collections prospectively when it adopted SFAS 116, it would separately report transactions involving collection items not previously capitalized. Descriptions of the collections, including information about stewardship policies and items deaccessed (removed from the collection), must be included in notes to the financial statements by organizations that do not capitalize their collections or that capitalize them prospectively.

Capitalization of works of art, historical treasures, and similar assets that are not collection items is required, even if those items are held by organizations that regularly maintain collections. Thus, if a museum does not capitalize its collections and it is given a work of art that it does not to add to its collection (perhaps because it duplicates other collection items), the museum would recognize that contribution and report the asset in its statement of financial position as a work of art held for sale.

Split-Interest Agreements

A split-interest agreement is an arrangement in which a donor transfers assets to a not-for-profit organization or to a charitable trust and requires the benefits of ownership of those assets be split among two or more beneficiaries. Charitable gift annuities, annuity trusts, charitable remainder unitrusts, charitable lead trusts, and pooled (or life) income funds are examples of split-interest agreements. The Audit Guide provides standards for reporting the initial gifts that create these funds and the annual adjustments necessary to report them properly. Accounting for split-interest gifts is a complex area; the following discussion is highly summarized and overly simplified.

Not-for-profit organizations should report their interests in irrevocable split-interest agreements. If another party, such as a bank, holds the assets, a not-for-profit organization recognizes its interest as a contribution and measures its interest at fair value, usually based on the present value of the cash flows to be received. If the not-for-profit organization holds the assets and is also a beneficiary of the agreement, it reports the fair value of the assets received from the donor as its assets and reports the actuarially computed present value of the payments to be made to other beneficiaries as its liability. The difference between the two amounts is the contribution received by the not-for-profit organization. Each year after, the liability to the beneficiaries is recomputed based on revaluations of the amounts to be paid, the expected lives of the beneficiaries, and other relevant actuarial assumptions.

The net assets resulting from most split-interest agreements are classified as temporarily restricted because they are subject to time restrictions and often purpose restrictions. The net assets are time-restricted either because the distributions are not yet due (when amounts are held by a third party) or because the contribution amount cannot be used by the not-for-profit organization until the death of the beneficiary or some other future specified date. However, the net assets are classified as permanently restricted if the donor has permanently restricted the organization's use of the assets. (For example, the donor requires that the not-for-profit organization use the remaining assets to create a permanent endowment fund at the end of the agreement.) Similarly, if upon the establishment of the agreement the organization can immediately spend the contribution portion without restriction, as is the case for some gift annuities, the net assets would be classified as unrestricted.

Revocable split-interest agreements are not recorded unless the not-for-profit organization holds the assets. Assets received by a not-for-profit organization that acts as trustee for a revocable agreement should be recognized as refundable advances at their fair value.

STATEMENTS OF POSITION

94-3   Reporting of Related Entities

SOP 94-3 provides guidance on reporting investments in majority-owned for-profit subsidiaries, investments in common stock in which the not-for-profit organization owns a 50% or less voting interest, and certain relationships with other not-for-profit organizations.

If a not-for-profit organization has a controlling financial interest in a for-profit organization (generally a majority voting interest), it follows the standards in ARB 51, *Consolidated Financial Statements,* as amended by SFAS 94, *Consolidation of All Majority Owned Subsidiaries.*

If a not-for-profit organization has significant influence over the operating and financial policies of the investee (generally owns 20% or more but less than 50% of the voting stock), it either follows the standards in APB 18, *The Equity Method of Accounting for Investments in Common Stock,* or, if permitted by the Audit Guide, reports the investment at fair value.

Different combinations of control and economic interest determine the appropriate accounting for relationships with other not-for-profit organizations, as shown in the following table. Control is defined for purposes of this SOP as the direct or indirect ability to determine the direction of management and policies through ownership, contract, or otherwise. Economic interest is defined for the purposes of this SOP as an interest in another entity that exists if (1) the other entity holds or utilizes significant resources that must be used for the purposes of the reporting organization, either directly or indirectly by producing income or providing services or (2) the reporting organization is responsible for the liabilities of the other entity.

Control?	*Economic interest?*	*Standards*
Yes, via ownership of a majority voting interest	Yes	Consolidate.
Yes, via ownership of a majority voting interest	No	Consolidate.
Yes, via majority voting interest in the board of the other entity, as a majority owner	Yes	Consolidate.
Yes, via majority voting interest in the board of the other entity, as a majority owner	No	Consolidation is prohibited, and disclosure required.

Control?	*Economic interest?*	*Standards*
Yes, via a contract or an affiliation agreement	Yes	Consolidation is permitted, but not required.
Yes, via a contract or an affiliation agreement	No	Consolidation is prohibited, and disclosure required.
No	Yes	Consolidation is prohibited, and disclosure required.
No	No	Consolidation is prohibited. No disclosure required.

In all cases, consolidation is prohibited if control is likely to be temporary or does not rest with the majority owner. If consolidation is prohibited but consolidated financial statements were presented in accordance with SOP 78-10, *Accounting Principles and Reporting Practices for Certain Nonprofit Organizations* (otherwise superseded), organizations may continue to consolidate the other organizations.

Certain disclosures are necessary if consolidated statements are not presented. If consolidated statements are not presented when consolidation is permitted, but not required, the not-for-profit organization must disclose the identity of the other organization, the nature of the relationship, and summarized financial data in addition to the information required by SFAS 57. If consolidation is prohibited, the not-for-profit organization must disclose the information required by SFAS 57, *Related-Party Disclosures.*

98-2   Accounting for Costs of Activities of Not-for-Profit Organizations and State and Local Governmental Entities That Include Fund-Raising

Many not-for-profit organizations solicit contributions as part of activities that also serve their program or management and general functions. For example, an organization that has a mission of reducing the incidence of cancer might conduct a direct mail campaign and include in an envelope a listing of lifestyle changes that will lessen the risks of cancer and a request for contributions. When a fund-raising activity is conducted in conjunction with an activity that serves a program or other support purpose, the activity is referred to as a joint activity.

SOP 98-2 establishes standards for reporting the costs of joint activities. It begins with the presumption that the costs of a joint activity should be reported as fund-raising expenses. To overcome that presumption, three criteria must be met: purpose, audience, and content. If all three of the criteria are met, the costs of a joint activity should be charged as follows:

- Costs identifiable with a particular function should be charged to that function.
- Joint costs should be allocated between fund-raising and the appropriate program or management and general function.

Joint costs are the costs of conducting joint activities that are not identifiable with a particular component of the activity. Joint costs might include the costs of salaries, professional fees, paper, printing, postage, event advertising, telephones, broadcast airtime, and facility rentals.

Determining whether all three criteria are met is complicated because the purpose and audience criteria have additional tests within them. The purpose test includes a call to action test, a compensation or fees test, a similar scale and same medium test, and an other evidence test. The audience criteria includes a prior donor test, an ability and likelihood to contribute test, and a need to use or reasonable potential for use test. Failure of one of the additional tests often causes the activity to fail the criterion.

If any of the three criteria is not met, all costs of the joint activity must be reported as fund-raising expense. "All costs" includes the costs that would have been considered program or management and general if they had been incurred in a different activity. There is an exception to the rule that all costs are charged to fund-raising expense if one or more of the criteria is not met. The costs of goods or services provided in an exchange transaction that is part of the joint activity are charged to cost of goods sold rather than fund-raising expense. For example, the costs of direct donor benefits, such as the value of items sold at a fund-raising auction or meals served at a fund-raising dinner, are not charged to fund-raising expenses.

SOP 98-2 requires that the method used to allocate the joint costs be rational and systematic and that it result in a reasonable allocation of costs. The method selected should be applied consistently given similar facts and circumstances. No particular method of allocation is required by the SOP, but three allocation methods are illustrated: the physical units method, the relative direct cost method, and the stand-alone joint-cost-allocation method.

Organizations that allocate joint costs are required to disclose the types of activities in which joint costs have been incurred, a statement that the costs have been allocated, and the total amount of joint costs allocated, and the portion of joint costs allocated to each functional expense category. The SOP also encourages disclosure of the amount of joint costs for each type of joint activity.

OIL AND GAS PRODUCING ACTIVITIES

PERSPECTIVE AND ISSUES

Oil and gas producing activities are those activities that involve the acquisition of mineral interests in properties, exploration, development, and production of crude oil, including condensate and natural gas liquids, and natural gas. Specialized GAAP does not address refining, marketing, or transportation issues. The successful efforts method of accounting adheres to a traditional historical cost basis. Property acquisition costs, whether the property is proved or unproved, are capitalized as incurred. For other costs incurred under this method a direct relationship between the costs incurred and specific reserves discovered is required before costs are capitalized. Under successful efforts, accounting costs that cannot be directly related to the discovery of specific oil and gas reserves are expensed immediately as incurred.

The use of the successful efforts method is preferred, but not required by GAAP. An oil and gas producing company is permitted to use the successful efforts method or, alternatively, a prescribed form of the full cost method permitted by the SEC. All enterprises are required to disclose the method used for accounting for costs incurred and the manner of disposing of capitalized costs. The SEC requires additional disclosures for publicly traded companies.

For an enterprise that uses the full cost method of accounting, assets being depreciated, depleted, or amortized are considered to be in use in the earning activities of the enterprise and, consequently, do not qualify for interest capitalization. However, assets employed in ongoing exploration or development activities but that are not yet engaged in earning activities and not presently being depreciated, depleted or amortized, are eligible for interest capitalization.

Exploratory wells or tests that are in progress at the end of the period present unique accounting issues. If, subsequent to the end of the period, but before the financial statements are issued, a well or test is found to be unsuccessful, the incurred costs, less salvage, should be expensed. Retroactively restated financial statements should not be issued.

Sources of GAAP	
SFAS	*FASB I*
19, 25, 69	33, 36

CONCEPTS, RULES, AND EXAMPLES

The following is a discussion of the recommended treatment of oil and gas activities as per SFAS 19. (Note that this treatment is recommended, but not required.)

The costs of the special types of assets used in oil and gas producing activities should be capitalized when incurred. Some examples include

1. Mineral interests in properties
   a. Unproved—Properties with no proved reserves
   b. Proved—Properties with proved reserves
2. Wells and related equipment and facilities
3. Support equipment and facilities
4. Uncompleted wells, equipment, and facilities

These costs should be amortized as reserves are produced and, along with lifting (production) costs, should become costs of production. Periodically, unproved properties should be evaluated for impairment. If impaired, a loss should be recognized.

Acquisition costs incurred to obtain oil and gas properties through purchase, lease, etc., should be capitalized.

Geological and geophysical costs, unproved properties' carrying costs, and the costs of dry hole and bottom hole contributions should be expensed. Drilling costs should be capitalized until a determination has been made as to the success of the well. If successful, these costs are transferred to uncompleted wells, related equipment, and facilities. The cost of drilling, less residual value, is charged to expense if proved reserves are not found.

Development costs are incurred in order to

1. Get access to and prepare well locations
2. Drill and equip development wells
3. Set up production facilities
4. Provide better recovery systems

These costs are capitalized as a cost in uncompleted equipment and facilities until drilling or construction is completed.

The cost of support equipment is to be capitalized and depreciated. This depreciation, along with other operating costs, is allocated to exploration, development, or production costs, as appropriate.

Production involves different costs ranging from lifting to field storage. These costs, together with depreciation, depletion, and amortization of capitalized acquisition, exploration, and development costs, are part of the cost of the oil and gas produced.

Unproved properties are reclassified to proved properties upon discovery of proved reserves. When proved reserves are found, the costs capitalized as uncompleted wells, equipment, and facilities are reclassified as completed wells, equipment, and facilities. Capitalized costs are to be amortized or depleted by the unit of production method. Estimated residual values must be considered when determining amortization and depreciation rates.

Any information that becomes available between the end of the period and the date when the financial statements are issued is to be considered in the evaluation of conditions existing at the balance sheet date. With respect to the costs of a company's wells, related equipment, facilities, and the costs of related proved properties, the provisions for impairment as outlined in SFAS 121 are applicable.

RECORDING AND MUSIC INDUSTRY
PERSPECTIVE AND ISSUES

SFAS 50 sets forth accounting and reporting standards for the recording and music industry. In this industry, business is transacted through contractual arrangements entered into by an owner (licensor) of a music master or copyright. The licensor grants the licensee the right to sell or distribute recordings or sheet music for a fixed fee paid to the licensor or for a fee based on sales. License agreements are modifications of the compulsory provisions of the copyright law. This section presents the proper accounting by both the licensor and the licensee for license agreements in the recording and music industry.

The industry is currently attempting to adapt its business models for copyright protection, product distribution, and artist compensation to new electronic distribution channels. The new business models that will inevitably evolve may require additional accounting guidance.

Sources of GAAP
SFAS
50

DEFINITIONS OF TERMS

Advance royalty. An amount paid to music publishers, record producers, songwriters, or other artists in advance of their earning royalties from recording or sheet music sales. Such an amount is based on contractual terms and is generally nonrefundable.

License agreements. Contractual arrangements entered into by an owner (licensor) of a master or music copyright with a licensee granting the licensee the right to sell or distribute recordings or sheet music for a fixed fee paid to the licensor or for a fee based on sales. License agreements are modifications of the compulsory provisions of the copyright law.

Minimum guarantee. An amount paid in advance by a licensee to a licensor for the right to sell or distribute recordings or sheet music.

Recording (or record) master. The master tape resulting from the performance of the artist. It is used to produce tapes for use in making cartridges, cassettes, and compact discs.

Royalties. Amounts paid to producers, songwriters, or other artists for their participation in making recordings and to sheet music publishers for their copyright interest in music. Amounts for artists are determined by the terms of personal service contracts negotiated between the artists and media companies and usually are determined based upon a percentage of sales activity and license fee income, adjusted for estimated sales returns. Royalties for publishing are based on the copyright or other applicable laws, but the requirements of the law may be modified by licenses issued by the publishers.

CONCEPTS, RULES, AND EXAMPLES

Accounting by Licensors

Revenues. A license agreement is considered an outright sale when the licensor has

1. Signed a noncancelable contract
2. Agreed to accept a specified fee
3. Transferred the music rights to the licensee, who is able to use them
4. Fulfilled all significant duties owed the licensee

When these conditions are met, the earnings process is complete and revenue may be recognized if there is reasonable assurance that the license fee is fully collectible.

In some cases the licensee pays a minimum guarantee, which is an amount paid in advance to a licensor for the right to sell or distribute recordings or sheet music. A minimum guarantee is first recorded as a liability and then amortized to income as the license fee is earned. If the amount of the fee that is earned is indeterminable, then straight-line recognition of revenue from the guarantee is required over the license period.

Example

A licensor receives a $10,000 minimum guarantee on a license agreement that spans a five-year period. The entry to record the receipt of cash is

Cash	10,000	
Liability under license agreement		10,000

The licensor will recognize revenue from the guarantee on a straight-line basis. At the end of each year of the license period, the licensor will record the following entry:

Liability under license agreement	2,000	
License fees earned		2,000

A licensor may charge fees for such items as free recordings beyond a certain number given away by a recording club. The amount of such fees is not determinable when the license agreement is made. Therefore, the licensor can recognize revenue only when the amount can be reasonably estimated or when the license agreement expires.

Cost of artist compensation. Royalties are paid to record producers, songwriters, or other artists for their participation in making recordings and to music publishers for their copyright interest in music. Amounts for artists are determined by the terms of personal service contracts negotiated between the artists and media companies and usually are determined based upon a percentage of sales activity and license fee income, adjusted for estimated sales returns. Publishing royalties are generally based on copyright or other applicable laws. Royalties paid to artists are recorded as a period expense of the licensor.

Advance royalties are amounts paid to music publishers, producers, songwriters, or other artists in advance of their earning royalties. Such royalties are based on contractual terms and are generally nonrefundable. Advance royalties are recorded as assets if the licensor expects that the artist's recording will be successful enough to provide for full recovery of the advance from future royalties due the artist. As royalties are subsequently earned by the artist, the capitalized advance is charged to expense. The advance must be apportioned between current and noncurrent assets according to how soon each portion is expected to be charged to expense. If it later appears that the advance will not be fully recovered from subsequent royalties earned by the artist, then the unrecoverable portion should be charged to expense in the period in which the loss becomes apparent.

Cost to produce masters. A master is the master tape resulting from the performance of the artist. The costs of producing a master include (1) the cost of the musical talent (musicians, vocal background, and arrangements); (2) the cost of the technical talent for engineering, directing, and mixing; (3) costs for the use of the equipment to record and produce the master; and (4) studio facility charges. Under the standard type of artist contract, the media company bears a portion of the costs and recovers a portion of the cost from the artist out of designated royalties earned. However, either party may bear all or most of the cost.

The portion of the cost that is paid by the media company is recorded as an asset if the company expects that sales of the artist's recording will be successful enough to provide for full recovery of costs. If this is not the case, then these costs should be expensed. Any amount capitalized should be amortized over the useful life of the recording in such a way that relates the costs to estimated net revenue to be realized. Costs to produce masters that are recoverable from the artist's royalties should be treated as advanced royalties by the media company.

Accounting by Licensees

When a licensee pays a minimum guarantee in advance, the guarantee is recorded as an asset and then amortized to expense according to the terms specified in the license agreement. If it later appears that the minimum guarantee is not fully recoverable through use of the rights received under the agreement, then the unrecoverable portion should be charged to expense.

Fees for which the amount is indeterminable before the agreement expires are sometimes stipulated in the license agreement. An example is a fee charged to a recording club for free recordings beyond a certain number given away. The licensee must estimate the amount of such fees and accrue them on a license-by-license basis.

REGULATED OPERATIONS

PERSPECTIVE AND ISSUES

Although various businesses are subject to regulatory oversight to greater or lesser degrees, as used in GAAP the term **regulated operations** refers primarily to public utilities, whose ability to set selling prices for the goods or services they offer is constrained by government actions. Generally, the regulatory process has been designed to permit such enterprises to recover the costs they incur, plus a reasonable rate of return to stockholders. However, given the political process of rate-setting by regulatory authorities, and the fact that costs such as those for plant construction escalated greatly during the past decade or so, the ability to recover all costs through rate increases has become less certain. For this and other reasons, specialized GAAP has been promulgated.

Sources of GAAP		
SFAS	*FASB TB*	*EITF*
71, 90, 92, 98, 101	87-2	92-7, 92-12, 93-4, 97-4

CONCEPTS, RULES, AND EXAMPLES

These accounting principles apply to regulated enterprises only if they continue to meet certain criteria, which relate to the intended ability to recover all costs through the rate-setting process. When and if these conditions no longer are met, due to deregulation or a shift to rate-setting which is not based on cost recovery, then application of the specialized GAAP is to terminate.

Asset Recognition

If certain costs are not recognized for current rate-setting purposes, but it is probable that the costs will be recovered through future revenue, then these costs can be capitalized even though a nonregulated enterprise would be required to expense these costs currently. Deferred costs can include an imputed cost of equity capital, if so accounted for rate-setting purposes, even though this would not normally be permitted under GAAP. Thus, the regulatory process can result in the accounting recognition of an asset that would not otherwise be recognized. If at any time it becomes apparent that the incurred cost will not be recovered through generation of future revenue, that cost should be charged to earnings. If a regulator subsequently excludes specific costs from allowable costs, the carrying value of the asset recognized shall be reduced to the extent of the excluded costs. Should the regulator allow recovery of these previously excluded costs or any additional costs, a new asset shall be recognized and classified as if these costs had been initially included in allowable costs.

Imposition of Liabilities

In other situations, the regulatory process can result in the accounting recognition of a liability. This usually occurs when regulators mandate that refunds be paid to customers, which must be accrued when probable and reasonably estimable, per SFAS 5. Furthermore, regulatory rates may be set at a higher level, in order to recover costs expected to be incurred in the future, subject to the caveat that such amounts will be refunded to customers if it later becomes apparent that actual costs incurred were less than expected. In such cases, the incremental rate increase related to recovery of future costs must be accounted for as a liability (unearned revenue), until the condition specified is satisfied. Finally, regulators may stipulate that a gain realized by the utility will be returned to customers over a specified future period; this will be accounted for by accrual of a liability rather than by recognition of the gain for accounting purposes.

Phase-in Plans

Special rules apply to so-called phase-in plans, as defined in SFAS 92. If a phase-in plan was ordered by regulators for a plant which had been substantially constructed before 1988, then all allowable costs which are deferred for regulatory purposes, subject to the phase-in plan, are also deferred for financial reporting purposes. However, imputed cost of capital permitted by regulators (in effect, interest on the deferred costs) cannot be capitalized for financial reporting. Specific criteria must be met in order to utilize phase-in accounting, and the method cannot be employed for plants not constructed until after 1987.

Abandonment

Accounting for abandonments is also stipulated for regulated enterprises. If an abandonment occurs or becomes probable, any costs which are probable of not being recovered should be written off as a loss. Furthermore, if the return on the investment that will be recoverable will not be equal to the normal rate of return, then an additional loss accrual must be recognized currently. This loss is measured by the difference between the projected future revenues, discounted at the enterprise's incremental borrowing rate, and the remaining costs to be recovered. The amount of loss to be recognized obviously depends on the enterprise's estimate of time to elapse until rate increases are effective, and the length of time over which the increases will remain in effect. These estimates may change over time, and the effect of revisions in the estimate will be reflected in earnings in the periods the new estimates are made.

The carrying value of the costs of an abandoned plant is increased during the period from the abandonment until recovery occurs through rate increases as promised by the regulatory authorities. If full return of investment is anticipated, the cost of abandoned assets is accreted at the rate (the enterprise's overall cost of capital) permitted for rate-setting purposes. If partial or no return on investment is expected, the asset value is accreted at the same rate that was used to compute the loss accrual, which is the enterprise's incremental borrowing rate. During the recovery period, the costs of the abandoned plant are amortized. If full return on investment is expected, this amortization should be computed on the same basis as is permitted for rate-setting purposes. If partial or no return is expected, amortization should be such as to provide a constant rate of return on the unamortized balance of the investment in the costs of the abandoned plant.

Deferred Income Taxes

Deferred taxes must be provided consistent with SFAS 109. There are no exemptions or special provisions for income tax accounting for regulated enterprises. Assets or liabilities related to future rate increases or decreases are temporary differences within the meaning of SFAS 109.

Accounting for Liabilities Related to Closure or Removal

Perhaps the most significant development arising from concerns about regulated enterprises is the proposed FASB statement that has been broadened in applicability to all types of entities. This proposal has, as its origins, concerns about the decommissioning costs for nuclear power generation plants, which was the sole focus when the project began in 1994. It later was expanded to address similar concerns applicable to industries having potential for environmental damage, such as offshore oil drilling and landfills. The project addresses all costs that relate to the retirement of a long-lived tangible asset and that are unavoidable as a result of either the acquisition, construction, or normal operation of that asset. The project does not address costs incurred as a consequence of improper use of the assets, or costs incurred over the assets' useful lives for operations or maintenance.

If the new standard is ultimately approved, unavoidable obligations will have to be recognized as liabilities and accrued when incurred. The time when these obligations will be deemed to have been incurred will generally be at the inception of the use of the related assets. Thus, the recorded amount of the assets will be grossed up to include another class of "costs" related to the usage thereof. Future periods' depreciation will include a pro rata share of the extra costs.

The proposal stipulates that the correct basis for measurement of the liability will be the expected present value of the cash needed to ultimately satisfy the obligation. The expected present value is the sum of the probability-weighted present values in a range of estimated cash flows (see SFAC 7 discussion in Chapter 1, Researching GAAP Problems). The goal is to estimate the amount that a willing third party would demand to assume the obligation. This assumes, of course, that the timing of these expenditures can be reasonably estimated—which is likely, given that by definition these are costs to be incurred upon closure or removal, and the choice of depreciable useful lives is similarly based on this same expectation as to timing. In estimating the future cash cost of closure or removal, factors such as future inflation, the effects of technology changes in the near term, efficiencies to be gained from moving down the learning curve, the impact of unforeseen circumstances which can be assumed from past experience, and internal costs related to the closure or removal activities, are all to be taken into account. Finally, in computing present value, the proposal states that the credit-adjusted risk-free rate, which is the rate on zero-coupon Treasury instruments that have maturities corresponding to the expected timing of the cash flows related to the closure or removal activities adjusted for credit standing of the entity, is to be used.

In the past, various methods were used to account for costs similar to those addressed in this proposal (although, in most cases, no accruals were being made at all). The proposal states that such alternatives as accruing extra depreciation expense (thereby ultimately causing the net book values of the assets in question to "go negative" and have credit balances, which implies that such a balance would be the amount of the net liability at the end of the assets' useful lives) would no longer be acceptable.

If adopted, the proposed statement would be effective for financial statements issued for fiscal years beginning after June 15, 2001.

Accounting for Deregulation and "Stranded Costs"

In recent years the utilities industries have been undergoing vast changes in the regulatory environment. The wholesale electricity markets were essentially deregulated in 1996, and the apparent intent is to fully deregulate public utilities entirely within the next several years. This will have significant effects on the financial reporting of many of the entities operating in these industries, since under GAAP many had recognized so-called regulatory assets and regulatory liabilities which will no longer be recognizable once full deregulation occurs. Also, certain costs may no longer be recoverable in a deregulated environment, transforming certain assets into so-called "stranded costs."

A consensus in EITF 97-4 has addressed the matter of deregulation. When deregulatory legislation has been enacted affecting all or a portion of the entity's operations, it should cease applying SFAS 71 to the affected operations. In cases in which the effects of deregulation are imposed by means of a rate order, such an order would have to be sufficiently detailed so that the entity would be able to determine how it will be affected. Regulatory assets would not, however, be immediately written off; instead, an evaluation of regulatory cash flows would be conducted to determine whether an impairment had occurred and to determine whether the portion of the business from which the regulatory cash flows are derived is still subject to SFAS 71. Only if the asset is impaired (applying SFAS 121 criteria) or if SFAS 71 is no longer applicable would the asset be written off before being recovered. Similarly, regulatory liabilities would not be written into income until the obligation is eliminated by the regulatory authority.

A related concern is whether the new regulatory assets or liabilities must be given recognition to reflect expenses and obligations that will arise from the portion of the business being deregulated. The same "source of cash flow" type of analysis noted above is to be applied to make these determinations. Thus, a cost or obligation is recognized as a regulatory asset or liability, respectively, once it is expensed or incurred after SFAS 101 is applied to that portion of the operations, if it has been designated for recovery or settlement, respectively, via regulated cash flows.

EMERGING ISSUES TASK FORCE CONSENSUS SUMMARIES

92-7 Accounting for Rate-Regulated Utilities for the Effects of Certain Alternative Revenue Programs

A consensus was reached regarding the treatment of additional revenues of rate-regulated utility companies that are to be billed in the future under alternative revenue programs. The EITF abstract identifies two types of alternative revenue programs, defined as Type A and Type B. The revenues from alternative revenue programs should be recognized when the events permitting billing of the revenues have occurred and three specific criteria that are discussed in the abstract are met.

The Task Force also notes that rate-regulated utilities recognizing revenues from an alternative revenue program that do not meet the conditions of this EITF must amend the plan or change the program to meet the conditions.

92-12 Accounting for OPEB Costs by Rate-Regulated Enterprises

If the regulator includes other postemployment benefits, (OPEB), costs in rates on a pay-as-you-go basis, the regulatory asset relating to the cost under SFAS 106 should not be recognized. The Task Force also reached a consensus that the regulatory asset for a rate-regulated enterprise should recognize the difference between SFAS 106 costs and the OPEB costs if future revenue will at least offset the deferred cost and meet four specific criteria. The four specific criteria are discussed in detail in the EITF Abstracts.

93-4 Accounting for Regulatory Assets

The Task Force reached a consensus that a rate-regulated enterprise that fails to initially meet the asset recognition criteria can recognize a regulatory asset for other postemployment benefits costs in a future period when applicable criteria are met. This consensus applies also to all regulatory assets recognized pursuant to SFAS 71 criteria.

Additionally, the Task Force noted that the carrying amount of the regulatory asset to be recognized should be reduced by any impairment that may have occurred.

TITLE PLANT

PERSPECTIVE AND ISSUES

SFAS 61 presents accounting and reporting standards for costs relating to the construction and operation of title plants. A title plant comprises a record of all transactions or conditions that affect titles to land located in a specified area. The length of time spanned by a title plant depends upon regulatory requirements and the time frame required to gather sufficient information to efficiently issue title insurance. Updating occurs frequently as documentation of the current status of a title is added to the title plant.

This pronouncement applies to enterprises such as title insurance companies, title abstract companies, and title agents that use a title plant in their operations. The standard provides that costs directly incurred to construct a title plant should be capitalized when the entity can use the title plant to do title searches and that such capitalized costs are not normally depreciated. The statement also requires that the costs of maintaining a title plant and of doing title searches be expensed as incurred.

Sources of GAAP
SFAS
61, 121

DEFINITIONS OF TERMS

Title plant. Consists of (1) indexed and catalogued information for a period concerning the ownership of, and encumbrances on, parcels of land in a particular geographic area; (2) information relating to persons having an interest in real estate; (3) maps and plats; (4) copies of prior title insurance contracts and reports; and (5) other documents and records. In summary, a title plant constitutes a historical record of all matters affecting title to parcels of land in a particular geographic area.

CONCEPTS, RULES, AND EXAMPLES

Acquisition Costs

The cost of constructing a title plant includes the cost of obtaining, organizing, and summarizing historical information pertaining to a particular tract of land. Costs incurred to assemble a title plant should be capitalized until the record is usable for conducting title searches. Costs incurred to construct a backplant (a title plant that antedates the time span of an existing title plant) must also be capitalized. However, an enterprise may capitalize only those costs that are directly related to and traceable to the activities performed in constructing the title plant or backplant.

The purchase of a title plant or an undivided interest in title plant (the right to its joint use) is recorded at cost as of the date acquired. If title plant is acquired separately, it is recorded at the fair value of consideration given. Backplant may also be purchased.

Capitalized title plant costs are not amortized or depreciated unless an impairment in the carrying amount of the title plant occurs. The following events or changes in circumstances, provided in SFAS 121, can indicate that the carrying amount may not be recoverable. An impairment may be indicated by the following circumstances:

1. Changing legal or statutory requirements
2. Economic factors, such as changing demand
3. Loss of competitive advantage
4. Failure to maintain an up-to-date title plant
5. Circumstances that indicate obsolescence, such as abandonment of title plant

The provisions of SFAS 121 apply to any such impairment.

Operating Costs

Costs of title plant maintenance and of conducting title searches must be expensed currently. A title plant is maintained through frequent, often daily, updating which involves adding reports on the current status of specific real estate titles and documentation of security or other ownership interests in such land. A title search entails a search for all information or documentation pertaining to a particular parcel of land. This information is found in the most recently issued title report.

Once a title plant is operational, costs may be incurred to convert the record from one storage and retrieval system to another or to modify the current storage and retrieval system. These costs may **not** be capitalized as title plant. However, they may be separately capitalized and amortized using a systematic and rational method.

Reporting Title Plant Sales

The sale of a title plant should be reported separately. The amount to be reported is determined by the circumstances surrounding the sale as follows:

Terms of sale	*Amount reported*
Sells title plant and waives all rights to future use	Amount received less adjusted cost of title plant
Sells undivided ownership interest (rights to joint use)	Amount received less pro rata portion of adjusted cost of title plant
Sells copies of title plant or the right to use it	Amount received

Note that in the last instance the amount reported is simply the amount received. In this case, no cost is allocated to the item sold unless the title plant's value drops below its adjusted cost as a result of the sale.

APPENDIX

DISCLOSURE CHECKLIST

The disclosure checklist presented below provides a quick reference to those disclosures that are common to the financial statements of most business enterprises. Selected references to items required by the SEC, for public companies only, are also incorporated.

DISCLOSURE CHECKLIST INDEX

General

    A. Basis of Reporting
    B. Accounting Policies
    C. Accounting Changes
    D. Related Parties
    E. Contingencies and Commitments
    F. Risks and Uncertainties
    G. Nonmonetary Transactions
    H. Subsequent Events, if Material
    I. Rights and Privileges of Various Equity Securities Outstanding
    J. Other Disclosures

Balance Sheet

    A. Cash and Cash Equivalents
    B. Receivables
    C. Marketable Securities
    D. Inventories
    E. Investments—Equity Method
    F. Other Investments
    G. Property, Plant, and Equipment
    H. Intangibles
    I. Accounting for Transfers and Servicing of Assets and Extinguishment of Liabilities
    J. Current Liabilities
    K. Deferred Tax Assets and Liabilities
    L. Notes Payable and Debt
    M. Financial Instruments and Derivatives
    N. Pensions and Other Postretirement Benefits
    O. Leases—Lessees
    P. Leases—Lessors
    Q. Stockholders' Equity

Income Statement

    A. Basic Disclosure
    B. Marketable Securities
    C. Income Taxes
    D. Extraordinary Items
    E. Discontinued Operations
    F. Interim Financial Information

    G. Segment Data
    H. Development Stage Enterprises
    I. Long-Term Construction Contracts
    J. Research and Development
    K. Sales Where Collection Is Uncertain
    L. Revenue Recognition When Right of Return Exists
    M. Other Reporting
    N. Foreign Currency
    O. Business Combinations and Consolidations
    P. Earnings Per Share

Statement of Cash Flows

    A. Basis
    B. Format

Statement of Comprehensive Income

    A. Format
    B. Disclosures

Specialized Industry GAAP

    A. Banking and Thrift Industries
    B. Broadcasting Industry
    C. Computer Software Costs and Revenues
    D. Franchisor Accounting
    E. Government Contracts
    F. Insurance Industry Transactions
    G. Mortgage Banking Activities
    H. Motion Picture Industry
    I. Oil and Gas Producing Activities
    J. Pension Funds
    K. Recording and Music Industry
    L. Regulated Operations

GENERAL

A. Basis of Reporting

1. Name of entity for which statements are being presented (if d/b/a different name than legal name, indicate both). _____

2. Titles of statements should be appropriate (certain titles denote and should be reserved for GAAP financial statements; other titles denote other comprehensive basis of accounting [OCBOA] financial statements). _____

3. Dates and periods covered should be clearly stated. _____

4. If comparative statements are presented, repeat footnotes from prior years to extent appropriate. _____

5. Differences between "economic" entity and legal entity being presented should be noted (e.g., consolidated or not? subsidiaries included and excluded, combined statements?, etc.) Disclose summarized financial information for previously unconsolidated subsidiaries. _____

6. For SEC reporting—identify new accounting principles not yet adopted and expected impact of adoption. _____

B. Accounting Policies

1. Description of business unless otherwise apparent from statements themselves. _____

2. Identify and describe significant accounting principles followed and methods of applying them that materially affect statements; disclosures should include principles and methods that involve

   a. Selection from acceptable alternatives. _____

   b. Principles and methods peculiar to the company's industry. _____

   c. Unusual or innovative applications of generally accepted accounting principles. _____

   d. Principles of consolidation or combination. _____

3. If there have been any material changes in classifications made to previously issued financial statements, these should be noted. _____

C. Accounting Changes

1. Nature and justification of change in accounting principle. _____

   a. The effect of the new principle on income before extraordinary items and on net income of the period of change. _____

   b. The cumulative effect of change on beginning retained earnings as a separate item. _____

   c. Unless specifically not required by a standard, disclose pro forma effects of retroactive application for both income before extraordinary items and net income; report pro forma amounts in both current and future reports for all periods presented that are prior to the change and that would have been affected; if income statement is presented for current period only, actual and pro forma amounts for immediately preceding period (also respective per share data). _____

   d. If the change does not involve a cumulative effect adjustment (e.g., when changing depreciation lives only for new acquisitions), describe change in method and its effect on income before extraordinary items and net income (also related per share amounts for the period of the change). _____

e. If required pro forma amounts cannot be computed or reasonably estimated for individual prior periods although the cumulative effect on retained earnings at beginning of period can be determined, explain reason for not showing pro forma amounts by period. _____

f. When the effect on opening retained earnings cannot be computed, (e.g., a change from FIFO to LIFO) report the effect of change on results of operations for the period of change; explain reason for omitting accounting of cumulative effect and disclosure of pro forma amounts for prior years. _____

g. If reinstatement of prior period reports is required under standard: state nature of and justification for change in accounting principle in period of change; report the effect on income before extraordinary items and net income for all prior presented (also per share amounts thereof); and disclose differences between opening balances of shareholders' equity accounts and balances previously reported. _____

2. For change in reporting entity, nature of change and reason for it; also, effect of change on income before extraordinary items and net income for all periods presented (also per share amounts). _____

3. For a change in accounting estimate, if the change affects several future periods (e.g., for change in useful lives of fixed assets), disclose the effect on income before extraordinary items and net income of current period (and related per share amounts). _____

4. For the correction of an error, disclose the nature of the error in previously issued statements and the effect of its correction on income before extraordinary items and net income (only in period of discovery and correction), with per share equivalents. _____

D. Related Parties

1. Nature of relationship and amounts due to or from related parties with significant terms and manner of settlement. _____

2. For each income statement presented, a description of and dollar amounts of transaction, including those to which no or nominal amounts are assigned, as well as guarantees or other terms which are needed for understanding of financial statement impact, and description of any change in terms. _____

3. Economic dependency (e.g., major customer, supplier, franchisor, franchisee, distributor, general agent, borrower, or lender) should be described and amount of transactions disclosed. _____

4. Nature and extent of related-party leases. _____

5. The nature of control relationship, even absent any transactions, of companies under common ownership or management control, if such could lead to operating results or financial position significantly different than what would have resulted if entities were autonomous. _____

6. Amount of investments in related parties. _____

E. Contingencies and Commitments

1. When accruals are **not** made because probable loss could not be estimated, describe the nature of the contingency. _____

2. Report the upper limit of range of estimates for cases in which lower limit is accrued because **no** best estimate exists. _____

3. The nature of reasonably possible losses and either the estimated amount of the loss or a statement that **no** estimate is possible. _____

4. Describe unasserted claims for which it is both probable that a claim will be asserted, **and** reasonably possible that an unfavorable outcome will result. _____

5. Report events occurring after balance sheet date that may give rise to a loss contingency, either via a footnote or by means of a pro forma presentation. _____

6. Gain contingencies may be disclosed (but not accrued), if described such that the likelihood of realization is not overstated. _____

7. Disclose guarantees of affiliates' obligations. _____

8. Disclose indirect guarantees of others' indebtedness. _____

9. Disclose material commitments, guarantees, and purchase obligations. _____

10. Describe any pending renegotiation of government contracts. _____

11. Pending litigation in which the entity is involved should be described, with gross potential losses and potential recovery (e.g., from insurance) separately identified. _____

12. Tax contingencies or disputes to which the entity is a party should be noted. _____

13. Unused letters of credit. _____

14. Environmental risks and liabilities should be described. _____

15. Accounts or notes receivable sold with recourse; other guarantees to repurchase receivables. _____

16. Unusual purchase or sales commitments. _____

17. Compensated absences or postemployment benefits that cannot be reasonably estimated but that otherwise meet criteria for accrual should be described. _____

F. Risks and Uncertainties

1. Nature of operations including description of major products, services, principal markets served, locations, and relative importance of operations in various businesses and basis for determination of relative importance (e.g., sales volume, profits, etc.). _____

2. Explanation that the preparation of financial statements requires the use of management's estimates. _____

3. Significant estimates used in the determination of the carrying amounts of assets or liabilities or in the disclosure of gain or loss contingencies when, based on information known to management prior to issuance of the financial statements it is at least reasonably possible that the effect on the financial statements of a condition, situation, or set of circumstances existing at the balance sheet date for which an estimate has been made will change in the near term due to one or more future confirming events **and** the effect of the change would be material to the financial statements. (If the estimate involves a loss contingency covered by SFAS 5, include an estimate of the possible loss or range of loss, or state such estimate cannot be made.) _____

4. Vulnerability due to concentrations in the volume of business with a particular customer, supplier, or lender; revenue from particular products or services; available sources of supply of materials, labor, or other inputs; and market or geographic area. (For concentrations of labor subject to collective bargaining agreements, disclose both the percentage of the labor force covered by a collective bargaining agreement and the percentage of the labor force covered by a collective bargaining agreement that will expire within one year. For concentrations of operations located outside of the entity's home country, disclose the carrying amounts of net assets and the geographic areas in which they are located.) _____

G. Nonmonetary Transactions

1. Nature of transaction.
2. Gain or loss and basis of accounting for assets transferred. _____
3. For advertising barter transactions

    a. Amount of revenue and expense recognized from advertising barter transactions. _____

    b. Volume and type of advertising surrendered and received (e.g., number of equivalent pages, broadcast minutes) that was not recognized in the income statement because the fair value was not determinable. _____

H. Subsequent Events, if Material

1. Adjust financial statements for conditions existing at balance sheet date. _____
2. Disclose for conditions subsequent to balance sheet (consider pro forma presentation); examples are: for sale of a bond or capital stock issue, purchase or sale of a business, settlement of litigation when event giving rise to claim occurred subsequent to balance sheet date, loss of plant or inventories as a result of fire or flood, losses on receivables resulting from conditions (such as a customer's major casualty) arising subsequent to balance sheet date, significant net realized and unrealized marketable equity security gains and losses after the date of the financial statements, substantial loans to insiders or affiliates, significant long-term investments, substantial dividends not in the ordinary course of business, loss contingencies arising after the date of the financial statements, or significant foreign currency rate changes after the balance sheet date and their effects on unsettled balances pertaining to foreign currency transactions. _____

I. Rights and Privileges of Various Equity Securities Outstanding

1. Show each class separately and any changes during the period. _____
2. Par value, assigned or stated value should be disclosed. _____
3. Liquidation preferences are to be stated. _____
4. Participations (for preferred classes) are to be disclosed. _____
5. Call, conversion, and exercise data are to be noted. _____
6. Redeemable preferred stock should be described. _____

J. Other Disclosures

1. Asset valuation allowances. _____
2. Pledged and encumbered assets. _____
3. Current and noncurrent classifications, if so utilized. _____
4. For derivatives, the hedging or trading objectives and policy. _____

BALANCE SHEET

A. Cash and Cash Equivalents

1. Segregate and classify the amount of restricted cash according to the nature of the restriction. _____
2. Compensating balances disclosed as to their nature and amount (if use of cash on balance sheet is not restricted, separate presentation on balance sheet is not required). _____
3. Overdrafts are to be presented as a current liability. _____
4. If uninsured balances are material, concentration of credit risk must be disclosed. _____
5. For SEC, foreign bank balances are to be distinguished. _____

B.   Receivables

1.   Receivables involving officers, employees, and other related parties separated as to the amount and nature of the transactions.   _____

2.   The amount of unearned finance charges and interest which has been deducted from the face amount of the receivables.   _____

3.   The amount and nature of pledged or assigned receivables and receivables sold without recourse.   _____

4.   The amount of the valuation allowance including the current period provision.   _____

5.   Credit balances reclassified as a current liability.   _____

6.   Concentrations of credit risk.   _____

7.   Transfers of receivables with recourse.   _____

8.   For impaired loans, disclose

    a.   For each balance sheet

        (1)   Investment in impaired loans.   _____

        (2)   Amount of allowance for credit losses.   _____

        (3)   Policy of income recognition for interest.   _____

    b.   For each income statement, disclose the average investment in impaired loans, interest income recognized and activity in the allowance for credit losses account.   _____

9.   For noninterest-bearing notes or inappropriate stated interest rates, disclose the discount or premium, the effective rate of interest and face amount, amortization for the period, and issue costs.   _____

10.   All other nontrade receivables (e.g., tax refunds, contract claims, etc.) are separately presented.   _____

11.   Significant concentrations of risk disclosed.   _____

C.   Marketable Securities

    For all classifications (trading, available-for-sale, or held-to-maturity), disclose the following information

1.   Fair value.   _____

2.   Gross unrealized gains.   _____

3.   Gross unrealized losses.   _____

4.   Amortized cost for each major security type.   _____

5.   Maturity date for those debt instruments held to maturity.   _____

6.   For each period for which the results of operations are presented, disclose

    a.   Proceeds from sales of available-for-sale securities and gross realized gains and gross realized losses on those sales.   _____

    b.   Basis on which cost was determined in computing realized gain or loss.   _____

    c.   Gross gains and gross losses included in earnings from transfers of securities from available-for-sale category into trading category.   _____

    d.   Change in net realized holding gain or loss on available-for-sale securities that has been included in separate component of shareholders' equity during the period.   _____

    e.   Change in net unrealized holding gain or loss on trading securities that has been included in earnings during the period.   _____

7.   For any sales/transfers from held to maturity classification, disclose

    a.   Cost of security.   _____

    b.   Realized or unrealized gain or loss. _____

    c.   Circumstances leading to decision to sell or transfer the security. _____

   8.   For SEC reporting—Substantial post-balance-sheet market decline. _____

D. Inventories

   1.   Basis of valuation (cost, lower of cost or market, etc.). _____

   2.   Cost flow assumption (FIFO, LIFO, etc.). _____

   3.   Classification (materials, work in process, etc.), with amounts of inventory in each. _____

   4.   Inventory accounting principles peculiar to a particular industry. _____

   5.   Pledging of inventories in borrowing agreements. _____

   6.   Product financing arrangements. _____

   7.   Accrued net losses on firm purchase commitments. _____

   8.   Liquidation of LIFO inventories and effects on income. _____

   9.   Lower of cost or market "losses," if material. _____

E. Investments—Equity Method

   1.   Name of each investee and the percentage of ownership of common stock. _____

   2.   Accounting policies with respect to each of the investments. _____

   3.   Difference between the carrying amount for each investment and its underlying equity in the investee's net assets and the accounting treatment of the difference between these amounts. _____

   4.   For those investments which have a quoted market price, the aggregate value of each investment. _____

   5.   If investments in investees are considered to have a material effect on the investor's financial position and operating results, summarized data for the investor's assets, liabilities, and results of operations. _____

   6.   If potential conversion of convertible securities and exercise of options and warrants would have material effects on the investor's percentage of the investee. _____

F. Other Investments

For equity and debt securities

   1.   Classification as a held-to-maturity or an available-for-sale investment. _____

   2.   Basis of accounting. _____

   3.   Any valuation accounts in stockholders' equity which reflect unrealized gains and losses and any income statement effects. _____

G. Property, Plant, and Equipment

   1.   Classes of assets. _____

   2.   The bases of valuation. _____

   3.   The methods of computing depreciation. _____

   4.   The amount of accumulated depreciation either by classes of assets or in total. _____

   5.   A description of and the amount of any assets pledged as collateral. _____

   6.   Capitalized interest cost

    a.   The total amount of interest cost incurred during the period. _____

    b.   The amount which has been capitalized. _____

   7.   Estimated costs to complete, for major construction. _____

   8.   Assets not used in the trade or business. _____

   9.   Capitalized preproduction costs related to long-term supply agreements. Aggregate amount of assets recognized

    a.   Pursuant to agreements providing for contractual reimbursement of pre-production design and development costs.   _____

    b.   Molds, dies, and other tools that the supplier owns.   _____

    c.   Molds, dies, and other tools that the supplier does not own.   _____

10.   Asset retirement obligations (ARO)

    a.   General description of ARO and the related long-lived assets.   _____

    b.   Description of how the fair value of the liability for ARO was determined.   _____

    c.   Funding policy, if any, for ARO.   _____

    d.   Fair value of assets, if any, that are legally restricted to satisfy the liability.   _____

    e.   If there is a significant change in the components of the obligation, reconciliation of the beginning and ending aggregate carrying amount of the liability separately showing the changes resulting from

        (1)   Additional liability incurred during the current period.   _____

        (2)   Settlements of the liability during the current period.   _____

        (3)   Accretion expense.   _____

        (4)   Revisions in expected cash flows.   _____

        (5)   Explanation of any significant changes in ARO not otherwise apparent.   _____

11.   Impairments

    a.   If impairment loss is recognized for assets to be held and used

        (1)   Description of impaired assets and situation surrounding impairment.   _____

        (2)   Amount of impairment loss and method of determining fair value.   _____

        (3)   If impairment losses are not reported separately or parenthetically, the caption where losses are aggregated.   _____

        (4)   The business segment affected, if applicable.   _____

    b.   In the case of assets to be disposed of

        (1)   The initial loss.   _____

        (2)   Gains or losses resulting from subsequent revision in estimates of fair value less cost to sell.   _____

        (3)   If they can be identified and to the extent they are included in entity's operations for the period, results of operations for disposed assets.   _____

        (4)   If not reported separately or parenthetically, caption where gains and losses are aggregated.   _____

        (5)   Description of the assets and situation surrounding disposal, the carrying amount of assets and expected date of disposal.   _____

        (6)   Results of operations for assets to be disposed of to the extent that those results are included in the entity's results of operations for the period and can be identified.   _____

        (7)   The business segment affected, if applicable.   _____

H.   Intangibles

1.   For each major class of intangible asset

    a.   Gross carrying amount.   _____

    b.   Accumulated amortization.   _____

    c.   Amortization expense for all periods presented.   _____

    d.   Aggregate amortization expenses for each of the five succeeding fiscal years as of the date of the latest balance sheet presented.   _____

e.   Method of amortization. _____

f.   A description of any intangible asset not being amortized, the total carrying amount as of the date of each balance sheet presented and the method used to estimate its fair value. _____

g.   With respect to goodwill

    (1) Changes in the carrying amount during the period including goodwill acquired, impairment loss recognized, portion included in the gain or loss on disposal of all or a portion of a reporting unit and, for entities reporting segment information, that information for each segment and any significant changes in the allocation of goodwill by segment. _____

h.   For each goodwill impairment loss recognized during any periods presented

    (1) Description of the facts and circumstances leading to the impairment. _____

    (2) Description of the reporting unit for which the impairment loss is recognized, the adjusted carrying amount of goodwill of that reporting unit, and the amount of the impairment loss. _____

    (3) If a recognized impairment loss is an estimate pending finalization, that fact and the reasons it has not been finalized and, in subsequent periods, the nature and amount of any significant adjustments made to the initial estimate of the impairment loss. _____

    (4) For entities required to report segment information, the segment to which the impaired goodwill relates. _____

    (5) In a period in which negative goodwill is recognized as an extraordinary gain, the information required for such gains (See "Income Statement—D. Extraordinary Gains" in this Appendix). _____

2.   In the year of acquisition, the following information as of acquisition date

   a.   For each class of intangible asset

    (1) A description of the assets and their recorded amounts. _____

    (2) Key assumptions and methodologies used to value them. _____

    (3) Description of amortization method and, if not straight-line, the reasons. _____

    (4) Weighted-average amortization period. _____

    (5) Any residual value assumed in determining the amount to be amortized (if significant in relation to the carrying amount of the intangible asset class). _____

   b.   A description and the carrying amount of any significant intangible asset presumed to have either a useful economic life greater than twenty years or an indefinite life, the useful life assigned, and the factors supporting that life. _____

   c.   With respect to goodwill

    (1) The amount of acquired goodwill. _____

    (2) The amount of acquired goodwill related to each segment (for entities required to report segment information). _____

    (3) The amount of acquired goodwill that is deductible for income tax purposes. _____

3.   R&D expenditures

   a.   The total research and development costs charged to expense for each period for which an income statement is presented. _____

   b.   For contractual agreements

(1) The terms of significant agreements under the R&D arrangements as of the date of each balance sheet presented. _____

(2) The amount of compensation earned and costs incurred under contract for each period for which an income statement is presented. _____

4. Deferred charges and other assets

a. Charges, segregated by type. _____
b. Carrying value of capitalized computer software. _____

5. Computer software

a. Capitalized value. _____
b. Amortization. _____
c. Write-downs to realizable value. _____

6. Capitalized direct-response advertising _____
7. For obligations to service financial assets

a. Amounts of servicing assets/liabilities recognized and amortized. _____
b. Fair value of items (methods and assumptions). _____
c. Risk and amounts of impairment. _____

I. Accounting for Transfers and Servicing of Assets and Extinguishment of Liabilities

1. For all servicing assets and liabilities

a. The amounts recognized and amortized during the period. _____
b. Fair value of such recognized items including methods and assumptions. _____
c. Risk characteristics of assets used to measure impairment. _____
d. Activity in the valuation allowance for impairment. _____
e. Assets set aside solely to satisfy payments of a specific obligation. _____

2. Other disclosures

a. Security required for repurchase agreements or security lending transactions. _____
b. Remaining debt outstanding previously treated as having been extinguished by in-substance defeasance, and a general description of the transaction. _____
c. Restriction on assets set aside to pay specific obligations. _____
d. Fair value of assets transferred, or description and reasons why fair value cannot be measured. _____

J. Current Liabilities

1. For accounts payable, disclose amounts that are

a. Trade. _____
b. Nontrade. _____
c. Related parties (affiliates; investees for which the equity method is used; employee trusts; principal owners; management, immediate families of owners and management; or any party capable of significantly influencing a transaction). _____

2. Callable obligations:
For long-term callable obligations containing a violation of debt agreement, report

a. A description of covenants violated. _____
b. In unclassified balance sheet, include surrounding circumstances with disclosure of long-term debt maturities. _____

    c.   Obligation that will be classified as noncurrent because it is probable that a violation of debt agreement will be cured within a grace period or a waiver has been obtained. _____

3.   Income taxes payable

    a.   Current portion. _____
    b.   Deferred portion. _____

4.   Notes payable

    a.   Description of note. _____
    b.   Classified by type

       (1) Trade creditors. _____
       (2) Bank. _____
       (3) Factors or other financial institutions. _____
       (4) Holders of commercial paper. _____
       (5) Related parties (see Accounts Payable, 1.c.). _____
       (6) Employees, underwriters, and promoters (other than related parties). _____

    c.   Describe assets used as security. _____
    d.   Interest rate. _____
    e.   Aggregate maturities and maturities for next five years. _____

5.   Other current liabilities

    a.   Accruals. _____
    b.   Advances or deposits. _____
    c.   Current portions of long-term liabilities. _____
    d.   Compensated absences. _____
    e.   Liabilities not recorded because amounts could **not** be estimated. _____
    f.   Short-term debt expected to be refinanced

       (1) Terms of new obligation incurred or expected to be incurred. _____
       (2) Terms of equity securities issued or expected to be issued. _____

    g.   Bank overdrafts. _____
    h.   Special termination benefits. _____
    i.   Credit balances in accounts receivable. _____
    j.   Terms, interest rates, collateral, and other significant information about the underlying obligation. _____

K. Deferred Tax Assets and Liabilities

1.   Classify as current if related to asset or liability that is current or will result in net taxable or deductible amounts next year. Otherwise classify as noncurrent. _____
2.   Total of deferred tax liabilities. _____
3.   Total of deferred tax assets. _____
4.   Report the valuation allowance for deferred tax assets, allocated pro rata between current and noncurrent deferred tax assets, and changes in allowance during the year. _____
5.   Deferred tax liabilities and assets attributable to different taxpaying components or to different tax jurisdictions should **not** be offset. _____

6. The approximate tax effect of each type of temporary difference and carryforward that gives rise to a significant portion of deferred tax liabilities and assets. For non-SEC reporting, disclose the types of temporary differences and carryforwards but may omit disclosure of the tax effects of each type. _____

7. The amounts and expected timing of reversals of deductible temporary differences. _____

8. Any portion of the valuation allowance for deferred tax assets for which subsequently recognized tax benefits will be allocated to reduce goodwill or other non-current intangible assets of an acquired entity or directly to contributed capital. _____

9. The amounts and expiration dates of operating loss and tax credit carryforwards for tax purposes. _____

L. Notes Payable and Debt

1. Notes and bonds

   a. The aggregate amount of debt shown as a long-term liability on the face of the financial statements net of the current portion due within one year and any discount or premium. _____

   b. The detail relating to each debt issue, including

      (1) Nature of the liabilities. _____
      (2) Maturity dates. _____
      (3) Interest rates (effective and stated). _____
      (4) Call provisions. _____
      (5) Conversion privileges. _____
      (6) Restrictive covenants (i.e., sinking fund requirements, restrictions on retained earnings, etc.). _____
      (7) Assets pledged as collateral (these assets are shown in the asset section of the balance sheet). _____
      (8) Amounts due to related parties including officers, directors, and employees, and terms of settlement. _____
      (9) Disclosure of notes or bonds issued subsequent to the balance sheet date. _____
      (10) Amounts of unused letters of credit. _____

   c. The current portion of the long-term debt is shown as a current liability unless other than current assets will be used to satisfy the obligation. _____

   d. Long-term debt is classified as current if the debtor is in violation of a debt covenant at the balance sheet date which

      (1) Makes the obligation callable within one year, or _____
      (2) Will make the obligation callable within one year if the violation is not cured within a specified grace period. _____

   e. The debt referred to in d. above need not be reclassified if either of the following conditions are met:

      (1) The creditor has waived or has subsequently lost the right to demand repayment for one year (or, if longer, the operating cycle) from the balance sheet date, or _____
      (2) It is probable (likely) that the violation will be cured by the debtor within the grace period stated in the terms of the debt agreement, thus preventing the obligation from being called. _____

2. Gains or losses resulting from the extinguishment of debt are to be aggregated and unconditionally classified as extraordinary items and the following information provided either on the face of the financial statements or in the notes:

    a. A description of the extinguishment transaction, including the sources of the funds used, if practicable. _____

    b. The income tax effect of the transaction. _____

    c. The per share amount of the aggregate gain or loss, net of tax. _____

3. Troubled debt restructurings

    a. Disclosures by the debtor

      (1) A description of the changes in terms and/or major features of the settlement.

      (2) The aggregate gain on restructuring and the related tax effect. _____

      (3) The aggregate net gain or loss on the transfer of assets recognized during the period.

      (4) The per share amount of the aggregate gain or loss, net of tax. _____

    b. Disclosures by the creditor

      (1) For the outstanding restructured receivables, the aggregate recorded investment. _____

      (2) The amount of commitments to lend additional funds to debtors owing receivables whose terms have been modified by restructurings. _____

      (3) The recorded investment amount for which impairment has been recognized, including the total allowance for credit losses related to those impaired loans, and recorded investments not requiring an allowance. _____

      (4) The activity in the allowance for credit losses account, including the balance in the allowance for credit losses account at the beginning and end of each period, additions charged to operations, direct write-downs charged against the allowance, and recoveries of amounts previously charged off. _____

      (5) The creditor's interest income recognition policy on impaired loans, including how cash receipts are recorded. _____

      (6) For each period of operation, the amount of interest income related to impaired loans, the average investment impaired and if practical, the amount of interest income using a cash-basis method. _____

4. Unconditional purchase obligations are to be disclosed, if all the following criteria are met:

    a. It is noncancelable, or cancelable only

      (1) Upon the occurrence of some remote contingency. _____

      (2) With the permission of the other party. _____

      (3) If a replacement agreement is signed between the same parties. _____

      (4) Upon payment of a penalty in an amount such that continuation of the agreement appears reasonably assured. _____

    b. It is negotiated as part of a supplier's product financing arrangement for the facilities that will provide the contracted goods or services or for costs related to those goods or services (e.g., carrying costs for contracted goods); and _____

    c. It has a remaining term in excess of one year. _____

    d. If the obligation fulfills the foregoing criteria and is recorded on the balance sheet, the following disclosures are required:

      (1) Aggregate amount of payments to be made. _____

    (2) Aggregate amount of maturities and sinking fund requirements for all long-term borrowings.   _____

  e. If the obligation is **not** recorded on the balance sheet, then the following footnote disclosures are required:

    (1) The nature and term of the obligation(s).   _____

    (2) The total amount of the fixed or determinable portion of the obligation(s) at the balance sheet date in the aggregate and for each of the next five years, if determinable.   _____

    (3) The nature of any variable components of the obligation(s).   _____

    (4) The amounts purchased under the obligation(s) (as in take-or-pay or through-put contracts) for each period for which an income statement is presented.   _____

M. Financial Instruments and Derivatives

1. The method and significant assumptions used to estimate fair value.   _____

2. If not practicable to estimate fair value, disclose pertinent information such as carrying amount, effective interest rate, and maturity and the reason why it is not practicable.   _____

3. Disclose all significant concentrations of credit risk arising from all financial instruments (except financial instruments of a pension plan and certain other financial instrument identified in SFAS 107), whether from an individual counterparty or groups of counterparties, including:

  a. Information about the (shared) activity, region, or economic characteristic that identifies the concentration.   _____

  b. The maximum amount of loss due to credit risk that, based on the gross fair value of the financial instrument, the entity would incur if parties to the financial instruments that make up the concentration failed completely to perform according to the terms of the contracts and the collateral or other security, if any, for the amount due proved to be of no value to the entity.   _____

  c. The company's policy of requiring collateral or other security to support financial instruments subject to credit risk, information about the entity's access to that collateral or other security, and the nature and a brief description of the collateral or other security those financial instruments.   _____

  d. The company's policy of entering into master netting arrangements to mitigate the credit risk of financial instruments, information about the arrangements for which the entity is a party, and a brief description of the terms of those arrangements, including the extent to which they would reduce the entity's maximum amount of loss due to credit risk.   _____

4. For companies that hold or issue derivative instruments that are not hedging instruments, disclose

  a. The purpose of the derivative activity.   _____

  b. The objectives for holding or issuing those instruments within a context needed to understand those objectives.   _____

  c. The strategies for achieving those objectives.   _____

5. For companies that hold or issue derivative instruments that are designated and qualify as hedging instruments, disclose the following:

  a. The objectives for holding or issuing those instruments within a context needed to understand those objectives.   _____

b. The strategies for achieving those objectives. _____

c. The entity's risk management policy for each of the types of hedges, including a description of the items or transactions for which risks are hedged. _____

6. For fair value hedges, disclose for derivative instruments, as well as nonderivative instruments that may give rise to foreign currency transaction gains or losses, that have been designated and have qualified as fair value hedging instruments and for the related hedged items

    a. The net gain or loss recognized in earnings during the reporting period representing (1) the amount of the hedges' ineffectiveness and (2) the component of the derivative instruments' gain or loss, if any, excluded from the assessment of hedge effectiveness, and a description of where the net gain or loss is reported in the statement of income or other statement of financial performance. _____

    b. The amount of net gain or loss recognized in earnings when a hedged firm commitment no longer qualifies as a fair value hedge. _____

7. For cash flow hedges, disclose for derivative instruments that have been designated and have qualified as cash flow hedging instruments and for the related hedged transactions

    a. The net gain or loss recognized in earnings during the reporting period representing

        (1) The amount of the hedges' ineffectiveness. _____

        (2) The component of the derivative instruments' gain or loss, if any, excluded from the assessment of hedge effectiveness, and a description of where the net gain or loss is reported in the statement of income or other statement of financial performance. _____

    b. A description of the transactions or other events that will result in the reclassification into earnings of gains and losses that are reported in accumulated other comprehensive income, and the estimated net amount of the existing gains or losses at the reporting date that is expected to be reclassified into earnings within the next twelve months. _____

    c. The maximum length of time over which the entity is hedging its exposure to the variability in future cash flows for forecasted transaction excluding those forecasted transactions related to the payment of variable interest on existing financial instruments. _____

    d. The amount of gains and losses reclassified into earnings as a result of the discontinuance of cash flow hedges because it is probable that the original forecasted transactions will not occur. _____

8. For hedges of the net investment in a foreign operation, disclose, for derivative instruments, as well as nonderivative instruments that may give rise to foreign currency transaction gains or losses under SFAS 52, that have been designated and have qualified as hedging instruments for hedges of the foreign currency exposure of a net investment in a foreign operation, the net amount of gains or losses included in the cumulative translation adjustment during the reporting period. _____

9. On the face of the balance sheet, in a statement of changes in equity or in the footnote, the following:

    a. The beginning and ending derivative gain or loss. _____

    b. The related change associated with the current period hedging transactions. _____

    c.   The net amount of any reclassification into earnings.   _____

    d.   In the year of initial adoption of SFAS 133 only, the amount of gains and losses reported in accumulated other comprehensive income and associated with the transition adjustment that are now being reclassified into earnings during the next twelve months following the date of initial application.   _____

10.   Except for those financial instruments specifically exempted under SFAS 107, as amended by SFAS 133, disclose (except for small, nonpublic entities as set forth in SFAS 133):

    a.   The fair value of financial instruments and related carrying amount for which it is practicable to estimate that value.   _____

    b.   The methods and significant assumptions used to estimate fair value of financial instruments.   _____

11.   If not practicable to estimate the fair value of a financial instrument or classes of financial instruments, provide

    a.   Information pertinent to estimating fair value of that financial instrument or class of financial instruments, such as carrying amount, effective interest rate, and maturity date.   _____

    b.   The methods and significant assumption used to estimate fair value of financial instruments.   _____

12.   For forward sales contracts, forward purchase contracts, purchased put options, and purchased call options that are indexed to, and potentially settled in, a company's own stock, disclose the gains and losses that are included in earnings.   _____

13.   Disclose any gains or losses on written put options that require net cash settlement or give the counterparty a choice of net cash settlement or settlement in the company's stock.   _____

14.   Disclose the accounting policy for the premium paid (time value) to acquire an option that is classified as held-to-maturity or available-for-sale.   _____

N. Pensions and Other Postretirement Benefits

1.   Defined benefit plans

    a.   Schedule reconciling beginning and ending balances of the benefit obligation, separately showing if applicable

        (1) Service cost.   _____

        (2) Interest cost.   _____

        (3) Contributions by plan participants.   _____

        (4) Actuarial gains and losses.   _____

        (5) Changes in foreign currency exchange rates.   _____

        (6) Benefits paid.   _____

        (7) Plan amendments.   _____

        (8) Business combinations.   _____

        (9) Divestitures.   _____

        (10) Curtailments.   _____

        (11) Settlements.   _____

        (12) Special termination benefits.   _____

    b.   Schedule reconciling beginning and ending balances of the fair value of plan assets, separately showing if applicable

    (1) Actual return. _____

    (2) Changes in foreign currency exchange rates. _____

    (3) Employer contributions. _____

    (4) Employee or retiree contributions. _____

    (5) Benefits paid. _____

    (6) Business combinations. _____

    (7) Divestitures. _____

    (8) Curtailments. _____

    (9) Settlements. _____

c.   Information on the funded status, amounts unrecognized in the balance sheet, and amounts recognized in the balance sheet including

    (1) Unamortized prior service cost amount. _____

    (2) Unrecognized net gain (loss) amount (those not yet reflected in market-related value should also be included). _____

    (3) Unamortized net obligation or net asset amount still remaining from that recorded at SFAS 87 and SFAS 106 date of initial application. _____

    (4) Accrued liabilities or prepaid assets, intangible asset and accumulated other comprehensive income (as a result of recording an additional minimum liability). _____

d.   Net periodic benefit cost recognized, separately showing

    (1) Service cost. _____

    (2) Interest cost. _____

    (3) Expected return on plan assets. _____

    (4) Amortization of unrecognized transition asset or obligation. _____

    (5) Recognized gains or losses. _____

    (6) Recognized prior service costs. _____

    (7) Recognized settlement or curtailment gain or loss. _____

e.   Amount in Other Comprehensive Income for the period due to a change in the additional minimum pension liability. _____

f.   Assumed weighted-average rates for

    (1) Discount rate. _____

    (2) Expected long-term rate on plan assets. _____

    (3) Compensation rate increase (if applicable for pay-related plans). _____

g.   Health care cost trend rate(s)

    (1) Used to measure expected costs of benefits covered by the plan (gross eligible charges). _____

    (2) Direction and pattern of change together with

        (a) The ultimate trend rate(s). _____

        (b) The time when that rate is expected to be achieved. _____

h.   The effect of both a 1% increase and a 1% decrease in the assumed health care cost trend rates on

    (1) Service and interest cost components aggregated. _____

    (2) Health care APBO (based on the substantive plan and while holding all other assumptions constant). _____

    i.   Other, if applicable
         (1) Employer and related parties
              (a) Amounts and types of securities included in plan assets.   _____
              (b) Approximate amount of annual benefits covered by annuity con-
                   tracts issued by the above.   _____
              (c) Any significant transactions with the plan.   _____
         (2) Alternative amortization methods used.   _____
         (3) Existence and nature of substantive commitments.   _____
         (4) Termination benefits recognized
              (a) Nature of event.   _____
              (b) Cost.   _____
    j.   If not otherwise apparent, an explanation of matters of significance in regard
         to changes in
         (1) Benefit obligation.   _____
         (2) Plan assets.   _____

2. Two or more defined benefit plans (pension, postretirement, or both)
    a.   Should provide most useful information
         (1) May be aggregated for pension and may be aggregated for postretire-
              ment plans.
              (a) If combined, plans where the accumulated benefit obligations are in
                   excess of plan assets should show
                   1] Aggregate benefit obligation.   _____
                   2] Aggregate fair value of assets.   _____
              (b) If combined, pension plans with APBO in excess of plan assets
                   should show
                   1] Aggregate pension benefit obligation.   _____
                   2] Aggregate pension fair value of assets.   _____
         (2) May be disaggregated in groups.   _____
    b.   Amounts recognized in the balance sheet separately
         (1) Prepaid benefit costs.   _____
         (2) Accrued benefit liabilities.   _____
    c.   US pension and OPEB plans and outside US plans may be combined unless
         benefit obligations outside the US are significant relative to the total and
         those plans use significantly different assumptions.   _____

3. Defined contribution plans
    a.   Amount of cost separate from defined benefit plans
         (1) Pension.   _____
         (2) Other postretirement.   _____
    b.   Description of nature and effect of significant changes affecting comparabil-
         ity.   _____

4. Multiemployer plans
    a.   Total amount of contributions without disaggregation.   _____

    b.   Description of nature and effect of significant changes affecting comparability. _____

    c.   In case of withdrawal, SFAS 5 applies. _____

5.   Nonpublic entities may elect the following in lieu of required disclosures:

    a.   Benefit obligation, fair value of assets, funded status. _____

    b.   Employer contributions, participant contributions, benefits paid. _____

    c.   Amounts recognized in balance sheet

       (1) Prepaid assets. _____

       (2) Accrued liabilities. _____

       (3) Intangible assets. _____

       (4) Accumulated other comprehensive income. _____

    d.   Net periodic benefit cost

       (1) Recognized in net income. _____

       (2) Recognized in other comprehensive income. _____

    e.   Assumed weighted-average rates for

       (1) Discount rate. _____

       (2) Expected long-term rate on plan assets. _____

       (3) Compensation rate increase (if applicable for pay-related plans). _____

    f.   Health care cost trend rate is

       (1) Used to measure expected costs of benefits covered by the plan (gross eligible charges). _____

       (2) Direction and pattern of change together with

          (a) The ultimate trend rate(s). _____

          (b) The time when that rate is expected to be achieved. _____

    g.   Employer and related parties (if applicable)

       (1) Amounts and types of securities included in plan assets. _____

       (2) Approximate amount of annual benefits covered by annuity contracts issued by the above. _____

       (3) Any significant transactions with the plan. _____

    h.   If applicable, significant nonroutine events, such as amendments, curtailments, settlements, combinations, and divestitures. _____

O. Leases—Lessees

1.   For capital leases, disclose

    a.   The gross amount of assets recorded under capital leases presented by major classes according to function or nature. _____

    b.   Future minimum lease payments in the aggregate and for each of the next five fiscal years with separate deductions made for executory costs (including any profit thereon) included in the minimum lease payments, and the amount of imputed interest needed to reduce the net minimum lease payments to present value. _____

    c.   Total of minimum sublease rentals to be received in the future under noncancelable subleases. _____

    d.   Total contingent rentals actually incurred for each period for which an income statement is presented. _____

     e.   Depreciation on capital leases should be separately disclosed.   _____

2.   For sale-leaseback transactions, disclose

     a.   In addition to requirements of SFAS 13 and 66, financials of seller-lessee shall describe terms of sale-leaseback transaction, including future commitments, obligations, provisions, or circumstances requiring or resulting in seller-lessee's involvement.   _____

     b.   Where seller-lessee has accounted for transaction by deposit method or as a financing

        (1)   The obligation for future minimum lease payments as of the date of the latest balance sheet presented in the aggregate and for each of the five succeeding fiscal years.   _____

        (2)   The total of minimum sublease rentals, if any, to be received in the future under noncancelable subleases in the aggregate and for each of the five succeeding fiscal years.   _____

3.   For operating leases having a remaining noncancelable term in excess of one year, disclose

     a.   Future minimum lease payments in the aggregate and for each of the next five fiscal years.   _____

     b.   Total of minimum rentals that will be received under noncancelable subleases.   _____

4.   For all operating leases

     a.   Present rental expense disclosing separately the amount for minimum rentals, contingent rentals, and sublease rentals.   _____

     b.   Rental payments for leases with terms of a month or less that were not renewed may be excluded.   _____

5.   General description required of lessee's leasing arrangements including, but not limited to

     a.   Basis of computing contingent rental payments.   _____

     b.   Existence and terms of renewal or purchase options and escalation clauses.   _____

     c.   Restrictions imposed by leasing agreements such as on dividends, additional debt, and further leasing arrangements.   _____

P. Leases—Lessors

1.   For sales-type and direct financing leases, disclose

     a.   Components of the net investment in leases including the following

        (1)   Future minimum lease payments to be received with separate deductions for amount representing executory costs (including any profit thereon), and the accumulated allowance for uncollectible lease payments.   _____

        (2)   Unguaranteed residual values accruing to benefit of lessor.   _____

        (3)   For direct financing leases only, initial direct costs.   _____

        (4)   Unearned interest revenue.   _____

     b.   Future minimum lease payments to be received for each of the next five fiscal years.   _____

     c.   Total contingent rentals included in income for each period for which an income statement is presented.   _____

2. For operating leases, disclose

   a. The cost and carrying amount (if different) of property leased or held for leasing, segregated by major classes of property according to function or nature, and the total amount of accumulated depreciation. _____

   b. Minimum rentals on noncancelable leases in the aggregate and for each of the next five fiscal years. _____

   c. Total contingent rentals included in income for each period for which an income statement is presented. _____

3. A general description of the lessor's leasing arrangements. _____

4. For an investment in leveraged leases recorded net of the nonrecourse debt, the net of the balances of following accounts shall represent the initial and continuing investment in leveraged leases:

   a. Rentals receivable, net of portion of rental applicable to principal and interest on nonrecourse debt. _____

   b. A receivable for amount of investment tax credit to be realized on transaction. _____

   c. Estimated residual value of leased asset. _____

   d. Unearned and deferred income consisting of

      (1) Estimated pretax income (or loss), after deducting initial direct costs, remaining to be allocated to income over the lease term. _____

      (2) Investment tax credit remaining to be allocated to income over lease term. _____

   e. For leverage leases, for each income statement presented, disclose

      (1) Pretax income from leveraged leases. _____

      (2) Tax effect of that pretax income. _____

      (3) Amount of investment tax credit recognized as income. _____

Q. Stockholders' Equity

1. The following should be disclosed:

   a. The sources of capital supplied to the firm _____

   b. The legal restrictions on the distribution of invested capital _____

   c. The legal, contractual, managerial, and financial restrictions on the distribution of dividends to stockholders _____

   d. The priorities of the classes of stockholders in a partial or final liquidation _____

2. Capital stock and additional paid-in capital

   a. For each class of stock, disclose

      (1) Par, stated, or assigned value. _____

      (2) Number of shares authorized, issued, and outstanding. _____

      (3) Number of shares held in treasury. _____

      (4) Conversion terms of preferred, if applicable, including call prices, rates, and dates. Additionally, the amount of redemption requirements for all issues of stock that are redeemable at fixed or determinable prices on fixed or determinable dates must be disclosed for each of the five years following the date of the latest balance sheet presented. _____

      (5) Changes in the number of shares authorized, issued, and outstanding during the year and changes in the equity accounts. _____

      (6) Liquidation values, if different than par, in the aggregate for preferred. _____

(7)　For preferred classes of stock, any dividend preferences, special privileges, etc.　　_____

(8)　Any unusual voting rights.　　_____

b.　The amount of cumulative dividends in arrears, per share and in aggregate.　　_____

c.　Aggregate securities issuable under rights or warrants, as well as their prices, and exercise and expiration dates.　　_____

d.　Any discount on capital stock.　　_____

e.　The amount of subscribed shares not yet issued.　　_____

f.　Deferred compensation expense offset against the paid-in capital account, "Stock options outstanding."　　_____

g.　Stock dividends distributable in total or at par or stated value with the excess included in additional paid-in capital. Also acceptable is deferment of their recording until issuance. However, disclosure is necessary in the notes.　　_____

h.　The amount of capital stock issued in business combinations (purchase or pooling) or agreements to issue additional shares at a later date.　　_____

i.　Transactions affecting equity subsequent to the date of the financial statements (recapitalization, sales of stock, etc.).　　_____

j.　Additional paid-in capital, listed by source, along with any changes during the period.　　_____

k.　Any changes in the capital accounts of partners or sole proprietors.　　_____

3.　Retained earnings

a.　Appropriation and segregation of retained earnings, as well as their nature, cause, and amount. Changes in these accounts should be disclosed.　　_____

b.　Nature and dollar amounts of restrictions on retained earnings (treasury stock, lease covenants, etc.).　　_____

c.　Date retained earnings for ten years following quasi reorganization.　　_____

d.　Increase/decrease results from combination by pooling of interests (revenues, expenses, extraordinary items, and net income).　　_____

e.　Prior period adjustments, net of tax and in gross. For correction of an error, in the period discovered, disclose

(1)　Nature of the error on previous statements.　　_____

(2)　Effect of correction on income before extraordinary items, net income, and related per share amounts.　　_____

4.　Dividends

a.　Dividends in aggregate and per share as well as the nature and extent of any restrictions on retained earnings limiting availability of dividends.　　_____

b.　The amount of dividends in arrears, per share and in aggregate.　　_____

c.　Dividends declared after balance sheet date, prior to opinion date, unless a long-established history of regular payment dates exists and the dividend is not abnormal in amount.　　_____

d.　For stock dividends and stock splits, disclosure of the amounts capitalized, per share and in total. Historical presentations of earnings per share should be restated in an equivalent number of shares so the figures are presented on a comparable basis.　　_____

5.　Treasury stock

a.　If treasury stock is accounted for by the cost method, present total cost of treasury stock as a deduction from total stockholders' equity. Disclose number of shares held in treasury.　　_____

b. If treasury stock is accounted for by the par value method, present par value of treasury stock as a deduction from par value of issued shares of same class. Any related additional paid-in capital from treasury stock is netted with corresponding additional paid-in capital without separate disclosure. Disclose number of shares held in treasury. _____

c. If treasury stock is accounted for by the constructive retirement method, disclose number of shares held in treasury. _____

6. Compensatory stock plans

   a. Plan description, including general terms of awards such as vesting requirements, maximum term of options granted, and the number of shares authorized for grants of options or other equity instruments. _____

   b. For each year for which an income statement is provided, state

      (1) Number and weighted-average exercise prices of the following options: those outstanding at the beginning and at the end of the year; those exercisable at the end of the year; and those granted, exercised, forfeited, or expired during the year. _____

      (2) Weighted-average grant-date fair value of options granted during the year and additional required disclosures if exercise prices of some options differ from the market price of the stock on the grant date. _____

      (3) Number and weighted-average grant-date fair value of equity instruments other than options, such as shares of nonvested stock, granted during the year. _____

      (4) Description of method and significant assumptions used during the year to estimate the fair value of options. _____

      (5) Total compensation cost recognized for stock-based employee compensation awards. _____

      (6) Terms of significant modifications of outstanding awards. _____

   c. For options outstanding at the latest balance sheet date, the range of exercise prices and the weighted-average remaining contractual life. _____

7. Employee stock ownership plans (ESOP)

   a. Description of the plan, including basis for determining contributions, groups covered, nature and effect of matters affecting comparability of information across periods. _____

   b. The basis for releasing shares by leveraged and pension reversion ESOP. _____

   c. Accounting policies pertinent to ESOP transactions. _____

   d. Compensation cost recognized during the period. _____

   e. Numbers of shares allocated, committed to be released, and held in suspense by the ESOP. _____

   f. Fair value amount of unearned compensation at year-end. _____

   g. Nature of any repurchase obligations and aggregate fair value thereof. _____

8. For SEC only, disclose

   a. Dividend payout restrictions. _____

   b. Stock subscriptions. _____

   c. Redemption requirements on redeemable stock. _____

   d. Separate classification for redeemable preferred stock. _____

INCOME STATEMENT

A. Basic Disclosures

1. Sales, costs, and expenses. _____
2. Income or loss before extraordinary items. _____
3. Extraordinary items. _____
4. Income taxes. _____
5. Discontinued segments. _____
6. Depreciation. _____
7. Interest expense. _____
8. Gain or loss from extinguishment of debt. _____
9. Foreign currency realized gains and losses. _____
10. Marketable securities gains and losses. _____
11. Research and development expenses. _____
12. S Corporation election—No income tax effect. _____

B. Marketable Securities

1. Proceeds from sales of available-for-sale securities and the gross realized gains and gross realized losses on those sales. _____
2. Basis on which cost was determined in computing realized gain or loss. _____
3. The gross gains and gross losses included in earnings from transfers of securities from the available-for-sale category into the trading category. _____
4. The change in net unrealized holding gain or loss on available-for-sale securities that has been included in other comprehensive income during the period. _____
5. The change in net unrealized holding gain or loss on trading securities that has been included in earnings during the period. _____

C. Income Taxes

1. State if entity is not subject to income taxes because income is taxed directly to owners. State the net difference between tax and book bases of assets and liabilities. _____
2. State amounts allocated to

   a. Current tax expense or benefit. _____
   b. Deferred tax expense or benefit (exclusive of the effects of other components listed below). _____
   c. Investment tax or other credits. _____
   d. Government grants (to the extent recognized as a reduction of income tax expense). _____
   e. The benefits of operating loss carryforwards. _____
   f. Tax expense that results from allocating certain tax benefits either directly to contributed capital or to reduce goodwill or other noncurrent intangible assets of an acquired entity. _____
   g. Adjustments of a deferred tax liability or asset for enacted changes in tax laws or rates or a change in the tax status of the enterprise. _____
   h. Adjustments of the beginning-of-the-year balance of a valuation allowance because of a change in circumstances that causes a change in judgment about the realizability of the related deferred tax asset in future years. _____

3. Amounts allocated to

a. Continuing operations. _____

b. Discontinued operations. _____

c. Extraordinary items. _____

d. Cumulative effect of accounting changes. _____

e. Prior period adjustments. _____

f. Gains and losses included in comprehensive income but excluded from net income. _____

g. Capital transactions. _____

4. Reconcile statutory tax rates to actual rates for significant items (nonpublic enterprises need only disclose the nature of significant reconciling items). _____

5. Amounts and expiration dates for operating loss and tax credit carryforward for financial reporting. _____

6. If consolidated return filed, separately issued financial statements should state

a. Amount of current and deferred tax expense for each income statement. _____

b. Tax-related balances due to or from affiliates for each balance sheet. _____

c. The method of allocating consolidated amounts of current and deferred tax expense and effects of any change in that methodology. _____

7. Cumulative effect of change (similar to change in accounting principle) for earliest restated financial statements. _____

8. When a deferred tax liability is not recognized because of the exceptions to comprehensive recognition of deferred taxes, the following information shall be disclosed:

a. A description of the types of temporary differences for which a deferred tax liability has not been recognized and the types of events that would cause those temporary differences to become taxable. _____

b. The cumulative amount of each type of temporary difference. _____

c. The amount of the unrecognized deferred tax liability for temporary differences related to investments in foreign subsidiaries and foreign corporate joint ventures that are essentially permanent in duration if determination of that liability is practicable or a statement that determination is not practicable. _____

d. The amount of the deferred tax liability for temporary differences other than those in c. above (i.e., undistributed domestic earnings, the bad-debt reserve for tax purposes of a US savings and loan association or other qualified thrift lender, the policyholders' surplus of a life insurance enterprise, and the statutory reserve funds of a US steamship enterprise) that is not recognized. _____

D. Extraordinary Items

1. Segregated and shown net of tax. _____

2. Adequate explanations of nature of extraordinary item(s). _____

3. Infrequent or unusual items shown separately although not extraordinary; not shown net of tax. _____

4. For adjustment of amounts reported in prior period that do not qualify as prior period adjustments, classify separately in same manner as original item, with year of origin, nature and amount. _____

E. Discontinued Operations

1. Assets and operations segregated in balance sheet and income statement, respectively. _____

2.   Gain/loss from disposal reported as separate category after continuing operations and before extraordinary items and cumulative effect of accounting changes.   _____

3.   Expected loss on future disposal to be accrued and reported.   _____

4.   Operating results up to measurement date distinguished from results from measurement date through disposal date.   _____

F.   Interim Financial Information

1.   Provide the minimum disclosures required by APB 28 when publicly traded entities report summarized interim financial information. These required disclosures are

     a.   Sales or gross revenues, provision for income taxes, extraordinary items, cumulative effect of a change in principle, and net income.   _____

     b.   Basic and diluted earnings per share.   _____

     c.   Seasonal revenues, costs, and expenses.   _____

     d.   Significant changes in income tax estimates.   _____

     e.   Discontinued operations and extraordinary, unusual, or infrequently occurring items.   _____

     f.   Contingencies.   _____

     g.   Effect of changes in accounting principles or estimates.   _____

     h.   Significant changes in financial position.   _____

2.   When summarized financial information is reported on a regular quarterly basis, the above disclosures should be presented for the current year and the current year-to-date (or preceding twelve months), with comparable data for the preceding year.   _____

G.   Segment Data

1.   General information on segments including:

     a.   Factors used to identify the enterprise's reportable segments, including the basis of organization (e.g., whether management has chosen to organize the enterprise around differences in products and services, geographic areas, regulatory environments, or a combination of factors and whether operating segments have been aggregated).   _____

     b.   Types of products and services from which each reportable segment derives its revenues.   _____

2.   The following about each reportable segment if the specified amounts are included in the measure of segment profit or loss reviewed by the chief operating decision maker:

     a.   Revenues from external customers.   _____

     b.   Revenues from transactions with other operating segments of the same enterprise.   _____

     c.   Interest revenue.   _____

     d.   Interest expense.   _____

     e.   Depreciation, depletion, and amortization expense.   _____

     f.   Unusual items.   _____

     g.   Equity in the net income of investees accounted for by the equity method.   _____

     h.   Income tax expense or benefit.   _____

     i.   Extraordinary items.   _____

3. Disclose the following about each reportable segment if the specific amounts are included in the determination of segment assets reviewed by the chief operating decision maker:

   a. The amount of investment in equity method investees. _____

   b. Total expenditures for additions to long-lived assets other than financial instruments, long-term customer relationships of a financial institution, mortgage and other servicing rights, deferred policy acquisition costs, and deferred tax assets. _____

4. An explanation should be provided of the measurements of segment profit or loss and segment assets for each reportable segment; at a minimum, these shall include the following:

   a. The basis of accounting for any transactions between reportable segments. _____

   b. The nature of any differences between the measurements of the reportable segments' profits or losses and the company's consolidated income before income taxes, extraordinary items, discontinued operations, and the cumulative effect of changes in accounting principles (if not apparent from the reconciliations); for example, accounting policies and policies for allocation of centrally incurred costs that are necessary for an understanding of the reported segment information. _____

   c. The nature of any differences between the measurements of the reportable segments' assets and the company's consolidated assets (if not apparent from the reconciliations); for example, accounting policies and policies for allocation of jointly used assets that are necessary for an understanding of the reported segment information. _____

   d. The nature of any changes from prior periods in the measurement methods used to determine reported segment profit or loss and the effect, if any, of those changes on the measure of segment profit or loss. _____

   e. The nature and effect of any asymmetrical allocations to segments; for example, an enterprise might allocate depreciation expense to a segment without allocating the related depreciable assets to that segment. _____

5. Reconciliations of the totals of segment revenues, reported profit or loss, assets, and other significant items to corresponding company amounts, as follows:

   a. The total of the reportable segments' revenues to the enterprise's consolidated revenues. _____

   b. The total of the reportable segments' measures of profit or loss to the company's consolidated income before income taxes, extraordinary items, discontinued operations, and the cumulative effect of changes in accounting principles. _____

   c. The total of the reportable segments' assets to the company's consolidated assets. _____

   d. The total of the reportable segments' amounts for every other significant item of information disclosed to the corresponding consolidated amount. _____

6. Company-wide disclosures (required for all companies subject to SFAS 131 including those companies that have a single reportable segment)

a. Revenues from external customers for each product and service or each group of similar products and services unless it is impracticable to do so. (The amounts of revenues reported shall be based on the financial information used to produce the enterprise's general-purpose financial statements. If providing the information is impracticable, that fact shall be disclosed.) _____

b. Revenues from external customers

(1) Attributed to the enterprise's country of domicile. _____

(2) Attributed to all foreign countries in total from which the enterprise derives revenues unless it is impracticable to do so. (If revenues from external customers attributed to an individual foreign country are material, those revenues shall be disclosed separately. Also disclose the basis for attributing revenues from external customers to individual countries.) _____

c. Long-lived assets other than financial instruments, long-term customer relationships of a financial institution, mortgage and other servicing rights, deferred policy acquisition costs, and deferred tax assets

(1) Located in the enterprise's country of domicile. _____

(2) Located in all foreign countries in total in which the enterprise holds assets unless it is impractical to do so. (If assets in an individual foreign country are material, those assets shall be disclosed separately.) _____

d. If providing the geographic information is impracticable, that fact shall be disclosed. _____

7. Major customers

If revenues from transaction with a single external customer amount to ten percent or more of an enterprise's revenues, disclose that fact, the total amount of revenues from each such customer, and the identity of the segment or segments reporting the revenues. _____

8. Earnings before income tax disclosures

Depreciation and amortization expense for each reportable segment, when the chief operating decision maker evaluates the performance of its segments based on earnings before interest, taxes, depreciation, and amortization. _____

H. Development Stage Enterprises

1. The financial statements should be identified as those of a development stage company and should include a description of the nature of the development stage activities. _____

2. The financial statements for the first fiscal year in which the company is no longer considered to be in the development stage should disclose that in prior years it had been in the development stage. If financial statements for prior years are presented for comparative purposes, the cumulative amounts and other additional disclosures required below need not be shown. _____

3. On the balance sheet, any cumulative net losses should be reported with a descriptive caption such as "deficit accumulated during the development stage" in the stockholders' equity section. _____

4. Report the cumulative amounts of revenue and expenses since inception. _____

5. Report the cumulative amounts of sources and uses of cash since inception. _____

6. Present in the statement of stockholders' equity all transactions since inception. _____

7. Disclose the date of each stock issuance in the statement of changes in stockholders' equity. _____

8. Disclose the basis for stock issued for other than cash. _____

I. Long-Term Construction Contracts

1. The method of recognizing income (percentage-of-completion or completed-contract). _____

2. If the percentage-of-completion method is used, the method of computing percentage of completion (e.g., cost-to-cost, efforts-expended). _____

3. If the completed-contract method is used, the justification for its use should be indicated. _____

4. Length of the operating cycle; if greater than one year, the range of contract durations should be disclosed. _____

5. The basis of recording inventory. _____

6. The effect of changes in estimates. _____

7. The accounting for deferred costs. _____

8. The accounting for general and administrative expenses. _____

9. Criteria for determining substantial completion (e.g., compliance with specifications, acceptance by customer). _____

10. Information on revenues and costs arising from claims. _____

J. Research and Development

1. Expenditures. _____

2. R&D arrangements.

   a. Terms including royalties, purchase provisions, license agreements and funding. _____

   b. Amounts earned and costs incurred each period for which an income statement is presented. _____

K. Sales Where Collection Is Uncertain

1. Method and justification of accounting for installment basis sales. _____

2. Yearly gross profit rates. _____

3. Contractual terms such as interest and repossession provisions. _____

4. Average length of installment contracts. _____

L. Revenue Recognition When Right of Return Exists

1. Basis for recognizing revenue and cost of sales. _____

2. Estimated amount of returns. _____

3. Description of return privilege granted to customers. _____

4. Length of time covered by the return privilege. _____

M. Other Reporting

1. Financing arrangements—Real estate and product financing. _____

2. Real estate sales. _____

3. Futures contracts. _____

4. Service sales transaction.

   a. The revenue recognition method used and its justification. _____

   b. Information concerning unearned revenues. _____

   c. Information concerning deferred costs. _____

   d. Periods over which services are to be performed. _____

N. Foreign Currency

1. Aggregate transaction gain or loss that is included in the entity's net income. _____

2. Analysis of changes in accumulated translation adjustments which are reported as other comprehensive income. At a minimum, the disclosures should include

   a. Beginning and ending amounts of the translation adjustments account. _____

   b. Aggregate adjustment for the period resulting from translation adjustments, and gains and losses from certain hedges and intercompany balances. _____

   c. Amount of income taxes for the period allocated to translation adjustments. _____

   d. Amounts transferred from the translation adjustments account and included in determining net income as a result of the (partial) sale or liquidation of the foreign operation. _____

3. Significant rate changes subsequent to the date of the financial statements including effects on unsettled foreign currency transactions. Rate changes subsequent to the balance sheet date are not incorporated into the financial statements for the period just ended. _____

O. Business Combinations under Purchase Accounting

1. Name and brief description of the acquired enterprise and the percentage of voting shares acquired. _____

2. The period for which the results of operations of the acquired enterprise are included in the income statement of the acquiring enterprise. _____

3. The cost of the acquired enterprise and, if applicable, the number of shares of stock issued or issuable, the value assigned to those shares, and the basis for determining that value. _____

4. Contingent payments, options, or commitments specified in the acquisition agreement and the accounting treatment that will be followed should any such contingency occur. _____

5. A condensed balance sheet disclosing the following for each major asset and liability caption of the acquired enterprise:

   a. The book values as reflected in the acquired enterprise's financial records at the date of acquisition before fair value adjustments. _____

   b. The fair values assigned at the date of acquisition. _____

6. For any purchase price allocation that has not been finalized, that fact and the reasons therefore and, in subsequent periods, the nature and amount of any material adjustments made to the initial allocation of the purchase price. _____

7. The amounts of

   a. Acquired goodwill. _____

   b. Acquired goodwill related to each segment (for entities that are required to report segment information in accordance with Statement 131). _____

   c. Acquired goodwill that is deductible for income tax purposes. _____

8. For individually immaterial business combinations which have been completed, if those combinations are material in the aggregate, disclose the following information

   a. The number of enterprises acquired and a brief description of those enterprises. _____

   b. The aggregate cost of the acquired enterprises, the number of shares of stock issued or issuable, and the value assigned to those shares. _____

   c. The aggregate amount of any contingent payments, options, or commitments and the accounting treatment that will be followed should any such contingency occur (if potentially significant in relation to the aggregate cost of the acquired enterprises). _____

    d.   The amounts of

        (1) Acquired goodwill. _____

        (2) Acquired goodwill related to each segment (for entities that are required to report segment information in accordance with Statement 131). _____

        (3) Acquired goodwill that is deductible for income tax purposes. _____

9.   For any material business combination completed **after** the balance sheet date but before the financial statements are issued, the information identified in items 1-7 above (unless not practible). _____

P.   Earnings Per Share

1.   For each income statement presented

    a.   Reconciliation of the numerators and the denominators of the basic and diluted per share computations for income from continuing operations. _____

    b.   Effect that has been given to preferred dividends in arriving at income available to common stockholders in computing basic EPS. _____

    c.   Securities (including those issuable pursuant to contingent stock agreements) that could potentially dilute basic EPS in the future that were not included in the computation of diluted EPS because to do so would have been antidilutive for the period(s) presented. _____

2.   Earnings per share amounts for income from continuing operations and net income, shown on the face of income statement for all periods presented. _____

3.   If applicable, per share amounts for discontinued operations, extraordinary items, and cumulative effect of an accounting change, presented either on face of income statement or in notes to financial statements. _____

4.   For latest income statement, provide a description of any transaction that occurs after end of the period but before issuance of financial statements that would have changed materially the number of common shares or potential common shares outstanding at end of period if transaction had occurred before end of period. _____

5.   Amounts should be restated when stock dividends, splits, or reverses occur after close of period but before statements are issued with appropriate disclosure. _____

6.   When operations of a prior period have been restated, earnings per share data also should be restated; the effect of the restatement, expressed in per share terms, should be disclosed in year of restatement. _____

7.   Disclose EPS for income from continuing operations when there are discontinued operations of a segment of a business. _____

STATEMENT OF CASH FLOWS

A.   Basis

1.   Definition of cash and cash equivalents adopted. _____

2.   Summarize noncash investing and financing activities _____

B.   Format

1.   Reconcile net income to net cash flow. _____

2.   If direct method used, display major categories of gross cash receipts and cash payments. _____

    a.   Cash receipts

        (1) Cash receipts from sale of goods or services. _____

        (2) Interest and dividends received. _____

        (3) Other operating cash receipts.   _____

  b. Cash payments

        (1) Payments to employees and other suppliers of goods or services.   _____
        (2) Income taxes paid.   _____
        (3) Interest paid.   _____
        (4) Other operating cash payments.   _____

  c. Reconcile net income or loss to net cash flow from operating activities.   _____

3. If indirect method used

  a. Present reconciliation of net income or loss to cash flow from operating activities, separately reporting all major items, either within the statement or in a separate schedule.   _____
  b. Disclose both interest and income taxes paid in a schedule following the statement or in the notes.   _____

4. Report cash flows from purchases and sales or maturities of trading securities under operating activities.   _____

5. Report cash flows from investing activities:

  a. Report separately cash inflows and outflows.   _____
  b. Report gross for each security classification in the statement of cash flows, the cash flows from purchases, sales and maturities of available-for-sale securities, and separately for held-to-maturity securities.   _____

6. Report cash flows from financing activities

  a. Report separately cash inflows and outflows.   _____
  b. Effect of exchange rate changes on cash balances held in foreign currencies shown separately on statement of cash flows.   _____
  c. Cash payments for debt issue costs.   _____

STATEMENT OF COMPREHENSIVE INCOME

A. Format Options

1. Continuation of income statement (preferred by FASB).   _____
2. Separate statement starting with net income.   _____
3. Part of statement of stockholders' equity.   _____

B. Disclosures

1. Total amount for comprehensive income.   _____
2. Amounts of other comprehensive income by type.   _____
3. Reclassification adjustment(s) for items included in net income also included in other comprehensive income in this period or prior period   _____

  a. Face of financial statement in which comprehensive income reported.   _____
  b. Notes to financial statements.   _____
  c. Gross display on face of financial statement or net display on face of financial statement and gross display in notes to financial statements except for minimum pension liability which does not have reclassification adjustments.   _____

4. Cumulative amounts of other comprehensive income by type

  a. Face of balance sheet.   _____

b.   Statement of changes in stockholders' equity. _____

c.   Notes to financial statements. _____

SPECIALIZED INDUSTRY GAAP

A. Banking and Savings Institutions

(See the AICPA Audit and Accounting Guide: *Banks and Savings Institutions*, 1999.)

B. Broadcasting Industry

1.   License agreements for program material not reported due to failure to meet the specified conditions. _____

C. Computer Software Costs and Revenues

1.   Amount of research and development costs charged to expense during the period. _____

2.   Amount of capitalized computer software costs amortized to expense during the period. _____

3.   Unamortized computer software costs at the end of the period. _____

4.   Amount of capitalized computer software costs written down to net realizable value. _____

D. Franchisor Accounting

1.   Nature of all significant commitments resulting from franchise agreements. _____

2.   Description of services not yet substantially performed. _____

3.   If collectibility is uncertain

    a.   Use of installment or cost recovery method. _____

    b.   Sales price of franchises including deferral of both costs and revenue. _____

    c.   Amounts originally deferred but later recognized due to resolution of uncertainty. _____

4.   Initial franchise fees segregated from other franchise fee revenue and contribution to net income of such initial fees. _____

5.   Saturation point of locations or other expectation of decline in future initial franchise fee revenue. _____

6.   Segregation of franchisor owned outlet revenues and expenses from other activities. _____

7.   Other

    a.   Franchises sold or purchased or operated. _____

    b.   Franchisor owned outlets. _____

    c.   Significant changes in the outlets during the period. _____

E. Government Contracts

1.   Contracts subject to renegotiation for which reasonable estimates are not determinable include

    a.   Reasons for inability to estimate. _____

    b.   Material uncertainties and significance thereof. _____

    c.   Basis for measuring renegotiation provision. _____

2.   For terminated defense contracts

    a.   Material facts and circumstances. _____

    b.   Disclose termination claims separately. _____

       c.   Report as sales separately.   _____

  3. Each federal, state, or local governmental unit

       a.   Treated as a single customer.   _____

F. Insurance Industry Transactions

  1. Liabilities for claims and claim adjustment expenses.

       a.   Basis for estimating liabilities.   _____

       b.   For short-term contracts carried at present value

           (1) Carrying amount.   _____
           (2) Discount rate used.   _____
           (3) Claim adjustment expenses.   _____
           (4) Consideration of anticipated investment income in determining if a premium deficiency exists.   _____

  2. Future policy benefits owed.

       a.   Methods and assumptions.   _____
       b.   Average rate of expected investment yields.   _____

  3. Capitalized acquisition costs

       a.   Nature.   _____
       b.   Method of amortization.   _____
       c.   Amount amortized during the period.   _____

  4. Reinsurance transactions

       a.   Nature, purpose, and effect of ceded transactions.   _____
       b.   Methods of income recognition on reinsurance contracts.   _____
       c.   Short-term contracts—Premiums from direct business, reinsurance assumed and ceded.   _____
       d.   Long-term contracts—Premiums and amounts assessed against policyholders, reinsurance assumed and ceded, premiums and amounts earned.   _____
       e.   Concentration of credit risk on reinsurance receivables and premiums.   _____

  5. Participating insurance

       a.   Relative percentage.   _____
       b.   Method of accounting for dividends.   _____
       c.   Amount of dividends.   _____
       d.   Additional income allocated to participating policyholders.   _____

  6. Statutory accounting practices

       a.   Statutory capital and surplus

           (1) Actual amount.   _____
           (2) Amount required by statute (if significant compared to actual).   _____

       b.   Statutory restrictions of the payment of dividends

           (1) Nature.   _____
           (2) Amount of retained earnings restricted.   _____

  7. Income tax disclosures.   _____

G. Mortgage Banking Activities

1.   Method used to determine lower of cost or market value—aggregate vs. individual loan basis.   _____

2.   Servicing rights capitalized during the period

   a.   Amount.   _____
   b.   Method of amortization.   _____
   c.   Amount of amortization for the period.   _____

3.   Fair value of capitalized servicing rights, including methods and assumptions used and explanation of reasons if not practical to estimate.   _____

4.   Risk characteristics for stratifying servicing rights in measuring impairment.   _____

5.   Changes in servicing rights valuation allowance.   _____

H. Motion Picture Industry

1.   The portion of the costs of completed films expected to be amortized during the upcoming operating cycle.   _____

2.   The components of film costs separately for theatrical films and direct-to-television product including

   a.   Released.   _____
   b.   Completed and not released.   _____
   c.   In production.   _____
   d.   In development or preproduction.   _____

3.   The percentage of unamortized film costs for released films, excluding acquired film libraries, expected to be amortized within three years from the balance sheet date. If that percentage is less than 80%, additional information should be provided including the period required to reach an amortization level of 80%.   _____

4.   For acquired film libraries

   a.   The amount of remaining unamortized costs.   _____
   b.   The method of amortization.   _____
   c.   The remaining amortization period.   _____

5.   The amount of accrued participation liabilities expected to be paid during the upcoming operating cycle.   _____

6.   The method of accounting for revenue, film costs, and exploitation costs.   _____

7.   The effect on income before extraordinary items, net income, and related per share amounts of the current fiscal period for a change in estimate that affects several future periods.   _____

I. Oil and Gas Producing Activities

   SFAS 69 requires publicly traded enterprises to disclose the following oil and gas producing data as **supplementary** (not part of the financial statements) information:

1.   Proved oil and gas reserves.   _____

2.   Capitalized costs.   _____

3.   Acquisition, exploration, and development costs.   _____

4.   Results of operations.   _____

5.   Standardized measure of discounted future cash flows relating to proved reserves.   _____

J. Pension Funds

1. The plan's accounting policies should disclose a description of methods and assumptions

    a. Used to determine fair value. _____

    b. Used to determine the actuarial present value of the accumulated benefit obligation (APVAPB). _____

    c. Changed during the current period. _____

2. The financial statements should disclose the following:

    a. Plan descriptions—Including vesting and benefit provisions. _____

    b. Significant plan amendment descriptions—Indicate if APVAPB does not include the effects of the amendments. _____

    c. Priority order of participants' claims to assets. _____

    d. Benefits guaranteed by Pension Benefit Guaranty Corp. _____

    e. Funding policy and any period changes. In addition, the following should make the disclosure indicated:

        (1) Contributory plan—Method of determining contributions. _____

        (2) ERISA—Whether minimum funding requirements were met. _____

    f. Disclosure of a minimum funding waiver or a request for one from the IRS is required. _____

    g. Policy concerning insurance companies and the purchase of contracts that are excluded from plan assets. Disclosure should be made of the amount of dividend income related to excluded contracts. _____

    h. Income status of the plan. _____

    i. Investments that are 5% or more of plan assets should be identified. _____

    j. Significant real estate or other transactions between the plan and the sponsor, the employer, or the employee organization. _____

    k. Infrequent or unusual events that occur between the benefit information date and the issuance of statements that would aid in the determination of the plan's ability to pay benefits. _____

K. Recording and Music Industry

1. Licensors

    a. Commitments to pay advance royalties in the future. _____

    b. Future royalty guarantees. _____

    c. Cost of record masters borne by the record company and capitalized as assets (disclose separately). _____

L. Regulated Operations

1. Refunds

    a. Effect on net income, when recognized in period(s) different than related revenue

        (1) Not recognized as an extraordinary item. _____

2. Discontinuation of specialized accounting

    a. Reasons for discontinuation. _____

    b. Portion of operations to which the discontinuation applies. _____

    c. Net adjustment reported as an extraordinary item. _____

GAAP

**INTERPRETATION AND APPLICATION OF
GENERALLY ACCEPTED ACCOUNTING PRINCIPLES**

2002 EDITION

SELF-STUDY
CPE PROGRAM

Unit I
Chapters 1-7

Unit II
Chapters 8-11

Unit III
Chapters 12-15

Unit IV
Chapters 16-23

JOHN WILEY & SONS, INC.

About This Course

We are pleased that you have selected our course. A course description that is based on the 2002 edition of *GAAP: Interpretation and Application* follows:

Prerequisites:	**None**
Recommended CPE credits:	**10 hours per unit**
Knowledge level:	**Basic**
Area of study:	**Accounting and Auditing**

The credit hours recommended are in accordance with the AICPA Standards for CPE Programs. Since CPE requirements are set by each state, you need to check with your State Board of Accountancy concerning required CPE hours and fields of study.

If you decide to take this course follow the directions on the following page. Each course unit costs $59.00. Methods of payment are shown on the answer forms.

Each CPE exam is graded no later than two weeks after receipt. The passing score is at least 70%. John Wiley & Sons, Inc. will issue a certificate of completion to successful participants to recognize their achievement.

Photocopy one copy of the answer sheet for each additional participant who wishes to take the CPE course. Each participant should complete the answer form and return it with the $59 fee for each self-study course.

The enclosed self-study CPE program will expire on December 31, 2003. Completed exams must be postmarked by that date.

Directions for the CPE Course

Each course unit includes reading assignments and objectives, discussion questions and answers, and a publisher-graded examination. For those units that you intend to have graded by the publisher, follow these steps:

1. Read the chapter learning objectives.
2. Study the respective chapter in the *2002 GAAP: Interpretation and Application.*
3. Answer the discussion questions and refer to the answers to assess your understanding of the respective chapter.
4. Study material in any weak areas again.
5. Upon completion of all chapters in a unit, do the publisher-graded examination for that unit. Record your answers by writing true, false, or a letter (a-e) on the line for that question on the answer form.
6. Upon completion of the examination, cut out the answer sheet, put it in a stamped envelope, and mail to the address below:

> GAAP CPE Program Director
> John Wiley & Sons, Inc.
> 7222 Commerce Center Drive
> Suite 240
> Colorado Springs, CO 80919

CONTINUING PROFESSIONAL EDUCATION: SELF-STUDY

UNIT I

OBJECTIVES

Chapter 1: Researching GAAP Problems

Studying Chapter 1 should enable you to:

- Understand the development of generally accepted accounting principles
- Differentiate between the levels of GAAP
- Understand the sources of GAAP for both business entities and state and local government
- Identify the authoritative publications of the FASB
- Distinguish between mandatory and preferable GAAP
- Describe and explain materiality
- Learn how to research established GAAP
- Learn how to use this book in researching answers to questions about GAAP

Read Chapter 1 and answer discussion questions 1 through 4.

Chapter 2: Balance Sheet

Studying Chapter 2 should enable you to:

- Understand the purpose of the balance sheet
- Define assets, liabilities, and equity
- Understand the limitations of balance sheets
- Understand the classifications on the balance sheet
- Learn about the disclosures that accompany balance sheets
- Learn about the form and measurement of items on the balance sheet

Read Chapter 2 and answer discussion questions 5 through 8.

Chapter 3: Statements of Income and Comprehensive Income

Studying Chapter 3 should enable you to:

- Understand the purpose of the income statement
- Understand the elements comprising the income statement
- Differentiate between the concepts of income
- Define revenues and the realization concept
- Explain the characteristics of expenses
- Learn the criteria for extraordinary items
- Define comprehensive income
- Learn about prior period adjustments
- Learn about special requirements for development stage companies
- Learn about other comprehensive income
- Learn about accounting for start-up costs
- Learn about restructuring costs

Read Chapter 3 and answer discussion questions 9 through 14.

Chapter 4: Statement of Cash Flows

Studying Chapter 4 should enable you to:

- Understand the purpose of the statement of cash flows
- Define cash equivalents
- Classify cash flows as operating, investing, or financing activities
- Describe the preparation of the operating activities section under the
  - Direct method
  - Indirect method
- Describe the preparation of the investing activities section
- Describe the preparation of the financing activities section
- Describe the disclosure of noncash financing and investing activities

Read Chapter 4 and answer discussions questions 15 through 19.

Chapter 5: Cash, Receivables, and Prepaid Expenses

Studying Chapter 5 should enable you to:

- Classify items as cash
- Describe the accounting for receivables
- Understand how bad debt expense is estimated
- Understand pledging, assigning, and factoring of receivables and the differences between them
- Understand the requirements of SFAS 140, *Accounting for Transfers and Servicing of Financial Assets and Extinguishment of Liabilities*
- Requirements for recognition of transfer
- Derecognition of liabilities

Read Chapter 5 and answer discussion questions 20 through 24.

Chapter 6: Short-Term Investments and Financial Instruments

Studying Chapter 6 should enable you to:

- Understand the accounting for short-term investments
- Classify short-term investments
- Describe derivative financial instruments
- Know the disclosure requirements for financial instruments
- Know the disclosure requirements for derivative financial instruments
- Describe the SFAS 140 amendment dealing with held-to-maturity securities of SFAS 115, *Accounting for Certain Investments in Debt and Equity Securities*
- Be familiar with SFAS 133 concerning derivatives and its tentative effective date

Read Chapter 6 and answer discussion questions 25 through 32.

Chapter 7: Inventory

Studying Chapter 7 should enable you to:

- Determine ownership of goods

- Identify inventoriable costs
- Understand differences in financial statement amounts among cost flow assumptions
- Understand the application of the dollar-value LIFO method
- Describe the lower of cost or market valuation method
- Discuss the acceptability and workings of estimation methods
- Gross profit
- Retail
- Account for purchase commitments
- Apply the LIFO conformity rule

Read Chapter 7 and answer discussion questions 33 through 39.

DISCUSSION QUESTIONS

1. What is the content of the conceptual framework pronouncements by the FASB?

2. What is GAAP and what are its sources?

3. What is the hierarchy of GAAP?

4. Discuss materiality.

5. Define the elements of a balance sheet.

6. What are the three conditions for an item to qualify as an asset?

7. What are the three conditions for an item to qualify as a liability?

8. Discuss some of the disclosures that accompany balance sheets.

9. What is the difference between the economic and accounting definitions of income?

10. What are the recognition criteria for revenue?

11. What is the realization concept?

12. What are the criteria for an event to be classified as extraordinary on the statement of income?

13. What is the difference between an "expense" and a "loss"?

14. Distinguish between comprehensive income and other comprehensive income and describe how comprehensive income is reported.

15. What information is provided for users in the statement of cash flows?

16. Under the indirect method of presentation, how should dividends received and income recognized from an investment accounted for under the equity method be treated?

17. Describe how to determine cash paid for interest.

18. During an accounting period some bonds were retired and new bonds were issued. How should these transactions be accounted for in a statement of cash flows?

19. Discuss the disclosure of a capital lease transaction in a statement of cash flows, both at inception and when payments are made under the lease agreement.

20. What is promulgated GAAP for accounting for cash and what are the criteria for inclusion?

21. Describe how receivables should be presented on the balance sheet.

22. What are two popular techniques used to estimate bad debts expense? Which is oriented toward the income statement and which is oriented toward the balance sheet?

23. Describe pledging, assigning, and factoring of receivables. Which is the most significant in terms of accounting requirements?

24. What is the basic accounting problem addressed by SFAS 140 and what is the principal issue?

25. What three categories are used to classify securities under SFAS 115 and how is each category valued?

26. What is the determination of current or noncurrent status for individual held-to-maturity and individual available-for-sale securities based on?

27. What is the balance sheet classification of trading securities and what items are included in income from continuing operations?

28. What value is used for transfers among the three categories used in SFAS 115?

29. How should the cash flows resulting from the sales, purchases, or maturity of securities be accounted for on the cash flow statement?

30. How does SFAS 133 recommend that derivatives be shown on the balance sheet?

31. What are derivatives?

32. SFAS 107 requires entities to disclose what basic information?

33. Under what circumstances does an entity not have ownership of goods in its possession?

34. Under what circumstances does the use of the LIFO cost flow assumption result in lower net income than FIFO?

35. How is the cost of a dollar-value LIFO layer determined for a manufacturer's inventory?

36. Describe the workings of the link-chain method.

37. Discuss the objective and implementation of the lower of cost or market valuation process.

38. Explain how dollar-value LIFO is applied under the retail method.

39. What are three ways of measuring the effect of a LIFO liquidation on net income under IRS requirements?

ANSWERS TO DISCUSSION QUESTIONS

1. The conceptual framework pronouncements cover the objectives of financial reporting, qualitative characteristics of accounting information, elements of financial statements, and recognition and measurement in financial statements.

2. GAAP is the conventions, rules and procedures that define accepted accounting practice and comes primarily from the FASB and its predecessors.

3. The hierarchy of GAAP consists of four levels specified in SAS 69 as establishing GAAP. These levels are: accounting principles promulgated by a body designated by the AICPA Council to establish such principles, pursuant to rule 203 (ET section 203.01) of the AICPA Code of Professional Conduct; pronouncements of bodies that are exposed for public comment prior to issuance; pronouncements of bodies that are not exposed prior to issuance; and industry or other general practices.

4. Materiality is both quantitative and qualitative. It involves the use of judgment in evaluating the significance and importance of events.

5. Assets (future economic benefits controlled by an entity), liabilities (probable future sacrifices of economic benefits from present obligations) and equity (residual interest in assets).

6. Assets provide probable future benefits in the form of cash flows, the benefit is restricted solely to the entity, and the benefit arose out of a past event.

7. Liabilities require probable future transfers of assets, the obligation cannot be avoided, and the event obligating the entity has previously occurred.

8. Disclosures include accounting policies, related parties, subsequent events, contingencies, and risks and uncertainties.

9. Accountants define income as that created by events subject to recognition criteria while economists use a wealth maintenance concept.

10. The four criteria are

   a.   The item must be defined as an element of financial statements.
   b.   The item must be measurable in monetary units.
   c.   Relevance.
   b.   Reliability.

11. Realization states that revenue is recognized only when the earning process is complete or virtually complete and an exchange transaction has taken place.

12. For an item to be extraordinary, it must have an unusual nature (e.g., abnormal and not related to ordinary activities) and be of infrequent occurrence (e.g., not expected to recur in the foreseeable future).

13. Both expenses and losses are decreases in assets or increases in liabilities, but expenses relate to the entity's central operations while losses involve peripheral transactions.

14. Comprehensive income is the change in equity of a business enterprise during a period from all transactions and other events and circumstances from numerous sources other than with owners. Comprehensive income includes net income and other comprehensive income. Under SFAS 130, changes in components of comprehensive income should be reported in the financial statements. Net income and other comprehensive income should be displayed as part of the income statement, a separate statement of comprehensive income where the beginning number is net income, or in a separate statement of changes in equity.

15. The statement of cash flows discloses increases and decreases of cash and classifies cash flows into operating, investing, and financing activities.

16. Dividends received increase cash and must be added to net income to arrive at cash from operating activities; income recognized must be deducted from net income because no cash was received.

17. Cash paid for interest is equal to interest expense plus a decrease (or minus an increase) in accrued interest payable less bond discount amortization (or plus premium amortization).

18. Bonds issued should be shown with the cash resulting therefrom and bonds retired should be shown with the cash used.

19. In the period of inception, a capital lease should be disclosed as a noncash financing and investing activity either following the statement or in the footnotes. As payments are made on the lease, part of each payment represents a principal reduction and part represents interest expense. The former is shown under financing activities and the latter in operating activities.

20. The promulgated GAAP for accounting for cash is ARB 43, chapter 3. To be included as cash in the balance sheet, funds must be represented by actual

coins and currency on hand or demand deposits available without restriction. It must be management's intention that the cash be available for current purposes.

21. Receivables should be presented at **net realizable** (i.e., realistically anticipated collectible) amounts.

22. The **percentage-of-sales** method is principally oriented towards achieving the best possible matching of revenues and expenses. **Aging the accounts** is more oriented toward the presentation of the correct net realizable value of the trade receivables in the balance sheet. Both methods are acceptable and widely employed.

23. Pledging is an agreement where accounts receivable are used as collateral for loans. The assignment of accounts receivable is a more formalized transfer of the asset to the lending institution. Factoring traditionally has involved the outright sale of receivables to a financing institution known as a factor. This category of financing is the most significant in terms of accounting implications.

24. The basic accounting problem addressed by SFAS 140 involves instances of possible continuing involvement through recourse, repurchase agreements, options generated, servicing, and collateral. The issue is whether the transfer has resulted in a sale or a secured borrowing.

25. SFAS 115 is GAAP regarding investments in all debt securities and in equity securities that have a readily determinable fair value. It classifies these securities into one of the following three categories:

    1. Held-to-maturity — Debt securities reported at amortized cost
    2. Trading — Debt and equity securities reported at fair value
    3. Available-for-sale — Debt and equity securities not classified as 1 or 2, reported at fair value

26. The determination of current or noncurrent status for individual held-to-maturity and individual available-for-sale securities is made on the basis of whether or not the securities are considered working capital available for current operations (ARB 43, ch 3A).

27. Trading securities are required to be carried at fair value on the balance sheet as current assets. All applicable interest and dividends, realized gains and losses, and unrealized gains and losses are included in income from continuing operations.

28. Fair value is used for transfers between categories.

29. Cash flows resulting from sales, purchases, or maturity of securities should be accounted for as follows:

     1. Trading — Operating activity
     2. Held-to-maturity — Investing activity
     3. Available-for-sale — Investing activity

30. SFAS 133 specifies recognition of all derivatives in the balance sheet as assets or liabilities measured at fair value. Derivatives could be specifically designated as hedges.

31. Derivatives are financial instruments that derive their value from changes in a benchmark based on stock prices, interest rates, mortgage rates, currency rates, commodity prices, or some other agreed-upon base.

32. SFAS 107 requires entities to disclose the fair value of all (recognized and unrecognized) financial instruments that it is practicable to estimate, including liabilities. Pertinent descriptive information as to the fair value of the instrument is to be disclosed if an estimate of fair value cannot be made without incurring excessive costs.

33. An entity does not have ownership of goods that are in its possession when goods are on **consignment** from another entity or the transaction is a **product financing arrangement.**

34. The LIFO cost flow assumption results in lower net income than FIFO in periods of rising prices. This result is obtained because higher costs are matched with revenue. When prices are declining the opposite result is obtained.

35. The amount of a dollar-value LIFO layer is determined for a manufacturer's inventory by expressing both beginning and ending inventory in base-year costs in terms of total dollars. The difference is the amount of the layer in base-year dollars. An index is calculated by dividing the ending inventory at current-year cost by the ending inventory at base-year cost. Finally, if a layer is added, the layer at base-year prices is extended at the current index.

36. Each period a link (index number for the period) is calculated which is determined by dividing the inventory priced at end-of-year prices by the ending inventory priced at beginning-of-year prices. Next, the current-year index number is multiplied by the cumulative index number to arrive at a new cumulative index number. This index is then used to restate the inventory to base-year cost by dividing the inventory in end-of-year dollars by the cumulative index. From this point, accounting for a decrement or increment is basically the same as the double-extension method.

37. The objective of the lower of cost or market valuation process is to determine the inventory amount (lower of cost or market) which most clearly reflects pe-

riodic income. A departure from the cost basis of pricing the inventory is required when the utility of the goods is no longer as great as its cost. The implementation of lower of cost or market requires that three steps be followed.

a. Determine market—where market is the replacement cost limited to the ceiling (net realizable value) or floor (net realizable value less normal profit)

b. Determine cost

c. Select the lower of cost or market for either an individual item or for the inventory as a whole

38. Under dollar-value retail LIFO the first step is to divide the ending inventory at selling price by a government published index number to arrive at a base retail amount which is compared to the beginning base retail amount. The difference is a layer to be added or a decrement to be removed. A layer added is determined by extending the layer at base-period retail by both the cost-to-retail ratio and the current year government published index number.

39. The three ways of measuring the effect of a LIFO liquidation on net income under IRS tax requirements are

a. The difference between actual costs of sales and what cost of sales would have been had the inventory been reinstated under the entity's normal pricing procedure.

b. The difference between actual costs of sales and what cost of sales would have been had the inventory been reinstated at year-end replacement cost.

c. The amount of the LIFO reserve at the beginning of the year which was credited to income (excluding the increase in the reserve due to current-year price changes).

UNIT I

PUBLISHER-GRADED EXAMINATION

True/False   1. Materiality is defined as the larger of 2% of revenues, 2% of expenses, or 5% of equity.

True/False   2. There are two broad categories of accounting principles: recognition and disclosure.

Multiple-Choice   3. All of the following types of entities must follow Statements issued by the FASB except
   a.   Regulated industries.
   b.   Local governments.
   c.   Not-for-profit organizations.
   d.   SEC registrants.

Multiple-Choice   4. The Emerging Issues Task Force
   a.   Is not recognized by the SEC as an authoritative source of GAAP.
   b.   Issues authoritative pronouncements for narrow issues of immediate interest.
   c.   Is an organization of accounting educators that do research about issues for which divergent accounting practices are developing.
   d.   Meets annually to advise the FASB about items that they should include in their agenda.

Multiple-Choice   5. The weaknesses of a balance sheet include
   a.   The values of certain assets are not recognized.
   b.   Estimates are used to value certain assets.
   c.   Liabilities are not reported using current market interest rates.
   d.   All of the above.

Multiple-Choice   6. The heading of a balance sheet includes all of the following except
   a.   The name of the entity.
   b.   The title of the statement.
   c.   The period for which the balance sheet reports transactions.
   d.   Words that indicate that another basis of accounting is used, if that is the case.

Multiple-Choice   7. All of the following generally are noncurrent assets except
   a.   Trading securities.
   b.   Patents.
   c.   Bond issue costs.
   d.   Equipment used in producing goods for sale.

Multiple-Choice   8. All of the following generally are noncurrent liabilities except
   a.   Capital lease obligations.
   b.   Pension obligations.
   c.   Long-term debt that is callable because a bond covenant has been violated.
   d.   Mortgage payable.

True/False   9. Generally, the amortization of an intangible asset is credited directly to the asset account, and not to a contra asset or valuation account.

Multiple-
Choice   10. Revenue can be recognized before it is realized in which of the following situations
   a. Production of commodities that trade in markets in which the ultimate realization of revenue is assured.
   b. As costs are incurred under the percentage-of-completion method.
   c. Both a. and b.
   d. Neither a. nor b.

Multiple-
Choice   11. All of the following must be reported net of tax **except**
   a. Extraordinary gains and losses.
   b. Discontinued operations.
   c. Adjustments of minimum pension liabilities.
   d. Change in accounting principles.

True/False 12. Extraordinary gains are either unusual in nature or infrequent of occurrence.

True/False 13. Gain on loss on the disposal of a segment includes the income or loss from its activities after the measurement date but before the disposal date.

True/False 14. If the disposal date occurs in the year after the measurement date, an expected gain on the disposal of a segment in the next year can be offset against a loss on the disposal realized in the current year as long as the net amount is zero or a loss (i.e., a net gain cannot be recognized until realized in the next year).

Multiple-
Choice   15. All of the following are examples of start-up costs **except**
   a. Costs of introducing a new product or service.
   b. Costs of conducting business in a new territory.
   c. Policy acquisition costs of an insurance company.
   d. Costs of pursuing a new class of customers.

True/False 16. Restructuring cost liabilities should include the incremental benefits that will be received by employees who will voluntarily terminate if it is probable that they will do so.

True/False 17. Expected gains on the sale of assets to be disposed of should be netted against the liability for exit costs.

Multiple-
Choice   18. Which of the following items would appear in the financing section of a statement of cash flows?
   a. Exercise of the conversion feature of a bond payable.
   b. Incurring a capital lease liability.
   c. Issuing stock in exchange for services rendered.
   d. Exercise of a stock option.

True/False   19. Noncash transactions should be included in the statement of cash flows as if the transaction had been a cash transaction. For example, the purchase of a building by the assumption of long-term debt should be reported as a use of cash for the purchase of a building and a source of cash from issuance of a mortgage note.

Multiple-   20. In a statement of cash flows, the sale of trading securities should be
Choice   shown as a
                    a.   Supplemental disclosure of a noncash item.
                    b.   A cash inflow from operations.
                    c.   A cash inflow from investing activities.
                    d.   A cash inflow from financing activities.

Multiple-   21. An available-for-sale stock with a cost of $2,000 is sold for $15,000
Choice   cash. The following information would be included in a statement of
                    cash flows
                    a.   An investing cash inflow of $15,000.
                    b.   An investing cash inflow of $13,000.
                    c.   A subtractive adjustment to compute cash from operating activi-
                         ties of $13,000.
                    d.   Both a. and c.

Multiple-   22. If the direct method of reporting operating activities is used, all of the
Choice   following classes of cash receipts and payments should be included
                    except
                    a.   Cash collected from customers.
                    b.   Interest and dividends received.
                    c.   Income taxes paid.
                    d.   Proceeds of short-term borrowings.

Multiple-   23. Company A has an investment in Company B that is accounted for
Choice   using the equity method. Company B paid dividends of $4,000 to
                    Company A during the year. Company A's share of Company B's net
                    income was $25,000. The adjustment of net income to arrive at cash
                    flows from operating activities is
                    a. $25,000 decrease.
                    b. $ 4,000 increase.
                    c. $29,000 decrease.
                    d. $21,000 decrease.

Multiple-   24. Which of the following statements about compensating balances is
Choice   true?
                    a.   An entity may be required to maintain a minimum amount of cash
                         on deposit to increase the yield on a loan from the bank.
                    b.   A compensating balance is not available for unrestricted use.
                    c.   If material, a compensating balance should be shown as a separate
                         line item on the balance sheet.
                    d.   All of the above.

Multiple-
Choice

25. If a note is issued in exchange for property, goods, or services and the rate on the note is not reasonable, what value should be used to record the note?
   a. The fair market value of the property, goods, or services.
   b. The market value of the note.
   c. Either a. or b., whichever is more clearly determinable.
   d. None of the above.

Multiple-
Choice

26. Which of the following arrangements is most likely to qualify as a sale under SFAS 140?
   a. Assignment of receivables.
   b. Pledging receivables.
   c. Factoring receivables with recourse.
   d. Factoring receivables without recourse.

Multiple-
Choice

27. Which of the following prevents a transfer from being accounted for as a sale?
   a. A transferee is allowed to pledge or sell assets only on the day that they are purchased.
   b. A transferor's right of first refusal on offers from third parties to purchase financial assets from the transferee.
   c. A requirement to obtain the transferor's approval to sell assets if that approval is not to be unreasonably withheld.
   d. The transferor prohibits sale of the transferred assets to its competitors.

Multiple-
Choice

28. When imputing interest on a note receivable whose interest rate is unreasonable, which rate should be used?
   a. The risk-free rate.
   b. The prime rate.
   c. The market rate for a borrower of similar credit standing under similar terms.
   d. None of the above.

Multiple-
Choice

29. Which of the following conditions must be present if a transfer of financial assets is to be reported as a sale?
   a. The transferred assets are beyond the reach of the transferor, its affiliates, and its creditors, even in bankruptcy proceedings.
   b. The transferee can freely sell or pledge the transferred assets.
   c. The transferor has not agreed to repurchase or redeem the assets before their maturity.
   d. All of the above.

Multiple-
Choice

30. If a transfer is accounted for as a sale, the transferor should do all of the following **except**
   a. Derecognize all assets sold.
   b. Recognize all new assets at their fair value.
   c. Recognize all liabilities incurred at their fair value.
   d. Recognize all retained interests at their fair value.

Multiple-Choice   31. Which of the following is **not** a transfer of financial assets subject to the provisions of SFAS 140?
  a.   Securitizations.
  b.   Transfers of receivables with recourse.
  c.   Repurchase agreements.
  d.   Transfer of an option to purchase commodities that cannot be settled in cash.

Multiple-Choice   32. When accounting for collateral on a loan that is not in default
  a.   The transferor shows the collateral as its asset and the transferee does not recognize the collateral received.
  b.   The transferee reports the collateral at fair value along with an obligation to return it except when it has pledged or sold the collateral.
  c.   The transferor reduces the amount of the loan by the fair value of the collateral transferred.
  d.   The transferee does not recognize the collateral unless it has the right to sell it.

Multiple-Choice   33. SFAS 133 requires
  a.   Standardized accounting for all freestanding derivatives, but those which are embedded in other instruments still are not to be accounted for.
  b.   Standardized accounting for both freestanding and embedded derivatives, but only if these are being used for hedging or other risk management purposes.
  c.   Standardized accounting for all freestanding and embedded derivatives.
  d.   Standardized accounting for freestanding derivatives, but only expanded disclosure regarding derivatives which are embedded in other instruments.

Multiple-Choice   34. Hedging can be any of the following types **except**
  a.   Cash flow.
  b.   Price level.
  c.   Fair value.
  d.   Foreign currency exposure.

Multiple-Choice   35. In order to use hedge accounting as defined by SFAS 133
  a.   The notional amount of the hedge must be within 5% of the actual amount of the underlying obligation.
  b.   The fair value of the hedging instrument must equal that of the underlying obligation at the inception of the hedge.
  c.   The entity must have defined the transaction as a hedge at inception and have a mechanism for measuring effectiveness each reporting period.
  d.   The hedge cannot be associated with investments classified as being held to maturity.

Multiple-
Choice

36. At the end of a year, goods that are in transit between a buyer and a seller are
    a. Carried in the inventory of the buyer.
    b. Carried in the inventory of the seller.
    c. Carried in the inventory of one of the parties based on the terms of sale.
    d. Carried in the inventory of the carrier who was contracted to deliver them.

True/False

37. The LIFO method of inventory valuation originates in US tax literature and is not covered by GAAP literature enforceable under the AICPA Code of Conduct.

Multiple-
Choice

38. Which of the following cost methods **is not** an acceptable method for valuing a LIFO increment?
    a. Actual cost of the goods most recently purchased.
    b. Actual cost of goods purchased during the LIFO base year.
    c. Actual cost of goods purchased in order of acquisition.
    d. Average unit of cost of all goods purchased during the current year.

Multiple-
Choice

39. Which of the following inventory pricing methods is **not** permitted by GAAP?
    a. First in, first out.
    b. Last in, first out.
    c. Latest purchase price.
    d. Weighted-average cost.

True/False

40. For interim reporting purposes, variances from standard costs may be deferred if expected to reverse before the end of the annual period.

GAAP 2002 CPE Course

UNIT I

Record your CPE answers on the answer form provided below and return this page for grading.

Mail to:

GAAP 2002 CPE Director

John Wiley & Sons, Inc., 7222 Commerce Center Drive, Suite 240, Colorado Springs, CO 80919

PAYMENT OPTIONS

☐ **Payment enclosed ($59.00 per Unit).**
(Make checks payable to John Wiley & Sons, Inc.)
Please add appropriate sales tax.
Be sure to sign your order below.

Charge my:

☐ American Express ☐ MasterCard ☐ Visa

Account number _____

Expiration date _____
Please sign below for all credit card orders.

Signature _____

NAME _____

FIRM NAME _____

ADDRESS _____

_____

PHONE ( ) _____

CPA STATE LICENSE # _____

ISBN 0-471-43888-X

SEE THE OTHER SIDE OF THIS PAGE FOR THE CPE FEEDBACK FORM.

UNIT I CPE ANSWERS

1. ___	2. ___	3. ___	4. ___	5. ___	6. ___	7. ___	8. ___	9. ___	10. ___
11. ___	12. ___	13. ___	14. ___	15. ___	16. ___	17. ___	18. ___	19. ___	20. ___
21. ___	22. ___	23. ___	24. ___	25. ___	26. ___	27. ___	28. ___	29. ___	30. ___
31. ___	32. ___	33. ___	34. ___	35. ___	36. ___	37. ___	38. ___	39. ___	40. ___

GAAP 2002 CPE Feedback

1. Were you informed in advance of the

   a. Course objectives? Y N
   b. Requisite experience level? Y N
   c. Course content? Y N
   d. Type and degree of preparation necessary? Y N
   e. Instruction method? Y N
   f. CPE credit hours? Y N

2. Do you agree with the publisher's determination of

   a. Course objectives? Y N
   b. Requisite experience level? Y N

   c. Course content? Y N
   d. Type and degree of preparation necessary? Y N
   e. Instruction method? Y N
   f. CPE credit hours? Y N

3. Was the content relevant? Y N

4. Was the content displayed clearly? Y N

5. Did the course enhance your professional competence? Y N

6. Was the course content timely and effective? Y N

How can we make the course better? If you have any suggestions please summarize them in the space below. We will consider them in developing future courses.

_____

_____

_____

_____

CONTINUING PROFESSIONAL EDUCATION: SELF-STUDY

UNIT II

OBJECTIVES

Chapter 8: Special Revenue Recognition Areas

Studying Chapter 8 should enable you to:

- Understand the unique elements in accounting for long-term construction contracts
- Explain revenue measurement under percentage-of-completion and completed-contract
- Understand the various methods used to measure progress under the percentage-of-completion method
- Explain revenue recognition methods for service sale transactions
- Differentiate between various revenue recognition methods when collection is uncertain
- Understand the criteria that must be met for revenue to be recognized when the buyer has a return right
- Explain the conditions for use of the full accrual method for real estate sales
- Understand the condition for profit recognition on retail land sales
- Understand the adequacy tests for a buyer's initial investment for real estate sale
- Learn about impairment of real estate operations
- Explain the unique conditions that must be met for a franchisor to recognize revenue on sale of a franchise

Read Chapter 8 and answer discussion questions 1 through 10.

Chapter 9: Long-Lived Assets

Studying Chapter 9 should enable you to:

- Determine the cost of fixed assets
- Calculate depreciation, depletion, and amortization
- Account for nonmonetary transactions
- Describe and record impairment
- Understand capitalization of interest
- Account for intangible assets and research and development costs

Read Chapter 9 and answer discussion questions 11 through 19.

Chapter 10: Investments

Studying Chapter 10 should enable you to:

- Understand accounting for marketable equity securities held as passive investments
- Understand accounting for debt securities held as investments

- Account for investments in common stock in which the investor has significant influence over the investee company
- Understand the difference between permanent impairments of investments and temporary declines in value
- Account for transfers of investments between portfolios
- Understand the deferred tax implications of investments in debt and equity securities
- Apply the equity method of accounting for intercorporate investments

Read Chapter 10 and answer discussion questions 20 through 26.

Chapter 11: Business Combinations and Consolidated Financial Statements

Studying Chapter 11 should enable you to:

- Understand and apply the differences between pooling of interest and purchase accounting for business combinations
- Allocate the purchase price of business acquisitions among tangible and intangible assets and liabilities, including goodwill and negative goodwill
- Understand and account for minority interests in business combinations
- Understand the circumstances when consolidated financial statements will be required
- Account for changes in ownership after initial acquisition of a subsidiary
- Account for contingent consideration paid in a business combination
- Understand the accounting for preacquisition contingencies
- Prepare combined financial statements

Read Chapter 11 and answer discussion questions 27 through 33.

DISCUSSION QUESTIONS

1. What are the two methods for recognition of revenue for long-term construction contracts?

2. What are the four types of pricing arrangements typical for long-term contracts?

3. How is progress toward completion usually measured under the percentage-of-completion method?

4. What conditions must be met for the recognition of contract revenue for claims?

5. What are the methods commonly used to measure performance for service sales transactions?

6. Under what circumstances should the installment method of revenue recognition be used?

7. Discuss the conditions for recognizing revenue when a customer may return the purchase.

8. Discuss the conditions for consummation of a sale for other than retail land sales of real estate.

9. What methods of income recognition should be used when the full accrual method of nonretail sales of real estate is not appropriate?

10. Discuss the accounting for amenities in connection with real estate operations.

11. GAAP regarding long-lived assets involves what primary determinations?

12. What is the basic requirement regarding asset impairment per SFAS 121?

13. What costs are recorded as part of the cost of fixed assets?

14. What are the basic requirements that must result from the method of depreciation chosen?

15. Identify the three types of nonmonetary transactions.

16. What is the general rule established by APB 29?

17. Recoverability of long-lived assets should be assessed under what circumstances?

18. In general terms, what portion of interest should be capitalized?

19. When intangible assets are purchased, what should their cost be?

20. What are the three categories of investments defined by SFAS 115, and what types of securities can be classified in each of these?

21. How does the accounting for available-for-sale securities differ from those classified as held-to-maturity?

22. What is the reason for reporting unrealized gains and losses on available-for-sale securities in the equity section of the balance sheet?

23. Are market declines in available-for-sale or held-to-maturity securities never reflected in earnings prior to the disposition of the investment?

24. Can an entity transfer securities between the portfolios, and if so, what would be the accounting implications?

25. How are impairments to the value of investments which occur after the balance sheet date to be accounted for?

26. Why is the equity method sometimes called "one-line consolidation"?

27. To be consistent with the concept underlying pooling-of-interests accounting, what would have to be true about the ownership interests in the companies participating in the pooling transaction?

28. In what situations will consolidated financial statements be required?

29. What is goodwill and what is "negative goodwill"?

30. What are preacquisition contingencies and how are they accounted for?

31. In a purchase business combination the price is paid in stock, with additional shares to be issued if the market price declines within one year. If the extra shares are issued, does the purchase price have to be adjusted?

32. If additional shares are given after a purchase business combination due to an "earn out" provision being met, will there be an adjustment of the purchase price?

33. Can a pooling be effected by means of a swap of common stock for preferred stock?

ANSWERS TO DISCUSSION QUESTIONS

1. The two methods are percentage-of-completion and completed-contract.

2. The four types of pricing are: (a) fixed price, (b) time and materials, (c) cost type, and (d) unit price.

3. Progress toward completion is usually measured by the cost-to-cost method, efforts expanded method, units of delivery method, or units of work method.

4. For claim revenue to be recognized
   a. The contract must provide a legal basis for the claim (or a legal opinion has been obtained).
   b. Additional costs were caused by unforeseen circumstances.
   c. Costs are identified.
   d. Evidence in support of the claim is objective and verifiable.

5. The methods commonly used to measure performance on service sale transactions are the specific performance method, the proportional performance method, the completed performance method, and the collection method.

6. The installment method of revenue recognition should be used when the length of the contract payment period or other such condition does not permit reliable estimation of uncollectibles.

7. When the right of return exists, recognition of revenue at the time of sale can only be met if
   a. The sale price is fixed or determinable.
   b. The buyer has paid or is obligated to pay.
   c. The buyer's obligation is unchanged by condition or theft of the product.
   d. The buyer has separate economic substance from the seller.
   e. The seller is not obligated to perform substantial future service.
   f. The amount of future returns can be reasonably estimated.

8. The conditions for a sale on real estate are met when the parties are bound by a contract, all consideration has been exchanged, permanent financing has been arranged, and all precedent conditions have been performed.

9. The methods of income recognition when the full accrual method cannot be used are
   a. Deposit.
   b. Cost recovery.
   c. Installment.
   d. Reduced profit.
   e. Percentage-of-completion methods.

10. Amenities that are to be sold, transferred, or retained should have all costs in excess of fair value charged as common costs, with the fair value treated as the asset.

11. GAAP regarding long-lived assets involves the determination of the appropriate cost at which to record the asset, the appropriate method to be used to allocate that cost over the periods benefiting, the measurement of impairment losses, and the accounting for assets to be disposed of.

12. SFAS 121 requires long-lived assets and certain identifiable intangible assets and any goodwill related to those assets to be reviewed for impairment whenever circumstances and situations change such that there is an indication that the carrying amount may not be recoverable.

13. All costs required to bring the asset into operating condition are recorded as part of the cost of the fixed assets. Examples include sales taxes, finders' fees, freight costs, installation costs, break-in costs, and set-up costs. Thus, any reasonable cost involved in bringing the asset to the buyer and incurred prior to using the asset in actual production is capitalized.

14. The method of depreciation chosen must result in the systematic and rational allocation of the cost of the asset (less its residual value) over the asset's expected useful life.

15. APB 29 governs the accounting for nonmonetary transactions. It identifies the following three types of nonmonetary transactions:
   a. Nonreciprocal transfers with owners
   b. Nonreciprocal transfers with other than owners
   c. Nonmonetary exchanges

16. The general rule established by APB 29 is that the accounting for nonmonetary transactions should be based on the fair values of the assets involved. The fair value to be used is that of the asset surrendered unless the fair value of the asset received is "more clearly evident."

17. Recoverability under SFAS 121 should be assessed under the following circumstances (among others):
    a. The asset market value decreases significantly
    b. The use of the asset is significantly changed in extent or manner
    c. Legal factors or business climate changes adversely affect asset value
    d. Regulator's adverse assessment or action
    e. Original expected costs are significantly exceeded
    f. A history of cash flow losses and continued asset losses are forecasted

18. The amount of interest to be capitalized is that portion which could have been avoided if the qualifying asset had not been acquired.

19. When intangible assets are purchased, their cost should be the cash or fair market value disbursed or the present value of the liability assumed in conjunction with the exchange. This amount represents the potential earning power of the intangible asset as of the date of its acquisition.

20. The three categories, or portfolios, of investments are trading, available-for-sale, and held-to-maturity. Marketable equity can be categorized in the first two portfolios only, while investments in debt securities may be in any of the three portfolios.

21. Available-for-sale securities are reported at fair market value, with unrealized gains or losses included in the equity section of the balance sheet; held-to-maturity investments are reported at amortized historical cost.

22. Reporting unrealized gains or losses in equity is done to avoid having periodic earnings affected by price changes which are, over the long run, expected to largely offset or net out. However, since fair value is used to report the asset, it was necessary (due to the double entry nature of accounting) to report these unrealized gains or losses in the financials, and the solution was to create a new contra equity or additional equity account entitled "accumulated other comprehensive income" for them.

23. "Other than temporary" declines in value must be reported in earnings in all instances. Once such a decline is recorded, the adjusted carrying amount is the new cost basis and any increases in value would be disclosed in the manner prescribed for the portfolio in question: as additional equity if the change in value affects available-for-sale securities; or as a footnote disclosure if it affects held-to-maturity investments.

24. Transfers are permitted when management intent changes, although transfers from the held-to-maturity category are expected to be rare, since such transfers call into question management's originally stated intentions and might preclude classifying future investments in debt securities as being held-to-maturity. Transfers between portfolios are to be accounted for similarly to arm's-length transactions between unrelated parties.

25. If the decline in value occurred after the balance sheet date but before the financial statements are issued, it would be disclosed if material, but would not be recorded since it was truly a "subsequent event." If, however, a "confirming event" revealed that the investment was impaired as of the balance sheet date, the decline in value would be formally recorded and reported in earnings for the period.

26. The equity method is similar to consolidation since the impact on the reporting entity's net income and net worth will be identical to what it would have been had full consolidation been effected. However, instead of reporting the investor's share of each revenue and expense item, the investor's share of the net income of the investee is reported in a single line (with certain limited exceptions).

27. Poolings of interests are based on continuity of ownership after the combination has occurred. The same group of shareholders that controlled the combining entities must survive as owners after the combination. They must also maintain their relative ownership interests. Originally, it was thought that the entities would have to be roughly the same in size so that neither would dominate the combined enterprise, but this has long been ignored and is **not** endorsed as a criterion in APB 16.

28. Under current rules, consolidated financial statements will be required if one entity owns over 50% of another, unless control is temporary or control is absent. The former "nonhomogeneity" exceptions no longer apply.

29. Goodwill is the excess of the price paid in a purchase business combination over the fair value of the net identifiable assets acquired. Negative goodwill is the excess of the fair value of the net identifiable assets acquired over the cost.

30. Preacquisition contingencies are uncertainties existing at the date of the purchase acquisition. If resolved within one year the purchase price is reallocated; if after one year, these are accounted for as current period events.

31. No. Contingencies based on market value of shares given in a purchase business combination do not result in adjustment of the purchase price if more shares have to be issued pursuant to the terms of the agreement.

32. Yes. The additional consideration will be considered part of the purchase cost; allocation to assets acquired may need to be adjusted.

33. Poolings require that only voting common stock be given in exchange for voting common stock of the other entity.

UNIT II

PUBLISHER-GRADED EXAMINATION

True/False   1.   Under the matching concept, amounts should be billed on contracts in progress in the period that the related costs are incurred.

True/False   2.   Construction-in-progress is not recognized as an asset on the financial statements of a contractor.

True/False   3.   If installment sales are incidental to the company, the realized gross profit from such sales is permitted to be shown as a single line item on the income statement.

True/False   4.   Under the cost recovery method, income is recognized pro rata as each dollar of cost is recovered.

Multiple-Choice   5.   Profit from real estate sales may be recognized in full when
   a.   A sale is consummated and the seller's receivable is not subject to future subordination.
   b.   The buyer's initial and continuing investments are adequate to demonstrate a commitment to pay for the property.
   c.   The seller has transferred to the buyer the risks and rewards of ownership, the transaction is, in substance, a sale, and the seller does not have substantial continuing involvement in the property.
   d.   All of the above.

True/False   6.   In accounting for sales of real estate, there are different percentage criteria that range from 5% to 25%, depending on the type of property sold, that are to be applied to judge the sufficiency of the minimum initial investment.

True/False   7.   Initial franchise fees and continuing franchise fees are always recognized as revenue by a franchisor based on the prices charged to the franchisees for the respective services.

True/False   8.   Preacquisition costs relative to operating real estate properties are analogous to start-up costs and are to be expensed as incurred.

True/False   9.   Under the installment method of revenue recognition, in a period in which no collections are made, there is no revenue recognized.

Multiple-Choice   10.   Which of the following is not an acceptable method of revenue recognition for a service transaction?
   a.   Specific performance method.
   b.   Partial performance method.
   c.   Collection method.
   d.   Completed performance method.

Multiple-Choice   11. According to GAAP, when an obligation is incurred to remove, reclaim, restore, or clean up property when a long-lived asset is taken out of service, that obligation
   a. Must be ratably accrued over the projected service life of the asset.
   b. Must be recorded when incurred, with adjustments as needed in subsequent periods.
   c. Is not reflected in the financial statements in most cases, since it is contingent on future events.
   d. Is a disclosure item, unless deemed to be remote in terms of likelihood.

Multiple-Choice   12. When an asset retirement obligation recorded in an earlier period is found to have been lessened due to changed conditions
   a. The reduction is accreted over the remaining estimated life of the asset.
   b. No recognition is given to the change in estimate, since it is a gain contingency which GAAP does not permit recognition of.
   c. The reduction, appropriately measured, is reflected immediately in earnings.
   d. It is ignored since, once recognized, asset retirement obligations are not to be remeasured for any reason.

Multiple-Choice   13. In computing the amount of asset retirement obligation to be recognized, the labor cost component of future clean-up costs should be based on
   a. Outside labor, even if the intent is to use the labor of staff employed at lesser cost than would be paid to outsiders.
   b. Whatever labor source is intended to be used, external or internal.
   c. Outside labor, unless, based on past behavior of the reporting entity, it can be shown that use of internal staff is at least probable.
   d. Labor costs as reported by government statistical data sources.

True/False   14. APB 29 prohibits recognition of gain on nonreciprocal transfers.

True/False   15. Interest should be capitalized on self-constructed assets, even if the company's outstanding borrowings are not collateralized by the constructed assets.

Multiple-Choice   16. Under the provisions of SFAS 142
   a. Intangible assets are no longer amortized, but must be tested annually for impairment.
   b. All intangible assets other than goodwill are amortized over no longer than twenty years.
   c. All intangible assets other than goodwill are amortized over no longer than forty years.
   d. None of the above are correct.

Multiple-   17. Which of the following is **not** considered to be an intangible asset?
Choice   a.   Organizational costs.
                   b.   Goodwill.
                   c.   Leasehold improvements.
                   d.   Patents.

True/False   18. A leasehold improvement made to a property with two years remaining on its lease is required to be amortized over that two-year period, even if the useful life of the improvement is more than two years.

True/False   19. Due to widely publicized abuses by large companies, purchased in-process research and development costs are now required to be capitalized and amortized over the same life as the goodwill related to the acquisition.

True/False   20. Costs incurred to operate a website, including training, administration, and maintenance, are to be capitalized during the site's start-up period.

Multiple-   21. Under the provisions of SFAS 142
Choice   a.   Goodwill is amortized over no longer than twenty years, unless it can be demonstrated that it has an indefinite life.
                   b.   Goodwill is tested for impairment when conditions indicate that an impairment may have occurred, but otherwise remains at its original cost.
                   c.   Goodwill is assumed to have indefinite life, and goodwill internally generated after a business combination can under some conditions be permitted to replace expired purchased goodwill on the balance sheet.
                   d.   Goodwill is tested for impairment regularly, in a way that assures that only the value of the purchased goodwill—and not any internally developed goodwill—can be placed on the balance sheet.

True/False   22. Having significant influence over another entity necessitates accounting for equity investments in the entity on a fair value basis.

True/False   23. Fair value information on passive investments must be provided for trading and available-for-sale securities; since held-to-maturity securities are accounted for at amortized cost, fair value information is not relevant.

Multiple-   24. The distinction between significant influence and control is that
Choice   a.   With significant influence, use of the equity method is always necessary, but with control, consolidation is optional.
                   b.   With significant influence, consolidation is optional, but with control, consolidation is always required.
                   c.   With significant influence, use of the equity method is presumed to be necessary, but with control, consolidation is always required unless temporary.
                   d.   With significant influence, use of the equity method is always necessary, but with control, consolidation is inappropriate unless majority ownership is also held.

| True/False | 25. | Transfers from the held-to-maturity to the available-for-sale portfolio of debt securities are made at amortized historical cost, with any changes in fair value from that date forward reflected in the contra or additional equity account. |

| True/False | 26. | Transfers of debt or equity securities from the available-for-sale portfolio to the trading portfolio results in immediate income statement recognition of unrealized gains or losses previously reported in the equity section. |

Multiple-Choice 27. When securities in the held-to-maturity portfolio are sold, this will
   a. Make it impossible to categorize any later securities acquisitions as being for the held-to-maturity portfolio.
   b. Make it very difficult, but not impossible, to categorize later securities as held-to-maturity.
   c. Necessitate marking all other securities in the portfolio to fair value and taking the gains and losses into earnings immediately.
   d. Necessitate marking all other securities in the portfolio to fair value and taking the grains and losses into other comprehensive income immediately.

True/False 28. Application of SFAS 115 to trading or available-for-sale securities will give rise to deferred tax assets or liabilities.

True/False 29. Equity method accounting is not required when the investee is not in an industry which is homogeneous with the investor's industry.

True/False 30. The amount of deferred tax to be provided on temporary differences arising in connection with equity method investments depends upon management's expectations regarding how the income will be realized.

True/False 31. Deferred taxes recorded in connection with unrealized gain or loss on securities which are classified as available-for-sale are reported in the income statement.

True/False 32. Mergers of entities under common control at the time of the transaction cannot be accounted for as purchases even if cash is paid.

True/False 33. While nonreciprocal transactions with shareholders are normally accounted for at fair value, in the case of spinoffs of major portions of a business entity to its shareholders the accounting should be based on book value, not fair value.

Multiple-Choice 34. Under the provisions of SFAS 141
   a. All business combinations will be accounted for as poolings of interest.
   b. All business combinations will be accounted for as purchases, unless among entities under common control.
   c. All combinations of businesses under common control will be accounted for as purchases.
   d. Business combinations will be accounted for as purchases, unless goodwill is involved, in which case they will be treated as poolings.

Multiple-
Choice

35. Under the provisions of SFAS 141 and 142
   a. When business combinations accounted for as purchases give rise to goodwill, amortization expense is to be presented net of taxes "below the line" (i.e., after operating income).
   b. When business combinations accounted for as purchases give rise to goodwill, amortization must be set forth separately within operating expenses.
   c. When business combinations accounted for as purchases give rise to goodwill, impairment is recognized in other comprehensive income rather than in the income statement.
   d. When business combinations accounted for as purchases give rise to goodwill, any impairment must be reported in the income statement as a separate caption within operating costs.

Multiple-
Choice

36. Under SFAS 142, impairment testing of goodwill is accomplished by applying a(n)
   a. Fair value approach.
   b. Entity-wide value assessment.
   c. Individual asset approach.
   d. Pooled asset approach.

Multiple-
Choice

37. Under SFAS 141, pooling
   a. Can only be used when all twelve of the highly restrictive criteria are met.
   b. Can only be used when the five newly established criteria are all met.
   c. Can only be employed to account for combinations of entities under common control.
   d. Cannot be used under any circumstances.

Multiple-
Choice

38. According to the new standards SFAS 141 and 142, goodwill is the
   a. Excess of the consideration paid in a purchase business combination over the underlying net assets' book values.
   b. Excess of the consideration paid in a business combination over the underlying net assets' fair values.
   c. Excess of the consideration paid in a business combination over the replacement cost of the identifiable tangible net assets acquired.
   d. Excess of the consideration paid in a business combination over the replacement cost of the identifiable tangible and intangible net assets acquired.

Multiple-
Choice

39. In a business combination accounted for as a purchase
   a. The allocation of purchase cost must be completed at the time of the transaction, with any later adjustments being reflected directly in stockholders' equity.
   b. The allocation of purchase cost must be completed at the time of the transaction, with any later adjustments being reflected in earnings.
   c. The allocation of purchase cost is made at the time of the transaction, with adjustments being made, if necessary, only until the end of the fiscal year in which the purchase occurs.
   d. The allocation of purchase cost is made at the time of the transaction, with adjustments being possible up to one year after the transaction.

Multiple-
Choice

40. Under SFAS 141, "bargain purchase" transactions
   a. Are no longer recognized.
   b. May still be recognized, but "negative goodwill" will no longer be given balance sheet recognition.
   c. Will be accounted for as poolings of interest only.
   d. None of the above.

GAAP 2002 CPE Course

UNIT II

Record your CPE answers on the answer form provided below and return this page for grading.

Mail to:

GAAP 2002 CPE Director

John Wiley & Sons, Inc., 7222 Commerce Center Drive, Suite 240, Colorado Springs, CO 80919

PAYMENT OPTIONS

☐ **Payment enclosed ($59.00 per Unit).**
(Make checks payable to John Wiley & Sons, Inc.)
Please add appropriate sales tax.
Be sure to sign your order below.

Charge my:

☐ American Express ☐ MasterCard ☐ Visa

Account number _____

Expiration date _____
Please sign below for all credit card orders.

Signature _____

NAME _____

FIRM NAME _____

ADDRESS _____

PHONE ( ) _____

CPA STATE LICENSE # _____

ISBN 0-471-43889-8

SEE THE OTHER SIDE OF THIS PAGE FOR THE CPE FEEDBACK FORM.

UNIT II CPE ANSWERS

1. ___	2. ___	3. ___	4. ___	5. ___	6. ___	7. ___	8. ___	9. ___	10. ___
11. ___	12. ___	13. ___	14. ___	15. ___	16. ___	17. ___	18. ___	19. ___	20. ___
21. ___	22. ___	23. ___	24. ___	25. ___	26. ___	27. ___	28. ___	29. ___	30. ___
31. ___	32. ___	33. ___	34. ___	35. ___	36. ___	37. ___	38. ___	39. ___	40. ___

GAAP 2002 CPE Feedback

1. Were you informed in advance of the

    a. Course objectives? **Y N**

    b. Requisite experience level? **Y N**

    c. Course content? **Y N**

    d. Type and degree of preparation necessary? **Y N**

    e. Instruction method? **Y N**

    f. CPE credit hours? **Y N**

    c. Course content? **Y N**

    d. Type and degree of preparation necessary? **Y N**

    e. Instruction method? **Y N**

    f. CPE credit hours? **Y N**

2. Do you agree with the publisher's determination of

    a. Course objectives? **Y N**

    b. Requisite experience level? **Y N**

3. Was the content relevant? **Y N**

4. Was the content displayed clearly? **Y N**

5. Did the course enhance your professional competence? **Y N**

6. Was the course content timely and effective? **Y N**

How can we make the course better? If you have any suggestions please summarize them in the space below. We will consider them in developing future courses.

_____

_____

_____

_____

CONTINUING PROFESSIONAL EDUCATION: SELF-STUDY

UNIT III

OBJECTIVES

Chapter 12: Current Liabilities and Contingencies

Studying Chapter 12 should enable you to:

- Record current liabilities
- Describe the accounting for due-on-demand obligations
- Account for short-term obligations expected to be refinanced
- Explain the accounting for compensated absences
- Describe, record, and disclose contingencies

Read Chapter 12 and answer discussion questions 1 through 9.

Chapter 13: Long-Term Debt

Studying Chapter 13 should enable you to:

- Record long-term debt
- Account for notes payable
- Amortize bond premiums and discounts
- Account for the extinguishment of debt
- Understand the requirements of SFAS 140 regarding extinguishment of liabilities
- Account for troubled debt restructurings
- Understand convertible debt issues

Read Chapter 13 and answer discussion questions 10 through 20.

Chapter 14: Leases

Studying Chapter 14 should enable you to:

- Know the definitions of terms used in accounting for leases
- Classify a lessee's lease as a capital lease or an operating lease using the four criteria specified in SFAS 13
- Classify a lessor's lease as operating or as a sales-type, direct financing, or leveraged lease using the same four criteria applicable to lessees and the two criteria applicable only to lessors
- Distinguish between sales-type and direct financing leases
- Account for each type of lessee's and lessor's lease that contains varying provisions
- Account for sale-leaseback transactions
- Account for leases involving real estate

Read Chapter 14 and answer discussion questions 21 through 30.

Chapter 15: Income Taxes

Studying Chapter 15 should enable you to:

- Understand the differences between the liability and deferred approaches to deferred tax accounting
- Understand the concept of temporary differences
- Determine the deferred tax assets and liabilities to be recorded by a company which has temporary differences
- Compute the allowance to be provided for deferred tax benefits which are not more likely than not to be realized
- Determine the allocation of income tax expense among captions on the income statement (intraperiod allocation)
- Understand the accounting for operating loss carryforwards
- Understand the exceptions to the deferred tax provisions required under GAAP

Read Chapter 15 and answer discussion questions 31 through 40.

DISCUSSION QUESTIONS

1. Define current liabilities.

2. How should the current maturing portion of long-term debt be classified on the balance sheet?

3. What principal pronouncement governs the accounting for short-term obligations expected to be refinanced?

4. SFAS 5 states that a loss contingency must be accrued if what two conditions are met?

5. SFAS 43 states an employer must accrue a liability for employees' compensation of future absences if what conditions are met?

6. What is the proper valuation of long-term debt?

7. When the rate on a note is **not** considered fair, how should the note be recorded according to APB 21?

8. What is the preferred method of accounting for a discount or premium arising from a note or bond?

9. What costs may be incurred in connection with issuing bonds and how are they accounted for?

10. What SFAS will provide the accounting and reporting standard for extinguishments of liabilities after December 31, 1996?

11. What is the exception to the general rule that all gains and losses from extinguishment, if material in amount, receive extraordinary item treatment?

12. In what two ways can a troubled debt restructuring occur?

13. When convertible debt is issued, what value is apportioned to the conversion feature?

14. Under SFAS 84, what is the accounting specified for an induced conversion of debt to equity?

15. Define minimum lease payments.

16. What are the differences between sales-type and direct financing leases?

17. Describe the accounting treatment in cases where the fair value of the property exceeds the present value of the property's minimum lease payments at the inception of the lease.

18. Over what period of time should a leased asset be amortized (depreciated)?

19. How should lessors and lessees account for rental payments that are specified in a lease on other than a straight-line basis?

20. Describe the lessor's accounting for initial direct costs in an operating lease.

21. Describe the lessor's accounting for initial direct costs in a direct financing lease.

22. How should lessees account for guaranteed residual values in a capital lease?

23. How does the seller-lessee account for a gain in a sale-leaseback transaction in which substantially all of the risks and rewards of ownership are retained by the seller-lessee?

24. How does the seller-lessee account for a loss in a sale-leaseback transaction in a case in which the sales price of the property is less than the book value and the fair market is greater than the book value?

25. What kind of continuing involvement indicates that a sale-leaseback of real estate transaction is a normal leaseback and, thus, sale-leaseback accounting treatment is appropriate?

26. What is the objective of the liability method of deferred tax accounting?

27. What are temporary differences?

28. How are the tax effects of temporary differences in the bases of assets acquired in purchase business combinations to be accounted for?

29. In measuring the tax effect of temporary differences, what tax rates should be utilized?

30. How is the valuation allowance for deferred tax assets determined?

31. How is the effect of changing tax rates on previously provided deferred tax assets and liabilities reported, and in what period?

32. What tax rates should be used to provide deferred taxes on undistributed earnings of equity method investees?

33. The "indefinite reversal" criterion of APB 23 was used to avoid the provision of deferred taxes on undistributed earnings of subsidiaries. Can this still be done, or must deferred taxes be provided?

34. How should income taxes be allocated among income from continuing operations, income from discontinued operations, extraordinary items and the cumulative effect of change in accounting principles?

ANSWERS TO DISCUSSION QUESTIONS

1. ARB 43, Chapter 3 defines current liabilities as those enterprise obligations whose liquidation is reasonably expected to require the use of existing resources properly classifiable as current assets or the creation of other current liabilities.

2. Currently maturing portion of long-term debt is shown as a current liability if the obligation is to be liquidated by using assets classified as current. However, if the currently maturing debt is to be liquidated by using other than current assets (i.e., by using a sinking fund which is properly classified as an investment) then these obligations should be classified as long-term liabilities.

3. SFAS 6 specifies when it is acceptable to reclassify a currently maturing debt to a long-term liability. Either post-balance-sheet financing or both management's intent and ability to refinance as demonstrated in an agreement that extends due date of the currently maturing debt beyond one year are required.

4. SFAS 5 states that a loss must be accrued if both of the following conditions are met:

    a. It is probable that an asset has been impaired or a liability has been incurred at the date of the financial statements.
    b. The amount of loss can be reasonably estimated.

5. SFAS 43 states that an employer must accrue a liability for employees' compensation of future absences if all of the following conditions are met:

    a. The employee's right to receive compensation for future absences is attributable to employee services already rendered.
    b. The right vests or accumulates.
    c. Payment of the compensation is probable.
    d. The amount of the payment can be reasonably estimated.

6. The proper valuation of long-term debt is the present value of future payments using the market rate of interest, either stated or implied in the transaction, at the date the debt was incurred. An exception to the use of the market rate of

interest stated or implied in the transaction in valuing long-term notes occurs when it is necessary to use an imputed interest rate (APB 21).

7. According to APB 21, when the rate on the note is **not** considered fair, the note is to be recorded at the "fair market value of the property, goods, or services received or at an amount that reasonably approximates the market value of the note, whichever is the more clearly determinable." When this amount differs from the face value of the note, the difference is to be recorded as a discount or premium and amortized to interest expense.

8. The effective interest method is the preferred method of accounting for a discount or premium arising from a note or bond, although some other method may be used (e.g., straight-line) if the results are not materially different.

9. Costs may be incurred in connection with issuing bonds. Examples include legal, accounting, and underwriting fees; commissions; and engraving, printing, and registration costs. Although these costs should be classified as a deferred charge and amortized using the effective interest method, generally the amount involved is such that use of the simpler straight-line method would not result in a material difference.

10. SFAS 140 provides accounting and reporting standards for extinguishments of liabilities.

11. Except for any gains and losses resulting from satisfying sinking fund requirements within one year of the date of the extinguishment (SFAS 64), all gains and losses from extinguishment, if material in amount, receive extraordinary item treatment (SFAS 4).

12. A troubled debt restructuring can occur one of two ways. The first is a settlement of the debt at less than the carrying amount. The second is a continuation of the debt with a modification of terms (i.e., a reduction in the interest rate, face amount, accrued interest owed, or an extension of the payment date for interest or face amount).

13. When convertible debt is issued, no value is apportioned to the conversion feature when recording the issue (APB 14). The debt is treated as nonconvertible debt.

14. Upon conversion, the debtor must recognize, under SFAS 84, an expense for the excess of the fair value of all the securities and other consideration given over the fair value of the securities specified in the original conversion terms. The reported expense should not be classified as an extraordinary item.

15. Minimum lease payments are the payments that the lessor/lessee is or can be required to make in connection with leased property. Minimum lease payments include:

a. Rent payments.
b. Bargain purchase options over the lease term.
c. Guarantee of residual value.
d. Failure to renew or extend penalties.

16. Sales-type leases occur when the lessor recognizes a profit or loss on the transaction in addition to interest revenue. This occurs when the fair value of the property differs from the carrying value. On the other hand, direct financing leases only have interest revenue to recognize in the transaction as profit or loss due to the cost of the item being the same as the fair value.

17. When the fair value of the property exceeds the present value of the minimum lease payments at the inception of the lease, the lease is classified as a sales-type lease. The present value of the property is booked as sales revenue and the excess of fair value over the present value (carrying amount) will be booked as unearned interest at the inception of the lease. Unearned interest will be amortized into income using the effective interest method, resulting in a constant periodic rate of return on the net investment. The journal entry to record the inception of the lease follows:

Lease Receivable	xxx	
Sales		xxx
Unearned Interest	xxx	
Cost of Goods Sold	xxx	
Inventory		xxx

18. The lessee will amortize (depreciate) the leased asset over the lease term unless title transfers or a bargain purchase option exists, in which case the lease is amortized (depreciated) over the useful life of the asset. The amortization (depreciation) method used should be consistent with the lessee's normal depreciation policy.

19. Generally, the total cash flows over the life of the lease should be recognized on a straight-line basis over the life of the lease. An alternative basis which is systematic and rational and is more representative of the time pattern of physical usage of the lease property may be used by lessors and lessees.

20. The lessor will amortize initial direct leasing costs over the lease term as the revenue is recognized for operating leases (usually straight-line).

21. The lessor will amortize the initial direct leasing costs over the lease term so that a constant periodic rate is earned on the net investment. The effect of the amortization is to reduce the implicit interest rate (yield) to the lessor over the life of the lease.

22. The guaranteed residual value is included in the minimum lease payments to reduce the periodic payments in cases where the property is to revert back to the lessor.

23. A gain on the sale of property in a sale-leaseback transaction is deferred by the lessee and amortized over the life of the asset at the same rate that the asset is being depreciated.

24. Such losses are termed artificial. A real loss would occur only if the fair market value were less than book value. Artificial losses shall be deferred and amortized as additional depreciation.

25. Active use of property in the seller-lessee's trade or business represents continuing involvement that does not preclude the use of sale-leaseback accounting.

26. The liability method has as its primary objective the presentation on the balance sheet of the best estimate of the amount of future tax benefits or the liability for future income taxes to be paid by the reporting entity. This is in contrast with the deferred method which was utilized by the earlier GAAP, APB 11, under which the principal goal was the matching of periodic revenue and expense on the income statement, with little concern about whether the deferred tax assets or liabilities represented actual claims or obligations.

27. Temporary differences include all differences between the tax and book bases of assets and liabilities; this definition includes timing differences as defined under prior GAAP, but also includes other differences.

28. Tax effects of differences in the bases of assets acquired in purchase business combinations are reflected as deferred tax assets or liabilities, and the assets acquired are "grossed up" for these differences in the purchase price allocation process. The formerly prescribed "net of tax" method is no longer acceptable.

29. Since deferred tax assets and liabilities should represent the amounts of benefits to be received or obligations to be settled when the temporary differences reverse, the tax rates expected to be effective at those times should be used, based on current law (not rumored tax rate cuts, for example).

30. The purpose of the valuation allowance is to reduce the net deferred tax asset to the amount which is "more likely than not" to be realized. This must be assessed at each financial statement date.

31. The effect of changing tax rates on previously provided deferred tax assets and liabilities must be reported as part of the current year deferred tax provision allocated to income from continuing operations, even if the deferred tax asset or obligation relates to items which did not affect income from continuing operations.

32. The tax rates to employ are dependent upon the method by which the enterprise intends to realize the earnings, as ordinary income or as capital gains, for example. This expectation may change from one period to the next.

33. SFAS 109 has eliminated the "indefinite reversal" exception to comprehensive interperiod income tax allocation. However, existing temporary differences for which deferred taxes were not provided under the indefinite reversal criteria prior to 1993 are exempt. Deferred taxes must be provided on all differences arising after that date.

34. Intraperiod tax allocation should be determined by a "with and without" approach, which means that tax on total income is compared to tax on income from continuing operations, with the marginal amount allocated to all categories other than continuing operations. Generally, the effective rate of the marginal items is applied to all such items, unless it is clear that some specific portion of the marginal tax provision belongs to one or another item.

UNIT III

PUBLISHER-GRADED EXAMINATION

True/False   1. Short-term obligations may be classified as noncurrent if the enterprise intends to refinance the obligation, and after the balance sheet date but before the balance sheet is issued the enterprise issues long-term obligations to refinance it.

Multiple-Choice   2. Which of the following are **not** compensated absences for which accrual is necessary?
    a. Vested vacation pay.
    b. Personal days that would be paid if the employee terminated.
    c. Paid sick days that accumulate but do not vest.
    d. Paid holidays if the right to payment is based on past service.

Multiple-Choice   3. Postemployment benefits other than pensions are accrued if
    a. The four conditions in SFAS 43 are met.
    b. The conditions in SFAS 43 are not met, but the conditions in SFAS 5 are met.
    c. Either a. or b.
    d. Postemployment benefits are not accrued until employees are terminated.

True/False   4. The effect of a fire that damages production facilities should be accrued as of the balance sheet date if the effect is material and the fire occurs after the balance sheet date but before the issuance of the balance sheet.

True/False   5. In general, an otherwise long-term debt should be classified as a current liability if a debtor has violated a debt covenant causing the debt to be callable by the lender.

True/False   6. Fair value amounts recognized for multiple swap, forward, option, and other unconditional or exchange contracts with a single party can be offset if the contracts were executed under a master netting agreement.

True/False   7. An entity that enters into a multiple-year retrospectively rated contract with an insurance company should recognize a liability to the extent that it has an obligation to pay additional cash as a result of the experience under the policy.

Multiple-Choice   8. If the estimated loss from a contingent event is within a range, the amount to be recognized as a liability is
    a. The top of the range.
    b. The average of the bottom and top of the range.
    c. The bottom of the range.
    d. None of the above are correct.

Multiple-Choice

9. Contingent liabilities are recognized if the amount of the liability can be reasonably measured and
   a. It is probable that a loss has been incurred.
   b. It is reasonably possible that a loss has been incurred.
   c. It is either probable or reasonably possible that a loss has been incurred.
   d. Contingent liabilities are disclosed, not formally recorded in the accounts.

Multiple-Choice

10. If reclassification of a short-term obligation as long term is based upon the existence of a refinancing agreement, each of the following must be true **except**
    a. The lender or investor is financially capable of honoring the refinancing agreement.
    b. The agreement is noncancelable and will not expire within one year of the balance sheet date (or one operating cycle, if longer).
    c. The proceeds of the refinancing agreement are received before the date that the balance sheet is issued.
    d. The replacement debt will not be callable except for violation of a provision of the refinancing agreement with which compliance is objectively determinable and measurable.

Multiple-Choice

11. Which of the following is a true statement?
    a. A bond that bears no interest will be issued at par.
    b. A convertible bond will yield less proceeds upon issuance than a similar bond without the convertible feature.
    c. A bond that has a stated rate that exceeds the market rate will be issued at a discount.
    d. A bond that has a stated rate that exceeds the market rate will be issued at a premium.

Multiple-Choice

12. Commitments to pay money at determinable future dates are subject to application of present value techniques and imputation of interest under APB 21, **except** for the following item(s)
    a. Normal accounts payable due within one year.
    b. Transactions between a parent and a subsidiary.
    c. Transactions where the interest rates are affected by a governmental agency.
    d. All of the above.

True/False

13. If the market rate is greater than the stated rate on a bond when it is issued, the bond will be issued at a premium.

True/False

14. The effective interest method is the preferred method of accounting for a discount or premium arising from a note or bond.

Multiple-Choice   15. If the effective interest rate method is used to amortize a bond premium, interest expense related to a bond with a balance of $10,000 and a stated rate of 12% that was issued when the market rate was 10% would be
    a. $1,000
    b. $1,200
    c. $1,500
    d. None of the above.

True/False   16. When a bond is issued between payment dates, the purchaser pays the issuer for the amount of interest accrued since the last payment date.

True/False   17. The legal fees, accounting fees, underwriting fees, commissions, and other costs associated with issuing bonds are commonly subtracted from the bond proceeds before computing the effective interest rate, in much the same way as a discount.

True/False   18. The amount of a guarantee obligation increases the loss or decreases the gain on an extinguishment of debt.

True/False   19. If a company offers an inducement to creditors to encourage conversion of convertible debt, the company should reduce the credit to additional paid-in-capital by that amount.

True/False   20. The effective interest rate method of amortization of a bond premium results in equal amounts of amortization in each period.

Multiple-Choice   21. Lessors may classify leases as
    a. Operating.
    b. Sales-type.
    c. Direct financing.
    d. All of the above.

True/False   22. From the standpoint both of a lessee and lessor, an operating lease may result in amounts recorded on the balance sheet if payments of the minimum rentals due under the lease vary over the term of the lease.

True/False   23. In the case of a lessee operating lease, the actual leased asset is not recognized on the lessee's balance sheet because the substance of the lease is that of a rental versus a transfer of the rights and obligations associated with the asset.

True/False   24. Lease accounting uses the term residual value in the same manner that fixed asset accounting uses the term salvage value.

True/False   25. From the standpoint of the lessor, a sales-type lease results in revenue being recognized from both interest and dealer's profit.

True/False   26. The sales price of the property in a sale-leaseback transaction is always fixed at the appraised value of the property on the date of the transaction.

True/False 27. If the fair value of the property at the time of a sale-leaseback is less than its undepreciated cost, the seller-lessee should defer the difference and amortize it over the term of the leaseback.

Multiple-Choice 28. Which of the following is an example of continuing involvement by a seller-lessee?
   a. An obligation or option to repurchase the property.
   b. A guarantee of the buyer-lessor's investment or debt related to that investment.
   c. Continuing to remain liable for an existing debt on the property.
   d. All of the above.

True/False 29. Leases involving only land are not subject to all four of the same criteria for capitalization as other leases.

True/False 30. In all leases that involve both land and building, the lease payments relative to each are to be treated separately.

Multiple-Choice 31. GAAP defines temporary differences as being (only)
   a. All differences in the tax and book bases of assets and liabilities with the exception of goodwill.
   b. All differences in the tax and book bases of assets and liabilities with the exception of those to which the "indefinite reversal" criterion can be applied.
   c. Revenues or expenses which are recognized in different years for tax purposes and for financial reporting purposes.
   d. All differences between "tax" and "book" income other than "permanent" differences.

True/False 32. The amount reported as a deferred tax asset, net of any allowance, does not necessarily represent the dollar actual amount of tax benefits the entity expects to receive in the future.

True/False 33. If deferred tax assets are recorded in connection with a purchase business combination, along with a 100% allowance account, and the allowance is properly reduced or eliminated later, the adjustment will first be used to eliminate goodwill recorded in the purchase, then other intangibles recorded, and finally to reduce the current period's tax provision.

Multiple-Choice 34. The deferred tax effects of a change in tax status from a C corporation to an S corporation can be reported as
   a. A change in reporting entity as defined by APB 20, with an adjustment to the opening balance of retained earnings.
   b. An adjustment to paid-in capital, since by assuming the tax burden directly, the shareholders have in effect made a contribution to the entity's permanent capital.
   c. Either an adjustment to the current period's tax provision, or an adjustment to paid-in capital.
   d. An adjustment to the current period's tax provision.

Multiple- Choice	35.	Taxes allocable to extraordinary items is determined by a. Allocating taxes to extraordinary items only if the entity is in a net taxable position for the reporting period. b. Applying statutory rates to the extraordinary items individually. c. Using a marginal approach to allocate tax effects to the extraordinary items versus ordinary income. d. Applying an average tax rate based on the entity's recent tax history.

Multiple- Choice	36.	The tax effects of prior periods' corrections are a. Reported only if the entity is in a net taxable position in the current year. b. Included "net" in other comprehensive income. c. Included in income from continuing operations. d. Allocated to retained earnings.

Multiple- Choice	37.	When a tax law has been amended such that a rate increase will take effect in a later period a. The new rate would **not** be used to compute the deferred tax provision in the current period, because there is no assurance that this will really take effect. b. The new rate would be used to compute the deferred tax provision in the current period. c. To deal with both uncertainty and conservatism, the deferred taxes should be computed using a blend of the old and new rates. d. The new rates should be used to compute deferred taxes only if past experience suggests that these will in fact be implemented as promised.

True/False	38.	The tax effect of net operating loss carryforwards should be given current recognition only if probable of ultimate realization.

Multiple- Choice	39.	**Intra**period tax allocation is a. Not permitted under SFAS 109. b. Accomplished by using a "with and without" or marginal approach for all items of income or expense other than continuing operations. c. Accomplished by allocating the total income tax provision proportionally to continuing operations and all other categories (discontinued operations, etc.). d. Accomplished by allocating taxes first to continuing operations, then to discontinued operations, extraordinary items, other comprehensive income, and corrections of prior periods, in that order, until the full provision has been accounted for.

True/False	40.	The tax effect of corrections of prior periods should be included with income from continuing operations.

GAAP 2002 CPE Course

UNIT III

Record your CPE answers on the answer form provided below and return this page for grading.

Mail to:

GAAP 2002 CPE Director

John Wiley and Sons, Inc., 7222 Commerce Center Drive, Suite 240, Colorado Springs, CO 80919

PAYMENT OPTIONS

☐ **Payment enclosed ($59.00 per Unit).**
(Make checks payable to John Wiley & Sons, Inc.)
Please add appropriate sales tax.
Be sure to sign your order below.

Charge my:

☐ American Express ☐ MasterCard ☐ Visa

Account number _____

Expiration date _____
Please sign below for all credit card orders.

Signature _____

NAME _____

FIRM NAME _____

ADDRESS _____

PHONE ( ) _____

CPA STATE LICENSE # _____

ISBN 0-471-43890-1

SEE THE OTHER SIDE OF THIS PAGE FOR THE CPE FEEDBACK FORM.

UNIT III CPE ANSWERS

1. ___	2. ___	3. ___	4. ___	5. ___	6. ___	7. ___	8. ___	9. ___	10. ___
11. ___	12. ___	13. ___	14. ___	15. ___	16. ___	17. ___	18. ___	19. ___	20. ___
21. ___	22. ___	23. ___	24. ___	25. ___	26. ___	27. ___	28. ___	29. ___	30. ___
31. ___	32. ___	33. ___	34. ___	35. ___	36. ___	37. ___	38. ___	39. ___	40. ___

GAAP 2002 CPE Feedback

1. Were you informed in advance of the

   a. Course objectives? Y N
   b. Requisite experience level? Y N
   c. Course content? Y N
   d. Type and degree of preparation necessary? Y N
   e. Instruction method? Y N
   f. CPE credit hours? Y N

2. Do you agree with the publisher's determination of

   a. Course objectives? Y N
   b. Requisite experience level? Y N

   c. Course content? Y N
   d. Type and degree of preparation necessary? Y N
   e. Instruction method? Y N
   f. CPE credit hours? Y N

3. Was the content relevant? Y N

4. Was the content displayed clearly? Y N

5. Did the course enhance your professional competence? Y N

6. Was the course content timely and effective? Y N

How can we make the course better? If you have any suggestions please summarize them in the space below. We will consider them in developing future courses.

_____

_____

_____

_____

CONTINUING PROFESSIONAL EDUCATION: SELF-STUDY

UNIT IV

OBJECTIVES

Chapter 16: Accounting for Pensions

Studying Chapter 16 should enable you to:

- Understand the accrual basis of accounting for pension costs
- Know the six components of net periodic pension costs
- Calculate net periodic pension costs
- Describe the accounting for settlements and curtailments
- Account for postretirement benefits other than pensions
- Know GAAP regarding deferred compensation contracts

Read Chapter 16 and answer discussion questions 1 through 8.

Chapter 17: Stockholders' Equity

Studying Chapter 17 should enable you to:

- Understand the natures of preferred and common stock
- Account for contributed capital and retained earnings
- Understand accounting for treasury stock transactions
- Account for stock, cash and property dividends
- Account for stock splits and reverse splits
- Account for quasi reorganizations
- Account for employee stock options and related compensation arrangements
- Understand the use of the options pricing models for employee stock compensation arrangements
- Understand employer accounting for ESOP plans

Read Chapter 17 and answer discussion questions 9 through 13.

Chapter 18: Earnings Per Share

Studying Chapter 18 should enable you to:

- Differentiate between basic and diluted earnings per share
- Describe the treasury stock method and the if-converted method, and explain when these methods are utilized
- Describe the components of income for which EPS must be computed
- Calculate the income from continuing operations available for common stockholders (numerator) for basic EPS and diluted EPS
- Calculate the weighted-average number of shares outstanding (denominator) for basic EPS and diluted EPS
- Describe the treatment of stock splits and stock dividends in calculating EPS
- Describe the required EPS disclosures

Read Chapter 18 and answer discussion questions 14 through 18.

Chapter 19: Interim and Segment Reporting

Studying Chapter 19 should enable you to:

- Understand the discrete and integral views of reporting on interim periods
- Know the recognition criteria in interim periods for revenues, product costs, direct costs, and other costs and expenses
- Describe required interim reporting disclosures
- Describe what is meant by the management approach
- Identify reportable operating segments
- Know the three 10% tests

Read Chapter 19 and answer discussion questions 19 through 25.

Chapter 20: Accounting Changes and Correction of Errors

Studying Chapter 20 should enable you to:

- Differentiate among changes in accounting principle, changes in accounting estimate, and changes in reporting entity
- Describe the three ways of reporting accounting changes: retroactively, currently, and prospectively
- Describe the accounting and reporting for a change in accounting principle that is reported in the income statement, including disclosures and pro forma calculations
- Identify the changes in accounting principles that are accounted for retroactively
- Discuss implementation of retroactive-type changes in accounting principle
- Explain how to account for a change in accounting estimate
- Describe how to disclose a change in reporting entity
- Describe how to correct errors in previously issued financial statements

Read Chapter 20 and answer discussion questions 26 through 31.

Chapter 21: Foreign Currency

Studying Chapter 21 should enable you to:

- Differentiate between translation of foreign currency transactions and foreign currency financial statements
- Apply the factors from SFAS 52 that shall be used in identifying the functional currency of the foreign entity
- Apply the current rate method of translating balances of a foreign branch or subsidiary
- Apply the remeasurement method of translating balances of a foreign branch or subsidiary
- Describe the reporting of unrealized translation gains or losses
- Describe the accounting for hedges under SFAS 52 and SFAS 133

Read Chapter 21 and answer discussion questions 32 through 35.

Chapter 22: Personal Financial Statements

Studying Chapter 22 should enable you to:

- Know which financial statements and the format thereof that constitute a set of personal financial statements
- Know the valuation bases for assets and liabilities

Read Chapter 22 and answer discussion questions 36 through 38.

Chapter 23: Specialized Industry GAAP

- Know the sources of specialized industry GAAP
- Know key concepts applicable to the more important specialized industries

Read Chapter 23 and answer discussion questions 39 and 40.

DISCUSSION QUESTIONS

1. What are the sources of GAAP in the pension area?

2. Net periodic pension cost consists of the sum of what five components?

3. What is a major difference between the accumulated benefit obligation and the projected benefit obligation?

4. What do plan assets include?

5. What are service costs?

6. In SFAS 87, how is the additional minimum liability recognized?

7. What three criteria must all be met in order to constitute a pension obligation settlement?

8. What standard establishes the standard for employers' accounting for other than pension postretirement benefits (OPEB)?

9. If the aggregate deferred compensation contracts with individual employees are not equivalent to a pension plan, what governs the accounting?

10. What is the distinction between paid-in capital and retained earnings, and why is this considered to be important in financial reporting?

11. Why are stock subscriptions receivable generally reported as a contra equity account?

12. What is the distinction between a stock dividend and a stock split, and what is the proper accounting for each?

13. How are "gains" and "losses" on treasury stock transactions accounted for, and what is the underlying accounting principle?

14. What is the approach to accounting for employee stock options underlying the new rules of SFAS 123? How does this differ from the old approach of APB 25?

15. Under the options pricing models endorsed by SFAS 123, what attributes give value to employee stock options?

16. What are tandem stock plans and what is the basic concept of accounting for these under APB 25 and SFAS 123?

17. What is the objective of accounting for a "quasi reorganization"?

18. In EPS calculations, why are shares issued during a period weighted so as to reflect the portion of a period that they are outstanding?

19. In calculating income available to common stockholders, how are dividends in arrears on cumulative preferred stock treated?

20. Explain the reason that stock splits or dividends are reflected in EPS as though they occurred at the beginning of the period and, in cases when comparative financial statements are presented, for all prior periods presented.

21. Discuss the rationale for the dual presentation of EPS (i.e., basic and diluted EPS) by companies with a complex capital structure.

22. Is it possible for the computations of basic EPS and diluted EPS calculations to yield the same EPS figure?

23. Describe the treasury stock method and the if-converted method.

24. Discuss the difference between the discrete and integral views of reporting on interim periods.

25. Describe the treatment of inventory market declines in interim financial statements.

26. On what basis shall reportable operating segments be reported?

27. How are changes in depreciation/amortization methods for long-lived assets accounted for if the change is adopted for all assets?

28. How must changes in accounting principle requiring the cumulative effect method be disclosed in the year the changes are made?

29. In what circumstances may cumulative effect not be determinable? How are these circumstances to be disclosed?

30. If the cumulative-effect-type of accounting change is made at an interim date, how is it accounted for on the financial statements?

31. Describe when a change in reporting entity occurs.

32. What are the factors to be considered by management when selecting the functional currency?

33. Under the current rate method of translation, which elements are translated at historical rates?

34. Compare and contrast the remeasurement method of translation with the current rate method.

35. Explain the accounting at the end of a reporting period if an entity has receivables and payables that are denominated in a foreign currency.

36. If the number of US dollars for each foreign currency unit increases between the transaction date and the balance sheet date, does the translation of receivables and payables denominated in the foreign currency result in gains or losses?

37. Can a commitment to purchase a trading security use hedging accounting?

38. What has SFAS 133 changed with regard to accounting for a net investment in foreign operations?

39. What basis of valuation should be used for liabilities in the statement of financial condition?

40. How should estimated income taxes related to unrealized gains and losses be measured in personal financial statements?

ANSWERS TO DISCUSSION QUESTIONS

1. SFAS 87, 88, and 132 are the sources of GAAP in the pension area.

2. Net periodic pension cost consists of the sum of the following five components:
   a. Service cost
   b. Interest cost on projected benefit obligation
   c. Expected return on plan assets
   d. Amortization of unrecognized prior service cost
   e. Recognized actuarial loss

3. The accumulated benefit obligation does not include an assumption about future compensation levels, whereas the projected benefit obligation does include such an assumption.

4. Plan assets include contributions and asset earnings less benefits paid. They must be segregated and effectively restricted for pension benefits.

5. The service cost component of net periodic pension cost is the actuarial present value of benefits attributed during the current period. Under SFAS 87, the plan's benefit formula is the key to attributing benefits to employee service periods.

6. In SFAS 87, the additional minimum liability is recognized by an offset to an intangible asset up to the amount of unrecognized prior service cost. Any additional debit needed is considered a loss and is shown net of tax benefits

(subject to the restrictions on recognition of deferred tax assets per SFAS 109) in other comprehensive income.

7. The following three criteria must all be met in order to constitute a pension obligation settlement:

    a. Must be irrevocable
    b. Must relieve the obligor of primary responsibility
    c. Must eliminate significant risks associated with elements used to effect it

8. SFAS 106 establishes the standard for employers' accounting for other (than pension) postretirement benefits (OPEB). This standard prescribes a single method for measuring and recognizing an employer's accumulated postretirement benefit obligation (APBO). It applies to all forms of postretirement benefits, although the most material benefit is usually postretirement health care.

9. If the aggregate deferred compensation contracts with individual employees are equivalent to a pension plan, the contracts should be accounted for according to SFAS 87 and 88. All other deferred compensation contracts should be accounted for according to APB 12, para 6.

10. Paid-in capital represents the permanent owners' investment in the corporation, which in most jurisdictions represents legal capital that is available for the protection of creditors. Retained earnings is the accumulation of the earnings of the corporation since inception, less dividend distributions. Historically this distinction has been important since it reveals the amount of capital that will continue to be available for the satisfaction of creditors' claims and is a measure of the cumulative success of the company over its entire history.

11. Subscriptions receivable are shown as offsets to subscribed stock to avoid an overstatement of the balance sheet simply as a result of promises to acquire shares that have yet to be substantiated by cash infusions. In rare cases (if the cash is collected after the balance sheet date but before the statements are issued) the receivable is shown as an asset, since it is known to have been collected.

12. Stock dividends and splits both are merely the change in evidences of ownership, without any distribution of assets from the company to the stockholders. However, stock dividends are generally viewed by the market as indications of earnings distributions and are typically small (no more than 20% to 25%), while splits are universally seen as being merely bookkeeping events. Stock dividends often do not affect the market price of the outstanding shares (or do not affect it in proportion to the extent of the dividend) while splits are usually accompanied by proportionate declines in market value. For these reasons,

stock dividends are accounted for as true dividends (retained earnings are transferred to paid-in capital) while splits do not affect retained earnings.

13. When treasury shares are resold for more than cost, the "gain" is credited to paid-in capital, while if the subsequent sale is for less than cost, the "loss" is charged to retained earnings (unless paid-in capital from prior similar transactions is available to absorb the loss). The principle is that an entity's transactions in its own equity cannot create income to be reported in the income statement or increase retained earnings, while losses will reduce retained earnings.

14. SFAS 123 adopts the "fair value" approach to measuring stock options, while the older APB 25 rules used the "intrinsic value" model. Under APB 25 most employee options did not give rise to accounting recognition of compensation expense, although clearly the purpose of granting options was to compensate employees. SFAS 123 rules will result in compensation expense in most cases. However, SFAS 123 is not mandatory, so companies may elect to continue to use APB 25.

15. The value assigned to options under the Black-Scholes and binomial models is a function of the spread between option price and market price at grant date, the risk-free discount rate, the expected market price growth rate, the expected volatility in stock price, and the expected dividends to be paid on the stock during the service period. For nonpublic companies, the minimum value model is similar but ignores the volatility of stock prices.

16. Tandem plans are simultaneous grants of stock options and stock appreciation rights or phantom shares, whereby the exercise of one cancels the other. Under APB 25, as amended by FASB Interpretation 28, the accounting is based on the expectation of which of the two will be elected by the holders, but under SFAS 123, the liability arising from the stock appreciation rights, if they can be settled in cash at the holders' option, is generally the basis for the accrual of compensation expense.

17. Quasi reorganizations were developed to deal with major, permanent declines in price levels, which would make it unlikely that an entity could recover the carrying value of long-term assets, and which result in recurring losses due to high amortization charges. Under those limited conditions, a write-down of fixed assets can be recorded, and the accumulated deficit in retained earnings absorbed against paid-in capital. For an extended period of time thereafter, retained earnings must be "dated" so financial statement readers are not misled about the entity's historical performance record. A quasi reorganization is an accounting, not a legal, process.

18. Shares issued during a period are weighted from the date of issuance because that is the period of time during which management had use of the resources to generate income.

19. Only the preferred dividends for one year would be deducted from net income; the amount of dividends for one year were deducted in each prior year.

20. The rationale for stock splits or dividends being reflected in EPS as of the beginning of the period, and in all earlier periods when comparative financial statements are presented, is to avoid distortion when comparing earlier periods' earnings per share amounts with later periods'; it would appear that earnings per share decreased, when in essence each shareholder's equity in the earnings of the enterprise are unchanged by a split or dividend.

21. The underlying basis for this presentation is conservatism. The range from basic to diluted EPS distinguishes between no dilution and potential dilution, thereby providing the users with the most factually supportable range of EPS possibilities. Diluted EPS considers all other dilutive securities (unless such exercise would be antidilutive).

22. It is possible for basic EPS and diluted EPS (DEPS) to be the same, if the other potentially dilutive securities in the DEPS calculation are antidilutive. However, to the extent dilutive securities exist the DEPS figure will always be lower than the basic EPS figure.

23. Generally the treasury stock method is used for options and warrants, while the if-converted method is used for convertible securities. Each method requires certain pro forma assumptions. The treasury stock method requires that EPS be computed as if the options or warrants were exercised as of the beginning of the period (or date of issuance, if later), and that the funds obtained from the exercise were used to purchase common stock at the average market price. The if-converted method assumes the conversion of preferential securities with convertible features (e.g., convertible bonds or convertible preferred stock) to common stock. This method recognizes (via a pro forma assumption) that these securities share in the earnings of the common shareholder. Thus the dividends or net income effects applicable to the preferential security are not recognized in the income available to common stockholders figure, and the weighted-average number of shares is also adjusted.

24. According to the integral view of interim reporting, the resulting earnings figures for an interim period should give users information concerning annual earnings; these numbers should predict annual earnings. On the other hand, the discrete view is that each reporting period should stand by itself; estimates and allocations should not differ from those used in annual statements.

25. Market declines expected to be restored are deemed temporary and do not require recognition. Ordinarily, only seasonal gains may be deferred.

26. SFAS 131 requires reporting of information about operating segments on the same basis that it is provided for internal evaluation by the chief operating decision maker.

27. The change requires a cumulative effect adjustment. Newly acquired identifiable long-lived assets will use the new method of depreciation/amortization. Long-lived assets already on the books will be adjusted based on the new depreciation/amortization method.

28. The nature of and justification for the change and the effect of the change on income before extraordinary items, net income, and related per share amounts shall be disclosed for all periods presented.

29. The cumulative effect might not be determinable in a change from FIFO to LIFO. Disclosure will be limited to showing the effect and per share effect of the change in the period of change. It will also be necessary to explain the reason for omitting accounting for the cumulative effect and disclosure of the pro forma results.

30. No cumulative effect of the accounting change should be included in the net income of the period. The prechange interim periods of the year in which the change is made should be restated to reflect the newly adopted accounting principle.

31. A change in reporting entity occurs when financial statements are prepared that represent a different or changed entity. An example is including the financial statements of a subsidiary in the entity's consolidated financial statements although it had been excluded in a prior period.

32. The factors are: effect of foreign entity's cash flow on parent, responsiveness of sales prices to exchange rates and global competition, location of sales market as reflected by currency in which denominated, country in which expenses incurred, source of financing, and volume of intercompany transactions.

33. Only stockholders' equity accounts are translated at historical rates.

34. Whereas all assets and liabilities are translated at current rates under the current rate method, only monetary assets and liabilities are translated at the current rate under the remeasurement method. Nonmonetary assets and liabilities use historical rates.

35. Each of the receivables and payables must be translated to US dollars using the spot rate at the balance sheet date. Differences between the translated amounts and the carrying amounts result in unrealized gains or losses.

36. If the number of US dollars per unit of foreign currency increases, there would be unrealized gains on receivables and losses on payables that are denominated in that foreign currency unit.

37. SFAS 133 does not permit the use of hedging accounting for a firm commitment to purchase a trading security.

38. The only change mandated by SFAS 133 is that the hedging instrument must meet the "effective" criterion.

39. Liabilities should be measured at the lesser of the discounted amount of cash to be paid or the current cash settlement amount.

40. Estimated income taxes should be measured as if the current values of assets and liabilities had been realized or liquidated, respectively, and the provisions of current tax law were applied.

UNIT IV

PUBLISHER-GRADED EXAMINATION

True/False   1.   The funding policy of a pension plan sponsor is an integral consideration in the accounting for pension costs.

True/False   2.   If the employer/plan sponsor historically has been more generous to employees who participate in a pension plan than is required by the written plan document, the pension accounting should take into account the benefits actually projected to be provided by the employer and ignore the legal document.

True/False   3.   Interest cost incurred as a result of the changes in the present value of the projected benefit obligation is exempt from inclusion in interest capitalized during a period and, in fact, is accounted for as pension cost in the financial statements.

True/False   4.   Net pension costs include the expected gain on plan assets irrespective of whether it is actually achieved during the period.

Multiple-Choice   5.   When a pension plan is amended and that amendment results in increases in plan benefits attributable to services provided by plan participants in the past, the change is accounted for as
    a.   A change in accounting principle.
    b.   A cumulative effect adjustment to beginning retained earnings.
    c.   A component of other comprehensive income.
    d.   A change of accounting estimate.

True/False   6.   The projected benefit obligation is a component of the accumulated benefit obligation.

True/False   7.   For entities that have more than one pension plan, the plans are permitted to be aggregated for the purpose of applying pension accounting.

Multiple-Choice   8.   An annuity or other insurance contract is excluded from the plan assets, the accumulated benefit obligation, and the projected benefit obligation if
    a.   It is valid and irrevocable.
    b.   It transfers significant risks to an insurance company unrelated to the plan sponsor.
    c.   There is no reasonable doubt as to the ultimate payment of the amounts due under the contract.
    d.   All of the above.

Multiple-Choice 9. In accounting for stock-based compensation, the difference between intrinsic value and fair value measures is that
  a. Using fair value, rarely will there be compensation recognized in connection with qualified stock option plans.
  b. No compensation cost is reported if the exercise price is above fair value at the date of grant, under the fair value method.
  c. Using intrinsic value, rarely will there be compensation recognized in connection with qualified stock option plans.
  d. Fair value measures must be used for reporting by publicly held entities, whereas either fair value or intrinsic value may be used for private entities.

Multiple-Choice 10. Dividends must be charged against retained earnings
  a. In all cases, whether these are normal (i.e., cash), stock, or liquidating.
  b. Only to the extent required by state corporation laws; otherwise, these can be charged to paid-in capital accounts.
  c. If there is a firm commitment to resell the shares to third parties as of the balance sheet date.
  d. None of the above are correct.

Multiple-Choice 11. Treasury shares may be reported on the balance sheet as an asset
  a. If acquired to facilitate an ESOP program.
  b. If acquired for a specific purpose such as making a scheduled contribution to a profit-sharing plan.
  c. If there is a firm commitment to resell the shares to third parties as of the balance sheet date.
  d. None of the above are correct.

True/False 12. Under **both** fair value and intrinsic value approaches to stock-based compensation, no compensation expense will be reported if options are granted with exercise prices at or above market price at grant date.

True/False 13. Dividends paid on **unallocated** shares held by an ESOP are reported as dividends rather than as compensation expense.

True/False 14. Dilutive securities are securities whose issuance provides liquidity in excess of specified amounts.

Multiple-Choice 15. For the purposes of earnings per share calculations, a stock dividend or split is accounted for
  a. As an adjustment to the weighted-average number of shares outstanding in the current period.
  b. As an adjustment to the weighted-average number of shares outstanding in the current and all prior periods presented.
  c. By ignoring its effect since it does not generate additional consideration for the company.
  d. The same way as cash dividends.

Multiple- Choice	16.	A company that has a complex capital structure a. Has issued more than one class of capital stock. b. Has issued voting and nonvoting stock. c. Has issued either debt securities, equity securities, or options which contain provisions which have the potential, if exercised, to reduce earnings per share. d. Has both common and preferred stock.
Multiple- Choice	17.	In computing basic earnings per share, the weighted-average number of common stock shares outstanding is computed a. Using the arithmetical median. b. Using the arithmetical mode. c. Using the arithmetical mean. d. None of the above.
True/False	18.	If a company reacquires its own stock, the number of shares reacquired should be excluded from earnings per share calculations at the date of acquisition.
True/False	19.	In general, revenue recognition for interim reporting purposes follows the same rules and conventions as are used for annual reporting purposes.
True/False	20.	A physical inventory must be taken at the end of a fiscal quarter when issuing financial statements for that quarter.
Multiple- Choice	21.	Repairs made in the first quarter that are expected to benefit the remaining quarters of the fiscal year should be accounted for as a. A charge against first quarter earnings. b. A deferred asset until the end of the fiscal year when it is reversed as a charge against annual earnings. c. A deferral during the first quarter which should be amortized to the other quarters on a systematic and rational basis. d. None of the above.
True/False	22.	All enterprises that present consolidated financial statements are required to separately report the results of "material identifiable segments."
True/False	23.	Although definitions of segments may be different in similarly organized companies, GAAP allows each company to apply management's judgment in determining its operating segments.
True/False	24.	Segment information reported externally must conform with information reported internally that is used to manage the business.
Multiple- Choice	25.	Which of the following is **not** one of the tests to determine whether a segment is reportable? a. Revenues test. b. Operating profit and loss test. c. Net income test. d. Assets test.

Multiple-   26. Accounting changes, as defined by APB 20, include
Choice
                           a.   Prior period adjustments.
                           b.   Cumulative effect adjustments.
                           c.   Changes in accounting principle.
                           d.   Changes in management precipitated by Board of Directors' actions.

True/False   27. Although it is an auditing standard, SAS 69 governs the acceptability of accounting rules by establishing a hierarchy that categorizes and ranks the different accounting standards currently in force.

True/False   28. When a company adopts a change in accounting principles, it adjusts net income in the year of change for the entire effect of the change on all prior years.

Multiple-   29. The pro forma effects of a change in accounting principle are to be disclosed
Choice
                           a.   In the notes to the financial statements.
                           b.   On the face of the income statement.
                           c.   In the notes to the financial statements or on the face of the income statement.
                           d.   In the notes to the financial statements and on the face of the income statement.

Multiple-   30. Which of the following changes in accounting principle require retroactive adjustment of all prior periods presented?
Choice
                           a.   Change from FIFO to LIFO.
                           b.   Change from accelerated to straight-line depreciation.
                           c.   Change in method of accounting for long-term contracts.
                           d.   None of the above.

True/False   31. When a company changes its method of depreciation for newly acquired fixed assets, no adjustment is required to the accumulated depreciation previously recognized on assets acquired in prior years.

True/False   32. Nonmonetary items are balance sheet items other than cash, claims to cash, short-term investments, and cash obligations.

Multiple-   33. Which of the following is **not** one of the criteria used to determine a company's functional currency?
Choice
                           a.   Cash flows.
                           b.   Sales prices.
                           c.   The denomination of its foreign letters of credit.
                           d.   Existence of intercompany transactions.

True/False   34. GAAP requires management to choose either the current rate method or the remeasurement method to translate financial statements with the choice depending upon which country's currency is the functional currency.

True/False   35. Monetary assets are translated identically under both the current rate method and the remeasurement method.

Multiple-Choice

36. Personal financial statements differ from those for commercial entities under GAAP because
    a. Extraordinary items are not set forth separately in personal financial statements.
    b. Deferred income tax accounting is not required for personal financial statements.
    c. Cash flow statements for personal financial statements do not have an "operations" category.
    d. None of the above are correct.

True/False

37. Personal financial statements report financial instruments at fair value but use historical cost for other types of assets (e.g., real estate).

Multiple-Choice

38. To the extent that estimated current values are used to prepare personal financial statements, these are measured with reference to
    a. Discounted future cash flows.
    b. Fair market values.
    c. Appraisal values.
    d. All of the above are correct.

True/False

39. Broadcasters are permitted to record program rights that extend over multiple years at the gross amounts to be paid even though this conflicts with the GAAP regarding imputing interest on long-term receivables and payables.

Multiple-Choice

40. Which of the following costs of internal-use software are to be capitalized?
    a. Conversion of data from previous system.
    b. Training of personnel.
    c. Programmer's salary.
    d. Internal operating manual production.

GAAP 2002 CPE Course

UNIT IV

Record your CPE answers on the answer form provided below and return this page for grading.

Mail to:

GAAP 2002 CPE Director

John Wiley and Sons, Inc., 7222 Commerce Center Drive, Suite 240, Colorado Springs, CO 80919

PAYMENT OPTIONS

☐ **Payment enclosed ($59.00 per Unit).**
(Make checks payable to John Wiley & Sons, Inc.)
Please add appropriate sales tax.
Be sure to sign your order below.

Charge my:

☐ American Express ☐ MasterCard ☐ Visa

Account number _____

Expiration date _____
Please sign below for all credit card orders.

Signature _____

NAME _____

FIRM NAME _____

ADDRESS _____

PHONE ( ) _____

CPA STATE LICENSE # _____

ISBN 0-471-43891-X

SEE THE OTHER SIDE OF THIS PAGE FOR THE CPE FEEDBACK FORM.

UNIT IV CPE ANSWERS

1. ___	2. ___	3. ___	4. ___	5. ___	6. ___	7. ___	8. ___	9. ___	10. ___
11. ___	12. ___	13. ___	14. ___	15. ___	16. ___	17. ___	18. ___	19. ___	20. ___
21. ___	22. ___	23. ___	24. ___	25. ___	26. ___	27. ___	28. ___	29. ___	30. ___
31. ___	32. ___	33. ___	34. ___	35. ___	36. ___	37. ___	38. ___	39. ___	40. ___

Copyright © 2001 John Wiley & Sons, Inc.

GAAP 2002 CPE Feedback

1. Were you informed in advance of the

   a. Course objectives? Y N
   b. Requisite experience level? Y N
   c. Course content? Y N
   d. Type and degree of preparation necessary? Y N
   e. Instruction method? Y N
   f. CPE credit hours? Y N

2. Do you agree with the publisher's determination of

   a. Course objectives? Y N
   b. Requisite experience level? Y N

   c. Course content? Y N
   d. Type and degree of preparation necessary? Y N
   e. Instruction method? Y N
   f. CPE credit hours? Y N

3. Was the content relevant? Y N

4. Was the content displayed clearly? Y N

5. Did the course enhance your professional competence? Y N

6. Was the course content timely and effective? Y N

How can we make the course better? If you have any suggestions please summarize them in the space below. We will consider them in developing future courses.

_____

_____

_____

_____

_____